THE ROUTLEDGE HANDBOOK OF NEOPLATONISM

The Routledge Handbook of Neoplatonism is an authoritative and comprehensive survey of the most important issues and developments in one of the fastest growing areas of research in ancient philosophy. An international team of scholars situates and re-evaluates Neoplatonism within the history of ancient philosophy and thought, and explores its influence on philosophical and religious schools worldwide. *The Routledge Handbook of Neoplatonism* is a major reference source for all students and scholars in Neoplatonism and ancient philosophy, as well as researchers in the philosophy of science, ethics, aesthetics and religion.

Pauliina Remes is University Lecturer in Philosophy at Uppsala University (Sweden). She is the author of *Plotinus on Self: The Philosophy of the "We"* (2007) and *Neoplatonism* (2008), and the editor of *Ancient Philosophy of the Self* (2008, with J. Sihvola) and *Consciousness: From Perception to Reflection in the History of Philosophy* (2007, with S. Heinämaa and V. Lähteenmäki).

Svetla Slaveva-Griffin is Associate Professor of Classics and a core faculty in the History and Philosophy of Science Program at the Florida State University. She has published on a wide range of topics in ancient philosophy, including *Plotinus on Number* (2009).

ROUTLEDGE HANDBOOKS IN PHILOSOPHY

Routledge Handbooks in Philosophy are state-of-the-art surveys of emerging, newly refreshed, and important fields in philosophy, providing accessible yet thorough assessments of key problems, themes, thinkers, and recent developments in research.

All chapters for each volume are specially commissioned, and written by leading scholars in the field. Carefully edited and organized, *Routledge Handbooks in Philosophy* provide indispensable reference tools for students and researchers seeking a comprehensive overview of new and exciting topics in philosophy. They are also valuable teaching resources as accompaniments to textbooks, anthologies, and research-orientated publications.

Available:

The Routledge Handbook of Embodied Cognition
Edited by Lawrence Shapiro

The Routledge Handbook of Neoplatonism
Edited by Pauliina Remes and Svetla Slaveva-Griffin

Forthcoming:

The Routledge Handbook of Global Ethics
Edited by Darrel Moellendorf and Heather Widdows

The Routledge Handbook of Contemporary Philosophy of Religion
Edited by Graham Oppy

The Routledge Handbook of the Stoic Tradition
Edited by John Sellars

The Routledge Handbook of German Idealism
Edited by Brian O'Connor, Michael Rosen, Hans Joerg Sandkühler, and David Wood

The Routledge Handbook of Philosophy of Well-Being
Edited by Guy Fletcher

The Routledge Handbook of Philosophy of Imagination
Edited by Amy Kind

The Routledge Handbook of Philosophy of Colour
Edited by Derek Brown and Fiona Macpherson

The Routledge Handbook of the Philosophy of Biodiversity
Edited by Justin Garson, Anya Plutynski, and Sahotra Sarkar

The Routledge Handbook of Philosophy of the Social Mind
Edited by Julian Kiverstein

The Routledge Handbook of Collective Intentionality
Edited by Marija Jankovic and Kirk Ludwig

The Routledge Handbook of Brentano and the Brentano School
Edited by Uriah Kriegel

The Routledge Handbook of Epistemic Contextualism
Edited by Jonathan Jenkins Ichikawa

The Routledge Handbook of Philosophy and Evolution
Edited by Richard Joyce

The Routledge Handbook of Modality
Edited by Otávio Bueno and Scott Shalkowski

THE ROUTLEDGE HANDBOOK OF NEOPLATONISM

Edited by
Pauliina Remes and Svetla Slaveva-Griffin

Routledge
Taylor & Francis Group

LONDON AND NEW YORK

First published 2014
by Routledge
2 Park Square, Milton Park, Abingdon, Oxon OX14 4RN

and by Routledge
711 Third Avenue, New York, NY 10017

Routledge is an imprint of the Taylor & Francis Group, an informa business

British Library Cataloguing in Publication Data
A catalogue record for this book is available from the British Library

Library of Congress Cataloguing in Publication Data
A catalog record for this title has been applied for

ISBN: 978-1-844-65626-4 (hbk)
ISBN: 978-1-315-74418-6 (ebk)

Typeset in Minion Pro and Frutiger by Kate Williams, Swansea.

Printed and bound in Great Britain by
TJ International Ltd, Padstow, Cornwall

Contents

v

Acknowledgements

The appearance of this volume would have been impossible without the support of many individuals and institutions. Besides the contributors, we wish to thank the anonymous reviewers for upholding the *Handbook* to the highest standards of scholarship and giving it all in their comments; Michael Chase, Simon Fortier and Coralie Seizilles de Mazanco for their help in translating certain articles from French; Carl O'Brien for translating Jens Halfwassen's chapter from German with the assistance of Thomas Arnold and Tolga Ratzsch; Marcaline Boyd and Amanda Richard for their editorial assistance; Steven Gerrard and the production team at Acumen for their vision, and patience, at every stage of the project; Tony Bruce and the production team at Routledge for their wholehearted welcome of the book into their Handbooks series; the Department of Classics and the Program in the History and Philosophy of Science at Florida State University; the Department of Philosophy at Uppsala University; the Alexander von Humboldt Foundation; Riksbankens Jubileumsfond, the Swedish Foundation for Humanities and Social Sciences, and its "Understanding Agency" Programme; the Florida State University Council on Research and Creativity; C. H. Beck for allowing here the appearance of an English translation of a chapter from Halfwassen (2004); University of Laval Press for allowing the appearance of a revised version of Finamore (2009); and University of London Press for allowing the appearance of an updated version of a chapter from Sorabji (2010). We are most in debt to the forgiving understanding of our families. But none of this would have been possible without a friendship that knows no limits and no borders, from the long Finnish summer days of Mikkeli to the cosy coffee houses of stormy Cardiff.

Pauliina Remes and Svetla Slaveva-Griffin

Abbreviations

This list includes only the standard abbreviations of main reference sources. For the full names of abbreviated individual titles, see "Authors and Works" in H. G. Liddell and R. Scott, *A Greek–English Lexicon*, with a revised supplement (Oxford, 1996) xvi–xxxviii, and L. P. Gerson, *The Cambridge History of Philosophy in Late Antiquity* (Cambridge, 2010) vol. 2: 966–82.

CAG H. Diels (ed.) 1882–1909. *Commentaria in Aristotelem Graeca*. Berlin: Reimer.

CHLGEMP A. H. Armstrong (ed.) 1967. *The Cambridge History of Later Greek and Early Medieval Philosophy*. Cambridge: Cambridge University Press.

CHPLA L. P. Gerson (ed.) 2010. *The Cambridge History of Philosophy in Late Antiquity*, 2 vols. Cambridge: Cambridge University Press.

CMG 1908–. *Corpus Medicorum Graecorum*.

CPF F. Adorno *et al.* (eds) 1995. *Corpus dei papiri filosofici greci e latini* III: Commentari. Florence: Olschki.

DK H. Diels & W. Kranz (eds) 1951–2. *Die Fragmente der Vorsokratiker*, 6th edn, 3 vols. Berlin: Weidmann.

DPA R. Goulet (ed.) 1989–2012. *Dictionnaire des philosophes antiques*, 5 vols & 1 suppl. to date. Paris: CNRS.

ET Proclus, *Elementatio theologica* = *Institutio theologica* = *Elements of Theology*.

NHC The Nag Hammadi Codices.

QAM Galen, *Quod animi mores corporis temperamenta sequuntur*. In I. Mueller (ed.) 1891. *Claudii Galeni Pergameni Scripta Minora*, Vol. 2. Leipzig: Teubner. Also Kühn, vol. 4, 767–822.

RE A. Pauly, G. Wissowa, W. Kroll, K. Witte, K. Mittelhaus & K. Ziegler (eds) 1894–1978. *Real-Encyclopädie der classischen Altertumswissenschaft*. Stuttgart: Metzler & Druckenmüller.

SVF H. von Arnim (ed.) 1903–5. *Stoicorum Veterum Fragmenta*, 4 vols. Stuttgart: Teubner.

Introduction: Neoplatonism today

Pauliina Remes and Svetla Slaveva-Griffin

In this day and age putting together a volume such as *The Routledge Handbook of Neoplatonism* is a celebratory event even when the publishers' catalogues are laden with state-of-the-art companions, guides and histories in every field. In the case of Neoplatonism, the appearance of such a volume is momentous as a "rite of passage" acknowledging that the discipline of late ancient philosophy has reached its full maturity. What, then, one may ask, is so timely and attractive in the study of Neoplatonism today?

The fates of Neoplatonism have changed in the past two decades. It has come out from the cupboard of intellectual oddities to become the fastest growing area of research in ancient philosophy. This new-found interest has yielded fruitful results for the understanding not only of Neoplatonism itself but also of the cultural vitality of ancient philosophy in late antiquity. In the constantly changing, fractured, world of intellectual and ideological allegiance in the period from the third to the sixth century CE, Neoplatonism was a stabilizing factor, of a kind, the unity and completeness of which cannot be underestimated. Developing a system that builds the impermanent physical reality, in even more impermanent historical times, into a self-sustained whole of cascading causal principles made Neoplatonism an enduring philosophical force. The scholarly attempt to grasp this system better, with its complexity and resilience, various interpretations and unfoldings, has turned Neoplatonic studies into a success story today.

The first steps of Neoplatonic research were naturally constrained by the intellectual circumstances in which Neoplatonic philosophy grew in the shadow of its two Classical predecessors – Platonism and Aristotelianism. From the point of view of scholarship narrowly concentrated on the *floruit* of Greek ancient philosophy in Athens in the late fifth and fourth centuries BCE, Neoplatonism can be easily seen as the unwanted stepchild of this period of Classical ancient philosophy which earnestly but inanely tries to dovetail with its illustrious ancestry. This point of view has for some time now been challenged by an ever-growing interest in the post-Classical period of ancient thought, with late ancient thinkers as the most recent area of exploration. Within Neoplatonic scholarship, the pioneering efforts sent a sustained series of intellectual waves throughout the twentieth century which incited translations, rethought interpretations, and charted new territories for future research.[1] Thanks to the avalanching success of these efforts today we understand better the philosophical phenomenon of Neoplatonism: its sources, overarching simplicity, internal complexity, methodologies, and interrelations with every corner of knowledge. Neoplatonism, comprehensively understood, can no longer be dismissed as an *in-vitro* offspring of Platonism, which attempts to work out the quirks of Middle Platonism, sprinkled with (anti)-Peripatetic zest and a few smears of Neopythagoreanism, Stoicism and, not to forget, religious mysticism. From an idiosyncratic and peripheral aftermath of Plato's philosophy, Neoplatonism grew to establish itself as the foremost philosophical venue of late antiquity.

There are three directions of research that have contributed most to the success of Neoplatonic studies in the twenty-first century. First, contemporary research seeks to unravel the psychological, ethical and political consequences of metaphysics, the heart of hearts of Neoplatonic philosophy. While research of metaphysical themes remains the backbone of scholarly work, more and more studies are interested in bridging the gap between ontology and other areas of philosophizing. This is directly connected to the second feature of present research, namely the rising attention to how the Neoplatonists understood the so-called sensible realm. Areas such as politics and natural philosophy that were previously considered neglected by these thinkers have become insurgent and vibrant today. Metaphysics continues to play a key role in these studies, but the centre of attention has shifted, from merely revealing the finesse of the Neoplatonic ontological hierarchy for its own sake to understanding the inherent interconnectedness of all parts of the philosophical system, including metaphysics. The emerging picture is thus more balanced as well as more relevant for human concerns.

Besides the more practical and this-worldly emphasis, recent research is marked, thirdly, by the substantial advance of both historical and philosophical interpretations. Historically, Neoplatonism is now treated as a continuation of the Classical and Hellenistic heritage rather than an introspective curiosity from late antiquity the main outcome of which is the conceptual firmament of Christian ideology. The picture of the relationship of Neoplatonism with other schools of thought, both philosophical and religious, is rapidly becoming more concrete. The philosophical purport of this is to see, for example, Neoplatonic metaphysical hierarchy – the proliferation of entities as well as levels – as a series of attempts to address philosophical problems detected or left behind by earlier thinkers such as Parmenides, Plato, Aristotle and the Stoics. In the same vein, the study of the relationship between metaphysics and theology or metaphysics and mathematics – to give just two pairs of examples among many – has outgrown the limitations of scepticism to reveal a sound philosophically based communication. Thereby the new research in metaphysics, mathematics and theology has become more and more problem-oriented rather than strictly descriptive. As a result, the writing of a commentary on a single work has been supplemented by the analytical explication of a particular problem or a concept, sometimes within a single author, at others across time and divergent views.

Before discussing, briefly, some particularities of Neoplatonism as currently understood, a few methodological points about both the term and the object of research it grasps are in order. As is well known today, the term "Neoplatonism" captures something less than a unified phenomenon in the history of philosophy, and comes with its own historical baggage. The first of these problems, the impossibility of marking the chronological bound-aries of the school, will be discussed in the subsequent section introductions, where, par-ticularly in the context of Parts I and VII, we explicate our take on the boundaries – or the lack thereof – regarding the philosophical movement known as Neoplatonism. Here we shall limit ourselves to contending that in this volume, the concept of "Neoplatonism" is explored, perhaps paradoxically, *not* primarily through Platonic or ancient means; that is, by searching one definition or essence behind its different permutations in various thinkers, contexts and centuries. Rather, our approach is closer to Wittgenstein's idea of family resemblance; that is, that a term's usages should be followed through "a complicated network of similarities, overlapping and criss-crossing" (Wittgenstein 1953: 66). When asked to author a contribution to a volume entitled *Handbook of Neoplatonism*, scholars know, in a pre-theoretical manner, what is meant by this request. They are efficient users of the term "Neoplatonism", confident in conveying shared meanings by using it them-selves. But shared meanings are hardly entirely fixed: in the articles submitted for this volume, for instance, the core elements of this movement and philosophy were sometimes understood differently, and opinions diverge as to what, exactly, counts as Neoplatonic. From the methodologies applied to the ancient sources to the understanding of their core motivation – social, spiritual or intellectual – the volume offers a multitude of diverse voices. Yet it cannot be denied that the contributions do paint, in their separate ways, a picture of something singular, albeit perhaps not paradigmatically so. It is our hope that this wealth of approaches is the best vehicle in charting the meaning and content of the term "Neoplatonism", and our only regret is the number of superb scholars, interesting approaches and research results that, for reasons of extension, did not make their way into the volume.

When it comes to the usage of the term "Neoplatonism" itself, it is here that the com-parison with the Wittgensteinian idea of "family resemblance" is challenged. The problem with the term is, arguably, today's blind adoption of it from a historical usage that we no longer recognize, much less agree with. The term was coined in the eighteenth-century German scholarship, where its history seems to be bound to the understanding of its rela-tionship to Middle Platonism. According to recent research, the division between Middle and Neo-Platonism was cemented by Joseph Brucker (in *Historia Critica Philosophiae*, 1742–67), who used the term to create a juxtaposition, where the former was seen as a genuine form of Platonism, whereas the latter played the role of a villain, representing a distorted or deteriorated interpretation of Plato (see Catana 2013). The following problem now arises: if we are to follow the different usages of the term all the way to its origins, is all resemblance and similarity thereby lost? And worse still, have we adopted, ahistori-cally, a tainted term, created for a quite different context, and unhappily for a purpose that challenges and mocks the very object to which it refers? For these kinds of reasons, the term is not used in the by now authoritative collection on late ancient philosophy, *The Cambridge History of Philosophy in Late Antiquity* (2010). The editor, L. P. Gerson, argues for this choice as follows (we shall provide a lengthy quote to be able to explicate in detail our own choice to retain this very term):

> Unfortunately, in the eighteenth-century the label was intended mostly as pejo-rative, and that situation has not changed much even today. It was assumed that "Neoplatonism" represented a muddying of the purest Hellenic stream. … We refer

throughout to "Platonism" or "late Platonism", or "Christian Platonism" when discussing Plotinus, his successors and those Christian thinkers who were in one way or another shaped by the dominant tradition in ancient philosophy. In doing so, we make no presumptions about fidelity or lack thereof to Plato's own philosophy. It is enough, at least initially, to recognize that there were varieties of Platonism, just as there were varieties of Christianity in our period, and varieties of various philosophical movements in earlier centuries.   (2010: vol. 1, 1–10, at 3)

Gerson's methodological points are forceful and have already turned out to be influential. When this *Handbook* and its title were conceived, we could not foresee that the field would advance so rapidly that by the time of publication we would be put in a position to defend not only the original title of the volume but the name of the field itself. And while we find this kind of development most exciting and reassuring in the longevity of our field, why are we, as editors, not simply adopting Gerson's well-thought and -argued stance, and choose to persist in our use of the term? The reasons can be divided into (i) linguistic, (ii) pragmatic, and (iii) interpretative. Let us comment on each in turn. (i) Is an originally pejorative term predetermined to retain its pejorative associations through history? Evidently not. A number of Finnish village names originate from once foul terms, often connected to female anatomy. The original connotation being lost, they are used with pride by the inhabitants of these villages. In our view, Neoplatonism has for some time undergone a similar ameliorative process. Few know that the prefix "Neo-" of the term once got its force from the juxtaposition with Middle Platonism. People use it, rather, merely to denote a new kind of interpretation of Platonism that emerged in Alexandria in the third century CE, partly from elements that were available in the intellectual and religious climate of the time, and partly directly connected to the historical Plato or his writings. We believe that abundant first-rate scholarship on late ancient philosophy, with Gerson's double volume as a paradigmatic example, is the best way to erase the last vestiges of the once pejorative meaning of the term. (ii) For pragmatic reasons, "Platonism" and even "late Platonism" seem deficient when compared with Neoplatonism. The term "Platonism" seems simply too wide, lending itself to a variety of usages that are for our purposes potentially misleading. Even "late Platonism" raises the question of how late exactly the topic under study is. While Gerson sets out to describe the whole of late ancient philosophizing and its relationship to Christian philosophy, we limit ourselves, in the *Handbook*, to one school of thought – or better, one movement, scriptural community, like-minded ways of doing philosophy. To be able to distinguish this branch from other branches of Platonism, be they earlier or later, is vital for the undertaking of this collection. Our object is the interpretation of Plato that gets its first full expression in the *Enneads* of Plotinus in the third century CE and continues in such central figures as Porphyry, Iamblichus, Proclus and many others.

The pragmatic worry is connected to (iii) an interpretative view already implicitly expressed above. We believe it is still philosophically valuable and perhaps also possible to try to distinguish Neoplatonism from other kinds of Platonism. That is, we do believe that the term on the cover of the book captures a phenomenon. Whether there is a true unity holding together different thinkers under the term "Neoplatonism", and whether this unity could be something stronger than a family resemblance, and described through a list of shared background assumptions, convictions or doctrines, is an interesting question. In a highly useful article, Gerson himself has given such a list for "Platonism": (i) the understanding of metaphysics as a hierarchy of intelligible and sensible layers of which the higher is the explanatory, as well as the better and more ontologically powerful; (ii) the top-down explanatory approach, in which the orientation of investigation is predominantly vertical, not horizontal; (iii) a commitment to the psychological as an irreducible explanatory category, and the connected dogma of the immortality and eternity of the soul. Further, all or at least most Platonists share the idea of (iv) cosmic unity and its explanatory role in everything, including personal happiness (Gerson 2005a). As a particular branch of Platonism, Neoplatonism should contain all these features, but be open for a more detailed description, identifying it as one subset of "Platonism". In general expositions, particularly Neoplatonic features are often identified as the following: further stratification of the explanatory intelligible realm above the sensible or physical realm; the idea that soul uniquely mirrors this stratification in its own nature and yet is capable of transgressing the limits of this stratification; a commitment to an absolutely unified source and origin of this stratified order, the One. To argue, however, for this or some other exhaustive list is not what we set out to do in this volume. With this list as a guiding but not terminating map, the reader is advised to read, absorb, and crisscross the chapters themselves.

With the above case in point, Neoplatonism today has reached a level of conceptual maturity from which it can reflect upon itself. The understanding of Neoplatonic thought has advanced so far as to allow and foster the critical re-examination not only of its vast accumulation of data but also its definitions, terminologies, methodologies, and internal and external relations. One distinguishing characteristic which exposes Neoplatonism as a particularly systematic, or holistic, way of thinking is that it operates within a closed system of principles, the full interrelations and explanatory possibilities of which are emerging, as you read this, in research. The newly inspired as well as the seasoned expert of late ancient philosophy will equally welcome the shift from the static and fractured presentation of the Neoplatonic worldview as a frozen slice through three vertically organized *hypostases* into a dynamic whole of interrelated ontological processes. This "animated" understanding of the Neoplatonic structure of the universe as a sequential causal proliferation of underlying principles of reality – from the One as an ultimate source of existence, which is beyond existence itself, to the imprint of a paradigmatic intelligible reality onto the physical realm at the level of the soul – grasps something that could be defined as an essential feature of Neoplatonism, its systemic self-sustainability.

The implications of this systematicity for pursuing different research questions are significant. Since Neoplatonism has holistically thought out its principles, it does not offer compartmentalized "chopped-up" kinds of knowledge concerning individual sciences but presupposes the systematic application of the same conceptual framework to all sciences. As a result, Neoplatonic studies do not call for an inter-disciplinary but an all-disciplinary perspective. This kind of uniformity merges the lines between Neoplatonism as philosophy and the other spheres of knowledge. The dynamic understanding of the Neoplatonic structure of reality has naturally carried over to a similarly dynamic and integrative understanding of all spheres of knowledge. The static division of Neoplatonic metaphysics, psychology, epistemology, physics, ethics and aesthetics has given way, at least among the majority of researchers, to a dynamic approach in which the specific parameters of the individual areas are understood as dependent on all elements of the philosophical system as a whole. We have also striven to follow this approach in the present collection, as will be explained in greater detail below. While we have still chosen to adapt some thematical division for the sake of organizational clarity, a closer look at it will discern its inherent fluidity.

On one hand, this cohesiveness has allowed us to chart, with precision, the major signposts of the conceptual territory of Neoplatonism. But at the same time, there is always a danger that it obscures the understanding of their particulars and ends repeating its central structural solutions regardless of the phenomena under investigation. In relation to this integrative approach, a future line of research is to assess how Neoplatonism pervades all spheres of knowledge and whether it forces its systematicity on them by compressing or comprising their particular essence.

The form of methodological sustainability found in Neoplatonism is distinct in comparison to other ancient philosophical models, and it may ultimately be responsible for the particularly robust kind of aftermath Neoplatonism has incited. Its systematic unity has the explanatory power either to absorb or to deflect external influence. The effectiveness of this power is best illustrated by the fact that Neoplatonism, we conjecture, is often either rejected wholesale by other systems or absorbed, if not as a whole, nonetheless more profoundly than most other philosophical systems. This unity seems to be the doctrinal armour with which it pervades the philosophical foundation of Christianity, for an example, and repels the conceptual advances of Gnosticism, for a counter-example. Whether Neoplatonism is truly a philosophical approach marked by particular difficulty in which any given part or idea can be separated from the system as a whole remains to be seen.

Neoplatonism favours a top-down approach for explicating reality as a sequence of causal ontological processes originating from an absolute hyper-intelligible starting point and dissipating into indefinite but not infinite physical multiplicity. Despite the ontological imperfection of the sensible realm and human nature, as its principal investigator, this top-down organization of reality can be substantiated only if the bottom can receive and thereby reflect higher ontological principles. This notion imports more than a hint of a bottom-up approach into how Neoplatonists themselves thought learning and knowledge-acquisition work. For Plotinus (*Enn.* I.3[20].1–2), the method which takes the human soul up necessarily starts from the realm of sense. For all those who are not yet ready philosophers, sensible beauties, proportions and harmonies provide a gateway to the true principles of reality behind them. With proper guidance, they can gradually progress from what is more concrete and particular to what is more abstract and general. The education of the advanced student, a philosopher with a "winged" soul, consolidates this upward movement by studying mathematics and finally dialectics (*Enn.* I.3[20].3). Dialectics itself proceeds through inspecting, dividing and collecting species and genera, presumably starting by working on their sensible exemplars, as Plato teaches in the *Sophist* and elsewhere, until it arrives in the understanding of correct divisions and their interrelations (*Enn.* I.3[20].4).[2]

This fully fledged universal dialectics, no longer dependent upon sensible order or particulars, then provides, as its next phase, the principles for the improved, enlightened study of that very same sensible realm, both nature and human beings, as well as their best possible life. The study of the sensible realm is the turning point in which the ontological process of descent reverts its direction upwards to its intelligible source. Existence then is a self-enclosed cycle in which the top-down proliferation of reality needs a bottom-up introspection. The philosopher's task is to penetrate and understand the top-down and bottom-up sides of the cycle, as the image on the cover implies. The symbolism of George Frederic Watts' *After the Deluge: The 41st Day* (1885–6) captures the most powerful motifs in this holistic understanding and still leaves room for the imagination to roam. The relation between the large fiery concentric circle looming large over the raw simplicity of physical matter, painted in progressively darker shades of green and brown, reveals its true meaning only after a careful consideration of the painting and its title. "After the Deluge", when all man-made clutter is wiped out, the true interconnected structure of the universe is revealed. In this new-found simplicity, there is no top-down without the bottom-up and vice versa.

There is one last general point we need to make before presenting the thematic organization of the *Handbook*. Alfred North Whitehead's famous quip that the Western philosophical tradition "consists of a series of footnotes to Plato" has worn out its lustre today and needs to be toned down (Whitehead 1979: 39). This is nowhere more evident than in the study of Neoplatonism, the very field which founds its identity upon the study of Plato. It is no exaggeration, unlike Whitehead's pronouncement, if we define the Neoplatonists as exegetes of Plato. Here it should suffice to mention Plotinus' self-reflection: "that these statements of ours are not new; they do not belong to the present time, but were made long ago, not explicitly, and what we have said in this discussion has been an interpretation of them, relying on Plato's own writings for evidence that these views are ancient" (*Enn.* V.1[10].8.10–14).[3]

Plato himself shares the same sentiment when he looks back to Pythagoras and even Prometheus to trace the origin of what he deems the fundamental question of philosophy, the relation between one and many (*Phlb.* 16c5–10). The ancient philosophers' conscientious styling of an incessant chain of authority, to which they belong, is their way of articulating the understanding that conceptual principles and even systems, explaining reality, do not come *ex nihilo*, from a vacuum of intellectual interaction. This is simply impossible and perhaps this, ultimately, is the silver lining of Whitehead's statement. But the question for any subsequent philosophical school is what to do with the tradition it aligns itself with and how to do it.

If Pythagoras is Plato's Homer, Plato is the Neoplatonists'. As with Homer, with Plato there is a large body of text inviting myriad ways of interpretation. The first exegetical task is formal; that is, it requires "fixing" the text(s), understanding their literary genre (as is most evident in Proclus' commentaries on the Platonic dialogues) and organizing them in some didactically or philosophically conducive way (*curriculum*). The latter gives rise to what we may call "purple" Platonic dialogues: the *Parmenides* for metaphysics, the *Timaeus* for physics, the *Republic*, the *Phaedrus* and the *Phaedo* for psychology and ethics. In his programmatic article "Plotinus at Work on Platonism", Dillon argues that Plotinus is "neither the faithful Platonist that he saw himself as being, nor yet the systematic philosopher that he has been presented as being by most modern authorities on him", but "a thinker with an open-minded, 'aporetic' approach to philosophy" (Dillon 1992b: 189). Each chapter in the *Handbook*, in its own way, shows that Dillon's thesis applies to all Neoplatonists, not only to Plotinus.

The thematic organization of the *Handbook* follows, in its own manner, the up-and-down direction of Plotinus' dialectics. Parts I and II, dealing with factual matters of sources, physical facilities, external interactions, methods and style of exegesis, build the ground from which Neoplatonism reaches the height of its philosophic system. The texts and archaeological remains are the two material sources from which our understanding of Neoplatonism must begin. Part III, devoted to metaphysics, tackles the core of the Neoplatonic system, the detailed articulation of which has long been the primary focus of scholarly attention. It further presents a genuine point of departure from which the Neoplatonic top-down understanding of reality unfolds sequentially through the intelligible realm and then the soul as presented in Parts IV and V respectively. Parts VI and VII continue to unfold: Part VI shows how the ethical human realm is guided by and dependent upon the very same causal and intelligible principles. It further completes a full circle by explicating how Neoplatonic ethics, political theory and aesthetics express and deal with the turning points for the upward journey back to the ontological top. This thematical organization places metaphysics, in a typically Plotinian fashion, in its centre upon which the other branches of philosophy depend. Plotinus' own understanding of the role of dialectics, then, brings together the higher and lower echelons of reality into a dynamic self-sustainable system. Thus we hope to bring into action the benefits of the new, improved understanding of Neoplatonism as an organically developed whole of interrelated ontological entities and processes. Part VII, featuring the main directions of Neoplatonic legacy, concludes the volume with another kind of unfolding, one through time, in history. This part is more conventional and only tangentially pertains to the broadly understood dialectical undertaking, but it is no less necessary. As its reader will quickly see, it effortlessly continues and at times even more boldly reinforces the same conceptual tensions the mainstream Neoplatonism so often grappled with.

Inspired by and indebted to the distinguished accomplishment of the comprehensively structured, multi-authored collections of *The Cambridge History of Later Greek and Early Mediaeval Philosophy*, edited by A. H. Armstrong (1967), its successor, the two-volume *Cambridge History of Philosophy in Late Antiquity*, edited by L. P. Gerson (2010), and *The Cambridge Companion to Plotinus*, edited by L. P. Gerson (1996), we have striven for continuity but also for distinction. The *Handbook* relies on the above-mentioned *Histories* to provide (a) the exhaustive, from A to Z, treatment of the historical and intellectual context of Neoplatonism, and (b) the individual profiles and import of its representatives and developments. For lack of space, we cannot strive, unfortunately, for a comparable coverage of different ancient thinkers and present-day scholars. The *Handbook* aims to complement the individual presentations in the two *Cambridge Histories* by examining concepts and themes across authors as well as philosophical or ideological systems.

Within each part, some articles diachronically trace a particular conceptual development or an argument, others synchronically treat a topic in a certain author or a philosophical group. As the description of the thematic designation of Parts III–IV above makes clear, this seemingly static compartmentalization does not strictly follow the canonic subdivision of the different philosophical branches. We have deemed it more suitable for presenting the essence of our subject and more beneficial for the reader to retain some of the thematically confluent authenticity of Neoplatonic thought. Pulling apart concerns that from our perceptive are either metaphysical, epistemological or belong to the philosophy of mind, for instance, gives structure and clarity to a handbook, but it does entail an element of force: the ancient, and particularly the Platonic way of treating philosophical dilemmas is not, of course, to divide the concerned areas in such a straightforward manner. On the contrary, one of the most notable features of Neoplatonic thought is the ease with which many of these themes are symbiotically discussed. Inevitably some themes will resist any simple categorization: the human is also the cosmic, the ethical the metaphysical, and vice versa. In other cases, the most recent interpretative advances have directed our designation of a particular area of thought. To this end, while Part III is conventionally titled "metaphysics", Part V is unconventionally titled "nature" – instead of "physics" – in commensuration with the impact the newest directions of research on the Neoplatonic views of the physical realm have commanded, as explained in the sectional introduction to that part.

The need for a thematically flexible organization is most evident in Part IV in which we found it impossible – and detrimental for the reader – to distinguish between topics of psychology, epistemology, language and cognition. For reasons of breadth and depth, the thematical organization of the *Handbook* has notably expanded the sections on sources and style (respectively Parts I and II) in comparison, for example, to the *Cambridge Companion to Plotinus* or many of the shorter introductions to the field. For the same reasons, the section on the legacy of Neoplatonic thought (Part VII) is more syncretic since these topics have been amply treated in the two *Cambridge Histories* mentioned above and elsewhere in more chronologically appropriate scholarly venues. Here we have limited our selection to highlighting three particular cases of Neoplatonic influence on the theological foundation of Christianity (West and East), Islam, and Judaism in step with the latest trends in their respective fields.

The collection comprises, besides the thirty-three articles themselves, sectional introductions for each part. We refer the reader interested to learn which articles are included in each part and how they hang together to these shorter but more detailed introductions. They are designed to explain the rationale, aims and main themes of each part and to provide hands-on, topical guidance for their individual content and particularities requiring special consideration. The *Handbook*, however, as a whole is more than the sum of its parts and it is the synergy created by all parts and chapters that, at least we hope, will give it a life and meaning of its own.

If we were asked to put together a collection of this kind, say, fifty years ago, the selection of topics and authors would have been, if not easy, pretty straightforward: you gather nearly everyone whose work has made an impact in the field. You then look at what they can do, what the emphasis of their work is, and maybe supplement that initial inventory with one or two pieces on places where you see true *lacunae* by trying to commission some entirely novel work or, if push comes to shove, by writing the missing bits yourself, in less than ambitious terms. Our situation was very different. For most sections, there was already a formidable number of scholars and views to choose from, some obvious, others with equal potential and originality. Besides the subconscious yet obvious reasons that always guide one's choices, we did consciously attempt to find scholars with fresh takes on a given topic, and, if possible, the latest contribution on a given subject. Their views build, of course, on those of their predecessors and contemporaries, importing to the volume the work of the whole Neoplatonic scholarly community. Further, we aspired to comprehensiveness not merely in terms of thematic coverage, but, more importantly, in terms of different styles, methodologies and scholarly voices. It goes without saying that we do not share all views aired in the volume but we take pride in providing a forum from which these views will take up a life of their own and will instigate new scholarly dialogues in the times to come. In reality, we did not ask for summaries of research. Instead we offered an opportunity to circulate new ideas or to defend a recently opposed view, or we opened a possibility of seeing one's more detailed work in a larger context. The extent to which we are grateful to the contributors cannot be underlined nearly enough: they have done what we asked and more.

The Routledge Handbook of Neoplatonism, as suggested by its title, is designed to be of use to both the newly inspired graduate or postgraduate who is still looking for the forest after seeing the trees or looking for the trees after seeing the forest, as well as for the expert who is interested to find in one place state-of-the-art discussions, diversity of views, sources for reference, and perhaps even kernels of new ideas. Having said that, it should be acknowledged that certain chapters, especially in the parts on metaphysics, psychology and epistemology, presuppose, more heavily than others, previous familiarity with the material. This is not a self-study guide to what Neoplatonism is but an edifice of what Neoplatonic studies are today. As hinted earlier in this introduction, the collection is for everyone who is interested in Neoplatonism, ancient philosophy and the rich intellectual history of late antiquity.

Here are some practical notes about how to use the volume and where to find more information, if needed. All dates in the *Handbook* are in the Common Era (CE) unless otherwise noted. The works of ancient authors are abbreviated, when available, according to the list of "Authors and Works" in H. G. Liddell and R. Scott, *A Greek–English Lexicon*, with a revised supplement (Oxford 1996), xvi–xxxviii. A more up-to-date list of primary sources in ancient philosophy, also organized by author, can be found in L. P. Gerson, *The Cambridge History of Philosophy in Late Antiquity* (Cambridge: Cambridge University Press, 2010) vol. 2, Appendix. The Greek terms are transliterated in the main body of text throughout the volume, with the exception of Chapter 9 where the original Greek is retained to facilitate the subject matter. Otherwise quotations from Greek are limited to the footnotes. The contributors have used major text-critical editions and translations, when available. The bibliographies for each chapter are compiled into one and placed at the end of the volume, rather than at the end of each chapter, not so much for reasons of economy of space, but with the intent to provide a somewhat comprehensive, although not all-inclusive, survey of Neoplatonic scholarship. Finally, we should clarify that, in an attempt to make the references to Plotinus' *Enneades* user-friendly for the reader familiar either with the chronological arrangement of the treatises or with Porphyry's (*Plot.* 4–6), we have adopted the common practice to list the chronological order of a treatise in brackets, immediately after the number of its position in Porphyry's arrangement. For example, *Enn.* I.1[53].1.1–2, from left to right, means *First Ennead* (I), treatise number one (1) in Porphyry's arrangement, the fifty-third treatise (53) in the chronological order, chapter one (1), lines one to two (1–2).[4]

NOTES

1. To name just a few of the most influential scholars: Armstrong, Beierwaltes, Bréhier, Cilento, Harder, Henry, Igal, MacKenna, Page, Rist, Schwyzer.
2. *Sph.* 253c–d; *R.* 531c–535a; *Phdr.* 265d–266a.
3. Armstrong's translation (1966–88: vol. 5, 41); Greek text according to Henry & Schwyzer (1964–82).
4. For more information on the history of the method of reference to Plotinus' *Enneades*, see Tarrant, below, in Chapter 2, note 16 (p. 28).

I

(Re)sources, instruction and interaction

INTRODUCTION

This part of the *Handbook* strives to reconstruct the *modus operandi* of Neoplatonism first as a philosophical school, with established curricula, forms of instruction and facilities, and second as a flagship philosophical system, which continuously interacts with the diverse intellectual and ideological environment of late antiquity. This overarching task is achieved by three tributary goals, consecutively centred on the practical questions of what Neoplatonists read, how and where they pursued philosophy, with what other philosophical or religious lines of thought they engaged and to what extent. The answers to each question, of course, cannot be exhausted on the pages of the individual chapters. Instead, the chapters severally outline the major framework and the most recent advances of their subject. In some cases, such as Tarrant's "Platonist curricula and their influence" (Chapter 2) and Reydams-Schils and Ferrari's "Middle Platonism and its relation to Stoicism and the Peripatetic tradition" (Chapter 4), they have done so through synthesis; in others, such as the interactions of Neoplatonism with Gnosticism in Turner's "Plotinus and the Gnostics: opposed heirs of Plato" (Chapter 5) and Indian thought in Adluri's "Plotinus and the Orient: *aoristos dyas*" (Chapter 6), through ample textual evidence.

The first question concerns the sources the Neoplatonists used to develop and establish their curricula. They were certainly conscious of the challenge of gathering, organizing and perusing centuries-old texts, which hark back to the "divine" Pythagoras, culminate in the Platonic dialogues and continuously undergo numerous exegetical permutations. But the Neoplatonists are not historians of philosophy, exclusively concerned with the preservation of the Platonic originals. Nor are they avid but uncritical readers. They are philosophers proper for whom doing philosophy entails both studying philosophy and teaching philosophy. The Neoplatonists' sources for studying the Platonic dialogues became their resources for doing philosophy. The exegetical and instructional aspects of their intellectual enterprise are entrenched in the organization of Neoplatonic curricula, tailored to the changing tastes of their times and their proponents. Thus we can distinguish specific traits in the curriculum under Plotinus, Porphyry, Iamblichus, Ammonius and Olympiodorus. It also inevitably includes a wide range of non-Platonic texts, from Aristotle and the Neopythagoreans to the Orphic sacred texts and the *Chaldaean Oracles*.

In addition to carefully designed Neoplatonic curricula, the innate relation between exegesis and instruction also gives rise to different philosophical discourses, some of which, like the commentaries, have taken the form of a separate literary genre. The Neoplatonists' mode of expression is rich and versatile, persistently trying to close the gap between word and idea, form and content. To this end, we have deemed it important to devote a separate section – Part II – to the most characteristic genres and styles of Neoplatonic literature.

The second question concerns the place and form of the Neoplatonists' actual instruction and philosophical activities. Until recently, Porphyry's *Life of Plotinus* and Marinus' *Life of Proclus* have been our sole sources for glimpsing the life of the Neoplatonic schools in Rome and Athens. As Sorabji's "The Alexandrian classrooms excavated and sixth-century philosophy teaching" (Chapter 3) presents, recent archaeological excavations at Alexandria have allowed us to conjoin text with mortar in creating a more realistic, even visual, picture of some physical details of Neoplatonic education. Although the "House of Proclus" on the Athenian Agora will most likely always remain a mystery, the twelve lecture halls of Alexandria, dating to the period between the late fifth and the sixth century, offer a sumptuous example for how much the study of Neoplatonism can benefit from the unexpected corner of material culture.

Third, as students and intellectual heirs of Plato, the Neoplatonists did not see themselves as confined in a vacuum. As we shall see throughout the *Handbook*, they were in a constant dialogue with diverse and oftentimes opposing philosophical and ideological trends. Neoplatonism is a dynamic, outspoken interlocutor, possessing both the flexibility and the resilience to absorb, co-opt, assess or deflect philosophical influences from both its Middle Platonic and Neopythagorean predecessors and from the anti-Platonic strongholds of the Peripatetics, Epicureans and, especially, the Stoics.

If the tenacity with which Neoplatonism establishes itself as a leading school in the complex philosophical environment of late antiquity seems inner-disciplinary and, in this sense, more narrow, its relation with the burgeoning religious trends of its time involves both outspoken refutation, in the case of Gnosticism and Christianity, and impassioned affiliation, in the case of the *Chaldaean Oracles* and other sacred texts. The expanse of this area of Neoplatonic studies and its substantial overlap with topics in metaphysics, psychology and legacy compelled us to highlight only the two sub-areas of Gnosticism and Indian thought, the notable advances of which have forced us to re-evaluate our previous understanding and have opened major areas of research. "Plotinus and the Gnostics: opposed heirs of Plato" (Chapter 5) shows that behind the open animosity between Plotinus and the Gnostics, there are subtle threads of conceptual cooperation that deserve a second look (the latest instalment is Narbonne 2011a). Similarly, our attempts to look farther east, past the birthplace of the *Chaldaean Oracles*, to the ever-elusive "Orient" have been persistent but also marginalized by our preconceptions of rationality, philosophy and spirituality. Our inclination to compartmentalize different modes of thought has already required from us, in the many faces of Neoplatonism, a great deal of adaptation. But, as presented in "Plotinus and the Orient: *aoristos dyas*" (Chapter 6), we still have a much longer road to travel.[1] By editorial decision, the length of the last two chapters is expanded in order to increase the visibility and accessibility of otherwise less known material to the general readership of the volume.

NOTE

1. To be fair, the inception of this road lies with the constellation of scholars in Baine Harris (1982) and continues brightly into the future with Gregorios (2002) and Adluri & Bagchee (2014).

Platonist curricula and their influence

Harold Tarrant

The philosophical texts that we study have a profound effect upon our approach to philosophy. Part of the reason for the existence of separate traditions in separate countries or separate universities is the ease with which one keeps returning to the texts that have left an earlier mark upon us, often with new insights. We tend to think of the texts that we have encountered early as being particularly important, and to have the desire to make some contribution to advancing the understanding of them. Hence today, because the vast majority of scholars have encountered the *Nicomachean Ethics* early in their study of Aristotle, this is the work that we hold to be important, the work to whose understanding we want to contribute. The "Aristotelian Ethics" means the *Nicomachean Ethics*. We may almost forget that three of its books are common to the *Eudemian Ethics*, that the other five books of that work are by no means obviously inferior, and that while it seems to lack a discussion of friendship it contains other material of some importance. As for the early *Protrepticus* and the suspect *Magna Moralia*, it is practically possible to ignore them. It is in the nature of any curriculum to open our eyes to certain things and to blind us to others, entrenching certain approaches and ensuring that the curriculum is self-perpetuating, though not inflexibly so.

The Iamblichian curriculum that dominated the later Neoplatonist schools remained virtually the same for several generations, and certainly had some influence in prompting the Neoplatonists to emphasize some facets of Plato and neglect others, seeing subtleties and ironies of certain sorts, and failing to see others. Nor did this curriculum arrive from nowhere, for it is itself the product of the mix of texts that Plotinus and Porphyry had made central to Platonist endeavours. Even in their case there had been no sharp change in direction, and many of their central Platonic texts had been the subject of commentaries in the centuries before Plotinus – commentaries being an important witness to the reading of the texts involved within philosophic schools.[1] It is therefore desirable to begin this discussion a little earlier than Neoplatonism, and to see the fortunes of the Platonic curriculum at that time.

PLATONIC TEACHING-ORDERS BEFORE PLOTINUS
AND THEIR NEOPLATONIC RECEPTION

Early in the imperial age, some two centuries before Plotinus arrived on the Roman scene, the issue of an appropriate Platonic curriculum began to be hotly debated. Philosophical texts were now becoming more widely circulated, and there was more expectation that one would be able to access large bodies of philosophical work. Philosophers who claimed to teach in a given tradition of philosophy were expected to have wide familiarity with its founder's works, and the ability to communicate the meaning of those works to those who sought either a creed by which to manage their daily lives, or at least a sufficiently broad perspective on the ideas of the philosophers to impress their peers. But the more widely the texts of a given author became available the more it became necessary to develop some guidelines regarding the order in which one might encounter them. For the busier pupils it might also be necessary to identify which were the "core" works that anybody should read, and which were so insubstantial, esoteric or enigmatic that all but the devotee could leave them aside. In these circumstances arranging some of the larger philosophical corpora was regarded as worthwhile scholarly activity.

At some time in the first century BCE Andronicus of Rhodes had tried to give shape to the Aristotelian corpus, and early in the next century Tiberius Claudius Thrasyllus arranged both the Democritean and the Platonic corpora into groups of four (known as tetralogies), thirteen in the former case and nine in the latter. It is widely believed that Thrasyllus built partly on previous ideas about the arrangement of the corpus, and represented his system as partially dependent on Plato's own intentions; but he also desired to facilitate a natural reading of the corpus, since it is likely that his work had a title with a similar pattern to his work on Democritus: *That Which Precedes the Reading of Democritus' Books*.[2] The first tetralogy was intended to show the nature of the philosophic life (Diogenes Laertius 3.57), and we may infer from a newly published papyrus that the second had an epistemological purpose throughout, beginning with the *Cratylus'* study of names, proceeding to the *Theaetetus'* removal of false ideas about knowledge, and concluding with the scientific methods introduced by the *Sophist* and the *Statesman* (see Sedley 2009). We are not offered a full explanation of any remaining tetralogies in extant ancient literature, though the presence of *Laws* in the ninth and final group is in general agreement with the tendency to see a correspondence between a desirable reading order and the order in which Plato had written, since the *Laws* was known to Plutarch (*de Iside et Osiride* 370f1) and others as stemming from the end of Plato's life.[3] The concluding position of the *Epistles* is also explained by their tackling Plato's life, mirroring the emphasis of Socrates' life in the first tetralogy and in the *Euthyphro* in particular (see here again anon. *Proleg.* 25). In conformity with Plato's own special interest in how education should begin, it is clear from Diogenes' account of the corpus (3.62) that much attention had been given to the proper starting point of a Platonic education. At least eleven candidates, of whom Diogenes mentions nine, seem to have had their defenders: *Republic, Alcibiades I, Theages, Euthyphro, Clitopho, Timaeus, Phaedrus, Theaetetus* and *Apology*, with Albinus *Prologue* 4 adding *Epistles* and the anonymous *Prolegomena* (24.20–22) adding *Parmenides*. The second, third, fifth and tenth of these are not even agreed to be genuine works of Plato today, though each stands at the head of a Thrasyllan tetralogy and each seems to be in some sense introductory. We know that *Euthyphro* (followed by *Apology*) was Thrasyllus' starting point, and we know why this group was treated first.[4] *Republic* (placed first by Aristophanes of Byzantium), *Theaetetus* and *Timaeus* could easily be chosen by anybody who thought precedence should be given to politics, epistemology and physics respectively, while the choice of *Phaedrus* may be linked with the claim that it had a youthful theme and was the first Platonic dialogue to have been written – while Plato was still deciding on whether or not he should write.[5]

There is evidence that intense interest in the arrangement of the corpus continued up until the middle of the second century CE, with Dercyllides (of uncertain date, but before Theon), Theon of Smyrna (in a work about the order of Plato's works and their titles), and Albinus (*Prologue* 3–6) all contributing. Galen's collection of synopses of the dialogues also implied an order, and had begun with five dialogues whose subject was of a "logical" character.[6] Already by the time of Albinus, however, there seems to have been less conviction that a rigid order was either recoverable or educationally desirable. Persons of different ability study Plato with different levels of intensity and for different reasons. In favourable conditions a programme of choice might consist of *Alcibiades I*, *Phaedo*, *Republic* and *Timaeus* (*Prologue* 5). However, this might suggest that large swathes of the corpus have no real part to play in contemporary education. To correct this impression Albinus goes on in the following chapter (6) to outline the different roles that may be played by dialogues of different "characters", with a special emphasis, it seems, on the roles of those dialogues that do not seem intent on communicating doctrine, the so-called "investigative dialogues" (*zētētikoi dialogoi*).[7]

One might with some justification ask how it was that these pre-Plotinian developments could have a significant impact upon the Neoplatonist curriculum, but it is noticeable that the only full treatment of the Platonic curriculum of the Neoplatonists begins by going back to these earlier times. Chapter 24 of the anonymous *Prolegomena to Platonic Philosophy* begins by rejecting three early approaches, two arrangements that are based on notional dates, either dramatic date (measured against Socrates' life) or the compositional date (measured against Plato's), and the tetralogical arrangement. The arguments for Plato's having begun with the *Phaedrus* and concluded with the *Laws* are briefly given, and it is noted that those who approach the corpus from the issue of dramatic date begin with the *Parmenides* where Socrates is still a youth, and conclude with the *Theaetetus*, set at a time when Socrates had been dead for a while.[8] As for the tetralogical arrangement, the author is able to confirm that Thrasyllus had attributed groups of four to Plato himself, who was supposed to have imitated the tragic sequences presented at the Dionysia, consisting of three tragedies and a lighter piece, usually a satyr play.[9] In chapter 25 the anonymous attacks the arrangement by pointing to the absurdity of treating the final member of the tetralogies as analogous to the lighter satyr play,[10] and noting that the arrangement includes the *Epinomis*, which, it is claimed, cannot have been written by Plato. He also denies that all four dialogues of the Platonic tetralogies had a single *skopos* or target as Thrasyllus had apparently claimed,[11] and as had been the case with early tragic tetralogies.

In the light of his criticisms of these predecessors of Neoplatonism one might have expected the anonymous author to show how his own preferred arrangement avoided them, but this does not seem to be a priority. He rejects the agreed *spuria*, *Sisyphus*, *Demodocus*, *Halcyon*, *Eryxias* and *Definitions*, and from the thirty-six works of the corpus he excludes the *Epinomis* following Proclus. Again following Proclus, the *Republic* and *Laws* are excluded, not because Plato did not write them, but rather because they involve many separate *logoi* and are not written in dialogical fashion: something that also leads to the exclusion of the *Epistles*.[12] He is left with a corpus of thirty-two dialogues, but claims that there is no need for them all, contenting himself with only the twelve selected by Iamblichus. These involved a group of ten (*Alcibiades I, Gorgias, Phaedo, Cratylus, Theaetetus, Sophist, Statesman, Phaedrus, Symposium* and *Philebus*)[13] followed by the two so-called "perfect" dialogues, *Timaeus* and *Parmenides*. We shall return to Iamblichus shortly, but it should already be obvious that we have not said anything about the Platonic corpus used by Plotinus and Porphyry. There is a gap in our knowledge of the Platonic curriculum, and this requires an explanation.

THE REJECTION OF CORPUS ARRANGEMENT

The early imperial attempts to find a satisfactory arrangement of the Platonic corpus were inspired partly by the desire to interpret Plato better and with a greater degree of confidence. Hence a reading order or, given a school context, a curriculum, would have been linked with an expectation of progress in the interpretation of an author who refused to address his readers directly. That expectation was never realized, and the number of dialogues in the thirty-six-work corpus could help to confuse issues rather than clarify them. Furthermore, there was a tendency for any such collection to somehow suggest that a work like the *Clitophon* should be taken just as seriously as the *Republic*, which followed it in the eighth tetralogy of Thrasyllus, even though the latter consisted of ten books, any one of them more than three times the length of the diminutive *Clitophon*. Perhaps even worse, it tended to suggest that the *Critias* was of similar importance to the weighty and highly popular *Timaeus*. Much of the corpus was really an optional extra, and key issues of interpretation were always going to be settled on the basis of a limited number of high-profile works read in virtually any order.

Plutarch of Chaeronea, whose active life spanned the late first and early second centuries CE, showed little or no awareness of the activities of the corpus organizers, and was clearly preoccupied with just a few of the Platonic dialogues, usually those that we should designate, albeit on the basis of flawed evidence, as "middle" or "late" period. It is no accident that these are the dialogues in which Plato most obviously tries to build up what might be called a body of doctrine. If the number of parallels between the texts of Plato and Plutarch's surviving work is anything to go by,[14] then it is clear that the *Timaeus* was for him pre-eminent, followed by the *Republic, Laws, Phaedrus, Symposium, Phaedo* and *Gorgias*. Though still important, *Theaetetus, Sophist, Cratylus, Statesman* and *Philebus* were used more selectively. It may be no accident that this list includes twelve out of the fourteen dialogues of the later Neoplatonist curriculum, omitting only the first (*Alcibiades I*) and last (*Parmenides*), which had not yet come to be regarded as philosophically important.[15] Of the remaining dialogues, it is clear that *Apology* and *Meno* exercised some influence, as did the *Epistles*: these last as historical sources, not as philosophically illuminating texts.[16]

While Plutarch had shown no discernible interest in any kind of ordering of the dialogues, and seems above all to have believed in wide-ranging critical reading, Albinus, presumably following in the footsteps of his teacher Gaius, argued strongly against allowing theories about the ordering of the corpus to influence the Platonic curriculum. Though the first three chapters of his *Prologue* contain largely traditional material, chapter 4 goes on to accuse Dercyllides and Thrasyllus of wanting to impose on the dialogues an arrangement dictated by the participating characters and the particular circumstances of their lives, which, though arguably useful for other purposes, fails to settle on a starting point and order for Platonic instruction. Indeed, he claims that there is no such starting point of Platonic discourse, because it is perfect and resembles the perfect shape: a circle. And a circle has no beginning. So the nexus between any such arrangement and the Platonic curriculum is therefore broken. Even so, chapter 5 goes on to make it clear that this does not mean that we can begin anywhere. Different starting points suit different pupils, according to their natural ability, their age, their motivation, their prior knowledge, and the leisure afforded by their particular circumstances. The ideal recruit will begin with the *Alcibiades I* (now coming into prominence), continue with the *Phaedo*, and proceed to the *Republic* and the *Timaeus*.

This brief curriculum starts with the same dialogue as Iamblichus', continues with his third dialogue, and ends with his eleventh. The *Republic*, though not numbered, was one that retained a special status outside the twelve among the Neoplatonists. The reasons offered by Albinus for these four to be studied would have been intelligible to the Neoplatonists too.[17]

We may also confirm the importance of these dialogues by looking at what can be known about the existence of hermeneutical works, particularly commentaries, in early imperial times. The principal sources for these are the third part of *Corpus dei Papiri Filosofici Greci e Latini* specifically devoted to fragmentary commentaries on papyrus, and the collection of Middle Platonist testimonia and fragments published by Adriano Gioè.[18] There is a papyrus fragment from this time of a commentary of the *Alcibiades I*, whose author also refers, like the anonymous papyrus commentator on the *Theaetetus* (35.10–12), to his own commentary on the *Timaeus*. The *Theaetetus* commentator also refers to works on the *Phaedo* (yet to be encountered by the reader, 48.9–11) and the *Symposium* (70.10–12). Perhaps the least expected papyrus commentary on Plato from this period is on the *Statesman*.[19] Several of the authors in the Gioè volume wrote commentaries or at least interpretive works on the *Timaeus*, but there was also a more limited exegetical work by Plutarch and a partial commentary by Galen. We are told by Suidas of a *Commentary on the Republic* by Potamo (s.v.) and by Onosander (s.v.) at the beginning of the period, but a complete lemmatic commentary would have been a huge undertaking, and Theon's *Commentary on the Republic* (*Expos.* p. 146) may possibly have been limited to the mathematical material. Prominent passages received special attention in Plutarch's *Platonic Questions* and in Theon's *Exposition*. Dercyllides wrote on the Nuptial Number from book VIII (Proclus, *in R.* II.24–5), and on the spindle and whorls of Myth of Er (Theon, *Expos.* p. 201), a myth that was treated by several others (Proclus, *in R.* II.96.10–15). As for the *Phaedo*, several of those Platonists covered in Gioè contributed to its exegesis, particularly Harpocration, who also interpreted the *Alcibiades I* and the *Phaedrus*. We know of a *Commentary on the Gorgias* by Calvenus Taurus. Alcinous' *Handbook of Platonism* pays close attention to many passages of *Timaeus*, *Republic*, *Phaedrus* and *Phaedo* as well as a range of other dialogues, and strangely includes a miniature interpretation of the *Cratylus* (6, 160.2–34).

The combined evidence confirms that *Alcibiades I*, *Phaedo*, *Republic* and *Timaeus* were of considerable importance in the Platonist schools (perhaps in ascending order), alongside other dialogues such as *Phaedrus*, *Gorgias*, *Symposium*, *Cratylus*, *Theaetetus* and

Statesman. Only four works closely studied by the Neoplatonists are missing from this list: *Sophist, Philebus, Parmenides* and (except for a few popular passages) *Laws.* The situation changes somewhat by the time of Plotinus.

PLOTINIAN CURRICULUM

Thanks to Porphyry's *Life of Plotinus* we know quite a lot about intellectual life in Plotinus' school at Rome, but one looks in vain for an indication of what Platonic works were studied. It is almost as if the centrality of Plato was assumed to be obvious, and in chapter 16 what particularly offended among the beliefs of Plotinus' gnostic adversaries was the claim that Plato failed to penetrate to the depths of the intellectual realm. So Plato was the inspired centre of Plotinian learning, and it is therefore to the Stoic and more particularly the Aristotelian elements in Plotinus that Porphyry feels the need to draw our attention (*Plot.*14). When we hear of works being read aloud within the school, it is not the classic works of Plato or Aristotle, but those of their recent admirers. The admirers of Plato included two who are often seen rather as Pythagoreans (Numenius and his companion Cronius) as well as three who seem to have been more purely Platonists (Severus, Gaius, Atticus), but Plotinus and Porphyry regarded Plato and Pythagoras as close allies, and Pythagoreans of the period frequently regarded certain parts of the Platonic corpus as excellent evidence for Pythagorean doctrine – including most obviously Timaeus' account of the physical world and various passages that discussed the nature and immortality of the human soul. If one takes Numenius, he is most likely to be referred to as a "Platonic" in contexts involving the interpretation of Plato,[20] and it is notable that the works of these people read in Plotinus' school are referred to as *hypomnēmata*, a term regularly but not exclusively used to designate commentary-like works. If commentaries and other interpretative works on Plato and Aristotle were regularly read in the school at Rome, this would tend to confirm that the gathering shared a close knowledge of the works interpreted. Many authors read there are known to us today primarily as Platonic and Aristotelian interpreters, including Severus on the Platonist side and Alexander of Aphrodisias among the Peripatetics.

The works of Plotinus themselves, though they seldom make exegesis their primary objective, demonstrate wide familiarity with the Platonic corpus.[21] It is perhaps a frustration to some that he seems not to worry about the interpretation of whole dialogues, but fastens rather upon a limited number of important passages to which he will often refer, as if the important thing was what the passages meant for him rather than what they meant within their dialogic context. Passages tend to be drawn from the same group of dialogues as had been of principal interest in the second century, but these have now been supplemented with *Sophist, Philebus* and, above all, *Parmenides,* with important metaphysical doctrine being drawn from all three. The *Parmenides* has risen in status compared with its standing for more orthodox second-century Platonists[22] because of the belief that its final part consists not simply in logical exercises or a study of Parmenides' One, but at least five separate studies devoted to separate metaphysical orders, beginning for Plotinus with studies of the One, Intellect and Soul. Hand in hand with the rise of the *Parmenides* went the conviction that certain passages in the *Epistles,* especially *Epistle* II 312e[23] and VII 341c, expressed core Platonic doctrines.[24] The *Parmenides* joins the ranks of dialogues on which commentary-like works were written by Plotinus' time, and fragments of a commentary dealing with the first and second hypotheses survived into modern times. It is sometimes attributed to Porphyry, who along with Plotinus' supporter Amelius is known to have interpreted the work.[25]

Plotinus, however, was not the kind of figure ever likely to try to impose any kind of rigid stamp upon what was studied in his own school. The idea of some fixed curriculum leading to ultimate enlightenment was foreign to him, and it was the thinking that one did for oneself rather than the thoughts that one learned from others that counted.

THE PORPHYRIAN CONTRIBUTION

While Porphyry chose to highlight the extent of Aristotelian content in Plotinus' thought, he was himself responsible for the key place that Aristotelian logic, and particularly the *Categories*, played in the curriculum of late antiquity. From his pen there survives a commentary on the *Categories* in "catechist" style, offering answers to the student's basic questions, and the *Isagoge*, an introduction to the study of that work. He is known, however, to have written a much fuller and more scholarly commentary on the work, and it is now argued that a substantial fragment of a commentary in the Archimedes Palimpsest is indeed from the longer commentary (see Chiaradonna *et al.* 2013). Porphyry's success in guaranteeing the *Categories* in particular a permanent place in the curriculum may be judged by the fact that a great many subsequent commentaries, either on the *Categories* itself or on his own *Isagoge*, survive from subsequent authors, many from less well-known authors such as Dexippus, Elias and David. Prior to Porphyry Platonists had often engaged with Aristotle, and particularly with his logic, but many had remained hostile.

Substantial fragments of Porphyry's commentaries on Platonic works, particularly the *Timaeus*, survive, including a half-page fragment from his *Commentary on the Philebus* preserved by Simplicius that confirms that dialogue as one that had become suitable material for commentary – and hence probably for teaching within the school. There are substantial remains also of his exegetical work on Homer and a *Commentary on Ptolemy's Harmonics*, in which we see his special interest in Pythagorean musical theory. It is not difficult to see that Porphyry was a wide-ranging scholar, whose interests, including his teaching interests, were not easily constrained by artificial limits. Many of these interests may well have been inherited from his earlier teacher Longinus rather than from Plotinus, but our ignorance regarding the chronology of many of his works makes certainty impossible.

Apart from Porphyry's setting the trend for the teaching of Aristotelian works, particularly the logical works, within Neoplatonic schools, he exercised considerable influence over the reception of his master Plotinus' works. Though he is usually seen as the founder of Neoplatonism, the works of Plotinus did not become a central text for later Neoplatonists, but it seems clear that Porphyry's activities in arranging, editing and even establishing the titles of the treatises were intended to help Plotinus rise to a special status within the curriculum. He discusses the principles of his arrangements very briefly in chapter 24 of the *Life of Plotinus*, and from this it is clear that he favours an arrangement that groups things in terms of related philosophic content, beginning with more basic topics and leading to those more advanced. Hence he had aimed to arrange Plotinus more along the lines of Andronicus' treatment of Aristotle and Theophrastus than along those followed by the Thrasyllan Platonic tetralogies, even though he favours groupings of a fixed number. Perhaps, like Albinus, he had thought of the tetralogies as having been organized according to too many non-pedagogic considerations, but he certainly rejected date of composition as a basis for his arrangement.[26] He was presumably committed to the inclusion of all available works by a promise made to Plotinus. The total number of treatises, however, was less precisely determined than Porphyry implies, since in some cases what are transmitted as two works could have become one (like Plato's *Timaeus* and *Critias*), for example, *Enn.* V.1[10] and *Enn.* V.2[11], while the treatise *Various Questions* (*Enn.* III.9[13]) might plausibly have been divided.

While Plotinus' own works failed to become a core part of the curriculum in this or any other arrangement, for which reason I hesitate to regard him as the founder of a new school, the Plotinian arrangement of Porphyry provides us with some convenient clues about what kind of Platonic curriculum he would have favoured. The overall progression moves from human life (which is most familiar to us), through natural science, to the highest levels of reality: soul, intellect and the One. This is not a rigid separation, for, as in Plato, a plurality of questions would be discussed, but the following points should be considered:

- To begin with works of a broadly ethical character would seem to agree with the fact that the first three dialogues of the later Plato curriculum were *Alcibiades I*, *Gorgias* and *Phaedo*.
- More particularly, to begin with *Enn.* I.1, a treatise on the true nature of the living being (and of the human being in particular) agrees with the fact that the first dialogue of the Platonic curriculum is *Alcibiades I*, with its argument that the true self is soul rather than either the body or the body–soul combination, and in particular that it is what is most valuable in the soul; that is, something quasi-divine. The indebtedness of this treatise to the *Alcibiades* 129–33 is evident. Fundamental here was the belief that the most basic learning was understanding who we are.
- To continue with a treatise *On the Virtues* agrees with the fact that the *Gorgias* and *Phaedo* were supposed to discuss the constitutional (or civic) and cathartic virtues respectively.
- To conclude with three treatises that include either "the Good", or "the One", or both in their titles agrees well with the fact that *Philebus* and *Parmenides* are the final dialogues of the two stages of the later curriculum.
- To devote two Enneads after the first to matters concerning the natural world, prior to the three metaphysical Enneads, agrees with Iamblichus' fundamental division of the dialogues of his curriculum into "natural" (or "physical") and "theological" ones.[27]

In these ways there was a certain basic correspondence between the Porphyrian arrangement of Plotinus' works and Iamblichus' subsequent arrangement of twelve selected dialogues of Plato. This is indicative of considerable agreement about the order in which the would-be Platonist should tackle the fundamental issues of Platonic philosophy.

IAMBLICHUS

While Porphyry wrote much that concerned Pythagoras and Pythagoreans, with Iamblichus it seems that the study of Pythagoreanism became basic to school concerns in a slightly more formal way (D. O'Meara 1989). Porphyry's interest in, and promotion of, the logical works of Aristotle also continued, and Iamblichus became one of the many commentators on the *Categories*, in which he departed much more sparingly from Porphyry than over many issues (Finamore & Dillon 2002: 6). Even so, his lasting contribution to the curriculum was in the formalization of those dialogues of Plato in which he thought the entire philosophy of Plato was summed up.[28] This is evident in the proem of Proclus' *Commentary on the Alcibiades* (11.18–21), where he praises the decision to give first place to the *Alcibiades* that contains the seeds of all, and mentions that it comes first in the group of ten ordered dialogues that precedes the two that sum it up (referring to *Timaeus* and *Parmenides*).

It is, however, chapter 26 of the anonymous *Prolegomena to Platonic Philosophy*, usually attributed to the sixth-century Alexandrian Platonist Olympiodorus or his environment, that sets out to give details of this curriculum. Though the details are obscured owing to careless copying, the basics are agreed. The curriculum consisted of a group of ten, *Alcibiades I,** *Gorgias, Phaedo,** *Cratylus, Theaetetus, Sophist,** *Statesman, Phaedrus,** *Symposium* and *Philebus,** followed by two "perfect" dialogues, *Timaeus** (in which all natural philosophy is crystallized) and *Parmenides** (in which all theology is crystallized). Those seven dialogues marked with an asterisk are known to have been the subject of Iamblichian commentaries, while the absence of evidence in the case of the other five cannot be taken as an indication of any omission on his part. The absence of extant later Neoplatonist commentaries on *Theaetetus, Statesman* and *Symposium* and the failure of Olympiodorus' *Commentary on the Gorgias* and Proclus' part-extant *Commentary on the Cratylus* to show an interest in named predecessors means there are few places where evidence of Iamblichus' exegesis could have been preserved.

A fundamental division distinguished "physical" from "theological" dialogues, with the *Timaeus* summing up and crowning the former, and the *Parmenides* capping the latter. The reconstruction of the damaged text offered by the Budé editors (Westerink *et al.* 1990: lxxii–lxxiii) labels only *Sophist, Statesman* and *Timaeus* as "physical", and only *Phaedrus, Symposium* and *Parmenides* "theological". It seems to me likelier that all dialogues regarded as involving *theōria* (i.e. all but the first three) fell under one of the two categories, so that *Cratylus* and *Theaetetus* were also seen as "physical", and *Philebus* (supposedly concerned with the Good itself) was also seen as "theological". The introductory position of the *Alcibiades I* is explained in terms of the primacy of self-knowledge over any other subject (*Alc.* 127d–134a), and the tenth position of the *Philebus* in terms of its dealing with the all-transcendent Good: the dialogue too must transcend the others in the group of ten.

It is the positions of intermediate dialogues that are obscured by textual difficulties: inaccuracies that have resulted in the complete omission of *Sophist* and *Statesman*. The author begins by suggesting that the Neoplatonists' five levels of virtue are relevant, enumerating natural, ethical, constitutional (or "civic"), cathartic and theoretic virtues. However, only *Gorgias* and *Phaedo* are closely connected with any of these levels, the former with constitutional virtues (dealing at civic level with inter-class relations, and at a personal level with the relation between the constituent parts of the human soul), and the latter with the cathartic virtues (dealing with the progressively unified soul of the philosopher who is practising leaving the body). That two of the five kinds of virtue should be associated with the curriculum does not explain the introduction of the topic. However, after the *Phaedo* the *Prolegomena* state that we move on to the cognition of reality, which occurs "through ethical virtue" (26.35), but it is recognized that "ethical" (*ēthikē*) is a misreading for "theoretic" (*theōrētikē*), and there follow one occurrence of the associated verb *theōrein* ("study") at 26.36 and a second case of the adjective *theōrētikos* at 26.42. It seems to me that all dialogues after the *Phaedo* are thought of as requiring theoretic virtues,[29] and that this is in fact why the student should be reading certain virtue-related texts *prior to* the study of physical and metaphysical reality.

It should also be noticed that the *Alcibiades* begins by recounting Alcibiades' natural advantages, not just of the body but also of the soul. Proclus (*in Alc.* 96.7–10; 101.8–16) has no difficulty in linking this passage with the shadowy natural virtues. These are not something any education can instil in the pupil, for he either has them or lacks them, but the dialogue seeks to have Alcibiades go beyond them and acquire some kinds of virtues, presumably involving practice and habituation.[30] This being the case, it appears that *Alcibiades* was standardly seen as requiring the pupil to adopt the ethical virtues,[31] *Gorgias* the constitutional ones, *Phaedo* the cathartic, and subsequent dialogues the state of purity that unleashes the theoretic virtues.[32]

When one looks at the overall content of the curriculum, one sees that the emphasis is still on what are seen as middle and late dialogues. The first two are those that one would most easily think of as "Socratic", while the *Cratylus* probably contains some relatively early material. No very short dialogues are present, nor any that are obviously aporetic. Somewhat surprisingly there is a marked overlap with the earlier part of Thrasyllus' tetralogical arrangement, from the final dialogue of tetralogy I to the first dialogue of tetralogy IV:

Iamblichian order	Tetralogy & no.
1. *Alcibiades I*	IV.1
2. *Gorgias*	VI.3
3. *Phaedo*	I.4
4. *Cratylus*	II.1
5. *Theaetetus*	II.2
6. *Sophist*	II.3
7. *Statesman*	II.4
8. *Phaedrus*	III.4
9. *Symposium*	III.3
10. *Philebus*	III.2
11. *Timaeus*	VIII.3
12. *Parmenides*	III.1

So tetralogy II is preserved intact, while the theological part of the curriculum consists of tetralogy III in reverse order! Only the *Gorgias* and the mandatory *Timaeus* are imported from different parts of the Thrasyllan corpus. While many explanations of this could be offered, it probably does illustrate how dialogues that had come to be closely associated within the curriculum tend to remain closely associated even when the reasons for linking them change markedly. The result is that the dialogues of tetralogies V–VII, which mostly set out to depict Socratic investigation without any great emphasis on doctrinal content, play a comparatively minor role in the formulation of late antique Platonism, and that Socrates himself, though much respected, is treated as rather less than the ideal philosopher. It is the author who is inspired, not the figure whose influence on Plato is today seen as central. It might also be said that the curriculum ensures that the ethical concerns, for which Socrates was famous and which characterize the first three dialogues, naturally become less central to Neoplatonist education.

Further, the weakening of the Socratic influence allows the rise of a different side of Plato, which was supposed to come from the Pythagoreans and their presumed allies, the Eleatics. One consequence of this was an emphasis, seen in Iamblichus' basic division between physics and theology, on the disciplines of natural philosophy and of theology, all of it with a significant mathematical element. Another was a tendency to see certain colourful passages in Plato, and particularly his myths, as veiled revelations, to be interpreted in a symbolic fashion. Traditional philosophic argument was not by any means neglected, but the revelatory passages were those that attracted the most concentrated hermeneutic activities (Jackson *et al.* 1998: 14–15).

There are several such revelatory passages in the *Republic*, and it is thus unsurprising that the *Prolegomena* speak of people who justified the inclusion of both *Republic* and *Laws* (26.45–7). Proclus certainly wrote a surviving "commentary" on *Republic*, but this consisted of a collection of essays on special topics rather than a conventional treatment, and it is said that he too "excluded *Republic* on account of its being a plurality of discussions (*logoi*), and *Laws* for the same reason" (26.7–9). Iamblichus' requirement that *everything* within a dialogue should have a single *skopos* or "target" made it almost impossible to interpret such large works in the expected manner, but *Republic* remained an influential text, and Olympiodorus would interpret the *Gorgias* with almost constant reference to it (Tarrant 1997). Proclus himself makes much reference to it to explain features of the introductory discussion of the *Timaeus* (Tarrant 2007: general index), on the ground that its discussion had been set two days before. Similarly, he cannot avoid taking account of the *Critias* that will follow the *Timaeus*. In such respects at least the curriculum did not exercise too rigid a control over Proclian scholarship.

PLATO AND ARISTOTLE AT ALEXANDRIA
UNDER AMMONIUS AND OLYMPIODORUS

The curious thing is that this curriculum is reported in a work thought to come from the school of Olympiodorus. In sharp contrast to the major Athenian Neoplatonists Proclus and Damascius, Olympiodorus is not known to have commented on any dialogues later than the *Sophist* in the curriculum. His extant commentaries are on the first two dialogues, while there is also a part of his *Commentary on the Phaedo*. The surviving work gives rise to little or no suspicion that the target dialogues were part of a curriculum whose crowning glory will be the *Parmenides*, or indeed any of the other dialogues that had been conceived by Iamblichus as theological. His teacher Ammonius had apparently been under intense pressure from the Christian authorities at Alexandria, and some kind of compromise may have been reached that enabled a truncated and non-theological curriculum to be taught (Jackson *et al.* 1998: 15–17; Watts 2006: 222–31). Even so, compromises on matters that are central and fundamental are seldom made, and it seems likely that Ammonius and Olympiodorus preferred to teach the non-theological, and indeed more Socratic part of the Platonic curriculum. Ammonius is today known for his work on Aristotle, and Aristotelian commentaries have also come to us under the name of Olympiodorus.

A major contribution to the Aristotelian curriculum seems to have stemmed from Ammonius, and we find an important discussion at *On the Categories* 5.31–6.22.[33] He starts by explaining why one should not begin with ethics, which he regards as a natural starting point, enabling the reader to prepare inwardly for the reception of other doctrines. Owing to the amount of formal logic in the ethical treatises, logical works must be read first, followed by ethics, physics, mathematics and theology. Apart from the introductory logic, the curriculum thus bears a close relationship to Iamblichus' Platonic one, leading through ethics and physics towards theology, and it is actually made explicit that all these branches of Aristotle's philosophy are there to help us rise to the first principle of all things. Hence Ammonius appears to be thinking of the Aristotelian Unmoved Mover as in some way corresponding to the Neoplatonic One.

If this is so, it is less difficult to imagine why the Platonic theological works were no longer essential for Ammonius and Olympiodorus, and in particular why they would no longer privilege the *Parmenides* which for Proclus had been the source of a highly complex polytheistic theology. The deep metaphysical interpretation of the *Parmenides*, whether Iamblichus' or Proclus', required a considerable leap of faith, so that Proclus' biographer Marinus retreated from it and Damascius continued to wrestle manfully with the puzzles that it posed. Perhaps it is unsurprising if it was quietly dropped in Alexandria.

CURRICULAR EXTRAS

The mention of an Aristotelian curriculum reminds one that the Neoplatonist curriculum seems always to have included non-Platonic elements, but that these had not always been constant. Aristotle himself was central to Proclus' personal education, and he is supposed to have read all the works over two years; of these he was personally taught the *de Anima* by Plutarch of Athens.[34] Yet Aristotle was often criticized by Proclus, now treated as betraying Platonic principles of causality (*in Tim.* I.7.10–16), now dismissed as a "dialectician" or master of syllogistic (*in Tim.* III.114.7, 115.10–14), now seen as one who is fond of quibbling (*phileris, in Tim.* III.130.3–24). Indeed, Proclus seems to have written a monograph against Aristotle's criticisms of the *Timaeus* (*in Tim.* II.278.27). Nor has Proclus left us any commentaries on Aristotelian works as his master Syrianus did on four books of the *Metaphysics*. However, his surviving mathematical works include a commentary on book I of Euclid's *Elements*, while there are fragments of one on the Chaldaean Oracles, on Plotinus, on Hesiod *Works and Days* and on the Orphic *Theogony*.[35] His commentaries and exegetical works, including reports of two on Homer and others on Aristotelian logical works, suggest that these authors could be studied under him.

That said, one should bear in mind that Proclus' extant works were pitched at very advanced students of whom much extra-curricular reading might be expected. The key "inspired texts" that are referred to repeatedly in his commentaries on Plato are Homer, various Orphic writings that he usually attributed to Orpheus ("the theologian") himself, and the Chaldaean Oracles. Because they are all thought to be in agreement with Plato when allegorically understood, they may be seen as important adjuncts to the Platonic curriculum, adjuncts that actually assist in bringing the reader to the appropriate conclusions. These texts, however, were less a part of the "curriculum", since there is no evidence that the pupil was being encouraged, as he would be in the case of Platonic texts, to enter into an ongoing debate about their real meaning. It is really a *prescribed way of reading them* that was being taught.

Given Proclus' range of interests, it is not strange that other Neoplatonists ventured to add other works to the curriculum. We possess, for instance, a work on the oratorical theorist Hermogenes attributed to Syrianus, while an interest in rhetoric is constantly visible in Olympiodorus' *Commentary on the Gorgias*. We also have a commentary on Epictetus' *Enchiridion* by Simplicius, whose Aristotelian commentaries are much studied for the light that they shed on Presocratic philosophy in particular. Just as scholars today will often move in unexpected directions in order to follow new lines of enquiry through, so too did scholars of antiquity. Being a philosopher was in most cases inseparable from being a scholar, and scholars may often find it desirable to introduce new texts for study.

CONCLUSION

In these circumstances what is remarkable is how little the Platonic curriculum changed, not just after Iamblichus, but even since Plutarch of Chaeronea. Though the fortunes of the *Parmenides* fluctuated as philosophers became more confident or more doubtful both of its depth and of their own ability to understand it, in most cases the same works remained important, being referred to again and again, and being the subject of increasingly challenging commentaries until the demise of the Athenian school in 529. The Iamblichian curriculum, though novel in what it set out to achieve, was not so novel in its content. Almost any Platonist in late antiquity would have viewed with amazement the modern appeal of the *Euthyphro, Apology, Crito, Charmides, Laches, Lysis, Protagoras, Meno* and *Ion* and at our modern attempts to extract some kind of Socratic or early Platonic philosophy out of them. Even today's obsession with the *Republic* would have seemed strange to many, given the fact that the *Timaeus* always remained supreme for them (cf. Annas 1999: 5), with or without its elusive consort, the *Parmenides*.

NOTES

1. See Sedley (1997) on the ways in which commentaries served the needs of contemporary pupils.
2. I have discussed Thrasyllus in Tarrant (1993), appending a collection of testimonies. The work on Democritus is mentioned at Diogenes Laertius 9.41 = Thrasyllus T18a.
3. For further testimony to the late position of *Laws* see anon. *Proleg.* 25, where it is also evident that it is accepted by Proclus when he argues that the *Epinomis* cannot have been Plato's own work.
4. We are told by Diogenes Laertius (3.57) that it was conceived as putting the philosophic life on display.
5. See Diogenes Laertius 3.38 and again anon. *Proleg.* 24.7–19, where the late position of the *Laws* is cited in relation to this same arrangement.
6. These are identical with the four dialogues to which Diogenes attributed a logical character (Diogenes Laertius 3.50: *Statesman, Cratylus, Parmenides, Sophist*) with the addition of *Euthydemus*. The placing of

logic at the head of the curriculum follows the priority given to the *organon* in the Aristotelian corpus of Andronicus, and has a parallel in the *Handbook of Platonism* of Alcinous (6.159.39–45), which might also include not only *Cratylus* and *Parmenides* but also *Euthydemus* as works with a purpose relating to logic. The *Euthydemus* is seen almost as Plato's manual of sophistic refutation, equivalent to Aristotle's *de Sophisticis Elenchis*.

7. These include, at the first stage, dialogues that make trial of young men (*peirastikoi dialogoi*), at the second those that "bring to birth" young men's ideas (*maieutikoi*), at the fourth stage the "logical" dialogues (*logikoi*) to enable us to bind fast the Platonic doctrines encountered at the third stage, and at the fifth the dialogues that teach us anti-sophistic tactics (*anatreptikoi* and *endeiktikoi*).

8. The arrangement clearly had to appeal here to the date of the introductory conversation, rather than to that of the main discussion, which is set just before the *Euthyphro*. Yet the introductory conversation of the *Symposium* might have been just as late, and that of the *Phaedo* also takes place after Socrates' death. One wonders whether such a reading order was intended to illuminate a Socratic rather than a Platonic education programme.

9. The author speaks of the fourth not simply as satyric (cf. Thrasyllus in Diogenes Laertius 3.56), but as directed towards pleasure. He further adds to our knowledge of the rationale for the arrangement by reporting that it was supposed to have an element of circularity, in so far as it began with a focus on Socrates' life and ended with Plato's.

10. The example used is that of the *Phaedo*, the fourth member of the first tetralogy, but he might just as well have pointed to the *Statesman*, which concludes the second. If anything, a non-serious element might more easily be detected in the initial dialogue of the tetralogies, but the original reference to the satyr play might have been to highlight the fourth play which had been ignored in the arrangement of Aristophanes of Byzantium, who had postulated Platonic trilogies (Diogenes Laertius 3.61–2). In the light of the author's avoidance of the term "satyric", one may also note that the fourth play was sometimes a more conventional tragedy, but somehow "pro-satyric", like the *Alcestis* of Euripides, which stood in fourth position and offered comic elements in its presentation of Heracles.

11. At Diogenes Laertius 3.57, the first tetralogy alone seems to be accredited with a common *hypothesis* (presumably the original word for which the Neoplatonic *skopos* is substituted).

12. In this case it is their direct and straightforward communication that excludes them; it is not the case that any of these works are ignored by Proclus, for the *Republic* is the subject of an exegetical work (in the form of separate interpretative essays), while many passages of *Laws* and the esoteric material in *Epistles* II, VI and VII remain important throughout Neoplatonism.

13. The increasing centrality of set speech in the *Phaedrus* and *Symposium* seems never to have threatened their status as "dialogues", partly no doubt because of their emphasis on an interplay of characters, but partly also because of a unity of thematic material that was seen to underlie them (though there was dissension in the former case about what that unity involved: see anon. *Proleg.* 21.3–22.4).

14. I judge by the useful tables of parallels in Jones (1916: 109–53).

15. It seems that the *Alcibiades* achieved greater importance over the second century, presumably because of its final section in which self-knowledge becomes central; exactly when the *Parmenides* became important is a matter of serious dispute, but its importance seems to be taken for granted by Plotinus and in Sethian gnostic treatises with which we are told he was familiar (J. D. Turner 2001; J. D. Turner & Corrigan 2010).

16. See Tarrant (1983: 77) = (2011: xii 5) on the fact that references to the philosophical digression of *Epistle VII* begin to appear only from the middle of the second century with Numenius, Justin Martyr and Celsus; this is also the period when the esoteric passage of *Epistle* II begins to appear. This does not mean that the esoteric passages were absent from the *Epistles* as Thrasyllus had known them, as I should certainly regard the allusion to *Epistle VI* 323d present in Porphyry's *Commentary of Ptolemy's Harmonics* p. 12 as part of Thrasyllus T23.

17. *Alc. I* is studied with a view to turning the pupil round to recognize what he should be caring for (i.e. his soul or true "self"); *Phd.* with a view to the recognition of what the philosopher's life is like and what expectation it is based on, thinking of the "practice of death" (related to the Neoplatonic "cathartic virtues") and the immortality of the soul; *R.* functions like a complete handbook of education in virtue (the Neoplatonists would no doubt specify "constitutional virtue", *politikē aretē*); and *Tim.* offers physics and theology (as for Proclus), leading to a knowledge of things divine, and the ability to follow our acquisition of virtue by likening ourselves to the divine.

18. Adorno *et al.* (1995); Gioè (2002). Also extremely useful is Dörrie & Baltes (1987–2008: vol. 3, sections 78–81).

19. The majority view is that the papyrus *Commentary on the Parmenides* is from the third century, and from an author close to Plotinus, but not surprisingly there is some uncertainty.

20. Cf. frag. 43 des Places (Iamblichus); Proclus also includes Numenius among "Platonics" at *in R.* II.96.10–15 (= Numenius, T21 [Leemans]; see also T4–5); similarly Cronius is referred to as a "Platonic" by Syrianus (*in Metaph.* 109.11 [Kroll]).

21. Koch (2013) has a full discussion of the Platonic dialogues read by Plotinus, his selectivity, and his exegetical approach. She deals with the topic under four heads: "Un corpus restraint", "Un corpus sans ordre de lecture", "Un corpus 'anthologique'" and "Un corpus 'énigmatique'."

22. Some, including myself (Tarrant 1993: ch. 6), Tardieu (1996) and Bechtle (1999), argue that it had already been important among Pythagorean interpreters of Plato, but evidence is tricky. New work is showing that Sethian Gnostics are likely to have anticipated many developments that some would attribute to Plotinus, including the developing importance of *Parmenides* and *Sophist*; see J. D. Turner (2001), Z. Mazur (2013). It is noteworthy that Proclus, while failing to name any earlier philosopher who adopted the metaphysical interpretation of the *Parmenides* (in fact he fails to name any interpreter in his *in Parmenidem*), nevertheless expresses surprise at *Platonic Theology* II.37 that Origen, being like Plotinus a pupil of Ammonias Saccas, rejected the Plotinian interpretation of the first hypothesis.

23. This passage had probably already risen to importance in Numenius (frag. 12.13 [des Places]).

24. It is noteworthy that *Enn.* V.1[10].8 begins by referring to the passage from *Epistle* II, alludes next to *Epistle* VI 323d, to the *Timaeus* and *Republic* VI–VII, and after referring to *Parmenides* B3 concludes by offering his interpretation of the first three hypostases of the *Parmenides*. The chapter is noteworthy for its insistence that the three Plotinian hypostases are not in fact his own doctrine, but that he was merely repeating what Plato demonstrates to be ancient opinion, a puzzling statement that Dillon (1992b: 189) shows must be heavily qualified.

25. Its common working vocabulary is, in fact, closer to that of Plotinus than to any other thinker known to me, including Porphyry. Since Plotinus' style is distinctive I would expect the work to have been written by somebody close to Plotinus, and possibly from the same background.

26. Porphyry gives the approximate date of composition at *Plot.* 4–6, and it is now common practice to refer to a treatise's position in this numerical order in brackets, immediately after Ennead and its internal position.

27. Anon. *Proleg.* 26.16–21; it appears later (26.41–2) that there may have been no intention to label all dialogues in one of these ways.

28. See Festugière (1969) for a classic treatment of late antique curriculum.

29. On the theoretic virtues, see Brisson (2006: 97–8); his principal focus is Porphyry's *Sententiae*, where the terminology has still not been formalized, but the critical thing is a level of virtue at which catharsis has been completed.

30. From 119a Socrates attempts to persuade Alcibiades that he must work at building further on his natural gifts. At 124e this concern, for which the recurrent term is *epimeleia* (119a, 123d, 124b, d, 128b, 129a, 132c; cf. also *epimeleisthai, epimeletēs*), must be one directed towards excellence (= "virtue", *aretē*), and this theme returns at 134b, continuing to the end of the dialogue. It is not made explicit that this concerns ethical rather than political virtues, but Neoplatonists were concerned to demonstrate that Socrates achieved some success in improving Alcibiades, whereas they might infer from the fragility of Alcibiades' progress that he did not acquire the constitutional virtues, which require above all the proper functioning of the various faculties of the soul.

31. As noted by D. O'Meara (2003: 64), however, Damascius (in Olymp. *in Alc.* 5) took the view that the *Alcibiades* related to what I have called "constitutional" or "civic" virtue.

32. *Catharsis* is essentially a *process* of purification, and hence the cathartic virtues are those demonstrated by the soul that practises this process; see Brisson (2006: 94–7).

33. The passage is printed in Sorabji (2004: vol. 3, 41).

34. Marinus, *Procl.* 12–13 = Sorabji (2004: vol. 3, 45).

35. For Proclus' works, see Gerson (2010: vol. 2, 957–8).

3

The Alexandrian classrooms excavated and sixth-century philosophy teaching

Richard Sorabji

It was announced in 2004 that the Polish archaeological team under Grzegorz Majcherek had identified the surprisingly well-preserved lecture rooms of the sixth-century Alexandrian school.[1] This was a major archaeological discovery.[2] Although the first few rooms had been excavated twenty-five years earlier, identification has only now become possible. By 2008, twenty rooms had been excavated. Twenty is the number of rooms reported by a twelfth-century source writing in Arabic, Abd el-Latif, but there may be more than twenty.[3]

Some of the rooms had been rebuilt after an earthquake, presumed to be that of 535, so they would have been there only in Philoponus' later years. But others are dated to the late fifth century, so belong to the time of his teacher, Ammonius. Even the later rooms may be a guide to the structure of the earlier ones. Further reconstruction or refurbishment in the late sixth to very early seventh centuries is suggested by the ceramic in the cement of one room.

One very good specimen of a room, which is illustrated here, has three tiers of seats in a horseshoe, enough to accommodate thirty students, with a professor's throne (*thronos*) elevated up six steps at the back of the horseshoe, and a stone stand out at the front of the horseshoe. One stand has a hole in it, which Majcherek takes to be for a lectern to be inserted. The speaker would have stood there. Twenty rooms of similar or smaller size could have accommodated four hundred to five hundred students. The stand is not found in most rooms, but the throne was eventually recognized in all, although it sometimes took the form of one step, or a block covered with plaster or in one case marble. In most rooms the tiers are rectangular rather than horseshoe shaped, and some rooms have only one tier of seats (see Figure 3.1).

The position of the stone stand for a lectern isolated in the front of the room gives us a sense of the extent to which the speaker, often a student, would have been exposed to interrogation from professor and students. We can also imagine many different tasks that a speaker might perform there. The different environment of Plotinus' Rome did not

Figure 3.1 The horseshoe lecture rooms of sixth-century Alexandria, recently excavated by Grzegorz Majcherek, with the professor's raised throne at the back and a lectern stand (photo: M.Krawczyk, PCMA, with permission of Grzegorz Majcherek).

necessarily have a room of the same structure. But we can imagine how the Alexandrian rooms could have been put to use, when we think of Porphyry, newly arrived as a student at Plotinus' seminar in the third century. He had to rewrite his essay three times, and face criticism from another research student, Amelius, until he was persuaded to change his view. We might picture a student reading out his revised essay at the stand, although it was actually Amelius who was asked to read aloud Porphyry's essay (Porphyry, *Plot.* 18.19). Plotinus also started his classes by having commentaries and texts read to him by a student.[4] At a very much earlier date, in Athens of the second century BCE, Carneades, the head of the Platonic Academy, had a student summarize his previous lecture at the beginning of the next, and criticized him for getting it wrong (Philodemus, *Acad.Ind.* (Herculaneum papyrus) col. xxii(35)–xxiii(2)).

The professor's throne or *thronos*, by contrast, being at the back, gave him a much less exposed position than the modern Western professor tends to have. Raffaella Cribiore has explained the throne or *thronos* very well.[5] Plato caricatures the Sophists at *Protagoras* 315c, when he has Socrates go to see the sophist Hippias of Elis holding forth on a *thronos*, with listeners sitting round him on benches (*bathra*). Plutarch comments that Socrates did not use a *thronos* nor set out benches (Plutarch, *An seni respublica gerenda sit* [*Moralia* X] 796D–E). Ammonius is caricatured in the work named after him, *Ammonius*, which is written by one of his Christian students, Zacharias. Ammonius is presented as being interrupted in a lecture on Aristotle's physics by his Christian students who refute him on the question of whether the universe had a beginning. Ammonius is represented as sitting on a high step or seat (*hypsilon bēma*) and expounding Aristotle's doctrine in a very sophistic and swaggering way, which suggests that Ammonius' lecture arrangements made a similar provision.[6] Cribiore suggests that the caricature is partly drawn from Plato's *Protagoras*. Mossman Roueché has pointed out to me an Ethiopic text, which reports that earlier in Alexandria, Hypatia, the woman mathematician murdered in 415, had been forced off a high seat or chair before being dragged away to her death (*Chronicle of John, Bishop of Nikiu*, ch. 84). Cribiore and Majcherek have drawn attention to the fourth-century rhetorician Libanius describing the terror of a rhetoric student required to deliver his composition in front of the teacher who sits frowning "on a high place (*hupsilou tinos*)" (Libanius, vol. 8, *Chreia* 3.7 [Foerster]). The tallest set of professorial steps surviving in the Alexandrian excavation is six steps high. Comparison has been made with the minbar of a later period, the flight of steps leading up to the speaker in Islamic mosques.

As regards the rounded shape, it has been pointed out that Elias, a prominent Alexandrian philosopher later in the sixth century, explains its purpose.[7] Seminar rooms (*diatribai*) are rounded so that students can see each other and the teacher. Philoponus also attaches importance to seeing the students' faces, to tell whether or not they have understood.[8] The layout seems to have been designed to ensure a lot of student participation. The curved student seating may already be reflected in a mosaic installed in Apamea, now in Syria, by Julian, Roman Emperor from 361 to 363, to commemorate his favourite pagan philosopher, Iamblichus. A mosaic preserved on the site shows Socrates surrounded by colleagues in a curve to either side of him. I have interpreted another of the mosaics in this school in the introduction to Sorabji (1990). I know of no evidence that the curved shape was still used in Islamic teaching, and Yahya Michot has drawn attention to Islamic pictures of disorderly seating.[9] But some orderly arrangement would fit with those cases for which it is reported that the Islamic professor put his best pupil and aspirant successor to sit next to him, demoting him if next year's entry contained an even better student (Watt 1972).

In 639, a little after the last-known professor of pagan Greek philosophy in Alexandria, a Christian building with a very similar structure was erected in another part of the Mediterranean world at Torcello, off the coast of what became Venice (see Figure 3.2). The bishop's throne is elevated up steep steps at the back of the apse in the middle of its curved wall, and to either side and a little lower is a horseshoe of six tiers of curved benches for the presbyters to sit on. The arrangement is extraordinarily like that in the seminar rooms of sixth-century Alexandria. It was once thought that Christians took the curved shape of the apse from Roman judicial courts sited in the curved apse of a basilica. But it now appears that Roman judicial courts were housed in various shapes of building with varied seating arrangements (de Angelis 2010: index). The shape, without the seating, was well known from other Roman buildings, and the baths of Constantine in Arles have been cited as a model for later Romanesque churches in Provence (Mullins 2011: 157). I think it more likely that the seating pattern arose when the familiar shape was seen by both pagans and Christians as useful for teaching. A Christian mosaic that has been dated to 410–17 from the apse of Santa Pudenziana in Rome shows Christ on a gilded throne surrounded by disciples in a horseshoe. I have been told that the performance rooms of Hadrian from 123, newly excavated near Santa Pudenziana, include one room with the

Figure 3.2 The tiered curved benches of the apse and the bishop's throne retain the same structure for teaching in Torcello Cathedral, founded in 639 just after the last-known commentator in Alexandria.

Figure 3.3 St Catherine refuting the Neoplatonists of Alexandria in their seminar room, portrayed in the Basilica of St Clement, Rome, which itself retains its bishop's throne in the apse, although choir stalls conceal the curved structure. Painting by Masolino da Panicale, 1425 (photo: Scala, Florence).

same horseshoe shape, central dais and tiered seats on a larger scale.[10] This surely might have influenced later mosaic. I am also told that the bishop's throne in the apse is still called "the high place" in Eastern churches.[11]

There is an even more unexpected continuity of design. One of the basilicas with a throne in the centre of the apse, dated by an inscription to a cardinal of 1108, is that of St Clement in Rome. But this is the very basilica that contains a fresco of 1425 depicting the structure of the sixth-century Alexandrian lecture rooms. The fresco by Masolino da Panicale shows St Catherine of Alexandria from the third century CE refuting an earlier generation of Alexandrian philosophers (see Figure 3.3). She had been summoned by the emperor Maximinus to answer them, but she had turned the tables on them. She is counting off the points against them on her fingers, while they look very refuted. The emperor is pictured seated in the professor's elevated throne,[12] while the professors are arranged like students on benches to either side. Catherine is in the open space where hapless students might normally be put through their paces. How did Masolino depict so accurately Alexandrian seminar rooms of a type only now brought to light by archaeology? Could the bishop's throne in the apse of the very basilica that he was adorning have given him the clue? The chief difference from Alexandria and Torcello is that he has portrayed the benches in front of the throne as straight. He may have based the straight benches on the straight-sided choir stalls, which by his day had been installed outside the apse in St Clement and separated from it by a canopied altar.

Another depiction, reproduced in Figure 3.4, is by Sodoma, from the first half of the sixteenth century, and is in Monte Olivetto Maggiore. It shows a similar structure in a

Figure 3.4 St Benedict (529, Monte Cassino) tiptoeing out of a sixth-century pagan seminar room to avoid being corrupted; detail from fresco by Sodoma (1477–1549) in Monte Olivetto Maggiore (photo: Scala, Florence/Ministero Beni e Att. Culturali).

lecture room of Philoponus' period. Here Philoponus' contemporary Saint Benedict is tiptoeing out of a seminar, so as to avoid being corrupted by the pagan professor, who is again at the back on an elevated throne, while the listeners are seated to either side.[13]

One of the excavated lecture rooms at Kom-El-Dikka has a unique structure. Four student tiers are facing each other, but instead of a complete horseshoe there is an apse, where we might have expected the professor's throne to be. The apse would accommodate only a few people, and is separated off by a low, curved wall in front, so that it is not easily visible from the closest of the student seats. The area cut off is roughly circular. My present inclination is to wonder if there could have been an aperture in the roof leaving the apse open to the sky for viewing the stars. Only the two banks of student benches would have needed roofing. There is a report by Simplicius about his former teacher in Alexandria, Ammonius, that he looked through a three-dimensional "astrolabe" and confirmed that the "fixed" star Arcturus had moved one degree from its supposedly fixed position over the previous hundred years.[14] Philoponus wrote the only extant ancient treatise on the astrolabe. In that treatise, he describes how delicately you have to hoist the instrument by its ring, shut one eye to make sure you are looking through both holes, angle it to the right plane, swivel its ruler, and mark your findings with charcoal or wax on its face.[15] You could not have done all this if hoisting it by hand. It must have required a very stable platform, and the low wall in the front of the apse or the ground in the centre of the apse would have supplied one. Only one student could look at a time, so the line of sight from the student tiers across to those queuing in the apse to take a look would not matter. Nor would it matter in those astronomy classes that were held at night. The one described in Philoponus' chapter 5 [Segonds] is held in the day, but that would not be true of Ammonius' observation of Arcturus. There are two excavated rooms with an apse, and Majcherek tells me that they alone face east–west. That would fit with the interest of astronomers in observing at sunrise and sunset.

Another anomaly in four of the lecture rooms is a trench, which only in one case shows signs of having had a lined bottom capable of holding water. I was at first reminded of Galen's dramatic demonstrations of animal vivisection, which might well have required a dry place to stow the animal before the vivisection. In Galen's case, dry stowage would have been needed afterwards as well, since he prided himself on stitching the animals back up alive.[16] But I am told that surviving medical texts of the period expound only anatomy, not "anatomical procedures". Only the latter would have involved vivisection. This could suggest that the classes too only described anatomy. On the other hand, it may be that the descriptive classes were the ones most often represented in books, because they were more elementary and easier to record in writing than vivisections.

I have mentioned above Zacharias' caricature of Ammonius' seminar in these lecture rooms. But he also wrote about his fellow student Severus, in the *Life of Severus*, which survives in Syriac. He there gives an eye-witness account of how in the mid-480s twenty camel-loads of pagan idols were transported after a raid on a secret temple of Isis at Menuthis and, before being burnt, were paraded by the Christians in Alexandria, together with imprecations against the Alexandrian professor Horapollo, with whom Damascius had possibly been studying rhetoric at this time, and who was accused of converting students to paganism. It has been suggested that it may be the burnt idols from this incident that were reported by Elizabeth Rodziewicz as having been found at a site close to the newly identified lecture rooms (Haas 1997: ch. 9, note 109; Athanassiadi 1999: 27–9).

This incident was to lead to a period of persecution of the Alexandrian philosophers, to whom I will now turn.

When the young Damascius first studied in Alexandria, he is described as wearing the rhetorician's (not the philosopher's) gown (tribōn). Talk of wearing the philosopher's gown is very common,[17] and, although the practice of wearing academic robes has been said to come to Europe from Islam (Watt 1972), I think the idea may have reached Islam from ancient Greek practice.

Damascius studied and taught rhetoric for nine years. His rhetorical studies were in Alexandria, where he was also in the circle of Proclus' pupil Ammonius for whose mother he delivered the funeral oration. He seems to have been in Athens shortly before the death of Proclus in 485, and some have suggested that he was teaching his rhetoric there. He may nonetheless have been back in Alexandria during the persecution of 488–9, from which he may have fled with Isidore, according to one reconstruction.[18] Influenced by Isidore, Damascius turned from rhetoric to philosophy and studied philosophy in Athens, perhaps around 492. But at some unknown time he studied Plato's philosophy along with astronomy back in Alexandria under Ammonius and Ammonius' brother Heliodorus. This is likely to have been before his dissent from Ammonius' political deal with the authorities there. Although later dates have been suggested, there would have been possible earlier occasions up to 489. Isidore was offered and declined the philosophy chair in Athens both in succession to Proclus and, at Damascius' urging, in succession to the next head, Marinus. It was eventually around 515 Damascius himself who became head of the Athenian Neoplatonist school, only to have it closed by the Christian emperor Justinian in 529.

The only notable pagan Neoplatonist who had stayed behind in Alexandria after the persecution of 488–9 was Ammonius, and Damascius accused him of doing a sordid deal, presumably after that date, with the Christian authorities.[19] I believe the deal may have kept philosophy going in Alexandria much longer than in Athens. It has been a mystery what the deal was, but I have argued that on his side Ammonius agreed to teach pagan Neoplatonism without emphasizing religious practice, while the Christian authorities on their side funded his teaching.[20] As regards the first side of the bargain, I cited Ammonius' commentary on Aristotle, in Int.1.6–11, where he claims to follow his Athenian teacher Proclus. But the strange thing is that Proclus had argued, page after page, for the natural character of divine names, by claiming the power of pagan priests to motivate the gods by the correct use of their names. Ammonius, at the corresponding point in his account, omits all mention of divine names and mentions only the natural force in magic of human names, and that as the opinion not of any Neoplatonist philosophers, but of an obscure Egyptian priest, Dousareios. As regards the funding of Ammonius' teaching, the evidence is not direct. The Christian authorities of Alexandria had funded the philosophy chair of his father, Hermeias, and on the father's death had made an unparalleled offer to his esteemed widow to fund the philosophical training of Ammonius, who went to study with Proclus at the pagan Neoplatonist school in Athens. The Christian authorities wanted Alexandria to remain a world centre for pagan learning, so long as Christian students were not being proselytized. But how was Ammonius to continue without funding? The lavish character of the school's rebuilding after the earthquake of 535 seems to me to confirm that the Christian authorities would have been willing to pay for the teaching of Ammonius and his successors. Ammonius' reticence about religious practice differentiated him from the devotional enthusiasm of Iamblichus, and of the Athenian school notably under Proclus, and I believe this gives truth to the controversial claim that the Alexandrian school was different in character from the Athenian.

Often philosophy teaching was privately arranged in antiquity. The extent of public provision for philosophy in Alexandria and the range of subjects will have been unparalleled for the time. It has been pointed out that in the capital at Constantinople, the emperor Theodosius II set up only one public philosophy post in 425, against twenty in grammar, eight in rhetoric and two in law.[21] Ammonius was in a better position in Alexandria. He taught all the leading philosophers of the sixth century: Philoponus, Simplicius, Damascius, Asclepius, Olympiodorus, as well as the mathematician Eutocius, his immediate successor. Two of these went on to edit Ammonius' lectures, three to teach in Alexandria, although only Eutocius and Olympiodorus held an Alexandrian chair of philosophy. Philoponus had probably started as a teacher of grammar, as his pagan enemy Simplicius liked to emphasize, but that would not have prevented him from teaching philosophy too. He would have been likely to do so under Ammonius and Eutocius, and Edward Watts has suggested that he may have delivered his polemical dissent from Proclus and Aristotle, when Olympiodorus followed Eutocius in the chair (Watts 2006: 244–5).

When Ammonius died some time before 526, Philoponus did not succeed him. His was by far the most brilliant mind. But it was pagan philosophy teaching that the Christian authorities wanted offered, and the curriculum was not Christian in philosophy or in any of the other subjects either. In Zacharias' fictional work, in order to get a discussion of the Christian belief in God's Creation, the students have to interrupt Ammonius' lecture on Aristotle's physics. Philoponus by contrast was not only a Christian, but was by a gradual process presenting Aristotle in a more and more unconventional way, with ideas of his own. He would not have fulfilled the role of continuing the heritage of pagan learning, and he was left free to publish his attack on the pagan beliefs of Proclus in 529, the year in which Damascius' school in Athens, where Proclus had taught, was closed.

Philoponus taught more subjects than philosophy and grammar, to judge from his writings. These include not only a massive philosophical output along with a grammatical treatise on Greek accents, but also two commentaries on Nicomachus' arithmetic, and the astronomical treatise on the astrolabe which is directed at students, telling them how to use it. The subjects taught in the school included philosophy, grammar, rhetoric, mathematics, astronomy and medicine, a wider range than the three provided for in Constantinople by Theodosius. The written commentaries, which reflect lectures on standard texts, have a similar structure in different disciplines, which suggests that the lectures also had patterns in common. Thus in law and medicine, as in philosophy, the commentaries can be divided into lectures (*praxeis*) about a text, which is quoted in lemmata or excerpts, and in which a statement of the doctrine (*protheōria, theōria*) of a passage is separated from a discussion of the exact wording of the passage (*lexis* in philosophy, *paragraphē* in law).[22] In medicine, as in philosophy, at the beginning of a course before the first text is broached, there are prolegomena, which cover a standard number of frequently asked questions, and discuss definitions of the discipline. The practice is also followed in both disciplines of advanced students writing up the seminar "from the voice of" the master.

Evidence has been assembled for a two-way interaction in which medical students were required to study logic and medical teachers taught some philosophy (Westerink 1964; M. Roueché 1999). Already in Zacharias' *Ammonius*, the doctor Gessius is treated as studying the issue whether the universe had a beginning, and Ammonius' philosophical pupil Asclepius says in his commentary on Aristotle's *Metaphysics* that the medical Asclepius was his fellow student. At the end of the sixth century, Westerink has commented, Pseudo-Elias' *Prolegomena to Philosophy* with *Commentary on Porphyry's Isagōgē* shows more competence in medicine than in philosophy (Westerink 1967).

The person who inherited Ammonius' chair of philosophy, Eutocius, is recorded as writing on the logical works of Aristotle, a politically safe subject. Most of his works were on mathematics, which was equally safe and had been a strong Alexandrian tradition. Eutocius was followed by Olympiodorus, who, more enterprisingly, wrote commentaries still extant not only on Aristotle's logical texts, but also on Aristotle's *Meteorology* and Plato's *Gorgias, First Alcibiades* and *Phaedo*. He was less cautious than Ammonius when, for example, in *Phaedo* he said that pagan priestcraft or theurgy could bring you to the pagan Neoplatonist ideal of mystical union with the divine world of intelligibles.[23] But Westerink has shown him going to great lengths to present to his Christian students pagan beliefs as analogous to Christian ones (Westerink 1990: 328–36).

Olympiodorus was still teaching in 565, but he is widely thought to have been the last pagan professor and to have been succeeded by Christians of whom three, Elias, David and Pseudo-Elias, confined themselves in their extant writings to Aristotle's logical works, whether or not Stephanus did also. They continued Ammonius' tradition of providing introductions to philosophy and to Aristotle, a tradition that strongly influenced the Greek-speaking Christians Maximus the Confessor and John of Damascus, and eventually, via Persian and Syriac, the Arabic tradition. Ammonius' skill had kept the Alexandrian school open into the seventh century, much longer than the one at Athens. As to whether the lecture rooms were still in use even in the late seventh century, despite the Persian and Arab invasions of 615/16 and 640, the archaeological evidence is not at present decisive.[24]

NOTE

1. Majcherek & Kolataj (2003); Majcherek (2004). There are web reports on Majcherek's excavation in Polish in *Histmag* for 19 May 2004 by Lord Lothar at www.histmag.org and in English in Al-Ahram for 20–26 January 2005 at http://weekly.ahram.org.eg by Jill Kamil.
2. I am very much indebted to Roger Bagnall and to Grzegorz Majcherek for making it possible for me to attend the conference held on 16–18 March 2005 at and near the site in Alexandria, and to invite Majcherek to speak at a conference on the classrooms and the use in general of classrooms held by myself and Charlotte Roueché at the Institute of Classical Studies in London on 26–27 April 2005. I learnt more from a conference addressed by Majcherek, and hosted by the Oxford Centre for Late Antiquity on 8 March 2008. I shall include with acknowledgement points made by others at the three conferences, as well as drawing on Majcherek's report and personal communication and my own impressions. The proceedings of the Alexandria conference are published in Derda *et al.* (2007).
3. I owe this information to Judith Mckenzie.
4. Porphyry, *Plot.* 14.10. This is the interpretation of the passive voice of *aneginōsketo autōi* in Snyder (2000), from whom I draw these examples.
5. In her paper "The School of Alexandria and the Rivalry Between Rhetoric and Philosophy", delivered at conferences on the excavation in Alexandria, in Budapest and at the Institute of Classical Studies in London, and to be published in a different paper in preparation, "The Conflict between Rhetoric and Philosophy and Zacharias' Ammonius".
6. Zacharias Scholasticus, *Ammonius*, or *de Mundi Opificio* (*Patrologia Graeca* vol. 85, cols 1028–9); Colonna (1973) lines 92–9, trans. Sebastian Gertz.
7. Elias, *in Porph.* 21.30: Majchrek acknowledges Elzbieta Szabat as having pointed this out.

8. Philoponus, *in Ph.* 7, 771.21–772.3, trans. from Arabic Lettinck, repr. in Sorabji (2004: vol. 1, ch. 6, a54).

9. Yahya Michot's talk at the Oxford conference of March 2008 (above, note 2).

10. I thank Susan Walker, Keeper of Antiquities in the Ashmolean Museum, Oxford, for this information.

11. I thank the art historian Christine Verzar for this information.

12. I thank Tony Kenny for the identification.

13. I thank Maurice Pope for showing me the reproduction and its relevance, which I had not foreseen on my pre-excavation visit to the frescos.

14. Simplicius, *in Cael.* 462.12–31, trans. Müller in Simplicius, *On Aristotle On the Heavens* 2.1–9.

15. Chapter 5 in Hase's text, reproduced by Segonds with French translation (1981); chapter 4 in Green's translation (1932).

16. Von Staden (1995). Von Staden tells me he thinks my suggestion is not impossible.

17. Damascius, *Isid.* 122D [Athanassiadi]; see also Epictetus, *Dissertationes* 4.8.12; Plutarch, *de Capienda ex Inimicis Utilitate* (*Moralia* II) 87a; *de Tranquilitate Animi* (*Moralia* VI) 467d; Eusebius, *de Martyribus Palaestinae* 52.

18. Athanassiadi (1999: 34–5), who agrees on dating with Tardieu (1990: 27–31).

19. Damascius, *Isid.*118B [Athanassiadi], referring to Rodiewicz (1991).

20. Sorabji (2005) and more briefly in the introductions to each volume of Sorabji (2004), under the heading "The commentators and Christianity". I plan to respond elsewhere to David Blank's disagreement in Blank (2010: 659–60) and Blank (2011). Van den Berg (2004: 1999) adds a reason why the deal on ritual would have been congenial to Ammonius.

21. *Cod. Theod.* XIV.9.3, which is repeated in the *Cod. Iust.* as 11.19.1, cited by Dennis Feissel in his paper at the Alexandria conference (above, note 2).

22. I am indebted for law to the paper by Simon Corcoran (2005), "Learning Law", and for medicine to the paper by Rebecca Flemming (2005), "Learning Medicine 1", at the London conference cited in note 2, whose proceedings were not published.

23. Olympiodorus, *in Phd.* 8, 2.1–20 [Westerink]. Other examples of his less compromising position are given in the magisterial introduction to Westerink (1990: 328–36).

24. This chapter is revised from the second edition of my *Philoponus and the Rejection of Aristotelian Science* (2010).

4

Middle Platonism and its relation to Stoicism and the Peripatetic tradition

Gretchen Reydams-Schils and Franco Ferrari

Middle Platonism is a name that, since Praechter, has been conveniently assigned to the period spanning the first century BCE and the beginning of the third century CE that witnessed the long transition (beginning with Antiochus of Ascalon) from the so-called sceptical phase of Plato's Academy to a more systematic kind of Platonism represented by Plotinus and his successors (Praechter 1909: 524; Dillon 1996a; Sharples & Sorabji 2007; Bonazzi & Opsomer 2009; Männlein-Robert & Ferrari forthcoming). Despite its usefulness, the label also constitutes a challenge for scholars because it covers such a wide range of authors, methodological approaches and views. Even the chronological boundaries of this period are fluid. For instance, the work of Porphyry, Plotinus' pupil, harks back to a number of features typically associated with this earlier strand of Platonism (Zambon 2002), and that of Calcidius, a fourth-century Latin author of a commentary on Plato's *Timaeus*, adopts a perspective that reflects a similar mode and owes a special debt to Numenius. And although a very important anonymous commentary on Plato's *Theaetetus* can be dated to this period with some confidence, the date of the anonymous commentary on Plato's *Parmenides* is much more contested, though it is often associated with Porphyry (Bechtle 1999) or with late Neoplatonism (Linguiti 1995).

The range of authorial voices during this period is extremely diverse. The Jewish-Greek writer Philo of Alexandria (*c*.30 BCE–*c*.50 CE) is steeped in views derived from Plato (Runia 1986). Authors such as Eudorus, Numenius and Calvenus Taurus (the last one of whom we learn about mostly through the writings of Aulus Gellius) are associated with Pythagoras (hence they are also called Neopythagoreans) and indicate a renewed interest during the period in potential connections between Plato and Pythagoras. Also included are philosophically trained "rhetoricians" such as Apuleius of Madaura and Maximus of Tyre, who are commonly considered as belonging to the Second Sophistic, and Galen, who weaves elements of Platonism into his medical works. The writings of this period include manuals, or succinct overviews, of Platonic doctrines, such as Alcinous' *Didaskalikos* and Apuleius' *de Platone et eius dogmate*; introductory works, such as the *Prologos* of

Albinus; and some extant evidence of commentaries, as with the anonymous commentary on Plato's *Theaetetus*. During this period, the most widely used form of commentary[1] focused on specific passages or themes, such as Plutarch's *On the Generation of the Soul in Plato's Timaeus*, dedicated to the interpretation of a single passage about the World Soul; Galen's commentary on the medical parts of the *Timaeus*; Aelian's commentary on the musical parts of the *Timaeus*; and Taurus' commentary on genesis in *Timaeus*. (The prominence of Plato's *Timaeus* is a point to which we shall return.) And an author such as Plutarch of Chaeroneia (46–120) is in a class of his own, given the range of interests within and the volume of his extant work.

In general, it is fair to say that after the sceptical phase in the history of the Academy, Middle Platonism represents a range of attempts to cull a more systematic set of doctrines from Plato's writings. Unfortunately, there are a number of crucial missing links in the extant evidence, and in some cases, earlier scholars have posited missing links, such as "a school of Gaius", for which we have little or no evidence (Dillon 1996a: 266–7). It is particularly unfortunate that we have so little information about Eudorus of Alexandria, who appears to have played an essential role in the transition to Middle Platonism (cf. Bonazzi 2005; Chiaradonna 2009a). Moreover, we do not have much information about *school* activity as such, and a number of texts hence appear to stand in something of a vacuum (Glucker 1978; Donini 1982).

But in spite of these lacunae, a careful examination of the extant texts reveals much about how Middle Platonist authors attempted to develop a philosophical system. As this chapter will show, Middle Platonists treated Plato and his works as highly authoritative and provided a unified reading of the Platonic corpus as a whole. To preserve this unity of Plato's thought, however, they also had to resolve dissension in the ranks of the Platonist tradition and reconcile the divergent interpretations that had occurred over time. Once this unity was secured, however, a further step was required to preserve truth claims, which entailed co-opting rival systems of thought as much as possible. Whereas Platonist responses to Aristotle and the Peripatetic tradition have received plenty of attention from scholars, much work remains to be done to understand the exact nature of the relationship between Platonism and Stoicism in this period, and to that end this chapter will examine three instances of such crossovers in greater detail. Finally, the chapter will turn to Plato's *Timaeus* as the focal text for Middle Platonism and reflect upon how this strand of Platonist thought anticipated later developments in so-called Neoplatonism.

If, as is claimed here, this phase in the history of Platonism is very much characterized by its attempt to come up with a more systematic "Platonism", this attempt rested on several developments. First, the authoritative status of both Plato and his works increased considerably in this period (Sedley 1997; Boys-Stones 2001), and ultimately this status was transferred to Platonist philosophical teachers, as can be seen in Porphyry's *Life of Plotinus*. The increasingly authoritative status of texts, as exemplified in the surging importance of commentaries, led to a *performative* use of such accounts, which implied that the very act of studying Plato's words amounted to engaging in the philosophical life and its turn to the life of the mind. Not all philosophical schools in this period adopted this mode, however. The Stoics, by contrast, posited a very different model for the relation between teacher and pupil, endorsing a less authoritative role for founders and teachers and relying on a more *instrumental* use of texts as merely pointing the way (Snyder 2000; Reydams-Schils 2011).

Second, the body of Plato's works had to make sense as a whole, and a highly unitary reading developed in which individual texts were interpreted in light of one another and potential contradictions were explained away. The Middle Platonists, following the principle *Platonem ex Platone saphenizein* ("to clarify Plato on the basis of Plato"), held that Plato's philosophy was coherent and systematic. This method of interpreting Plato had two important corollaries: it created groupings of Plato's works and an order in which the texts should be read. Attempts to produce such groupings were recorded by both Diogenes Laertius and Albinus. In his life of Plato, Diogenes (third century) paid witness to the division of those works into groups of three texts (Diogenes Laertius 3.61–2) and of four texts, the latter attributed to Thrasyllus (3.56–61) and still used today (Tarrant 1993). Moreover, both Diogenes (3.49) and Albinus (*Intr.* chs 3 & 6) presented a diaeretic grouping based on Plato's alleged method of which traces also survive, as when we discuss the so-called aporetic works of Plato.

In conjunction with these groupings, both Diogenes Laertius and Albinus offered advice on the best order in which to read Plato's works. Diogenes Laertius recorded (3.62) that "some start with the *Timaeus*", and Albinus reported considerable debate about this matter. Taurus described the course of study that "Pythagoras" had devised (Aulus Gellius, *Noctes Atticae* 1.9) before admitting any pupils, Pythagoras would examine their physiognomies to find out whether they were suitable for philosophy; after an initial period of at least two years of silent listening to expositions, in which they would be mere auditors (*akoustikoi*), pupils would embark on a more active course of study as adepts of the sciences (*mathēmatikoi*); and they would end with physics, as the study of the world (*mundi opera*) and the principles of nature (*principia naturae*). Both the diaeretic division and the reading order involved a systematic approach: all of Plato's works were viewed as part of one and the same project, and as all contributing to the construction of a philosophical system (F. Ferrari 2010).

In addition to its advice on curricula for different types of students, the anonymous commentary on the *Theaetetus* (1.1–4.27) also attests to the tradition of so-called *prolegomena* schemata; that is, preliminary issues to be settled before one embarks on a detailed study of one of Plato's works, such as the purpose of the work, its division into chapters, and the reasons for choosing certain characters as spokespersons (Mansfeld 1994). In Theon of Smyrna's work (second century), we find another type of preliminary work, a survey of mathematical knowledge (*Expositio rerum mathematicarum ad legendum Platonem utilium*) that Theon claims to have written on behalf of those who had not been trained since childhood in the mathematical sciences necessary to understand Plato's work and to gain access to other forms of knowledge.[2]

It was, however, not merely the unity of Plato's works that needed to be established, but also a unity within the tradition of interpreters of Plato and in philosophical truth. The sceptical phase of the Academy, with Arcesilaus and Carneades as its main representatives, posed a major challenge to both of these projects. The attempts of these "Academics" to undermine dogmatism, and Stoic doctrine in particular, could be seen as having overreached, leaving no room for any truth claims. As a result, any return to a more systematic interpretation of Plato would have had to come to terms with this phase of the Academy as a potential major break in the tradition. A central aspect of Plutarch's work consists precisely of an attempt to keep "Academics" and "Platonists" together as belonging to one and the same tradition, and to maintain the continuity of Platonism (Opsomer 1998; Bonazzi

2003). In a lost work titled "On the Unity of the Academy Since Plato" (n. 63 Lamprias Catalogue), Plutarch tried to demonstrate that the Platonic tradition is unified and that the sceptical approach, if rightly interpreted, could be considered a part of this tradition. A prevalent strategy of the period was to limit the application of scepticism to just one area that all Platonists considered problematic for truth claims, that of sense-perception. In his *de E apud Delphos*, for instance, Plutarch tried to demonstrate that a sceptical attitude towards the validity of sense-perception is compatible with the metaphysical assumptions about the nature of Being and God.

But not everyone adopted this approach. Numenius, for instance, used the image of Pentheus' body being torn limb from limb to attack Plato's successors in the Academy (the generations of Platonists whose quarrels, according to Numenius, ruined his legacy) in a treatise called, should we miss the point, "On the Stand-Off between Plato and the Academics" (frags 24–8 [des Places]). In this invective, Numenius also emphasized the connections between Plato and Pythagoras, lampooning the shameful behaviour of other schools and trying to shame earlier Platonists by pointing to the unity in the Epicurean ranks. Numenius, however, still had some respect for the first generations of Platonists, notably for Speusippus and Xenocrates, and if Nemesius' rendering of Numenius' views is accurate, he could even bring himself to cite Xenocrates (frag. 4b [des Places] = Nemesius 2, 8–14 [Morani]).[3]

The very notion of philosophical truth was at stake in the struggle to produce unity among Plato's followers. The sceptical Academy had notoriously exploited the disagreement among different schools of thought to recommend a suspension of judgement. To escape this deadlock, thinkers had to establish as much common ground as possible between the different systems in a dynamic of co-optation. That is, they tried both to integrate aspects of rival systems and to subjugate those to their own dominant frame of thought. Antiochus of Ascalon has traditionally been credited with the first major attempt of this kind, but similar attempts had been made in the Stoic camp by, for instance, Panaetius (Sedley 2012) and Posidonius (Reydams-Schils 2013). Their integration of Platonic elements, as that by the later Seneca, should not be seen as a kind of thoughtless "eclecticism" or as a major concession to Platonic thought, but rather as part of a strategy against sceptical attacks that was intended to preserve a rich sense of truth. Similarly, Middle Platonist attempts at integrating views from rival schools of thought do not diminish the originality of these attempts. On the contrary, the many variations among these attempts demonstrate that considerable ingenuity was required to create a more or less seamless fabric of thought.

In Plotinus' work, we can see a highly advanced mode of such co-optation that leaves the Epicureans as the main outsiders. Aristotle and the Peripatetic tradition rank second after Plato, and their presence is felt most strongly in Plotinus' analysis of the function of intellect (*nous*). As Karamanolis has put it, "Platonists used Aristotle as a means of accessing Plato's thought" and

> did so in three main ways: (*a*) Aristotle's reports on Plato's views were taken as preserving Plato's teaching; (*b*) those views of Aristotle which were found also in Platonic dialogues were taken as recasting doctrines of Plato in a more systematic form; (*c*) Aristotle's developments, mainly in logic, were often thought to be prefigured in Plato.   (2006: 28)

Compared to Aristotle, according to Plotinus, the Stoics rank lower; as metaphysical chickens, and in their version of the categories of reality, they are the target of considerable scorn by Plotinus because they radically reject any notion of transcendence and consider their active divine principle to be corporeal (*Enn.* V.9[5].1; VI.1–3[42–4]). Nevertheless, in his own analysis of the more dynamic aspects of soul, the universe and nature, Plotinus co-opted major traits from Stoicism, too.

In the period before Plotinus, as is to be expected, this hierarchy of co-optation was still much more fluid and contested. (We should also recall that although we know very little of their authors, major commentaries on Aristotle's work had also been composed during that time, the most important being the works of Alexander of Aphrodisias.) Most of the extant fragments of Atticus, for instance, are devoted to a polemic against the Peripatetic tradition, and indirectly against those Platonists who wanted to posit a harmony of thought between Plato and Aristotle. (Lucius and Nicostratus are two other examples of a critical attitude towards Aristotle.)

Similarly, an ongoing polemic against Stoicism allowed for different degrees of co-optation. The Stoics were suspect to Platonists for four principal reasons. First, as alluded to earlier, their immanent physics posited a divine active principle that is completely intertwined with matter and the *kosmos*, with its cycles of ordering and destruction, and thus denied the independent existence of any higher intelligible reality. Second, they held the view that anything that has real being, including the active principle and the soul, has to be corporeal (with the corollary that, according to them, the soul is mortal). Third, they proposed a monist view of the human soul as opposed to psychologies that posited a range of semi-independent conflicting powers (as in Plutarch's *de Virtute Morali*). And fourth, they viewed providence and fate as determining not only all aspects of the *kosmos* but as controlling human beings as well (Reydams-Schils 1999).

That Platonism co-opted elements from other systems of thought has been amply studied and documented. However, much more work remains to be done, especially regarding Stoicism, to understand more fully how the co-opted Stoic traits ended up transforming Platonic thought from within, like stowaways not that carefully stowed away after all. That is, scholars still have a tendency to take the polemical language of co-optation too much at face value. Given that Plato's *Timaeus* in particular helped to shape Stoic thought in its earliest phase, the influence of the Early Academy in that process has been much overestimated in recent scholarship (Reydams-Schils 2013). Furthermore, the philosophers of the Middle Platonist era had to put considerable effort into reclaiming a cosmology onto which major Stoic accretions had grafted themselves (Reydams-Schils 1999; Köckert 2009; F. Ferrari 2012). Given that in antiquity, reading a text implied reading it together with its interpretive tradition, there could be no complete return to Plato's own account as such. Cicero's translation of Plato's *Timaeus*, for instance, betrays the influence of debates among the schools of Hellenistic philosophy that were so central to his thought that they coloured his very reading of the *Timaeus* (Lévy 2003). Similarly, Philo of Alexandria's use of the *Timaeus* itself shows many traces of a Stoic influence (Reydams-Schils 1999: 135–65).

That this influence could be pervasive and transformative and yet easy to overlook can be demonstrated by the following three examples.

CALCIDIUS ON THE HUMAN SOUL

A first example is taken from psychology (Reydams-Schils 2006: 187–91). Instead of focusing on the polemics about the structure of the soul, and in spite of establishing a clear hierarchy (in ascending order) between the Stoics, Aristotle and Plato, Calcidius uses a doxographical schema that was also quite common in antiquity: a kind of master list of rational and irrational soul functions that tried to accommodate as many Platonic, Aristotelian and Stoic elements as possible. Despite variations in the manner in which different authors compiled such lists, the basic underlying approach was the same: to use the dual distinction of rational and irrational soul components in order to establish a common ground between different schools of thought, and thus to avoid the need for a suspension of judgement on this crucial topic. By the time Porphyry became interested in this model (see, for instance, frag. 253 [Smith] = Stobaeus 1.49.25a [Wachsmuth & Hense]), it already had a well-established tradition of its own. We can also find this approach in the work of Philo of Alexandria, for instance (Reydams-Schils 2002; see also Alexander of Aphrodisias, *de An.* 94.7–100.17).

The presence of such a master list can be detected in Calcidius' work in that the lists of soul functions attributed to the different thinkers throughout the commentary regularly combine elements of different origins. Thus Calcidius uses the Stoic connection between soul and "natural" *pneuma* (by which Chrysippus may have actually meant *pneuma sumfuton*, not the so-called "nature" level in the Stoic scale 773–89) to highlight that the soul, with its ruling part and seven instrumental parts, also directs the vital *pneuma* as well as nutrition, growth (*adolendo*) and motion (these latter functions gesture towards Peripatetic accounts: *Comm.* ch. 220). The Peripatetic list of soul functions under the heading of the appetitive soul includes "anger" and "desire", which were, of course, key notions in Platonic psychology. And to close the circle, in Calcidius' account of the Platonic soul functions, the senses have been promoted considerably: their headquarters, so to speak, are right next to the rational principle, because they are its "companions and messengers" (*comitesrationis et signi<feri>*, *Comm.* ch. 331, 245.7–8), in a precise echo of the Stoic passages Calcidius has chosen. According to this reading,[4] the senses largely take over the auxiliary role of spirit as the natural ally of reason. In this manner, Plato's epistemology is transformed to allow more room for doxastic reason and to yield a fruitful and harmonious cooperation between sense-perception and reasoning (which, to say the least, would be called into question by many Platonic passages), and thus more in line with Peripatetic and Stoic perspectives.

Another harmonizing feature in the treatise is Calcidius' attempt to prepare the ground for the view he ends up endorsing: there are two principles in a human soul, one that he calls *id ipsum animantis*, which we have in common with other living things, and another that he calls the principle (part or power) of the "rational soul". Even in his rendering of the first view in his doxography, which according to him assigns no specific location to the soul's principal part, Calcidius already draws his reader's attention to a distinction between the contributions of the heart and the head (*Comm.* ch. 214). The Hebrews' position, he goes on to argue, could have been salvaged if they had paid attention to a distinction embedded within their own views: that between the rational and the irrational soul, with the latter containing the appetites. The Stoics, according to Calcidius, also distinguish between a "natural" principal soul power in animals and a "rational" ruling principle in humans. According to other Stoic sources *pneuma* allegedly manifests itself as "cohesion" in lifeless things, as "nature" in plants, as "soul" in animals, and as "rational soul" in human beings. Thus Calcidius' distinction, if it were genuinely Stoic, would create problems for the difference between "nature' and "soul" in the Stoic system (compare this to *Comm.* ch. 54, 102.19–20). From one perspective, cohesion, nature, soul and rational soul are all manifestations of nature in its most general Stoic sense, but in that case it would not make sense to contrast "rational" with "natural", as Calcidius does, because the "rational" would be "natural" too. From another perspective, "nature" is a specific Stoic usage for plants, but, unlike Calcidius here, Stoics distinguish between "nature" and "soul", and so the notion of a non-rational, natural soul principle would become problematic. Stoic usages of the label "nature" would thus be either too general or too specific to fit Calcidius' purpose, and he is thus blurring Stoic distinctions in this passage. By plant-ing traces of Plato's alleged position within other views, the doxographer here sends an implicit message, made explicit elsewhere in the commentary, that Plato had managed not only to find the truth, but also to retrieve the insights of other thinkers so as to come up with the most complete account.

Calcidius' version of the master list runs through his entire commentary. In the treatise on fate, for instance, he renders the scale of being as follows:

> Therefore, because they partake in corporeality, there is between men and beasts and other things lacking life, a fellowship and participation in bodily phenom-ena, and if humans have birth, nourishment and growth in common with others, sense-experience (*sentire*) and impulse (*appetere*), finally, are common only to humans and animals lacking speech and reason. Now desire (*cupiditas*) and spirit (*iracundia*), in the case of animals, whether wild or tame, are irrational impulses (*appetitus inrationabilis est*, Latin uses singular here), in the case of a human being, however, whose characteristic it is to devote his mind to reason, they are rational [impulses]. The impulse (*appetitus*) to reason, to understand, and to know the truth is proper to a human being, who is at the greatest distance from desire and spirit; for the last-mentioned qualities can also be seen in mute animals, even to a much sharper degree; however, the perfection of reason and intellect is proper to a human being and god alone.
> (*Comm.* ch. 182, 209.16–210.4, trans. Den Boeft, modified; see also *Comm.* ch. 137)

This scale of beings clearly combines Stoic, Peripatetic and Platonic features. The first level consists of corporeality, which humans also share with lifeless things; the next level, presumably that of plants, includes birth, nourishment and growth; animals and humans share sense-perception and "impulse" (*appetitus*, more on this below), with the latter also covering spirit and appetite; and finally, unique to human beings and the gods is reason (which here is also a kind of *appetitus*).

Let us take a closer look at Calcidius' attempt to read the distinction between rational and irrational into Stoic psychology and its doxographical ancestry:

> He [Chrysippus] defines the inner deliberation of the mind as follows: "The rational power is an inner motion of the soul." For even mute animals have a principal power of soul, by the means of which they discern food, imagine, avoid

traps, overcome obstacles and emergencies, and recognize necessity, but this is not a rational power, rather, it is a natural one; of mortal things only a human being has the use of the good principle of mind, that is, of reason, as the same Chrysippus says ... [next quotation].   (*Comm.* ch. 220, 233.13–19)

The lines in this passage between the two quotations from Chrysippus are Calcidius' interpretation, and the wording of the section as a whole also indicates that he sees a connection between what he calls the natural soul principle in animals and the lower vital functions, which for a Stoic would fall under the "nature" heading in the scale of being. What falls under the non-rational or natural soul principle in the quoted passage is what the Stoics would have called "representation" (*phantasia*) and impulse (*hormē*), which an adult human being, according to the Stoics, would have in common with pre-rational children and irrational animals; in adult human beings, another function, assent, manifests itself with the advent of reason.

The alignment between human and animal perception and impulse, leaving out reason and assent, appears to have figured in polemics against the Stoics (as in Plutarch *Adv. Col.* 1122C–D, with the Academic claim that we do not need assent to explain human action). Both Alexander of Aphrodisias (*de Fato* 181.13–182.20 = LS 62G) and Nemesius (291.16 = LS 53O) also try to erase the differences between human and animal psychology that appear in Stoicism, this time by attributing assent to both. But such an alignment by no means remained confined to polemics; as we see in Philo and Calcidius, it also became a doxographical tool wielded to harmonize different psychologies.

In a passage from Cicero, it has to be noted, a Latin phrase such as *appetitus impellit ad agendum* is ambiguous enough to refer both to Stoic impulse and Platonic desire (*epithymia*), glossing over the fact that impulse's "obedience" to reason in Stoicism is fundamentally different from Platonic desire's submission:

Souls' movements are of two kinds: one belongs to thought, the other to impulse. The sphere of thought is principally the investigation of truth, while impulse is the stimulus to action. So we must take care to use thought for the best possible objects, and to make *impulse obedient to reason*.
    (*Off.* 1.132, included among fragments of Panaetius, frag. 88 [van Straaten]; see also *Off.* 1.101)

Calcidius makes good use of the same ambiguity in his master list and tells us that for him both spirit and desire are types of *appetitus* (244.14) (even though he assigns an *appetitus* even to reason).

Yet such a harmonizing move did not need to come at the expense of the important realization that, according to the Stoics, human representation and impulse do not merely co-exist with reason, but are transformed by it: whatever adult human beings do falls under the reign of reason, whether it is used correctly or not. Calcidius' entire claim about the importance of doxastic reason rests on such a realization. And he transposes this realization even onto his rendering of Platonic psychology, as when he claims that spirit and appetite are of a higher order in humans than in animals, precisely because in human beings, these are meant to serve reason and hence are rationalized to some extent (*Comm.* ch. 182, quoted above, and *Comm.* ch. 187, 212.10–14).

ALCINOUS ON GOD

A second example of co-optation pertains to the divine principle. Alcinous' account of divine agency has many Peripatetic traits.[5] The Forms are said to be the thoughts of God (that is, God thinks himself, and the product of his thought are the transcendent Platonic Ideas); this divine agency is said "to act on [the intellect of the whole heaven] while remaining itself unmoved … as the object of desire moves desire" (*Intr.* 164.23–6), and Alcinous posits an eternal universe (Reydams-Schils 1999: 199–201). Clearly reflected in this view is Aristotle's notion of the highest god as an Unmoved Mover who thinks himself. Yet Alcinous also describes his highest god in strongly relational terms, as "caring" for the universe. One feature of his description of the divine stands out in particular: "by his own will he has filled all things with himself" (*Intr.* 164.42–165.1, trans. Dillon). This is a rather odd description of a transcendent divinity, and a wording that would seem more appropriate for the Stoics because of their highly developed notion of divine Providence. The *Timaeus* itself mentions only that the Demiurge "wanted everything to be as much alike to himself as possible" (*Ti.* 29e3) and keeps the universe together by his will (*Ti.* 41b4). Some parallel passages from other authors focus on the account of God holding the universe together through his will (cf. Philo, *Her.* 246 and Atticus, frag. 4, 67–71; 93–5). Others place the claim in a Stoic context by connecting it primarily to Providence (cf. Pseudo-Plutarch, *de Fato* 572F; Calcidius, *Comm.* ch. 205.3–5 and Marcus Aurelius, *Noctes Atticae* 6.40; 9.1). And the prominence of the theme of Providence in later Platonist writers, which goes much beyond what the *Timaeus* itself has to offer on this score, was largely due to a Stoic influence. The "will of God" remains but a touch of the brush in the overall picture presented by this Middle Platonist handbook, yet it is unmistakably there, to the point of creating an unresolved tension in Alcinous' views of the divine (see below).

PLUTARCH ON MATTER

A third example comes from Plutarch and concerns the principle of matter (Reydams-Schils 1999: 193–6). Whereas other Platonists vehemently rejected the Stoic notion of a corporeal matter, Plutarch fully integrated this notion into his ontology. In his *de Animae Procreatione in Timaeo* (1013C), he distinguishes implicitly between three levels of matter: (a) matter as "corporeal substance" (*sōmatikē ousia*, *de An. Procr.* 1014C, E, 1017A, 1023A); (b) matter as sensible "straightaway", tangible and visible when "by participating in and simulating the intelligible it has got shape", which happens in the pre-cosmic phase (*de An. Procr.* 1014C; 1016E); and (c) matter as acquiring motivity (and imagination, *de An. Procr.* 1014C; 1017A; 1023D; 1024A) through soul inhering in it (an irrational, disorderly soul, in the pre-cosmic phase, a view that assumes that all self-motion requires a soul).

Plutarch's distinction between matter's corporeality and its sensibility – if somewhat ambiguous because features under (a) arguably could be related to (b), or vice versa – acquires its full meaning from the perspective of Stoic doctrine. Given that sensible features such as visibility and tangibility result from a rudimentary participation in the intelligible, accounting for matter as body without these features would be difficult without making a connection with the Stoic view of the principle of matter *qua* body as passivity and being without quality (*apoion*). Furthermore, just as the Stoics claimed that the passive and the ordering principles always concur in reality, so Plutarch could posit a distinction between matter as corporeal and as sensible and yet claim that in reality matter always has sensible features that result from its participation in the intelligible, however minimally (this, we take it, is the force of "straightaway", at *de An. Procr.* 1013C). The intelligible realm, however, unlike the Stoic active principle, remains essentially transcendental, which leads to the quandary of participation.

The notion of a corporeal matter occurs not only in contexts in which Plutarch engages in a polemic against the Stoics but runs through the entire treatise of *de Animae Procreatione in Timaeo*. Furthermore, Plutarch restates the same view in the *Quaestiones Platonicae* (3, 1001D–E). Finally, it becomes clear why Plutarch used only one side of a type of regress-argument against the Stoic view of corporeal principles: because he himself accepts some form of corporeal matter, he tackles only the notion of a corporeal active principle, implying that it too would contain matter, but does not use the matching argument against a corporeal matter *qua* matter (*de Communibus Notitiis*, 1085Cff.). Other Platonists, such as Alcinous (as in *Intr.* ch. 8) or Calcidius (as in *Comm.* chs 294, 311, 319), do not fail to accuse the Stoics of creating a contradiction in terms by positing matter as a body without quality (*soma apoion*), because for them to be a body implies a forming principle that bestows the quality of corporeality. It is striking that in his extant works, Plutarch does not use this argument of self-contradiction against the Stoics, not even in the *de Stoicorum Repugnantiis*. To Plutarch, matter as body has qualities not because to be body necessarily entails being qualified, but because matter as body is always *also* sensible owing to its participation in the intelligible. Positing an intrinsically corporeal matter is a genuine and fundamental concession to the Stoic theory of the principles.

The three examples cited above – Calcidius on the structure of the human soul, Alcinous on divine agency, and Plutarch on matter – reveal a very complex interplay between Platonic, Peripatetic and Stoic elements. To say merely that a certain common language of philosophy had been developed by this period, in which many terms were integrated without necessarily carrying all the connotations that they had in their original context, is hermeneutically naïve: on the contrary, thinkers' ongoing polemical exchanges counted on the persistent presence of such connotations even while engaged in attempts at co-optation. Similarly, to posit that for Platonists "Platonic doctrines" constituted the dominant frame of reference, while true enough in itself, can underestimate the transformative effect of co-opted notions from other currents of thought.

In Platonism from Plotinus onwards, and especially in the fully developed philosophical curriculum that Iamblichus devised, the pinnacle of Platonism is arguably constituted by the *Parmenides* and a reading of that dialogue that increasingly focuses on a hyper-transcendent level of reality. In the earlier phase of Platonism, as we have seen, the role of focal text around which many of the debates centred was reserved for the *Timaeus*. Alcinous, for instance, structured his handbook around the divisions first between practical and theoretical philosophy and dialectic as covering the art of reasoning, with the category of practical philosophy further divided into ethics, household management ("economics" in its ancient, etymological sense) and politics, and of theoretical philosophy into mathematics, physics and theology (P. Hadot 1979). His expositions on theology and especially on physics are dominated by the framework provided by the *Timaeus*.

The *Timaeus*, however, had left its readers with many puzzles that demanded answers. Is the "beginning" of the ordering of the world by the Demiurge to be taken literally (as

Atticus and Plutarch did), or is it merely a metaphor that Plato uses for pedagogical purposes to convey a causal, atemporary dependence, as the majority of the Platonists appear to have held? How are the different "ordering" forces represented by the Demiurge, his model in intelligible reality, the lower gods, and the World Soul related to one another (Opsomer 2005)? Another very important question concerned the relationship between the Demiurge, his model, and the idea of the Good, to which the Middle Platonists presented a range of solutions. According to Plutarch (and Atticus), the Demiurge of the *Timaeus* and the Good of the *Republic* are identical, whereas according to Numenius (and perhaps Alcinous), Demiurge and Good are two different principles: the idea of the Good (identified with the One) is the First God, the principle of Being (i.e. of the world of Forms), whereas the Demiurge is the second God, the principle of the sensible cosmos (frags 16; 17; 19; 21 [des Places]). Also left unanswered was how such notions as Monad and Dyad, Limit and Unlimited, fit with the *Timaeus* account.

To what extent, if any, has the World Soul in the *Timaeus* been affected by a connection with matter (the tradition's designation of the "receptacle" from Aristotle onwards)? Given that matter as a principle is co-eternal with God, a view that was put into question from Plotinus onwards, how does this dualism affect the existence of evil? The most interesting solution to the problem of the origin of evil may be that of Plutarch and Atticus, both of whom think that matter cannot be the principle of evil because it is devoid of all quality: "What is without quality and of itself inert and without propensity Plato cannot suppose to be cause and principle of evil" (Plutarch, *de An. Procr.* 1015A). Thus the cause of evil (that is, disorder) must be found in the principle of a pre-cosmic chaotic movement of matter (i.e. in the irrational pre-cosmic soul; see also the above discussion of Plutarch's notion of matter). According to Plutarch, matter and pre-cosmic soul are two different principles: "In fact, while Plato calls matter mother and nurse, what he calls the cause of evil is the motion that moves matter"; that is, the irrational soul (*de An. Procr.* 1015E). In addition to the complex issue of matter, during this period several other central concerns arose from Plato's *Timaeus*, including how human freedom relates to divine Providence and fate and how the lower, irrational and mortal soul parts affect the human being as a whole.

Given the complexities that arise in defining the strand of Platonism predating Plotinus, the exact relationship between Middle Platonism and Neoplatonism is difficult to establish, but the category of *Vorbereitung* ("preparing the way") may be of some use here (cf. Theiler 1934). Middle Platonist authors seem to have anticipated several principal features of Neoplatonist tendencies, including (a) the rediscovery of transcendence (world of Ideas and Demiurge); (b) the establishment of a hierarchical structure of reality, which is represented as a succession of ontological levels (One or first God, transcendent Forms, Demiurge, immanent Forms, Soul, demons, sensible bodies, matter, and so on); (c) the rejection of the Hellenistic (Stoic) conception of *apatheia* and a renewed interest in the Platonic-Aristotelian theory of *metriopatheia*; and (d) the formulation of the *telos* as assimilation to God (*homoiōsis theōi*). Nonetheless, acknowledging that Middle Platonism prepared the ground for what is now commonly referred to as Neoplatonism should not obscure the original contributions of this current of thought, in all its multifaceted variety.

NOTES

1. For a list of commentaries, see Dörrie & Baltes (1987–2008: vol. 3, §§77–81).
2. Petrucci (2009). For the Neoplatonic development of mathematics in relation to metaphysics, see Slaveva-Griffin (Chapter 13), below.
3. The image is also used by Atticus, frag. 1 [des Places], Clement of Alexandria, *Strom.* 1.13.57.1–6 [Migne], and Calcidius, *Comm.* ch. 246, 256.14–16 [Waszink]. The latter, unlike Numenius, rejects the Old Academy, too.
4. This reading, which is also present in Philo of Alexandria's works, could have derived some support from Plato *Lg.* 964e–65a.
5. On this section, see now also the detailed discussion with bibliography in Dörrie & Baltes (1987–2008: vol. 7.1, §188.1).

5

Plotinus and the Gnostics: opposed heirs of Plato

John D. Turner

Throughout the first half of the twentieth century the majority of scholars have tended to see the relationship between Plotinus and the Gnostics as primarily adversarial (see Porphyry, *Plot.* 16), and characterized by Plotinus' philosophical critique of specific gnostic doctrines, which is explicit in his anti-Gnostic treatise (*Enn.* II.9[33]) and the other three treatises of the so-called *Großschrift* (*Enn.* III.8[30], *Enn.* V.8[31] and *Enn.* V.5[32]), surfacing also at other points throughout the rest of his treatises. But with the appearance of Hans Jonas' dissertation, *Gnosis und spätantiker Geist* (Jonas 1934–93), Joseph Katz's essay "Plotinus and the Gnostics" (Katz 1954), Cornelia de Vogel's essay "On the Neoplatonic Character of Platonism and the Platonic Character of Neoplatonism" (de Vogel 1953), as well as Henri-Charles Puech's essay "Plotin et les Gnostiques" (Puech 1960), scholars began to emphasize fundamental similarities between Plotinian and gnostic metaphysics that were thought to stem from their shared environment in the religio-philosophical climate of opinion typical of late antique Alexandria. Since then, additional proponents of this view have arisen, including the present author,[1] but not without the vigorous objection to Jonas' hypothesis by Armstrong, who maintained that "the thought of Plotinus is profoundly un-Gnostic and anti-Gnostic" (Armstrong 1978: 113).

In the latest study of the relation between Plotinus and the Gnostics, Jean-Marc Narbonne observes that over the course of a roughly twenty-five-year teaching career in Rome beginning during the years 244–6 and ending abruptly in 269, Plotinus developed a number of positions reflecting confrontations with a multitude of issues. This career was marked by several decisive events and many quarrels, among which the battle with the Gnostics certainly took precedence.[2] Indeed, Porphyry's *Life of Plotinus* tells us that a number of gnostic apocalypses circulated in his Roman seminar, principally treatises of the so-called Sethian or "classical" Gnostics, especially the Nag Hammadi treatises *Zostrianos* and *Allogenes*. According to Porphyry, Plotinus himself was said to have refuted these treatises many times in his courses, even going so far as to write his own critique in

Enn. II.9[33] and mandating even more thoroughgoing refutations of them by his principal disciples, Amelius and Porphyry, during the years 263–8, but the conflict continued until the demise of the seminar in 269, since some of those close to Plotinus – whom he called "friends" – had fallen under the spell of the rival doctrine and were defecting (*Enn.* II.9[33].10.3–6). From his first days in Rome, Plotinus was surrounded not so much by scholastic Platonists, but by Platonizing Gnostics whom he considered for some time to be his friends (Narbonne 2011: 68–9). This suggests that he regarded them as belonging to the same group as did he and his disciples, namely to the partisans of "Plato's Mysteries" (Puech 1960: 182–3).

Rather than merely dressing up their mythologies with a superficial smattering of Greek philosophical terminology, the Platonizing Gnostics have turned out to be genuinely innovative interpreters of ancient philosophical traditions, and had a far greater degree of intellectual agency with respect to contemporaneous academic philosophy than is usually supposed. Right alongside Plotinus, these Gnostic interpreters were reading and commenting upon the very same texts as he did. They were activist contemplatives who were spreading a doctrine of salvation that competed with Plotinus' own and who shared with him several presuppositions, even if certain particular themes made them radical opponents. Indeed, Plotinus' interpretation of Plato shows itself to be very conscious of this direct competition; as Plotinus states himself, "in general they [the Gnostics] falsify Plato's account of the manner of the [world's] making, and a great deal else, and degrade the great man's teachings" (*Enn.* II.9[33].6.24–6).[3]

This chapter offers, first, a description of gnostic and early Neoplatonic metaphysics, and second, using this as a background, a summary of Plotinus' critique of gnostic doctrines, especially in his treatise *Against the Gnostics* (*Enn.* II.9[33]). Third, since Plotinus mainly criticizes gnostic thought for its unacknowledged and "falsifying" appropriation of Plato's teaching, this chapter will conclude with a comparison of Plotinus and the Gnostics as exegetes of Plato's dialogues. The reader should be aware that the discussion of these issues here is a work in progress, intended to point the way towards future research rather than to offer a comprehensive treatment.

GNOSTIC AND EARLY NEOPLATONIC METAPHYSICS

One of the novel developments in the transition from the rather static ontologies typical of Middle Platonism to the dynamic emanationism of Plotinus, and subsequent Neoplatonism is the doctrine of the unfolding of the world of true being and intellect from its source in a transcendent, only negatively conceivable ultimate unitary principle which is itself beyond being: first, an initial identity of the product with its source, a sort of potential or prefigurative existence; second, an indefinite procession or spontaneous emission of the product from its source; and third, a contemplative visionary reversion of the product upon its own prefiguration within its source, in which the product becomes aware of its separate existence and thereby takes on its own distinctive form and definition.[4] The later Neoplatonists named these three stages *permanence* or *remaining*, *procession* and *reversion*, and – like the Sethian Platonizing treatises – often characterized the three successive modes of the product's existence during this process by the terms of the noetic triad of Existence or Being, Life and Intellect.

Although Plotinus has often been credited with being the first major philosopher to elaborate such a scheme, it is clear that similar models of dynamic emanation are beginning to develop in gnostic thought, some of which chronologically precedes Plotinus. The main difference is that, whereas for Plotinus, only the spontaneous efflux from the One, but not the One itself, knows or reflexively acts upon itself, for most gnostic models, the supreme principle is capable of reflexive self-knowledge, which knowledge or thought becomes the second principle. Thus in Valentinian thought, at the beginning of the *Tripartite Tractate*, the ineffable Father has a thought of himself, which is the Son (*Tripartite Tractate* [NHC I.5] 56.16–57.3), and in Clement of Alexandria's account of the Valentinian system of Theodotus, the Unknown Father is said to emit the second principle, the Monogenes-Son, "as if knowing himself".[5] Similarly, in both *Eugnostos the Blessed* and its nearly identical but Christianized version, the *Sophia of Jesus Christ*, the divine Forefather sees himself "within himself as in a mirror", and the resultant image is the second principle, the Self-Father.[6] In Hippolytus of Rome's account of Simonian doctrine, the pre-existent first principle abides in absolute unity, but gives rise to an intellectual principle through self-manifestation: "manifesting himself to himself, the one who stood became the second".[7]

Plotinus' familiarity with gnostic thought is probably based on a number of gnostic sources, some lost and some extant. Among the latter, the most important original gnostic compositions are present in the fourth-century Coptic papyrus library from Nag Hammadi, in particular the Platonizing Sethian treatises from codices VII, VIII, X and XI, and from codex I, the Valentinian treatise *Tripartite Tractate*. The metaphysical schemes of these gnostic treatises, owing in no small part to their similarity to his own, not only invited his criticism, but also probably made positive contributions to his thought.

The following survey of the metaphysics of dynamic emanationism and ontogenetic production in original gnostic sources begins with the somewhat less complex schemes in the *Tripartite Tractate* and proceeds to the more complex schemes found in the Sethian Platonizing treatises.

THE METAPHYSICS OF THE *TRIPARTITE TRACTATE*

In the *Tripartite Tractate*, the generation of all reality other than the supreme principle begins with the generation of a second principle, the Son, when the ineffable Father has a thought of himself:[8]

> For it is truly his ineffable self that he (the Father) engenders. It is self-generation, where he conceives of himself and knows himself as he is. He brings forth something worthy of the admiration, glory, praise, and honour that belong to himself, through his boundless greatness, his inscrutable wisdom, his immeasurable power, and his sweetness that is beyond tasting. It is he himself whom he puts forth in this manner of generation, and who receives glory and praise, admiration and love, and it is also he who gives himself glory, admiration, praise, and love. This he has as a Son dwelling in him, keeping silent about him, and this is the ineffable within the ineffable, the invisible, the ungraspable, the inconceivable within the inconceivable. This is how he exists eternally within himself. As we have explained, by knowing himself in himself the Father bore him without generation, so that he exists by the

Father having him as a thought – that is, his thought about himself, his sensation of himself and … of his eternal self-standing.

(*Tripartite Tractate* 56.1–57.3, trans. Thomassen in NHC [Meyer])

The ambiguity in the self-reflexive pronouns, which can refer to either the Father or the Son, resembles similar ambiguities in Plotinus' language of ontogenesis through self-contemplation, where the ambiguity of antecedents is necessary, since the object of the self-perception of both the first and the second principle are one and the same; that is, the second principle is always prefiguratively present in the first. For example, in *Enn.* V.1[10].7, the subject of self-perception can be properly called neither One nor Intellect, but is rather a subject that starts out as the One, but by perceiving itself, ends up as Intellect:

But we say that Intellect is an image of that Good; for we must speak more plainly; first of all we must say that what has come into being must be in a way that Good, and retain much of it and be a likeness of it, as light is of the sun. But Intellect is not that Good. How then does it generate Intellect? Because by its return to it it sees: and this seeing is Intellect.   (*Enn.* V.1[10].7.1–6)

Moreover, the *Tripartite Tractate* or something much like it seems to have been decisive for central images in Plotinus' theory of emanation by providing a clear antecedent for the theory of undiminished giving. Compare the images from pages 51, 60, 68 and 74 of the *Tripartite Tractate*:[9]

The Father is singular while being many …. That singular one who is the only Father is in fact like a tree that has a trunk, branches, and fruit.

(*Tripartite Tractate* 51.8–19)

The aeons existed eternally in the Father's thought and he was like a thought and a place for them. And once it was decided that they should be born, he who possesses all power desired to take and bring what was incomplete out of … those who [were within] him. But he is [as] he is, [for he is] a spring that is not diminished by the water flowing from it.   (*Tripartite Tractate* 60.1–15)

For the Father produced the All like a little child, like a drop from a spring, like a blossom from a [vine], like a …, like a shoot …, so that they needed [nourishment], growth, and perfection.   (*Tripartite Tractate* 62.6–13)

the true aeon also is single yet multiple …. Or, to use other similes, it is like a spring that remains what it is even if it flows into rivers, lakes, streams, and canals; or like a root that spreads out into trees with branches and fruits; or like a human body that is indivisibly divided into limbs and limbs – main limbs and extremities, large ones and small.   (*Tripartite Tractate* 74.1–18)

with Plotinus' image of the One as a spring in which all rivers have their source or as the life of a great plant, eternally giving and yet self-standing:

What is above life is cause of life, for the activity of life which is all things is not first; it itself flows forth, so to speak, as if from a spring. Imagine a spring that has no other origin; it gives itself to all the rivers, yet is never used up by the rivers, but remains itself at rest; the rivers that proceed from it remain all together for a while before they run their several ways, yet all, in some sense, know beforehand down what channels they will pour their streams. Or: think of the life coursing throughout some huge plant while its origin remains and is not dispersed over the whole, since it is as it were firmly settled in its root: it is the giver of the entire and manifold life of the tree, but remains unmoved itself, not manifold but the origin of that manifold life.

(Enn. III.8[30].10.3–14, trans. Armstrong, with alterations)

In all of these passages, the subject of discussion is the emergence of multiplicity from a sole source, wherein the product emanates from its source but the source remains undiminished. Although these common images of water and plants can be found *individually* in Macrobius and the *Corpus Hermeticum*,[10] they are *all* to be found in the *Tripartite Tractate*.

Another of the *Tripartite Tractate*'s points of contact with Plotinus' thought is its account of the divinely willed creation of the physical cosmos (*oikoumenē*) – despite its deficiency – by the *logos*, the last of the aeons emanated from the Father, as not only necessary and willed by the supreme Father, but also a product of *natural*, not artificial, wisdom:

It came upon one of the aeons that he should undertake to reach the inconceivability of the Father, and to give glory to it as well as to his ineffability. It was a Word belonging to the unity, [although] it was a singular Word that arose out of the union of the members of the All, nor was it from him who had brought them forth – for he who has brought forth the All [is] the Father. For this aeon was one of those who had been given wisdom, with ideas first existing independently in his mind so as to be brought forth when he wanted it. Because of that, he had received a natural wisdom enabling him to inquire into the hidden order, being a fruit of wisdom.[11] Thus, the free will with which the members of the All had been born caused this one to do what he wanted, with no one holding him back. Now, the intention of this Word was good, because he rushed forward [to] give glory to the Father, even though [he] undertook a task beyond his power, having desired to produce something perfect, from a union in which he did not share, and without having received orders.   (*Tripartite Tractate* 75.17–76.12)

In this respect, Corrigan has argued that, like Plotinus, this author too avoids the notion of a fallen and culpable personal agent behind the world's creation.[12] The *Tripartite Tractate* should be compared with Irenaeus' account of Ptolemy's Valentinian cosmogonic myth, in which Sophia plays the role of the (Indefinite) Dyad as an outbreak of passion, but, perhaps since she is not here credited with the natural wisdom possessed by the *Tripartite Tractate*'s *logos*, she is viewed merely as the culpable cause of multiplicity.[13]

THE METAPHYSICS OF THE SETHIAN PLATONIZING TREATISES

While the *Tripartite Tractate* clearly presupposes a scheme of dynamic emanation presented largely in metaphors of flowing, growth and even embryology, the equivalent scheme in the Sethian Platonizing treatises is explicitly articulated as an interaction within transcendental triads that form the links between the ultimate source and its products.

The most widely known treatise in the large corpus of the so-called Sethian or classic gnostic literature from Nag Hammadi is the *Apocryphon of John*. According to its initial theogony, the supreme Invisible Spirit emanates an overflow of luminous water in which he then sees a reflection of himself; this self-vision then becomes the second, intellectual, principle, Barbelo, the divine First Thought. In turn, Barbelo contemplates the same luminous water from which she had originated in order to generate the third principle, the divine Autogenes as the "First Appearance" of the Invisible Spirit's first power.[14] Within this corpus, the four "Platonizing Sethian" treatises – *Zostrianos*, *Allogenes*, the *Three Steles of Seth* and *Marsanes* – occupy a special place, especially since Porphyry's *Life of Plotinus* 16 tells us that two of them – *Allogenes* and especially *Zostrianos* – were studied and critiqued at length by Plotinus and other members of his philosophical seminar in Rome during the years 265–58. Indeed, Plotinus' own critique in *Enn.* II.9[33].10 seems actually to cite *Zostrianos* 10.1–20,[15] which raises the question of the extent to which the doctrines he read in these Sethian texts may have made positive contributions to his own metaphysical philosophy.

The metaphysical hierarchy of the Platonizing Sethian treatises is headed by a supreme and pre-existent Unknowable One, often called the Invisible Spirit.[16] As in Plotinus, this One is clearly beyond being, and can be described only in negative terms mostly derived from the second half of Plato's *Parmenides*, especially its first hypothesis (137c–142a).

Below the supreme One, at the level of determinate being, is the Barbelo Aeon, conceived along the lines of a Middle Platonic tripartite divine Intellect. It contains three ontological levels, conceived as sub-intellects or subaeons of the Barbelo Aeon: one that is contemplated (*nous noētos*), called Kalyptos or "hidden"; one that contemplates (*nous noeros* or *theorētikos*), called Protophanes or "first appearing";[17] and one that is discursive and demiurgic (*nous dianooumenos*), called Autogenes or "self-generated".[18]

At the highest level, Kalyptos contains the paradigmatic ideas or authentic existents, each of which is a unique, uncombinable paradigmatic form.[19] At the median level, Protophanes contains "those who are unified"; that is, the contemplated ideas that are "all together"[20] with the minds that contemplate them, apparently to be distinguished both from ideas of particular things (in Autogenes) and from the uncombinable authentic existents in Kalyptos.[21] At the lowest level, Autogenes would be a demiurgic mind (*nous dianooumenos*) who shapes the individuated realm of Nature below him according to the forms in Kalyptos that are contemplated and made available to him by Protophanes (the *nous theorētikos*).[22] As the equivalent of the Plotinian Soul, Autogenes analyses these forms in a discursive fashion (as a *nous dianooumenos*), and thus comes to contain the "perfect individuals", the ideas of particular, individual things, as well as individual souls.[23] Somewhat like the three Gods or Intellects of Numenius, the first God is inert and so in some sense "hidden" from all else except the second who contemplates the ideal forms in the first, while the third God is merely the lower demiurgical aspect of the second when he directs his attention downwards to impose these Forms on matter to produce the perceptible cosmos. While the first God gives rise to nothing, the second God both contemplates *and* creates.[24]

But, whereas Numenius, as noted above, offers a "static" ontology that does not account for the process by which his three Gods come into being, a number of gnostic thinkers were developing schemes by which a hierarchy of transcendental beings emanated from a single source by a process of dynamic emanation, perhaps derived from Neopythagorean speculation on the generation of the dyad and subsequent multiplicity from the monad.[25] In the case of the theologians behind the Sethian Platonizing treatises, a bit of reflection on the significance of the names Kalyptos, Protophanes and Autogenes would suggest that they could designate not just the ontological levels of the Barbelo Aeon, but rather the dynamic process by which the Barbelo Aeon gradually unfolds from its source in the Invisible Spirit: at first "hidden" (*kalyptos*) or latent within the Spirit as its prefigurative intellect, then "first appearing" (*prōtofanēs*) as the first moment of the Spirit's separately existing thought or intelligence, and finally "self-generated" (*autogenēs*) as a fully formed demiurgical mind, perhaps equivalent to the rational part of the cosmic soul that operates on the physical world below in accordance with its vision of the archetypal ideas contained in the divine intellect, Protophanes.[26]

Nevertheless, when it came to working out the actual dynamics of the emanation of the Barbelo Aeon, the Platonizing Sethian treatises ended up employing a completely different and distinctive terminology to account for the emergence of the Barbelo Aeon from the supreme Invisible Spirit, namely the noetic triad of Being, Life and Mind.

Indeed, Plotinus himself had employed such a triad, although only hesitatingly as a means by which the One gives rise to something other than itself, as in the generation of intellect from a trace of life emitting from the One.[27] However, just as the Sethians confined the Kalyptos–Protophanes–Autogenes triad to their second hypostasis Barbelo, Plotinus mostly confined the function of the noetic triad almost entirely to his second hypostasis, Intellect, where it is used to argue that Intellect is not merely a realm of static being, but is instead living and creative thought.[28]

By contrast with Plotinus' implementation, in the Platonizing Sethian treatises, the noetic triad appears as an entity called the Triple Power of the Invisible Spirit, which functions as the intermediary means by which the supreme Invisible Spirit gives rise to the Aeon of Barbelo. It is composed of the three powers of Existence (*hyparxis* rather than *to on*, Being), Vitality (*zōotēs* rather than *zōē*, Life) and Mentality (*nootēs* [or Blessedness in *Zostrianos*] rather than *nous*, Intellect), and serves as the emanative means by which the supreme Unknowable One generates the Aeon of Barbelo in three phases. (1) In its initial phase, the Triple Powered One is a purely indeterminate Existence (*hyparxis* or *ontotēs*), latent within and identical with the supreme One; (2) in its emanative phase it is an indeterminate Vitality (*zōotēs*) that proceeds forth from One; and (3) in its final phase it is a Mentality (*nootēs*) that contemplates its prefigurative source in the supreme One and, thereby delimited, takes on the character of determinate being as the intellectual Aeon of Barbelo.[29]

These Sethian treatises present several variations in the ontological relationship between the Unknowable One and/or Invisible Spirit, his Triple Power and the Barbelo Aeon. Thus, somewhat like Plotinus, the *Three Steles of Seth* tends to portray the Triple Power as a dynamic structure inherent in the second principle Barbelo (but also in the supreme One),[30] while *Zostrianos* tends to portray it as the Invisible Spirit's inherent threefold power. On the other hand, *Allogenes* and *Marsanes* tend to hypostatize the Triple Power by identifying its median processional phase (e.g. Vitality, Life, Activity)[31] as a quasi-hypostatic "Triple-Powered One" (or Triple-Powered Invisible Spirit) interposed between the supreme Unknowable One and the Aeon of Barbelo, although in its initial and final phases it actually *is* these two.

It is significant that the anonymous Turin *Commentary* on Plato's *Parmenides* also employs this triad in a derivational context. According to the sixth fragment of the *Commentary* (*Anon. in Parm.* 6.10–26) there are two "Ones": a first One whom the *Parmenides*' first hypothesis describes as altogether beyond the realm of determinate being, and a second One, the prototype of all true, determinate being, to be identified with the "One-who-is" of the second Parmenidean hypothesis. In each phase of the unfolding of the second One or Intellect from the first One, a distinct modality of the Intellect predominates at a given phase. First, as a pure infinitival Existence (*einai* or *hyparxis*), Intellect is a purely potential Intellect identical with its prefiguration in the absolute being (*to einai*) of the first One. In its final phase, it has become identical with the determinate or participial being (*to on*) of Intellect proper, the second hypostasis; it has now become the hypostatic exemplification of its "idea", the absolute being (*to einai*) of the One. The transitional phase between the first and final phases of Intellect in effect constitutes a median phase in which Intellect proceeds forth from the first One as an indeterminate Life.

Middle Platonic and Neopythagorean sources prior to the anonymous *Commentary*, the Platonizing Sethian treatises, and to Plotinus himself seem to offer no explicit implementation of such a process of contemplative self-generation. Various Neopythagoreans certainly derived a dyadic second principle from a primal Monad,[32] but not from the Monad's self-cognition, and, except for Moderatus and Philo of Alexandria, their second principle is not generally an Intellect. And when Middle Platonists – for whom the supreme principle is generally an Intellect rather than a hyperontic One – apply the Aristotelian (e.g. *Metaph.* 1072b13–14) notion of a self-contemplative Intellect thinking the Platonic Forms as its own thoughts, the self-contemplation of the supreme principle does not give rise to a hypostatically distinct secondary principle; indeed, it is sometimes unclear whether the object of contemplation is or is not hypostatically distinct from the thinking subject. In the extant fragments of the anonymous *Parmenides Commentary* the doctrine of generation through contemplative self-reversion is more implied than clearly elaborated: the two Ones are here related by participation, but it is never clearly stated that the second One unfolds dynamically from the self-conception of its prefiguration in the first One.[33] All this suggests that Plotinus and the author of the *Commentary* may be indebted to gnostic thinkers for various details of their metaphysics of dynamic emanation and perhaps even the Being–Life–Mind triad itself.

PLOTINUS' CRITIQUE OF GNOSTIC DOCTRINE

Enn. II.9[33], perhaps completed in the year 265, is the only treatise in the *Enneads* where Plotinus explicitly and at length criticizes his contemporaries whom Porphyry identifies as Gnostics, whose erroneous opinions threaten to mislead the intimate members of his own circle.

Points of disagreement with extant gnostic treatises

Plotinus is critical in general of the Gnostics' unnecessary multiplication of hypostases, since he regards the supreme One as entirely transcendent to Intellect; there is no being that exists between them as mediator, nor may one distinguish between a higher intellect in repose containing all realities (*onta*) and a lower one in motion, or a One in act and another One in potency (*Enn.* II.9[33].1). Nor may one distinguish between an intellect at rest, another that contemplates them and another demiurgic mind (or soul) that reflects or plans (*Enn.* II.9[33].6), as did Numenius and even Plotinus himself on one occasion (*Enn.* III.9[13].1). This partitioning is reflected in many sources, including the fragments of Numenius' *On the Good* and the *Chaldaean Oracles*, but most clearly in the doctrine of the Kalyptos, Protophanes and Autogenes levels of the Barbelo Aeon as found in all four Platonizing Sethian treatises.[34]

With even greater vehemence, Plotinus attacks doctrines found principally in *Zostrianos*, especially its teaching on Sophia (*Zostrianos* 9.16–11.9). Of course, he agrees that a certain wisdom (Sophia) presides over the making of everything (*Enn.* V.8[31].5): the primal wisdom is "neither a derivative nor a stranger in something strange to it", but is constantly consubstantial with true being and thus with Intellect itself, not a derivative of it (*Enn.* V.8[31].5). But he attacks the idea that Soul or Sophia – the two are certainly distinct, since Plotinus is able to ask whether both descended together or one was the instigator of a shared transgression (*Enn.* II.9[33].10.19–24) – declined and illuminated the darkness, producing an image (*eidōlon*) in matter, which in turn produced an image of the image (but see Plotinus' own version of this in *Enn.* III.9[13].3). His opponents apparently describe this illumination as a downward tendency of the soul itself (as Sophia in the *Apocryphon of John* and Valentinian sources) or as a luminous efflux, which does not diminish the magnitude or station of its source (as in *Zostrianos* 9.16–11.9). The image of the soul, we hear in one place, is reflected in the darkness, and then the image of that image, pervading matter, assumes the shaping and ordering functions of the Platonic demiurge (*Enn.* II.9[33].10.25–33). Unlike Nature's "tranquil vision" of the things above (*Enn.* II.9[33].2; cf. *Enn.* III.8[30].4, 8.6) this creator figure pursues not true being, but only images thereof (*Enn.* II.9[33].10.25–27). Since he is incapable of the full and instantaneous apprehension either of the true soul or of its primary reflection – which the Gnostics call his mother (*Enn.* II.9[33].12.10) – he works from his own reason and imagination in a chronological succession (since the other elements must await the preparation of fire, *Enn.* II.9[33].12.13–15). To such a claim that "there was within her (i.e. Sophia) no pure, original image" (*Zostrianos* 9.10–11, NHC [Meyer]), Plotinus elsewhere objects that "there is in the Nature-Principle itself an ideal archetype of the beauty that is found in material forms" (*Enn.* V.8[31].3.1–3). Indeed, in *Enn.* II.9[33].10, Plotinus actually cites about eleven lines from *Zostrianos* (*Enn.* II.9[33].10.19–33 ≈ NHC *Zostrianos* 9.17–10.20).[35]

Another clear point of contact with *Zostrianos* (and *Marsanes*) is Plotinus' critique of the nomenclature of the psychic aeonic levels extending below the Barbelo Aeon, namely the Repentance, Sojourn and Aeonic Copies (*Enn.* II.9[33].6.6–7),[36] which he characterizes as "terms of people inventing a new jargon to recommend their own school". Then Plotinus continues with what seems to be his fundamental criticism – the Gnostics plagiarize and then falsify Plato:

They contrive this meretricious language as if they had no connection with the ancient Hellenic school, though the Hellenes knew all this and knew it clearly, and spoke without delusive pomposity of ascents (*anabaseis*) from the cave and advancing gradually closer and closer to a truer vision (*thean alēthesteran*). Some of their ideas have been taken from Plato but others – all the new ideas they have brought in to establish a philosophy of their own – are things they found outside the truth. For the judgments too, and the rivers in Hades and the reincarnations come from Plato. And the making a plurality in the intelligible world – Being and Intellect and the other Maker and the Soul – is taken from the words in the *Timaeus*, for Plato says: "The maker of this universe thought that it should contain all the forms that intelligence discerns contained in the living being that truly is" (39e7–9). ... And in general they falsify Plato's account of the making and a great deal else, and degrade the great man's teaching as if they had understood the intelligible nature, but he and the other blessed philosophers had not .... They themselves have received from them what is good in what they say – the immortality of the soul, the intelligible universe, the first god, the necessity for the soul to shun fellowship with the body, the separation from the body, the escape from becoming to being – for these doctrines are there in Plato. (*Enn.* II.9[33].6.7–43)

Plotinus' major criticisms are thus directed at gnostic interpretation of Plato's *Timaeus*, at its un-Hellenic failure to respect the beauty and divinity of the cosmos and its gods and its multiplication of divine agencies or hypostases, as well as any suggestion of interruption in the continuous generation of reality from the primal source or of any downward declination of divine beings, especially the World Soul.

Points of agreement with extant gnostic treatises

On the other hand, Plotinus does not seem to attack the general scheme of the unfolding of the divine world implemented in these treatises. In the case of the *Tripartite Tractate* discussed earlier, he accepts the principle of undiminished giving. In the case of the Platonizing Sethian treatises, he accepts the notion of the traversal of vitality or life from its source in the supreme deity until its realization in the hypostasis of Intellect (*Enn.* III.8[30].8–10; VI.7[38].17.13–26; cf. *Allogenes* 49.5–21 and note 27). He also accepts the notion that spiritual beings – the Platonic ideas as minds united with their objects of thought – are simultaneously present in their entirety as "all together" in the Intellect (*Enn.* V.8[31].7–9), which *Allogenes* and *Zostrianos* expressed by the phrase "those who are united" (in Protophanes),[37] and the *Tripartite Tractate*'s characterization of the aeons in the Pleroma:

His offspring, the ones who are, are without number and limit and at the same time indivisible. They have issued from him, the Son and the Father, in the same way as kisses, when two people abundantly embrace one another in a good and insatiable thought – it is a single embrace but consists of many kisses. This is the Church that consists of many people and exists before the aeons and is justly called "the aeons of the aeons." ... These [are a] community (*politeuma*) [formed] with one another and [with the ones] who have gone forth from [them and] with the Son, for whom they exist as glory. (*Tripartite Tractate* 58.21–59.16)

In the matter of the practice of mystical ascent, Plotinus seems to accept the notion that, through a series of contemplative self-withdrawals into the aspirant's primordial self, the One's self-image in us is elevated to silent union with God through contemplation, a technique extensively narrated in *Allogenes* (cf. also *Zostrianos* 44.1–5):

> There was within me a stillness of silence, and I heard the Blessedness whereby I knew [my] proper self. And I withdrew to the Vitality as I sought [myself]. And I joined it and stood, not firmly but quietly. And I saw an eternal, intellectual, undivided motion, all-powerful, formless, undetermined by determination. And when I wanted to stand firmly, I withdrew to the Existence, which I found standing and at rest. Like an image and likeness of what had come upon me, by means of a manifestation of the Indivisible and the Stable I was filled with revelation; by means of an originary manifestation[38] [61] of the Unknowable One, [as though] incognizant of him, I [knew] him and was empowered by him. Having been permanently strengthened, I knew that [which] exists in me, even the Triple-Powered One and the manifestation of his uncontainableness. [And] by means of a originary manifestation of the universally prime Unknowable One – the God beyond perfection – I saw him and the Triple-Powered One that exists in them all. I was seeking the ineffable and unknowable God of whom – should one know him – one would be completely nescient, the mediator of the Triple-Powered One, the one who subsists in stillness and silence and is unknowable.   (*Allogenes* XI.60.14–61.22)

Compare Plotinus' description of contemplative vision through withdrawal into one's prenoetic, primordial self, which, rather than "originary manifestation", he denominates as the "first life" (see also note 27) in *Enn.* III.8[30].9.29–39:[39]

> What is it, then, which we shall receive when we set our intellect to it? Rather, the intellect must first withdraw, so to speak, backwards, and give itself up, in a way, to what lies behind it – for it faces in both directions (*dei ton noun hoion eis toupisō anachorein kai hoion heauton aphenta tois eis opisthen autou amphistomon onta*); and there, if it wishes to see that First Principle, it must not be altogether intellect. For it is the first life, since it is an activity manifest in the way of outgoing of all things (*Esti men gar autos zōē prōtē, energeia ousa en diexodōi tōn pantōn*); outgoing not in the sense that it is now in process of going out but that it has gone out. If, then, it is life and outgoing and holds all things distinctly and not in a vague general way – for [in the latter case] it would hold them imperfectly and inarticulately – it must itself derive from something else, which is no more in the way of outgoing, but is the origin of outgoing, and the origin of life and the origin of intellect and all things (*archē diexodou kai archē zōēs kai archē nou kai tōn pantōn*).

Plotinus likewise accepts, but does not further develop the technique of "learned ignorance" found in *Allogenes*, by which the mystical aspirant knows the One by "unknowing" him,[40] as in *Enn.* VI.9[9].7.16–22:[41]

> abandoning all external things, she [the soul] must revert completely towards the interior, and not be inclined to any of the external things, but un-knowing

(*agnoēsanta*) all things – both as she had at first, in the sensible realm, then even in that of the forms – and even "un-knowing" himself (*agnoēsanta de kai auton*), come to be in the contemplation of that one; and, having come together and having had as it were sufficient intercourse with that, must come to proclaim the communion up there, if possible, also to another.

Besides this mixture of acquiescences, objections and corrections, it may be that Plotinus' encounter with the Gnostics also caused him to tighten up on his own doctrines;[42] for example, in *Enn.* III.9[13] he once toyed with a tripartition of the divine Intellect based on an interpretation of Plato's *Timaeus* (esp. 39e) that is very similar to that of Numenius and the Sethian Barbelo Aeon, but later explicitly rejects it in *Enn.* II.9[33].6. In *Enn.* VI.6[34] *On Numbers*, produced immediately after his antignostic treatise, he changes the order of the triad Being–Life–Mind occasionally applied to the unfolding of the Intellect from the One (based on his interpretation of the first two hypotheses of the *Parmenides*) in some of the earlier *Enneads* to the order Being–Mind–Life, and restricts its presence to the internal structure of Intellect.[43]

In sum, gnostic sources such as the Sethian Platonizing treatises and the *Tripartite Tractate* may have had a decisive influence on some of the most distinctive features and images of Plotinus' thinking. In fact, not only was gnostic thought a genuine forerunner of, and "Platonic" competitor with, some of those features of Platonic interpretation habitually thought to be distinctively Neoplatonic, such as the Being–Life–Mind triad, but also of major features of Plotinus' thought, not only because these ideas were part of a shared milieu, but also because Plotinus was involved in a dialogue with them for virtually the whole of his writing career.

PLOTINUS AND THE GNOSTICS AS EXEGETES OF PLATO'S DIALOGUES

As exegetes of Plato's dialogues, neither Plotinus nor the Gnostics concerned themselves with the main questions of a given dialogue, but centred their attention on specific affirmations – often in the form of isolated assertions – that supported the exegetes' own central metaphysical concerns, rarely paying attention to their original context.[44] Rather than following the letter of the Platonic text, each succeeded in producing and developing a new form of thinking, Plotinus in the service of explicating what he thought to be the actual intention of Plato's philosophy, and the Gnostics in the service of undergirding the authority and efficacy of their mythological revelations. As a result, in various places Plotinus uses important images or ideas from Plato which are clearly shared by the Gnostics in their portrayal of (a) intelligible reality, (b) their analysis of the modes of Being and Non-Being, (c) their use of the dialectical method of collection and division, and (d) their portrayal of the ascent and descent of the soul in the reincarnational cycle.

Intelligible reality

Both Plotinus and *Zostrianos* draw on Plato to describe the content of the intelligible world. In *Enn.* V.8[31], Plotinus describes the "true earth" and "true heaven":[45]

but the gods in that higher heaven, all those who dwell upon it and in it, contemplate through their abiding in the whole of that heaven. For all things there are heaven, and earth and sea and plants and animals and men are heaven, everything which belongs to that higher heaven is heavenly … for it is "the easy life" (cf. *Il.* 6, 138) there, and truth is their mother and nurse and substance and nourishment – and they see all things, not those to which coming to be, but those to which real being belongs, and they see themselves in other things (*heautous en allois*); for all things there are transparent, and there is nothing dark or opaque; everything and all things are clear to the inmost part to everything; for light is transparent to light.   (*Enn.* V.8[31].3.30–36)

Zostrianos offers a similar vision of intelligible reality, but without the Plotinian theme of mutual transparency:[46]

> At each of the aeons I saw a living earth, a living water, luminous [air] and an [unconsuming] fire. All [these], being simple, are also immutable and simple [eternal living creatures], possessing a variety [of] beauty, trees of many kinds that do not perish, as well as plants of the same sort as all these, imperishable fruit, human beings alive with every species, immortal souls, every shape and species of intellect, gods of truth, angels dwelling in great glory with an indissoluble body [and] ingenerate offspring and unchanging perception. (*Zostrianos* VIII.48.3–26)

In their portrayal of the realm of Intellect as containing the intelligible archetypes of physical realities such as earth, sea, animals, plants, men and gods, both Plotinus and *Zostrianos* draw upon the visions of the upper world enjoyed by the gods and those souls who "follow" them in two of Plato's most famous myths, *Phaedo* 109d–114c and *Phaedrus* 247a–249c.[47]

The modes of Being and Non-Being

Zostrianos further describes the contents of the Kalyptos Aeon – the topmost level of the intelligible Barbelo Aeon – using terminology derived from Plato's *Timaeus*, *Sophist* and *Parmenides* to show that it contains the archetypes of the entire realm of reality extending from the divine light itself all the way down to chaotic matter:

> It is there that all living creatures are, existing individually, although unified. The knowledge of the knowledge is there as well as a basis for ignorance. Chaos is there as well as a [place] for all of them, it being [complete] while they are incomplete. True light [is there], as well as enlightened darkness [i.e. intelligible matter] as well as that which truly is non-existent [i.e. gross matter], that [which] is not-truly existent [i.e. souls], [as well as] the non-existent ones that are not at all [i.e. sensibles].
> (*Zostrianos* VIII.117.1–14)

Here, the Kalyptos Aeon contains the archetypes of all polarities, ultimate knowledge and ignorance, unordered chaos and organized place (that is, the receptacle, cf. *Ti.* 52a8–b5), "true light" and "that which is truly non-existent" (*ontōs ouk on*, namely gross matter), "that [which] is not-truly existent" (*to ouk ontōs on*, souls as source of motion and change) and the sensible entities that are moved by them, "the non-existent ones that are not at all" (*ouk ontōs on*). These same categories or modes of being appear as well in *Allogenes* XI.55.17–30:

> Then [the mother of] the glories Youel spoke to me again: ["O Allogenes], you [shall surely] know that the [Triple-Powered] One exists before [those that] do not exist, [those that exist] without [truly] existing and those that exist, [and those that] truly exist. [And all these] exist [in Divinity and Blessedness and] Existence, even as non-substantiality and non-being [Existence]."

In *Enn.* I.8[51], "On what are and whence come evils", Plotinus employs similar propositional categories to identify matter as the ultimate source of evil:

> If, then, these (the One, Intellect, and Soul) are what really exists and what is beyond existence (*ta onta kai to epekeina tōn ontōn*), then evil cannot be included in what really exists or in what is beyond existence; for these are good. So it remains that if evil exists, it must be among non-existent things, as a sort of form of non-existence (*en tois mē ousin einai hoion eidos ti tou mē ontōs on*), and pertain to one of the things that are mingled with non-being (*tōi mē onti*) or somehow share in non-being. Non-being here does not mean absolute non-being (*mē on de outi to pantelōs mē on*) but only something other than being (*heteron monon tou ontos*); not non-being in the same way as the movement and rest which affect being, but like an image of being or something still more non-existent (*all' hōs eikōn tou ontos ē kai eti mallon mē on*). The whole world of sense is non-existent in this way, and also all sense-experience and whatever is posterior or incidental to this, or its principle, or one of the elements which go to make up the whole which is of this (non-existent) kind. (*Enn.* I.8[51].3.1–13)

Similarly, in *Enn.* III.6[26], Plotinus compares gross matter to Plato's receptacle and nurse of becoming; they are like a mirror in which visible things appear and remain, but the mirror itself is invisible and thus, in comparison to the not-truly existent images which participate in the truly existent forms, does not really exist:[48]

> If, then, there really is something in mirrors, let there really be objects of sense in matter in the same way; but if there is not, but only appears to be something, then we must admit, too, that things only appear on matter, and make the reason for their appearance the existence of the real beings, an existence in which the real beings always really participate, but the beings which are not real, not really; since they cannot be in the same state as they would be if real beings did not really exist and they did. (*Enn.* III.6[26].13.50–55)

The ultimate source of these categories of being – which become virtual Neoplatonic definitions of intermediate metaphysical entities – are traditional propositional categories taken from Plato's *Sophist* and *Parmenides*.[49] In the *Parmenides* Plato uses them to examine Parmenides' assertion of the unity of the universe and his claim that it is impossible to speak of "what is not". In the *Sophist*, he uses them to show that the false teaching of the

Sophists is equivalent to saying "what is not", a reality which – contrary to Parmenides – turns out to be intelligible after all.

In the *Parmenides*, both being and non-being can be the subject of both affirmations and negations, while in the *Sph.* 238c, which distinguishes the copulative and existential senses of "be" ("not to be x" does not mean "not to exist"), regards "that which is not" (*to mē on auto kath' auton*) as beyond all predication, discourse and thought. Thus the absolute One of the first hypothesis and the "One that is not" of the fifth hypothesis are both beyond all predication, discourse and thought. On the other hand, according to the *Sph.* 240b1–13, Forms are that which truly exists (*ontōs onta*) and are the object of thought, while copies are not that which truly is (*ouk ontōs onta, ouk onta ontōs*), and thus cannot be the object of thought. According to *Sph.* 254d, the supreme category is *to on* while *to mē on* is indeterminate and may or may not really be non-existent (*to mē on hōs estin ontōs mē on*).

In the process, the *Sophist* presents a new theory of the Form of Being and its relation to the other most comprehensive forms, but without arranging them into a hierarchy of metaphysical levels of reality as did subsequent interpreters, such as the authors of *Zostrianos* and *Allogenes*, and later on other Neoplatonist philosophers and patristic thinkers, notably Marius Victorinus. The use of these logical categories indicates that these gnostic authors were students of Plato's dialogues, not only of the popular protology of the *Timaeus*, but also of comparatively more abstruse dialogues such as the *Sophist* and *Parmenides*.

Dialectic

For Plotinus, dialectic is the science of intelligible reality, conceived on the model of the dialectical method of Plato's late dialogues, the *Sophist*, *Statesman* and *Philebus*, which employs methods of collection, division and definition in order to induce contemplation of the Ideas as the contents of the divine Intelligence.

> [Dialectic] is the science which can speak of everything in a reasoned and orderly way, and say what it is and how it differs from other things and what it has in common with those among which it is and where each of these stands, and if it really is what it is, and how many really existing things there are, and again how many non-existing things, different from real beings … feeding the soul in what Plato calls "the plain of truth," using his method of division to distinguish the Forms, and to determine the essential nature of each thing, and to find the primary kinds, and weaving together by the intellect all that issues from these primary kinds, till it has traversed the whole intelligible world; then it resolves again the structure of that world into its parts, and comes back to its starting-point; and then, keeping quiet … it busies itself no more, but contemplates, having arrived at unity.   (*Enn.* I.3[20].4.2–18)

A similar implementation of dialectic is found in three of the four Platonizing Sethian treatises. In *Marsanes*, the preliminary stages leading to Marsanes' vision of the supreme principles are occupied by discursive dialectic reasoning, specifically the same technique of collection and division:

For I am he who has [intelligized] that which truly exists, [whether] individually or [as a whole], by difference (*kata diaphoran*, cf. *R.* VI.509d–511e). [I knew] that they [pre]-exist [in the] entire place that is eternal: all those that have come into existence, whether without substance or with substance, those who are unbegotten, and the divine aeons, as well as the angels and the souls without guile and the soul-[garments], the images of [the] simple ones [souls?]. And [afterwards they] were mixed with [those (i.e. their bodies) that were distinct from] them. But [even the] entire [perceptible] substance still resembles the [intelligible substance] as well as the insubstantial. [I have known] the entire corruption [of the former (the perceptible realm)] as well as the immortality of the latter. I have discriminated (*diakrinein*, cf. *Soph.* 253d–e) and have attained the boundary of the partial, sense-perceptible world [and] the entire realm of the incorporeal essence. (*Marsanes* X.4.24–5.21)

A similar procedure emerges in *Zostrianos* as an interpretation of a celestial "baptism":[50]

And if one understands their origin, how they are all manifest in a single principle, and how all who are joined come to be divided, and how those who were divided join again, and how the parts [join with] the wholes and the species with the [genera] – when one understands these things – one has washed in the baptism of Kalyptos. (*Zostrianos* VIII.23.6–17)

Similarly, dialectic activity prefaces Allogenes' contemplative ascent:

I was able – even though flesh was upon me – to hear from [you] about these things. And because of the teaching that is in them, the thought within me distinguished things beyond measure from unknowable things. Therefore I fear that my wisdom has become excessive. (*Allogenes* XI.50.9–17)

These Platonizing treatises have here drawn again from Plato's dialogues, in this case, the *Phaedo*, *Sophist* and perhaps the *R.* 509–11. In *Phdr.* 265d–266c, Plato distinguishes two kinds of dialectic: an ascending or "synoptic" (*R.* 537c) dialectic that moves (by recollection) from idea to idea to the supreme idea, and a descending, "diairetic" dialectic that moves from the highest idea and by division distinguishes within the general ideas particular ideas until one reaches ideas that do not include in themselves further ideas. One thus moves from multiplicity to unity and from unity to its expressed multiplicity:[51]

Now I myself, Phaedrus, am a lover of these processes of division and bringing together (*diaireseōn kai synagōgōn*), as aids to speech and thought; and if I think any other man is able to see things that can naturally be collected into one and divided into many, him I follow after and walk in his footsteps as if he were a god. And whether the name I give to those who can do this is right or wrong, God knows, but I have called them hitherto dialecticians (*dialektikous*). (*Phdr.* 265b3–266c1, trans. Fowler)

THE ASCENT AND DESCENT OF THE SOUL

Already in *Enn.* II.9[33].6.10–16 Plotinus had recognized that gnostic teaching on the plight of the human soul was drawn from Plato: "Some of their ideas have been taken from Plato … the judgments too, and the rivers in Hades and the reincarnations come from there." The revelation of Ephesech in *Zostrianos* 44.1–46.31 offers a particularly convincing example (see Z. Mazur 2013):

> [44] Now the person that can be saved is the one that seeks itself and its intellect and finds each of them. And how much power this [type] has! The person that has been saved is one who has not known about these things [merely] as they [formally] exist, but one who is personally involved with [the] rational faculty as it exists [in him]. He has grasped their [image that changes] in every situation as though they had become simple and one. For then this one is saved who can pass through [them] all; [he becomes] them all. Whenever he [wishes], he again parts from all these matters and withdraws into himself; for he becomes divine, having withdrawn into god. …
> [45] When this one repeatedly withdraws into himself alone and is occupied with the knowledge of other things, since the intellect and immortal [soul] do [not] intelligize, he thereupon experiences deficiency, for he too turns, has nothing, and separates from it [the intellect] and stands [apart] and experiences an alien [impulse] instead of becoming a unity. So that person resembles many forms. And when he turns aside, he comes into being seeking those things that do not exist. When he descends to [or: happens upon] them in thought, he cannot understand them in any other way unless [46] he be enlightened, and he becomes a physical entity. Thus this type of person accordingly descends into generation, and becomes speechless because of the difficulties and indefiniteness of matter. Although possessing eternal, immortal power, he is bound in the clutches of the body, [removed], and [continually] bound within strong bonds, lacerated by every evil spirit, until he once more [reconstitutes himself] and begins again to come to himself.
> Therefore, for their salvation, there have been appointed specific powers, and these same ones inhabit this world. And among the Self-generated ones there stand at each [aeon] certain glories so that one who is in the [world] might be saved alongside [them]. The glories are perfect living concepts; it is [im-]possible that they perish because [they are] patterns of salvation, that is to say, anyone receiving them will be rescued to them, and being patterned will be empowered by this same [pattern], and having that glory as a helper, one thus passes through the world [and every aeon].   (*Zostrianos* VIII.44.1–22; 45.12–46.15)

According to *Enn.* IV.8[6], "The descent of the soul into bodies", the lower part of Soul in its desire to break away in isolation from its higher part in communion with Intellect inevitably becomes buried in the body.[52]

> The individual souls, certainly, have an intelligent desire consisting in the impulse to return to themselves springing from the principle from which they came into being, but they also possess a power directed to the world here below … and they are free

from sorrow if they remain with universal soul in the intelligible … for they are then all together in the same [place]. But they change from the whole to being a part and belong to themselves, and, as if they were tired of being together, they each withdraw into each of their individual selves. Now when a soul does this for a long time, fleeing from the All and standing apart in distinctness, and does not look towards the intelligible, it has become a part and is isolated and weak and preoccupied and looks towards a part and in its separation from the whole it embarks on one single thing and flies from everything else … it has left the whole and directs the individual part with great difficulty; it is by now applying itself to and caring for things outside and is present and sinks deep into the individual part. Here the so-called "molting" (*Phdr.* 246c) happens to it, and "the coming to be in the fetters of the body," since it has missed the immunity which it had when it was with the universal soul … and so, having fallen, it is caught and engaged with its fetter, and acts by sense because it is being prevented from acting according to intellect, and is said to be "buried" and "in a cave," but, when it turns to intelligence, it is freed from its fetters and ascends, and started upon the contemplation of reality by recollection: for, in spite of everything, it always possesses something transcendent in some way.   (*Enn.* IV.8[6].4.1–29)

These passages are clearly built on a reading of Plato's dialogues, the *Phaedrus'* myth of reincarnational cycles, the *Phaedo's* myth of post-mortem punishments, and the *Republic's* myth of the ascent from the Cave. One's ability to see the simplicity and unity of the ideal forms whose images comprise the furniture of the world guarantees its salvation,[53] since one can withdraw at any time from the world of images and inhabit the transcendent domain of the rational part of the soul that not only travels with the gods, but in fact is itself divine:

The lovers of knowledge, I say, perceive that philosophy, taking possession of the soul when it is in this state, encourages it gently and tries to set it free, pointing out that the eyes and the ears and the other senses are full of deceit, and urging it to withdraw from these, except in so far as their use is unavoidable, and exhorting it to collect and concentrate itself within itself, and to trust nothing except itself by itself and that thing itself among existing things which soul itself intelligizes by itself.   (*Phd.* 83a–b)

Yet despite the soul's ability to withdraw from the world of images into itself and intellectually assimilate to the divine realm, it still lives in the world and inevitably becomes occupied with other matters, with the result that its intellection becomes inhibited. Such souls experience a cognitive deficiency, "a loss of wings" (*Phdr.* 246; 249); they are dragged down from the heights (*Phdr.* 248a–b; cf. *Phd.* 81c–d; 109e) away from unity by appetition for the physical delights that do not have true existence. The result is the reincarnation of the soul in the realm of becoming.[54] In spite of its immortal power, the soul is caught in the reincarnational cycle, bound in the clutches of a physical body, temporarily freed at death, and then rebound in another reincarnation (*Phd.* 81d; 83d), lost in suffering (*Phd.* 108b), in the indeterminateness of formless matter (cf. *Phlb.* 41d).

While there is a strong similarity between Plotinus' and *Zostrianos'* appropriation of Platonic teaching, it is clear that for Plotinus the point of departure is *Zostrianos'* announcement of the availability of certain "glories" as divine helpers that ensure the ultimate salvation of souls, a notion that has no warrant in the thought of either Plato or Plotinus.

CONCLUSION

The preceding instances of the interpretation of key elements of Plato's teaching by both Plotinus and gnostic authors, particularly those of the Sethian Platonizing treatises, demonstrate that these gnostic authors were thoroughly immersed in the dialogues of Plato. While the gnostic authors fail to acknowledge Plato as the originator of these teachings and instead ascribe them to divine revelation, one cannot escape the conclusion that the common knowledge of their readers would have grasped allusions to these dialogues – some popular and some not so popular – in their understanding of these treatises as not only divinely revealed but as reinforced by the traditional wisdom of "the ancient philosophy".

NOTES

1. J. M. Robinson (1977), J. D. Turner (1980, 1986, 2000a, 2000b, 2001, 2004, 2006, 2007), Jufresa (1981), Böhlig (1981), Abramowski (1983), Pearson (1984), Sinnige (1984), Attridge (1991), Bos (1994), Bechtle (2000) and Corrigan (2000, 2001), Narbonne (2008) and Z. Mazur (2010).

2. Narbonne (2011: 115–16). As early as 2001, Corrigan (2001: 42) stated: "I propose that we should be alive to the real possibility that all of the treatises after the *Großschrift*, especially those with cognate interests such as VI.7[38] and VI.8[39], will bear similar traces of such a dialogue. In which case, and in the sense we have specified, Plotinus is certainly influenced by the Gnostics, for some of his most mature thought is shaped by an implicit conversation with them."

3. All translations of Plotinus' *Enneads* are based on Armstrong (1966–88).

4. Cf. *Enn.* V.2[11].1.8–13: "It is because there is nothing in it that all things come from it: in order that Being may exist, the One is not being, but the generator of being. This, we may say, is the first act of generation: the One, perfect because it seeks nothing, has nothing, and needs nothing, overflows, as it were, and its superabundance makes something other than itself. This, when it has come into being, turns back upon the One and is filled, and becomes Intellect by looking towards it. Its halt and turning towards the One constitutes Being, its gaze upon the One, Intellect. Since it halts and turns towards the One that it may see, it becomes at once Intellect and Being."

5. Clement of Alexandria, *Excerpta ex Theodoto* 7 [Casey]: ὡς ἂν ἑαυτὸν ἐγνωκώς, ... προέβαλε τὸν Μονογενῆ.

6. *Eugnostos* (NHC III.3) 74.21–75.12: "The Lord of the Universe is not rightly called 'Father' but 'Forefather.' For the Father is the beginning (*or* principle) of what is visible. For he (the Lord) is the beginningless Forefather. He sees himself within himself, like a mirror, having appeared in his likeness as Self-Father, that is, Self-Begetter, and as Confronter, since he is face to face with the Unbegotten First Existent. He is indeed of equal age with the one who is before him, but he is not equal to him in power." Also 72.10–11: "It looks to every side and sees itself from itself." Cf. The *Sophia of Jesus Christ* (NHC III.4) 98.24–99.13 & 95.6. Unless noted otherwise, translations of Nag Hammadi treatises are taken from Meyer (2007).

7. Hippolytus, *Ref.* VI.13 [Marcovich]: φανεὶς γὰρ αὑτῷ ἀπὸ ἑαυτοῦ ἐγένετο δεύτερος.

8. See also the *Valentinian Exposition* (NHC XI.22.31–9), where it is unclear whether the generation of the second principle is due to the second thinking the first or the first thinking the second.

9. This and the following observation on the *Tripartite Tractate* I owe to Kevin Corrigan in Corrigan & Turner (2012).

10. Macrobius, *Somn. Scip.* 2.6.23 [Willis]: "fons ... qui ita principium est aquae, ut cum de se fluvios et lacus

procreet, a nullo nasci ipse dicatur". Cf. *Corpus Hermeticum* IV.10 [Festugière]: ἡ γὰρ μονάς, οὖσα πάντων ἀρχὴ καὶ ῥίζα, ἐν πᾶσίν ἐστιν ὡς ἂν ῥίζα καὶ ἀρχή.

11. Coptic: ετβε πεει αϥϫι ⲛⲛⲟⲩⲫⲩⲥⲓⲥ ⲛⲥⲟⲫⲓⲁ ⲁⲧⲣⲉⲩϥⲁⲧⲣⲧ ⲛⲥⲁ ⲡϣⲙⲓⲛⲉ· ⲉⲧⲉⲏⲡ ⲣⲱⲥ ⲉⲅⲕⲁⲣⲡⲟⲥ ⲛⲥⲟⲫⲓⲁ ⲡⲉ· This natural wisdom is specified in 75.27–30 as a "wisdom each of whose thoughts are preexistent", suggesting that this natural wisdom was based on its possession of the divine ideas.

12. Corrigan (2001: 49): "Take, for example, the following passage from 5.8[31].5.4–8 where Plotinus traces *all* products of art or nature back to the wisdom of Intellect: 'the craftsman goes back to the *physical wisdom* (σοφίαν φυσικήν) according to which he has come into existence, a wisdom which is no longer composed of theorems, but is one thing as a whole (ὅλην ἕν τι), not the wisdom made into one out of many components, but rather resolved into multiplicity from one.' Plotinus implicitly emphasizes that this recognizably traditional view concerns *physical* wisdom (not manipulative or artificial thinking), evidently with the purpose of excluding *any* fallen, demiurgic Sophia who seeks to contract or reconstruct the world in a discursive manner." It is striking that the *only* extant parallels for Plotinus' usage of *physikē sophia* are Alexander of Aphrodisias' *in Metaph.* 266.2–18 [Hayduck] on Aristotle, *Metaph.* 1005b1–2 (itself an indirect parallel) and the *Tripartite Tractate*.

13. Irenaeus, *adversus Haereses* 1.2.2.13–23 [Doutreleau & Rousseau]: "The last and youngest aeon of the Duodecad emitted from Man and Church, that is Sophia, rushed forward (προήλατο) and experienced a passion apart from her consort 'Willed' (ἔπαθε πάθος ἄνευ τῆς ἐπιπλοκῆς τοῦ [συ]ζυγοῦ τοῦ Θελητοῦ). This passion originated among those associated with *nous* and Truth, but erupted in this errant aeon (ἀπέσκηψε δὲ εἰς τοῦτον τὸν παρατραπέντα), on the pretext of love, but actually of presumption (πρόφασιν μὲν ἀγάπης, τόλμης δέ), since she lacked the communion with the perfect father (διὰ τὸ μὴ κεκοινωνῆσθαι τῷ Πατρί) enjoyed by *nous*. The passion is the search for the father, for she wished as they say to comprehend his magnitude. Since she was unable to do this because she had undertaken an impossible task (διὰ τὸ ἀδυνάτῳ ἐπιβαλεῖν πράγματι), she was in deep distress."

14. *Ap. Jn.* BG 8502.2 (cf. also NHC II.1, III.1, IV.1) 26.1–30.4: "For it is he (the Invisible Spirit or Monad) who contemplates himself in his own light that surrounds him, which is he himself, the source of living water .... The fountain of theSpirit flowed from the living luminous water and provided all aeons and [27] worlds. In every direction he contemplated his own image (εἰκών), beholding it in the pure luminous water that surrounds him. And his Thought (ἔννοια) became active and appeared and stood at rest before him in the brilliance of the light. She [is the Providence (πρόνοια) of the All] the likeness of the light, the image of the invisible One, the perfect power Barbelo .... [29] Barbelo gazed intently into the pure Light, [30] and she turned herself to it and gave rise to a spark of blessed light, though it was not equal to her in magnitude. This is the only-begotten (μονογενής) one, who appeared from the Father, the divine Self-generated One (αὐτογενής), the first-born Child of the entirety of the Spirit of pure light."

15. This dependence was first discovered by Michel Tardieu (2005).

16. From certain earlier Sethian treatises (*Apocryphon of John*, the *Trimorphic Protennoia* and the *Gospel of the Egyptians*), the Platonizing treatises have inherited a tendency to identify the supreme deity by the somewhat Stoicizing name "the Invisible Spirit". While the *Three Steles of Seth* (VII.125.23–5) calls this supreme pre-existent One a "single living Spirit", *Zostrianos* identifies this One as "the Triple Powered Invisible Spirit". On the other hand, *Allogenes* tends to distinguish this One from both the Invisible Spirit and the Triple-Powered One, while *Marsanes* supplements them all with a supreme "unknown silent One".

17. Cf. Phanes, *Orphicorum Hymni* 52.5–6 [Quandt]; *Papyri Magicae* IV.943–4 [Preisendanz & Henrichs]; cf. Orphic *Argonautica*, line 16 [Dottin]: Φάνητα ... καλέουσι Βτοτοί· πρῶτος γὰρ ἐφάνθη.

18. Cf. Codex Bruce, *Untitled* 242.24–253.2 [Schmidt & MacDermot]: "Moreover the power that was given to the forefather is called first-visible because it is he who was first manifest (πρωτοφανής). And he was called unbegotten because no one had created him. And he was (called) the ineffable and the nameless one. And he was also called self-begotten (αὐτογενής) and self-willed because he had revealed himself by his own will." On the demiurgic activity of Autogenes, see *Allogenes* XI.51.25–32: the Barbelo Aeon is "endowed with the divine Autogenes as an image that knows each one of these (individuals), acting separately and individually, continually rectifying defects arising from Nature".

19. See *Allogenes* XI.46.6–35 [Meyer]. In *Zostrianos* 82.8–13 Kalyptos emerges as the second knowledge of the Invisible Spirit (the first being Barbelo), "the knowledge of his knowledge"; in 119.12–13 Kalyptos is associated with "his ἰδέα".

20. Coptic ⲣ̣ⲓⲟⲩⲛⲁ.Cf. *Enn.* IV.1[42].1.5–6: "There the whole of Intellect is all together and not separated or divided, and all souls are together" (ἐκεῖ δὲ (i.e. ἐν τῷ νῷ) ὁμοῦ μὲν νοῦς πᾶς καὶ οὐ διακεκριμένου

οὐδὲ μεμερισμένον, ὁμοῦ δὲ πᾶσαι ψυχαί); V.8[31].10.16-22: "the gods individually and together (οἱ θεοὶ καθ' ἕνα καὶ πᾶς ὁμοῦ), and the souls who see everything there and originate from everything ... are present there (in the intelligible realm) so long as they are naturally able, but oftentimes – when they are undivided – even the whole of them is present." Cf. *Corpus Hermeticum*, frag. 21 [Nock & Festugière]: "The preexistent one is thus above those that exist and those that truly exist, for there is a preexistent one through which the so-called universal essentiality of those that truly exist is intelligized together, while those that exist are intelligized individually (προὸν [ὂν] γάρ ἐστι, δι' οὗ ἡ οὐσιότης ἡ καθόλου λεγομένη κοινὴ νοεῖται τῶν ὄντως ὄντων καὶ τῶν ὄντων τῶν καθ' ἑαυτὰ νοουμένων)."

21. Cf. the status of Plato's "mathematicals" *apud* Aristotle, *Metaph.* 987b14-18; 1080a11-b14.

22. These functional distinctions within the divine intellect were justified by a reading of *Timaeus'* (*Ti.* 39e) doctrine of a transcendent model contemplated by a demiurge who then orders the universe in accord with the model: "According, then, as Reason (the Demiurge) perceives Forms existing in the Absolute Living Creature (the Model), such and so many as exist therein did he deem that this world also should possess," reflected in Numenius (Frags. 11, 13, 15, 16 [des Places]), Amelius (Proclus, *in Ti.* I.306.1-14; I.309.14-20; I.431.26-28), and the early Plotinus (*Enn.* III.9[13].1, but rejected in *Enn.* II.9[33].1).

23. Coptic ⲕⲁⲧⲁ ⲟⲩⲁ. Originally Aristotle's distinction (cf. Michael Psellus, *de Anima et Mente* 68.21-2 [O'Meara]: ἔτι ὁ νοῦς ὁ πρακτικὸς περὶ τὰ μερικά, ὁ θεωρητικὸς περὶ τὰ καθόλου); in *Enn.* III.9[13].1.26-37 this third hypostasis is called Soul and the products of its discursive thought are many individual souls. For Plotinus, the equivalent of Autogenes is Soul: its highest level dwells in Intellect (the equivalent of Protophanes) and contains all souls and intellects; it is one and unbounded (i.e. having all things together, every life and soul and intellect), holding all things together (πάντα ὁμοῦ), each distinct and yet not distinct in separation (ἕκαστον διακεκριμένον καὶ αὖ οὐ διακριθὲν χωρίς, *Enn.* IV.4[22].14.1-4). On individuals in Plotinus, see Blumenthal (1966, 1971b).

24. Cf. Bechtle (2000: n. 74): "Barbelo really is equivalent to mind. ... Barbelo corresponds to Numenius' second mind. Insofar as the second mind is participated in and used by the first, i.e. insofar as the second mind is prefigured in the first and thus is the first in a certain way, we have Kalyptos. Insofar as the Numenian second mind is identical with the third and acts through the third it can be compared to Autogenes. *Stricto sensu* the second mind as second mind is comparable to the Protophanes level of the Sethians."

25. For these thinkers, the Monad becomes a Dyad by a process of self-doubling (διπλασιασμός, ἐπισύνθεσις ἑαυτῇ: Theon of Smyrna, *Expositio* 27.1-7; 100.9-12 [Hiller]; Nicomachus, *Intro. Arith.* 113.2-10 [Hoche]; Sextus Empiricus, *Hyp. Pyrrh.* 3.153 [Mutschmann]; *M.* 10.261 [Mutschmann & Mau]; Hippolytus, *Ref.* 4.43), or begetting [Iamblichus] *Theol. Arith.* 3.17-4.7 [de Falco & Klein]), or by division (διαχωρισμός: [Iamblichus], *Theol. Arith.* 5.4-5; 8.20-9.7; 13.9-11), or by ἔκτασις or progression from potentiality as in a seed (ἐπέκτασις in Nicomachus *apud* [Iamblichus] *Theol. Arith.* 3.1-8; 16.4-11; Pseudo-Clementine, *Homilies* 224:34 [Rehm & Irmscher]: κατὰ γὰρ ἔκτασιν καὶ συστολὴν ἡ μονὰς δυὰς εἶναι νομίζεται; cf. *ibid.*: 234:18 ἀπ' αὐτοῦ εἰς ἄπειρον ἔκτασιν), or by receding from its nature (κατὰ στέρησιν αὐτοῦ χωρεῖν: Moderatus, *apud* Simplicius, *in Ph.* 230.34-231, 27 [Diels]; *recedente a natura sua singularitate et in duitatis habitum migrante*: Numenius, frag. 52 [des Places]), or by flowing (ῥύειν, ῥύσις: Sextus Empiricus, *Adv. Math.* 3.19; 3.28; 3.77; 7.99; 9.380; 9.381; 10.281). See also the testimonia on Eudorus, *apud* Simplicius, *in Ph.* 9.181.10-30 [Diels], Alexander Polyhistor *apud* Diogenes Laertius 8.24.7-25.10, on Archaenetus, Philolaus and Brotinus *apud* Syrianus, *in Metaph.* 165.33-166.6 [Kroll], and on Pseudo-Archytas *apud* Stobaeus, *Anth.* I.41.2.1-50 = 1.278-9 [Wachsmuth & Hense]. Hippolytus shows that the Simonian *Megale Apophasis* (*Ref.* 6.18.4-7) – like the Valentinians (*Ref.* 6.29.5-6) – used the concept of emanation (προβολή, προέρχεσθαι) of a Dyad pre-existing in the Monad. Also in the Sethian Platonizing treatises, one finds the notion of self-production by self-extension (*Marsanes* X.32.5-33.2; *Allogenes* XI.45.22-4), by division (*Three Steles of Seth* VII.121.25-123.14), as well as by ἔκτασις (in *Enn.* VI.6[34] Plotinus calls it ἀπόστασις which also very well picks up the idea of dynamic ontologies [*Zostrianos* VIII.81.1-20], self-contraction [*Allogenes* XI.45.22-4], and self-withdrawal [*Marsanes* X.9.1-21]). On Plotinus' version of dynamic ontology, see Slaveva-Griffin (Chapter 13), below.

26. In *ad Candidum* 14.11-14, Victorinus hints at a similar progression: "For what is above ὂν is hidden (cf. Kalyptos) ὄν; indeed the manifestation (cf. Protophanes) of the hidden is generation (cf. Autogenes), since ὂν in potentiality generates ὂν in act." In an earlier version (2000), Corrigan raised the possibility of an echo of the Sethian figures Kalyptos, Protophanes and Autogenes in *Enn.* V.5[32].7.31-5: "Thus indeed Intellect, veiled (καλύψας) itself from all the outer, withdrawing to the inmost, seeing nothing, beholds

– not some other light in some other thing but the light within itself alone, pure, suddenly apparent (φανέν), so that it wonders whence it appeared (ἐφάνη), from within or without, and when it has gone forth, to say 'It was within; yet no, it was without.'"

27. For example, VI.7[38].17.13–26: "Life, not the life of the One, but a trace of it, looking toward the One was boundless, but once having looked was bounded (without bounding its source). Life looks toward the One and, determined by it, takes on boundary, limit and form … it must then have been determined as (the life of) a Unity including multiplicity. Each element of multiplicity is determined multiplicity because of Life, but is also a Unity because of limit … so Intellect is bounded Life."

28. Justified by Plato, Sph. 248e–249b: "Are we really to be so easily persuaded that change, life, soul and intelligence have no place in the perfectly real (παντελῶς ὄν), that is has neither life (ζωή) nor intelligence (νοῦς), but stands aloof devoid of intelligence (φρόνησις)?" and Ti. 39e: "the Nous beholds (καθορᾷ) the ideas resident in the veritable living being (ὅ ἐστι ζῷον); such and go many as exist therein he purposed (διενοήθη) that the universe should contain". Intellect is not a lifeless being, but an act (Enn. V.3[49].5.33–44; cf. II.4[25].3.36; II.9[33].6.14–19; V.5[32].2.9–13; VI.9[9].9.17). This restriction perhaps owes to his aversion to Middle Platonic and even gnostic theologies that multiply the number of transcendental hypostases beyond three.

29. For example, Zostrianos 81.6–20: "She (Barbelo) [was] existing [individually] [as cause] of [the declination]. Lest she come forth anymore or get further away from perfection, she knew herself and him (the Invisible Spirit), and she stood at rest and spread forth on his [behalf] … to know herself and the one that pre-exists."; Allogenes 45.22–30: "For after it (the Barbelo Aeon) [contracted, it expanded] and [spread out] and became complete, [and] it was empowered [with] all of them, by knowing [itself in the perfect Invisible Spirit]. And it [became an] aeon who knows [herself because] she knew that one"; XI.48.15–17: "it is with [the] hiddenness of Existence that he provides Being, [providing] for [it in] every way, since it is this that [shall] come into being when he intelligizes himself"; Allogenes 49.5–26: "He is endowed with [Blessedness] and Goodness, because when he is intelligized as the Delimiter (D) of the Boundlessness (B) of the Invisible Spirit (IS) [that subsists] in him (D), it (B) causes [him (D)] to revert to [it (IS)] in order that it (B) might know what it is that is within it (IS) and how it (IS) exists, and that he (D) might guarantee the endurance of everything by being a cause for those who truly exist. For through him (D) knowledge of it (IS) became available, since he (D) is the one who knows what it (IS; or he, D?) is. But they brought forth nothing [beyond] themselves, neither power nor rank nor glory nor aeon, for they are all eternal." Cf. Apocryphon of John, cited above, note 14, where the living waters of the baptismal rite have become a transcendent emanation of luminous, living and self-reflective thinking.

30. Cf. the Three Steles of Seth 123.18–26: "Because of you (Barbelo) is Life: from you comes Life. Because of you is Intellect: from you comes Intellect. You are Intellect: you are a universe of truth. You are a triple power: you are a threefold; truly, you are thrice replicated, O aeon of aeons!" with 125.25–32: "You (the preexistent One) are a single, living spirit. How shall we say your name? It is not ours to say! For, it is you who are the Existence of them all. It is you who are the Life of them all. It is you who are the Intellect of them all."

31. Allogenes 66.30–38: "From the One who constantly stands, there appeared an eternal Life, the Invisible and Triple Powered Spirit, the One that is in all existing things and surrounds them all while transcending them all."

32. See above, note 22.

33. See the arguments of Z. Mazur (2005: 14): "It seems more likely that the anonymous Parmenides Commentary is vaguely using an already existing gnostic doctrine of contemplative self-reversion to explain the relationship between the Ones of the first two hypotheses of the Parmenides. After all, the author does seem to be familiar with the Chaldaean Oracles; why not Gnostics also? The clearest instances of such doctrine are contained in the pre-Plotinian gnostic Platonizing treatises Zostrianos and Allogenes. Even if one grants that the anonymous Parmenides Commentary implies a doctrine of primordial self-reversion, it still seems unlikely that Plotinus adopts this idea solely from his use of the Commentary or its equivalent. If it were read in Plotinus' circle, it may also have influenced the schemes of primordial self-reversion and Being–Life–Mind triads in the Platonizing Sethian treatises, but this still would not account for widespread instances of the motif of primordial self-reversion, not only in Plotinus' earlier treatises, but also in other and perhaps earlier gnostic systems, such as those attributed to Simon Magus and Basilides, which may have influenced Plotinus well before his contact with the Platonizing Sethians in his immediate circle. But this would also require the anonymous Parmenides Commentary or a contemporary equivalent to have informed a number of disparate early gnostic systems in addition to the Platonizing

Sethian treatises, but without having left a trace of its doctrine in contemporaneous Neopythagorean or Platonic sources."

34. Corrigan (2000; cf. 2001: 60) raised the possibility of an echo of the Sethian figures Kalyptos, Protophanes and Autogenes in Plotinus' treatment of the veiling, "first appearing" and "self-appearing" of intellect in *Enn.* V.5[32].7.31–5: "Thus indeed Intellect, veiled (καλύψας) itself from all the outer, withdrawing to the inmost, seeing nothing, beholds – not some other light in some other thing but the light within itself alone, pure, suddenly apparent (φανέν), so that it wonders whence it appeared (ἐφάνη), from within or without, and when it has gone forth, to say 'It was within; yet no, it was without.'"

35. Cf. *Enn.* II.9[33].10.19–32: "For they say that *Soul declined to what was below it, and with it some sort of 'Wisdom,'* whether Soul started it or whether Wisdom was a cause of Soul being like this, or whether they mean both to be the same thing, and then they tell us that the other souls came down too, and as members of Wisdom put on bodies, human bodies for instance. But again *they say that very being for the sake of which these souls came down did not come down itself, did not decline, so to put it, but only illumined* (supplied form to) *the darkness, and so an image from it came into existence in matter. Then they form an image of the image somewhere here below, through matter or materiality* or whatever they like to call it – they use now one name and now another, and say many other names just to make their meaning obscure – *and produce what they call the Maker, and make him revolt from his mother and drag the cosmos which proceeds from him down to the ultimate limit of images*" with *Zostrianos* 9.17–10.20: "*When Sophia looked [down], she saw the darkness, [illumining it] while maintaining [her own station], being [a] model for [worldly] things, [a principle] for the [insubstantial] substance [and the form]less form [...] a [shapeless] shape. [It makes room] for [every cosmic thing ...] the All [... the corrupt product. Since it is a rational principle that persuades] the darkness, [he sows from his] reason. Since it [is im]possible [for the archon] of [creation] to see any of the eternal entities,* [10] *he saw a reflection, and with reference to the reflection that he [saw] therein, he created the world. With a reflection of a reflection he worked upon the world, and then even the reflection of the appearance was taken from him. But Sophia was given a place of rest in exchange for her repentance. In consequence, because there was within her no pure, original image, either pre-existing in him or that had already come to be through him, he used his imagination and fashioned the remainder, for the image belonging to Sophia is always corrupt [and] deceptive. But the Archon – [since he simulates] and embodies by [pursuing the image] because of the superabundance [that inclined downward] – looked down.*" This dependence was first discovered by Tardieu (2005).

36. Plotinus lists them as μετάνοιαι, i.e. of Sophia; ἀντίτυποι, i.e. the Archon's counterfeit aeons; and παροικήσεις; cf. J. D. Turner (2001: 109–11, 558–70) and Codex Bruce, *Untitled* 263.11–264.6 [Schmidt & MacDermot]. Cf. also the "alien earth", *Enn.* II.9[33].11 with the "ethereal earth" of *Zostrianos* 5.10–29; 8.9–16; 12.4–21, etc. (perhaps the moon, as in Macrobius, *Somn. Scip.*1.11.7). He also rejects the sort of magical incantations and sounds found in the Platonizing Sethian treatises generally (*Enn.* II.9[33].14.2–9; cf. *Zostrianos* 52; 85–88; 118; 127.1–6; *Allogenes* 53.32–55.11; *Allogenes* VII.126.1–17; *Marsanes* 25.17–32.5). Yet this criticism is offset by his own quasi-incantational etymologies in *Enn.* V.5[32].5: "this power (of the One) sees and in its emotion tries to represent what it sees and breaks into speech, sounds which strive to express the essential nature of the universe produced by the travail of the utterer and so to represent, as far as sounds may, the origin of reality" and even by the appeal to non-discursive Egyptian hieroglyphs in *Enn.* VI.8[39].6.

37. Cf. "those who are unified", *Allogenes* XI.45.7–8, 46.21, 48.6–8, 55.14–15 and *Zostrianos* VIII.21.10–11: "undivided, with living thoughts" and 116.1–6: "All of them exist in unity, unified and individually, per-fected in fellowship and filled with the aeon that truly exists."

38. ογ͞μ͞ν͞τ`ⲁⲟⲣ͞ⲡ ͞ⲛⲟⲩⲱ͞ⲛ͞ϩ ⲉⲃⲟⲗ ~ *prophaneia*.

39. Cf. *Enn.* V.8[31].11.1–8: "Further, one of us, being unable to see himself, when he is possessed by that god brings his contemplation to the point of vision, and presents himself to his own mind and looks at a beautified image of himself; but then he dismisses that image, beautiful though it is, and comes to unity with himself, and, making no more separation, is one and all together with that god silently present, and is with him as much as he wants to be and can be."

40. *Allogenes* 60.38–61.8: "As if I were incognizant of him, I [knew] him [i.e. the Unknowable One] ... I knew the (Triple Powered One) that exists in me." Cf. also the anonymous *Parmenides* commentary, frags. II and IV and Porphyry, *Sent.* 25: "By intellection (κατὰ νόησιν) much may be said about that which transcends intellect (τοῦ ἐπέκεινα νοῦ), but it is better contemplated by incognizance than intellection (θεωρεῖται δὲ ἀνοησίᾳ κρείττονι νοήσεως)."

41. Cf. also *Enn.* VI.9[9].6.50–52; VI.7[38].39; V.3[49].12.48–53.

42. As suggested by Puech (1960: 184): "Il est plus significatif encore que la crise marquée par la rédaction du traité II 9 ait conduit, semble-t-il, Plotin à modifier l'expression de certaines de ses thèses antérieures, de celles qui, précisément, pouvaient prêter à confusion et paraître le rendre solidaire des gnostiques" ("It is even more significant that the crisis marked by the redaction of treatise II.9 had apparently led Plotinus to modify the expression of certain of his previous theses, precisely those which could have given rise to confusion and appear to show his solidarity with the Gnostics").

43. The order Being–Mind–Life (*Enn.* III.6[26].6.21–8; VI.6[34].6.15.1–3, 8.17–22; V.3[49].5.30–35) seems to derive from the influence of the *Ti.* 39e and *Soph.* 248e–249b cited above, note 28, and is used mainly in "noological" contexts where the structure of Intellect and its relation to Soul as locus of animation is of uppermost concern, while the order Being–Life–Mind (*Enn.* V.4[7].2.39–44; V.9[9].2.21–5; V.5[32].1.32–8, 2.9–13; VI.6[34].8.9–15, 18.29–36; VI.7[38].2.19–21, 16.6–22, 17.6–43), possibly based on the *Parmenides*, is used mainly in derivational contexts where the relation of Intellect or determinate being to its indeterminate, unitary source is of uppermost concern. But it is also possible that Plotinus moved in this direction in response to the Sethian Existence–Vitality–Mentality triad that *Allogenes* tended to present as an intermediate quasi-hypostatic figure, the Triple-Powered One, to which he may have objected as implying an unnecessary intermediate hypostasis between the One and Intellect (i.e. the Barbelo Aeon).

44. See the observations of Schwyzer (1970) concerning Plotinus' interpretation of the *Philebus*.

45. Cf. also *Enn.* III.8[30].1–8; VI.2[43].21–22; VI.7[38].1–12.

46. Cf. also *Zostrianos* 55.13–26 and 113.1–114.19; *Zostrianos* 116.1–6.

47. Cf. also *Grg.* 523a–6c and *R.* 614b–621b.

48. *Enn.* III.6[26].13.50–55: Εἰ μὲν οὖν ἔστι τι ἐν τοῖς κατόπτροις. καὶ ἐν τῇ ὕλῃ οὕτω τὰ αἰσθητὰ ἔστω· εἰ δὲ μὴ ἔστι. φαίνεται δὲ εἶναι. κἀκεῖ φατέον φαίνεσθαι ἐπὶ τῆς ὕλης αἰτιωμένους τῆς φαντάσεως τὴν τῶν ὄντων ὑπόστασιν. ἧς τὰ μὲν ὄντα ὄντως ἀεὶ μεταλαμβάνει. τὰ δὲ μὴ ὄντα μὴ ὄντως. ἐπείπερ οὐ δεῖ οὕτως ἔχειν αὐτὰ ὡς εἶχεν ἄν. τοῦ ὄντως μὴ ὄντος εἰ ἦν αὐτά.

49. The significance of these various combinations of negative terms is clarified by Proclus, *in Ti.* I.233.1–4: "Accordingly certain of the ancients call the noetic realm 'truly existent', the psychic 'not truly existent', the perceptible 'not truly non-existent', and the material 'truly non-existent'" (διὸ καὶ τῶν παλαιῶν τινες ὄντως μὲν ὂν καλοῦσι τὸ νοητὸν πλάτος. οὐκ ὄντως δὲ ὂν τὸ ψυχικόν. οὐκ ὄντως δὲ οὐκ ὂν τὸ αἰσθητόν. ὄντως δὲ οὐκ ὂν τὴν ὕλην). According to Tournaire (1996: 63), the predicate ὂν means innately organized (intelligible or psychic), οὐκὂν means innately unorganized (sensible, material), while the qualifier ὄντως signifies what is stable or stabilized (intelligible or material), and οὐκ ὄντως signifies perceptible or intelligible reality subject to change; cf. P. Hadot (1968: vol. 1, 147–211) and Henry & Hadot (1960: vol. 2, 712). In Marius Victorinus, *ad Candidum* 11.1–12 [Henri & Hadot] one finds the sequence *quae vere sunt, quae sunt, quae non vere non sunt, quae non sunt, quae non vere sunt, vere quae non sunt*. These terms and distinctions seem to originate with Plato; for example, in the *Sph.* 240d9–240a1 and 254d1 there is the series ὄντως ὄν. οὐκ ὄντως οὐκ ὄν. ὄντως μὴ ὄν, and in the *Prm.* 162a6–b3 there is the series εἶναι ὄν. εἶναι μὴ ὄν. μὴ εἶναι μὴ ὄν. μὴ εἶναι ὄν. In *de Caelo* 282a4–b7 (reflected also in the *Categories*), Aristotle makes similar distinctions, using ἀεί instead of ὄντως. An attempt to invoke the same categories also occurs in a revelation cited in Codex Bruce, *Untitled*, 237, 20–23 [Schmidt & MacDermot]: "And when Phosilampes understood, he said: 'On account of him are those things which really and truly exist and those which do not exist truly. This is he on whose account are those that truly exist which are hidden, and those that do not exist truly which are manifest.'" Here the categories alternate between modes of being (ὄντως ὄν, both absolute and "hidden" being, intelligibles and perhaps souls) and non-being (ὄντως οὐκ ὄν, both absolute and visible non-being, matter and perhaps sensible bodies), rather than exclusively between modes of non-being. Cf. also *Melchizedek* NHC IX.6.12–14; 16.18–19.

50. Largely in response to the metaphysical puzzlements that drive him to despair just prior to his ascent: "How can beings – since they are from the aeon of those who derive from an invisible and undivided self-generated Spirit as triform unengendered images – both have an origin superior to Existence and pre-exist all [these] and yet have come to be in the [world]? How do those in its presence with all these [originate from the] Good [that is above]? What sort [of power] and [cause, and] what is [the] place of that [one]? What is its principle? How does its product belong both to it and all these? How, [being a] simple [unity], does it differ [from] itself, given that it exists as Existence, Form, and Blessedness, and,

being vitally alive, grants power? How has Existence which has no being appeared in a power that has being?" (*Zostrianos* VIII.2.25–3.13).

51. The same dialectical procedure is further described in the *Sph.* 253d–e: "[Stranger:] Shall we not say that the division (διαιρεῖσθαι) of things by classes and the avoidance of the belief that the same class is another, or another the same, belongs to the science of dialectic (διαλεκτικῆς … ἐπιστήμης)? [Theaetetus:] Yes, we shall. [Stranger:] Then, surely, he who can divide rightly is able to see clearly 1) one form pervading a discrete multitude, and 2) many different forms contained from without by one higher form; and again, 3) one form unified into a single whole and pervading many such wholes, and 4) many forms, existing only in separation and isolation. This is the knowledge and ability to distinguish (διακρίνειν κατὰ γένος ἐπίστασθαι) by classes how individual things can or cannot be associated with one another. [Theaetetus:] Certainly it is. [Stranger:] But you surely, I suppose, will not grant the art of dialectic to any but the man who pursues philosophy in purity and righteousness. [Theaetetus:] How could it be granted to anyone else? [Stranger:] Then it is in some region like this that we shall always, both now and hereafter, discover the philosopher, if we look for him."

52. Already in his earliest treatise (*Enn.* I.6[1]) Plotinus held that, although the soul's share in the governance of the world requires its descent into the body, the embodied soul nevertheless becomes like a stranger clothed in ugly and alien garments, and must seek her return to her homeland where her father lives (*Enn.* I.6[1].8.16–21); to find this homeland is for the soul to turn inward and find itself (*Enn.* I.6[1].5.53, 8.4, 9.21–2).

53. *Phdr.* 249c: "For a human being must understand an utterance according to its Form, collecting into a unity by means of reason the many perceptions of the senses; and this is a recollection of those things which our soul once beheld, when it journeyed with God and, lifting its vision above the things which we now say exist, rose up into real being."

54. *Phdr.* 248c–d: "And this is a law of Destiny, that the soul which follows after God and obtains a view of any of the truths is free from harm until the next period, and if it can always attain this, is always unharmed; but when, through inability to follow, it fails to see, and through some mischance is filled with forgetfulness and evil and grows heavy, and when it has grown heavy, loses its wings and falls to the earth, then it is the law that this soul shall never pass into any beast at its first birth, but the soul that has seen the most shall enter into the birth of a man."

6

Plotinus and the Orient: *aoristos dyas*

Vishwa Adluri

One form it was previously, which again became fourfold …

(*Mahābhārata* 12.321.16c)[1]

In his *Vita Plotini*, Porphyry tells us that, at the age of twenty-seven, Plotinus was seized by a passion for philosophy. Plotinus searched long for a teacher until he finally met Ammonius in Alexandria:

> From that day he stayed continually with Ammonius and acquired so complete a training in philosophy that he became eager to make acquaintance with the Persian philosophical discipline and that prevailing among the Indians. As the Emperor Gordian was preparing to march against the Persians, he joined the army and went on the expedition; he was already in his thirty-ninth year, for he had stayed studying with Ammonius for eleven complete years. When Gordian was killed in Mesopotamia Plotinus escaped with difficulty and came safe to Antioch.
>
> (Porphyry, *Plot.* 3.14–23)[2]

Scholars have long wished to investigate the relationship between Plotinus and the Indian system of thought, but such research was limited to historical research or philosophical speculation.[3] Thus far, no specific Indian text has been suggested where such a "system" – one that bears the closest resemblance to Plotinian thought – could be found.[4]

In this chapter, I introduce such a text: the *Nārāyaṇīya*, found in the *Mokṣadharmaparvan* or the soteriological portion of the Indian epic, the *Mahābhārata*. In eighteen short chapters,[5] this text contains a combination of elements that were also essential for Plotinus' thought:

- a soteriology oriented towards the One;[6]
- difficulty of seeing and describing this One;
- levels of Being;
- intense erotic love and its relationship to the One;

- an ontological hierarchy that serves upward as a soteriology and downward as a cosmology.

The entire discussion, moreover, displays a keen understanding of the properties of number, such as the completely transcendent one, the Indefinite Dyad, and the cosmological resonances of the numeric series 1, 2, 3, ...[7] A more relevant "Plotinian" Indian text cannot be wished for, nor does one exist.

The method I follow in this chapter is straightforward. I will present the text,[8] its basic structure and philosophical project, and argue for why the *Nārāyaṇīya* provides a good basis for Plotinian–Indian comparative study. My discussion is divided into six sections. I first introduce the *Nārāyaṇīya* and then discuss relevant aspects of number in Greek philosophy from Pythagoras to Plotinus; thereafter, I return to philosophy of number in the *Nārāyaṇīya*.[9] In two concluding sections, I then address the question of Plotinus' Orientalism. The first of these reviews Bréhier's reasons – made in his 1928 classic work *La philosophie de Plotin*, translated into English as *The Philosophy of Plotinus* (1958) – for attributing Oriental influences to certain aspects of Plotinus' thought; the second then examines Bréhier's sources for making these claims.[10] Finally, I return to the question of Plotinian–Indian comparisons in the conclusion.

THE *NĀRĀYAṆĪYA*

The *Nārāyaṇīya* occurs in the *Śāntiparvan*, the twelfth major book of the *Mahābhārata*. The *Śāntiparvan* contains three sections: the *Rājadharmaparvan* (on the law of kingship), the *Āpaddharmaparvan* (on the law of emergencies) and the *Mokṣadharmaparvan* (on the praxis of salvation). The *Nārāyaṇīya* appears in the last of these sections and marks the culmination of the epic's cosmological, soteriological and literary programme.

The immediate context of the *Nārāyaṇīya* is an extended dialogue between the fallen Kuru patriarch Bhīṣma and the victorious king Yudhiṣṭhira regarding the various forms of *dharma*.[11] This text is distinguished by the glorification of Nārāyaṇa[12] as the supreme reality. It includes the divine sage Nārada's visit to the mystical island Śvetadvīpa (or the "White Island") where Nārāyaṇa reveals himself in his universal form (*viśvarūpa*, 12.326.1c). The text is interesting as it provides not only a well-developed theology but also philosophical discussions on ontology, cosmology, etymology, divinity and ritual. A summary of the various descents of the One Being (*ekaṁ puruṣaṁ*, 12.326.31c) Nārāyaṇa into the cosmos can be found here[13] – a theme that is richly developed in later sectarian texts, the *Purāṇas*.

Although a spate of philological scholars have insisted that the doctrine of Nārāyaṇa was introduced into the text by later dogmatic philosophico-religious interpolators,[14] and that the text is nothing more than a transparent attempt to import "theology" into the *Mahābhārata*, a closer view reveals matters to be much more complex. The *Nārāyaṇīya* articulates a sophisticated philosophy of number, which, to be sure, is oriented towards the One Being called Nārāyaṇa here, but the text is anything but dogmatic. The difficulty in conceiving the one reality, the difficulty of articulating it and achieving it are problems the text struggles to articulate. These difficulties – along with the difficulties the very conception of *one reality* creates for cosmology in terms of how, then, such a plurality (as is implied in the idea of cosmology) can exist – are exposed in this text. To be sure, the text does recommend certain practices conducive to this vision, but I am chiefly concerned here with the philosophical problem of the One and its relation to the many. Although Nārāyaṇa is said to be this One, owing to his infinity, this conception appears with all the attendant philosophical problems. Nārāyaṇa must be the One, but also the several levels between the One and the many. Thus: a dyad, a doubling, a pair, a fourfold. These are the emanations of the One (note that this series always proceeds through doubling). At the head of the many is a series of numbers: one, two, three (*eka, dvi, tri*). The One of the former progression (that is, of the series which proceeds through ontological doubling) and the one of the numerical series are quite different. Throughout, the text attempts to hold together these two senses of "one" in their irreducible difference.[15] The dyad, more-over, appears to be assigned a liminal role between the simple One and the many.[16]

This brief overview of the text already shows that number is the key concept in terms of which the *Nārāyaṇīya* must be understood. Before we look more closely at the *Nārāyaṇīya*, however, it is pertinent to recall the significance of number in Plotinian thought.

SIGNIFICANCE OF MULTIPLICITY FROM PYTHAGORAS TO PLATO

From the early Presocratics through Pythagoras and Plato, Plotinus inherits the central function of the philosophy of number in explaining both the multiplicity of beings and the relation of this multiplicity to the One.[17] Slaveva-Griffin distinguishes three central philosophical functions fulfilled by number in ancient philosophy:

- a cosmogonic function that "searches for the origin of multiplicity from some physical or metaphysical source";
- a cosmological function that "searches for a way to explain the innumerable diversity of material world in an orderly fashion"; and
- an epistemological function that "attempts to comprehend the visible and invisible constituents of the universe in a rational form" (Slaveva-Griffin 2009: 4).

Number is the crucial concept that mediates both between the move from the One to the many (cosmogony) and from the many to the One (cosmology). It allows these two to be held together in their irreducible tension. An epistemological investigation into the properties of numbers is thus not an enquiry undertaken for its own sake, but an attempt to understand the structure of reality in its outward pull away from the One and its inward pull towards the One.[18] Besides the problem of the relation of the cosmogonic and the cosmological properties of number, however, there is a further problem that arises in rela-tion the One: this is the problem of the polysemy of the term "one", which Plato discusses in the *Parmenides*.

Pythagorean elements are interspersed throughout Plato's dialogues, especially the *Timaeus* and *Philebus*, which Slaveva-Griffin discusses, and the *Laws, Theaetetus* and the *Republic*, which Rist (1967) analyses. However, I will focus here primarily on Plato's dialogue *Parmenides*. While the *Timaeus* and *Philebus* focus on cosmogonic and cosmo-logical themes and the latter three texts on the challenges to monism arising out of the problem of evil, the *Parmenides* is explicitly and technically ontological, setting for itself an investigation into the one, unity and multiplicity. The dialogue lists eight hypotheses, of which only the first two are of relevance to us here in the Plotinian framework. The first hypothesis, which speaks of the unity of the one as absolute, is most closely related to Parmenides' *Peri Physeōs*. This conception of the One insists on its absolute, pure and simple unity and excludes any predicates – including the predicate that it is one! Plato felt this last deduction of the first hypothesis to be self-contradictory, and thus introduced the second hypothesis, which is of most relevance to our discussion. This second hypothesis introduces sophistication or qualification (one can hardly call it difference) into the One.[19] The One, according to the deductions of this hypothesis, consists of both unity and being: *to hen* and *ousia, to einai* or *to on*. Slaveva-Griffin shows convincingly how this qualification of the One, "as unity and multiplicity interact at an ontological level, especially as represented in Plotinus' concepts of the Indefinite Dyad and Intellect" (Slaveva-Griffin 2009: 6). In support, she cites Simplicius, *Metaphysics* 187a: "Alexander says that 'according to Plato the One and the Indefinite Dyad, which he spoke of as Great and Small, are the Principles of all things and even the Forms themselves' … It is very likely that Plato made the One and the Indefinite Dyad the Principles of all things, since this was the doctrine of the Pythagoreans whom Plato followed at many points."[20] Note, however, that Plato does not elaborate on the Indefinite Dyad as such, but the 'unwritten doctrines' of Plato, the *agrapha dogmata*, attest to this notion.[21] Whatever the actual relationship between Plato's written and unwritten doctrines may be, we can accept with reliable confidence that the concept of the Indefinite Dyad played a role in Plato's conception of the "many" (Krämer 1990; Dillon 2003; Guthrie 1978: 418–42; Slaveva-Griffin 2009).

After Plato, the next thinker to consider is Speusippus, who renames Plato's One and the Indefinite Dyad as One and Multiplicity (*plēthos*). He constructs a conceptual system in *de Communi Mathematica Scientia*.[22] Slaveva-Griffin writes:

> According to this system, the first level of reality that derives from the union of a One and Multiplicity is the first principle of number, which in turn unites with multiplicity once again to produce the sequence of numbers and geometrical figures … the One imposes limit and quality into Multiplicity, being infinite divisibility …. Aristotle interprets multiplicity quantitatively as multiplicity of units and number as a composition of units, while Speusippus and, in retrospect, Plato view them as ontologically primal.   (2009: 7)

Rist (1965: 330–31) approaches the same issue from an ethical rather than an ontological point of view, relying heavily on Aristotle. Rist's ethical approach clarifies some of the background behind the issues of One, multiplicity and the Dyad, and how Aristotle's materialistic interpretations of number were stirring debate, but Rist makes the same error as Aristotle of confusing one as a simple, undifferentiated one with one as the first of a series.[23] To add to the problem of rescuing Parmenidean (or Platonic) monism, intellectual debates did not fail to exploit the analytic avenues opened. Thus, Rist takes Theophrastus' comment on this Pythagorean structure seriously, and asserts that unlike the later Milesians, Pythagoras was a dualist. Here it is important for us that Rist's interpretation explicitly hinges on the fact that "they [i.e. Plato and Pythagoras] … make a kind of opposition (*antithesin tina poiousin*) between the One and the Indefinite Dyad" (*ibid.*: 332).

In contrast to Rist's views, I would like to suggest that there is an alternative way to think of the Indefinite Dyad in Plato, namely through holding apart the different sense of "one", as is the case in the *Nārāyaṇīya*.[24] As we have seen, the text distinguishes between two main senses of one: the One Being, which is without a second and yet somehow engenders a procession through doubling, is different from the one of the series *eka*, *dvi* and *tri*. Retaining this distinction between two senses of one, we can now better address the problem as defined by Rist. First, we should note that in the *Nārāyaṇīya*, the One does not become the many; it remains distinct from the numeric series identified with cosmology: Ekata, Dvita and Trita are the sons of the Creator; yet, when sage Nārada arrives at Śvetadvīpa, wishing to behold the One, he sees the entire cosmos of Becoming contained within the One. The Creator's sons are less fortunate and are told that the One is seen through the dyadic beings of Śvetadvīpa being seen. Curiously, when Nārada returns to the Bādari hermitage of Nara-Nārāyaṇa, the sages, who were formerly a pair, now appear exactly as the dyadic beings of Śvetadvīpa. Distinguishing between the simple One and one as the first in a series would thus allow us to posit the Dyad without necessarily reverting to a dualistic ontology.[25]

With Xenocrates, we find a new way to conceive the relation of unity to multiplicity: Xenocrates genders the first two principles of the Monad and the Dyad: the Monad is considered masculine, and described as the Intellect. The Dyad is female, properly conceived of as the Indefinite Dyad owing to it containing multiplicity and unlimitedness.[26] The "World Soul" is created through the union of these male and female first principles.[27]

With these comments on the significance of number in Greek philosophers, I would now like to turn to the *Nārāyaṇīya*.

PHILOSOPHY OF NUMBER IN THE *NĀRĀYAṆĪYA*

Although the *Nārāyaṇīya* appears to propound a number of doctrines, giving it a very diverse appearance, the text is actually held together by a very small number of philosophical themes. Key among these is the relation of the One to the many, as it ultimately contains the solution to King Yudhiṣṭhira's incipient question regarding "infallible heaven": since all of Becoming is subject to passing-away, this will require an ascent, in the intellect, to the One. Let us see how. The text opens with a question concerning the highest divinity; King Yudhiṣṭhira asks:

> A householder or a student, a hermit or a mendicant,
> If one wishes to obtain perfection, what god ought he adore?
> How indeed can he obtain infallible heaven and [beyond it,] the ultimate good?
> By following which injunction ought he to sacrifice to the gods and ancestors?
> When liberated, where does one go? And what is the nature of liberation?
> Having attained to heaven, what must one do so as not to fall?
> Which god is the god of gods and the ancestor of ancestors?
> And what transcends even him? Tell me all this, O grandfather!
>
> (*Mahābhārata* 12.321.1–4, my trans.)

This question inaugurates a set of themes that inform the structure of the *Nārāyaṇīya*. Yudhiṣṭhira's question circumscribes an area of philosophical enquiry. Part of the question is critical; it wants to separate the subject from *āśrama*s, stages of life, and by implication *varṇāśramadharma*, the articulation of life according to one's social function and age.[28] Moreover, the question also separates out the attainment of heaven, and with it all finite goals, however lofty they may be. Specifically, the question is one of transcendence beyond heaven; it is what I have elsewhere called double transcendence, where heaven constitutes the first transcendence (see Adluri 2012a).

The question is one of perfection (*siddhim āsthātum icchet*, 1c), ultimacy (*niḥśreyasaṁ param*, 2a) and also permanence articulated by concerns with stability (*dhruvam*, 2a) and immunity to fall (*na cyavate*, 3c). This set of ultimate concerns is posited in a twofold theoretical perspective, which can be named "cosmological–soteriological".[29] The cosmological aspect is the enquiry into the "god of gods" and the ancestor of ancestors and what goes beyond even that. Thus the question will seek a stepwise progression up to the creator god, and beyond that to the ontological concept of the "One". This manifold question requires a manifold answer, but the essence of the question and the purport of the answer remain the ineffable One.[30] The unity of the *Nārāyaṇīya* is the problem of the One.[31] Thus, although Bhīṣma in his response touches upon many themes (including a visit by the divine sage Nārada to the mystical island Śvetadvīpa to view the One Being, here called Nārāyaṇa), these all pertain to the central and abiding question of this text: what is the relationship of the One to the many? It is this that makes the *Nārāyaṇīya* the paradigmatic text for studying the relationship of Neoplatonism to Indian thought.[32]

In response to Yudhiṣṭhira's enquiry, Bhīṣma states that the questions the king has raised concern a great mystery, but he knows of an ancient narrative (*itihāsaṁ purātanam*, 12.321.7a) concerning a conversation between sage Nārada and Nārāyaṇa. Sage Nārada, realizing that the highest Being has become *four* (*ekā mūrtir iyaṁ pūrvaṁ jātā bhūyaś caturvidhā*, 12.321.16c), goes to seek out *two* of these four, Nara and Nārāyaṇa. These two are a *pair*. When he reaches their retreat, he is surprised to find them engaged in worship. Surprised, Nārada asks Nārāyaṇa about the deity to whom he sacrifices: "You are glorified as the unborn, the sempiternal, the sustainer, regarded as immortal and unsurpassable. … To whom today do you sacrifice? – which god or which ancestor – we know not!" (12.321.24–6). Nārāyaṇa tells Nārada about a still higher form of his, known as Kṣetrajña (the Knower of the Field) or as Puruṣa (the Person or the Self). From this masculine Being proceeds the Unmanifest, Prakṛti, the womb of all beings.[33] Nārāyaṇa tells the sage that they worship Prakṛti "as deity and as parent", and, beyond her, the Self. This Self, however, is not attainable except through intense intellectual effort (*jñānayoga*).[34] Through this practice, unified souls (*ekāntin*s) reach their goal of entering into the Self.[35]

Learning that the One is higher than the four, Nārada sets out to behold that highest Being. He describes his preparation (purification, austerity, truthfulness, study of the Vedas, devotion to God, and one-pointedness) and then sets out, via Gandhamādana, to Mount Meru.[36] From the summit, he spies a wondrous site: Śvetadvīpa, or the "White Island", a luminous abode inhabited by beings that are "Transcending senses and abstaining from food … unwavering and very fragrant … with tongues they lick the one who faces the universe, the sun" (12.322.8–12). But the most interesting thing about these beings is that they are *dyadic*. For example, each of these radiant beings is endowed with *four* testicles, *sixty-four* teeth, and *one hundred* lines on the soles of their feet. A clear numerology is being worked out here (with the usual number of testicles, teeth, etc. being doubled).

The text then tells us how, before Nārada arrived there, the three sons of the Creator, Ekata, Dvita and Trita, had previously come there to view the One Being. In spite of their *askesis* they failed, because they lacked intense love or *bhakti*. Literally translated, the names Ekata, Dvita and Trita mean *Oneness*, *Twoness* and *Threeness*. Nārada is luckier, but the vision he is granted of the One is a *multiplicity*, a vision of the "form of all beings": *viśvarūpa*. This One Being, surprisingly, shimmers in various colours and is glorified with numerous names. The *simple One*, he is told, is beyond this cosmic form and is ineffable and incomprehensible. But the discourse that follows insists that cosmology and soteriology are intimately linked, and that the One being is to be *experienced* (rather than *viewed*) *through exclusive and unwavering love* or *bhakti*, and a philosophical system for this is expounded.

Even though scholars have long argued that *bhakti* is nothing more than a cult-emotive phenomenon, it is important to note that the *Nārāyaṇīya* does not so much recommend the practice of *bhakti* as it presents a philosophical argument for *bhakti* as a cognitive, epistemological-ontological stance towards the One.[37] More importantly for my thesis here is to see that love or *bhakti* represents the soteriological "way up" from the many to the One corresponding to the cosmogonic "way down" from the One to the many. The significance of *bhakti* for our topic can be seen from the way *bhakti* relates to the project of the *Nārāyaṇīya* of universalizing the soteriological philosophy of the *Upaniṣads*. Biardeau has argued that *bhakti* does not simply replace sacrificial and Upaniṣadic values, but "englobes"[38] these within a hierarchy of values.[39] Thus, instead of seeing *bhakti* as a dogmatic, irrational element in the text, we must see it as central to the *Nārāyaṇīya's* ontological, philosophical and numerological concerns.

Within the *Nārāyaṇīya's* philosophical ontology, *bhakti* plays a crucial role in the soteriological ascent. This is evident from the way Nārada, whose role as Nārāyaṇa's pre-eminent *bhakta* is well established from an early phase of Indian thought, becomes the paradigmatic figure of the narrative of ascent. Nārada's journey to the White Island follows strict numeric order. He goes from the many beings to the One, guided by the question of who that highest Being is. First, he is introduced in the text as someone who has "wandered all the worlds" (*nāradaḥ sumahad bhūtaṁ lokān sarvān acīcarat*, 12.321.14a) and, when he arrives at the Bādari hermitage, he also wonders, "this is the complete abode in which all the worlds are established, / With the devas, asuras, gandharvas, ṛṣis, kinnaras, and the snakes" (12.321.15c–16a). Then, thinking, "One form it was previously, which again became four-fold" (*ekā mūrtir iyaṁ pūrvaṁ jātā bhūyaś caturvidhā*, 12.321.16c), he desires to know who that highest Being is, whom the pair Nara-Nārāyaṇa worship. Thereafter, he goes from the pair to the dyadic beings of the White Island. When he arrives at the island, he is initially unable to view the One, as we might well expect. But the problem of the impossibility of actually "viewing the One" is elegantly side-stepped in the myth because when the One Being indeed manifests to him, it is precisely in the form of the universe! The emphasis here is on the ascending path of salvation and the numeric leap between the many and One, with special emphasis on the dyad. The accomplished dyadic beings are able to constantly behold the One, and salvation, in their case, seems to be a clear understanding of the dyadic nature of being an individual and being One.[40]

Not only the way up to One (soteriology) but also the way down from the One to the many (cosmology) is mythically inscribed in the narrative of the journey to the White Island.[41] But whereas the way up is singular, the way down is of two kinds: the series of number denoting procession, and the second series, which denotes multiplicity.

The universe progresses according to the numeric order of one, two, three. But the same cannot be said of the *One, which is nevertheless reflected in the multiplicity of the universe*. Thus, the text refers to two additional series of "descent" of the One: the first is the *vyūha*s or hypostases of the One, the second his *avatāras* or incarnations. The logic of the reflection of the One in the universe is, as is the case of all reflections, one of duplication.[42] The text mythically sets up the following steps for such a "descending reflection" of the One in the many:

1. Nārāyaṇa is, first, the "eternal Soul of the universe"; that is, one without a second.
2. Along with Nara, he forms a pair; that is, the one of a pair.
3. Nārāyaṇa is one of the fourfold of division, which is still not the same as the one of the numerical series (note that the number three, which constitutes the first genuine multiplicity, does not occur here).

There is no doubt here that the One is proceeding not through a numerical progression of the One to two and then to three. The fourfold form unambiguously points to doubling: one, two, four. The distinction we made earlier between duplication and numeric progression is borne out, the latter belonging exclusively to a cosmology. This fourfold duplication via the dyad is called the *vyūha* doctrine. But when the One manifests *theistically* in the universe, Nārāyaṇa takes on a soteriological form as Hari or Kṛṣṇa and these descents are then listed as incarnations or *avatāras*. Thus, the way up is *bhakti*, while the way down is cosmogonic procession for the universe and the One is reflected in it as the *vyūhas* and somehow theistically descends into the cosmos as *avatāra*. If we lay this out schematically, then we see that there are three senses of one, each heading a different series, as shown in Table 6.1.

This dyadic logic has parallels in Neoplatonic thought. Although Rist has argued that once Plato grants the Dyad he abandons his commitment to a philosophical monism, matters are obviously much more complex. The Dyad seems to function in an entirely different ontology than in the numeric series of one, two, three. In the *Nārāyaṇīya*, when Nārada returns from viewing the One on Śvetadvīpa, Nara-Nārāyaṇa, who were formally a pair, now appear to him as a dyad. But the crucial experience he has undergone in the meantime has been divine grace, the complement to *bhakti*, and it is this that enabled him to see the One.[43] The dyad, then, is not a merely *logical and theoretical* construction in the scheme of procession from the One to the many, but, it seems, a necessary step to

Table 6.1 The three series of "one" in the *Nārāyaṇīya*'s philosophical ontology.

Procession	Vyūha doctrine	Cosmology
ONE	ONE (as Vāsudeva)	MANY
One: Nārāyaṇa	Pradyumna	One: Ekata
Double: Nara-Nārāyaṇa pair	Saṃkarṣaṇa	Two: Dvita
Fourfold: Nara-Nārāyaṇa plus Hari and Kṛṣṇa	Aniruddha	Three: Trita

preserve the *relationship* of the One to the many, thus making the soteriological goal of the system of emanation feasible.[44]

In contrast, the sons of the Creator are said to have failed to see the One because they lacked the necessary *bhakti*. Although we could interpret this theistically as a doctrinal commitment to "devotion", such an interpretation risks missing out on the philosophical and ontological significance of the concept. Although usually translated as "devotion" or "love", *bhakti* derives from the root *bhaj* which has a rich range of semantic meanings including "to divide", "to distribute", "to allot or apportion to", but also "to grant", "to bestow", "to furnish", "to supply" and "to obtain as one's share", "to receive as", "to partake of", "to enjoy" and "to possess" (Monier-Williams 1899, s.v. "*bhaj*"). It is thus implied in the very act of the reversal of the process of exteriorization through which the fall away from the One occurs.[45] Rather than bespeaking merely the loving relation of the devotee to his or her god, *bhakti*, then, becomes a basic term for explicating the relationship of the One to the many. More importantly, we should note that *bhakti* is placed entirely on the side of the series that proceeds by ontological doubling (the leftmost column of Table 6.1). The cosmological series (the rightmost column) is cut off from the One not because it is a multiplicity, but because it is unable to intuit the One in this multiplicity. Nārada's *bhakti* precisely consists in seeing the One *even when the vision he is granted is that of all forms* (*viśvarūpa*). On returning to the Bādari hermitage, he is questioned by Nara-Nārāyaṇa about whether he was able to see the One and he tells them that, when he saw the One, he also saw the two of them by the god's side (12.331.38a). Thereupon Nara and Nārāyaṇa, in turn, reveal to Nārada that he was beheld by them on Śvetadvīpa (12.332.22a)! Thus, it is not just Nārada who beheld a multiplicity in the body of the One, but that multiplicity existed and was part of the One. But in the meantime, the vision of the One in its numeric possibilities has had the effect of rendering Nārada single minded (12.331.51c) and he declares his intent to spend his days in *askesis* at the hermitage of the two gods and they worship him in turn.[46]

It is thus clear that we should be on our guard against easy dismissals of the *Nārāyaṇīya* as a theological work without any philosophical significance. In spite of its mythological presentation, the text does not simply recommend a form of ritual or worship of a particular sectarian deity. Rather, in the very depictions of Nārada's journey, the vision of the One, and its complex quartets and triads of beings the text is struggling to articulate deeper ontological, cosmological, anthropological and ethical concerns. Thus, Greek thought is more theological than we are comfortable with, and Indian theology is more philosophical than we are accustomed to believe.

PLOTINUS' ORIENTALISM

According to Wolters (1982), the theory of an Oriental source for Plotinus' thought, especially concerning the One, can be traced back to the work of Bréhier. Wolters specifically has in mind Bréhier's argument, made in his *The Philosophy of Plotinus*, that, "we find at the very center of Plotinus' thought a foreign element which defies classification. The theory of Intelligence as universal being derives neither from Greek rationalism nor from the piety diffused through the religious circles of his day" (Bréhier 1958: 116). It is not necessary here to trace the further reception of this thesis in Neoplatonic studies, except to note that what is at stake in the debate is not the possibility of Hellenistic, Alexandrine or Jewish influence upon Plotinus, but, specifically, *Indian* philosophy as a source of influence on Plotinus (see Gregorios 2002).

As Gregorios notes, the problem of Plotinus' "Orientalism" is not the problem of Plotinus' Oriental sources, which are, in any case, not in doubt among scholars,[47] but the question of whether there is a specifically foreign element in Plotinus' thought, and that means an element *alien* to the spirit of Greek rationality (or, at least, to that spirit as it was understood in nineteenth-century philosophy). Here is where an engagement with Bréhier's thesis might profitably begin. Specifically, we shall ask how Indian philosophy was understood by Bréhier such that it could appear as the counter-concept to Greek rationality.[48] Further, we shall ask what it reveals about our own philosophical prejudices that Plotinus' thought of the One could appear inconsistent with his systematic philosophy and why, when it comes to the choice between these two, we are quicker to surrender the former (seeking a foreign origin for it) than the latter.

Concerning Plotinus' thought of the One, Bréhier argues that "the source of the philosophy of Plotinus" must be placed "beyond the Orient close to Greece, in the religious speculation of India, which by the time of Plotinus had been founded for centuries on the Upanishads and had retained their vitality" (Bréhier 1958: 117). At the outset, he rejects Greek and Near Eastern philosophy as the source of this thought, as he considers it incompatible with Plotinus' systematic philosophy (identified with the hypostases of the Soul and Intelligence). Thus he speaks of a "double aspect" to "Plotinus' notion of Intelligence", comprising "an articulated system of definition notions" and a "universal being in [which] … every difference is absorbed". Whereas the former is conducive to "a knowledge of the world and [holds] that reality can be grasped through reason", the latter seeks only "the mystical ideal of the complete unification of beings in the Godhead" (*ibid.*: 106). The former is the product of "Plotinus' exegesis of … Plato, Aristotle, and the Stoics" (*ibid.*). The origins of the latter, in contrast, lie in "new mental habits, born of religious beliefs the origin of which is in the Orient, outside of Hellenism" (*ibid.*: 107).

Bréhier develops the contrast between these two systems along three lines: (1) concerning the way Plotinus addresses the problem of the constitution of individual consciousness, (2) concerning the relation of the individual soul to the One, and (3) the way Plotinus conceives of the universal character of Soul.

Concerning the first, Bréhier argues that "the Plotinian concept of the relation of the individual to the universal being" is "quite different" (from the Greek concept). "It is no longer a rational unity which he is seeking but a mystical unification in which individual consciousness is to disappear" (*ibid.*: 110). This has both epistemological and ethical consequences. Epistemologically, we are no longer dealing with "a rational knowledge but [only] with an experience". "The 'true knowledge' of which Plotinus speaks … is only an immediate intuition of beings" (*ibid.*). Ethically, the Plotinian ideal of ecstatic union with the One "differs in principle from all the philosophical systems and religions of his time because of the almost complete absence of the idea of a mediator or savior destined to bring man into relation with God …. The very idea of salvation, which implies a mediatory sent by God to man, is foreign to him" (*ibid.*: 112).

Concerning the second, Bréhier argues that Plotinus, "in piling up contrasts between the reality accessible to Intelligence and the boundless reality in which ecstatic love loses itself", ultimately ends up "sever[ing] every bond which connected the first with the second" (*ibid.*: 156). The result is a hypertrophied intellectualism in which (according to Bréhier) no bridge is possible between the rationalism of the Plotinian system and its suprarational mysticism (*ibid.*: 148). Indeed, Bréhier argues that Plotinus, by premising his entire system upon the principle of the One, jeopardizes his entire systematic project (*ibid.*: 154).

Finally, concerning the third, Bréhier argues that Plotinus' understanding of Soul defies rational explanation. All difference being "absorbed" in "universal being", the "distinction between subject and object [too] comes to an end". In place of an "articulated system of definite notions", a "knowledge of the world", we find only the "mystical ideal of the complete unification of beings in the Godhead" (*ibid.*: 106). Thus, through a kind of hypertrophied intellectualism, Plotinus' rational philosophy ultimately goes over into its very antithesis: mere intuition and mere feeling of oneness with the totality of beings. "Intellectualism", says Bréhier poignantly, "has destroyed itself through its own exaggeration" (*ibid.*: 103).

The contrast between rationalism and irrationalism is absolute as Bréhier understands it (*ibid.*: 158; cf. also 156). Further, by destroying the notion of difference, irrationalism simultaneously makes ethics impossible. "Knowledge of the self possesses no ethical character in [Indian] philosophy" (*ibid.*: 128). It impinges upon the relation of the individual to the supraindividual reality. Although a "subject of knowledge", the self in this conception "nevertheless experiences nothing pertaining to the life of a moral person". Hence, the relation of this person to God cannot be "the trusting attitude of the faithful believer". "The ascetic is merely endeavoring to remove every veil that separates him from Brahman" (*ibid.*: 128–9). Irrationalism replaces (the desire for) knowledge with "an obscure emotion, a vital feeling without form, [or] an intangible *Stimmung*". "Real knowledge consists then not in classifying forms and in grasping their relations, but, on the contrary, in going beyond every finite form". Thus Bréhier argues that *brahman* (and *mutatis mutandis* the Plotinian One) is "not an object of knowledge". Even if knowledge of a certain kind is necessary to attain it, "this knowledge has nothing to do with understanding and erudition": "Knowledge of the Veda is required to lead to it. Meditation and ascetic practices are required. The identity of the self with the universal being is not a rational conclusion reached by the intellect, but a sort of intuition due to the practice of meditation" (*ibid.*: 125).

The philosophical system motivated by a yearning for unity is "opposed to the Hellenic and Judeo-Christian ideal". "In opposition to Greek philosophy", it implies "no attempt at a rational explanation of things". The connection between (the desire for) rational explanation and creation is very strong as Bréhier sees it. He argues that in the philosophical speculations of the Indians,

> what corresponds to rational explanation is at best a theory of emanation, which Oldenberg points out as a tendency in the philosophy of the Upanishads. Things will be only the unfolding and expansion of forces that are united in the universal being. This dynamism, the notion of the development of one and the same life, is very far from the rational order of forms sought by the Greek philosopher.
>
> (*Ibid.*: 128)

Finally, in its insistence on the identity of the individual and the whole, mysticism destroys the possibility of (rational) religion. Not only is "the very idea of salvation, which implies a mediator sent by God to man" (*ibid.*: 112) "foreign" to Plotinus, but "piety, in the usual sense of the word", is also "absent in him" (*ibid.*: 113).

Mysticism, understood as the longing for union with the One or for a trans-personal experience of the One, thus leads step-by-step away from the goals of rational (Greek) philosophy. It is in this sense that it introduces an "Oriental" element into Plotinus' thinking. Bréhier sees this longing as paradigmatically embodied in the philosophical speculation of the *Upaniṣads*: "The common and rather monotonous theme of all the Upanishads is that of a knowledge which assures the one possessing it peace and unfailing happiness. This knowledge is the consciousness of the identity of the self with the universal being" (*ibid.*: 123). Hence, if we detect an Oriental element (in the first sense) in Plotinus' thought, it must follow that there is an Oriental element (in the second sense) in his thought. The question of Plotinus' Orientalism thus becomes the question of the irrationalism of Indian philosophy.

BRÉHIER'S SOURCES

Although scholars have rarely raised the question of the sources of Bréhier's views of Indian thought, it is not difficult to show that Bréhier is, in fact, recapitulating a debate concerning the charge of pantheism filtered through the work of the leading German Indologist of the day, Hermann Oldenberg (1854–1920). Thus, we should first look at Bréhier's reliance upon Oldenberg and then at the historical context of Oldenberg's own work, especially as this was influenced by the *Pantheismusstreit* of the nineteenth century.

In his book on Plotinus, Bréhier cites only two sources for Indian philosophy. The first is Deussen's translation of the *Upaniṣads* (Deussen 1897); the second is Oldenberg's introductory text on the philosophy of the *Upaniṣads* (Oldenberg 1915). This constitutes the sum total of his knowledge of Indian philosophy. He is neither aware of the *Upaniṣads* first hand nor that there are complex debates concerning their correct interpretation and ultimate purport within the Indian tradition nor that the philosophy of the *Upaniṣads* is not simply reducible to a pantheistic or monistic doctrine. To be sure, the *Upaniṣads* speak of an ultimate reality known as *brahman* (a neuter singular term meaning "being"), but they do not arrive at *brahman* dogmatically. Further, it is by no means clear that by positing *brahman* or by upholding it as the ultimate real they imply a denial of phenomenological reality; that is, the universe of change and plurality. Thus, Bréhier is clearly following not the texts themselves (which always require an exegete, no less than Plotinian philosophy requires a master), but a naïve (and polemically motivated) reading of Indian thought when he presents Indian philosophy as the counter-concept to the rational philosophy of the Greeks. In this, he follows the lead of the German scholars, whom he explicitly thanks for "singularly increas[ing] our knowledge of the philosophy of India through their translations and commentaries" (Bréhier 1958: 123). Further, the idea of commonality between Plotinus and Indian philosophy is not Bréhier's own, but was suggested to him by these thinkers.

> Along with the names of Spinoza and Schelling, it is that of Plotinus which occurs most often in the works of Deussen and Oldenberg. Identity in the philosophy of Schelling, the union of the soul with God in the intellectual love in Spinoza, are

conceptions closely related to the identity of the self with the universal being in
Plotinus. They are found in the Upanishads.   (Bréhier 1958: 123)

Of the two, Oldenberg is by far the more important for Bréhier's work, both in terms of
the number of references to his work and the central place assigned to his work. Deussen,
by contrast, plays a relatively minor role. Bréhier only occasionally cites his translation of
the *Upaniṣads* in support of a point made in Oldenberg. Indeed, Bréhier does not appear
to have read the *Upaniṣads* independently. As he notes:

> The state of mind implied by such an idea has been described very definitely by
> Oldenberg: "In India," he writes, "the sense of personality does not acquire its
> full force. Moreover, a permanent and positive existence within fixed limits is not
> attributed to things. This is because, for Indian thinkers, life is not dominated by
> activity, which is conditioned by the individual and fixed nature of resisting objects.
> What prevails is the impatience of an intellect which cannot grasp rapidly enough
> a unity through the knowledge of which the entire universe is known …. The eye is
> closed to appearances and their color and detail. One seeks to understand how the
> vital stream, which is unique in all things, springs forth from its obscure depths."
>   (*Ibid.*, 123)[49]

Bréhier's reliance on secondary sources is problematic inasmuch as neither Deussen nor
Oldenberg were philosophers. Their grasp of Indian philosophy was weak and filtered
through Orientalist lenses. Neither had studied Neoplatonism in depth. By training,
both were Sanskritists. In addition, Deussen had studied some classical philology, but
Oldenberg's specialization was what he called "the comparative study of religions". While
Deussen made some efforts to learn Indian philosophy first hand (developing a friendship
with Swami Vivekananda, for example), Oldenberg neither knew nor cared for Indian
intellectual traditions. Indeed, he was frankly dismissive of the tradition, which he labelled
as "Indian-knowledge [Inderwissen]" (Oldenberg 1906: 5). Deussen and Oldenberg also
had only the haziest ideas about Western philosophy. Drawing their ideas about philosophy from the prevailing Kantianism of the time, they understood philosophy to mean systematic philosophy and rationalism as opposed to mysticism and to pantheism. From the
perspective of their Western, nineteenth-century presuppositions, the *Upaniṣads* (which
appear to preach a doctrine of identity with the One) seemed the most obvious instantiation of a non-rational, experiential philosophy urging the loss and merging of individual
consciousness into the One. The contrast they drew between philosophy and religion,
which Bréhier also borrows from them, was a relic of nineteenth-century neo-Kantianism.
In ancient philosophy, there was no systematic distinction between philosophy and theology. As recent scholarship has shown, Platonic philosophy relied upon many sources,
including the mystery religions, and its epistemological concerns cannot be separated
from soteriological ones (see, above all, the articles in Adluri 2013). The same holds true,
perhaps to an even greater degree, of the Neoplatonic tradition.[50]

   Philosophically, too, Oldenberg could not appreciate the complexity or depth of the
Upaniṣads, which he held rather to be evidence of the rise of pantheistic doctrines in
India, occluding the original rationalistic and monotheistic spirit of Aryan religion. In his
book *Die Lehre der Upanishaden und die Anfänge des Buddhismus* (Oldenberg 1915), he

propounded a four-stage development of Indian thought: (1) primitive worship of natural forces, leading to (2) the development of ritual techniques and magical incantations for controlling these forces; thereafter to (3) ideas of the unity and connectedness of all beings; and, finally, (4) to the emergence of a mature philosophy centring in the question of the relationship of the plurality of beings to *brahman* or the One. This development contrasted with what Oldenberg, borrowing a page from Comte, saw as the natural evolution of human culture: from fetishism to polytheism and, finally, to monotheism. In the first phase, Oldenberg saw the incipient beginnings of a monotheistic religion, especially with the emergence of Vedic deities such as Indra:

> There is Indra – originally, it appears, a storm god – fond of intoxicants, ready for war and conqueror of foes. Agni – Fire – the divine friend and guest of humans. Varuna – in prehistoric times, as one may suppose, a moon god – the one who sees through and punishes even the most deeply hidden sins.   (*Ibid.*: 12)

To be sure, alongside simple feelings of awe and reverence, there also existed commerce between humans and gods:

> The effective means of securing the grace of these gods for oneself are, closely related to each other, prayer and sacrifice, in which – the main idea of Vedic sacrifice at least may be expressed thus – the human gives to god so that he may give to him in turn, [he may] spare and protect him.   (*Ibid.*: 12–13)

Yet, under the influence of the Brahmans, ideas of reciprocity gave way to control and reverence for the gods to the domination of the priestly caste. As Oldenberg notes:

> in these gods [that is, the Vedic deities], the element of personhood, which, previously, in human existence and therefore also in religious existence played a minor role, begins to celebrate its triumph. Naturally, [it was] not an uncontested triumph, and even less was it a final triumph.   (*Ibid.*: 13)

Gradually, with the rise of Brahmanism, Indian thought took a different turn:

> The turn towards magic instead of the worship of gods becomes even more pronounced, as succeeding generations of Brahmans, who now possessed a completed system of sacrificial rituals and prayers, now took up the next task, of explaining all this [that is, the sacrificial ritual, gods, being and existence] in their own way so as to secure all power in the hands of the knower. …
> Here we have reached the point where we encounter the Brahmanic science of sacrifice, which requires our attention as the foundation and breeding ground of the great pantheistic speculation.   (*Ibid.*: 16)

Concerning pantheism, Oldenberg raises all the charges already familiar to us from the preceding section against it: pantheism is opposed to the spirit of rationality, it is antithetical to the true religion (which Oldenberg, in keeping with the climate of his time, considered, naturally, to be Christian monotheistic faith), it is destructive of individuality and individual responsibility, and, finally, it does not permit the development of an appropriate feeling of dependence and devotion towards God. Indeed, Oldenberg associates pantheism with the Brahmans' desire to feel themselves superior to the (intra-cosmic) gods and coeval with the godhead. Finally, there is the ethical aspect of power, control and riches which accrue to one who can thus command the gods.

From ethnographic and sociological perspectives as well, Oldenberg saw pantheism as a fatal choice. Although the earliest Aryan races had had an intimation of the notion of personhood, both at the level of the human and at the level of the deity, under the influence of the climate and racial admixture, they lost interest in a personal (and ethical) religion. For instance, Oldernberg argued that

> many think of the higher classes of the Aryan Indians, who, as is well known, entered India from Iran perhaps a thousand years earlier, as not as yet all too seriously affected by racial admixture with the despised dark skinned aboriginals: even today, in many places Brahmans of a purely or almost purely white type have preserved themselves.   (*Ibid.*: 4)

However,

> the nature and the climate of India, the easy domination of the native population, the absence of great historical battles created an atmosphere of undisturbed peace for the Brahmans. There flourished the tendency to reflection, to nurturing complicated knowledge, to the play of a fantasy that lost itself ever more uncontrollably in monstrosity and the monstrous.   (*Ibid.*)

It is not necessary to trace further here how Oldenberg sees the development of pantheism in India from the earlier to the later *Upaniṣads* and from the later *Upaniṣads* to the earlier and later schools of Sāṃkhya philosophy. This periodization of Indian culture, as I have argued elsewhere, becomes problematic once one sees that it is based upon an *a priori* theory of Indian history and not sustained by objective historical investigations. In any case, the salient point for us is not the later history of philosophical pantheism in India, but to understand the narrative of origins surrounding this concept – a narrative that first explains why pantheism was seen as a *corruption* rather than an *enrichment* of Indian thought.

Unaware of these issues or of the *Pantheismusstreit* that is at the back of Oldenberg's criticisms,[51] Bréhier ends up transferring the full weight of Oldenberg's antiphilosophical prejudices into Plotinian–Indian studies. In doing so, he completely overlooks the fact that the thought of the One, in Plotinus no less than in Indian philosophy, is rigorously grounded in the principle of non-contradiction. It is not, as he so eloquently says, the destruction of intellectualism through its exaggeration, but the principle of all explanation and intellection, and has been so in the Western tradition since Parmenides.[52] To reject Plotinus' Orientalism is therefore only a partial solution; in truth, anyone wishing to reject this aspect of Plotinus' thought must then also go back to Plato and Parmenides and explain how and why Being should not be a criterion of knowledge.[53]

CONCLUSION

The question of Plotinus' Orientalism thus cannot be settled by geographic or historical investigations, because the question is fundamentally not a positive question. It is a
conceptual question inasmuch as it pertains to our *definitions* of "Occidental" (or "Greek"
or "Western") and "Oriental". And these are terms, as Gregorios rightly sees, that are not
defined in terms of geographic boundaries, but in terms of intellectual, cultural and political identities.[54] But, as I have shown in the positive portion of my chapter, there is another
way to read Indian philosophy: one that begins not with *a priori* ideas of philosophy and
narratives of historical decline, but with an enquiring, philosophical mind.

Although the field of *Mahābhārata* studies is not without its own problems,[55] there is
much to be gained by a philosophical comparison of Plotinian thought with the Indian
epic. Hitherto, the majority of scholars have focused on the different schools of Vedānta,
but these philosophical schools are highly systematic and technical, responding to various
internal dialogues and debates. The *Mahābhārata*, in contrast, undertakes a fresh and
highly original response to the problem of the One and the many. Further, whereas the
Upaniṣads were esoteric texts, and thus guarded within a lineage of pedagogical succession,
the *Mahābhārata* was freely circulated and actively propagated. Its popular form makes it a
much more likely candidate than the *Upaniṣads* for discussion in ports such as Alexandria.
The epic therefore offers us a fresh perspective for investigating the question of Plotinus'
relationship to Indian thought. The *Nārāyaṇīya*, in particular, does not merely offer a "parallel" to Plotinus' work, one that can serve as a locus for further research. In presenting
these dyadic beings, the *Nārāyaṇīya*, as I have shown, provides a way for us to understand a
very obscure component of Neoplatonist philosophy: the Indefinite Dyad. By focusing on
substantive philosophical topics and on specific texts, we make much greater headway than
when we rely on broad crosscultural comparisons and jingostic prejudices.

What emerges, then, once we set aside our prejudices regarding Indian thought, is that
a philosophical reflection on number appears to encounter similar kinds of problems in
both Plotinus and the Indian text. These problems, which now need to be taken up in
future research, may be summarized as follows:

- The One as the ultimate *archē* or principle.
- The unity of the One is a problem, closely tied to cosmogony and cosmology and thus
  multiplicity.
- The unity of the One is also essential, as it offers the very rationale for a soteriology.
- Both in the Greek and in the Indian texts discussed here, cosmogony is the exact
  obverse of a soteriological ascent.
- Multiplicity is conceived of primarily as capacity for division, and secondarily as
  numeric progression.
- The Dyad as the first tremor (!) in the One is a complex, obscure but inescapable step
  in the relationship between the One and the many.
- Gender as an ontological category that allows us to conceptualize the relation of the
  One and the many in their unity and difference.

Finally, it bears repeating that studies of Indian and Neoplatonic thought, even if comparative, cannot simply rely on the presentations of traditions found in the work of the

doxographers. Even when doxographers are not motivated by the kinds of ideological agendas as Oldenberg and the entire German text-historical school (for instance, Paul Hacker) were, their work is insufficient to penetrating the philosophical proximity of these traditions. It has been well said by Abrams that

> Characteristic concepts and patterns of Romantic philosophy and literature are a displaced and reconstituted theology, or else a secularized form of devotional experience, that is, because we still live in what is essentially, although in derivative rather than direct manifestations, a Biblical culture, and readily mistake our hereditary ways of organizing experience for conditions of reality and the universal forms of thought. (1973: 65)

Nowhere is this perhaps as true as in philosophy, where nineteenth-century prejudices still impair our ability to enter into dialogue with the ancients. From Garbe to Oldenberg and Hacker, the history of Indological writing on Indian philosophy has been a history of error, where Kantian systematic philosophy was made normative for philosophy in general and all Indian schools evaluated and arranged as they approximated or failed to approximate this ideal.[56] But if we begin again, with Parmenides and Plato (and Plotinus) rather than with the nineteenth-century philologist-historians, we find that the two philosophical cultures are closer than they initially appear. It is in this sense that I wish to describe the relationship of Plotinus to the Orient in terms of the *aoristos dyas*.

ACKNOWLEDGEMENT

I would like to thank Joydeep Bagchee for his assistance with the research into Bréhier's sources, especially his translations of Oldenberg. I also wish to thank the editors of the volume, Svetla Slaveva-Griffin and Pauliina Remes, for their careful reading and philosophically inspiring comments. I gratefully acknowledge the assistance of my advisor, Dr Madhavi Kolhatkar, with the translations of the text.

NOTES

1. My translation; the numbers refer to the Critical Edition text by Sukthankar (1933–66); thus, "12" refers to the *parvan* or major book (the *Śāntiparvan*), "321" to the *adhyāya* or chapter in that book (in this case, the first chapter of the *Nārāyaṇīya*, which occurs from chapter 321 to 339 in the *Śāntiparvan*), "16" to the verse in that chapter and "c" to the hemistich.
2. All translations of Plotinus heareafter are taken from Armstrong (1966–88).
3. For a recent and fairly balanced view, see Lacrosse (2001). Older treatments, especially of the basic points of philosophical proximity identified by scholars, can be found in Wolters (1982) and Tripathi (1982).
4. Among the candidates proposed have been the *Upaniṣads* (either individually or as a group), the *Bhagavadgītā*, Buddhist texts such as the *Uttaratantra* or *Ratnagotravibhāga* and Abhidharma literature; for general discussion, see Hatab; for the *Upaniṣads* as source of influence, see Rosán (1982) and also Armstrong & Ravindra (1982); for the *Bhagavadgītā* as source of influence, see Sharma (1982); for the *Uttaratantra* or *Ratnagotravibhāga* as source of influence, see Wallis; and on Abhidharma literature, see Rodier (1982). All are in Baine Harris (1982). However, discussions of these texts rely on broad comparisons of the two traditions or on finding specific parallels between Neoplatonism and one or more texts. A rigorously Plotinian text in terms of its structure has not been proposed as yet.
5. As Hiltebeitel (2011a) notes, the number eighteen is significant. The *Mahābhārata* and the *Bhagavadgītā* are both divided into eighteen sections, either books (as in the case of the *Mahābhārata*) or chapters (as in the case of the *Bhagavadgītā*). Further, the great war lasts eighteen days and eighteen armies are said to take

part in it. The number eighteen has canonical significance in the Northern Recension, which organizes the epic into eighteen *parvans*; the Southern Recension, by contrast, features twenty-four *parvans*. In the Northern Recension texts, the *Bhagavadgītā*, which occurs in Book Six of the epic (the *Bhīṣmaparvan*), and the *Nārāyaṇīya*, which occurs in Book Twelve (the *Śāntiparvan*), divide the text into three sections of six books each. This triadic division, as I have argued elsewhere, is significant: the *Bhagavadgītā* represents the apex of the *pravṛtti* or cosmological narrative of the epic, the *Nārāyaṇīya* the culmination of its *nivṛtti* or soteriological trajectory.

6. Plotinus, *Enn.* V.3[49].17 and Augustine, *Confessions* 1.1.1 both attest to this quest for simplicity as the dominant concern of the philosophical enterprise.

7. The *Nārāyaṇīya* does not use the term "Indefinite Dyad", of course. But, as I demonstrate in the course of this chapter, it is clearly acquainted with the concept of the dyad as a stage intermediate to the One and a true plurality. In any case, what is essential for us here is *not* the question of primacy, whether historical or intellectual, but to learn to see the philosophical problems the two texts or traditions are struggling with. In this, reading the *Nārāyaṇīya* alongside the *Enneads* and the *Enneads* alongside the *Nārāyaṇīya* can be a way of illuminating *both*.

8. *Nārāyaṇīya*, *Mahābhārata* chapters 12.321–39; an English translation (of the Vulgate) can be found in Ganguli (1891); a more recent French translation (also of the Vulgate) is available in Esnoul (1979). I am currently completing a translation of *Nārāyaṇīya* based on the text of the Critical Edition. All translations in this chapter are my own.

9. There have been relatively few studies on number as compared to other Plotinian topics. Here I rely on the work of Slaveva-Griffin (2009) and Radke (2003) for making number central to my enquiry.

10. We should take Bréhier's work seriously, because, as Wolters shows in his article (see note 3 above), the thesis of Oriental influence on Plotinus goes back to Bréhier. Bréhier first articulated the thesis in his 1921–2 lectures at the Sorbonne and publicized it in 1928 (English trans. 1958). Wolters notes that, prior to Bréhier's work, "every leading Plotinus scholar of the twentieth century downplay[ed] any but Greek factors in accounting for the development of Plotinus's thought" (Wolters 1982: 296). Thus, the question of Bréhier's sources for making these claims plays a not insignificant role in how we approach the question of Plotinus' Orientalism.

11. The term *dharma* (variously translated as "law", "ordinance", "duty", "virtue", etc., see Monier-Williams 1899, s.v. "*dharma*") refers primarily to prescribed duties, obligations and/or laws within a definite social order. However, it is also hypostatized to an abstract concept, to Law or Justice personified, and, ultimately, into a cosmic principle and a deity. But here what Yudhiṣṭhira specifically has in mind is the *dharma* of the four classes and that appropriate to each of the four stages of life (student, householder, forest dweller and renunciate) or *varṇāśramadharma*. The question concerns the duties and actions proper to each stage of life so as to attain the final good.

12. Nārāyaṇa first appears as a name of the Puruṣa (the Primal Being or the Primal Man) in *Śatapatha Brāhmaṇa* 12.3.4.1 and 13.6.1.1 (Puruṣa Nārāyaṇa). Biardeau traces the name to Puruṣāyaṇa in the *Praśna Upaniṣad* (6.4) based on the synonymy of *nara* and *puruṣa* which permits the substitution of one by the other; the term may then mean "made of those who direct themselves toward Nara/Puruṣa". In the *Mahābhārata*, Nārāyaṇa is often used, doubtless because of its etymological and philosophical richness, as the name of the Supreme Being and two etymologies are proposed for the name. One etymology links him to the primeval waters on which Viṣṇu/Nārāyaṇa is said to sleep during the stage of cosmic reabsorption (cf. *Mahābhārata* 3.187.3: *āpo nārā iti proktāḥ saṃjñānāma kṛtaṃ mayā / tena nārāyaṇo 'smy ukto mama tad dhy ayanaṃ sadā*); the other, to mortal man of whom he is the refuge or shelter (*Mahābhārata* 12.328.35ab: *narāṇām ayanaṃ khyātam aham ekaḥ sanātanaḥ* and see also 12.328.35c–e linking both notions). See Biardeau (1991) and, on the notion of periodic periods of emission and absorption of the universe from the One, see note 29 below.

13. The text discusses two types of manifestations, which have become famous in later literature as the four *vyūhas* (*caturvyūha*) and the ten *avatāras* (*daśāvatāra*). The *Nārāyaṇīya* contains the earliest reference to the *caturvyūha* doctrine, although the text does not refer to Nārāyaṇa's forms by this name (with the exception of 12.336.53, where Vaiśampāyana mentions that some worship Nārāyaṇa as having one form, others as having two, others as having three, and yet others as having four forms [*caturvyūha*, 53d]). Rather, Nārāyaṇa is spoken of as being of quadruple form (*caturmūrtiḥ*, 12.321.8a; cf. also 12.326.67c and 12.327.95c); although of one form previously, he has become fourfold (*ekā mūrtir iyaṃ pūrvaṃ jātā bhūyaś caturvidhā*, 12.321.16c; cf. also 12.326.93a: *caturmūrtidharo hy aham*). These forms are referred

to as his Vāsudeva, Saṁkarṣaṇa, Pradyumna and Anniruddha forms and identified with the *kṣetrajña* (the knower of the field), *jīva* (soul), *manas* (mind) and *ahaṁkāra* (ego), respectively. Collectively, these entities are referred to as his fourfold form (*mūrticatuṣṭayam*, 12.326.43e). The *caturvyūha* doctrine becomes famous in later texts and iconography, especially those attributed (I believe, mistakenly) to the Pāñcarātra sect. (Because references to Nārāyaṇa's fourfold forms in the *Nārāyaṇīya* often occur in conjunction with root *bhū* plus the prefix *prādur* meaning "to become manifest", it is also common to refer to the manifestations as Nārāyaṇa's *prādurbhāvās* and the doctrine as the *prādurbhāvā* doctrine.) However, there is no doubt that the intellectual roots of the later practice of depicting Vāsudeva in fourfold form can be traced back to the *Nārāyaṇīya*; see Srinivasan (1979). The *Nārāyaṇīya* again provides us with the earliest list of the ten incarnations of Nārāyaṇa, but whereas the *vyūhas* have a role in cosmogenesis (at the end of the fourfold division of Nārāyaṇa, Brahmā the creator appears and, acting under Nārāyaṇa's direction, creates the universe), the incarnations are intracosmic events. This difference in status is also reflected in the word "*avatāra*" which is derived from *avataraṇa* meaning"descending, alighting" (from *avatṛ* meaning "to descend"); see Kuiper (1979).

14. See the articles in Schreiner (1997). For my criticisms of this approach, see Adluri (forthcoming).

15. Indian philosophy knows of several senses of "one". *Brahman* is said to be *ekam eva advitīyam* (one only, without a second; *Chāndogya Up.* 6.2.1); in the Puruṣa Sūkta hymn of the Ṛg Veda, we find a reference to "that One" (*tad ekam*, RV 10.9.3), who is prior to the distinction between being and non-being; RV 1.164.46 also refers to truth being one only (*ekam sat*). Likewise, the *Nārāyaṇīya* is rich in usages of "one", including references to Nārāyaṇa as *ekaṁ puruṣaṁ* (12.326.31c), to Rudra and Nārāyaṇa as "one being manifesting as two" (*sattvam ekaṁ dvidhākṛtam*, 12.328.24a), and to Nārāyaṇa as the One (*ekaṁ*, 12.328.35c, 12.339.9c).

16. In chapter 3, the three sages Ekata, Dvita and Trita (whose names literally mean "Oneness", "Twoness" and "Threeness") are unable to see the One, but they are told that the One Being is seen through the dyadic beings of Śvetadvīpa being seen (12.327.47c); likewise, when Nārada returns to the Bādari hermitage, having seen Nārāyaṇa in his universal aspect, Nara-Nārāyaṇa, who were formally a pair, now appear to have the characteristics of the Śvetadvīpa dyadic beings (12.331.25c–30a).

17. Slaveva-Griffin (2009: 3–4): "From the sixth century B.C.E. to the fifth century C.E., from the early Presocratics to the late Neoplatonists, every philosophical school has striven to explain the tangible order of multiplicity. … The understanding of the universe as a unity of one and many begins with the early Presocratics' search for the primary originative substance (*archē*) as the source and the unifying element of physical reality. Next, the Pythagoreans postulate that numbers organize the universe in one harmonious unity, which is interwoven by unlimited (*apeira*) and limiting (*perainonta*) elements."

18. The *Nārāyaṇīya* refers to these two aspects of reality as *pravṛtti* and *nivṛtti dharmas*. The question of their interrelation is a major theme not only of this text but also of the Sanskrit epic as a whole.

19. For an interesting solution to this problem, see Miller (1986). Miller argues that the "contradiction" in fact calls for a philosophical "decision".

20. Simplicius, *in Metaph.* 187a; translated and cited in Slaveva-Griffin (2009: 6, n. 16).

21. Although nowhere in the *Parmenides* is the *aoristos dyas* mentioned, this has not prevented scholars from seeking to associate the term with Plato. Szlezák (2010) reviews the evidence for ascribing a Platonic origin to the term, including the testimony of ancient authors.

22. Merlan (1953: 98–140) argues that chapter 4 of this work is a fragment of Speusippus; his claim has been widely accepted (the exception being Tarán). For Dillon's defence of Merlan against Tarán, see Dillon (1984; 2003: 41–2).

23. Rist (1965: 332), and see *ibid.*: 331: "If we enquire into the precise reason for the positing of the Dyad, we are faced with at least apparent difficulties. Merlan points out that in Apuleius and Plutarch passages can be found which suggest that some Platonists were asking themselves, What is the principle of differentiation within the Ideal World? and, under Aristotelian influence, were giving the answer, Matter. But this was not apparently Plato's reason for introducing the Dyad in the first place. The problem of the distinction between Ideas seems to have caused him little inconvenience; although as early as the *Protagoras* he was concerned about the relation of various virtues with one another (329d–333b). The difficulty which Plato seems rather to have wished to solve is the old Parmenidean one about the origin of plurality itself. The first hypothesis of the second part of the *Parmenides* shows that if Unity be understood in the strict Parmenidean sense and be considered entirely in isolation, then nothing whatever can be said of it. Presumably, therefore, in the world of reality as well as the world of λόγοι, if the

Platonic Good, or One, be considered by itself, then for all that it is the source of Being in some sense (*R.* 509), yet no other Beings (Forms) can exist unless there is some kind of substrate or ἐκμαγεῖον (*Met.* 988), or what you will, in the intelligible world, in which or on which the One can impose itself as Limit upon the Unlimited. Aristotle's whole account of the Idea-Numbers depends on the assumption that Plato expects that by positing the One and the Dyad he can account for the existence of more than one Form. He does not deal with the question: What is the difference between Forms? He contents himself with explaining that there is a difference between Forms, that there are, say, two Forms, the Ideal Two and the Ideal Three, and that these are not merely two different names referring to the same thing."

24. Plotinus was also interested in this problem and proposes a solution along the lines of the *Nārāyaṇīya* in *Enn.* VI.6[34].9 where the problem of the confusion between the arithmetical and ontological conception of the Indefinite Dyad is clarified and solved by introducing a distinction between substantial and monadic number. I thank the editors for this clarification.

25. Incidentally, this solution was already suggested by some Middle Platonists (Eudorus, Pythagoreans *apud* Sextus Empiricus, *Math.* 10). I thank an anonymous reviewer for pointing this out.

26. See Plutarch, *de An. Procr.* 1012d–1013b and *de Def. Orac.* 409e; cf. Dillon (2003).

27. This is important for us, because unimpeded by a masculine biblical monotheism, Indian thought fully exploits the distinction, enantiomorphism and unified dualism of gender. The male–male pair of Nara and Nārāyaṇa already sits in dynamic tension with the Puruṣa-Prakṛti male–female pair in the cosmogony of the *Nārāyaṇīya*. But once the One is gendered in relation to the many, and moreover deified, how is the One, as simple and untouched by predicates, to be described? Indian texts provide two solutions. First is the identification of the One as feminine. This ascendancy of the feminine is seen in a later text known as the *Devī Purāṇa*, where the One is primarily female. Second, in the more abstract philosophical systems, the One is *de facto* male, and matter is considered subordinate and feminine. While one simplistically attributes the empirical malfeasance of gender, seen across all cultures, to ontology, the reality depicted in texts shows an unmistakable playfulness regarding gender, deploying its uses in ontology with utmost seriousness. Thus, we already have a gender reversal in the *Nārāyaṇīya*. Arjuna and Kṛṣṇa, manifestations of Nara and Nārāyaṇa, also "switch" genders in the epic; Arjuna in the *Virāṭaparvan* and Nārāyaṇa in the *Ādiparvan*.

28. Indian thought traditionally divides social functions into four *varṇa*s (literally, "colours", but used with the general meanings of "kind, sort, character, nature, quality"): royal (military), sacerdotal, commercial or agricultural, and the menial classes. The *varṇa* scheme is crossed with a second social division, *āśrama* or the articulation of life according to age, to produce the concept of *varṇāśramadharma*. For a good survey of the concept, see Klostermaier (2007: 288–97); a comprehensive treatment can be found in Kane (1941).

29. These two concerns are ultimately one for Indian thought, for, as Biardeau (1968: 39) has shown, cosmology is but the reverse of the process of reabsorption by which a *yogin* absorbs the sensory world into himself. In Indian thought, the Puruṣa himself is conceived of as a *yogin*, specifically "un yogin cosmique, un *mahāyogin*" who lets the world emerge periodically from himself by turning outward. One consequence of this conception, as Biardeau correctly noted (1968: 109), is that "individual salvation [now] has to be integrated into this rhythm [of the periodic emission and reabsorption of the universe by the Puruṣa] and must also translate in its own way the hierarchy of the values which the successive levels of the cosmogony brought to light". Cosmology and soteriology are thus intimately connected in the *Nārāyaṇīya*, just as, in Plotinus, the soul's ascent cannot be understood independently of the process of emanation by which it descends.

30. When Nārada initially asks Nārāyaṇa about whom he sacrifices to, Nārāyaṇa responds that this topic is not to be revealed (*avācyam*), the secret of the eternal self (*ātmaguhyaṁ sanātanam*, 12.321.27a). It is said to be subtle (*sūkṣmam*), inconceivable (*avijñeyam*), unmanifest (*avyaktam*), immovable (*acalaṁ*), permanent (*dhruvam*, 12.321.28a), and transcending the senses and the primordial elements (*indriyair indriyārthaiś ca sarvabhūtaiś ca varjitam*, 12.321.28c). Earlier, Bhīṣma had said that this secret could not be stated by logic alone (*na hy eṣa tarkayā śakyo vaktum*, 12.321.5c), but was to be had through divine grace (*devaprasādād*, 6a) alone. Nārāyaṇa, too, confirms that it can be revealed only to one of devoted mind (*bhaktimataḥ*, 12.321.27c).

31. The demonstration of the unity of being is ultimately based on the principle of non-contradiction, and is a well-known aspect of *Mahābhārata* ontology. See *Gītā* 2.16: *nāsato vidyate bhāvo*.

32. The *Nārāyaṇīya* sees knowledge of the One not only as the ultimate import of this text, but explicitly as

the goal of all previous texts, including the Vedas (see lines 12.321.41a–42c). Thus, there is good reason to take the *Nārāyaṇīya* not as an isolated example, but as the fulfilment of a long tradition of a philosophical ontology, whose roots are to be found in the monistic speculations of the Vedas, especially the *Puruṣa Sūkta* and *Nāsadīya Sūkta* hymns of the *Ṛg Veda* (*ṚV* 10.90 and 10.129) and, of course, the *Upaniṣads*.

33. The exact passage reads: "From him [Puruṣa] has arisen the Unmanifest, composed of the three guṇas, O best of the twice-born. / Unmanifest, established in manifest forms, She who is Prakṛti unchanging. / Know her to be the womb of us both. He who is the soul of all subtle and corporeal being, / Is worshipped by us both. He indeed is the one who is conceived as deity and as parent. / There is thus no other parent or deity beyond him, O twice-born one" (*Mahābhārata* 12.321.29e–31a).

The change of gender (from the masculine Puruṣa to the feminine Prakṛti and back to the masculine Puruṣa) is also in the original and appears intentional; Puruṣa and Prakṛti, the male and female principles, appear to be conceived of as a dyad. Note also that *brahman* as an impersonal term for the One is a neuter singular noun, but, when conceived theistically as the Supreme Being Nārāyaṇa, is represented as male. In cultic and theurgic practice, God often appears either as male with a female consort or, less often, explicitly as the androgyne (for example, Śiva as Ardhanārīśvara), where the distinction between the male and female aspects is often interpreted as the difference between Being and its State of Being. Thus Indian thought in general is well aware of gender as a way of thinking about the unity, difference and co-belonging of the One and the many.

34. Literally, the text says that he "can be viewed by the discipline of knowledge" (*dṛśyate jñānayogena āvāṁ ca prasṛtau tataḥ*, 12.321.40a).

35. Literally, the text says that to those who are established in oneness with him even in this world (*ye tu tadbhāvitā loke ekāntitvaṁ samāsthitāḥ*, 12.321.42a), he, that Being (*taṁ* [*puruṣaṁ*], 12.321.41a), grants the supreme state (*ādyaṁ gatiṁ*, 12.321.41c): they enter into him (*te taṁ praviśanty uta*, 12.32142c).

36. Every aspect of Nārada's journey, beginning with his double ascent from Mount Gandhamādana to Mount Meru, is significant. As Mabbett notes (1983: 66), Mount Meru is "much more than a feature on the cosmographic map. A map is a misleading metaphor, for a map is two-dimensional. Meru rose up in a third dimension; in doing so, it pierced the heavens; in piercing the heavens, it transcended time as well as space; in transcending time it became (in Mus's sense) a magical tool for the rupture of plane. This is evident in the many layers of symbolism that exchange Meru for the cosmic man, for the temple at the center of the universe, for the office of kingship, for the *stūpa*, for the *maṇḍala*, and for the internal ascent undertaken by the tantric mystic. Meru is not, we must recognize, a place, 'out there', so to speak. It is 'in here'."

37. Under the influence of the text-historical school, *bhakti* was rapidly demoted from a philosophical concept to a sociological category. This view of *bhakti*, which I call the "cult-emotive approach", wherein *bhakti* stands in stark contrast to the rational enterprise of systematic philosophies, especially Advaita Vedānta, does not allow us to fully frame the question of love for the One *or* to appreciate the symbolic and philosophical genius of the epic. Seen from the "cult-emotive" perspective, *bhakti* appears as a state of irrational passion or rapture, while the crucial ontological insight into the relation of the One and the many encapsulated in it is lost. A better way to regard *bhakti* is that proposed by Biardeau (1989: 15), who has argued that "Orthodox Brahmanism, which is closer to the Revelation, is not the ancestor of modern Hinduism; it is its permanent heart, the implicit model for or/and against which *bhakti*, tantrism and all their sects have been constituted". In contrast to the excesses of the German historico-critical approach, nearly all of which is now of merely antiquarian interest, Biardeau provides a superb theoretical framework for understanding *bhakti*. She sees *bhakti* as essentially a philosophical structure, integrating the enduring cosmological and soteriological questions as developed within the texts of the tradition. Her insights have been developed further in the work of Hiltebeitel (2011b), who makes a rigorous case for the *Mahābhārata* as a work of *bhakti* through and through.

38. The term is Biardeau's; see Biardeau & Malamoud (1976).

39. Biardeau (1989: 27) rightly draws attention to the cognitive, intellectual aspect of *bhakti*; *bhakti* cannot be reduced to mere religious fervour (*ibid.*: 114) or a feeling directed towards one monotheistic god, especially the sectarian gods (Biardeau 1989: 107–8; 1968: 104, n.1). Biardeau & Malamoud (1976: 89) question and reject both the discontinuity between *smṛti* sectarianism and Upaniṣadic traditions as well as those allied with Brahmanic sacrifice (*ibid.*: 89–106, see also 89, n. 1). Boldly breaking with nearly two centuries of entrenched prejudices regarding *bhakti*, Biardeau demonstrates the wide-ranging significance of *bhakti* within Hinduism. For her, rather than speaking of a "*bhakti* religion", it makes more sense to

speak of a "universe of *bhakti*" (Biardeau 1989: 79–80), where *bhakti* is to be understood as a cognitive framework for a set of values. Thus, she notes of *bhakti* that it constitutes "a grandiose edifice, stupefying in its coherence and unity" (*ibid.*: 106).

40. In this latter sense, number is being understood ontologically, not arithmetically. The dyadic beings are somehow able to bridge individuality with identity or oneness, which they of course do through their intense love or *bhakti* for the One. The soteriology the epic proposes, therefore, is very much a matter of what is practicable and experienceable here and now and thus with this elucidation of *bhakti* Yudhiṣṭhira's opening question (how are members of *all* four classes and not just the Brahman renunciate to experience salvation?) is answered.

41. This is of course mythic; the actual experience of this is repeatedly stated to be a matter of philosophical praxis involving both discriminative intelligence (Sāṃkhya) and certain kathartic practices which form part of Yoga.

42. In reflection, there is always a doubling of the original: as original and its image. This property of reflection comes in use for explaining the process of emanation of the world from the One, especially for a monistic ontology such as Advaita Vedānta, which cannot acknowledge that the One (as cause) undergoes a real transformation in producing the universe (its effect) (this is the *pariṇāmavāda* of the Sāṃkhya school). Rather, Advaita will either argue for the world as an illusory transformation of the cause (*vivartavāda*) or as a reflection produced by the One (*pratibimbavāda*), a reflection of course having no real existence independent of its original. In this context it is interesting to note that Plato too uses the language of images and mimesis (see *R.* 595a–598d and *Ti.* 37d) to describe the generation of the cosmos. For a discussion of the former, see my "Warrior and Art Critic: Plato's *Republic* 10", paper presented at the 7th Annual Conference of the International Society for Neoplatonic Studies, Krakow, Poland, 2009.

43. This is expressed repeatedly in the text, with varying emphasis on the element of grace (*devaprasāda*) (12.331.14a: *devaprasādānugataṁ vyaktaṁ tat tasya darśanam*) or *bhakti* (12.332.3: *nāsya bhaktaiḥ priya-taro loke kaś cana vidyate / tataḥ svayaṁ darśitavān svam ātmānaṁ dvijottama*).

44. The dyad is not simply inserted in between the One and the many as some sort of ad hoc abstract solution to bridging the difference or gap between them. Rather, the epic seems to see dyadic existence as a real, existent possibility: as the Śvetadvīpa narrative shows, it is that state in which a direct experience of the One (while still being other than the One, but liminally so) becomes possible. Without these beings, neither would Nārāyaṇa appear nor would Nārada's soteriological journey to the One be complete. Thus, the dyad becomes a necessary step for making the soteriological goal of the system of emanation possible.

45. Obviously, there are certain parallels to the Plotinian *tolma* here, but these must remain the subject of a future paper.

46. A careful and close reading of the text thus refutes the Orientalist prejudice that *bhakti* is a relationship of subordination to a god experienced as higher and as absolutely other. Instead, as I have been arguing, it becomes the principle of organization of the left-hand side of the table, where the one's various manifestations are not at odds with the idea of its unity.

47. Ammonius Saccas, Nemesius and Philo are all Oriental philosophers, whose influence upon Plotinus is attested to in his own writings.

48. Curiously, Armstrong (1936), who otherwise rejects Bréhier's arguments for Indian influence upon Plotinus, nonetheless accepts the latter's thesis of an opposition between a "rational" and an "irrational" element in Plotinus' thought.

49. Bréhier cites and translates Oldenberg (1915: 39).

50. A different approach to refuting Bréhier was undertaken by Rist, who argued that the mysticism of Plotinus was of the *theistic* sort (by which he meant that the soul, even when it attains union with God, does not lose its self-identity). According to Rist, since the mysticism of the *Upaniṣads*, in contrast, is of a monistic nature, the question of the *Upaniṣads* as a source of influence upon Plotinus can be set aside. See Rist (1967: 214, 229).

51. Although Oldenberg may have been responsible for framing the evolution of Indian philosophy in terms of the pantheism debate, he was not responsible for the debate itself, whose origins lie, rather, in the *Pantheismusstreit* of the nineteenth century. Herling (2009: 89) offers a useful summary: "In essence, the so-called *Pantheismusstreit* began when minor philosopher F. H. Jacobi revealed a confession made by Lessing, one of the leading lights of the German Enlightenment, late in his life: he (Lessing) was committed to the philosophy of Spinoza, and in the discourse of the day, that made him a pantheist, an irrationalist, and (ultimately) an atheist .... Reactions to Lessing's confession piled up quickly (Mendelssohn and Kant

himself were famous respondents). Jacobi himself clearly had a philosophical agenda in making the revelation public: he was inspired (like Herder) by his friend Hamann and by his own Lutheran commitment …. The key point is that Jacobi thought all philosophical perspectives, including those of the *Aufklärer*, ended in Spinozist pantheism if the centrality of faith and revelation did not undergird them: only faith and revelation could provide the transcendent anchor for reason, lest it slip off into the mechanistic determination of a Leibniz or Spinoza, and subsequently into the dangerous thought that God is everywhere (and thus nowhere)."

52. Similarly, Ciapalo (2002) argues, against Bréhier, that even though Plotinian thought culminates in the mystical, nondual experience of union with the One, there is no reason to seek Oriental sources for it; "Plotinus' account of the final stage of the soul's ascent to and unification with the One … [is] the conclusion of a long and careful deductive argument whose major premise is that first principle mentioned earlier – to be real is to be one" (*ibid.*: 76). For him, "what is most interesting" about Plotinus' thought "is that he is thoroughly Greek in his approach to philosophical problems. Namely, he is eminently rational" (*ibid.*: 77). If he is nonetheless "led by the relentless application of his logic to eventually draw conclusions that themselves defy complete penetration by human reason" (*ibid.*) this is not, as Bréhier thought, rooted in his Orientalism, but in the "fundamentally universal" nature of human experience.

53. As Schmitt (2012) has recently argued, the concept of rationality of ancient philosophy was based upon the insight that, in order to be known, a thing had to be some definite thing, and that means some *one* thing. It is in this sense that Platonic philosophy considered both being and unity to be the most fundamental criteria for knowledge. Modernity, however, rapidly sets itself apart from this *Seinsphilosophie*. Instead, it proposes that the criterion for something to be known is its conformity to its representation in consciousness.

54. In Oldenberg's case, Indian philosophy in general, and the *Upaniṣads* in particular, offered a convenient mirror to reflect back cherished ideas of the critical nature of Orientalist scholarship. Filtered through the lenses of his nationalism and Aryanism, the history of India appeared as a history of terminal decline, ending only with the advent of Western critical scholarship. For a more comprehensive look at Oldenberg's work, especially as concerns the latter portion of the claim, see Adluri & Bagchee (2014).

55. For a good overview of the history of *Mahābhārata* scholarship, see Hiltebeitel (2012); also Adluri (2010).

56. For my comments on Garbe's work, see my online review of Nicholson on H-Net (Adluri 2012b).

II

Methods and styles of exegesis

INTRODUCTION

Since 1987, the inaugural year of the *Ancient Commentators on Aristotle* project, some aspects of the form and method of Neoplatonic discourse have received more attention than others. To this end, Part II has two main goals: (i) to present the versatile methods of Neoplatonic discourse, ranging from formal commentaries to letters, from introductions to philosophy and summaries, and (ii) to showcase two outstanding styles of Neoplatonic writing in two distinctive scholarly approaches to them. The first goal reflects the boom in the study of the forms of Neoplatonic exegesis, especially that of the philosophical commentary. The second makes pioneering steps towards systematic presentation of the two most distinguished styles of Neoplatonic discourse: the hypo-ordered larger-than-life elegance of Plotinus' thought and the hyper-ordered dialectical purity of Proclus' exegesis. In their turn, the two styles are presented by two different approaches (philological and analytical respectively) not because the styles lend themselves to the particular approach but because we want to show how productive these approaches can be and how much future work is in store with them.

The leading method of Neoplatonist engagement with philosophy can be most broadly defined as hermeneutical in nature, by both the Neoplatonists' own reflection and our modern evaluation. It is impossible here not to call to testament, as in Chapter 1, above (p. 7), Plotinus' much-quoted self-assessment in *Enn.* V.1[10].8.11–15 that: "these statements of ours are not new; they do not belong to the present time, but were made long ago, not explicitly, and what we have said in this discussion has been an interpretation of them, relying on Plato's own writings for evidence that these views are ancient" (trans. Armstrong).

It is most likely that any late ancient philosopher who has made his primary occupation the study of Platonism in all of its late antique hues, including Christian, would subscribe to Plotinus' conscious awareness of the highly hermeneutical nature of this philosophical enterprise. The statement is quite revealing but also deceptively simple. It is revealing in so far as it defines the three key elements in building the Neoplatonist philosophical identity: the antiquity of the studied ideas; the obscurity of these ideas; and the need of interpretation. Neoplatonic philosophy is exegetic philosophy, but underneath the simplicity of the straightforward sequential linearity (antiquity – obscurity – necessity of exegesis) there is a rich and complex matrix of dialectical analysis and synthesis, perspicacity, alacrity, originality and inventiveness.

To engage with philosophic ideas, for the Neoplatonists, means to engage with philosophical text, more extensively and explicitly with the Platonic corpus and the works of Aristotle that are most relevant to it, and less so and certainly more implicitly with the opposing conceptual or ideological trends. The Neoplatonic curricula, despite their relative fluidity, as presented in Tarrant's chapter (above, Chapter 2), canonically stabilize the texts and make them available for exegetical and didactic purposes. The Neoplatonists continue, to a great extent, the methodological work begun by the Middle Platonists, as outlined in the chapter by Reydams-Schils and Ferrari (above, Chapter 4). As Baltussen's chapter on the "Aristotelian commentary tradition" (Chapter 7) presents, the Neoplatonists do not deliberately develop and subsequently use the form of the commentary because it is the literary genre proper for this kind of philosophizing, but as a natural "by-product" of the centuries-long and multifarious dialogue between teachers and pupils when the pupils of today are the teachers of tomorrow. This intellectual lineage shapes the immediacy with which the ancients engage with the text and allows for great diversity, as amply illustrated by the two-volume collection on *Philosophy, Science and Exegesis in Greek, Arabic and Latin Commentaries* (Adamson *et al.* 2004). It should not remain unnoted that the Neoplatonic analytical method of exegesis is also heavily influenced by Aristotle, particularly in the development of the commentary tradition, as evidenced by the eponymous title of the first chapter in this part.

In addition to the development of the commentary as a genre, the deeply educational nature of the Neoplatonist engagement with philosophy fosters other major forms of discourse. Among these are the high-profile texts of Plotinus' *Enneads*, Porphyry's *Launching Points to the Intelligible*, Iamblichus' *On the Mysteries* or the most pedagogically oriented *Protrepticus*, Proclus' *Platonic Theology*, Damascius' *On the First Principles*. The diversity of the non-commentary forms of Neoplatonic exegesis, as Smith demonstrates in his treatment of "The non-commentary tradition" (Chapter 8), shows the broad professional and public appeal of Neoplatonic thought, aside from the detailed specialized examination and interpretation of the Platonic texts. Porphyry's *Letter to Anebo* and *Letter to Marcella*, the *Introduction to Aristotle's Categories* (*Isagoge*), the summary of his *Launching Points to the Intelligible* (*Sententiae*), and his treatise *On the Abstinence from Eating Animal Food* (*de Abstinentia*) testify the wide "genre" repertoire even of only a single author. The outreach appeal of some of these works, in which the heavy core of Neoplatonic metaphysics is judiciously presented, if at all, in a simplified form, should not be considered as Neoplatonism "light" but as a testament to the Neoplatonists' surprisingly high sense of civic duty and their constant attempt to engage, *pace* the tempting portrait of their "otherworldliness",[1] with their social environment.

The diverse methods of Neoplatonic exegesis naturally lead to diverse and at times rather different styles of expression. The study of Neoplatonic stylistics is one of the first areas of exposure to Neoplatonic thought and paradoxically at the same time one of the least recognized areas "in print". The stylistic and even methodological remarks, with the notable exception of Proclus, can be found compartmentalized either at the end of the introductions to the translations of individual works or in the footnotes pointing out the quiddity of specific argument. While we are all too aware of the inherent relation between form and content in some Neoplatonic authors, this area of research still awaits the harvest of its fruits.

Bréhier's famous comparison of Plotinus' style to "a living thought" – full of twists, turns and evocative energy – captures both the allure and the obstacle this kind of style presents. Brisson's chapter on "Plotinus' style and argument" (Chapter 9) lays out, exhaustively and with the humbling expertise of one who has overseen, with Jean-François Pradeau, the new French translation of Plotinus' *Enneads*, the facts of Plotinus' complex thought, more often confined to "off the cuff" remarks of his mind-boggling style (Brisson & Pradeau 2002–10). Brisson unravels the peculiarities of Plotinus' style and presents them as the symbiotic product of his origin, education, place of living, preference for the question-and-answer lecture-type discourse, peculiar attitude towards writing, and the fate of his works in the hands of his most devoted pupil, Porphyry. This kind of holistic presentation, coupled with numerous systematically organized observations of style and language, vividly demonstrates why Plotinus' thought, despite its complexity, opens the door to a new form of Platonism which revitalizes the final period of ancient philosophy prior to its reincarnation in Medieval philosophy.

Almost at the other extreme of philosophic discourse from Plotinus stands Proclus' much-celebrated "geometrical method" of crafting philosophical arguments to the state of a stylized perfection. Martijn's comprehensive examination of Proclus' method of argumentation in "Proclus' geometrical method" (Chapter 10) reveals a highly nuanced picture which is built on the principles of the different forms of geometrical presentations (axioms, postulates, proofs and theorems) but which acquire their real philosophical meaning only through Proclus' consistent infusion of dialectic and didactic tools, respectively definitions, hypotheses, scientific understanding, thought and knowledge. Ultimately for him, the structure of knowledge reflects the structure of reality and thus the order of philosophical argumentation should correspond to the order of that reality. Although the geometrical method closes the gap between written word, analytical conception and the higher orders of reality, Martijn shows that even then it does not work so perfectly well for the study of metaphysics as for that of mathematics. The logical and dialectical focus of his geometrical method raises questions about the epistemological value of language, but above all, attempts to present the complexity of Neoplatonic metaphysics within reach of human thought.[2]

NOTES

1. For more on the charges of otherworldliness, see Corrigan (Chapter 24), Stern-Gillet (Chapter 25), Remes (Chapter 28) and O'Meara (Chapter 29), below.
2. Discussed explicitly in Ahbel-Rappe (Chapter 11), van den Berg (Chapter 16) and Gerson (Chapter 17), below, and generally in Part III on metaphysics.

7

Aristotelian commentary tradition

Han Baltussen

NATURE AND BACKGROUND OF ANCIENT PHILOSOPHICAL COMMENTARY

It is fundamental to our understanding of commentary as a genre that they respond to another text, often called the 'base text'. Ancient commentaries have sometimes been characterized as "secondary texts", but the label is likely to cause some misconceptions about how we should understand the nature of commentary (Sluiter 2000). It is preferable to read "secondary" as "using another text as its starting point" rather than as "unimportant", "subservient" or "unoriginal".[1] In what follows I hope to show that the commentary in late antiquity defies such facile descriptions. Philosophical commentary required certain conditions for it to develop and thrive. And instead of being a philological activity, like most modern commentaries tend to be (producing a set of disparate notes to a text), philosophers would comment within a specific ideological setting and almost always to serve a higher purpose (understanding and truth); in other words, they were created in response to the school founder's writings (a "canon") and were didactic in purpose. Given the peculiar nature of the works it will be helpful to spend some time clarifying the background of philosophical exegesis, especially among the Peripatetics. After that I turn to the main part of the analysis, in which I clarify the methodology and evolution of the commentaries on Aristotle.

While the earliest formal commentaries were probably written in the first century BCE, several important stages of exegetical evolution preceded it, and contributed important technical elements to the exegetical strategies. It will be worthwhile to look at these briefly. For a long time literacy was the privilege of very few in a predominantly oral world. But that did not mean lack of sophistication (see Richardson 1975, 1992, 1993; Havelock [1966] 1982; Ong 1982; Thomas 1992). Allegorical and cosmological interpretations from the sixth and fifth century BCE already distinguished between literal and non-literal reading, when they attempted to uncover the (supposed) deeper meaning of Hesiod's didactic poetry or Homer's epics or lyric poetry (e.g. *hermēneus* "interpreter", *Ion* 530c). The philosophers also engaged with these texts, now also available in written versions. Their focus was on explaining the world distinct from Homer. They began to evaluate language and syntax, and conceptual analysis (e.g. Protagoras invented names for parts of speech, frag. 80a [DK] = Diogenes Laertius 9.53–4). Moving away from the religious reading of the universe in which gods determined everything, natural philosophers started questioning certainties, considering alternatives and inventing new forms of discourse, which would drive philosophical analysis of the world (Most 1999). Heraclitus (frag. 101 = Diogenes Laertius 9.1) first drew a sharp contrast between information (*polymathia*, a quantitative notion) and the right interpretation of the world (*noos*, "understanding", a qualitative notion). Within 250 years of its introduction writing became the vehicle of elaborate explanatory accounts, even if it came initially in the traditional guise of poetry (Parmenides, Empedocles and Xenophanes use Homeric hexameter).

THE RISE OF THE RUNNING COMMENTARY: 100 BCE–200 CE

It is in the fifth and fourth century BCE that clear evidence for a second-order discourse in philosophical circles is found. The Sophists, Plato and Aristotle are the main contributors to this new frontier. Verbal cunning and more systematic analyses, assisted by written notes, would raise awareness of the process of thought and argumentation, leading to an increase in semantic stability *and* differentiation combined with a greater self-conscious perspective. Terms for types of exegetical writings began to draw distinctions between comments (*hypomnēmata*) and preparatory notes (*hypomnēmatika*) (Dorandi 1991). In the relatively short period of one hundred years, this trend helped crystallize certain well-worn techniques among rhetoricians and emerging philosophical argument into what was to become philosophical commentary.[2] It had become a methodical evaluative scrutiny of existing philosophical views with the purpose of pushing forward the search for the truth. Formalization was the next logical step.

The first ancient philosophical commentary (taken in a formal sense) does not appear before the first century BCE. It is commonly thought to arise in the first century BCE/ CE, but there exists in fact little agreement on this issue. Should we agree with Dillon who has placed it "in the generation of Eudorus [first century BCE] that the tradition of *formal* commentary on both Plato and Aristotle seems to begin" (Dillon 1996a: 437, emphasis added)? He also considered the third century BCE, thinking of "Crantor who wrote 'the *first formal commentary*' as a Platonist on a work of Plato".[3] Still other views are more implicit: in his magnificent overview of the Aristotelian tradition, Moraux simply starts his chapter "Die Ältesten Kommentatoren" with Andronicus (first century BCE) (Moraux 1973). J. Barnes refers to Theophrastus' and Eudemus' works as "interpretations or exegeses of Aristotle, in a loose sense", but qualifies this by stating: "*there is no reason to believe* that they wrote *commentaries* on his writings" (J. Barnes *et al.* 1991: 5, emphasis added). This must be correct given what we know about their work (philosophical and complementary rather than purely exegetical), and the characteristics of later exegetical writings bear this out. Elsewhere J. Barnes is close to Dillon: "philosophical commentaries go back at least to the third century BCE; and there were probably Aristotelian commentaries by the first century BCE".[4]

The discussion often suffers from incomplete evidence and a lack of clarity in definition (e.g. scholars speak of commentary next to *formal* commentary), while the emergent nature of the genre is usually ignored. The seeds of the commentary tradition were already sown in the pre-Platonic literary tradition.[5] Plato himself clearly exploited an existing *practice* of clarifying text in the discussion of a poem of Simonides in his *Protagoras* 339a–348c. This is a prime example of incipient commentary, as it incorporates features found in the Homerists and Sophists. The core elements seem to be already well known: Socrates claims to know the author's intention (*boulēsis*), uses grammatical arguments to prove points, and proposes different ways of illustrating the hidden meaning of the poem (347a). The episode also includes two prototypes of hermeneutical principles concerning the importance of authorial consistency (341e1–2, later labelled "clarifying Homer from Homer")[6] and the notion of an overall purpose of the poem rather than just interpret words or phrases. Even if we allow for an element of parody in Plato's representation of these practices, it had to contain certain realistic features to be plausible and credible for his audience.[7]

It is fair to say that a new dynamic arose with the *Anonymous Commentary on Plato's Theaetetus* (first century BCE?). While the early instances of exegesis were either compositional (by bards who reinterpreted existing stories into a new format), polemical (such as the reactive accounts in natural philosphy by the Presocratics) or selective (partial comments on one work such as Crantor's on Plato's *Timaeus*), the *Anonymous Commentary on Plato's Theaetetus* was the first visible case of an elucidation of a Platonic work by a "convert" keen on defending the Platonic position (a case of apologetics). What we have here is a supporter of Plato writing a "running commentary", who in fact applies a variety of outlooks, some of which he may no longer be fully aware of.[8] In other words, the work presents a continuation of the Platonic style of exegesis present, *in statu nascendi*, in the *Protagoras*, itself composed of established practices and innovative moves. Yet in spite of its syncretistic perspective, the intention of this commentary is to offer a genuine *Platonic* interpretation, regardless of whether we judge it successful. By now the central text has gained so much authority that it can no longer be challenged (at least not openly). It is here that we see the philosophical canon establish itself and the importance of an "agreed" written version of the founder's views.[9]

RUNNING COMMENTARY ON ARISTOTLE: 200 BCE–550 CE

Platonist commentaries on Aristotle's works began with Porphyry (*c.*300 CE).[10] As a student of Plotinus (*c.*210–275 CE), he had been involved in the exegetical activities of Plotinus' classes, in which Plato, Aristotle and other works were discussed. But Plotinus famously also included the exegetical comments of Alexander of Aphrodisias (*c.*200 CE) in his own explications (Porphyry, *Plot.* 14). Alexander was regarded as *the* commentator on Aristotle, setting the standard for the line-by-line running commentary for centuries to come. Plotinus' approach thus started a tradition of an inclusive attitude towards previous commentaries on Plato and Aristotle. The late Platonists (Neoplatonists) thus took on board Peripatetic (Andronicus, Eudorus) and Middle Platonist precedents (e.g. Anon., *in Tht.*) as well as the first clear examples of the running commentary by the Aristotelians Aspasius and Alexander of Aphrodisias.[11]

With Plotinus as the founder of a new exegetical style producing a new philosophy, Platonism would be the dominant school of thought for the next four hundred years. Starting with Plotinus, a new curriculum was designed and then developed further by his pupil and biographer Porphyry, marking a new stage in the history of Greek philosophy. More importantly, an educational context became the ideal environment to nurture exegetical activities of "canonized" texts: curiously Aristotle became the introduction to Plato, and commentary on both authors the preferred mode of philosophical education. This approach to the two scholarchs of related, but still different, philosophical persuasion was based on the idea that their views could be brought into harmony. As Sorabji puts it, "Not for the only time in the history of philosophy … a perfectly crazy position (harmony) proved philosophically fruitful" which would lead to new ideas; the result was "an amalgam different from either of the two original philosophies" (Sorabji 1990: 5). Gerson's explanation for this perspective is persuasive: "Platonists, for the most part, did not regard Aristotle as an anti-Platonist."[12]

In the Platonic commentaries many of the emerging reflexes and topical themes we saw above (e.g. analysis of words and concepts, creative exegesis, making explicit connections with other texts) remain part of the approach. The idea of "tradition", of placing oneself in a line of interpreters, bestows both authority and continuity upon one's activity. But within the teaching context a more formalized methodology had been established, and the complexity of levels of commentary with it: we should think of a complex texture or fabric rather than just accumulated layers (like Russian dolls). In other words, they are complex documents to be read with considerable care and knowledge of the ideological frame of mind with which they were written.[13]

By distinguishing a fixed set of standard questions for opening the discussion of a text, the late Greek commentators established a structure for teacher–student interaction *and* a lucid and sensible philological approach to difficult texts.[14] These so-called preliminary questions deal with important issues such as (a) authenticity, (b) place in the corpus, (c) utility and (d) purpose – the basis for detailed page-by-page, sometimes line-by-line, commentary (Mansfeld 1994: 10–11). Clearly this required a scholarly environment and the habitual use of books. It also reflects the focus on a body of writings regarded as a fixed set of texts representing an authoritative body of knowledge used in teaching; that is, a canon. Concerns about a canon started in the first century BCE, and once established, a fixed set of texts would stimulate the writing of commentary.

Closer to the last stage of the most elaborate commentary, we find Syrianus, the Athenian teacher of Proclus (d. 475 CE), who determined much of the commentary style in the fifth and sixth century CE (D'Ancona 2002: 208–11). He adopted Alexander's method of providing a *lēmma* (literally a "snatch" of text) for commenting, and this format becomes the norm, in spite of several other forms of presentation. For instance, lecture notes ("from the master's voice", *apo phōnēs*, e.g. Proclus' *Timaeus* commentary is based on a record of Syrianus' teaching), discussion divided into *theōria* and *lexis* (Olympiodorus), or interpretive paraphrase (Themistius).[15] Interestingly, as in earlier periods, the text commented upon is said to use intentional "unclarity": while in the past Orpheus and the poets were said to provide messages in riddles, Aristotle is now said to use intentional unclarity so as to fend off the uninitiated (Ammonius, *in Cat.* 7.10–11 [Busse]). Such self-legitimization of the commentator's task will inevitably lead to expansive supplementation as the main tool for clarification (Sluiter 2000). No wonder that the written commentaries soon grew longer and longer.

Proclus (c. 412–85 CE) also contributed several new strategies for exegesis.[16] He was "chosen by Syrianus as 'the heir capable of inheriting his vast learning'" (Dodds 1963: xxiii, quoting from Marinus, *Procl.* 12). He set out the principles of late Platonism in two major works, using mathematics as a structuring device in the one. Such an elaborate scheme of a highly intellectual nature may seem unpromising for the common man, but it was not unprecedented. Plato had set an example with his *Timaeus*, synthesizing much of the preceding tradition in natural philosophy. Proclus was far more systematic, with the ambition to embrace the sum of Platonist thought on the universe and with a clear spiritual objective in mind: to offer a convincing and comprehensive form of salvation. This shows in more than just his strictly philosophical works. The hymns that he wrote (traditionally seen as "mere" expressions of religious fervour) can in fact be considered as philosophically meaningful contributions (Saffrey 1992; van den Berg 2001). The influence of Proclus is acknowledged by Simplicius in his *Physics* commentary: "those after Proclus up until our time almost all follow Proclus not only on this point, but on all other issues" (*in Ph.* 795.11–13 [Diels]).[17]

Proclus' contributions to the commentary format concern especially the use of a demarcation of passages to be read (*praxeis*) and a clear division between general exegesis (*theōria*) and specific exegesis (*lexis*).[18] His commentary on the *Timaeus* is a monumental work, which has absorbed much of the foregoing tradition.[19] But he was operating in an increasingly hostile environment, in which Christianity, now the official religion of empire, began to encroach on pagan territory and create formal and informal practices which would marginalize the pagan ideas and rituals. Once he went into exile for one year due to tensions in Athens and spent time in Lydia studying religious customs there (Marinus, *Procl.* 15). His staunch defence of paganism brought on risks when he expressed "direct criticism" of Christian doctrine.[20]

Our last important witness for the methodology of Aristotelian commentaries is the sixth-century Platonist Simplicius (*c.*480–540 CE). In writing his long commentaries on Aristotle Simplicius is following these examples, while philosophically still following the tradition established by Plotinus. In his works he manages to review and incorporate most Platonist commentaries written up to his day. Simplicius respectfully refers to Proclus as "the philosopher from Lycia and the teacher of my teachers" (*in Ph.* 611.11–12, cf. 795.4–5). He mentions Proclus mostly for the methodical refutation of objections and attacks to Plato's thought by Aristotle and others. He probably used a work by Proclus "who wrote a book, solving the objections" (*biblion ... tas enstaseis dialyōn*, *in DC* 640.24–5).

Simplicius' works serve our purpose well, because they provide exceptionally good evidence for understanding the late Platonist commentary style.[21] His commentaries are a source for exegetical and didactic practices, and also inform us about Greek philosophy from the Presocratics to his own day. They also form an important moment in the transition from late antiquity to the Middle Ages. But most importantly, they show us a distinctive stage of the interpretation of Aristotle and Plato.

Simplicius is important because from our modern perspective his scholarly method is quite reliable: he is unusually self-conscious of his approach and thoughtful in his assessment of text, manuscripts and an astounding range of sources (see Chase 2003: 8; Baltussen 2008). He also uses quotation far more often than most other commentators. He gives further evidence for the animosity between Platonists and Christian intellectuals. Since Iamblichus (third century CE) a greater emphasis on religion had resurfaced.

It could range from strong ritualistic approaches, such as Proclus' theurgy, to more theological concerns about theodicy and the creation of the world (Simplicius, Philoponus). The lively school context in which Platonism is held with a strong conviction, as a way of life, thus resembled a religious initiation. Not surprisingly, there are significant parallels with Christian exegetical strategies, which is at least in part a sign of their common Greek stock (Mansfeld 1994). But the rivalry between Christian and pagan positions is even more significant, as both parties strove to win the hearts and minds of men by arguing *in books about books*, with authoritative texts at the core. But as the official state religion, Christianity would threaten the pagan schools supported by worldly authority and ultimately cause the closing of Plato's Academy in Athens in 529 CE by Emperor Justinian.

Among the many references to his commentator predecessors Alexander of Aphrodisias (*c*.200 CE) is by far the most-quoted source in Simplicius.[22] Simplicius calls him the "most knowledgeable of Aristotle's exegetes".[23] Alexander's surviving works show him as a patient and meticulous thinker and commentator, firmly making use of the Aristotelian tradition, without agreeing with everything Aristotle wrote.[24] Simplicius represents the more recent Platonist outlook in which Aristotelianism and Platonism were brought closer together on important issues, with occasional Stoic ideas thrown in. Simplicius' use of his sources plays an important role in this and already illustrates well his skill and innovation in clarifying Aristotle. The weaving of many different voices into the fabric of his commentaries may be compared with the writing of a symphony – an image Simplicius would have liked, since one of his aims is to show there exists agreement (Greek: *symphōnia*) between Plato and Aristotle. He will variously use paraphrase and quotation; about these two modes he expresses specific views (and here he is not typical of the Neoplatonic school): first, how to use them, and second, what role they can fulfil.

In his commentary on Aristotle's *Categories* Simplicius acknowledges debts to earlier exegetes. Using a topos of modesty, he claims that he merely wants to copy and expound Iamblichus' commentary.[25] He gives a clear idea of his intentions and aims as a commentator (*in Cat.* 7.23–32 [Kalbfleisch], trans. Chase):

> The worthy exegete of Aristotle's writings must not fall wholly short of the latter's greatness of intellect (*megalonoia*). He must also have experience of everything the Philosopher has written, and must be a connoisseur (*epistēmōn*) of Aristotle's stylistic habits. His judgement must be impartial (*adekaston*), so that he may neither, out of misplaced zeal, seek to prove something well said to be unsatisfactory, nor, if some point should require attention, should he obstinately persist in trying to demonstrate that [Aristotle] is always and everywhere infallible, as if he had enrolled himself in the Philosopher's school. [The good exegete] must, I believe, not convict the philosophers of discordance by looking only at the letter (*lexis*) of what [Aristotle] says against Plato; but he must look towards the spirit (*nous*), and track down (*anichneuein*) the harmony which reigns between them on the majority of points.

This description of the natural talents of an exegete (with similarities to those found in the Anon. *in Tht.*, e.g. col. IX.25–X.12 [Bastianini & Sedley]) are still sound today: he advocates impartiality, a broad familiarity with the works and their style, and, remarkably, a capacity to distinguish between the letter and the spirit of the text.[26] But virtue and hard work are also relevant, as well as an interest in learning by "frequent … in-depth examination of Aristotelian concepts" (*ibid.*).

The high frequency of references to Alexander in Simplicius' commentaries is statistically significant.[27] His works play a major role in Simplicius' elucidations, and a few different types can be distinguished. Alexander certainly provides a helpful exegesis of Aristotle and often entails *agreement*. Simplicius is clearly looking for enlightenment from his predecessor-colleague for understanding Aristotle's arguments better. Even if we grant that some rhetoric may be involved, often the consultation of an authority is genuine and will lead to further discussion of possibilities and textual details. For instance, at *in Ph.* 434.36 the position of Aristotle is propped up by Alexander's comments, which are brought in without qualifier: "Now he [Aristotle] wishes to provide clear examples of things reciprocally changed in initiating change and at the same time, as Alexander says, to separate off the divine body from being reciprocally changed and affected." Such brief interjections ("as Alexander says") are frequent and often signal agreement – giving an example of the argument from authority. Moreover, Alexander will serve to back up Simplicius' argument. Based on agreement, this move resembles an argument from authority, in that Alexander's view is invoked for confirmation and/or is placed in opposition to that of "others".[28] A correct understanding of a text is the basis for offering clarifications. In addition, the polemic against Philoponus about the eternity of the world is a well-worn part of exegesis (Hoffmann 1987). Here the strategy is to declare the opponent an inferior exegete: he has misunderstood a passage (a comment made possible on the basis of Alexander's interpretation). Two things stand out: (a) the emphasis is on text and its polysemy; (b) he now uses a secondary text, making this polemic a tertiary phenomenon where previous interpretations become part of the overall discourse of how to understand Aristotle.

Two further points can be made regarding the influence of Alexander. Alexander is often mentioned in connection with a variant in the manuscript tradition, an important link to the scholarly discussions of different lines of transmission. Finally, many references represent direct quotations. Even when Alexander's view is criticized and/or rejected, *he is quoted anyway*. In a considerable number of cases Simplicius will give quotations where *disagreement* with Alexander is expressed.[29] Although many Alexandrians quote ancient sources when they disagree, Simplicius deviated from this habit by quoting both categories; that is, if he agreed or disagreed. This puts him slightly above the usual suspicion of presenting a distorted narrative, which might have induced him to keep references to views he disagrees with very brief. Such a procedure would allow a critic to suppress evidence and present only as much material as is needed for a convincing refutation of the opponent.[30] It seems plausible to put this down to respect for Alexander's views.

In sum, Alexander is seen as both an authoritative interpreter and source for ammunition against others. Thus an Aristotelian commentator is given pride of place at the heart of Platonist commentaries. That he is also criticized shows how Simplicius has a mind of his own, despite his heavy reliance on others. Yet most of the time he seems to keep up the pretence of merely passing on the wisdom and insight from his predecessors (again, the "*topos* of modesty": Sluiter 2000: 200). The abundant sources and his scholarly method may well indicate that his works did not originate in the classroom, even if they may have been intended for such use. The later Alexandrian commentary tradition (Elias, David, Stephanus) tried to consolidate by writing *prolegomena* to the study of Plato and Aristotle, and their work is reflected in later compendia (Sorabji 1990: 20).

CONCLUDING REMARKS

The late antique commentary was a form of philosophical activity: it arose out of the teacher–student interaction during the reading of a preferred body of texts, which became a canonized corpus. Platonist exegesis of Aristotle's works was intended to prepare the minds of students for the more important ideas of Plato. This inversion of the historical relation was justified with traditional and doctrinal arguments: after the moral training (reading Epictetus' *Handbook*) the "smaller mysteries" of Aristotle's works would lead from a better understanding of words and concepts (*Categories, On Interpretation*) and the physical world (*Physics, On the Heavens*) to the metaphysical understanding of Plato's philosophy.

With the rise of commentary in the first century BCE, among both Platonists (Anon., Lucius, Nicostratus) and Peripatetics (Eudorus, Boethus, Xenarchus), philosophical progress would be determined by these factors: a self-conscious embedding within a recognized tradition (philosophy) viewed as a cooperative undertaking with the purpose of finding the truth while exploring the meaning of many views on the truth. Commenting on others is thereby *subordinated to* the quest for knowledge and understanding, and the conveying of truths *once established* would entail teaching *by way of* commentary. Every period would have their "own" Plato or Aristotle, and commentary was part of that process of renewal. The label "Neoplatonism" fails to take that into account, operating with a flawed notion of purity of the tradition. In the Platonic tradition it is a deliberate continuation and passing on of an "established" philosophical truth, yet it also involves creative interpretation.

The ancient philosophical commentary, in its formal and fully mature form, is thus not so much a deliberate choice of "genre" as a *natural by-product* of this ongoing dialogue between pupils and colleagues, past and present. This also explains the sheer size of the works, with their multifarious chorus of voices in multi-layered documents of unprecedented length. The commentaries often have an overarching aim, ideologically framed by an institutionalized learning process, which lacks the irksome features of modern commentary such as fragmentation, parallelomania and the reference-book function (Gibson 2002). Thus they could stand on their own feet as valuable and valued contributions to science and philosophy.[31]

NOTES

1. From the perspective of interpretation "which takes control and … remakes its object in the very act of its subservience" McCarty (2002: 363) has declared the commentary "primary".
2. For the former, see Nehamas (1990); for the latter, Mansfeld (1986).
3. *Ibid.*: 43, emphasis added. An even earlier commentary of the third century BCE is on a poetic text with religious and cosmological content (Betegh 2004).
4. J. Barnes (1992: 270); see also Falcon (2012). Historical and literary writings at the time are also of interest: "commentary on the *Royal Diary* of Alexander", *c.*335 BCE (Hammond 1987); "the first attested commentary on a text, Aristophanes's *Plutus*, [was] by Eratosthenes's pupil Euphormius" *c.* third/second century BCE (Wilson 1969: 370, ignoring the Derveni papyrus, "published" in 1967); "the first commentary on a prose author: Aristarchus's commentary on Herodotus", second century BCE (Wilson 1969: 371).
5. For a fuller discussion, see Baltussen (2004 [with further literature], 2007).
6. The seminal paper on the *Homerum ex Homero* principle is Schäublin (1977). Recent observations on the topic can be found in Mansfeld (1994), Sluiter (2000), Baltussen (2004).

7. I give a more elaborate argument for this in Baltussen (2004). Cf. Yunis (2003), Kahn (2003).

8. Elements in the exegesis show him to be a product of his time: his syncretism is clear in Stoic and Peripatetic notions merging with the Platonist perspective (Bastianini & Sedley 1995; Sedley 1997).

9. The earliest successors (Speusippus, Xenocrates) are still in the midst of establishing what the canonical Platonic view is. It is indicative of the importance and influence of Plato's system that his corpus is one of two to survive complete. This also holds for the other: that of Plotinus.

10. Karamanolis (2004, 2006).

11. The philosopher-doctor Galen (129–216/19 CE) added further dimensions to commentary and some of his work was known to Simplicius, but there is no room here to describe his contribution.

12. Gerson (2005b: 270). He also rightly emphasizes that "to be in harmony … must be sharply distinguished from the view, held by no one in antiquity, that the philosophy of Aristotle was identical with the philosophy of Plato" (ibid.: 271).

13. Sorabji (1990: 15): "Evidently, the theological motive of the Neoplatonic curriculum and the pressure to harmonize Plato with Aristotle creates dangers, if the commentaries are read as straightforward guides to Aristotle, without due allowance being made."

14. These have been well studied recently: see I. Hadot (1987; 2002: 167–76), Mansfeld (1994), Blumenthal (1996a), J. Barnes (1992, 1999).

15. Most commentaries in theōria and lexis are lemmatic, but not all of them are apo phonēs, i.e. notes taken at a lecture. I owe this point to the anonymous reader.

16. This section is based on Baltussen (2008: ch. 5).

17. Cf. I. Hadot (2001: xlvii ff.), Dodds (1963), J. Barnes (1992).

18. Lambertz (1987: 1–2), who distinguishes between lecture notes (Vorlesungsnachschriften) and commentary proper (von den Exegeten selbst redigierten Kommentare, which Proclus himself calls hypomnēmata); cf. Dillon (1973: 54), Festugière (1963), Lamberz (1987).

19. See most recently Cleary (2006: 147): "it is clear that Proclus is conscious of standing at the end of a long tradition of interpreting Plato's Timaeus that goes right back to the Academy, and obviously this tradition dominates his whole interpretation of the dialogue". Now translated by Tarrant & Baltzly (2007–2013).

20. Dodds (1923: xxviii n. 4) adds examples from Damascius, Isid. 48.11ff., 92.26ff. and Simplicius, in DC 370.29. Cf. Watts (2004, 2006).

21. As was most recently pointed out by Chase (2003: 8). But this has been a growing consensus for some years now: cf. I. Hadot (1987); Tarán (1987: 246–7) who mentions two of the four points; de Haas (2001); Baltussen (2002).

22. It is not easy to provide a number: a search on the Thesaurus Linguae Graecae (version E, © University of Irvine California) for "Alexand(r)-" offers around 700 instances, only giving explicit occurrences of the name (and all its cases).

23. My translation; see Simplicius, in Ph. 80.15–16 and 707.33–4.

24. On certain issues he diverged from Aristotelian orthodoxy, such as the immortality of the soul: see Moraux (1942), Sharples (1987).

25. J. Barnes (1992). Cf. below, note 30.

26. This distinction was the basis for most ancient strategies of allegorical reading (pagan or Christian; Chase's use of the Pauline formulation of the dichotomy ["letter" and "spirit", 2003: 23] is slightly misleading). There was also the philological and rhetorical tradition (status de scripto et sententia).

27. Above, note 22.

28. For example, Simplicius, in Ph. 521.10, τῶν παλαίων "thinkers of old" in opposition to the νεώτεροι "moderns, upstarts", a contrast already popular in Galen (c.129–216/19 CE).

29. There is a notable parallel in later commentators of the early Renaissance, where reference to Alexander is dictated mostly on account of disagreement (Fazzo 1999: 48).

30. Simplicius has been imputed with such an approach regarding Alexander on the basis of recently found marginalia of a Paris manuscript, and in this case that verdict seems justified (Rashed 1997). That assessment should not be generalized, since at least according to modern standards the quoting of dismissed views has merit. These important fragments are from Alexander's lost commentary on Aristotle's Physics.

31. In this essay I have drawn on a number of my earlier works on the topic published between 2002 and 2010, but much has been revised, added or rearranged in order to make it fit the current volume's purpose.

8

The non-commentary tradition

Andrew Smith

The practice of writing commentaries on the works of Plato and Aristotle had begun in an early period and was one of the main occupations of professional Platonists and Aristotelians in the two centuries leading up to the time of Plotinus. But handbooks and treatises on particular topics were also produced.[1] More popular philosophical writing aimed at the general public was invariably in the form of essays or orations, such as those of Plutarch, Maximus of Tyre or Apuleius. Philosophical ideas were extensively employed by Philo of Alexandria in his works of biblical exegesis, while a specialist such as the medical writer Galen wrote treatises on particular philosophical topics which touched on medicine.[2]

PLOTINUS

Plotinus is something of an exception in so far as his published work is only in the form of treatises on particular philosophical problems even though the issues often begin with or closely involve philosophical texts, particularly of course Plato. His seminars too were based on the reading of a philosophical text, but this simply formed the basis of further enquiry and is to be clearly distinguished from the formal exposition of a continuous text, which came to be the general practice.

The *Enneads* of Plotinus are difficult to fit into any particular philosophical genre. According to Porphyry's introduction to his edition of the *Enneads* Plotinus was very reluctant to commit any of his teaching to writing and Porphyry claims the credit for encouraging him to do so. His comments on Plotinus' method of composition are revealing: he apparently wrote in a continuous manner without revising his work (Porphyry, *Plot.* 8). It also seems that the written treatises reflect closely the style of his teaching. Not that they are in any sense transcripts of the seminars which he conducted, but that they reflect the spirit of open discussion and relentless examination of theories, which were

115

the mark of his teaching style. Porphyry relates, for example, how on one occasion when he himself raised questions about the relationship of soul to body Plotinus allowed the discussion to go on for three days despite the protestations of a member of the seminar who preferred to be given straightforward presentations by Plotinus himself.[3] The briefest encounter with any treatise of the *Enneads* will provide examples of passages in which Plotinus appears to be debating with interlocutors who hold opinions different from his own or who present objections. These may sometimes be identifiable as the views of Stoics, Epicureans, Peripatetics or even of other Platonists. Sometimes Plotinus seems to be putting forward objections of his own to help clarify or progress the analysis. Although this often makes for difficult reading since it is sometimes not altogether clear which views Plotinus himself holds, it does present us with a lively philosophical discourse which is aporetic and exploratory. It may be this that Porphyry refers to when he says that Plotinus applied the "mind of Ammonius", his teacher.

Another feature of his seminar style recorded by Porphyry is the reading of recent philosophical texts as starting points for a discussion or exposition of important themes.[4] His discussion of time, for example, in the treatise on "Eternity and Time" commences with a review of the theories of earlier philosophers, particularly that of Aristotle (*Enn.* III.7[45].7–10). The basic assumption behind this practice is his conviction that there is a *philosophia perennis* which is to be found, of course, in Plato, but which needs expounding and elucidating, as he explains in *Enn.* V.1[10], where he says that "these statements of ours are not new … but were made long ago, not explicitly, and what we have said in this discussion has been an interpretation of them, relying on Plato's own writings for evidence that that these views are ancient". In fact, this entire treatise illustrates very clearly how Plotinus positions his own thought in the history of philosophy. After exploring and stating the nature of the three primal hypostases, the One, Intellect and Soul, he finds them expressed in Plato (*Enn.* V.1[10].8.1–2); but he affirms that the Presocratics (Parmenides, Anaxagoras, Heraclitus and Empedocles) also had some insight into them, as did Aristotle (*Enn.* V.1[10].8.15–19. For the Presocratics, see Stamatellos 2007). It remains his task to make more explicit and elucidate what Plato has already proposed. We should also acknowledge the use by Plotinus of Stoic ideas, and throughout the *Enneads* the evidence of a productive encounter with Aristotle (for an example of this, see A. Smith 2004).

Lastly, we should not ignore the practical nature of Plotinus' teaching and writings. As for all ancient philosophers, philosophy is not a merely theoretical study, but has practical implications for the conduct of our lives. It is particularly important for Plotinus to express this since he is not presenting his students with ethical precepts but with what might to us seem abstruse metaphysical ideas, which are far removed from the conduct of our everyday lives. But for him the discovery of the primary principles of the universe is co-terminous with the discovery of our real selves; and spiritual progress can only be made when we rediscover and take ownership of our real inner self. Philosophical enquiry provides the way to do this (see Schniewind 2003). Many of the treatises are in fact structured around this principle of self-discovery. *Enn.* V.1[10], for example, begins with the encouragement to look within ourselves to discover what sort of entity we are. This discovery will then lead us to the primary principles themselves, which we can identify with those found in Plato and adumbrated in other philosophers. He then returns to the individual (*Enn.* V.1[10].11–12), who has within him these principles; and he finally encourages us to turn inwards to rediscover them within ourselves and live by them. It is in exhortatory passages like this that Plotinus comes closest in style and spirit to Plato as opposed to the often more Aristotelian terseness of close analysis and exposition, which characterizes much of the *Enneads*. *Enn.* I.6[1], "On Beauty", provides another example of a treatise which combines close analysis, in this case of the concept of beauty, and an exposition of the ascending levels of reality, which culminates in an appeal to turn within ourselves. A further dimension to this may be found in *Enn.* VI.9[9], where Plotinus attempts to delineate the nature of the One and our relationship to it. The One is beyond Being and Intellect; it cannot be spoken of or reached by our reasoning powers. But Plotinus still attempts to say what can be said of it, even if that will fall short of capturing its nature. His treatment oscillates constantly between reasoning about the One and invoking personal experience of it, an experience that transcends reason and intellect (for an analysis of this treatise, see A. Smith 1992). He appeals to his students to approach the One themselves to attain this personal experience, but at the same time not to abandon entirely the use of reasoning, since it is only by way of reasoning that we reach the point of transition to what is above reason. These passages illustrate both the way in which Plotinus constantly reviews a difficult topic, viewing it from different angles,[5] and also his intense awareness that he is sometimes exploring the furthest reaches of metaphysics on the borderline between what is and is not accessible to reason, what is timeless (eternal) and what is in time.

Plotinus' treatises are not a formal exposition of his philosophical system, although some of the treatises do contain most of the elements of his metaphysical world. Rather, they deal with major issues, which arise from an attempt to understand the writings of Plato and the tradition of Platonic interpretation. They often cover the same problems but from different angles, and where there appear to be contradictions, these can often be resolved by a consideration of the differing contexts within which they arise. The edition of his treatises which we possess, the *Enneads*, is a construct of Porphyry, who in editing the text was intent on giving it a certain pedagogical order, moving from ethical and this-worldly issues, to soul, intellect and finally the One. A further complication was his division of the work into six books of nine treatises (nine being for him of theological significance: three triads), which necessitated the splitting and repositioning of some of the treatises. To overcome this artificial arrangement it has become popular to print and read the treatises in their original chronological order of composition, which Porphyry thankfully has carefully recorded for us. This has the merit of restoring split works and highlighting the transitions from topic to topic, but throws little light on any possible development of Plotinus' thought, as he did not begin writing until his maturity.

From the time of Porphyry onwards ever-increasing attention was paid both within the schools of the Neoplatonists and in their publications to the reading and careful commentary of Platonic texts. By the time of Iamblichus a carefully ordered programme of Platonic texts was in place. But the activity of the philosophers of the schools continued to require other forms of communication. By means of letters, exhortatory works, general introductions, compendia, polemical treatises and large-scale comprehensive works they engaged with the society in which they lived, with their fellow philosophers and with their students.

LETTERS

The letter as a means of communicating philosophical ideas was a long-established tradition before the Neoplatonists. We hear of letters of Pythagoras and of other Pythagoreans. And, of course, there are the surviving letters of Plato himself. Like those of the Pythagoreans, the letters of Plato are mostly later compositions (probably only *Ep.* II and VII are genuine and these are apologies rather than doctrinal expositions or hortatory epistles), but would have been accepted as genuine by the Neoplatonists. There is evidence, too, for letters of Aristotle, Theophrastus and other Peripatetics (e.g. Strato) as well as the fragmentary remains of important doctrinal letters of Epicurus. From a later period we hear of letters of Carneades (Diogenes Laertius 4.65) and of Apollonius of Tyana, and we have the curious collection of so-called letters of Socrates and the Socratics, composed probably in the first century BCE or CE. Nor should we forget the Roman tradition exemplified especially by Seneca.

In Neoplatonic circles the letter was used by philosophers in a variety of ways, from a straightforward means of communication as in the correspondence of Porphyry with his former teacher Longinus, which accompanied the manuscripts of Plotinus, to letters of a purely literary kind (Porphyry, *Plot.* 19). Porphyry's *Letter to Anebo* falls into the latter category. This letter, addressed to the Egyptian priest Anebo, professes to raise a number of problems with him about the nature of Egyptian religion. There is little reason to suppose that Anebo is a real person and that the letter-form is anything more than a literary device to accommodate Porphyry's enquiries. His *Letter to Marcella*, however, though it is not simply a private letter and was probably meant for a wider audience, does have the characteristics of a personal communication, of a husband to his wife, and is given a realistic setting, his necessary absence on a special mission (Porphyry, *Marc.* 4). The letters of Iamblichus, too, fall into this category and there is no reason to suppose that the addressees or the occasions for communicating with them are fictitious. In fact one of them, Sopater, even wrote his own philosophical letters, one of which, addressed to Himerius, has been preserved.

The philosophical content of these letters is characterized by its practical nature and by its simplified presentation of Neoplatonic ideas, simplified in the sense that there is avoidance of technical terminology and of more abstruse metaphysical concepts. Porphyry's *Letter to Marcella*, for example, does not mention the One and presents a much simplified metaphysical foundation for its exhortation to raise the soul towards the divine. Such simplicity is exactly what is needed in what is a protreptic or exhortation to philosophical reflection. Moreover, there is no need in these first stages to go any further than Intellect. We will see that a similar restriction applies to his *Sententiae*, which also have little to say about the One. The letters of Iamblichus, too, are expressed in a popular and restricted philosophical palette. Their themes are also ones that are concerned with ethical conduct in this world. Topics touched on include justice, self-control, courage, wisdom, and virtue in general. Iamblichus deals with practical or civic virtue but concentrates rather more on a higher level of what we might think of as internal virtue and which he calls purificatory. Behind this we can detect the standard Neoplatonic grades of virtue which first appear in Plotinus (*Enn.* I.2[19]), are systematized by Porphyry (*Sent.* 32) and further refined by Iamblichus and Proclus (see Marinus, *Procl.* 3). Fate and providence also figure prominently. This is clearly a subject area of practical interest, although it is treated at a relatively high metaphysical level. Again, these are topics which called for Plotinus' attention and which later prompted special treatises from Proclus,[6] no doubt motivated by the practical needs of those trying to lead the philosophical life. But it is striking that more theoretical subjects, such as dialectic, are not neglected by Iamblichus. Thus, while these letters, some of which are addressed to figures identifiably involved in politics and administration, clearly avoid complex technical discussion they are not merely exhortatory but encourage their addressees to construct for themselves a securely based philosophical foundation for the challenge of living a good life.

These letters remind us that the Neoplatonists, just as much as other philosophers in the ancient world, were primarily concerned about what we might call the spiritual welfare of their followers, whether students within their schools or adherents seeking advice in the practical affairs of their private and public lives.

INTRODUCTIONS TO PHILOSOPHY

We have already mentioned the introductory nature of works such as the *Letter to Marcella*. The task of introducing students and others to the philosophic life was promoted by a variety of publications. On the technical side there are introductions to logic such as the *Isagoge* of Porphyry, which was intended to be read before attempting to tackle (with the aid of commentaries) the logical works of Aristotle. Iamblichus' *Protrepticus* is intended to persuade people to turn to philosophy. And the various *Lives of Pythagoras* are also cast as introductions to the philosophical life, which must begin with ethical training even before the basic metaphysical groundwork is laid. It is important to understand that Platonists considered it essential to have a sound ethical formation and discipline before embarking on philosophical studies, which in turn strengthen that foundation to enable the soul to rise eventually beyond the realm of mundane ethical conduct. There has been a tendency to denigrate the Neoplatonists for their apparent neglect of ordinary human life in favour of the life of contemplation. It is true that they were not primarily interested in the technical discussion of ethics, but that is not to say that everyday ethics did not play an important role in their concept of the philosophical life. Their attention to this, however, was achieved more through example and precept than theoretical discussion, and in this they relied greatly on tradition by adopting ideas from Stoicism[7] and from the Pythagorean tradition. The accounts of Pythagoras written by Porphyry and Iamblichus in fact serve as models of how to live one's life. This is particularly the case with Iamblichus, whose work bears the title "On the Pythagorean Life" though it is cast in the form of a life of Pythagoras. It was intended to be followed by the reading of the *Protrepticus*, which contained readings from Pythagoras, Plato and Aristotle; the course then continued with volumes on particular aspects of Pythagorean philosophy before the reading of the dialogues of Plato (and the treatises of Aristotle).

Porphyry's work probably has something of the same aims as that of Iamblichus, but is differently conceived. It formed part of the first book of his four-book *Philosophical History*, extant only in fragments, which unfortunately makes it difficult to discern the intention and scope of the work as a whole. The *History* seems to have covered Greek philosophy from the beginning up to the time of Plato. Book II included Empedocles. Book III seems to be dedicated to Socrates and Book IV to Plato. Given the extensive treatment of Pythagoras which must have occupied a large part of Book I, it looks very much as if the work as a whole expressed a Platonic view of the history of philosophy with a strong emphasis on the connection between Plato himself and the Pythagorean tradition. Compared with Iamblichus, Porphyry's treatment is far more academic. He generally cites his sources and, for example, gives different versions of the origin and early life of Pythagoras, whereas Iamblichus is more content with a straightforward narrative. But great attention is also paid to Pythagoras' way of life: his ethical conduct, abstinence from eating flesh, his generally ascetic lifestyle, all of these supported by exemplary stories and instructive precepts. There is a stress on the community life, which he encouraged. And although Platonic schools such as those of Plotinus and Iamblichus do not seem to have been as organized and idealistic as Pythagoras' community, they were nevertheless identifiable communities with a common purpose and an atmosphere of mutual support. The sort of ascetic life that Porphyry describes in his life of Plotinus could be seen as based on the Pythagorean model. And it is in this context that one must understand Porphyry's *de Abstinentia*, a treatise written to encourage a member of the school not to give up on his vegetarian diet, which is just one of the means by which we can avoid the distractions caused by the body through overeating and heavy meat consumption, which slows down the body and impedes the operations of the soul.

But we should not forget that the Pythagorean contribution to Neoplatonism through the Neopythagorean revival was far more than just in the realm of ethics and lifestyle. According to Porphyry (*Plot.* 47), Pythagoras can teach us to rise beyond the body to the incorporeal world. Through the medium of mathematics, which are seen as symbols for the Forms, we can rise to the intelligible realm, and even to the One and the Indefinite Dyad. It is this same contribution of Pythagoreanism, which moves Iamblichus to compose a series of works on Pythagorean mathematics and metaphysics and to acknowledge the symbolic nature of Pythagorean precepts, which leads us to what is beyond normal human understanding (*Plot.* 23.103). And yet the main appeal of these "lives" of Pythagoras is to those who wish to make the necessary adjustments to the way they conduct their lives that will lead to the beginnings of the philosophical life. The admonitions are practical and concern not only human relations on an intimate scale (true friendship) but also within the fabric of the structure of society within the city. The detailed account of Pythagoras' political engagement (*Plot.* 27) is another indication of the importance placed by these Platonists on everyday political realities and the contribution to them which the philosopher can make.

SUMMARIES

Another genre is that of what we might call formal summaries of philosophical thought, such as the *Sententiae* of Porphyry and Proclus' *Elements of Theology* and *Elements of Physics*. There are indications of a considerable tradition in the production of such summaries, particularly among Platonists. Their use is primarily pedagogical. The *Curiae Doxai* of Epicurus provide an early example. The short sayings were evidently meant to be learnt by heart and absorbed into one's lifestyle by constant repetition. The handbook of Arius Didymus is more like a work of reference, while Alcinous' *Handbook of Platonism* and the *Platonic Doctrines* of Apuleius are examples of what must have been a widespread phenomenon of easily digested and condensed accounts of what had become a systema-tized formulation of Plato's thought. When we turn to the Neoplatonic contributions that we have mentioned, we see that although they are each very different in scope they have in common an attempt to express basic philosophical concepts in a formal manner. They all lead the mind in a particular direction, from a starting point to a finish. In this sense they may be said to belong to the genre of "introductions". The two works of Proclus are very formal in their construction and move the reader from basic to more complex proposi-tions in an almost geometrically inspired logical sequence. The structure and purpose of Porphyry's *Sententiae* is more difficult to discern. But it, too, as its full title, *Philosophical axioms (sententiae) which lead to the Intelligibles*, implies, is intended to lead the soul towards the intelligible world. The fact that it survives in an incomplete form and that some of its sections may have been reordered makes it difficult to assess its intent. But recent analysis of its contents helps us to make more sense of its aims (see D'Ancona 2005). The individual "*sententiae*" vary in length from a few lines to several pages, each of them consisting of a skilfully contrived mosaic of ideas from the *Enneads* of Plotinus, composed of long or short citations, summaries, verbal reminiscences and short phrases. It is also noticeable that the "*sententiae*" become longer as the work progresses, beginning with very short definitions and leading in the end to more expansive and striking passages.[8] Porphyry would appear to have drawn largely on three key treatises from the *Enneads*: *Enn.* III.6[17], *On Impassivity*, *Enn.* V.3[49], *On the Knowing Hypostases* and *Enn.* VI.4–5[22–3], *The Presence of Being Everywhere*. The material presented serves very closely the theme of "leading" the reader "towards the intelligibles" which, as we have noted, is the inten-tion expressed by the title of the work: we are first taught about the nature of the soul's relationship to body, the fact that it is, in its innermost nature, not corrupted by body, that we can and must return to this aspect of ourselves which expresses itself at its highest level in our intellect. This return to our real self is a return to Intellect and the power of true Being. The ultimate principle, the One, is clearly mentioned (e.g. in *Sent.* 10 and 43 (p. 54.8 [Lamberz])), but plays no major role in the main argument which is clearly concerned with the ascent of the soul up to the level of Intellect. In this it corresponds very well with the sort of limited spiritual ascent that is expressed in other works of Porphyry, such as *de Abstinentia* and *ad Marcellam*, which advocate a return to Intellect without any reference to the One. This content suggests Porphyry's concern to find a form of "salvation", which is open and meaningful to more than the most elevated philosopher,[9] and we should in no sense read into this that he had abandoned the doctrine of the transcendent One or its importance as the ultimate goal of the philosopher. Much of the material concerns the sharp distinction that is to be made between corporeal and incorporeal reality, and their relationship. Hence the substantial use of *Enn.* VI.4–5[22–3], a treatise in which Plotinus seems to lay aside for a moment all hierarchical distinctions of level in the intelligible world in order to concentrate on the examination of the way in which the incorporeal is present to and expresses itself in the realm of three-dimensional extension. We might recall here, too, Porphyry's concern with the relationship of soul and body, an issue which he raised in Plotinus' seminar.[10] Although, in the *Sententiae*, Porphyry does not seem in essence to differ fundamentally from Plotinus, we may detect at times a hardening of position and lack of flexibility, due perhaps to the conciseness of the format he has chosen. But on at least one occasion he does follow a line of argument which seems to have been of only marginal interest to Plotinus and which may be a concession to more popular sentiment.

In *Sent.* 29, he introduces the notion of the astral body, a sort of quasi-corporeal entity, to account for the concept of the soul being in Hades as a place, after its separation from its earthly body. Porphyry probably introduced this concept because it would have been familiar to readers in the context of the descent of the soul through the planetary spheres.

One of the longest sections is taken from Plotinus' treatise on the virtues. It is fully in place here as it traces the ascent of the soul in its passage from its more embodied encounter with virtue to the level of intellect, which strictly is above virtue or rather is the level of the models of virtue. If we had a full text of the *Sententiae*, we might be able to claim with more certainty that this section is central to the plan of the work. As it is we must be content with saying that the section on the virtues plays a pivotal role in emphasizing the core purpose of the work as a means of leading the soul through philosophical reflection to disengage itself from the world and return to its true self in Intellect. Finally we may notice Porphyry's choice in *Sent.* 40 of a long passage from *Enn.* VI.5[23] in which Plotinus addresses and exhorts his listener/reader directly in the second person. All of these elements contribute to the exhortatory nature of this work.

Brief mention should be made of Sallustius' *On the Gods and the Universe*. This short work, which shows the influence of Iamblichus, is a handbook, for educated people who did not have the time to attend philosophy lectures (see chapters i and xiii). It aims to provide them with a correct understanding of the nature of the gods and their role in the universe and to lead them to union with the divine. The topics cover the different types of mythical representation of the gods, the hierarchy of reality, providence, fate, the nature of the human soul, virtue and the origin of evil. Particular attention is paid to the indestructibility of the universe, to sacrifice and the transmigration of souls. Without entering into the complexities of Neoplatonic metaphysics, Sallustius addresses in Platonic terms what he perceived to be the main intellectual issues facing educated pagans in the fourth century.[11]

Proclus' *Elements of Theology* is quite different. Unlike the *Sententiae* and the work of Sallustius, which serve the practical purpose of aiding, in an immediately applicable and practical way, the relative novice in his ascent to the divine, the *Elements of Theology* aims to set out the basic metaphysical principles of Neoplatonism in a logical order of propositions, to each of which is assigned a demonstration. This *a priori* deductive system is inspired by the methods of Euclidean geometry. The resultant text is highly concise and technical, lacking in any kind of ornamentation or personal exhortation. Proclus' concern is to set out the metaphysical structure of reality rather than the descent and return of the individual soul. "Theology" in this sense means what Aristotle would term "first philosophy", the ultimate causes of things. It is the only systematic presentation of Neoplatonism that we possess and, although few, if any, of its basics precepts are not already contained in Plotinus' *Enneads*, the precise arguments used in their support are sometimes not found in Plotinus. Almost inevitably in a work of such complexity, there are deficiencies and possible clashes with what Proclus says elsewhere, but that may be due to a wish to exclude unnecessary details[12] or possibly because he continued to revise and adjust the work throughout his lifetime (the view of Steel 2010: 636). Propositions 1–112 present the basic principles that underlie Neoplatonic metaphysics: for example, the One and the Many, procession and reversion, time and eternity, while propositions 113–211 apply them to explicate the levels of reality from the One to Soul. Although the text is bare and lacks any reference to authorities, there are frequent hidden assumptions, drawn particularly of course from

Plato, which render the arguments less cogent than they at first appear. Moreover, some of the arguments are circular. Nevertheless, this remains an important source of reference for understanding the most basic principles of Neoplatonic metaphysics which, when used together with his more expansive analyses in other works, can illuminate and provide a different perspective from Plotinus' more aporetic approach to key issues.

The *Elements* represents one side of Proclus' attempt to express what is central to Platonism; the other, and we might say more comprehensive, statement of Platonism is found in his grand project of a *Platonic Theology*. This work is monumental, voluminous, full of references to the most important authorities, Plato, the *Chaldaean Oracles* and the Orphics, not least appeals to a sense of personal religious experience, something which is completely absent, though not inconsistent with, the *Elements of Theology*. This work, like all of Proclus' major compositions, except perhaps the *Elements*, does not survive in its complete form; but its surviving six books still comprise some 680 pages of text in the Budé edition. The intention of the project is to identify a distinctive Platonic theology in the dialogues of Plato and to integrate this with both traditional theology and the theology of the *Chaldaean Oracles* and the Orphics; in other words, to produce a grand synthesis of Hellenic theology based on Plato.

Proclus begins by making a clear distinction between natural theology or metaphysical theology and the sort of theology expressed through myth, symbol and divine inspiration, all of which may be found in Plato. In fact, he argues, his predecessors had failed to analyse Plato's theology properly because they based their assessments on an uncritical compilation of every passage in which Plato mentions the gods. The correct procedure is to identify the metaphysical principles that underlie his theology, and the primary source for this is the *Parmenides*, which is to be understood not as an exercise in logic but as a metaphysical exposition of the structure of reality. The hypotheses of the *Parmenides* not only provide the basic structure of the Platonic world – the One, Intellect, Soul, body and matter – but detailed attributes of each order, most particularly of the transcendent orders, and may then be described as presenting theology "dialectically" (Proclus, *Theol. Plat.* I.4 [I.17.20]). Like Iamblichus before him, Proclus identifies divinity closely with unity, but although the One is the ultimate cause of unity, the unity which comes to be shared in by what we term gods is to be found at a lower level, intermediate between the utterly transcendent One which cannot be participated and Intellect. The key, Proclus argues, is to be found in his master Syrianus' interpretation of the second hypothesis of the *Parmenides*. This hypothesis, which in general is to be interpreted as expressing the multitude in unity of the intelligible world, is to be interpreted as also expressing the unities or henads whose properties can be shared by what is below them; and these are the ultimate determiners of gods not only at the level of intellect but at lower levels too. Thus the whole hierarchy of gods, right down to the gods, daemons and heroes who dwell on the earth, finds its origin in the henads expressed in the second hypothesis of the *Parmenides*. Having established this principle it remains then to gather the common attributes of the gods to be gleaned from the other dialogues of Plato, mainly *Laws*, *Republic*, *Phaedrus*, *Phaedo* and *Cratylus*, and then to assign to the different levels of gods[13] what is said in the various dialogues, whether by divine inspiration (*Phaedrus*), symbolically (*Gorgias*, *Symposium*, *Protagoras*) or through images (*Timaeus*, *Politicus*). Into this schema can then be inserted the authorities of the *Chaldaean Oracles* (divinely inspired), Orphic literature (symbolic) and Pythagoras (use of images).

It would be wrong to think that the idea of henads was devised simply as a means of explaining the presence of divinity throughout the universe and reconciling polytheism with the monism of the Neoplatonic system. The concept of henads also had a purely metaphysical function in Proclus' system, for it could be argued that it provided a necessary intermediary to bridge the gap between Intellect and the One. The assertion of a completely transcendent One is probably one of Plotinus' most striking philosophical innovations. It clearly troubled later generations. Porphyry seems to have grappled with the problem and Iamblichus found his solution in positing two Ones, a solution which Proclus rejected. But in rejecting it, he had to face the same problem. The divine henads provided one approach, which also had the advantage of helping to integrate religious and natural theology.

CONCLUSION

Both Plotinus and his successors claimed their title of Platonists largely because of the centrality of the Platonic corpus in their conduct of the philosophical life. The close examination of Platonic texts and the compilation of commentaries as aids in the interpretation of these texts were distinguishing features of Platonism from Porphyry to the end of the Neoplatonic schools. But, as we have seen, other forms of philosophical activity and other kinds of published work were of at least equal importance in promoting the worldview of these late Platonists. And not the least impact of this non-commentary tradition is the influence it had on the Arabic tradition where direct treatises on philosophical topics were of greater interest than the text of Plato himself.

NOTES

1. Thrasyllus wrote a prolegomena to reading Plato, Severus a treatise on the soul, Origen (the Platonist) wrote on *daimones* and a work entitled *That the King Alone is Creator*. The Aristotelian Alexander of Aphrodisias, in addition to his extensive commentaries, composed a number of treatises on special topics.
2. For example, *The Errors of the Soul*, *The Faculties of the Soul Follow the Mixtures of the Body*, *On Demonstration*, *The Best Doctor is Also a Philosopher*.
3. Porphyry, *Plot.* 8.13. In ch. 3, he tells us that Plotinus encouraged his students to ask questions and that this often led to a lack of order in the seminars.
4. In Porphyry, *Plot.* 14, Severus, Cronius, Numenius, Gaius and Atticus are mentioned, along with the Aristotelians Aspasius, Alexander and Adrastus. See Armstrong (1957) for a good example of Plotinus' use of Alexander of Aphrodisias.
5. There is a similar approach in *Enn.* VI.4–5[22–3] where, in exploring the way in which incorporeal being relates to body, he presents us with a series of different viewpoints from which to approach the problem.
6. *de Providentia et Fato et Eo Quod in Nobis*; *de Decem Dubitationibus Circa Providentiam*; *de Malorum Subsistentia*.
7. As, for example, Simplicius' commentary on Epictetus' *Enchiridion*.
8. For example, *Sent.* 7 has two lines, *Sent.* 29 has 43, *Sent.* 40 (on intellect) has 78. *Sent.* 32 (on virtues) has 159 and could have been a centrepiece of the work as a whole.
9. As expressed, for example, in *de Regressu Animae* as reported by Augustine. Cf. Porphyry, frags 283–302 [Smith] and especially frag. 302 [Smith]. According to Augustine, Porphyry, though intent on discovering such a way to "salvation", admitted that he had not yet found it.
10. Porphyry, *Plot.* 13.
11. Sallustius is probably to be identified with Sallustius, the friend of the emperor Julian to whom Julian

dedicated his *Oration* 4 and 8. His treatise may then be seen in the context of Julian's attempted pagan revival in 363.

12. See Dodds' introduction to the edition, with translation and commentary (1963: xv–xviii). This edition is still the best introduction to Proclus' metaphysics.
13. Intelligible, intellectual, hypercosmic, encosmic, divine souls, angels, daemons and heroes.

9

Plotinus' style and argument

Luc Brisson

THE CONTEXT

The *Life of Plotinus and the Order of his Books* was written by Porphyry more than thirty years after the death of Plotinus. Porphyry first evokes the memory of his stay in the School between 263 and 268. He relies subsequently on the testimony of Plotinus himself for the period between 212 and 246, on that of Amelius, Plotinus' most senior disciple at Rome, for the period between 246 and 263, on his own eye-witness reports for the period between 263 and 268, and finally on that of Eustochius for the circumstances and date of Plotinus' death. He then gives us several indications concerning his editorial work.

The information Porphyry provides us on Plotinus' personal life is rather meagre, for the master did not like to talk about it. We do, however, learn a great deal about Plotinus' activities: his philosophical position, audience, teaching method, writing practices. All these details allow us better to understand Plotinus' style and manner of argumentation.

Biography

Plotinus is said to have been born in 205, and, according to some testimonies extraneous to the *Life of Plotinus*, it would have been at Lyco, identified with Lycopolis, a town of Upper Egypt corresponding to modern Assiout.[1] We know nothing about his family, which need not, however, have been of Egyptian origin. Plotinus is a name of Latin formation, and Plotinus himself displays a lack of knowledge of the workings of hieroglyphic writing (see *Enn.* V.8[31].6). His family must have been a wealthy, cultivated Roman family, which had relations at the highest level. At the time, the offspring of wealthy families were handed over to a nursemaid right from their birth, and this was the case with Plotinus. He received a good education: he went to a schoolmaster since the age of seven, and at twenty-seven he was in Alexandria with Ammonius, who was to be his philosophy teacher. All indications are that if Plotinus joined the court of the emperor Gordian III in his expedition against the Persians, it was because his family (probably high civil servants) had strong connections with the imperial court. At the age of twenty-seven, Plotinus launched into philosophy (*Plot.* 3.6–14) at Alexandria. If he was indeed born in 205, this "conversion" must have taken place in 232. From this time on, he remained with Ammonius for a total of eleven years, thus until 243. Practically nothing is known of this Ammonius and his school, which can be explained by their "Pythagorean" attitude to communication: Ammonius wrote nothing (*Plot.* 20.36), and his disciples had to keep his doctrines secret (*Plot.* 3.24–7). Under Ammonius, who had taught Longinus (*Plot.* 20.36–8), Plotinus had Herennius and Origen as his fellow disciples, and all three had made a pact not to reveal the doctrines that Ammonius had set forth to them (*Plot.* 3.24–30).

It was to familiarize himself with the philosophy of the Persians and the Indians that Plotinus joined the court of Gordian III, the eighteen-year-old emperor who was launching an expedition against the Persians. The army left Rome in the spring of 242, but it was not until the good weather of the following year that it marched into combat, after having assembled at Antioch. Since Plotinus left Ammonius in 243, one can imagine that it was at Antioch that he joined the emperor's court. The following year, however, the emperor died at Zaitha, probably assassinated: this is what one may suppose when we learn that Plotinus owed his safety only to his flight to Antioch (*Plot.* 3.21–2). A few months later, probably in the spring of 244, he left Antioch to come to Rome (*Plot.* 3.23–4). He was then forty years old, and the accession to power of Philip the Arab, who was accused of the death of Gordian III, did not present problems for him. Amelius attached himself to Plotinus two years after the latter's arrival at Rome (*Plot.* 3.38–41). As Longinus implies (*Plot.* 20.32–3), Amelius was Plotinus' disciple and assistant as soon as he opened his school at Rome in 246.

Plotinus, assisted by Amelius for twenty-four years, was not a holder of an imperial chair, nor was he a head of a private institution. He provided open instruction to all, without any institutional character; that is, without structures based on law and custom. This explains why when Plotinus left Rome (at the same time as Amelius), the school dissolved. Yet this did not prevent Plotinus from having an influence on the Platonists who taught in the great intellectual centres of the empire, particularly Apamea and Athens. At Rome, he lived in the house of Gemina, a woman of the aristocracy who had been won over to philosophy (*Plot.* 9.2), and who may have been the widow of Trebonianus, emperor from 251 to 253. His school seems to have been under the protection of the emperor Gallienus himself and of his wife Salonina (*Plot.* 12.2). In the summertime, he continued his teaching in another place (*Plot.* 5.3–5), probably in Campania, on the property of Zethus (*Plot.* 2.18–20), which had previously belonged to Castricius (*Plot.* 7.22–4).

Anyone who wished could attend Plotinus' classes (*Plot.* 1.13–14), as Porphyry remarks when drawing up an inventory of students at the beginning of chapter 7, distinguishing the simple auditors (*akroatai*) from the disciples (*zēlōtai*). Among the former, we must distinguish the painter Carterius (*Plot.* 1.13–14), several senators (*Plot.* 7.29–30), and even people who were far from agreeing with Plotinus, whether they were Gnostics such as Adelphius and Aquilinus (*Plot.* 16.1–9), a financial civil servant like Thaumasius (*Plot.* 13.12–17), the rhetorician Diophanes (*Plot.* 15.6–17), or even Origen, his former fellow disciple under Ammonius (*Plot.* 14.20–25). Among Plotinus' disciples one finds women, including Gemina and her daughter (*Plot.* 9.1–5). Among the men, one finds in the first place those who devoted themselves exclusively to philosophy: Amelius and Porphyry; then some physicians: Paulinus of Scythopolis (*Plot.* 7.6), Eustochius of Alexandria (*Plot.*

7.8) and Zethus (*Plot.* 7.17–24), who was of Arab descent. There was also the poet Zoticus (*Plot.* 7.12), and several senators, including Castricius Firmus (*Plot.* 7.24–9), Marcellus Orrontius (*Plot.* 7.31), Sabinillus (*Plot.* 7.31) and Rogatianus (*Plot.* 7.32). Finally, there was only one representative of the business echelon, Serapion of Alexandria (*Plot.*7.46–7), who receives a negative portrayal.

The instruction dispensed by Plotinus consisted of two aspects: exegetic and dogmatic. In his classes, exegesis, which occupied a considerable place (*Plot.* 14.10–18), constituted only the initial part of the exposition of a doctrine inspired by that of Ammonius (*Plot.* 14.15–16), and, through him, by Numenius. Plotinus' doctrine could be characterized as Platonism strongly permeated by Stoicism, which it combated and interpreted through a Neopythagorean grille (*Plot.* 20.71–3). Plotinus was even accused of having plagiarized Numenius; the testimony of Porphyry (*Plot.*13–14) coincides with that of Amelius on this point (*Plot.* 3.35–8). Plotinus avoided any rhetorical elaboration in his classes (*Plot.* 18.4–5) and favoured discussion over systematic exposition, which disconcerted Porphyry upon his arrival at the school (*Plot.* 18.8–19) and was the subject of complaint on the part of some auditors, such as Thaumasius (*Plot.* 13.1–10). Although he pronounced some words poorly, Plotinus was an excellent pedagogue. All these qualities were accompanied by a genuine competence that extended to domains other than philosophy: "He had a complete knowledge of geometry, arithmetic, mechanics, optics and music, but was not disposed to apply himself to detailed research in these subjects" (*Plot.* 14.6–10); "He studied the rules of astronomy, without going very far into the mathematical side, but went more carefully into the methods of the casters of horoscopes. When he had detected the unreliability of their alleged results he did not hesitate to attack many of the statements made in their writings" (*Plot.* 15.21–6).[2]

The written work

For ten years, from 244 to 253, Plotinus contented himself with not writing anything. It was in 254 – the first year of the reign of Gallienus – that he began to write. Thus, when Porphyry arrived in 263, he discovered twenty-one treatises.

During the period when Porphyry remained with him, that is, a bit more than five years, from 263 to 268, Plotinus wrote twenty-four treatises. Porphyry's stay with Plotinus ended sadly: a personal problem, a theoretical opposition between Porphyry, who admired Aristotle, and Plotinus, who had just written the treatises *On the Genera of Being* against Aristotle, or emotion inspired by the perspective of the emperor's overthrow and its consequences for the life of the school? No one can say. Towards the fifteenth year of the reign of Gallienus, that is, shortly before the emperor's assassination, Porphyry, suffering from melancholy, was seized by a desire to commit suicide. Plotinus sensed this, and prescribed that Porphyry retire to Sicily (*Plot.* 11.11–19). Porphyry left for Lilybaeum, where he received the last nine treatises written by Plotinus.

Towards the end of August 268, the emperor Gallienus was assassinated, and Claudius, a soldier of Illyrian origin called "the Goth" because of his success against the peoples by that name, was chosen to succeed him. Whether or not Claudius was an accomplice in this assassination, we may assume that his accession to power had repercussions in the political class that provided support for Plotinus and formed his entourage. Amelius left Rome in the first year of the reign of Claudius (*Plot.* 3.41–2); that is, in 269. In 270, at the time of Plotinus' death, Amelius was in Apamea (*Plot.* 2.32–3). On the way, he brought copies of Plotinus' treatises to Longinus (*Plot.* 19.32), who was then in Phoenicia, probably in Tyre. Plotinus, gravely ill, also left Rome around the same time, at the end of a stay that lasted a full twenty-six years (*Plot.* 9.20–21).

Plotinus continued to write in his Campanian retreat, and in 269 sent five treatises to Porphyry, who was in Sicily at the time. Then, at the beginning of the second year of Claudius, that is, in 270, he sent him the last four treatises he was to write. This was shortly before his death, for Plotinus died in Campania, at the end of the second year of Claudius (*Plot.* 2.29–32), probably from the consequences of tuberculosis that affected his respiratory tract, if we can believe the description given by Porphyry (*Plot.* 2.5–15).[3]

The Porphyrian edition of the *Enneads*

The *Life of Plotinus*, which must have been preceded by a portrait of the master, is an introduction to the new edition that Porphyry had just carried out of the treatises he collected for the occasion into six Enneads, or groups of nine. We can assume that this classification was inspired by numerological considerations, which were quite natural in a Neopythagorean context that was highly sensitive to the symbolism of numbers. Two is the first even number and three the first odd number; six comes from the multiplication of two by three, and nine from the multiplication of three by itself. All this leads one to believe that Porphyry divided some treatises in such a way as to arrive at the number fifty-four. Evidence for this includes the fact that *Enn.* IV.4[28] begins in the middle of a phrase from *Enn.* IV.3[27], together with the brevity of several other treatises: *Enn.* IV.2[4], IV.9[8], V.2[11], III.9[13], II.2[14], I.9[16], II.6[17], V.7[18], IV.1[21], II.8[35], II.7[37], I.5[36], IV.6[41], III.3[48] and I.7[54]. In addition, *Enn.* III.9[13] presents a kind of free-for-all thematic mixed bag.

Porphyry claims to have begun his editorial work during Plotinus' lifetime:

> This, then, is my account of the life of Plotinus. He himself entrusted me with the arrangement and editing of his books, and I promised him in his life-time and gave undertakings to our other friends that I would carry the task. So first of all I did not think it right to leave the books in confusion in order of time as they were issued.
>
> (*Plot.* 24.1–6)

This is certainly also implied by the last lines of the *Life of Plotinus*. Yet this edition was not published until 300–301. Thirty years passed between Plotinus' death in 270 and Porphyry's systematic edition. We may assume that in the course of this period a chronological edition was in circulation. This is confirmed by Eusebius' division (*EP* XV.22 [des Places]) of *Enn.* IV.7[2], which differs from that of Porphyry, and the fact that Eusebius (*EP* XV.10) preserves a passage on the soul as *entelechy* that is not to be found in the manuscripts of the *Enneads*. In this context, it is likely that what is called the "edition of Eustochius" (on the basis of a scholium to *Enn.* IV.4[28].29.55) must have been the copy given by Plotinus on his deathbed to the doctor Eustochius, the only disciple who was with him at the time.[4]

Porphyry divided the six *Enneads* which he constituted from Plotinus' work into three volumes. In fact, these were three codices, books composed as quaternions, or sections containing four folios folded in two, resulting in eight folios and sixteen pages, bound together and attached to wooden covers. The *Enneads* occupied three of these "books", the first one including the *Life of Plotinus* by Porphyry as an introduction, which was itself probably preceded by the portrait of Plotinus made by Carterius.[5]

The first volume, which comprises treatises with a primarily moral theme, contains the first three *Enneads*. The second volume contains the fourth *Ennead*, which includes the treatises concerning the soul. Finally, the third volume comprises the treatises that deal with the One. In short, this classification, whose numerical combination must have delighted any Neopythagorean, proposes an anagogical reading order that, in a pedagogical perspective, enables one to rise from the sensible world towards the One, by way of the Soul and the Intellect.

After arranging the treatises in this way, Porphyry proceeds to explain the nature of his remaining work on the edition (*Plot.* 26.28–37). There seem to be traces of summaries and résumés of arguments (for instance, in the final chapter of *Enn.* III.1[3] and *Enn.* IV.3[27].5.15–19). In addition, there are some indications for the existence of Porphyrian commentaries on the *Enneads*, be they Porphyry's *Sentences* or the (pseudo-)*Theology* attributed to Aristotle, which are made up of paraphrases in Arabic, perhaps of Porphyrian origin,[6] of some parts of the last three *Enneads*.

THE QUALITY OF THE GREEK LANGUAGE

The translator of Plotinus who is familiar with Plato's language cannot help but be disappointed by the quality of the language of the *Enneads*. At the time of the Roman Empire, the language used by intellectuals, and particularly by philosophers, was Greek. This is why Plotinus taught and wrote in Greek, even though, as we have seen, his mother tongue was not, in all probability, Greek: in view of his origins, Plotinus must have been a Latin speaker.[7] This lack of familiarity with Greek language, added to his problems with pronunciation, must have made his speech produce a less than perfect impression. As far as writing is concerned, he did not try to form his letters carefully or separate his words; what is more, since his sight was poor, he did not reread what he had written at the first attempt. Most of these orthographical errors have, however, disappeared from the works that have come down to us, largely as a result of Porphyry's editorial work. In pointing out his work of correction, Porphyry shows himself to his best advantage. Nevertheless, it was a job well done, for the only real typographical mistake in the *Enneads* is found at *Enn.* IV.7[2].8[5].4, in a passage that appears only in Eusebius,[8] who must have possessed Plotinus' uncorrected manuscripts, which had belonged to Eustochius. The mistake testifies to the state of the text prior to the edition of the *Enneads*. Thus, the text that has come down to us is not faulty.

But Plotinus' language is not that of the purists either, such as the Atticists who claimed to follow the great authors, especially Plato and the orators. It borrows considerably from common language, teeming with elements from the Attic and Ionian dialects.[9] This can be explained by the fact that Plotinus' treatises reflect an oral instruction, in which discussions between the master and his audience were customary. As proof, one may cite the frequency of the particle ἤ, used as a marker of dialogue in Plotinus, which is different from its use in the traditional philosophical style after Aristotle. Here, Plotinus meets up in a sense with Plato's practice as an instrument of education;[10] he thereby finds himself a prisoner of a particular state of the language.

The grammar

In order to give an honest description of Plotinus' grammar, one must avoid appreciating Plotinus' language on the basis of modern grammars. The *Enneads* reflect a state of the Greek language that is dated (first half of the third century CE) and situated in space (the Rome of politicians and intellectuals who came from every corner of the Empire). Moreover, Plotinus did not, it seems, intend to create a literary oeuvre. First, let us consider a few particularities of his grammar.

Phonetics and morphology

As far as phonetics is concerned, there is very little that is bizarre, although there are some unexpected forms: ὑγίεια (*Enn.* VI.1[42].10.28), ὑγεία (*Enn.* III.2[47].8.40 [a later form, condemned by the Atticists]), τέλεος (*Enn.* I.8[51].5.7), τέλειος (*Enn.* I.8[51].4.29); instead of the usual οὐδεν, μηδέν, ἀεί, one finds οὐθεν (*Enn.* V.6[24].6.28, *Enn.* IV.4[28].13.14), μηθέν (*Enn.* II.5[25].1.14), αἰεί (*Enn.* IV.7[2].8³.10). Different forms co-exist for nouns and pronouns: the Attic declension υἱέος (*Enn.* V.8[31].13.11) is used instead of υἱοῦ; but the Attic second declension is maintained with ἵλεως, ἵλεων (*Enn.* I.4[46].12.8) and with νεῷ (*Enn.* V.1[10].6.12); hesitation between νεῷ and ναῷ (*Enn.* VI.9[9].11.19); νοῦς has as its nominative plural either νόες (*Enn.* VI.7[38].17.27) or νοῖ (*Enn.* VI.2[43].22.27); Attic crasis ἅτερος for ὁ ἕτερος (*Enn.* I.5[36].4.1).

The same holds true for morphology. For adjectives and adverbs, the comparatives and superlatives are usually fashioned in the traditional way; however, one finds a considerable number of original expressions,[11] some of which are pleonastic.[12] The use of cases is sometimes surprising.[13] Plotinus makes little use of the dual, except for δύο and ἄμφω.[14] As far as verbs are concerned, he uses either pure (Attic) forms or ordinary (common) forms,[15] verbs in -νυμι being the most irregular.[16] The ποῖ that is common in Hellenistic Greek is replaced by ποῦ.[17] Plotinus also has a notable tendency to substantivize other parts of speech, as is often the case in philosophical language.[18]

Syntax

One also finds a certain number of peculiarities on the level of syntax, especially as far as questions of agreement, articles, nouns, pronouns, negation and the verbal system are concerned. A masculine or feminine subject is often found with a neuter predicate.[19] In addition, subjects in the neuter plural often govern a singular verb, as is quite regular in classical Greek. Singular and plural may be found alongside one another in asyndeta, or groups of words without combining particles.[20] One notes a hesitation as far as the gender of the first principle is concerned: sometimes it is masculine, and sometimes neuter (*Enn.* V.1[10].6.40–53). Plotinus also speaks of the intellect[21] and of the soul[22] in the neuter. This variation indicates the difficulty encountered by a philosopher who uses terms that in ordinary language are attributed a gender that overlaps with sexual categories (masculine or feminine), whereas such differences are no longer in force in philosophical language. The use of the article with an interrogative or indefinite pronoun (for instance, τὸν μέν τινα νοῦν, *Enn.* II.9[33].1.26) is reminiscent of Aristotle;[23] one notes this particularly original formulation: "he must come ... to Beauty, and not only to some particular beauty" (οὐ τό τι καλὸν μόνον, *Enn.* I.3[20].1.33). From time to time, one finds a noun lacking an article with an attribute or an apposition with the article (*Enn.* IV.1[21].1.6; IV.3[27].2.22). The pronouns ἑαυτῶν or αὐτῶν are used as pronouns for the first or the second person plural (*Enn.* V.1[10].6.10; VI.2[43].19.23); likewise, αὐτῷ is used for the second person singular (*Enn.* I.6[1].9.17).

The use of moods and tenses in the verbal system often features peculiarities. The imperative sometimes has a concessive sense (*Enn.* VI.1[42].10.28). The future may feature several values, whether unreal or potential; it may also express the expectation of an event. Irreality and potentiality are manifested in the main clause by means of ἄν.[24] This ἄν may be repeated; nevertheless, one notes several errors concerning the use of the conjunction ἕως, indicating a future event with the subjunctive but without the necessary ἄν;[25] in contrast, ἵνα ἄν ᾖ is surprising (*Enn.* IV.4[28].4.17). The uses of ἵνα are often unusual; ἵνα may be construed with subjunctive and optative in the same phrase.[26] What is more, it often features a meaning that is not final ("in order that") but consecutive ("so that").[27]

The use of negation is also highly particular: one often finds μή where one would expect οὐ,[28] although οὐ should be reserved for objective negation. One often finds οὐδέ ... οὐδέ where one expects οὔτε ... οὔτε (*Enn.* III.4[15].5.9). In addition, Plotinus makes frequent use of participial constructions, even when one expects an inflected verb (*Enn.* III.7[45].1.7–16); likewise, one finds a genitive absolute (including one without a subject) whereas a simple genitive is expected (*Enn.* II.9[33].17.16). Tenses are sometimes combined in an odd way: "But behold Intellect, pure Intellect, and look upon it with concentrated gaze (ἀτενίσας, an aorist participle), not seeing it (μὴ δεδορκώς, perfect participle) with these bodily eyes of ours" (*Enn.* VI.2[43].8.7). The same holds true of cases (*Enn.* III.2[47].14.4).

Phrase construction

The difficulties are most appreciable at the level of the construction of phrases and their coordination. It seems clear that this is a consequence of the oral nature of the discourse Plotinus is writing down. Informed listeners may be content with allusive or even incomplete phrases. In addition, the coordination of these phrases seems to them automatic, as it were.

The verb "to be" (ἐστίν, εἰσίν, ὄντος, etc.) must often be supplied (*Enn.* V.9[5].10.18; I.1[53].5.17; III.9[13].1.11). The correlation between τὸ μέν and τὸ δέ is not always to be found.[29] One often does not find οὐ before οὐδέ (*Enn.* IV.7[2].3.6). It is not unusual for εἴτε to lack a consequent term (*Enn.* IV.8[6].2.5). The indefinite pronouns τις or τι are often lacking; what is worse, sometimes a word is omitted and the context provides no clue about what it is: "and admitted that the stars (ἀστέρες is lacking) contribute (διδόντες) a great deal corporally to the constituents of the body" (*Enn.* III.1[3].6.5–6). One often comes across phrases with a subject in the accusative and a verb in the infinitive, although no declarative verb is to be found in the vicinity.[30] One even finds an infinitival construction in a subordinate clause introduced by ὅτι: "because (ὅτι) it is bodily and a qualified body it is subject to every sort of change and has (ἴσχειν) every variety of desire" (*Enn.* IV.4[28].21.5–6). This led Kirchhoff to correct the reading of all the manuscripts in this instance, which have ἴσχειν, into ἴσχει. In some cases, a translator must supply δεῖ,[31] and in others ἀνάγκη.[32]

Plotinus makes frequent use of ellipses. Several phrases lack a predicate, which must be supplied with the help of the context: "Let us assume, then, that there is a mixture. But, if this is so, the worse element, the body will be improved and the other element, the soul, will be made worse. The body will be improved by sharing in life, the soul made worse by sharing [μεταλαβόν is missing] in death and unreason?" (*Enn.* I.1[53].4.1–4). A bit further on, we find this verbless phrase, which also lacks a predicate: "But if we assume it to be like [missing] the shape of an axe imposed [missing] on the iron" (*Enn.* I.1[53].4.20–21). Sometimes, even a word is lacking, which must be supplied: for instance, "It is called 'without quality' (ἄποιος) because it has in its own right none of the qualities (τῶν ποιοτήτων) which (ἃς) it is going to receive and which [αἵ is missing] are going to be in it as their substrate, but not in the sense that it has no nature at all" (*Enn.* I.8[51].10.2–5).

Word placement is sometimes erratic in Plotinus: "and many adequate (καὶ πολλοὶ καὶ ἱκανοὶ) demonstrations (λόγοι) have been set down (καταβέβληνται) which show it" (δεικνύντες τοῦτο, *Enn.* III.2[47].1.4–5); compare this with the word order in Plotinus: καὶ πολλοὶ καὶ ἱκανοὶ καταβέβληνται δεικνύντες τοῦτο λόγοι. This seems to be a trace of orality in the discussion. There is a large number of parentheses, indicating an aside remark within a response; a striking example is found at *Enn.* III.6[26].6.24–32.

The entire third chapter of *Enn.* VI.8[39] is constructed as an anacoluthon. The answer to the question raised[33] begins with two participles, ἀναγαγόντες (line 2) and θέμενοι (line 3), which is understood in the following part of the phrase (εἶτα ἐν λόγῳ ὀρθῷ), without any inflected verb being found in the vicinity.[34] Then, in order to explain ἐν λόγῳ ὀρθῷ, at line 4, a parenthesis opens that ends at line 21. The point is to identify will with reason, which is necessarily right, since it pertains to science, and because of this can give an account of itself. Indeed, if one cannot give an account of a representation that is a right opinion, how can one say that it depends on us?[35] Even more, this parenthesis contains within itself an anacoluthon (lines 10–13) that is a definition of representation in the strict sense,[36] a definition that is followed by a parenthesis (lines 13–16) explaining in what sense representations vary as a function of the body's humours.[37] After having accounted for the identification of will with right reason (lines 16–21),[38] the phrase begins again with ἀναγαγόντες, and ends at line 26[39] with φήσομεν παρεῖναι, coordinated with δώσομεν of line 23, which seems to indicate the oral nature of this phrase. Note that the most recent editors, Henry and Schwyzer, eliminate two members of the phrase as glosses: [εἶναι δώσομεν] (line 24) and [ὅσοι νῷ καὶ ὀρέξει τῇ κατὰ νοῦν ζῶσι] (lines 25–6). These glosses do not belong to Plotinus, but indicate the difficulty a reader of Greek mother tongue had in understanding this phrase. What can one say of the difficulties encountered by a modern translator!

Style

It is hard to speak of Plotinus' style in general, because it is necessary to make distinctions as far as the quality of writing is concerned. Those made by Porphyry have no other goal than to show himself in a favourable light. The treatises Plotinus wrote during Porphyry's stay at the school (263–8) are more extensive and powerful, in terms of style and argumentation, than those he found upon his arrival, while the final ones testify to the decline in the sick master's strength (*Plot.* 6.30–37). In contrast, the distinction made by Schwyzer between classes and lectures seems more relevant. Indeed, one notes that although all Plotinus' treatises are related to his teaching, some are better written than others, when discussion gives way to lengthy expositions; but one ought not to be too systematic in this area.

In any case, Plotinus was hard to understand, even to his contemporaries. We find two testimonies in favour of this impression in the *Life of Plotinus*. First, there is the letter in which Amelius defends Plotinus against the accusations of plagiarism of which he was the victim on the part of the philosophers of Athens: Plotinus plagiarizes Numenius of Apamea, robs the Christians, and is a big blowhard (πλατὺς φλήναφος, *Plot.* 17.16–24). Although Amelius considers that the Athenian philosophers react in this way to show "their glibness (εὐστομία) and readiness of speech (εὐγλωττία)", in the commentary Porphyry gives of this letter he admits some of these facts, and tries to explain them (*Plot.* 18.1–9).

In Porphyry's words, Longinus, "who was the greatest literary critic of the time", then residing at Apamea, did not understand him, and attributed his difficulties to the poor quality of the manuscripts in his possession (*Plot.* 19.20–26). Porphyry's comment is that if Longinus, influenced by ignorant people, considered Plotinus to be an unimportant author, it was because he was ignorant of Plotinus' usual way of expressing himself (*Plot.* 20.1–9). How can we explain this?

Longinus judged his contemporaries' writings by the standard of the epideictic speech, which enabled orators to display their virtuosity. This kind of speech had to follow the rules of rhetoric; that is, it had to present a complex but obvious structure, giving preference to counterbalancing and ample phrasing. As Porphyry testifies, however, Plotinus' works must be placed in relation to his lectures. They therefore maintained the qualities and defects of oral style. Plotinus is hard to read, because he expresses himself allusively, as is normal in front of a group of well-informed listeners. His writings are therefore characterized by particularly condensed expression: he loves concision and subtlety.[40] In addition, since his expositions are often interrupted by questions that raise objections or demand technical clarifications, his phrase is uneven, since it accumulates explanations and remarks layer upon layer, like a layer cake.

Vocabulary

In his choice of philosophical terminology, Plotinus was, as is quite natural, influenced by Plato, Aristotle and the Stoics. It should be noted, however, that he even takes over forms from the poets: ἀγλάισμα,[41] ἀριπρεπής,[42] προσεννέπειν,[43] which indicates the high proficiency in Greek literature. He also invents many new words by means of (a) an ἀ-privative ἄζων,[44] ἄογκος,[45] ἀσκέδαστος,[46] αὐλότης;[47] by adding a suffix: αἴνιξις,[48] δυνάμωσις,[49] φρόντισις;[50] or (b) a prefix: παμπρόσωπον,[51] ἐκοτάζω,[52] πολυπραγμόνησις.[53] He also creates a variety of compounds with αὐτό: αὐτογῆ,[54] αὐτοδέκας,[55] αὐτοουσία,[56] while he creatively ascribes a new meaning to others: ἄθεος,[57] ἐπίνοια,[58] ἐπικοσμέομαι.[59]

He also takes up the etymological speculations of the *Cratylus* and the Stoics. For the Stoics, it was the same λόγος that expresses itself in language and serves to produce nature. Such a conception was compatible with Cratylus' position in his namesake dialogue, since this position inflects etymology in the direction of an allegorical interpretation. Here are a few examples. In the soul, the discursive capacity (διάνοια) is acquired by means of the intellect (νοῦς) (*Enn.* V.3[49].6.20). Justice (Δίκην) thrones alongside Zeus (Δία, *Enn.* V.8[31].4.41–2). In the Intellect, all realities are filled with life (ζωῆς) and are boiling (ζεόντων).[60] In the heavens, the gods (θεῶν) always contemplate (θεῶνται, *Enn.*

V.8[31].3.28). The world (κόσμος), whose etymological origin is connected with order and therefore with beauty, is associated with the verb that signifies "to embellish" (ἐπικοσμεῖν, *Enn.* IV.3[27].14.1–5). We also find a play on words concerning eternity: "For 'eternity' is derived from 'always existing' (αἰὼν γὰρ ἀπὸ τοῦ ἀεὶ ὄντος, *Enn.* III.7[45].4.42–3)." The term is explained as follows: "but there, Plato says, is the archetype, which 'has the form of good', because it possesses the Good in the Forms (ἐκεῖ δὲ τὸ ἀρχέτυπον τὸ ἀγαθοειδές φησιν, ὅτι ἐν τοῖς εἴδεσι τὸ ἀγαθὸν ἔχει, *Enn.* VI.7[38].15.9–10)." The body (σῶμα) must have its salvation or its conservation (σῴζοιτο) assured, as in the *Cratylus*.[61] The names of the gods are also of etymological interest to him. He says of Pandora (Πανδώρα) that "Aphrodite gave her something and the Graces, and different gods gave her different gifts, and she took her name from the gift (δώρου) and all the givers (πάντων τῶν δεδωκότων)" (*Enn.* IV.3[27].14.8–10), while with regard to Apollo, he says: "This is why the Pythagoreans symbolically indicated it to each other by the name of Apollo, in negation of the multiple (ἀποφάσει τῶν πολλῶν)"(*Enn.* V.5[32].6.28). Plotinus recalls the etymological analysis of Kronos, whom he assimilates to the pure Intellect, proposed by Plato in the *Cratylus*: "and let him see pure (ἀκήρατον) Intellect presiding over them, and immense wisdom, and the true life of Kronos (Κρόνου), a god who is fullness (κόρου) and intellect (νοῦ)".[62] We also find explained the relation between Aphrodite (Ἀφροδίτη) and grace (ἁβρόν) (*Enn.* III.5[50].8.17); between Eros (Ἔρως) and vision (ὁράσεως) (*Enn.* III.5[50].3.15); and between Hestia (Ἑστία) and rest (ἔστη) (*Enn.* V.5[32].5.16–18). This interest in the interpretation of divine names must be associated with the practice of allegory. Plotinus associates his metaphysics and psychology with mythology, in which he finds the broad outlines of his thought expressed in an allusive way (Brisson 2004: 74–81).

In Ouranos, Kronos and Zeus, Plotinus sees a mythical transposition of the three main hypostases of his system (cf. P. Hadot 1981a). There can be no doubt that Ouranos represents the One, but this correspondence is more presupposed than it is developed (*Enn.* III.8[30].11.33–45). In contrast, the correspondence between Kronos and the Intellect is the subject of several developments in the first treatise of the fifth *Ennead* (see above). Most of the details describing the relations between Zeus and Kronos are taken into account in this interpretation. Thanks to a ruse thought up by Rhea, Zeus, the last of Kronos' sons, escapes his father, who has been swallowing his children. This detail is to be understood as follows: the Intellect, filled with Intelligibles, engenders the Soul as its last offspring, who is to transmit to the outside an image of its father and its siblings who have remained with their father.[63] As the hypostasis Soul, Zeus can be assimilated to the Demiurge, who sets the universe in order and guides it (*Enn.* IV.4[28].9.1–18). By extension, he can also be assimilated to the World Soul (*Enn.* IV.4[28].10.1–4, 10.4–29), and even to human souls (*Enn.* IV.3[27].12.6–19). We can continue, however, and descend even further along the scale of realities. In the last chapter of the treatise *On the Impassibility of the Incorporeals* (*Enn.* III.6[26].19.25–41), he, basing himself on the name "Mother" given to the receptacle in the *Timaeus* (51a4–5), assimilates matter to Cybele, considered as "Mother of the gods". Finally, for Plotinus, the "Great Mother", as sterile as the eunuchs that escort her, personifies inert matter, while ithyphallic Hermes represents the divinity that distributes the spermatic reasons (λόγοι σπερματικοί) that generate the sensible world.

There is one domain, however, in which myths intervene constantly: that of the soul in general. It is no accident that the example that best illustrates this is the myth of the birth of Eros, as told by Socrates in Plato's *Symposium*. Plotinus gives various interpretations of this famous myth. In his treatise *On Love* (*Enn.* III.2[47]), almost entirely devoted to the myth of the birth of Eros, Plotinus begins by recording the various versions Plato gives of the genealogy of Eros. In the *Phaedrus* (242d–e), Eros is the son of Aphrodite; but in the *Symposium* (203c), he is born of Poros and Penia. This duality can be explained by the fact that there are two Aphrodites (*Smp.* 180d–e). One is the celestial Aphrodite, daughter of Ouranos or Kronos; she is therefore the hypostasis Soul, who, by uniting with Kronos in uninterrupted contemplation, gives birth to Eros; that is, the higher Soul (*Enn.* III.5[50].2). The other Aphrodite, born of Zeus and Dione, embodies the soul of the sensible world. She engenders a second Eros, who is her vision. Within the world, this Eros presides over marriages and helps well-disposed souls to recollect the Intelligibles (*Enn.* III.5[50].3). Finally, since each individual soul, even that of animals, is an Aphrodite, it engenders its particular Eros, which corresponds to its nature and merits. Hence, there are three kinds of Eros: a universal Eros, a cosmic Eros, a plurality of individual Erotes. The first is a god, whereas the two others are demons (*Enn.* III.5[50].4). Finally, Plotinus associates another myth with that of the birth of Eros: the myth of the loves of Eros and Psyche. Psyche, of course, is the soul, and her intimacy with Eros is a sign that the love of the One-Good is connatural to her (*Enn.* VI.9[9].9.28–34).

Many other examples could be given.

Figures

If Porphyry insists on the fact that Plotinus "was completely free from the staginess and windy rant of the professional speech-writer" (τῷ πάσης σοφιστικῆς αὐτὸν σκηνῆς καθαρεύειν καὶ τύφου, *Plot.* 18.5–6), it is probably, as Bréhier (1924: xxvi–xxviii) thought, in order to distinguish him from the orators of his time, and from the philosophers who sought an elevated style. This does not prevent Plotinus from being familiar with and using a few rhetorical tropes.

Anaphora is a figure of style consisting in repeating a word or even a syntagma in verses, phrases, or sets of phrases or verses. Here are a few examples: "able in this way to pray alone to him [the One] alone" (μόνους πρὸς μόνον, *Enn.* V.1[10].6.11 [see also *Enn.* I.6[1].5.57; VI.9[9].11.51; VI.7[38].34.7–8]); "Now when light of this kind [the light of the stars] stays on high, in the place in which it is set, pure in the purest region (καθαροῦ ἐν καθαρωτάτῳ), what kind of outflow could there possibly be from it?" (*Enn.* II.1[40].8.1–2); "this is what it thinks, a dim thing dimly and a dark thing darkly (νοεῖ ἀμυδρῶς ἀμυδρὸν καὶ σκοτεινῶς σκοτεινόν), and it thinks without thinking (καὶ νοεῖ οὐ νοοῦσα)" (*Enn.* II.4[12].10.30–31). This stylistic figure is found rather often in Plotinus, who uses it to highlight terms and hence ideas.

One finds many alliterations: "The soul of the All [that is, its lowest part] would be like the soul in a great growing plant, which directs the plant without effort or noise (ἀφόνως … καὶ ἀψόνως)" (*Enn.* IV.3[27].4.27).[64] Another example: "for since the soul is one nature in many powers, sometimes the whole of it is carried along with the best of itself and of real being, sometimes the worse part is dragged down (καθελκυσθὲν) and drags (συνεφελκύσασθαι) the middle with it; for it is not lawful for it to drag down (καθελκύσαι) the whole" (*Enn.* II.9[33].2.6–9).

Anaphora may even be discerned in this second example. It should be noted that alliteration was a very characteristic trope for Gorgias and the Sophists. Plotinus does not hesitate to make use of plays on words: "We must understand, too, from this that this nature is time, the extent of life of this kind which goes forward in even and uniform changes progressing quietly (ἐν μεταβολαῖς προιὸν ὁμαλαῖς τε καὶ ὁμοιαῖς ἀψοφητὶ προιούσαις), and which possesses continuity and activity" (*Enn.* III.7[45].12.1–3).

Plotinus makes frequent use of antithesis, especially in the form of oxymorons, which aim at bringing together two terms (a noun and an adjective), which their meaning should keep separate, in a formulation that seems to be contradictory. This is the only way to conceive what is unlimited: "One will conceive it as the opposites and at the same time not the opposites" (τὰ ἐναντία ἅμα καὶ οὐ τὰ ἐναντία, *Enn.* VI.6[34].3.28). The Soul is compared to a circle whose centre is the Intellect: "For the soul of this kind is a noble thing, like a circle fitting itself round its centre, the first expansion after the center, an unextended extension" (διάστημα ἀδιάστατον, *Enn.* IV.4[28].16.22); the Soul is also compared to such a circle in the preceding treatise (*Enn.* IV.3[27].17.12); and for the oxymoron, see *Enn.* V.8[31].9.20 and *Enn.* VI.5[23].8.32. Another beautiful example in support of the Soul's "unextended extension" is found in ἀσχημάτιστα σχήματα, the "unfigured figures" of intelligible numbers (*Enn.* VI.6[34].17.25–6).

Several times, Plotinus makes use of correction and rectification. *Enn.* V.2[11], *On the Generation and Rank of Things that Come After the First*, aspires to be a commentary of a phrase from Plato's *Parmenides*, a phrase taken out of context which Plotinus wants to make say something quite different from Plato. The beginning of the treatise is also a good example of the use of correction and rectification:

> The One is all things and not a single one of them (Plato, *Prm.* 160b2–3); it is the principle of all things, not all things (ἀρχὴ γὰρ πάντων, οὐ πάντα, ἀλλ᾽ ἐκείνως πάντα), but all things have that other kind of transcendent existence; for in a way they do occur in the One (ἐκεῖ γὰρ οἷον ἐνέδραμε); or rather they are not there yet, but they will be (μᾶλλον δὲ οὔ πω ἐστίν, ἀλλ᾽ ἔσται). (*Enn.* V.2[11].1.1–3)

In *Enn.* VI.7[38], Plotinus takes up the same idea, but he situates himself in another viewpoint: "If then all the other things exist before it, it would already be affected by them; but if they do not, then this Intellect generated them all (εἰ δὲ μὴ ἔστιν, οὗτος τὰ πάντα ἐγέννα), or rather was them all (μᾶλλον δὲ τὰ πάντα ἦν)" (*Enn.* VI.7[38].13.27–8).

Use is also made of paraenesis (exhortation) and prosopopoeia (representation of a voiceless being as speaking or acting). When he launches into an exhortation, Plotinus uses the second person singular form. We find two examples in the treatises *On Providence*. One of them is classic:

> Then, again, all these kinds must be brought together under the one genus "living creature"; then also the things which are not living creatures must be classed by their kinds, and then included in the one genus "non-living"; then both together, if you like (εἰ βούλει), must be included in being; and then in that which makes being possible. (*Enn.* III.3[48].1.15–19)

The other leads to a prosopopoeia: "Since, then, what has come into being is the whole universe, if you contemplate this, you might hear (τάχα ἂν ἀκούσαις) it say" (*Enn.*

III.2[47].3.19–20). There then follows the speech given by the world, which goes on for more than twenty lines in Henry and Schwyzer's edition. At *Enn.* III.8[30].4.3–14, it is Nature who explains how she fashions things by contemplating. Similar prosopopoeias are found in other treatises. The Intellect speaks at *Enn.* V.5[32].7.35; the discursive part of the Soul (*Enn.* V.3[49].3.4); while in chapter 13.24, it is the Intellect. What is more, Plotinus often uses prosopopoeia as a counter-example, justifying on several occasions the impossibility for such and such a reality to pronounce anything at all, such as sensation (*Enn.* VI.4[22].6.15), time (*Enn.* III.7[45].12.38) or matter (*Enn.* III.6[26].15.28), or else even to emphasize the uselessness for a star to express itself in words (*Enn.* IV.4[28].7.14).

Images: comparisons and metaphors

In rhetoric, "image" is a generic term that includes comparisons and metaphors. The former compares two elements that contain a common characteristic or an analogy between that which is compared and that to which it is compared by means of a comparative word or phrase: "as", "like", "similar to", "it seems" and so on. A metaphor is a comparison without a comparative term, the most condensed form of an image. This direct assimilation of that which is compared and that to which it is compared may create images that are surprisingly dense. It is often hard, however, to distinguish between these two kinds of figure. Plotinus constantly uses images in his exposition and sometimes even repeats the same image or the same metaphor within the same treatise (Bréhier 1955).

Here, based on the work of Ferwerda (1965), is an incomplete inventory of the images Plotinus uses in the *Enneads*.

1. Mathematical figures: point, line, circle and sphere. The Intellect is around the One like a circle of which it is the centre (*Enn.* I.7[54].1.24); the Soul, as we have seen, is a sphere whose centre is the Intellect (see above p. 137). Some images refer to the sensible world, resembling a sphere, which the soul penetrates from all sides (*Enn.* V.8[31].9.4 (a thought experiment)).
2. Springs and water; river water, spring water. All the rest flows forth, as from a spring, from that which is its principle (*Enn.* III.8[30].10.5): One, Intellect, Soul.
3. Light (Beierwaltes 1961) essentially represents the intelligible, which permeates everything, and which, when it becomes exhausted, becomes the darkness in which matter consists (*Enn.* IV.3[27].9.20–27). Into this darkness constituted by matter, the lower part of the World Soul deposits the reasons that correspond to the Forms in the soul, in order to produce bodies. The latter can thus be considered shadows, since a shadow is a parcel of darkness endowed with a form. The light of the sun and stars is also involved when other subjects are dealt with, particularly colour.
4. Fire and heat are associated with the vegetative soul. This is why when death occurs, a human being's higher soul, associated with sunlight, immediately leaves the organic body, in which the vegetative soul, ensuring its organic functions, persists for a certain time, as is shown by the growth of hair and nails (*Enn.* IV.4[28].29.3–7); its action is therefore associated with the heat produced by sunlight.
5. Walking, motion and paths are most often associated with the soul's motions as it methodically acquires knowledge, making its way towards virtue, or rises back up towards its principle.[65]

6. Family and amorous relations: father, mother, seed, love and union are associated with procession from a principle considered as the father.[66] Conversion is associated with amorous union with the principle (*Enn.* VI.7[38].26.23), and all souls are sisters (*Enn.* II.9[33].18.16).
7. Nature: the lowest part of the World Soul is compared to the life that animates plants.[67] Several animals are mentioned, particularly birds with their feathers and wings, associated with the soul;[68] horses, associated with the parts of soul, as in the *Phaedrus*; and worms, bugs and snakes. The same holds true for mud and filth, which are associated with impurity, and for the body.[69]
8. The parts and activities of the human body, which is a miniature world, are naturally associated with those of the body of the world. The sense of touch is associated with intuition, the eye and vision with the intellect's contemplation of the intelligible. In contrast, sleep and dreams are related to sense knowledge.[70]
9. Trades and techniques are often called into service: the action of the lower part of the soul is described with the features of a farmer; the intellect and discursive thought are compared to a judge and a legislator; the soul is the pilot of the world's body, which is described as a ship.[71] Matter is like the bitter deposit left by wine, while its size varies like that of a piece of clothing, embellishing it without modifying it; since Plato and Aristotle, wax and seals serve to describe the effect of sense impressions on the soul.[72]
10. Reason (λόγος) governs the World Soul and must govern ours, as in a city that is not given over to the whims of corporations or a tumultuous assembly.[73] Life in this world is assimilated to a wrestling match or sports competition; the relations between unity and multiplicity are often referred to an army led by a general.[74] Order in the universe and in human beings is compared to a person who rules a household, whose beauty he ensures; the parts of the soul are assimilated to those of science, which remains one despite the diversity of its species. The theatre and actors are often called upon. The same holds true of dance and chorus, and of the music evoking the course of the heavenly bodies. Finally, the Intellect, and especially the One, are described within a religious context.[75]

Metaphor is an essential figure for Plotinus, for he is led to describe the incorporeals with a language intended to describe the world of bodies: One, Intellect–Intelligible, Soul, matter. The power and beauty of Being charm all the things that depend on it.[76] The intelligible is known in the mode of the sensible, for it is possible to rise back up from the sensible towards the intelligible.[77] Reasonings are already in extension and motion. Being stimulates, strikes and produces in the soul a representation concerning being. Even when "plunged" within the sensible, the Intellect remains autarchic.[78] The soul leans forward, manifests audacity, and springs forth out of the all.[79] When fatigued, the soul becomes heavy, and sometimes it experiences the pains of childbirth.[80] The One accords its favours to that which comes after it.[81] It manifests will.[82] The power contained in the One enables it to give even what it does not have.[83] The Intellect becomes heavy as it becomes multiple, and the soul advances.[84] The Intellect sees the Good, goes back on its tracks, hides itself, and is full of strength.[85] God is known by the imprint of himself he leaves behind.[86] The life of the sage is not "scattered" in sensation.[87] We engender time by thought.[88] Geometers draw figures while contemplating.[89] What is sensible slides over matter, and matter is thrown out of being.[90]

In short, Plotinus has a good knowledge of rhetoric, of which he makes broad use. One can even wonder whether Porphyry's insistence in wishing to separate his teacher from rhetoric[91] represents a tendency of the time, against which he wants to react, given that he was a student of Longinus, author of a treatise on rhetoric. Philo of Alexandria already protested against a possible confusion between a philosophical treatise and a speech intended to display one's rhetorical abilities.[92] Epictetus often reproaches his students for the rhetorical nature of their interventions.[93] Perhaps Plotinus is also following them. In any case, although the level of his language is quite mediocre on a strictly grammatical and basic syntactic level, Plotinus reveals himself as a virtuoso when he undertakes to express himself in a colourful way: his inventiveness on the level of images and metaphors is remarkable. He surprises the reader, inspiring emotion and hence adherence. This is probably what earned him fame: his success in making Platonic rationalism moving.

ARGUMENTATION

The first difficulty encountered by whoever seeks to define argumentation in Plotinus resides in the impression of disorder that reigns in most of Plotinus' shorter treatises that take up canonical scholastic themes, to the rhythm of an open discussion between the master and his disciples. This impression is attenuated in the treatises or groups of treatises that deal with questions of major importance, for instance: *Enn.* III.6[26], *On the Impassibility of the Incorporeals*; *Enn.* IV.3–4[27–8], *On Difficulties Concerning the Soul*; *Enn.* VI.1–3[42–4], *On the Kinds of Being*; *Enn.* VI.6[34], *On Numbers*; *Enn.* VI.7[38], *How the Multiplicity of the Ideas Became Established, and on the Good*; *Enn.* VI.8[39], *On the Voluntary and on the Will of the One*, and perhaps also *Enn.* III.7[45], *On Eternity and Time* and *Enn.* V.3[40], *On the Knowing Hypostases and on What is Beyond*. Even here, difficulties subsist: *Enn.* III.6[26] is divided into two parts: chapters 1–5 deal with the soul's impassibility, while chapters 6–13 are on matter. *Enn.* VI.7[38], for its part, deals with three themes: chapters 1–15 examine the relations between the intelligible and the sensible world; chapters 16–35 focus on the relations between the One and the Intellect; and chapters 36–42 deal with the question of whether the supreme hypostasis thinks. One conclusion thus becomes inescapable: one never finds a systematic exposition of a major question in Plotinus.

We can therefore understand Plotinus' use of argumentation. Argumentation must be distinguished from both demonstration and proof. Demonstration starts out from arbitrary axioms, and, by applying rules that are known to all, seeks to reach a conclusion. To demonstrate is to establish the truth of a proposition by "logical" means. Proof, for its part, seeks to establish a concrete, empirical fact, by means of an experimental verification in physics, or a direct or indirect testimony in a judicial context. To argue, finally, is to exhort a person to do something, by showing that the consequences of such an action entail some good, particularly ethical. Strictly speaking, there is no proof in Plotinus. Although some of the rules of demonstration are known to him, he does not really have recourse to demonstration. He therefore restricts himself to argumentation.

The use of τεκμήριον and τεκμαίρεσθαι is rarely found in Plotinus, and always in a context involving a verification in the sensible. People who weep and moan provide a proof of the existence of evil in the world; the fact that certain functions persist in a corpse – the growth of hair and nails, for instance – is the proof that the lower part of the soul is active in them.[94] The fact that the memory of pleasant things is not itself pleasant provides the proof that one must distinguish between memory and desire; the fact that there is an inner beauty shows that beauty is concerned with form, not with mass.[95] Astrology lacks proof, whereas the spectacle of the universe is proof that order reigns within it.[96] There is no proof that memory belongs to the union of the soul and body.[97]

As far as demonstration is concerned, Plotinus is aware of the procedures set forth by Plato, Aristotle and the Stoics. In *Enn.* I.3[20], *On Dialectic*, he rapidly evokes logic, which is interested only in propositions and syllogisms: only part of it is useful (*Enn.* I.3[20].4.19–24), but it remains at the level of language. In *Enn.* VI.1–VI.3[42–4], *On the Kinds of Being*, he provides a lengthy treatment of the Aristotelian and Stoic categories, only to reduce them to the sensible world, since the only real "categories" that concern the intelligible are the five Great Kinds of the *Sophist*. In the field of methodology, moreover, Plotinus maintains only the Platonic dialectic. Yet he shows originality in this domain as well; he does, of course, evoke the methods of collection and division used in Plato's *Statesman* and *Sophist*, which serve to distinguish between the various kinds (*Enn.* I.3[20].4.10–14), but these methods lose the heuristic orientation they had in these two dialogues, to become, in agreement with a certain interpretation of *Republic* VI, the *Phaedrus* and the *Symposium*, a path for rising back up to the Intelligible, and thence as far as the One (*Enn.* I.3[20].4.14–19).

Most often, Plotinus makes use of argumentation, but in a particular sense. His goal is to bring the reader (as he had done for his listening audience) to subscribe to the Platonic position in every area. The aim was no longer to display originality, but to point out a truth already set forth by Plato, by comparing it to the competing positions of Aristotle, the Stoics, and sometimes even of Epicurus and the Sceptics. One must admit, however, that Plotinus had only an indirect relation to Plato and Aristotle, for even if he read them directly, he did so through the interpretative filter of the interpreters who preceded him. Yet we must go further. For Plotinus, leading his readers to adhere to Platonic thought features an ethical dimension. Such an adherence implies a way of life that must lead to the goal set for all Platonists: that is, assimilation to the divinity, understood as contemplation of the intelligible, and hence to happiness. This project is reflected in the reading order Porphyry proposed in his classification of the *Enneads*.

In fact, the interpretation of Plato proposed by Plotinus cannot be reduced to an academic exercise. Its goal is to introduce the reader to a way of life, as was the case for the Epicureans and the Stoics. The argumentation Plotinus deploys seeks to demonstrate the superiority of this way of life over that which was proposed by other philosophers, and even by the Christians, who were on the way to becoming a social majority. Above all, dialectic and knowledge constitute the highest degree of virtue, as is emphasized in the last chapter of *Enn.* I.3[20], *On Dialectic*, which immediately follows the treatise *On the Virtues*: "Dialectic (διαλεκτική) and theoretical wisdom (σοφία) provide everything for practical wisdom (φρονήσει) to use, in a universal and immaterial form" (*Enn.* I.3[20].6.12–14). There can be no question here of reducing Plotinus to the status of a preacher who uses the instruments of rhetoric to persuade his audience, but it must be admitted that he turns even logic and dialectic into instruments in the service of a happy life, oriented by a knowledge that enables the soul to return towards its principle. We can therefore understand why Neoplatonism very quickly became the only philosophical adversary to Christianity.

To understand the thought of Plotinus, it must be re-situated within its time, when philosophy had become a way of life. The regularity and permanence one had to find in the sensible world in order to be able to talk about it, think about it, and act upon it, were ensured by the activity of the Soul, which derived from the Intellect, which emanated from the One. Plotinus provided a coherent vision of this system, with a view not only to showing his superiority over other philosophical systems and Christianity, but to ensuring for each human being who lived in conformity with that world-vision a happiness consisting in becoming similar to the divinity; that is, in becoming perfect in so far as was possible. Plotinus' style and argumentation must be placed within this context, lest they be misunderstood. By his qualities as an author, Plotinus made attractive and engaging the original interpretation of Plato that he developed throughout his work.

ACKNOWLEDGEMENT

I am most grateful to Michael Chase who translated this chapter in English and who made many valuable comments on my interpretations.

NOTES

1. Eunapius, *Vit. Soph.* III.1.1–2, p. 5.18–20 [Giangrande]; Pseudo-Elias, *in Isag.* 27.3 [Westerink]; David, *in Porph.* 91.23–6 [Busse]; *Suda* Π 1811, t. IV, p. 151, 23 [Adler].
2. For instance, *Enn.* II.3[52]. Hereinafter translation of the *Enneads* is according to Armstrong (1966–88), with slight modifications.
3. On this controversial diagnosis, see Grmek (1992).
4. Goulet Cazé (1982, 1992) in answer to Brisson (1992). See also D'Ancona (2007).
5. For other examples of portraits of an author in the beginning of an edition, see Martial, *Epigrams* IX.47, XIV.186; Galen, III, p. 776 [Kühn].
6. For an exposition of views on this subject, see *DPA* (1989: I.241–90).
7. We know nothing about Plotinus' family, but the comparative frequency of the names *Plotinus* and *Plotina* in Latin seems to point in this direction.
8. Porphyry reads ψυχικοῦ instead of φυσικοῦ in Eusebius: see Henry (1938: 120).
9. The sections of this work are based on Schwyzer (1951, esp. 512–30; 1978: 321–3).
10. The translation of Plotinus' complete works under the direction of Brisson & Pradeau (2002–10) insisted strongly on this point.
11. Ἀγαθοειδέστερον (*Enn.* VI.7[38].22.33); ἀγαπητότατον (*Enn.* VI.7[38].30.30); αἰτιώτατον (*Enn.* VI.8[39].18.38); ἀθροωτέραις (*Enn.* III.7[45].1.4); ἀνθρωπινωτέροις (*Enn.* II.9[33].9.9).
12. Such as μᾶλλον αὐταρκέστερον (*Enn.* III.5[50].1.47); μᾶλλον ἀπαθέστερον (*Enn.* III.6[26].9.19).
13. In "about her (= Aphrodite), one can ascertain that she is a god and not a daemon" (ἣν δὴ καὶ θεόν … οὐ δαίμονα, *Enn.* III.5[50].2.25), we have the relative in the feminine gender, although θεόν remains masculine; "there are, in the world, many Aphrodites, which have come into being in it as daemons" (καὶ Ἀφροδίτας ἐν τῷ ὅλῳ πολλάς, δαίμονας ἐν αὐτῷ γενομένας, *Enn.* III.5[50].4.18–19). Here the phrase γενομένας δαίμονας is feminine, although only a masculine form is known of the noun; likewise, μάγος is feminine (*Enn.* I.6[1].8.18) although only masculine forms are known.
14. But one finds ἀνθρώπους δύο (*Enn.* VI.6[34].16.16) and δύο φιλοῦντας (*Enn.* II.3[52].4.15).
15. For instance, διατιθεῖσι instead of διατιθέασι (*Enn.* VI.1[42].12.29).
16. For instance, ἐδείκνυον (*Enn.* V.1[10].9.32) and μιγνύων (*Enn.* IV.3[27].7.10).
17. *Enn.* V.1[10].4.12; V.2[11].2.12; V.3[49].10.19; V.5[32].19.20.
18. Τὸ εὖ (*Enn.* I.4[46].2.29); τὸ ὧδε καὶ ὧδε (*Enn.* VI.4[22].13.4).

19. For instance, ψυχὴ δὲ νῷ καλόν (*Enn.* I.6[1].6.27); οὐχ ὁρατὸν γῆ (*Enn.* II.1[40].6.21).
20. For instance, ἓν πάντα (*Enn.* V.3[49].15.23); ἕκαστα τὰ ἄλλα (*Enn.* VI.8[31].13.4).
21. For instance, τὸ (= τὸ ἀγαθόν) δ᾽ ἐστίν ἀν ἐνδεές ... δοὺς ἐξ αὐτοῦ νοῦν (*Enn.* I.8[51].2.4–6); πρὸς αὐτὸ (= the Intellect, neuter) βλέπει ... ζωῆς γὰρ αἴτιος (= the Intellect, masculine) (*Enn.* I.6[1].7.11).
22. At *Enn.* IV.7[2].13, ἡ ψυχή is spoken of first in the neuter (lines 4–8), then as feminine (lines 9–20).
23. See τὸ τὶ μέγεθος (Aristotle, *Pol.* III.12.1283a4).
24. One must be very cautious with the use of ἄν, many occurrences of which must have been added by scribes in order to normalize the text.
25. For example, *Enn.* I.3[20].5.4; I.8[51].13.24; II.4[12].5.5; III.8[30].10.22.
26. *Enn.* I.8[51].15.26; II.1[40].7.3; III.6[26].14.33.
27. *Enn.* VI.7[38].10.5; VI.8[39].17.26.
28. *Enn.* V.8[31].3.10; IV.7[2].83.24; III.2[47].12.4; III.5[50].15.10.
29. *Enn.* IV.3[27].4.3; IV.9[8].4.10; VI.1[42].7.31.
30. *Enn.* I.4[46].14.12; II.1[40].3.14.
31. *Enn.* I.4[46].14.12; II.1[40].3.14; II.9[33].5.1; III.6[26].2.62; III.7[45].9.33; IV.4[28].1.22; V.8[31].6.17; VI.7[38].35.20.
32. *Enn.* I.1[53].6.5; III.8[30].9.37.
33. *Enn.* VI.8[39].3.1–2: "We must therefore enquire about these matters: for [in doing so] we are already also coming near to our subject of discourse, the gods."
34. *Enn.* VI.8[39].3.2–4: "Well then, we traced back what is in our power to will, and then placed this in the context of discourse, and then of correct discourse."
35. *Enn.* VI.8[39].3.4–10: "but perhaps we ought to add to 'correct' that it belongs to rational knowledge; for if someone had a right opinion and acted on it he would not indisputably have the power of self-determination if he acted, without knowing why his opinion was right, but led to his duty by chance or some representation; since when we say that representation is not in our power, how can we put those who act by it in the class of the self-determined?"
36. *Enn.* VI.8[39].3.10–12: "But we do say this about the representation which one can properly call representation, that which is roused by the experiences of the body."
37. *Enn.* VI.8[39].3.12–16: "(for being empty, or again full, of food and drink in a way gives the representations shape, and one who is full of semen has different representations, and so it is according to the qualities of the bodily fluids)".
38. *Enn.* VI.8[39].3.16–21: "and we shall not class those who are active according to representations of this kind among those whose principle of action is self-determined; therefore, we shall not grant to bad men, who do most things according to these, either having something in their power or voluntary action, but we shall grant voluntary action to one whose doings depend on the activities of Intellect and who is free from bodily affections".
39. *Enn.* VI.8[39].3.21–6: "We trace back what is in our power to the noblest principle, the activity of Intellect, and shall grant that the premises of action derived from this are [εἶναι has been transposed from the gloss at line 24] truly free, and that the desires roused by thinking are not voluntary, and we shall say that the gods who live in this way have self-determinations."
40. As Macrobius writes in *Somn. Scip.* 2.12.7 [Willis]: "Plotinus magis quam quisquam verborum parcus."
41. *Enn.* III.5[50].9.9 from Aeschylus, *A.* 1312.
42. *Enn.* II.3[52].8.7 from Homer *Il.* VIII.556, also cited in the Oracle of Apollo, *Plot.* 22.51.
43. *Enn.* II.9[33].18.18 from Aeschylus, *A.* 242 and Euripides, *Hipp.* 793, *Tr.* 50, *Or.* 428.
44. *Enn.* III.4[15].1.7; III.6[26].6.26: "being lifeless".
45. *Enn.* VI.1[42].26.29; VI.4[22].5.14; VI.6[34].8.9: "without mass".
46. *Enn.* VI.5[23].8.36: "not being scattered".
47. *Enn.* I.2[19].7.5: "immateriality".
48. *Enn.* VI.8[39].19.14: "speaking with a hidden meaning".
49. *Enn.* IV.6[41].3.30: "empowering".
50. *Enn.* IV.3[27].4.25: "care".
51. *Enn.* VI.7[38].15.26: "all faces".
52. *Enn.* II.7[37].2.7: "exude".
53. *Enn.* VI.3[44].23.4: "curiosity".
54. *Enn.* VI.7[38].11.35: "the earth as such".

55. *Enn.* VI.6[34].5.39–40 & 14.49: "the decad as such".
56. *Enn.* VI.8[39].12.8 & 14: "being as such".
57. *Enn.* V.3[49].17.33: "without seeing".
58. *Enn.* VI.6[34].6.36: "afterthought".
59. *Enn.* IV.3[27].14.2: "further set in order".
60. *Enn.* VI.7[38].12.23; see Aristotle, *de An.* 1.2.405b28.
61. *Enn.* IV.4[28].22.30–31; see Plato, *Cra.* 400c7.
62. *Enn.* V.1[10].4.8–10; see Plato, *Cra.* 396b6–7.
63. *Enn.* V.1[10].7.35–6; cf. also *Enn.* V.5[32].3.20–24.
64. Note, moreover, the magnificent image that assimilates the world, which is a living being, to a tree containing the soul that makes it live (*Enn.* IV.3[27].4.26–31; for another occurrence of this image, see *Enn.* III.3[48].7.10–16).
65. Knowledge, *Enn.* I.3[20].3.3; virtue, *Enn.* VI.9[9].4.14–15; rises back up, *Enn.* I.6[1].8.22.
66. *Enn.* V.9[5].4.9–11; VI.1[10].1.1.
67. *Enn.* IV.3[27].4.26, 8.45, 13.16; VI.7[38].22.15; IV.4[28].1.29, 11.11, 32.31, 40.13.
68. All these passages refer to *Phdr.* 246c: *Enn.* I.3[20].3.2; I.8[51].14.20; V.3[49].4.13; II.9[33].4.1; III.3[27].7.19; IV.8[6].1.37; VI.9[9].9.24.
69. Horses, *Enn.* II.3[52].13.15–16; III.3[48].1.12; worms, bugs and snakes, *Enn.* IV.4[28].4.26–33; mud and filth, *Enn.* I.6[1].5.42–4; body, *Enn.* VI.7[38].31.26.
70. Body of the world, *Enn.* III.2[47].3.14, 3.38, 7.6, 7.37; III.3[48].5.3, 6.4, 6.34; touch, *Enn.* II.1[40].6.9; eye and vision, *Enn.* I.8[51].5.19; II.4[12].5.9; IV.4[28].5.9, etc; sleep and dreams, *Enn.* III.6[26].5, 10, 18, 25, 6.68, 7.41; V.5[32].11.19.
71. Farmer, *Enn.* II.3[52].16.33; II.4[12].16.13; IV.3[27].4.31; judge, *Enn.* VI.4[22].6.9; legislator, *Enn.* V.9[5].5.28; ship, *Enn.* III.4[15].6.48; IV.3[27].17.23, 21.6.
72. Wine, *Enn.* II.3[52].17.24; clothing, *Enn.* III.6[26].18.20; embellishing, *Enn.* III.6[26].11.20.
73. World Soul, *Enn.* IV.4[28].39.12; our soul, *Enn.* II.9[33].7.5; whims, *Enn.* IV.4[28].17.23; VI.4[22].15.23.
74. Wrestling match, *Enn.* III.2[47].5.4; IV.3[27].32.27; army, *Enn.* II.3[52].13.29; III.3[48].2.4.
75. Person who rules a household, *Enn.* I.2[19].1.42; I.6[1].2.25, 3.6; II.9[33].18.3; V.5[32].4.31; theatre, *Enn.* III.2[47].11.13, 15.21, 33, 43, 16.8, 35, 17.18, 35, 18.22; dance and chorus, *Enn.* IV.4[28].8.46, 33.6, 34.28, 35.13; Intellect and the One, *Enn.* I.6[1].7.6, 19; 8.2; V.3[49].14.9; V.5[32].11.12; VI.9[9].11.13, 18, 30.
76. *Enn.* VI.6[34].18.48.
77. The sensible, *Enn.* I.4[46].10.14; the intelligible, *Enn.* II.9[33].16.33–56.
78. Reasonings, *Enn.* VI.9[9].5.12; Being, *Enn.* VI.6[34].12.5; Intellect, *Enn.* VI.7[38].9.44.
79. Leans forward, *Enn.* IV.4[28].3.1–3; III.3[27].15.1; audacity, *Enn.* V.1[10].1.4; springs forth, *Enn.* VI.4[22].16.29.
80. Fatigued, *Enn.* IV.8[6].4.10–12; heavy, *Enn.* IV.3[27].15.6; childbirth, *Enn.* IV.3[27].13.31.
81. *Enn.* V.3[49].15.24.
82. *Enn.* VI.8[39].13.38.
83. *Enn.* VI.7[38].15.20.
84. Multiple, *Enn.* III.8[30].8.33; advances, *Enn.* VI.9[9].3.4.
85. Sees, *Enn.* VI.7[38].41.33–5; tracks, *Enn.* III.8[30].9.29; hides, *Enn.* V.5[32].7.31–3; strength, *Enn.* VI.2[43].21.8.
86. *Enn.* V.8[31].11.15.
87. *Enn.* I.4[46].10.32.
88. *Enn.* III.7[45].11.7.
89. *Enn.* III.8[30].4.9.
90. What is sensible, *Enn.* III.6[26].14.23; thrown out of being, *Enn.* II.5[25].
91. Porphyry, *Plot.*13, 18.
92. Philo, *Life of Moses* II.212; *Questions on Genesis* IV.92.
93. Epictetus, *Dissertationes* II.1.29–33.
94. Evil in the world, *Enn.* III.2[47].15.60; lower part of the soul, *Enn.* IV.4[28].29.8.
95. Memory & desire, *Enn.* IV.3[27].28.19; beauty, *Enn.* V.8[31].2.24.
96. Astrology, *Enn.* III.1[3].5.25; order reigns, *Enn.* III.2[47].13.18.
97. *Enn.* IV.3[27].26.12.

10

Proclus' geometrical method

Marije Martijn

An old chestnut in Proclus research is "the geometrical method". This notion refers, of course, to Euclid's method in his *Elements*. In Proclus, it is primarily associated with the presentation of the basics of Neoplatonic metaphysics in the *Elements of Theology*, a work which in different ways summons the *mos geometricus*. Although it has become clear that Proclus does not exactly follow Euclid's method of presentation in his *Elements of Theology* (see § "First case: *Elements of Theology*" below), the importance of the suggestion that he does cannot be underestimated: it is this chestnut which is primarily responsible for the rehabilitation of Proclus' thought in the past century. Taylor, when writing a defence of Proclus in 1918, states: "We have learned that the Neo-Platonists were neither magicians nor emotionalist *schöne Seelen*, but systematic philosophers addressing themselves to the philosopher's task of understanding the world in which he lives as seriously as Aristotle or Descartes or Kant." His main evidence for this thesis is Proclus' *Elements of Theology*, as displaying a "manner and method" similar to those of "the great rationalists", rather than "ecstasies and other abnormal psychological wonders" (A. E. Taylor 1918: 605–6).

The key terms in Taylor's analysis are "systematic", "seriously" and "rational". And the names of Aristotle, Descartes and Kant summon the same image: of serious, systematic, rational and methodic philosophers striving for true understanding of the world. As a vindication of Neoplatonism against verdicts of mysticism and vagueness, such a statement works quite well. It does not, however, tell us what Proclus' geometrical method is, or what its aims are.

The same criticism holds for most descriptions of Proclus' supposed method in the *Elements of Theology*, or of the stereotype *more geometrico* has become. The general, but too limited, picture is that it moves from principles to their consequences, via deduction – it is a "synthetic" method of "a priori" deduction (Dodds 1963: xi), or an "axiomatic-deductive" method,[1] or also a "hypothetical deductive" method.[2] However, as Lloyd says (concerning Galen, but it holds for anyone subscribing to mathematics as an ideal of science), "quite what that ideal comprises is more difficult to pin down than is generally recognized" (G. E. R. Lloyd 2005: 110).

In the following, we will try to capture how Proclus himself understands the "geometrical method". The chapter falls into four parts, not counting the introduction: "The elements of *Elements*" contains an analysis of Proclus' description of "Elements" in his commentary on book I of Euclid's *Elements*, "Methods of geometry" an overview of the relevant methods of geometry as identified by Proclus, "Are Proclus' *Elements* written *more geometrico*?"[3] discusses the two cases of *Elements* among Proclus' own works: the *Elements of Theology* and *Elements of Physics*, and "*More geometrico* in the commentaries" three cases of "geometrical method" in Proclus' Platonic commentaries. As we will see, there are four aspects in which the earlier-mentioned descriptions of Proclus' geometrical method fall short: first, they ignore the *didactic aim* the *mos geometricus* has for Proclus. Second, they focus on its *synthetic* side, but, as we will see, *analysis* is just as important.[4] Third, they lack a reference to the necessary metaphysical background of the method. And finally, there is not one geometrical method: in different contexts the method is elaborated differently.[5]

For reasons of space, we will not go into the details of Proclus' sources of inspiration. Let me merely point out that Euclid cannot be Proclus' only source,[6] mainly because in this work there are no hypotheses, and it does not reveal ontological causal relations, which is, however, one of the main reasons for Proclus to use the method in the first place (cf. Harari 2008). Among possible other sources are Zeno, the method of hypothesis from Plato's *Phaedo*, the hypotheses of the *Parmenides*, the description of geometry in the *Republic*, the classical model of science of Aristotle's *Posterior Analytics*,[7] and Iamblichus and Syrianus.[8]

THE ELEMENTS OF *ELEMENTS*

Assuming that for Proclus *more geometrico* means "in the manner of Euclid's *Elements* (*stoicheiōsis*)", the best place to start a proper assessment of the method as he sees it is his analysis of the title "Elements".[9] That analysis is part of a discussion of the two aims Proclus distinguishes in the work, one with reference to the subject matter (*kata ta pragmata*), namely constructing the five regular solids or "cosmic figures", and one with reference to the student (*kata ton manthanonta*, in Eucl. 71.20–26):[10]

> Of the aim of the work with reference to the student we shall say that it is to lay before him an elementary exposition (*stoicheiōsis*, as it is called) and a method of perfecting his thinking (*teleiōsis tēs dianoias*) for the whole of geometry. If we start from the elements, we shall be able to understand the other parts of this science; without the elements we cannot grasp its complexity, and the learning of the rest will be beyond us. The theorems that are simplest and most fundamental and most like first hypotheses are assembled here in a suitable order (*taxis prepousa*), and the demonstrations of other propositions take them as the most clearly known and proceed from them. ... Such a treatise ought to be free of everything superfluous, for that is a hindrance to learning (*mathēsis*); the selections chosen must all be coherent and conducive to the end proposed, in order to be of the greatest usefulness for scientific understanding (*epistēmē*); it must devote great attention both

to clarity and to conciseness, for what lacks these qualities confuses our thought (*dianoia*); it ought to aim at the comprehension of its theorems in a general form, for dividing one's subject too minutely and reaching it by bits make knowledge (*gnōsis*) of it difficult to attain.

(*in Eucl.* 71.4–75.5, trans. Morrow, slightly modified)[11]

From this passage and the rest of the discussion, it is quite clear that the term *stoicheiōsis* should be understood as functioning primarily in a *didactical* context (D. O'Meara 1989: 171; Nikulin 2003: 195). It is this context which determines what a good *stoicheiōsis* is according to Proclus: any work which presents the basics of a science and trains our discursive intellect,[12] and which provides us with the basic tools to further elaborate the parts of the science that are not described (cf. *in Eucl.* 71.22–3). It does so by bringing together in a suitable or proper order primary theorems and demonstrations from them.

The proper order, as Proclus finds it in Euclid's *Elements*, follows a particular sense of *stoicheion* as the simplest thing into which the composite can be divided,[13] where that which is "more of the nature of a principle" (*archoeidestera, in Eucl.* 73.8) is the element of that which is "placed (*tetachmenōn*) in the account of the result" (i.e. the conclusion, 73.8–9) – or, as he later describes it: "that from which everything else proceeds and into which it resolves" (*analuetai,* 73.18). Note that this latter aspect of resolution already hints at the presence of analysis in Proclus' geometrical method (see below in this section); moreover, the starting points that *have* to be distinguished are the definitions/hypotheses,[14] not the axioms and postulates.[15] This shows from Proclus' remark that a geometer has to distinguish between starting points and what follows from them, *because* geometry is a hypothetical science – as opposed to the only unhypothetical science, that is, metaphysics, which provides the principles to the other sciences (*in Eucl.* 75.5–14).[16] This also implies, as we will see, that any *Elements* of metaphysics does not distinguish principles.[17]

It is difficult, says Proclus, to properly select and order the elements (*in Eucl.* 73.15–18). The proper ordering should not contain anything superfluous, should be coherent and to the point, clear and concise, and have a high level of universality in the theorems. These characteristics are emphatically each connected to a didactic aim (*didaskalia*) of the text: learning (*mathēsis*), scientific understanding (*epistēmē*), our thought (*dianoia*) and knowledge (*gnōsis*) respectively.[18] All proofs should "result from the principles", that is, use nothing other than the foregoing,[19] and anything that seems to be missing either can be derived using the given methods, or is too complex for the present purpose, or can be composed on the basis of "given causes".[20] This implies that hidden assumptions, that is, assumptions that have not been explicitly stated as deriving from a definition or argument, should be avoided.

In sum, then, any *Elements* is a concise *introductory teaching*, which, for didactic reasons, consists of *first principles* (if any) and *derivations* (or deductions), presented in the proper *order*:[21] any deduction should be made using only the principles and what has already been established.

So far, Proclus' description of what makes a good *stoicheiōsis* matches modern descriptions of *more geometrico* quite well, except for the emphasis on didactics. Today the axiomatic method tends to be seen in a context of justification (Beierwaltes 2007: 82–3); that is, of showing how certain propositions are true because they are grounded by ultimate ones, which are considered as already known to be true.[22] But that is not its primary aim

for Proclus: grounding, as well as coherence, consistency, clarity, being to the point, conciseness and universality, are all subordinate to the didactic aim of the text.[23]

If anything, Proclus' view is closer to the context of discovery sometimes related to the
axiomatic method (De Jong & Betti 2010: 193). For Platonists, discovery should of course
be understood in the *Meno*'s sense, that is, as *anamnēsis*, and hence as part of the didactic
aim of science. And although it is not in the foreground in the description of what makes
a good *stoicheiōsis*, it does play an important part in Proclus' "geometrical method": and
this is where the analytic side comes in.

Proclus' motivation for emphasizing the proper order is primarily epistemological: he
who does not follow it upsets all cognition by putting together things that do not belong
together (*in Eucl.* 75.23–5). Behind the epistemological motivation, however, lies the well-
known assumption of ancient epistemologies that the structure of knowledge reflects that
of reality.[24] As a consequence, the order of presentation of knowledge should follow the
order of reality: cause and immediate effect belonging together, but not cause and more
remote effect. It is telling in this regard that Proclus, in one of the first pages of his first
prologue, already speaks of the "principles" of mathematics from which everything else
comes forth in the "proper order", in the context not of epistemology, but of metaphysics:

> To find the principles of mathematical being (*ousia*) as a whole, we must ascend
> (*animen*) to those all-pervading principles that generate everything from them-
> selves: namely, the Limit and the Unlimited. For these, the two highest principles
> after the indescribable and utterly incomprehensible causation of the One, give
> rise to everything else, including mathematical being (*physis*). These principles
> bring forth all other things collectively and transcendentally, and the things which
> proceed receive their procession in appropriate degrees and in the proper order
> (*metrois tois prosēkousi kai taxēi tēi prepousēi*).
>
>   (*in Eucl.* 5.14–24, trans. Morrow, modified)

This ontological order is the very same order we have seen Proclus advocate in the presentation of knowledge.[25] There is an important caveat to be made here, however, with regard
to the didactical context of *Elements*. In a Platonic schema of *anamnēsis*, the direction in
which the teacher takes the student is up, in an analytic movement from consequences
to causes, from participations to Forms, from the many to the One, from composite
to elements – not down, in a synthesis from the first principle to its consequences. As
Proclus says in the quoted passage, "we must ascend". Whenever that which is, to use an
Aristotelian distinction, most clear and familiar by nature (*physei*) is not most clear and
familiar with respect to us (*hēmin*, *Phys.* 1.1.184a16–18); that is, when the first principles
in the order of reality are not the starting point or "the point of entry" in the order of
knowledge, analysis leading to the first principles is necessary.[26]

It is significant in this context that in his discussion of the ordering of material in a
stoicheiōsis, Proclus explicitly mentions *reductio* or proof *per impossibile* and analogic
reasoning (*in Eucl.* 73.20–22). The fact that he notes the occasional omission of these
two methods suggests that he considers them to be more or less standard components of
the geometrical method. And indeed, in Proclus' own works, as in Euclid, they are (see
§ "Methods of geometry" below). A reason for their separate mention might be that they
are closely related, for Proclus, to the crucial analytic, ascending aspect of the method.

When we turn to his own applications of the geometrical method, we see that, rather than (synthetically) starting from principles and moving to consequences, as Euclid does, they indeed commence with a short analytic move from principles to even higher principles (see §§ "Are Proclus' *Elements* written *more geometrico*?" and "*More geometrico* in the commentaries" below).

METHODS OF GEOMETRY

To understand in what manner Proclus' *more geometrico* includes the analytic road to principles as part of *anamnēsis*, let us take a closer look at the relevant methods of geometry. Proclus is hardly interested in the various operations on figures and ratios; that is, the constructive work (drawing a straight line between points, describing a circle, dividing and compounding figures, etc.).[27] He considers the constructions a necessary, but inferior and preparatory part of geometry, more closely related to the perceptible than to the Forms, and better at home in productive, than in theoretical science.[28] Instead, as a Platonist he prefers the theorems and their demonstrations concerning the essential properties of geometrical entities (*in Eucl.* 77.11–12).

The primary methods involved, then, are the dialectical methods needed for direct, syllogistic demonstration (in Barbara) on the basis of first principles: division of genera into species and definition "in the case of the first principles", and demonstration "in the case of their consequences", to show how the more complex proceeds from the simpler.[29] But of course, Proclus also involves the fourth dialectical method, analysis, "to revert again to the [simpler]" (*in Eucl.* 57.25–6) – the method, that is, which shows how the (until then) unknown is actually "resolvable" into known principles, thereby affirming (*thetikai*) those principles.[30] Analysis is the "upward" method; that is, the method that brings the student to knowledge of causes. As shown below, in his application and recognition of "the geometrical method", Proclus tends to give analysis a special place and to emphasize other geometrical methods and formulae which contribute to or signal this upward direction (see §§ "Are Proclus' *Elements* written *more geometrico*?" and "*More geometrico* in the commentaries" for examples).

Take, for example, the two methods Proclus mentioned as sometimes omitted from the presentation of *Elements*: indirect demonstration *per impossibile* (*tropos di' adynatou*), and demonstration by *analogia*. The former starts from *diaeresis*, dividing the genus proposed for examination into its species, and eliminating the parts irrelevant for the proof, and then refutes the contrary of what is sought on the basis of its impossible consequences, indirectly establishing the truth of the thing sought (*in Eucl.* 211). Although it is as such not specified among the four dialectical methods, it is, of course, a very dialectical method in the sense that it is part of the actual practice of Socratic dialectic as the refutation of false opinions. It is analytic, to the extent that it proves the higher on the basis of the lower (cf. Heath 1956: 140).

The method of *analogia*, that is, demonstration using proportional relations, draws conclusions using the common notion "if four entities are proportional, they will also be proportional alternately"; that is, the alternation of equal ratios (A:B = C:D).[31] The mathematical variety of this method is closely related to the metaphysical one (for Proclus they are the same method on different levels of reality) (the same goes for the literary variety:

see Martijn 2010a: ch. V). In metaphysics, the proportional relations between cause and effect guarantee the continuity of emanation, and as a consequence, in epistemology, they guarantee the possibility of reversion of the soul.[32]

A related method is geometrical conversion (in Eucl. 69.19–24): the exchanging of (parts of) theorems (described at in Eucl. 251.24–259.14 & 409.1–17). Theorems consist of a hypothesis and a conclusion, in the sense of an antecedent and a consequent, for example, "if in a triangle two angles are equal, the sides which subtend the equal angles will also be equal". This method is not a method of demonstration, but it is part of demonstration to the extent that it generates theorems, which can be demonstrated and used as premises in subsequent demonstrations. Geometrical conversion is a crucial element of Neoplatonic argumentation, because it is based on the fact that the relation between the subject in the antecedent and the attribute in the consequent is primary and per se (in modern terms: the propositions are actually double implications). As a consequence, and as opposed to logical conversion, it renders universal affirmative propositions (cf. Heath 1956: 256). This method is importantly related to analysis, to the extent that, for analysis to be possible, propositions need to be unconditionally convertible[33] – one of the reasons, no doubt, why geometry has its paradigmatic role.

As mentioned above, even some at first sight superficial geometrical practices and formulae contribute to "the geometrical method". Although they are not all considered necessary components of good Elements, Proclus does use them in his applications of the geometrical method, as well as when referring to it in the commentaries. Anticipating the results of the case-studies in the following sections, let me mention the most important ones. First is the division of the work into separate propositions and, within them, the division of the mathematical proposition into enunciation, setting-out, definition of goal, construction, proof and conclusion.[34] Of the latter, most important for our purposes is the repetition or reformulation of the "enunciation" at the end of the demonstration, by way of conclusion, and the corresponding formula quod erat demonstrandum (hoper edei deixai etc.). For Proclus they indicate the two directions of geometry; that is, from starting point to end and back.[35] Second is the use of imperatives signalling postulations, as a sign of the didactic or dialectical context;[36] third, the corollary (porisma), that is, an extra result of the demonstration of another theorem, or a "lucky find",[37] as indicating the synthetic side of Elements and the completability of a system; fourth, variables as signs of the universality of the demonstrations, another requirement of good Elements;[38] fifth, "a fortiori" (pollōi ara meizōn/pleon), a formula which Proclus identifies as originating in geometry (see below) and which refers to the method of demonstration by analogia:[39] owing to analogic relations between layers of reality plus the principle that a cause has a property to a higher degree (cf. ET prop. 18), it is possible to ascend to causes on the basis of knowledge about the caused;[40] and finally, "geometrical necessity" (geōmetrikai anankai): this is in itself not an aspect of methodology, but Proclus does connect it to the method of demonstration, and ascribes it to (the drawing of) conclusions. The source of the necessity differs from one context to the next: in in Eucl., it is said to be due to the subject matter of geometry,[41] and in non-geometrical contexts, to the universality of demonstration (in Ti. I.346.31–347.1, see below, § "First case: physics and the commentary on the Timaeus"), or to the logical relation between premises and conclusion (see below, § "Second case: metaphysics and the commentary on the Parmenides"). These three features are interrelated, and are necessary conditions for any ascent to causes.

ARE PROCLUS' *ELEMENTS* WRITTEN *MORE GEOMETRICO*?

First case: *Elements of Theology*

In his famous and influential introduction to metaphysics, entitled the *Elements of Theology* (*Stoicheiōsis Theologikē*), Proclus sets out his metaphysics in 211 propositions, each followed by what looks like a demonstration, or at least an elaboration supporting it.[42] In roughly the first half of the work (props. 1–112), the fundamental oppositions of Neoplatonic metaphysics (between unity and plurality, cause and consequent, etc.) are introduced (see also Dodds 1963: x). In the second half, these oppositions are elaborated with regard to the ontological hierarchy consisting of the henads (props. 113–65), intellects (props. 166–83) and souls (props. 184–211). Within each of these subsections, the propositions are roughly ordered from the ontologically prior to the posterior.[43] For example, the first proposition about the henads regards their overall unity, the last one regards the lowest, encosmic henads.

The title and form of the *Elements of Theology* indicate that the method of exposition Proclus chose for this work follows Euclid's example. And, as said above in the introduction, this is how the work is traditionally viewed. On the other hand, that view has been challenged. On the face of it, the primary demands of a *stoicheiōsis* are met: the work starts from a principle – in a broad sense – and works its way down in the proper order. Moreover, within the argumentation for the propositions, we find the methods Proclus regards as standard (although not always used) components of geometrical *Elements*: indirect demonstration *per impossibile* is very frequently used (props. 1, 5, 22, etc.); the method of analogy for reasoning on the basis of the similarity of different levels of reality is both argued for and used.[44] And finally, Proclus uses some of the above-mentioned primarily geometrical practices and formulae, repeating or reformulating the "enunciation" at the end of the demonstration by way of conclusion (e.g. prop. 1, 2, 7, etc.; the formula *quod erat demonstrandum* does not occur, but we do find comparable expressions at props. 6 and 25),[45] and he often gives corollaries.[46]

Whether the *ET* contains anything superfluous, and is coherent, to the point, clear and concise, is to some extent a matter of taste. Compared to Proclus' other works, however, the *ET* is a model of parsimony, to the great relief of Dodds (1963: xi). This shows most of all from the fact that it does not contain any appeal to philosophical or religious authorities. Proclus does not inform us what the work is about, or what his aim is (besides the telling title), but this is just another aspect of its conciseness. Proclus' intention seems quite clear, since, as Lowry (1980: 90) says, "all the fat is trimmed away". Likewise, although completeness is here a relative term, the *ET* seems at least intended to be complete – as an introduction to theology or metaphysics; that is, to true causes – in the sense that it discusses all transcendent levels of reality.

On the other hand, one can easily criticize the *ET qua stoicheiōsis* (Lohr 1986: 59–60). It has often been argued that the *ET* only *ostensibly* follows the Euclidean example. One of the main arguments adduced for this modification is the absence of definitions or other starting points in Proclus' introduction of metaphysics (cf. D. O'Meara 1989: 197). For him, however, this would not be a convincing argument, since, as we saw, the separate treatment of starting points belongs to hypothetical sciences. But metaphysics is an unhypothetical science (see also Nikulin 2003: 200–201). Stronger arguments have been adduced, however. For example, the argumentations are not flawless: the "demonstrations" are quite often elaborate repetitions of the enunciation, phrases from Plato or Oracles are presented as *a priori* truths, and the work contains some logical errors (Dodds 1963: xi–ii). Second, "it is not obvious that there is a real dependency between [the propositions] as there is, for instance, between propositions of Euclid book I".[47] That dependency does exist in the sense that the lower hypostases, discussed in later propositions, *metaphysically* depend on earlier ones, but the concomitant logical dependence should be reflected in the argumentations, as it is in Euclid. And finally, the *ET* seems to violate the criterion of "proper order" in different ways. Most interesting is the fact that the first proposition, "Every manifold in some way participates in the one", is not the most fundamental one (see also Gerson & Martijn forthcoming). On the basis of parallels with *in Prm.*, it has been shown that not the first, but the fourth proposition is the foundation of all the others. The first four propositions form a short dialectical analysis, followed by a synthetic ordering of propositions derived from the first principle (D. O'Meara 2000: 285–88; Opsomer 2013). The first proposition can be read as a general characterization or even something resembling a definition of the manifold, as always containing some "one", either in its parts considered separately or in the manifold as a whole. The subsequent argument "demonstrates" the first proposition by showing that "the ultimate constituents of any plurality … need to be atomic" (Opsomer 2013). Proclus then goes on to show that, since any manifold is both one and not one (prop. 2), it is different from, posterior to and dependent on oneness. Before there can be "many", there has to be "one" (prop. 5). Moreover, this "one" has to be "the one itself" (prop. 4), which is separate from the thing that becomes "one" by participation, as well as from the "one" which it participates in (prop. 3). It is not until the fifth proposition that Proclus has concluded to the necessity of the One by itself, prior to a plurality of participated ones, on the basis of the general characterization of the manifold expressed in the first proposition. Thus the *ET* follows the geometrical method, but commences with a short analysis,[48] based on what is technically speaking not a definition of "manifold", although it does resemble one, and which functions as a "point of entry" or "cognitive pilot", directing our thought to the un-hypothetical principle.[49]

Second case: *Elements of Physics*

The *Elements of Physics*, Proclus' presentation of the necessity of an incorporeal unmoved mover on the basis of Aristotle's physical works, is closer in form to Euclid than is the *ET* (cf. D. O'Meara 1989: 197). Apart from propositions, demonstrations using reductions (Nikulin 2003: 185) and corollaries, which we find also in the *ET*, the *Elements of Physics* moreover uses definitions, variables and formulae such as imperatives for postulations and the formula *quod erat demonstrandum*:[50] a phrase Proclus otherwise uses only in his commentary on Euclid.

On the other hand, it is less of a *stoicheiōsis*, as it does not obey the criteria of "proper order" in two respects: (a) it is not complete, since, contrary to what its title promises, it does not treat all of physics, but only certain aspects of motion and change (D. O'Meara 1989: 197). More damaging is that it could nonetheless be complete regarding its apparent aim, that is, showing the necessity of an unmoved mover, but it is not, since: (b) like the *ET* it contains hidden premises.[51]

Let us, however, again consider Proclus' supposed intention and tentatively put forward a thesis the confirmation of which actually requires detailed analysis of the *Elements of*

Physics. Since its demonstrations lead upwards from bodies in motion to knowledge of the cause of corporeal motion, what the introduction of physics gives us is a version of the geometrical method, which is *primarily analytic.*[52]

Proclus' own *Elements*, then, are both written *more geometrico*, but this does not mean that they obey all criteria, nor does the method come down to the same in both cases. The latter goes also for the geometrical method as it occurs in the Platonic commentaries. There is not one "geometrical method", but its details depend on the science or subject matter at hand.

MORE GEOMETRICO IN THE COMMENTARIES

In commenting on Plato's text, Proclus often imposes a structure on it, which we would qualify as logical. In some dialogues, however, he himself identifies it as a geometrical structure, or describes elements of it in terms borrowed from Euclid (we will only look at explicit references to geometry in connection with methodology). The extent to which he does this differs from one commentary to the next, depending on the given structure and subject matter of the dialogue in question, and ranging from an occasional remark to an extensive "elementification".

First case: physics and the commentary on the *Timaeus*

On one extreme we find the commentary on the *Timaeus* in which, more than in any other commentary, Proclus labels the method applied by Plato as "geometrical".[53] There are obvious reasons for the strong presence of the geometrical method in this commentary. First of all, the main speaker of the dialogue, Timaeus, is a Pythagorean, so it is no surprise to find Proclus emphasizing the presence of mathematics in its various guises in the commentary. Second, there is a clinching argument for Proclus to think of geometry as a methodological paradigm in the context of the *Timaeus*, and that is that philosophy of nature, like geometry (but unlike dialectic), is a hypothetical science (Martijn 2010a: 90–99).

The geometrical method is very present in this commentary, but only in a specific part of it: not the comments on the passages of the dialogue which already contain geometry (*Ti.* 31b–32c and 34b–36b),[54] but those on the *prooemium* (*Ti.* 27d5–29d3), in which Timaeus sets out the principles of his cosmology. The prooemium seems already to have a "geometrical" (in the sense of hypothetico-deductive) structure (Finkelberg 1996; Runia 1997), but Proclus takes it to extremes: to answer the general problem of cosmology (whether the universe is "becoming"), Plato, says Proclus, presents a kind of division, "a *distinction* of two genera (Being and Becoming), in order for the exposition to proceed as from geometrical hypotheses to the examination of the consequents" (*in Ti.* I.226.24–7); he "*defines* the always Being, assuming that it exists, as the geometer defines the point, assuming its existence", because "[philosophy of nature] is also a *hypothetical* science and its hypotheses should be assumed before the demonstrations" (*in Ti.* I.228.26–229.3, cf. *in Ti.* I.236.15, 30), and "the geometer would no longer be a geometer if he discussed his starting points" (*in Ti.* I.236.33); he then "truly according to the geometrical method presents ... *axioms* after the definitions" (*in Ti.* I.258.12–13), introducing the efficient and paradigmatic causes of Becoming; he presents another axiom which "imposes a name on the subject in a geometrical fashion": that is, "the heavens or the cosmos" (*in Ti.* I.272.10–11); he shows "*demonstratively* that the cosmos has become, from the definition, according to the *conversion* of the definition: for geometers also use such proofs" (*in Ti.* I.283.15–18); and subsequently demonstrates, among others with a *reductio*, the necessity of the demiurgic and paradigmatic causes of the cosmos; finally, in what Proclus with hesitation calls "the fourth demonstration", he recognizes analogic reasoning, namely "geometrically adding the alternate 'as Being is to Becoming, so truth is to belief'" (*in Ti.* I.345.3–4).[55] Definitions, hypotheses, axioms, demonstrations, conversion, proof *per impossibile* and analogy, just as in Euclid:[56] the intention is clear.

An important additional feature of Proclus' exegesis of the prooemium is that, in the presentation of the "axioms", Proclus discerns a short analytic ascent to the causes of Becoming (*Ti.* 28ab; *in Ti.* I.258.9–272.6). Elaborating the axioms into a number of syllogisms (also involving *reductio*), he shows that on the basis of the definition of Becoming one has to conclude the necessity of the demiurgic and paradigmatic causes.[57] As in the *ET*, then, the "geometrical method" involves a short analysis leading to the principles of the science being presented. This analysis fits Proclus' view of the *Timaeus* as a "teaching" (*didaskalia*) (see Martijn 2010a: esp. 84–5 & ch. V).

The harvest of the analysis is that the universe as "most beautiful object" was made after a "most divine paradigm" by "the best maker", that is, the demiurgic and paradigmatic causes of Becoming. Proclus buttresses this harvest using a number of *reductiones*, to conclude with yet another reference to geometry: "let these … statements be laid down as demonstrated by 'geometrical necessity', as they say".[58] The geometrical necessity of the conclusions, which Proclus explains as due to their universality and the intelligibility of the transcendent (*in Ti.* I.346.31–347.1), highlights what he considers the summit of the *Timaeus*.

Second case: metaphysics and the commentary on the *Parmenides*

For Proclus, the *Parmenides* is Plato's only entirely theological or metaphysical dialogue, and as a consequence the only completely dialectical one (*Theol. Plat.* I.7–10, cf. I.4.18.20–24). When we run into demonstrations, divisions, analyses or definitions, we need not think of geometry, as these are primarily dialectical methods.[59] Any references to the geometrical method may be no more than metaphors for logical certainty. For example, Proclus first introduces geometry at a crucial point, namely in the description of the method of the *Parmenides*: "The method of the arguments proceeds through the most precise powers of reason, … firmly establishing each of the matters at hand 'by geometrical necessity' (*geōmetrikais anankais*, *in Prm.* 645.11–16). Perhaps Proclus here merely mentions geometry, rather than logic, to avoid giving the impression that the *Parmenides* concerns logic: instead, he takes it to be the metaphysical dialogue which derives all of reality from a first principle, the One.[60]

Other references to geometry, however, show that there is more to it. The second mention does not occur until the second half of the dialogue, in Proclus' comments on what he considers the final stage of analysis, after the maieutic first half of the dialogue: the first hypothesis. From Parmenides' One-Being his audience ascends to the One itself, using a common notion (the One is not many, functioning as what we called a "cognitive pilot"), as in geometry.[61] Later references concern the presence of self-evident starting points and the subsequent synthetic order of reasoning in Parmenides' investigation of the hypotheses.[62]

Furthermore, the expression "by geometrical necessity" is used on two more occasions, to emphasize that the *taxis* of demonstration; that is, posterior following from prior, imitates the ontological hierarchy (*in Prm.* 1132.22–5, 1162.22). Interestingly, the very same point is made in the one and only reference to the geometrical method in the *Platonic Theology*, concerning the method of the *Parmenides*: by his mode of demonstration (*ho tropos tōn apodeixeōn*), says Proclus, that is, using the least possible number of simplest and best-known starting points, or common notions, to derive an increasingly complex plurality of conclusions, Parmenides provides an intellectual paradigm (*paradeigma noeron*)[63] of the order of geometry or the other *mathēmata*.[64] This order of reasoning is "necessary" (*anankē*), because of a *necessary* (*anankē*) correspondence between the order of demonstration and the causal order of reality: *logoi* carry an image "of the things which they interpret" (*Ti.* 29b4–5).[65] To conclude, the main two purposes of the geometrical method in this commentary seem to be (a) to emphasize the analysis leading to the first principle and (b) to emphasize the subsequent metaphysical aim of the dialogue; that is, deriving lower levels of reality from the One, synthetically presented according to the order of reality.

Third case: ethics and the commentary on *Alcibiades I*

The commentaries in which the geometrical method plays no part are those on *Republic* and *Alcibiades*. Although Proclus analyses parts of both dialogues almost *ad nauseam* in terms of syllogistic reasoning – using reductions, syllogisms in Barbara, definitions, axioms or common notions, conversions, necessary conclusions, which are then used as premises for further deductions, corollaries and expressions such as *a fortiori* – he either never (*in R.*) or hardly (*in Alc.*) mentions geometry.[66] *In R.* does not contain any reference to the geometrical method. This absence is surprising, considering the importance of geometry and its methods in the *Republic*. Likewise, it is interesting that in *in Alc.* we find only some references in passing. For our purposes, some brief comments on *in Alc.* suffice.

For Proclus, the primary aim of the *Alcibiades*, self-knowledge, is ethical, and the dialogue concerns the refutation of false opinions. It does not contain an orderly presentation of reality – with one exception (see below). The method suitable for the ethical aim, Socratic dialectic (*in Alc.* 169.12–171.5), is of course similar to that of geometry – it involves analysis and synthesis (*in Alc.* 179.14–180.2), as well as common notions and something like postulates (premises agreed upon with the interlocutor) (*in Alc.* 175.24–176.6) – and elsewhere, as we saw, Proclus explicitly compares lower dialectic, using hypothetical starting points and scrutinizing their consequences, to geometry (see note 62). Not, however, in the *Alc*. Perhaps this is because for Proclus the *Alcibiades* is not only an ethical dialogue, but also an introduction to all of philosophy: ethics, (meta)physics and *logic* (*in Alc.* 11.3–14). So naturally, Proclus uses the comments on methodology to emphasize its contribution to logic. For example, when presenting syllogisms in Barbara (which, incidentally, contribute to the metaphysical content of the dialogue), for example, "everything just is beautiful, everything beautiful is good, therefore everything just is good", he explains what first-figure syllogisms are (*in Alc.* 318.16–319.1).[67]

Nonetheless, there are two interesting references to geometry as a methodological paradigm. The first, quoting Aristotle, emphasizes the paradigmatic necessity of geometry (cf. *in Ti.* and *in Prm.*), but as opposed to ethics. Necessity is here related not to the method of demonstration itself, but to the knowability of the subject matter:[68] Socrates'*oimai*, "I think" (*Alc.* 103a), does not express ignorance, but awareness of the lack of necessity concerning knowledge of human affairs (or more specifically "other minds"). This confirms our suspicion that the ethical aim of the dialogue in part explains the absence of the geometrical method: ethics is not a demonstrative science.

Elsewhere in the commentary, we find the remark "*a fortiori*, as the geometers would say".[69] The expression *a fortiori* refers to the power of analogy, allowing us to draw conclusions concerning higher levels of reality on the basis of knowledge of the lower. Proclus uses "*a fortiori*" quite frequently, but only in *in Alc.* is it explicitly called geometrical. Perhaps that is simply due to the introductory role of the *Alcibiades* in the Neoplatonic curriculum: Proclus may not expect his readers to make the connection. On the other hand, this remark comes at a crucial point: it is attached to what is the metaphysical core of the dialogue for Proclus, and the only presentation of the order of reality it contains, namely the proportional relation "base lover : divine lover = nature : soul".

CONCLUSION

We can conclude from the above that there is not one "geometrical method" in Proclus. Different sciences or contexts ask for different varieties of a method that derives conclusions from the relevant kinds of starting points. Moreover, there is far more to the method than starting points and derivations. The main aim of the method, according to Proclus, is didactic. As a consequence, it contains not only synthetic, but also analytic elements. And the metaphysical background of the geometrical method requires that the order of presentation of knowledge corresponds to the causal order of reality.

Geometry provides an ideal methodological paradigm, better than either dialectic or empty logic (*in Cra.* 1.11), because of the geometry's intermediate position in between the sensible and the intelligible.[70] It combines a rigid structure reflecting the order of reality with the power of reversion to higher levels of reality. Rosán rightly sees Proclus' focus on the geometrical method as motivated by "the sense of beauty that is inherent in the absolute necessity of a rigorous and all-pervading system".[71] But the system itself is not the be-all and end-all of the geometrical method: it is what it represents, and what you can do with it.

NOTES

1. G. E. R. Lloyd (2005: 118), on "the geometrical method" in Galen.
2. A. E. Taylor (1918: 606–7). Cf. Oeing-Hanhoff (1971: 233), who explains the *mos geometricus* as "mathematisch-synthetische Methode".
3. This section owes a lot to D. O'Meara (1989: 177–9, 196–8).
4. In the following, "analysis" does not refer to geometrical analysis. On Proclus' ignoring of Euclid's application of that method in structuring a proof, see Netz (1999: 293–4). On the notion of "analysis" relevant in this chapter, see below, note 26.
5. This is also clear from O'Meara's excellent analysis of the role of geometry in Proclus' work (D. O'Meara 1989), to which this chapter owes a lot.

6. Note that Hathaway (1982) quite unconvincingly maintains that Proclus *unconsciously* adopted Euclid's method. Cleary (2000a: 88) takes the *ET* to have Aristotle, *not* Euclid, as its model.

7. I use "science" here in the sense of "grounded knowledge" or "scientific understanding" (i.e. *epistēmē*), not in the narrow sense of one of the "natural sciences". On the classical model of science in Proclus and in general see Martijn (2010c), De Jong & Betti (2010), Betti *et al.* (2011).

8. On Iamblichus as a possible source of Proclus and the difference between the two in the relation between the methods of geometry and those of dialectic, see D. O'Meara (1989: 170, 172–3). On Syrianus, see Ierodiakonou (2009b).

9. *In Eucl.*, second prologue, chapter 7. On Proclus' commentary on Euclid, see further Szabó (1965), Breton (1969), D. O'Meara (1988), Bechtle & O'Meara (2000), Helbig (2000), Nikulin (2002), Bechtle (2006), Lernould (2010). I thank Jan Opsomer for his valuable suggestions concerning components of the geometrical method.

10. At the end of the commentary on book I, Proclus seems to have reduced the aim of the book to the former (*in Eucl.* 431.15–432.19, esp. 432.5–9). Possibly, at the end of the book, Proclus is less interested in the method used and more in the subject matter, or perhaps he changed his mind with regard to the primary aim of the *Elements*, but that does not affect his views on the nature of the method used.

11. On this passage, see also Nikulin (2003).

12. *Dianoia* has to refer to discursive intellect, rather than "understanding" (Morrow).

13. Morrow's translation here seems a bit sloppy. The focus of Proclus' analysis slides from the order of presentation of knowledge (foundation vs. derived knowledge) to the order of ontological composition (elements vs. composite), possibly because of an influence of Aristotle's definition of *stoicheion* in *Met.*1014a.26–1014b.15. For other references to Aristotle, see Heath (1956: 116).

14. On the relation between these two in *in Eucl.*, see Martijn (2010a: 91).

15. For reasons of space this chapter does not contain a discussion of the role of the axioms or common notions, i.e. the self-evident starting points of geometry, in the geometrical method. For examples see below §§ "First case: physics and the commentary on the *Timaeus*" and "Second case: metaphysics and the commentary on the *Parmenides*".

16. This impression is reinforced by the remark further on that Euclid *had* to distinguish (ἔδει διαστείλασθαι, *in Eucl.* 75.27) starting points from consequences, and that he does just that, and "thereafter also" (ἔπειτα καὶ, *in Eucl.* 76.4) distinguishes between axioms, hypotheses/definitions and postulates – but not that he *had* to.

17. Metaphysics does not have any (discursive) starting points, cf. *in Prm.* 702.9–11.

18. This seems to me a case of *variatio* for purposes of emphasis, rather than a meaningful distinction of different forms of cognition resulting from different aspects of the method.

19. Proclus criticizes Apollonius several times because the proofs he presents involve later theorems, which makes them unsuitable for an introduction (ἀλλοτρίαν … τῆς στοιχειώσεως), *in Eucl.* 335.16–336.8, 280.4–11 & 282.24–283.3. Note that Proclus often refers to Euclid as "the author of the *Elements*" when he discusses the proper order of the work. An interesting case in point is *in Eucl.*193.1–9 (with *in Eucl.* 339.11–344.8): Proclus rejects the indemonstrability of the fifth postulate (and hence its status as a postulate), but postpones talk about its demonstration until the time is right (Morrow refers to *in Eucl.* 364.13 & 371.10). Cf. *in Eucl.*162.8, 248.4, 310.17, 321.9–20, 326.12, 334.3.

20. αἰτίων τῶν δεδομένων, i.e. probably principles, rather than Morrow's "from traditional premises". The disjunction seems to be non-exclusive, as the three examples apparently overlap.

21. *In Eucl.* 75.10–14. We find these elements also in other writers using the term *stoicheiōsis*, albeit not all at once. Suda mentions introductory teaching, order and conciseness (Σ 1241 = Photius, *Lexicon* 540 [Porson]); Porphyry also mentions introductory teaching (*in Cat.* 134.28 [Busse]); and Pseudo-Galen focuses on the order "from elements to end", that is, from the principles to what is sought (*Definitiones Medicae* 356.4–15 [Kühn]). Cf. Epicurus, *Her.* 37 [Arrighetti].Thanks to Jan Opsomer for pointing me to these passages.

22. Cf. De Jong & Betti (2010: 193–4); Betti *et al.* (2011: 2). Alternatively, justification may be related to coherence and consistency of the subject, cf. Nikulin (2003: 193–5).

23. Cf. D. O'Meara (1989: 171), who speaks of "pedagogical virtues". Note that these are properties which Proclus even tries to give to his own commentary: see *in Eucl.* 200.11–18. Cf. *in Eucl.* 429.9–15.

24. On this and a related issue in Proclus, that *texts* reflect reality, see Martijn (2010a: chapter V).

25. The same parallel is present in Proclus' reading of Platonic dialogues. See Martijn (2010a: 276–80).

26. Analysis is too complex a notion to do it justice here. Let me merely point out that although Proclus' concept of analysis in *in Eucl.* is far from precise, context allows us to choose the most relevant notion from the many ancient varieties. Beaney (2003) divides analysis into three main varieties (with many subspecies): decomposition of a complex into simples, regression or working back to first principles, and transformation/interpretation of a statement to a correct logical form; Oeing-Hanhoff (1971) distinguishes, among the ancient varieties, mathematical analysis, practical analysis of an aim to its means of realization, logical analysis into figure and mode, analysis of conclusions to their premises, conceptual analysis, material analysis, grammatical analysis, erotic analysis and astronomical analysis. Proclus clearly has in mind regression, or analysis of conclusions to their premises, which for him also means analysis of effects to their causes. For further references on analysis in Proclus, see Martijn (2010a: 133–4). Note that the above oversimplifies the relation between reality and knowledge in Proclus. See also Martijn (2010b: 159).
27. See, for example, the treatment of *Post.* I–III at 185.1–187.28, and the description of geometrical procedures at 57.9–58.3.
28. Constructions are needed in the "problems", which are inferior to the theorems. See *in Eucl.* 209.10, 243.13–25, 79.3–11.
29. *In Eucl.* 57.18–26. On the dialectical methods in mathematics in general, see *in Eucl.* 42–3; on analysis and synthesis see moreover *in Eucl.* 8, 255; on division and collection, *in Eucl.* 12–15, 19, 318; on definitions, *in Eucl.* 131, 178; on demonstration, 33–4. See also D. O'Meara (1989: 171–3).
30. Cf. *in Eucl.* 211.19–21, 242–3, 255.18. See also Beierwaltes (1979: 250 and note 20, 262). Analysis is also one of the methods for finding *lemmata* (propositions which are used to establish other propositions, but themselves need to be demonstrated), next to division and something resembling *anginoia* (cf. Aristotle, *An. Post.* I, 34) – intuition, which is not really a method, but a "talent" (ἐπιτηδειότης), or "nature" (οὐ μεθόδοις … τῇ φύσει, *in Eucl.* 211), and consists in "seeing" on the basis of as few principles as possible. This is the primary task, not of *dianoia*, discursive thinking, but of its summit, *logos* or a kind of *nous* (e.g. *in Ti.* I.246.20–248.6).
31. For Proclus' explanation of the method, see *in Eucl.* 254.21–256.8. *Analogia* does not occur in the *in Eucl.* often, as it is not introduced by Euclid until book V (and applied in plane geometry in book VI). Cf. *in Eucl.* 9.4 for the common notion and *in Eucl.* 405.1–406.9 for an application.
32. Note that the method can go both up and down the ontological ladder. On *analogia* in Proclus, see the insightful discussions in Gersh (1973: 83–90) and Beierwaltes (1979: 65, 153–7).
33. Heath (1956: 139). On related issues, see further de Haas (2011) and Harari (2008).
34. On this feature see Netz (1999), who shows that Proclus imposes this structure on Euclid.
35. On enunciation and conclusion, see *in Eucl.* 203.1–210.25, esp. 210.5–16.
36. For example, (*ek/pros-*)*keisthō*, as at *in Eucl.* 190.6, 274.10, etc.
37. Different from *porisma* in another sense, namely of a problem whose solution requires not only construction or theory but also discovery: see *in Eucl.* 212.12–17, 301.22–305.16.
38. On logical variables as a sign of universality, invented by Aristotle, see Łukasiewicz (1951: 7–8).
39. Cf. Cleary (2000a: 77). Damascius uses the expression in this manner quite often, e.g. *Pr.* I.58.15 [Westerink & Combès].
40. Another formulaic element, which we will not go into, is the use of the second person. A practice of geometry that we do not find in any of Proclus' texts is the use of diagrams.
41. Cf. *in Eucl.* 26.10–27.10. Cf. *in Alc.*, see below, § "Third case: ethics and the commentary on *Alcibiades I*".
42. On the *Elements of Theology* as an exposition *more geometrico* see also D. O'Meara (2000).
43. In the manuscripts, the propositions are distinguished, but not called propositions. The division into subsections is Dodds', not Proclus', but it is justified by the content.
44. What Dodds calls the "supplementary theorems on causality" (esp. props. 97, 108 & 110) describe the metaphysical basis for the method. Many other propositions use it (explicitly, e.g. props. 113 & 164, cf. 100, 139, or more often implicitly, e.g. 105, 155, 197). Note that in general the analogies do not move up, but down the ontological ladder, fitting the overall direction of the *ET*.
45. As such a non-geometrical feature of *ET* for D. O'Meara (2000: 286), but not for Proclus.
46. More precisely, he uses formulations which elsewhere signify corollaries (e.g. "From these things it is also clear that …", props. 14, 22, etc., cf. prop. 26, where he merely adds a further conclusion).
47. Cleary (2000a: 68). He is referring to logical, not ontological, dependency.
48. Another seeming violation of the "proper order" is noted by Lowry (1980: 94): Neoplatonic metaphysics

is not just a hierarchy of hypostases, but it also involves metaphysical processes responsible for the relations existing within the hierarchy. These processes are described in props. 7–112. Against Lowry I would say that since these processes are in a sense caused by the first principle(s), the proper order is largely maintained.

49. For a similar case of such "cognitive pilots", cf. Martijn (2010a: chapter III, esp. 106).

50. D. O'Meara (1989: 177–8). The formula ὅπερ ἔδει δεῖξαι occurs ten times, nine in book I (cf. ὅπερ ἔδει ποιῆσαι, Inst. Phys. I.9 [Ritzenfeld]), and the tenth as the very last sentence of the work, to emphasize the grand conclusion that there is an unmoved mover.

51. Opsomer (2009: 193–203). Nikulin (2003: 195) mentions that, as in the ET, Proclus does not distinguish different kinds of starting points (definitions, axioms, postulates). Such a distinction, however, is not among Proclus' criteria of stoicheiōsis.

52. Thus, pace Martijn (2010a: 216) and D. O'Meara (1989: 177–9), the mos geometricus here does not only serve "to reinforce Aristotle's argumentation by imposing a syllogistic rigour".

53. On this topic, see also Lernould (2001, 2011), Martijn (2010a: ch. 3).

54. Proclus' book III on body and soul of the world respectively. On these passages, see also Martijn (2010a: 166–204). Proclus' comments on Ti. 53b–55c (on the regular polyhedra) are not extant.

55. On this last passage, see Martijn (2010a: 255–61). Cf. in Ti. II.13.8.

56. On references to "geometrical necessity", see below.

57. On the syllogistic structure of this passage, see Martijn (2010a: 115–32); Lernould (2001, 2011). On the analytic aspect, see Martijn (2010a: 118, 123, 131–2).

58. in Ti. I.331.29–332.9. The reference is to R. 458d5, where we find geometrical vs. erotic necessity.

59. Theol. Plat. I.9.40.1–18. See also Proclus' explanation of the dialectical methods (in the context of an argument for the necessity of the Forms) at in Prm. 980–83 [Steel].

60. On the polemics concerning the aim of the Parmenides (logical exercise or theology), see Theol. Plat. I.9–10 (34–46) and in Prm. 630.11–645.6.

61. In Prm. 1092.21–1094.13 with 1079.4–20. See also D. O'Meara (2000: 282–3).

62. In Prm. 1099.29–1100.8, 1140.16–18, 1151.28–1152.11, cf. 1195.21–1960.1, 1206.1–25. The description of lower dialectic contains a rather different reference to geometry: like geometry, Zeno's lower dialectic has hypothetical starting points (in Prm. 701.21–702.11), as opposed, of course, to the non-hypothetical nature of Parmenides' higher dialectic (in Prm. 1033.30–1034.29, re. R. 533b6c).

63. "Intellectual paradigm" probably refers to the dialectical order as discursive yet rooted in intellect (nous), owing to the intuition of principles. Cf. in Prm. 701.24–6, see also above.

64. Theol. Plat. I.10 45.19–46.2. On this passage, see also A. C. Lloyd (1990: 16–17) and Cleary (2000a).

65. Theol. Plat. I.10 46.2–22, cf. above, § "The elements of Elements".

66. See in Alc. 11.18–18.10, esp. 15.1–18.10, in R. beginnings of essays 3, 4, 13, 15, 17 and considering its title probably also 2, which is not extant.

67. In the preceding pages, Proclus emphasized that the dialogue contains ethics, theology "and all of philosophy, so to speak" (in Alc. 315.1–318.15).

68. In Alc. 23.8, quoting Aristotle, EN 1094b26 and Plato, Ti. 29b3–d3.

69. In Alc. 134.15. He also identifies a "geometrical corollary" (in Alc. 217.8). Cf. the formula at in Alc. 216.21, similar to that introducing corollaries in ET.

70. Partially explained by Nikulin (2003: 195). See further Cleary (2000b).

71. Rosán (1949: 227). On the beauty of mathematics, see Martijn (2010b). On Proclus as a systematic philosopher, see Beierwaltes (2007), Gerson & Martijn (forthcoming).

III

Metaphysics and metaphysical perspectives

INTRODUCTION

The changing fates of Neoplatonism, from a late esoteric appendage to the Classical period of ancient philosophy to an up-and-coming vibrant field, is ostensibly a result of the advances we have made in understanding Neoplatonic metaphysics, the heart of hearts of Neoplatonism. The goal of this part is to present the status quo of Neoplatonic metaphysics today from three main perspectives: its principal conceptual network, its main proponents, and the latest directions of research. In almost all cases, in a typical Neoplatonic threefold fashion, the findings of the three perspectives come together in a single point revealing the defining role of metaphysics for Neoplatonism.

To understand Neoplatonism means to understand Neoplatonic metaphysics. This approach has guided our studies for a long time and has revealed a complex conceptual structure that has left us more often than not scraping for answers and, refusing to admit defeat, willing to start from scratch again and again. But charting the main conceptual structure of Neoplatonic metaphysics (the first perspective above) as a hierarchical organization of three underlying principles of existence – until recently commonly known as "the hypostases" of the One, Intellect and Soul and as of lately referred to as "layers", "causal priority/posteriority" or "stops" of reality – has sketched very "dimly", to borrow the Neoplatonists' own expression, the main contours of their metaphysical map. But this map remains a map; that is, a two-dimensional representation of entities and not a "real-time" model of how these entities work. The further exploration of the main pillars on this map has required scholars to zoom in (i) microscopically into their internal structure and (ii) macroscopically into their interrelations. The results have unravelled a dynamic holistic system or, to borrow again from the Neoplatonic linguistic repertoire, a system which is "boiling with life".

Thus Neoplatonic metaphysics is transformed from the study of the edifice of reality to the study of the underlying (causal) processes of reality. It becomes a study of the inner- and interrelations between the individual components and processes in the universe. And here comes the second perspective. Working out the complexity of these relations, constantly trying to develop a more accurate operating model, requires a Promethean stroke of genius in combination with Sisyphean determination. In this respect, it is necessary to view Neoplatonic metaphysics not only as a result of Plotinus' ingenuity and labour, but also as a series of the combined Promethean–Sisyphean efforts of all Neoplatonists. Among them are scholarchs of the stature of Porphyry, Iamblichus, Proclus and Damascius and the studiousness of Philoponus, Olympiodorus, Stephanus of Alexandria and, not to forget, the anonymous commentators.

Metaphysics is the study of the invisible relations in *what there is*, the universe, from the supra-celestial bodies to human psychology. Consequently Neoplatonic metaphysics relates to every aspect of the human condition: rational, irrational, scientific, epistemological, cognitive, psychological, religious, aesthetic and so on and so forth. This observation introduces the third perspective, which brings to light the latest directions of research in the study of metaphysics and demonstrates its defining role for Neoplatonism.

Given the "global" approach to Neoplatonic metaphysics and especially the intimate relation between metaphysics and ethics, today's editors of a comprehensive volume on Neoplatonism may well entertain the possibility of organizing the presentation of the core divisions of Neoplatonic philosophy in the *Handbook* according to the organization of the

Neoplatonic curricula (symbolically presented in Porphyry's arrangement of Plotinus' *Enneads*). This means to start from ethics, to proceed to physics, then to psychology, and to culminate in metaphysics. The editors of this volume were enticed by the anagogical authenticity of this organizing method, its originality (in comparison with the more standard organization from metaphysics to physics, to ethics, to aesthetics), and by intellectual curiosity about the benefits the new perspective may yield. After weighing what is the single most crucial point from which the rest of Neoplatonic philosophy falls into place, however, the choice landed once again on metaphysics. The thematic parts of the *Handbook* start with metaphysics not because it has been traditionally the most complex and studied branch of Neoplatonic philosophy but because it is the cornerstone or the linchpin for all other areas of Neoplatonic thought. If a philosophical system postulates an intelligible reality as the paradigm, rational principle, or cause (depending on the preferred viewpoint) of the physical world and a single transcendent principle as a source of this intelligible reality, it naturally follows that every aspect of this philosophy is but metaphysics.

The presentation of metaphysics opens with Ahbel-Rappe's chapter on "Metaphysics: the origin of becoming and the resolution of ignorance" (Chapter 11), which outlines the course of Neoplatonic metaphysics from Plotinus to Damascius in parallel with the development of the two main types of Neoplatonic metaphysical discourses (constructive and deconstructive or apophatic). Ahbel-Rappe explains and attempts to bridge the gap between metaphysics as an abstract form of relational, propositional or dialectical reasoning of *a priori* postulates and the individual who, by using this reasoning, pushes the limits of rationality and resorts to a more contemplative form of knowledge. The Neoplatonic solutions – or the lack thereof – of this *aporia* depend on the angle of examination and range from contemplative productivity in Plotinus, to causality in Proclus, to a sober reminder of the limits of our all too human comprehension, in Damascius.

In his "Metaphysics of the One" (Chapter 12), Halfwassen addresses the central question – and problem – of Neoplatonic metaphysics: the relation between the One and many which is further subsumed in the tension between the One, as the productive principle of existence and the basis of being and thought, and the One which is absolutely homogenous, self-sufficient and transcendent. Plotinus' concept of the One is founded on the principle that everything that is conceivable, from the monolithic oneness of Being to the fragmented coherence of Many, has unity. This unity ontologically precedes and founds even the subjective positioning of Thought. Our knowledge of the universe then depends on our ability to understand; that is, to ascend, through a *henological reduction* and intellectual contemplation, to the absolute One as pure unity and an object of negative theology. These themes are further elaborated in Part IV dealing with language, epistemology and psychology.

Slaveva-Griffin's chapter on "Number in the metaphysical landscape" (Chapter 13) presents the aspect of Neoplatonism most heavily endorsed by all shades of Platonism and Pythagoreanism: the much acclaimed and debated relation between mathematics and metaphysics, from Plotinus to Iamblichus, Syrianus and Proclus. This aspect explains the structure of the intelligible realm and the physical world as an orderly progression from the One to many which is not measured by quantitative changes in magnitude and multitude, but by the dynamic, ontologically correspondent, nature of number. Throughout its many permutations, the Neoplatonic concept of number explicates the inner relations of the intelligible, the conceptual tension between the transcendent One and the productive One, the proliferation of the grades of reality and the relation between ontology and theology. Ultimately, the question about the relation between number and metaphysics is a question about the relation between number and substance as the primary kind of being, and the relation between number and the soul as a mediator between the intelligible realm and the physical world. This chapter introduces the major metaphysical topics of substance and matter, treated respectively in the ensuing two chapters, as well as the larger themes of cognition, epistemology and psychology in Part IV.

Moving from the dynamic relations between the different layers of reality to a more topical treatment of a single concept, Chiaradonna's chapter on "Substance" (Chapter 14) presents the nature, development and latest research questions of this fundamental concept of Neoplatonic metaphysics. The initial difficulty concerns which criteria to use in determining the primary nature of substance. Is it a primary subject of all other things and, if it is, should it be equated with matter, which is addressed in the following chapter? Is it a primary formal cause in the structure of corporeality? Is it a primary self-subsistent principle of motion? Or is it a primary intelligible essence separate from its physical phenomenalization? The gradualist nature of Neoplatonic metaphysics allows the opportunity for various interpretations and solutions to the problem.

Narbonne's chapter on "Matter and evil in the Neoplatonic tradition" (Chapter 15) examines the place and role of the ontologically opposite corollary of metaphysics: matter. The concept of matter and its counterpart, the principle of evil, are inseparable concomitants of any discussion of Neoplatonic metaphysics. As the zero-grade of ontological substantiation, matter is the conceptual negative of being or Form as the full grade of ontological substantiation. As such, matter possesses the ontologically unredeemable qualities of poverty, passivity, plasticity, indefinability, unlimitedness, unmeasuredness, lack of order and thus intrinsic evil (O'Brien 1971, 1998, 1999; Corrigan 1996a). Depending on their tolerance of the idea of dualism, the Neoplatonists offer different explanations of the presence and origin of matter and evil in the structure of the universe. Groundbreaking research in this area has allowed us to understand better the delicacy with which the later Neoplatonists – in comparison to Plotinus' linear negation of matter – treat the physical world as exemplified in the concept of "enmattered forms" (Opsomer 2001; Opsomer & Steel 2003; Phillips 2007; Narbonne 2009). In this respect, even the discussion of matter and evil pertains to the domain of metaphysics, while it looks ahead to the focal presentations of physics and ethics, in Parts V and VI, respectively.

11

Metaphysics: the origin of becoming and the resolution of ignorance

Sara Ahbel-Rappe

ORIENTATION: THE LANGUAGE OF METAPHYSICS

Neoplatonic metaphysics does more than tell a story; it is illocutionary as well as indexical, in so far as it tells us how to see the world and how things got to their present state, and offers a corrective for our current condition, namely ignorance.[1] Neoplatonic metaphysics seeks to explain appearances (the world) in a way that simultaneously calls that very thing – the world – into question. Accordingly, the metaphysical discourses of Neoplatonism move in two directions: they are constructive, affirming and revealing a vision of reality that is not yet in evidence. Plotinus attracts the reader into the project of uncovering that reality by offering instructions (see Rappe 2000) in how to work with the text or doctrine: "Shut your eyes and change to and wake another way of seeing";[2] "Let there be in the soul a shining imagination of a sphere";[3] "One must not chase after it, but wait quietly til it appears" (*Enn.* V.5[32].8.4). These discourses are also deconstructive and apophatic. Plotinus assists his reader in denying and removing a vision of reality that is already too much in evidence: "How to see this? Take away everything!"[4]

Neoplatonic metaphysical treatises often catalogue primary and secondary principles (an approach that contemporary scholarship also emphasizes).[5] The assumption is that reality is graded and that some things are prior to, that is, are more real, than other things. Yet it could well be that in its refusal to downgrade appearances, the phenomenal world, to *mere* appearance, Neoplatonism runs the concurrent risk of relying overmuch on the explanatory apparatus of cause and effect. Addressing itself to the reader *qua* soul (*Enn.* VI.4[22].14.16: "Who are we?") (see Remes 2007), this kind of discourse seeks to explain the place of the soul in terms of the larger reality, the causes or first principles, whose product it is. But if the reader takes up a position of being or identifying with soul, and metaphysics is a description of how the soul returns to the first principles, then the very point of metaphysics, as a corrective to what the Neoplatonist sees as extopic or exotic – the embodied, separate self and its temporally defined existence[6] – is lost. For this reason, the language of Neoplatonic metaphysics is best understood as promissory, offering a glimpse of reality, a prelude to genuine knowledge.[7]

It would not be going too far to suggest that Neoplatonic metaphysics, as a discursive construction, is ancillary to a discipline of contemplation that is not in itself confined to or even concerned with causal explanations. To the extent that Neoplatonic philosophy and its study rely on arguments for a first principle, these in themselves do not constitute the end product of this philosophy. Accordingly, it may be very tempting to reduce Neoplatonic metaphysics to an explanatory system that achieves consistency, complexity and flexibility over time, but its purpose can never be reduced to the creation of such a system. No matter how rooted in the authority of Platonic exegesis or in the systematic interpretation of Platonic texts, the greatest truth on which Neoplatonic metaphysics relies is none other than the direct reality of the person who approaches it in search of the truth.[8] Therefore, paradoxically, the purpose of Neoplatonic metaphysics, orienting the student towards the real, often breaks in on or is at times in tension with its existence as a self-standing explanatory discourse.

THE CENTRAL PROBLEM OF NEOPLATONIC METAPHYSICS: ONE OR MANY?

Given that Neoplatonism directly bases its entire philosophical outlook on the positing of a transcendent unity, the One beyond being,[9] it makes sense that the dialectic of One and Many forms a nucleus within Neoplatonic metaphysics as it develops over the centuries. Plotinus and the Neoplatonists subsequent to him locate the difficulty over the derivation of all things from the One as the central problem in metaphysics:

> But [soul] desires [a solution] to the problem which is so often discussed, even by the ancient sages, as to how from the One, being such as we say the One is, any-thing can be constituted, either a multiplicity, a dyad, or a number; [why] it did not stay by itself, but so great a multiplicity flowed out as is seen in the real beings and which we think correct to refer back to the One.   (*Enn.* V.1[10].6.3–8)[10]

Briefly, the puzzle can be described as follows: if the One, which by definition lacks multiplicity, differentiation, qualities, attributes and even being, is the highest and most complete identity, then how do the Neoplatonists account for the proliferation of various kinds of being, the very fact that there is life, mind, intelligence in all of their diversity? If we say that all of these beings are "from" the One, then what causes their departure from this ultimate identity? If the One is the cause of all beings, and this causality is conceived as a participation of all things in the One, then the transcendence of the One is compromised at the outset. And yet if the One remains isolated in its transcendence, this raises the question of how it communicates reality to any of the other aspects of being.

From its inception, then, Neoplatonic metaphysics faces a dilemma: either all that is must ultimately reside within the One or else the One produces whatever else arises as outside of itself. To choose the first option allows a solution that implies that there is something in the One that is not the One. The second option places emphasis on the causal powers of the One. The problem with the first option is that whatever is in the One is simply One; how can there be distinctions in the primordial unity? The problem with the second option is that it entails the diminishment of effect with respect to its cause (otherwise, lesser realities would be equivalent to the One),[11] and we will have no way to account for the origin of this unlikeness: how can absolute unity give rise to multiplicity in the first place?

In what follows, I attempt to survey a variety of answers to this dilemma, tracing a dialectical path through the history of Neoplatonic metaphysics. Plotinus inaugurates a tradition of responses to this dilemma in terms of his most fundamental intuition: that the One's productivity is contemplative by its very nature.[12] His metaphysics of light[13] emphasizes the place of self-knowledge, self-revelation and theophany in understanding the relationship between world and principle. By contrast, Proclus' metaphysics of eternal being emphasizes the structures and hierarchies of the intelligible order, unfolding along the lines of a causality or of a transfer of power (*dynamis*, the capacity to effectuate reality). Power (as we find it in Proclus' system) represents both a departure from a greater reality and the production of a lesser reality.[14] Thus to bring about the effect is to reveal a possibility that it was latent within the higher order; it is to diminish that same order as well as to augment it.[15] Given these fundamental tensions operating in the Proclean metaphysics of being, later Neoplatonists went on to treat them through a perspective that skirted the problem of being altogether. Damascius rather institutes a metaphysics of non-being,[16] in his insistence on a radical return to the origin, conceived not as One or Good, but as the Ineffable, as the unconditioned ground of reality, the first principle that does not just underwrite the metaphysical enterprise as such, but simultaneously seeks to tame the arrogance, so to say, of that very enterprise. These three kinds of discourse, of light, of being, and of emptiness or of non-being, then, reveal the creative directions or orientations that together constitute some of the wealth of Neoplatonic metaphysics.

PLOTINUS' METAPHYSICS OF LIGHT

The causal role of the One as source of all subsequent stations of the real is rooted, for Plotinus, in the contemplative nature of the One's activity, if it can be said to have an activity (Plotinus speaks variously about this possibility).[17] Uniquely among all Neoplatonic thinkers, Plotinus emphasizes the relationship between One and Intellect as the first dimension of the manifest world, exploring the continuities and affinities between the One as what Plotinus calls "pure light" and "eternal awakening"[18] and Intellect as the actualization of that "light". By contrast, for Proclus, the intelligible realm, the realm subsequent to the One, is first conceived in terms of Being. By dwelling for a moment on this contrast between Plotinus and Proclus, who inverts the Plotinian order of Intellect and Being, understanding that the objective formations of Being take priority over their status as living intellects, we come to understand the inaugural point of this metaphysical tradition as a whole.

Plotinus employs three different models for understanding Intellect's relationship to the One (thereby anticipating Proclus' metaphysics of procession, remaining and reversion): the inchoate Intellect; the actualized Intellect; and the hyper-Intellect.[19] Most often he characterizes the first movement, procession, as a "shining out", or an "irradiation" (*perilampsis; epilampsis*). For example, in *Enn.* V.1[10].6.26–9, he discusses the emergence of the intellect from the One as *perilampsis*, the "effusion of light", which circumradiates the sun.[20] Plotinus is inclined to front the *Republic*, its images of the Good as source of intelligibility, and the epithet, *agothoeides* ("having good as its nature"; "affinity with the good", e.g. *Enn.* VI.7[38].15.9, 16.5) (Bussanich 1988), as the primary textual authority for his understanding of the derivation of Intellect from the first principle.[21]

This metaphor, the sun and its radiance as applied to the first principle ("the first activity flows from it like a light from the sun", *Enn.* V.3[49].12.40), invites interrogation: into what does this One, the first principle, shine? Into what place does its radiance arrive? The implications portend a paradox: at the very beginning of manifestation, the One has nowhere else to shine; nothing other than itself to illuminate. Plotinus writes in the same essay, still developing this metaphor of circumradiant light, "the One does not push away its outshining from itself" (*Enn.* V.3[49].12.44). So at the very inception of the One's procession, even before Intellect arises, there is a question that defies the metaphor and the metaphysical theory that undergirds it. If we are speaking about the One, by definition there can be nothing external to it; the outshining is not something that can function outside the One. Therefore the One, in giving rise to manifestation, is thereby engaged in (a paradoxical) self-disclosure; in functioning as the ground of all things, the One does no more than reveal itself to itself, discovering even as it gives rise to its own infinite possibilities. Plotinus writes of the One's own self-absorption as follows: "Now nothing else is present to it, but it will have a simple concentration of attention on itself. But since there is no distance or difference in regard to itself, what could its attention be other than itself?" (*Enn.* VI.7[38].39.1–4).

In a well-known text, Plotinus offers the most compressed of creation stories: in it, he employs the Platonic language of images and alludes to the *Republic*, certainly, but most importantly he assimilates the generation of the intelligible world to the act of vision, in keeping with the contemplative foundation of the One's activity:

> But we say that Intellect is an image of that Good; for we must speak more plainly; first of all we must say that what has come into being must be in a way that Good, and retain much of it and be a likeness of it, as light is of the sun. But One is not Intellect. How then does it generate Intellect? Because by its return to it, it sees (*heōra*): and this seeing is Intellect.   (*Enn.* V.1[10].7.1–6)[22]

The last sentence, translated neutrally above, is one of the most controversial in all of the *Enneads*, and can be more tendentiously translated as: "Because by Intellect's return to it [the One] [Intellect] sees",[23] or alternatively as "Because by turning to itself the One sees". At stake in the differences between these translations is the purported agency of the One. The second possibility faces the difficulty that the One cannot undergo a reversion to itself, when it has never been described as having proceeded. The first possibility faces the difficulty that the Intellect has not yet arisen in the first place; this translation would seem to defer, rather than offer, any explanation for its origin. Again, to say that Intellect just is equivalent to the seeing of the One suggests the opposite of what has just been said: the One precisely is not Intellect (and it is because the One is not Intellect that the question asked here is "how does the One generate Intellect?") As the ambivalences are built into the Greek and the grammatical subject of the verb, *heōra* ("sees"), is entirely irrecoverable, of necessity we ask who is doing the seeing: is it Intellect or the One? In hinting that the One turns towards or into itself, that it enjoys a form of self-awareness that yet reverberates as a separate identity in Intellect, Plotinus offers an account of the relationship between One and Intellect. As I will try to suggest in what follows, Plotinus wants to make clear that the intelligible world does not obscure the One's nature; instead, its very function is to allow the One to fully recover its own nature.

The procession of Intellect is equivalent to inchoate Intellect, an outflow that is the external activity of the One; yet Intellect also has its own (internal) activity, which it realizes when it reverts to the One and actualizes itself as a knowing principle in relation to an object of knowledge. Plotinus describes this process in the following passage:

> But how, when that [sc. One] abides unchanged, does intellect come into being? In each and every thing there is an activity which belongs to the *ousia* [the being of something] and one which goes out from the *ousia*, and that which belongs to *ousia* is the activity which is each particular thing, and the other activity derives from that first one, and necessarily follows it in every respect, being different from the thing itself.   (*Enn.* V.4[7].2.27–30)[24]

Here we have a description of the self-determination of Intellect as a separate hypostasis. According to Plotinus, the internal activity of an entity is identical to the *ousia*, the being or essence of that thing, whereas what that internal activity consists in is actually a contemplation of or reversion towards what is higher (A. C. Lloyd 1987). In the case of the One itself, there can strictly be no activity in it, since it is beyond essence, nor is there anything higher for it to contemplate. The One, then, contemplates itself, and yet it cannot do so inasmuch as the One is not an object of thought. Therefore, in the One's turning towards itself, Intellect emerges. To the extent that the One initiates this self-directed activity, it gives rise to a phase of intellect known as "inchoate" Intellect.

In order to find language for the notional distinction between the One as thinking itself and the One as quasi-object of its own thought, Plotinus' astute reading of Plato's *Parmenides* plays an important role: Plato distinguishes the consequences of the assertion that the One is, both for the One itself and for others (cf. the so-called fourth hypothesis). In Plato's *Prm.* 156b6–159b, we read: "If the One is, what are the consequences for the others?," which is elaborated further at 157b5–7: "We have next to consider what will be true of the others, if there is a One. Supposing then, that there is a One, what must be said of the things other than the One."

The internal act of a given reality is, in some sense, what it is in itself; the external act is how it is for others. But in saying this much, we have already altered the nature of the One: the One cannot be something in itself, since this of course implies containing its own activity, its own *ousia*, which, Plotinus indicates, is not present in the One. And yet, in containing itself, it will be subject to the distinction between self and other, between the container and what is outside of that container. It is in this sense that scholars have made a point of emphasizing that, whenever the Intellect reverts to itself, that is, whenever inchoate intellect "sees" the One, what it sees must be an image of the One.[25] Thus inchoate Intellect functions as a kind of intelligible matter, whereas the image of the One functions to limit, define and actualize the Intellect proper.[26] He reaches back into Aristotelian[27] metaphysics, physics and psychology. Here the One (either in itself or as seen by the Intellect) becomes the object of the Intellect's vision or intellection; it is the reality or existence that actualizes or makes real Intellect's apprehension of its object. In so conceiving its object, Intellect actually generates Being or beings: "in seeing that it had offspring and it was directly conscious of their generation and their existence within it" (*Enn.* VI.7[38].35.33).[28]

Above I suggested that there are Plotinian analogues for Proclus' more precise scheme of procession, reversion and remaining.[29] We have already discussed procession and reversion as they relate to the genesis of Intellect. "Remaining in the cause" implies that the external activity that becomes the effect does not exhaust the cause; this feature of the causal triad is allowed, in Proclus' metaphysics, through the law of undiminished giving, captured in *ET* prop. 75, according to which the cause transcends the effect. In Plotinus' case, however, we are more concerned with the nature of Intellect as it manifests both the capacity to create, through its intellection, the realm of being, and through its transparency, so to speak, the capacity to remain free of that same creation.

We encounter the hyper-intellectual phase (equivalent to remaining in the cause) of Intellect in Intellect's ascent back to the One, into union with the One.[30] This aspect of the Intellect is what Plotinus calls the loving Intellect (*nous eron*) or the inebriated Intellect (*nous methystheis*, *Enn.* VI.7[38].35.25):

> [Intellect then has one power] by which it looks at what transcends it by a direct awareness (*epibolē*) and reception, by which also before it saw only, and by seeing acquired intellect and is one. And that first one is the contemplation of Intellect in its right mind, and the other is Intellect in love, when it goes out of its mind "drunk with the nectar".   (*Enn.* VI.7[38].35.19–25, trans. modified)

Astonishingly, Plotinus tells us that the hyper-noetic intellect does not think (*Enn.* VI.7[38].35.30) (see Bussanich 1988: commentary *ad loc.*): that there is an Intellect that remains without thought. Moreover, this side of Intellect always belongs to it: "Intellect always has intellection and always non-intellection" (*Enn.* VI.7[38].35.30). The loving Intellect in discovering the Good finds that it sees the Good not as its object, but rather it becomes a seeing that has no object: "while the vision fills his eyes with light it does not make him see something else by it, rather the light itself is what is seen" (*Enn.* VI.7[38].36.20). This is the hyper-noetic phase of Intellect, which encounters the Good as its very own nature (light). Whether or not the inchoate Intellect and the Intellect in love are one and the same Intellect, it is clear that Plotinus' language often leads us to link the two aspects.[31] For example, O'Daly (1973: 166) quotes *Enn.* VI.9[9].4.29–30: "when someone is as he was when he came from him, he is already able to see as it is the nature of that God to be seen". Here at least it would seem that Plotinus emphasizes the simultaneity of the two phases of Intellect, which we might call before and after procession, which constitute together what Plotinus calls the One's self-arrival. Intellect then proceeds, remains in, and reverts to its cause, the One, simultaneously. When Intellect returns to the One as loving Intellect, it rediscovers its capacity to know, even when there is no object of vision. Hence, in releasing all the objective conditions, it no longer exercises intellection. In *Enn.* III.8[30].9.29, we learn that Intellect takes a backward step from its identity as Intellect: "the intellect must return, so to speak, backwards, and give itself up."

The intimacy that Plotinus insinuates between the Intellect and the One tells us a great deal about the nature of Intellect or wisdom and its objects. The nature of wisdom is to be empty: as Plotinus tells us, that kind of Intellection is non-intellection. The inward motion of the One, its own self-permeation or arrival within itself, is recuperated eternally, as the Intellect continually remains grounded in the One, entirely unconditioned. Intellect originates in this openness, freed from all objects – profoundly contrasting with the proliferation of beings that is for Plotinus the other, generative side of Intellect. In looking to the Good, Intellect thus is thinking, eternally generating its prolific offspring; in discovering itself as the Good, Intellect is not thinking, eternally free; as Plotinus puts it, "about to see (*emelle noein*)" (VI.7[38].35.33). The upshot of this discussion is that always and everywhere, Plotinus emphasizes the contemplative ground of the metaphysical enterprise as such: first and foremost, because reality is none other than the One's own self-disclosure. Further, the nature of wisdom or Intellect as it arises from the ground of this fundamental reality is empty – utterly without content or distinctions, located nowhere and with no object. Only by encountering wisdom in this pristine form can metaphysics be understood – as a contemplative realization, not as an explanation. Of course, this kind of intimate assimilation between the One and Intellect is not just the initial phase of the Intellect's emergence from the One. It has simultaneously achieved its proliferation in the plurality of beings, in the world of forms, and in the multiplicity of Intellects, all derived from its differentiation from the One. But it never loses the capacity to become transparent, free from objects, free to give rise to objects.

PROCLUS' METAPHYSICS OF BEING

In moving towards Proclus' metaphysics of Being and away from Plotinus' metaphysics of light, we necessarily turn away from the affinity of the One and Intellect. For Proclus, as we have already had occasion to note, what arises immediately after the realm of the One is not primarily understood as Intellect, but as Being, which Proclus explores in the terms of a series of investigations into principles of causation. In the interests of coherence, explanatory consistency and fullness, he develops an account, in the *Elements of Theology*, that seeks to derive the entire ontological order from one fundamental axiom: "Every plurality participates somehow in unity" (*ET* prop. 1).

In studying Proclus' metaphysics of Being, we turn away from what we saw in Plotinus was a heavy reliance on the *Republic* to focus on the *Philebus* as an important source text for Proclus. Proclus associates the three principles of *Phlb.* 27d, limit, unlimited and mixed (*peras*, *apeiron* and *mikton*), with the first stages in the devolution of reality after the One.[32] In the metaphysics of Proclus, *peras* and *apeiron* constitute a dyad after the One, becoming conduits of unity and multiplicity, and introducing the possibility of reality outside of the ineffable first principle. The third nature, the *Philebus*' Mixed, introduces a subsequent stage of development, which Proclus and Iamblichus understand as the intelligible world, or the realm of Being.[33] Thus the three kinds of Plato's *Philebus* are the fulcrum around which reality proliferates and the hidden fullness of the One pours forth into the world of manifestation.[34]

For Proclus, *peras* and *apeiron* are related to a Pythagorean interpretation of Plato's *Philebus*. This interpretation functions as the basis for his explanation of how the world of multiplicity, expressed as the gradations of Being, arises from the absolute One. The dyad therefore constitutes a manifestation of the hidden or latent power of the One, that is, its all-possibility. As Van Riel has demonstrated, Proclus actually coins a word, *ekphansis* ("manifestation"), as a way to display the relationship between the Dyad (*peras* and *apeiron*) and the One.[35] The nature of the One is revealed or is made manifest in what for Proclus constitutes the first Dyad which he calls, in a manner that might remind us of Plotinus, an *ekphansis*, "a showing forth of the nature of the One".[36] Essentially, for Proclus *peras* and *apeiron* function like form and matter; their product, a synthesis of the infinite power of the One together with the unity of the One, is a compound; that is, Being. Therefore, the One has, as it were, elements that in some sense share its realm; by denying that there is any potency, any *dynamis*, in the One, Proclus must transfer this function to the primal limit that functions with the primal limitlessness to, in a sense, produce the realm of Being (*PT* III.9.31).[37]

Proclus defines the One as the cause of all things, as causing that which it itself does not possess, through the doctrine according to which "every cause properly so-called transcends its effects" (*ET* prop. 75). Another important source text for this principle, at least in so far as it applies to the metaphysics of the One, is the *Parmenides*, the interpretation of which, he tells us, is owing principally to Syrianus. Proclus says of the One, "everything then, which is negated of the One proceeds from it. For it itself must be no one of all other things, in order that all things may derive from it" (*in Prm.* VI.1077.29–31 [Steel]). Proclus suggests that all that the second hypothesis of the *Parmenides* asserts is denied by the first, and indeed, that the very negations of the first hypothesis actually cause the corresponding positive assertions to be found in the second hypothesis (*in Prm.*VI.1075).Thus the One produces by means of negations; this is very strange language, and it may seem to be much less satisfactory than even Plotinus' metaphorical accounts of generation, which refer to the undiminished giving of the One, of its giving birth.

In addition to using the *Philebus* and the *Parmenides* as his source texts, Proclus' interests in the logic of causation extend further into a series of principles that formalize Platonist intuitions concerning image and archetype, matter and form, and the reciprocity of the Good with respect to all other members of reality. Form acts as cause and image imitates that form (*Phd.* 74e1); the Good extends providential care in the form of introducing Being and intelligibility (*R.* 508e), and acting as the teleological goal of every soul (*Smp.* 205a5). Proclus then fuses the fundamental Platonic relationship, between the Form and its image, with the Aristotelian conception of the transmission of cause, to create a causal principle that pulls his system in two competing directions. This principle, that the cause is necessarily greater than the effect (*ET* prop. 75.1–2: "Every cause properly transcends its resultant."), relies both on the explanatory capacity of causes to bring about realities that express (imitate or revert to) their sources, and on the Platonic axiom that the image is less real than the archetype.[38]

Above we saw that in the metaphysics of Plotinus (at least the initial stages of reality's expansion), not only is there an emphasis on the affinity between Intellect and the One, but the activity of Intellect flows in two directions: the shining out and the self-arrival, two sides of the same act, so that there is no departure from the nature of the One, a perspective that Plotinus underscores in his metaphors that convey the undiminished giving of the One (the inexhaustible font; the radiance of the sun). The Intellect, for Plotinus, reverts upon the One, refracting the light of the One into an infinite series of intuitions, each intuition discovering its object as fully real, as the eternal ground of its own capacity to discern reality. For Proclus, too, the entire procession of effects from their original cause flows backwards towards the source in a circuit that ultimately allows the lower to function as the mirror of the higher. Proclus describes this circuit most succinctly in *ET* prop. 35: "every effect simultaneously proceeds, remains, and reverts to its cause".

How, then, does the cause return to or revert upon its effect? We have glimpsed the Platonist intuitions that inform Proclean metaphysics in *mimēsis*, the imitation of the cause (the effect preserves likeness with the cause), and in *eros* (the effect has an erotic disposition towards union with the cause). But in order to understand the process of reversion in greater detail, it is necessary to discuss the vertical and horizontal gradations that allow both differentiation and ranking among similar kinds of reality and distinction and hierarchy between superior and subordinate kinds of realities. For Proclus, multiplicity, the proliferation of effects from their causes, can be studied as internal and external, as uniform and hetero-form procession, or as horizontal and vertical procession. In a way that might put us in mind of Plotinus' theory of two acts, Proclus refers "to procession and multiplication as the external activity of an entity, and reversion and unification as its internal activity" (A. C. Lloyd 1987: 33).[39] At *ET* prop. 108, Proclus sketches these two kinds of profusion: "Every particular member of any order can participate the monad of the rank immediately superjacent in one of two ways: either through the universal of its own order, or through the particular member of the higher series which is co-ordinate with it in respect of its analogous relation to that series as a whole" (*ET* prop. 108).

This sentence is imposing and sounds quite abstract, but a simple example might illustrate these two kinds of procession. Suppose that Intellect proceeds horizontally into various lesser forms of intellect (the demiurgic and human intellects). Suppose further that Intellect also proceeds vertically (declines) into a lesser hypostasis, Soul, while the Soul hypostasis itself proceeds horizontally into the various members of that hypostasis.

Here we have two successive transverse series or strata of reality proceeding from their respective "monads" or universal terms, Soul and Intellect: thus we have two kinds of procession, one, for example, of Soul from Intellect (vertical) and one, for example, of World Soul from Soul (horizontal). What then accounts for the "declination", as Proclus terms it, from One to Intellect, from Intellect to Soul, and from Soul to body? Proclus will need

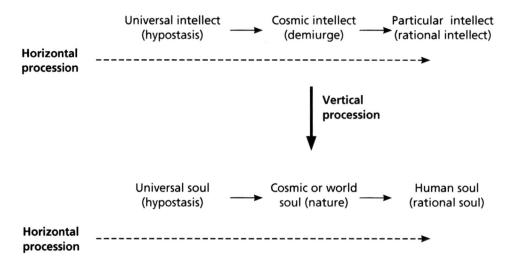

Figure 11.1 Vertical and horizontal procession.

to invoke the principle that the cause is greater than the effect, together with the principle that every multiplicity participates in a unity that is prior to it.

Now, each member of these series can revert in each of two ways: vertically (Soul reverts to Intellect), or horizontally (Soul reverts to or within its own hypostasis, becoming in a sense most profoundly itself). Either way, Intellect's reversion to the One (and we saw this in the case of Plotinus' inchoate Intellect reverting to the One and becoming actualized Intellect) does not result in the disappearance of Intellect. Instead, the stage of reversion enables the effect to become most distinctively itself: it achieves its essence, its definition, its formal nature, by engaging in the internal act that is most appropriate to itself. For Proclus, reversion to the cause takes place according to the three channels or aspects of the intelligible order: Being, Life and Intellect. Thus, reversion to the cause results in the complete realization of, for example, the human soul as a living, intelligent being possessed of self-knowledge and fully cognizant, as well, of its eternal source.[40]

We see that not only does Proclus suggest that the One is the cause of all things, and that every cause transcends its effects, but he also provides a "circular" model of causation according to which, "every effect remains in its cause, proceeds from it, and reverts upon it" (*ET* prop. 35).[41] He discusses this spiritual circuit in his *in Prm.* 620, when he reminds the reader that "every plurality exists in unity". Thus, when it comes to understanding the fundamental relationship between the transcendent principle and its manifestations, Proclus insists that there is an unparticipated aspect of each and every hypostasis, including the One. Moreover, the primary sense of the hypostasis is its subsistence as what Proclus calls a "whole before the parts" (*ET* prop. 67).

Yet the strength of Proclus' system is also perhaps its weakness: the terms of the procession can never be reversed, as reversion itself entails a strengthening of identity with respect to the being that reverts to the higher, receiving its good and fulfilling its nature through that very reversion. Proclus' soul, in reverting to its ultimate source, the One, is able, according to the metaphysics of Proclus, to realize a kind of unification with the divine, an act that takes place when the soul actualizes its own "centre", as Proclus calls it, but reverts to the transcendent. As he describes this process in the *in Prm.*, Proclus suggests that the formal boundaries between soul and first principle in fact strengthen the soul in its otherness, its ontological station apart from that principle:[42] "We must awaken the One in us in order that we might be able, if it is permissible to say this, to know somehow what is like [us] with what is like [that], within the parameter of our own ontological station (*taxis*)" (*in Prm.* 1081.5).

Here we glimpse a moment that breaks free of merely metaphysical discourse: earlier in the passage Proclus warns us that this knowledge can never occur through merely discursive capacity. Nevertheless, Proclus emphasizes the ontological distance between the One in us and the One *qua* transcendent principle. The upshot is that even this highest form of knowledge, when the soul awakens the faculty that is most akin to the one, also at the same time recommits the soul to its identity as other than the One; as ontologically inferior and as eternally, even irremediably, belonging to a different order or rank. In *ET* prop. 31, Proclus repeats what is essentially Plotinus' understanding concerning procession and reversion: procession grants existence; reversion grants essence. As we saw, the reversion to the One in Plotinus' philosophy allows Intellect to become not the One, but rather itself: the Indefinite Dyad, intelligible matter, is defined through its object, the One as determined or conditioned by the very nature of Intellect. Likewise, the reversion to the cause allows the effect, in Proclus' philosophy, to realize its own highest nature; to become more itself.

Yet Neoplatonism is not just an exegetical metaphysics that attempts to reify the hypotheses of Plato's *Parmenides*. This manifestation of the One in all things is, ultimately, just the life of the soul, as it undertakes the journey of awakening to its source in the One, and also its cosmic mission of returning the multiplicity back into the source. We have seen that Plotinus' metaphysics opens the door, through its emphasis on the affinities between Intellect and the One, and through its insistence on the simultaneous capacity of the Intellect to give rise to the world of Being and to remain free of all objects, to a realization: the entire world of manifestation is none other than the self-disclosure of the One. Proclus' metaphysics of Being, though it reiterates and formalizes the ontological principles of Platonism and the model of procession employed by Plotinus, rather emphasizes a hierarchical world: the soul visits, as it were, its source in the One. It catches a glimpse of that ultimate principle but accepts its place in the cosmic chain.

DAMASCIUS' METAPHYSICS OF NON-BEING

It is now time to confront how the Neoplatonic tradition after Proclus engaged with the paradoxical implications of Proclus' system, and with the paradoxes inherent in the very postulation of Being as a product of two principles: the indefinite flow of power and the fixity of that power (*apeiron* and *peras*) in the eternal self-determination of Being. For this task, we turn to the work of Damascius, the last scholarch of the school, who in his *Problems and Solutions Concerning First Principles* reveals a systematic tendency to criticize the developments of Proclus' metaphysics by introducing and fundamentally elevating the prior interpretations of the influential third-century Syrian philosopher, Iamblichus, *vis-à-vis* scholastic questions. For example, although Damascius sympathizes with Proclus' and Plotinus' insistence on the transcendent simplicity of the One, he does so to the extent that he is not actually content to call the One "the One". Instead, it has no name – perhaps it can be called the Ineffable (*arrhēton*).

Damascius launches his *Problems and Solutions* by calling into question Proclus' derivation of all things from the One. In the rest of the work, he advances what is both a critique of Proclus' theory of causation at the level of the Ineffable, the highest principle, as well as a positive account of the One. Therefore, Damascius, like his more recent predecessors, once more responds to what we saw was Plotinus' initial enquiry – why does the One, which lacks all attributes, flow forth, so to speak, as "all things"? "Is the so-called One Principle of all things beyond all things or is it one among all things, as if it were the summit of those that proceed from it? And are we to say that 'all things' are with the [first principle], or after it and [that they proceed] from it?" (*Pr.* I.1.1–9).

As demonstrated in the first part of this chapter, Plotinus leaves the fecundity of the One largely unexplained – he relies on metaphors that imply the infinite generosity of the One coupled with its infinite power. Proclus, of course, assumes this much when he writes that "every manifold in some way participates [in] unity", but has some difficulty in explaining how the One is something in which all things participate. Again, as we saw, he arrives at a compromise solution when he suggests that there are principles in the realm of the One, the primal pair consisting in limit and the unlimited, that bring about the realm of Being as their product. This solution does not satisfy Damascius, and much of the *Problems and Solutions* is devoted to a discussion of the One. For him, the word "One" will imply "all things". The One includes all things by its very nature, and so there are actually three names for the One: the One (*hen*), the One-all (*hen-panta*) and the Unified (*hēnōmenon*).

Throughout his discussion of the first principles, however, Damascius maintains a much more aporetic stance than Proclus. Even if he suggests doctrinal innovations, his very manner of couching them is more often than not obscured by what he understands as the problematic nature of metaphysical discourse proper. For example, in discussing the causality of the One, he asks:

> What follows after this discussion is an inquiry into whether there is a procession from the One into its subsequents, and of what kind it is, or whether the One gives no share of itself to them. One might reasonably raise puzzles about either position. For if the One gives no share of itself to its products, how has it produced them as so unlike itself, that they enjoy nothing of its nature?   (*Pr.* I.99)

On the other hand, Damascius wants to claim that no such procession is possible, given that procession implies distinction (the distinction between what proceeds and what does not proceed) and therefore, there can be no procession from the One:

> Every procession takes place together with distinction, whereas multiplicity is the cause of every distinction. Distinction is always the cause of multiplicity, whereas the One is before multiplicity. If the One is also before the One in the sense that the One is taken as one without [others], then a fortiori the One is before the many. Therefore the nature of the One is entirely without distinction. And therefore the One cannot proceed.   (*Pr.* I.100)

After posing the *aporia* concerning transcendence in the opening sections of the work, as well as his general criticism of Proclus' understanding of Being as the product of the intelligible realm, Damascius launches a sustained enquiry into the meaning of Proclus' spiritual circuit in so far as it relies on the concepts of "procession" and "reversion", by revealing what are at least on the surface the fallacies entailed by Proclus' solution of circular causation:

> What is it we mean when we say, "remaining in the cause"? Something must be either first or third, so that it cannot be the processive if it is still that which remains. Does remaining mean that what proceeds has its origin in the cause? But this is absurd: cause must be prior; effect is subsequent. Perhaps the cause remains while the effect proceeds?   (*Pr.* II.117)

But now the whole idea of remaining in the cause is trivialized, and amounts to no more than the tautology that the first is not the second, and so forth. Again, Damascius critically examines the structure of procession, showing that reversion is part of a unified triad, in which the three moments act together to define the nature of a hypostasis, but at the same time, reversion is also dissolution or undoing of the very effects achieved through the process of procession. How is it possible for reversion to assume these very different functions? He also points out that "reversion" is ambiguous between something which achieves its own definition from an inchoate state, and something which returns to a higher source or to its cause.

Damascius' innovations in the realm of metaphysics are actually implied both by Proclus' complete theory of cyclical creativity and indeed by Plotinus earlier, as, for example, when he says at *Enn.* VI.5[23].7.1–2: "for we and what is ours go back to real being and ascend to that and to the first which comes from it".

The spiritual circuit, the return of all to the One and especially the soul's special function as a conduit of this return, is the crucial premise of Neoplatonism in so far as it constitutes a religion. What, after all, is the place of the human self in this cosmic drama of the One's radiance and of attaining to the goal of wisdom, which is to uncover a vision of the whole? The soul's destiny is to return to the One, not just in the sense that the soul will develop wisdom or knowledge but also in the sense that the soul becomes instrumental in the completion of the spiritual circuit. Yet how the soul accomplishes this very journey is exactly the problem entailed by the system that, as it were, underwrites it. This anxiety pervades Damascius' criticisms.

In attempting to undermine the metaphysics of Being developed by Proclus, Damascius will appear to be a David, flinging shots against the over-towering system of Proclus: he can sound even more scholastic, almost pointlessly refining the language of metaphysics in order to bring down a creative edifice that, after all, remains a celebration of the divine nature of Being, of the sanctity of the cosmos as a whole, as well as a truthful indication of where the good of the intelligent beings, inhabiting that cosmos, actually lies. All this, as we have seen, is in keeping with fundamental Platonic axioms. Yet in my view, Damascius also performs a crucial role in the tradition he inherits. We can see that he shifts the perspective of his metaphysics: he struggles to create a metaphysical discourse that accommodates, in so far as language is sufficient, the ultimate principle of reality. After all, how coherent is a metaphysical system that bases itself on the Ineffable as a first principle? Instead of creating an objective ontology, Damascius writes ever mindful of the limitations of dialectic, and of the pitfalls and snares inherent in the very structure of metaphysical discourse:

> If, in speaking about [the Ineffable], we attempt the following collocations, viz. that it is Ineffable, that it does not belong to the category of all things, and that it is not apprehensible by means of intellectual knowledge, then we ought to recognize that these constitute the language of our own labors. This language is a form of hyperactivity that stops on the threshold of the mystery without conveying anything about it at all. Rather, such language announces the subjective experiences of *aporia* and misapprehension that arise in connection with the One, and that not even clearly but by means of hints.   (*Pr.* I.8.11–16)

Beyond the discourse of metaphysics lies the empty ground of wisdom, rooted in the unconditioned reality that is the One. It is for this reason, perhaps, more than any petty academic rivalries or obsessions with scholasticism that Damascius, as the last of the scholarchs, reminds us of the limitations that beset all metaphysical discourse. At the cost of originality, he shadows Proclus and attempts to undo the great edifice of the metaphysics of being, in order to return his reader to the intellect that does not grasp being. In closing his work, Damascius clarifies the relationship between individual and the first cause, the One or Good, perhaps pleading for a return to Plotinus' metaphysics of light: "The way the individuals are contained in that nature and the way they are differentiated from it is like the light of the sun, which forever remains both in its own commonality and also is distributed individually to each being, because the sun contains a single illuminating cause of all the individual eyes" (*Pr.* I.96).

Contemplation, the direct self-realization of the nature of the One as permeating the ground of one's own Intellect; the awareness of the pristine nature of wisdom that does not grasp being as something outside of itself, this is the fundamental ground that Damascius attempts to uncover beneath the overarching, byzantine structure of Proclus' metaphysics of being. So Damascius says of contemplation, the only compelling human enterprise for him: "We attempt to look at the sun for the first time and we succeed because we are far away. But the closer we approach the less we see. And at last we see neither [sun] nor other things, since we have completely become the light itself, instead of an enlightened eye" (*Pr.* I.85).

ACKNOWLEDGEMENT

My sincerest thanks to the editors of this volume, Svetla Slaveva-Griffin and Pauliina Remes. Their vision for the volume as a whole as well as their investment in the details of each article, including my own, is commendable. I would also like to thank the careful comments of an anonymous reviewer of this chapter, whose criticisms improved the article immeasurably.

NOTES

1. Neoplatonic texts address the reader as one who earnestly strives to assimilate the truths under discussion, cf. the instructions cited in notes 2–5 below. Plato's texts themselves share this assumption about ignorance on the part of the audience/reader: "Strange prisoners". "They're like us" (*R.* 515a.2).
2. *Enn.* I.6[1].8.26: ἀλλ' οἷον μύσαντα ὄψιν ἄλλην ἀλλάξασθαι καὶ ἀνεγεῖραι, ἣν ἔχει μὲν πᾶς, χρῶνται δὲ ὀλίγοι. All translations from the *Enneads*, hereinafter, are according to Armstrong (1966–88), with modifications or otherwise specified.
3. *Enn.* V.8[31].9.4: Ἔστω οὖν ἐν τῇ ψυχῇ φωτεινή τις φαντασία σφαίρας ἔχουσα. πάντα ἐν αὐτῇ.
4. *Enn.* V.3[49].17.38: Πῶς ἂν οὖν τοῦτο γένοιτο; Ἄφελε πάντα.
5. *Enn.* V.2[11].1.1: "The One is all things and not a single one of them; it is the principle of all things, not all things, but all things have that other kind of transcendent existence; for in a way they do occur in the One." Also Damascius, *de Principiis* 1.1: "Is the so-called 'One Principle' of all things beyond all things or is it one among all things, as if it were the summit of those that proceed from it? And are we to say that 'all things' are with the [first principle], or after it and [that they proceed] from it?" All translations of *de Principiis* are from Ahbel-Rappe (2010). An exemplary approach to the metaphysics of Proclus via the dialectic of one and many may be found in Steel (2010).
6. *Enn.* IV.8[6].1.1: "Often I have woken up out of the body to my self and have entered into myself."
7. Cf. Syrianus, *in Metaph.* 4.27–32: "For by the analytical method wisdom grasps the principles of being, by the divisional and definitional method the substances of all things, by the demonstrative inferring the essential properties of substances. This however is not the case with substances, which are the most simple and properly speaking intelligible, for these substances are entirely that which they are. For this reason they cannot be defined or demonstrated, but are grasped only by apprehension."
8. *Enn.* VI.5[23].7.1–6: "For we and what is ours go back to real being and ascend to that and to the first which comes from it, and we think the intelligibles; we do not have images or imprints of them. But if we do not, we are the intelligibles. If then we have a part in true knowledge, we are those; we do not apprehend them as distinct within ourselves, but we are within them."

9. Cf. Proclus, *ET* prop. 1: "Every multiplicity participates a Unity." In *Enn.* V.1[10], Plotinus interprets the three initial hypotheses in the second half of Plato's *Parmenides* as adumbrating his own metaphysical doctrine, according to which reality has different levels, which are, for Plotinus, the One, Intellect and Soul. He refers the first hypothesis ("if the one is", *Prm.* 137c4) to the One beyond being, the transcendent source of all.

10. On Plotinus' metaphysics of the dyad, see Slaveva-Griffin (2009).

11. Cf. Proclus, *ET* prop. 30: "If, on the other hand, it should remain only without procession, it will be indistinguishable from its cause, and will not be a new thing, which has arisen while the cause remains."

12. Cf. Plotinus' description of the One as (*Enn.* VI.8[39].16) "an eternal awakening … super-intellection". He explains that the One's activity, its productivity, is "like being awake with nothing else to wake it", and that "Intellect and intelligent life" "are identical with it". Therefore, he concludes, Intellect and wisdom and life "come from it and not from another" (*Enn.* VI.8[38].16.35–8, trans. Dillon & Gerson).

13. As I explain in the next section, Plotinus relies heavily on the *Republic*'s analogy of the sun to discuss the contemplative dimensions of metaphysics: everywhere intellect is characterized by "*theōrein*". Cf. *Enn.* V.1[10].6.28.

14. Cf. Proclus, *ET* prop. 75: "Every cause properly so called transcends its resultant."

15. Proclus, *ET* prop. 30.25: "For if it is a new thing, it is distinct and separate; and if it is separate and the cause remains steadfast, to render this possible it must have proceeded from the cause."

16. Cf. Damascius, *Pr.* I.18: "'Nothing' has two meanings: one is transcendent, the other is not. In fact the [word] 'one' also has two meanings, as the limit for example of matter and as the first, or what is before being. Therefore 'not being' also [has two meanings], as not even the one as limit, and as not even the first. In a similar way the unknowable and Ineffable have two meanings, as that which is not even the limit of conception, and that which is not even the first."

17. In using the heading for this section, I owe much to Beierwaltes (1961). For Beierwaltes, light is not merely a metaphor when used to describe Intellect, but can only succeed as an image of Intellect "because there is a presence of the original in the image" (*ibid.*: 342, my trans.). On the activity of the One as contemplative, Emilsson (2007: 71) cites V.4[7].2.15–9: "the One is not like something senseless; all things belong to it and are in it and with it, it being completely able to discern itself. It contains life in itself and all things in itself, and its comprehension of itself is itself in a kind of self-consciousness in everlasting rest and in a manner of thinking different from the thinking of Intellect" (trans. Emilsson). Cf. also *Enn.* VI.7[38].39.1–4, quoted below, where Plotinus talks about the One's "concentration" on itself.

18. *Enn.* V.3[49].17.30–39: "this [light] is from him and he is it; we must think that he is present when, like another god whom someone called to his house he comes and brings light to us: for if he had not come, he would not have brought the light. So the unenlightened soul does not have him as god; but when it is enlightened it has what it sought, and this is the soul's true end, to touch that light and see it by itself, not by another light, but by the light which is also its means of seeing. It must see that light by which it is enlightened: for we do not see the sun by another light than his own." *Enn.* VI.8[39].16: "an eternal awakening … super-intellection".

19. For example, in *Enn.* III.8[30].9.31, Plotinus explicitly tells us that Intellect is "*amphistomos*" (facing in two directions); possibly he means remaining in the One as well as proceeding from the One: τὸν νοῦν οἷον εἰς τοὐπίσω ἀναχωρεῖν καὶ οἷον ἑαυτὸν ἀφέντα τοῖς εἰς ὄπισθεν αὐτοῦ ἀμφίστομον ὄντα. "Intellect approaches as it were from behind and as it were lets go of itself into what is behind it, as it faces in two directions." Cf. Bussanich (1988) and commentary *ad loc*.

20. *Enn.* V.1[10].6.26–9: Πῶς οὖν καὶ τί δεῖ νοῆσαι περὶ ἐκεῖνο μένον; Περίλαμψιν ἐξ αὐτοῦ μέν, ἐξ αὐτοῦ δὲ μένοντος, οἷον ἡλίου τὸ περὶ αὐτὸ λαμπρὸν ὥσπερ περιθέον.

21. Plotinus continually turns to and adapts freely the language of *R.* 509a.3, especially emphasizing the affinity between the One and Intellect: Ὅ τι οὖν ἐγέννα, ἀγαθοῦ ἐκ δυνάμεως ἦν καὶ ἀγαθοειδὲς ἦν, καὶ αὐτὸς ἀγαθὸς ἐξ ἀγαθοειδῶν, ἀγαθὸν ποικίλον.

22. *Enn.* V.1[10].7.5–6: Πῶς οὖν νοῦν γεννᾷ; Ἢ ὅτι τῇ ἐπιστροφῇ πρὸς αὐτὸ ἑώρα.

23. Following Bussanich (1988: 37). Both alternatives present problems: the abrupt change of subject ἑώρα, if the subject is Intellect (which has not yet been created!) defies explanation. For a thorough analysis of this passage, see Atkinson (1983), A. C. Lloyd (1987) and Bussanich (1988), all of whom offer commentaries on this text.

24. Ἐνέργεια ἡ μέν ἐστι τῆς οὐσίας, ἡ δ' ἐκ τῆς οὐσίας ἑκάστου· καὶ ἡ μὲν τῆς οὐσίας αὐτό ἐστιν ἐνέργεια ἕκαστον, ἡ δὲ ἀπ' ἐκείνης, ἣν δεῖ παντὶ ἕπεσθαι ἐξ ἀνάγκης ἑτέραν οὖσαν αὐτοῦ.

25. Cf. A. C. Lloyd (1987: 176) who cites *Enn.* III.8[30].8.31–2: "Intellect is not contemplating it [the One] 'as one.'" "[In V.3{49}.11]… Intellect tried to grasp the One as simple but found itself with something else."

26. On Plotinus' philosophy of the Dyad, see Slaveva-Griffin (2009). Plotinus reaches into Pythagorean conceptualization through his reading of the *Philebus*' Dyad, *Peras* and *Apeiron*.

27. A. C. Lloyd (1987: 163) cites Aristotle's theory (*de An.* 431b2–5): "The faculty of thinking then thinks the forms in the images, and as in the former case what is to be pursued or avoided is marked out for it, so where there is no sensation and it is engaged upon the images it is moved to pursuit or avoidance" (trans. Ross). Bussanich discuses this theory (1988: 224) and cites *Enn.* V.6[24].5.15: ἀγαθὸν καὶ ὡς ἀγαθὸν καὶ ἐφετὸν αὑτῷ γενόμενον νοεῖ καὶ οἷον φαντασίαν τοῦ ἀγαθοῦ λαμβάνον.

28. For Lloyd, the object of the inchoate Intellect's vision is the image of the One; this doctrine is consistent, he maintains, with Aristotle's psychological theory, according to which intellect can become aware of *ousia* via *phantasia*. Cf. Bussanich (1988: 231–3) for a discussion of A. C. Lloyd (1987).

29. Again, cf. Proclus, *ET* prop. 30: "All that is immediately produced by any principle both remains in the producing cause and proceeds from it."

30. A. C. Lloyd (1990: 170) has argued that these phases, the mystical union with the One and the procession of the Intellect or generation of Intellect, are parallel moments in Plotinus' metaphysics. P. Hadot (1986: 243) also assimilates the two: inchoate and hyper-noetic Intellect are the same. Bussanich (1988: 234–5) argues vigorously against this interpretation.

31. On this controversial topic, see Trouillard (1955: 46); O'Daly (1973: 164); Bussanich (1988: 233).

32. As Dillon (2003) has shown, it is conceivable that Pythagorean interpretations of this part of the *Philebus*, according to which the indefinite or *apeiron* functioned as a dyad that acted upon the One or first principle, resulting in the development and elaboration of the order of primary beings, already figured into the Early Academy. For Proclus on the *Philebus*, see *PT* III.9.

33. Being forms the apex of the intelligible triad, which is as it were composed of two elements – the limit and the unlimited – that constitute its parts; hence its equivalence to the Platonic "mixed". Cf. *ET* prop. 89: "all true Being is composed of limit and infinite" and prop. 90: "prior to all that is composed of limit and infinitude there exist substantiality and independently the first Limit and the first Infinity".

34. Following is the Greek text of the *Philebus* 27d.6–10, as printed in the Oxford Classical Text, with the bracketed words indicating a textual variant; some editors print the neuter form of this phrase, as opposed to the masculine gender; thus the Mixed in this line refers either to the mixed life or to the mixed *qua* ontological kind: Καὶ μέρος γ' αὐτὸν φήσομεν εἶναι τοῦ τρίτου οἶμαι γένους· οὐ γὰρ [ὁ] δυοῖν τινοῖν ἐστι [μικτὸς ἐκεῖνος] ἀλλὰ συμπάντων τῶν ἀπείρων ὑπὸ τοῦ πέρατος δεδεμένων, ὥστε ὀρθῶς ὁ νικηφόρος οὗτος βίος μέρος ἐκείνου γίγνοιτ' ἄν "We will, I think, assign it to the third kind, for it is *not a mixture of just two elements* but of the sort where all that is unlimited is tied down by limit. It would seem right, then, to make our victorious form of life part of that kind" (trans. D. Frede).

35. Van Riel (2001: 144) points out, "Plato says that the god has 'shown' *peras* and *apeiron*" at *Phlb.* 23c.9–10. Proclus substitutes the word δεῖξαι with ἐκφαίνειν.

36. *PT* III.9.36.17–19: Ὅσῳ δὴ τὸ ποιεῖν τοῦ ἐκφαίνειν καταδεέστερον καὶ ἡ γέννησις τῆς ἐκφάνσεως, τοσούτῳ δήπου τὸ μικτὸν ὑφειμένην ἔλαχε τὴν ἀπὸ τοῦ ἑνὸς πρόοδον τῶν δύο ἀρχῶν. "To the extent that making is inferior to manifesting and production is inferior to manifestation, by so much the mixed has received an inferior procession from the One than the Dyad."

37. See Chlup (2012: 78–9) on the limit and unlimited as the primary fund for every existent.

38. Cf. A. C. Lloyd (1976): "The analysis of Proclus's proof confirms on more formal grounds the fairly obvious hypothesis that the principle of the cause being greater than its effect is the result of superimposing more Platonism on a transmission theory of causation." For Lloyd it is obvious that the transmission theory can be traced to Aristotle. He cites *GA* 734a30–32, so that the Form, or conformation, of B would have to be contained in A.

39. A. C. Lloyd (1990: 98) goes on to cite the example of *PT* V.18.283–4. The demiurge addresses the younger gods and his words are described "as the external activity of the intellect; for they 'make the indivisible proceed to divisible existence'".

40. On the soul's reversion to intellect, see Chlup (2012: 86–7), quoting *ET* prop. 70.8–19.

41. The classic work on this is Gersh (1973); now see the excellent treatment in Chlup (2012: 62–82).

42. On the ontological boundaries of the soul in its contact with the One, see the discussion of Chlup (2012: 174–84).

12

The metaphysics of the One

Jens Halfwassen

THE ONE AS THE BASIS FOR BEING AND THOUGHT

> It is by the One that all beings are being, both those which are primarily being and those which are in any sense said to be amongst beings. For what could anything be if it was not one? For if things are deprived of the One which is predicated of them, they are not those things. (*Enn.* VI.9[9].1.1–4)[1]

Plotinus' programmatic treatise *On the Good or the One* begins with these words. It summarizes the basis of his "philosophy of the One" (*Enn.* VI.9[9].3.14), as he essentially characterizes his own thought in the shortest possible way. Let us analyse this claim in more detail.

First, unity is the most essential condition for the Being and the conceivableness of all things. This insight cannot be reasonably disputed. Whatever we think of as existing, we already think of it as a unity. In fact, we can only *think* of such things which are a unity in some way: what is not one in any way does not exist with regard to thought. Parmenides had already formulated this idea and Plato had made it the basis of his philosophy. He had pointed to the etymology of the Greek word for nothing (*ouden*) as "that which is not one" (*oude hen, R.* 478b; cf. *Prm.* 166c), which is adopted by Plotinus (*Enn.* V.2[11].1.1). What is not one is nothing. Therefore everything which is, is necessarily one and in such a manner that it only *is*, for the very reason that it is *one*.

That something is, is based on the fact that it is one: therefore unity is the *reason* for Being, the existence of all things, but not only that. Secondly, *what* something is it also owes to its character as a unity, since if it were not one, it would no longer be that which in each case it is. Whatever something is, it is also that only because, and in so far as, it is a unity. It always contains its essence as a *unified* essence. Without a unitary character, it would be undefined and what is completely undefined is neither something, nor does it exist at all, nor can it be thought. Unity is therefore the basis of Being, not only in the sense of existence, but at the same time also in the sense of being what it is, the essence or the definition of every defined entity. That is valid for *all* conceivable classifications. Unity is consequently also the reason for the "thinkability" of all classifications and of conceivable entities by means of their being defined. So, third, unity turns out to be not only the ontological basis for existence and essence, but also the epistemological basis for our understanding of existence and essence.

Since unity is the basis for everything that is at all conceivable, therefore even its apparent opposite, the Many, in so far as it can be conceived of, is itself contingent upon the One: "For if it has not become a unity, even when it is composed of many, one can in no way say of it that it is" (*Enn.* V.3[49].15.12–14). In fact, we always of necessity think the Many as a unity, that is to say as a *united* multiplicity and that means as a united whole, which is formed from many elementary unities, so that the conception of the Many *presupposes* unity in a double sense, that is, the unity of the totality of a multiplicity, just as much as the unity of each one of its individual components. At the conclusion of his *Parmenides*, Plato illustrated that a radically disunited multiplicity cannot be conceived of, that it is absolutely nothing and therefore is not many (*Prm.* 165e–166c). Therefore nothing can oppose the One, because even multiplicity is only conceivable as a unity and therefore always presupposes the One. As a basis for the conceivability and definition of everything, including multiplicity, the One is without opposition or beyond it. As that which is detached from any opposite, it is the Absolute (*apolyton, Enn.* VI.8[39].20.6).

No one can dispute that everything which can be conceived of, can only be conceived of as a unity, because everything which is conceivable must be defined and definition is only possible as a unity. However, this insight can be interpreted in different ways. That unity, therefore, because it is the necessary condition for all thought, is the basis for Being, that is, for the existence and essence of all entities as Plotinus hypothesizes, only follows if one presupposes that the structure of Being fundamentally corresponds to the structure of our thought. This unity of thought and Being was first expressed by Parmenides (frag. 3). Plato had also referred to it with the sentence "that which entirely 'is' is entirely knowable, and that which in no way 'is' is in every way unknowable" (*R.* 477a [Shorey]). This differs from an Aristotelian approach in that the ground for being as well as knowability indeed transcends being and knowability, as we will see below. However, it is precisely here that an objection might be suggested. One could perhaps argue, just like Kant, that unity is the highest principle of our reasoning faculty, by means of which we order reality according to unitary points of view, because we could not grasp them otherwise (CpR B §16). However, it does not necessarily follow from this requirement of unity on the part of our thought that reality by itself, independent of our thought, must be a unity and must be ordered according to a unitary perspective. For Kant, the final basis for unity of our thought-forms is the unity of the thinking Self, the unity of subjectivity; self-consciousness first *places* the unitary perspective in its thought, through which it apprehends and orders the diversity of the world, as it is present in perception. Therefore, it produces itself the unitary nature of its classifications and of the thoughts formulated through them via subjective synthesis – according to Kant. Unity for him, then, is only a subjective principle, not the basis of Being.

Interestingly, Plotinus also poses the question whether Thought[2] itself first spawns unity, without which nothing can be thought: when Thought transmits that which is obtained by perception to us, "even though it is a multitude, it does not permit it to be a multitude, so that it somehow even here makes unity apparent, either by imparting unity itself, which multiplicity does not have, or by recognising unity lying in order by means of its acute vision and uniting the reality of the many to this unity" (*Enn.* VI.6[34].13.19–23, trans. O'Brien).

He, then, clearly formulates the alternatives: to interpret our thought's requirement for unity either subjectively, as a consolidation of Thought itself, or realistically and ontologically, as the perception of the unitary character of Being itself, which reveals itself in its orderliness. In the second case, it is Thought which again extracts the unitary nature of the order, so that Plotinus at no point disputes the impossibility of transcending subjectivity or the contribution of Thought itself to our presupposition of unity.

Which alternative should be chosen? Plotinus provides a quasi-transcendental analysis of the conditions for the possibility of our thought. This ensures the ontological significance of our conceptual anticipation of unity and simultaneously means that our fundamental classifications of Thought are stable in reality. Plotinus' argumentation runs as follows: if we can only think, in so far as we already presuppose unity, where both that which is thought and the intellective act (*noēsis*) encompassing it must possess a unitary character, then that which is presupposed by each intellective act from its very beginning cannot itself be the *product* of an intellective act which presupposes it. An intellective act originally positing unity would not be unitary before this position and would therefore be nothing, and thus not be a thought either. The One presupposed by every intellective act as a condition for taking place does therefore not rest upon the subjective positioning of Thought itself, but rather necessarily precedes all subjective unifying actions of Thought:

> If, then, it is not possible to think anything without the One how is it possible for that not to exist without which it is not possible to think or speak? For it is impossible to say that it does not exist of something, without which one cannot think or say anything at all. But that which is needed everywhere for the coming of existence of every act (*noēsis*) and content of thinking (*logos*) must be there before (*prohyparchein*) content and the act of thinking: for this is how it can be brought to contribute to their coming into existence.   (*Enn.* VI.6[34].13.43–9)

Our thought's requirement for unity itself proves that the One is the necessary condition for all our thinking and hypothesizing; with its abolition thinking itself would be suspended. The One is not a *product* of our thought, not posited by it, since every intellective act is itself only possible if the One has been *presupposed*. The One is therefore more primordial than Thought and is its principle; on account of its need for unity, Thought finds in itself the necessity of always requiring its principle. The logical priority of the One before the implementation of Thought, which from its very beginning requires unity, ensures for Plotinus the ontological validity of our intellective anticipation of unity. Since the One is also always presupposed before everything which conceivably contains Being, the ontological priority of the One before Being is by this means simultaneously revealed, which proves that the One is the principle of Being: "But if it is needed for the existence of each and every substance – for there is nothing which is not one – it must exist before substance and initially generate Being" (*Enn.* VI.6[34].13.50–51; cf. Halfwassen 2004: 59–97; Gabriel 2009: 184–310).

Plotinus' argumentation demonstrates that the One as the principle of Thought precedes and makes possible every implementation of subjective thinking and in this way it itself cannot be what is posited by our thought. However, does it also demonstrate that reality itself is based on unity and is structured as a unity? Here the sceptical argument is suggested that Plotinus does not demonstrate the unity of Thought and Being, as it is so understood, but rather always presupposes it. However, a scepticism which questions the affinity of the fundamental structure of our thought with the fundamental structure of Being enmeshes itself in self-contradiction. If the anticipation of unity which first makes thinking possible and therefore precedes it should not be sufficient to ensure the ultimate unity of reality, then one must concede the possibility that reality by itself, independently of our thought, might also consist of a disunited multiplicity of disconnected individual things. However, it is precisely this assumption which claims already unitary classifications of thought, such as actuality, multiplicity or individual things, as stable reality. By doing so, it already presupposes the stability of reality attained by our classifications of thought; that is, the anticipations of reality which make it possible. Therefore it presupposes the argument which it wants to dispute. However, a presupposition which is presupposed even when attempting to deny it cannot be disputed. Therefore the One is not only the basis of Thought, but also, owing to our thought having a foundation in reality, it is necessarily the basis for Being.

As the *basis* for Being and Thought, the One precedes both. This absolute priority of the One also shows itself in the fact that while we can think all entities and even Being itself only as a unity, we must on no account always think the One as connected to Being. We can of course conceive of non-Being. So, for example, we can think of Non-Being as different from Being, Becoming as the intermediary between Being and Nothing and even of Nothing itself as the complete lack of Being; and by this means we think of Non-Being, Becoming and Nothing, in each case, as a unitary constitution. In contrast, we cannot think of anything, without simultaneously thinking of it as a unity. The One is therefore prior to Being, just as it is prior to Thought. The One is the Absolute and is not contingent upon Being or Thought and it is presupposed in and before all Being, just as in and before all Thought, and does not allow itself to be thought away.

The absolute nature of our presupposition of unity has a series of metaphysically significant implications, which form the structural principles of Neoplatonic philosophy:

(a) Unity enables the differentiation of Being and Non-Being. Admittedly, we think of "Being" and "Non-Being" to an equal extent as unitary constitutions, but in thinking of Non-Being, we do not conceive of any positive content, no "what" or "something" of its own, but rather simply the *negation* of Being. Every positive content, every "what" or "something" which can be attributed to Being, must have a positive, unitary character: "so that it is being when it is one in some way" (*Enn.* VI.6[34].1.20). Being, for Plotinus, primarily signifies determination, that something is made into something and not merely actual existence. So content implies determination. In contrast, Non-Being is indeterminate, which is non-being on account of its lack of determination. As the basis of all determination, the One is the principle of Being, which endows it with all its determination and by this very means makes it a being and preserves it in Being: "For all that is not one is kept in being by the One and is what it is by this One" (*Enn.* V.3[49].15.11–12).

(b) Furthermore, unity is the measure which makes the differentiation of various grades of Being possible. If the unity of something is the basis of its Being, then every "something" is also a being to the extent that it is one. A higher degree of unity at the same time signifies a higher degree of Being; the more unified something is, the more "being" it is (*mallon on*, *Enn.* VI.9[9].1.26–8). For example, the Soul, the principle of unity of the organism in which it lives, is not only more unified, but on this account participates more in Being, than the bodily organism which it renders into a unity. In contrast to the organism, which is generated when the Soul endows it with unity, and passes away when it loses its unity, the Soul always exists and is imperishable (cf. *Enn.* IV.7[2]). Only the henological approach of his philosophy allows Plotinus (as it already allowed Plato) to posit the graduation of Being; that is, the differentiation between different grades and levels of Being. Unity as the basis of Being generates the "ontological comparative" and in this way also forms the foundation of the Theory of Ideas, in conformity with the unitary nature of something participating more in Being than its individual realization. Since the unitary classification "justice" or the unitary classification "courage" possess a higher degree of unity than the many different cases of just or courageous behaviour, as Ideas they also possess a higher, more substantial or "more being" Being than these. It is only unity which makes the multiplicity of its instantiations into what they are.

(c) If multiplicity is the concept opposed to the One, then the relationship of unity to multiplicity forms the foundation of our thinking and all its classifications, including the foundation of Being; it is also prior to the opposition between Being and Non-Being. Plato saw the ultimate and most original principles in the One and the Many. However, since multiplicity is only possible and conceivable as a unity, it always presupposes the One; conversely the One does not presuppose the Many. The relationship of unity to multiplicity is therefore fundamentally asymmetrical and from this fundamental asymmetry, Plotinus obtains the motif of ascent and the notion of the transcendence of the absolute One, which determines his entire philosophy.

THE ASCENT TO THE ABSOLUTE

The relationship of unity to multiplicity determines the ontological structure that is foundational for all entities, irrespective of whether they are intelligible and eternal or manifestly appearing and changeable. All Being is only because and in so far as it is a unity. However, because of that, it is simultaneously Being and One, and if it is twofold, then it is a multiplicity (Plato, *Prm.* 142b–144e). However, that multiplicity is itself only possible as a united multiplicity, the unity-endowing One is therefore always presupposed, therefore the One and Many do not have equal priority and power as principles of Being, but rather the One as the basis of all multiplicity is the sole absolute principle, the origin of everything (*archē pantōn*, *Enn.* VI.9[9].5.24). Plotinus arrives by this means at his monistic interpretation of Plato's theory of principles with all its bipolarity of unity and multiplicity which determines Being (cf. *Enn.* V.1[10].5.6–19).

As the basis for all multiplicity, the One necessarily *transcends* all multiplicity. This thought is central for Plotinus. If the One is the reason for all multiplicity, then it cannot be present in multiplicity as the One, as itself, and merge into this presence. While it sustains, by means of its presence, the Many in Being, it cannot, however, merge in this presence with the Many, but rather it remains by itself above it as a unity *beyond* multiplicity. Otherwise, on account of its immanence in the Many, it would itself be a multiplicity; it would be divided into multiplicity and would therefore no longer be the One or the origin of unity, which holds multiplicity together as a unity and by this means makes it possible:

> For, from what has been said, it is not correct to divide the One up into the many, but rather to bring back the divided many to the One, and that One has not come to these many, but these because they are scattered have given us the impression that also that has been taken apart, as if one were to divide what controls and holds together into parts equal to what is controlled.   (*Enn.* VI.4[22].7.3–9)

The question of how the One can be the basis of multiplicity, without in this process nullifying itself as One, had already occupied Plato. It comprises the basic problem of the Theory of Ideas: how can an Idea be the basis for the multiplicity of its many instantiations and still remain a unity itself (*Prm.* 131b–e; cf. *Phlb.* 15b)? Plotinus answers this fundamental question of Platonism exactly as Plato had previously answered it: "But there is a need for the One, from which the many derives, to exist *before* the Many" (*Enn.* V.3[49].12.9–10). The basis cannot, then, itself have the character of the thing which it serves as a basis for. As the origin of multiplicity, the One itself is no longer a multiplicity, but rather it is the basis for multiplicity, precisely because it as a unity itself remains itself beyond multiplicity. The basis, then, remains always transcendent in relation to the thing which it is a basis for and it is a basis for it precisely by means of its transcendence:

> And this is no wonder. Or yes, it is a wonder how the multiplicity of life came from what is not multiplicity and the multiplicity would not have existed, if what was not multiplicity had not existed before the multiplicity. For the origin is not divided up into the All, for if it were divided up it would destroy the All too; and the All could not any more come into being if the origin did not remain by itself different from it.   (*Enn.* III.8[30].10.14–19)

Plato was the first to state the transcendence of the basis in relation to what it is a basis for, by means of which it is foremost the basis (*Smp.* 211b; *R.* 509b; *Test. Plat.* 50, 52; cf. also *Phdr.* 245d; *Ti.* 37d, 42e), and his nephew, Speusippus, had formulated it in all its essentials: "The origin is never of the same kind as that which it is the origin of" (frag. 72; cf. also *Test. Plat.* 55b).

From the transcendence of the One over the Many, by means of which it is the basis for the Many, there originates throughout all of Plotinus' philosophy a movement of ascent. It is understood as a *henological reduction*; that is, as a return movement (*anagōgē*) of multiplicity in each of its shapes to the unity upon which it was based at any time, in the process of which multiplicity is transcended to the One (cf. Halfwassen 1992: 57–61):

> Therefore, too, we go back everywhere to *one*. And in each and every thing there is some *one*, to which you will trace it back, and this in every case to the *one* before it, which is not simply one, until we come to the simply One (*haplōs hen*); but this cannot be traced back to something else. But if we take the *one* of the plant – this is its abiding origin – and of the *one* of the animal and the *one* of the soul and the *one* of the universe, we are asking in each case what is the most powerful and really valuable in it.   (*Enn.* III.[30].8.10.20–26)

The henological reduction is therefore comprehended in three stages: (1) from the individual phenomena to the Ideas; (2) from the world as the unity of all phenomena to the unity of all Ideas (the One-Being); (3) from the unity of Ideas (the One-Being) to the absolute One, which is absolutely devoid of multiplicity, and therefore no further reduction is possible. This movement of ascent, its stages and its methods follow Plato's Theory of Principles:

1. From the manifest multiplicity of individual things, the first step leads to the respective Idea from which they derive their unity, for example, from many plants to the Idea of the plant, the "One of the plant". For Plato already the most general and most fundamental classification of the Ideas was that they were the basis of unity for the multiplicity of their instantiations (R. 476a, 479a, 507b, 596a; Prm. 131b–c, 132a–d, 133b, 135b–d; Phlb. 15a–b); Aristotle defines the Ideas in the same terms as Plato as a "one over the many" (hen epi pollōn), because as a unity it transcends the multiplicity of its instantiations (Met. 990b7–13, 1079a3–9; APo. 77a5). Therefore when Thought in a multiplicity recognizes the unity of a shared classification, an Idea must always be set *above* this multiplicity as the transcendent basis of unity in multiplicity (see also On the Ideas, frag. 3).

2. However, unity in multiplicity is not only the basic condition of every individual entity. Since this condition is common to all entities, it already merges all particular entities into a unity, which is once again a unity in multiplicity; that is to say, the unity of the world or the universe (pan), of the entirety of the world. The unity of the entire world equally presupposes a transcendent basis of unity as a unity in multiplicity, which merges all individual things into the unity of the world's totality. This basis for the unity of the entire world is no longer a particular Idea, but rather the totality of the Ideas, which encompasses all individual Ideas, the cosmos of the Ideas, which Plato called the "One-Being" (hen on) in the Parmenides; it is the totality of all Ideas, just as the world is the totality of all instantiations (Ti. 30c–31b; cf. 92c). As the unity of all Ideas, the One-Being transcends all individual Ideas, which it contains in itself as its moments.

3. The character as a unity in multiplicity, which requires the reversion to a transcendent basis of unity, defines not only individual instantiations and the world as a totality, but also the Ideas and the One-Being as a totality. Admittedly, every Idea is a unity, but it is not an absolutely simple unity, which is completely devoid of multiplicity and which cannot be further analysed, but rather every Idea contains as a definable essence a multitude of moments of its own nature, which are indicated in its definition. For example, the Idea of Man contains in itself the Ideas of "Life", "Reason" and "Community" which are essential to man's nature. As the unity of the multiplicity of the moments of its nature every Idea is a number (cf. Enn. VI.6[34]). In this sense every Idea is also a "unity from many" (hen ek pollōn): that is, the unity of the entire totality of its moments, as Plato defines them in the Parmenides (157c–e). That is most especially true for the One-Being as the totality of all Ideas. Admittedly as the all-encompassing unity of the totality of Being, it enjoys a higher degree of unity than any particular Idea. However, it contains all given Ideas within itself as its moments and, just like every other Idea, it is thereby a unity, which contains multiplicity in itself. As a unity with immanent multiplicity or as a "One-Many" (hen polla, Plato, Prm. 144e5;

often cited by Plotinus, e.g. *Enn.* V.1[10].8.26), the One-Being thereby also presupposes a transcendent basis for its own unity. As the totality of the Ideas, however, the One-Being is no longer a unity alongside other unities, but rather the unity of the absolute totality, outside of which there exists nothing, the total unity (*hen panta*, *Enn.* III.6[26].6.23; V.3[49].15.23). The basis of its unity is by this means the absolute or simple One, the One itself, which as *pure unity* is absolutely devoid of multiplicity and for which therefore a further basis is neither required nor possible. The simple One is by this means the Absolute, by which the ascent to the ultimate Principle ends; it is the aim of the ascending movement towards a point of origin, beyond which it is not possible to proceed further.

Furthermore, it is important in principle that this ascent is understood as a movement of abstraction (*aphairesis*), so that it does not lead to a deflation of thought, but rather continuously to a higher plenitude of essence from one level to the next. The abstraction is to be understood as a liberation from multiplicity and from the finitude and changeability of the many things, which is contingent upon multiplicity. It is the revelation of the unity which serves as the basis for multiplicity, but which is hidden by it. The reversion to the One is to be understood, then, as a successive removal of all multiplicity, and at the same time it attains, to the extent to which multiplicity is removed, to a continuously higher, more intense and more concentrated plenitude; the plenitude increases with simplicity. Therefore, since the One is the basis of Being, all plenitude, which is obscured by multiplicity, is found in unity. For example, while the Idea of the plant is recognized by means of looking beyond all individual plants and their particular properties, it is not an empty product of abstraction like our general concept "plant", but rather it is that by means of which all individual plants are plants at all, by participating in it; that is in its unitary nature. Accordingly, the One-Being is also not the emptiest and most general concept which we can form, but rather the very embodiment of the plenitude of Being (Halfwassen 2004: 68–79).

Certainly, when it is necessary to go beyond this epitome of the plenitude of Being to the absolute One, which contains no multiplicity and therefore also no positively conceivable content, then there arises the paradox that the Absolute, which is the basis for everything, can only be thought of as nothingness (*Enn.* III.8[30].10.26–35). Plotinus does not conceal this paradox in any way. It preserves in itself the highest notion of Platonism: the pure transcendence of the Absolute and its interpretation by means of a strict negative dialectic or *negative theology*. One can speak of "negative theology" here to the extent that "theology" in the ancient sense, since Aristotle, signified a theory of principles. "Negative theology" means the exclusion of the Absolute as the definitive principle and point of origin by denying all positive attributes. It is thereby not implied that the transcendent Absolute, the One itself, can be conceived of as God and even less so as a personal God of any kind; it is rather that the One itself is "more than God" (*Enn.* VI.9[9].6.12–13). The very conception of God is included in that which a strict negative theology transcends. "What one says of God is insufficient for me: that which is beyond divinity is my life and my light", says Angelus Silesius in terms of Neoplatonic negative theology (in *The Cherubinic Pilgrim*: Angelus Silesius 1986: I.15). It was in exactly this sense that Ps-Dionysius Areopagite, a student of Proclus, coined the term "negative theology" (*apophatikē theologia*) around the year 500.

ABSOLUTE TRANSCENDENCE AND NEGATIVE THEOLOGY

Negative theology is the attempt to think of the Absolute as absolute transcendence. Its starting point is the notion that the Absolute must be conceived of as a *pure unity*. However, if pure unity is to be consistently conceived of, then it strictly denies all classification, because any classification which can be conceived of at all would lead it into multiplicity. As that which is detached from all multiplicity and all determination, the One is itself *pure transcendence*, absolutely *beyond everything* (*epekeina pantōn*, *Enn.* V.1[10].6.13; V.3[49].13.2; V.4[7].2.39–40). Plotinus stresses this repeatedly. Particularly illuminating is his first detailed explanation of the absolute transcendence of the One in the early *Enn.* V.4[7]:

> For there must be something simple before all things, and this must be other than all the things which come after it, existing by itself, not mixed with the things which derive from it, and all the same able to be present in a different way to the other things, being really one and not a different being and then one; for it is false even to say of it that it is one and there is "no concept or knowledge" [Plato, *Prm.* 142a] of it; it is indeed also said to be "beyond Being" [Plato, *R.* 509b]. For if it is not to be simple, outside all coincidence and composition, and the true and absolute One, it could not be a first principle (*archē*); and it is the most self-sufficient (*autarkestaton hapantōn*), because it is simple and the first of all.   (*Enn.* V.4[7].1.5–13)

The Absolute is the absolutely simple (*pantē haploun, Enn.* V.3[49].11.27). Consequently, everything which is not absolutely simple, that is every unity, which in some way still contains multiplicity in it, presupposes the absolutely simple as its origin, and is dependent upon it, because every unity which is limited by multiplicity is only a unity at all by means of the absolutely pure unity. The pure unity, which, as an absolute simplicity, strictly excludes any form of multiplicity from itself, is the purer nature of the Absolute. Absolute simplicity signifies the removal of every multiplicity, including any conceptual multiplicity and by this means the exclusion of any ontological structure, whatever its nature, which always implies a conceptual composition. Moreover, by this means, it equally signifies the removal of any determination, since determination, on the one hand, implies something *to which* it comes and *of which* it is a determination and, on the other hand, it is by this conceptually distinguishable from that "something" of which it is a classification or essence. Every determined "something" allows itself to be separated into the thing determined and the determination, and in this way already demonstrates a composition, an ontological structure as the relationship of a multiplicity of at least conceptually distinguishable moments. For that reason, the absolute unity of the One itself excludes every determination and every structure from itself. Therefore any possibility of relation of the Absolute to itself or to others is excluded, since any relationship to itself or to others presupposes at the very least a conceptual differentiation of relata. Since every determination places the thing determined in relationship to itself or to others, the absolutely simple is also absolutely without determination; that is, it is also not only undeterminable for us, but rather *it is by and for itself beyond all determination*. Pure simplicity itself is therefore also not the determination of the Absolute; rather it is correctly understood as the absolute *negation* of all determination. Absolute simplicity which is understood *in this manner* is the pure concept of the Absolute, which can only be thought of negatively. However, the pure transcendence of the Absolute is contained in this absolute simplicity, correctly understood as the negation of all determination. By means of its pure simplicity the Absolute is completely removed from everything, so it is "beyond everything" (*epekeina pantōn, Enn.* V.1[10].6.13), and by this means it is also "before everything" (*pro pantōn, Enn.* V.4[7].1.5), "above everything" (*hyper panta, Enn.* V.5[32].13.33) and "different from everything" (*pantōn heteron, Enn.* V.4[7].1.6). The point of Plotinus' negative theology is to express this.[3]

Even referring to the Absolute as "the One" is improper and metaphorical, because the Absolute is not a unity in the sense that things which are in Being have a positive character of unity, which determines a single thing, itself conceptually distinguished from unity. *Pure* unity in contrast means the negation of all determination and all Being; it means that the One is not even conceivable *as a unity* in affirmative concepts. Plotinus stresses this emphatically: "This marvel of the One, which is not existent, so that 'one' may not here also have to be predicated of something else, which in truth has no fitting name but if we must give it a name, 'one' would be an appropriate ordering way of speaking of it, not in the sense of something else and then one" (*Enn.* VI.9[9].5.30–33).

The term "the One" should instruct *us* to transcend all multiplicity and all determination in thought: in reality it targets the "Super-One"; in order to conceive of this, Thought must transcend itself and its own unitary thought (*Enn.* VI.9[9].6.1–15). The Absolute is the One, not in any positively determined sense of unity, but rather only in the negative sense, that it is beyond all multiplicity (*Enn.* V.5[32].6.24–34). Therefore, the name of the One, which is most suitable to the negative content of the Absolute, leads to the insight that the Absolute is in reality unspeakable (*arrhēton, Enn.* V.3[49].13.1; cf. Plato, *Ep.* VII.341c). There is no denotation which is suitable to the One; one can say nothing concerning it at all, because the twofold structure of predication, which always says something about something, is fundamentally inappropriate to the pure unity of the Absolute. We can say nothing about what the Absolute is, but rather what it is not (*Enn.* V.3[49].14.6–8; VI.8[39].8.4–8), because the Absolute is not a "what" or a "something" (*ti*), but rather it is before everything which is a "what" (*Enn.* V.3[49].12.51–2; *pro tou ti*). We therefore have neither knowledge nor insight of the Absolute (*Enn.* V.3[49].14.2–3; VI.9[9].4.1–2), for all knowledge (*epistēme, gnōsis*) is directed at the "what" or the essence of a thing, and intellection (*noēsis*) – the highest form of knowledge – intuitively encompasses this essence in a simple gaze of Intellect. Plato for this reason denied the Absolute any determination, Being and a unitary character, alongside knowability, sayability and the ability to be designated (*Prm.* 142a).

Plato summarizes the absolute transcendence of the Absolute in the formula that it "transcends essence in dignity and surpassing power" (*epekeina tēs ousias presbeia kai dynamei hyperechontos, R.* 509b; cf. also *Test. Plat.* 50). After Plato, the absolute transcendence of the One was most strongly stressed by his nephew and first successor as head of the Academy, Speusippus: it is beyond Being and also beyond the Good and the Beautiful (frag. 72 [Isnardi Parente]). In this way, it is also "beyond Intellect" (*epekeina nou*), as Aristotle formulated it, following Plato and Speusippus (*On Prayer*, frag. 1; cf. Plato, *R.* 508e–509a; Speusippus, frag. 89 [Isnardi Parente]). Transcendence above being, "beyond Being" is, however, the most precise and at the same time the most all-encompassing expression for the pure transcendence of the Absolute, because "Being" is not simply a classification alongside other classifications, which must be excluded from the Absolute; rather it forms a *foundation* for all other classifications and represents the *epitome* of all determination. Furthermore, "Being" (*ousia*) in a concise sense does not simply signify that something is and exists, but rather it refers to the plenitude of essence, in which something completely is what it actually is; the final and actual fruition of Being is therefore no particular essence, but rather the One-Being as the absolute epitome of the entire plenitude of Being. In this sense, Being is the totality of all determination, which lacks nothing – no conceivable classification and no conceivable degree of Being (*Enn.* III.6[26].6) (see Halfwassen 2002: 504–11). However, the plenitude of Being, the epitome of all determination, is *not* the Absolute; the One-Being is not the First Principle, but rather the Second, after the One itself. Therefore, the transcendence of the One above Being signifies its transcendence over the totality. "Its product is already all things. But if this product is all things, that Principle is beyond all things: therefore 'beyond being'" (*Enn.* V.4[7].2.39–40). Because of the significance of this transcendence of Being as transcendence above the totality, Plotinus repeatedly cites the Platonic phrase "*epekeina tēs ousias*" (on at least thirty-one occasions, which makes it by far the most repeated citation in Plotinus' oeuvre).

That Being is not only the foundation, but rather also the epitome of all determination is connected to its classification as an *eidos*, which was developed by Plato and which his most important students, Speusippus, Xenocrates and Aristotle, developed further in different directions (see Krämer 1973). *Eidos* – which literally means "aspect, appearance, shape, form" – refers to the *constitution* of Being. What does not possess constitution of nature is therefore not Being. As the origin of all constitution, the One itself cannot be anything constituted and therefore does not possess any character of Being at all. Exactly by means of its transcendence over all constitution of Being, it allows constitution and by this means Being as the totality of all constitution:

> Since the substance (*ousia*) … is form (*eidos*) … and not the form of some one thing, but of everything, so that no other form is left outside it, the One must be without form (*aneidon*). But if it is without form it is not a substance, for a substance must be some one particular thing, something, that is, defined and limited, but it is impossible to apprehend the One as a particular thing: for then it would not be the principle, but only the particular thing which you said it was. But if all things are in that which is generated [from the One], which of the things in it are you going to say that the One is? Since it is none of them, it can only be said to be beyond them. But these things are beings (*ta onta*) and being (*to on*): so that it is "beyond being" (*epekeina ontos*). This phrase "beyond being" does not mean that it is a particular thing – for it makes no positive statement (*thesis*) about it – and it "does not give it a name" [Plato, *Prm.*142a] but all it implies is that it is "not this". But if this is what the phrase does, it in no way comprehends the One.
>
> (*Enn.* V.5[32].6.1–14)

Plotinus here makes it clear what absolute transcendence actually means: it does not signify that Being as one component, and the One as its ulterior origin as the other, together make up the whole, but rather it means that "which is detached from *every* totality and transcends it", as Proclus later formulates it (*in Prm.* 1107.32–3). The Absolute does not allow itself to be assembled with Being in a totality which encompasses both of these,

Being and the Absolute, but rather it always transcends any such horizon of totality (Huber 1955: 58–60). Being is already the totality of that which can be thought of as determined. The transcendence of the Absolute above Being is therefore not a determination of what the Absolute is or is not, but rather it is the rejection of all determination. Transcendence, therefore, does not contain any positing; that is, it is no longer a positive observation of something, but rather the rejection of all meaning. However, it performs the rejection of all conceivable meaning in such a way that it at the same time supplies the *direction* in which this rejection is to be understood. That is, the Absolute is in no way lacking that which is negated from it, but rather is superior to it. Transcendence is therefore the assertion of something which exceeds everything that permits itself to be thought of and that permits assertions to be made of it; it is therefore not a "something" any longer. It is an assertion that even retracts itself as an assertion in order by this means to *point to* what transcends every positive assertion, to what in truth is absolutely unsayable (*Enn.* V.3[49].13.1–6). The semantic form of the assertion about transcendence and its character as illustrative of what goes beyond everything therefore surpass mere negation. The special feature of the assertion concerning transcendence remains in the fact that its absolute semantic excess and its absolute conceptual negativity are mutually dependent: the rejection of everything targets what surpasses everything and which is beyond everything and exactly that does not allow itself to be expressed in any other way except through the negation of all that which it surpasses. The Absolute is nothing in exactly this sense: "It is certainly none of the things of which it is origin; it is of such a kind, though nothing can be predicated of it, not being (*on*), not substance (*ousia*), not Life, as to be above all of these things" (*Enn.* III.8[30].10.28–31).

The Absolute is "nothing from the All, rather before All" (*Enn.* III.8[30].9.53–4) so that it must not be said of it that "it neither is the 'it is' (*to estin*)" (*Enn.* VI.7[38].38.1), "it is not (*ouk esti*)" (*Enn.* VI.7[38].38.11), "we take even the 'is' away from it" (*Enn.* VI.8[39].8.14), therefore "it also does not exist (*oude hypestē*)", but rather it is "before all existence (*pro hypostaseōs*)" (*Enn.* VI.8[39].10.35–6) and "beyond Being" (*hyperontōs*)" (*Enn.* VI.8[39].14.42). "And if you can take hold of it after taking away Being (*to einai*), you will greatly marvel" (*Enn.* III.8[30].10.31–2). This transcendence of Being, however, can only be implemented to the extent that Thought can also transcend itself along with Being. The goal of transcending Thought is then ultimately *ekstasis*, the stepping out of Thought out of itself (*Enn.* VI.9[9].11.23).

PLOTINUS' MYSTICISM: *EKSTASIS* AS THE SELF RISING ABOVE THOUGHT

Plotinus' mysticism of *ekstasis* emerges from the absolute transcendence of the One. This connection is important. One completely misunderstands Plotinus, if one assumes that his philosophy is a subsequent attempt to understand a mystical experience of unity. His mysticism would then stand at the beginning of the theory. What can be referred to as Plotinus' mysticism is rather the reverse: the *consequence* of his theory of the Absolute as pure transcendence, as it was developed. Plotinus himself stresses this repeatedly (*Enn.* VI.9[9].4).

Even the term "mysticism" is utterly ambiguous and can cause misunderstanding. It is derived from the verb "*myein*", which means to close one's eyes, just like during initiation into the mysteries. If one applies the expression "mysticism" to Plotinus, one must first steer clear of any association with irrationality and obscurantist emotional experience. For Plotinus it has nothing to do with being in a state of trance or Dionysian experiences. Plotinus only speaks of "*myein*" once (*Enn.* I.6[1].8.25) and by this means the complete turning away of consciousness from every relation to the sensible world, by which means consciousness is entirely concentrated upon itself. The goal of this collection and concentration on what is internal is the unclouded clarity and brightness of Intellect. This is not an emotional experience, but rather purely intellectual; emotions – even of a Dionysiac-ecstatic sort – are a connection with the external world, which should be discarded by consciousness. The concentration of consciousness upon itself is furthermore not unification with the Absolute, but only the first, if crucial, step towards it.

Through this "mystical" self-contemplation of what is internal to us, "another vision" is activated in us, a purely intellectual form of seeing, which, according to Plotinus, is accessible to every person, but only a few are aware of it (*Enn.* I.6[1].8.25–7). A non-discursive, and therefore not linguistically composed, form of thinking and recognizing is meant by this, which perceives the thing recognized in a simple glance of the Intellect with a single blow, that is, an intuitive display of the whole at once, which at the same time is of absolute and indisputable evidence, and in its implementation the thinking or contemplating consciousness does not stand opposite what is contemplated as a "subject" which is differentiated from its "object", but rather fuses with it and becomes a unity. Johann Gottlieb Fichte, Friedrich Hölderlin and Friedrich Wilhelm Joseph Schelling later spoke of "intellectual contemplation", because in it what is perceived is present at once as a totality, just like with vision; not sensibly, but rather purely intellectually. Plotinus speaks of a "gazing" (*thea*) or "contemplation" (*theōria*), but mostly of "intellection" (*noēsis*); this term was used by Plato and Aristotle, in order to distinguish intuitive from discursive recognition. This intuition, the highest form of recognition, is the manner in which the absolute Intellect can recognize and think itself as the very plenitude of Being. Who actualizes it is therefore one with the absolute Intellect, the basis of our soul and our thinking consciousness, into which consciousness reverts, when it concentrates perfectly upon itself. The act of intellectual contemplation is therefore the transformation of consciousness into the Intellect as our true or actual Self: our "becoming Intellect" (*noōthēnai*, *Enn.* VI.7[38].35.4; VI.8[39].5.35) (see Beierwaltes 2001: 97–114). It is the highest ascent of our self-consciousness and at the same time the most perfect removal of boundaries, so that it can no longer distinguish itself from other things as something fixed, which it itself is not. For that which it contemplates and that with which in its contemplation it becomes a unity, is not an individual thing, but rather the plenitude of Being, which is the contemplating Intellect itself:

> Often I have woken up out of the body to myself and have entered into myself, going out from all other things; I have seen a beauty wonderfully great and felt assurance that then most of all I belonged to the better part; I have actually lived the best life and come to identity with the divine and set firm in it. I have come to that supreme actuality (*energeia ekeinē*), setting myself above all else in the realm of Intellect. Then after that rest (*stasis*) in the divine, when I have come down from Intellect to discursive reasoning (*logismos*), I am puzzled how I ever came down.
>
> (*Enn.* IV.8[6].1.1–9)[4]

Intellectual contemplation is a genuine philosophical form of mystical experience. It is an experience of all-encompassing unity, in which the Self knows its identity with the All-Unity of Intellect. It does not have any irrational connotations, since its structure and its necessity can be argumentatively demonstrated, even when it no longer understands itself argumentatively and deductively, but rather as a stepping out from discursivity and by this means also from the temporality and the sayability of our usual consciousness and conscious thought. It is the basis of our self-consciousness, since only through it can the Self truly and immediately know itself as a unity (cf. *Enn.* V.3[49].3–5); in this respect Plotinus agrees with German Idealism after Kant. The experience of unity from intellectual contemplation, the awakening to oneself, is a "standing still in the divine" (*Enn.* IV.8[6].1.7), that is to say in the absolute Intellect, because it is no longer a movement of searching, but rather an eternal discovery of the plenitude of Being and the eternal knowledge within it, since it has stepped out of time. For Plotinus, however, it is not an experience of the Absolute. Plotinus requires of the thinking and seeing of the Absolute that it also surpasses even the noetic contemplation of Intellect, the fulfilment of the search of Thought for Being. Just like thought, in order to obtain its fulfilment in Intellect, it must step outside of its relationship to the external world, which is transmitted via the sensible, so it must also go beyond Intellect, in order to reach the Absolute in its pure transcendence, so it must transcend everything which is conceivable: "but just as he who wishes to see in intelligible nature (*noētē physis*) will contemplate what is beyond the perceptible if he has no mental image of the perceptible, so he who wishes to contemplate what is beyond the intelligible will contemplate it when he has let all the intelligible go" (*Enn.* V.5[32].6.17–20).

The absolute transcendence of the One demands from Thought the detachment of everything which is thinkable, as is accomplished by negative theology. However, this contains a fundamental paradox. How can one abolish all thinkability from Thought, without thereby at the same time abolishing Thought itself? And when the abolition of thinkability can be understood only as the self-abolition of thought, then how is a self-abolition possible which is not a self-annihilation or self-destruction of reason? Plotinus' theory of *ekstasis* arises from this very paradox and is his response to it. As pure transcendence, the Absolute withdraws and becomes unreachable for Thought. Thought reaches absolute transcendence only by means of leaving itself, through transcending itself, in which Thought – outpacing itself – perfects itself and is not destroyed, to the extent that it is no longer Thought, but rather surpasses Thought as "Super-Thought" (*hypernoēsis, Enn.* VI.8[39].16.32). "Ekstasis" refers to this self-transcendence of Thought. Plotinus' *ekstasis* is, then, the consequence of the pure transcendence of the Absolute.

Plotinus repeatedly stresses that the absolute transcendence of the One is not only transcendence of Being, but rather it is at the same time also transcendence of Intellect and transcendence of knowledge: "Then since it is beyond Being (*epekeina ousias*), it is also beyond all activity (*epekeina energeias*) and beyond Intellect and Thought (*epekeina nou kai noēseōs*)" (*Enn.* I.7[54].1.19–20, trans. O'Brien). From this it equally follows that the One itself "does not think" (*Enn.* V.6[24].2.2); for this reason "it does not perceive itself" (*Enn.* III.9[13].9.12–13), "it does not recognise or think itself" (*Enn.* VI.9[9].6.46), "it does not know itself" (*Enn.* V.6[24].6.31), but rather "it is also raised above self-consciousness (*synaisthēsis*) and every intellective act" (*Enn.* V.6[24].5.4–5). From the transcendence of the One above Intellect, and consequently above every form of Thought, of recognition and of consciousness, arises the problem of how we can then reach the Absolute, the goal of the entire ascent. Certainly, from Thought's requirement for unity we can ultimately postulate an absolute basis for pure unity beyond all Thought and all Being. However, such a conclusion concerning the origin of all unity is still not an attainment of the Absolute, but rather only what points beyond Thought itself. This pointing beyond Thought itself is still not a fulfilment of the search for the Absolute. The Absolute appears in its pure transcendence to be unattainable, "For again, since knowledge of other things comes to us from intellect, and we are able to know intellect by intellect, by what sort of sudden and simple intuition (*epibolē athroa*) could one grasp this which transcends the nature of Intellect?" (*Enn.* III.8[30].9.19–22). Plotinus' answer runs as follows:

> The perplexity arises especially because our awareness of that One is not by way of reasoned knowledge (*epistēmē*) or of intellectual perception (*noēsis*), as with other intelligible things, but by way of a presence (*parousia*) superior to knowledge. The soul … must therefore run up above knowledge and in no way depart from being one, but one must depart from knowledge and things known and from every other, even beautiful, object of vision.   (*Enn.* VI.9[9].4.1–10)

Thought constitutes itself through its anticipation of unity. The vision of the One itself is the fulfilment of the anticipation of unity, which first makes all Thought and knowledge possible.This fulfilment is only possible to the extent that one transcends every form of unity, which continuously characterizes knowledge, even in its highest form as intellectual contemplation. At the same time it is determined through its intentionality: it is always directed towards what it wishes to thematically perceive. This intentionality of Thought is first made possible through its anticipation of unity, which therefore precedes its intentionality; at the same time it endows Thought with the structure of a unity in divisiveness, which is fundamental for our entire objective consciousness. Therefore, in order to perceive something thematically, we must think of what has been perceived as the unity of something determined; as what is determined, however, is not simply one, rather it is at the same time differentiated from the Thought perceiving it and from all other determined things. The thematic perception of something is always the perception of something that is differentiated from the perceiver himself within a horizon of determinations, in which the perceived is first constituted as *one* determinate thing, through being delimited from other determinate things appearing in the same horizon.[5] I grasp something always as "this and not that"; therefore I grasp it at the same time as being determined but also as different from myself. The intentionality of thought for this reason leads to the self-division of Intellect into thinking and thought, knowledge and known, subject and object. This division, however, is not absolute. Therefore I can only grasp something when it stands in my horizon and so forms a unity with me.

The thematic perception of something always signifies two things: the differentiation and division of perceiver and thing perceived, as well as the collective comprehension of both in a unity, the unity of a collective horizon. This horizon of unity makes all thematic perception possible, but it makes it possible to the extent that as a mere horizontal unity it contains distinctions in it – in particular the distinction between thing perceived and perceiver. The unitary horizon itself is by this means co-present in all thematic perception, but never thematically as such. Only in *noēsis* proper, that is, intellectual contemplation, Thought encompasses this whole structure, the object, its horizon and the knowing Self.

However, first, it does so in a non-objective or non-objectifying way and, second, the whole structure remains a unity of differentiated elements.

Pure unity beyond all differentiation and beyond all multiplicity is in no way thematically knowable; that is, it can never become the explicit theme of any epistemic thought, because it always transcends the unitary form of knowledge, the unity with differentiation in itself, which also constitutes *noēsis*. It itself therefore does not know about itself, it does not know or think itself, because this would already be a division of unity in itself and therefore a removal of the absolute or pure unity of the One itself (*Enn.* VI.9[9].6.42–52; VI.7[38].38–9). However, according to Plotinus that does not mean that it is unattainable for us. As the absolute basis of all unity, which first allows every unity in differentiation, the One rather is ever-present to us (*Enn.* VI.9[9].8.33–45); however, in a presence which is higher and prior to all knowledge. Prior to knowledge is Thought's anticipation of unity, which first allows all knowledge and consciousness; in this original anticipation of unity the One in us is actual. In order to notice the operative presence of the One in us, we must therefore take back the intentionality of our consciousness, in which the unity of Intellect becomes divided, to the original anticipation of unity, which makes all Thought possible, without itself being saturated Thought or the thematic perception of anything. This original unity in our thought, which precedes all self-differentiation, "the First of Intellect" (*Enn.* VI.9[9].3.27), is that in us in which and through which the Absolute is present for us; Proclus refers to it as "the One in us" (*to en hēmin hen, in Prm.* 1072.8) (see Beierwaltes 1979: 367–82).

We notice the presence of the Absolute, when we turn back to undifferentiated unity, which is the basis of our thought, so that we in no way step outside of unity, as already occurs, when we attempt to thematize it as a unity: "But when the soul wants to see by itself, seeing it only by being with it and being one by being one with it, it does not think it yet has what it seeks, because it is not different from what is being thought" (*Enn.* VI.9[9].3.10–13). The experience of unity with the Absolute is then not a conscious act, in which the Absolute would be thematically conscious of us, but, as the retraction of the Intentionality constituting all thematic consciousness into the unity antecedent to all differentiation, it remains prior to consciousness. As the most intensive experience of unity, however, it is not unconscious and not less, but rather *more* than all consciousness: Plotinus refers to it as "something like being awake (*hoion egrēgoris*) when the wakener was not someone else, a wakefulness and a thought transcending thought (*hypernoēsis*) … his waking transcends substance and intellect and intellectual life" (*Enn.* VI.8[39].16.31–4).

The self-perception of the unity of Thought in intellectual contemplation includes the knowledge that it is the anticipation of the undifferentiated pure unity, the anticipation of the absolute One, which first makes possible Thought as a unity: "But he who has learnt to know himself will know from whence he comes" (*Enn.* VI.9[9].7.33), "for in turning to itself it turns to its principle" (*Enn.* VI.9[9].2.35–6). In order to experience the presence of the One, the premise is the withdrawal of the intentionality of Thought and Vision into that most original unity in Thought, which first makes all Thought possible. This, however, is itself no longer Thought, but the basis for it. The Intellect, which withdraws to its own original and simple unity, is no longer self-conscious Intellect, but rather only a pure, pre- and supra-conscious implementation of unity: "ignoring all things (as it did formerly in self-perception but then in the realm of Forms) and even ignoring itself, it comes to be in the contemplation of that One" (*Enn.* VI.9[9].7.18–21).

Plotinus also speaks of a "loving Intellect" (*nous erōn*), which he distinguishes from the "thinking" or "rational" Intellect (*nous emphronos*, *Enn.* VI.7[38].35). Love, *eros*, is a longing for unity, which is prior to all attaining thematic consciousness of something; it is the longing for undifferentiated unity, since it reaches fruition as a fusion with the beloved in an indistinguishable unity, which obliterates all differentiation. At the same time, love as the free transcendence over itself is the traction towards transcendence, which leads to self-transcendence. The "loving Intellect" is the Intellect which transcends all otherness and therefore all intentionality of Thought, which removes itself to the undifferentiated simple unity which is the basis for all Thought. The Intellect which reverts to its original unity is no longer Intellect, but rather only simple, pure unity. Since pure unity excludes every otherness from itself or from others, it is no longer distinguished from the Absolute when therefore there is no otherness, the things which are not other are present to each other: "That One, therefore, since it has no otherness is always present, and we are present to it when we have no otherness; and the One does not desire us, so as to be around us, but we desire it, so that we are around it. And we are always around it, but do not always look to it" (*Enn.* VI.9[9].8.32–5).

This glance at the Absolute, whose presence first renders us possible, on account of which it is inalienable from us, is not an intentional seeing but rather an undifferentiated union with the Absolute which extinguishes the distinction between both, "for it was not really seen but united to him" (*Enn.* VI.9[9].11.5–6).

> But perhaps one should not say "will see" but "was seen", if one must speak of these two, the seer and the seen, and not both as one – a bold statement. So then the seer does not see and does not distinguish and does not imagine two, but it is as if he had become someone else and he is not himself and does not count as his own there (in absolute transcendence), but has come to belong to that (the Absolute) and so is one, having joined centre to centre.   (*Enn.* VI.9[9].10.12–17)

Therefore, the union is also inexpressible (*dysphraston*, *Enn.* VI.9[9].10.19), because language in its differentiated structure fundamentally fails to match the experience of undifferentiated, absolute unity. Therefore everything which can be said about it is a dark inkling and mere hints about what is really unsayable (*Enn.* VI.9[9].11.27).

The union with the Absolute is at the same time the most exalted experience of transcendence: it reaches "by transcending everything (*tō hyperbanti panta*) absolute transcendence" (*Enn.* VI.9[9].11.35). This includes the transcendence of the Self "and he himself was not there … but he was as if carried away or possessed by a god (*enthousiasmos*) in a quiet solitude and a state of calm (*erēmos*)" (*Enn.* VI.9[9].11.11–13). The union is therefore no longer a vision, but rather a stepping out of oneself (*ekstasis*), a radically simplifying transformation (*haplōsis*) to absolute simplicity and a total dedication of oneself (*epidosis hautou*) to absolute transcendence (*Enn.* VI.9[9].11.23). This transcendence of the self, however, is not a rejection of the self, but rather the surpassing fulfilment of the search for Self: transcending the Soul comes "not at something else, but to itself, and in this way since it is not in something else, it will not be in nothing but in itself, but when it is in itself alone and not in being, it is in that, for one becomes not substance but beyond substance" (*Enn.* VI.9[9].11.38–42).

The most original, undifferentiatedly simple unity in the foundation of our thought, in which the Absolute beyond Being is present, is as such not Being, but rather transcendence above Being. It is the basis of our Self, for which reason its transcendence above Being is not the extinction of selfhood, but rather its fulfilment. The Self, which transcended all determination of Thought and therefore also Being, steps out of itself, because as an undifferentiated pure unity, it is no longer the Self, but rather nothing as a pure unity and for this very reason it is one with the One itself. In this experience of absolute transcendence, what transcends reaches its goal as an "escape in solitude to the solitary" (*Enn.* VI.9[9].11.51), as is expressed by the famous concluding formula with which Plotinus' programmatic treatise *On the Good or the One* ends. Having started from the One as the ground of existence and essence – the Good from which Being springs – we have now arrived at the One as the ultimate goal of Thought – the Good as the end to which Thought finally returns.

ACKNOWLEDGEMENT

The editors are most grateful to Carl O'Brien for translating this essay from German, with the assistance of Thomas Arnold and Tolga Ratzsch.

NOTES

1. Unless otherwise noted, translations of the *Enneads* are by Armstrong (1966–88), occasionally modified.
2. "Thought" is capitalized here and throughout the article for the following reasons. The everyday term "thought" (a) is wide enough regarding the kind of activity subsumed under it (over and against the more narrow "intellect"), and (b) implies activity rather than being a faculty or property (unlike "mind" or – again – "intellect"). However, usually as we employ the term "thought" we still conceive of it as an activity of someone (a person) or something, i.e. some active entity behind the activity of thought itself, some subject. In capitalizing the term we keep the conceptual width and the dimension of activity, but want to draw attention to the fact that we are dealing with "pure" thought in Plotinus.
3. Plotinus also appeals to Plato, namely to the negative dialectic of the first hypothesis of his *Prm.* 137c–142a; see Halfwassen (1992: 298–405), Dodds (1928), Horn (1995b).
4. On this passage, see also Aubry (Chapter 20) below.
5. Applying the notion of horizon in this context is no illegitimate usage of modern terminology; cf. Hinske (1974).

13

Number in the metaphysical landscape

Svetla Slaveva-Griffin

The question of the relation between number and metaphysics forms one of the sharpest conceptual divides between Plato and Aristotle. Consistently throughout his dialogues, Plato envisions number as a building block of the universe: from the arithmetical psychogony in the *Timaeus*, to the mixture of Limit and Unlimited in the *Philebus*, to the second hypothesis in the *Parmenides*, to the Indefinite Dyad in the "unwritten doctrines".[1] The systematic pursuit of number earns Plato the recognition that he "Pythagorizes".[2] In his own words, the significance of Pythagoras' teachings equals only Prometheus' gift of fire to humanity (*Phlb.* 16c5–10). Aristotle, on the other hand, negates any ontological value to number. His anti-Platonic polemic in the *Metaphysics* rejects the idea of number as an intermediary ontological class between sensibles and non-sensibles, and the conception of the Indefinite Dyad as the originating principle of substantiation.[3] For Aristotle, number is simply intellectual abstraction of empirical experience.

The title of this chapter itself declares on which side of this Platonic–Aristotelian divide the Neoplatonists stand. Despite Aristotle's virulent criticism, Plato's view of number finds fertile soil to grow and flourish in the propitious climate of Neopythagorean philosophy and the exact sciences in late antiquity. This chapter examines the Neoplatonists' expansive interest in the constitutional role of number and maps the metaphysical landscape according to the ontology of number in the thought of its most avid proponents: Plotinus, Iamblichus, Syrianus and Proclus.

The times have passed when one could cautiously study the "relation" between number and metaphysics with the palpable intent to preserve the analytical purity of Neoplatonism from the shadow of numerological mysticism. In the last three decades, the concept of number has grown out of its cast as "the ugly duckling" in the study of Neoplatonic ontology.[4] Our advanced understanding of its Neoplatonic treatment requires restating the question about the relation between number and *being* directly, without its Aristotelian baggage.[5] The recent trend of taking Neoplatonic metaphysics, in its dazzling diversity, as a dominant framework which integrates all other philosophical branches, including physics, psychology and ethics, makes the re-examination of the import of number timely and relevant. If we welcome the assessment of Chiaradonna and Trabattoni – as we should – that "physics is but a part of metaphysics", we should also agree that this is even more so true in the case of mathematics.[6]

NUMBER THEN AND NOW

To the Neoplatonic mind, the beauty and multiplicity of the visible world are but pale imperfections of the beauty and order of its invisible underlying principles. As Linguiti elicits in Chapter 22, below, physicality, as if an optical illusion, distorts the holistic perfection of the intelligible principles. Seeking to understand the paradigm of the natural world, the Neoplatonists, following their Platonic predecessors, grapple with ways to transgress the illusory knowledge gathered by the senses. Just as in everyday empirical demonstrations such as when we look at a spoon in a glass of water from below and it appears crooked, so, from a Neoplatonic perspective, do observation and examination of physicality obscure and misinform our understanding of the true essence of reality.

Now, if we look at the same spoon from above, it does not appear crooked any more but only slightly magnified. The top-down approach yields a more accurate perception of the spoon and as long as we take into account the magnifying effect of the water, we acquire a better understanding of its shape. The example illustrates why the Neoplatonists prefer the top-down approach for learning about reality.[7] As long as we realize the impermanency and the ontological inferiority of physical reality in comparison to its intelligible model – just as we realize the magnifying distortion in the appearance of the spoon in the water – we can grasp the Neoplatonic view of the natural world as "a sort of 'physical instantiation' of metaphysical principles", albeit distorted and illusory.[8] In Plotinus' words, "even here below a thoughtful life is majesty and beauty in truth, though it is dimly (*amydrōs*) seen" (*Enn.* VI.6[34].18.22–4; cf. VI.6[34].8.11).

Rilke's statement that "we are the bees of the invisible" resonates with the principal Neoplatonic view that our human task is to find the origin of that which surrounds us, to understand the truth of absolute existence and, especially in regard to humanity, to restore our ontological kinship with the divine.[9] Like the bees, we labour, purposefully, to collect all possible data from physical reality in order to understand systematically and comprehensively its underlying principles.

For scientists – ancient as well as modern – the honey the bees collect is the quantifiable information measuring every physical property. According to Michael Psellus' report, Iamblichus understands sensation as "solid number" (Psellus, *On Ethical and Theological Numbers* 18–19 [O'Meara]). Syrianus attributes to Iamblichus the even more modern view of number as "the 'place' of the universe which may be regarded as empty when taken by itself", but when taken phenomenally, the Monad, with its generation of numbers, does not seem to leave "any place empty, filling as it does all arithmetical receptacles with an uninterrupted succession of numbers".[10] Syrianus' own contribution to the understanding of arithmetical numbers involves the idea of number as the matter upon which the soul imposes the form of the particular number it inherits from the intelligible.[11]

From both phenomenological and epistemological perspectives, we try time and again "to rectify" the perception of the "crooked" spoon in the water by measuring all of its quantifiable aspects and by theoretically modelling, based on the collected data, the "perfect spoon".[12] But even then, regardless of how many times we measure the length, width and weight of the spoon, the numbers do not produce absolute but approximate measurements which, for practical purposes, "are good enough" to our senses. Statistical data and mathematical analysis provide a way out for us to quantify the physical world but ultimately they do not furnish true understanding of the inner workings of reality and leave us reaching out to theoretical modelling, speculation and dialectical enquiry.[13] This is where the jobs of the scientist and the philosopher converge.[14] This convergence is best summarized in Socrates' advice to the budding mathematician Theaetetus to follow the example of mathematical proof in searching for "a single formula that applies to the many kinds of knowledge" (*Tht.* 148d4–7).[15]

Mathematics studies the relation between number and multiplicity and as such it intersects with one of the main domains of philosophy: the study of one and many in the structure of the universe. Rilke's metaphor about the bees and the invisible acquires a stunningly literal meaning in Socrates' examination of the question in the *Meno*. While searching for a single definition of virtue, he encounters a "swarm" (*smēnos*) of examples. Baffled by this plurality, he observes:

> I seem to be in luck. I wanted one virtue and I find that you have a whole swarm
> of virtues to offer. But seriously, to carry on this metaphor of the swarm suppose
> I asked you what a bee is, what is its essential nature (*peri ousias hoti pot' estin*),
> and you replied that bees were of many different kinds ... what is that character in
> respect of which they don't differ at all, but are all the same?
>
> (*Men.* 72a4–b2, trans. Guthrie)

With Socrates, the Neoplatonists also look for the single essence (*ousia*) of things that are many. Multiplicity, discrete or continuous, is the first most apparent feature of physicality. If unexamined, it appears chaotic, random and infinite. But for Socrates and the Neoplatonists, behind the overwhelming diversity of physical magnitude and multitude, there is a permanent intelligible order. The concept of number is in the privileged position to be both "the honey the bees collect" when measuring the quantifiable properties of multiplicity and "the bee" itself in modelling the paradigm of reality.

The philosophical debate whether number is quantifiable or ontological in nature is still ongoing. The modern permutations of the Platonic–Aristotelian divide are many, from Kant's utilitarian arithmetic, to Frege's view of number as *a priori* analytic judgement, to Field's nominalism.[16] The latest Aristotelian instalment in it is Leng's (2010: 258–60) defence of mathematicals as "representatively useful fictions" of mathematically stated hypothesis of empirical theories. Her premise supports Quine's quip that "[t]he philosopher and the scientist are in the same boat" (Quine 1960: 3). Quine's boat can be happily named "Naturalized Ontology", in Leng's phrase, and it is sailing away from the Platonic paradise of understanding numbers not only as expressions but also as constituents of underlying ontological principles (Leng 2010: 36–43).

In late antiquity, Quine's boat would still have had scientists and philosophers on board. They would have been a quite diverse crew whose differences, however sharp, would not have led to mutiny. Even in Euclid's *Elements*, the absence of specific treatment of the relation between number and ontology is not strong enough to make an *ex silentio* argument for his rejection of the idea. Anyone acquainted with the common Neoplatonic analogy of point–line–circle for visualizing and explaining the structure of the universe would recognize the Platonic and Neoplatonic sub-context of the opening entries in the *Elements*.[17] A stronger ontological flavour of the Euclidian definition of point is detected in Moderatus' distinction between a monad as the first principle of number (*tōn arithmōn archē*) – homogenous and indivisible – and the arithmetical number one as the principle of enumerating individual things (*tōn arithmētōn archē*).[18] Taken even further, Moderatus' conception of number as "a system of monads" (*systēma monadōn*), which progresses from a monad into multiplicity and regresses from multiplicity into a monad,[19] finds its fully developed metaphysical parallel in the Neoplatonic view of procession (*proodos*) and return (*epistrophē*) as the ontological movement of intelligible substantiation.[20] It foreshadows the future Neoplatonic understanding of the ontological dynamics between one and many microscopically in the individual substantiation of beings, macroscopically in the Monad of the Supreme Living Being and supra-cosmically in the absolute unity of the One as the foremost originative principle of existence transcending existence itself.

It is unnecessary to look for possible tension between Euclid's strictly arithmetical treatment of number and Moderatus' ontologically suggestive definition of number.[21] The physical and metaphysical dimensions of the concept are mutually informative even when a philosopher or a mathematician still favours one over the other because the other, although absent, saliently remains in the background of discussion.

At the same time hard-core Neopythagoreans like Nicomachus toy with ways to articulate sharper terminological differences in the entangled fabric of the concept. In his *Introduction to Arithmetics*, Nicomachus talks about intelligible number (*noētos arithmos*) and scientific number (*epistēmonikos arithmos*). The former operates at the cosmological level: "In the thought of this demiurgic god", there is intelligible number (*noētos arithmos*) which is completely immaterial (*aulos*), eternal (*aidios*) "according to which … everything is completed: time, motion, heavens, stars, revolutions of all kinds". The latter "embraces the essence of quantity, …odd and even".[22] This explanation does not, explicitly or implicitly, distinguish the scientific number from the intelligibles nor does it connect the scientific number with its physical representations, as one familiar with the later Neoplatonists' "Platonized" interpretations of Nicomachus may expect.[23] Instead, it seems that this kind of number is still part of the intelligible and Nicomachus is working out here the conceptual difference between its cosmological role and its intrinsic property of expressing quantity.[24] Nicomachus' search for "the essence of quantity" in scientific number (*ousian … tēs posotētos*, *Ar.* I.6.4) and its proper place among the universals faintly anticipates Plotinus' principal question about number; that is, how it relates to primary substance (*ousia*). Nicomachus' notion of *ousia* in the definition of scientific number does not share the Neoplatonic meaning of the term, but it does mark an evolutionary stage between Socrates' use of the term in the *Meno* (72b1), cited above, and its fully fledged Neoplatonic content by juxtaposing the questions of essence of being and essence of quantity.[25]

NUMBER IN PLOTINUS' METAPHYSICS

Plotinus' understanding of number stands out in its simplicity in comparison, as we will see, with the later developments of the concept in Iamblichus, Syrianus and Proclus. He conceives of two kinds of number: substantial (*ousiōdēs*) and monadic (*monadikos*). The former, non-discursive and non-quantitative, belongs to the intelligible realm. The latter, discursive and quantitative, measures or enumerates the physical world (*Enn.* V.5[32].4–5; VI.6[34].9). The two are in a Form-and-image relation.

Underneath this simplicity, there are four undercurrents foreshadowing the future evolution of the concept: Aristotelian, Platonic, Neopythagorean and genuinely Plotinian. The Aristotelian undercurrent is recognized in the initially crude distinction between intelligible and arithmetical number. Plotinus' singular treatment of number in *Enn.* VI.6[34] offers an anti-Aristotelian defence of Plato's stance.[26] It systematically refutes Aristotle's misconceptions of the "number of infinity", the Indefinite Dyad and the nature of the arithmetical number as intellectual abstraction by soul. Ultimately, Aristotle's terms for the intelligible and the mathematical number – respectively formal (*eidētikos*) and arithmetic number (*arithmētikos*) – are reconstructed and renamed as substantial (*ousiōdēs*) and monadic number (*monadikos*).[27]

The anti-Aristotelian and pro-Platonic undercurrents in Plotinus' view are, of course, given. His most original work on the concept does not concern Plato's exoneration but his concentrated effort on explicating the nature of substantial number. Instead of focusing on the relation between intelligible and monadic number (as one would if following the Platonic–Aristotelian divide), he shifts his attention to the relation between number and substance (*ousia*). It is in this aspect that the Neopythagorean undercurrent in his concept is most visible (Charles-Saget 1980: 9–17, 52; Slaveva-Griffin 2009: 42–53). Because the ultimate Neopythagorean answer to the question of how number relates to the One is the equation of number with the One as the Father and the Monad, Plotinus has to work out a solution in which the One, as the Neoplatonic first originative principle of existence, retains its transcendence even when it comes to the origin and role of number in the intelligible:[28] "For number is not primary: The One is prior to the dyad, but the dyad is secondary, and originating from the One, has it as definer, but is itself of its own nature indefinite; but when it is defined, it is already a number, but a number as substance (*arithmos hōs ousia*); and soul too is a number" (*Enn.* V.1[10].5.6–9).

Plotinus' solution to the problem is this (cf. *Enn.* V.5[32].4; VI.6[34].9). Since the One is prior to any existence, the One is ontologically superior to the Indefinite Dyad – the principle of potentiality – and the substantial number. The Indefinite Dyad, however, is not ontologically superior to number but the two of them form an ontologically equal pair in which the One defines the Dyad and this defined Dyad is number "as substance" (*arithmos hōs ousia*). The Indefinite Dyad and the substantial number are the two sides of the same ontological process. The Dyad as an absolute principle of potentiality is indefinite by nature but, as a recipient of the productive power of the One, it is limited and thus defined by "number as substance". Number – and not the Indefinite Dyad – orders intelligible multiplicity.

What does Plotinus mean by "number as substance" and why should there be a relation between number and substance? If he is going to argue that number in the intelligible does not have anything in common with arithmetical number in the physical world: first, he has to deny its association with quantity, and second, if number is going to participate in the intelligible, he has to explain how it relates to substance as a primary kind of being.[29]

Plotinus' first answer – concerning quantity – is Platonically straightforward. The main characteristic of intelligible existence is incorporeality and the main characteristic of incorporeality is the complete lack of quantity.[30] Even the Form of quantity (*eidos hē posotēs*, *Enn.* II.4[12].9.7) itself is bodiless and thus without quantity.[31] Physical quantity and the arithmetical number are excluded from the intelligible.

The second answer – about the relation between number and substance – is in the heart of Plotinus' ontological work on number. Insisting that the One is not number, he is quick to explain that "number has an existence from itself" but also that "substantial number is that which continually gives existence (*to einai aei parechōn*)".[32] If number is the defining expression of the One onto the Indefinite Dyad, then number must be intrinsic to substance:

> And certainly the beings were not numbered at the time when they came to be; but it was [already clear] how many there had to be. The whole number therefore, existed before the beings themselves. But, if numbers were before beings, they were not beings. Now number was in being, not as the number of being – for being was still one – but the power (*dynamis*) of number which had come to exist divided being and made it, so to speak, in labour to give birth to multiplicity. For number will be either the substance or the actual activity of being (*energeia*), and the absolute living being is number, and Intellect is number (*to zōion auto kai ho nous arithmos*). (*Enn.* VI.6[34].9.22–9)

The passage explicates what Plotinus means by number acting "as substance", cited earlier (*Enn.* V.1[10].5.6–9, above, p. 204).The relation of number to substance is such that number is its power (*dynamis*) and actuality (*energeia*). On this account, he does not call this kind of number "intelligible" (*noētos*) with Nicomachus, nor "Formal" (*eidētikos*) with Aristotle, nor even "true" (*alēthēs*) with Plato, but "substantial" (*ousiōdēs*).[33]

As power and actuality, substantial number then permeates the structure of the intelligible in four specific aspects: Being is "unified number" (*to on arithmos hēnomenos*),[34] Intellect is "number moving in itself" (*nous arithmos en heautōi kinoumenos*), beings are "number that has unfolded outward" (*ta onta arithmos exelēligmenos*) and the Complete Living Being is "encompassing number" (*to zōion arithmos periechōn*).[35] These four aspects converge in Plotinus' definition of existence as "separation from the One" (*apostasis tou henos*) (*Enn.* VI.6[34].1.1; Slaveva-Griffin 2009: 42–53). The beginning of the centripetal motion in Intellect is thinking itself, which makes its first ontological stop at the "unified number" of Being through the self-moving/thinking number of Intellect. Then it unfolds outwardly into the individual beings, just to fold itself inwardly as the "encompassing number" of the Complete Living Being. Since all these are only aspects of the activity of substance as number, they are ontologically equidistant from the One (see Corrigan [Chapter 24], below). Together the four aspects of substantial number compose the map of Plotinus' metaphysics.[36]

Since for Plotinus there are only two layers of reality, excluding the transcending One, he is concerned only with two kinds of number: substantial and monadic. His concept of monadic number is deliberately straightforward Platonic, rejecting the Aristotelian notion of abstraction and underplaying the Neopythagorean idea of intermediacy. Since the monadic number pertains to the physical world, it is an image of substantial number. This is perhaps the reason why Plotinus does not busy himself with the subject of mathematicals – a well-established Platonic *topos*, which flourishes in the later developments of the concept – as intermediary entities between the intelligible and the physical world.[37] Plotinus understands Plato's "true number" to mean "number as substance" which "has an existence from itself and does not have its existence in the numbering soul" (*Enn.* V.5[32].4 and *Enn.* VI.6[34].4.21–3 respectively). The notion of intermediateness between the two layers of the structure of the universe is carried out by the concept of Soul, the third underlying principle of existence, which he conspicuously leaves out from having a specific aspect in the substantial number (Slaveva-Griffin 2009: 112–30; Maggi 2010: 89–93).

The internal complexity of substantial number reflects the dynamic relations within the intelligible. The non-linear nature of the concept, contrary to its physical counterpart, creates tension with its monolithic surface. This opens the door for future conceptual proliferation, the seed for which is already planted by the Neopythagoreans, but it could not grow to fruition without Plotinus' metaphysics.

NUMBER IN IAMBLICHUS' METAPHYSICS

The first signs of proliferation of the concept are found in Iamblichus. His strong interest in a more precise stratification of reality focuses on the outer edges of the ontological ladder by positing, respectively at the top and at the bottom, a divine number superseding the intelligible and a self-moved number superseding the physical. Thus the divine number (*theios/theologikos*) leads the catagogical sequence of intelligible/eidetic number (*noētos* or *eidētikos*), intellectual number (*noeros*), self-moved number (*autokinētos*) and physical number (*physikos*).[38]

This variegated complexity differs starkly from the two-toned nature of the concept in Plotinus. It obviously suits better Iamblichus' pronounced Neopythagorean interests. With the Pythagoreans around Hippasus, he views number "as the first paradigm of creating the universe" and mathematicals as useful for understanding both "physical and theological matters" (*physika ē theologika*) (*In Nic.* 10.20–21; *Comm. Math.* 92.19–20). But matters of ontological considerations are equally important to him (Shaw 1995: 33; 1999: 129; Van Riel 1997: 44–5; Maggi 2012: 83). While Plotinus says that all gods are in the intelligible, without further elaboration, Iamblichus sorts out the intelligible paradigm to fit in the ontologically superseding gods.[39] He shares the Pythagorean view that divine number "is fitted to the substance of the gods and power, order and activities" and commends the search for "which numbers are similar (*syngeneis*) and related to which gods (*homophyeis*)".[40] For him, the last question reveals a genuine – and not symbolic – ontological affiliation between numbers and gods.

In Iamblichus' ontological ladder, the divine number is succeeded by the intelligible/eidetic number (*Comm. Math.* 64.1–2). This kind of number, he clarifies, is contemplated in harmony "with the purest substance", the substance of the intelligible realm.[41] Unfortunately, he is not as specific as we would have liked him to be about the ontological relation of this kind of number with soul in the way he is about the relation between the divine number and the gods. His only assertion is that it concerns "the self-moving substance (*autokinētos ousia*) and the eternal rational principles (*aidioi logoi*)" (*Comm. Math.* 64.4–6). It is not clear, however, how this kind of number, if it concerns soul, is different from its successor, the self-moved number (*autokinētos*). If we accept O'Meara's judicious association of the self-moved number with soul, as the so-called psychic number,[42] the self-moved number completes the sketch of Iamblichus' metaphysical map.[43]

For him, the kinds of number are altogether ontologically different and do not express the internal relations of the intelligible realm. While Plotinus focuses exclusively on the inner workings of substantial number within their ontological environment, Iamblichus is interested in ironing out the conceptual wrinkles surrounding the relation of number with what is beyond and what immediately succeeds the metaphysical realm. The difference in their approaches yields different results, with not much ground for comparison.[44] There are still two observations worth making.

First, Plotinus time and again carefully dances around the question about the relation between number and the One. The crux of the problem lies in his understanding of the One as simultaneously comprising the ideas of being the first originative principle of all existence as well as of transcending all existence.[45] Iamblichus separates the two ideas into an Ineffable One that is beyond existence and One that oversees a dyad of Limit and Unlimited.[46] The latter is responsible for mixing Limit and Unlimited in the production of the Unified (*to hēnōmenon*), which, in its turn, is responsible for the existence of the intelligible (Iamblichus, *in Ti.* frag. 7 [Dillon]). This Unified is conceptually closest to Plotinus' "unified number" as an aspect of substantial number, expressed in Being (see above, p. 205). But while Plotinus insists on keeping the unified number of Being separate from the One, although he considers it ontologically superior to the multiplicity of beings, Iamblichus delegates the absolute unity of the Unified to the productive power of the One. He diffuses the tension between ontological superiority and intelligibility, detected in Plotinus' "unified number" of Being, by distancing the Ineffable One from the productive unified One.[47]

Second, Plotinus defines Intellect as number "which moves in itself" (*arithmos en heautōi kinoumenos*) in the intelligible, while Iamblichus talks about "self-moved" number (*autokinētos arithmos*) as ontologically successive to the intelligible (see above, p. 205). Iamblichus' placement is ontologically more accurate in the context of the Pythagorean and Platonic notion of soul as number moving in itself (Xenocrates, frags. 181–2). It also makes Plotinus' concept of Intellect as "number moving in itself" stand out. There is also a difference in the understanding of agency. In his view of Intellect as substantial number moving in itself, Plotinus emphasizes the active agency of motion in Intellect while Iamblichus does not determine the agency of motion in his self-moved number: it is only secondarily implied through its association with soul.[48]

The reason for the above differences stems from and demonstrates the principal difference between Plotinus' and Iamblichus' view of number. We have already noted that the primary focus of Plotinus' treatment of number lies exclusively on the place of number in the intelligible. By transposing the traditional idea of a self-moving number from the Soul to the Intellect, Plotinus conveys successfully the characteristic of Intellect as self-thinking and thus completes the map of the intelligible as charted by the four aspects of substantial number.

Plotinus conspicuously skirts the question of intermediacy between the two kinds of number and since this is where the role of soul comes to play, it does not receive a corresponding aspect in substantial number. Although he does say that soul is number "if it is a substance", the modality of his statement betrays his hesitation. The duality of soul, with its descended and undescended part, makes soul unsuitable to his understanding of substantial number. Soul's relation with the physical world precludes it from gaining a place among the aspects of substantial number and therefore from receiving more attention in his treatment of substantial number.[49]

Iamblichus, on the other hand, as we have already seen, is interested exactly in the upper and lower edges of the intelligible and their relation with their adjacent realities. His placement of the self-moved number after the intelligible number portrays his commitment to the idea of soul and mathematicals as intermediaries between the metaphysical and the sensible. He embraces the Pythagorean stand on the analogical use of number in understanding the structure of the universe and expands the system of different kinds of number to all echelons of reality. Iamblichus' number, as put by Maggi (2012: 80), is omni-extensive.

An indicator of this omni-extension is his equally profuse interest in the physical applications of number. The physical number represents the principles that are mixed in bodies (*enkekramenoi logoi tois sōmasi*), enmattered rational principles (*enyloi logoi*) and enmattered images (*enyla eidē*) (*Comm. Math.* 64.8–12; Psellus, *On the Physical Number* 1–98). They are explicitly distinguished from mathematical numbers (Sheppard 1997). The former "is seen in common concepts", while the latter "is found in the lowest things, generated and divided in bodies".[50] The terminological difference between Iamblichus' physical number and Plotinus' corresponding monadic number reflects Iamblichus' openly Neopythagorean agenda in examining the physical structure of the universe. Since for him mathematics busies itself with describing the nature (*physiologein*) of things in generation, he busies himself as well to enumerate the pervasive presence of number in nature (*Comm. Math.* 64.17–18).

The copious conceptual proliferation of number in Iamblichus embodies his attempt to sharpen the contours of the metaphysical realm, with specific attention to its periphery. With the help of Proclus' *Commentary on the Timaeus*, we can note that, for Iamblichus, numbers "are symbols of divine and ineffable truths" (*in Ti.* II.215.5–7).

NUMBER IN SYRIANUS' METAPHYSICS

Almost a century after Iamblichus, Syrianus joins Quine's boat sailing the deep Platonic waters of metaphysics (D. O'Meara 1989: 119–41; Wear 2011). Two examples from his hermeneutical work on Homer suffice to illustrate his intolerance for Aristotle's obstinate failure to accept Plato's ontological view of number. To characterize the depth of Aristotle's arrogance in the matter, Syrianus quotes Poseidon's rebuke of Zeus' threat to destroy him: "excellent though you may be, you have spoken defiantly".[51] And, to expose the futility of Aristotle's criticism, he adduces Hektor's puzzlement at Glaukos' accusation of cowardice for not fighting Ajax: "why did a man like you speak this word of annoyance".[52]

The quotations point the direction of Syrianus' interest in number. With Plotinus' anti-Aristotelian fervour, he fully extends the Platonic model of substantial and monadic number to interlink consecutively all levels of reality (*in Metaph.* 83.14–26; D. O'Meara 1989: 132; Longo 2010: 623–4). At the same time, with Iamblichus' Neopythagorean passion, he directly correlates numbers with the Forms by supposing the Forms as causes the ontological effects of which are measured, analogically, by corresponding numbers (*in Metaph.* 103–4; 134.22–6). Thus the map of Syrianus' universe is charted successively

by divine/henadic (*theios* or *heniaios*), intelligible (*noētos, eidētikos* or *ousiōdēs*), intellective (*noeros*), psychic (*psychikos*), mathematical (*mathēmatikos*) and physical number
(*physikos*).[53]

The Iamblichian structure of this scale is apparent but of most interest to us is what
Syrianus does with it. He begins by clarifying the conceptual stratigraphy at the top of
the ontological hierarchy. He reformulates Iamblichus' Ineffable transcendent One into
a simple unparticipated One, which "is not co-ordinate with anything", "related to itself"
and "superior to being".[54] In the same vein, he understands Iamblichus' productive One
as a participated One which "is co-ordinate with the unlimited dyad".[55] The latter presides
over the cosmic principles of Limit (*peras*), causing unity and sameness, and Unlimited
(*apeiria*), causing procession and multiplicity (*in Prm.* frag. 5 [Wear]).

Parting further from Iamblichus, Syrianus equates the participated One with Limit and
envisions the first relation between Limit and Unlimited as the Unified (*to hēnomenon*).[56]
Thus construed, the Unified constitutes the henadic realm, which is responsible for bridging the gap between the unparticipated transcendent One and the intelligible realm.
Regardless of whether the Unified consists of the henads or is the totality of the henads,
in any case the Unified and the henads enact the productive power of the participated One
in the emanation of Intellect (Wear 2011: 8–9).

Plotinus, almost two centuries before Syrianus, calls the henads holding places
(*protypōsis*) "for beings which are going to be founded on them".[57] Iamblichus, who is
most often credited with the origination of the concept, places the henads at the level of the
participated One and not at the level of the Unified as Syrianus does.[58] Visually speaking,
if we were to discern nuances in the internal stratigraphy of the One, the henads occupy
the lowest ring of the One in its participated aspect. They represent the absolute unities
of beings before they have unfolded, to use Plotinus' language, into the intelligible and
thus they are supra-noetic (Wear 2011: 8). By inserting what could be called a henadic
realm or even a henadic number between the One and the intelligible, Syrianus brings
to fruition the long-term project of Plotinus and Iamblichus to explain how exactly the
One imparts its generative power to Intellect without compromising its absolute unity
and transcendence.

"Syrianus," as felicitously put by Wear, "postulates a new layer of reality for every difficulty he finds in the text of the *Timaeus*" (*ibid.*: 4). This, we should add, is true for Plotinus
and Iamblichus. The consecutive Form-and-image relation between the kinds of number
constructs a tightly knit map of reality in which the outer edges of the metaphysical further
emerge: first, through a more specific articulation of the concept of henads, and second,
through an elaborate account of the intermediary status of numbers (D. O'Meara 1989:
133). Concerning the latter, Syrianus sharpens the distinction between mathematics and
theology found in Iamblichus. Both arithmetical numbers and geometrical figures are
ontologically innate to soul and this kinship allows them to reveal, more than analogically,
the higher realities.[59]

NUMBER IN PROCLUS' METAPHYSICS

The Neoplatonist who first comes to mind on the subject of number and metaphysics is
Proclus, both with his *Commentary on the First Book of Euclid's Elements* and his exhaustive

opus reaching farther than the mention of a single title. In his thought, number outgrows the restrictive division between physical and metaphysical to embroider holistically the fabric of the universe. For Proclus, as for Plotinus, the real meaning of the Platonic axis between physics and metaphysics is primarily ontological. Sensitive to the elevated status of dialectics, Proclus, unlike Iamblichus and perhaps even Syrianus, draws the unexpected conclusion that mathematics veils, not unveils, the hidden principles of reality.[60] Number fossilizes and thus distorts the ever-flowing universal processes. How does Proclus reach such a profoundly different but still programmatically Neopythagorean conclusion?

Recent studies of Proclus' metaphysics have ever so sharply delineated the distinction between "theologizing mathematics and theology or dialectic proper".[61] The heart of the matter for Proclus is that the Greek term *analogia*, despite its connotation of "vagueness" in English, authentically in Greek denotes "precision", particularly in mathematical con-texts.[62] The material world is informed by mathematics not only because arithmetic and geometry quantify, measure, and spatially relate or mentally extrapolate physical proper-ties but also because mathematicals occupy a middle ground between the intelligible and the sensible. But the elements of precision and intermediacy do not suffice to convince him that mathematicals unequivocally reveal the true principles of existence: "For the reasons (*logoi*) that govern Nature are not receptive of the accuracy or the fixity of math-ematicals. …Therefore it is not possible to consider physical things arithmetically."[63] To finish the job of mathematics, Proclus employs the method of "analogical reasoning" (even when expressed *more geometrico*), built upon the premise that the mind puts together the similarities between different objects from different layers of reality not because of its dialectical capacity but because the layers themselves are ontologically related.[64]

His realism about the constraints of mathematicals in the study of the natural world inherits a certain Plotinian nuance. With the four aspects of substantial number, Plotinus completely divorces number from mathematics and physicality in order to explain the dynamics within the intelligible. Proclus too sees, on his own terms, the main constraint of mathematicals in that they do not enact but freeze, in a frame, the self-sustainability of both the intelligible and the living organism of the universe:

> There is the first proportion through which nature puts harmony into its own works and through which the Demiurge organizes the universe (*logos*) running through itself primarily and then through all things … sympathy or co-affection (*sympatheia*) comes to be among all the things in the cosmos, inasmuch as all things are guided by one life and a single nature.   (*in Ti*. II.24.2–7)

This life consists of individual instantiations of the tripartite cycle of *procession* (*proodos*), *remaining* (*monē*) and *reversion* (*epistrophē*) re-enacted at each ontological level.[65] The physical world, including the crooked spoon we mentioned in the beginning of the chapter, actively participates, according to its own ontological purpose, in the constant cycle of energy which builds the universe. Every element in this dynamic system, even the seemingly lifeless spoon, in order to exist, imitates actively its higher emanating principles (Chlup 2012: 67).

The centre of this dynamic metaphysics is Proclus' concept of the henads which crowns his predecessors' unceasing efforts to grasp and resolve the tension between ontology and transcendence. The concept explicates – as much as possible for an ineffable and unknowable entity – what Iamblichus and Syrianus refer to as divine number (*theios arithmos*) (*ET* prop. 123). The caption of *ET* prop. 113 states: "the whole series of gods (*theios arithmos*) has the character of unity" (*heniaios*).[66] The proposition demonstrates Proclus' principal conceptual change in the term "number" to denote, in "a broad, non-mathematical sense", a series, group or class (D. O'Meara 1989: 205). More specifically, this divine number does not express the ontologically informed but still mathematically analogical idea of gods as a procession of numbers, but the altogether non-mathematical idea of causation in which the gods are absolutely unitary henads "pre-subsisting" at the level of the One:

> For if the divine series (*theios arithmos*) has for antecedent cause the One, as the intelligible series (*noeros*) has Intellect and the psychical series (*psychikos*) Soul, and if at every level the multiplicity is analogous (*analogon*) to its cause, it is plain that the divine series has the character of unity (*theios arithmos heniaios estin*), if the One is God.   (*ET* prop. 113.2–5, trans. Dodds, modified)

The first two lines of the passage run as the inventory lists of the different kinds of number found in Iamblichus. A closer look, however, does not discern an inventory of the ontological variations of number but an analytical map of the series of ontological causations (divine, intelligible and psychical) substantiating the three principal layers of reality. The passage unfolds around the key word "analogous" which explains the relationship between multiplicity and its source, more accurately cause. By "analogous" Proclus does not mean a mathematical "fitting", as Iamblichus would say, between the different kinds of number and their ontological match but an intrinsic kinship.

Since the One is the immediate antecedent cause of the divine series containing the henads, the divine series therefore has to be akin to the One and since the One is unitary, the divine series too has to be unitary: "Thus if a plurality of gods (*plēthos theōn*) exist, this plurality must be unitary" (*heniaion esti to plēthos*).[67] "Unitary" here particularly means the unmediated closest possible relation to the One (*to hēn*) and differs distinctly from the idea of "brought together multiplicity", conveyed by the term "unified" (*hēnomenon*).[68] It is precisely from their closest proximity to the One that the henads derive their name. At the level of the One, they are indistinguishable from the One and in this sense unitary (*heniaios*): they "share nature with the One", are "one-like, ineffable, supra-essential and altogether similar to its cause".[69] From the levels proceeding from the One, however, they appear as many.[70] From this upward perspective, Proclus abandons the language of mathematics in their description. They are not a series of a monad, dyad, triad and so on, but "paternal", "generative", "perfect", "protective", "zoogonic" (*ET* prop. 151–5). In other words, they are life giving. To understand the full extent of their primary ontological role, we should put them in the spotlight of Chlup's metaphor of the productive power of the One as "a chewing gum bubble coming out of our mouth and yet being only kept in existence by the constant stream of air we are blowing into it".[71] The henads are the "constant stream of air" which keeps the bubble of the universe alive.

Proclus' dynamic model culminates in the Platonic enterprise in explicating the structure of the universe. If we are to redirect Socrates' wish in the *Timaeus* from gazing at the distinctive physical qualities of "magnificent-looking living organisms" to gazing at them alive in their original ontological environment, Proclus – not Critias or Timaeus, Iamblichus or Syrianus – fulfils Socrates' wish completely, about ten centuries later.[72]

For the Neoplatonists the bottom-up approach of examining reality is illusory to the naked eye and the Platonically uninformed mind. As Plato professes at the end of the *Timaeus*, the birds "descended from innocent but simpleminded men, men who studied the heavenly bodies but in their own naïveté believed that the most reliable proofs concerning them could be based upon visual observation" (*Ti.* 91d6–e1, trans. Zeyl). Starting with Iamblichus, the later Platonists indefatigably strive to close the gap between the applied sciences of mathematics and its ontological dimension.[73] From the quantifiable heterogenic multiplicity of the physical world, to the unquantifiable homogenic multiplicity of the metaphysical realm, to the highest productive principle of existence, the Neoplatonists embody to an absolute degree Rilke's vision that "we are the bees of the invisible". The metaphysical landscape is the meadow from which they purposefully and laboriously collect the essence of life, from the "crooked" spoon to the divine henads.

NOTES

1. Respectively *Ti.* 34b10–36d7, *Phlb.* 16c5–10, *Prm.* 142b1–151e2.
2. Pseudo-Plutarch, *Placita Philosophorum* 887c4; Eusebius, *PE* XV.37.6.3; Cicero, *de Fin.* 5.87.4–9. Cf. Burkert (1972: 15).
3. *Metaph.* 987a29–988a17; 1085b5. Cf. Syrianus, *in Metaph.* 187a. On Aristotle's position, see Annas (1976); Turnbull (1998: 74–82).
4. It has received special attention in the works of D. O'Meara (1975, 1989), Charles-Saget (Bertier, Brisson & Charles-Saget *et al.* 1980), Horn (1995a), Nikulin (1998a, 1998b, 2002), Radke (2003: 234–41), Slaveva-Griffin (2009), Maggi (2009, 2010).
5. To be fair, Aristotle's rejection of Plato's view is one of the catalysts behind the Neoplatonists' interests in the concept and should not be completely omitted. If this is not apparent in Iamblichus and Proclus, it is certainly so in Plotinus and Syrianus.
6. Chiaradonna & Trabattoni (2009: 14). The latest instalment is Wilberding & Horn (2012).
7. Although the top-down approach easily lends itself to the idea of hierarchical vertical organization of the ontological layers and has dominated the discussion of Neoplatonic ontology for quite some time (Wagner 1982b; 2002: 301), it is more accurate to think of them as simultaneous horizontal threads. The idea of vertical hierarchy is a "side effect", intrinsic to logical thinking. The constraints of the up-and-down approach have long been noted in D. O'Meara (1996) and freshly reinstated by Linguiti (Chapter 22) and Corrigan (Chapter 24), below.
8. Chiaradonna & Trabattoni (2009: 5). For a more redeeming view, see Martijn (2010a: 297–302).
9. Rilke (1963: 157) in B. Mazur (2003: 4, 235). For a timely critique of the anthropocentric focus in the study of metaphysics and rationality, see Corrigan (Chapter 24), below.
10. Syrianus, *in Metaph.* 149.31–150.4, hereafter trans. O'Meara. This view anticipates most, if not all, developments in modern science and physics, not the least the binary language of computing.
11. *In Metaph.* 13–14, 133.4–14. See Mueller (2000); Dillon & O'Meara (2006: 3).
12. An ancient example for the misleading nature of the senses is the famous Epicurean claim that the sun is only as big as we perceive it.
13. *Enn.* V.1[10].5.10–13: "masses and magnitudes are not primary: these things which have thickness come afterwards, and sense-perception thinks they are realities. Even in seeds it is not the moisture which is honourable, but what is unseen: and this is number and rational principle." Hereafter the Greek of the *Enneads* follows Henry & Schwyzer (1964–82); the translation, with alterations, follows Armstrong (1966–88). For a more utilitarian approach, see August Comte in Serres (1982: 85): "For in renouncing the hope, in almost every case, of measuring great heights or distances directly, the human mind has had to attempt to determine them indirectly, and it is thus that philosophers were led to invent mathematics."
14. Syrianus, *in Metaph.* 13–14, 27–32: "For either astronomers and all mathematicians, and indeed all physical philosophers, must give up hope of scientifically demonstrating any proposition, and abandon the idea that proofs derive from the causal principles, not just of the conclusion, but of reality itself, or, as long as

both of these is maintained, it must be the case that the causal principles of all things that are produced both in the heavens and in the whole of nature pre-exist in some kind of universal reason-principles."

15. Cornford's translation (1935). Cf. *R.* 510b–11b, 522c, 534a; also D'Ooge (1926: 23–6), D. O'Meara (1989: 17–23). For an anagogical interpretation of mathematics and geometry, see *Epinomis* 990c–91b, and Vitrac & Rabouin (2010). Burnyeat (1987) is sceptical but admissive of the idea.

16. Respectively, van Atten (2012: 4); Frege (1950: 99); Field (1980). For a recent reassessment of the status quo of pure mathematics, see Pincock (2012: 279–99).

17. Def. 1: Σημεῖον ἐστιν, οὗ μέρος οὐθέν. Def. 2: Γραμμὴ δὲ μῆκος ἀπλατές. For Plato's possible influence on Euclid's replacement of Aristotle's term στιγμή for line with σημεῖον, see Heath (1956: 4). Cf. D'Ooge (1926: 48–52).

18. Theon, *Expos.* p. 18, lines 3–8. Cf. Stobaeus, *Anth.* I.21. See Dillon (1996a: 346–50), Mueller (2000), Slaveva-Griffin (2009: 42–6).

19. According to Iamblichus, Thales first defines the monad (*in Nic.* 10.9). See Bulmer-Thomas (1983: 384).

20. Plotinus, *Enn.* V.2[11].1.7–21; Proclus, *ET* prop. 30.12–14, 33.1–6, 35.1–2, 39, 42. There is also a strong ontological resonance in his conception of the monad as a complete privation of multiplicity (στερηθεῖσα), onlyness (μονή) and stability (στάσις), Theon, *Expos.* p. 18, lines 7–8. Cf. Stobaeus, *Anth.* I.21. See Dillon (1996a: 350).

21. The passage of time from Euclid to Moderatus has not diluted but condensed the ontological notions in the concept.

22. *Ar.* I.6.6–12, trans. D'Ooge. See also Helmig (2007: 140). A distant echo of Nicomachus' idea of revolutions (ἐξελιγμοί) is found in Plotinus' concept of beings as "number which has unfolded outward" (ἐξεληλιγμένος ἀριθμός), *Enn.* VI.6[34].9.30. Below, p. 205.

23. Such as by Philoponus and Asclepius, but not Iamblichus. See Helmig (2007: 140–42).

24. On the relation between scientific number and the true objects of philosophy, see Helmig (2007: 141–2).

25. A further distillation of the future ontological layers of the concept is found in Nicomachus' threefold definition of number as "a combination of units" (μονάδων σύστημα), "limited multiplicity" (πλῆθος ὡρισμένον) and "a flow of quantity made up of units" (ποσότητος χύμα ἐκ μονάδων συγκείμενον) (*Ar.* I.7). For the ontological relation between χύμα and ὕλη, see *Enn.* VI.7[38].12.19–26.

26. Number is also mentioned in passing in *Enn.* 5.1[10].5, V.5[32].4–5, VI.2[43].13.31.

27. *Enn.* VI.6[34].2, 4, 9.34–5, 17; Aristotle, *Metaph.* 1086a2–5; 1083b16–17. See Slaveva-Griffin (2009: 58–68, 93).

28. *Enn.* V.5[32].4.16–18: The One "does not even belong to the category of substantial (οὐσιώδης) number and so certainly not to that which is posterior to it, the quantitative number". I amend here Armstrong's rendering of οὐσιώδης as "substantial", not "essential", in light of its reoccurrence, a few lines below, which Armstrong also translates with "substantial".

29. Narbonne's treatment of matter and evil in Plotinus below (Chapter 15) amply justifies Plotinus' position on number here. For the nature of *ousia*, see Chiaradonna (Chapter 14), below.

30. *Enn.* II.4[12].9.2–4: "Certainly that which exists is not identical with that which has quantity. … One must regard all bodiless nature as altogether without quantity." See Slaveva-Griffin (2009: 109–12).

31. *Enn.* II.4[12].9.5–7: "For quantity itself is not a thing which has quantity; that which has quantity is that which participates in quantity; so it is clear from this, too, that quantity is a form." Consequently geometrical figures in the intelligible are also without quantity and as such they are "unfigured figures" (ἀσχημάτιστα σχήματα, *Enn.* VI.6[34].17.25–6).

32. *Enn.* V.5[32].4.18–19; Cf. *Enn.* VI.6[34].4.21–2. The verb παρέχω means "cause" when referring to incorporeal entities, as in the quoted phrase, and "produce" when referring to sensible things.

33. Νοητὸς ἀριθμός appears only once in Plotinus (*Enn.* V.9[5].11.13); ἀληθὴς οὐσία (*Enn.* VI.6[34].8.10) distantly echoes Plato's ἀληθὴς ἀριθμός. See Horn (1995a: 235–6).

34. *Enn.* VI.6[34].9.29–32. Plotinus' "unified number" of Being is an early prototype of the Unified in Iamblichus and Syrianus: see below, pp. 207–8 and 209, respectively. It finds a parallel in the concept of Protophanes in "the Platonizing Sethian" Treatises: see Turner (Chapter 5), above.

35. Horn (1995a: 235). For *exelēligmenos*, see above, note 22.

36. These four aspects also correspond to the four primary kinds of substance: the "unified number" of being corresponds to rest, the "number moving in itself" of Intellect to motion, the "number unfolded outward" of beings to otherness, the "encompassing number" of the Complete Living Being to sameness. Cf. the originative principles of number in Nicomachus, *Ar.* II.17.1; 18.1; 19.1; 20.2. On the relation between

substantial number and the primary kinds, see Slaveva-Griffin (2009: 95–130); on the relation between substance and the primary kinds, see Santa Cruz (1997: 105–18).

37. This does not mean that Plotinus discounts the importance of mathematics in the philosopher's training in dialectics, see *Enn.* I.3[20].3.6–10. Also Maggi (2009: 57–61).

38. According to *Comm. Math.* 63.23–64.14. There is no specific order for the different kinds of number in Psellus, *On the Physical Number* and *On Ethical and Theological Arithmetic*. He also refers to intelligible number variously as *noētos, noeros, ousiōdēs, eidētikos, On the Physical Number* 4–5.

39. *Enn.* V.8[31].9.15–17. Aside from the use of θεολόγοι (*Enn.* III.5[50].2.2, 8.22), the term or its derivatives do not occur in the *Enneads*.

40. *Comm. Math.* 63.24–9: θεώρημα πρῶτόν ἐστι τὸ θεολογικόν, τῇ τῶν θεῶν οὐσίᾳ καὶ δυνάμει, τάξει τε καὶ ἐνεργείαις συναρμοζόμενον. With D. O'Meara (1989: 79) and contrary to Maggi (2012: 80), I take the lines to refer to divine number and not to all mathematicals in general.

41. It is, at times, distinguished from the intellectual (*noeros*) number. The intelligible number represents the ontologically prior numbers in the intelligible, while the intellectual number belongs to the ontologically secondary demiurgic activities, associated with soul. Syrianus, *in Metaph.* 140.10–15. See D. O'Meara (1989: 79).

42. At times it is also followed by yet another kind of number of even more obscure and problematic nature, the hypostatic number. It is absent from *Comm. Math.* 63–64 and is mentioned only passingly in Psellus. D. O'Meara (1989: 79) speculates a possible identification with mathematical number which is not on Iamblichus' list either. Maggi (2012) omits it also.

43. Xenocrates, frags. 181–5. It is tantalizing, in view of his commentary on the *de Anima*, that Iamblichus does not explicitly identify the self-moving number with Soul here. We do not have a strong enough reason here to suspect any possible influence of Plotinus' treatment of soul in relation to substantial number. But the reluctance of both Plotinus and Iamblichus on the matter is conspicuous and merits further investigation. See Slaveva-Griffin (2009: 112–18), and D. O'Meara (1989: 62), followed by Maggi (2010: 172).

44. But we should note that Iamblichus' comment on the relation of intelligible number to the purest substance supports Plotinus' choice of naming this kind substantial and not intelligible or eidetic.

45. *Enn.* I.8[51].2–5; III.8[30].10; V.5[23].4.6–7, 5.2–11; VI.7[38].32.21–3.

46. As documented in Proclus, *in Prm.* 1114.1–10 and Damascius, *Pr.* I.87.8–10. For a detailed discussion, see Halfwassen (1996).

47. Dillon (1993: 50–53) even argues that Iamblichus makes the productive One an object of intellection, thus placing it closer to Plotinus' "unified number" of Being. See Wear (2011: 9).

48. D. O'Meara (1989: 79) also renders it as self-moved.

49. When counting, soul externalizes the internal non-quantitative number into a specific quantitative expression (*Enn.* VI.6[34].16.47–54). See Slaveva-Griffin (2009: 114–30).

50. *On the Physical Number* 6–8. In Psellus, the physical number is associated with each one of the Aristotelian causes and not with the Aristotelian view of numbers as abstractions from material quantity.

51. Syrianus, *in Metaph.* 13–14, 170.27 in relation to Aristotle, *Metaph.* 1088b35–89a7. Cf. *Il.* XV.185 [hereafter Lattimore's translation with alterations].

52. Cf. *Il.* XVII.170. Manolea cautions that, while Syrianus is openly scornful of Aristotle's take on the Platonic concept of number, his "tone does not exclude the respect he feels for Aristotle" (2004: 222–3). Other Homeric quotations with similar purpose include Syrianus, *in Metaph.* 13–14, 168.9–12; 168.35–8; 194.5–9. For a complete discussion, see Manolea (2004: 218–31).

53. Most characteristic references are found in *in Metaph.* 122.31–2; 130.24; 142.27; 146.9.

54. *In Prm.* frag. 4.5; *in Metaph.* 11.29, 165.33. Wear (2011: 247–9).

55. *In Prm.* frag. 12.4–5; *in Metaph.* 11.30. Wear (2011: 316–18).

56. *In Prm.* frag. 11. Iamblichus' Unified supersedes Limit. There is even a touch of Plotinus' "unified number" in Syrianus' idea of a specific power (*dynamis*) between the Unified and Being.

57. *Enn.* VI.6[34].10.2–4 and 20–29. See Horn (1995a: 248–50). Plotinus' role in this development has been overlooked, see Slaveva-Griffin (2009: 91–2, 94, 113). Most recently Mesyats (2012: 161–2) partially acknowledges Plotinus' contribution. For the history of the debate about the origin of the idea of the henads, see Wear (2011: 9) and Longo (2010: 620).

58. According to Dillon (1993: 50), the One-Being, including the multiplicity of the henads, coincides, in Iamblichus, with the highest level of Intellect and is thus object of intellection.

59. *In Metaph.* 82.20–25, 4.29–5.2. D. O'Meara (1989: 131, 133, 135).

60. *In Ti.* IV.15: "By way of concealment of the words Plato used mathematicals, as veils (παραπετάσμασιν) of the truth about reality, as the theologians use their myths, and the Pythagoreans their symbols: for in images one can study the paradigms, and through the former make a transition to the latter," trans. Martijn (2010a). Cf. Iamblichus' somewhat mechanical view of numbers "fitting" the corresponding layers of reality, *Comm. Math.* 63, above, note 40. See Martijn (2010a: 197).

61. D. O'Meara's phrase (1989: 204). Also see Martijn (2010a: 186–92); Steel (2010: 635); Chlup (2012: 47–111).

62. As Martijn argues (2010a: 190–91) with support from Gersh (1973: 87) and Baltzly (2007).

63. *In Ti.* II.23.29–33. For analysis, see Baltzly (2007: 69).

64. *In Eucl.* 51.9–56.22, 78.20–79.2. On *phantasia* and mathematical projection, see Sheppard (1997); Martijn (2010a: 190). On the strong didactic and dialectic foundation of Proclus' much-famed "geometrical method" of exposition, see Martijn (Chapter 10), above.

65. *ET* prop. 35.1–2: "Every effect remains in its cause, proceeds from it, and reverts on it" (trans. Dodds). See Steel (2010: 639–41); Chlup (2012: 62–82).

66. By translating *arithmos* as number, Dodds interprets the syntactical function of *theios* attributively. But the agreement between the two words also suggests a conceptual entendre between "number of the gods" and "divine number".

67. *ET* prop. 113.8–9, although the absolute unity of the henads still drives from within, not from the One (*ET* prop. 114). See Dillon (1972, 1993); D. O'Meara (1989: 82–3, 204–7); Butler (2005, 2008); Chlup (2012: 114). Cf. Iamblichus, *Myst.* 59.1–60.2.

68. *ET* prop. 115: "Being, Life and Intelligence are not henads but unified groups" (οὐχὶ ἑνὰς ἀλλ᾽ ἡνωμένον). See Chlup (2012: 115–16).

69. *PT* III.3.12.21–23. Cf. *ET* prop. 115.

70. *ET* prop. 64: At the level of the One, the henads are self-complete (αὐτοτελεῖς), when contemplated from below, they are irradiating (ἐλλάμψεις). This is another way of looking at them respectively as non-participating (ἀμέθεκτος) and participating entities (μετεχόμεναι, μεθεκταί) (*ET* prop. 116). See Mesyats (2012: 152–3).

71. Chlup (2012: 67) continues: "By way of analogy, all of our world is such a 'bubble' that may seem steady and firm at first sight, and yet would immediately burst and collapse if the higher levels stopped pumping their energy into it. Luckily enough, such a thing can never happen, for the energy flows from the higher levels as a spontaneous by-product of their perfection."

72. *Ti.* 19b. As suggested by Smith in Chapter 8 above and by Steel (2010: 652), for Proclus, the conceptual culmination of number in the henad even becomes a tool of ideological defence of pagan polytheism against Christian monotheism.

73. See above, p. 202. The Neoplatonists' effort prompts Psellus to note (*On the Physical Number* 2–3) the great diversity (*poikilia*) of number which ever expands the map of ontological realities.

14

Substance

Riccardo Chiaradonna

THE BACKGROUND

"Substance" stands for the Greek *ousia*.[1] The philosophical meaning of *ousia* is that of a primary kind of being which is opposed to what "is" in a secondary or derivative sense. Hence Plato's Forms are characterized as *ousia* (as opposed to their sensible copies) and the same holds for Aristotle's first category (as opposed to the secondary categories which depend on *ousia*). The Stoics too adopted the notion of *ousia* and applied it to the material passive principle (as opposed to the *logos*). This is a very sketchy description and raises several thorny issues. Saying that *ousia* is a primary kind of being in fact leaves open the question of which criteria to adopt in order to define priority. *Ousia* might be taken to be prior in so far as it is a primary subject for all other things (and this would clearly privilege matter as a candidate for primary substancehood), or rather a primary and self-subsistent principle of motion (such as Aristotle's unmoved mover), or again a primary formal cause within the structure of corporeal beings (such as Aristotle's hylomorphic form) or, finally, a primary stable and invariant essence that is separate from its physical instantiations (such as Plato's Ideas). The philosophical interest of the Neoplatonic debates on "substance" lies in their highly creative incorporation of these questions within the distinctive framework of late antique gradualist metaphysics.

Furthermore, "priority" is not the only problematic issue at stake, as the very notion of "being" in ancient philosophy is contentious. It is controversial whether we should identify Plato's *ousia* with what exists primarily (this would involve the controversial notion of degrees of existence) or rather with what is *F* in a primary (i.e. stable and invariant) sense. A possible way out from this difficulty would be that of regarding the very distinction between "to exist" and "to be *F*" (something like the later scholastic distinction between existence and essence) as inadequate for grasping how ancient philosophers, and Plato in particular, conceived of "being": for the ancient way of understanding "being" entails that "existence" is always "being something" and that there is no concept of existence as such

216

for subjects of indeterminate nature.[2] When we come to Aristotle, the issue becomes even more puzzling because different accounts of *ousia* co-exist in his *corpus*. In the *Categories*, Aristotle presents the particular subjects of properties (e.g. the individual human being, the individual horse) as primary *ousiai*. Furthermore, he does not mention the distinction between form and matter and conceives of universal species and genera (e.g. human being, animal) as secondary *ousiai* (*Cat.* 5.2a11–19). In the *Metaphysics*, instead, form is regarded as primary *ousia* within a hylomorphic account of physical realities. Unlike what happens in the *Categories*, substancehood and subjecthood are no longer straightforwardly equated in the *Metaphysics* (*Metaph.*1029a7–b30). In the *Metaphysics* form is that which makes a composite substance what it is. Hence form can be seen as primary substance (*Metaph.*1037a28–30), even if it is in matter and cannot exist apart from it. In turn, the Stoics identified *ousia* with the passive cosmic material and unqualified principle (Diogenes Laertius 7.134 [*SVF* I.85] and 150 [*SVF* I.87]). This was probably a polemical move against Plato and Aristotle's previous identification of *ousia* with form: the very concept of *eidos* has no place in Stoic corporealist ontology.

It was necessary to recall this intricate background since late antique views on *ousia* can only be properly assessed against the previous tradition; and this is hardly surprising given the overall exegetical character of late antique philosophical debates. Plotinus' tripartite treatise *On the Genera of Being* (VI.1–3[42–4]) laid the basis for subsequent accounts.[3] In the first part of his treatise Plotinus provides a critical overview of the Peripatetic (*Enn.* VI.1[42].1–24) and Stoic (*Enn.* VI.1[42].25–30) theories of categories. The second part (*Enn.* VI.2[43]) contains an account of the intelligible genera (being, movement, rest, identity and difference), which illustrates Plotinus' distinctive interpretation of Plato's *Sophist*. The third part (*Enn.* VI.3[44]) focuses on genera in the sensible world and Plotinus' discussion is again full of references and allusions to the previous tradition (in particular to Peripatetic theories). Plato, Aristotle and the Stoics, then, provide the background of Plotinus' account, but further aspects should be considered. No philosopher later than Epicurus is mentioned in the *Enneads*, although Plotinus was fully aware of the post-Hellenistic debates on Plato and Aristotle. Porphyry (*Plot.* 14.4–14) reports that commentaries on Plato and Aristotle were read in Plotinus' school and recent scholarship has increasingly shown that Plotinus' views are based not only on Plato and Aristotle, but on the readings of Plato and Aristotle developed from the first century BCE onwards.

Simplicius connects Plotinus' critical account of Aristotle's categories with that of two previous interpreters: Lucius (a very enigmatic figure whose identity and chronology are still an open question) and Nicostratus (whom scholars from Praechter onwards have identified as the second-century Platonic philosopher mentioned in a Delphian inscription).[4] At *in Cat.* 73.15–28, Simplicius says that Lucius, Nicostratus and Plotinus raised objections against Aristotle's list of categories (genera), since it is unclear whether it is meant to apply to sensible objects alone, or to all beings.[5] This remark is further expanded: either the intelligible and the sensible genera are the same, or they are partly the same and partly different. If the genera are different, Aristotle's list is incomplete, for it omits intelligible beings; if instead the genera are the same, we should assume that intelligible and sensible items are synonymous (i.e. that they share the same name and essence: see Aristotle, *Cat.* 1a6–12). But this cannot be the case, for intelligible and sensible items form an ordered series where the intelligibles are prior (in so far as they serve as models), whereas the sensibles are posterior (in so far as they are copies). Members of such series do not share the same essence and therefore cannot be species under the same genus.[6] Aristotle's division, however, cannot be rescued by resorting to the other hypothesis either, for if the genera are homonymous (i.e. if they are applied to intelligible beings in a sense different from that which pertains to sensible objects), Aristotle's division is incomplete, since he did not specifically address the question of the intelligibles. Furthermore, it would be odd to find genera such as *paschein* and *pros ti* in the intelligible world (for these genera appear to be incompatible with the distinctive mode of being of intelligible, *per se* existent and incorporeal beings). Perhaps only some genera in Aristotle's list apply to both the intelligible and the sensible world, whereas others are peculiar to one ontic level – yet Aristotle did not make this distinction (Simplicius, *in Cat.* 73.26–7). Apart from some details, the lines from Simplicius just paraphrased closely correspond to Plotinus' overture in *Enn.* VI.1[42].1, where after explaining that his discussion will be focusing on beings and their principal divisions, he addresses his general criticism to Aristotle's list of categories (note however that Plotinus does not mention Aristotle, but refers to a group of philosophers: this might suggest that Plotinus' target is Aristotle and his interpreters). The conclusion drawn by Plotinus is identical to that in Simplicius: his opponents' list of genera cannot be seen as an exhaustive division of beings, for they omitted intelligible beings (*Enn.* VI.1[42].1.30: *ta malista onta paraleloipasi*).[7]

Ousia occurs both in Plotinus and in Simplicius (see Simplicius, *in Cat.* 73.20; Plot. *Enn.* VI.1[42].1.24, 26), but it is doubtful whether it refers to substance here. For this puzzle is not limited to *ousia*/substance as the primary kind of being, but rather refers to the essence or nature proper to items in each category (hence not only to substance, the primary genus, but also to quality, quantity, etc.). This broad sense of *ousia* should not be confused with its narrower sense as primary being. A rigid distinction between the two senses, however, would not be completely justified either. For when Plotinus argues that "it would be absurd for *ousia* to mean the same thing when applied to primary beings and those which come after them" (*Enn.* VI.1[41].1.26–7), his words can also easily be read as referring to *ousia* as primary being. Plotinus would then be suggesting that *ousia* (i.e. that which "is" primarily – see the remarks above) cannot be a unique genus that covers both intelligible and sensible items. In *Ti.* 27d Plato describes the sensible realm as that which becomes, but never is, and Platonists before Plotinus sometimes hesitated to apply the term *ousia* to the world of bodies: for *ousia* as such is intelligible (*ousia noētē*: see Plut., *Def. Orac.* 428B–C) (see Dörrie & Baltes 1987–2008: vol. 4, sections 103.0a–103.4). As we shall see below, in the *Genera of Being* Plotinus develops this position and argues that *ousia* is only properly referred to intelligible being, whereas what is improperly called *ousia* in the sensible realm does not satisfy the requirements of primary being and hence is *ousia* only homonymously.[8]

Ousia refers unambiguously to Aristotle's first genus/category in another puzzle that Simplicius ascribes to Nicostratus and Plotinus at *in Cat.* 76.13–17 (see VI.1[42].2.2–8). Again, both Nicostratus and Plotinus are said to raise an objection against the view that *ousia* is a single genus. For if *ousia* were a common genus over sensible and intelligible items, this genus would be prior to them and predicated of both. Hence *ousia* would be neither incorporeal nor corporeal, for otherwise what is corporeal would also be incorporeal and vice versa. The only way to make sense of this argument is to regard the highest genera as beings (i.e. the most general beings that comprise all existing items under them), and "corporeal" and "incorporeal" as mutually exclusive and jointly exhaustive properties of beings. Given these premises, a highest genus has to be either incorporeal or corporeal: *tertium non datur*. But this does not really suffice, because Nicostratus and Plotinus further suggest that an incorporeal genus cannot be predicated of sensible items and that a corporeal genus cannot be predicated of intelligible items. Hence *ousia* cannot be a single genus over intelligible and sensible entities. It is not easy to see why this should be the case, for qualities predicated of bodies were commonly regarded as incorporeal by both Platonic and Peripatetic philosophers (who diverged from the Stoics on this issue): accordingly, there would be nothing strange in predicating an incorporeal genus of a body. In order to rescue Nicostratus' objection, we might perhaps suppose that the "incorporeal" versus "corporeal" dichotomy was a cursory way of referring to a more sophisticated alternative opposing separate incorporeal (i.e. intelligible) beings on the one side and both bodies and their immanent incorporeal features on the other side. The distinction between separate and immanent incorporeals is fully developed by Porphyry, but traces of it can also be found in the previous tradition; hence it could well be in the background of Nicostratus and Plotinus' discussions.[9] If sensible genera (those predicated of bodies) are conceived of as immanent incorporeals, whereas intelligible genera are regarded as separate incorporeals, then a highest genus predicated of both sensible and intelligible items should be neither a body (for according to Platonic and Peripatetic philosophers bodies are not predicated of anything), nor an immanent incorporeal (for immanent incorporeals are predicated of sensible items, but not of intelligible ones); nor should it be a separate incorporeal being (for separate incorporeals are not predicated of bodies), something which would be quite impossible. This interpretation would perhaps rescue Nicostratus and Plotinus' objection, but it remains speculative.

Whatever might be the case, Nicostratus and Plotinus' overall approach is sufficiently clear: Aristotle's general division of genera/categories, and Aristotle's *ousia* as the primary genus in this division, are assessed against the Platonic metaphysical distinction between the intelligible and the sensible world. This critical approach can be seen as a predictable Platonic criticism that opposes Plato's "two world theory" to Aristotle's views on sensible substance and categories (see J. Barnes 2005: 43–8). This conclusion, however, requires further qualifications. It is worth noting that this critical approach is typical of the Platonists in the second century CE who debated on the harmony between Plato and Aristotle. What we know of the early Platonic-Pythagorean reception of Aristotle's *Categories* in the first century BCE (e.g. from the *testimonia* on Eudorus of Alexandria in Simplicius, or from Pseudo-Archytas' treatise on categories) points instead to a different direction. At that early stage, Aristotle's categories were probably incorporated within a Platonic-Pythagorean doctrinal framework: some of Aristotle's views were indeed criticized or adapted, but the distinction between intelligible and sensible beings was not used against his division. Rather, Pseudo-Archytas suggests that Aristotle's first category was initially regarded as including both sensible objects and Ideas.[10] Nicostratus' and Plotinus' remarks about how intelligible and sensible beings can be ranked under the same genera probably reflect a later phase in the reception of Aristotle's philosophy.

Another aspect is worth noting. We know from Simplicius (*in Cat.* 82.6–7; 90.31–3) that according to Alexander of Aphrodisias, Aristotle's account of primary and individual substance in the *Categories* can also be applied to the separate intelligible Form; that is, the prime mover (unlike Aristotle, Alexander regards the unmoved mover as a Form separate from matter) (see Guyomarc'h 2008). Thereby Alexander possibly aimed to counter

Nicostratus' objection that Aristotle neglected intelligible beings in his account of catego-ries.[11] This fact reveals how puzzling Plotinus' remark that Aristotle omitted *ta malista onta* really is: for there are obviously intelligible substances in Aristotle's philosophy (i.e. the unmoved movers, Alexander of Aphrodisias' separate Forms) and it would seem misleading to reject Aristotle's account of substance on the ground that it leaves out the intelligibles. Either Plotinus (and Nicostratus before him) deliberately ignored Aristotle's account of intelligible beings, or Plotinus and Nicostratus did not regard Aristotle's theory of intelligible *ousia* as capable of answering their criticism. Whatever we might think of Nicostratus, Plotinus was certainly familiar with Aristotle's theology but, rather surpris-ingly, does not mention Aristotle's intelligible movers in his treatise *On the Genera of Being*. Why so? Simplicius is again helpful in solving this predicament, for at *in Cat.* 73.19–21 he specifies that Lucius, Nicostratus and Plotinus argued that intelligible and sensible items cannot share the same *ousia*, since they form an ordered series where the intelligibles are paradigms whereas the sensibles are copies. Hence these Platonic opponents of Aristotle did not merely assess Aristotle's division of genera against the distinction between intelli-gible and sensible beings (which would indeed leave the question of the intelligible movers open); rather, they assessed Aristotle's account against a precise view of intelligible and sensible beings; that is, the *Platonic* view of the intelligibles as models and primary beings, according to which sensible objects are merely copies of the intelligible *ousiai*.

This approach is obviously misleading, since Aristotle did not omit Plato's Ideas, but rejected this theory and developed a different account of *ousia*. Even Alexander of Aphrodisias, who held a strongly essentialist reading of Aristotle which converges with Platonism on several issues, rejected Plato's separate Forms.[12] In Nicostratus' and Plotinus' criticism as reported by Simplicius, Aristotle's views on genera and substance are ulti-mately assessed against a Platonic philosophical background rejected by Aristotle and his followers. Aristotle is criticized for not being a Platonist. This ideological, rather than genuinely philosophical, criticism fits well into the second-century debate on the harmony between Plato and Aristotle and recalls Atticus' vehement anti-Aristotelian polemics.[13] Whatever might be the case with Lucius, it is extremely likely that Nicostratus shared Atticus' anti-Aristotelian approach. Certainly, Plotinus took this criticism as the starting point of his enquiry about substance and categories and incorporated Nicostratus' puzzles into his discussion. Yet, as we shall see in the next section, this schematic Platonic criticism is not Plotinus' last word on this issue and his discussion of Aristotle's *ousia* is actually far more sophisticated.

PLOTINUS

Plotinus' account of Aristotle's sensible substance in *Enn.* VI.1[42] ends with a general critical remark: his opponents' view does not make clear the concept and the nature of sub-stance (*tēn ennoian tēs ousias kai tēn physin*, *Enn.* VI.1[42].3.22). This remark can indeed be seen as a restatement of the criticisms already raised by Nicostratus and incorporated by Plotinus in the immediately preceding chapters. For a Platonist, the real nature of primary being coincides with that of Platonic paradigmatic intelligible beings. Since Aristotle did not focus on these, he did not explain what the nature and concept of substance really are. Plotinus, however, does not stop at that and most interestingly comes to this critical conclusion after a detailed scrutiny of some questions *internal* to the Peripatetic theory of sensible substance. This is a crucial move and one that characterizes Plotinus' distinctive approach. The discussion starts at *Enn.* VI.1[42].2.8, where Plotinus, immediately after paraphrasing the objections raised by Nicostratus, says that he will now focus on "the substances here below themselves". First he refers to the Peripatetic distinction between matter, form and composite within *ousia*, and asks what can be common to these (*Enn.* VI.1[42].2.8–10). Then he argues that according to his opponents these are all substances, but form is said to be substance more than matter is. Plotinus agrees, but adds that others (the Stoics?) would say that matter is more substance (*Enn.* VI.1[42].2.12). Another puzzle is connected to the distinction between primary and secondary substances: what can be common to them, if secondary substances derive their name of "substances" from primary ones (*Enn.* VI.1[42].2.12–15)? Then Plotinus claims that it is impossible to explain what *ousia* is (*ti estin hē ousia*, *Enn.* VI.1[42].2.15). Invoking the proper characteristic of "being that which is one and numerically the same which is able to receive contraries" (Aristotle, *Cat.* 4a10–11, trans. Ackrill, adapted) does not suffice for this purpose (*Enn.* VI.1[42].2.16–18). Chapter 3 of *Enn.* VI.1[42] begins with a further remark: one might perhaps include all divisions of *ousia* (intelligible *ousia*, matter, form and composite) within the same genus by conceiving this genus not as a common synonymous predicate, but as a hierarchical unity of provenance from a single principle. Hence intelligible *ousia* would be a primary one, whereas the other things (*ta alla*) would be *ousia* to a second-ary and lesser degree (*ab uno* relation): something like the genus of the Heraclids (*Enn.* VI.1[42].3.1–4) (for further details, see Chiaradonna 2002: 227–71). As we shall see below, this solution was actually adopted by later commentators in order to answer Nicostratus' and Plotinus' objections. Plotinus, however, is sceptical, for if this were the case, everything should be included in *ousia*, since all beings derive from substance (*Enn.* VI.1[42].3.5–7). Indeed, one might reply that there are two kinds of derivation: that within the genus of substance and that of other beings from substance (*Enn.* VI.1[42].3.7–8). But Plotinus further remarks that this does not solve the problem, if we do not grasp what is the most essential thing (*to kyriōtaton*) about substance, which enables other things to derive from it (*Enn.* VI.1[42].3.8–10). What Plotinus provides in the following lines is a succinct scru-tiny of the ways in which Aristotle and his commentators attempted to grasp the genus of substance and clarify its nature. Plotinus mentions some standard Peripatetic ways of referring to sensible substances such as being a *tode ti* or being a primary subject (*Enn.* VI.1[42].3.12–16). Very interestingly, at *Enn.* VI.1[42].3.16–19 Plotinus paraphrases a Peripatetic argument according to which features that are constituent "parts" of their substantial subjects (in Plotinus' example, Aristotle's secondary substances) are them-selves substances, whereas accidents such as "white" are predicated of (and inherent in) subjects independent of them (Alexander of Aphrodisias uses this argument in order to explain why form is not inherent in body as an accident).[14] The conclusion mentioned above comes after this section. Plotinus argues that one might well say that those listed by his opponents are peculiar properties of substance that only demarcate substance by comparison with other things (*pros ta alla*, *Enn.* VI.1[42].3.20). This, however, is not yet enough to define *ousia* as one genus, nor does it make clear the concept and nature of substance in itself (*Enn.* VI.1[42].3.21–2).

Here, as elsewhere, Plotinus' discussion is developed as an internal criticism of Aristotle.[15] Plotinus argues that Aristotle's account of *ousia* is not only incomplete (for one should *supplement* Aristotle's sensible *ousia* with Plato's separate substance), but also self-refuting: while Peripatetics claim that *ousia* has a primary status over what depends on it, they cannot ground this priority, as they are unable to conceive of *ousia* adequately and in itself.[16] According to Plotinus, the only satisfying way to make sense of priority is the Platonic one, which makes *ousia* metaphysically separate from the whole structure of sensible being. Hence the *ousia* of *x* must not be something primary and essential in sensible particulars (i.e. something in sensible particulars which makes them what they are), but must rather be an extra-physical and self-subsisting principle which acts as an essential cause for that which it is the *ousia* of. While the Peripatetics recognize that *ousia* must be prior and separate, what they actually provide is instead a mere descriptive inventory of sensible items, in which some proper features are demarcated from all others and factually referred to substance. They do not give any genuine reason for this claim and do not provide any appropriate account of substance.[17] Plotinus' final remark that his opponents cannot make of *ousia* a genus is best understood against the background of his distinction between genera and categories (*Enn.* VI.1[42].1.15–18; VI.1[42].4.51–2; VI.1[42].9.25–32; VI.1[42].10.41). Plotinus' point is that categories are mere factual collections of items bereft of any internal unifying principle (from this perspective, Plotinus' critique is somewhat similar to Kant's famous remark about the rhapsodic character of Aristotle's list). A genus, by contrast, should collect the multiple items under it in a properly unified way; but according to Plotinus only real intelligible and paradigmatic genera can ground this kind of unity (for they are both genera and principles: see *Enn.* VI.2[43].2.10–14). The Peripatetic list of proper features of substance does not satisfy this requirement and does not allow us to grasp what *ousia* is in itself. Hence, Plotinus' criticism leads to the conclusion that in order to ground Aristotle's ontic distinctions sufficiently, one should transgress the boundaries of Aristotle's philosophy and endorse another view, that of Platonic intelligible beings.

Very interestingly, the previous debate within the Peripatetic tradition could suggest Plotinus' conclusions. As noted above, two different accounts of substances are present in Aristotle's *corpus*. We know from Simplicius (*in Cat.* 78.4–20) that Boethus of Sidon, one of the early commentators of Aristotle in the first century BCE, relied on the account of the *Categories* (where substance is conceived of as a primary subject) and assessed the distinction between matter, form and composite, which Aristotle presents "elsewhere", against the background of that account. Boethus' conclusion was very clear: whereas matter and composite satisfy the criteria for substancehood established in the *Categories*, form cannot do so and lies outside substance, since it is inherent "in matter", which is a substantial subject different from form.[18] Alexander of Aphrodisias' later essentialist view of substance was at least partially developed as a response to the earlier rival Peripatetic ontology set out by Boethus (this interpretation is developed extensively in Rashed 2007). Alexander did not reject the account of substance in the *Categories*, but attempted to make it compatible with the ontic priority of essential form established in works such as *Metaphysics* and *On the Soul*. As noted above, Alexander emphasized that form is not in matter "as in a subject" (i.e. form is not inherent in body in the same way as an accident such as "white" inheres in its substantial subject) but is rather a constituent part of the substantial subject. Since it is a constituent part of substance, form is itself *ousia*. This status is shared by all sensible essential features, most notably by the specific *differentia* whose status Alexander (rather problematically) equates to that of form.[19] Plotinus is familiar with the "parts of substance" argument (see above), but Alexander's response would not be sufficient according to him: for claiming that some features of sensible objects have substantial priority over all others does not suffice to adequately ground this priority. The question remains open of how a selection of substantial features can be made within a Peripatetic philosophical view: for example, how we can select those qualities of sensible objects which are constituent *differentiae*. Plotinus' answer would be that such selection lacks any proper ground within a Peripatetic approach, since both *differentiae* and accidental qualities are qualitative features of sensible objects, which share the same status and therefore cannot be sufficiently distinguished. Accordingly, Plotinus argues in *Enn.* VI.2[43].14.18–19 that constituent features of sensible and qualified *ousia* do not apply to substance "as such" (*holōs*).[20] Furthermore, Plotinus raises the same kind of criticism against the Stoics at *Enn.* VI.1[42].25–30. He argues that their corporealist view makes it impossible to really distinguish God as the active principle from *ousia*/matter. God would in fact be nothing but "matter in a certain state" (*hylē pōs echousa*, *Enn.* VI.1[42].27.7) and the only way out of this predicament would be to regard God as an incorporeal and formal principle metaphysically distinct from matter (*Enn.* VI.1[42].26.10–15).

Claiming that Aristotle's *ousia* cannot have any primary ontic status leaves the question open of how to grasp *ousia* adequately and in itself. Plotinus tackles this problem in the second part of the *Genera of Being*, where he focuses on genera in the intelligible world. In the first chapter, Plotinus recalls what he takes to be Plato's view on being. He thus opposes real paradigmatic and intelligible being to what others think is being, but should instead be called "becoming" or even "not being" (*Enn.* VI.2[43].1.20, 24). Plotinus' agenda is set out at *Enn.* VI.2[43].1.30–33: first he shall enquire on true being "on the assumption that it is not one";[21] afterwards he shall say something "about becoming and what comes to be and the universe perceived by the senses" (see *Enn.* VI.3[44]). True being is the perfectly unified and interconnected world of Forms, which Plotinus famously conceives of as thought-activities of the non-discursive divine Intellect. Plotinus' programme of grasping what *ousia* is in itself entails, then, that we understand the nature of the intelligible paradigmatic being appropriately and without applying to it categories only appropriate for the sensible world. This is what Plotinus actually says in *Enn.* VI.2[43].4, where he opposes the nature of bodies and that of intelligible substance as two mutually exclusive domains. The investigation of intelligible substance and its genera entails that we remove all features that belong to bodies (*Enn.* VI.2[43].4.12–17).

This programme takes it for granted that we can get an adequate understanding of the essence proper to divine, intelligible being. This is the positive side of the approach negatively set out in *Enn.* VI.1[42].3, where Plotinus claims that Aristotle and his followers do not make clear what the nature and concept of substance really are. As Plotinus argues in *Enn.* VI.5[23].1–2, our soul should grasp intelligible beings through the principles appropriate to them and without making use of principles only appropriate for understanding the nature of bodies. Plotinus' metaphysics may thus be viewed as an over-ambitious science of divine being "as such" (see Chiaradonna 2011). In fact, both bodies and intelligible beings entail multiplicity, but according to Plotinus of two radically different kinds: for bodies are made of quantitative and extensional parts which are one outside the other, whereas intelligible beings make a perfectly interpenetrated whole where parts are neither quantitative nor mutually external.[22] The crucial point raised by Plotinus in *Enn.* VI.2[43] and *Enn.* VI.5[23] is that we cannot grasp the intelligible kind of multiplicity by taking the corporeal kind of multiplicity as a starting point (hence Plotinus' infrequent use of the *via analogiae* in the treatises *On the Genera of Being*). The theory of supreme genera developed in *Enn.* VI.2[43] is in fact Plotinus' most sophisticated attempt to outline how the distinctively intelligible non-discursive kind of multiplicity is structured (esp. *Enn.* VI.2[43].7–8 and 19–22).

One might indeed ask how we come to this science of intelligible being, since our soul's discursive cognitive activity is ordinarily directed to "external" sensible objects (*Enn.* V.3[49].4.15–16), and these cannot be used as a starting point for our knowledge of intelligible substance. The answer lies in Plotinus' view of our self: for our self is not only embodied, but is directly connected with the eternal, non-discursive and intelligible Intellect through the highest part of our soul.[23] Accordingly, our soul is always acquainted with true being, although we are ordinarily not conscious of this fact. This approach emerges in *Enn.* VI.2[43].5–7, where Plotinus argues that we come to grasp genera in real being by focusing on the soul and how it is structured. His point is that there is a set of concepts, such as substance and life (*Enn.* VI.2[43].7.2), which we discover in our soul and grasp appropriately when we turn our cognitive power away from bodies. It is crucial that these concepts pertain *primarily* to the intelligible realm. Hence they are not predicates of the sensible world, which we apply analogically to the intelligible one; rather, they are aspects that characterize intelligible being in itself and are only derivatively (homonymously) applied to the sensible world (*Enn.* VI.3[44].2.2). It is by reflecting on these concepts proper to the intelligible that we "discover" the five supreme genera that, as noted by Remes (2007: 145), are "the necessary condition of Intellect's life and act of thinking". Therefore, Plotinus' notion of substance in itself is *toto caelo* different from that which the Peripatetics refer to bodies and their constituent features. Plotinus' substance coincides in fact with the incorporeal and non-discursive nature of the Intellect that we discover within us by removing all categories appropriate to bodies and by reflecting on how our intelligible soul is structured.

This position entails several problems and the question of how we can grasp directly and adequately the nature of divine, intelligible being is certainly a crux in Plotinus' philosophy. Here I will not focus on this issue, but will recall another set of problems which pertain to Plotinus' account of substance. If the nature of substance coincides with intelligible being, the status of sensible particulars becomes difficult to assess (on Plotinus' account of sensible particulars, see Remes 2007: 35–55). As noted above, Plotinus refrains from describing sensible objects as *ousiai* in *Enn.* VI.2[43].1. Substance can neither be a body nor something "in bodies" like Aristotle's essential and enmattered forms. But this leaves open the question of how to regard sensible particulars. If their *ousia* is a self-subsisting principle external to them, the conclusion can hardly be avoided that sensible particulars are in themselves mere unstructured wholes in which nothing is essential. In *Enn.* VI.3[44].8 Plotinus actually seems to reject the Peripatetic view that some features are constituent of bodies, for they make each body the (kind of) entity which it is, whereas other features are merely extrinsic accidents. The Peripatetic distinction between *differentiae* and accidents tends to vanish in Plotinus' physical world and sensible particulars emerge as mere "conglomerations of qualities" which the causal activity of the *logos* (their intelligible forming principle) produces in matter (*Enn.* VI.3[44].8.27–37; VI.3[44].15.24–38; see Kalligas 2011). Elsewhere, however, Plotinus appears to hold a different position, since he establishes a hierarchy between constituent and accidental properties within sensible particulars and maintains that constituent features are activities that derive from the *logos*, whereas accidents have a different origin (which Plotinus however does not specify) (see esp. *Enn.* II.6[17].2.20–26). While some ingenious attempts have recently been made to reconcile Plotinus' accounts of the status of sensible particulars, I am inclined to think that the question must remain open (see Karamanolis 2009). It is difficult to avoid the impression that Plotinus' accounts reveal an internal tension, for either he is conceiving of sensible particulars as endowed with an internal structure, which corresponds to a hierarchical order among their properties (but this comes too close to the notion of "essential property", and according to Plotinus sensible particulars are not endowed with essences), or he is conceiving of sensible particulars as integrally unstructured and qualitative wholes, where "completing" and "extrinsic" properties cannot be opposed (but this apparently jeopardizes an adequate explanation of sensible particulars, and Plotinus does not appear willing to abandon the idea that some properties are more "important" than others).[24]

PORPHYRY AND LATER NEOPLATONISTS

As noted above, Plotinus' account of substance laid the ground for later Neoplatonic discussions. This, however, does not mean that Plotinus was unanimously followed. Certainly some crucial features of his approach were preserved: this holds for his discussion of Aristotle's ontology against the background of Platonic metaphysics and for his in-depth first-hand reading of both Aristotle's treatises and the previous commentators (in particular Alexander of Aphrodisias). From this perspective, Plotinus can really be seen as the founder of Neoplatonism. Plotinus' most distinctive ideas (e.g. his internal criticism of Aristotle and the non-analogical account of intelligible *ousia*), however, had a difficult reception from Porphyry onward. In his extant works on the *Categories*, Porphyry never overtly criticizes Plotinus, but his overall programme of harmonizing Aristotle with Plato can hardly be seen as a prosecution of Plotinus' distinctive approach.[25] What emerges from Porphyry's short commentary on the *Categories*, from the *testimonia* on his extensive lost commentary *ad Gedalium* in seven books and from other texts is a different overall view.[26] Unlike Plotinus, Porphyry has no hesitation in incorporating Peripatetic theses within his Platonic philosophy. This was possibly part of Porphyry's overall project of establishing a unitary Hellenic tradition of thought in opposition to the Christians. Indeed, Porphyry's attitude was not unprecedented, and Platonists before Plotinus had already incorporated Aristotle's views within their philosophy. While Plotinus can be seen as building on the anti-Aristotelian position of Nicostratus, Porphyry is closer to such Aristotelizing Middle Platonists as Alcinous (see Zambon 2002: 295–338). This is only part of the story, however, for Plotinus uses Nicostratus' criticism as a starting point, but develops his discussion of Aristotle in a highly distinctive way, and Porphyry does not merely incorporate Aristotelian tenets within his philosophy, but engages in extensive commentary work on Aristotle's treatises, drawing from previous Peripatetic commentators such as Boethus, Herminus and Alexander. Porphyry, therefore, was not merely an Aristotelizing Platonist: in addition to that, he was the first Platonic commentator of Aristotle (see Karamanolis 2004).

In his commentaries on the *Categories*, Porphyry follows the standard Peripatetic interpretation according to which the "object" (*prothesis, skopos*) of Aristotles' treatise is not things/beings as such, but words that "signify" things (*pragmata: in Cat.* 58.18–20;

59.17–18).[27] Plotinus is not mentioned, but Porphyry's distinction between the enquiry carried out in the *Categories* and that on being and its genera certainly appears un-Plotinian, if not anti-Plotinian (*in Cat.* 59.30–33). Since the *Categories* deal with words that signify things, and not with things as such, it is inappropriate to assess Aristotle's list as if it were a complete division of beings and their fundamental kinds. It has been argued that Porphyry aimed to separate logic from metaphysics and discussed the former as a metaphysically (or even philosophically) neutral subject.[28] This is only partially true, however, since ontology is far from being absent in Porphyry's logical works. Still, what we find in Porphyry's works on the categories is not his fully developed Platonic ontology; rather, it is a simplified and partial ontology limited to sensible particulars and their immanent features. For Porphyry conceives of categories as words that signify things, and our language in his view refers primarily to the sensible world (*in Cat.* 91.7–12, 91.19–25). Not only that, but words are "messengers of things" and derive their basic mutual differences from the latter (*in Cat.* 58.23–9). Hence the division of categories reflects the basic ontic distinctions of (sensible) things. This isomorphism between language and sensible objects explains why beings are (at least indirectly) included in the enquiry in question. Porphyry's discussion of *ousia* is part of this approach. From both his short commentary and what we know of his longer one the following picture emerges: Porphyry basically followed the Peripatetic account of sensible *ousia* as developed by Alexander of Aphrodisias. Significantly, Simplicius (*in Cat.* 78.20–24 = frag. 58 [Smith]) reports that Porphyry criticized Boethus' equation of the immanent form with the non-substantial categories. Hence Porphyry regards both sensible particulars and their constituent features, such as specific *differentiae*, as substances (*in Cat.* 95.31–96.1). Aristotle's view that sensible particulars are primary substances is explained by the subject matter of the *Categories*: for sensible particulars are the primary object of our language and are then regarded as primary substances, even if Aristotle himself elsewhere takes intelligible substances as primary (*in Cat.* 91.14–26).

The difference from Plotinus' critical discussion of Aristotle's sensible *ousia* could not be greater. Porphyry actually regarded Aristotle's account of the sensible world as incomplete (since it had to be supplemented with Plato's separate and paradigmatic principles: see Simplicius, *in Ph.* 10.32–5 = frag. 120 [Smith]), but not as inconsistent. In Porphyry's view, Aristotle and his followers provide a satisfying account of sensible *ousia*, which can be fully incorporated within Platonism since it is the lower part of a larger metaphysical framework that includes Plato's transcendental principles at its top.[29] In this way, Aristotle's *ousia* becomes part of Porphyry's concordant Platonism. This holds for the Stoic views on substance and quality too, which Porphyry attempted to adapt and incorporate within his Aristotelian–Platonic framework (see Simplicius, *in Cat.* 48.11–15 = frag. 55 [Smith]). It is difficult to avoid the impression that Porphyry's approach is philosophically less interesting than Plotinus' critical discussion of Aristotle. Porphyry's programme, however, is both subtle and very interesting from a historical point of view. Through his commentaries on Aristotle, Porphyry in fact established a central aspect of late antique philosophy, and his view of the harmony between Plato and Aristotle was shared (to different extents) by all subsequent Neoplatonists. The influence on posterity of Porphyry's programme was thus immense and, rather ironically, his interpretation of Aristotle's *Categories* was crucially important for Christian late antique and Medieval authors (see Erismann 2011).

Iamblichus, the second great Neoplatonic commentator, developed Porphyry's programme in a distinctive way. Iamblichus' commentary is lost, but a good deal of information about it is provided by Dexippus (a disciple of Iamblichus: Simplicius, *in Cat.* 2.25–9)
and Simplicius, who rely on their predecessor.[30] Simplicius (*in Cat.* 2.9–14 [Kalbfleisch])
says that Iamblichus followed Porphyry closely, but, unlike Porphyry, applied his "intellective theory (*noera theōria*)" on all levels. This expression refers to the metaphysical account of intelligible beings, which had a key position in Iamblichus' exegesis
(Dillon 1997; Taormina 1999). In addition to that, Simplicius says that Iamblichus took
Aristotle's *Categories* to be inspired by Archytas' Pythagorean teaching (i.e. by Archytas'
apocryphal treatise on categories, which Iamblichus thought to be authentic).[31] As far as
we can judge, this attitude was different from that of Porphyry, who basically followed
Peripatetic views when interpreting Aristotle. For example, Iamblichus, unlike Porphyry,
interpreted Aristotle's theory of substantial predication from the perspective of the
Neoplatonic theory of derivation, thus regarding substantial predication as the logical
expression of the metaphysical relation in virtue of which physical objects partake in separate *ante rem* forms (see Simplicius, *in Cat.* 52.9–18; Chiaradonna 2007b). Iamblichus
pushed his reading of Aristotle along Platonic–Pythagorean lines so far that (as David/
Elias, *in Cat.* 123.2–3 reports) he did not refrain from assuming that Aristotle was not
opposed to Plato on the theory of Ideas. This was indeed an extreme interpretation and
one that remained isolated: even Athenian Neoplatonists did not follow Iamblichus on
this issue.[32]

Simplicius' response to Nicostratus and Plotinus at *in Cat.* 76–7 is a good example of
Iamblichus' approach. Against Nicostratus and Plotinus' critique, Simplicius first retorts
that it is not correct to assess Aristotle's view against the background of intelligible substances, for Aristotle did not intend to focus on the intelligibles in the *Categories*, and
Archytas (the Pythagorean archegete of the teaching on categories) confirms this interpretation (Simplicius, *in Cat.* 76.19–23). This is the first part of Simplicius' reply, but he
soon provides a much more metaphysical response which aims to show that Aristotle's
view on *ousia* is actually perfectly compatible with the Platonic–Pythagorean teaching,
for *ousia* is an intelligible genus/principle from which metaphysically lower *ousiai* derive
(Simplicius, *in Cat.* 76.25–77.4). Simplicius (*in Cat.* 77.4–13) takes Aristotle's division of
ousiai in *Metaph.* 1069a30–b2 to confirm this view and, again, the Pythagorean Archytas is
mentioned in support of Aristotle. Hence Aristotle's account of *ousia* is ultimately rescued
by regarding *ousia* as a hierarchical unity of derivation, which conforms to Platonic metaphysics (Simplicius, *in Cat.* 77.14–15). This is a very impressive response, but it is worth
noting that Plotinus' main objections against Aristotle remain unanswered: for example,
Simplicius/Iamblichus does not explain why this hierarchical genus does not also include
all other items that derive from substance. Furthermore, the main requirement set out
by Plotinus – that of grasping what intelligible being is in itself – is in no way fulfilled
by Iamblichus/Simplicius, who argues instead that Aristotle's account of *ousia* and categories makes it *analogically* possible to grasp what intelligible beings are (Simplicius, *in
Cat.* 74.22–75.9). Dexippus (*in Cat.* 41.25–7) claims that intelligible beings are incomprehensible to us and "ineffable" in themselves. Hence we apply the name *ousia* to them
metaphorically, based on what is familiar to sense-perception. Plotinus' account of *ousia*
is thus completely reversed.

NOTES

1. This translation raises some puzzles which I will not go into here: see Arpe (1941). The term *ousia* is probably impossible to translate adequately and all solutions are ultimately unsatisfying: see M. Frede & Patzig (1988: vol. 2, 16–17). *Faute de mieux*, here I will make a rather free use of "substance" and "essence", and will often transliterate the Greek word.

2. See Kahn (1976: 333, repr. in 2009: 72). It has been suggested (with different emphases) that a distinctive notion of "existence" or "act of being" can be found among late antique philosophers (e.g. in Plotinus' account of *energeia* as the *hypostasis* of the One at VI.8[39].20.9–15, in "Porphyry"'s view that *einai* is prior to *on* and *ousia* at *in Prm.* XII.21–35 and in the late Neoplatonic use of *hyparxis*). See the accounts in P. Hadot (1973, repr. in 1999: 71–88); Gerson (1994: 3–14); Corrigan (1996b). For further qualification, see Chiaradonna (2012a).

3. On Plotinus' *Genera of Being*, see Wurm (1973); Strange (1987); A. C. Lloyd (1990: 85–97); Gerson (1994: 79–103); Horn (1995a); Corrigan (1996a); de Haas (2001); Chiaradonna (2002, with a *status quaestionis* at pp. 15–40). Two annotated translations are Isnardi Parente (1994) and Brisson (2008). There are several recent overviews of the Neoplatonic debate on the categories. See, in particular, Sorabji (2004: vol. 3, 56–127), with a very useful selection of sources, and Tuominen (2009: 202–17).

4. On Lucius and Nicostratus, see Moraux (1984: 528–63) and the collection of *testimonia* in Gioè (2002). The pre-Plotinian debates on the *Categories* are now extensively discussed in Griffin (forthcoming).

5. This ontic interpretation of Aristotle's categories as (the highest and non-reducible) genera that are intended to account for all beings can be seen as problematic and influenced by Plato's metaphysics. Note, however, that Aristotle regards *ousia* and categories as genera or "kinds" in *APo.* A 1.402a23–5; B 1.412a6. In his commentary on *Metaph.* 1003b21, Alexander of Aphrodisias describes Aristotle's categories as "genera of being" (*in Metaph.* 245.34–5).

6. Simplicius, *in Cat.* 73.19–21: καὶ πῶς ἔσται κοινωνία τῆς αὐτῆς οὐσίας, ἐν οἷς τὸ πρότερον ἔστιν καὶ τὸ ὕστερον, καὶ τὸ μὲν παράδειγμα, τὸ δὲ εἰκών; That items forming an ordered series cannot be under the same genus is an Academic argument used by Aristotle against Plato (Aristotle, *Metaph.* 999a6–13; *Eth. Nic.* A4, 1096a17–23; *Eth. Eud.* A8, 1218a1). See A. C. Lloyd (1962). Here Nicostratus and Plotinus turn this argument against Aristotle.

7. Translations from Plotinus are taken from Armstrong (1966–88), with some slight changes. The Greek text is that of Henry & Schwyzer (1964–82).

8. These remarks can be compared with what Slaveva-Griffin (2009: 98–9) notes about the difficulties residing in the concept of "number" (*Enn.* V.5[7].4–5; VI.6[34]). On the one hand, "number" is a genus concept whose species are the substantial (intelligible and non-quantitative) and the monadic (quantitative) number. On the other hand, number is primarily substantial number, whereas monadic number imitates substantial number as its ontological paradigm.

9. Porphyry, *Sent.* 19 and 42. See Chiaradonna (2007a). In his reply to Nicostratus and Plotinus, Simplicius mentions the distinction between two kinds of *asōmata* (*in Cat.* 77.28–30). The distinction is actually present in some sections from the *Enneads*: see e.g. *Enn.* IV.2[4].1.33–41.

10. See "Arch." *Cat.* 30.23–31.1 [Thesleff]. On this early debate, see Chiaradonna (2009a).

11. This would not be an isolated case. The recently discovered *Categories* commentary in the Archimedes Palimpsest (most probably, a long section from Porphyry's *ad Gedalium*) shows that Alexander's famous view on universals as accidents of definable natures was the response to a puzzle raised by Nicostratus (Chiaradonna *et al.* 2013).

12. On Alexander's approach to Plato's Forms, see Lefebvre (2008). On Alexander's essentialism, see Rashed (2007).

13. On Atticus' polemics, see Moraux (1984: 564–82). Predictably enough, Atticus argued that Aristotle's ten categories have no pertinence to Plato's philosophy (Eusebius, *PE* XV.iv.19 = frag. 2 [des Places]). See J. Barnes (2003: 336 ["Additional Note [G]: Platonists and Aristotle's 'categories'"]).

14. See Alexander of Aphrodisias, *Quaest.* I.8.17.17–22; I.17.30.10–16; I.26.42.24–5; *Mant.* 122.4–12. Plotinus mentions the "parts of substance" argument in *Enn.* VI.3[44].5.10–25 too (see Chiaradonna 2008a). On this argument in Alexander, see Rashed (2007: 42–52).

15. Some interpreters are inclined to read Plotinus' account of categories as a dialectical discussion whose aim is to incorporate (rather than reject) Aristotle's theory: see (with different emphases) Strange (1987);

Horn (1995a); de Haas (2001). According to such interpretations, Plotinus' and Porphyry's approaches would be basically similar. For a criticism of this view, see e.g. J. Barnes (2008).

16. Schiaparelli (2010) provides an in-depth account of Plotinus' criticism of Aristotle's views on form and definition in *Enn.* II.7[37].3 and VI.7[38].2. She argues that according to Plotinus, "the Aristotelian doctrine about real definitions is not wrong, but it is incomplete. It is likely that Plotinus wants to add that in some cases, namely when we want to explain how things are at the level of the sensible world, we cannot simply refer to something like definitions that indicate the essence" (*ibid.*: 488). I agree with this reading and would only suggest a different nuance. As I would put it, according to Plotinus Aristotle's doctrine is ultimately wrong and self-refuting *precisely because* it is incomplete: for it is impossible to make sense of things in the sensible world if one omits their essential and intelligible causes.

17. Aristotle's concept of natural priority in the *Metaphysics* has recently been interpreted as involving priority in "what is" something (A is prior to B if and only if A can be what it is independently of B being what it is, while the converse is not the case: see Peramatzis 2008). Plotinus would probably argue that we cannot establish a hierarchy of items like this within the sensible realm. His discussion of Aristotle's soul (*Enn.* IV.7[2].8⁵; IV.3[27].20–21) is revealing, for Plotinus claims that the distinction between soul and body cannot be grounded adequately, if the soul is conceived of as a hylomorphic form. The same holds with Plotinus' discussion of Aristotle's constituent *differentia*, for (a) the selection of those predicates of sensible *ousiai* which can count as *differentiae* lacks any adequate ground (*Enn.* VI.3[44].8.27–37, 10.12–28); and (b) these predicates could in no way qualify "substance as such" (i.e. intelligible substance: see *Enn.* VI.2[43].14.18–19, discussed below).

18. Simplicius' passage is translated with a commentary in Sharples (2010: 77–8, 86–8). On Boethus' ontology, see now Rashed (2013).

19. For a discussion, see again Rashed (2007: 53–79, 104–17 [with a commented French translation of Alexander's texts on specific *differentia* preserved in Arabic]).

20. See *Enn.* VI.2[43].14.18–22: Νῦν δὲ λέγομεν οὐκ οὐσίας ὅλως εἶναι συμπληρωτικὰ τὰ τῆς τινὸς οὐσίας· οὐ γὰρ οὐσίας προσθήκη γίνεται τῷ ἀνθρώπῳ καθὸ ἄνθρωπος εἰς οὐσίαν· ἀλλ' ἔστιν οὐσία ἄνωθεν, πρὶν ἐπὶ τὴν διαφορὰν ἐλθεῖν, ὥσπερ καὶ ζῷον ἤδη, πρὶν ἐπὶ τὸ λογικὸν ἥκειν. These lines are difficult and my previous account in Chiaradonna (2002: 137–42) stands in need of revision. Here Plotinus is probably suggesting that the properties of a particular (sensible and qualified) substance are not constituent of substance as such (οὐσίας ὅλως), i.e. of intelligible substance. See Lavaud (2008: 101 ["la substance considérée absolument"]) and Helmig (2006: 266 n. 30 ["die Substanz schlechthin"]), who provide the correct reading of ὅλως as going together with οὐσίας (cf. the similar expression ἡ κίνησις ἢ ὅλως κίνησις at *Enn.* VI.1[42].16.16–17, where Plotinus refers to motion as an actual intelligible principle of corporeal extensional and quantitative motion). However, I do not agree with other aspects of Lavaud's interpretation and would still take τὰ τῆς τινὸς οὐσίας at *Enn.* VI.2[43].14.19 to refer to the properties of sensible and qualified substances (see *Enn.* VI.2[43].15.1–2). The remarks in Lavaud (2008: 102 n.1) do not seem persuasive to me. Instead, I agree with the reading provided by Helmig (2006: 265–6). I would argue that when Plotinus says that the properties of sensible and particular substances are not constituent of substance as such, he is not suggesting that there are *other* properties, different from the sensible ones, which are constituent of intelligible *ousia*. Rather, he is suggesting that the subject/property distinction is in itself incapable of accounting for how the perfectly unified intelligible being is structured (*Enn.* VI.2[43].15). From this perspective, the very distinction between constituent and accidental qualities is irrelevant, and Plotinus' *megista genē* cannot in any way be seen as predicates of intelligible being (for they are neither essential nor accidental predicates). Hence motion is neither something accidental to substance nor something which contributes to its completion: rather, it is "substance itself" (*Enn.* VI.2[43].15.10). I would like to thank Stephen Menn for his comments on my previous interpretation of this passage.

21. The One is above being and is bereft of any kind of multiplicity (even that of intelligible genera). Plotinus distinguishes the status of the One from that of genera: see *Enn.* VI.2[43].10.20–23.

22. On Plotinus' talk of the "non-quantitative" dimensions of substance, see e.g. *Enn.* IV.4[28].16.22, *diastēma adiastaton* and *Enn.* VI.6[34].17.24–5, *aschēmatista schēmata*. See on this the discussion in Slaveva-Griffin (2009: 95–103). A challenging account of Plotinus' views on extension and bodies can now be found in De Risi (2012). The reference work for Plotinus' theory of the non-discursive Intellect is Emilsson (2007).

23. On Plotinus' dual theory of the self, see Remes (2007). It is controversial whether according to Plotinus our soul has a direct cognitive access to the world of intelligible Forms, independently of sense-perception.

I tried to develop the interpretation set out here in Chiaradonna (2011, 2012b). For a different account, see Gerson (1994: 177–80).

24. I would now qualify what I wrote in Chiaradonna (2002), and would be more prudent in describing the radical anti-essentialism in *Enn.* VI.3[44].8 as Plotinus' last word on the status of sensible objects.

25. For a different account, see the contributions mentioned above, note 15.

26. On Porphyry's interpretation of Aristotle, see Evangeliou (1988) and Karamanolis (2006: 243–330). Porphyry's extant short commentary on the *Categories* has been newly re-edited after Busse's classical C.A.G. edition: see Bodéüs (2008). The *testimonia* on Porphyry's great commentary *ad Gedalium* in seven books (see Simplicius, *in Cat.* 2.5–9) are collected in A. Smith (1993 [45T–74F]). A substantial section from this work (corresponding to the commentary on *Cat.* 1a20–b24) is probably preserved in the Archimedes Palimpsest: see Chiaradonna *et al.* (2013).

27. For an English translation of Porphyry's commentary, see Strange (1992). On Porphyry's semantics, see A. C. Lloyd (1990: 36–75); Van den Berg (2008); Griffin (2012).

28. This reading has been developed in different ways by Ebbesen (1990) and J. Barnes (2003). Criticism in Chiaradonna (2008b).

29. I developed this reading in Chiaradonna (2007a, 2007b).

30. Fragments in Dalsgaard Larsen (1972). The relation between Dexippus and Simplicius' sources is intricate. P. Hadot (1974, repr. in 1999: 355–82) argued that Dexippus follows Porphyry's *ad Gedalium* rather than Iamblichus, but this conclusion has been questioned by Dillon (1990: 75 n. 13) and Luna (2001: 774). Be that as it may, Dexippus did not entirely follow his master's Pythagorizing interpretation. On Dexippus see now J. Barnes (2009). Several studies and translations have recently been devoted to Simplicius' *in Cat.* Luna (2001) is fundamental.

31. See above, note 10.

32. Here I can only sketchily outline Proclus' position. Some recent works have shown that Proclus attempted to incorporate and adapt elements of Aristotle's hylomorphism within his own physics and metaphysics (see Opsomer 2009). However, Proclus was far from unreservedly positive in his overall assessment of Aristotle. In particular, in his commentary on the *Timaeus* Proclus regards Aristotle's causal explanation of the physical world as inferior to that of Plato, on account of the fact that Aristotle confined his research to "subservient" physical causes, i.e. matter and enmattered forms, leaving out the most fundamental causes that transcend the physical world, i.e. the efficient and productive cause (the Demiurge), the paradigmatic cause (Ideas) and the final cause (the Idea of the Good) (see on this Steel 2003). Despite their very different emphases (critical vs. concordant), Proclus' position is, from this perspective, closer to that of Porphyry than to that of Plotinus, for Proclus does not reject the view that Aristotle's causal theory may be applied to the physical world (although it must be supplemented with Plato's superior causes): hence, we find no trace in his writings of Plotinus' internal criticism of Aristotle. On Proclus' account of enmattered essential form, see esp. *in Ti.* II.25.6–9 [Diehl] with the discussion in Helmig (2006). On the different meanings of *ousia* in Proclus' commentary on the *Timaeus*, see Baltzly (2007: 37 n. 3).

Matter and evil in the Neoplatonic tradition

Jean-Marc Narbonne

In the Platonic tradition, the role of matter as a possible source of evil is closely linked to earlier discussions on the subject, especially those of Plato and Aristotle.[1] But there exists a fundamental difference between the Neoplatonic treatment of this subject and its Classical sources, namely, *the derivative character of matter*. Indeed, beginning with Plotinus – and already before him in some other traditions such as Neopythagoreanism, gnosticism and the *Chaldaean Oracles*[2] – matter is no longer an originative principle as was the case up to the Middle Platonism of Numenius, but an entity derived from another principle. From that point on, the classic opposition between Matter and Form, more or less acute depending on the author (but sometimes harshened to a form of radical dualism, as one can observe in Plutarch or Numenius), took on a different meaning, one which neither Plato nor Aristotle could have foreseen. Indeed, in the case where matter is a produced reality, the relationship between matter and form can be either one of relative cooperation, or one of relative opposition. But when matter and form each have an independent origin, any opposition between them tends to be seriously accentuated.

Now, this type of *extreme dualism*, based on two autonomous and equally primordial principles, is well known to Aristotle and is in fact attributed by him to most of his predecessors (cf. *Ph.* I.5–6) – while he himself holds that two opposite principles must necessarily "act on a third thing different from both" (*Ph.* 189a25–6), since he believes that "contraries are mutually destructive" (*Ph.* 192a21–2) – but especially to Empedocles, who offered, according to Aristotle, the most radical version of it:

> But since the contraries of the various forms of good were also perceived to be present in nature – not only order and the beautiful, but also disorder and the ugly, and bad things in greater number than good, and ignoble things than beautiful, therefore another thinker introduced friendship and strife, each of the two the cause of one of these two sets of qualities. For if we were to follow out the view of Empedocles, and interpret it according to its meaning and not to its lisping

expression, we should find that *friendship is the cause of good things, and strife of bad*. Therefore, if we said that Empedocles in a sense both mentions, and is the first to mention, *the bad and the good as principles*, we should perhaps be right.

(Aristotle, *Metaph.* 984b32–985a9, trans. Barnes)[3]

To find another dualism as radical as this one in the Greek philosophical writings, one must look to much later authors connected with Middle Platonism, such as Atticus, Plutarch, Numenius, Cronius, Harpocration or Celsus.[4] The most interesting text in this respect[5] is probably the one we find in Plutarch's *Isis and Orisis*:

Inasmuch as Nature brings, in this life of ours, many experiences in which both evil and good are commingled, or better, to put it very simply, Nature brings nothing which is not combined with something else, we may assert that it is not one keeper of two great vases who, after the manner of a barmaid, deals out to us our failures and successes in mixture, but it has come about, *as the result of two opposed principles and two antagonistic forces*, one of which guides us along a straight course to the right, while the other turns us aside and backward, that our life is complex, and so also is the universe; and if it is not true of the whole of it, yet it is true that this terrestrial universe, including its moon as well, is irregular and variable and subject to all manners of change. For it is the law of Nature that nothing comes into being without a cause, and if the good cannot provide a cause for evil, *then it follows that Nature must have in herself the source and origin of evil*, just as she contains the source and origin of good. The great majority and the wisest of men hold this opinion: they believe that there are two gods, rivals as it were, the one the Artificer of good and the other of evil. These are also those who call the better one a god (*theon*), and the other a daemon (*daimona*).

(*de Isid. et Osirid.* 369b1–d7, trans. Babbitt)[6]

As we noted, a radical dualism of this sort is by definition excluded from an integral emanative system such as the one advocated by our Neoplatonic philosophers. For them, the challenge will consist in trying to explain how evil, defect, monstrosity and irregularity can appear inside a structure emerging from, and governed by, a unique and wholly good principle. Whence comes evil, if there exists no independent principle of evil? Whence come defects, if all realities come from a unique principle which can produce only good things and which may in no way be held responsible for evils? To resolve these questions, many avenues were explored by the philosophers of antiquity. Though we cannot here analyse each of these avenues in detail, we may say that two fundamental attitudes may be drawn from these approaches, one attempting to preserve a strong dualism inside a monist context, and the other attempting to minimize as far as possible the presence of evil, and so any opposition to the Good, within the whole universe. The first option is, for the most part, the position of Plotinus, who goes so far as to conceive of a substance of evil inside the whole, which, taken globally, is still governed by the Good. The other option, although its foundations were laid by Iamblichus, is represented largely by the position of Proclus, who in fact undertook a detailed refutation of Plotinus' stance. We will examine each of these views successively before offering our own assessment of the debate as a whole.

MATTER AND EVIL IN PLOTINUS

The model of *Timaeus* 50c–51b: matter as pure receptivity and impassibility

The ultimate source of Plotinus' analysis of the role of matter in the sensible cosmos is without doubt the *Timaeus*, more precisely the following passage where Plato describes the nature of the *receptacle* (*chōra*) in relation to the sensible copies appearing in it:

> Now the same account holds also for that nature which receives all the bodies. We must always refer to it by the same term, for it does not depart from its own character in any way. Not only does it always receive all things, it has never in any way whatever taken on any characteristics similar to any of the things that enter it. Its nature is to be available for anything to make its impression upon, and it is modified, shaped, and reshaped by the things that enter it. These are the things that make it appear different at different times. The things that enter and leave it are imitations of those things that always are, imprinted after their likeness in a marvelous way that is hard to describe. This is something we shall pursue at another time. For the moment, we need to keep in mind three types of things: that which comes to be, that in which it comes to be, and that after which the thing coming to be is modeled and which is the source of its coming to be. It is quite appropriate to compare the receiving thing to a mother, the source to a father, and the nature between them to their offspring. We also must understand that if the imprints are to be varied, with all the varieties there are to see, this thing upon which the imprints are to be formed could not be well prepared for that role if it were not itself devoid of any of those characters that it is to receive from elsewhere. For if it resembled any of the things that enter it, it could not successfully copy their opposites or things of a totally different nature whenever it were to receive them. It would be showing its own face as well. This is why the thing that is to receive in itself all the [elemental] kinds must be totally devoid of any characteristics. … In the same way, then, if the thing that is to receive repeatedly throughout its whole self the likenesses of the intelligible objects, the things which always are – if it is to do so successfully, then it ought to be devoid of any inherent characteristics of its own. This, of course, is the reason why we shouldn't call the mother or the receptacle of what has come to be, of what is visible or perceivable in every other way, either earth or air, fire, or water, or any of their compounds or their constituents. But if we speak of it as an invisible and characterless sort of thing, one that receives all things and shares in a most perplexing way in what is intelligible, a thing extremely difficult to comprehend, we shall not be misled. And insofar as it is possible to arrive at its nature on the basis of what we've said so far, the most correct way to speak of it may well be this: the part of it that gets ignited appears on each occasion as fire, the dampened part as water, and parts of earth or air insofar as they receive the imitations of these.
>
> (*Ti.* 50b5–51b6, trans. Zeyl)

One is struck, in this long description, by the absolute inalterability of the receptacle itself, which, on the one hand, receives everything, but remains, on the other hand, completely unaltered throughout the process; that is, it is not modified in any way by what goes in and comes out of it. The receptacle does not deviate from its own nature (*Ti.* 50b9) and never assumes the Form which it receives (*Ti.* 50b9–51a1), therefore remaining *unformed* (*amorphon*) and above all, "outside all Forms" (*pantōn ektos eidōn, Ti.* 50e4–5; 51a3–4). Accordingly, the receptacle remains "an invisible and characterless sort of thing" (*Ti.* 51a8) and the most one dare say of it is that this third kind of being, alongside the Ideas and the copies themselves, constitutes a *place* (*chōra*) and that this place is *incorruptible*, and consequently eternal, as its task is exclusively to "receive all things" (*Ti.* 52b1–2). Yet it remains itself unknown, and is only apprehensible "by a kind of bastard reasoning that does not involve sense perception" (*Ti.* 52b2–3).

In all treatises, Plotinus tried to adhere as closely as possible to this fundamental Platonic conception. Accordingly, matter is assigned all possible negative predicates, and is described as being sterile (*agonos*),[7] unreceptive (*adektos*),[8] disgracious and ugly (*aischron, aischra, aischos*),[9] disordered (*akosmētos*),[10] unmixed shortage (*akratos elleipsis*),[11] unilluminated (*aphōtiston, alampes*),[12] irrational (*alogon*),[13] without size (*amegethes*),[14] immeasurable (*ametros*),[15] unmixed (*amiges*),[16] without share in goodness (*amoiros*),[17] unformed (*amorphon, aschēmosynē, ameres, aneideon*),[18] without colour (*amydra, achrous, amydron*),[19] unchangeable (*analloiōton*),[20] indestructible (*anōlethros, aphthartos*),[21] invisible and indeterminate (*aoriston/aoristia, aoraton*),[22] impassible (*apathēs/apathes/apatheia*),[23] infinite (*apeiron/apeiria*),[24] unqualified (*apoios/apoion*),[25] uncorporeal (*asōmatos*),[26] alterity in itself and evil in itself (*autoeterotēs, autokakon*).[27]

Plotinus, of course, retains the Aristotelian word "matter" (*hylē*), a word absent from Plato in its technical sense. Yet Plotinus' use of this word is far removed from its original Aristotelian sense, since Plotinian matter is no more that *out-of-which* (*ex hou*) things are made (like a statue is made, say, *out of wood*), as it was for Aristotle, but simply the *that-in-which* (*en hōi*) the copies find themselves. Moreover, Plotinian matter is even less real than the Platonic receptacle itself, in so far as it is no longer a *space* or some *physical extension* existing prior to the arrival of the different copies, as was the case with the Platonic *chōra*. Rather, matter, for Plotinus, must receive not only all the qualities from the Form, but even size itself, which the Form will communicate to it upon entry. In other words, matter receives its extension from an intelligible determination, that is, the Form, so that one can say that matter in and of itself possesses no proper dimension or extension. As Plotinus himself puts it, matter is "receptive of extension" (*diastēmatos dektikē*), or the "receptacle of size" (*hypodochē megethous*) (*Enn.* II.4[12].11.18–19, 37–8), but itself without size (*amegēthes*) (*Enn.* II.4[12].12.23). This surprising doctrine, possibly Chrysippean in origin (*SVF* II.536.b), exposed in two special developments within his corpus (*Enn.* II.4[12].8–12; III.6[26].16–18), transforms matter into a sort of empty concept, although not a pure nothingness, which is precisely the judgement Plotinus himself attempts to counter:

> So here in the material world the many forms must be in something which is one; and this is what has been given size, even if this is different from size. … So, then, matter is necessary both to quality and to size, and therefore to bodies; and it is not an empty name (*kenon onoma*) but it is something underlying, even if it is invisible and sizeless.
> (*Enn.* II.4[12].12.6–24)[28]

In fact, to say that matter is deprived of size amounts to saying that matter is in itself *in(de)finite* (of no *definite* size), since Plotinus, influenced here by the *Philebus*, holds that matter *per se* is unlimitedness and indefiniteness (*apeiron*) (*Enn.* II.4[12].15–16), this indefiniteness having no other option than to adapt itself to the conditions imposed by what comes to it: "But matter is indefinite and not yet stable by itself, and is carried about here and there into every form, and since it is altogether tractable (*euagōgos*) becomes many by being brought into everything, and in this way acquires the nature of mass" (*Enn.* II.4[12].11.40–43). In all those contexts, Plotinus insists on the constraint imposed on matter by the Forms: "And that which makes matter large (as it seems) comes from the imaging in it of size, and that which is imagined in it is sized in this world; and the matter on which it is imagined is *compelled to keep pace* (*anankazetai synthein*) with it, and submits itself to it all together and everywhere" (*Enn.* III.6[26].17.31–5). And here again: "But matter, which has no resistance, for it has no activity, but is a shadow, *waits to endure passively whatever that which acts upon it wishes.*"[29]

In this context, the image of matter as a *mirror* might help us understand this confusing statement about the *impassibility* of matter. Plotinus, as we just saw, maintains that matter *endures passively* whatever wishes to act upon it. But in the very same treatise, he professes that matter is impassible (*apathes*) (*Enn.* III.6[26].7.41).How are we to resolve this apparent paradox? Here again, the central inspiration comes from the *chōra* itself which, as we just saw, never undergoes a change of condition or state (*Ti.* 50b9), "for while it is always receiving all things, nowhere and in no way does it assume any shape similar to any of the things that enter into it" (*Ti.* 50b9–51c1). In the same way, Plotinus' matter receives everything without being affected by anything, since matter is comparable to a *mirror* in which the copies as reflections of the Ideas appear: "For one must not call presence or putting on shape 'being affected'. If one said that mirrors and transparent things generally were in no way affected by the images seen in them, he would be giving not an inappropriate image. For the things in matter are images too" (*Enn.* III.6[26].9.14–19).

Matter, then, receives without being altered (*Enn.* III.6[26].10–11) by what it receives, and therefore receives in an impassive fashion or, to put it otherwise, it participates without participating (*Enn.* III.6[26].14.21–2), and the change one can notice in it remains in fact *exterior* to it (*ektos*, as Plato had already written), since matter remains "alone and isolated" (*monon kai erēmon*) (*Enn.* III.6[26].9.37). And of course, matter is not affected either by the change of size or volume it endorses: "But matter, all the same, keeps its own nature and makes use of this size as a kind of garment, which it put on when it ran with it as the size in its course led it along."[30]

A final point to consider is that the copy and matter do not really benefit from each other in what might be termed their sort of "external exchange". Since matter has no affinity with what comes to it, the result is that "neither does that which enters it get anything from it, nor does matter get anything from what comes into it" (*Enn.* III.6[26].15.10–11). It is not only *impassible*, but also sterile (*agonos*), since it does nothing beyond offering itself as the place in which everything occurs. In this way, its existence appears minimal, or even empty. To quote Armstrong's well-known quip, matter seems not only impassible, but impossible.[31]

The model of *Timaeus* 52d–53b: necessity and disorder

The paradox of Plotinian matter is that while it represents extreme weakness and poverty, it is also the most belligerent opponent possible of Form. Because of its profound foreignness, its radical impassivity and its inalterability, matter remains what it was since its origin, and escapes definitively the work of the Good. Its extreme sterility, however, does not preclude any activity on matter's part. Indeed, Plotinian matter is surprisingly active, although this activity amounts to nothing more than the undermining of Form. In this respect, Plotinus once again aligns his position with the text of the *Ti.* 52e, which holds that the Nurse of Becoming, "owing to being filled with potencies that are neither similar nor balanced, in no part of herself is she equally balanced, but sways unevenly in every part, and is herself shaken by these forms and shakes them in turn as she is moved". The presence in the *chōra* of these dissimilar and unbalanced powers stems from the fact that the cosmos itself is the result of two orders, as indicated at *Ti.* 48a: "For, in truth, this Cosmos in its origin was generated as a compound, from the combination of Necessity and Reason." However, as we know, many followers of Plato saw in this need for combination and this random cause (*Ti.* 48a7) the true source of evil according to Plato.[32]

Perfectly plastic on one hand, matter, on the other hand, is in complete opposition to the Good. It is not merely neutral but active, a principle of evil actively opposed to the Good principle, so that it can be said, as Plotinus teaches in *Enn.* I.8[51], that the Good and Evil are two competing principles: "the principles are double, one of evil things, one of good things".[33] How is this possible? How can one conceive of an opposition, in a single cosmos, of two substances independent of each other, as when Plotinus explains that "the substantial reality of the divine is contrary to the substantial reality of evil" (*Enn.* I.8[51].6.46–7)? How can there be two wholes opposed to each other, as when we read that this "whole, too, is contrary to the whole" (*Enn.* I.8[51].6.43–4), and how did they come to this antithetical situation? The responses of Plotinus to these different questions are exceptionally complex, and have often been misunderstood, not only by modern interpreters, but also by his immediate successors.

First, it must be understood that matter may constitute a whole, and even a very bad one, as its nature is infinite and undefined, and that it embodies in this way the native disorder. This analysis is based not only on the *chōra* of the *Timaeus*, but on the *apeiron* in the *Philebus* (24c–d). For Plotinus, matter "must be called unlimited of itself, by opposition to the forming principle; and just as the forming principle is forming principle without being anything else, so matter which is set over against the forming principle by reason of its unlimitedness must be called unlimited without being anything else" (*Enn.* II.4[12].15.33–7). The same teaching is to be found later in *Enn.* I.8[51]: "Indefiniteness and unmeasuredness and all the other characteristics which the nature of evil has are contrary to definition and measure and the other characteristics present in the divine nature" (*Enn.* I.8[51].6.41–3). However, it is known that this indefinite nature is intrinsically evil, because any improvement would destroy its condition: "For if it really participated and was really altered by the good it would not be evil by nature" (*Enn.* III.6[26].11.41–3).

Second, one might ask how there could be two wholes opposed to one another. The response of Plotinus is to place one of the two wholes in internal opposition to the other whole. The whole of evil is opposed, but from inside, to the whole of the Good which encompasses it externally. Evil-matter is thus a heterogeneous whole within Being itself. This is shown schematically in Figure 15.1.

By means of this approach, Plotinus retains the benefits of mixed dualism (evil does not come from the first principle, but exclusively from the second; evil manifested as real force, although it remains less than the force of the Good; each individual has the responsibility, through the exercise of the virtues, to get closer to the first principle and flee from

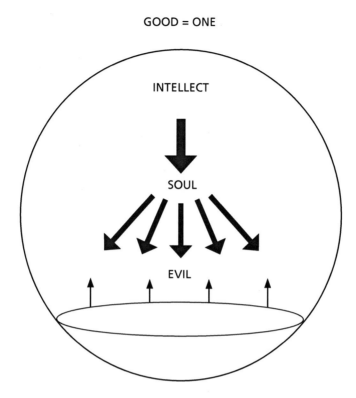

Figure 15.1 Structure of evil-matter.

the second) and monism, since the whole remains overall a good whole, in spite of the presence in it of a bad element, both limited and impregnable.

The evil cannot be totally outside of being (because there is no such outside), but it cannot be inside either, since it is radically opposed to being: so it is both inside and outside, inside but *as an outsider* (cf. *Enn.* III.6[26].14.18–25). This is why Plotinus is able to compare the evil with a prisoner bound with golden shackles. Evil is always present, threatening and real, but it is still contained within the limits of the Good: "But because of the power and nature of good, evil is not only evil; since it must necessarily appear, it is bound in a sort of beautiful fetters, as some prisoners are in chains of gold, and hidden by them, so that though it exists it may not be seen by the gods" (*Enn.* I.8[51].15.23–5).

Placed between the two poles, each individual is therefore tasked, through philosophical activity, to break free of the attraction exercised by evil and go back to his homeland. The recognition of the presence of primary evil in matter is not an encouragement to inaction or pessimism, but an appeal to courage and reflection. Since each individual does not himself embody primary evil, and since primary evil also does not exist beyond the material level, optimism remains possible for everyone, providing one does one's best to escape the worst. Inherently bad action is therefore not directly human, but the initiative of matter itself, the first unmixed Evil (*to prōton kai akraton kakon, Enn.* I.8[51].12.5), which is Evil *per se* (*autokakon, Enn.* I.8[51].8.42, 13.9), and which Plotinus somehow *personifies*. This personification of the role of matter in Plotinus' analysis, we cannot fail to notice, represents the most crucial difference with the description of the receptacle in the *Timaeus*, because Plotinian matter is not only a blind corrupting factor, as in Plato, but something which presents itself as *intentionally bad*. Of the *chōra*, one could say (even though Plato himself does not say so) that it is bad as one says that "the weather is bad", but not in the sense that one "acts badly" or "pursues bad ends". But of the Plotinian matter, one is no longer so sure, as the description of the battle between Soul and matter here below in *Enn.* I.8[51] reflects:

> There is matter in reality and there is soul in reality, and one single place for both of them. ... But there are many powers of soul, and it has a beginning, a middle and an end; and matter is there and *begs* it and, we may say, *bothers* it and *wants* (*thelei*) to come right inside. ... This is the fall of soul, to come in this way to matter and to become weak, because all its powers do not come in action; matter *hinders* them from coming by *occupying* the place which soul holds and *producing a kind of cramped condition*, and *making evil* what it *has got hold of* by a sort of theft – until soul manages to escape back to its higher state. So matter is the cause of the soul's weakness and vice: it is then itself evil before soul and is primary evil.
>
> (*Enn.* I.8[51].14.27–51)

In this description, aside from the explicit designation of matter as something evil *per se* and principle of all evils, several verbs reflect matter's autonomous action against the Soul. Both of these ideas are clearly absent from the vocabulary of the *Timaeus*.

Finally, how have these two wholes come to this reciprocal situation? Plotinus rejects the original dualism and he categorically refuses the possibility that evil comes from divine realities above. Hence, the only solution for him was to make the primary evil *responsible for its own emergence*. The primary Good does not yield the primary Evil. Rather, among the primitive otherness, which emanates from the first Good, there is something which has escaped from above *by itself, as if of its own initiative* (see *Enn.* VI.1[42].1), and has pursued its flight towards the lower world. Facing this escape and this flight, the role of the Soul has been to catch up with the infinite matter and to envelop it from the exterior in order to stop its flight. From then on, situated in the very depths of the world, the Evil-infinite-matter is the counter-principle, admittedly with limited power, but eternally acting, and to which the different powers of the soul will confront each other in their descents. Briefly outlined, this is the principle of Plotinus' solution. A detailed analysis of several passages relating to this emergence of matter allows for a reconstruction of Plotinus' solution to the problem of evil.[34]

Assessment of Plotinus' position on evil

The benefit of Plotinus' position on evil is that it enables an account of a genuine opposition between the beneficial and harmful acts in the sensible world. It is indeed possible in certain cases to let oneself be overcome by the corporeal passions, which take root in the blind and brutal force of matter. Moreover, it is because we are beings composed of matter and Form that vice is possible. As Plotinus mentions, the Idea of the axe does not cut, it is only the physical axe that cuts (see *Enn.* I.8[51].8.11–14). The will to possess in excess, to dominate and to subjugate finds its source in a blind, savage and insatiable

want. In certain cases, the soul can let itself be governed by its inferior parts, by the passions, which rise unordered out of the material components of the body. This possibility
depends on an exterior force which comes from below and which is completely real, as
Plato's *Phaedo* had already suggested when evoking the body.[35] In this sense the evil-matter
is not simply a lack or a privation of something: it is a positive force, which, in certain
cases, can become dominant and pervasive. If the inferior can at times prevail over the
superior, it is because the inferior, dynamically speaking, disposes of a power that is not
only real – and that is thus not simply a lack or an absence – but at times superior to what
is axiologically superior to it. It is in this sense that Plotinus can speak of a struggle between
two antithetic principles, even if it is evident that the principle of evils exerts a power on
the whole inferior to that of the principle of goods.

There is, however, a flaw, or weakness, in Plotinus' position, which lies in his absolutiza-
tion of the role of matter as source of evil. Indeed, were we to take literally the assertion
according to which "matter is the cause of the soul's weakness and vice: it is then itself
evil before soul and is primary evil" (*Enn.* I.8[51].14.49–51), then not only could we no
longer differentiate one soul from another, but there would also no longer be any point
in advocating virtue and practising of philosophy. For if matter is the exclusive cause
not only of physical, but also of psychic flaws, such as weaknesses of the soul, then there
no longer exists a differential factor between the souls, and we would fall into a sort of
absolute materialism.

Yet I do not believe that this reflects the definitive position of Plotinus on the subject.
Certainly, he insists on not reproducing the gnostic pattern according to which the fall of
the soul in the sensible world is fundamentally due to a flaw within the soul itself (*Enn.*
II.9[33].12–14). The truth, for Plotinus, is that radical evil exists (it is the infinite-matter),
that the flaws exist *before us* (*pro hēmōn tauta*) (*Enn.* I.8[51].5.27–8) in matter, and that
consequently, the lack of good (*elleipsis tou agathou*), which arises in the soul, cannot be
the first evil. Otherwise, he thinks, "the nature of evil will no longer be in matter but prior
to it" (*Enn.* I.8[51].5.4–5), which would place its origin squarely with the primary divine
principles, including souls, a gnostic thesis which Plotinus wishes to avoid at all costs.[36]
That being said, Plotinus' fundamental conviction is that despite the determining influence of the matter, "there is an 'escape from the evils of soul' for those who are capable of
it, though not all men are" (*Enn.* I.8[51].5.29–30).

MATTER AND EVIL IN PROCLUS

It is well known that the Plotinian views on matter and evil have, since late antiquity,
been subject to numerous criticisms. Moreover, even Plotinus' immediate Neoplatonic
successors did not follow him on this subject. Plotinus himself is partly to blame for this,
as a few of his theses were articulated in a manner that could lead to confusion. Such is
the case when he speaks of an opposition between the two principles of matter and the
Good, as if they were two equivalent poles.

Proclus reproaches him for this in the *de Malorum Subsistentia* 31:

> But if matter is evil, we must choose between two alternatives: either to make
> the good the cause of evil, or to posit two principles of beings. ... Now, if matter

stems from a principle, then matter itself receives its procession into being from the good [and cannot, accordingly, be evil *per se*]. If, on the other hand, matter is a principle, then we must posit two principles of beings which oppose each other, *viz.* the primary good and the primary evil. But that is impossible. For there can be no two firsts.   (*DMS* 31.6–14, trans. Opsomer & Steel)

Proclus offers the same criticism regarding the professedly absolute action of the matter on the soul: "If souls are drawn by themselves, evil for them will consist in an impulse towards the inferior and the desire for it, and not in matter. … If, on the other hand, souls are drawn by matter …, where is their self-motion and ability to choose?" (*DMS* 33.15–25). The problem to which Proclus alludes here is real, even if, as we have argued above, it is possible to find in Plotinus at least a partial solution to this difficulty.

Admittedly, Proclus concedes that it is indeed here below, where matter is to be found, that evil appears (*DMS* 51.40–46), and where individual fallen souls, endowed with material bodies, are to be found (*DMS* 23–4, 28). It does not follow, however, that this is the cause, and even less the sole cause, of the disorder with which we are constantly confronted here below, as this finds its origin not at the level of the receptacle itself, as Plotinus falsely believes when reading *Ti.* 30a2–6, but already in the unlimitedness created by God, as shown by the *Phlb.* 26c4–27c1. In short, according to Proclus, there is no reason to make matter, which derives from a good principle, evil in itself by giving it the status of principle.[37]

In Proclus' eyes, the only judicious solution is to posit that there is no unique evil in itself. Instead, there are various evils that afflict equally various beings, evils, which are like accidents, deviations of realities that are *a priori* good. The technical term to denote such an accident is *parypostasis*, which can be translated as an *adventitious existence*: "For the form of evils, their nature, is a kind of defect, an indeterminateness and a privation (*ellipsis*, *aoristia*, *sterēsis*); their *mode of existence* (*hypostasis*) is, as it is usually said, more like a kind of *adventitious existence* (*parypostasis*)" (*DMS* 49.7–10, slightly modified).

Such an explanation, however, gives rise to a grave difficulty for Proclus, namely that of explaining how what is simply a *lack* or a *privation*, and thus inferior to that which it opposes, can have the strength to modify or contaminate a being that is superior to it. In other words, what in his system can play a role comparable to that of the recalcitrant receptacle of the *Timaeus*, or of the malignant matter of Plotinus? Is evil really only an absence, a lack, or a progressive exhaustion of the Good, incapable of retaliation? The *dualism* that opposes evil-matter to the Good which we have seen in Plotinus will no doubt be suppressed by Proclus in favour of a new form of dualism, a dualism of privations. In this new dualism, we suddenly find opposed, on the one hand, privations which are only privation, that is to say pure absences, or lacks, and on the other hand, privations which, curiously, may only be described as *incomplete privations*. These *incomplete privations* are not "altogether impotent and inefficacious" (*impotentes omnino et inefficaces*), but reveal themselves capable of opposing the Good. These special privations are in fact forms of *negative possessions*, which are capable not only of turning on their positive counterparts, but also of prevailing over them:

Evil is indeed privation, though not a complete privation. For being coexistent with the very disposition of which it is privation, it not only *weakens* this disposition by its presence (*illum quidem debilem facit ipsius presentia*), but also *derives* power and form from it (*ipsum autem assumit*[38] *potentiam et speciem ab illo*). Hence, whereas privations of forms, being complete privations, are mere absences of dispositions, and do not actively oppose them, privations of goods actively oppose (*adversantur*; *machontai* [Isaac]) the corresponding dispositions and are somehow contrary to them. For they are not altogether impotent and inefficacious; no, they are both coexistent with the powers of their dispositions, and, as it were, led by them to form and activity. (*DMS* 52.2–10)

Here, Proclus seems caught in a sort of contradiction, inasmuch as this privation of the second type (i.e. the privation that is not purely privation) must *already be in possession* of a certain power to be capable of weakening its positive counterpart, of fighting against it, and of deriving its strength from it; and yet, at the same time, *it must not itself already possess any strength*, if it is indeed true that its strength comes entirely from its adversary. This *non-privative privation* must then at once possess, and not possess, the strength with which we credit it. The situation is comparable to that which one can notice in the argument *causa sui*, which also rests upon an initial contradiction. Indeed, in order to cause oneself, it is necessary to both not be, so that one requires a cause, and yet to be already, so that one is capable of causing oneself. Hence, the same thing must at the same time, and from the same point of view, *be and not be*, which is evidently a contradiction. Likewise, in Proclus, if evil is *de facto* "unwilled, weak and inefficacious (*involitum et debile et inefficax*)" (*DMS* 54.7), it is hard to conceive by what means it could, as Proclus claims, not only borrow its strength from its adversary against its will, but also succeed in defeating it! This is what seems to occur when he writes: "Likewise in souls, evil, when it vanquishes good, uses the power of the latter on behalf of itself. That is, it uses the power of reason and its inventions on behalf of its desires" (*DMS* 53.14–16; see also 7.35–42, 38.13–25). This autonomous power of retaliation, or even of quasi-rational calculation, which is suddenly granted to evil by Proclus, echoes, in a certain way, the attitude of Plotinus, which seems, at first glance, equally contradictory. Plotinus, on the one hand, presented matter as a pure principle of receptivity, denuded of power, and on the other hand, suddenly granted matter a capacity for action *contra* Form and what comes close to resembling a "will" to fight against it. The language employed here by Proclus indeed is highly reminiscent of that of Plotinus. According to Proclus, this special privation "weakens the disposition by its presence" (*illum quidem debilem facit ipsius presentia*, *DMS* 52.5–6), which is exactly what Plotinus says about its active principle of evil: "matter is present, begs it and bothers it"; "matter darkens the illumination, the light from that source, by mixture with itself, and weakens it"; "matter's presence has given soul the occasion of coming to birth" (*Enn.* I.8[51].14.35–6, 40–42, 53–4).

This ultimately contradictory approach we find in both authors seems to be not the sign of a simple inconsistency in their analyses, but the reflection of a sort of antithesis inherent to any study of the concept of evil. On the one hand, the Good cannot be the cause of evil, and Plotinus and Proclus both agree with Plato on this fundamental point. On the other hand, the efficiency, and even the refinement, of the means we see employed in certain bad actions compels us to abandon the conception of evil understood as simply a digression from, or an attenuation of, the Good. For how else shall we understand the relative autonomy of evil and its, at times, surprising capacity for action? Yet, to speak of

Evil as simply a *pure contrary*, as if it occupied a rank equal to that of the Good, is evidently unjustified, and Proclus was, in this regard, right to criticize Plotinus' formulations. Evil is not a contrary, but rather, a *subcontrary*. Consequently it can, according to Proclus himself, possess a certain power: it is not simply privation and lack. This, of course, gives rise to the question of whence evil derives its power and how it comes to acquire it thence. Is it that power is somehow bestowed upon it (although it is impossible that the Good itself should positively empower evil), or because evil siphons off the power of its host? But if the latter is the case, how does evil manage to do this if it has no power of its own?

In sum, we note that Plotinus and Proclus do not end up with widely divergent results, despite the considerable differences in their respective approaches. Admittedly, Plotinus roots all the particular evils in a unique primary evil, while Proclus objects to the existence of any positive evil, for which he substitutes singular evils understood as defects or absences. But even Proclus cannot hold himself to such a lifeless representation of evil.[39] This explains the sudden emergence in Proclus' writings of these privations of a new kind, in truth harmful powers, stemming from who knows where, but suddenly capable of real obstructions and even of partial victories.

In short, Plotinus and Proclus both undertake, in their own way, a task that is as necessary as it is problematic,[40] namely to account for tensions and oppositions which arise in the sensible, while at the same time trying to preserve the innocence of the gods, and the idea of the fundamental goodness of the whole.

ACKNOWLEDGEMENTS

I should like to thank Simon Fortier and Svetla Slaveva-Griffin for their help in the translation and revision of this essay.

NOTES

1. For other contemporary perspectives on Plotinus' theory of material evil, see Corrigan (1996a), O'Brien (1999), D. O'Meara (2005), Schäfer (2002). For further information concerning our own interpretation of this theory, see Narbonne (2006, 2007). For other perspectives on Proclus and the relationship of his theory of evil to that of Plotinus, see Opsomer (2001, 2007), Phillips (2007), Fortier (2008), Skliris (2008).
2. This might be the case of Moderatus who, according to Porphyry's Περὶ ὕλης, as reported by Simplicius (*in Ph.* 230.34–231.24 = frag. 236 [Smith]); a good account of the issues regarding this text is found in Dörrie & Baltes (1987–2008: vol. 4, sections 4, 122, 176–8, 477–85), would also have taught that matter is both evil and derivative at the same time, as well as for the *Chaldaean Oracles* (frag. 34, 88 [des Places]; cf. Psellus, *Hypotyp.* 27, p. 75.34 [Kroll]).
3. Greek of the italicized sections in order of appearance in the passage: τὴν μὲν φιλίαν αἰτίαν οὖσαν τῶν ἀγαθῶν τὸ δὲ νεῖκος τῶν κακῶν and τὸ κακὸν καὶ τὸ ἀγαθὸν ἀρχάς. See also *Metaph.* 1075b1–7.
4. For Atticus, cf. Proclus, *in Ti.* I.391.10 [Diehl]; for Numenius, frag. 52 [des Places]; for Numenius, Cronius and Harpocration, cf. Iamblichus, *de An.* 375.6–15 [Wachsmuth & Hense]; for Celsus, cf. Origen, *Cels.* 4.65; 8.55 [Bader].
5. Owing to our uncertainty concerning the date of the text and its fidelity to Numenius himself, one can draw no definite conclusion from Calcidius' *in Ti.* (*c.*295–9), which lend to Numenius, as an heir of Pythagoras, a very malicious view of matter and of its role in the constitution of the world. On this, see Dillon (1994: 156–7).
6. Greek of the italicized sections in order of appearance in the passage: ἀλλ᾿ ἀπὸ δυεῖν ἐναντίων ἀρχῶν καὶ δυεῖν ἀντιπάλων δυνάμεων; δεῖ γένεσιν ἰδίαν καὶ ἀρχὴν ὥσπερ ἀγαθοῦ καὶ κακοῦ τὴν φύσιν ἔχειν; and τὸν μὲν ἀγαθῶν, τὸν δὲ φαύλων δημιουργόν.

7. *Enn.* III.6[26].19.25.
8. *Enn.* III.6[26].13.25.
9. *Enn.* II.4[12].16.24; III.6[26].11.27; I.8[51].5.23; 9.12–13.
10. *Enn.* IV.3[27].9.17.
11. *Enn.* I.8[51].4.24.
12. *Enn.* II.4[12].5.35; 10.19.
13. *Enn.* VI.6[34].11.32; VI.3[44].7.8.
14. *Enn.* II.4[12].10.1, 11.4, 13, 12.23.
15. *Enn.* I.8[51].3.25–9, 38, 4.27.
16. *Enn.* III.6[26].15.9.
17. *Enn.* I.8[51].4.22.
18. *Enn.* II.4[12].2.3–4, 10.18, 23; II.4[25].4.12; III.6[26].7.28–9; I.8[51].3.14; 8.21.
19. *Enn.* II.4[12].10.27, 12.29; II.5[25].5.21.
20. *Enn.* III.6[26].10.26–7.
21. *Enn.* II.5[25].5.34; III.6[26].10.11.
22. *Enn.* II.4[12].2.4, 10.14, 11.37, 12.23, *passim*; III.6[26].7.14.
23. *Enn.* III.6[26].6.7, 7.3, 41, 12.26, etc.
24. *Enn.* II.4[12].7.16, 17, 15.4; III.6[26].7.8; I.8[51].6.42.
25. *Enn.* II.4[12].7.11, 8.1–2, 10.2, 13.7; I.8[51].10.1.
26. *Enn.* II.4[12].9.5; III.6[26].6.3.
27. *Enn.* II.4[12].13.18; I.8[51].8.42;13.9.
28. Hereinafter the translation of the *Enneads* is according to Armstrong (1966–88).
29. *Enn.* III.6[26].18.28–30: ἀναμένει παθεῖν ὅ τι ἂν ἐθέλῃ τὸ ποιῆσον.
30. *Enn.* III.6[26].18.19–21. This passage refers to the peculiar Plotinian thesis according to which matter adopts the volume, which Form imposes on it as it descends. For further discussion, see Narbonne (1993: 224–60), Brisson (2000).
31. Armstrong (1966–88: vol. 3, 207): "Some readers may feel, by the time they reach the end of the treatise, that Plotinus has made matter not only impassible but impossible."
32. Cf. Festugière (1986: xiv): "d'Albinus à Numénius, de Plotin à Porphyre, c'est quasi un dogme reçu que la matière est agitée de mouvements désordonnés avant l'intervention du Démiurge et que, par suite, l'origine du mal est dans la matière comme telle."
33. *Enn.* I.8[51].6.33–4: ἀρχαὶ γὰρ ἄμφω, ἡ μὲν κακῶν, ἡ δὲ ἀγαθῶν.
34. *Enn.* II.4[12].15; II.5[25].4, 5; III.6[26].7, 13; VI.6[34].1–3; IV.3[27].7. For an analysis, see Narbonne (2011: 11–54).
35. Plato, *Phd.* 66c: "Because the wars, the discords, the battles, to elicit them there is nothing else than the body and its covetousness."
36. *Enn.* II.9[33].13.27–9: "one must not consider evil as nothing else than a falling short in wisdom, and a lesser good always diminishing".
37. On this point, Simplicius based himself on and developed Proclus' position, *CAG* volume 8, part 5, pp. 109, 5–20: "But surely, Plotinus says, not-substance is in general opposed to substance, and the nature of evil is contrary to the nature of good, and the principle of the worse things to the principle of the better ones. These are to be divided thus: if not-being, which we oppose to being as its contrary, does not subsist anywhere in any way, then it will not have any relation to anything else, given that it is nothing. If, on the other hand, it exists as a determinate being, then it is wrongly said to be cut off in all respects from that which is, *since it participates in it* (sc. in that which is). But if they i.e. being and not-being are separate as two substances, they will have being itself as one. If, however, they are separately transcendent (*exeiremenai khoristos*) because of an eminent otherness (*ekbebekuian heteroteta*), i.e. the Form of Otherness, then they will not share the relation of contraries since they have nothing in common with one another. And if, as is usually said, not being is produced out of being, just as the sensible is produced from the intelligible and the material from the divine as if the ultimate were produced from the first, *how can it* sc. *non-being enjoy contrariety with it* sc. *being, in the sense of being in all respects separated from it, given that it* sc. *non-being has its entire existence from it* i.e. *being? How will not being, which has no ratio of either comparison or opposition towards being, but falls away to extremity as nothing, be contrary to it as to the very cause that produced it, a contrariety which causes it to be equal to that which was supposed to be its contrary?"* (trans. de Haas & Fleet).

38. In the Greek text reconstituted by Isaac Sebastocrator (cf. *Procli Diadochi Tria Opuscula* [Boese 1960]), the Greek term is προσλαμβάνει. This term, which might also be rendered as *taking to oneself* or *attracting to oneself*, is indeed a very forceful way to describe the counteraction of this special privation!

39. One can also sense this fundamental difficulty in the secondary literature, as, for example, in Steel's (1998) treatment of this problem, where he states at one point that in "Proclus' elaboration of the doctrine [of evil] all dualistic explanations are completely eliminated" (p. 83) and closes his analysis by saying that, owing precisely to this special privation, "evil and good are in fact two opposite powers – and here lies the truth of the dualistic position – the one set in action against the other" (p. 101).

40. I therefore largely agree with Phillips' following conclusion (2007: 267): "The great Neoplatonist project in formulating their doctrines of evil, to affirm the existence of evil while also placing it squarely within God's providential control of the cosmos, and achieving both of these aims while still removing God from any and all responsibility for evil's existence, does take a radically different course after Plotinus' doctrine, but nonetheless is betrayed by essentially the same difficulties throughout. To be sure, Proclus refines some of the rougher edges on Plotinus' doctrine, yet is for all that none the more successful finally in reconciling these two perhaps irreconcilable concepts." Proclus is even less successful when one takes seriously into account, as we have attempted to do here (in so far as we are aware, for the first time), the curious double concept of privation that he surreptitiously introduces as a substitute for Plotinus' analysis.

IV

Language, knowledge, soul and self

INTRODUCTION

One of the particularities of Neoplatonic philosophy is its conception of the soul and its relationship to *what there is*, to metaphysics. Both living and cognitive capacities are explained through the soul's intimate relationship with the essence of reality. For the Neoplatonists, the soul is, as it were, a window to the entire cosmos and metaphysical realm, through its likeness and natural connection to them. Combining, as can be noted in several chapters of this volume, Platonic and Aristotelian influences, the Neoplatonic soul functions both as a principle of different living functions and that of powers of cognition, being an intermediary in between the higher and perfect ontological realities and the sensible and bodily realm. According to Plotinus, a human being, and her soul, stretches all the way from her connection to the body through the hypostasis Soul and Intellect to touch her ultimate source, the One. This explains our capacities, from desire and other living functions to perception, language and concept-formation, discursive thinking, as well as knowledge and moral instinct. While the later Neoplatonists came to question this part of Plotinus' anthropology, they did retain, in mediated ways, the human soul's innate capacities of approaching what is perfect or divine.

Given the central role that the soul plays in Neoplatonic philosophy, both in metaphysics and cosmology as well as philosophical anthropology and theories of cognition and knowledge – not to mention the frequency with which late ancient commentators wrote on Aristotle's *de Anima* – it is somewhat striking how little concentrated research literature we find on this notion. Admittedly, there is widespread agreement on general axes along which these topics are discussed by Neoplatonists: that the metaphysical top-down approach also pervades what they say about soul, its powers and possibilities, and that this top-down direction nonetheless leaves room for refined accounts of not just intellection but even embodied functions.[1] In the case of Plotinus the situation is, further, relatively good: there are strong studies on both sense-perception and intellection in the *Enneads*, and other aspects and powers of the soul are a topic of increasing scholarly attention.[2] But even Plotinus scholarship suffers from central lacunae. The ontology of the soul, and the precise relationship between the higher and the lower soul are far from clear. Is the lower soul part of the World Soul or an unfolding of the individual, rational soul? How does *phantasia* work in Plotinus? How to square Plotinus' undeniable top-down directionality with his more Aristotelian-reminiscent remarks on how learning and dialectic begins with our experiences? And so on. In the case of other central figures, such as Iamblichus and Proclus, there is simply quantitatively less on offer.[3]

This section cannot hope to be encompassing. Rather, it has three ambitions. First, we wish to provide alleys to those aspects of Neoplatonic theories about soul and cognition that exhibit their particular, "Neoplatonic" take on the issue. Second, we aim to fill some of the gaps in the research literature. Finally, it is our aim to show some discussions where Neoplatonists exerted an undeniably detailed, subtle or original approach.

In Plato, famously, knowledge is explained with the help of the natural, inborn connection of human rational soul to the real beings, the Forms. These are either something the soul has learned in a previous existence, or internal to the soul. Combining this with the Aristotelian understanding of both perceptual and rational states of the soul as reception and identity with the object received, Neoplatonists came to emphasize innateness: language learning, concept-formation[4] and knowledge acquisition are enabled by the soul's innate powers to grasp being, powers that the soul receives from the hypostasis Intellect. This is their top-down approach. Plotinus postulated an intellect (an individual copy or instantiation of the Intellect) in each and every human soul. While we may not be – and mostly cannot be – aware of this intellect's functioning within us, it explains how we are capable of intellection, of knowledge. It also governs – mediated and unfolded – lower forms of thinking, how we may perceive the rational organization in nature, and even the way we form, for instance, words, as we see in van den Berg's "The gift of Hermes: The Neoplatonists on language and philosophy" (Chapter 16). It is this structural correspondence, as it were, between the organization of the world and that of the mind, that grounds our thinking and knowledge of the former.

The challenge for anyone sharing this picture is to explain, first, why and how we are simultaneously in possession of this knowledge, yet find it so laborious, at times impossible, to become aware of it. And why did the soul, if it has this divine origin, ever come to be imperfect and in the body in the first place?[5] Second, as becomes clear in van den Berg's chapter, even the early Neoplatonists admitted that the soul also engages in concept-formation of the Aristotelian type, namely abstraction. Thereby the question of relationship between such mental contents that are innately specified, and those that arise from interaction with the external world (from down upwards, as it were), becomes pressing. As Gerson explicates in his "Neoplatonic epistemology: knowledge, truth and intellection" (Chapter 17), Plotinus suggests that the Intellect does function as a rule-giver to the discursive forms of ordinary thinking, but the details of how this happens remain somewhat obscure. Yet undeniably the theory fares well in one respect: it provides a very clear answer as regards justification and grounding of knowledge. Knowledge consists, in an Aristotelian manner, of an identity between the knower and the known. As Gerson argues, only this kind of identity between the thinking mind and an immaterial (as opposed to material) object capable of this identity can satisfy what the Neoplatonists require from knowledge, namely infallibility. The Neoplatonists conceive of infallibility as a kind of second-order awareness: you not only know, but also know that you know. This awareness arises out of the unmediated, non-representational unity and identity between the thinking mind, its activity and objects of thinking.

The later Neoplatonists came to deny that the soul would literally exist on all levels of the hierarchy, and posit it more firmly on its own level proper and closer to human beings. In the famous wording of Proclus, "Every particular soul, when it descends into temporal process, descends entire: there is not a part of it which remains above and a part which descends" (*ET* prop. 211). Iamblichus is the originator of later Neoplatonic conceptions of the soul that differ substantially from their Plotinian-Porphyrian predecessor. In his "Iamblichus on soul" (Chapter 18), Finamore illuminates the ways in which Iamblichus read Plato and combined him with Aristotle, and arrived at the specifically Iamblichean take on the soul, its unity, powers and place within the cosmos. Iamblichus retains the Plotinian idea of an intellect within each human soul, but no longer thinks that it can survive human descent into body intact. It cannot ground infallible knowledge – only the Intellect itself can. The philosophical challenges in this Neoplatonic variety are slightly different. When the strict identity relationship between the knower and the object known is lost for an embodied human being, knowledge as both an epistemological notion and a cognitive, psychological state has to be explained in some other manner. Nonetheless in later Neoplatonism, too, the connection to the higher levels of being is innate and natural for the soul.

Besides the less well-known Iamblichean theory of the soul, the details of the Peripatetic influences on Neoplatonism bring us further from completely charted waters. While everyone who has read Porphyry's *Life of Plotinus* knows that Alexander of Aphrodisias was read and commented in Plotinus' school, the content of his influence is still under examination. On a close reading of Alexander's position and Plotinus' critique of it, Schroeder's "From Alexander of Aphrodisias to Plotinus" (Chapter 19) guides the reader into the ways in which Plotinus builds both his discussion of the physics of illumination in perception and the analogical relationship between the One and that which it illuminates and thus makes intelligible. In causation as well as epistemology, Plotinus turns Alexander's dualistic discussions into a monism where illumination as well as intellection are looked on exclusively, as it were, from above.

One philosophical thematics in which the Neoplatonic philosophers are likely to go well beyond any of their predecessors and competitors are self-reflexive relations. In here, too, they build upon the Classical and Hellenistic background, upon the Socratic call for self-knowledge, upon the both Platonic and Aristotelian question on whether the perceiver also perceives that she perceives, and the Peripatetic worry of whether the thinker thinks that he thinks. As was already mentioned, the Neoplatonists conceive of infallible knowledge through a self-reflexive relation of the knower also knowing that she knows. This part contains two studies that concentrate on this area in different ways. Aubry's "Metaphysics of soul and self in Plotinus" (Chapter 20) reveals how Plotinus is capable of separating a notion of self from the notion of soul by elaborating on self-identification. Unlike soul, the self is "that which searches, examines and decides these questions: whatever can it be?" (*Enn.* I.1[53].1.9–11). Plotinus' originality lies in the conceptual distinction between a reflexive subject and that of a subject of attribution.

In "Perceptual awareness in the ancient commentators" (Chapter 21), Lautner explores a temporally later discussion on a cognitively more basic level of self-reflexivity, the notion of perception of perception. Like Schroeder, he follows a thread from Alexander of Aphrodisias to Neoplatonism, the Neoplatonic commentators. What we can witness is a rich and intricate discussion in which perceptual awareness is sometimes located in another faculty or the soul as a whole, sometimes seen as included in the perceptual act itself. In this Neoplatonic discussion, surprisingly many of the elements in today's philosophical treatments on awareness and self-awareness are anticipated: the division between awareness of the object ("content") and of the activity of perceiving; the question of whether the latter is included in the former or not; and if it is not, whether the higher order awareness is conceptual or perceptual in nature.

NOTES

1. The situation will certainly change in the near future because of the availability of interesting source materials in Sorabji (2004–2005), the translations of some key primary texts (especially the commentaries on Aristotle's *de Anima*) in the *Ancient Commentators on Aristotle* series, as well as other similar advances within scholarship, like the new translation projects of Plotinus by Parmenides Press (English), Cerf (French) and Edizioni Plus (Italian).
2. Here the list of scholarship is actually longer than can be given in this context. Some of the important examples include: Blumenthal (1971a), Emilsson (1988, 2007), Gurtler (2005), Schiaparelli (2009), Kalligas (2011), Chiaradonna (2012b).
3. Steel (1978, 1997a) and the translation and commentary of Iamblichus' *de Anima* by Finamore & Dillon

(2002), for example, are crucial. Cf. e.g. Opsomer (2006a, 2006b), Gritti (2008), Perkams (2008); on Proclus, Chlup (2012) is also useful in general.

4. There is a new, important study on concept-formation by Helmig (2012).

5. For more discussion on the soul's presence in the body, see Kalligas (2012).

16

The gift of Hermes: the Neoplatonists on language and philosophy

Robbert M. van den Berg

Ever since young Socrates decided that philosophers should search the truth in words (*logois*) rather than through empirical observations (Plato, *Phd.* 99e4–100a3), Platonists have always stressed the essentially linguistic nature of philosophy. Hermes, the god traditionally associated with language because he is the messenger (*hermēneus*) of the gods (cf. Plato, *Cra.* 407e5–408b3), became their patron deity. Neoplatonists invoke him at the beginning of their treatises, since he is "the god who is in charge of words" (*theos ho tōn logōn hegemōn, Hermēs*) as Iamblichus puts it at the beginning of *On the Mysteries of the Egyptians* (1.4). In a similar vein, Ammonius thanks this "god of *logos*" for any success that he may have as an interpreter (*hermēneus*) of Aristotle's *Peri Hermeneias* at the beginning of his commentary (1.11). Proclus almost affectionately refers to him as "our lord Hermes" (*in Cra.*117.68.12), because he is the "chorus-leader of philosophy", who by means of philosophy and dialectic takes us to the Good itself (*Theol. Plat.* VI.22.98.147). In short, "Hermes, i.e. language (*logos*), is common to all, as the proverb has it", Simplicius (*in Epict. Ench.* 132.40–41 [Dübner], my trans.) explains, because we all share the capacity for discursive reasoning and language (*logos*) that underlies philosophy.

This chapter will not be about anything like a "Neoplatonic philosophy of language" for the simple reason that there is no such thing. Neoplatonists usually discuss language in the context of logic or dialectic. They are mainly interested in language as a tool for philosophical investigation. They inherited this instrumental approach to language from their intellectual forefathers, Plato and Aristotle. In the *Cratylus* (388b–390d), his most substantial discussion of language, Plato describes *onomata* – literally "names", both of individuals and of things in general – as the instrument (*organon*) of the Platonic dialectician. Aristotle likewise discusses language especially in his so-called *Organon*, the collection of his logical treatises, in particular in the *Categories* and *de Interpretatione*. All three texts were part of the standard Neoplatonic curriculum. Students first turned to the *Organon*, starting with the *Categories* and the *de Interpretatione*, in order to master logic as an indispensable tool for doing philosophy and next moved on to study a selection of

Plato's dialogues, including the *Cratylus*.[1] They were thus exposed both to an Aristotelian account of logic and language and a Platonic one.

These two accounts by no means run parallel to each other. Plato's views about language reflect his metaphysical theory. *Onomata* refer primarily to the Forms. The particulars derive both their nature and their name from the Form that causes them. Thus, in the passage alluded to above from the *Phaedo*, it is stated that "each of the Forms exists and that other things, while they share in them, are called after these (*tēn epōnymian ischein*)" (*Phd.* 102b1–3). This Platonic theory of top-down eponymy is alien to Aristotle's world-view in which there is no place for an intelligible realm that is in some sense more real than the sensible one. For Aristotle true being coincides with a particular substance (*tode ti*) in the sensible world. Names therefore refer primarily to physical objects, not to intelligible Forms. Plato had devised a special sort of intellectual discipline to deal with the intelligible Forms, called dialectic. The dialectician divides reality up "at the joints" (*Phdr.* 265e); that is, he tries to define each Form by distinguishing it from all other Forms. According to the *Cratylus* (388b–390d), the dialectician uses *onomata* as an instrument to instruct us about reality, for he assigns a name to each Form that he distinguishes and takes care that that name is somehow appropriate; that is, that it is a telling name that reveals something about the nature of its object.[2] An example of this dialectical use of names can be found, for example, in the *Sophist* (218d8–221c5), where the Eleatic stranger illustrates the dialectic method by defining "angling". He does so by distinguishing it from all other sorts of hunting, making up appropriate names for various types of hunting for which there does not yet exist a Greek name as he goes along. In Platonic dialectic, then, names summarize the outcome of a dialectical process and are therefore important. Aristotle, on the other hand, is especially interested in syllogistic logic, as he develops it in the *Organon*. Syllogisms are about combinations of true propositions. Propositions consist of combinations of words, which can be either true or false, in contrast to the individual words that make up the proposition (cf. *Cat.* 2a4–10). What matters to Aristotle, therefore, is not the individual word, but the sentence in which various words are combined. Moreover, Aristotle was a linguistic "conventionalist". He holds that the relation between words and their objects is the result of arbitrary acts of baptism. A dog, for example, is called a dog because we have agreed to call it thus. Plato, on the other hand, is a linguistic "naturalist". He holds that words should somehow reflect the nature of their objects. This raises problems for the project of harmonization of Plato and Aristotle, as we shall see below (§ "Words as symbols"). What both philosophers have in common, though, is an epistemological optimism that may strike the modern reader as naïve: language makes the external world accessible to us, the existence and knowability of which is never questioned.

This chapter will be concerned with the reception of Platonic and Aristotelian ideas about language and its function as a philosophical tool by the Neoplatonists, in particular with the question of how they dealt with the tension between the two accounts.[3] As the reader will have noticed by now, the term "Neoplatonism" is misleading in that it suggests some sort of doctrinal unity. In fact Neoplatonists were very happy to disagree with one another on a good many issues, language included. In many cases, those disputes are related to the question of whether or not Platonic and Aristotelian philosophy can and indeed should be harmonized. We shall start our survey with Plotinus, who has no qualms about criticizing Aristotle. Next we shall move on to the ancient commentators on the *Categories* and the *de Interpretatione*, such as Porphyry, Iamblichus, Dexippus and

Ammonius, who, not surprisingly, tend to harmonize the Aristotelian and Platonic perspectives. Finally we will move on to the only ancient commentator on the *Cratylus* we know of, Proclus, who, like Plotinus before him, was far more critically disposed towards Aristotle.

PLOTINUS

For Plotinus human language (*logos*) reflects the intelligible realm of Intellect. He holds that the human soul is "an image of Intellect" (*Enn.* V.1[10].3.7); that is to say, that just as the Intellect is made up of the intelligible Forms, so the soul is made up of emanations of these Forms. Plotinus calls the sum of these emanated Forms *logos* and the individual emanated Forms *logoi*.[4] It is no coincidence that he uses in this context the same word (*logos*) that is also used to designate language. We should think of the emanation of these Forms from Intellect, that is, of the causation of soul, as the uttered thought (*logos prophorikos*) of Intellect; in other words when Intellect causes Soul it "speaks out" its thoughts.[5] The philosophical soul that wants to examine these emanated Forms imitates this action of Intellect. The soul, since it consists of the emanated *logoi*, already knows them passively. In order to actualize this knowledge, it has, as it were, to split itself up in an examining subject and an object of examination. In order to achieve this, soul projects its *logoi* in order to view and examine them as something different from itself. Plotinus describes this process of projection in terms of uttering a thought (*propherein*) and the taking-in-hand (*procheirisis*) of the *logoi*, a term which derives from the simile of the aviary in the *Theaetetus*.[6] Philosophical thought thus takes the form of some sort of *dialogue intérieur* of the soul with itself in which it actualizes its innate knowledge of the Forms. Language on this level points to a weakness of the human soul. The soul of the true sage will coincide with the Intellect of its soul and will thus know the Forms in a direct intuitive way. It will not need to articulate them discursively as happens in discursive philosophical thought. Discursive thought of the soul is but an imperfect imitation of the intuitive contemplation of Intellect, which we may subsequently translate in spoken language. As Plotinus puts it in a famous comparison:

> As the spoken word [*en phōnēi logos*] is an imitation of that in the soul, so the word in the soul is an imitation of that in something else: as the uttered word [*ho en prophorai*], then, is broken up into parts as compared with that in the soul, so that in the soul as compared with that before it [i.e. Intellect], which it interprets.
> (*Enn.* I.2[19].3.27–30, trans. Armstrong)

For Plotinus, then, language refers primarily to actualized versions of the *logoi* that make up the human soul, not to our thoughts of particular objects in the physical world. This fits the chief purpose of language, at least in the context of Platonic dialectic: to help us to orientate our soul towards the contemplation of the intelligible Forms, away from the material realm. In the end the aim of philosophical language is to abolish itself. The soul that has ascended to the intelligible contemplation of the Forms will have transcended discursive thought and language altogether (as Heiser [1991: 6–9] has rightly pointed out). Hence Plotinus' interest in language is limited and it comes as no surprise to find that he is not interested in the question of how this view of language can be related to that of the Aristotelian *Organon*. Peripatetic logic is at best some sort of a necessary preliminary to the study of philosophy, but nothing more than that. It is best dealt with as swiftly as possible (*Enn.* I.3[20].4).

THE NEOPLATONIC COMMENTATORS ON THE *CATEGORIES*

Physical substance as the primary object of language

In contrast to his teacher Plotinus, Porphyry spent much time and energy on the *Organon*, and the *Categories* in particular. Plotinus had been very critical of this particular work: he had faulted Aristotle for positing that what is called being "most strictly, primarily and most of all" (*ousia hē kyriōtata te kai prōtōs kai malista legomenē*) is an individual sensible object (*Cat.* 2a11–14), a "something" (*tode ti*), and not Platonic intelligible being.[7] Porphyry argued that Plotinus' criticism misses the point of the *Categories*. The Aristotelian categories are not about the structure of intelligible reality – in that case Plotinus' criticism would be justified – but about significant words in so far as they signify (*sēmainein*) particular things around us:

> I claim that once man himself had come to be able to indicate and to signify (*dēlōtikos kai sēmantikos*)[8] the things around him, he also came to be able to name and indicate each thing by means of words. Thus his first use of linguistic expressions came to be to communicate each thing by means of certain words and expressions. In accordance with this relation between words and things, this thing here is called a "chair", that a "man". (*in Cat.* 57.20–25, trans. Strange)

Porphyry here applies the Aristotelian epistemological principle that we proceed from what is better known to us to what is better known *per se* to the development of language.[9] As we have seen, in the *Phaedo* and elsewhere Plato suggests that names refer primarily to the Forms because these are more real. Porphyry, being a Platonist, would, of course, not wish to deny that the Forms are more real than their physical participants, yet his point is that our order of discovery is the inverse of the ontological order. We first come to know the physical objects around us, and only much later the intelligible objects of philosophical speculation. It is therefore only logical to assume that we first named the things in front of us, and only later the metaphysical reality. Thus, when Aristotle says that a particular is "most strictly, primarily and most of all" a being, his point is that the *word* "being" is primarily used to designate individual objects, not that individual *objects* are more real than intelligible being.

Later generations of commentators on the *Categories* will refine Porphyry's statement that the *Categories* deal with words that signify things in the sensible world. Words do not refer directly to objects, but to our concepts of them. In Ammonius' formulation: "Aristotle's aim, then, is to treat not simply nouns and verbs, but rather the first application of simple words signifying (*sēmainōsi*) simple things by means of simple concepts" (*in Cat.* 11.7–12.1, trans. Cohen & Matthews). Ammonius' concepts or thoughts (*noēmata*) are not the same as those of Plotinus. As we have seen, Plotinus holds that language refers to the *logoi* in our soul and therefore indirectly to the intelligible Forms. This is not the case for the type of concept that Ammonius has presently in mind. He describes them (9.9) as "later-born" (*ta hysterogenē*). The term "later-born" is used by Neoplatonists to describe concepts that we derive from sensible things by means of abstraction (cf. Sorabji 2004: vol. 3, 135–7). They are called thus to distinguish them from the concepts associated with the *logoi* in our soul: whereas we are born with the latter, we develop the former only after studying the sensible world. Those later-born concepts based on abstraction are clearly inferior to the concepts that are based on our *logoi* and that hence go back on the Forms themselves. They only yield a sketch of the true nature of things, known as a "conceptual definition" (*ennoēmatikos logos*) as opposed to more advanced philosophical analysis, which produces a so-called "essential definition" (*ousiōdēs logos*). The point is not so much whether or not Neoplatonists like Porphyry and Ammonius accept the existence of Plotinus' type of concepts – they do – but rather whether we should start our philosophical investigations from the later-born concepts or not. Porphyry and Ammonius, working on the Aristotelian principle that we proceed from what is better known to us towards what is better known *per se*, believe we should do so; Plotinus does not.[10]

From the fact that for Porphyry language refers primarily to physical objects, we should not conclude that according to Porphyry and the many other commentators on the *Categories* words refer uniquely to concepts based on abstractions from physical objects. His point is rather that especially the first words to be coined, the so-called first use of linguistic expressions, referred to physical objects. As he goes on to explain, once we coined expressions "as the primary tokens for things, man began to reflect upon these expressions that had been posited from another point of view" (*in Cat.* 57.29–31, trans. Strange) and started to differentiate between nouns (*onomata*) and verbs (*rhēmata*). Porphyry refers to the first round of naming in which the various things and actions received their names as the first imposition (*prōtē thesis*), and to the introduction of words like "noun" and "verb" as the second imposition (*deutera thesis*). According to the Neoplatonic commentators on the *Organon*, the *Categories* dealt with the first imposition and *de Interpretatione*, about which more below, with the second.

Synonymy and homonymy

Before we get to *de Interpretatione*, let us first reflect on the fact that regardless of whether one follows the Platonic or Aristotelian model of naming, we use one and the same name to designate two apparently different things. We apply the *onoma* "man", for example, both to the individual Socrates and to the Form Man. How can this be? Neoplatonists discussed this issue in the Aristotelian terms of synonymy and homonymy. Aristotle (*Cat.* 1a1–12) defines synonymy as two things sharing both the same name and the same definition. A man and an ox are both called "animal" since they are both self-movers equipped with sense-perception. In the case of homonymy, two otherwise different things share the same name, but not the same definition. We may say of an ox and of a picture of an ox that it is an "animal", but in this case, two different definitions apply. In the first case, we are dealing with an animal in the sense of a self-mover equipped with sense-perception; in the second case with a picture of such a self-mover. Both Plotinus and Porphyry seem to agree that in the case of an intelligible and a sensible entity sharing the same name, we are dealing with homonymy. Porphyry is now confronted with a problem: Platonic philosophy is about metaphysical reality and if language refers primarily to the sensible realm it may be less suited to express metaphysical reality. He and those following in his wake bite that bullet. They hold that what we call intelligible being is actually something that cannot be properly captured in words. Intelligible reality becomes ineffable. As Dexippus, a commentator on the *Categories* who is believed to be much dependent on Porphyry, puts it:

> So, since (intelligibles) are ineffable, he [Aristotle] uses the same name "being" (*ousia*) metaphorically of them, making them knowable through things sensible and perceived by us. For sensible being will be homonymous with intelligible being, representing it only by analogy, but it will be synonymous with physical being, representing it by its very composition.   (*in Cat.* 41.25–30, trans. Dillon, adapted)[11]

If the intelligible Forms are ineffable, this does not mean that we call the Form Man "man" for no good reason at all. We are not dealing here with what Porphyry calls "homonymy by chance". It is, for example, pure chance that the name "Paris" applies both to the son of Priam and the French capital. Porphyry (*in Cat.* 65.21–66.21) distinguishes this type of homonymy from other cases of homonymy in which the homonymy is not coincidental. Most important among these in the present context is homonymy from analogy (*kat' analogian*). Porphyry gives the example of the word "source" (*archē*): one can speak of the unit as the source of number, of the point as the source of a line, or of a spring as the source of a river. The definitions of a unit, point and spring are not identical, yet the word "source" is not applied to them by chance: for as the unit is to a number, so the point is to a line and the spring to a river. Dexippus and many others refer to homonymy by analogy as metaphor, even though Porphyry (*in Cat.* 66.29–67.26) objects that in the case of a metaphor a thing already has a name of its own to which subsequently another name is added, whereas this is not the case for homonyms.[12] But what does guarantee that "being" somehow metaphorically "grasps" the right intelligible entity? Apparently, we have to trust Aristotle's authority until we gain a full understanding of intelligible reality that allows us to see for ourselves why it makes sense to apply the term "being" metaphorically to the intelligible.

Most Neoplatonic commentators on the *Categories* were happy to take over Porphyry's solution. Not so, however, Iamblichus. He tries to bring the *Categories* in line with Platonic metaphysics. His commentary has been lost, so that we have to rely on Simplicius who in his own commentary reports on Iamblichus' very peculiar interpretation of the *Categories*, his so-called *noera theōria* (intellective interpretation).[13] Iamblichus apparently read the *Categories* as an ontological treatise rather than as a logical one. In his view the Aristotelian categories used to describe the physical world have metaphysical causes, and in his commentary he set out to reveal these intelligible origins of the categories. His discussion of the category "being-in-a-position", as preserved by Simplicius (*in Cat.* 339.36–340.12), gives us a good impression what his *noera theōria* was like. The expression "being-in-a-position" applies primarily to the intelligible: "in the strictest sense (*kyriōtata*) everything is said to be positioned in god, since all that comes after him is comprehended in him". Contrast this to the position of Dexippus, who would have said that the expression "everything is in God" is an analogy or a metaphor, which compares the ineffable relation of all things to God to physical things kept together in some physical container. In other words, Iamblichus here adopts the Platonic top-down perspective on naming. One would perhaps expect that if "being-in-a-position" applies primarily to the intelligible, it applies to the sensible only analogically. This, however, is not the case. Iamblichus claims explicitly that "the same account (*logos*) of being-in-a-position runs through all these cases, namely of one thing being limited within another" (*in Cat.* 340.8–9). Admittedly it means something different for one body to be in another than it means for our thoughts to be in our soul, because bodies are physical objects and thoughts and soul are not, yet this does not do away with the fact that the same definition of "being-in-a-position" applies to all these cases. Iamblichus thus comes close to describing the relation between the intelligible and the sensible in terms of synonymy.

DE INTERPRETATIONE

Language and Aristotelian logic: the assertoric sentences

Aristotle begins his *de Interpretatione* with a series of definitions, including that of the "assertion" (*apophansis*). As we have seen above, according to Neoplatonic commentators, *de Interpretatione* deals with the so-called "second imposition"; that is, with nouns and verbs, and in particular with their "interweaving" (*symplokē*) into simple assertions; that is, into sentences that claim that something is the case. They are therefore either true or false – in contrast to other types of sentences, such as exclamations, commands, questions and wishes – and therefore of interest to the philosopher who searches the truth. As Ammonius puts it: "Aristotle does not instruct us in this course about every simple sentence, but only about the assertoric – and rightly so, for only this type of sentence is receptive of truth and falsity, and under this type fall demonstrations, for the sake of which the whole course in logic has been composed by the Philosopher" (*in de Int.* 2.21–5, trans. Blank). Ammonius is obviously right about the logical nature of *de Interpretatione*, but sometimes he pushes this idea a bit too far, for example, when he explains the fact that Aristotle only mentions nouns and verbs, whereas grammarians distinguish between eight different parts of a sentence (*in de Int.* 11.1–7). Ammonius replies that nouns and verbs suffice to construct an assertoric sentence, while overlooking the fact that in Aristotle's day nouns and verbs were the only two types of words that were distinguished, the other six being a later invention.[14]

However this may be, it is sufficiently clear that for Aristotle and Ammonius assertoric sentences are far more important than isolated words, since individual words can be neither true nor false, whereas assertoric sentences are. As such, this idea is not typically Aristotelian: it can be been traced back to Plato's *Sophist* (262d13–263d4). One would thus expect that all Neoplatonists would accept its logical consequence: that names in isolation are neither true nor false. This was not the case though. Socrates in the *Cratylus* (385b–d) had (falsely) argued that, from the fact that assertions can be true or false, it follows that the same goes for their constitutive parts; that is, individual names. As we shall see, Proclus in his commentary on the *Cratylus* is therefore inclined to attach more philosophical importance to names than to assertoric sentences and syllogistic logic.

Words as symbols

The fact that assertoric sentences are true or false plays a role in the discussion whether language refers to things or to our thoughts of these things. The Peripatetic commentator on Aristotle, Sosigenes, a teacher of Alexander of Aphrodisias, for example, had argued that names refer to things rather than to thoughts. As Dexippus in his *Commentary on the Categories* (7.8–8.23) had been quick to point out, the things themselves are neither true nor false. We may, however, hold false or correct beliefs about things, when we combine certain thoughts incorrectly, for example, when we combine the thought of a woman with the thought of Socrates into the thought that "Socrates is a woman". From this it follows that language is an expression of our thoughts of things, rather than of things directly. This is good Aristotelian doctrine, as appears from a famous passage from *de Interpretatione*:

> Now spoken sounds are symbols of affections [*pathēmatōn symbola*] in the soul, and written marks symbols of spoken sounds. And just as written marks are not the same for all men, neither are spoken sounds. But what these are in the first place signs of – affections in the soul – are the same for all; and what these affections are likenesses of (*homoiōmata*) – actual things – are also the same.
>
> (Aristotle, *Int.* 16a3–8, trans. Ackrill)

Aristotle's line of thought seems sufficiently clear. He believes that somehow we all share a similar concept (an "affection in the soul") of, for example, a horse (the actual thing). This is because our concept of "horse" faithfully reflects the actual horse. When we want to express our thoughts to one another, we do so by means of *symbola*. We just happen to have agreed that a certain bit of sound – "horse" in English, "Pferd" in German, "cheval" in French – refers to our concept of horse. It is precisely because spoken words are a matter of convention that they can be different in different languages. What goes for spoken words goes for the writing that we use to record the spoken. Egyptian hieroglyphs, cuneiform script, Latin letters: they are all different because they are a matter of convention, but ultimately they communicate the same concepts.

All Neoplatonists were happy to agree that language expresses our concepts or thoughts about things, whatever these may be. The real problem is Aristotle's claim that language is solely a matter of convention: "I say 'by convention' [*kata synthēkēn*] because no name is a name naturally [*physei*] but only when it has become a symbol. Even inarticulate noises (of beasts, for instance) do indeed indicate something (*dēlousi ti*), yet none of them is a name [*onoma*]" (*Int.* 16a26–9, trans. Ackrill, adapted). Aristotle's explicit denial of speech to animals is interesting in its own right, especially because Porphyry, who is usually happy to follow Aristotle, disagrees, at least implicitly, with him on this account. In *de Abstinentia* (3.3.1–8) he defends at some length the idea that animals too have language. What I wish to focus on in the present context, though, is the fact that Aristotle describes spoken words as symbols based on convention. This is in apparent contradiction with the *Cratylus* (390d–e), where Socrates defends the claim that names are in a way natural (*physei*). If one maintains that Plato and Aristotle are in harmony, then, this passage calls out for an explanation.

Ammonius (*in de Int.* 20.1–30) begins by explaining the difference between the terms "likeness" and "symbol". A "likeness" is an image of a thing. Now, images of Socrates will all resemble him, for each portrait will represent him as a bald man with a snub nose and bulging eyes. If names were likenesses all names would more or less sound the same. Symbols on the other hand can be very different: both the sound of a trumpet and a torch that is thrown can signal the attack. Since the same concept can be indicated by words that sound very different, words are symbols rather than likenesses. The symbols do not arise naturally: admittedly making sounds comes to us naturally, but we should think of these sounds as matter (*hylē*) which we subsequently turn into words when we articulate these sounds in a certain way by use of our linguistic imagination (*lektikē phantasia*), just as a carpenter turns the natural material wood into some sort of artifact, while using his imagination. Therefore, words are a matter of convention, not a product of nature. In support of his case, Ammonius points to people who are deaf from birth: such people make noises, since it is natural to do so, yet they do not pronounce proper words because they were unable to learn the linguistic conventions. Since linguistic correctness depends on convention, the way in which ordinary language-users use the language is norma-tive. This explains, for example, why commentators like Porphyry and Dexippus worry about the fact that Aristotle violates ordinary usage (*synētheia*) when he uses the Greek word *katēgoria*, normally used to denote the speech of the prosecution against someone, in a new outlandish way (*xenizein*) to refer to his categories (Porphyry, *in Cat.* 55.3–14; Dexippus, *in Cat.* 5.30–6.26). The commentators explain that Aristotle, since he was dis-cussing new things for which there did not yet exist an appropriate terminology, needed to stretch the ordinary meaning of existing words (*metachrēsis*).

So far, so good. But how can this be squared with Socrates' claim that words are correct by nature and not by convention? Ammonius (*in de Int.* 35.13–37.27) draws a distinction between two ways in which names can be "by nature": either they are likenesses produced by nature, comparable to shadows and reflections in water and mirrors, which appear spontaneously, that is, naturally, or they are likenesses, produced by humans, that fit the nature of the things named by them. It is, for example, no coincidence that the Greek word for sea, *hē thalassa*, is feminine and the Greek word for river, *ho potamos*, masculine: the way in which rivers flow into the seas that receive them is analogous to the sexual rela-tions between men and women.[15] When Aristotle denies that names are "by nature", he means that words are not naturally produced likenesses. He would not deny, however, that name-givers coin words in such a way as to fit the nature of the object named, as appears from the fact that in various places Aristotle tries to show that names befit their objects. Ammonius has a point here: Aristotle is indeed interested in etymology, which suggests that he does not assume that names are completely arbitrary linguistic tokens. We shall see below, however, that Ammonius' teacher, Proclus, does not agree with this attempt to harmonize Plato and Aristotle.

THE *CRATYLUS*

Language and Platonic dialectic

As we have seen above, in the context of Aristotelian syllogistic logic, the natural focus is on the (assertoric) sentence as the primary linguistic unity. These sentences are the build-ing blocks of syllogistic arguments aimed at demonstration. Platonic dialectic, on the other hand, favours individual *onomata* because they encapsulate the research by the wise dia-lecticians of old. "And so the end of their contemplation became for us the starting-point for the discovery of the intellection of things", as the Alexandrian Neoplatonist Hierocles (*in CA* 25.3, trans. Schibli, adapted) puts it.[16] What Hierocles means by this is that by care-fully etymologizing those names, that is, by tracing the reasons why the wise named the things as they did, we learn a lot about intelligible reality. The idea that we can teach and learn through etymology derives from the lengthy etymological section that makes up a significant portion of the *Cratylus*. Ironically, most modern scholars believe, with good reason, that the whole point of the etymological section is to disqualify etymology as a means of philosophical investigation, for as Socrates (439b–d) points out, we cannot be sure that the name-givers had arrived at a proper understanding of reality.[17]

The place of the *Cratylus* in the standard curriculum of twelve Platonic dialogues that had been designed by Iamblichus reflects this idea of names as the starting point of our ascent towards the intelligible. The anonymous *Prolegomena to Platonic Philosophy* (26.34–9) describes the *Cratylus* as the first dialogue in which the reader is introduced to the study of reality (*ta onta*) after dialogues such as the *Gorgias* and the *Phaedo* that were intended as a moral preparation for this study. The *Cratylus* does not deal with reality directly, as do subsequent dialogues, but does so through names. Even though we may assume that the *Cratylus*, since it was part of the curriculum, was frequently discussed in Neoplatonic schools, Proclus' commentary on it is the only one we know of. It has come down to us in the form of a collection of excerpts from notes that an anonymous student of his lectures on that dialogue took down and discusses the dialogue up to *Cratylus* 407c, when the last note of the commentary breaks off mid-sentence.[18]

Words as images

Proclus starts off his commentary by discussing the aim (*skopos*) of the dialogue. The dialogue reflects on the issue of correctness of names in order to demonstrate the "generative activity and the assimilative powers" of the human soul. Proclus' interpretation of Socrates' position on the correctness of language is roughly that names are correct if they are faithful images of intelligible reality. Correctly given names thus testify of the human ability to know the Forms and to create likenesses of them. Just as the divine Demiurge generates the physical cosmos as an image of the intelligible cosmos, in a like manner the human name-giver constructs names that are images of his knowledge of the intelligible Forms. The dialogue encourages us to turn our attention away from the physical realm towards the intelligible and thus promotes both self-knowledge and knowledge of the intelligible.

Proclus stresses this anagogic aspect of the *Cratylus* by comparing Platonic dialectic to Aristotelian logic:

> [T]he *Cratylus* is logical and dialectical, not, however, in the manner of Peripatetic dialectical methods, which are unrelated to reality [*ta pragmata*], but in the manner of the great Plato. ... This sort of dialectic is said by him to be the "capstone of mathematics" (Plato *R.* 534e) and to lead us upwards to the one cause of all things, the Good. ... For the analytical method of the Peripatos, and its main part, dem-onstration, are easy to master and very clear for everybody who is not completely confused and has not drunk much water from river Lethe.   (*in Cra.* 2.1.10–2.4)

Proclus can thus be seen to adopt Plotinus' rather critical attitude towards Aristotle. Unlike Porphyry and others who seek to harmonize Aristotle with Plato, Proclus insists on the differences between the two philosophers.[19] As we have seen above, Ammonius tries to square the Aristotelian idea of *onomata* as *symbola* and the Platonic idea of *onomata* as likenesses, by arguing that Aristotle called them *symbola* because they are not likenesses in the way that images (*eikones*) are, yet that Aristotle too assumed that *onomata* were not completely arbitrary symbols. Proclus simply rejects the Aristotelian account of names as *symbols* and insists on the point that names are likenesses precisely in the sense that they are like images, constructed by wise name-givers:

> And just as theurgy by means of certain symbols and ineffable tokens makes the statues here into images of the gods and makes them suitable for the reception of the illuminations from the gods, in the same manner the legislative art too by means of that same assimilative power makes names into statues of the things, depicting the nature of things by means of various sounds, and once it had fashioned these, it handed them over to the people to use them. (*in Cra.* 51.19.12–19)

Proclus compares names of intelligible reality to the animated statues that played an important role in theurgy, the religious rituals that the Athenian Neoplatonic school of Proclus regarded as an essential means to come in to contact with and ascend to the divine. As this passage suggests, philosophy and religion were intimately intertwined for Proclus and his followers, as appears also from the fact that he is especially interested in divine names.

Divine names

One of the most striking aspects of Proclus' commentary on the *Cratylus* is the close attention that Proclus pays to the etymologies of divine names. To us, this may seem to be an irrelevant topic in a philosophical discussion, but it was not so to Proclus and his circle. For them the ultimate goal of philosophy was to establish a Platonic theology; that is, a systematic account of how reality is derived from the ultimate principle. This principle, the One, together with other intermediate causes that derive their existence from the One (e.g. the Henads, Being, Intellect), are divine. They correspond to the gods and goddesses of traditional mythologies, such as the theogonies of Hesiod and Orpheus, and other sources of revealed theological wisdom like the *Chaldaean Oracles* (see e.g. Saffrey 1992). Thus for Proclus studying the etymology of divine names is part of his metaphysical project, as appears from the fact that many of the etymologies of divine names that we know from the commentary on the *Cratylus* reappear in Proclus' monumental work the *Platonic Theology* (see e.g. Proclus, *Theol. Plat.*1.5.25.18–32). Proclus distinguishes various types of divine names. The first division is that between the names by which the gods call themselves and man-made divine names. Some of the man-made divine names are the product of divine inspiration, whereas others are the product of scientific knowledge and in some cases even of opinion. The god-made divine names are, as one would expect, of the highest value, both because they contain important theological information and because we use them to invoke the gods in theurgical rituals. They thus help us to return to the divine (see e.g. *in Cra.* 71.31.29–32.5). This is not to say that all gods can be named. The One cannot be named, because any name is composed of various letters. Different letters represent different aspects of the nature of the object named. Thus, any name attributed to the One would thus, wrongly, suggest that the One is a plurality (Proclus, *in Prm.* VII.508.89–509.97). Likewise, the very first intelligible gods that are close to the One cannot be named because of their extreme degree of unity (*in Cra.* 71.32.23–5). Their world, which transcends that of speech, is that of silence (*sigē*).[20] The name "one" does not refer to this ineffable first principle, but to our concept of it, which consists in our natural desire for oneness.

Human names

As we have just seen, divine names are the ultimate illustration that names are "by nature" – just think of the explanation of the name "Hermes" alluded to at the start of this chapter – rather than the product of arbitrary imposition and linguistic conventions, as he believes Aristotle maintains. Proclus is, however, willing to make one concession to Aristotle. Naturally, correct names are correct because they are made on the basis of the name-giver's knowledge of intelligible reality. In some cases of naming, however, such knowledge is not available. Proclus has especially the names of individuals in mind. The parents who name their children cannot rely on the sort of reliable knowledge that the philosopher has at his disposal about the unchanging universal Forms when inventing names. The former names are therefore rather the product of arbitrary imposition, or baptism as we would now say. Even in these cases, however, most names will eventually turn out to match the character and behaviour of their bearers, be it sometimes in unexpected ways. Taking an example from Plato's *Cratylus* (394e), Proclus (87.42.4) mentions the case of Orestes. When Agamemnon named his son thus, he may have done so hoping that his son would later in life rush forwards (*orouein*); as it turned out it was an appropriate name for someone who would kill his own mother, since the name suggests brutality, normally associated with uncivilized mountain (*oros*)-dwellers. Proclus explains such cases as the result of Chance (*tychē*), which he understands as some daemonic or divine power, not as some blind force that operates randomly.

Proclus on the issue of homonymy/synonymy

Proclus, like all other Neoplatonists (cf. pp. 255–7 above), was confronted with the issue of homonymy/synonymy which he approaches from his top-down perspective on naming. His discussion of the question in his commentary on Plato's *Parmenides* (4.849.13–853.9) reads like a criticism of Porphyry's Aristotelian approach to language. Proclus begins by calling Parmenides' statement (130e6) "that the Forms have given their names as well as their being to the things in this world" "a remark of genius and well worthy of Platonic principles" (trans. Morrow & Dillon). He explicitly rejects the bottom-up view of naming that we encountered in the commentaries on the *Categories*, according to which "names have their origin in perceptible things; for these, being before everybody's eyes, are the first to have received specific names, and from them, by the use of certain analogies, the wiser men set names for invisible reality" (*in Prm.* 849.17–21, trans. Morrow & Dillon).

His own take on the matter, that the visible things are named after their intelligible causes, brings Proclus to the much debated issue of synonymy and homonymy. Proclus himself prefers to describe the relation between Forms and particulars in terms of homonymy, be it of a very unusual type. He rejects the view that in, for example, the case of the name "man", the name man is a single name that is ambiguously applied to two different objects. Rather, the name "man" is only seemingly the same in the case of the intelligible and the sensible man. As we shall discuss below in some more detail, Proclus, in keeping with Plato's *Cratylus*, assumes that a name is in some way a likeness of its object. This likeness becomes apparent when one etymologizes that name. Proclus assumes that one can etymologize a given name in different ways – his example is the double etymology of *eros* in *Phaedrus* 238c and 252b – and that the different etymologies point to different types of objects, intelligible and sensible ones. In order to clarify his point, Proclus compares these seemingly identical names to two similar portraits of Athena by two different artists. One artist has simply copied the famous statue of Athena by the sculptor Phidias, the other has been inspired by an epiphany of the goddess. On superficial inspection, the two portraits may seem similar. The one based on the epiphany, however, will make a special impression of the viewer, whereas the other is doomed to remain just a frigid likeness of a lifeless statue: "In the same way the word 'man', though applied to the two objects, is not in the same way a likeness of both; in the one case it is the likeness of a paradigm, in the other case the likeness of a likeness, the image of an image" (*in Prm.* 282.6–9).

But why does Proclus claim that names are primarily a likeness of intelligible reality and only secondarily of the sensible thing? One could, after all, imagine that, as Porphyry suggests, mankind first made names for physical objects that it was familiar with, and only later turned its attention to the names of intelligible objects, even though these are ontologically speaking prior to the sensible instances. The reason for this is that Proclus follows Plato's idea that names are first and foremost the instruments of the Platonic dialectician that he uses to divide up reality:

> For in general, since we use names because we want to indicate distinctions in thought between things and distinction and unmixed purity is to be found in these (i.e. the Forms), but not in those (i.e. physical objects), the names we use will be suitable primarily to the former, not to the latter that contain a considerable mixture of opposite qualities, such as white and black, equal and unequal and the like. (*in Prm.* 852.16–22, trans. Morrow & Dillon, adapted)

When we say "black", we mean "black", not some mixture of black and its opposite white. Since particular instances of blackness will never be one hundred percent black, it follows, Proclus thinks, that the concept of "blackness" to which the name "black" refers is related to the Form blackness rather than to (an abstraction of) particular instances of impure blackness.

Proclus thus appears to distinguish between two types of language: language that refers to the intelligible realm and language that refers to the physical world. I suggest that we may equate the latter type of language with the type of language that, according to Porphyry and others, the *Categories* is about. As we have seen (p. 258), Porphyry and others had worried about Aristotle's outlandish use of the Greek language, referred to as *xenizein*. In his commentary on the *Alcibiades* (258.21–259.21), Proclus discusses the opposite of *xenizein*, *hellēnizein*, which we may translate roughly as "using the Greek language correctly". Proclus distinguishes between three types of *hellēnizein*: the first type of correctness consists in upholding the Greek custom (*synētheia*) of naming things, "for example to refer to this thing as '*xylon*', to that thing as '*anthrōpos*', to another thing as '*hippos*' and so forth". This recalls the discussions of language in the commentaries on the *Categories* according to which language refers to particular objects, while the commentators insist on the need to respect the ordinary usage (*synētheia*) of language; that is, to stick to linguistic conventions. Passing over the second form of *hellēnizein* swiftly, that of the grammarians, Proclus next describes the third form of *hellēnizein* as giving naturally correct names to all things, the task that the *Cratylus* assigns to the name-giver/dialectician. Proclus' point is apparently that the layman and the philosopher, even though they will both use the same word, for example, *xylon* to refer to wood, will do so in different ways. The layman will do so because he has been taught to call particular instances of a certain stuff thus, the philosopher because he understands the nature of wood and why *xylon* is an appropriate name to designate such a nature.

CONCLUSION

The Neoplatonists derived their ideas about language and its role in philosophy predominantly from Aristotle's *Categories* and *de Interpretatione* and Plato's *Cratylus*. Plato's dialectic and his ideas about language are firmly bound up with his famous doctrine of metaphysical Forms, whereas Aristotle's rejection of that theory is reflected in his views on language and logic. Different strategies of how to cope with the tensions between the Platonic and Aristotelian account yielded different ideas about language. Some simply took sides. Plotinus, for example, seems to have gone with Plato, whereas Porphyry, at least as far as we can tell from his commentary on the *Categories*, was apparently happy to restrict himself to expounding Aristotle's views. Others tried to combine the Platonic and Aristotelian perspectives. As we have seen, Iamblichus made an original, if not necessarily convincing, attempt to square Platonic metaphysics with the Aristotelian *Categories*, whereas Ammonius tried to interpret away Aristotle's claim that language is meaningful by convention only and that names are nothing but symbols, in order to be able to harmonize it with Plato's claim that names are meaningful by nature. Proclus, on the other hand, did not so much try to harmonize Plato and Aristotle, but rather tried to separate them and accord them their own domain. Aristotle's entire philosophy, his logic and ideas about languages included, bears on the physical world of particulars, that of Plato on the intelligible realm of Forms. This move allows him to keep both Plato and Aristotle aboard without conflating them, yet also entails a degradation of Aristotelian philosophy to at best a preparation for Plato's. One did not have to see the relation between Aristotle and Plato in this way, though. Simplicius, one of the last Neoplatonists, fully recognized the differences between Plato and Aristotle:

> The reason [i.e. of the fact that Aristotle seemingly contradicts Plato] is, I believe, that Aristotle, on the one hand, most of the time wants to preserve the conventional meaning of the words (*hē synētheia tōn onomatōn*) and constructs his arguments on the basis of what is evident to the senses. Plato, on the other, frequently despises such things, but gladly hastens back towards intelligible contemplation.
>
> (*in Ph.* 1249.13–17 [Diels])

According to Simplicius, however, these different approaches need not be a problem. Quite the contrary: Aristotle's and Plato's approaches perfectly supplement each other, and thus help us to arrive at a better understanding of reality.[21]

NOTES

1. In the Athenian Neoplatonic school, for example, young Proclus was first made to study "all the works by Aristotle" before he embarked upon "the mystagogy of Plato" (Marinus, *Procl.* 13.1–10).
2. I here read this section from the *Cratylus* in a way that fits the Neoplatonic interpretation of it. I do not, of course, wish to suggest that this is the only possible way of reading this passage, on which see now the recent commentary by Ademollo (2011: 95–114).
3. For an extended version of much of what I have to say in this chapter, see van den Berg (2008). For a first orientation on the topic of language in Neoplatonic authors, see also the useful collection of texts in Sorabji (2004: vol. 3, 205–49).
4. On *logos* and *logoi* in Plotinus, see Brisson (1999).
5. Plotinus borrows the term *logos prophorikos* from the Stoics who distinguish between *logos endiathetos* (internal speech, the thoughts that someone may have in mind, but has not yet expressed) and *logosprophorikos* (expressive speech, the actual utterance of these thoughts) and reinterprets it in Neoplatonic metaphysical terms of a plurality that emanates from a unified source. On the Stoic origin of these terms, see, for example, Porphyry, *Abst.* 3.2: "According to the Stoics there are two kinds of *logos*, the internal (*endiathetos*) and the expressive (*prophorikos*)", trans. G. Clark 2000: 80.
6. Cf. Plotinus, *Enn.* III.8[30].6.21–5; Plotinus' analysis of the actualization of knowledge is equally inspired by Aristotle's psychology (see esp. *de An.* 2.417a21–417b28). On the term *procheirisis* and its antecedents, see further van den Berg (2010).
7. Cf. Sorabji (2004: vol. 3), for relevant primary texts and secondary literature.
8. There exists a subtle difference between "indicate" and "signify": even the unarticulated sounds of animals may indicate (*dēloun*) something, yet only articulated human speech actually signifies (*sēmainein*) something (cf. Aristotle, *Int.* 16a26–9, quoted in § "Words as symbols" below).
9. Cf. e.g. Aristotle, *APo.* 71b33–72a5.
10. On these two *logoi*, see, in addition to Sorabji (2004: vol. 3, 135–7), Kotzia-Panteli (2000). Admittedly, Plotinus's views of language may seem at first sight untenable. Note, however, that Plotinus' position is soundly Platonic. In *Phaedo* 74b–e, for example, Socrates argues that we cannot develop a concept of equality by just looking at equal sticks and stones (i.e. at things that are better known to us). We are able to recognize the imperfectly equal sticks and stones as equal because we already possess an innate notion of equality associated with the Form Equality itself. Cf. e.g. *Enn.* I.6[1].3.1–5: we recognize a beautiful thing as such because we relate it to the form (*eidos*) of Beauty that we have in ourselves. For Plotinus' rejection of the Aristotelian principle that we should start from what is better known to us, see Chiaradonna (2002: 276–7).
11. Chiaradonna (2002: 263–71) gives a useful discussion of this text as part of his illuminating analysis of the notion of *analogia* in Plotinus and other Neoplatonists (Chiaradonna 2002: 227–305).
12. On homonymy/synonymy, cf. Sorabji (2004: vol. 3, 230–35).
13. On Iamblichus' *noera theōria*, see further Dillon (1997).
14. Ammonius' oversight hardly comes, of course, as a surprise: no Neoplatonic exegete ever followed a historical approach.
15. But note that, as an anonymous reader observes, other Greek words for sea happen to be masculine (e.g. *ho pontos*).
16. On Hierocles, cf. most recently Schibli (2002) (and further Kobusch [1976] and I. Hadot [1978]). On the beneficial working of the wise man's contemplation, cf. D. O'Meara (2003: 73–81).
17. For a recent overview and evaluation of the scholarship on the etymological section of the *Cratylus*, see Ademollo (2011: 237–56).
18. The commentary has been translated by Duvick (2007).
19. On the critical attitude of the Athenian Neoplatonic school (Syrianus, Proclus) towards Aristotle, see, for example, Saffrey (1987) and D'Ancona (2000).
20. *In Cra.* 71.32.28. Proclus derives the term *sigē* (silence) from the *Chaldaean Oracles*, cf. *Theol. Plat.* IV.9.30.12–31.5.
21. On Simplicius' attempts to harmonize Aristotle with Plato by arguing that they supplement each other, see I. Hadot (1978: 148) and Hoffmann (1987); for the passages quoted above, see esp. Hoffmann (1987: 213).

17

Neoplatonic epistemology: knowledge, truth and intellection

Lloyd P. Gerson

Neoplatonic epistemology generally is rooted in the Platonic–Aristotelian account of knowledge (*epistēmē*) and belief (*doxa*), reflection on the materialist challenge to this account by the Stoics, and a response to the later Pyrrhonian arguments against the very possibility of wisdom, the central pretension of all "dogmatists".

Since Neoplatonists saw no essential difference between Plato and Aristotle regarding fundamental epistemological matters, they felt free to draw on both in order to meet the challenges posed by their opponents. The central challenge comes from materialism: first, for Plato and Aristotle, probably from Atomists and then later, more powerfully, from the Stoics themselves. The present chapter will focus on the fundamental elements in the integration of the Platonic-Aristotelian account into the larger Neoplatonic metaphysical framework.

In *Timaeus*, Plato explains the nature of this challenge (see *Ti.* 51c–e). He argues as follows: if knowledge is different from true belief, then separate Forms must exist, for these are the objects of knowledge.[1] But Forms are immaterial entities; hence, materialism is false. Clearly, what requires scrutiny is the assumption that knowledge is something distinct from true belief and the further assumption that knowledge is exclusively of immaterial entities. As it happens, the reason for both assumptions is identical: knowledge is infallible or unerring.[2] Knowledge is different from true belief because the latter does not have this property even though a true belief is, by definition, not false. Infallibility differs from truth as a property of a belief because one might have a true belief and yet not know that it is so. One might have it by accident, so to speak. By contrast, infallibility is the impossibility of error; that is, the knower cannot be in a state of knowing and at the same time not realize that he is in this state. Given the infallibility of knowledge, we can see at once that there cannot be knowledge of material entities or, stated otherwise, that knowledge can only be of immaterial entities. This is so because a material entity must be outside of the intellect, and so whatever is in the intellect must be merely a representation of that putative material object of knowledge. But there is no way to guarantee infallibility in the representation of anything. That is, there is no entailment from "S has a representation of p" to "S knows p". The only way that infallibility is possible is if the objects of knowledge are immaterial entities such that they can actually be present to the intellect, a presence that does not, of course, preclude their presence to other intellects, too.

Aristotle in *de Anima* comes to the same conclusion via a somewhat more circuitous path (*de An.* 3.3.427a17–b7). He is arguing against materialists who maintain that sense-perception and thinking – the genus of which knowledge is a subspecies – are the same sort of thing, namely a kind of physical change in the cognizer produced by an external physical object. He argues in reply that thinking must be different from sense-perception because thinking can be *false* whereas sense-perceptions are true (*de An.* 3.3.427b11–14). If thinking were a mere physical change, then there could be no falsity in thinking only the presence or absence of the change. But the faculty which is capable of falsity is identical with that which is capable of truth. To be capable of a false belief it is necessary to have an immaterial intellect, for a false belief (or a true one) requires that (a) a subject of that belief be present in the intellect. Assume, like the materialist, that what is in fact present is a representation of the external physical object. In order to have the belief, one must then (b) cognize something universal in the attribution of a predicate to that subject. If this were not so, then falsity would not be possible because no one could have the false belief that "A is B" where "A" and "B" are representations of different physical objects. The predicate in the judgement or belief must be understood universally if the claim of predicative identity is to be made. The cognition of a universal could not be a bodily or material state, since every one of these has determinate particularity. So, to believe that "this is a dog" is to cognize "dog" universally, but universal cognition is not exhaustible by a particular instantiation or representation. That is, cognition of universals requires their non-representational presence. So, belief requires an immaterial intellect. But belief could not be possible unless one is capable of knowledge; that is, the presence of an intelligible object in the intellect and the awareness of its presence (*de An.* 3.4.429a24–9). In a belief, the cognition of a universal is not an example of knowledge. But such cognition is not possible unless knowledge is possible, too.

The presence of the intelligible object in the intellect for Plato is a "possessing" (*kektēsthai*); the awareness of its presence is a "having" (*echein*) (*Tht.* 197b–d). For Aristotle, "possessing" becomes "first actuality" and "having" "second actuality" (*de An.* 3.4.429b5–9). Knowledge in the primary sense is the "having" or the "second actuality". It is absolutely crucial for grasping this account that we recognize that the subject in which the intelligible object is present is identical with the subject which is aware of that presence. This is, of course, only possible if the subject is immaterial. So, fully actualizing knowledge or having it requires that the knower know himself, at least in so far as he is an intellect.[3] That is, knowledge is self-knowledge.

In this light, it is not difficult to see why Plato insists that knowledge must be infallible. To maintain that it is coherent to say, "I know but I may be mistaken" is to use the word "know" in a way significantly different from the way that Plato uses the verbal forms of the word *epistēmē*. It is to make knowledge a form of belief, something that Aristotle accepts no more than Plato.[4]

The Academic Sceptic Arcesilaus deserves a brief mention in this context, since it is he who, in his attack on Stoic epistemology, was the first after Aristotle to see the essential connection between knowledge, immaterialism and infallibility. As Arcesilaus showed, if the Stoic claim to knowledge rests on "presentations" (*phantasiai*) then, since there is no such thing as false knowledge, there must be some criterion for distinguishing knowledge from a false belief. But presentations leading to the one or the other may be indistinguishable.[5] From this it follows that one cannot know unless one is certain or infallible, but the grounds for claiming knowledge can never in principle be conclusive. Hence, knowledge is not possible. The materialist Stoics had no way of countering this argument.[6]

More important for our purposes is the argument found in Sextus Empiricus that is directed not against materialists exclusively but against all dogmatists; that is, against all those, immaterialists included, who maintain that knowledge must be infallible. As Sextus so clearly sees, if knowledge is to be infallible, then, as noted above, the subject in which the knowable object is present must be identical with the subject who is aware of its presence. But then,

> If intellect (*nous*) grasps itself, either it is as a whole that it will grasp itself or not as a whole, but using some part of itself for this. It will not be able to grasp itself as a whole. For if it grasps itself as a whole, it will as a whole just be the grasping and, in grasping, since the grasping is the whole [that is, all there is of it], it will not be that which is grasped. But it is the height of absurdity that the grasping should exist but not that which is grasped. Nor can intellect use some part of itself for this. For how does the part itself grasp itself? If as a whole, the object sought will be nothing; if with a part, how will that part in turn cognize itself? And so on indefinitely. So, grasping is without a beginning (*anarchon*), since either there is no first subject to be found to do the grasping or else there will be no object to be grasped.
>
> (Sextus Empiricus, *M*. 7.310–13)[7]

Sextus' argument is intended to drive a stake through the heart of any dogmatic pretension to knowledge precisely because all dogmatists recognize that knowledge must be infallible. So, even if we grant the immateriality of the putative knower, if it can be shown that infallibility is not possible, then there can be no knowledge and the dogmatists' quest for wisdom is vain.[8]

PLOTINUS

In one of the very few passages in the *Enneads* in which Plotinus seems to take notice of Sextus or at least of Pyrrhonian Sceptics, he actually responds to this argument or to one very much like it. He asks, "Must that which thinks itself be complex in order that, with one part of itself contemplating the others, it could in this way be said to think itself, on the grounds that were it altogether simple, it would not be able to revert to itself, that is, there could not be the grasping of itself?" (*Enn*. V.3[49].1.1–4, trans. Dillon & Gerson).[9]

The reply made by Plotinus is to the effect that self-thinking would not be possible if the complexity of the intellect were bodily complexity; that is, if it had parts outside of parts or extension.[10] In that case, knowledge would not be possible because infallibility would not be possible. Knowledge would in that case consist in one "part" of the intellect monitoring or otherwise taking cognizance of the state of another part. As we have seen, there can be no infallibility in this case. So, the intellect must be immaterial and knowledge must be the self-reverting awareness by the intellect of its own state (*epistrophē pros heauton*). Infallible cognition is indistinguishable from "having" the truth, in Plato's terminology (see *Enn.* V.3[49].5.19–26; V.3[49].8.36). Like Plato, Plotinus clearly identifies the activity of intellect, *noēsis*, with *epistēmē* or *sophia* (*Enn.* I.2[19].7.3; cf. *Enn.* V.9[5].5.30, quoting Aristotle). He takes knowledge as the paradigm of cognition and all other types of cognition as imitations or inferior versions of this. But, again, following Plato, he maintains that these inferior types of cognition would not be possible unless we were the sorts of creatures capable of the highest type. Indeed, unless we already do possess knowledge, modes of cognition like discursive reasoning would not be available to us. As Plotinus puts it, we reason discursively by the "rules" (*kanones*) that we have from Intellect (*Enn.* V.3[49].4.15–17). These rules are not themselves the intelligibles or Forms; they are representations (*typoi*) of them.[11] It is difficult to know precisely what Plotinus means to indicate here, but perhaps the simplest interpretation is that the rules or representations are elementary logical principles which are a necessary condition for thinking at all.[12] What distinguishes these rules from mere signs is their universality. Animals can react to signs, but they cannot cognize universally. Only with such rules can we think at all and cognize universally.

The need for access to "rules" is owing to the fact that we possess "undescended intellects".[13] Briefly, the claim is based on the argument that since intellect and intelligibles are inseparable, the separateness of the one from the sensible world entails the separateness of the other. What this means is that our access to intelligibles is at the same time access to our own undescended intellects. The possibility of access is accounted for by our embodied souls being images of their paradigms, the undescended intellects.

So, following Aristotle, the paradigm of thinking is self-thinking: "In general, thinking seems to be an awareness (*synaisthēsis*) of the whole with many things coming together into that which is identical, whenever something thinks itself, which is thinking in the principal sense" (*Enn.* V.3[49].13.13–15; cf. *Enn.* II.9[33].1; 5.6.1).

The rather obscure phrase "many things coming together into that which is identical" is firmly embedded in Plotinian metaphysics wherein the first principle of all, the One or the Idea of the Good, is absolutely simple or one or self-identical. Intellect, the second principle of all, is, as Plotinus says, minimally complex; that is, it is a one–many (see e.g. *Enn.* V.4[7].1.1–21). It is unavoidably complex because the One is uniquely simple. Its complexity consists in the facts that (a) there must be some distinction between intellect and intelligible, and (b) there must be a multiplicity of intelligibles to account for all the multiple genuine cases of sameness in the world. So, the "many things coming together into that which is identical" are the intelligibles or Forms with which Intellect is eternally cognitively identical; that is, they make it to be what it is by "informing" Intellect while Intellect is simultaneously eternally aware of this information (see *Enn.* V.8[31].4.4–12; cf. Procl., *ET* 52).

Accordingly, every image or inferior form of thinking constitutes an act of identification, in two phases, so to speak. Consider belief. To engage in the type of thinking that is belief is to affirm that, say, A is B, where "A" stands for the subject and "B" for an instance of the universal property or attribute that is predicated of it. Plotinus takes the "is" in this predicative judgement to be an act of identification, saying that B names one thing that A is. Of course, the identity may be accidental or adventitious. But the judgement or belief is an act of thinking that two things are, in a way, one. The second phase of this sort of thinking is the awareness of one's own intellect being qualifiedly identified by; that is, identical with this belief. This is a qualified identity since the object cognized here, that is, the subject of the belief and its identity with an instance of the predicate, cannot identify or inform the intellect the way an immaterial entity can. A belief stands to knowledge or thinking in the "primary sense" roughly analogous to the way an instance of a Form or intelligible stands to that Form itself. Embodied thinking always occurs by imaging the perfect thinking of Intellect, the locus of intelligibility.

The Pyrrhonian argues that if we do not have a criterion for distinguishing true beliefs from false beliefs, there is no more reason to believe a proposition p is true rather than false. In other words, rational belief would not exist. But we can never have a criterion, for that would have to provide a means of distinguishing appearances that guarantees that they are appearances of reality from appearances that are deceptive. But there is no entailment from "s appears to me thus and so" to "s really is thus and so". How could there be such an entailment so long as we distinguish appearance and reality? But if we do not distinguish them, not only will it follow that all appearances are true, but any effort to explain appearances will fail; there will be nothing to explain. Philosophy and science will be pointless activities.

Plotinus' response to the Pyrrhonian objection is that if we do not *right now* know eternal truths, we are incapable of any higher cognition, perhaps nothing more than sense-perception and imagination. But if we are capable of higher cognition, including, say, a belief that there are no rational beliefs, then we must have access to eternal truth. The desiderated criterion for true belief is our possessing knowledge of eternal truth. The proof that we possess such knowledge is that if we did not possess it, we could not understand our own belief claims, regardless of whether these are true or false. So, Plotinus responds to the Pyrrhonists by hewing to the Platonic-Aristotelian account of knowledge and refusing to accept the assumption that the criterion of knowledge or rational belief must somehow consist in showing how sense-perception or appearance provides entailing evidence for the truth of belief.

It is crucial for Plotinus' argument that our access to our intellects – whether these be undescended or not – is necessarily also access to intelligibles. That is, the intellect must be cognitively identical with these intelligibles or, as he puts it in a treatise the first part of which is devoted to the problem, they must not be "external" to it.[14] If our access to our intellects were only access to a power, say, like using our muscles to lift something, then we would not have access to eternal truth, but only to some sorts of cognitive images or representations of the truth. But then the problem raised by the Pyrrhonists would be replicated at the level of the intelligible realm. In the first chapter of *Enn.* V.5., Plotinus wants to show that, given that intelligibles or Forms must exist if we are to explain sameness in difference in the sensible world, these intelligibles cannot be external to Intellect.

> But the greatest objection is this. If, indeed, one were to grant that these intelligibles are totally external to Intellect, and then claim that Intellect contemplates them as such, it necessarily follows that it does not itself have the truth of these things and that it is deceived in all that it contemplates: for it is those intelligibles that would be the true reality. It will contemplate them though it does not have them, instead receiving reflected representations of them in a kind of cognition like this. Then, not having true reality, but rather receiving for itself reflected representations of the truth, it will have falsities and nothing true. If, then, it knows that it has falsities, it

will agree that it has no share in truth. But if it is ignorant of this as well, and thinks that it has the truth when it does not, the falsity that is generated in it is double, and that will separate it considerably from the truth.

This is the reason, I think, that in acts of sense-perception truth is not found, but only belief, because belief is receptive,[15] and for this reason, being belief, it receives something other than that from which it receives what it has. If, then, there is no truth in Intellect, an intellect of this sort will not be truth nor will it be truly Intellect, nor will it be Intellect at all. But there is nowhere else for the truth to be.   (*Enn.* V.5[32].1.50–68; cf. *Enn.* V.3[49].5.21–5)

The last line of this passage reveals the underlying strategy in this argument. Truth must exist in Intellect if intellection is to be possible. If intellection is not possible because truth does not exist there, then, as we have seen, no higher cognition is possible, including belief.

The truth that is in Intellect is ontological truth, a property of being in relation to an intellect.[16] What Plotinus is disputing is the claim that what is in Intellect is only semantic truth; that is, a property of putative propositional representations of being. Suppose that the *ne plus ultra* of cognition were true belief. Then reality, the "truth makers" for true belief, would be external to all cognizers. In that case, the highest form of cognition would not be knowledge, for knowledge is infallible, and infallibility in the cognition of representations is not possible. But if there is no knowledge, then, as we have seen, there is no belief, or at least no true belief as distinct from false belief.

The explanation of why we must have access to Intellect, or to our own intellects, if we are to have higher cognition is essentially the same as the explanation of why we must have access to intelligibles. But if the explanation is the same, then this must be because Intellect and intelligibles are inseparable; that is, intelligibles are not external to the Intellect. The only way that ontological truth can be internal to Intellect is if being is internal to Intellect. If ontological truth is not internal to Intellect, then even the claim that we are representing reality is a sort of bluff. For the very idea of representation assumes a reality independent of that representation. But if intelligibles are not internal to Intellect, then the reality is completely inaccessible and claims to represent it are empty.

The internality of intelligibles to Intellect is the condition for what we do as embodied intellects. If I grasp, say, a mathematical truth, that is, if I see the truth of a mathematical proposition, I am not doing what Intellect does eternally, but I am doing something that I could not do if Intellect, and my own undescended intellect, were not eternally cognitively identical with intelligibles. Plotinus agrees with Aristotle (and Plato) that all our embodied cognition requires images.[17] But he insists further that only those with intellects can recognize the images for what they are because an image is only graspable as an image in relation to its intelligible paradigm.

The ability to cognize images as images is closely connected to the general principle enunciated above that thinking is essentially, that is, paradigmatically, self-thinking. In self-thinking, there are no images or representations. There is cognitive identity with intelligibles. In the inferior or derived modes of cognition, there is also cognitive identity, but because there are images, this identity is qualified. And because the identity is qualified, it is easy to confuse the cognitive state with representations – including propositional representations – of it. In contemporary epistemological parlance, the things I know and believe are propositions; according to the Platonic model, my knowledge or belief are expressed in propositions, which are representations of my cognitive state. It is because I know or believe that I make such representations either to myself or to others. Even in the case of belief, however, there is qualified self-thinking, my awareness of the state I am in. I cannot be unqualifiedly cognitively identical with anything that is materially constituted. But I cannot cognize anything without some form of self-thinking.

The non-propositional and non-representational nature of primary or paradigmatic thinking follows from its perfect cognitive identity with all that is intelligible.[18] This cognitive identification is also an activity (*energeia*). Accordingly, all of its inferior images, that is, all types of cognition, are images of this activity. For example, when I am in a belief state, I am, in my awareness of being in this state, not only identical with myself as informed by an instance of an intelligible, but I am also engaged in an activity which consists in identifying the predicate of the judgement with the subject. When I believe that "A is B" I cognize "B" as naming one of the things that is that which "A" names. Even though A is not necessarily B, its contingent identity with B is how the belief is represented to myself. The identity represented in a necessary proposition is, of course, closer to the paradigmatic state, indeed closer to the absolutely self-identical first principle of all. To see two (or more) things as one is the essence of higher cognition. At the level of Intellect, all intelligibles are seen in this way.

In order to complete this picture, it is necessary to emphasize that the paradigm of cognition is not, for Plotinus, as it is for Aristotle, identified with primary being or a first principle of all. In short, Intellect is not the Unmoved Mover. This needs to be stressed because the cognitive identity in Intellect is not perfect identity. Intellection, that is, self-thinking, could not be what the first principle of all consists in since all thinking is complex. The first principle of all can neither engage in cognition nor be cognized, at least in so far as cognition is understood as the presence of an intelligible in a cognizer and the awareness of that presence. The problem that this poses for Plotinus is that since all things desire the Good, that is, the first principle, how else could Intellect attain this Good but by engaging in intellectual activity, thinking itself as all that is intelligible? Plotinus' implicit response to this is to maintain that the Good is virtually all things including all that is intelligible.[19] It is virtually all things roughly in the way that "white" light is virtually the spectrum. Intellect "has" the Good in the best way possible; it knows all that the Good is virtually.

PORPHYRY

Porphyry, pupil of Plotinus and editor of his *Enneads*, wrote voluminously in defence of the Platonic system as articulated by his master. In his work, *Launching Points to the Intelligibles* (*Aphormai pros ta noēta, Sententiae*), Porphyry collects and more or less briefly comments on a number of passages from the *Enneads* collectively intended to orient the embodied human person in the direction of the first principle of all. On the matter of our return to the One, Porphyry seems to regard the activity of intellection as only the penultimate stage of ascent.

On the subject of that which is beyond Intellect, many statements are made on the basis of thinking, but it may be immediately contemplated (*theōreitai*) only by means of a nonthinking (*anoēsiai*) superior to thinking; even as concerning sleep many statements may be made in a waking state, but only through sleeping can one gain direct cognition (*gnōsis*) or comprehension for same is known by same, because all cognition consists in assimilation (*homoiōsis*) to the object of cognition.   (*Sent.* 25 [Lamperz], trans. Dillon & Gerson)

This portentous passage takes up, however briefly, several remarks made by Plotinus to the effect that even if there is no cognitional access to the One, nevertheless there must be some way of attaining it since, ultimately, it is the source of our being. Plotinus addresses the point in his treatise *On Nature and Contemplation*:

Since cognition of other things comes to us through Intellect, and we are able to know Intellect by means of intellect, by what sort of simple grasp (*epibolēi athroai*) could one get hold of (*aliskoito*) that which is by nature beyond Intellect? We shall say to the one to whom we have to explain how this is possible that it is by sameness in us.   (*Enn.* III.8[30].9.19–23; cf. *Enn.* V.3[49].14.1–6; V.6[24].6.32–5)

So, it is owing to the fact that we are images of the first principle that we can assume that it is possible somehow to attain some kind of union with this. Plotinus elsewhere connects the attainment of the One with the "greatest study" (*megiston mathēma*) of the Idea of the Good in *Republic*.[20]

Yet what this "nonthinking superior to thinking" is remains quite obscure. It is highly plausible that Porphyry has in mind what he reports in his *Life of Plotinus*, namely that Plotinus "attained" (*etychē*) the goal of union with the One four times in his life (*Plot.* 23.16–17). But we cannot suppose that achieving this goal could consist in the obliteration of the self, given that it occurred four times.[21] More important, since the One is absolutely simple, there can be no union with it, something that would evidently compromise its unqualified simplicity. It seems more likely that what Plotinus achieved was awareness that the One is all things – virtually. For present purposes, what is most important is the explicit limitation of intellection to intelligibles and its situation within the overall metaphysical, psychological and ethical framework of Platonism. Embodied human life is located on a sort of axis, one terminus of which is the One or the Good and the other terminus is totally unformed matter, as close to absolute non-being as it is logically possible to get. All human action, including thinking, is judged by Platonists from Plotinus onwards as orienting a person towards one terminus or the other. Knowledge, therefore, has a specific goal which is union with the One as far as possible. That is, knowledge is supposed to be transformative in the specific sense that by recovering the activity of our undescended intellects we unify the self, which is otherwise "dispersed" as a result of embodiment.

Porphyry thematizes the idea of reversion to our source as a cognitive enterprise in this way: "Everything that generates in virtue of its essence generates something inferior to itself, and everything that is generated reverts (*epistrephei*) by nature towards that which has generated it" (*Sent.* 13.1–2).

This passage generalizes the claim made by Plotinus that Intellect, after it has been generated by the One, reverts to the One and becomes Intellect when it looks at it; that is, when it seeks the Good (*Enn.* V.2[11].1.9–10). Our nature is rational, and reversion is accomplished by cognitive activity, certainly in the practical sphere when we act virtuously, but even more so as we engage in thinking that is disengaged from bodily desires.

That human progress consists in a reversion and that this reversion is primarily cognitive activity is explained ultimately by the One as producer of all things and, hence, virtually all things. Reflection on even the lowest type of human cognition gives an indication that our goal or good consists in a process of unification. For as we have seen, we could not have beliefs if we were not the sorts of beings to be able to have knowledge; that is, able to identify cognitively with intelligibles and to be aware of this identification (cf. Porphyry, *Sent.* 43.25–35 [Brisson]). Because all things desire their own good, and because the good of each individual is the same, namely the Good that is the unique absolutely simple first principle of all, our good is attained by progressing in the direction of the Good, and this progress consists in nothing but becoming knowers.

PROCLUS

Proclus' *Elements of Theology* is a kind of *summa* of systematic Platonism. It draws heavily on Plotinus, whom Proclus called "the exegete of the Platonic revelation", and those between Plotinus and himself – especially Porphyry, Iamblichus and his own teacher Syrianus – to set out the principles that integrate the various elements of the hierarchical metaphysics that is Platonism.

Plotinus anticipates Proclus in identifying reversion to the Good with "reversion to oneself" (*epistrophē eis hauton*) in the case of Intellect.[22] But the centrality of this idea for Platonism, especially when applied to embodied human life, only becomes clear in the works of Proclus and his successors.[23]

The first claim made in this regard is that "all things that are able to revert to themselves are incorporeal" (*ET* 15). Following Plotinus in his claim that thinking is essentially self-reverting, Proclus concludes that the subject of thinking must be incorporeal. The reason for this is that a body has parts outside of parts, and if (a) the presence of an intelligible and (b) the awareness of that presence are distinguishable, as they must be, then they would have to be attributable to different parts of the putative corporeal soul. But in that case, (b) would have to become the new (a) and there would have to be a (c) that is aware of the presence of the intelligible in the new (a).

Next, "all that is able to revert to itself has an existence separable from all body" (*ET* 16). If the subject of thinking were only immaterial in the anodyne way that, say, a property of a body is immaterial, then it could not be self-reverting. For the activity of self-reversion could not occur in that whose existence is dependent on a body. This is so because the self-reversion requires that there be one subject that is both the subject of the information by the intelligible and the subject that is aware of this information. But the subject of the putative immaterial property is a body.[24]

Finally, "everything which is primarily self-moving is able to revert to itself" (*ET* 17). That which is "primarily self-moving" is the soul (*ET* 20.8–11). This does not quite amount to the conclusion that the cognition that is essentially self-reverting is an activity of the soul as such, for as Proclus points out, if that were the case then all things with soul would be capable of thinking (*ET* 19). So, then, how is the type of soul that is capable of thinking distinguished from the types that are not? Proclus' answer to this question is to argue that self-movers are not uncaused, but must have their cause in an unmoved mover (*ET* 20.13–18). Intellect is such a mover, eternally active (*aei … energōn*) without change.[25] The souls of human beings do not have thought essentially; they can participate in it. The souls of animals cannot participate, perhaps because their souls are in fact properties of bodies. That is, they are not immaterial entities.

Commenting on the nature of the World Soul in Plato's *Timaeus*, Proclus says,

> From this it is clear that self-reversion is self-cognition and cognition of all the things in it, as well as those things that come before it and those that result from it. It seems, then, that all cognition is nothing other than reversion upon what is cognized and a self-appropriating (*oikeiōsis*) or harmonizing (*epharmosis*) with it. Because of this, truth is also the harmony of the one who cognizes in relation to the thing that is cognized. But since reversion is twofold – being in one sense a reversion upon the Good, but in another sense a reversion upon being – the organic (*zōtikē*) reversion of all things comes to be in relation to the Good, while the cognitive reversion takes place in relation to being. For this reason, the one reversion when it has been achieved is said to possess the Good, but when the other has been achieved it is said to possess being (each of these being the object of the reversion in question). And to arrive at the truth (*alētheuein*) is the grasp (*katalēpsis*) of being, whether it be in the identical thing which grasps it, or in what is prior to it, or in what comes after it.   (*in. Ti.* 3.286.32–287.11)

This passage makes a number of important points, especially the distinction between "cognitive reversion" and "non-cognitive reversion". All living things revert to the Good which is just Proclus' technical way of saying that they all desire the Good by desiring the good of each. Of course, this is true for us as well. But, uniquely, we are also capable of a cognitive reversion to being, and this is self-reversion. This is primarily the way *we* possess the Good.[26]

The self-appropriating or harmonizing with the truth, which is later described as "arriving at it", is the awareness of the cognitive identity of oneself and intelligibles or being that are present to the intellect. We note further that the grasp of being is variously of that which is in constitutive of Intellect, namely the Forms, or prior to Intellect, namely the One or Good, or that which is posterior to Intellect, namely images or *logoi* of the Forms in Soul or in nature. Thus, Proclus acknowledges the grades of the self-reversion that thinking is.

SCHOOL OF AMMONIUS

Ammonius, son of Hermias, was an Alexandrian pupil of Proclus, and later immensely influential within his own school, which included Asclepius of Tralles, Simplicius, Olympiodorus, and the Christian philosophers John Philoponus, David, Elias and Stephanus. Abstracting from the mostly subtle differences among the views of these philosophers, I focus here on their treatment of an epistemological problem left by the rejection by virtually all later Platonists of Plotinus' argument that our intellects are undescended.[27]

It is ultimately a problem that arises from the systematization of Platonism. The problem, as first encountered in *Meno*, and then solved there and in *Phaedo*, is how it is possible for embodied persons to acquire knowledge. The solution is that "having" knowledge is possible because we already "possess" it owing to our disembodied life prior to embodiment. We need only recollect it. With the systematization of Platonism by Plotinus, however, it emerges that our embodied intellects do not possess this knowledge, for intellect could only "have" knowledge; that is, eternally actualize it by being cognitively identical with all that is intelligible. That is, there is no way for embodied intellects to "possess" it; what we possess are only images of the intelligibles. Hence, since intellect is necessary for all higher cognition, we must somehow have access to our undescended intellects.[28] The undescended intellect is the stand-in for the Platonic embodied intellect that "possesses" knowledge as a result of its previous disembodied life. Rejecting the idea that our intellects are undescended, Ammonius and his followers were led to reflect on how our *descended* intellects operate in relation to intelligibles and hence how knowledge is possible for embodied persons.[29]

The groundwork for the non-Plotinian solution to this problem is provided by Proclus, who makes a distinction between Forms considered in themselves and Forms considered as intentional objects of intellect.[30] Since Intellect is cognitively identical with all intelligibles, Platonists are obliged to account for the fact that all sensibles with any measure of intelligibility must partake of Intellect without necessarily having intellectual properties; that is, without cognition of any sort. Indeed, all the Forms are united in their cognition by Intellect so that participation in them without cognition reveals a problem. It does not quite solve the problem to note that everything receives its prior principles according to its own capacity and so things without immaterial intellects cannot receive Intellect *qua* knower; they can only receive it *qua* Form or Forms.[31] This might explain why chairs do not think, but it does not explain how those individuals manifestly capable of thinking are able to access intelligibles at the same time as they are *descended*; that is, separated from Intellect and so inferior to it in the metaphysical procession.

We might suppose that for the followers of Ammonius, Intellect can do for the embodied person what for Plotinus the undescended intellect does. But this cannot be quite right either. For Plotinus, in his systematic expression of Platonism, argues that we must not merely "possess" knowledge but we must "have" it as well, even though it is not the embodied person who has it. For the followers of Ammonius, we can only possess it by means of our pre-embodied encounters with Forms (Ammonius, *in Cat.* 37.11–12; Philoponus, *in de Intell.* 16.83–96, 38.84–9). But we do not possess the Forms themselves; rather, we only possess *logoi* of them in ourselves (Ammonius, *in Metaph.* 89.17–20). These are obscured by our embodiment.

What are these *logoi* supposed to be? Are they the same as the "rules" or "laws" that Plotinus says we have in our embodied intellects coming from Intellect? Perhaps, but the scant supply of examples suggests rather that they are universal concepts employed in propositional judgements. If we put this doctrine together with the rejection of the undescended intellect, and add that much of the discussion of the *noera eidē* is conducted within commentaries on Aristotle's *de Anima*, the possibility occurs that Ammonius and his school are appealing to Aristotle's active intellect to account for embodied higher cognition.[32]

In Philoponus' commentary on Aristotle's *de Anima* book 3.4–8, extant only in the translation of William of Moerbeke and known as *de Intellectu*, Philoponus fairly clearly takes this strategy. In his commentary on chapter 5, he sets out the elements of the solution.[33] First, he argues against Alexander of Aphrodisias and others that the active intellect is not to be identified with the divine intellect. Accordingly, the passive and active intellects are one, operating as principles of matter and form in the embodied person. Second, having already argued that the intellect pre-exists embodiment, and that intellect is the place of forms, he claims that the embodied intellect does possess; that is, already knows these forms.[34] Third, he follows Aristotle in maintaining that we are not aware of the presence of forms owing to bodily impediments (de Intellectu 33.87–8, 40.30–43, 57.68–9). Finally, what the active intellect does is actualize the forms present in intellect.

This actualization, however, is not the identification of the intellect with the intelligibles, as it is for Plotinus in the undescended intellect (de Intellectu 36.68–9). Rather, the actualization is of a representation of these intelligibles, specifically, a *ratio cognitiva* ("*gnōstikos logos*").[35] What these representations are exactly is not so easy to ascertain. Philoponus writes,

> Since the *rationes* of all things are in the soul, the *rationes* of the better things which are superior to it [are in the soul] in the form of representations (*eikonice*), the *rationes* of less good things which are posterior to it [are in the soul] as exemplars, when it actually produces the *rationes* which are in it, it actually becomes what they are either in a representative way or in an exemplary way, as we say that the image of Socrates becomes what Socrates is or that the *ratio* in the art of building becomes what the house is. (*de Intellectu* 83.37–48, trans. Charlton)

So, the actualization of the intelligible or intelligibles in the intellect is a representational state. The object of knowledge is the content of the representation, not the intelligible itself.[36] The knowledge is the identification of the intellect with the act of representing. So, presumably, when one understands or "sees" the truth of a proposition, the actualization of the intellect is this state of understanding.

Philoponus does not address the sceptical challenge posed by Sextus and faced by this account, but it is not too difficult to see how he might do so. Even though we know representations, we do not have to adduce a criterion whereby we can distinguish good representations from bad ones, for these representations are in effect actualizations of what we are potentially. We no more have to justify our claim to know a mathematical theorem than we have to justify our claims to possess cognitive powers when we are in fact actualizing them. When Plato in *Parmenides* has Parmenides sharply reject the claim that Forms are concepts and that knowledge of Forms is thus knowledge of concepts, he is assuming that concepts (*noēmata*) are purely representational and so not necessarily derived from the Forms themselves (*Prm.* 132b–d). By contrast, Philoponus seems to be relying on the doctrine of recollection as the basis for the claim that what is in the embodied intellect potentially is the Form cognitively; that is, in the way that Aristotle explains knowledge.[37] Representation, then, becomes actualization (cf. Ps.-Philoponus, *in de An.* 539.34–5).

Despite the differences among Platonists in accounting for knowledge, there is a deep underlying consistency in orientation. Knowledge, like digestion or pregnancy, is assumed to be a natural state. This naturalistic epistemology is, however, considerably removed from its contemporary counterpart. For the natural state of knowing is held to be an infallible mental state only available to intellects, the fundamental property of which is immateriality. All cognition, from the highest to the lowest, is mapped onto a hierarchical, integrated metaphysics. The epistemology is mostly unintelligible apart from the metaphysics, and vice versa. The epistemology and the metaphysics provide the framework for the various Platonic accounts of the facets of embodied human existence.

NOTES

1. The word is *nous*, not *epistēmē*, though they seem to be used synonymously. Cf. *R*. 534a4 with 511d6–e5.
2. See *R*. 477e6–7 where the property of knowledge is *anamartēton*. At *Tht*. 152c5–6 the property is *apseudes*.
3. Cf. *de An*. 430a4–5; 3.5.430a19–20; 3.6.430b25–6; 431a22–3; *Metaph*. 12.9.1074b38–75a5.
4. See *APo*. 1.33.88b30–37. Cf. 1.8.75b24; 1.18.81b5–7; *Metaph*. 7.15.1040a1–2; *EN* 6.3.1139b19–24. Plato, *Tht*. 187a1–201c7, argues that if true belief were knowledge, then false belief would not be possible. But since false belief is possible, true belief is not knowledge. This is because knowledge is (a) the presence of the knowable and (b) the awareness of its presence. If condition (a) alone is met that is not false belief; if neither (a) nor (b) are met, then there is not false belief either since there would be no object of belief.
5. See Cicero, *Acad*. 2.40; cf. Sextus Empiricus, *M*. 7.402–10. Sextus attributes this argument to Carneades, not to Arcesilaus.
6. Sextus, *M*. 7.252, says that the Stoics tried to counter the argument by adding the criterion "of such kind as could not come from that which does not exist". In other words, they wanted to guarantee the distinctness of the "graspable presentations" (*katalēptikai phantasiai*) as experienced by the knower from that experienced by the mere believer. But this can hardly be correct: there can be no such externalist criterion of infallibility, even if there can be an externalist criterion of truth.
7. See Gerson (2009: 124–33). All translations of texts are those of the author unless otherwise noted.
8. See also *PH* 2.70–72 for the *reductio* argument that the truth or falsity of representations is "ungraspable" (*akatalēptikos*); that is, indeterminable.
9. On the essential self-reflexivity of knowledge in Plotinus, see Kühn (2009).
10. See *Enn*. V.3[49].1.8–9 where it is sense-perception that cognizes "bodily nature" (*tou sōmatos physin*).
11. See *Enn*. V.3[49].2.10, 12 (*typoi*); *Enn*. V.3[49].3.12, "traces" (*ichnē*). At *Enn*. V.3[49].4.2, Plotinus uses the metaphor of "laws" (*nomoi*). See Emilsson (2007: 207–13). Plotinus may also have in mind the *megista genē* of the *Sophist*, namely being, identity, difference, motion and rest.
12. At *Enn*. V.3[49].3.8–9, normative rules are included, i.e. the rules that give us the ability to judge something good or bad. Perhaps such judgements are a function of judgements of unity; that is, the more unity, the better something is.
13. See *Enn*. VI.4[22].14.16–22; IV.8[6].4.31–5; IV.8[6].8; IV.7[2].13 for Plotinus' claim that our intellects are "undescended", a claim that most later Platonists rejected. On the undescended intellect, see Szlezák (1979: ch. 4).
14. See *Enn*. V.5[32], *That the Intelligibles are not External to the Intellect*.
15. Taking the word for belief, *doxa*, as derived from the word for "receive", *dechomai*.
16. At *R*. 508e1, the Idea of the Good provides truth to Forms and knowability (*gignōskesthai*). Cf. *R*. 509b5.
17. Aristotle's insistence that there is no thinking without images (see *de An* 3.7.431a17, 432a9, *Mem*. 1.449b31–450a1), is, I assume, a Platonic point. Thinking for Plato is *logos* in the embodied soul, and *logos* is or contains images. See *Tht*. 189e4–190a6; *Sph*. 263e3–8. The paradigm or principle of thinking is *epistēmē*, which is non-imagistic. For that reason it is the prerogative of the separate intellect, not its embodied manifestation. See Plotinus, *Enn*. V.1[10].6.45–6; V.1[10].3.8–10; V.1[10].7.42 for the sense in which Soul is a *logos*; that is, an image of Intellect. At *Enn*. V.3[49].3.44–5 Plotinus concludes his discussion of our identity as discursive reasoners with the pronouncement: "sense-perception is our messenger, but Intellect is our king", referencing Plato, *Phlb*. 28c7. We can only recognize the messenger for what it is if we acknowledge the king.
18. See *Enn*. V.5[32].1.50–68 where the argument is that if the intelligible were external to intellect, then intellect would have only representations of the (ontological) truth, not the truth itself. Such representations would include propositions. On non-propositional thought in Plotinus see A. C. Lloyd (1969–70), Sorabji (1982), Beierwaltes (1985), Emilsson (2007).
19. See *Enn*. III.8[30].10.1; IV.8[6].6.11; V.1[10].7.10–11; V.4[7].1.23–6; V.4[7].2.38; VI.9[9].5.36.

20. See *Enn.* VI.7[34].36.3–6 with *R.* 505a2. Cf. *Enn.* VI.7[38].40.1–4; VI.9[9].11.22–5. In this passage (VI.7[38].36.4) Plotinus says "either cognition or touching" (*eite gnōsis eite epaphē*) which I take it is not in contradiction to the claim that the One is beyond intellection. I suppose that the first alternative indicates "knowing" the One by knowing all Forms and that the second alternative indicates a super-intellective activity.

21. On the self in relation to the One see O'Daly (1973), Bussanich (1988), Remes (2007).

22. See *Enn.* VI.9[9].2.36. Cf. VI.9[9].7.28–34; V.3[49].6.39–43; V.6[24].5.16–19.

23. See Gerson (1997a), Chlup (2012: 142–4). On the identification of self-reflexivity with recollection, see *in Alc.* 13.12–6 [Segonds].

24. See Ps.-Simplicius, *in de An.* 211.1–8, where the point is made that self-reversion is necessary for an affirmation of the truth of what is present in the intellect. One cannot have a belief without believing that it is true, but one cannot believe one's belief is true unless one engages in self-reversion.

25. Proclus here follows Aristotle in distinguishing *energeia* from *kinēsis*, though the distinction has its root in Plato, who distinguishes the unique motion that is *kinēsis nou* from all others in *Lg.* 897d3.

26. Cf. *ET* 158. See *in Prm.* 1047a1–24, on the One as the *archē* of all cognition.

27. The only other Platonist who embraced Plotinus' argument for an undescended intellect is apparently Damascius, whose resultant heterodox epistemology cannot be treated here.

28. When Plotinus says at *Enn.* V.3[49].3.44–5, "sense-perception is our messenger, but intellect is our king", he is referring to the intellect that is "over us", like a king, namely the undescended intellect. This intellect is explicitly said to be "separate" (*chōristos*) in the line above. Proclus, *in Ti.* II.251.18–19, quotes this line but interprets it differently since he rejects the idea of the undescended intellect. Cf. *ET* 211; *in Prm.* 948.18–38.

29. One additional major consequence of the rejection of an undescended intellect is the felt need for some alternative means of access to the intelligible realm. Theurgy or pagan sacramentalism is, beginning with Iamblichus, motivated in part by this rejection. I shall not deal with this here.

30. See *ET* 176, 178; *in Prm.* 776.10. At *in Ti.* II.325.7–8 Proclus says that everything in the Living Animal is in the "intelligible mode" (*noētōs*) and in the Demiurge in the "intellective mode" (*noerōs*). Cf. 323.21; 418.6–10.

31. See *ET* 57, 12–13: "for even that which is soulless, in so far as it partakes of Form, partakes of Intellect or of the productive working of Intellect".

32. Cf. Ps.-Simplicius, *in de An.* 41.31–42.3. See Perkams (2008).

33. See *de Intellectu* 42.91–53.84 [Verbeke]. Cf. Ps.-Simplicius, *in de An* 244.39.41.

34. Philoponus, *de Intellectu* 38.84–39.43, is aware that Aristotle insists that the soul is mortal and does not pre-exist embodiment. But he notes, accurately enough, that Aristotle distinguishes intellect (or the "rational soul") from soul, *de An.* 2.2.413b26, and seems to want to say in chapter 5 that intellect both pre-exists embodiment and that it continues to exist post-embodiment. Cf. Proclus, *ET* 190; Ps.-Simplicius, *in de An.* 42.20–22.

35. See *de Intellectu* 9.11–12, 32.57. Charlton thinks that *cognoscibiliter* translates *gnōstikōs*, but this might well be synonymous with Proclus' *noerōs*. Cf. *in de An.* 111.19, 596.9; Porphyry, *Sent.* 42.12, *noeros logos*.

36. See *in de An.* 2.7–12. These are variously called "concept" (*conceptus*) and "theorem" (*theōrēma*).

37. See *in A Pr* 464.25–465.2. Cf. Ammonius, *in Cat.* 37.11–12. For Aristotle's usage see *de An.* 3.4.427a27–9. In this regard, Philoponus is hearkening back to the Middle Platonic position. See e.g. Alcinous, *Didask.* 155.26–9 [Whittaker], where embodied concepts (*physikai ennoiai*) have as objects expressions of the primary intelligibles (*prōta noēta*) that are stored up in the soul (*enapokeimenē*). Alcinous is, of course, not arguing against Plotinus' undescended intellect, but rather the Stoic materialist conception of knowledge.

18

Iamblichus on soul

John F. Finamore

Iamblichus of Chalcis (*c*.245–*c*.325 CE) was third in the succession of major Neoplatonic philosophers (after Plotinus and his pupil Porphyry), was possibly the student of Porphyry himself (and certainly knew him), and was the founder of his own school in Apamea in Syria. He is noted especially for bringing religious ritual (theurgy) into Neoplatonism. His *de Mysteriis* is a refutation of the more moderate Neoplatonism of Porphyry. In it Iamblichus argues for a correct kind of magic ritual to be used in practising his brand of Platonism. Iamblichus established a hierarchy of divinities from the One down through the realm of Nature, all of which were essential in the human being's ascent to the gods.[1]

Central to Iamblichus' philosophy is his doctrine of the soul. The human soul straddles two worlds (the realms of the Intelligible and of Nature) and can operate in both. Human souls descend to live a life on earth, but their real home is in the Intelligible World of the Forms. Through the help of the intermediary divinities, human souls re-ascend to the Intelligible and regain their proper abode. The human soul is the central character in this drama, and its purification through philosophy and ritual is central to its eventual ascent.

As in other areas, Iamblichus' philosophy of the soul had a large impact on later Neoplatonists. We are lucky enough to have large sections of his *de Anima*, preserved by John Stobaeus. His *de Mysteriis* and fragments from his Platonic commentaries also shed light on Iamblichean psychology, but the most important fragments are preserved by the author of the commentary to Aristotle's *de Anima*, who may or may not be Simplicius,[2] and by Priscianus of Lydia. We will consider all of these sources as we examine Iamblichus' unique doctrine of the soul.[3]

THE PLATONIC BACKGROUND

Plato laid the groundwork for all later Platonic conceptions of the soul: its immortality, punishment or reward in Hades, transmigration after death, affinity to the eternal Forms and involvement in the world of nature, and partition into different "parts". Plato was a dynamic thinker, often trying new ideas in various dialogues, criticizing earlier doctrines, and honing these doctrines carefully. The earliest and most important exposition of his beliefs occurs in the *Phaedo*. There the human soul is opposed to the body but nonetheless straddles the two worlds of pure thought and of corporeal existence. The soul is akin to the Forms – incorporeal, eternal, and capable of being purified and living apart from the body. In the *Phaedo*, it is the body that causes harm to the soul, and the philosopher is urged to undergo a kind of death, withdrawing as much as possible from the body and enjoying to the degree possible separate, incorporeal thought (*Phd.* 66a–68b). The body is a kind of tomb into which the soul is plunged and from which it must extricate itself to practise philosophy properly (*Phd.* 82e). In the underworld myth, philosophers after death live happily on the highest, purest reaches of earth, free from all bodies (*Phd.* 114bc). In order to attain this outcome, we must divest ourselves of all bodily influences and live a properly ascetic life.

In the *Republic*, however, Plato reconsiders the nature of the soul and finds that it itself contains a nature that is opposed to philosophical engagement. Famously, Plato divided the soul into three aspects (rational, spirited and irrational).[4] These three aspects demonstrate again the soul's intermediary nature, with the rational part capable of thought and the two lower parts connecting the soul more closely to the body and the physical world. In book 4, Plato establishes the three parts by showing that each of the parts can hold desires that are at odds with other parts. If two parts hold mutually contradictory desires (e.g. when the irrational part desires drink and the rational part opposes drinking), then the two parts must be separate (*R.* 436a–441c). The result is that the soul is not opposed to the body but rather to itself – or to a separate part of itself. In the choice of lives at the end of the Myth of Er in book 10, disembodied souls make bad choices because of past lives, and these choices (since they are not fully rational) involve the other two parts of the soul besides the rational (*R.* 619b–620d). Thus, even the disembodied soul has three parts.

This conception of the tripartite disembodied soul is taken up again in the *Phaedrus* myth (*Phdr.* 246a–257a), where the human soul is compared to a charioteer (the rational part) struggling to control two horses, one noble (the spirited part) and one recalcitrant and demanding (the irrational part). In this myth the whole soul is immortal, but it falls into a body because of the bad influences of the horses. The philosophical charioteer has the best (but still incomplete) control of the two horses. This myth clearly concerns the soul in its disembodied state at the beginning of a 10,000-year period at the very time when it has a chance to contemplate the Forms. The 10,000-year period is divided into ten 1,000-year periods, during which the soul is born and reborn into different bodies. If the soul can lead a philosophical life three times in a row, it can escape the cycle of births, but only for that 10,000-year period. It must descend again at the beginning of the next period. Thus, unlike the *Phaedo* myth (where the philosophical soul lives bodiless forever), in the *Phaedrus* rebirth is a constant process that begins anew every 10,000 years.

In the *Timaeus*, Plato re-conceives the soul's journey into body. There are still three aspects of the human soul (rational, spirited and irrational), but now they are conceived as separate souls, not parts of souls. The Demiurge creates the highest soul, the rational, and it alone is immortal. The younger gods create the lower two souls (or, perhaps, two aspects of a single soul), and these are mortal (*Ti.* 41a–44c). They house the souls in different parts of the body (*Ti.* 69b–71a). After death, the rational soul of the philosopher returns to its star (*Ti.* 42b). Plato does not make it clear if it must descend again. The lower souls perish with the body. The conception is therefore quite different from that of the earlier dialogues.

What remains constant throughout all of these dialogues is the soul's intermediate nature. The soul belongs properly to the world of the Forms, and its home is there – bodiless, contemplating eternal truths. It also lives for a time in the world of becoming, and it must live as purely as possible there to re-ascend to the Forms. The *Timaeus* stresses the intermediary nature of the rational soul via its very composition. The Demiurge fashions the rational soul from Being, Sameness and Difference of two types: not just of the Intelligible variety but rather blended with what is divisible and of the world of generation (*Ti.* 35a–36b). Thus, the soul has in its very make-up aspects of both worlds and can therefore be active in both realms. It is in this sense intermediary.

In the *Timaeus*, Plato also differentiates between the Cosmic Soul, which was blended first from these three elements, and the human soul, which was blended later from the same three elements but in a less pure state (*Ti.* 41de). The Demiurge fashioned these and then handed over the rest of creation (the lower two souls and the body) to the younger gods (i.e. the planetary gods, which the Demiurge had also fashioned). Thus, there is a clear differentiation between the immortal rational soul (fashioned by the Demiurge) and the other mortal parts (fashioned by the gods). It is the rational soul that is constructed from the intermediary Being, Sameness and Difference, and so it is that soul alone that is not only immortal but also intermediary between the Forms and Nature.

IAMBLICHUS INTERPRETS PLATO

Iamblichus, like all later Platonists, had to make sense of what Plato had written. In particular, he had to allow for the soul to be tripartite yet ultimately single and partless. The *Timaeus* gave him a way to do so, but the shadow of the *Republic* and its tripartition had to be handled as well. Unlike modern interpreters of Plato, Iamblichus could not appeal to a conception of Plato changing his opinion in different dialogues or trying on different hats. For Iamblichus, all the dialogues must espouse a single Platonic doctrine.

Iamblichus presents his solution in sections 10–13 of his *de Anima*. He begins by distinguishing the soul's essence from the powers it exerts (see Taormina 1993). A soul's essence is single,[5] while its powers are multiple. The powers of the soul include what it does: nourishing, perceiving, imagining, thinking, and so on. Its essence is the very nature of the soul, the life it leads while using its powers. Further, since the soul lives a double life – one in the body and one separated from it – it follows that its singular essence is split and that it brings forth different powers in each phase. Powers that are appropriate for the embodied soul (perception, say, or the functions of living in a body) would be inappropriate for the disembodied soul. It is, however, the same soul that exhibits these powers (section 10). The soul, then, has a continuum of powers. Following the *Timaeus*, priority is given to its disembodied powers – when the rational soul is separate from the body – but one cannot ignore the powers of the embodied soul, which differ from those of the disembodied.

Why do they differ? In section 11, Iamblichus argues (again using the *Timaeus* as his foundation) that the embodied soul has three parts that operate in three areas of the body. In *Ti.* 69c–70b, Plato said that the rational part resided in the head, the spirited in the chest, and the desiderative near the stomach. Iamblichus here accepts this description and adds that the rational soul itself has multiple powers that cover these lower functions. Thus the rational soul exhibits its powers through the body and the lower souls, and each of what for Iamblichus are two souls (rational and irrational) has its own place in the body complex.[6] The soul has parts when it is embodied, but these are separate from and used by the rational soul. The powers that are actualized in the lower souls and body originate in the rational soul, but the rational soul requires the lower parts to actualize them.[7]

Although Iamblichus uses the *Timaeus* for the basis of his doctrine of the soul, he still must account for the tripartition of the soul in the *Republic* and *Phaedrus*. He does so in section 12, following an older doctrine that he shares with Porphyry.[8] Both Porphyry and Iamblichus conclude that Plato's division of the soul was made for the sake of explaining the four virtues. For them, Plato's was a pedagogical move, not a philosophical doctrine. Thus the teachings of the *Republic* (and by extension the *Phaedrus* as well) are reduced to pedagogical analogies. They are true as far as they go, but the complete truth is that the soul has very many powers, more than tripartition suggests. Iamblichus combines Aristotle's psychic powers (nutritive, perceptive, imaginative, desiderative, rational) with Plato's two lower souls, and he thereby makes the whole conglomerate one that is necessarily attached to the soul/body complex. The rational soul itself is a separate entity.

If the rational soul is the source of the powers exhibited through the lower souls in the body, what is the status of these lower souls? Plato in the *Timaeus* makes it clear that the lower souls are mortal, but Iamblichus took a different view. Interpreting Plato's use of the word "mortal" in a liberal fashion as "related to mortal matters", he argues that these lower souls (though distinct from the rational soul) were in themselves immortal (Dillon 1973: 373–4). Further, Iamblichus accepted the existence of an immortal, ethereal vehicle of the soul, which housed the rational soul in its descent from the Intelligible and to which the lower souls were also attached. For Iamblichus, this whole complex (rational soul, irrational soul and vehicle) was immortal.[9]

A thorough discussion of the vehicle and its role in philosophy and theurgy is impossible here (see Finamore 2013). Briefly, the vehicle is the seat of the *phantasia* in the soul. It is therefore responsible for such things as our memory and our collection of perceptible images through which rational discursive thought is possible. It can also receive images through the rites of theurgic ritual, and these in turn become part of the ascent ritual which frees our rational soul from our bodies and raises it to higher levels of being. The vehicle's immortality therefore guarantees that our personality (including especially our philosophical nature) is our permanent possession.[10] Thus, after death, the soul leaves the body with its irrational soul and vehicle attached. What made us who we were on earth (our memories, our idiosyncrasies, our previous judgements) remain with us. As we enter Hades for punishment or reward, we are the same individual that we were before. Only the body is left behind.

Iamblichus' reassessment of Plato's doctrines is now coming into focus. Having collapsed the two mortal parts of the soul (desiderative and spirited) into a single irrational soul and having imported Aristotle's concepts of nutrition, perception and desire into that irrational soul and of *phantasia* into the psychic vehicle, he now maintains the immortality of all the soul elements. In *de Anima* section 13, he writes that these lower powers (i.e. the vehicle and irrational soul) continue to exist after the soul's separation from body. In *Myst.* VIII.6 he cites an Egyptian belief that human beings have two souls: one deriving from the Intelligible and the other from the planetary gods; that is, the rational and desiderative/ spirited souls as described in the *Timaeus*. The irrational soul causes us to be adaptable to the world of generation, but the rational soul is the one by which we intellegize and reunite with the Intelligible. We have already seen that the higher soul works through the lower. We can now also see that Iamblichus' solution helps bring the *Republic* and *Timaeus* into a kind of harmony. After the separation of soul and body and after the rational soul has ascended to the Intelligible (and perhaps higher, to the realm of the One itself), the soul returns to its irrational soul and vehicle. It thus has the same guiding control over these lower structures as it had had in its previous life. Thus, the rational soul can retain its own personality both in Hades (when it makes its own choice for its next life) and in the next life. There is, therefore, continuity between the various earthly lives of philosopher-theurgists.[11] Looked at from the perspective of the *Phaedrus*, we can control our problematic horses just as well as we could before in our previous existence.

There is one more preliminary point to be made here. We have seen that Plato differentiated two sorts of souls: divine and human. The Neoplatonic universe was more complex. In books I, II and III of the *de Mysteriis*, Iamblichus distinguishes various kinds of soul between the planetary gods and human beings, including especially angels, daemons, heroes and purified human souls. These souls each exist in separate *taxeis* or ranks. They cannot metamorphose into each other. Once a human soul, always a human soul – and so too for the other ranks. The higher ranks of souls are useful for human ascent, but they (like the planetary gods) are separate from us. Human beings are near the bottom of the hierarchy. Our ascent requires that we master our lower souls and become philosophically and theurgically purified and also that we engage the help of the higher ranks to raise us to the gods.[12]

SIMPLICIUS AND THE IAMBLICHEAN INTERMEDIATE SOUL

Iamblichus lays out his own doctrine of the soul and its intermediary nature in *de Anima* sections 6–7. In section 6, he (rather unfairly) places previous Platonists into a single camp: Numenius, Plotinus, Amelius and Porphyry all fail to mark the distinctions between various kinds of soul, and indeed even between Intellect and soul.[13] In section 7, he gives his own view: the human soul is an intermediary between Intellect above and the world of becoming below. It is distinct from Intellect and all the superior classes (angels, daemons, heroes, etc.), but is connected to them (above) and to generation (below). On the face of it, Iamblichus is not asserting anything new or revolutionary. All Platonists (including those he had mentioned in sect. 6) thought that the human soul was intermediary in just this way.

For Iamblichus' unique position on the soul, we must turn to the commentary on the *de Anima* of Aristotle that comes down to us under the name of Simplicius. The commentator tells us that Iamblichus not only thought that the soul was an intermediary but also that it had a double essence.[14] The soul is in its very essence both Intelligible (when it is engaged

in intellegizing apart from the body) and generated (when it is engaged in bodily activities). Proclus later rejected this idea, saying that the soul changed in its activities but not
in its essence.[15] Iamblichus' doctrine was more radical. Even as we are engaged in lower-
level activities concerned with matters down here, our soul is still essentially intelligible;
when it is engaged in pure thought above, it is still essentially involved in generation. As
the commentator says, the soul "does not simply remain but simultaneously both remains
what it is and becomes" (*in de An.* 90.4–5).

This doctrine is consciously associated with Aristotle's active and passive intellect.
Simplicius quotes Aristotle's words from III.5 that the active intellect, once it has been
separated, is what it is; that is, immortal (*de An.* 430a22–3) (quoted again and more fully
at *in de An.* 77.10–11). He can then argue that the rational soul differs from the rest of the
soul, which is necessarily tied to the body.

Although the rational soul is separate, it also forms a natural union[16] with the other
psychic powers (and therefore with the body to which they are attached) because of the
lives it projects in its inclination outside of itself (*in de An.* 77.9–10). This inclination is, of
course, a part of the life-drama of a human soul. As Iamblichus tells us, the soul, *qua* mean,
exists on two levels. In its descent it comes to live the embodied life, projecting and activat-
ing its lower powers. Later in the commentary, Simplicius writes, following Iamblichus,
that when the soul is dissipated and slackened,[17] it sinks down towards what is secondary.[18]
This slackening is part of the soul's dual essence in Iamblichean theory. That is to say, the
soul is essentially what it is before and after the slackening. Both essences belong to the
soul, and both essences are one. Returning to our passage, we move from this psychic
declension with its associated secondary lives to the kind of union it forms with the body.
It is not a structure of contiguous parts,[19] such as corporeal parts would form, but a union
appropriate for incorporeal entities, soul and body unified without division, one undivided
whole (*in de An.* 77.12–15). Simplicius is imagining a thorough interpenetration of immaterial soul with body. It is not a cobbled together composite, but a unified whole with the
incorporeal soul everywhere infused into the corporeal substrate.[20] If the union of soul and
body is unified in this way, he tells us, then the union of the separated and the unseparated
souls must be even finer (*in de An.* 77.17–19), no doubt because it is the compound of two
incorporeal substances. He qualifies the kind of inseparability he has in mind:

> Even if some [forms of life] are inseparable [from the body], the other is separable
> but because of its standing apart from itself and its inclination to what is outside of
> it, it is somehow inseparable and joined together with the other [lives]; it actualizes
> common activities in the whole of itself but separate activities by itself, since it is tran-
> scendent in relation to the other [lives]. (*in de An.* 77.19–23 [Hayduck], my trans.)

The human soul exists on various levels from the nutritive faculty below to rational soul
above.[21] Of all of the various levels, only one is separable from the body, that of the rational
soul. Mindful, however, of Iamblichus' dictum that the soul is a mean between intellect
and nature, and that it descends whole and changes thereby in its very essence (not just
in its powers or activities), Simplicius is careful not to cast the rational soul's separation
as permanent or even stable. In this composite of soul and body, the role of the lower
powers (the two mortal lower souls in the *Timaeus*) is to be permanently involved with
the body. They are inseparably linked, and yet they are still soul. Just as they are closely

intertwined with body, so too the rational soul is intertwined with them and these two psychic entities also form a compound. Thus, through this connection, the higher soul can be said to act with the lower soul in controlling the body. Nonetheless, this is only one aspect of the higher soul's life since it, unlike the lower, can live separately, however unstably and impermanently.

As Simplicius presents it, Iamblichus' doctrine makes the human soul schizophrenic. It is trapped in a twilight zone between pure contemplative thought and bodily activities. It can never fully embrace either extreme, but it lives in the middle. Returning to our passage, we can see how far Iamblichus' doctrine has affected Simplicius. Even the connection between higher and lower soul is schizophrenic in this sense. *Qua* embodied, the rational soul exists at that level, its ability to contemplate harmed and its activities demoted. *Qua* intellect, it lives separately and purely. But it can live neither life completely nor forever. Such is the fate of the human soul.

We can obtain a glimpse of the underlying Iamblichean doctrine in frag. 86 of Iamblichus' *Timaeus* commentary. There, Iamblichus is explicating *Ti*. 43a2–6. The younger gods have received the immortal soul from the Demiurge and have now borrowed fire, air, earth and water from the cosmos. The gods "glue together what they have taken into the same [mass], not with the indestructible bonds with which they themselves are held together but welding them together with thick rivets invisible because of their smallness, making each body one from all" (*Ti*. 43a2–4, my trans.).

Iamblichus interprets the "thick rivets" as "the union of the reason principles in nature" and the "welding together" as "their demiurgic coherence and union". Thus, Iamblichus sees the rivets as metaphorical. The gods connect soul to body by placing *logoi* in the soul. These would, of course, be *logoi* relating to the body and to the irrational powers. They would, in fact, make the higher processes of the immortal soul more attuned to the composite life of soul and body, with its concomitant irrational necessities. This union, which Simplicius described as a total infusion of soul and body, Iamblichus similarly explains as a *synochē* and *henōsis* granted from the creator gods. These words are intended to express the close union involved, as remarked by Plato when he says that the bond, though inferior to that in the gods themselves, nonetheless accomplishes a unity from multiplicity.

We now come to another problem, first articulated by Carlos Steel.[22] Simplicius (*in de An*. 313.1–30) reluctantly disagreed with Iamblichus' interpretation of the two intellects in 3.5. Whereas he sees the two intellects at work in the human soul, Iamblichus sees them as external, as in fact the transcendent Intellect and that participated by soul. So, to understand what Iamblichus thought, we must leave Simplicius behind and turn instead to Priscianus' *Metaphrasis in Theophrastum*.

Priscianus discusses intellect from *Metaphrasis* 25.27–37.34. The beginning of this section of the *Metaphrasis* is missing in the manuscripts. As Huby (1993) has argued, Priscianus makes use of Iamblichus' theories of the soul in this treatise, borrowing materials from Iamblichus (probably from his *de Anima*) to use in responding to problems raised by Theophrastus.

In the opening of this section as we have it (*Metaphr*. 25.27–27.7), Priscianus is concerned with the concept of the potential intellect that he has found in Theophrastus. He paraphrases Theophrastus: "One must take 'potentially' analogically in regard to the psychic intellect, as [it is] related to intellect in actuality, that is to the separated intellect" (*Metaphr*. 26.5–7 [Bywater], my trans.).

As Huby notes, it is difficult to decide if the term "psychic intellect" is from Theophrastus.[23] Like her, I find it doubtful. This seems an Iamblichean – or certainly Neoplatonic – phrase referring to the intellect in soul, which is to be contrasted with pure Intellect, and that indeed is how it is used here. Whatever distinction Theophrastus might have made, we have here a Neoplatonic one between transcendent Intellect and the intellect-in-soul.[24]

Priscianus then considers how this psychic intellect may be considered as "potential" (*Metaphr.* 26.12–23), and in so doing uses Iamblichean vocabulary with which we have already become familiar. Looking to Aristotle's comment at 429a27–9 that the intellect is the place of the forms potentially, Priscianus says that the psychic intellect is of this sort (*Metaphr.* 26.12–14). The problem for this intellect arises in the soul's inclination towards what is partial (*Metaphr.* 26.15–16). As we saw in the *de Anima* commentary, this declension leads the soul away from its intellectual activity and towards generation. Priscianus repeats the vocabulary of *in de An.* 241.9, using the verb *chalasthai* of the soul in this declension, saying that in the descent from the Intelligible "the connection between the two realms is somehow slackened and is not precise as was its unity in the separated [Intellect]" (*Metaphr.* 26.19–20).[25] Thus this passage echoes the Iamblichean doctrine of the soul's median position, existing in two realms and constantly torn between them. The descent causes essential changes in the soul itself, making it weaker and more attuned to the world of generation. Here, in Priscianus, we concentrate specifically on its deterioration *vis-à-vis* the Intellect. He stresses, therefore, the soul's need for the actualizing transcendent Intellect (*Metaphr.* 26.20–23): "Therefore for purely indivisible knowledge [the soul's intellect] itself has need of the Intellect that actually perfects, and the intelligible objects in it [i.e. in the psychic intellect] have need of the illumination of the separated intelligible objects so that its intelligible objects might be perfected [and so be] perfect."

Thus, the transcendent Intellect *qua* active intellect always has the intelligible objects actually, but the human soul possesses them only intermittently when it is actually in contact with the Intellect itself, for at that time the soul's intellect is actualized by the transcendent Intellect while the intelligible objects that are always in the actual Intellect become actualized in the psychic intellect as well.[26] Unfortunately for the human soul, this experience is necessarily temporary, and it descends again, becomes weakened thereby, and associates itself with life in the body. It is in this way, Priscianus says (*Metaphr.* 26.26–9), the psychic intellect is potential.

So far Priscianus has been talking as if there were only two levels under consideration: transcendent Intellect and the intellect in our souls. Later (*Metaphr.* 32.25–34.28), when he expounds the teachings of Iamblichus and Plutarch of Athens, whom he calls the "genuine interpreters" of Aristotle (*Metaphr.* 32.34), he adds the intermediate level of Intellect-participated-by-soul. Thus we have the three moments of the Intellectual Triad: Unparticipated Intellect, Participated Intellect, and Intellect in participation.[27] The last two moments of this triad cognize intelligible objects by using the *logoi* contained in them.[28] The actual intellect knows all things too but on a higher level, and thus the other two lower intellects know them in a secondary fashion (*Metaphr.* 33.7–17). Thus, it is clear that what the actual intellect does immediately, purely, and from a higher perspective, the other two intellects do in a less pure fashion, dependent on *logoi*.

After defining "actuality" as "indivisible unity" (*henōsis ameristos*) and "unified perfection" (*hēnōmenē teleiotēs*) of the Unparticipated Intellect and its objects (*Metaphr.* 35.4–5), he turns to "potentiality". Characteristically of Iamblichus (as we have seen), it involves a declension to a lower level and the resultant lack of wholeness. Priscianus defines "potential" as "involving a union with otherness and a descent into what is somehow determined and perfected" (*Metaphr.* 35.8–9). Thus, the resulting union is less cohesive. Intellect and intelligible object are no longer identical, but there is some otherness and the perfecting comes from outside rather than from the intellect itself.

Priscianus admits that this kind of potential union is more appropriately applied to the psychic intellect, which he describes in Iamblichean terms as having a "slackened" (*kechalasmenēn, Metaphr.* 35.14) union with its objects and thus dependent on the transcendent Intellect (*Metaphr.* 35.12–15).[29] Thus, as we have seen, the human soul is in its essence slackened and therefore incapable of complete union with the intelligibles and, further, in need of the transcendent Intellect for any union whatsoever.

What is striking is that the median intellect, the one participated by soul, is also slackened (*Metaphr.* 35.16–17). He says, "It is participated in because of its descent, it is suspended from its unifying and completely indivisible determinate, and it is perfected by it in its essence" (*Metaphr.* 35.17–18). As a mean term, it is lower ranked than the transcendent intellect and thus the human soul can participate in it, and moreover it is inferior to that intellect which provides its determinacy and perfection (two things which we saw the transcendent Intellect providing for itself). Nonetheless, this is a higher intellect than that in the soul, and *qua* intermediary, it is proximate to the transcendent Intellect, and therefore Priscianus is at pains to explain its potentiality. It is, he says, still closely related to the transcendent Intellect and perfects itself through it in a secondary way and is united with it in a secondary way (*Metaphr.* 35.19–23).[30]

The importance of the role of the Intellect in the life of the soul can be seen as well in frags 55 and 56 of Iamblichus' *Timaeus* commentary.[31] Iamblichus is interpreting *Timaeus* 36c2–5, where the Demiurge has split the soul ingredients into two and formed them into two circles: the Circle of the Same and the Circle of the Different. Iamblichus takes the novel approach that these circles refer not to the soul (as one would expect) but to intellect. He is able to do so because Plato had written that the motion was "carried *around*" (*periagomenē, Ti.* 36c3) and not carried *in* the soul (frag. 55.5–6), and it is the realm of the Intellect that surrounds the soul. Further, Iamblichus characterizes the motion of the Circle of the Same (which he associates with the transcendent Intellect in frag. 56) as a "motionless motion" (frag. 55.11–12), which exists in a unified way (55.12), is uniform (55.13), and is one and indivisible (55.13–14). The soul, on the other hand, is a self-moved motion (55.12–13) and dyadic (55.13), and divides and multiplies itself (55.14). As these epithets show, the relation between the transcendent Intellect and the psychic intellect here expressed is in harmony with that in Priscianus. The Intellect is more unified and hence more pure; the soul more divided.

In frag. 56 Iamblichus says that the Circle of the Same (the outer circle and the transcendent Intellect) contains (56.5) the World Soul and the individual souls[32] and is unmixed with them (56.6), while the Circle of the Different (the Participated Intellect) is *in* the souls (56.6), and is mixed with and directs them (56.7). It is because of this arrangement that the Whole Soul actualizes in a stable fashion and is unified with the Demiurge himself (56.8–9).

We can now see why Iamblichus located these circles higher and why he interpreted the active and passive intellects in *de An.* 3.5 as he did. Given his conception of the soul, as a mean whose higher and lower activities show that the soul is, in its very essence, a changeable mean between Intellect and Nature, the soul requires external aid to be able to function stably. On its own, it cannot attain the heights of the Intellect. It is marred in its very nature, destined to fall. Thus, without an active role for the realm of Intellect, the life of the soul is doomed to roaming the lower depths of the cosmos. For this doctrine, Iamblichus was able to find the textual support he needed in the two most important philosophers in the Neoplatonic canon, Plato and Aristotle.

CONCLUSION

Iamblichus' doctrine of the soul fits well with other tenets of his philosophy. As Plato prescribed, the human soul is intermediary between the unchanging world of the Forms and the ever-changing world of becoming. Like every Platonist before him (including some he himself criticized for not making the distinction clearly enough), Iamblichus taught that the soul was intermediary and took part in both realms at different times. This ability to live two lives, as it were, also aided in Iamblichus' religious philosophy. The Iamblichean metaphysical universe is a complex place. Above the Forms and the Intelligible is the One itself.[33] Below the Intellect are a series of psychic intermediaries (visible gods, angels, daemons, heroes, purified human souls). The human soul was placed far apart from the One and Intellect, adrift in the world of becoming. The soul could not ascend back to its Intelligible home without divine aid. Such aid was available through sacred rites and theurgical practices. As Iamblichus makes clear in *Myst.* V.18, the largest segment of humanity is held down by nature, is subject to fate, and never rises.[34] Other human beings can and do make progress through theurgical ascent. Such souls could be trained and purified so that, starting with the lowest intermediaries (heroes, daemons, etc.), the soul could begin to separate itself from its body and rise towards the gods.

The theurgic rites unlock the harnessed higher powers of the soul: its higher, separated life. In *de An.* section 48, Iamblichus notes that the human soul possesses "a disposition, good in form, similar to that of the gods in intellect" (*de An.* 72.7–8). This is the psychic equivalent of Intellect, what we find Iamblichus equating with Aristotle's passive intellect in his *Timaeus* commentary. This disposition is obviously not a fully formed intellectual principle, but it does offer the potentiality of the soul's union with the Intellect itself. That this disposition is "good in form" (*agathoeidē*) shows that the principle is also useful for ascending beyond the Intellect to the One. Iamblichus distinguishes the One of the Soul from the soul's intellect (*in Phdr.* frag. 6.2–3). Thus there are present in the soul the powers that can, with the help of theurgy, bring the human soul into union with the Intellect and the One.[35]

The relationship between psychology, metaphysics and religious ritual works out in the following manner. The human soul has capacities for union with the Intellect and One, but these are buried in the human soul. Most of humanity never ascends beyond discursive thought, and so the potential for ascent comes to naught. Those few who can rise higher require the help of theurgists, ritual and divine intermediaries. Through these the soul is freed from the body and rises higher, eventually rising to the Intellect itself. The intellective faculty in the soul has the potential for pure thought. The Intellect itself possesses the objects of thought actually. The process follows Aristotelian principles: what is potential must be brought into activity by something actual. This psychic faculty, then, is actualized by Intellect, which provides fully actualized Intelligible objects to those existing only potentially in the human soul. At this point, the soul lives its highest life, engaging in pure intellection. Even as it does so, the soul is slipping back into its lower condition. The psychic intellectual capacity cannot hold, and the soul begins to project its lower powers, ready to descend and work at a lower level. This is Iamblichus' unique doctrine. The soul, even when at its highest, slips and falls. Conversely, when a soul that can ascend is engaged in acts in generation, it also is raising itself higher. The soul has both aspects essentially, and both aspects exist in it simultaneously. There is an ever-present tug upwards and downwards.[36]

ACKNOWLEDGEMENTS

A large part of the section "Simplicius and the Iamblichean intermediate soul" appeared earlier in Finamore (2009). I wish to thank University of Laval Press for allowing me to include it here. I also wish to thank the editors, Svetla Slaveva-Griffin and Pauliina Remes, and the anonymous reader for their comments and suggestions.

NOTES

1. There is a complex interweaving of ancient ritual in Platonism before Iamblichus. Various earlier Platonists – such as Plutarch and Apuleius, to name two – accepted the role of magic and religion into Platonic philosophy. The *Chaldaean Oracles*, a collection of Platonically inspired writings that claimed to have been received from the soul of Plato by a certain Julian in the time of Marcus Aurelius, contained a rite of the ascent of the soul that Iamblichus later adopted. Outside of Platonism, the Hermetic and gnostic texts contained their own versions of ascent rituals; it is unclear how much Iamblichus read of these non-philosophical texts (and perhaps he read none of them at all). In the *de Mysteriis*, he did attack the kind of magic that we find in the magical papyri (the sort that involves forcing daemons and the souls of the recently dead to work the will of the conjurer) and substituted instead the theurgical rite in which human beings cooperated with gods and other divinities. On the role of theurgy in Iamblichean philosophy, see especially Shaw (1995); cf. Finamore (2013: 347–54).

2. There is a long debate over whether the author of the *de Anima* commentary and Priscianus are the same person. Steel (1978) championed the view; Blumenthal (1982, 1990, 1996a, 2000) was always doubtful, sometimes arguing that Simplicius himself wrote it and sometimes an unknown other Neoplatonist; I. Hadot (2002) has argued for Simplicius as its author, and see also I. Hadot (1978: 193–202; 1982: 46–67; 1990: 290–94). I have argued (Finamore & Dillon 2002: 18–24) that the author is neither Priscianus nor Simplicius. Perkams (2005, 2008) tries to show that the author of the commentary is Priscianus, but his arguments do not rule out the possibility that the author is Simplicius himself. Most recently, De Haas (2010: 759–60) has surveyed the evidence, and considers the question still open, although we should "respect the unanimous attribution of the manuscripts" that the author is Simplicius. Although we cannot decide the authorship question beyond a doubt, the contradictory positions of the two philosophers on the two intellects (see below) indicate that the author of the *de Anima* commentary is not Priscianus. I. Hadot's (2002) stance that the similarities between Simplicius and Priscianus are caused in part by the two authors' reliance on the same commentary of Iamblichus is enticing. This reliance would also explain the commentator's differences in style from other works of Simplicius and his use of vocabulary and technical terminology not found in his other works.

3. For the *de Anima*, see the edition of Finamore & Dillon (2002), where the Greek text and English translation are provided along with commentary. For the *de Mysteriis*, see Clarke *et al.* (2003) and most recently Saffrey & Segonds (2013). For the *de Anima* commentary, see the appendix to Finamore & Dillon (2002).

4. For a fuller discussion of the role of the soul in the *Republic* and *Phaedrus*, see Finamore (2005). See also Lorenz (2006: esp. 160–62) and G. R. F. Ferrari (2007: esp. 196–200).

5. Iamblichus introduces the concept of simplicity/singleness twice in section 12. He writes that Plato says that the soul has an incomposite essence (*asynthetos ousia*, 34.4) and Aristotle a simple essence (*haplē ousia*, 34.5). As we shall see later, the simple essence is also dual, but its binary nature is in itself unitary.

6. Strictly speaking, Iamblichus collapses the two Platonic lower souls into a single soul that he denominates

"irrational". For the Platonic precedent, see *Ti.* 69e4: τὸ τῆς ψυχῆς θνητὸν γένος, referring to both lower souls. For more on Iamblichus' irrational soul, see below.

7. See also my discussion in Finamore & Dillon (2002: 100–12).

8. See Porphyry, "On the Powers of the Soul", frag. 253.11–18 [Smith] (= Stob. 350.19–25). See also Finamore & Dillon (2002: 113–14); Finamore (2011: 3–5); and Perkams (2006: 169–71).

9. Iamblichus, *de Anima* section 13; *in Tim.* frags 81, 84. For the vehicle, see Kissling (1922) ; Dodds (1963: 313–21); Dillon (1973: 47; 1987: 898); Finamore (1985: 1–6, 11–27, 144–55).

10. For the role of theurgy in Iamblichean philosophy, see Finamore (1985: esp. 125–55; 2013) and Shaw (1995: esp. 129–228).

11. There would be continuity as well among the various lives of those who were not saved by philosophy and theurgy. For them, the mistakes that they made in one earthly life would be repeated in the next unless they turned to and followed the Platonic path.

12. For the distinct roles of these "Superior Classes" of souls and the differences among them, see Finamore (2010).

13. For a good overview of Iamblichus' strategy and his oversimplification of his predecessors' doctrines, see Dillon's notes in Finamore & Dillon (2002: 88–91).

14. *In de An.* 89.33–90.25 (= frag. C in Finamore & Dillon 2002: 234–7).

15. *ET* 191: "Every participated soul has an eternal essence but an activity in time." Cf. Perkams (2006: esp. 181–2); instead of one soul that undergoes substantive change, Proclus adopted multiple souls that were each individual substances. On the distinction between essence and activity in the soul, see Steel (1997a: 296–7).

16. σύμφυσις, 77.12. Compare Iamblichus, *de An.* sect.10, where he writes that Plato thinks that the psychic powers are "naturally conjoined (*symphytoi*, 34.3) with the soul".

17. διαφορεῖσθαί πως καὶ χαλᾶσθαι, 241.9.

18. See Simplicius 240.33–241.26, where he cites Iamblichus for this view. See the notes of Finamore & Dillon (2002: 256–8). The commentator mentions in this passage not only the descent (*neusis*) but also projection. He also quotes Aristotle, *de An.* 430a22–3.

19. The phrase is: ἡ σύμφυσις οὐ κατὰ συνέχειαν (77.12–13). The unified compound is not "continuous" in the sense that it is not like atoms placed side by side to create a whole compound.

20. Thus, the whole soul senses through the sensitive faculty (78.29–30), as we saw in Iamblichus' *de Anima*. The whole soul is involved "because each power is naturally united with the whole in an indivisible way" (79.30). It is this σύμφυσις of irrational powers with the whole soul that puts the whole soul over the whole body. See Urmson & Lautner (1995: 177 n. 310). See also 78.31–3: the whole soul holds the body together "by means of the lives that are inseparable from it because of their indivisible natural union in the whole"; and 79.29–34: various psychic powers (such as the vegetative, sensitive and rational) are of the same kind as each other and the whole "because of their inseparable natural union with each other". Looking at the larger cosmic significance, since the World Soul holds the same relation to the physical cosmos (its body), only without any slackening of its nature, the World Soul is fully united with the cosmos and so extends through it completely everywhere. The distinction is related to Plato's doctrine in the *Timaeus* that the World Soul's ingredients are purer than those of the individual souls. There is a general weakening that occurs down the ranks of soul, and the human soul therefore undergoes more "slackening"; that is to say, it more readily undergoes a fall into matter and an association with it, even to the point of identifying its essence with the material world.

21. On the bifurcation of the lowest phase of the soul between the body prepared for ensoulment and the ensouled body, see Blumenthal (1996a: 103–5). For the commentator's "multiplying levels", see Blumenthal (1982: 78; 1990: 308–9).

22. Steel (1978: 142–54). The "problem" arises only for those (such as Steel) who want to say that the author of the two works is Priscianus. Simplicius' radical break with Iamblichus shows one alternative to the question of how the human soul acts. For Iamblichus and Priscianus, the human soul is fundamentally attached and involved with the Intellect, and the soul's intellegizing depends in large part on the interaction of the Intellect itself. The author of the *de Anima* commentary sees the human soul as more independent. It does not seem likely to me that this fundamental contradiction in beliefs could exist in a single philosopher even over two separate works written at different times. Priscianus, a Neoplatonic contemporary of Simplicius and fellow student of Damascius, opted to follow Iamblichus; Simplicius chose another path.

23. Huby & Steel (1997: 64 n. 313). As she points out, Steel (1978: 148 n. 25), accepts it as Theophrastean. Huby points out that the term is found in Simplicius as well, which would point to Iamblichus as a common source.

24. For more on the relationship between the human rational soul with its intellectual component and Intellect itself, see Finamore (1997: 166–73).

25. On the verb χαλᾶσθαι, see Huby's note in Huby & Steel (1997: 64 n. 318). She there cites Steel (1978: 66 n. 53) for the words' first occurrences in Priscianus, Simplicius and Damascius. It is clear, however, that the word occurs in Iamblichean contexts and should be associated with him. See Finamore & Dillon (2002: 256). Cf. *Metaphrasis* 27.15, where Priscianus uses the verb again in a similar context.

26. For the rational soul's departure from the Intellect and its actualization by it, see 27.14–29. To have a clearer notion of how radical Iamblichus' doctrine is, consider it in relation to Plotinus' doctrine that the human soul is always intellegizing.

27. For these three moments in a triad in Iamblichus, see *in Tim.* frag. 54.6–7 and Dillon's note (1973: 335; cf. 33). On Priscianus here, see Huby in Huby & Steel (1997: 66 n. 362). For what follows in Priscianus (29.26–31.24), see Huby (1993: 10–12). As she shows, the remainder is about the individual soul, even though he has made this triple division here. She also shows how the passage is based on Iamblichean doctrines. For such triads in Simplicius, see Blumenthal (2000: 138 n. 296).

28. Huby, in Huby & Steel (1997) 68 n. 393, thinks that Priscianus "leaves it unclear whether the participated intellect and the rational soul are one and the same", but the tenor of this section of the commentary shows that he differentiates them both. The evidence from Iamblichus' *Timaeus* commentary (below) will verify this fact.

29. See also 35.15–16: the *chalasmos* is clearer with respect to the soul.

30. Cf. Priscianus' remarks at 35.29–36.5, where he again stresses the Participated Intellect's median nature. It is involved in a descent (so that the psychic intellect participates in it) and is actualized by the transcendent Intellect. He repeats the language of "perfection", saying that "it is connected to the First [Intellect] and is perfected by it, or rather it perfects itself through it [i.e. through the transcendent Intellect]".

31. Steel (1978: 143) has introduced passages from Simplicius' *Categories* commentary that show that Iamblichus in his commentary also stressed the role of active intellect in the soul's thinking.

32. For the "two souls" mentioned here being the World Soul and the individual souls "taken as a whole", see Dillon (1973: 337).

33. For Iamblichus' doctrine of three moments in the Realm of the One, see Dillon (1973: 29–33; 1987: 880–85).

34. *Myst.* V.17.223.8–12. See my discussion in Finamore & Dillon (2002: 161–3).

35. On these two psychic elements, see my note in Finamore & Dillon (2002: 211), Finamore (1997: 166–73), and Dillon (1973: 254). In *Myst.* V.22.230.14–231.2, Iamblichus claims that union with the One is rare and occurs only in advanced age. Clearly, advanced training in theurgy is required and, of course, takes time.

36. If the soul's ascent to the One is parallel to its ascent to Intellect, then this dual essence is also apparent in the ascent to the One. In this case, there are no objects to be actualized (because we are rising above the realm of Forms and of thought itself to pure unity without differentiation). The One – certainly the One Existent, the lowest of the Iamblichean Ones (see Dillon 1973: 31–3) – actualizes the potentiality in the One of the Soul; see *in Phdr.* frag. 6 and Dillon's note (1973: 254). The soul then experiences the complete unity of the One. The forces at work within the soul towards its declension can be overridden only by the One itself. In itself, the soul is helpless and dependent on the One.

19

From Alexander of Aphrodisias to Plotinus

Frederic M. Schroeder

PORPHYRY ON PLOTINUS' USE OF HIS SOURCES

In his *Life of Plotinus* Porphyry lists the authors who were read in the school of Plotinus and includes "Alexander" among the Peripatetics who were studied (*Plot.* 14.13).[1] Most scholars identify this figure as Alexander of Aphrodisias, although there are other candidates.[2] This chapter will, in any case, offer internal evidence for Plotinus' specific engagement with the text of Alexander. Earlier, in the beginning of the same chapter, Porphyry cautions us as to Plotinus' use of such texts:

> In writing he is concise and full of thought. He puts things shortly and abounds more in ideas than in words; he generally expresses himself in a tone of rapt inspiration, and states what he himself really feels about the matter and not what has been handed down by tradition. His writings, however, are full of concealed Stoic and Peripatetic doctrines. (*Plot.* 1.14.1–5)[3]

Clearly, Porphyry would convince us that Plotinus absorbs his erudition into his own broad philosophical vision. Concerning Longinus, Plotinus observes: "Longinus is a scholar (*philologos*) but certainly not a philosopher (*philosophos*)" (*Plot.* 14.19–20). As his story of Plotinus' criticism of Longinus reveals, Porphyry clearly sees Plotinus as more the philosopher than the philologist. This preference for philosophy over philology on the part of Plotinus accords well with his original, creative and philosophical attitude towards his sources. Scholars have expressed a range of opinion that varies from great optimism to extreme scepticism in seeking the sources of Plotinus in Alexander (see Schroeder 1984: 240–42; Sharples 1987: 1220–23).

A CRUX IN ALEXANDER *DE ANIMA* 88.26–89.6

On a minimal interpretation of the notoriously difficult chapter, *de Anima* 3.5., Aristotle sees in play in his noetic doctrine the categories of potency and act that are at work in his ontology.[4] The Active Intellect (or Productive Intellect) acts as the efficient cause for potential intelligibles to become actual intelligibles, even as light is the efficient cause for colours to change from being potential colours to being actual colours. Some are convinced that Aristotle may have had in mind the analogy of the sun and the Good in *Republic* 508a4–509b10 where, even as the sun is the cause of both being and being visible to the visible objects in the sensible world, so is the Good the cause both for being and for being intelligible in the intelligible realm.[5] We shall be asking whether Alexander and Plotinus interpret *de Anima* 3.5. with reference to the Platonic analogy.

We shall, later in this chapter, be examining the influence on Plotinus of Alexander's understanding of the Aristotelian Active Intellect and the analogy of light. We shall begin our study of Alexander's reception of the Active Intellect together with the analogy of light in Aristotle with the presentation of an important crux of interpretation. It is important to keep in mind that Alexander, in exploring the role of the Active Intellect in causation, concentrates on the Active Intellect, not as intellect, but as intelligible.

At *de Anima* 88.26–89.6 Alexander states a general principle:

> For in all things that which is especially (*malista*) and eminently (*kyriōs*) what it is is the cause for other things of being such as they are. For that which is especially visible, such as light, is the cause for other things of their being visible and that which is especially and primarily good is the cause for other good things of their being good. For other things are judged good by their contribution (*synteleiai*) to this. Indeed that which is especially and by its own nature intelligible is, it is reasonable to maintain, the cause of intellection of other [intelligibles]. Such an entity would be the Active Intellect.[6]

Merlan remarks:

> The causal relation is of the type "whatever is eminently some kind of being imparts this kind of being to everything which is less eminently the same kind of being"....
> It is obvious that Alexander presents a very particular type of causation. It is as close to what is causality in Neoplatonism as possible.   (1969: 38–9)

Moraux (1942: 90–92) argues that this principle of causation is well expressed by the medieval maxim: *Propter quod alia, id maximum tale* ("that on account of which other things possess a certain quality itself holds that quality supereminently"). This maxim he misconstrues to mean that that which holds a quality supereminently is the cause of that quality in something else. As A. C. Lloyd (1976: 150) properly observes: "Alexander was not at that point trying to prove the *existence* of something supremely intelligible." Thus Alexander is not reasoning from the existence of, for example, good things to the necessary existence of a supreme good. Rather he is assuming the existence of that principle (e.g. a supreme good) and stating that all other goodness is to be derived from it. The statement is not a conclusion, but a premiss, of argument. Moraux, in misinterpreting the maxim, correctly interprets the passage at hand (Schroeder 1981: 222). The doctrine expressed by the formula that that which holds a quality supereminently is the cause of that quality in other things is, in any case, to be found in Aristotle and hence need not be regarded as Platonic.[7]

It is significant that in the case of goodness Alexander adds the rider: "Other things are judged good by their contribution (*synteleia*) to this." This addition is significant because it represents a departure from the apparent monism of causation in the passage. The effect contributes to its causation. Donini sees Alexander here as applying a contribution of good things to the Good that is not accorded to a contribution by visible things to visibility or intelligibles to intelligibility. He thinks that Alexander shrinks from the Platonism of positing a supreme Good from which all goods are derived by participation. He sees such contribution as modifying the principle that that which is eminently what it is is the cause of that quality in something else. Alexander is distancing himself from Middle Platonism (Donini 1974: 46–8). If we may rescue Alexander from the charge of special pleading, that is, that he is advancing the argument concerning contribution on the part of good things to goodness simply in order to dissociate himself as an Aristotelian from Platonism, we should do so.

To understand the contribution on the part of good things to the Good it is germane first to enquire why anyone would wish to see Platonic (let alone Middle Platonic or Neoplatonic) overtones in this passage. Let us for the moment confine ourselves to the passage's account of goodness (*de An.* 89.2–4) (Merlan [1969: 38–9] focuses upon the instances of visibility and intelligibility). We are aware that Aristotle criticized the Good of Plato's *Republic* on the grounds that "good", since it is predicable in different senses in different categories, cannot serve as a genus in which other goods participate. Therefore the Good cannot function as the formal cause of goodness.[8]

Bergeron and Dufour properly, in their commentary on Alexander's *de Anima*, argue that, while the Good may not be the formal cause of goodness, it is the final cause.[9] If this is the case, we need discover no Platonism in the present passage. To put it another way, Aristotle is not rejecting the Idea of the Good (he equates the Good with the God of *Metaphysics* 12),[10] but is identifying the Good as the final cause.[11] While Bergeron and Dufour elsewhere consistently translate *synteleia* as "contribution", and the verb *syntelein* as "contribute", they in this instance elect to translate the noun as "association", as in a community organized around a common goal (*de An.* 89.4) (Bergeron & Dufour 2008: 349–50). Even in this case, there is surely "contribution" of some kind: the members of the community must contribute something to their common good. As I remark in my review of their commentary:

> Alexander argues that, whereas the lower phases of the soul exist for the sake of survival, the disposition (*hexis*) of intellection contributes (*suntelei*) not to survival, but to well-being (81.15–16). Thus the *hexis* of intellection is judged good by its contribution to goodness. Also, by stating that language contributes to the best social life for man, Alexander is claiming that in this way it is being evaluated for its contribution to goodness (49.23–5; cf. 93.17–20 for a similar use of *synergein* and contribution to goodness). What is more, it would seem that contribution is an important theme in Alexander's psychology generally. Alexander states (75.24–6) that each lower stage of soul contributes (*syntelein*) and has as its end the higher state that develops from it.   (Schroeder 2010: 85)

Bergeron and Dufour (2008: 350) contend that their translation of *synteleia* as "association" is supported by Aristotle, *Metaphysics* 1075a11–22. There Aristotle asks whether the good exists as something self-sufficient, or whether it is immanent in the order of the universe, or both. It is both, as in the instance of an army: the good is present both in the order of the army and in the general, but especially in the general (as source of order). All things "are ordered together (*syntetaktai*) toward one thing" (*Metaph.* 1075a18–19). It is of interest that Pseudo-Alexander glosses *syntetaktai* with the verb *suntelein*, not in the sense of "association", but of "contribution" towards the completion of the cosmos on the part of components that are not equal in dignity (*in Metaph.* 715.8–9).[12] From this discussion we may see that the appropriate translation of *synteleia* at Alexander, *de Anima* 89.4 is not "association", but "contribution".

Aristotle's example of the general and the army would well illustrate Alexander's concept of contribution. The general is eminently good (at victory). The soldiers are also good in a lesser degree. Yet they make their own contribution towards victory. In the psychological hierarchy of Alexander, each phase contributes to the good of the higher phase. The notion of contribution also sits well with the idea that the supreme good is not the formal, but the final, cause of goodness. The soldier (or the lower phase in the hierarchy of soul) aspires to and contributes towards the *finis* or goal of goodness. Alexander's use of *synteleia* may owe a debt to Aristotle's *Nicomachean Ethics* I.4.1096b29 where Aristotle, maintaining that "good" is not a univocal term, yet seeks a commonality of meaning whereby things are good by contributing to the good as one end.[13] Thus Alexander's use of *synteleia* in the sense of "contribution" is compatible with the view that the Good is final cause.

Yet Aristotle shows himself to be a Platonist.[14] While he rejects the Good as formal cause, he does recognize the same transcendent and metaphysical principle as final cause. Thus he applies to the Good his own classification of causes: clearly the Good is neither a material nor an efficient cause. Since it is not the formal cause, it remains for it to be the final cause as indeed it is. Thus Aristotle accepts the Platonic Good as adapted to his own philosophy. As was noted above, scholars have seen the analogy of the Active Intellect to light in Aristotle, *de An.* 3.5 as drawing its inspiration from the analogy of the sun to the Good in *Republic* 508a4–509b10.[15] Alexander in following Aristotle on the Good as final cause is, like Aristotle, a faithful Platonist. However, there is nothing in this passage that would invite us to see anything that is (in the words of Merlan) "as close to what is causality in Neoplatonism as possible".[16]

ALEXANDER ON THE PHYSICS OF ILLUMINATION

Aristotle defines light as the act of the diaphanous *qua* diaphanous. The diaphanous is that which is, like air, water or transparent solids, visible, not in itself, but through the colour of something else. Colour, which is by nature visible, sets in motion that which is diaphanous in act. Aristotle speaks also of another visible object which, he says, shall remain nameless, but is clearly phosphorescence (*de An.* 2.7.418a27–8; 419a2–6). Light is not a body and is not an emanation from a body, either fire or another luminous body, but is the presence (*parousia*) of fire or something like fire in the diaphanous (*de An.* 2.7.418a26–418b17).

As we have seen, Alexander, in drawing the analogy of the Active Intellect to light in Aristotle, *de An.* 3.5, says that light, which is eminently visible, is the cause of visibility for other things (89.1–2). To understand the analogy of light, it is surely worthwhile to explore what Alexander says, not about light as the term of an analogy, but about natural light itself in the process of illumination. In pages 42–4 Alexander explores the physics of light. Alexander here, in the treatment of the physics of light, as in his analogy of light, says that light, which is supremely visible, is the cause for other things of their being visible (44.13–15). (There are some objects, such as the divine body, fire and phosphorescent objects, that are by nature luminous.[17] We shall define "illumination", for the purposes of the present discussion, as a process in which a source of light illumines an object that is not itself a source of light.)[18]

The sensible objects that belong to sight are colours and objects that can be seen in the dark (e.g. phosphorescent objects). The latter are not properly colours because they do not fit the definition of colours as that which may move the diaphanous in act. We translate the word *diaphanēs* as "diaphanous" or "transparent". Examples of diaphanous objects are air, water and such solids as do not contain their own colour, but when moved by colours can serve as a medium through which vision may perceive colours. These become diaphanous objects when they are illumined (42.4–11).

Alexander then considers the question of how colour comes to be in light and light comes to be in the diaphanous (42.19–43.4). He begins with a negative statement: light is not an emanation. This denial doubtless springs from the conviction that light is incorporeal, as he explains at 43.11. (Both in his view that light is not an emanation and that it is incorporeal he follows Aristotle, de An. 2.7.418b13–17.) However, in addition to the denial of corporeality, Alexander is thereby rejecting the hypothesis that light is the effect uniquely of its source. He also denies that light is the form, the diaphanous the matter, of illumination, so that the diaphanous as matter would receive the light as its form. Similarly, colour is not the form that is received by the diaphanous in act as the matter that would receive that form (42.18–22).

Alexander then offers a proof that light is neither an emanation nor a formal cause. He says that "when those things are withdrawn" that cause colour and light to be in the diaphanous, then colour and light also disappear. We may suppose the reasoning to be: if light is an emanation, then we might expect something luminous to remain after withdrawal of the source of illumination (as something remains heated if fire is withdrawn). If light is the form of the diaphanous, then that form would abide after its causes were removed. Let us examine more closely the phrase "when those things are withdrawn".[19] What is included in "those things"? Alexander specifies that if that which illumines[20] is not present, then light disappears from the diaphanous and if those things that induce colour[21] are withdrawn, then colour retires from the diaphanous. He later says that light comes about in the diaphanous by the presence (*parousia*) of fire or the divine body.[22] This presence he interprets in terms of relation (*schesis*):[23] for, he argues, light comes about through the relation between the source of illumination and the illumined object. For light is incorporeal, and for this reason the generation of light is atemporal (43.8–11). It would seem reasonable to conclude that "those things" include both the source of illumination and the source of colour.

Having rejected the hypotheses concerning emanation and formal cause, Alexander says that light comes about in the diaphanous because there is a certain change (*tis … kinēsis*) from both.[24] By "both" he means both the source of light and the source of colour.[25] Alexander proceeds to specify that the change in question is in accordance with presence construed as relation (as we have seen, relation between the source of illumination and the illumined object [the diaphanous]).

Alexander offers an example: it is on the same model that things are seen in mirrors. The mirror would qualify as exemplifying the definition that the diaphanous solid is without its own colour (42.7–8). The mirror (*qua* reflecting surface, not *qua* its material substrate) borrows colours from other things. When someone stands before the mirror, that person is the source of light and colour. The mirror is the diaphanous object that receives light and colour. A sort of change arises from the presence of the sources of light and colour. As we have seen, the presence of the source is construed in terms of relation. This means, of course, that the source of light is a necessary, but not a sufficient cause of illumination because illumination proceeds from the presence of the source in accordance with the relation between the source and the illumined object.

Illumination then produces a "kind of change" (*tis … kinēsis*) in the illumined objects. The only kind of change that we can imagine here would be qualitative change (since it cannot be a change of size or place).[26] Yet Alexander, as we have seen, qualifies "change" here as "a kind of change". The qualifying *tis* ("kind of") indicates that he cannot be content simply with qualitative change.

The reason for this discontent is revealed from a study of texts beyond Alexander's *de Anima*, the *in de Sensu* and the "How according to Aristotle sight comes about". In Alexander, *in de Sensu* (132.2–6),[27] we read:

> For air and the diaphanous are not illumined through change (*kinēsis*), but all at once the diaphanous and the illumined come about from that which is potentially diaphanous and illumined, passing from a state of not having to a condition of having, not through receiving and being affected (*kineisthai*). For it is by relation (*schesis*) and presence of the source of light toward that which is by nature to be illumined that light is brought about.

Alexander further contrasts the illumination brought about by this relation with the causation of sound and scent both of which require a transition (*diadosis*) and change (*kinēsis*) taking place in time (132.14–15). The *kinēsis* that is excluded here is an alteration that takes place over time through a medium (*sc.* air). When Alexander at *de Anima* 43.1–2 speaks of illumination as *tis kinēsis* the function of the indefinite pronoun is to exclude communication through a medium over a length of time. We should recall that Aristotle says of light at *de An.* 2.7.418b14–17 that it is "neither fire nor corporeal at all, nor an emanation from any body (for it would in that case be a kind of body), but the presence of fire or something of that nature in the transparent". Alexander remarks at *de Anima* 42.20–21 that light is not an emanation from a source of light. The incorporeal nature of light forbids that light be transmitted through a corporeal medium. Alexander in the *de Anima* 43.10–11 says: "For it is in relation to the source which is capable of illumining and those things that are capable of being illumined that light is. For light is not a body" (cf. Schroeder & Todd 2008: 665). Illumination then produces a kind of change (*tis kinēsis*) in the illumined objects. Since light is incorporeal, change cannot be transmitted either through space or in time, but must take place all at once.

There is another text which Accattino and Donini (1996: 181–2) think, because of its affinities with the *in de Sensu*, may reflect the thought of Alexander: the treatise in the *de Anima Mantissa* entitled "How according to Aristotles sight comes about" (143.4–18) also denies that illumination and visibility require an alteration (*alloiōsis*) defined as a change that comes about in time and involves a transition. Illumination rather comes about by the presence (*parousia*) of the luminous source and its relation (*schesis*) with the illumined object. The relationship is compared to that of two objects that are externally, but not internally, related (being on the left of or being on the right of). We have seen that in the *in de Sensu* sight and sound involve a communication over distance and in time. The *in de Sensu* excludes light from such communication. Doubtless the intent of this treatise is also to exclude such communication (Accattino & Donini 1996: 181–2). Sharples (2004: 127) is of the view that the relationship described by the imagery of being on the left or on the right would signify a "Cambridge change"; that is, a change in which the externally related objects (the source of light and the illumined object) would remain unaffected.

Significantly, in the passage which we discussed above in which Alexander considers the presence of light in terms of relation (*de An.* 42.19–43.11), Alexander uses the image of mirrors. If the source of light and colour (in this case reflection) is removed, there is no illumination (reflection). Now the word *katoptron* can refer not just to a mirror as artefact, but to any reflective surface (Schroeder 1980: 55 n. 58). The mirror or reflective surface is not altered *qua* bronze, silver, water, and so on, but *qua* reflective surface. So when Alexander speaks of how the illumined object is not affected by the illumination, he does not mean that there is no effect. Rather, the reflective surface is changed in the sense that when the object before the mirror stands in a relation with the reflective surface, that surface reflects the source of the reflection. This same pattern of relation will apply to instances of illumination other than reflection. We also need not think that illumination *is* the relation between the source and the illumined object (see further Schroeder & Todd 2008: 666). Rather, that relationship is the condition of illumination taking place.

We are now in a position to see why Alexander refers to the change that takes place as "a kind of change" (*tis ... kinēsis, de An.* 43.1–3). To speak, for example, of qualitative change would entail a contradiction of the denial that illumination involves *kinēsis* in the *in de Sensu*. This denial applies to the corporeal substrate of illumination. Yet the surface of the substrate allows illumination to take place without any change to the substrate itself. The pronoun *tis* is introduced in order to show that *some kind* of change is taking place, namely in the case of mirrors, *what* is being reflected, for example, now one person, then another (considered as sources of reflection in colour and illumination).[28]

Alexander also says that when something can in act (*kat' energeian*) appear through (*diaphainisthai*) what is diaphanous, then the diaphanous is eminently what it is and achieves its perfection (*teleiotēs*) and native form from light as far as it is diaphanous (43.5–8). This statement implies that the diaphanous is not just eminently visible when it is illumined, but confers visibility on things that are seen through it. Thus light, when it comes to be in the diaphanous, confers illumination on everything in its field that is capable of being illumined. As we have seen, the diaphanous cannot be a medium in the sense in which air is a medium through which sound or scent are communicated over a distance and through an interval of time. Light is incorporeal and exists as pure activity (*energeia*).

We have seen that Alexander gives as examples of the diaphanous transparent things, air, water and solids that do not have their own colour. Later he extends the definition of the diaphanous to things that have their own colour. Every body that is receptive of colour shares more or less in the quality we call "diaphanous" (44.20–21, cf. 45.5–19). With this extension of the term, "diaphanous" would seem to mean not simply "transparent", but "capable of being illumined or of appearing in the diaphanous medium".

Furthermore, there are two kinds of the diaphanous. The first is indefinite, and light is the act of the indefinite diaphanous *qua* diaphanous (44.13–15). The second is definite and its limit is colour. There are, in the case of objects that have a definite diaphanous character, two limits, one *qua* physical object, the surface, and another limit *qua* coloured, which is colour (45.20–46.1; cf. Aristotle, *Sens.* 3.439a28–33). Alexander also establishes a hierarchy among diaphanous objects. The source of light (e.g. fire) is white and white is the colour of light at its purest. That white becomes mingled with other colours in the diaphanous medium. In objects with their own colour, the presence of earth can impede the purity and luminosity of colour (45.5–19). So in the diaphanous there are hierarchical distinctions based on purity. We may ask whether the expansion of the definition of "diaphanous" leaves it lacking in meaning.

Generally there seem to be a number of contradictions in Alexander's account of the physics of light. We shall see that Plotinus sees these contradictions as arising from Alexander's failure to think through properly the consequences of the incorporeal character of light. If light is incorporeal and not transmitted through air or some other diaphanous medium, then why is there need for a diaphanous medium at all? And why compound the problem by expanding the definition of "diaphanous" to that which is capable of appearing through a diaphanous medium? Alexander interprets the presence (*parousia*) of the source of illumination in terms of the relationship (*schesis*) between the source of illumination and the illumined object. According to my interpretation (which resists the notion of "Cambridge change"), the word "relation" (*schesis*) does describe a spatial relation between the source of light and the illumined object: if I am correct in this, why should location be so important for the generation of an entity that is incorporeal and timeless? (Plotinus, as we shall see, regards light as the act of a luminous body *qua* luminous [i.e. not *qua* corporeal] directed externally.)

PLOTINUS ON THE PHYSICS OF ILLUMINATION

Plotinus says (*Enn.* IV.5[29].6.27–31[29]): "But, just as life, being an activity (*energeia*), is activity of the soul (*psychēs ... energeia*), and if something, body for instance, is there, it is affected, but life also exists if this something is not there, what would prevent this being so also in the case of light, if it is a kind of activity?" In the case of life, that is an activity of the soul, life abides whether the body lives or dies (cf. *Enn.* IV.5[29].7.55–60). So the illumined object is immaterial to the existence of light. If the object is illumined, then it is illumined, but light remains an activity that is independent of the object being illumined. The context is provided by a discussion of whether air is necessary to the existence of light. Since light is essentially an activity, it does not require air as a medium (*Enn.* IV.5[29].6.1–17). We may note that Plotinus' position is opposite to that of Alexander, who uses air as an example of the diaphanous, and that for Alexander, light is the act of the diaphanous *qua* diaphanous. Clearly for Plotinus the diaphanous, while it may be illumined, is not essential to the existence of light. This is his argument:

But the activity within the luminous body, which is like its life, is greater and is a kind of source and origin of its [outward] activity; that which is outside the limits of the body, an image of that within, is a second activity which is not separated from the first. For each thing that exists has an activity which is a likeness of itself, so that while it exists that likeness exists, and while it stays in its place the likeness goes far out.   (*Enn.* IV.5[29].7.13–19)

Thus the emanation of a second activity from the primal activity of its source is an expression of a more general principle.[30]

Despite his principal disagreement with Alexander, Plotinus expresses his view on light in language that is reminiscent of what we have already encountered in Alexander:

The light from bodies, therefore, is the external activity of a luminous body; but the light in bodies of this kind, bodies, that is, which are primarily and originally of this kind, is altogether substance, corresponding to the form of the primarily luminous body. When a body of this kind together with its matter enters into a mixture, it gives colour; but the activity by itself does not give colour, but only, so to speak, tints the surface, since it belongs to something else and is, one might say, dependent on it, and what separates itself from this something else and is, one might say, dependent on it, and what separates itself from this something else separates itself from its activity. But one must consider light as altogether incorporeal, even if it belongs to a body. Therefore "it has gone away"[31] or "it is present"[32] are not used of it in their proper sense, but in a different way, and its real existence is as an activity. For the image in a mirror must also be called an activity: That which is reflected in it acts on what is capable of being affected without flowing into it; but if the object reflected is there, the reflection too appears in the mirror and it exists as an image of a coloured surface shaped in a particular way; and if the object goes away, the mirror-surface (*to diaphanes*) no longer has what it had before, when the object seen in it offered itself to it for its activity.   (*Enn.* IV.5[29].7.33–49)

We can see that Plotinus and Alexander agree that light is incorporeal (even if it is derived from a body). Yet Alexander defines light as the perfection of the diaphanous *qua* diaphanous. This is not the case for Plotinus, for whom light is the procession of light as a secondary act derived from the primary act of the luminous body. Alexander denies that light is an emanation or efflux from fire or the divine body. In this he is, as we have seen, avoiding the implication that light is corporeal. For Plotinus light does flow from its source, but in such a way that corporeality is avoided (even if the luminous body from which it proceeds is corporeal). Light as secondary activity flows from the primary activity of the source. For Alexander, illumination is caused by the presence (*parousia*) of the source of light in accordance with the relation (*schesis*) of the source of light and the object of illumination. Whereas Alexander then, in seeking to avoid the corporeal character of light, denies that it is an emanation from a source of light, Plotinus, while also denying that light is bodily, affirms that light is an emanation from a luminous source.

The words "when a body of this kind enters into a mixture ..." (*Enn.* IV.5[29].7.37–8) are rather opaque. Plotinus is distinguishing between (a) the internal activity of the luminous body; (b) the secondary activity of light that proceeds from the luminous body; and (c) the product of the secondary activity. What, we may ask, enters into a mixture with what? At *Enn.* IV.5[29].7.49–62 Plotinus says that life flows from the upper soul. He then entertains the question of whether the life in the body (distinct from these activities of soul) is not the product of the activity of life, rather than that activity itself? Similarly, the light that is mixed with bodies is a product distinct from the light that flows from the luminous source. The products of illumination may disappear but not the activities that make them. Now the light that is the first and internal act of the luminous body is the essence of the luminous body *qua* luminous body. Yet the body is, apart from being a luminous body, a body with matter that can be "mixed up with" other bodies in the sense that it causes them to be illumined. As such it gives colour. By this Plotinus must mean that the light itself is without colour, but the body *qua* body (not *qua* luminous body) conveys colour. Thus a red rose placed in front of a mirror conveys the light from the source that illumines it into the mirror. But the colour red it possesses *qua* body, and this colour appears *per accidens* in the mirror. So Plotinus is uncomfortable with "gives colour". It rather tints the surface of the illumined object. The secondary light that proceeds from the illumined body is in no way affected. The tint on the surface of the illumined body is absent from[33] the secondary act of illumination. Thus Plotinus does not accord to colour the importance attached to it in Alexander, for whom it is that which renders light visible (see § "Alexander on the physics of illumination" above). He also avoids the apparently contradictory notion that colours can be transparent by the fact of appearing through a diaphanous medium.

In the case of reflection, Plotinus begins by saying that the image of the figure that causes the appearance in the mirror is an activity which proceeds from its cause without (corporeal) emanation. Yet because light is incorporeal, the words "it has gone away" (*apelēlythe, Enn.* IV.5[29].7.42; cf. Alexander, *de An.* 43.22–3: *apelthontōn; synaperchetai; apelthoi*) and "it is present" (*parestin, Enn.* IV.5[29].7.42; cf. Alexander, *de An.* 43.1: *pareiē*) are not appropriate. The presence of the source is not, as in Alexander, defined in terms of its relation with the object to be illumined. When the figure that causes the appearance in the mirror is removed, the image does not appear. Yet the secondary activities of light and reflection continue and the light is not cut off from its source. When Plotinus says that the image of the figure that causes the image is an activity, what he means is that that figure is projecting an image whether there is a mirror there to receive it or not. This idea expresses the more general notion of emanation that everything that exists projects an external activity that is an image of itself. Yet the tincture of colour on the surface of the mirror is cut off from that activity, however much it is dependent upon it. It is a product of that activity. Similarly, the light that proceeds from the luminous body *qua* luminous is projected whether or not it illumines a body as object of illumination.

The presence of the source in Plotinus is not defined in terms of its relation to the illumined object. The presence of the source is defined in terms of the secondary activity of illumination that proceeds from itself as primary activity. If something is thereby illumined, then it is illumined. Thus when a person (as source of light and colour) steps away from the mirror, the image in the mirror disappears. This does not mean that the image no longer exists. On the general principle stated above, everything that exists projects such an image of itself. Like Alexander, Plotinus speaks of what happens when the source of light, colour or reflection "goes away". Yet the only relevance of the presence or absence of the mirror is to whether that image *appears*. Similarly for illumination in general, presence (or absence) do not interfere with illumination as such, only whether this or that object is illumined. Alexander's account of illumination has two elements: (a) the definition of light; and (b) an account of the genesis of light. For Plotinus these two elements coincide. For Alexander, with reference to the second element, the object of illumination is a necessary, if not sufficient, condition for illumination. In this sense, the object of illumination makes its own contribution to illumination.[34] For him the source of light is both the necessary and sufficient condition for illumination. In other words, Plotinus entertains a monistic, and Alexander a dualistic, theory of illumination.

THE EVOLUTION OF INTELLECT IN ALEXANDER

In the *de Anima* Alexander presents an account of the ontogenetic evolution of the human intellect which culminates in the abstraction of intelligible forms from their material substrate. These forms exist in the act of their being thought by the human intellect. On the other hand, he sets forth the view that the Active Intellect (equated with the Aristotelian God of *Metaphysics* 12), being the supreme intellectual object, is the cause of the existence of the intelligibles. We may seek to reconcile these two apparently contradictory accounts.

The first phase of intellect in Alexander is the potential intellect (*dynamei nous*) otherwise known as the material intellect (*hylikos nous*). The description of the first phase as potential intellect would seem to contradict the notion that it is capable of abstracting form from its material substrate, conserving concepts, and knowing. Donini argues, with respect not to the intellect, but to the soul generally, that by *dynamis* Alexander means not potentiality, but power to do and action in what Aristotle describes as first entelechy (an example of which is knowledge we have when asleep as opposed to the knowledge we actually use when awake) (*de An.* 2.1.412a–b1) (see Donini 1970; Alexander, *de An.* 9.15–27; 15.29–16.10; 24.18–25.2). I have applied Donini's reasoning to the rational soul, showing that by potential intellect Alexander understands not a passive faculty, but a first entelechy. The function (*energeia*) of reason proceeds as a second from a first entelechy. That Alexander refers to the first phase of intellect as material intellect would also suggest an unwanted passivity. However, the potential intellect is material in the sense that it receives the *hexis* or fixed disposition of intellection (Schroeder 1982; Alexander, *de An.* 81.22–82.3). In the case of the irrational soul the terms *dynamis* and *hexis* are used interchangeably (Schroeder 1982; Alexander, *de An.* 26.30–32). In the human being they are separated. All human beings progress to the grasp of the universal and knowledge through synthesis of similar perceptions (*koinos nous*) (Schroeder 1982; Alexander, *de An.* 82.26–8; 82.5–15). In the human being, the second stage of intellectual evolution, the *hexis* or fixed disposition of intellection, is enjoyed by the sage alone.[35] The *hexis* in turn is, in its relation with the third phase, or active intellect, a first entelechy analogous to the person who knows something as contrasted with the second entelechy (the active intellect), analogous to the person who uses that knowledge.[36]

At *de Anima* 89.17–18 Alexander boldly equates the Active Intellect of Aristotle, *de An.* 3.5 with the God of Aristotle, *Metaphysics* 12 who is "thought of thought" (1074b34–5).[37] Alexander argues that the Active Intellect is cause for all the intelligibles:

If there were not something that is intelligible by nature, nothing intelligible would come to be, as has already been remarked. In all cases in which one principle is primarily something and another secondarily, that which is secondarily derives its being from that which is primarily. What is more, if such an Intellect should be the First Cause, which is cause and principle of being for all the others, it would be productive (*poiētikos*) in the sense that it is the cause of being for all the intelligibles.   (Alexander, *de An.* 89.6–11)

Alexander establishes two classes of intelligible object: transcendent and immanent. The immanent forms are potential intelligible objects and become intelligible objects when the human mind abstracts them from their material substrate. The transcendent form or forms are free of a material substrate and are addressed by the Active Intellect equated with the Aristotelian God (87.24–88.3).[38] The phrase "all the intelligibles" includes both immanent and transcendent form.[39]

We have, then, two accounts of the genesis of immanent intelligible forms. In the first the potential intellect (regarded as first entelechy) abstracts potentially intelligible forms from their material substrate and renders them both existent and intelligible in act. Merlan insists that the immanent intelligibles "exist only in the act of intelligence that abstracts them from their matrix" (Merlan 1967: 118; Alexander, *de An.* 87.24–88.3). He also observes, "In other words, they exist qua intelligible only in and through the act of intelligizing them" (Merlan 1967: 118; Alexander, *de An.* 90.2–9; 19–21). In the latter, the cause of intelligibility is that which is supremely intelligible which causes intelligibility in other things by being itself eminently intelligible. So it is that that which is supremely intelligible is by that fact the cause of intelligibility for other things. We may ask how these two accounts are to be reconciled (on which see Sharples 1987: 1207–8).

We shall recall that Alexander says (89.2–4) that that which is eminently good is the cause of goodness for other things. That eminently good principle is not the formal, but the final cause of goodness. Alexander adds that other things are judged good by their contribution (*synteleia*) to goodness. We saw that the notion of contribution makes great sense in that *synteleia* describes generally the contribution made by a lower level of the soul to a higher level (75.24–6). The potential intellect is also a phase of the human soul. That phase has its function prepared by sensation as it abstracts forms from matter, compares and conserves them, and knows them. The Active Intellect, engaged in thinking the transcendent forms, is the final cause of the intelligibility and being of the immanent intelligibles. It is so by being eminently intelligible. Yet the ontogenetic evolution of the human soul contributes, phase upon phase, to the intelligibility and existence of the immanent forms. We have seen that the *hexis* of intellection contributes to goodness by promoting not just survival, but well-being (81.15–16). If we understand intelligibility and the growth of intellect as goods, then we may see how the evolution of intellect contributes to a good end, *namely* intelligibility. Thus in the cases both of goodness and of intelligibility the principle that that which is eminently p is the cause of p in other things is not compromised by the notion of contribution on the part of other things.

We may return to the case of light. The source of light is inherently both luminous and visible. Yet it also causes luminosity and visibility in an object of illumination when the conditions of presence of the source and relationship between the source and the object of illumination are realized. The illumined object makes its own contribution to illumination in the sense that it is a *sine qua non* of illumination (of course, this contribution does not follow the pattern of final causation observable in the genesis of goodness and intelligibility). In the analogy of the Active Intellect to light, even as the source of light is inherently luminous and visible, the Active Intellect (equated with God) is inherently intelligible. The conditions of presence and dependence necessary for intellectual illumination are met when the human intellect abstracts forms from matter and, by its progress, brings these forms into the appropriate relationship with the Active Intellect. That omega point of noetic illumination takes place within the human soul.[40] We know that light makes colours visible. To colours may correspond the potential intelligibles which, when illumined (in the sense of rendered intelligible), become actually intelligible. The act of intellectual illumination that takes place when the Active Intellect cooperates with the human intellect to render actual the immanent intelligibles manifests efficient causation (in addition to the final causation that we have already discussed). Nyvlt argues that Alexander, in thus presenting efficient as well as final causation, differs from Aristotle, for whom his God operates alone by final causation, and prepares the way for Plotinus for whom the upward path of the soul is final causation, while emanation from the One is efficient causation (Nyvlt 2012: xi, 2, 5, 6, 8, 206, 226, 235, 237–40).

We have seen that intelligibility and goodness are produced by final causation. Yet illumination does not involve final causation. Rather, intellectual illumination intervenes at the end of the progress of the mind towards its final goal to actualize the potential intelligibility of the second order of intelligibles as the human mind abstracts these from matter. Intellectual illumination is a form of efficient causation contextualized by an overall pattern of final causation.

THE ANALOGY OF THE ACTIVE INTELLECT TO LIGHT IN PLOTINUS

Rist is persuaded that Alexander's identification of the Active Intellect with God would have been attractive for Plotinus.[41] In Aristotle, *de Anima* 3.5.430a12 the Active Intellect functions *tōi poiein panta*.[42] Plotinus may interpret these words to mean "by making (creating) everything". Such an interpretation may be at work in *Enn.* VI.8[39].19.16–19: "But he, being principle of substance, did not make (*epoiēse*) substance for himself but when he had made it left it outside of himself, because he has no need of being, he who made it." The One, in its production of Intellect, would then function as Active Intellect (Rist 1966b: 90). Since Intellect is the first principle to emanate from the One and everything else goes on to emanate from Intellect, the One "makes everything".

Plotinus applies the analogy of the sun to the production of Intellect from the One and describes the One as "by its own light bestowing intelligibility on the things that are and on Intellect" (*Enn.* VI.7[38].16.30–31). The hypostasis of Intellect proceeds from the One as "a radiation from it while it remains unchanged, like the bright light of the sun which, so to speak, runs around it, springing from it continually while it remains unchanged" (*Enn.* V.1[10].6.28–30). Plotinus goes on to state the principle that everything that exists produces an image of itself as archetype of its existence (*Enn.* V.1[10].6.30–34). It is in the following chapter that Plotinus states his monistic view of the genesis of natural light. There is then symmetry between the emanation of natural light from its source and the analogy of light in which the Intellect emanates from the One as light from its origin. The One, in producing Intellect, plays a role which is comparable to that of the Active Intellect in Alexander which is the ultimate cause of intellection. Yet the discussion is removed from the sublunary sphere altogether as the one hypostasis begets another as light is generated from the sun. It is significant for the Platonism of Plotinus that, where Alexander engages in an analogy of the Active Intellect to light, Plotinus' analogy refers to the sun (Plato, *R.* 6.508a4–509b10). Where Plotinus unites the definition of light and the account of its genesis, Alexander divides them. Plotinus differs also from Alexander in making the source of light its unique cause. For Plotinus, then, the One is the unique cause of everything. By emanation it acts as efficient cause in producing Intellect. It in turn acts as final cause in serving as the goal of our return or conversion to itself.[43]

We have examined above how Alexander (*de An.* 88.26–89.6) states the principle that that which is eminently p is the cause of p in other things. It is clear that such a principle does not inform Plotinus' analogy of the Active Intellect to light. Indeed, the One is not, in its own nature, intelligible (*noēton*), but is "intelligible for another",[44] that is, the hypostasis of Intellect (*Enn.* V.6[24].2.10). Generally, the problem in Plotinus is how the One produces that which it does not have (cf. *Enn.* V.3[49].15.35–6, 7.15.18–20; VI.7[38].17.1–6). Thus Merlan is surely incorrect in the view we examined above that we are in Alexander as close to causality in Neoplatonism as possible (Merlan 1969: 38–9).

There is a suggestion that the role of the One as source of Intellect would be repeated mimetically at lower levels. Thus Plotinus speaks of the intellection of the human soul as a "state (*hexis*) of the soul, which is one of the things which derive from Intellect" (*Enn.* I.1[53].8.1–2).[45] Here we have Alexander's word *hexis* but described not in terms of ontogenetic evolution, but as gained from Intellect which is superior to the soul. Plotinus describes the chain of reality extending from the One to the sensible world as: "like a long life stretched out at length; each part is different from that which comes next in order, but the whole is continuous with itself, but with one part differentiated from another, and the earlier does not perish in the later" (*Enn.* V.2[11].2.26–9).

Blumenthal comments: "These words are interesting. They contrast with Aristotle's view that the lower faculties are always present if the higher ones are, and exemplify the different approaches of the two philosophers: Plotinus in discussing any part of this world tends to look down on it from above" (1972: 26 n. 19). We have seen that Aristotle argues against the Platonic Good as the formal cause of goodness by observing that "good" is predicable in different senses in different categories. "Life" is also not predicable in a generic sense as it bears different meanings at different stages of the soul's development. For Aristotle, focal meaning occupies an intermediate position between synonymy (demanded by generic predication) and equivocation. A p-series of terms predicated by focal meaning demands a pattern of cognitive priority. Thus "healthy" may refer to the maintenance, creation or symptom of health. "Medical" could describe the medical art, the practitioner, his function, his instrument, and so on.[46]

Plotinus agrees with Aristotle (*EN* 1.4.1095a18–20; cf. *EE* 2.10.1219b1–2) that we may equate living well (*to eu zēn*) with well-being (*eudaimonia*). Where Aristotle's context is ethical (to live *well*), Plotinus begins his enquiry in a biological context (to *live* well). If a creature has the good appropriate to its grade of life, it may be said to live well. Aristotle denies that well-being may be situated lower than humanity because lower stages of life are incapable of contemplation (*EN* 10.8.1178b20–32). Ultimately Plotinus agrees with this idea. The senses of "good" and "life" are predicated homonymously (in the sense appropriate to *pros hen* predication) of the various grades of life in the *scala naturae*. Contemplation, at the summit of this hierarchy, is the truly good life (*Enn.* I.4[46].1–3).

(Plotinus argues [*Enn*. VI.2[43].17] that the Good is not a genus, but is predicated by focal meaning of different entities within the hierarchy of being).

Plotinus then predicates the words "life" and "good" in a descending p-series which extends from the Good through Intellect and Soul to the sensible world by focal meaning. In this way he meets Aristotle's critique of the Platonic Good by a use of Aristotelian argument.[47] He is, in effect, agreeing with Aristotle that the Good is not the formal cause of goodness because it is predicated in different senses in different categories. The same difference of perspective may be seen as existing between Alexander and Plotinus, with Plotinus looking at Alexander's world from above.

CONCLUSIONS

The fundamental difference between Plotinus and Alexander is that, where Alexander is a dualist, Plotinus is a monist. The distinction is manifested in their different accounts of the physics of light. It is also at work in their respective epistemologies. It is clearly apparent in Plotinus' attack on the physics of illumination in Alexander. For Alexander, the presence of the source of light and the relation between the source and the illumined body are both necessary (though each is not in itself sufficient) conditions for the genesis of illumination. In Plotinus the source of light is the sole cause for illumination. It is less clear in the Plotinian response to Alexander's epistemology. In the dualistic account of Alexander the Active Intellect is, in its cooperation with the human intellect, the efficient cause for the abstraction of form from matter, and the Active Intellect is the final cause of that evolution of the human mind that progresses to that moment. If Alexander is a source for Plotinian epistemology, Plotinus has traced a labyrinthine path from Alexander's position to his own, which is quite different. In the monistic version of Plotinus, the One (corresponding to the Active Intellect in Alexander) is the efficient cause of Intellect. It is also the final cause of the return of Intellect (and ultimately of our return) to the One. Alexander also differs from Plotinus in that the intelligibility of his highest principle may be predicated (in a lesser degree) of intelligible forms in the sublunary world. For Plotinus his highest principle, while it is the cause of intelligibility, is not in itself intelligible: thus Plotinus accepts a greater degree of transcendence and incommensurability.

NOTES

1. The text of the *Life of Plotinus* is to be found in volume 1 of Henry & Schwyzer (1964–82), *Plotinus*: line references are to this text.
2. Becchi (1983: 90) identifies "Alexander" here with Alexander of Aegae who was one of the teachers of Nero and composed commentaries on the *Categories* and *de Caelo* of Aristotle. I might suggest another candidate. We have now an inscription for a statue dedicated by Alexander of Aphrodisias to his father Alexander, also a philosopher, from the rich site of Aphrodisias in Caria. On the assumption that Alexander's father was also a Peripatetic, perhaps the "Alexander" in Porphyry is not the familiar commentator, but his father; for the epigraphic evidence see Chaniotis (2004).
3. Trans. Armstrong. Porphyry's *Life* is included in Armstrong's translation, *Plotinus*, vol. 1. Translations of Porphyry, *Life of Plotinus* and Plotinus are taken from Armstrong.
4. References to Alexander, *de Anima* are to the Bruns edition.

5. Cf. Hicks (1907: 501); Sprague (1972); Moraux accuses Alexander for his lack of Aristotelian orthodoxy in his use of the Platonic analogy: Moraux (1942: 92 n. 2) and Donini (1974: 43 & n. 100).

6. Translations of Alexander are mine.

7. Cf. *Metaph.*993b24–6; *APo* 1.2.72a29–30 and Accattino & Donini (1996: 288). For a thorough review cf. Sharples (1987: 1207–8).

8. *NE* 1.4.1096a17–1097a14 and *EE* 1.8.1217b1–1218b27.

9. Bergeron & Dufour (2008: 350–51) and especially Aristotle, *Metaph.*1075a11–15; cf. Accattino & Donini (1996 : 291–2), especially their treatment of *EE* 1.1218b7–27.

10. *Metaph.* 1072a26–b1, b10–11, b18–19 & b30–4; 1074b25–6, b33–5 & 1075a8–10; 1075a11–15 & a37, and Bergeron & Dufour (2008: 350–51); cf. Gerson (2005b: 260–61).

11. *Metaph.*1075a11–35; Bergeron & Dufour (2008: 350–51); cf. Aristotle, *Metaph.* 983a31–2; 984b11–14; Gadamer (1978: 101; 1986: 174).

12. However, there is no reason to believe that the Ps.-Alexander consulted Alexander's commentary on *Metaphysics* 12: see Sharples (2002: 5 and n. 22).

13. πρὸς ἕν ἅπαντα συντελεῖν; cf. Gadamer (1978: 89–90; 1986: 151–2) for the relationship between this passage and the analogy of attribution in *Metaphysics* 3.2.

14. Much controversy surrounds the question of Aristotle's Platonism. For bibliography on the question of whether Aristotle is, or is not, a Platonist, see Gerson (2005b: 12–15). Gerson himself affirms the Neoplatonic view that there is a harmony between the philosophy of Plato and Aristotle.

15. Cf. note 5 above.

16. Merlan (1969: 38–9). Of course, other schools may share with Platonism the ethical axiom that everything strives for the good. Platonism requires a transcendent or superordinate Good with respect to which all good things are ordered and this principle is adopted by Plato, Aristotle and Alexander. Such a transcendent principle could not be operative in Stoicism because the Stoics reject the Platonic Theory of Forms and refuse to hypostatize universals, cf. Sedley (1985); for a useful treatment of the Stoics on the subject of the good (in its relation to nature), cf. M. Frede (1999).

17. Alexander, *de Anima* 46.1–6; *in de Sensu* 45.26–46.3; the treatise "How according to Aristotle sight comes about", *Mantissa* 143.35–144.23; Accattino (1992: 58–9).

18. Accattino (1992: 59) (cf. Accattino & Donini 1996: 183) objects to my notion of illumination as a joint effect of the source of light and the illumined object (Schroeder 1981) that it would not explain the luminosity of the source of light itself or of objects that are themselves luminous. However, I am speaking not simply of light, but of illumination in the sense defined above.

19. ἀπελθόντων γοῦν τῶν ταῦτα ἐμποιούντων (*de An.* 42.22).

20. τὸ φωτίζον (*de An.* 43.1).

21. τὰ χρώννυντα (*de An.* 42.23).

22. Cf. Aristotle, *de An.* 2.7.418b16: πυρὸς ἢ τοιούτου τινὸς παρουσία.

23. I wrote (Schroeder 1981: 217–18 n. 11): "παρουσία is interpreted in terms of σχέσις, not vice versa. If παρουσία describes only the presence of source to the product, then σχέσις will be redundant." I should perhaps have written "to the object of illumination" rather than "to the product". Accattino (1992: 56 n. 50) interprets me to mean that παρουσία is the more particular, σχέσις the more general term. Accattino prefers to construe relation as the more general and presence as the more particular term. He refers to Alexander, *in de Sensu* 134.11–19, where relation is exemplified by the father and son (a more general term) while presence is represented by spatial location (a more particular term). I am not sure what Accattino is getting at here. I did not intend to differentiate between the two terms as general and specific so much as to say that relation is epexegetic of presence. Accattino proceeds to argue that, if presence were the more general term, Alexander would not have written at *de An.* 42.2–3 κατὰ παρουσίαν καὶ ποιάν σχέσιν. He adds that the καὶ would have explanatory sense. Quite so: the one phrase *explains* the content of the other. Bergeron & Dufour (2008: 179) agree with me.

24. ἀπ' ἀμφοτέρων (*de An.* 43.2).

25. I earlier construed "both" to mean "both from sources of colour and light and coloured or illumined objects" (Schroeder 1981: 217). Accattino (1992: 57) prefers the proximate referents. Cf. Accattino & Donini (1996: 182–3). To concede this point is not to disturb my larger argument, cf. Schroeder & Todd (2008: 664).

26. Aristotle, *de An.* 2.8.419b10–11 speaks of colour as τὸ κινητικῷ εἶναι τοῦ κατ' ἐνέργειαν διαφανοῦς; cf. Aristotle, *Ph.* 8.7.260a26–8 for *kinēsis* as change either of size, quality or place.

27. For Aristotle's denial that light involves *kinēsis* cf. *Sens.* 6.446a28–30.

28. Accattino (1992: 53–5) (cf. Accattino & Donini 1996: 180–81) observes that Aristotle at *de Anima* 2.7.418a31; 419a10–11 and 13–14 states that colour moves the diaphanous in act (at *de An.* 418a31: πᾶν δὲ χρῶμα κινητικὸν ἐστι τοῦ κατ᾽ ἐνέργειαν διαφανοῦς). Alexander feels he has to use κίνησις out of piety towards Aristotle. The addition of the qualifying τις to κίνησις at Alexander, *de An.* 43.1–2 is intended to alleviate the embarrassment of using a word that, as we have seen, he condemns elsewhere. My interpretation preserves Alexander from this kind of misplaced loyalty.

29. Reference is to the Henry & Schwyzer *editio minor*. All line references are to this edition.

30. On this doctrine of the double act see Rutten (1956); A. Smith (1974: 6–13); Schroeder (1986, esp. 192–3; 1992: 32–3); Narbonne (1994: 61–79); F. Ferrari 2002; Emilsson (2007: 22–68).

31. Τὸ "ἀπελήλυθε" (*Enn.* IV.5[29].7.42); cf. Alexander, *de An.* 42.22–3: ἀπελθόντων … συναπέρχεται … ἀπέλθοι.

32. Τὸ "πάρεστιν" (*Enn.* IV.5[29].7.42); cf. Alexander, *de An.* 43.1: παρείη.

33. ἄπεστιν.

34. Although that contribution cannot follow the pattern of final causation observed with respect to the role of contribution in the genesis of goodness and intelligibility.

35. Schroeder (1982); Alexander, *de An.* 82.6–11; the *hexis* is also described as *epiktētos* ("acquired") (*de An.* 82.1).

36. Cf. *de An.* 85.25–86.6. For the derivation of these three phases of intellection from Aristotle, *de Anima* cf. Bergeron & Dufour (2008: 341).

37. Papadis (1991a; 1991b: 348–65) calls this identification into question. For my reasons for rejecting his arguments, see Schroeder (1997a: 114 n. 31).

38. Cf. *de An.* 87.24–88.3; 89.13–15; 90.2–11; 90.20–21 and Merlan (1969: 16–17). For an account of the alternation between plural intelligible forms and a single intelligible form, cf. Sharples (1987: 1209–11). Sharples points out that the discussion of plural intelligible forms at 87.24–88.16 precedes the introduction of the Active Intellect, so that we need not think that Alexander sees plural intelligible forms as the proper objects of the Active Intellect. What is more, "the discussion of pure forms at 87.24–88.16 precedes any mention of the active intellect, and seems intended to introduce the notion of pure form in a general way, preliminary to the argument at 88.17 ff. that the active intellect is a pure form" (1211). See Accattino & Donini (1996: 283–4); Bergeron & Dufour (2008: 344–5). Merlan (1967: 120) sees in the thinking of the transcendent intelligible in Alexander the source of Plotinus' doctrine that the intelligibles are not outside the hypostasis of Intellect (the subject of *Enn.* V[32].5).

39. Bergeron & Dufour (2008: 351–3) *pace* Accattino & Donini (1996: 292).

40. Nyvlt (2012: 202–5) expresses agreement with my interpretation of the genesis of intelligibility and the way in which it follows the analogy of illumination in Alexander. Bazán (1973: 478–85) argues that the Active Intellect furnishes the light by which the human intellect performs the abstraction of form from matter. Moraux (1978: 300–301) argues *contra* that the *hexis* of intellection must exist before it can conceive of the Active Intellect. Sharples (1987: 1208 n. 108) agrees with Moraux but falsely attributes Bazán's view to me (Schroeder 1981, 1984). I am arguing that the illumination of the immanent forms takes place after their abstraction.

41. This section shall prescind from discussing the influence of the *de Intellectu* on Plotinus because I am convinced both that Alexander of Aphrodisias is not the author of that work and that Plotinus influences the *de Intellectu*. Cf. Schroeder (1982, 1997a); Schroeder & Todd (1990: 6–22; 2008).

42. Rist (1966a: 10; 1971 reprint: 508) interprets these words to mean making things of one kind things of another.

43. On the subject of emanation and conversion see Schroeder (1986; 1992: 24–65).

44. νοητὸν ἑτέρῳ.

45. In context, Plotinus is asking how we are related to Intellect and then clarifies that he is not speaking of "the state of the soul which is one of the things which derive from Intellect, but Intellect itself". Nevertheless, he implies that there is such a state of the soul, etc.

46. Cf. Aristotle, *Metaph.* 1003a33–b4; 1061a1–5; cf. A. C. Lloyd (1962: 67; 1990: 76–8).

47. See Schroeder (1997b) where this question is discussed in close philological argument.

20

Metaphysics of soul and self in Plotinus

Gwenaëlle Aubry

One of the great singularities of the philosophy of Plotinus consists in thinking of the self[1] for its own sake and, in particular, in producing a concept of it different from that of soul.[2] This philosophical breakthrough is inseparable from the discovery of immediate reflexivity; that is, the subject's ability to apprehend itself independently of its relation to an object or to another subject.[3] In Plotinus, however, this reflexivity occurs only in an interrogative form, which can be read, in particular, in *Enn.* I.1[53] and *Enn.* VI.4[22]. In other words, it does not, as in Descartes, assume the form of an intuition by means of which the subject, grasping itself as consciousness, would, at the same time, have an evident revelation of its essence. In *Enn.* I.1 and *Enn.* VI.4, the two reflexive questions serve as preludes to two enquiries involving the concepts of soul and human being, but also manifesting the irreducibility of the self to either of them. It is precisely this irreducibility that will interest us: we will see how Plotinus, although he seems to think of the self by means of the connected notions of soul and human being, but also of individual or even of consciousness, ceaselessly produces and renews a gap between them and the self. It is on the gap between soul and self that our attention will focus more particularly, both because it carries the others along with it, and because these two concepts are also susceptible of different meanings in Plotinus: just as he allows levels of the soul, so he is also prepared to accept levels of the self. And yet, they do not coincide. The self properly so called, which Plotinus refers to as the *hēmeis*, is distinct both from the essential or separated soul and from the soul linked to the body. Situated rather than defined, it cannot be substantified. To use Plotinian terminology, the *hēmeis* is neither god nor animal, but rather the power to become either one. These two possible and exclusive identifications depend on the orientation it gives to its consciousness. Consciousness therefore does not appear, as it will in Descartes, as a revelation of identity, but as a means of identification.

I should like to point out not only this irreducibility of the "self" to the soul, but also the fundamental role it plays in the Plotinian system: to show how it is that by which Plotinian metaphysics integrates an ethics, or, again, that by which the necessity of procession leaves room for the free choice of conversion.

DEGREES OF THE SOUL AND THE METAPHYSICS OF PROCESSION

The separated soul

Another singular aspect of the philosophy of Plotinus is that it affirms the existence of a separated soul,[4] which remains in the Intellect and alien to both the powers and the passions of the body. This doctrine was to be rejected by the later Neoplatonists, particularly Iamblichus and Proclus (Steel 1978), but it occupies a fundamental place in Plotinian thought. Thus, we shall have to enquire into the connection articulating it with the other singular point in Plotinus: his conception of the self.

This separated soul is the object of an experience that can be said to be foundational, and which is described in the first person in *Enn*. IV.8[6]:

> Often, awakening from my body to myself, having become external to everything else and internal to myself, contemplating such a wonderful beauty, certain then more than ever, that I belong to the higher world, activating the best life, becoming identical to the divine, and establishing myself in it, having attained this supreme activity and established myself above every other intelligible, when, after this rest in the divine, I descend from the Intellect to reasoning, I wonder how I could ever have descended in this way, and now again, how my soul was ever able to come to be inside a body, if it is such as it appeared by itself, even though it is in a body.
>
> (*Enn*. IV.8[6].1.1–11)[5]

As it is described here, this experience is at the same time that of a separation from the body – designated as an "awakening" – and of a presence to oneself. Nevertheless, it includes a flip side, or negative aspect: the experience of the "descent" or of falling back into the body, which, even more than the experience of separation, inspires astonishment, to the point of serving as prelude to one of the guiding questions of Plotinus' philosophy: "How I could ever have descended in this way, and now again, how was my soul ever able to come to be inside a body?" (ll. 8–10). When formulated in this way, this question is consonant with the reflexive questions of other treatises which will be discussed below: if the Plotinian subject grasps itself only in an interrogative form, that is, not as something obvious but as something strange, it is because it undergoes the experience of several modes of relation to itself. The problem that then arises is that of which one defines it properly.

Through successive equivalences, the experience of self described by the first lines of *Enn*. IV.8 is also presented as an experience of the "divine" and of the "Intellect" (*nous*). Such, then, is the apparently paradoxical thesis that Plotinus maintains: the separate soul is divine, and yet it is in us; it is an intellect, but also a soul, or again, more precisely, it is "being-soul", the essential soul, simultaneously pure form and pure *energeia*.[6] In *Enn*. V.3[49], Plotinus formulates this paradox in yet another way: strictly speaking, the intellective soul cannot be counted among the parts of the soul, and yet, it is indeed ours (*hēmeteron*); in fact, he continues, "it is ours without being ours. ... It is ours when we use it; it is not ours when we do not use it".[7] Here the distinction, to which we shall return, is already indicated between the soul and the self understood as "us", or as *hēmeis*. By "soul", *Enn.* V.3 here means *dianoia*, the soul that is not intellective but discursive, which, as Plotinus writes, "we always use", unlike the first one.[8] The inaugural lines of *Enn.* IV.8 described nothing other than the negative experience of the "descent" into the body as being that of the Intellect's falling back into reasoning. Intellective thought, *noēsis*, thus appears as essential activity, *energeia*, or else as the life of the separate soul (cf. *Enn.* V.3[49].8.30–57; I.1[53].13.5–8). Like the total Intellect, and each of the intellects of which it is composed, the higher soul is characterized by intuitive thought; that is, by the simultaneous, inarticulated and non-propositional grasp of a complex content – comparable to a glance that embraces all the features of a face in a single vision (cf. *Enn.* IV.4[28].1.21–5; Emilsson 2007: 185–91).

We can remain strangers forever to this essential mode of being and thinking: or, as treatise *Enn.* V.3[49] says, we possibly never make use of it. *Enn.* V.1[10] opens with the acknowledgement of this fundamental ignorance: "Yet what can it be that has brought it about that the souls forget the god who is their father, and that they are as ignorant of themselves as they are of him, although they are parts that come from above, and in general belong to him?" (*Enn.* V.1[10].1.1–3).

The soul's forgetfulness of the Intellect is also a forgetting of its own intellective origin – an origin that nevertheless has not come and gone, nor does it belong to a mythic past, but that remains in a state of unperceived presence. This forgetfulness is characteristic of pre-philosophical consciousness. Unaware of its dignity, soul is fascinated by externality: the body, the sensible. Narcissistic, it prefers its reflection to itself, ignorant of the fact that without it, this reflection, which is merely the effect of its power, could not subsist (cf. *Enn.* I.6[1].8.8–16; P. Hadot 1976). In order to tear the soul away from this mirage, it must be restored in its self-esteem; that is, recalled to the divine that it harbours. The *gnōthi seauton* which, for Plotinus as for Plato, serves as a prelude to philosophy, thus signifies, as much as "Know yourself", "Know your worth" and "Become once again what you are" – and what in truth you have never ceased being, but of which you have lost awareness (cf. Verbeke 1997; Aubry 2007).

One must ask, however, what exactly is the status of this self that is rediscovered in the Intellect and the experience of which was described in *Enn.* IV.8? What remains in it of the personal self, the concrete, incarnate individual? That it is identical to the essential soul, so be it: but can it, as such, still be described as an individual?

Distinctions are necessary here, which manifest the complexity of the Plotinian thought of the self: in the first place, this essential self constituted by the separated soul must indeed be distinguished from the *hēmeis* and from what we may call the biographical subject; that is, the bearer of a history, a memory, and the form of consciousness that is linked to them.[9] In *Enn.* IV.3[27], Plotinus thus develops the singular theory of the two memories: two distinct memories correspond to the separated soul and to the soul linked to the body, one that preserves the intelligible trace of the object, the other, the sensible trace (*Enn.* IV.3[27].31.28–31). Freed from the body, the soul preserves the memory of its friends, its children and its fatherland for a while; then, gradually, it forgets them: "The good soul is forgetful. … It is light and by itself" (*ibid.*: 32.18–21). This is why Socrates, having risen back up to the intelligible, does not recall that he has done philosophy (*Enn.* I.4[46].1.5), nor even when he contemplates that it is he, Socrates, who contemplates (*ibid.*: 2.1–3).

Like memory and individual history, consciousness disappears in the Intellect. More precisely, it gives way to a feeling of presence in which the duality between subject and object is abolished. In this state, Plotinus writes, we are "only potentially ourselves" (*Enn.* IV.4[28].2.5–8). We merge with that which we contemplate: "The self (*autos*) is all things and both are one" (*ibid.*: 2.22). In the Intellect, then, we are no longer "we", but we are beings: "both what is ours and we are brought back to being" (*Enn.* VI.5[23].7.1). Here, none can say "it's me up to this point" (7.15).[10]

This state in which the subject no longer experiences itself as such, but in its unity with being and with the others, is nevertheless designated by Plotinus as the site of its greatest proximity to itself, at the same time as it is genuine self-knowledge: "Being in this way, we are more than anything conscious of ourselves (*hautois synetoi*), and we acquire knowledge of ourselves as we make ourselves one" (*Enn.* V.8[31].11.31–3). Thus, *synesis* is opposed to the reflexive consciousness which, just as *dianoia* fragments the contents of *noēsis*, divides what was grasped as a unity into a duality:[11] "This identity is a kind of immediate sense (*synesis*) and consciousness of the self (*synaisthēsis hautou*), which itself must take great care not to distance itself from itself, by wanting to sense too much" (*Enn.* V.8[31].11.23–4). This, then, is what P. Hadot (1997: 40) has called "the paradox of the human personal self": it is when we are least aware of ourselves that we are most ourselves.

Still, the question arises of what the subject, thus identified with the intellective soul and unburdened of all biographical content, then grasps of itself. At this essential level, can we still speak of identity? Of individuality? This question joins another controversial one: that of whether or not Plotinus accepted the existence of Forms of individuals.[12] This problem cannot be dealt with here for its own sake.[13] However, an attentive reading of the texts shows that Plotinus does indeed admit an intelligible principle of distinction between individuals which, however, cannot be identified with a Form, but must be identified, in the first place, with the original distinction between intellective souls (cf. *Enn.* IV.3[27]. 8.15–16; V.8[31].10.1–18), and then with the *logos* that is associated with them.[14] To each soul-intellect is added a *logos* that contains not only the essential qualities of Man as such (*Enn.* II.6[17].1.17; VI.1[42].20.19–20), but also – and this is the originality of the Plotinian thesis – the differences, which are not just specific, but also individual (*Enn.* V.7[18].1.21, 1.23, 3.5–6; V.9[5].12.5–11).

This principle of individual distinction must, of course, be distinguished from the concrete individual. Yet it is not the negation of that individual, but rather its foundation. The paradox of the Plotinian personal self is thus illuminated: if, for Plotinus, one is never more oneself than when one is no longer conscious of oneself, this is because the subject identified with its essential soul is not abolished in the universal. Rather, it is identified with the very source of its individuality; that is, with the singular viewpoint of its intellect upon the total Intellect, as well as with the *logos* that bears the power of its own becoming.

At this point, then, one can indeed identify the separated soul, the soul as *ousia*, and the essential self. Although the essential self is already individuated, it is not merged with the conscious, incarnate biographical self. As we shall see, it is nevertheless, for the Plotinian subject, a possible identity. Indeed, the notion of a separated soul orients Plotinian ethics, which has no other goal than to transform this constant but ordinarily unperceived presence into a conscious presence. Far from being immediate or mechanical, this transformation is given as a demanding, normed itinerary, whose various stages correspond to various degrees of virtue: the civic virtues, which are those of the soul still connected to the body; the cathartic virtues, by the exercise of which it separates itself from the body; finally, the contemplative virtues (I.2[19]). This ethical itinerary, and we shall return to this point, is inseparably a trajectory of consciousness, which gradually turns away from the body to orient itself towards the separated soul. Several of Plotinus' treatises allow this itinerary not only to be seen, but to be carried out. They can be read as efficacious texts, which aim to bring about this mutation of consciousness. This is the case with *Enn.* I.1[53] (see Aubry 2004), but also with *Enn.* IV.8[6] which, opening with the inaugural experience of the fall from *noēsis* to *dianoia*, ends with the evocation of the separated soul; or again with *Enn.* V.1[10], whose structure is rather close, since it leads from the souls' forgetfulness of their divine origin to attention (*prosokhē*); that is, to that form of consciousness that knows how to leave itself open to the "voices from above" (*Enn.* V.1[10].12.12–20).

In truth, then, the Plotinian beyond is very close: to reach it, it is enough to make oneself deaf to the tumult of the body, to release oneself from narcissistic fascination. For Plotinus, Odysseus represents the anti-Narcissus: he is the one who was able to resist the spells of the sensible, the charms of Circe and of Calypso (*Enn.* I.6[1].8.18–20). Yet the Plotinian Odyssey is a return to something that is always-already-there, which is the locus in us of a divine autarky, lucidity and happiness.

The lower powers of the soul and *dianoia*

Yet we must now return to the question of *Enn.* IV.8[6].1.9–10: "How could my soul ever come to be inside a body?" This question, ordinarily designated as being that of the descent of the soul, must, in fact, be formulated more precisely:

- First, because, strictly speaking, for Plotinus the soul does not descend. What descends, or mixes with the body to animate it, is the power, the *dynamis*, that emanates from the separated soul.
- In its confrontation with the body and with temporality, *noēsis* is transformed into *dianoia*. This is the moment by which the soul is truly constituted *qua* soul, in its difference from the Intellect. As such, it participates, like the first, in the necessity of procession.
- The descent can be considered as a fall or a fault only when *dianoia* and the consciousness linked to it, forgetful of the separated soul, are completely oriented towards the body.

One must therefore distinguish between these various moments of procession by seeing what concepts of the soul and what concepts of the self correspond to them, and how the distance between them designates the very locus of Plotinian ethics.

Dynamis *and "Descent"*

As early as chapter 2 of *Enn.* IV.8[6], Plotinus states a principle: "It is not a bad thing for the soul to provide the body with the power of good and being, since it is not true that all providence applied to lower reality prevents this providential agent from remaining in what is best" (2.24–5).

This principle applies, in the first place, to the mode of government of the World Soul. For the higher part of this soul "is situated above the heaven, sending its lowest power within it" (2.32–3). In this way, the World Soul is "always directed toward those things, setting this universe in order with a power that is completely detached" (2.52–3). Here it clearly appears that the World Soul does not "descend". What is "sent" into the world is not it, but its "lowest power" (*dynamis*). Yet it is precisely because the World Soul does not descend that it is able to govern the universe, to set it in order into a cosmos, a beautiful totality. This point of doctrine is explicitly formulated elsewhere, for instance, at *Enn.* IV.3[27].6.21: "The souls that incline toward the intelligible world have a greater power"; or else *Enn.* II.9[33].2, where one reads that the World Soul governs "simply by looking at what is before it, thanks to its wonderful power. The more it devotes itself to contemplation, the more it is beautiful and powerful" (15–16).

This description of the mode of governance of the World Soul is nothing other than an application of the Plotinian model of causality. This states that from every being in act (*energeiai*) there necessarily emanates an active, productive power (*dynamis*), which in turn is the cause of a new being and a new act. This model applies first to the causality of the One-Good, which, although it is perfect, is beyond act.[15] However, it also holds, beyond the first principle, for all of procession, so that one can deduce from it the main features of such procession: necessity (causality is not the result of a choice), continuity (*dynamis* ensures the sustained presence of the cause to the effect, which it transcends), and degradation (the effect is inferior to its cause, and is, in turn, the source of a diminished power) (e.g. *Enn.* V.4[7].1.23–8). This is the model that dictates here Plotinus' affirmation that the power of the World Soul is all the greater the more intense its act of contemplation is.

Yet the same model also holds for the individual soul. As we have seen, the separated soul is also an *energeia*, a perfect and impassible act of contemplation. It is therefore, as such, at the beginning of an emanated power. For the individual soul as for the World Soul, however, Plotinus emphasizes that it is this power, this *dynamis*, and *not the soul itself*, that descends and is mixed with the body. This is why the Aristotelian definition of the soul as first entelechy of the body[16] must be opposed by the assertion that the soul is itself in act, already *entelekheia*, without the body, and that only for this reason there can be a body. Thus, the *synamphoteron*, that is, the living body, is not a mixture of body and soul, but only of the body and the power emanated from the soul. If it exists, Plotinus writes, it is "by the mere presence of the soul, not because this soul itself gives itself to the couple, but because it creates the nature of the animal from the qualified body and from a kind of light it gives" (*Enn.* I.1[53].7.1–4). Thus, one must answer the Gnostics that "it is not because the soul inclines that it produces, but rather because it does not incline" (*Enn.* II.9[33].4.6–7).

It is at the conjunction of the powers emanated from the World Soul and the separated individual soul that the organic compound is constituted – or again, that the "man without qualities" present in the Intellect will be transformed into a concrete particular. Once again, however, two moments must be distinguished here: the power emanated from the World Soul constitutes what Plotinus calls the "living body", or else the "qualified body".[17] By this, one must understand the body endowed with the vegetative power, and with an inferior form, not yet individualized, of sensation.[18] To this living body, *Enn.* VI.4[22] also attributes an *epitēdeiotēs*, or a disposition to receive such-and-such a soul.[19] However, the "qualified" body does not really become an individual body until the power that comes from the individual soul is added to the power emanated from the World Soul. The World

Soul still has a role to play in this conjunction: it is she who "distributes" individual souls, like dancers in a choreography, into one animated body or another (cf. *Enn.* VI.7[38].7.10; IV.3[27].12.17–19, 37–9). Yet a spontaneous motion is added to this determination.[20] Indeed, Plotinus writes of the divine soul that it "leaps (*hoion exethoren*), as it were, out of the all into a part" (*Enn.* VI.4[22].16.29–30). This is when it becomes the soul *of* a body. And it is within this relation that particularization must be situated: whereas it was only potentially particular in the Intellect,[21] the soul becomes particular in act.

The constitution of the dianoia

Here, however, a difficulty must be illuminated. If the higher soul does not descend, if only its emanated *dynamis* is mixed with the body, how should we understand Plotinus' words that the soul "leaps" towards its own body? The answer is that this motion is what constitutes the soul *qua* soul, in its difference from the Intellect, or again that by which *noēsis* is modified into *dianoia*. Indeed, *dianoia* is the result of the encounter of intellective thought with time. It deploys the immediacy and totality of intuition into successive moments, to respond to the demands of the body, of action, and of a life diffracted by temporality (*Enn.* III.7[45].11). Thus, it must be considered "the sign of a diminishment of the Intellect" (*Enn.* IV.3[27].18.1–7): and it is indeed this diminished, less intense, less lucid life that was attested by the liminary experience of *Enn.* IV.8. At the same time, however, this weakening does not affect the separated soul, and constitutes the soul in its proper function of animation and organization of the sensible. Thus, the soul's dianoetic constitution is still inscribed in the order of procession. Still in *Enn.* IV.8, Plotinus emphasizes its necessity: "The function of the more rational soul is to think, but not only to think. What would differentiate it from the Intellect? For it has added something else to the fact of being intelligent, such that it did not remain Intellect" (3.21–4). Once again, it is this necessity that is indicated by the insistence on the soul's "double nature" and its "amphibious" character (*Enn.* IV.8[6].4.31–5; cf. also *Enn.* IV.7[2].13).

Thus, no more than the gift of power in which animation consists can the soul's relation to the particular body be truly considered as a "descent" or a fall. It is, of course, a distancing, or a secession from the intelligible totality: as such, however, it constitutes the soul in its proper nature, and therefore always participates in the order of procession.

The situation of the hēmeis

At this point, then, one sees the various levels of the soul becoming arranged; that is, always according to the order of procession: the higher soul; its lower powers, which are mixed with the body; and, intermediary between the separated soul and the animated body, *dianoia*.

The question then arises of whether, and to what extent, these levels of the soul can be made to correspond to levels of the "self". We have seen that the separated soul could be identified with the essential individual. Yet what about the soul (or, more precisely, the soul's powers) that is (or are) mixed with the body, and the *dianoia*?

Plotinus raises this question explicitly, in the reflexive form of questioning by the *hēmeis* of its own identity:

> We, however. ... Who are "we"? Are we "that one", or are we that which has approached [to "that one"], and is subject to becoming in time? ... It is true that

now another man, who wanted to exist, has added himself to that man, and once he found us ... he attributed himself to us, and he added himself to that man who we were originally ... and thus we have become both, and more than once we are no longer who we were before, and we are the one that we then added on to ourselves, when the man we were stops being active, and, in a way, stops being present.

(Enn. VI.4[22].14.16–31)

This text describes the *hēmeis* as the "couple" (*to synamphō*) of two men, who are precisely the separated soul and the animated body. It also appears, however, that the *hēmeis* cannot be identified with either of them: both are in it, without either of them being it, properly speaking. Nor do they constitute it as elements, but, rather, as alternating and alternative presences that are also "activities": when we are the second man, it is because the first one "stops being active".

We see here, once again, what is singular about Plotinian reflexivity: the act by which the subject grasps itself reveals to it not its identity, but its duality. Through it, it does not attain itself in its essence (the separated soul, the first man), but in its difference from the latter. This structure is also found elsewhere. Thus, in *Enn.* I.1[53], one reads yet another reflexive question: after enumerating the various contents of interiority, from the passions to *noēsis*, by way of opinion and reflection, Plotinus asks: "That which searches, examines and decides these questions: whatever can it be?" (1.9–11). Once again, however, this question does not preside over the unification of the various inner contents. If the *hēmeis* is able to apprehend them without mediation, it does not discover itself as what unifies them, to the very degree to which it is conscious of them. At first, it grasps itself only as this multiplicity, not as what totalizes it: "*polla gar hēmeis*", Plotinus thus writes, "we are several" (*Enn.* I.1[53].9.7). Thus, *Enn.* I.1[53] will initially distribute this multiplicity between three distinct terms: the separated soul, the soul that uses the body, and "a third thing made up of the soul and the body"(1.2–5; Cf. Plato, *Alc.* 130a). This movement seems to attest an oscillation between two conceptions of the subject: the reflexive subject and the subject of attribution (the logical or ontological substrate). What in fact appears, however, is that once again the reflexive subject – the *hēmeis* – does not allow itself to be reduced to the subject of attribution. It cannot be identified with any of the three terms among which *noēsis*, reflection, opinion and passions are distributed. It is distinct both from the soul when alone, or separated, and from the compound of soul and body. As far as the "soul using the body" (*Enn.* I.1[53].3) is concerned, the question is more complex. Still in *Enn.* I.1[53], Plotinus lists the operations that are at the foundation of the soul's power (*hēgemonia*) over the animal: reflection, *dianoia*, opinion, *doxa*, notions, *noēseis*; and he concludes by saying, "and this is precisely what we are, above all (*malista*)" (7.16–17). Here we see that the *hēmeis* is not identified with the soul using the body, nor even with *dianoia*, but is simply situated on the same level as these. And this situation is presented as dominant, but not as exclusive. This is why Plotinus specifies, shortly afterwards: "The '*hēmeis*' is thus twofold: either one takes the beast into account, or else one considers only what is already above it" (10.5–7). The surprising "above all" (*malista*) at the end of Plotinus' phrase can be explained as follows: the *hēmeis* can also be situated higher or lower than *dianoia*, according to whether it identifies with the animate body or the separated soul, with the second or the first man. Although it is there "above all", it can also be elsewhere.

We thus see, to conclude on this point, that if the essential self can be identified with the separated soul, on the other hand the *hēmeis*, or reflexive subject, must be distinguished both from the latter and from the body animated by the powers that proceed from it. The separated soul and the animal, the first and the second man, are in it without being it. The consciousness by which it grasps itself does not grant it access to its identity, but only to this constitutive duality and to the various inner contents that can be referred to it. The *hēmeis* can only be situated at a level intermediary between the two men, or else between the separated soul and the living compound, but this situation is itself mobile, so that the *hēmeis* cannot be strictly identified with the *dianoia* either. We must now see how this dynamic character of the Plotinian subject is what constitutes it as the subject of ethics.

THE IDENTIFICATION OF THE *HĒMEIS* AND THE ETHICS OF CONVERSION

The *hēmeis* and the levels of the soul

Like *Enn.* I.1[53], *Enn.* V.3[49] underlines both the proximity and the difference between the *hēmeis* and *dianoia*. The *hēmeis* is here designated as "the main part of the soul intermediary between two powers" (*Enn.* V.3[49.].3.35–8). The rest of the treatise will identify these two powers as sensation and intelligence. One might therefore be tempted to read an identification here between the *hēmeis* and the soul *qua* soul; that is, the *dianoia*. A bit earlier in the treatise, however, Plotinus writes, as we have seen, that intelligence belongs to us, but not to the soul.[22] *Hēmeis* and soul are thus distinguished here, and they are so in that some powers can be attributed to the *hēmeis* that cannot be attributed to the soul: it would make no sense to say of *noēsis* that it "belongs to the soul", since the latter, as we have seen, is constituted *qua* soul, that is, as *dia-noia*, the deployment within time of an intuitive content, only in its difference from the *nous*. Thus, *Enn.* V.3[49] makes an additional distinction between the self-knowledge of *dianoia* and that of the *hēmeis*; for *dianoia*, to know itself in its essence is to know itself as coming from the Intelligence, but also as distinct from the latter; for the *hēmeis*, in contrast, to know itself is to know the Intelligence as constituting its essence (4.23–30). The *dianoia* is an image of the Intelligence, and this is what constitutes it as such. The *hēmeis*, for its part, is what can actualize the Intelligence as one of its powers.[23]

This also holds true for sensation: here again, one can say of it that it is "ours" – but not that it belongs to *dianoia*, nor to the median part of the soul, since it is to the animated body that it must be attributed: "It is agreed that sensation is considered to be always ours – indeed, we always sense – whereas for the Intellect, there is room for doubt, because we do not always use it and because it is separated" (*Enn.* V.3[49].3.39–41).

The terminology here is very close to that of *Enn.* VI.4[22]: like the two men, the two powers that correspond to them (one, sensation, defining the animal, the other, intelligence, defining the separated soul), are the subject of an alternative "usage". Just as *Enn.* VI.4[22] designated "us" as being adventitious man "more than once", so, here, it is said that we "always sense". And just as the first man was said to be "inactive" when the second man is active in us, so here it is said that "we do not always use it". The parallelism between those fomulations is worth noticing, even though the vocabulary of usage substitutes for that of activity.

If the *hēmeis* cannot be identified with the median part of the soul, any more than with the separated soul, it is because, unlike the soul, it is not the subject of definitional powers.

Whereas the separated soul has *noēsis* as its essential act, the median part of the soul is constituted as *dianoia*, and the living body is the subject of sensation and passions, the *hēmeis*, for its part, is what can make use in turn of either one of these powers.

Hēmeis and consciousness

In this irreducibility of the *hēmeis* to the various levels of the soul, we may see an effect of Plotinus' discovery of the difference between subject-consciousness and subject-substrate.

That the *hēmeis* is not a substance follows from the fact that for Plotinus, only the separated soul can be said to be *ousia*. The animated body itself, like every sensible reality, cannot be said to be such (see Chiaradonna 2002). However, the fact that the *hēmeis* is not the substrate of definite operations either results from the connection Plotinus establishes between it and consciousness. This connection is more intimate than the one between *hēmeis* and *dianoia*; and it is precisely, as is shown by the following text, that by virtue of which the *hēmeis* cannot be identified with a part of the soul, but rather with what Plotinus calls "the total soul":

> Everything present in the soul is not for that reason conscious, but … it reaches "us" when it reaches consciousness.[24] When one of the soul's activities is exercised without communicating anything to consciousness, that activity does not reach the total soul. It follows that "we" know nothing of this activity, because "we" are connected to consciousness (*meta tou aisthētikou*), and "we" are not part of the soul, but the total soul.   (*Enn.* V.1[10].12.5–10)

It is thus this connection with consciousness that brings it about that the *hēmeis* cannot be identified with one level of the soul but is, at least in principle, that to which these levels are all present, and which totalizes them. Nevertheless, this text must be read together with those from *Enn.* VI.4[22] and *Enn.* V.3[49], already cited, which designated the two men – and with them *noēsis* and sensation – as presences or activities that are not simultaneous, but alternating and alternative. This implies that we should further elucidate the link between the *hēmeis* and consciousness.

Consciousness and identification

A passage from *Enn.* I.1[53] sheds light on the formulation, still vague, of *Enn.* V.1[10]: "'we' are linked to consciousness". Here, precisely, the question is raised of the degree to which the *hēmeis* can not only be associated with *dianoia*, but even identified with the separated soul: "Are we not also what is prior to this part (that is, the middle part of the soul)?" The answer is as follows: "Yes, as long as we become aware of it: for we do not always use all that we have, but only when we orient the middle part upwards, or in the contrary direction; must we not say that we make use of all that we make pass from potentiality or disposition to act?" (*Enn.* I.1[53].11.4–8).

Even more than as the subject of consciousness, the *hēmeis* appears here as what presides over its orientation "upwards, or in the contrary direction" – in other words, towards the first or the second man, towards intelligence or towards sensation. This realization is at the same time described as a "making use" and an actualization. Yet it is also that by which what was merely "ours" becomes "us". Thus, "we are also" what is superior to the middle part of the soul – that is, the separated soul – when we become aware of its presence in us: in other words, this realization is inseparably an identification. Consciousness is therefore not so much constitutive of identity as it is a condition for identification. We are not what we are aware of: quite the contrary, we become what we *become* aware of. If the reflexive question ends up in the acknowledgement of a duality, becoming aware, for its part, is equivalent to the choice of an identity.

Consciousness and conversion

There is nothing necessary about such a process. As we have said, consciousness, in its pre-philosophical stage, is spontaneously directed downwards; this is why Plotinus writes in *Enn.* V.3[49] that "we always sense". Yet it depends on us to prolong or to reverse this orientation, and this is the point at which Plotinian ethics enters the picture. As we have seen, the gap between the soul and the Intellect, its union with the body, is not by itself a "fault" or a "descent", but participates in the movement of procession. There is a fault only when the government (*hēgemonia*) of the body becomes exclusive concern (*kēdemonia*) for it. Entirely swallowed up by the body, under the sway of narcissistic illusion, consciousness then becomes incapable of reflecting the other activities of the soul and other powers of the *hēmeis*: Plotinus compares it to a broken "mirror", in which "discursive reason and Intelligence exercise their activity without reflection" (*Enn.* I.4[46].10.17–19). It is this same image of the mirror that is broken, or such that one can see oneself in it only as fragmented – the "mirror of Dionysus" – which elsewhere comes to express the soul's fascination with its own body and its descent into it (*Enn.* IV.3[27].12.1–2). In fact, it is in this bad orientation of consciousness, both obsessed and troubled by the body, that the true "descent" must be seen.

The necessary process of particularization, by virtue of which the essential "self" becomes an incarnate "self", then yields to the risk of parcelization: the subject, completely merged with its body, cuts itself off from the others, entering into that regime of division, of mutual inhibition, which characterizes corporeal reality (cf. *Enn.* III.6[26].6.33–64); but it no longer has access to its own totality, either. Thus, as early as *Enn.* IV.8[6], the Platonic drama of the descent is retranslated by Plotinus in epistemic terms: the descent must be understood, above all, as the forgetfulness by the soul of its intelligible rootedness; that is, as the obliteration of some of its faculties, the deactivation of some of its powers (cf. *Enn.* IV.8[6].8.1–13; I.8[51].14.44–6).

The point, then – and this, as we have said, is the movement obeyed by several Plotinian treatises – is to recall the subject to the consciousness of all the powers it bears within itself in order that, ultimately, it may be able to direct its attention towards the separated soul. In other words, the goal is still to give rise to a trajectory of consciousness whose various moments would be the following: pre-philosophical consciousness, fragmented, narcissistic, which has no other object than its own body (*kēdemonia*); the totalizing consciousness by which the *hēmeis* discovers that all the powers of the soul are "its own"; selective consciousness (*prosokhē*), oriented towards the separated soul alone; finally, the pure presence (*synesis*) in which all duality between the intellect and its object is abolished.

This trajectory of consciousness is inseparably an epistemic and an ethical trajectory: *Enn.* V.3[49] and *Enn.* I.1[53] thus manifest that the constant activity within us of the separated soul is the necessary condition for such everyday cognitive operations as judgement. Indeed, the latter is the placing in relation of the imprints, or *typoi*, issuing forth from sensible things, with the *typoi* issuing from the intelligible forms (*Enn.* V.3[49].2– 3.11; I.1[53].7.9–16, 9.18–23); that is, the notions (*noēseis*). True reasoning can then be defined as the "activation of notions" (*Enn.* I.1[53].9.21). This process of the actualization of notions is also what Plotinus calls "reminiscence", by which he defines cathartic virtue (cf. *Enn.* I.2[19].4.19–25; IV.3[27].25.30–3; V.3[49].2.7–14).

In this way, the movement of conversion is the reverse of that of procession: the degradation of powers is reversed into an actualization of the potential; that is, of the traces left in us by higher realities.[25] However, while procession is necessary, conversion is contingent, depending as it does on the choice of the *hēmeis*, who can remain forever cut off from its intelligible origin and its essential identity.[26]

In conclusion, then, we see that the association of *hēmeis* with consciousness prohibits the identification of it with any specific level of soul. At the same time, Plotinus thus provides himself with a graduated conception of the subject, since he distinguishes between the *hēmeis* and the intelligible "self". It is in the latter – identical to the pure *ousia*, that is, the separated soul – that the foundation of individuality resides, together with the most intense life and an unalterable happiness. We have tried to show what was singular about these two theses, already in themselves. But the strength of Plotinus' thought also resides in their articulation: in the affirmation both that something of us remains "up above", so that happiness is a very close presence, and that it can nevertheless escape us, since this presence must still be actualized, and this actualization depends on a choice. Whereas his successors Iamblichus and Proclus were to deny the existence of the separated soul and to delegate conversion to theurgical ritual or to a purely cognitive process (see Westra 1987), Plotinus, for his part, is able to conceive both the permanent, impersonal subject and the ethical subject defined as what makes the choice of its identity.

ACKNOWLEDGEMENT

I would like to give all my thanks to Michael Chase for his translation.

NOTES

1. Emphasized by Henri Bergson (2011), the fundamental role of Plotinian thought in the constitution of the notion of "Self" is curiously undervalued in genealogies such as those of Vernant (1989), C. Taylor (1989) or Foucault (2001). For recent re-evaluations, see Remes & Sihvola (2008), as well as Aubry & Ildefonse (2008).
2. This point was already noted by Dodds (1960). Let us specify at the outset that the notion of "self" is understood here in a broad sense, including both what is called in French "le moi" and "le soi"; that is, both the biographical, incarnate individual and the impersonal and/or essential identity.
3. Plotinus thereby distinguishes himself from both Plato and Aristotle, who accept reflexivity only *qua* mediated by an object or by another subject. Cf. especially Brunschwig (1983, 1996).
4. It has become frequent in the secondary literature to designate this soul as "undescended". We will see below how this designation is inadequate, in so far as, strictly speaking, the soul never "descends" for Plotinus.
5. Translation is that of P. Hadot, retranslated by M. Chase.

6. Cf. I.1[53].2.2, 6, 8. On the problem of the demarcation between soul and Intellect, cf. Blumenthal (1993b, 1996b).

7. *Enn.* V.3[49].3.23–9: Ἀλλ'οὐ ψυχῆς μὲν φήσομεν, ἡμέτερον δὲ νοῦν φήσομεν ….

8. *Ibid.*: 3.28.

9. If this distinction between the levels of the self structures the foundational works of P. Hadot (1980) and O'Daly (1973), contemporary research has, partly under the influence of the "philosophy of mind", been mainly interested in this essential level (see Rappe 1996; Gerson 1997b). Remes (2007) reconstructs the question of the continuity between the essential self and the concrete personal self.

10. εἶτ'οὐκ ἔχων ὅπη αὐτὸν στήσας ὁριεῖ καὶ μέχρι τίνος αὐτός ἐστιν.

11. Cf. *Enn.* V.8[31].11.5–12. See, along the same lines, *Enn.* IV.3[27].30.7–14, where consciousness is associated with discourse, *logos* and with imagination, *phantastikon*, as well as *Enn.* I.4[46].10.21–34, where Plotinus writes: "Acts of consciousness risk weakening the acts they accompany, whereas if they are not accompanied by consciousness, acts are more pure, having more intensity and life."

12. The debate is abundant: see, in particular, Rist (1963, 1970), Armstrong (1977), Blumenthal (1966, 1998), Gerson (1994: 139–51), Kalligas (1997), Morel (1999), Petit (1999), Nikulin (2005), Remes (2005; 2007: 32–59).

13. It is discussed in Aubry (2008a), of which I take up the conclusions here.

14. Cf. *Enn.* VI.7[38].5.2–3 (with the commentary of P. Hadot [1987: 214]).

15. On the subversion of the Aristotelian couple of potential and act implied by this model, and its application to the first principle, see Aubry (2006).

16. Aristotle, *de An.* II.1.412a19–414a28. On this progressive definition, see Ackrill (1979).

17. ζωωθὲν τὸ σῶμα; τὸ σῶμα τοιοῦτον/τοιόνδε. On the Plotinian terminology of the soul–body union, see Aubry (2004: 378–80).

18. The texts do not all agree on this point. Some (*Enn.* VI.4[22].15) suggest that it is the individual soul that, at birth, endows with sensation the body already animated by the World Soul; others (*Enn.* I.1[53].8.18) explicitly make sensation an effect of the World Soul. This conflict may be reduced, however, in so far as Plotinus distinguishes two forms of sensation: one, purely mechanical, is the pure reception of a *pathos* by the living body; the other, active and conscious, would already be a perception (as is well known, Greek has only one word, *aisthēsis*, for sensation and for perception). One may assume that the former is an effect of the World Soul, the latter of the individual soul.

19. *Enn.* VI.4[22].15.2. On this notion of *epitēdeiotēs*, see Aubry (2008b).

20. That is, neither constrained nor fully free. Cf. O'Brien (1977), D'Ancona (2003), Aubry (2012).

21. *Enn.* VI.4[22].16.36: οἶον δυνάμει τότε τὸ μέρος οὖσα.

22. *Enn.* V.3[49].3.23–4: οὐ ψυχῆς … ἡμέτερον δέ ….

23. On the irreducibility of the *hēmeis* both to the separated soul and to *dianoia*, may I refer to my reply (Aubry 2008c: 118 n. 29) to Chiaradonna (2008c). See also Lavaud (2002).

24. Here, *aisthēsis*. We also find the term *antilēpsis* at line 12. On the Plotinian vocabulary of consciousness, see, for an attempt at classification, Schwyzer (1960), A. C. Lloyd (1964), Warren (1964).

25. On the way in which the equivocity of *dynamis* (its twofold meaning of power/potentiality) comes to express in Plotinus the reciprocity of procession and conversion, cf. Aubry (2006).

26. For this reason, I see in the *hēmeis* not a "pure potentiality" (as Tornau [2009] reproached me), but a power of choice and self-determination. On this link between *hēmeis* and *proairesis*, cf. Aubry (2004: 302–4); in the same sense, see Sorabji (2006: 119) as well as O'Daly (1973: 49).

21

Perceptual awareness in the ancient commentators

Péter Lautner

Most Neoplatonists were convinced that the perceptual activity of the senses is a conscious activity, including even the reception of primary sense-qualities such as colours and sounds. This means that we cannot perceive anything unless we are aware of the specific impact exerted by the sense-object upon the sense-organ. The commentators can also rely on the doctrine found in Aristotle's *Physics* 7.2, according to which what is distinctive of perceptual alterations is that the subject is aware of them.[1] The problem with that discussion was that it did not explain why some alterations rather than others involve awareness. Why are we supposed to think that sense-perception implies awareness whereas other forms of qualitative change do not? For this reason, the discussion seemed to leave mysterious the possession by the sense-organs of the capacity to perceive. Moreover, an important part of the awareness involved in sense-perception is that we are aware not only of the specific impact, but also of the perceptual activity of our sensory power. The root of the problem is exposed in Aristotle's *de Anima*. In 3.2, Aristotle insists that we do perceive that we perceive. He seems to take it for granted that our perceptual system is capable of grasping its own operations. At the beginning of *de Anima* 3.2, he presents the following aporia:

> Since we perceive that we see and hear, it must either be by sight that one perceives that one sees or by another [sense]. But in that case there will be the same [sense] for sight and the colour which is the subject for sight – so that either there will be two senses for the same thing or {the sense} itself will be the one for itself.
>
> (425b12–16, trans. Hamlyn)[2]

The distinction between perception and perception of perception – perceptual consciousness – is here taken for granted, and the fact that a subject perceives that he perceives is something that calls for explanation. In principle, the problem posed by *Physics* 7.2 is now resolved. On the account of the *de Anima*, in order for the subject to be aware of a perceptual alteration, he has to exercise the full capacity for sense-perception which includes the working of both the particular sense in question and the perceptual system as a whole. It implies that not only are the particular sense-organs altered by their proper objects but that the central sense, located in the heart, is also working. Perception of external sense-objects is not the same as perceptual awareness but, as is clear from Aristotle's explanation of insensitivity in sleep, it requires it (see *de Somno* 2.455a33–b1, b8–12). If the controlling sense-organ, and hence the common perceptual power, is not operative, the particular senses will not be capable of getting activated either. Although the organ of touch, for instance, will presumably still have the capacity to be heated and cooled when the subject is asleep, such changes do not produce perception because the subject temporarily lacks the capacity to perceive his perceptions. The possession of this capacity depends not on the condition of the particular sense-organs but on that of the central organ, the heart, which controls the entire process at the level of physiology as well. On the other hand, Aristotle also raises the possibility that it is the same particular sense that is capable of perceiving both its primary objects and the act of perceiving them.

The commentators in late antiquity share Aristotle's conviction that perception is not the same as perceptual awareness. But that seems to be the only point on which they agree, since – as far as our sources allow us to say – they put forward considerably different theories on the reflexivity of the perceptual system. The main thrust of their arguments was not just the seemingly technical issue of how to apprehend the activity of the senses. At stake was the unity of the soul. If the different kinds of reflexive activities in the soul – such as perceptual awareness and awareness of thinking or feeling – did not have a common root, then some philosophers were afraid that the unity of the self would be broken, since different reflexivities might not comply to a hierarchical structure, with the principle of self-consciousness on the top.

The best start for our discussion might be to turn to a survey we come across in one of the commentaries. The survey forms a part of a commentary on Aristotle's *de Anima* book 3 and the manuscripts ascribe it to Philoponus, but the authorship is doubted.[3] For convenience, I shall call the commentator Pseudo-Philoponus. He takes Aristotle to deny that the central sense has any activity of its own. Aristotle wants the particular senses to lay hold both of the things subject to them and their own activities too. The visual sense apprehends both the colours; that is, the sense-objects peculiar to it, as well as the act of seeing. He launches harsh criticism at Aristotle for the above assumption. Before doing so, however, he mentions three interpretations on the matter. One of them emphasizes the role of the common sense, the second attributes perceptual awareness to the rational soul, whereas the third ascribes it to the so-called attentive faculty. The commentator's procedure is all the more important because the original sources containing these explanations are lost.

ALEXANDER OF APHRODISIAS

Of the three views expounded there, one is set forth by Alexander of Aphrodisias.[4] In his commentary on the *de Anima*, he thinks that the five particular senses grasp the sense-objects that are their subjects, and the common sense (*koinē aisthēsis*) grasps both the subjects and their activities.[5] Although the commentary has not survived to us, we have

Alexander's own *de Anima*, a kind of rehearsal of Aristotle's work with some important modifications. Here he makes the same point on perceptual awareness and the argument might also be fairly similar. We read that:

> It is by this common sense that we perceive ourselves seeing and hearing and exercising each sense. For one who is seeing perceives himself seeing and one who is hearing perceives himself hearing. For it is not by some other capacity besides [common][6] sense that we perceive ourselves perceiving. For we do not see that we are seeing nor hear that we are hearing, since seeing is not visible, nor hearing audible. Rather, it is the activity of the first, controlling sense faculty which is called "common" by which awareness (*synaisthēsis*) of perceiving accrues to those who perceive.   (*de An.* 65.2–10)[7]

Alexander's argument is quite Aristotelian in its vein.[8] If the proper object of sight is colour, then it would be hard to see how it is possible that the visual sense apprehends its own activity too. The activity is not coloured and therefore it cannot be the object of sight. To illustrate the working of the common sense, Alexander used a metaphor that was to exert great influence on the Neoplatonists, beginning with Plotinus (*Enn.* IV.7[2].6.89). He likens it to the centre of a circle from which the particular senses as radii branch off (63.9–10). The reason why he adopted the new metaphor of the circle may have been to emphasize the multiplicity of sensations and the central role of common sense power in our perceptual system. It also shows that the central sense is not a sum of the particular senses. Rather, it stands apart from the particular senses just as the centre differs from any points on the circumference. Common sense also seems to coordinate the particular senses in so far as it connects them to one another, which leads to some characteristic functions of its own, such as perceiving the common sense-objects (such as size, shape and motion) and the workings of the particular senses.[9]

In another text (*Quaestiones* 3.7) attributed to him, however, Alexander – if he is the author – gives a very different account on the same matter.[10] The aim of the argument is to show why sense-perception involves perceptual awareness. Unlike Aristotle, then, Alexander does not take it for granted that we perceive that we are perceiving. The argument from the perception of primary sense-objects to perceptual awareness serves to account for this thesis which will be much disputed in later times. He offers three points that deserve attention. First, he refers to Aristotle in saying that sight is capable of perceiving not only colours and coloured things but also the privation of them, for every sense perceives the privation of its objects. It is by sight that we perceive both light and darkness (92.23–7). The author also assumes that Aristotle accepted that the act of seeing itself is in a way coloured. This must be so if seeing comes about when the sense-organ receives the form of the thing seen without the matter that underlies it. As a sign of this he refers to after-images (*aisthesis* and *phantasia*); often, when the thing perceived has departed, there still remain behind in the senses certain sensations and images of them (92.27–31). Third, in the final argument, he claims – on Aristotelian grounds (*de An.* 3.2.425b26–426a4) – that the actuality of the thing perceived and of the sense are one, differing only in account, since a sense at work is constituted by the possession of the form of the thing perceived without its matter, whereas the thing perceived in actuality is nothing but its form being possessed without its matter (92.32–93.23). Its form is possessed by the sense receiving it. According to a general principle of change, formulated in *Physics* 3.3 (202a21–b5), the change produced by some cause is always in the thing that is changed. Consequently, as a kind of qualitative change, sense-perception takes place in the perceiving subject. Moreover, sense-perception implies perceptual awareness because sense-perception is a reception of sensible forms coming from without. Perceptual awareness comes about when the sense apprehends the sensible forms in itself and, on account of this, fulfils its function as sense. We perceive the change within ourselves. The two processes are one, differing only in account. For it is by receiving the form from the things perceived, which are outside, that we apprehend them, but it is by the sense having the form of the things perceived in itself that perceptual awareness comes about. To take the example of seeing, we see something in virtue of apprehending the perceptible's form. By apprehending the form the sense of sight sees and at the same time it comes to see itself seeing (93.15–18). On this account, sense-perception is intimately linked to a certain kind of awareness. In sense-perception, we simultaneously apprehend both the thing perceived and the activity of the sense in relation to the thing perceived. Perceptual awareness is tied to the fact that in sense-perception we must be aware of the reception of external influence. Hence the reflexive nature of sense-perception is somehow included in the activity of grasping the primary objects of sense-perception.

How shall we harmonize the two accounts?[11] After all, it seems that in the *de Anima*, Alexander emphasizes the role of common sense power, whereas in *Quaestiones* 3.7 he derives perceptual awareness from the general nature of sense-perception. My suggestion is that the two accounts are complementary. The *Quaestiones* offer a general account of how perceptual awareness is possible. The reception of sensible forms requires awareness. Following Aristotle, Alexander assumes that this kind of awareness belongs to the perceptual faculty. It is not the rational faculty that such a task has been assigned to. In the *de Anima*, Alexander specifies the thesis by pointing out that perceptual awareness comes about by virtue of the activity of the centre of our perceptual system. It may remain unclear as to what arguments led him to dismiss the possibility that the particular senses might be able to grasp the activity of their own. There seem to be two points that could not have been accepted, for different reasons, and they also marked the limits within which Alexander's argument must have moved. On the one hand, he accepted the Aristotelian thesis that perceptual awareness is the task of the perceptual system. On the other hand, he might have had doubts about the ability of the particular senses to grasp their own activities. Even if the act of seeing is somehow coloured (*de An.* 92.27–31), there must be a difference between the perceiver and the perceived. The difference is within the perceptual system and lies between the particular sense and the common sense power.

PLUTARCH OF ATHENS

Going back to Pseudo-Philoponus, we find two other approaches. One is by Plutarch of Athens who was the first head of the Athenian school of Neoplatonists. At first sight, Pseudo-Philoponus' report seems to be puzzling. First, he says that on Plutarch's view it is the function of the rational soul to know the activities of the senses. This happens by virtue of the inferior part of the rational soul, which is opinion (*doxa*) (464.23–30: part of Source 29 in Taormina 1989), for opinion, which is the most common and inferior part of the soul, joins the rational to the non-rational. On this account, Plutarch charges a single rational capacity with the task of being aware of perceiving. It turns out very quickly, however, that the claim is badly established. Pseudo-Philoponus relies on some more recent philosophers who took Plutarch to task for making *doxa* apprehend the activity of the senses. The core of the criticism was that as the inferior part of the rational soul, *doxa* would not be capable of grasping the operations of the higher rational capacities. If we want a single power responsible for all sorts of awareness, as the critics obviously do, we must find a capacity which has a certain – cognitive – control over all the conscious activities of the soul. Later on, Pseudo-Philoponus himself responds that he has never come across the view that *doxa* is the centre of awareness in Plutarch. Instead, he connects Plutarch's position to that of Alexander. Both of them suggested that it is the common sense that has the function of perceiving that we are perceiving.[12] Pseudo-Philoponus rejects this by arguing that as a sense, the common sense cannot apprehend activities because these do not fall under the particular senses and the common sense is after all capable of grasping nothing but sensibles. Activities are not of this kind.

At first sight, Plutarch's explanation of perceptual awareness is ambiguous. The emphasis may not be on the partial issue of how we can perceive that we are perceiving, but on preserving the unity of the human soul. For, as Pseudo-Philoponus points out, *doxa* cannot be the faculty of apprehending that our senses are at work. Such a kind of reflexive activity must have one source, otherwise the unity of the soul will be in danger. But *doxa* cannot be this source because it cannot apprehend the activities of higher faculties, such as intellect and discursive reason. It is a general rule that, in the order of the faculties of the soul, the activities of the higher cannot be grasped by the lower. In fact, *doxa* could perform such a task on itself or on spirit (*thymos*) and thus also on sense-perception, but is not able to apprehend the activity of the intellect or discursive reason; it is fully disqualified from being the only reflexive activity in the soul. Following this line of argument, we should point to the intellect, the highest capacity in our soul, as the indirect source of perceptual awareness. This would rule out that beasts are aware of the activity of their senses. But Plutarch does not insist on this explanation; instead he also joins Alexander in attributing perceptual awareness to common sense.

What conclusion can we draw here? The most important is that the common sense cannot be entirely distinct from the particular senses. It cannot be a distinct sense over and above the particular senses. If it were distinct altogether Plutarch would have to confront the difficulties he faced in discussing the supposed role of *doxa*. As a higher, rational capacity doxa cannot be the centre of reflexivity and if we separate the seat of perceptual awareness from sense-perception proper we have to ask for an extra capacity to grasp the activity of this capacity. To illustrate the relation of common sense to particular senses we can thus return to Alexander's reinterpretation of Aristotle's simile of the point and limit into the simile of the centre of a circle and its radii. The centre is different from the particular senses but it depends on them. There is no other cognitive source for the common sense power except for the particular senses. They furnish it with the information it shapes further by division and combination.

It is not quite clear what prompted Plutarch to adhere to this double account of perceptual awareness. How to reconcile the two accounts? Perhaps he simply changed his mind. That is certainly a possibility. In that case, we have to say that the change did not exclude the former position from his successors' minds and, consequently, there were two doxographical traditions on Plutarch's view on the human soul.[13] There may also have been problems in transmission of the text with the result that either the more recent commentators or Pseudo-Philoponus misconstrued Plutarch's position. Alternatively, one might say that the divergence between the two accounts is not overwhelming. We have to bear in mind that for Iamblichus the human soul is permeated by the intellect in a way that sense-perception itself becomes rational.[14] Moreover, at Athens Iamblichus was the greatest authority after Plato.[15] If our perceptual system is rational, then the gap between common sense and *doxa* does not represent the gap between the non-rational and the rational element in us, which thus includes the whole perceptual activity as well.[16]

PROCLUS AND DAMASCIUS

Let us look at the final group referred to in Pseudo-Philoponus' doxography (464.30–465.17). The so-called "more recent" commentators criticized Plutarch's theory and suggested that it is the function of the attentive part (*prosektikon*) of the rational soul to apprehend the activities of the senses.[17] They credited the rational soul with six powers, among them the attentive, the task of which was to stand over what happens in human being and say "I exercised intellect", "I thought", "I became spirited", and so on. In general, this attentive capacity ranges over all the powers of the soul.[18] For this reason, it presides over the perceptive power as well, and this is why I am able to say that "I see", "I hear", and so on. They insisted on this claim because on their view this was the way to preserve the unity of the human soul. It seems that they held the attentive part responsible for self-consciousness in general, since it is by virtue of this attentive part that we are able to say that "I think" or "I see". Pseudo-Philoponus does not name the philosophers representing this group but we know that Proclus and Damascius, one of Proclus' successors at Athens, were of this view.[19]

In Proclus' commentary on the *Parmenides* we find a detailed exposition of the thesis.[20] On discussing the conative powers in the soul and using a slightly modified version of the Aristotelian division into appetite, spiritedness and rational choice, he says that there must be a single vital principle which presides over them. Hence perceptual awareness arises not from the perceptual system, but from a rational capacity. To emphasize reflexivity, Proclus uses the term "awareness" (*parakolouthein*) to maintain that the attentive capacity is following all the other activities and cooperates with them.[21] To some extent he could rely on his predecessors, most notably Plotinus.[22] Thus perceptual awareness is endowed with two functions. It moves the soul towards all these objects and at the same time enables us to say that "I have appetite", and so on. The unitary principle is also responsible for the capacity of saying "I am perceiving", "I am reasoning" and "I will". It seems that Proclus connects the two functions, which implies that reflexivity of this sort has a guiding force as well. It not only works as a capacity of registering certain kinds of psychic activities but also directs them. Direction can take two forms: either moving the capacities in the right direction so that we desire the right thing, for instance, or moving us, human beings, towards the goals set by the conative powers. In the latter case it would be an extra moving force in us, along with appetite, spiritedness and rational choice. I have not found any evidence in Proclus for such a conception.[23] However, the passage may allow for another explanation as well: the attentive capacity seems to check the direction of desires. It is said to give the nod (*synepineuein*) to desires and live along with them. If the gesture of giving a nod is to be taken at face value then the function of the attentive capacity is to let the various desires aim at the right goal. Awareness is endowed with a controlling function as well, then, which may or may not be efficient in directing desires. The double function of the attentive capacity, not mentioned in Pseudo-Philoponus' doxography, connects awareness to guidance and, hence, evaluation. The source for evaluation, just as for attention, is the high position of the capacity in the soul. It belongs to the rational capacities. Proclus says that it presides over the *sensus communis*, and is prior to opinion, desire and rational wish.[24] In sum, it is closer to the intellect (*nous*) that is the transmitter of truth in the soul.

Proclus also lays great emphasis on the singular nature of the attentive capacity. If it were manifold, we would not be able to say that "I desire" and "I perceive".[25] Furthermore, the attentive capacity is not only singular but also partless. This is why in each case it can say "I" and "I am active". From a Neoplatonic point of view it may be interesting to note that this "I" is not only a bearer of rational capacities. It cannot be identified with intellect or discursive reason (*dianoia*) since it is also the bearer of sense-perception and appetite. We might say that, for Proclus, sense-perception is a very complex phenomenon, but it still contains elements or stages, such as perception of pleasure and pain, which are clearly not rational.[26] Appetite and spiritedness lack such complexity; they only can listen to reason without being rational themselves (see *in Ti.* 1.250.20; 3.355.14–15). Since the "I" covers both appetite and spiritedness, along with sense-perception and some purely rational capacities, we may conclude that reflexivity is constitutive of the "I", and since reflexivity extends to non-rational capacities as well, the "I", too, is intimately related to certain non-rational elements in us. Perceptual awareness does not seem to be essentially different from other reflexive activities; there is no mention made about the possibility that all the first-order activities such as desire and opinion are apprehended in different ways.[27]

On the other hand, elsewhere Proclus proposed another theory which might contradict the one we find expounded in the *Parmenides Commentary*. In the commentary on the *Timaeus* he distinguished four strata of sense-perception, with the highest one being a kind of internal perception (2.83.16–84.5). This is the context where Proclus also mentions *synaisthēsis*. The term has a chequered career, but here it does not seem to me to refer to reflexive self-awareness. Rather, it might be a joint-perception which serves to apprehend motion and time, and as a consequence, to perceive the affections that are produced in the perceiver.[28] Hence *synaisthēsis* may refer to something non-conceptual.[29] For this reason, it differs from any rational capacity. If we want to clarify the relation between *synaisthēsis* and the activity of the attentive part of the rational soul, there seem to be two marks that are relevant. First, the attentive part is verbal; it says that "I perceive" or "I desire", whereas *synaisthēsis* is not tied to the usage of words. Second, the attentive part apprehends activities exclusively; it grasps that the senses are working. By contrast, *synaisthēsis* apprehends content as well; it also grasps the affections produced in the perceiver. Perception of motion is linked to perception of affections but is directed both to inward and outward motions. Hence perception of motion is not directed to the perceiving subject as a perceiving subject. Apprehension of the perceiving subject as a perceiving subject is too specific a task for *synaisthēsis* to complete. That can be done by the attentive part solely.

In Damascius' commentary on the *Phaedo*, we have explicit references to attention as a separate capacity. The commentary has survived to us in two versions, each devoting a passage to explain the phenomenon (*in Phd.* 1.269–72; 2.21–2). The explanations are very similar. In both passages, the line of thought starts with a fairly specific question. What is the reason why we do not know, when recollecting, that it is a recollection? It happens many times that recollection comes up as a newly acquired knowledge and we are not aware that we are recollecting. As a matter of fact, it is easier to recollect something than to know that we are recollecting. The latter requires a more specific knowledge. As a consequence, the act of recollection does not involve the awareness that we are recollecting, although it certainly involves the awareness that something is coming up in our mind. We are aware that something goes on in our mind but we cannot specify it; it can be a sort of discovering, thinking of something new, but it equally can be an act of recollecting. The problem is subtle and Damascius tries to solve it with reference to the attentive part of the soul (*to prosektikon*). Accordingly, we fail to know that we are recollecting because the attentive part does not focus on the activity of recollection. The reason is that attention is easily diversible, since its direction varies constantly. As an awareness, that is, knowledge of the activities of the soul, attention is tied to the subject's reversion upon oneself, whereas other kinds of knowledge are directed towards external objects.[30] One might perhaps say that attention zigzags, which causes an occasional failure to realize that we are recollecting. Beasts also have recollection, which means only that they can recall past memories, not that they have any specific knowledge of the Forms.[31] Their memories might pop up again, but they do not reflect on them either. The reason for this lack is that they are devoid of any trace of rationality. They are not endowed with the attentive capacity, not even in a downgraded form.

There are three points to be emphasized here. First, it seems that Damascius distinguishes two levels of attention: at one level we can be aware that we think of something, at the other level we can qualify the activity in question and say that we are recollecting, and not thinking of something new. The diverted focus of attention may only be responsible for the failure at the latter level. Second, unlike Proclus, however, Damascius thought that reflexivity has two sources. The attentive part is directed towards all the cognitive activities only, whereas reflection on desiderative activities requires another activity. It is called *syneidos*, *joint-cognition*. We are aware of our feelings, emotions and desires by virtue of a certain joint-cognition. This joint-cognition may not be responsible for the arousal of the various conative activities, since they are raised by memory or *synaisthēsis*, *joint-perception*.[32] It seems, therefore, that the main shift within the human soul lies between the cognitive and the appetitive capacities, not between the rational and the non-rational ones.[33] Third, the division between the two forms of reflection raises the problem of the unity of the reflective capacity. Damascius does not deal with it in the commentary, although it is of crucial importance, since the dual structure of reflexivity endangers the unity of the subject. He might have suggested a derivational structure to make sure that awareness of the appetitive activities depends on the attentive. The problem was clear both to Proclus and Pseudo-Philoponus.

PSEUDO-PHILOPONUS

We need some sort of transition here. Pseudo-Philoponus agrees with all three interpretations to a certain extent and offers a detailed justification for each one.[34] His text contains the most elaborated arguments for the *prosektikon* theory, and against Aristotle's assumptions. First of all, he fully agrees that there is not a sixth sense of which the task is to come to know that we see or hear. The reason for agreeing with this, however, is not that the same sense is capable of apprehending both its peculiar objects and its own activity. When it comes to the denial of a sixth sense, Aristotle's explanation in de Anima 3.1 can be accepted. By contrast, the commentator criticizes him bluntly for the claim that it is the same sense that perceives and realizes that it is perceiving. Aristotle attempted to prove the point by saying that sight, for example, does not grasp colour only, but also light and dark, to which the commentator replies that sight apprehends only colour, and it knows others by denial, by their not being colour, and is not affected by them. We come to know our activity in a way which is very different from the way we know things by denial, however.

It is also absurd to say that activity is coloured in any way. Activity is incorporeal and incorporeal entities cannot have colours. Furthermore, Pseudo-Philoponus thinks it is impossible that the same sense should know that it sees. He develops an argument to the effect that, if it can revert to itself (this is what perceptual awareness means to him), the power of perception is both immortal and incorporeal. In order to get to know that it sees, the visual sense should revert to itself after having seen the colour. If, however, it reflects on itself it also has an activity which is separate from matter, which implies that it has a being separate from matter. Therefore it must be both immaterial and incorporeal. Separation is limited, however, since without grasping a perceptible object the activity of perceptual awareness cannot exist. Moreover, the senses are not eternal, since they are tied to bodily organs. Therefore, they cannot revert to themselves. As a consequence, it is the rational part of the human soul to apprehend that we are perceiving. It is the attentive part that has this job.[35] The thesis clearly goes against the Aristotelian assumptions, since in the de Anima Aristotle did not envisage the possibility that perceptual awareness might be due to reason. It is not quite clear how to explain the status of the attentive part. Does Pseudo-Philoponus think that it is an independent part or faculty of the rational soul, which might mean that it can be defined without reference to other rational faculties, or is it just a well-described function of reason? It seems as if he tends to favour the first option. He uses the attribute of the "more recent" commentators without any reservation, which implies that he accepted that the attentive power is a part of the rational soul. It has the function of grasping every psychic activity. Perceptual awareness is just one part of its activity.[36] It is true that Pseudo-Philoponus uses such terminology very rarely. Indeed, except for this doxographical digression he makes use of the term "attentive" only once (555.12); he says that Plato used to call "intellective cognition" (noera gnōsis) attentive. He must have drawn on some doxographical report, since the term does not occur in Plato's works, as they have come down to us. Neither is there any passage in the dialogues – to my best knowledge – where some cognate of prosektikon turns up in a similar context. The commentator justifies the claim by saying that if the subject stating "I thought" and the subject stating "I fed" were different, then one may reasonably say that it would be as if I perceived this and you perceived that. It recalls the Trojan Horse model in the Theaetetus. In any case – independently of any historical reliability – in Pseudo-Philoponus' use, attention seems to be a phenomenon which applies to a broader range of rational activities in the soul, not only to a single one.

Pseudo-Philoponus' last argument emphasizing the inability of the sense to perceive its own activity is particularly striking when we turn to the texts of fellow philosophers at Athens. Moreover, against the background offered by the conceptions of Proclus and

Damascius, it is also interesting to see that other Athenian commentators were of a different view. The commentators were Damascius' younger contemporaries and their conceptions show internal discrepancies in the school that, in this case, seemed to be an upshot
of their diverging allegiance to Iamblichus.

PSEUDO-SIMPLICIUS

We have a commentary on Aristotle's *de Anima* that has been attributed to Simplicius by
the manuscripts. Doubts have been raised on the authorship, which I will not discuss now.
But much in it seems to me to show clearly that the text cannot be by Simplicius, although
I am still a little bit puzzled as to whom we have to attribute it to. For convenience, again,
I shall call the author "Pseudo-Simplicius".[37] We also possess a work by Priscian of Lydia
who paraphrases Theophrastus' views on the soul and also adds some remarks and corrections which are – as far as we can say with some certainty – based on Iamblichus' views.

Unlike Pseudo-Philoponus and the "more recent" commentators, Pseudo-Simplicius
strongly insists that our perceptual power is capable of apprehending the activities of the
soul. On the other hand, he agrees with Pseudo-Philoponus that, properly speaking, reflexivity is the function of the rational soul. But that does not lead him to the conclusion that
the perceptual system is not capable of grasping the activity of its own. He gets support
from Iamblichus who claims that our rationality penetrates as far as sense-perception.[38]
He takes it for granted that the perceptual system is endowed with such a capability, and
tries to find an explanation for those characteristics. He comes to the conclusion that
sense-perception is rational in so far as it can revert to itself. The argument for the thesis
is somewhat obscure, although there might be some possibility to reconstruct it, since the
following argument reflects the structure of the relevant section in Proclus' *Elements of
Theology* (167). What is perceiving cognizes itself – this is the starting point emphasizing
the conscious nature of sense-perception. For this reason it reverts to itself, which is
nothing but a formula expressing awareness. It cannot have bodily characteristics, since
every body which has different parts of itself in different places would never be able to turn
its attention to itself entirely. There would always be a spatially distinct part taking cognizance of another spatially distinct part. The activity of perceptual awareness is gathered
together and becomes undivided, while every body is divided. Thus perceptual awareness
belongs to a power, the rational soul, which is entirely independent from the body.[39] This
line of thought is quite interesting. On the one hand, the commentator does his best to
maintain the Aristotelian thesis that perceptual awareness is a function of the perceptual
system itself. On the other hand, he uses Iamblichus' doctrines – and perhaps Iamblichus'
proofs – to argue for the thesis. Unlike Aristotle, he is convinced that sense-perception
retains features that characterize the rational faculties. By "rationality", he may not mean
that the content of sense-perception is propositional, but only that the activity of the
perceptual system mirrors the activity of the intellect in so far as it is capable of reverting
to itself. It is because of this feature that the perceptual system is capable of grasping the
activities of its own.[40]

How does he resolve the particular problem posed by Aristotle's account? How to
describe the mechanism of perceptual awareness in detail? If a sense is to grasp its own
activity, then the activity itself should possess the peculiar features which the sense is

able to grasp. First, the commentator takes Aristotle to support the claim that the sense is primarily cognitive of its primary object – sight is of colours, hearing is of sounds – but that does not exclude the possibility that it can cognize other things as well, although in a different way. Perception of darkness is a proper case in point (this had already been noted by Aristotle: see *de An.* 426b31–427a9). In the act of perceiving, the sense is capable of making the judgement even when, though it tries to perceive, there is nothing around to be perceived. We may illuminate this point with the help of a thought experiment. Imagine that we enter a dark room from a sunny place. We do not see anything, although we are pretty sure that our visual sense is working. In this case, we judge by sight that it is dark. We do not see anything, but we can be sure that our visual sense is working in a way; it is trying to perceive something, without success.[41] We cannot say that we see. For this reason, our awareness is not of seeing, but of trying to see and failing to do so. This implies that by the act of attempting to perceive we can also judge/discriminate the fact that our senses are working. Hence our senses have a certain kind of independence, since the activity of the senses does not consist of receiving a sensible form only. On trying to expound this, the commentator turns to the analysis of sight, and draws attention to a distinction between two ways of apprehending light (189.19–21). The first happens through the perception of colours; it is when we perceive colours that have light falling on them. Thus we perceive light incidentally. The second happens when we perceive light on its own – when we see the air as it is lit. Perception of darkness is not perceiving in either – direct or indirect – way. On seeing something, sight perceives itself acting, which is due to its rational nature. By seeing nothing, it also has to grasp something, since it is not inactive. We are aware that we do not see anything, but as awareness is always additional to some activity, there must be an activity of which we are aware. This is a kind of perception where the only thing our visual sense perceives is its being at work (perception must have an object). Taken in this way, seeing in darkness might appear a borderline case, but the commentator feels free to generalize the point; each act of perception involves both a perception of a proper object (colour) and a perception of the act of perceiving. This latter is a special kind of grasp, since in many cases – such as the one suggested by the example – perceptual awareness consists in perceiving that the sense is trying to perceive something, unsuccessfully.

To prove the case more forcefully, Pseudo-Simplicius discusses another solution to the problem raised by Aristotle on perceptual awareness (189.28–33). He focuses on the involvement of primary objects of sense-perception in perceptual awareness. Again, take the example of sight. The primary objects of sight are colours. We see things in so far as they are coloured. Seeing, however, as every kind of sense-perception, is a reception of forms without the underlying matter. For this reason the sense itself also, in a way, becomes coloured, as being coloured it can also be the object of seeing, which is of course an actuality. Thus the visual sense perceives itself in the act of perception; that is, in the reception of visual form. The commentator takes Aristotle to apply the term "reception" to signify the functioning of the sense-organ, not to that of the sense itself. Reception of visual form does not mean that the sense itself gets coloured as a result of an affection. The sense actualizes colours, and is not affected by them. It actualizes colours not by producing them, but by discriminating them.[42] In order to preserve the general impassibility of human sense-perception (and that of the soul in general),[43] the commentator describes the process in which the sense-organ receives the form of the objects. These forms are received by the sense actively; the sense only makes the appropriate discrimination. This is why perceptual awareness is inevitable in the process of sense-perception. The sense grasps its own act of discriminating. This argument is strikingly different from the previous one, since it relied on the extreme case of seeing no colours, whereas the latter is based on the ordinary process of sense-perception, and heavily influenced by Neoplatonic notions.

PRISCIAN OF LYDIA

Like Pseudo-Simplicius, Priscian of Lydia was also against the assumption that a distinct part of the rational soul is responsible for perceptual awareness, and joins those who ascribe it to the perceptual system. The approach in his treatise on Theophrastus' views on sense-perception and intellect, however, slightly differs from Pseudo-Simplicius in so far as he did not discuss the possibility of perceiving the vain effort of the sense to perceive. In the wake of Iamblichus, he affirms the rational nature of sense-perception.[44] The rational nature extends as far as to the particular senses, which gives the ground of his criticism of Theophrastus' thesis that perceptual awareness is due to the common sense power. He does not see any crucial difference between the particular senses and the common sense, since he regards the latter as a synthesis and concentration of the former. Furthermore, just like Pseudo-Simplicius and many other Neoplatonists, he also insists on the active nature of the sensory power. But we find an interesting shift here, since he says that the individual sense perceives its own activity *in a way*.[45] To see the importance of the modifying clause we have to realize that the particular sense seems to perceive that it is perceiving because it is a part of the perceptual system, or more precisely, because it is connected to the common sense power. It would not be capable of performing such a task on its own.[46] Thus Priscian ascribes perceptual awareness to *sensus communis*. He thinks that, owing to the common power, we are able to perceive that we are perceiving. His emphasis is on the capacity of perceiving both the activity and the inactivity of the senses (22.11–14). It seems paradoxical that a sense can perceive its own inactivity. This Priscian tries to resolve by saying that the common sense power, as it were, transcends its specific activity and inactivity. Hence the sensory power seems to be endowed with a two-stage model of perception: the first stage is directed towards the sensible objects whereas the second apprehends the first. So far, this is a commonplace in the Greek epistemological tradition. The novelty is that there is no such dependence between the two stages that the second would work only if the first works, too. From this point of view it has its own independence. Furthermore, the commentator does not say that the particular sense works even if it does not perceive anything. It is not the effort that is perceived during second-order perception. The common sense power apprehends the inactivity of the particular senses, which means that it apprehends the stillness of the sense.

ACKNOWLEDGEMENTS

Parts of the infant version of the paper were delivered in October 2011, in Fribourg, and I am indebted to the audience, especially to Filip Karfík and Martine Nida-Rümelin for important clarifications. I also owe much to Pauliina Remes, Svetla Slaveva-Griffin and the anonymous referee for their insightful remarks. My study was supported by the Hungarian Research Fund (OTKA), project number 104574.

NOTES

1. See *Ph.* 244b15, commented on both by Simplicius (*in Ph.* 1059.23–29) and Philoponus (757.15–20); see the Arabic paraphrase of his *in Ph.* VII, edited by Abû l-Husayn al-Baṣrî in the first half of the eleventh century, preserved in a Leiden manuscript (MS Leiden Or. 583) and translated into English by Paul Lettinck (1994).

2. The problem was touched upon, very abruptly and without further thoughts, in Plato's *Charmides* 167a–169c.

3. The literature abounds: for good summaries, see Charlton (2000: 1–10) and Perkams (2008: 237–9), both opting for Stephanus of Alexandria (*floruit* 610) as the author.

4. Given the confines of my contribution, his views will not be discussed at length. The only reason I shall talk about him in this context is that his theory of the soul exerted enormous influence on those authors in late antiquity who were thinking about the soul philosophically.

5. According to the report in Pseudo-Philoponus' *in de Anima* 3.464.20–23.

6. The word "common" (κοινή) in line 6 has been inserted by Ivo Bruns (1887), the editor of the Greek text, with reference to the medieval Hebrew translation, on which see his Preface xiv–xv. We can follow Accattino & Donini (1996: 234) who reject the inclusion by pointing out that the text is perfectly understandable as it stands in the Greek manuscripts.

7. Translated by Sorabji (2004: 148–9), slightly modified. The account recalls Aristotle's *de Somno* 2.455a15–22. Caston (2012: 33) argues that συναίσθησις does not mean self-awareness, although it refers to it; primarily, it has the meaning of "being aware of something while perceiving something else" (*ibid.*: 34). The examples he adduces concern joint-perception of another object, whereas perceptual awareness implies perception of a mental act.

8. See *de An.* 3.2.425b12–25, although Alexander is explicit in attributing to the *sensus communis* the capacity to perceive the activities of the particular senses: see Accattino & Donini (1996: 234).

9. As a late antique parallel to Alexander's notion, especially in the use of the metaphor of centre and radii, one might be tempted to refer to Themistius. But even if he uses the metaphor in order to clarify the operation of the perceptual system, he does it for different purposes. On his view, a particular sense is able to perceive that it is perceiving, hence there is no need for a common sense power to do that job (his *in de An.* 83.21–35). He employs the metaphor to emphasize the role of common sense in distinguishing different types of perceptual qualities, such as telling the difference between white and sweet.

10. For the authorship of the treatise, see Bruns (1892: viii), assuming that the text could form a part of a continuous commentary. Sharples (1994: 3 n. 23; 134 n. 270) has found the claim lacking decisive evidence.

11. Caston (2012: 41) doubts if the two accounts can be reconciled. On his view, it is possible that one account was discarded in favour of the other at some later stage. Later on (*ibid.*: 48–9) he adds that the crucial difference is that in the *Quaestiones* the explanation of perceptual awareness turns on sameness of perceived object and perceiving subject and as such applies equally to perception and thinking, whereas in the *de Anima* it turns on the disanalogy in their objects; it applies to thinking only. The disanalogy might be not so sharp if we take into account that forms – intelligible and perceptible alike – must be in the soul in order that a cognitive activity get going, irrespective of their origins.

12. I have argued for an interpretation in Lautner (2000) which I summarize here with small revisions. Of the two accounts attributed to Plutarch, the second seems to me to be the one held by Plutarch, which implies that the "more recent" commentators misinterpreted his position. Blumenthal (1975: 134–6) and Taormina (1989: 91–2) think that both positions were held by Plutarch. They envision some kind of developmental evolution of Plutarch's view, and assume that he held the former view at the end of his career. There may be a possibility of reconciling the two positions and regard the change as a shift in aspect, but to do so we must have a clearer account of the relation between *doxa* and *sensus communis*. If *doxa* concerns the physical world exclusively, as it seems, and the perceptual system contains propositional elements – seeing not a colour only but also that something is the case – then such a link can be established. In lack of textual evidence, however, I do not think we can say too much about the issue in Plutarch. Furthermore, If Blumenthal and Taormina were right, it is curious that Ps.-Philoponus never came across the *doxa* theory in Plutarch: see Tornau (2007: 124–5). I owe this point to the anonymous referee.

13. This may imply that the more recent commentators did not use the doxographical material in Alexandria. As the most probable candidates for the title were Proclus and Damascius, the material at Athens might have been different from that in Alexandria from this point of view too.

14. *Apud* Ps.-Simplicius, *in de An.* 173.1–7; 187.35–9. In fact, the rational soul pervades human beings to the extent that the human body will be rationally arranged, which, of course, reflects Plato's views in the *Timaeus*.

15. Again, Pseudo-Simplicius called him the best judge of the truth (*in de An.* 1.12–14).

16. These philosophers must have understood this as going very well with the *sensus communis* business – one power that gathers the information from different modalities. I owe this note to one of my referees.

17. It is unclear who was the first of the Platonists to posit such an independent capacity. Proclus referred to Atticus (*in Ti.* 2.306.1–2 = frag. 36 [Des Places]), who might have been the earliest exponent of the theory.

18. There is a puzzle here, since the thesis implies that the attentive part stands over the vegetative activities as well. But it is not easy to see how one can be aware of (not know about!) one's metabolic processes. On the other hand, both Damascius and Proclus employed examples referring to what we call "mental" activities.

19. See Westerink's extensive note to Damascius' *in Phd.* 1.271 (Westerink 1977: 162–3). He mentions that "the more recent" commentators cannot be identified because the references in Proclus and Damascius did not come from commentaries on Aristotle's work. Perhaps by "commentators" Pseudo-Philoponus did not mean commentators of Aristotle's *de Anima* exclusively.

20. 957.28–958.11 Cousin (= 4c10 in Sorabji 2004). The passage does not contain the term προσεκτικὸν μέρος, but the function described here fits in with what Pseudo-Philoponus ascribes to the "more recent" commentators. Furthermore, Proclus assumes that we have a fifth rational capacity, called προσοχή, beside intellect, discursive reason, opinion and rational choice (*in Phil. Chald.* 4.55–6 = 211.1–4 [Des Places]), and the extant remains of his, partial or not, commentary on the *Enneads* do refer to the προσεκτικὸν μέρος: see § 16 in Westerink (1959: 7).

21. "Following" translates παρακολουθοῦν. Παρακολούθησις and its cognates were used by the commentators to refer to various phenomena. Sometimes they refer to attention (see *in Alc.* 336.13: εἰ δὲ βούλει τοῖς ῥήμασι παρακολουθεῖν ἀκριβῶς, see also *in Prm.* 621.21, 1099.11). Sometimes they allude to consciousness (e.g. *in Remp.* II 93.10). Elsewhere, however, and especially in the *Parmenides Commentary*, they refer to following an argument or a process (*in Alc.* 170.7; *in Prm.* 676.8, 1071.17, 1088.35, 1099.11), not a state. This is the reason why I think that the term "consciousness", with all its modern connotations, does not fit perfectly to the field of παρακολούθησις. If "awareness" is a better way of putting it, we should use that term.

22. Plotinus used it in making a distinction between minimal or perceptual consciousness and a second-order awareness of one's thoughts or actions. See *Enn.* I.4[46].9.14–25; 10.22–8; IV.3[27].26.40–46. For further references and clarifications, see Remes (2007: 98 n. 7, 112, 119–22). How deep the late Neoplatonists' knowledge of the *Enneads* was is an intricate question. Sometimes, as in the case of Philoponus and Damascius, their knowledge seems to be superficial at best, but Proclus wrote a commentary on some texts of Plotinus' work.

23. In *in Prm.* (927.15–18) Proclus mentions that attention (προσοχή) is certainly concentrated by enthusiasm (προθυμία), if not raised by it. As enthusiasm seems to be a kind of desire, attention may be subordinate to desire from this point of view.

24. "Rational wish" translates βούλησις, which, in the wake of the *Nicomachean Ethics*, cannot be regarded as an independent faculty, rather a kind of motivational force which works in accordance with the precepts of reason.

25. It seems as if Proclus were relying on the Trojan Horse model in the *Theaetetus*.

26. See the fourfold division of sense-perception in *in Tim.* 2.83.16–84.5.

27. This is not the place to pursue the both general and very nuanced issue of self-reflexion in Proclus, which supposes that the subject must return to itself (ἐπιστροφή), i.e. its origin. This kind of activity is more than simple introspection: see Steel (2004: 237).

28. See also 3.8.28–9.2. I have argued for this point in Lautner (2006: 119–22). Baltzly (2009: 266–71), on the other hand, argues that in order to show that the highest form of sense-perception is given to human beings as well, not only to the cosmos, we have to explain how human sense-perception can meet the requirement of apprehending the sensible essences of things (2.84.17–18). It can only apprehend the activities of the sensible things (1.293.1–5). This is true, and my claim must be modified accordingly. However, the case is still to be clarified, since the apprehension of the cosmos seems to include both sense-perception and opinion (καὶ ὁ κόσμος οὖν ὄψις τέ ἐστιν ὅλος καὶ ὁρατὸν καὶ ὄντως αἰσθήσεικαὶ

δόξῃ περιληπτὸν τῇ ἑαυτοῦ αἰσθήσει καὶ τῇ ἑαυτοῦ δόξῃ, 2.84.8–10). Since the goal of opinion is to apprehend substances (οὐσίας, 1.248.11–12; 293.3), it seems as if the cosmos, too, perceives substances owing to its opinative element. The expression "*whole* perception" (ὅλη αἴσθησις 2.84.15–16, emphasis added) might indicate that it is a complex activity containing many partial acts. By describing the δόξα λογική as a kind of sense-perception (2.83.7–8) Proclus perhaps suggests that there is no sharp division between the two capacities.

29. Baltzly (2009: 270) suggests that, by using this term, Proclus wants to say that the cosmos' perception of itself is "not localized into individual sense-objects or divided into distinct sense-faculties. It is rather more like our awareness of the totality of our own bodies." I would add that it seems to be tied to opinion intimately, which might indicate that, in the case of the cosmos, the whole process is propositional.

30. I cannot discuss the issue of reversion (ἐπιστροφή) here. It is a central tendency or dynamism of every being, implying a return to its true self, which originates from a higher entity. For a useful discussion, see Gerson (1997a) and Perkams (2008: 285–99); the latter also compares ancient and some more modern notions.

31. Here Damascius treats ἀνάμνησις in the same way as Aristotle does in *Mem.* 2. Hence Damascius does not require that this kind of memory must be directed towards any transcendent entity exclusively.

32. In *in Phil.* 161.5; 163.5, Damascius admits that ἐπιθυμία can be twofold: one comes about by virtue of anticipation through memory, the other by συναίσθησις alone. My suggestion is that συναίσθησις means here a kind of joint-perception, an additional movement of the soul which is linked to sense-perception which gives rise to appetite. It may not mean awareness or consciousness in general.

33. The same distinction between προσεκτικόν and συνειδός is also made by Olympiodorus (*in Alc.* 23.16–17), but he does not seem to have much to say about the precise working of perceptual awareness.

34. *In de Anima* 465.31–467.13. Pseudo-Philoponus' agreement with Proclus is all the more interesting, since it is well known that elsewhere he fiercely criticized his Athenian predecessor.

35. As he spells it out in 466.27–8: ὥστε οὐκ ὀρθῶς λέγει Ἀριστοτέλης, ἀλλ' *ὡς εἴπομεν* τοῦ προσεκτικοῦ ἐστι τῆς ψυχῆς τὸ γινώσκειν τὰς ἐνεργείας τῶν αἰσθήσεων (emphasis added). See also 465.33–4.

36. Here I have to disagree with Bernard's important analysis stating that "self-awareness is neither self-contained, nor a faculty" (1987: 160), but an ability of the ultimate cognizing faculty, the reason. The disagreement might only be in terminology. Pseudo-Philoponus accepts that the προσεκτικόν is a part of the rational soul, along with other parts. Of course, it depends on other parts and "soul" (the αἰσθητική soul mentioned in 549.29–31, 595.36, 598.10), but that should not be a disqualifying factor. After all, in certain circumstances, discursive reason can also depend on the perceptual power for its content derived from the physical world.

37. For a useful overview on the question of authorship, see Steel (1997b: 103–41) and Perkams (2005; 2008: 150–55), both of whom think that the author is Priscian of Lydia, a fellow philosopher at Athens who joined Simplicius and other Athenian Neoplatonists in the exile to Persia after 529.

38. 173.1–7 and 187.35–9, the latter containing an explicit reference to Iamblichus. This is why he thinks that perceptual consciousness is a specific feature of human beings (187.27).

39. 187.30–36. "Perceptual awareness" translates here συναίσθησις (177.32; 181.23; 188.4; 189.24, 25, 27). It refers to a kind of joint-perception (or simultaneous perception – see Blumenthal 2000). The capacity belongs to the perceptual power, but is rational, as all the perceptual power is. Literally, we perceive that we are perceiving even if this perception, as all the others, is a rational activity. This is the capacity that enables us to perceive that something is good or true (211.11). I. Hadot (1997: 74) understands the term as a kind of "irreflexive conscience". Certainly, it refers to a kind of awareness, but it must also be somehow reflexive since it is tied to ἐπιστροφή.

40. Hubler (2005: 310) stresses that Pseudo-Simplicius and Pseudo-Philoponus achieved the same general result, since both divorced perceptual awareness from the non-rational soul. This is certainly true in so far as perceptual awareness is a rational activity since it manifests reversion. But the views of Pseudo-Simplicius and Pseudo-Philoponus diverge, since the latter ascribed it to a faculty of the rational soul itself, whereas the former keeps it within the confines of sense-perception.

41. 189.20–28. As the commentator puts it: ὡς καὶ τὴν συναίσθησιν οὐχ τῆς ὁράσεως εἶναι, ἀλλὰ τῆς πείρας οἷον ἀποτυγχανούσης (emphasis added). This kind of distinction may remind us of Themistius' distinction in his *in de Anima* 83.24–5 where he says that we perceive that we are not seeing/hearing anything by the very same sense by which we also perceive that we are seeing/hearing.

42. 189.34: ἀλλ' ἐνεργεῖ τὰ χρώματα οὐ ποιητικῶς ἡ ὄψις ἀλλά κριτικῶς. Blumenthal (2000: 126 n. 124)

takes the term κριτικῶς to refer to the perceptual faculty as making judgements about what happens in the sense-organs. It is not quite clear what kind of judgement is involved here. The opposition of productive and discriminative ways of actualizing may point to an activity through which the sense cannot create impressions but is able to discern different impressions/changes in the sense-organ. The difference may be individual or by type. On the other hand, κριτικῶς was connected to συνετικῶς (166.5, see also 166.17). The primary meaning of the latter term may not be "in a conscious way" but perhaps "comprehensively", in so far as it refers to a combination of the various perceptual alterations. The ambiguity in the Greek term is mirrored in the English "comprehensively", to mean both "with understanding" and "in a holistic way". Discernment and comprehension are the two ways in which the senses work: see also Priscian's *Metaphrasis* 7.16.

43. For the Neoplatonists, impassibility of the soul means that the causal processes are always from upwards. The soul cannot be subject to changes caused efficiently by bodily processes. The soul cannot receive πάθη. In sense-perception it means that the sense does not receive anything; it judges the qualitative change in the sense-organ. Plotinus has already emphasized it; see *Enn.* IV.3[27].3.23, 26.8; IV.4[28].22.30–33; IV.6[41].1.1–2. This has been taken over by the commentators.

44. He does not say this explicitly but it is obvious from the direct connection between sense-perception and λόγος (meaning notion or reason-principle): see e.g. 3.22–3.

45. 22.3–4: ἑκάστη πως συναισθήσεται ὅτι αἰσθάνηται. See also I. Hadot (1997: 63–6), who sees here and other passages in Pseudo-Simplicius and Priscianus a transition from σύνεσις to συναίσθησις, which signals a change from an ontological point of view, since συναίσθησις belongs to the perceptual power which is an essentially non-rational faculty. It is difficult to see to what extent sense-perception is rational or non-rational in these commentators. There are explicit statements that it is pervaded by the rational soul, and the perceptual power works with λόγοι.

46. 22.14–20. By contrast, Pseudo-Simplicius seems to accept that the particular sense is capable of perceiving its activity.

V

Nature: physics, medicine and biology

INTRODUCTION

Physics, or the study of nature, is the fastest-growing area in Neoplatonic studies in the last two decades, if not even before. There is one principal reason, with two opposite effects, for this most welcome development: metaphysics. The constitutive role of metaphysics as the Neoplatonic "science" of a hierarchically organized universe, shaped and governed "from above", casts a long shadow over the role of the physical world in such a highly structured universe which, in turn, has cast an even longer shadow over the scholarship on the subject. In this sense, metaphysics is the proverbial stepmother of physics which at an initial, perfunctory, glance degrades the significance of the natural world to a mere passive receptor of higher underlying principles or causes. This imbalance of ontological value between the metaphysical and physical realms (to stick with the Neoplatonic order of priority) has naturally affected the scholarly evaluation of the Neoplatonists' contribution to what is called today the "natural sciences", to the extreme of denying any research in them. This is the negative side of the story.

The positive side of the story includes our expanding understanding of Neoplatonic metaphysics as an organically sustainable system which does not consist of entities caught, with their incorporeality and unchangeability, in some kind of permafrost of intelligible existence, but of two-way dynamic processes which unfold downward to instantiate the physical world and revert upward to confirm the ontological "goodness" of this instantiation. In this holistic sense, the physical world, with all its imperfection and fragmentation, is the feedback of the metaphysical realm. In fact, it is the only feedback there is about it, and the speed of this realization is increasing rapidly. The growing interest in redeeming the value of the Neoplatonic understanding of nature, in its material impermanent diversity, is also a direct result of the ever-increasing availability of new text-critical editions and translations of Neoplatonic works. To mention only a few examples, there are the commentaries (multiple in some cases) on Aristotle's *Physics, Metereology, Generation and Corruption*, Euclid's *Elements*, Ptolemy's *Almagest*.[1] The higher visibility afforded by these texts leads to their prompt contextualization but also raises questions about our interpretation of already established texts. The growing number of individual and collected studies in this respect is noteworthy.[2]

Linguiti's "Physics and metaphysics" (Chapter 22) responds to the urgent call for assessing the changing landscape of Neoplatonic physics and adjusting our understanding of it. In this vein, even a text such as Plato's *Timaeus*, upon which Neoplatonic metaphysics is built, shows that the scales of metaphysics and physics are not so categorically tipped in favour of divine order but, in fact, are balanced between the effects of this divine order and the natural processes of the physical entities and organisms involved in them. For the later Neoplatonists and especially Proclus, there is explicit continuity between the transcendent causes, governing the cosmos, and the various levels of entities within this cosmos. Without the latter, the transcendent causes would be ineffectual. Thus even nature is construed as a metaphysical principle, which consists of a series of micro-natural principles (*physiologiai*) corresponding to all levels of physical reality, from mathematics to biology.

The interest in the "natural sciences" is matched by equally contagious enthusiasm for the "life sciences". Our increased knowledge of the Galenic corpus and the rapid appearance of new texts, translations and studies of medical treatises from every period of antiquity steadily introduce medical and biological themes in Neoplatonic scholarship.[3]

Wilberding's "Neoplatonism and medicine" (Chapter 23) forcefully dissipates the tradi-tional view of the Neoplatonists' neglect of the human body as a biological entity. Just as in the case of physics, our understanding of Neoplatonic metaphysics will be unrealistically skewed if we deny that the Neoplatonists see any philosophical value in the body, not to mention, in light of their complex understanding of Soul. The body, as part of the physical world, is an instantiation of the same higher governing principles. In fact, from both the physical and the metaphysical perspective, the body offers a microcosmic working model of the universe and, even from this viewpoint alone, its value is priceless.

The Neoplatonic value of "life" – its inherent "good" and "right" – is the subject of Corrigan's "Humans, other animals, plants and the question of the good: the Platonic and Neoplatonic traditions" (Chapter 24). Corrigan tests the Neoplatonic attitude towards what may seem overly modern sensibility of, to use his quip, "thinking globally but acting locally", which seeks to uncover and preserve the value of life in all organisms. It turns out that, for the Neoplatonists, biology, as everything else in the cosmos, has an intelligible nature and reflects the principle of the supreme "good". Although expected, this discovery is still humbling for our modern and post-modern Cartesian worldviews. The Neoplatonic understanding of biological diversity is inclusive rather than exclusive in proffering drasti-cally different models of rationality.

NOTES

1. Here we cannot overestimate the impact of the *Ancient Commentators on Aristotle* project as a whole, and the second volume (dedicated to physics) of Sorabji (2004–2005).
2. Wagner (1996, 2002a, 2002b), Lernould (2001), Chiaradonna & Trabattoni (2009), Martijn (2010a), Wilberding & Horn (2012).
3. Tieleman (1998), Sharples & van der Eijk (2008), Gill *et al.* (2009), Wilberding (2011).

22

Physics and metaphysics

Alessandro Linguiti

SOME BASIC TENETS

For the Neoplatonists, as for the members of other philosophical schools in antiquity, the primary objects of physics – or natural philosophy – are bodies and their movements. Because of the very assumptions of their own philosophy, however, unlike other thinkers, the Neoplatonists are almost exclusively interested in the metaphysical causes of the physical world. Consequently, they never examine natural phenomena *iuxta propria principia*, so to say, but rather concentrate on causes, or principles, which differ by nature from physical bodies, in that they are incorporeal, immaterial, "spiritual" and located in an order of reality that is not the same as the one allotted to bodies. These causes belong in fact to a "superior", more elevated order, which is usually described by the metaphor of "verticality", much favoured by the Neoplatonists, hence the widespread use of the formula "vertical causation" to describe the "metaphysical" character of causes acting upon the physical world "from above".[1] On this account, the physical world, that is, the world of physical bodies, appears to be the outcome of incorporeal forces that transcend it, as well as the domain in which these forces operate.

This is clearly in harmony with the premises set out by Plato in the *Timaeus* and in book X of the *Laws*, where the focus is on immaterial principles like the Forms, the Demiurge and the World Soul as true causes of the sensible realm, and where, conversely, "physical" causes like bodies and bodily interactions are depreciated as merely "auxiliary" causes.[2] But unlike the *Timaeus* – or, better, unlike what a possible reading of the *Timaeus* suggests – the Neoplatonists do not conceive of the natural world order as something at the same time having divine origin and capable of autonomous functioning. In the *Timaeus*, as Broadie lucidly explains, bodies and natural systems are described by Plato

> as indeed the effects of divine and world-transcending Reason, but also as genuinely *natural* entities or systems with their own natural modes of working. Thus the

gods fashioned the complex respiratory and metabolic systems in mortal animals, but it is clearly the mortal animals themselves that will be breathing in and out, or undergoing the stages of the metabolic cycle. There is no divine agent doing the animals' breathing or digesting or growing for them ... the cosmic system and the physical systems within it are *both* natural in their working *and* divinely caused.

(2010: 75–6; original emphasis)

According to Plotinus and his followers, on the contrary, the physical world never emancipates itself from its metaphysical causes, which relentlessly and pervasively keep on operating within it. For the Neoplatonists, the way a natural being is and acts thoroughly depends on its formal principle, or *logos*, which never loses contact with its metaphysical origin; that is, Nature or the lower Soul (see below).

Moreover, sensible effects are in an asymmetrical relation with their intelligible causes, given that for the Neoplatonists the superior, that is, the cause, can subsist and be thought of without the inferior, that is, the effect, whereas the reverse is not true. Nonetheless, this has no bearing on the fact that the effect follows *necessarily* its cause. So viewed, the realm of Becoming is no longer in opposition to the realm of Being, but is rather its necessary manifestation, albeit only on the "phenomenal" level. According to the Neoplatonists, in other words, the natural order – degraded as it may be – is still the divine order itself, modulated into its corporeal facets; that is, extensiveness, plurality, distinction, separation in space and time, hostility, indigence, and so on:

> For from that universe which is one this universe comes into existence, which is not truly one; for it is many and divided into a multiplicity, and one part stands away from another and is alien to it, and there is not only friendship but also enmity because of the separation, and in their deficiency one part is of necessity at war with another.
> (*Enn.* III.2[47].2.1–6)[3]

This line of reasoning undermines the validity of the "axiom" of the two worlds, which are so often adduced to portray the standard Platonic attitude. Wagner writes with reference to Plotinus (but the same could safely be maintained with regard to any other Neoplatonist):

> Plotinus speaks at times as if there were, on the one hand, a sensible world and, on the other hand, an intelligible world, even though in fact there is just the single vertical order and its various levels of reality – the sensible world being just its lowest level, a final image or manifestation of its substance and its principles.[4]

All this marks a great distance from the philosophical physics (that is, physics based more on theoretical assumptions than on the empirical scrutiny of phenomena) of the rival schools. Admittedly, according to the Stoics too, natural philosophy tallies much with theology, but the way the Stoics conceive of God or the divine, that is, as bodily causes immanent in the only existing world, has little to share with the Neoplatonic view. Even more evident is the distance between Neoplatonic physics and the explanations provided by the Atomists, who are inclined to exclude any presence in the world of effective incorporeal causes: consequently, the Atomists interpret all phenomena merely in terms of the mechanical interactions of bodies, which have their own principle of movement in themselves. The expression "horizontal causation" – the very opposite of Neoplatonic "vertical causation" – perfectly suits the kinds of explanations given by the Atomists; the same can be said, with some qualification, of the way in which Aristotle and his followers account for the sensible world. Indeed, leaving aside the theological implications of the doctrine of the unmoved mover, Aristotelian physics is essentially a philosophy of nature *iuxta propria principia*, without recourse to transcendent powers. According to Aristotle and his followers, the principle, or "nature", that rules bodies is totally internal to them, and does not come from outside; it exists together with the sensible thing it resides in – as a sort of property – and ceases to exist when the sensible thing ceases to exist. Also in this case the process of causation can be adequately defined as "horizontal", on the grounds that what causes alterations in bodies is internal to the bodies themselves, and homogeneous with them. It is true that the Aristotelian form (*eidos*) – which ultimately is responsible for formal, efficient and final causation – is, as such, incorporeal (*Ph*. II.7); in physics, however, form should not be considered in isolation from the bodily compound it constitutes together with the material cause (which is also "nature", although to a lesser degree than form: *Ph*. II.1).[5]

In keeping with such guidelines, in what follows I shall try to clarify in which ways Neoplatonic thinkers (Plotinus and Proclus above all) have characterized the sensible world, explained its ontological status, as well as its functioning, by invoking extra-physical causes, and accordingly recommended a fitting method of enquiry. Before this, however, it may be useful to recall that the Neoplatonic conception of the natural world has been for a long time largely neglected by scholarship. To tell the truth, at the end of the nineteenth century Baeumker (1890) sharply discerned the metaphysical presuppositions of the Neoplatonic philosophy of nature, and some decades later Bréhier made his lasting contributions in the field.[6] Yet as recently as twenty-five years ago Blumenthal (1987: 560) could safely remark that "apart from the problems of matter and evil it is still true that the sensible world, in itself, remains a neglected area of Plotinus' philosophy" (and this holds *a fortiori* true for the other Neoplatonists). Since then, however, much has changed, also because scholars are realizing that even a "metaphysical" approach like the Neoplatonic one can significantly contribute to clarifying crucial notions such as those of "cause", "movement", "matter", "body", "quantity", "quality", "space" and "time".

Let us consider, in this regard, the seminal books by Sorabji devoted to basic concepts in ancient philosophy, as well as his *Sourcebook* on physics in the series "The Philosophy of the Commentators".[7] Another influential scholar is Wagner, an author of valuable essays and the editor of the book *Neoplatonism and Nature* (see Wagner 1982a, 1985, 1986, 1996, 2002a, b). It is also worth mentioning, even in a brief survey such as this, the lively debate concerning the status of sensible substance in Plotinus,[8] as well as the many path-breaking suggestions contained in P. Hadot's (2004) *Le voile d'Isis. Essai sur l'histoire de l'idée de nature*. More recently, two valuable conference proceedings and a remarkable book on Proclus have visibly attested to the increasing interest in the topic of the Neoplatonic philosophy of nature.[9] Actually, the reputation of the Neoplatonists as philosophers chiefly interested in the spiritual causes of the physical world (Intellect, Soul, Providence, Nature, incorporeal reason-principles, etc.) has not really been challenged by these studies; nonetheless, after delving deeper into many questions and opening new promising perspectives, scholars now tend to agree that the value of Neoplatonic physics should be assessed not from its attempts to work out a coherent conception of reality – in this respect, the

Neoplatonists would indeed appear to have been successful – but rather from its capacity to give rational explanations of the many natural phenomena in all of their complexity and multiple aspects (and in this respect they were probably less successful). The focus of our enquiry, then, must be the modalities in which characteristics and relations of the intelligible order are brought by incorporeal causes into the physical world, mainly envisaged as a set of interacting bodies.[10]

FEATURES OF THE SENSIBLE WORLD

For all Platonists sensible bodies are, strictly speaking, devoid of *hypostasis*, that is, of any substantial reality, and thus merely provided with an illusory and deceptive kind of being: "wishing (*scil.* Plato) to show the emptiness of substantial being in the things of sense and the great area which there is of mere appearance" (*Enn.* III.6[26].12.10–11).[11]

All that can be attributed to bodies is just a feeble, dependent subsistence, in so far as they are the final and weakened effect – although a necessary one, as already noted above – of superior incorporeal causes, to which they totally owe their existence, as well as the modes of their being. For these reasons, bodies possess an unstable nature, as such doomed to impermanence and dissolution:

> but the true wakening is a true getting up from the body, not with the body. Getting up with the body is only getting out of one sleep into another, like getting out of one bed into another; but the true rising is a rising altogether away from bodies, which are of the opposite nature to soul and opposed in respect of reality. Their coming into being and flux and perishing, which does not belong to the nature of reality, are evidence of this.   (*Enn.* III.6[26]6.71–7)[12]

In addition to that, the most characteristic way in which Plotinus refers to the sensible substance (*ousia aisthētē*), that is, the body, is as a "conglomeration of qualities and matter", deprived of any autonomous substantiality.[13] In open polemic against Aristotle, in fact, Plotinus often refuses to admit the full presence of any substantial principle within sensible compounds, so that the very name "substance" cannot rightfully be applied to bodies.[14] The point is that in sensible things, according to him, there is no real composition of formal principles (that is, the *logoi*, or reason-principles) on the one hand and matter (*hylē*) on the other hand. Compared to the *chōra* of the Platonic *Timaeus* or Aristotelian matter, matter actually plays a very marginal role within Plotinus' view of the sensible world. In the *Enneads* it is often described as pure non-being, characterized by privation, sterility and an utter lack of life; it is not even a substrate able to receive in itself the incorporeal formal principles, and as a consequence of this, these latter are not really situated in matter. As stressed in the remarkable treatise *On the Impassibility of the Bodiless* (*Enn.* III.6[26].6–19), the formal principles have no true interaction with matter, and are not even able to model or alter it in any way: matter only acts as a sort of inert mirror, by means of which the formal principles produce an illusory and precarious reflection of themselves. This deceptive image is the body.[15]

Proclus, on his part, looks more favourably to the hylomorphic scheme inherited from Aristotle, and largely exploits it to explain the ontological status of sensible things (see

Opsomer forthcoming). Nonetheless, he too sticks to a negative conception of corporeal reality, by denying the existence of a specific metaphysical principle for bodies. In fact, whereas according to Proclus there are henads of incorporeal entities, such as Nature, Soul and Intellect (which are respectively participated in by individual natures, souls and intellects), there is no henad of the Body at all.[16] Particular bodies thus have no henad which they can participate in, and this clearly hints to their lack of real existence; a point firmly maintained by Proclus.[17]

This does not imply, however, that according to the Neoplatonists bodies have no distinctive properties. On the contrary, they exhibit extension, mass, size, dimensions, resistance, divisibility, movement, and so on; nevertheless, it must always be borne in mind that all these qualities have their full and authentic reality in the ideal causes of bodies, and that whatever is to be found in bodies is just a more or less pale reflection of transcendent archetypes (see below). This does not amount to saying that the properties of bodies are entirely epiphenomenal, but rather that they are the means by which the incorporeal powers get their shape in the world of extended realities. Indeed, taken in themselves bodies reveal a total lack of power; that is, complete inertia or passivity. Any form of energy or dynamism, as well as any causal efficacy, belongs exclusively to incorporeal beings, as Proclus proclaims in a lapidary statement: "The proper nature of all bodies is to be acted upon, and of all incorporeal beings to be agents, the former being in themselves inactive and the latter impassible."[18] The reference is presumably to book X of Plato's *Laws* (896a–897b), where a major distinction is proposed between self-moving incorporeal entities on the one hand, and bodies moved by something else on the other hand. Be that as it may, the point is often stressed elsewhere by Proclus and by other Neoplatonists.[19] Let us consider, for instance, *Enn.* IV.7[2].3, where the permanence in being of bodies is said to be due solely to the Soul, or Porphyry's *Sentences*, where the main focus is both on the contrasting properties of corporeal things and their incorporeal causes. Particularly striking is the inversely proportional relation between mass or volume (*onkos*), typical of extended bodies, and power (*dynamis*), typical of incorporeals:

> That which is greater in volume is lesser in power, if one compares it, not to similar classes of thing, but to things different in kind in virtue of otherness of essence: for volume is in fact a sort of departure from itself and a fragmentation of power. In consequence, what is transcendent in power is alien to all volume, for power is at a maximum when it has withdrawn into itself, and it is in giving power to itself that it acquires the strength that it is proper to it. Hence body, in proceeding towards volume, departs just so much in diminution of power from the power of incorporeal real being, as real being is not emptied into volume, remaining as it does in the greatness of the power conferred on it by its freedom of volume. Even as, then, real being, in respect of volume, is free from magnitude and volume, so the bodily, in comparison to real being, is weak and powerless; for what is greatest in respect of the greatness of its power is alien to volume, while what is greatest in greatness of volume is deficient in power.   (*Sent.* 35.39.13–40.6 [Lamberz])[20]

CAUSES AND GENESIS OF THE SENSIBLE WORLD

Let us consider now more closely the causes that, acting from "above", determine the very existence of sensible things, along with their features.

The first item to mention is obviously the One, the highest and most universal cause for all the Neoplatonists (for instance, *Enn.* VI.9[9].1.1–17). In Aristotelian terms, we might say that the One is endowed with a causality both efficient and final: being identical with the Good, the One is on the one hand – according to the Platonic analogy of the sun – *diffusivum sui*, that is, the producer of everything; and on the other hand the final end of everything, the universal aspiration to the Good being nothing else than an aspiration to unity.[21] For these reasons Plotinus and his followers, though sticking in principle to the doctrine of the ineffability of the One, do not hesitate in several contexts to name it "Good", "God", "cause", "principle", "foundation", and so on.[22] It is not possible, however, to ascribe to the One causal functions of other kinds, that is, material or formal/paradigmatic functions – at least not directly: for these are peculiar to principles, like matter and the Forms, which, though deriving from the One, are different from the One.[23]

Paradigmatic causality, then, belongs to the Forms, which the Neoplatonists unanimously assign – yet not always at the same level – to the hypostasis immediately after the One; that is, Being-Intellect or the intelligible hypostasis, as it is most frequently called.[24] Between the intelligible Forms and the sensible particulars, however, there are several subsequent levels, each of which consists of its own formal structures and is a more or less distant "image" of the archetypal Forms contained in the intelligible hypostasis. This proliferation of levels of Forms enables the Neoplatonists to bypass some of the paradoxes of participation recorded by Plato in the *Parmenides*, on the one hand by preserving the transcendence of each Form, and on the other by securing the presence of a formal structure – a "representative", so to say, of the transcendent Form – in each sensible particular. The origin of such a multiplication of levels of Forms may be traced back to Plato himself, who in the *Timaeus* distinguishes between the Form itself and the Form in the sensible thing, describing this latter as a "copy" or "image" of the former.[25] It was the late Neoplatonists, however, who fully developed this tendency, finally positing a six-level hierarchy of Forms, or Ideas, with some levels internally exhibiting even further subdivisions.[26]

For our purposes, it is enough to reflect on the simpler quadripartite hierarchy of ideal levels put forth by Plotinus: the first stage is represented by the Forms-Minds constituting the second hypostasis, the second by the Forms contained in the higher Soul (defined as "primary *logoi*"), the third by the "traces" of the Forms (or "secondary *logoi*") present in the lower Soul or Nature,[27] and the fourth by the enmattered *logoi*, which finally give shape to the sensible bodies as their ultimate formal principle.[28] Proclus, too, while subscribing to the aforementioned sixfold partition, adopts a similar quadripartite scale:

> Those which exist primarily exist in and for themselves, Socrates says, and are in the rank of intelligibles. ... The forms in soul have their being in a secondary way, in respect of perfection; and thus are likenesses of the intelligibles. ... The forms in nature are likenesses even more, i.e. they are likenesses of likenesses. ... The forms in sensible things are last of all and they are images only, for the Forms end their

procession at what is unknowable and indeterminate. There is nothing after them, for all the reason-principles reach their final term in sensible things.

(*in Prm.* I.627.4–14 [Steel], trans. Morrow & Dillon)

The only forms which enter in a more or less problematic composition with matter,[29] then, in order to generate bodies, are the last reason-principles (*logoi*, as in Plotinus), placed at the bottom of the hierarchy; this implies that "demiurgy" does not belong to the archetypal and transcendent Forms, but rather to a principle ranked below in the metaphysical hierarchy, which the enmattered forms or *logoi* ultimately originate from.[30]

We are now in a better position to understand Proclus' classification of the causes of the sensible world, as it is spelled out in the prologue of his *Commentary on Plato's Timaeus*. Here Proclus points to the material cause (i.e. matter as receptacle) and to the formal cause (the immanent form; that is, the last *logos*) as mere "auxiliary" or "secondary" causes (*synaitia*).[31] These secondary causes are subordinate to the true causes; that is, the ones transcending the physical world: the Demiurge, as genuine efficient cause (see note 28); the ideal models which the Demiurge gazes at, as paradigmatic causes; the One-Good, the goal of all that is generated, as final cause.[32] Consequently, the true philosophy of nature must focus on these three causes, with which Plato deals at length in the *Timaeus*.[33]

Some further topics must now be considered, in order to better comprehend the ontological character of the sensible realities according to the Neoplatonists. Let us start with the difference between the status of the *logoi* in Nature and that of the *logoi* in sensible compounds; this is explained by Proclus in the frame of the Plotinian doctrine of the double activity, according to which the *logoi* when abiding in Nature correspond to her activity *of* the essence, and when proceeding outside Nature correspond to her activity *from* the essence:[34]

Twofold are the acts and the powers of the gods. Some abide with the gods themselves, act in relation to them and have as their own goal the degree of reality (*hypostasis*) unique and unified with the essence; others, instead, proceed from the first acts and powers, display their effective power in relation to inferior realities and exist together with the many who receive them and with their essential specific character as well. And since there are two kinds of acts and powers, the second kind depends on the preceding one, determines itself in relation to the former and receives its own peculiar existence according to the former. For there is need that, everywhere, the acts proceeding outside be images of the acts which abide inside, unravel their compact indivision, multiply their unification and divide their indivisibility.

According to this explanation, the act of Nature is twofold: one abides in Nature, who, thanks to it, keeps herself, as well as the rational principle in her, together; the other one proceeds from Nature, and thanks to it the bodies are filled by all these natural powers which, moved by Nature, affect each other and are affected by each other in a natural way. (*Theol. Plat.* V.18.64.3–20)

These *logoi*/acts which abide in Nature are thus models of the *logoi*/acts that proceed outside her, and the characteristics of the model change fundamentally in the process of shaping the sensible world: all that in the model, or cause, was unitary and indivisible becomes plural and divisible in the copy, or effect. The qualities and properties of the effect, that is, the bodies, are thus different from the qualities and properties of the cause: *faciens non est tale, quale factum* (Proclus, *de Prov.* 8.13–15). Therefore, we must always keep in mind that the status of "physical" properties in the causes, that is, in the *logoi* inside Nature, is a different one from that of "physical" properties in the effects; that is, in bodies. Heaviness, lightness, warmth, coldness and so on in the incorporeal principles are admit- tedly the causes of the corresponding properties in bodies, but are not really comparable to them.[35] The least that can be said is that such properties are not heavy, light, warm or cold in the way bodies are heavy, light, and so on; and this, for the same reason, is why the Platonic idea of White cannot be "white" in the same way as a wall is "white" (see *Enn.* II.4[12].9; I.2[19].6; VI.6[34].17).

Let us turn now to another point. Plotinus, as is well known, fitted the generation of natural beings into the scheme of the causal power of contemplation, *theōria*, straightfor- wardly equated with *poiēsis*. Especially in *Enn.* III.8[30], contemplation amounts to that by means of which all levels of reality after the One are produced. The coming into being of Being-Intellect and, after it, of the hypostatic Soul, the World Soul and the physical world is in each case the consequence of an act of vision or contemplation (*theōria, Enn.* III.8[30].4, 7). Being-Intellect stems from the One because an indistinct power, eternally flowing from the highest source, reverts to the One in order to contemplate it: only at this point does Being-Intellect become what it really is, which is to say a stable and harmoni- ous community of Forms that think themselves. The Soul derives from Being-Intellect in an analogous way: out of superabundance, a noetic energy, similar to light, flows from a higher principle and then reverts to its origin in order to contemplate it; as a result of this vision, a new level of reality arises – the Soul as the first image of the intelligible order. All subsequent levels of reality come into being by a similar process: even Nature, the lower limb of the World Soul, engenders bodies by means of its unconscious thinking, a sort of dim and dreamlike contemplation. The point is that the final *logos* in itself does not have sufficient energy to revert to its source, Nature; therefore it limits itself to producing bodies through its feeble contemplation (*Enn.* III.8[30].4.1–14). Strangely enough, this set of theses, even though not explicitly rejected, is not really taken up again by any Neoplatonist in antiquity: we have to wait for the Platonism of the Renaissance and Modern Age to find a revival of this extremely fascinating theory according to which the body is ultimately to be conceived as the result of an unconscious act of thinking.[36]

THE NEOPLATONIC SCIENCE OF THE PHYSICAL WORLD

As is to be expected, once measured against the standards of modern science, Neoplatonic physics does not appear to be very "scientific" – if at all (and the same, indeed, can be said more or less of all ancient physics). First, it does not share the basic assumption of the uniformity of reality, not only on the grounds of the contrast between the intelligible world on one hand and the sensible one on the other, but also because of the essential difference between celestial and terrestrial spheres within the sensible world;[37] second, it does not avail itself of experimental procedures; and third, it leaves scanty room for empirical observations, sharply subordinated as they are to the speculative knowledge of the intelligible world. As far as this last point is concerned, it is true that Plotinus and his followers assign some value to the ascending method of moving from sensible images up to their intelligible models by means of "reminiscence". At the end of the first chapter of *Enn.* III.7[40], *On Eternity and Time*, Plotinus indeed seems to value the ascending path as much as the descending one, according to which the properties of sensible realities ought instead to be deduced from those of intelligible ones:

> And first we should enquire about eternity, what sort of thing those who make it different from time consider it to be, for when we know that which holds the position of archetype, it will perhaps become clear how it is with its image, which the philosophers say time is. But if someone, before contemplating eternity, should form a picture in his mind of what time is, it would be possible for him, too, to go from this world to the other by recollection and contemplate that of which time is a likeness, if time really has a likeness to eternity.
> (*Enn.* III.7[45].1.16–24, trans. Armstrong; see Chiaradonna 2003: 221–50)

Nonetheless, elsewhere in the treatise, the "anamnestic" and inductive track is not beaten much at all; and this is mainly for one reason: as causes are greater than their effects, the study of images alone cannot lead to a correct knowledge of their models. Plotinus, in fact, advises against transferring the characteristics of sensible things onto their intelligible models, by taking these latter as a sort of reinforced version of the former. The way a Form possesses – or, to be precise, *is* – a given property is not the same as that in which a sensible thing possesses the same property; and this is enough to discredit a cognitive method, which moves upwards (see p. 350; *Enn.* II.4[12].9; I.2[19].6; VI.6[34].17). The right *modus operandi* consists instead in knowing intelligible realities according to their own principles:

> But when, on the other hand, one engages in reasonings about the intelligibles, the right way would be to take the nature of substance about which one is concerned and so establish the principles of one's reasonings, without passing over, as if one had forgotten, to the other nature, but applying one's mind to that intelligible nature by means of itself.
> (*Enn.* VI.5[23].2.19–23; see also *Enn.* VI.6[34].8.7–8; Chiaradonna 2009b: 33–8)

Much to our disappointment, Plotinus does not explain the true modalities of this knowledge of intelligible items, which is supposed to operate entirely within the intelligible world. The least we can say is that the doctrine of the so-called "undescended soul" must somehow be involved. According to him, the highest and most divine part of the human soul never descends into the body, but always remains in the second hypostasis, that is, Being-Intellect, where it is stably engaged in the contemplation of the intelligible Forms. This part of us, as it seems, knows in exactly the same way as the Forms-Minds know; that is, thanks to a kind of intellectual intuition (*noēsis*) that in an extra-temporal instant grasps all the intelligibles in their mutual relation. This kind of knowledge is thus superior to rational thinking (*dianoia*), which performs its action in time and is able to grasp only partial connections among the intelligibles.[38] As a consequence of this, Plotinus' cognitive attitude is prevalently anti-empiricist: sense-data, taken in themselves, are to be discarded, and we must turn instead to our inner self, in order to discover the presence of the intelligibles within us.[39] Thanks to the undescended soul, in fact, we are in standing intimacy with the intelligible order and its items, the Forms, even if we are not aware of it.[40]

For these reasons, as it seems, Plotinus sticks to the *deductio* of the characteristics of sensible things from those of their intelligible models as the *via regia* in his philosophical physics. This is what we found at the beginning of *Enn.* III.7[45], and that we can also find in *Enn.* II.7[37].3, where even "corporeality" is taken as a form, impressed on matter by an incorporeal rational principle; this evidently means, once again, that the proper clue to understanding sensible corporeality lies in ideal corporeality. Plotinus' epistemological project is thus eminently "rationalistic", which is to say based on deductive inferences leading from intelligible principles all the way down to natural phenomena. Given that in the Neoplatonic view everything (except the One and, perhaps, the Forms themselves) is an effect of an intelligible cause, such a method should in principle be capable of accounting for everything in the world.

A fuller treatment of the topic, combined with some interesting theoretical developments, is to be found in Proclus' *Commentary on Plato's Timaeus*.[41] Proclus obviously shares the opinion that the sensible world is a copy of the intelligible one, ultimately depending upon its transcendent causes, but this does not imply for him that the natural world is a negligible object of study or that physics is valuable only if it is reduced to metaphysics. Proclus is in fact very interested in stressing the continuity between the transcendent causes of the cosmos on the one hand, and the various orders of beings that they give origin to within that cosmos on the other. Moreover, for Proclus, Nature, as a metaphysical principle, exists not just at one specific ontological level, but as a chain or series. For these reasons the Platonic philosophy of nature, *physiologia*, is presented by Proclus in different ways depending on what level of nature is being investigated. As Martijn (2010a: 297) succinctly puts it:

> Mirroring Nature itself, philosophy of nature consists in fact in a number of hierarchically and serially ordered phases of *physiologia*, namely theological *physiologia*, which analyzes the universe into its transcendent causes, mathematical *physiologia*, which through reasoning by *analogia*, using ontological images, leads to insight in body and soul of the universe, empirical *physiologia*, which concerns the phenomena in the sky, and biological *physiologia*, treating of the informed living body.

The pivotal role of the intelligible causes and their study is clearly not at stake, because the higher up in the hierarchy a *physiologia* is ranked, the more important it is, and because all the *physiologiai*, including the lowest one, are valuable especially in so far as they can function as introductions to theology. Nevertheless, according to Proclus, each of them, within the limits of its specific domain, has a partial but significant autonomy as far as its subject matter and methods are concerned.[42]

NOTE

1. The expression "vertical causation" has been in vogue since the seminal papers by Wagner (1982b) and J. Barnes (1983)
2. See Plato, *Ti.* 46c–e, 68e–69a; *Laws* 10.896b–897b.
3. All translations of Plotinus' *Enneads* hereinafter are according to Armstrong (1966–88).

4. Wagner (2002a: 301), but see too the much earlier work of Drews (1907: 330).

5. It is worth adding that the Neoplatonists conceived of Nature (or of the Soul, which Nature originates from) mainly as a universal principle, presiding over the physical world as a whole. This view is certainly very distant from the Aristotelian way of thinking, according to which "nature" has mostly a distributive meaning: the singular nature of each single entity. As is well known, even when Aristotle employs "nature" in its general sense, he almost always means the weak order of the collection as opposed to the strong order of the system. See, among others, Siorvanes (1996: 145): "Aristotle rejected both the notion of a soul for the cosmos and the need for a single principle for the world as a whole."

6. In the past century, Émile Bréhier was probably the scholar who had the best insight into Plotinus' conception of the physical world; see especially the appendix "Le monde sensible et la matière" in Bréhier ([1928] 1961: 189–207).

7. See Sorabji (1980, 1983, 1988, 2004: vol. 2) who constantly highlights the contribution of late antique philosophers.

8. Bréhier's stances have been examined again, sometimes critically and sometimes with positive appraisals, by Corrigan (1996a) and Chiaradonna (2002). As far as the ontology of the sensible realities is concerned, we must not forget the valuable work of Wurm (1973) and Horn (1995a).

9. See Chiaradonna & Trabattoni (2009), Martijn (2010a), Wilberding & Horn (2012). On the same subject, see also Lernould (2001).

10. There are some interesting hints in Fattal (1998), Brisson (2000), Linguiti (2009).

11. This passage is well commented on by Fleet (1995: 215–16).

12. See also *Enn.* IV.7[2].3.19; 8.44–5; II.1[40].1.7–8, 24–5; 2.5–6, 3.1–2; and I.8[51].4.1–5.

13. See *Enn.* VI.3[44].8.20, well commented upon by Chiaradonna (2002: 126–46); according to Brisson (2005: vol. 1, 115–16), Porphyry agrees with Plotinus on this point.

14. See *Enn.* VI.3[44].2.2–4, 5.1–3; and again Chiaradonna (2002: 111–17).

15. See also below, note 29, on Plotinian "pseudo-hylomorphism".

16. This point has well been grasped by Siorvanes (1996: 123–5) and Rosán (1949: 116).

17. See especially Proclus, *Theol. Plat.* III.6. The body is still a being (ὄν), but it cannot be ranked as a reality, because it is not self-substantiated and is thoroughly subject to external forces.

18. Proclus, *ET* prop. 80, 74.27–8 [Dodds]. See also Plotinus, *Enn.* VI.5[23].11.5–11.

19. See esp. Proclus, *Theol. Plat.* I.14.61.23–62.1; III.6.20.9–21.21 [Saffrey & Westerink]; *de Prov.* 10 [Isaac]. Cf. J. Barnes (1983) and Steel (2002b: 81–4).

20. Dillon's translation in Brisson (2005: 819). The parallels between Porphyry's *Sentences* and Plotinus' *Enneads* on the one hand, and Proclus' *Elements of Theology* on the other hand are insightfully studied by D'Ancona (2005: 139–275).

21. *Enn.* I.7[54].1.21–4; VI.2[43].11.19–26; VI.5[23].1.8–18.

22. A few examples: "Good" (Plotinus, *Enn.* II.9[33].1; V.5[32].12–13; VI.7[38].16.27; Proclus, *ET* 12); "God" (Plotinus, *Enn.* II.9[33].6.39; V.3[49].7.1; Porphyry, *Sent.* 31); "cause" (Plotinus, *Enn.* V.5[32].13.35–6; VI.8[39].18.38; Porphyry, *Sent.* 14.13; Proclus, *ET* 12); "principle" (Plotinus, *Enn.* III.8[30].9.38–42; V.3[49].15.27; V.4[7].1.23; V.5[32].11.10; Porphyry, *Sent.* 43.1; Proclus, *ET* 12); "foundation" (Plotinus, *Enn.* V.6[24].3.7). For a valuable discussion of the attributes of the One, see Gerson (1994: 15–41).

23. On the different forms of derivation of matter from the One, see Van Riel (2001).

24. Whereas Plotinus thoroughly equated Being and Intellect in maintaining that Forms are also Minds, Iamblichus and the later Neoplatonists conceived of the second hypostasis as a more differentiated structure. For them, Being (the intelligible cosmos) is prior to Intellect (the intellective cosmos), and in the sphere of Being the first rank is not occupied by the Forms: at its summit there is rather undifferentiated Being, which is the cause of the pure and simple existence of things; then there is the power of Being, and only at the third level do we find the Intelligible Paradigm, that is, the sum of the Forms, which are the causes for things of their being something determined (see Proclus, *Theol. Plat.* III.14.51.20–52.11).

25. See *Ti.* 51a1–c5. Several Middle-Platonic thinkers echo this distinction, naming ἰδέα the transcendent Form and εἶδος the Form related to matter; see e.g. Alcinous, *Didasc.* IV.155.39–42 and n. 63 *ad loc.* by Whittaker (1990: 85) and especially Seneca, *Epist.* 65 (on this fundamental text, see Dörrie & Baltes (1987–2008: vol. 4, sections 116.1, 118.1).

26. With reference to Proclus, *in Prm.* IV.969.9–971.7 and III.803.5–805.22 [Steel]. Steel (1987: 124) has established the following ranking of forms: (1) intelligible; (2) intelligible-intellectual, subdivided into: (a) established in a secret and ineffable manner at the summit of the intellectual gods; (b) cohesive; (c)

perfective; (3) intellectual in the genuine sense, subdivided into: (a) established at the summit of the intel-lectual gods; (b) generative; (c) demiurgic; (4) assimilative; (5) transcendent and supracelestial forms; (6) cosmic, subdivided into: (a) intellectual; (b) psychical; (c) physical; (d) perceptible, to be distinguished in their turn into immaterial forms and material ones (i.e. existing as "enmattered" in the sensible compound).

27. For the Plotinian identification of *physis* with the lowest stages of the Soul, and more precisely of the World Soul, see esp. *Enn.* IV.4[28].13.3–4; III.8[30].4.14–16 and Martijn (2010a: 27 n. 40, with bibliographical references).

28. See esp. *Enn.* II.3[52].17–18; *Enn.* V.9[5].6; VI.7[38].5; III.5[50].9. Plotinus clearly adapted the Stoic theory of seminal reason-principles (λόγοι σπερματικοί) to a Neoplatonist framework; see Witt (1931).

29. According to Plotinus (see above, p. 346), sensible things do not result from a genuine composition of matter and form, and for this reason some scholars have described his stance as "pseudo-hylomorphic"; see on this Linguiti (2007).

30. According to Plotinus, the *logoi* stem from the Nature conceived of the last fringe of the Soul (above, note 26). Unlike Plotinus, Proclus kept Nature separate from Soul (see Martijn 2010a: 27–35) and placed the origin of the *logoi* in Nature or Fate (for the substantial equation of Nature and Fate in Proclus, see Linguiti 2009). As is well explained by Opsomer (forthcoming), Proclus envisages several demiurgic principles, but the Demiurge in the full and proper sense is the third deity of the first intellective triad.

31. See note 2 above.

32. See Proclus, *in Ti.* I.2.29–3.13, 4.1–5. Seneca had already maintained that Plato had added a fifth cause to the four Aristotelian causes, namely the paradigmatic one (*his quintam Plato adicit exemplar, Epist.* 65.7). In his *Commentary on Plato's Timaeus*, Proclus takes into account even a further, sixth cause, that is, the instrumental one (*in Ti.* II.357.13–15), probably following in Porphyry's footsteps (see Simplicius, *in Ph.* 10.35–11.3 [Diels]).

33. As Falcon (2011) rightly remarks, the Neoplatonists overtly proclaimed the superiority of the Platonic doctrine of causes against Aristotle.

34. As is generally known, the two kinds of activity (of the essence/from the essence) were clearly distin-guished by Plotinus (see *Enn.* V.4[7].2; V.1[10].6–7). For both Plotinus and Proclus the *logoi* of the Nature are unable to "convert" towards their origin (see e.g. *in Ti.* I.12.25–7). On the way they act, see also Proclus, *in Prm.* III.792.16–795.6 [Steel].

35. See Proclus, *in Ti.* III.274.32–275.4: "When Nature too moves masses by the material and corporeal powers that she has put in these, like earth by means of heaviness and fire by lightness, what would be surprising about that?" and *de Prov.* 13.22–5: *omne enim corpus cogitur et facere quodcumque facit et pati quodcumque patitur, calefacere aut calefieri et infrigidare aut infrigidari*; see also Martijn (2010a: 35–8). The references to heaviness and lightness, as well as to the becoming hot or cold of bodies, can be traced back to the list of physical properties contained in Plato's *Laws*, in the well-known passage stating the priority of the Soul and of its functions with regard to bodies: "Soul drives all things in Heaven and earth and sea by its own motions, of which the names are wish, reflection, forethought, counsel, opinion true and false, joy, grief, confidence, fear, hate, love, and all the motions that are akin to these or are prime-working motions; these, when they take over the secondary motions of bodies, drive them all to increase and decrease and separation and combination, and, supervening on these, to heat and cold, heaviness and lightness, hard-ness and softness, whiteness and blackness, bitterness and sweetness, and all those qualities which soul employs, both when, in conjunction with reason, it runs aright and always governs all things rightly and happily, and when, in converse with unreason, it produces results which are in all respects the opposite" (*Lg.* X.896e8–897b4, trans. Bury).

36. Consider, for example, Leibniz's notion of the body as formed by immaterial and spiritual atoms (the "monads"), characterized by a blurred and confused perception.

37. The Platonic philosophers of the imperial age made two major concessions to Aristotle as far as cosmology was concerned: for along with the notion of natural place, they also accepted the division of the physical world into a celestial and a terrestrial sphere.

38. On the difference between discursive and non-discursive thought in Plotinus, see Emilsson (2007: 176–213).

39. For an illustration of this anti-empiricist attitude, see Slaveva-Griffin (Chapter 13), above.

40. A valuable introduction to the Plotinian doctrine of the "undescended soul" can be found in Szlezák (1979: 167–205); Chiaradonna (2009b: 81–115); also Aubry (Chapter 20), above. The most significant passages are *Enn.* IV.7[2].13.1–13; IV.2[4].12–13; IV.8[6].4.30–31, 8.1–6, 8.17–18; IV.3[27].12.4–5; II.9[33].2.4–10.

41. Well analysed by Martijn (2010a). See also the useful review of the book by Baltzly (2011).
42. The research for this paper was carried out in the framework of the co-financed research project PRIN MIUR 2009: "Post-Hellenistic Philosophies from Antiochus to Plotinus".

23

Neoplatonism and medicine

James Wilberding

Prayer is indeed good, but while calling on the gods a man should himself lend a hand.   (de Diaeta 4.87)[1]

Up until fairly recently, a majority of scholars might have balked at the suggestion that Neoplatonists had any serious interest – let alone any contribution to make – in the natural sciences and in particular in ancient medicine. This reaction reflects a rather uncharitable view of the Neoplatonic project, according to which the sensible world fails to warrant any sustained scientific investigation on account of its being a mere image of the true object of investigation, namely the intelligible cosmos, with the result that Neoplatonists focused their attention on other pursuits.[2] In fact, as scholars are now coming to see, things are the other way round: the sensible cosmos is a particularly worthy object of study precisely because it is an image of the intelligible cosmos. As a result Neoplatonic natural philosophy is currently receiving a level of attention that it has not enjoyed for centuries.[3]

Nevertheless, one might suspect that medicine is a domain of investigation that is particularly ill suited to Neoplatonic philosophers, and it is best that we confront this suspicion at the outset. At the core of this concern is a view analogous to the one captured above: the true object of care for a Neoplatonist is one's soul; one's body is at best an object of indifference and at worst an obstacle to one's philosophical ascent. Why, then, should a Neoplatonist engage with a field whose goal is the health and preservation of the body? To begin with, this argument can also be turned on its head – given that the ill health of the body can impede philosophical progress the Neoplatonic philosopher *should* concern himself with the health of the body,[4] and the fact is that there is considerable evidence that a significant number of Neoplatonists *did* concern themselves with the health of the body.

When one looks beyond the illustrious front line of Neoplatonism – Plotinus, Porphyry, Iamblichus, Proclus and perhaps Damascius[5] – one discovers among the company of lesser-known Neoplatonists many who were themselves physicians. In a few cases we are even in the privileged position of possessing writings of these physicians, for example, of Oribasius of Pergamum (fourth century),[6] Pseudo-Elias (seventh–eighth century?)[7] and – still somewhat controversially – Stephanus of Athens (c. sixth–seventh century?).[8] Unfortunately, in the cases of most physicians no writings have been recorded, let alone handed down to us. Already in Plotinus' school in Rome, for example, there were three physicians, though we know very little about them – Eustochius of Alexandria (third century),[9] Paulinus of Scythopolis (third century),[10] Zethus the Arabian (third century)[11] – and later there were a number of physicians and/or iatrosophists associated with the two famous schools of Neoplatonism in Athens and Alexandria, notably: Iacobus Psychrestos (sixth century),[12] Gessius (fifth–sixth century),[13] Agapius of Athens and Alexandria (fifth–sixth century),[14] John of Alexandria (sixth–seventh century),[15] and a certain Asclepius (sixth century).[16]

Perhaps the most intriguing of these figures is a certain Asclepiodotus of Alexandria and Aphrodisias.[17] Already at an early age in his native Alexandria, Asclepiodotus is reported to have been intensely interested in the empirical study of natural science (*Isid.* 80A). In addition to displaying both serious talent and interest in music and mathematics (*Isid.* 85A–C; cf. Duysinx 1969), he studied medicine with Iacobus Psychrestos in Alexandria (*Isid.* 85D–E) and went on to achieve celebrity for his medical abilities. One notable achievement was the re-establishment of "the long-lost use of white hellebore".[18] Asclepiodotus studied philosophy under Proclus with great success: not only did Simplicius praise him as Proclus' best student (*in Ph.* 795.13–14) and Olympiodorus refer to him as the "great philosopher" Asclepiodotus (Olympiodorus, *in Meteor.* 321.26 [Stüve]), but Proclus himself dedicated his *Commentary on the Parmenides* to Asclepiodotus, saying that he was a dear friend and has "a mind worthy of philosophy".[19] Regarding the scope of Asclepiodotus' interest in philosophy, the reports diverge a bit. On the one hand, Damascius is very critical of his understanding of the divine heights of philosophy presented in the *Chaldaean Oracles* and the Orphics, limiting his praise to Asclepiodotus' talents in natural philosophy.[20] If taken at face value, we might now be inclined to reverse Damascius' value judgement and give Asclepiodotus credit for a more cautious – perhaps a more Galenic? – attitude towards speculative metaphysics.[21] On the other hand, this empirically minded picture of Asclepiodotus is belied by a great deal of evidence that he was a committed believer and practitioner of magic and religious mysteries.[22] The reports about his writing appear to reflect the same tendencies, for we know that he composed hymns to the gods (*Isid.* 87B), as well as a commentary on Plato's *Timaeus*, whose focus appears to have included the third, more medical part of the dialogue.[23] Unfortunately, his writings have not survived.

And beyond these physicians there are any number of individuals who have various claims to a background in both Neoplatonic thought and medicine, without necessarily ever having been practising physicians. Some Neoplatonic commentators and philosophers, for example, reveal more than a passing interest in medicine,[24] as is particularly clear in the cases of Olympiodorus (sixth century),[25] Elias (sixth century),[26] David (sixth century or later),[27] Priscian (fifth–sixth century)[28] and John Philoponus (sixth century),[29] and while we know very little of Proclus' successor Marinus, he is reported to have followed Galen's theories.[30] Beyond this circle one can find a number of Neoplatonism enthusiasts with various degrees of medical training or interest, such as Nemesius of Emesa (fourth century),[31] Eunapius of Sardis (fourth century)[32] and Julian the Apostate (fourth century).[33] Further, there are also a number of pseudonymous treatises in late antiquity that either deal with or touch upon medical issues and that show clear Neoplatonic influence. In embryology, for example, there are Pseudo-Galen's *de Spermate*[34] and *an Animal sit quod est in Utero*[35] and Pseudo-Iamblichus' *Theologoumena Arithmeticae*.[36] And the interaction between the two areas continues in various forms well beyond late antiquity.[37]

Far from being an object of neglect, then, the study of medicine generated a great deal of interest among Neoplatonists; so much interest, in fact, that a comprehensive examination of this intersection of disciplines is simply not feasible here. As there has already been some work assessing the interaction between philosophy and medicine in Alexandria in the sixth and seventh centuries,[38] in what follows I shall therefore be focusing on two central figures of Neoplatonism, Plotinus and Proclus, as these are thinkers whose relation to medicine has received the least amount of scholarly attention. It will be shown that although these Neoplatonists did not view themselves as medical specialists, they did respect medicine as an indispensable discipline. This is made possible by their views on the nature of health and disease, which they closely associated with the body's humours and temperaments. At the same time, they were also convinced that their own unique philosophical training put them in a position to promote or even restore health – both in themselves and in others – in one of two ways, either through the dietetic commitments inherent to the philosophical life or through what we might describe as more "supernatural" means, such as prayer and magic. While this last claim would seem *prima facie* to be in tension with their aetiology of health and disease and their recognition of the efficacy of traditional medical practice, this tension existed within the medical tradition long before the rise of Neoplatonism, and Neoplatonists developed metaphysical theories aimed at resolving it.

MEDICAL TRAINING AND INTERESTS

Porphyry's *Life of Plotinus* and Marinus' *Life of Proclus* shed crucial light on their respective subjects' attitudes to and backgrounds in medicine, which allows us first of all to conclude that neither studied medicine. Both biographers give thorough, if somewhat hagiographical, accounts of their masters' educations, and in neither case is any mention made of medical studies.[39] Moreover, both relate to us that when major medical issues arose within their respective schools, both engaged the services of physicians rather than attempting to treat the patients themselves. In Plotinus' case, he himself suffered from an undetermined chronic illness,[40] and appears to have been treated by his own student Eustochius,[41] and Proclus is reported to have spared no expense in bringing and exhorting physicians to care for the members of his school who had fallen ill.[42] Given, however, the presence of so many physicians in their respective schools, we should expect both Plotinus and Proclus to have some familiarity with medical issues as well as at least some limited exposure to medical texts.

In their written works we can find evidence of this exposure. Plotinus' discussion of the physiological seats of the three parts of the soul in *Enn.* IV.3[27].23, for example, clearly reveals Galenic influence.[43] For whereas Plato located reason in the brain, and the spirited and appetitive parts of soul somewhat indistinctly in the chest and the belly respectively,[44] Galen lent more precision to this doctrine by locating the latter two parts in the heart and the liver respectively, and supported this refined theory with anatomical data that had been established since Plato's death. The discovery by Herophilus and Erasistratus that the nerves are the pathways of sensation and voluntary motion and have their origin in the brain, for example, served as empirical evidence for the correctness of Plato's view that reason is seated in the brain (see Solmsen 1961), while the differentiation, dating back to

Praxagoras, of the arteries and the veins, with the former having their origin in the heart and the latter in the liver, provided further support for the locations of the spirited and appetitive parts of soul (*ibid.*: 177–94). All of this is found again in Plotinus,[45] though he does not quite integrate it into a fully developed physiological psychology.[46] Moreover, Plotinus also appears to agree with the Galenic thesis that the soul follows the temperaments of the body, as long as this thesis is not misunderstood as claiming the *identity* of the soul with the temperaments, as well as the corollary that environmental factors can influence one's soul via the body's temperaments.[47] And as we shall see below, Plotinus' brief remarks on the aetiology of disease and health appear to reveal further influence of medical texts.[48]

Proclus' debt to the medical tradition is more difficult to assess, as the second half of his *Timaeus* commentary, which would have covered the more medical material in the *Timaeus*, has not been preserved, apart from two Greek fragments[49] and a short section of his comments on *Ti.* 89e–90c that has been preserved in Arabic.[50] This is all the more disappointing, as this Arabic section appears to reveal that Proclus was indeed making use of Galen in his commentary on this material. For example, directly after repeating the Galenic localization of the three parts of the soul in the brain, heart and the liver,[51] Proclus offers by way of support a consideration that is reminiscent of Galen's *That the Faculties of the Soul Follow the Mixtures of the Body* (*QAM*): "This is shown by the damages befalling these organs as well as by their [appropriate] remedy. For when damage occurs to the brain, this harms the faculty of reason, and when there occurs damage to the faculty of reason, we give medical treatment to the brain; and things are analogous with the other two parts."[52]

Elsewhere Proclus also makes a certain preoccupation on his part with Galen's *QAM* clear.[53] Further, in this same section Proclus' rather curious description of the contributions of the activities of the spirited and appetitive parts to the health of the body – the appetitive part is said to be responsible for attracting what is helpful and the spirited part for repelling what is harmful – bears a striking similarity to Galen's integration of the powers of attraction and repulsion in the preserved fragments of his own commentary on the *Timaeus*.[54] Proclus also refers occasionally to examples of medical practice and procedures to underline a point, which might – but need not necessarily – indicate some discussions with the physicians in his school.[55] Overall, however, we can say that Proclus shows a very limited interest in medicine in his writings, as can be seen by the paucity of his references to central anatomical concepts and key physicians,[56] as well as by the use he does make of medical authors. To take one example, in his lengthy discussion of nuptial arithmetic in his commentary on Plato's *Republic* 546a–547a, Proclus sees an opportunity to examine the much discussed issue of the duration of pregnancy in humans, and in particular to defend the traditional views on the possibility of seven-month pregnancies and the impossibility of eight-month pregnancies.[57] He begins by reporting the view of "Herophilus and many other highly regarded [physicians]" – and this is to my knowledge the only reference to Herophilus in the surviving Neoplatonic texts – that the ancient belief in the possibility of the seven-month pregnancy is erroneous and the result of a miscalculation of the date of conception.[58] Proclus' response is not exactly what one would expect of a philosopher with serious interests in medicine: he simply appeals to the authority of the Pythagoreans, the Orphics, Zoroaster, Empedocles and others who do accept this belief.[59]

There is certainly a case to be made for Porphyry's having had a much more thorough familiarity with medicine and biology, since it is now generally accepted that Porphyry was the author of the epistolary treatise *To Gaurus on How Embryos are Ensouled* (*ad Gaurum*), in which embryology is discussed in some detail. As this text has received a considerable amount of attention recently,[60] there is no need for a detailed examination here. Let us simply note that while Porphyry does make use of medical texts to support his position that the soul enters the offspring at birth, he makes little attempt to actually engage with the medical tradition. Not only is there no evidence of first-hand experimentation and anatomy, but even the textual source material found in the *ad Gaurum* is very limited; it is drawn almost exclusively from the Hippocratic *de Natura Pueri*,[61] though like Plotinus and Proclus, Porphyry does implicitly accept Galen's refinement on the locations of the three parts of the soul.[62] It can also be seen in how he takes certain contentious views for granted. He simply assumes, for example, that there is no female seed, and he gives no indication that he is even aware of the controversy surrounding this issue (see Wilberding 2008). The same could be said about the order of the formation of the organs. All of this suggests that Porphyry has familiarized himself a little with Hippocratic embryology, but that his overall relationship to medicine is comparable to that of Plotinus and Proclus.

AETIOLOGY OF DISEASE AND HEALTH

As we have now seen, despite their somewhat cursory engagement with medical theories, Neoplatonists generally held medicine to be an efficacious and often necessary means for maintaining and restoring the health of the body, which already suggests a certain level of naturalization in their views on the aetiology of disease and health. Indeed, the pre-eminent historian of medicine Ludwig Edelstein congratulated the Neoplatonists for precisely such a naturalized aetiology (with some qualifications, as we shall see below) on the basis of a passage in Plotinus, in which he criticizes his gnostic contemporaries for boasting of the power to cure people afflicted with diseases, which for them were either identical to or closely associated with the presence of demons within the body:[63]

> Those who consider the matter carefully will not be fooled into thinking that *diseases have any other causes* than exhaustion, excess and deficiency of nourishment, decay, and in general processes that have their starting point either inside or outside [of the body]. And the treatment of diseases makes [this] clear. For the disease is passed down and out [of the body] when the stomach is emptied or a drug is administered, and so too when blood is let, and fasting has also cured patients.   (*Enn.* II.9[33].14.17–23)[64]

Here Plotinus, who is likely drawing on an unidentified medical source,[65] appears simply to rule out supernatural causes of disease,[66] and although he does not offer a sustained discussion of the nature of health, this aetiology fits well with what he does tell us about health, for he appears to adopt the traditional view of health being a function of the temperaments of the body,[67] and he places great emphasis on the medical benefits of sound regimen. Regimen, having long been a central part of traditional medicine, formed the core of Pythagorean medicine (as well as of Plato's discussion of medicine in the *Republic*), and Porphyry's account of Plotinus' life shows his commitment to a form of Pythagorean regimen.[68] That such a regimen benefits one's health is made clear in the *Enneads*[69] and depicted rather vividly in the anecdote, related in Porphyry's *Life of Plotinus*, of a certain student of Plotinus named Rogatianus, who by his "renunciation and indifference to the needs of life" adopted the Pythagorean regimen and thereby cured himself of arthritis.[70] This understanding that health and disease can be controlled by the natural properties found in nourishment and elsewhere underlies Plotinus' acknowledgement of the influence that region and climate can have on the body and the soul.[71]

Those familiar with the subsequent development of Neoplatonism will be quick to point out Edelstein's fallacy in generalizing about the aetiology of disease for *all* Neoplatonists on the basis of what Plotinus says.[72] For with Iamblichus demonology, theurgy and magic take on an increased importance in Neoplatonic thought, and he makes no secret of his belief that demons can cause diseases and incantations can cure them (Iamblichus, *Myst.* 2.6 and 5.16). For this reason two points deserve special emphasis. First, despite what he says in the passage above, even Plotinus was prepared to accept that demons exist and that magic and prayer are efficacious both as causes and remedies of diseases.[73] Second, even post-Iamblichean Neoplatonic philosophy does in fact to a large extent retain this empirically oriented account of health and disease.

Proclus, for example, also follows the medical tradition in associating health and disease with the harmonious relation of the body's humours:

> For disease arises from the asymmetry of what is introduced – with this or that [foreign] thing assimilating itself to this or that organ and destroying the proportion between that part and the remaining parts from which we will then be composed. Through this, an excess and deficiency of the humours insinuates itself.   (*in Ti.* II.62.32–63.4, trans. Baltzly)[74]

Proclus, however, does not appear to be entirely content with the traditional identification of health with the "symmetric" or harmonious mixture of the humours, for such an identification would make health posterior to the body and its states. He therefore inverses this causal relation in the sequel:

> For it is requisite for the health that truly is to be prior to the generated kind of health, this being in a singular manner. Such is the case with the health of the universe. For generally if *health is the cause of symmetry among the elements*, it is necessary that health be present in the highest degree in the universe in which the symmetry of the elements is present to the highest degree.   (*in Ti.* II.63.11–16)[75]

Given that symmetry is a kind of unity, this inversion is exactly what we should expect of Neoplatonists, who refer all forms of unity in the sensible world to higher causes. This inversion is significant, for as we shall see below, it will help Proclus develop a more unified account of the various causes – including supernatural causes – of health, but for now let us direct our attention to the down-to-earth emphasis he places on the natural properties in the body. For by placing this focus on the humours and temperaments, Proclus gives us an account of health and disease that is wholly compatible with traditional medical practice, which seeks to maintain and restore the natural state of the body and its temperaments by a variety of physical means, e.g. diet, drugs, surgery and bloodletting.[76] And as in Plotinus' case, this commitment to the efficacy of medical practices is borne out by the weight he accords to regimen – Proclus' student and biographer repeatedly stresses his "intolerably harsh" diet[77] – which again occupied a prominent position in ancient medicine, as well as by his acknowledgement of the medical advantages and disadvantages of various environmental factors.[78] Proclus, in fact, even appears to have recognized that certain diseases are genetically inherited.[79]

THE ADMISSION OF THE SUPERNATURAL IN MEDICINE

There is certainly no denying, however, that supernatural channels play a much greater role in Proclus' thoughts on medicine and healing than in Plotinus', as is accurately reflected in his biography. Marinus relates two separate occasions on which Proclus was healed from an incurable ailment after encountering a son of Asclepius in his dream,[80] and he also experienced waking visions of Asclepius and his sons.[81] In other episodes, Proclus is presented as taking a more active role: through chanting and praying to Asclepius he is able to alleviate pain and even cure disease (Marinus, *Procl.* 17, 20 and 29; see note 42). (Indeed, through these frequent references to Asclepius, Marinus appears to be suggesting that just as Plotinus' personal *daemon* turned out to be a god (Porphyry, *Plot.* 10.23–5), so too does Proclus' turn out to be none other than Asclepius himself.) Marinus never mentions Proclus invoking a daemon to cure a disease, but Proclus himself appears to signal the efficacy of this practice.[82]

This admission of the supernatural into the domain of medicine would seem to undermine Edelstein's praise of the Neoplatonists for their rejection of medical "superstition", but a brief look at the medical tradition shows that this admission is hardly unique to Neoplatonism. Prayer and divinely inspired dreams or visions, for example, not only are a core element of the traditional cults of Asclepius[83] but also find some recognition within the Hippocratic corpus.[84] Even Galen, the champion of a down-to-earth approach to Greek medicine, repeatedly calls attention to his own somnial encounters with the divine (on Galen's conception of the divine, see M. Frede 2003). He tells us that he owes his career in medicine to a dream that his father Nicon had when he was a boy, in which Asclepius directed him to educate his son in medicine,[85] and that he himself received divine advice in dreams. It was a dream that persuaded him to rewrite a section of his treatise *de Usu Partium* on the eye;[86] a dream of Asclepius that encouraged him not to join Marcus Aurelius on a dangerous campaign;[87] and two clear dreams sent by Asclepius that instructed him on how to treat a life-threatening illness that he was suffering from.[88] Thus, Galen can call himself a "worshipper" of Asclepius and justify his belief in the existence of gods because "they are revealed in divination and dreams … and indeed I have experienced it myself".[89]

When it comes to incantations and magical charms and amulets, by contrast, one certainly discovers clear expressions of scepticism and intolerance in the Hippocratic corpus and in Galen (Nutton 2004: 266–71), but even here there is important common ground. For although Galen vehemently protests the efficacy of magic, he was a firm believer in there being natural powers of sympathy in the world. Indeed, much of his physiology and pharmacology rests on principles of sympathy (Keyser 1997). Yet all that Neoplatonists wish to admit under the term "magic" are the causes and effects governed by principles of cosmic sympathy.[90] The disagreement would seem to concern only the exact parameters of sympathetic causation, whether spoken words or music, for example, can generate a physical effect in the world.[91]

Edelstein, backing away a bit from his earlier praise, seeks to drive a larger wedge between the theories of sympathy subscribed to by physicians and those of the Neoplatonists, urging that whereas the former are "proved by experiments" (Edelstein 1937: 232), the latter "explained sympathy not by physical but by psychic causes" (*ibid.*: 235). Thus, he concludes that "effects which were in earlier times natural and empirical later became mysterious" (*ibid.*). Edelstein is certainly right about Neoplatonists demonstrating comparatively little interest in experimentation, but his criticism seems to miss the critical point that the two groups were working on different sets of questions. Whereas a physician is looking to determine the concrete particulars of sympathy – which substances possess which powers – the Neoplatonists were mostly interested in the metaphysical conditions for sympathy; that is, given the concrete particulars of sympathy (whatever these might be), what must the nature of reality be like such that these sympathy relations can obtain at all? That is to say, while physicians were appealing to a theory of sympathy in order to explain particular phenomena, Neoplatonists were seeking to explain the efficacy of sympathy itself. Viewed from this perspective, the Neoplatonists were aiming at making the world less mysterious, not more so. "Psychic" and other higher causes were introduced to eliminate what would have been seen as gaps in older medical theories. Whereas the author of the Hippocratic *de Morbis Popularibus* VI, for example, was content to say that nature is unintelligent and yet "does what needs to be done without having received any education or instructions" and to leave it at that,[92] the Neoplatonist will fairly complain that some account must be given of how an unintelligent principle can consistently manoeuvre the physical world in intelligent ways.[93] Thus, the Neoplatonists bring in "psychic" and other higher causes to account for its intelligent activity.

As we saw above, Proclus maintains that the harmonious state of the body's humours must, like all unitary states in the sensible world, be referred to a higher cause. In ordinary cases, the proximate cause of this harmonious state will be either the body's own vegetative soul or the physician's art of medicine (cf. Plotinus, *Enn.* III.3[48].5.29–32). But Proclus is not content to let the story end there, since some explanation is required not only for how the vegetative soul knows how to regulate the body's humours so reliably, but also for how two very different causes can share the same power and know-how: both the art of medicine and the vegetative soul generate health in the body. But this is not all. As we have now seen, the extraordinary cases must also be accounted for. For the dreams, prayers and visions, which the medical tradition was content to leave as loose ends, all would seem to involve some communication of medical knowledge and/or causal efficacy. Indeed, Neoplatonists would expand the list of *explananda* even further to include why certain individuals are particularly gifted in the art of healing, why certain places and certain substances (e.g. plants) have curative powers, and why the universe as a whole, which is itself a living thing, never grows ill. Proclus reasonably sees all of these questions as related. After all, they are all concerned with explaining why the single power to heal is instantiated in many different things in so many different ways. This is in some sense, then, the classic one-over-many problem of Platonism, and Proclus simply adopts the approved solution: he posits a series of higher causes to account for the entire spectrum of medical knowledge and power that appears to be flowing into the world.[94] He has this series, which he describes alternately as both a series of the causes of health and a series of the causes of the art of medicine,[95] culminate in the Demiurge, and he invokes this series to explain the entire catalogue of medical phenomena, not only dreams and visions but also the enduring health of the universe,[96] the healing powers of daemons,[97] the healing powers of certain places,[98] material substances with curative powers such as plants,[99] and the innate talent of certain individual practitioners.[100] The upshot of positing this series of causes is a unified theory of medical causation that allows Proclus to conclude that when he is praying to Asclepius he is tapping into the same source of medical knowledge as the common physician.[101]

CONCLUSION

What does Neoplatonism have to do with medicine? The answer to this question will vary according to the scope of one's understanding of both medicine and Neoplatonism. In its history Neoplatonism has had an extremely large sphere of influence, which ensured a significant amount of interaction between the fields of medicine and Neoplatonic philosophy. This interaction produced not only Neoplatonic philosophers with a considerable education in medicine, but also practising physicians who had been educated in Neoplatonic schools of philosophy. Viewed more narrowly, it is still possible to discern a clear, though limited, interest by core Neoplatonists in certain aspects of medicine. Plotinus and Proclus, the most celebrated members of the movement and the foci of this study, did not practise medicine, though perhaps it would be more accurate to say that they *did* practise medicine, but only in a qualified sense, as they are both firm believers in the health benefits of regimen, practising strict regimens themselves and encouraging others to do so as well. Yet, they do not appear to have enjoyed any noteworthy training in traditional medicine, nor is there any evidence that they had first-hand experience of anatomy, and the anatomical knowledge that they did acquire from medical texts or discussions with their students does not figure very prominently in their accounts of humans and other living beings. But even if they did not fully engage with medicine in this straightforward empirical sense, they certainly did lay claim to other varieties of medical knowledge; that is, the art of living in a healthy manner (regimen) and the art of healing by higher causes.[102] Above all of this it is possible to detect an underlying interest in the *philosophy* of medicine. After all, Proclus' series of causes of health is meant to address the problem of how a diverse set of medical phenomena can be accounted for in a systematic manner, and in positing these causes Proclus could credibly describe himself as merely saving the widely accepted phenomena. One result of this systematic philosophy of medicine is that Proclus can see himself via his prayers and chants as tapping into the same font of medicine as physicians, but this admission of higher-order medicine should not be seen as in any way invalidating or eclipsing common medical practice.[103] They knew full well that the body's state could be and often needed to be administered by the physician's art.

NOTES

1. The Hippocratic *de Diaeta* 4.87 (218.21–2 [Joly] = 6.642 [Littré]), on which Nutton (2004: 66) comments: "This is not a rejection of the gods, but a demarcation of spheres of effective action. These spheres may overlap."

2. Zeller's content-header on the first page of his discussion of Plotinus' natural philosophy sums up his view in three words: "no scientific research". Underneath, he insists that because for Plotinus the sensible world is only an obfuscation of the intelligible, "he necessarily must have lacked both the sensibility and the capacity to research the laws of the physical world" (*mußte ihm notwendig für eine Erforschung der physikalischen Gesetze ebenso der Sinn wie auch die Fähigkeit abgehen*) (1868: 619). Zeller's view still has traction, as can be seen in Föllinger (1999: 255), but for a recent reassessment of Zeller's view, see Wilberding & Horn (2012).

3. The relevant studies are too numerous to list, but one might gain a first impression of this new work from Sorabji (2004–2005: vol. 2), Chiaradonna & Trabattoni (2009) and Wilberding & Horn (2012).

4. See e.g. Porphyry, *Abst.* 1.53.2 = 127.10–12 [Nauck].

5. The attributions to Damascius found in several manuscripts of commentaries on the Hippocratic *Prognosticon* and *Aphorisms* are inaccurate. See Westerink (1964: 173–4) and the *Dictionnaire des philosophes antiques* (*DNP*) 2.591–3.

6. Editions of Oribasius' surviving works have been published in the series *Corpus Medicorum Graecorum*. The *Suda* attributes works to him that are possibly distinct from the surviving works and possibly philosophical in nature. He was the physician and friend of Julian the Apostate, who was himself a propagator of Neoplatonic thought. Historians of medicine generally consider him to be a mere medical encyclopedist, but Eunapius (*VS* 21 = 87.16–89.17 [Giangrande]), perhaps hagiographically, characterizes Oribasius also as a model philosopher. Temkin observed that "nothing is known about his philosophical views" (1991: 214), but more recent research is beginning to reveal that Neoplatonism did indeed make its way into Oribasius' medical thought, though the full extent to which it did so remains unclear. Boudon-Millot & Goulet (*DPA* 8.803–4) point out that the Platonic theory of *anamnēsis* plays a role in his theory of medical research, and Metzger (forthcoming) has shown how Oribasius' commitment to Neoplatonism influenced his views on the *ephialtēs* affliction (*Synopsis ad Eustathium* VIII.2).

7. See Westerink (1967: xv), who concludes that Pseudo-Elias is probably a professor of medicine lecturing on logic, though his "philosophical knowledge is of the flimsiest". Wolska-Conus (1989: 69–82) argues that Pseudo-Elias is to be identified with Stephanus of Athens. See below.

8. The main controversy surrounding the physician Stephanus of Athens is whether he is to be identified with the philosopher and commentator Stephanus of Alexandria, the author of a commentary on Aristotle's *De Interpretatione* (*CAG* volume 18, part 3). A second and related controversy is whether Stephanus of Alexandria is the author of a commentary on the third book of Aristotle's *de Anima* that has come down to us under John Philoponus' name (*CAG* volume 15, pp. 446–607). Wolska-Conus (1989, cf. 1992) has argued most extensively and persuasively for both identity theses, and further arguments have been added regarding the second controversy by Charlton (2000: 1–15) and Tornau (2007). Not all scholars are convinced – e.g. Lautner (1992) and M. Roueché (1999: 154) – but if there is a majority consensus on this issue, it is one of cautious acceptance of Wolska-Conus' thesis. Even if a single thinker is responsible for these philosophical and medical commentaries, it remains to be seen whether Stephanus is a key figure for the integration of medicine into Neoplatonic thought: first, because he does not appear to have enjoyed a thorough Neoplatonic education (Perkams 2008: 279), and second, because it is difficult to find any expressly Neoplatonic elements in the medical commentaries (see Westerink's list of philosophical topics found in the medical commentaries (1964: 171), none of which is specific to Neoplatonism).

9. There is no evidence of any writings. See Porphyry, *Plot.* 2.12–13, 23–31, 7.8–12 and Brisson *et al.* (1982: 81). Porphyry has high praise for Eustochius, who appears to have completed an edition of Plotinus' treatises prior to the *Enneads*, the edition produced by Porphyry thirty years after Plotinus' death. Grmek's claim (1992: 338) that Eustochius gave up medicine to study philosophy strikes me as an over-interpretation of *Plot.* 7.10–12. We are told that Eustochius cared for Plotinus towards the end of his life.

10. There is no evidence of any writings. See Porphyry, *Plot.* 7.5–7 and 7.16–17, and Brisson *et al.* (1982: 102). Porphyry reports that he was a poor student of philosophy.

11. There is no evidence of any writings. See Porphyry, *Plot.* 7.17–24, and Brisson *et al.* (1982: 82).

12. There is no evidence of any writings. A physician and philosopher held in the highest regard by his

contemporaries, in particular for his medical training and success, Iacobus was associated with the Neoplatonic school in Athens at least on a practical level: he treated Proclus (Damascius, *Isid.* 84J [Athanassiadi]) and might have been familiar with Isidore of Alexandria (*Isid.* 84E). The evidence for any theoretical commitment to Neoplatonism is lean and mixed: he was a pagan and praised by Isidore as having an "Asclepian" soul (see below, note 100), and he apparently had a holy aura – so much so that he was ridiculed by some of his contemporaries for being a holy man and not a doctor (*Isid.* 84E). Moreover, one of his students, Asclepiodotus of Alexandria, was also counted among Proclus' best students (Simplicius, *in Ph.* 795.13–14 [Diels]; see below). At one point Damascius implicitly ascribes to Iacobus a commitment to Pythagorean rules of healing with its emphasis on regimen (*Isid.* 84D with Athanassiadi's note *ad loc.*), but this commitment is partly called into question in *Isid.* 84J, where Iacobus is reported to have prescribed mallow to Proclus, despite a Pythagorean prohibition against consuming mallow (Iamblichus, *VP* 109 = 63.6–8 [Deubner–Klein]; and see Athanassiadi's note *ad Isid.* 84J). See Keyser & Irby-Massie (2008: 429–30) and *DPA* 3.821–3.

13. There is no evidence of writings. Gessius was a celebrated teacher and practitioner of medicine in Alexandria, and he is reported to have studied philosophy under Ammonius of Alexandria. As Athanassiadi puts it, Gessius was "an important figure in the philosophical life of Alexandria ... and a pillar of the Hellenistic resistance". See Damascius, *Isid.* 128, *DPA* 3.477–8, and now Watts (2009).

14. Although the *Suda* and older scholarship (including *DPA* 1.63 but still Keyser & Irby-Massie [2008: 40]) distinguish between Agapius of Athens and Agapius of Alexandria, these are two definite descriptions of the same person (see Athanassiadi 1999: 257 n. 278). After his initial studies in "letters, medicine and philosophy" in Alexandria, Agapius moved to Athens where he was admitted to Proclus' school towards the end of the latter's life. After Proclus' death Agapius was taught by Proclus' successor Marinus (Damascius, *Isid.* 107). He later returned to Alexandria and worked with the physician Gessius (see above). Following the Great Persecution, he moved to Constantinople where he set up a philosophical school and taught among others John Lydus, who described Agapius as both the "last" and the "first" of Proclus' students (John Lydus, *de Mag.* 3.26).

15. Little can be said about John. Two commentaries on Hippocratic treatises have come down to us under the name John of Alexandria – *in Hipp. Epid.* VI [Duffy] and *in Hip. Nat. Puer.* [Bell *et al.*], both in *CMG* 11.1.14 – although there are some questions as to whether the same John of Alexandria is the author of both (see Pormann 2003). Assuming common authorship, these texts reveal that John had considerable exposure to Platonism. He works Plato into his commentary on several occasions (e.g. *in Hipp. Nat. Puer.* 146.16–32 and *in Hipp. Epid.* VI 44.21–3), and he integrates some Platonic vocabulary throughout (e.g. God is twice referred to as "the Demiurge" [*in Hipp. Epid.* VI 60.31 and *in Hipp. Nat. Puer.* 164.39] and Nature is described as "holding the reins" [ἡνιοχεῖ] at *in Hipp. Nat. Puer.* 134.13. Cf. also *ad in Hipp. Epid.* VI 60.29–34 [Duffy]). His exposure to Neoplatonism in particular becomes clear when he invokes numerological considerations to explain the duration of the embryo's first formation (*in Hipp. Nat. Puer.* 164.37–166.23; cf. 134.22–4 and 148.1–5) and cites at another point the *Chaldaean Oracles* (*in Hipp. Epid.* VI 60.34; cf. *Chald. Or.* 22.3 [Des Places]).

16. A student of Ammonius, though not to be confused with the Asclepius of Tralles, who was also a student of Ammonius and preserved his lectures on Aristotle's *Metaphysics* (*CAG* volume 6, part 2). The Asclepius in question has been described as "the most prominent physician of the first half of the 6th century" (Westerink 1964: 175) and was the teacher of Stephanus of Athens (*ibid.*: 172). There appears to be a consensus that Stephanus uses the description "the new commentator" to refer to this Asclepius (*ibid.*). If this is right, it possibly reveals an at best limited regard for Neoplatonism (and Galen). For according to Stephanus, this "new commentator" returned to the Peripatetic position on the location of the *hēgēmonikon* in the heart (*in Hipp. Progn. Comm.* III 256.32–258.3 [Duffy]). This Asclepius composed a commentary on the Hippocratic *Aphorisms* (see Westerink's introduction in *CMG* 11.1.3.1.17–23 [1985–95]).

17. See Martindale (1980: 161–2), Goulet (1989–2012: vol. 1, 626–32), C. Roueché (1989: 87–93), R. R. R. Smith (1990: 153–5), Athanassiadi (1999), Watts (2010: *passim*). These accounts vary somewhat on account of the fact that there are very clearly two individuals named Asclepiodotus and associated with Aphrodisias, who are both active in the same circles. As a result, there is disagreement over which Asclepiodotus is meant in some of the fragments.

18. *Isid.* 85D. In this connection it is interesting that Proclus himself once refers to the medical application of hellebore (*in Ti.* I.377.17–20 [Diehl]), which may be an indication of some discussion between Proclus and

Asclepiodotus on medical issues, though what Proclus says is very general and might simply be inspired by Plato's *Euthydemus* 299b.

19. Proclus, *in Prm.* 618.12–14 [Steel]. Proclus apparently also called Asclepiodotus back to Athens at one point, thinking that he might be a suitable successor, though he ultimately decided otherwise (*Isid.* 99); cf. Watts (2006: 115–16).

20. *Isid.* 85A. His characterization of Asclepiodotus as "packing everything together and bringing it down to the level of the physical world" is undoubtedly meant as a criticism. R. R. R. Smith (1990: 154) is probably right about Damascius inventing or exaggerating "deficiencies" in order to have Isidore's star shine that much brighter. As Athanassiadi points out (1999: 213 n. 220), it is hardly likely that Proclus would have dedicated his commentary on the *Parmenides* to someone incapable of understanding the highest pinnacle of philosophy.

21. J. Freudenthal (1896: 1642, esp. ll. 17–25).

22. *Isid.* 81–2, 86 and 96, and Zacharias Scholasticus, *Life of Severus* p. 17 [Kugener].

23. Olympiodoros, *in Meteor.* 321.26–9. Cf. Dörrie & Baltes (1987–2008: vol. 3, sections 223–4).

24. See Westerink (1964), Todd (1977), Duffy (1984), M. Roueché (1999). For the dubious attributions of two medical works to Simplicius, see Baltussen (2010: vol. 2, 713).

25. Westerink (1964: 172; 1976: 27) points out Olympiodorus' very frequent use of Hippocrates, a fact best explained in his view by concluding that Olympiodorus must have lectured on Hippocrates. M. Roueché (1999: 155) rejects this conclusion but agrees that Olympiodorus does display an "unusual degree of interest in medicine".

26. Westerink (1964: 172–3) and M. Roueché (1999: 154).

27. Westerink (1962: xx–xxiv; 1964: 173–4).

28. See de Haas (2010).

29. For Philoponus' knowledge and use of Galenic medical ideas, see Todd (1984) and van der Eijk (2006: 1–4 and the notes [*passim*, e.g. 138 n. 226]). It remains uncertain whether Philoponus actually composed commentaries on medical texts. The Arabic tradition has attributed as many as seventeen commentaries on medical texts to him, but this appears to be due, at least in part, to the confusion resulting from the fact that there are a number of different individuals named "John the Grammarian", "John of Alexandria" and/or "John Philoponus". See Pormann (2003) and now *DPA* 5a.554–63. Of these, the strongest case for our Philoponus' authorship has been made for a commentary (of which only a fragment survives) on the eleventh book of Galen's *de Usu Partium*, as argued by Strohmaier (2003) and endorsed by van der Eijk (2005: 134 n. 371) and Pormann (2003: 249).

30. See *Isid.* 97I, though Marinus happily relates a number of miracle healings in his *Proclus*. See below.

31. See the introduction to Sharples & van der Eijk (2008), which discusses the questions surrounding his knowledge of medicine and his commitment to Platonism (including very close connections to Galen's work).

32. Eunapius studied under the philosopher Chrysanthius (*VS* 6.1.6 = 18.10–11 [Giangrande] and 23.1.1 = 90.21–4 [Giangrande]), who in turn was a student of Iamblichus' successor Aedesius (*VS* 5.1.11 = 12.10–13 [Giangrande] and 6.1 = 17.8–18.13 [Giangrande]). At the end of his *Lives* Eunapius boasts that he is not without experience in medicine (οὐδὲ γὰρ ἄπειρος ἦν ἰατρικῆς ὁ ταῦτα γράφων [*VS* 100.12–13 Giangrande]) and reports how he vetoed the doctors' orders to subject Chrysanthius to a bloodletting procedure and thereby preserved his life (*VS* 23.6 = 100.7–20 [Giangrande]).

33. Julian's commission of both Oribasius' epitome of Galen and his epitome of ancient physicians demonstrates a clear interest in medicine. See also R. B. E. Smith (1995: 236 n. 74).

34. The surviving text (in Latin) remains without a critical edition, but a solid first orientation can be won from the English translation and commentary of a Middle English translation of *de Spermate* in Pahta (1998). On the Neoplatonic influence, see now Slaveva-Griffin (2014).

35. Wagner (1914). An English translation may be found as an appendix in Kapparis (2002: 201–13). Keyser & Irby-Massie (2008: 339) go so far as to suggest that the author is either Iamblichus or one of his students. It would seem, however, that the views advanced in the *an Animal sit* on the nature and generation of the soul are, in certain points at least, incongruous with much of Neoplatonic thought (e.g. *pneuma* appears to be introduced not as a mere vehicle of the soul but as its substance, cf. 166.3–4 [Wagner], where the soul is said to be nourished by *pneuma* won from the digestion of nourishment).

36. De Falco & Klein (1975), with the English translation by Waterfield (1988).

37. To take just a couple of examples, there is good reason to believe that Michael of Ephesus was a physician

(Praechter 1906: 863–4; Ierodiakonou 2009a: 187–94), in addition to being influenced to some extent by Neoplatonism (Steel 2002a, D. O'Meara 2008). Likewise, there is evidence that Michael Psellus, another very prolific Byzantine Neoplatonist, had a considerable medical background and was even a practising physician (see Volk 1990). For some connections btween Neoplatonism and medicine in the Renaissance, see Pagel (1985).

38. See the studies referred to in notes 24–9. As editions of the surviving texts continue to appear we can expect more studies on the role that Neoplatonism played in the medical doctrines of this period.

39. Porphyry credits Plotinus with having studied all the schools of philosophy plus astronomy (*Plot.* 15.21–6) and with having "complete knowledge" of geometry, arithmetic, mechanics, optics and music (14.7–10). Marinus presents Proclus as a *Wunderkind* who, after a brief (*Procl.* 8) but apparently very successful (*Procl.* 11) encounter with rhetoric, mastered all of Aristotle in two years, before turning to Plato and higher philosophy (*Procl.* 13), and who had a special knack for mathematics and logic (*Procl.* 4 and 9). He takes pains to emphasize Proclus' training and subsequent brilliance in politics (*Procl.* 14–16).

40. See Porphyry, *Plot.* 2. The nature of this illness has been the subject of much discussion. See Grmek (1992), Edwards (2000) and Slaveva-Griffin (2010: 104–10) for the most recent discussions.

41. *Plot.* 2 reports Plotinus' reaction to an unnamed physician's (presumably Eustochius) suggestions for treatment. More on this below. In light of the fact that Plotinus himself made use of medical help, one must be careful not to exaggerate his disregard for bodily health (*Enn.* III.2[47].5.6–7). He is concerned about his health, but he is not willing to pursue his health at all costs. See below on Plotinus' commitment to regimen.

42. See Marinus, *Procl.* 17. Todd's (1984: 104 n. 12) claim that Marinus reports at *Procl.* 17 that Proclus "had some medical skill" is presumably based on Guthrie's (1925) misleading translation of καὶ τὶ καὶ αὐτὸς ἐν τούτοις περιττότερον εἰσηγεῖτο as "and himself suggested some more efficacious remedy". Cf. Edwards' more accurate translation (2000: 83): "and in these circumstances he himself did something extra". Marinus is alluding to prayer and ritual, on which see below. Likewise, when Proclus applies a liniment to his ailing foot, it is because he has been "advised by certain people" (συμβουλευθεὶς παρὰ τινῶν) to do so (*Procl.* 31).

43. For what follows, see Tieleman (1998).

44. See Plato, *Ti.* 69c–71a together with 73b–d. It is often said that Plato himself located the spirited part in the heart (Cornford 1935: 282; Nutton 2004: 117). This view might be right (cf. *Ti.* 70a7–b3 and 70d4), but it is hard to square with Plato's claims that the marrow and the brain have been created to be the seat of the soul (*Ti.* 73b–d). See also Johansen (2004: 150–52).

45. Although Plotinus never explicitly mentions the arteries, his remarks about the fine and pure blood being sent out from the heart (*Enn.* IV.3[27].23.42–6) appears to reflect Galen's differentiation of the arteries from the veins by the *pneuma* present in the former. See Tieleman (1998: 322).

46. Although Plotinus has the distinction of being the only Neoplatonist in our group who explicitly attempts to include the nerves in his account (Sorabji 2005: vol. 1, 59–60), he fails to make clear what role they play in his physiology, given that in his view the soul is already present as a whole throughout the body. See Emilsson (1988: 105–6) and Morel (2002: 218). Outside of *Enn.* IV.3[27].23 Plotinus makes no appeal to the nerves or the particularly pure blood associated with the arteries.

47. See *Enn.* I.8[51].8.28–38; I.8[51].14; III.1[3].5.24–7; III.1[3].6.5–10; III.1[3].8.14–20; IV.3[27].23.42–7; IV.3[27].26.12–14; IV.4[28].20.28–36; IV.4[28].21; IV.4[28].28.17, 40–52; IV.8[6].2.42–5. See Boys-Stones (2007a: 120–1), who also suggests that at *Enn.* 4.3[27].7.22–5 Plotinus might be implicitly referring to Galen's reading of the Hippocratic *de Aere Aquis Locis* in his QAM 57.14–62.22 [Mueller] = 4.798.6–803.12 [Kühn]. Plotinus' commitment to the environmental corollary is also witnessed in his advice to Porphyry in *Plot.* 11.12–17, on which see below.

48. *Enn.* II.9[33].14.17–36 and *Enn.* IV.4[28].45.47–9, discussed below.

49. See *DPA* 5b.1576. Neither fragment deals with medical issues.

50. The *editio princeps* of this passage has recently been completed by Arnzen (2013), which also provides an English translation and notes. The (unedited) passage has previously been translated into French in Festugière (1966–8: vol. 5, 241–8) and German in Pfaff (1941: 53–60).

51. Other passages confirming this account of localization include *in R.* I.254.14 [Kroll]; *de Prov.* 16.9 and 23.11–14 [Isaac]. Cf. *in Ti.* III.242.17–19 and *de Decem Dub.* §52.5–10 [Isaac]. But see below, note 59.

52. Proclus, *in Ti. ad* 89e3–90a2, trans. Arnzen (2013). For Galen, see QAM 39.14–22 [Mueller] = 4.776.17–777.9 [Kühn]; 44.2–4 [Mueller] = 4.782.4–6 [Kühn]; 48.5–12 [Mueller] = 4.787.6–13 [Kühn]; 67.8–16

[Mueller] = 4.808.5–12 [Kühn]; 78.23–79.4 [Mueller] = 4.821.2–6 [Kühn]. Cf. Porphyry (?), *in Ti.* frag. 86 = 102.26–34 [Sodano] and Porphyry, *AG* 15.5 = 55.25–8 [Kalbfleisch].

53. See Proclus, *in Ti.* III.349.21–30 (the only reference to Galen by name in the surviving corpus); *in Prm.* 1014.22–8, *in R.* I.222.14–15; I.249.21–3; *in Alc.* 226.19–22 [Segonds]. As Boys-Stones (2007a: 121) points out in his commentary on the *Republic*, Proclus seems prepared to concede this Galenic thesis only with the qualification that this is true of the uneducated alone who have not been instructed in philosophy (*in R.* I.222.14–15; cf. Olympiodorus, *in Gorg.* 49.6.11–13 [Westerink]), but in this Arabic passage Proclus appears to be taking things a bit further. See also *in R.* II.63.8–14.

54. For Proclus, see his comments on *Ti.* 89e3–90a2 in Arnzen (2013), and cf. Proclus, *in Ti.* I.33.31–34.2 and I.40.6–8 and Hermias, *in Phdr.* 194.9ff. [Couvreur]. For Galen, see *in Ti.* 11.15–20 [Schröder]. Whereas Galen allocates both powers of attraction and repulsion to the appetitive part of soul, Proclus associates the latter power with the spirited part. Proclus does not clearly state that the object of repulsion is inappropriate *nourishment*, but this seems likely given the context.

55. The three medical examples in *de Decem Dub.* 59.54–8 are clearly taken over from Plutarch *Mor.* 559e–f. It seems likely that Proclus, *in Alc.* 155.4–6, is inspired by Plato's *Ti.* 89c7–d1, though cf. Olympiodorus *in Alc.* 54.10–15 [Westerink] who makes a similar point with explicit reference to Hippocrates. Proclus' remark about the importance of the καιρός in medicine (*de Decem Dub.* 51.1–8) might be inspired by a Hippocratic text (*Aph.* 1.1), and see Proclus' remark about hellebore in note 18, above. The most common example that one encounters is that a surgical inspection of an ulcer should be performed prior to treating it in order to ascertain the nature of the disease: *in Alc.* 119.12–16; *in R.* I.103.7–11; *in Ti.* I.380.10ff.; *Mal.* 59.15–17 [Isaac]. Other examples include *in Alc.* 304.12–15 (which need not necessarily be in tension with *in Alc.* 155.4–6); *in Alc.* 175.13–15 and *in Ti.* I.320.17–21. And see below on Proclus' aetiology of disease.

56. According to the *Thesaurus Linguae Graecae* Proclus refers to the heart (καρδία) only twenty-eight times, the liver (ἧπαρ) five times, the brain (ἐγκέφαλος) three times, and the lungs (πλεύμων, πνεύμων) three times; even blood (αἷμα) only turns up seven times in the surviving corpus. One must also bear in mind that many of these references are either only in the broadest sense medical or (especially in the case of the heart) not medical at all (e.g. in the case of blood four of the seven references – *in R.* I.290.21; *in R.* II.111.21; *Hymni* 5.13 [van den Berg]; *Epigrammata* 2.5 [Vogt, p. 34] – are not medical). I have not found any clear instance of νεῦρα in the sense of "nerves" or of ἀρτηρία in the sense of artery. Proclus refers to Galen by name once (see above, note 53), Hippocrates of Cos four times (*in Alc.* 120.14, on which see Segonds [1985 *ad loc.*]; *in Alc.* 254.15 (very general reference); *in Ti.* II.28.24 (a quote from *de Natura Hominis*); *in Eucl.* 38.26 [Friedlein] (probably a reference to *de Aera Aquis Locis*), with at least one unnamed reference occurring at *de Decem Dub.* 51.4–5.

57. Proclus, *in R.* II.31.22ff. and cf. *in R.* II.59.6ff. For some background on the issue, see Hanson (1987).

58. Proclus, *in R.* II.33.9–14 = Herophilus frag. 198 [von Staden]. Von Staden remarks that "the textual basis for attributing this view to Herophilus is flimsy" (1989: 299).

59. Proclus, *in R.* II.33.14ff. This might be compared to Proclus' explanation of the preservation of Er's body during his after-life experience (*in R.* II.113.6ff.). He begins with the physiological explanation that a kind of vital fire is preserved in the area of the heart, as is the case with hibernating animals (*in R.* II.113.13–19 and 117.8–9), but then adds that demonic powers are also preserving the body (*in R.* II.117.24–6). Note that his passing remark about the bonds of soul being in the marrow (*in R.* II.113.15–16 and 125.9–11) is drawn from the *Timaeus* and somewhat in tension with his nods elsewhere to Galen's localization of the tripartite soul (see above, note 51). A further quite interesting case of Proclus combining medical and mystical ideas is to be found in *in R.* II.186.15–19, in which Proclus appears to invoke a theory according to which impure fluid from the brain can impair one's eyesight in such a way that one is no longer in a position to see *daimons* and cosmic powers (cf. Olympiodorus, *in Phd.* 13.15 [p. 179, Westerink], and Iamblichus, *VP* 163 [92.13–14, Deubner & Klein] with the emendation suggested by Dillon & Herschbell). The medical side of this combination – about impure fluid from the brain affecting sight – is hinted at in Galen (*in Hipp. Aphor. Comm.* 17B.615.4 [Kühn]; *in Hipp. Prorrhet. Comm.* 35.6–7 [Diels] = 16.554.4–5 [Kühn]; *de Sectis* 31.7–10 [Helmreich] = 1.104.5–7 [Kühn], and it appears to be taken in the psychological direction by Stephanus (*in Hipp Aph.* 3–4 198.6–14 [Westerink]; *in Hipp Prog.* 104.3–14 and 270.15–31 [Duffy]), who suggests that this fluid can have negative affects on the *phantasia*. See also Michael of Ephesus, *in GA* 112.27–9 [Hayduck]. I would like to thank Philip van der Eijk for bringing some of these passages to my attention.

60. See Wilberding (2008, 2011), Brisson *et al.* (2008), Brisson *et al.* (2012).

61. See esp. *AG* 2.2 (34.20–35.9 [Kalbfleisch]) and 10 *passim* (46.12–48.8 [Kalbfleisch]) with notes *ad loc.*

in Wilberding (2011) and Brisson *et al.* (2012). One remark (*AG* 3.4 [37.6–7 Kalbfleisch]) appears to be drawn from a source outside of the Hippocratic corpus (see Brisson *et al.* 2012: 229).

62. *AG* 13.6 (53.8–10 [Kalbfleisch]), and cf. his remark about bile's effect on the meninges in *AG* 15.5 (55.25–8 [Kalbfleisch]), which shows that he too accepts a version of the thesis that the soul follows the temperaments of the body. In light of *AG* 13.6, it would seem that Porphyry, *in Ti.* frag. 56 (103.2–33), in which the third part of the soul is not located in the liver, should not be attributed to Porphyry. Interesting in this regard is also Porphyry, *Quaestionum Homericum ad Iliadem Pertinentium Reliquiae* 1.214.7–16 [Schrader] (*ad* 16.315), though the attribution to Porphyry has been called into question by Erbse (1960: 17–70) and by MacPhail (2011), who does not include it in his recent edition.

63. See Edelstein (1937: 220–21, cited according to Temkin & Temkin [1967] 1987). On the claims of the Gnostics, cf. Brakke (2010: 65). Tatian, whom some scholars consider to have been a Gnostic and who taught in Rome until probably 172 CE, advances a view in *Oratio ad Graecos* 16–18 similar to that presented by Plotinus here.

64. A similar sentiment can be found in *Enn.* III.2[47].8.39–40, where Plotinus suggests that when it comes to achieving health, prayer is no ersatz for healthy living and medical treatment.

65. The passage goes well beyond Plato's *Ti.* 82a1–7. Dufour, in Brisson & Pradeau (2002–10) *ad loc.*, suggests that Plotinus' source might be the Hippocratic *de Natura Hominis* 9 (188.3–10 [Jouanna] [6.53.4–11 Littré]) or Galen's commentary on it (57.22–58.6 [Mewaldt] = 15.110.1–10 [Kühn]). Cf. the similar ideas in *Aph.* 2.22 (4.476.6–8 [Littré]) and *Flat.* (104.8–105.4 [Jouanna] = 6.92.8–14 [Littré]). There are also striking parallels to Stobaeus, *Anth.* IV.37.14.61–7 [Wachsmuth & Hense], which is part of a text that according to Kudlien (1968: 29–30) is "typical of the university medicine of the time [*viz.* 3rd C. CE] and may have originated in the third century".

66. See also *Enn.* I.8[51].8.3–7 and *Enn.* IV.4[28].45.47–9.

67. *Enn.* IV.7[2].8^4.14–17, and see above on Plotinus' view on the temperaments.

68. We are told that Plotinus reduced the quantity of his sleep and food intake (Porphyry, *Plot.* 8.21, 23.3; cf. Porphyry, *Abst.* 1.27.2–5 = 104.25–105.20 [Nauck] and 4.4.1 = 243.14–26 [Nauck]; Iamblichus, *VP* 13 = 10.10–18 [Deubner & Klein]; *VP* 69 = 39.3–22 [Deubner & Klein]; *VP* 187 = 104.3–14 [Deubner & Klein]; *VP* 226 = 121.18–122.1 [Deubner & Klein]; Diogenes Laertius 8.19), and observed a vegetarian diet (Porphyry, *Plot.* 2.3–5; cf. Porphyry, *Abst.* 1.3.3 [87.4–11 Nauck]; Iamblichus, *VP* 108–9 = 62.10–63.13 [Deubner & Klein]). Cf. Plotinus' claim (*Enn.* III.1[3].1.34) that one's diet can affect embryological outcomes. On Pythagorean regimen, see Wöhrle (1990: 39–45).

69. Plotinus, *Enn.* II.9[33].14.11–13 and see above, note 47. Cf. *Enn.* III.1.2.5–6; Iamblichus, *VP* 264 [141.19–142.9 Deubner & Klein].

70. Plotinus praised Rogatianus as an example for others. Porphyry, *Plot.* 7.31–46, cf. Porphyry, *Abst.* 1.53.2–4 = 127.10–128.4 [Nauck].

71. See Plotinus, *Enn.* II.3[52].14.30–33; III.1[3].5.24–33; IV.3[27].7.22–4. We may witness this belief being put into action in Porphyry, *Plot.* 11.12–17, when Plotinus diagnoses the cause of Porphyry's illness as black bile and, as a remedy, suggests living for a period of time in a different region.

72. "This statement proves that even the latest philosophical system of antiquity, the one which is generally held responsible for so much superstition of the ancients, rejected the demonological explanation of diseases categorically" (Edelstein 1937: 221).

73. On demons, see Plotinus, *Enn.* I.6[1].7.20; II.1[40].6.54; IV.3[27].18.22–3; III.5[50].6.38–43. On magic, see *Enn.* IV.4[28].40–44, esp. *Enn.* IV.4[28].43.7–10. See also Porphyry, *Plot.* 10, where Porphyry relates what happened when Plotinus himself was attacked by a magician (he suffered only minor discomfort). For the role of demons in medicine in another pre-Iamblichean Platonist, see Porphyry, *Abst.* 2.38–9 [167.3–169.10 Nauck].

74. Note that in light of Galen's criticism (*PHP* 504.17–20 [De Lacy] = 5.678.6–10 [Kühn]) of Plato (*Ti.* 82a1–7) for conceiving of health as a harmony of *elements* instead of *humours*, it is significant that Proclus here opts for the latter. Concurring passages on the nature of disease and health include: *in R.* I.38.9–12; *in Cra.* 174 = 99.8–11 [Pasquali]; *in Cra.* 176 = 100.13–18 [Pasquali].

75. Note that it was common to consider the elements in the case of the universe as analogous to humours in the case of human beings (e.g. Galen, *de Humoribus* 19.485.1–2: ὅπερ ἐν κόσμῳ στοιχεῖον, τοῦτο ἐν ζῴοις χυμός).

76. Proclus, *in Alc.* 213.10–12; *in Ti.* I.159.17, and see above on Proclus' employment of physicians.

77. See Marinus, *Procl.* 3 and 26. Marinus even blames Proclus' deteriorating health on the harshness of his

diet (*Procl.* 30). Like Plotinus, Proclus was also a vegetarian (*Procl.* 12 and 19; cf. *in Ti.* III.241.3–5), even to the point of disobeying doctors' orders (Damascius, *Isid.* 84J; cf. Porphyry, *Plot.* 2.1–5), and reduced his amount of sleep (*Procl.* 22 and 24). He also appears to have abstained from sexual intercourse (*Procl.* 17 and 20), as Plotinus likely did as well. On the importance of regimen for health, see Proclus' comments on *Ti.* 89e1–2 in Arnzen (2013).

78. See Proclus, *in R.* II.62.21–63.6; *in Ti.* I.99.13–17; I.107.14ff.; I.139.31; I.162.11ff.; *de Decem Dub.* 36.11–14.
79. Marinus relates (*Procl.* 31) that Proclus was concerned that he had inherited arthritis, and cf. e.g. *in Ti.* I.99.17; I.396.10ff.
80. His condition in *Procl.* 7 is described as ἀνιάτως διακειμένου and in *Procl.* 31 as genetic (and so presumably incurable).
81. See *Procl.* 30 and 32, though these visions were not accompanied by any curative experience and are apparently recounted to demonstrate Proclus' "affinity" to Asclepius. Proclus refers to these visions in *in Alc.* 165.26–166.7. See also the account of the bird (presumably no vision) in *Procl.* 31.
82. See Proclus, *in Prm.* 826.15–18 and *in Ti.* I.158.21–3.
83. See T382–454 in Edelstein & Edelstein (1945: vol. 1, 194–261) along with (1945: vol. 2, 139–58).
84. See *de Diaeta* 4.87 (218.14–22 [Joly] = 6.640.16–642.10 [Littré]) and 4.93 (230.11–12 [Joly] = 6.662.8–9 [Littré]). The author of *de Morbo Sacro* is more critical of prayers for health, but see van der Eijk (2005: 45–73, esp. 71) and Nutton (2004: 64–6, 110–13).
85. Galen, *de Libris Propriis* 88.13–17 [Mueller] = 19.69.7–11 [Kühn] and *Methodi Medendi* 9.4 = 10.609.8–11 [Kühn].
86. See Galen, *de Usu Partium* 2.93.5ff. [Helmreich] = 3.812 [Kühn].
87. Galen, *de Libris Propriis* 99.9–11 [Mueller] = 19.19.1–3 [Kühn].
88. See Galen, *de Curandi Ratione per Venae Sectionem* 11.314.18–315.7 [Kühn], with *de Libris Propriis* 99.9–11 [Mueller] = 19.19.1–3 [Kühn] and *de Propriis Placitis* 58.1–21 [Nutton].
89. Galen, *de Propriis Placitis* 58.1–21 [Nutton] and *de Libris Propriis* 99.11 [Mueller] = 19.19.3 [Kühn]. And see further Nutton (2004: 279).
90. See Plotinus, *Enn.* IV.4[28].40.1–4. Theurgy is to be distinguished from magic in that it appeals to still higher causes. See below on Proclus' series of medical causes and Clarke *et al.* (2003: xxvii).
91. Iamblichus (*Myst.* 3.9) maintains that music can "displace the temperaments or dispositions of the body".
92. *De Morbis Popularibus* VI.5.1 = 5.314 [Littré].
93. Indeed, this complaint was not unfamiliar to Galen, who in his aporetic discussion of the identity of the agent responsible for forming the embryo objects to the solution that it is the vegetative soul on account of the fact that the process of formation reveals a great deal of wisdom and this soul is bereft of reason (*de Foetuum Formatione* 104.16–20 [Nickel] = 4.700.6–12 [Kühn]).
94. See Proclus, *in Ti.* I.158.2–164.22; II.62.31–64.10; *in Cra.* 174 (and cf. §164); *in R.* II.117.19–119.2.
95. It seems fairly clear that these two series are to be identified. In *in Ti.* II.62.31ff., Proclus describes this series in terms of health and labels this cause in the Demiurge "the font (πηγή) of health"; in *in Cra.* 174, he describes the same series in terms of medicine and labels the cause in the Demiurge "the intellectual power of medicine" (99.20 [Pasquali]). And cf. *in R.* I.69.6–9 and II.153.25–27.
96. *In R.* I.69.6–9; *in Cra.* 174 = 99.18–21 [Pasquali]; *in Ti.* II.63.9–17. Cf. *in R.* II.153.25–7.
97. *In Ti.* I.158.18–23; *in Cra.* 174 = 98.29–99.4 [Pasquali]; *in R.* II.117.19–119.2.
98. *In Ti.* I.163.5ff. and III.140.27–8. And see above, note 78.
99. This is how I understand the ὕλαι καὶ ὄργανα referred to in *in Ti.* I.158.20. For plants, *in Cra.* 174 (99.3 [Pasquali]).
100. Proclus, *in R.* II.118.10–14 and 153.25–7; *in Ti.* I.163.5ff.; *in Alc.* 32.20–33.4. Cf. Olympiodorus, *in Phd.* 7.4.4–5 [Westerink] and Damascius, *Isid.* 84E, where Isidore is reported to have thought that Iacobus Psychrestos (see above, note 12) had an "Asclepian" soul.
101. Cf. Proclus, *in Cra.* 176 (100.13–17 [Pasquali]) and Plotinus, *Enn.* IV.4[28].42.9–10.
102. See John of Alexandria, *in Hipp. Epid. VI* 104.6–9, where John distinguishes this art of healing by higher causes as a different kind of medicine (which can be learned in six months!).
103. What Nutton (2004: 306) says to sum up the Christian attitude towards medicine in the later Roman Empire applies equally well to the Neoplatonic attitude: "The medicine of Galen and the medicine of Christianity were, for the most part, regarded as complementary: medical skills and herbs came from God, and were to be valued as such, but a total reliance on human intervention unaided by prayer and faith in God was foolish and unspiritual."

24

Humans, other animals, plants and the question of the good: the Platonic and Neoplatonic traditions

Kevin Corrigan

A major contemporary problem that troubles characterizations of Neoplatonism is its hierarchical structure, a structure that, in the assessment of many critics, privileges human beings over other animals and plants, as well as mind, soul and rationality over body.[1] This has been partially responsible for the domination of human interests over those of other species, on the one hand, and for the chimera of intrinsic goods based upon the categorical imperatives of rational duty and virtue, on the other.[2] Human beings are intrinsic "goods" and have "rights" because they are rational and can make agreements. Other animals, by contrast, can make no rational agreements and are made to serve us. For Stoics and Epicureans, according to Porphyry's account, "[w]e cannot act unjustly towards creatures which cannot act justly towards us" (*Abst.* 1.6.89, trans. G. Clark). Christian exegesis of Genesis 1:26 apparently just reinforced the pagan view that animals are made "for us", just as masters should rule slaves, men should rule women and adults children (S. Clark 2011: 36).

From another perspective, while human beings may be regarded as having intrinsic "rights" by contrast with irrational animals and plants,[3] the Platonic tradition, it is often argued, eliminates the value of individual things for their own sakes and makes us respect or love others not for themselves but only for the sake of Forms or the Good beyond Forms (see e.g. Vlastos 1981; Dover 1980: 113). So, on the one hand, this hierarchical view makes human beings disproportionately important and subordinates animals and plants to our interests and, on the other, it seems to eliminate individuality for its own sake in favour of abstract universality. Let me be clear. These criticisms are widespread and powerful, but, in my view, false and profoundly misguided, since Neoplatonism generally, and the Platonic tradition it inherits, is remarkably enlightened on the very issues for which it is criticized. The real issue is how we can provide a more balanced assessment of these negative pictures both of individual human beings and of other animals and plants in light of the demonstrable strengths of Neoplatonism. But we cannot do this without establishing a broader framework and taking into consideration the problematic nature of the Platonic "Good".

One broader problem with theories of rights, intrinsic goods and hierarchy for think-ing about the ancient world generally is that such theories are embedded implicitly within modern paradigms of rationality and operate in the sphere of the rational universalizability of principles and axioms, however much these principles (different versions of the categori-cal imperative) may derive from ancient models (Stoicism or Cicero, *de Officiis*) (see e.g. Glei 1999). This is why recent attempts to detect animal rights theories in ancient thought (e.g. Sorabji 1995a; see also Sorabji 1993: 134–57) or to build such theories upon modern neo-Aristotelian underpinnings (e.g. Nussbaum 2000, 2003, 2006) are either necessarily inconclusive (as in Sorabji's case)[4] or rationalistic and modern (as in Nussbaum's call for a capabilities theory to cover human beings and other animals or in Fineman's [2008] case for a theory of vulnerability and preferences). Rights extended to other animals and plants on the basis of human rationality alone risk being empty extensions, while a blank-cheque notion of justice in which everything has rights risks being even emptier.

What I want to suggest here is that the ancient Platonic principle of the Good should be a starting point for any such considerations: a starting point that may be as fruitful for us as it was for Socrates in *Republic*, books 6–7, but just as already always forgotten and strange as it proved for his interlocutor, Glaukon, in book 6 (*R.* 509c) – fruitful, not in terms of developing a modern ethical theory somehow dependent upon or derived from the Good, but rather of seeing what role it might have played both in the thought of Plato and Aristotle and in subsequent ancient practice. This is, in part, precisely what I propose to do – and it is important, since the dimension of the Good, in the ancient sense, seems to have been entirely lost for the modern and contemporary worlds.

The Good in *Republic* 6–7 is, in fact, not a "rational" principle as such, for it is non-propositional and beyond being and thought (*R.* 509b6–10). In other words, if rational-ity is taken to be the criterion by which we parse the world of nature, then the Good too must be excluded from consideration: an absurd consequence, in fact. Yet, at the same time, Socrates represents the Good not simply as the theoretical ground of everything but as *the* most practical and useful good of all: without it, nothing is truly beneficial (*R.* 504e–505b). It is, according to Socrates, the regulative ground of all our judgements, dimly glimpsed or "divined" in all our experience (from perplexity [*R.* 505d11–e2; 506a6] to sex – the latter, at least, according to Aristophanes in the *Symposium* [*Smp.* 192c–d]); and it is also what provides both the power and means of seeing, feeling or thinking anything (*R.* 508e–509b). In short, the Good is that by which the *best state* or capacity of anything is felt, seen, imagined or thought reflexively.[5] Nussbaum's theory of capacities, despite its Aristotelian resonance, misses this dimension entirely. This is somewhat strange, since Aristotle, despite his somewhat different view of the Good (*EN* 1.6), actually bases a theory of the "goods" of all animal species upon a "good" which goes beyond them all (*EN* 6.7: on this passage, see below). This is not an empty "placeholder" as it might seem for us, I suggest, but for Plato and Aristotle the non-rational, but practical ground of all desire, thought and perception: in the case of Plotinus later, the ground not so much of thought and life (although it is also their ground too) as of *all* existence, including the bare being of ourselves, other animals, plants and stones (*Enn.* VI.7[38].23.22–4). What it is therefore for anything to be a "good" or to be in the best state of its potentiality or capacity – no matter how rudimentary – is a function of this non-rational, but reflexive activity of the Good, at once a cause and a condition of practical usefulness, creative art and reflexive thought, as well as of the barest existence. This dimension of the Good has been somewhat eclipsed in the modern world but it was the ground of a much broader view of the kinship[6] of all animals, plants and things in the ancient world than has been possible until the most recent times. It is also, I shall argue here, a dimension that does not commit the ancients to unnecessary hierarchical thinking, to "intrinsic good" theories or to the erasure of the importance of individuals.

In this chapter I shall briefly outline some of the theoretical and practical consequences of this vision in the ancient Pythagorean–Platonic tradition with particular emphasis upon four figures after Plato (424/423–348/347 BCE) and Aristotle (384–322 BCE): Theophrastus (371–287 BCE), Plutarch (46–120 CE), Plotinus (204–70 CE) and Porphyry (234–305 CE) [with a coda from Pseudo-Dionysius (late fifth–early sixth century CE) and Proclus (412–85 CE)]. My focus here is not to give either a history of such thought or a survey of the growing body of contemporary scholarship but rather to highlight what I take to be some major insights of this tradition, to reject some common mistaken impressions and to provide different ways of looking at a lost, but, I think, still significant achievement of the human spirit.[7]

It seems to me that the Neoplatonists were prepared, as the modern phrase has it, to think globally and act locally. To be a philosopher or a scientist – a lover of wisdom or knowing – in this sense was to live a certain kind of life:[8] to renounce any form of money or property, to care for everything in the universe to the best of one's ability[9] and to live a life of scientific enquiry and prayerful contemplation. Plotinus lived in the house of a Roman woman, Gemina (*Plot.* 9). He owned nothing. Young boys lived in the house too and he apparently helped them with their multiplication tables. He was celibate, and did not himself eat animals or use medicines with animal content (*Plot.* 2.3–5). He ate, drank and slept little, but accepted the social responsibilities of friendship, acted as an arbitrator in legal disputes, and took seriously his financial and educational duties as guardian for children whose fathers had died (*Plot.* 7 and 9). He even wanted to found a city based on philosophical principles, a "Platonopolis", as did Plato himself, but the venture fell through. In other words, he was committed to an ecological programme of some definite sort and took seriously the sustainability issues involved in setting up a modest economic civic programme based on vegetarianism.

In this he was following a long tradition that was in some ways more radical than the contemporary animal rights movement. Pythagoras and Empedocles (although all traditions about the life and work of Pythagoras are contested) argued that animals are akin to human beings not only because they are made of the same elements but also because souls may be reincarnated as either human or other animals. Killing and eating animals was thus equivalent to murder and even cannibalism (cf. G. Clark 2000: 123 n. 11 & 12). In other words, kinship was based upon similarity of biological structure and reincarnation. In fact, Empedocles believed that there was a golden age of friendship between humans and animals, before the rise of Strife.[10] Animal sacrifice was, on this basis, seen as a perversion of an original state of friendship. Furthermore, according to Cicero, both Pythagoras and Empedocles gave not only kinship but legal rights to all animals: "those great and learned men, Pythagoras and Empedocles, declare that all living creatures have the same legal status, and proclaim that inexpiable penalties threaten those by whom a living creature is harmed".[11] Empedocles appears to have gone further and extended such status even to plants and the elements, for he proclaimed that he had been "a boy and a girl and a bush and a bird and a fish" (frag. 117b [DK]) and, according to Sextus Empiricus

(*M.* 8.286), Empedocles held that *all things* are rational, not just animals but also plants, writing explicitly, "Know that all things have wisdom and a share of thought".[12]

What exactly "wisdom and a share of thought" (*phronēsin … kai nōmatos aisan*) meant was a problem for later thinkers. As Sorabji has argued, Aristotle and subsequent writers accused Parmenides, Anaxagoras, Empedocles, Democritus and even Homer of not distinguishing intelligence (*phronēsis*) from perception (*aisthēsis*) or other aspects of soul.[13] Anaxagoras ascribes mind or *nous* to everything, great and small, in some places, but, Aristotle complains, elsewhere *nous* in the sense of *phronēsis* appears not to belong to all animals and not even to all human beings.[14] There thus arises the clear distinction between humans and other animals on the basis of a distinction between understanding, or higher-order intelligence, and perception, a distinction that can be found in Alcmaeon, Anaxagoras himself, Protagoras, Plato and, of course, Aristotle.[15]

What gets my interest here is not so much the wedge between humans and other animals (and plants, not to mention the elements) based on a sharper distinction between thought and perception that is characteristic of Aristotle's mature thought.[16] Glimpses of this can also be found in Plato, particularly the occasional denial of reason to other animals and the question whether or not (true) beliefs can be ascribed to the non-rational parts of soul (Sorabji 1993: 9–12). My focus is rather upon an important line of thought present in Plato, Aristotle and the later Platonic tradition, which I shall call the inclusive, intelligible nature of biology.

A first part of this intelligible biology can be found in Plato's *Timaeus*, where all living creatures are said to be parts of the inclusive intelligible model upon which the Demiurge frames the many species of the sensible cosmos:

> let us suppose the world to be the very image of that whole of which all other animals both individually and in their tribes are portions. For the original of the universe contains in itself all intelligible beings, just as this world comprehends us and all other visible creatures. For the god, intending to make this world like the fairest and most perfect of intelligible beings, framed one visible animal comprehending within itself all other animals of a kindred nature.   (*Ti.* 30c–31a)[17]

Any interpretation of this famous passage must surely involve an inclusive intelligible design running through all species even prior to the rational deliberative design of the Demiurge, for the Demiurge is represented as looking towards a pre-existent intelligible paradigm. In part, it is true, this is related to Plato's notion of reincarnation, as we can see in *Ti.* 76e: "For those who were constructing us knew that out of men women should one day spring and all other animals" (90e–91a). In part, again, it reflects a cyclical view of inter-species transformation, as at *Ti.* 90e–92c, especially 92b–c: "Thus, both then and now, living creatures keep passing into one another in all these ways, as they undergo transformation by the loss or gain of intelligence or unintelligence" (*nou kai anoias, Ti.* 92c1–3).

However, it also reflects two further important features of Platonic thought: first, the view that animality includes everything living, both animals and plants, and on the basis of a shared elemental structure:

> Blending it [the nature of the mortal, human living creature] with other shapes and senses they engendered a substance akin to that of man, so as to form another

living creature: such are the cultivated trees and plants and seeds which have been trained by husbandry and are now domesticated among us; but formerly the wild kinds only existed, these being older than the cultivated kinds. *For everything, in fact, which partakes of life may justly and with perfect truth be termed a living creature* (*zōon men an en dikēi legoito orthotata*) … Wherefore it lives indeed and is not other than a living creature, but it remains stationary and rooted down owing to its being deprived of the power of self-movement.   (*Ti*. 77a3–c5, emphasis added)

Plants then are also "animals" or living creatures.[18]

Second, there is the view that each animal species has its own good, or specific *aretē* with its own dynamic capacity: "Moreover, the habit and statue of the goddess [Athena] indicate that in the case of all animals, male and female, that herd together, every species is naturally capable of practicing as a whole and in common its own proper excellence (*tēn prosēkousan aretēn hekastōi genei pan koinēi dynaton epitēdeuein pephyken*)" (Plato, *Criti*. 110b5–c2). This suggests an important corollary to the intelligible biology of the *Timaeus*, namely that there is a peculiar good fitted to each species of which the species is capable. So there is a hint of a capacity theory that relates to individuals but that is holistic and specific in nature. In other words, every species has its own particular good or goods, dependent not upon human rationality, but related to the "habit and statue" of the goddess (in the language of the *Critias*) or to the providential creativity of the Demiurge (in the language of the *Timaeus*).

It seems to me that this inclusive intelligible biology founded upon divine design or goodness, on the one hand, and specific natural capacities or best fittedness, on the other, is hinted at in a highly significant way in the *Nicomachean Ethics*, no matter how much Aristotle might otherwise deny intellect and reason to other animals (see notes 13 and 14). In Aristotle, this takes the form of a viewpoint beyond that of human practical intelligence in which the good of all species has to be included. What is the goodness of soul except its conformity to the ultimate end of all best activity? What is this ultimate end? If it is only practical intelligence (*phronēsis*), then it will be a purely human activity, but there are other things in the universe that are higher and more important than the human being and, therefore, *sophia* or philosophic wisdom must be a more comprehensive viewpoint than the merely human. Speculative/philosophic wisdom includes the good of all things, as Aristotle puts it:

[Wisdom (*sophia*) is scientific knowledge] of the highest things, we say; for it would be strange to think that the art of politics, or practical wisdom (*phronēsis*) is the best knowledge, since a human being is not the best thing in the world. Now if what is healthy or good is different for human beings and for fishes, but what is white or straight is always the same, any one would say that what is wise (*sophon*) is the same but what is practically wise (*phronimon*) is different; for it is to that which observes well the various matters concerning itself that one ascribes practical wisdom, and it is to this that one will entrust such matters. This is why we say that some even of the lower animals have practical wisdom, namely, those which are found to have a power of foresight (*dynamin pronoetikēn*) with regard to their own life. It is evident also that philosophic wisdom (*sophia*) and the art of politics cannot be the same; for if the state of mind concerned with a human being's best interests is to be called philosophic wisdom, there will be many philosophic wisdoms; there will not be one concerned with the good of all animals, but a different philosophic wisdom about the good of each species.   (*EN* 6.7.1141a20–35, trans. McKeon, adapted)[19]

We are here at the heart of a perhaps paradoxical vision that leads almost directly to Plotinus. For Aristotle, Mind or *nous* in the primary sense is separate from everything, but it also "includes/embraces everything" especially in so far as the desire to understand the world and ourselves *as we are* – that is, as *being* – is already a divine understanding itself.[20] Part of that understanding is the life of practical intelligence, but the deeper part is an understanding that goes beyond the merely human perspective to embrace the good of everything. To become fully human, therefore, we paradoxically have to be able to transcend a merely human perspective. Divine understanding, namely that of the apparently solitary Unmoved Mover or the Good, as Aristotle also terms it, is the proper threshold for understanding the goods of all things (animals, plants, blood and elements included). If, then, from a human perspective, the human being is to be distinguished by mind and rationality from the rest of nature, nonetheless, from the perspective of *sophia*, the human being has to be able to transcend specific interests – including purely human rationality – in order to grasp the good of nature in its broadest and most divine form. In other words, exactly as we will find in Plotinus, through many intermediaries including Alexander of Aphrodisias, mind should not belong to us only; we should belong instead to it, even to the point of our not being entirely human any longer; mind is both "ours" and not "ours" (cf. Plotinus, *Enn.* V.3[49].3.26–7, 4.25). And if this is so, then while other animals and plants may not have or possess mind or reason, they must belong to the dimension of divine mind, a belonging that enables Aristotle (with Heraclitus) to say even of the lowliest parts of animals that there are deities here too (see Aristotle, *PA* 1.6).

Precisely how this can be so is, of course, a problem for the interpreters of Aristotle, as it also is for the Stoics and Epicureans, who reject any notion of animal "rights" or of a broader view of animality. Only human beings naturally "belong" with each other (are *oikeioi*)[21] according to the Stoic ideal of a world-wide city (Cicero, *Fin.* 3.62–8) of fellow-citizens. Instead of some intelligible biology, the Stoics change the otherwise concrete biology of Aristotle, according to whom all living things are animate and plants have "nutritive soul"; that is, they are alive and grow (Aristotle, *de An.* 413a20–b10). The Stoics, instead, hold that the activity of the nutritive soul in plants is not soul really, since plants have neither impressions nor impulse or desire; instead, plants cohere by nature or *physis*. And for the Stoics and Epicureans, justice extends only to rational beings, not to non-human animals, for only rational beings can act justly and be treated with justice. Justice is an agreement for mutual advantage, according to an Epicurean argument, and no mutuality on the basis of justice is possible between human beings and animals. Besides, animals endanger us by being predators or by the fact that, if we do not kill them, they will reproduce at an alarming rate and overwhelm the environment and eat all the food.[22] Yet Epicurus himself advocated vegetarianism on the grounds that meat-eating was unnecessary and harmful to health; and Lucretius perhaps tries to harmonize Empedocles and Epicurus in so far as domestication of animals involves a sort of implicit (or lesser) contract of mutual advantage of protection from wild animals between domestic animals and human beings (cf. Campbell 2008: 16–21). Indeed, the Stoics famously suggested that dogs could reason syllogistically (at least virtually [*dynamei*]): in the course of following a scent, for instance, a dog approaching a fork in the trail eliminates trail *a* and *b* and immediately goes down trail *c*.[23] So, despite the Stoic and Epicurean rejection of a rational contract, the picture remains more complex.[24] How far, then, can explicit or implicit rationality extend and how can the broader perspective of *nous* or *sophia* really embrace the goods of all things with practical consequences for ordinary action?

Plotinus and Porphyry in late antiquity answer these questions in illuminating ways, precisely because they see that the cosmos, instead of being an independent body or a body that possesses a mind, is utterly pervaded by the dimensions of soul and mind, dimensions rooted and grounded in the Good itself. In fact, intellect cannot hold the power it receives from the Good and so breaks it up into its own defective, but variegated good-formed vision with the result that "it is good from many good-formed [parts], a good richly varied" (*Enn.* VI.7[38].15.24–5). For Plotinus, one major problem bequeathed from Plato is to overcome the apparent domination of rationality valorized by the (mythical) representation of the Demiurge deliberating or taking thought, and a second problem is the apparent absurdity of including wild animals in the intelligible paradigm of the *Timaeus*.

To counter the first problem, Plotinus argues that Plato cannot mean that the Demiurge actually reasons or deliberates because such a representation of rationality in any form of creation is a *defect*, not an achievement. Reason is necessary to work things out after the fact; understanding grasps reality all at once without the need to work things out. In other words, divine understanding of plants, animals and even the elements does not depend on, or even embody, discursive rationality (*dianoia*, *logismos*, etc.). The creative principles in things or *logoi* are rational only after the fact.[25] Understanding (*noēsis*) is prior to rationality. In other words, at this point in history, human rationality stops being the dominant paradigm for understanding human relations with other animals and plants. This is an immensely important moment in the history of thought!

To counter the second problem – how can *nous* embrace the goods of all things? – Plotinus develops a rather sophisticated, variegated view of intelligence. In *Enn.* VI.7[38].9–10, he poses the problem of the apparent absurdity of including some animals in the *Timaeus*' Living Creature before offering his own innovative response:

> But someone will say, "I grant the valuable living animals, but … how could the cheap and irrational ones [be there in the Complete Living Creature]?" … Now, there …, intelligence (*to noein*) is different in man and in the other living creatures, and reasoning is also different (*to logizesthai*); for there are present somehow also in the other living creatures many works of deliberate thought (*polla dianoias erga*). Why then are they not equally rational? And why are human beings not equally so in comparison to each other? But one must consider that the many lives, which are like movements, and the many thoughts should not have been the same, but different … in brilliance and clarity. … For just as any particular life does not cease to be life, so neither does an intellect of a particular kind cease to be intellect … since the intellect appropriate to any particular living being does not on the other hand cease to be the intellect of all, of man also, for instance, granted that each part, whichever one you take, is actually all things, but perhaps in different ways. For it is actually one thing, but has the power to be all; but we apprehend in each what it actually is; and what it actually is, is the last, so that the last of this particular intellect is horse … as the powers unfold they always leave something behind … and

as they go out they lose something … and in losing different things different ones find and add on something else because of the need of the living being … nails … claws and fangs.   (*Enn.* VI.7[38].9.1–44)[26]

Here intelligence, far from being a single rationality or monolithic paradigm, as it tends to be in the modern world, is more like a variegated continuum of different intensities of organized life that allows for a sort of natural selectivity, of which we see only the last manifestation. There is a kind of geological depth to each species that prevents us from recognizing that each is, in fact, a holographic representation of a much larger intelligible organism which manifests design or purpose without a designer or deliberative agent. All animals have reason or implicit rationality in such different ways that the barriers are porous. Even human beings are not all equally rational. In fact, we are more "life-kinds" than separated rigidly into different human and other-animal species.[27]

But what does it really mean to think in terms of what is "good" or "best" in relation to other life-kinds, animals and plants? Plotinus gives a plausible answer to this question as a function of natural capacities in one of his later treatises, *Enn.* I.4[46].1:

Suppose we assume the good life (*to eu zēn*) and well-being (*to eudaimonein*) to be one and the same; shall we then have to allow a share in them to other living things as well as ourselves? If they can live in a way natural to them without impediment, what prevents us from saying that they too are in a good state of life?… But if anyone dislikes the idea of extending some degree of well-being to the other living things – which would involve giving a share in it even to the meanest, because they too are alive and have a life which unfolds to its end-first of all, why will it not seem absurd of him to deny that other living things live well just because he does not think them important? Then, one is not compelled to allow to plants what one allows to all other living beings; for plants have no perception (*aisthēsis*). But there might perhaps be someone who would allow well-being to plants just because they have life; one life can be good, another the opposite, as plants too can be well (*eupathein*) or badly off, and bear fruit or not bear fruit.   (*Enn.* I.4[46].1.1–26)

Among the give-and-take of different possibilities, Plotinus clearly makes a case for the well-being even of plants on the basis of life-capacities such as fruit-bearing.[28] He also seems to come close to the idea that such well-being is not an "extension" or a human valorization of life so much as a well-being *for* and *of* plants themselves, which we are able to recognize. This puts the emphasis on the goods of individuals and species *for themselves* rather than upon any extension of rights or of "justice" derived from any supposed monolithic human rationality. This is an important statement in the history of thought and accords well with Plotinus' view that the Good is the most fundamental presence in and to everything (*Enn.* V.5[32].12): as he puts it in *Enn.* VI.7[38].23, "But what does it [the Good] make now? Now too it preserves them and makes the thinking things think and the living things live, breathing in intellect, breathing in life, and if anything cannot live, it makes it be." This suggests that the existence of everything, but especially of stones, rocks and the elements, is rooted directly in the power of the Good. There is in Plotinus a real way of thinking non-hierarchically about everything, since the power of the Good is not abstracted from things through a hierarchy of soul and intellect but rather grounded in and for everything *directly* in such a way that soul and intellect are co-enfolded in that direct creativity.

Of course, we must also acknowledge – alongside this – that the ancient tradition was somewhat divided on the question of plants and even on transmigration of humans into other animals. Porphyry holds that eating the fruits of plants is not like killing animals. We do not hurt plants or crops by taking them (*Abst.* 3.26.12, 18.2, 19.2) or sheep by shearing them, and we may take honey as a reward for looking after bees (*Abst.*13.2). Plato, as we saw above, holds that plants are "living creatures" and have perception of pleasure and pain, but neither belief (*doxa*) nor reasoning (*logismos*) (*Ti.* 77b–c). And the transmigration of souls was used as an argument against meat-eating, not plant-eating (Plutarch, *de Esu Carnium* 998c; cf. Plato, *Ti.* 91d–92c; *Phd.* 81d–e).

As Sorabji has pointed out, Plotinus, and other Platonists, considered "remote control" options in which the human soul, or its separable (intellectual) part, does not actually enter the animal body (Sorabji 1993: 188–93; also G. Clark 2000: 125–6). How we are to understand this is a real difficulty. Is it simply a question of what will later be called the ghost-in-the-machine syndrome, according to which "lower" realities (like bodies on one interpretation of Descartes) are manipulated by "higher" invisible entities? Or should we see such "remote control" options as an integral part of the intelligible biology based upon the "good" in Platonism and Aristotelianism, according to which in the view from nowhere, or from the threshold of the Good, the goods of all things reside? I tend to favour the latter view. But does this mean that "lower" things such as other animals, plants and stones are in the immediate care of higher principles – as in Iamblichus, "the primary beings illuminate the lasts, and immaterial things are present immaterially [theurgically] to the material" (*Myst.* V.23.232.11–12) or as in Proclus, one can see "the lasts in the firsts and the firsts in the lasts" (trans Copenhaver); but if so, at least in Iamblichus, and against Porphyry, this unifying theurgic care is compatible with animal sacrifice. Whatever the case, Porphyry is said by Augustine to have argued that a human soul could not be reincarnated in an animal (*Civ. Dei* 10.30), but he may have considered different possibilities, just as Plotinus also suggests that the individual soul articulates the pre-existent outline prepared for it in matter and, in doing so, becomes what it shapes – either beast or human (*Enn.* I.1[53].11.9–15; VI.7[38].6–7) – or again that there is transmigration from human to other animal and plant existence, and Plotinus has an intriguing "ent-like" (cf. Tolkien) way of putting it:

> and in many ways we live like plants, for we have a body which grows and produces; so that all things work together but the whole form is human being in virtue of its better part. But when it goes out of the body, it becomes what there was most of in it … those who lived by sense alone become animals. … But if they did not even live by sense along with their desires, but coupled them with dullness of perception, they even turn into plants; for it was this, the growth-principle, which worked in them, alone or predominantly, and they were practising to become trees.
> (*Enn.* III.4[15].2.9–24; cf. G. Clark 2000: 125–6)

So there appear to be several different views of transmigration in Plotinus and Porphyry that perhaps cannot be easily reconciled. Nonetheless, the overall practical attitudes to the well-being of animals and plants are strikingly clear in both of them, in line with a tradition that goes back to Pythagoras and Empedocles through the great figures of Theophrastus (*c*.371–*c*.287 BCE) and Plutarch of Chaeronea (*c*.45–120 CE), in whose work some of "the central arguments developed by contemporary animal-rights philosophers relating to intellect and sentience in non-human animals" are already adumbrated (Newmyer 2006: 104). Among Porphyry's many sources is Plutarch who wrote two dialogues, *On the Cleverness of Animals* (or *Whether Land or Sea Animals are Cleverer*) (see on this Gilhus 2006: 45–52; Newmyer 2006: 31–47, 73–5) and *Beasts are Rational*, and two further treatises *On the Eating of Flesh* (I and II) (collected in *Moralia* 12), in which he argued that reason and intellect are distributed in different degrees throughout the animal kingdom and that the eating of animals is one of the least pleasing human customs, a custom that ignores proper consideration of natural justice in favour of cruelty, luxury and excess. Indeed, Plutarch provides a damning picture of animal "husbandry" practices that is worth citing if only because it poignantly anticipates the forced-feeding, chain-production practices of our own age (that one can and should abhor even if one is not a vegetarian). If we have to kill an animal at all, Plutarch argues, we should do so "from hunger, not as a luxury":

> but in pity and sorrow, not degrading or torturing it – which is the current practice in many cases, some thrusting red-hot spits into the throats of swine so that by the plunging in of the iron the flood may be emulsified and, as it circulates through the body, may make the flesh tender and delicate. Others jump upon the udders of sows about to give birth and kick them so that, when they have blended together blood and milk and gore (Zeus the Purifier!) and the unborn young have at the same time been destroyed at the moment of birth, they may eat the most inflamed part of the creature. Still others sew up the eyes of cranes and swans, shut them up in darkness and fatten them, making the flesh appetizing with strange compounds and spicy mixtures.   (*Moralia* 996F–997A, trans. Cherniss & Helmbold)

This is a striking observation of the ethical problems involved in luxury and systemic cruelty that deserves proper acknowledgement, but, of course, it is in Porphyry's great work on abstinence from flesh-eating that we come closest to a rudimentary theory of animal and plant rights.

As Osborne reminds us, we should not accept Porphyry's work uncritically. Porphyry addresses philosophers and his view that meat-eating is surplus to requirements and a luxury is not necessarily correct in the diet of ordinary people living on the land and growing their own food (Osborne 2007: 237). We should not blind ourselves to the connection between vegetarianism and luxury in our own society, she argues, and to the practical implications of alternative lifestyles. Nonetheless, Porphyry's *de Abstinentia* is an extraordinary, far-sighted work for any age. It is not simply a defence of Pythagoras and Pythagorean doctrine (cf. D. O'Meara 1989: 28). Porphyry conducts a powerful comparative analysis of the rejection of animal-killing in the earlier Greek golden age and among the Egyptians, Jews, Indians and Persians. Following Theophrastus, *On Piety*, he argues, against the otherwise compelling tradition of animal sacrifice, that such sacrifice is a perversion of the older custom of gathering, cultivating, sacrificing and eating plant foods. This perversion occurred only because in times of war and starvation human beings took up cannibalism, for which animal sacrifice became a substitute. The gods, however, prefer simplicity: "divinity considers rather the quality (*ēthos*) of the sacrificers than the quantity (*plēthos*) of the sacrifice" (*Abst.* 2.15).

Yes, on Porphyry's thesis against animal sacrifice, vegetarianism, in contrast to a meat diet, demands minimal attention from the soul and therefore helps to liberate the soul imprisoned in the body: a dubious thesis, for some, simply wrong (Osborne 2007: 237); for others, defensible. But the context Porphyry establishes and some of his major arguments are more plausible. The kinship (*to syngenes*) of all animals is older than aggression: barley and grain antedate meat offerings (*Abst.* 2.19–29.148–59). The best sacrifice is, instead, a pure heart/mind (*Abst.* 2.34.163–4). Kinship can be based upon fellow-feeling, sensitivity and a similar sensory/structural apparatus rather than upon rationality.[29] At the same time, on the question of spoken language (*Abst.* 3.3–6), Porphyry argues that each species has its own understanding that is just noise to others (*Abst.* 3.3.188–90), that the complexity and diversity of other animal speech shows it has meaning (*Abst.* 3.4.190–91), and that animals don't speak human language either because they are not taught or because they are impeded by their vocal organs (*Abst.* 3.4.191–2). At any rate, it is simply prejudice or shortsightedness only to call our speech language and dismiss all other forms of communication (*Abst.* 3.5.192–3). After all, the gods communicate silently and animals are closer to this form of communication than we are (*Abst.* 3.5.192). Moreover, people who know and live with animals recognize their calls and are recognized in turn (*Abst.* 3.5.193–4). On the question of inner *logos* or understanding (*Abst.* 3.7–15), Porphyry argues that animals are like us in perception and organization, but that their forms of perception surpass our own (*Abst.* 3.7–8.195–8), that they have memory (*Abst.* 3.10.200) and are not completely deprived of *logos*.[30] As in the case of Plotinus, rationality in this sense admits of different degrees (*Abst.*3.8.197–8) with the result that each species has its own particular wisdom (*Abst.* 3.8–11.196–201). Furthermore, just as the gods do not need to learn, so animals too can be rational without needing to learn (*Abst.* 3.10.199–200); and yet they are also taught by nature or learn through each other or through us. In addition, animal groups observe justice (*to dikaion*) to each other;[31] indeed, the reciprocal needs of humans and other animals establish an innate justice between us; and if someone claims there is no connection (*schesis, koinōnia*) or contract between us and other animals, we may plausibly reply that we do not make contracts with every human being, yet this does not make other human beings non-rational. In fact, the relation between us and other animals is often the reverse of what we claim, for they *domesticate us* rather than we them![32] So far, there is a theory of natural justice, and a sense of kinship based more upon sensory and structural similarities than direct similarity of reason but little question of rights. On the other hand, justice and reason are not a matter of extending human privileges but rather of recognizing capacities, strengths and vulnerabilities as based on the natures of other animals.

So at *Abst.* 3.1–2, Porphyry does argue for "extending" justice to other animals but this is on the basis of underlying capacities in animals:

> Moving on to the discussion of justice, since our opponents say that it should extend to beings like us and therefore rule out the irrational animals, let us present the view which is true and also Pythagorean, by demonstrating that every soul is rational in that it shares in perception and memory. Once that is proved, we can reasonably … extend justice to every animal. … It is self-love which leads them

to say that all the other animals without exception are non-rational, meaning by "non-rationality" complete deprivation of *logos*. But if we must speak the truth, not only can *logos* be seen in absolutely all animals, but in many of them it has the groundwork (*hypobolē*) for being perfected.   (*Abst.* 3.1–2)

Furthermore, we rightly *feel* the distress of other animals, but the basis for justice is *their* nature: "It is the nature of animals to have perceptions, to feel distress, to be afraid, to be hurt and therefore to be injured" (*Abst.* 3.19). And this involves not so much *our* recognition of *their* plight as an understanding that their perception and memory respond to a different but recognizable form of *logos in* them:

> But let us suppose that perception does not need intellect to do its job. But when perception has made the animal aware of the difference between appropriate and alien and has gone away, what is it in them that now remembers and is afraid of painful things[?] … let us not say that if beasts think (*phronein*) more sluggishly and are worse at reflection (*dianoeisthai*), they do not reflect or think at all, or even have a *logos*; but let us say that they have weak and turbid *logos*, like blurred and disturbed vision.   (*Abst.* 3.22–3; cf. *Enn.* VI.7[38].7.29–31)

At the same time, Porphyry clearly avoids making these different forms of *logos* in other animals a founding criterion from which to derive justice, because we spontaneously recognize many examples of justice in animal groups, and because we can see that these are grounded in specific capacities for the good (*aretē*) in each; that is, in rational dispositions or skills (*entrecheia*), that should not be erased because of other considerations, such as a lack of predictable stability in some animal natures.

> Who does not know how animals that live in groups observe justice towards each other? Every ant does, every bee. … In every creature there is evident a particular virtue to which it is naturally disposed, but neither nature nor the consistency of the virtue takes rationality away from them; and that is the point which must be proved if the acts of virtues are not also appropriate to rational aptitude.[33] If we do not understand how an animal acts because we cannot enter into their reasoning, we shall not therefore accuse them of non-rationality. No one can see the intellect of God. … One might be surprised at those who derive justice from reason, and say that animals which are not in our society are savage and unjust, but do not extend justice to those that are in our society. Just as for humans life is over when society is taken away, so also for animals. Birds and dogs and many of the quadrupeds, such as goats, horses, sheep, donkeys, mules, perish if they are deprived of human society. Nature that created them has made them need humans and has also made humans need them, establishing an innate justice in them towards us and in us towards them.   (*Abst.* 3.11–12)

The analogy between human justice and animal justice is, therefore, more like an innate natural bond of mutual justice between all species that Porphyry argues cannot be simply "for us"; instead, other animals are naturally "like us, not for us": "If they say that not everything came into being for us …, then in addition to the great confusion and unclarity of the distinction, we still do not escape injustice, because we set upon and treat harmfully creatures which were born in accordance with nature like us, not for us" (*Abst.* 3.20).

The statement that animals are like us, but not for us, is an important anticipation of one of the major principles of modern thinking about other animals. Consequently, Porphyry concludes (reporting Theophrastus), just as we say that all human groups are related to one another by having the same ancestors or food, customs and race in common, so too is the kinship between all animals strongly grounded in physiology and common psychosomatic structure:

> Thus also we posit that all human beings are kin to one another, and moreover to all the animals, for the principles of their bodies are naturally the same ... I mean for instance skin, flesh, and the kinds of fluids that are natural to animals. We posit this the more strongly because the souls of animals are no different, I mean in appetite and anger, and also in reasoning and above all in perception. Just as with bodies, so with souls: some animals have them brought to perfection, others less so, but the principles are naturally the same in all. ... If it is true that the origin of characteristics is like this, then all species have intelligence (*phronousi*), but they differ in upbringing and in the mixture of their primary components. The race of other animals would then be related and kin to us in all respects, for all of them have the same foods and breath ... and show that the common parents of all are heaven and earth. (*Abst.* 3.25)

Just as we saw above that Plutarch pulls no punches when it comes to the abuse of animals in the pursuit of mindless luxury, so Porphyry too compares human beings in many ways unfavourably with animals. Whereas animals feel goodwill even for their eventual slaughterer who nurtures them for his own sake, not theirs, "humans conspire against no one so much as the person who nurtures them; there is none for whose death they pray more fervently" (*Abst.* 3.13.3). Against the argument that eating plant food is no less killing than eating animal food, Porphyry responds that it "is not the same kind of taking, for it is not from the unwilling. If we let them be, they themselves let fall their fruits, and the taking of fruit does not entail the destruction of plants as when animals lose their souls" (*Abst.* 2.13).

What is fascinating, then, to see in Porphyry's *de Abstinentia* is the following: (1) an irenic tradition that Porphyry claims to be immemorial, namely, the view, however well or ill founded, that we have not always lived by bloodshed and as carnivores; (2) an extended "legal" tradition based not on social contract but on family-relatedness between humans and animals as belonging to one household or *oikos* – or, in other words, a real *ecological* relatedness, based on "justice" rather than "rights",[34] or, again, (3) a form of ecology that arises powerfully out of the dimensions of soul-intellect grounded in the Good and that has immediate practical repercussions not least of which are questions of sustainability, economic stability, moral coherence, and the overall quality of life for humans and non-humans in an ecosystem where each *needs* the other.[35]

But there is something still more telling in Porphyry's work. The *de Abstinentia*, it seems to me, implies a broader understanding (even if elsewhere in his writings Porphyry takes a harsh view of other groups)[36] that tolerance of other religions/nations or species is *not enough*, for it entails a standpoint of false superiority and an unwarranted management model. Other peoples and other species have needs and rights that have to be acknowledged for our benefit and *for theirs*. In this spirit, Porphyry comes very close to a theory of rights, if such a theory is to be grounded not on our preferences or agency, but on the worth or nature of animals themselves, and on individual animals, not simply groups or species.[37] Furthermore, although Porphyry is eager to press-gang everything he can into the service of his own argument, his methodological practice in undertaking such a comparative study is to allow ourselves to be transformed by the superior practices of other religions, nations and times if only we can overcome the unthinking prejudices inculcated in us by narrower social, political, moral and religious forms. Passive tolerance is insufficient, but active tolerance too is not enough. We have to be open to the superiorities we find in other peoples – and in other species (see note 32). And so his collection of materials from different sources on the Egyptians, Indians, Jews and others is an impressive indication that authentic experience and humane practice may be found anywhere – among Brahmans, Essenes and so on – rather than belonging to any single tradition exclusively.

What we find here and in later Neoplatonism is a cosmic attitude and an attentiveness to the lives of animals and of plants that have been almost entirely lost and that provide good evidence for supposing that modern negative views about hierarchy and the elimination of the importance of individuals (whether humans, other animals or plants) are simply misguided. As D. Turner has pointed out in relation to Pseudo-Dionysius:

> there could be little more mistaken than to conceive of the One as the being which tops off the ascending scale of beings, ontologically closer to those next to it than to those lesser beings down the scale. … For each and every being the relation of its existence to its creating cause has the same immediacy. God has brought Cherubim and worms into existence in acts of creative causality which are, for want of a better word, "equidistant" from their effects.
>
> (1995: 30–31)

We therefore have to emphasize, and not elide the tension between hierarchical scale and a radical anti-hierarchical creative immediacy in Neoplatonism. This tension is perhaps nowhere more striking than in two passages from Pseudo-Dionysius: "When we talk of yearning, whether this be in God or an angel, in the mind or in the spirit or in nature, we should think of a unifying and commingling power which moves the superior to provide for the subordinate, peer to be in communion with peer, and subordinate to return to the superior" (*de Divinis Nominibus* 713a–b).[38]

This providential care of superior for subordinate is,[39] in fact, an intimate paradoxical coincidence of opposites – transcendence and immanence – in which the divine longing for *all* created things is manifested:[40]

> And in truth it must be said too that the very cause of the universe, in the beautiful, good superabundance of his benign yearning for all is also carried outside of himself in the loving care he has for everything. He is, as it were, beguiled by goodness, by love, and by yearning and is enticed away from his transcendent dwelling place and comes to abide within all things, and he does so by virtue of his supernatural and ecstatic capacity to remain, nevertheless, within himself.
>
> (*de Divinis Nominibus* 712a–b)[41]

This is a remarkable passage which, in my view, demonstrates the immediacy of the "Good" to everything, and in language that cannot be reconciled in a simple-minded way with any hierarchical thinking that supposedly does away with the radical importance, and even novelty, of individuals, for it is the Divine Thearchy itself which is said to be "enchanted", "beguiled" or "bewitched"[42] by goodness, love and yearning so that it is led down to dwell in everything without ever going out of its own dwelling. Here we find a dimension of sympathy, co-feeling, co-inherence: in the *pathos* of human beings, other animals or even plants, the *pathos* of God is or can be manifested.[43] It makes little sense, then, to berate Platonism for a blanket failure to recognize individuals when its careful articulation of the fullest recognition of individuals is, in fact, one of its major achievements. Individuals emerge as individuals most fully in the ecstatic love of God.

But we can still ask: does the Good's love of the goodness in everything *really* include other animals and plants, or does "everything" mean only those faithful "good" ones who can be included in ecclesiastical and celestial hierarchies? On balance, I think that "everything" really does mean everything for later Neoplatonism, and I suggest that we can see exactly this in a remarkable passage from Proclus' *On the Hieratic Art*, which looks so weird to the modern eye as to make us aware that we are dealing with an almost entirely lost ancient sensibility, a sensibility that conspicuously includes plants. Proclus writes:

> Just as in the dialectic of love we start from sensuous beauties to rise until we encounter the unique principles of all beauty and all ideas, so the adepts of hieratic science take as their starting point the things of appearance and the sympathies they manifest among themselves and with the invisible powers. Observing that all things form a whole, they laid the foundations of hieratic science, wondering at the first realities and admiring in them the latest comers as well as the very first among beings; in heaven, terrestrial things according both to a causal and to a celestial mode and on earth heavenly things in a terrestrial state.
> (*de Sacrificio et Magia* 148.1–10 [Bidez], trans. Copenhaver)

The example he gives is the heliotrope and its *prayer*:

> What other reason can we give for the fact that the heliotrope follows in its movement the movement of the sun and the selenotrope the movement of the moon, forming a procession within the limits of their power, behind the torches of the universe? For, in truth, each thing prays according to the rank it occupies in nature, and sings the praise of the leader of the divine series to which it belongs, a spiritual or rational or physical or sensuous praise; for the heliotrope moves to the extent that it is free to move, and in its rotation, if we could hear the sound of the air buffeted by its movement, we should be aware that it is a hymn to its king, such as it is within the power of a plant to sing.   (*de Sacrificio et Magia* 148.10–18)

The thought that a heliotrope prays and that, if we could only hear the sound of the air buffeted by its movement, we would be able to hear what is within the power of a plant to sing, makes clear, however weird it might appear, that even plants are their own individual "goods" whose goodness coheres most fully in their hymn to a higher Good, a relatedness it is possible even for us, as it were, to overhear.

In sum, while the ancient world has a multiplicity of different, often contradictory views about the relation of human beings to other animals and plants, and while Aristotle tends to deny reason, on the one hand, and the Stoics and Epicureans to deny contractual relations, on the other, to other animals, there is another complex tradition running through ancient thought from Pythagoras, Empedocles, Plato and Aristotle into early and later Neoplatonism that is based upon the Good of the *Republic*, reflects the intelligible biology of the *Timaeus*, and the more inclusive role of *sophia* (by contrast with that of *phronēsis*) in Aristotle's *Ethics*. I have argued that the Platonic Good does not commit the ancients to unnecessary hierarchical thinking, to "intrinsic good" theories or to the erasure of the importance of individuals. Instead, hierarchical thinking has to be kept in tension with the anti-hierarchical immediacy of the Good's presence to everything; and if species or kinds are parts of an intelligible biology based in Plato and Aristotle, individuals must arguably be parts of that biology not only in the intelligible world of Plotinus, where good-formedness is characteristic of each form,[44] but especially in the providential care and love of the Good in Proclus and Pseudo-Dionysius, where individuals – all animals and plants – are to be found in their fullest focus, even to the extent that the Good itself is enthralled by them. The practical results of this focus, I have argued, can be seen in the thought of Theophrastus, Plutarch, Plotinus and, above all, Porphyry, who makes the case for an immemorial tradition, according to which we have not always lived by bloodshed or as carnivores, and for a real *ecological* relatedness, based on "justice" rather than "rights" and on mutual need without undue romanticism. Porphyry, for instance, argues cogently that we may kill other animals that jeopardize our security, but this should not be our mindless practice with all animals; and, at the same time, he is thoroughly realistic about the real limitations of human nature.

On balance, therefore, while we find elements of a language of rights from Cicero to Porphyry, we do not find any fully articulated theory of animal and plant rights in the ancient world. We do, however, find claims based upon justice as well as upon the goods of, and capacities for, the flourishing of animals and plants that are highly significant and practical in their own right. Above all, we find the recognition of perspectives other than our own, whether those of the Good in Plato or of *sophia*, based upon the proper flourishing of species in Aristotle, or of the best functioning of other animals *for themselves* and not for us, in Porphyry. The recognition is, of course, our own in the light of what is good or best, but it is not simply a question of our own preference or projection, but rather a claim grounded in the features of things themselves, whether vulnerabilities, shared sensitivity, together with structural, physiological and psychosomatic similarities, or developmental capacities. I suggest that we can talk about such claims in the following ways. We can recognize them in so far as animals and plants possess developmental capabilities that are features of their natures, and not just of our projections. We can recognize them in so far as there is a range of the goods of things (other than those of human beings) that are good for their own sakes (and not just for our sakes). And we can recognize them in so far as these goods, while certainly dependent upon the Good itself, are not simply good for the sake of that Good – as if their goodness were to belong only to it – but rather, in so far as their goodness belongs to them genuinely, however much it may also be a gift, so that we are compelled to recognize this gift as both inherent to them and radically interconnected with other goods.

Finally, what is striking about Neoplatonism (especially by contrast with our contemporary world) is that not only do we find different models of rationality: to be precise, a continuum of different intensities of life-kinds manifested throughout nature; and not only do we find many examples of design without rationality; but, even more important, rationality ceases to be the dominant paradigm for determining whether things are meaningful at all. Intellect, in fact, is not "rational" in any modern sense, although it is supremely meaningful, one might claim; and the One or the Good is even less "rational" than Intellect; and so it is perhaps appropriate that the Good, or what will later be for Nicholas of Cusa both the *maximum* and the *minimum*, should be both the source and the refuge of all things, living and non-living, that is, animals, plants, the simplest existences, and even the barest possibilities in which no rational analysis could reasonably discern any genuine potential or dream anything other than hope.

NOTES

1. In this chapter my primary focus will be more upon rationality than upon the mind/soul–body relation. For a treatment of the latter, see Corrigan (2009a: esp. 37–51).
2. The word "hierarchy" is particularly associated with the work of Pseudo-Dionysius the Areopagite (see Hathaway 1969; D. Turner 1995: 26–49; Corrigan & Harrington 2004), but the term picks up and recapitulates for a Christian context the descending order of Neoplatonic "hypostases" – the One, Intellect and Soul – in Plotinus and Porphyry, and the more complicated levels of existence in Iamblichus and Proclus, and especially the theory of "chains" we find in Proclus, with "a god presiding as a 'monad' over an elaborate chain of angels, daemons, souls, living things and even inanimate objects, which receive the influence of this god as a dominant factor in their existence" (Dillon 1973; cf. Wallis [1972] 1995: 151–3).
3. For evaluation of this claim in connection with the principal terms and related concepts involved – for example, human rights, natural law, justice (Gr. *dikaiosynē, dikē/to dikaion*; Lat. *iustitia, aequitas*) in accordance with what is appropriate (Gr. *kat' axian*; Lat. *dignum*) or "right/obligation/appropriate" (Gr. *to prosekon*; Lat. *ius*) and kinship, belonging or *oikeiosis* – see Sorabji (1993: 134–57). For the ancient academy, justice is a "*hexis* that gives each his share according to his worth" (Plato, *Def.* 411d–e), and this appears in Roman thought under the formula *suum cuique tribuere* (Cicero, *Leg.* 1.6.19; *Off.* 3.5.15; Ulpian, *Dig.* 1.1.10). Cf. *Brill's New Pauly Encyclopedia of the Ancient World. Classical Tradition* (2006–11): vol. 3, 1224–26. On the question of rights specifically, see also note 37 below.
4. For a judicious evaluation of the evidence for and against, see especially Sorabji (1993: 208–19).
5. By "reflexively", I mean that the Good is the principle by which we are able to conceive the best state of anything, a principle disclosed in the acts of seeing or thinking themselves, just as in seeing we see the light of the sun, according to Socrates' analogy in *Republic* books 6–7, and in thinking objects of thought we think of them as "good-form" (*R.* 508d–509b). For the conception of Forms as ideals or "what should be" and for understanding the Form of the Good as overcoming the modern dichotomy between being and value, see Ferber (1989: 30–33); and cf. Gonzalez (1998: 209–44).
6. "Kinship" is in this case primarily designated by the Greek word *oikeiotēs* and cognates, a network of terms that is used by Plato (esp. *Republic* 8–9), Aristotle and others, especially the Stoics. Theophrastus argued for an *oikeiotēs* or relatedness between humans and animals (see Porphyry, *Abst.* 3.25); for the history of *oikeiōsis*, see Long (1996a), Sorabji (1993: 122–33) and G. Clark (2000: esp. 124 n. 17).
7. I am particularly indebted to the many works of S. Clark (most recently 2011: 35–60); G. Clark's translation and useful notes of *Porphyry: On Abstinence from Killing Animals* (2000); Sorabji (1993); among other recent works are the following: Cassin & Labarrière (2000), Heath (2005) , Steiner (2005), Gilhus (2006), especially the chapter on soul and reason, Newmyer (2006), Nussbaum (2006), Osborne (2007) and Beauchamp & Frey (2011).
8. The classic work on this theme is, of course, that of P. Hadot (1981b [English trans. 1995], 1995: 280).
9. This is, in fact, the model articulated in Plotinus' view of intellect (*nous*): all in all, all in each, and each in all. For one conspicuous example, see *Enn.* V.8[31].4. Cf. Porphyry, *Plot.* 2 (on Plotinus' last words).
10. Frags 130b, 128b, 137b [DK]; Sedley (2005: 331–71); Campbell (2008: 6–8).
11. *Rep.* 3.11.19: "non enim mediocres viri sed maxumi et docti, Pythagoras et Empedocles, unam omnium animantium condicionem iuris esse denuntiant, clamant que inexpiabilis poenas impendere iis a quibus violatum sit animal", trans. G. Clark (2000: 123 n. 12).

12. Frag. 110b [DK]: πάντα γὰρ ἴσθι φρόνησιν ἔχειν καὶ νώματος αἶσαν, trans. G. Clark (2000: 125). Aristotle, in fact, calls Empedocles' claim that justice involves not killing anything that has life a "law of all things" "according to nature" "that extends without break through wide-ruling aether and boundless earth" (*Rh.* 1.13.1373b1–17, my trans.).

13. Sorabji (1993: 8–9); Aristotle, *Metaph.* 1009b12–31; Theophrastus, *Sens.* 23; Aetius 4.5.12 (*Dox. Graec.* 392.4–7).

14. Aristotle, *de An.* 404b1–6; 405a8–16; 427a19–29.

15. Alcmaeon, frag. 1a [DK] (Theophrastus, *Sens.* 25); Anaxagoras, frag. 21b [DK]; Plato, *Prt.* 321d, 322a; *Phd* 96b; and Sorabji (1993: 9–16).

16. For passages in Aristotle, see Sorabji (1993: 12–16, 17–20, 30–40, 50–51, etc.). One passage, sometimes ascribed as a fragment to Aristotle's early thought (from Iamblichus, *Protr.* 36.7–13), according to which animals have small glints of *phronēsis*, and *logos* – Sorabji argues (1993: 15–16) – is most likely from Porphyry.

17. Hereinafter the translation of the *Timaeus* is according to Jowett.

18. Cf. Proclus, *On the Hieratic Art*, on the heliotrope, below; and on similarities of constituent elements and nourishment, see *Ti.* 80d6–e2: "And it is owing to this [the work of fire and breath in bodily respiration] that in all living creatures the streams of nutriment course in this way through the whole body. And inasmuch as these nutritive particles are freshly divided and derived from kindred substances – some from fruits, and some from cereals, which god planted for us for the express purpose of serving as food, they get all varieties of colors because of their commingling."

19. The passage concludes: εἰ γὰρ τὴν περὶ τὰ ὠφέλιμα τὰ αὑτοῖς ἐροῦσι σοφίαν, πολλαὶ ἔσονται σοφίαι· οὐ γὰρ μία περὶ τὸ ἁπάντων ἀγαθὸν τῶν ζῴων, ἀλλ' ἑτέρα περὶ ἕκαστον (*EN* 6.7.1141a29–32).

20. While the Unmoved Mover is transcendent or separate from everything, it is also immanent in its own way, as Aristotle suggests at the beginning of *Metaph.* 1075a11–15: Ἐπισκεπτέον δὲ καὶ ποτέρως ἔχει ἡ τοῦ ὅλου φύσις τὸ ἀγαθὸν καὶ τὸ ἄριστον, πότερον κεχωρισμένον τι καὶ αὐτὸ καθ' αὑτό, ἢ τὴν τάξιν. ἢ ἀμφοτέρως ὥσπερ στράτευμα; καὶ γὰρ ἐν τῇ τάξει τὸ εὖ καὶ ὁ στρατηγός, καὶ μᾶλλον οὗτος· οὐ γὰρ οὗτος διὰ τὴν τάξιν ἀλλ' ἐκείνη διὰ τοῦτόν ἐστιν; and it also explicitly "embraces everything" according to traditional wisdom in *Metaph.* 1074a38–b3: παραδέδοται δὲ παρὰ τῶν ἀρχαίων καὶ παμπαλαίων ἐν μύθου σχήματι καταλελειμμένα τοῖς ὕστερον ὅτι θεοί τέ εἰσιν οὗτοι καὶ περιέχει τὸ θεῖον τὴν ὅλην φύσιν.

21. For the Stoic view of *oikeiōsis* in this context, see Sorabji (1993: 122–33).

22. S. Clark (2011: 10–11). On contract in Roman law and on animals as enemies to each other and to humans, see Gilhus (2006: 22–36).

23. For context and interpretation of this, see Sorabji (1993: 20–21).

24. S. Clark makes a good sense of this complexity (2011: 35–60).

25. For *logoi*, see Corrigan 2004 (112–16) and also esp. *Enn.* V.8[31].5–7.

26. Hereinafter the translation of the *Enneads* is according to Armstrong (1966–88), with adaptation.

27. S. Clark (2011: 52), especially: "Evolutionary change is no great surprise for either Platonists or Aristotelians."

28. I recognize that this passage is aporetic and partly directed to unfolding difficulties in Aristotle's notion of well-being, but I find it nonetheless significant that Plotinus actually poses the question and takes it seriously by recognizing a range of different intensities of goodness of life in animals and plants (*Enn.* I.4[46].3), even if he is ultimately to restrict well-being in the most authentic sense to the life of Intellect.

29. See e.g. *Abst.* 3.19.2: "It is the nature of animals to have perceptions, to feel distress, to be afraid, to be hurt and therefore to be injured"; and in Sorabji (2004–2005: vol. 1, 360–61).

30. Cf. *Abst.* 3.8: "Aristotle says that animals with keener perceptions are wiser (*phronimōtera*)"; cf. *EN* 1141a25–8; *HA* 608a16; and for caution in ascribing intellectual activity to animals, see G. Clark (2000: 169 n. 423).

31. *Abst.* 3.11–12.200–202, especially: "Just as for humans life is over when society is taken away, so also for animals."

32. *Abst.* 3.12–13.202–203: "the one vice they do not have is hostility to someone of goodwill: their response in every case is total goodwill. … But humans conspire against no one so much as the person who nurtures them; there is no one for whose death they pray more fervently"[!].

33. *Abst.* 3.11: ἐξέχει γὰρ ἐν ἑκάστῳ ἰδία τις ἀρετὴ πρὸς ἣν πεφυσίωται, οὔτε τῆς φύσεως οὔτε τοῦ βεβαίου διὰ τοῦτο ἀφαιρουμένου αὐτῶν τὸ λογικόν· ἐκεῖνο γὰρ ἐλέγχειν δεῖ, εἰ μὴ τὰ ἔργα ἀρετῶν καὶ λογικῆς ἐντρεχείας οἰκεῖα.

34. *Abst.* 1–4: "our opponents say that justice is confounded … if we treat as family (*oikeios*) the other beasts which are in no way related to us, instead of using some for work and some for food and regarding them as of another kind, without rights in our community as they are without rights of citizenship" (ἔκφυλα καὶ ἄτιμα τῆς κοινωνίας καθάπερ πολιτείας νομίζοντες).

35. *Abst.* 3.12.3: "Nature that created them has made them need humans and has also made humans need them, establishing an innate justice in them towards us and in us towards them."

36. See e.g. his famous work *Against the Christians*.

37. These are the conditions Sorabji (1993: 156–7) suggests for any theory of animal rights, and one might well argue that Porphyry's *de Abstinentia* amply fulfils these conditions.

38. Pseudo-Dionysius, *de Divinis Nominibus* 713a–b: Τὸν ἔρωτα, εἴτε θεῖον εἴτε ἀγγελικὸν εἴτε νοερὸν εἴτε ψυχικὸν εἴτε φυσικὸν εἴποιμεν, ἐνωτικήν τινα καὶ συγκρατικὴν ἐννοήσωμεν δύναμιν τὰ μὲν ὑπέρτερα κινοῦσαν ἐπὶ πρόνοιαν τῶν καταδεεστέρων, τὰ δὲ ὁμόστοιχα πάλιν εἰς κοινωνικὴν ἀλληλουχίαν καὶ ἐπ᾽ ἐσχάτων τὰ ὑφειμένα πρὸς τὴν τῶν κρειττόνων καὶ ὑπερκειμένων ἐπιστροφήν.

39. As in Proclus, divine providential love is at root a love that recalls everything to itself, an *eros pronoētikos/epistreptikos*, that is also a function of our love for each other (cf. Proclus, *in Alc. I* 54–6).

40. With Iamblichus, and certainly Proclus and Pseudo-Dionysius, we encounter the unfolding of a remarkable view of divine love that is implicit in earlier Platonism and not simply a reaction, I suggest, to Christian influence, namely the view that God's love involves a kind of radical divine vulnerability, a longing that pierces all created life. On this, see Corrigan (2012).

41. Pseudo-Dionysius, *de Divinis Nominibus* 712a–b: Τολμητέον δὲ καὶ τοῦτο ὑπὲρ ἀληθείας εἰπεῖν, ὅτι καὶ αὐτὸς ὁ πάντων αἴτιος τῷ καλῷ καὶ ἀγαθῷ τῶν πάντων ἔρωτι δι᾽ ὑπερβολὴν τῆς ἐρωτικῆς ἀγαθότητος ἔξω ἑαυτοῦ γίνεται ταῖς εἰς τὰ ὄντα πάντα προνοίαις καὶ οἷον ἀγαθότητι καὶ ἀγαπήσει καὶ ἔρωτι θέλγεται καὶ ἐκ τοῦ ὑπὲρ πάντα καὶ πάντων ἐξῃρημένου πρὸς τὸ ἐν πᾶσι κατάγεται κατ᾽ ἐκστατικὴν ὑπερούσιον δύναμιν ἀνεκφοίτητον ἑαυτοῦ.

42. See also Agathon's speech in the *Smp.* 197e, where such a notion of enchantment is first broached.

43. Especially on the "pathetic god": see Corbin (1969).

44. Where everything that can be fitted to a *logos*, including bodies and matter, Plotinus claims, must be included (see *Enn.* VI.2[43].21–2, esp. 21.29–59).

VI

Ethics, political theory and aesthetics

INTRODUCTION

From the contemporary point of view, ethics is often centrally concerned with behaviour or conduct. Morality is understood as principles about right or wrong, principles that are effected and govern our life with one another, in a group or society. Further, some theorists today see these principles as being shaped entirely by that same society. There are many profound ways in which ancient philosophy – and Neoplatonism – differ from this picture. First, the whole idea of ethics as some kind of a search for or a collection of principles of moral behaviour may be intrinsically foreign to the ancient philosopher. In antiquity, the emphasis lies in the virtuous character capable of adapting to different circumstances and situations – a view which has, of course, given rise to the contemporary reactionary movement within ethics, virtue ethics. Talk about moral obligations is rare in antiquity, whereas a lot of space is devoted to therapy of emotions and other means of character improvement. Second, in so far as some moral principles are discussed, the search is for principles that would be unqualifiedly true. That is, many ancient philosophers (apart from Cynics and Sceptics and, according to one interpretation, Artistotle) are ethical realists. Neoplatonists are also ethical realists but of a special and radical kind. Goodness is an objective feature of being, a crucial and existing aspect of the metaphysical system, present in different degrees on all its levels, and to be traced all the way to the primary cause, the origin of its derivation, the One. While the relationship of goodness in the sensible realm to the higher kind of goodness it imitates may be tricky (both ontologically and episte-mologically), it is only that relationship which ensures that the former truly qualifies as goodness, and not mere apparent goodness. Third, as Stern-Gillet argues forcefully in her "Plotinus on metaphysics and morality" (Chapter 25), to understand Neoplatonic ethical treatises one must let go of the modern and contemporary expectation that ethics centrally deals with how to reconcile an inherently dangerous self-interest (or, better, self-partiality) and other-interest. It does not preoccupy itself with what duties we have to other people and how these are in conflict with our own interests, or how we should minimally treat other people well, in a way that would ensure common good.

In Neoplatonism, the crucial axis is not between the self and the other – rather, it is between the higher and the lower, between the origin of all goodness and the lack of it, between that which is immaterial and that which is the body, as already discussed, at onto-logical and cosmological levels, by Chiaradonna and Narbonne above respectively in their chapters on "Substance" (Chapter 14) and "Matter and evil in the Neoplatonic tradition" (Chapter 15). The often-called "denigration" of the body in Platonism has to be understood in its proper context. While undoubtedly singular in its emphases, it should also be seen as a continuation of the Classical and Hellenistic discussions on the invulnerability of true happiness and goodness, as a state worth striving for.[1] In doing so, it also provides room for further developments within conceptualizing independence, autonomy and freedom.

Collette-Dučić, in his "Plotinus on founding freedom in *Ennead* VI.8[39]" (Chapter 26), introduces the Neoplatonists' interest in the concept of human freedom in the larger metaphysical framework of the question about the free will of the One. Again, we will see Plotinus working on both levels at the same time, explicating the freedom of the One in parallel with that of the human individual. As Collette-Dučić points out, Plotinus' real interest lies in the question of the freedom of individuals, and in showing how that resides in goodness and self-knowledge. Collette-Dučić's contribution shows us, further, how subtly Plotinus engages in philosophizing with his Stoic predecessors, as well as the extent to which there would seem to be quite a wide agreement concerning the nature of freedom between the two camps. In Adamson's "Freedom, providence and fate" (Chapter 27) we continue with the same theme and see how one central motivation in Neoplatonic philosophizing is in grounding human freedom in the face of different challenges posed to it. From Plato's *Phaedo* and *Timaeus* onwards, Platonists had struggled to define and limit the causes that they considered mechanistic from such causation that is organized towards a goal, towards goodness. The latter is understood as more crucial because it has more explanatory value for the thing/action caused. In the late ancient period, in which the Stoic discussions on determinism already belonged to at least the advanced philosophical syllabus, the further challenges posed to autonomy were acutely perceived. Adamson's chapter operates through explicating the ways in which the Neoplatonists divide fate and providence, subjecting the human to the latter but saving her from the former. As Adamson puts it, "autonomy or freedom is compromised not by the absence of multiple options, but by the threat of determination from outside". And it is precisely the body, and what the embodiment brings with itself, through which human beings encounter external determination.

The question of how deep a hostility all this brings towards the embodied life, its activities and objects, has been the subject of lively discussion. This is the famous question of the extent of otherworldliness and possible ascetism of Neoplatonism.[2] It is perhaps fair to say that in the past, the predominant reading underlined the causal primacy, both efficient and teleological, of the immaterial realm and activities connected with that realm, as well as the undeniable hostility shown in the sources as regards bodily objects and beauty, and the embodied activities connected with them. More than vestiges of this approach remain, and rightly so, given the rhetorically powerful passages about the insignificance, ugliness and risky nature of everything connected with the body – the danger of external determination mentioned above. However, it is equally undeniable that a view, with its own textual backing, in which the two aspects of reality are seen in a more balanced relationship is emerging. This interpretative line tries in different ways to explicate why neither spirituality nor belief in the causal predominance of the higher, intelligible level of reality, and ultimately the One, needs to lead to trivialization and turning away from the bodily. Ethical and political themes cannot be considered separated from the metaphysical system governing Neoplatonism as a whole, but when one starts to tease out their implications in these areas, one quickly notes how much more material the sources contain than initially envisioned.

In this volume, the latter interpretative option is testified in three different discussions. First, in "Action, reasoning and the highest good" (Chapter 28), Remes contrasts Plotinus' more straightforward top-down approach as regards both the explanatory and value hierarchy between intellection and action to the Stoic, Epictetan approach explicated and further elaborated by Simplicius. At least as regards those still progressing in their quest for virtue and knowledge, acting on moral principles is as important as the principles themselves. In fact, putting virtue into action is the reason for which moral principles are learned in the first place. This call to act morally contains two goals the co-suitability of which the Neoplatonists did not see a reason to argue: the improvement of the person's surroundings, and of her own soul. Because acting improves the state of the agent, through virtuous action the agent further improves her character.

According to a view that has been even more persistent than the one claiming that the Neoplatonists had no ethics to speak of,[3] there really is no Neoplatonic political theory. In his "Political theory" (Chapter 29), O'Meara draws on that part of his work which simply proves this view wrong (D. O'Meara 2003, and numerous articles). His studies show that Neoplatonists had a theory of what political science concerns, divided this further into legislative and judicial branches, and theorized over how practical and political reasoning differs from theoretical intellection. The top-down approach is visible in, among other things, their heavy inclination to treat political constitutions through different kinds of ideals (following, of course, already the Kallipolis of Plato's *Republic*). Sociability, or friendship, is understood as one imitation and unfolding of the unity present on higher levels of being, and thus, again, not in contrast with care of one's own virtue or ascent to intelligible origin, but as intimately connected with it.

Concerning aesthetics, the situation has been slightly different. The Neoplatonists have long had a recognized place within aesthetic theory. In many circles within the history of Western philosophy, Plotinus has been credited as the inventor of the idea of this worldly beauty as an imitation or unfolding of a transcendental source (see e.g. Kuisma 2003). While real beauty lies in the intelligible, the sensible objects may transmit some of this beauty by symbolic or mimetic relationship with the origin. In her "Plotinus' aesthetics: in defence of the lifelike" (Chapter 30), Vassilopoulou situates Plotinus' remarks about beauty within different approaches in aesthetics. She brings to the fore especially Plotinus' notion of "lifelikeness". The role of beauty in art is not simply to reproduce any combination of qualities considered harmonious and hence beautiful. Beauty captures something else, the formative force that not merely organizes, but also moves and governs change, a dynamic presence of the soul in bodies. A good work of art, even one that is two-dimensional and not moving, captures some of this internal power, some of its life. Living things (and lifelike things) are beautiful because they display the activities characteristic of the higher levels, the life of the Soul, the life of the Intellect, as present in the sensible world.

Besides the interrelations with many topics in Part III on metaphysics, this section connects with Part IV as regards especially the ethical implications of psychology visible in Schroeder (Chapter 19) and Aubry (Chapter 20).

NOTES

1. Studies now considered classic are e.g. Nussbaum (1986) and Annas (1993). For Neoplatonism, see also Bussanich (1990).
2. Chapter 25, by Stern-Gillet, offers plenty of references for this discussion.
3. Examined critically, for instance, by Schniewind (2003).

25

Plotinus on metaphysics and morality

Suzanne Stern-Gillet

> When compulsory passions and actions come in the way virtue has not in its supervision
> wished that they should occur … even among these it preserves what belongs to itself
> and brings it back up to itself, even in the world below.
>
> (Plotinus, *Enn.* VI.8[39].6.10–14, trans. Armstrong, modified)

A DEBATED ISSUE

Ethics is a constituent part of most philosophical systems. Plato, Aristotle, the Stoics, Aquinas, Spinoza and Kant all have an ethical theory, which is organically linked to the other parts of their system. Is Plotinus' philosophy, undeniably systematic though it is, an exception to this general rule? The fact that learned students of Neoplatonism have raised the question is evidence enough that the question does arise. That is perplexing enough. More perplexing even is the fact that these same scholars should have come to two diametrically opposed answers despite being in broad agreement on the meaning of the relevant passages in the corpus. It would seem therefore that it is not so much the meaning of these passages as their interpretation in the broader doctrinal context of the *Enneads* that is the object of scholarly disagreement.

The controversies arising from this disparity of views have recently intensified to such an extent that it would be true to say that the nature of Plotinus' ethics is currently one of the most earnestly debated issues in the field. Since no particular viewpoint has so far appeared to be gaining the upper hand, it is perhaps not surprising that the controversy shows no sign of dying down. This chapter is an attempt to advance the debate by identifying the assumptions on the nature of ethics that have given rise to it and to take a fresh look at a range of passages in the *Enneads* with a view to formulating an answer less narrowly beholden to the assumptions in question.

THE PROBLEM

At one time – not so long ago – scholars who considered the question tended for the most part to disparage whatever ethical reflections they conceded were to be found in the *Enneads*. Some went as far as denying that Plotinus had an ethics at all. To document in detail the many critical, if not downright derogatory, accounts of the nature of Plotinus' ethical reflections would far exceed the space of this volume, and a brief summary of the criticisms that have been directed at Plotinus' ethics will therefore have here to suffice.

These criticisms fall into three broad categories. The first and most frequently alleged ground of criticism is that Plotinus consistently downplayed what we moderns take to be the very core of the moral life, namely concern for the needs and entitlements of others. In 1921 René Arnou, for instance, rebuked Plotinus for advocating "a certain form of *egoism* masquerading as disinterestedness" (Arnou 1921: 44, my trans., emphasis added) and, in 1996, John Dillon issued a similar complaint: "[the] single-minded pursuit of union with God which is Plotinus's only approved form of ethical activity does not really leave much room for that concerned interaction with our fellow men which constitutes the traditional arena of ethics". Plotinus' ethics, Dillon concluded, in being "addressed to the late antique sage", offers little "practical guidance to the common man".[1]

A second ground of criticism levelled at Plotinus' ethical reflections is that they are essentially "negative". Such negativity, in Paul Plass' opinion, "comes to the surface most clearly at two points: Plotinus' devaluation of conventional virtue and the nature of his own metaphysical ethical principles" (Plass 1982: 244). For Richard Bodéüs the negativity is most apparent in Plotinus' conception of the process of purification which he would have the incarnate soul undertake prior to beginning her ascent to the Intelligible. Since the purifying soul is a soul that frees herself, so far as possible, from the influence of the body, it follows that the Plotinian moral life, in Bodéüs' estimation, consists in making oneself insensitive to the suffering of the body, "one's own and, even more, that of others".[2] It is to become "a person, so to speak, entirely different" from the compound of body and soul that most human beings take themselves to be (*ibid.*: 257).

Third and last comes the complaint, as put forward by Rist in his seminal 1967 study, *Plotinus: The Road to Reality*, that Plotinus' thought on ethical matters is "somewhat contradictory":

> The theory of the self-sufficiency of the sage should preclude him from all communal interests except that of teaching, while the theory of the union of the self with the One and the submerging of our own lives and activities in the life and activity of the One should lead to an outgoing attitude of the personality in the form of creativeness at all levels. ... Theoretically such care should distract the soul; but again theoretically it would enable the soul to perform its functions to the full.[3]

In spelling out what he described as the "somewhat contradictory" aspects of Plotinus' ethical reflections, Rist paved the way for attempts by later scholars to argue that Plotinus, far from neglecting the domain of ethics, as we moderns conceive it, had included teaching in the activities of the sage and had countenanced the view that union with Intellect and the One should result in "an outgoing of the personality in the form of creativeness at all levels".

All in all, therefore, for one reason or another, the received interpretation at the end of twentieth century tended to be that Plotinus' ethics was one-sided or otherwise unsatisfactory. Matters, however, were soon to change; received interpretations invite dissent, and this particular received interpretation proved no exception. Latterly, a number of scholars have argued that Plotinus' ethics, far from being as one-sided and otherworldly as had previously been supposed, does include norms of other-regarding conduct and, consequently, that ethics and political philosophy do form an integral part of it. In the defence of this thesis, they have adopted a variety of strategies and approaches.

A common line of defence consists in turning to the detail of Porphyry's eulogistic account of his master's life to back the view that concern for the needs of others is an integral aspect of his ethics. Thus, most notably, Andrew Smith has professed to find in the *Vita Plotini* (9.5–22), no less than in various passages in the *Enneads*, enough evidence to substantiate his claim that Plotinus offers "a practical ethical code" or "a meaningful theory of practical ethics".[4]

Most attempts to find other-regarding norms in Plotinus' philosophy, however, have been carried out through the detailed exegesis of his own writings. In his reconstruction of Neoplatonic political thinking, from Plotinus to al-Farabi, Dominic O'Meara has identified in the *Enneads* a small number of passages which, in his view, do contain a political philosophy *in ovo*. The principle of emanation and reversion, as well as the broad concept of contemplation worked out in the tractate *On Nature and Contemplation and the One* (*Enn.* III.8[30].4.31–46), do, in his estimation, provide a theoretical background against which Plotinus can, and does, justify the life of action. More specifically, political engagement can proceed from, and be an image of, mystical union in so far as "union with the One *must* involve sharing in its metaphysical fecundity, its nature as the self-giving and self-communicating Good". As the Good is metaphysically fecund and nourishes the lower levels of reality, so the Neoplatonic philosopher, after communing with the Good, may, very properly, O'Meara claims, "descend to political matters as a consequence and expression of the union reached with the One".[5] Moral expertise and legislative activity, so O'Meara assures us, although they are not the highest manifestations of contemplation, are nonetheless worthy derivative exercises of it.

Alexandrine Schniewind, for her part, pursued a suggestion mooted by Rist in 1967 that the ethical function of the Plotinian sage (*ho spoudaios*) is, for the most part, to teach. As described in the tractate *On Well-Being* (*Enn.* I.4[46]) (Schniewind 2000 and, mainly, 2003), the *spoudaios* identifies himself with his higher self, holds onto the One or Good as his goal and succeeds, in so far as a human being can, in mastering the weaknesses attendant upon his soul's temporary association with the body. Far from being entirely disengaged from ordinary human concerns, the sage, in Schniewind's phraseology, also "teaches", "inspires" and is "a model for" others. To motivate "ordinary human beings" (*epieikēs anthrōpoi*) to rise above the "common life of body and soul" (16.9), he carefully tailors his pedagogical methods and inspirational guidance to the level and capacities of his audience. In this particular tractate, so Schniewind argues, we get a glimpse of Plotinus' own pedagogical practice: chapters one to four are addressed to the large and philosophically untutored audience who attended the meetings of the school, chapters five to eleven to the inner circle of disciples, and chapters twelve to sixteen to the closest few who, like Porphyry himself,[6] were entrusted with the master's writings and could therefore rightly be described as his assistants.[7]

In her circumspect attempt to identify an ethics of concern in the *Enneads*, Pauliina Remes focuses on the noetic life rather than the final *unio mystica* to back her claim that an ethical theory, albeit one of a highly abstract nature, is built into the very fabric of the *Enneads*. The purified soul's ascent to the Intelligible, in the course of which she divests herself from particularities of all kinds, enlarges the self and enables it to grasp "essences and the real nature of things" (Remes 2006: 15; see also Remes 2007). Those who have suc-cessfully undertaken such a process of conversion, Remes argues, gain "a global standpoint that [is] directed to the perfection of the entire *kosmos*, not on the happiness of any one part of it.While social virtues are not constitutive of the good, the cosmological point of view renders the well-being of the world as a whole the *telos* of an individual life" (2007: 19). Remes concludes that the ethical theory that she finds in the *Enneads*, far from being a variety of ethical egoism, is more aptly described as an "ethics of disinterested interest".[8]

HIDDEN (AND NOT SO HIDDEN) ASSUMPTIONS

What can we learn from these diverging viewpoints? Quite a lot or disappointingly little, depending on how one looks at them. While the debate itself shows that both parties to the disagreement do, as often as not, share a number of basic assumptions about the nature and foundations of ethics in general, the assumptions in question stand in the way of getting a clear view of Plotinus' ethics. The reason is that they reflect, for the most part, a miscel-lany of theories on the nature of ethics that had currency in the latter half of the twentieth century and proceed from the anti-foundationalist conviction that it is futile to search for the grounds, metaphysical or other, of moral value.[9] Although some of these assumptions have since been called into question, modified or altogether discarded, they nonetheless appear to have retained a hold on the minds of specialists in ancient thought. Ploughing their own different, though neighbouring, furrow, they have been content to leave such assumptions, as well as the theories from which they proceed, largely unacknowledged and unexamined. It is my claim that those modern assumptions and theories hinder the interpretation of Plotinus' own ethical reflections, which themselves proceed from very different assumptions. Accordingly, I shall take my first task to be that of identifying the modern assumptions that have been brought to the study of Plotinus' ethics, with a view to showing why, and in what ways, they are likely to divert attention from what lies at its very core. This should clear the ground and enable me to consider afresh a number of relevant Plotinian passages.

  According to the first assumption (hereafter the "basic" assumption), the function of ethics is to lay down principles whose application is expected to promote the common good by counterbalancing the interests of all those likely to be affected by the decisions and actions that human beings commit themselves to in the course of their daily life. This basic assumption is itself rooted in the belief, whether consciously held or not, that self-partiality is a fundamental human trait which, as such, must be held in check if human beings are to show due concern for each other and for those other forms of life which share the planet with them. So understood, moral principles are the rudder which prevents, or minimizes, whatever conflicts of interests would otherwise arise. So understood, the specific task of ethics is to counteract the limitations of human sympathies and thus to alleviate "the human predicament" (in the terminology of Warnock 1971: 71) by protecting the entitlements of all those with whom the moral agent has the kind of dealings likely to require guidance in that respect. As Kurt Baier famously put it: "The very *raison d'être* of a morality is to yield reasons which overrule the reasons of self-interest in those cases when everyone's following self-interest would be harmful to everyone. Hence moral reasons are superior to all others" (Baier 1965: 150).

Far from coming alone, the basic assumption gives rise to a second assumption, namely that, *pace* Kant, for example, there cannot be duties to oneself. Indeed, if the function of ethics is to counteract the limitations of human sympathies, it follows that the concept of obligation (or duty) is essentially other-directed. Even if those who are committed to the basic assumption do not take a contractual (or contractarian) view of moral obligation, they are, even so, likely to argue that the notion of obligation (or duty) to oneself is well nigh incoherent or hopelessly ill-conceived.[10] It is incoherent in the sense that obligations and entitlements are correlative and that, in the case of putative obligations to self, there cannot, strictly speaking, be an entitlement corresponding to the obligation.[11] It is ill-conceived in the sense that duties to oneself, if they are to have moral significance, need to be mediated through, or be derivative upon, duties to others.[12] These objections owe their force, not only to the conception of morality as essentially other-directed, but also to the assumption that selfhood is broadly coextensive with moral agency. Outside the framework of these assumptions, they lose their compelling force. Since Plotinus' concept of higher selfhood as normative differs significantly from the one that lies at the basis of the objections latterly levelled at self-regarding duties, particular care must be taken not to project the theoretical background to these objections onto the interpretation of the ethical views put forward in the *Enneads*.

The above two assumptions, in turn, are likely to give rise to a third one. Those who, being committed to the basic assumption, take the function of ethics to be the promotion of the common good are likely to extend to reflexive notions such as self-fulfilment, self-regard and self-love the kind of suspicion that they harbour on the subject of duties to oneself. Such moral attitudes, they are prone to argue, are at best of peripheral relevance to ethics and at worst a mere garb destined to give superficial respectability to a form of psychological egoism which sanctions the promotion of the agent's self-interest at the expense of those with whom he has dealings (see e.g. Arnou 1921: 44). This third assumption is likely to account for the predilection, shared by many an apologist of Plotinus' ethics, for citing Porphyry's pious report in the *Vita Plotini* of the devoted care with which his master looked after orphaned children (see e.g. A. Smith 1999).

All three assumptions, especially when they remain below the level of critical awareness, cloud the examination of Plotinus' ethics by generating questions to which the text of the *Enneads* can provide no clear or incontrovertible answers. The reason is that the assumptions in question are foreign to the thinking of a philosopher whose overriding aim – not to say his sole aim – was to convince his disciples of the truth of the metaphysical system he developed in the *Enneads*. There is no need in the present context to rehearse in detail the central tenets of his metaphysics, all of which are as familiar to those who criticize Plotinus' ethics as to those who defend it: the One as cause of all things and universal object of desire, the distinction between internal and external activity, the formation of Intellect, the stages in the descent of Soul, the generation of matter, the double selfhood of human beings and the complementarity of the processes of emanation and reversion.[13]

There are, however, aspects of Plotinus' metaphysics which bear more directly than others on the ethically charged reflections contained in the *Enneads*. These reflections, like other aspects of Plotinus' philosophy, cannot be fully understood in isolation from their doctrinal context. While it is commonly assumed that Kant's *Groundwork to the Metaphysic of Morals*, for instance, can profitably be studied by those who are largely untutored in the complexities of the first *Critique*, Plotinus' ethical reflections are almost unintelligible unless placed within the metaphysical background that alone can give them significance. This is all the more so in that, although questions of ethics frequently intrude in Plotinus' thinking on a host of other matters, they are only occasionally dealt with as such, as in tractates *Enn*. I.2[19] and *Enn*. I. 4[46]. If, therefore, we are to take the full measure of Plotinus' ethical teachings and avoid projecting upon them the assumptions described above, all of which stem from the view that the main function of ethics is to give us reasons to counter our innate self-partiality, we must first turn to those elements of Plotinus' metaphysics that render otiose the formulation of narrowly conceived other-regarding norms.

METAPHYSICS AND MORALITY

Plotinus' description of the emanation and return of the Soul is the anchor point of his ethics. Since this is the most puzzling, if not the most paradoxical, part of his system, the first task that confronts the would-be student of Plotinus' ethics is to understand how he accounts for the emergence of moral norms in a metaphysical process that he consistently characterizes as timeless and necessary. And, as if this was not paradox enough, he makes compliance with the moral norms in question part of the purificatory process that enables individual human souls to return to their ontological priors. The lack of symmetry between Plotinus' account of the descent of Soul and that of her return is perplexing. Why, the reader may ask at this point, is the ascending soul a soul who ascends of her own initiative while the descending soul is a soul who complies with "a law" inscribed in her nature?[14] In this section I shall consider the two paradoxes raised by Plotinus' presentation of the soul as a reality whose descent is necessary, but whose return, on the part of one of her manifestations, is a matter of moral understanding and agency.

Soul, as we know, is a hypostasized logical "moment" or "stage" in a necessary process of emanation which begins with the perfect unity and goodness of the One and ends with the non-being and abjectness of matter. More internally complex than her priors, Soul descends in stages. The World Soul, issuing forth from Intellect, generates, in turn, individual human souls and nature in its various manifestations. As the emanative process runs out of power, lifeless matter is produced. Though necessary, the descent of individual souls into body, which is a *sine qua non* condition of the fulfilment of their mission in the world of sense, is compatible with their ascent to the higher realities from which they proceed and in which their highest element remains. But if descent is a stage in a metaphysical process which brooks no exception, ascent is a moral ideal, which, as such, may prove to be beyond the reach of souls too weak to resist the demands that corporeality makes upon them. To come within reach of this moral ideal, so Plotinus teaches, embodied human souls must be attentive to the imprints of the higher realities that they bear within themselves. The moral life, therefore, as he conceives it, is a life consistently inspired by the knowledge that our soul, while being herself, is also an image (*indalma*) of higher realities and that she will find that her perfect (*teleia*) and true (*alēthinē*) life is in the intelligible realm (*Enn*. I.4[46].3.33–7). Let us now look at some of the philosophical difficulties encountered on the way to this conclusion.

As an intermediary between the two higher hypostases and the world below, Soul, in Plotinus' famous phrase, is an "amphibious reality", a reality with a twofold nature and role.[15] Although an emanant of *Nous*, Soul never altogether leaves her prior; although the World Soul and human souls do descend, they leave something of themselves in the Intelligible Principle (*Enn.* IV.8[6].8.2–3). By her very nature, therefore, as Plotinus often reminds us, Soul belongs to the higher world. On the other hand, as a separate hypostasis, whose function is to generate and govern the sensory universe, it is also part of Soul's nature and ontological mission to attend to the world that she has generated. For an incarnate soul, this means, *inter alia*, ministering to the needs and wants of the particular body to which she is joined. While it is appropriate that incarnate souls should do so, the caring role is not without risks, since the body, immersed as it is in the material world, proves to be, more often than not, a distracting presence for the soul by repeatedly presenting her with occasions for forgetting her higher nature. As Plotinus conceives it, self-forgetfulness takes the form of moral lapses. The introduction of morality, which itself presupposes some degree of freedom, raises the paradoxes mentioned above. If, as we shall see, Plotinus shares our modern assumption that freedom from certain constraints – external or internal – is a condition of voluntary action,[16] the question arises as to how he can ascribe moral responsibility to human souls for doing what is in accord with their amphibious nature and metaphysical mission.

Plotinus' choice of words is partly responsible for the paradoxes. His heavy reliance on images and metaphors imparts a degree of conceptual fuzziness to terms that philosophers such as Aristotle had taken care to define or circumscribe. Partly as a result, Plotinus' key terminology is not infrequently at odds with later philosophical usage. His concepts of voluntariness and necessity are cases in point, being both equivocal and bearers of connotations foreign to later thinkers. While these thinkers, for the most part, take the concepts of voluntariness and necessity to be antithetical, Plotinus refused the antithesis and claimed that the descent of the soul was both necessary and voluntary. Was he inconsistent in doing so? Since the paradox entailed by the use of contradictory terms to describe one and the same metaphysical process would affect the consistency of the Plotinian system as a whole, the matter fully deserves the careful consideration that it has received over the last few decades. The vast and highly polemical literature that has grown around the issue has led to a better understanding of Plotinus' idiosyncratic concept of necessity.[17] As a key feature in a system that purports to account for the derivation of the many from unity, Plotinian necessity would be classified by modern philosophers of logic as a metaphysical necessity with a *de re* modality, true of all possible worlds. So much is in accord with Plotinus' own comparison of necessity to a "law" (*nomos*) inscribed within the soul, a law "which does not derive from outside the strength for its accomplishment, but is given to be in those who are subject to it, and they bear it about with them" (*Enn.* IV.3[27].13).[18] Working its way from within the nature of what is subject to it, Plotinian necessity, as applied to the descent of soul, precludes deliberation and choice as well as the operation of external causes.

Necessity, so understood, is compatible with voluntariness (*to hekousion*) if "voluntariness" is taken to denote the spontaneous and unreflective yielding to a natural impulse, yearning or in-built tendency. Necessity is not compatible with voluntariness if voluntariness is taken to refer to actions properly so-called; that is, "doings" or "undertak-
—ings" resulting from deliberation and choice and carried out in the absence of external constraints or in spite of them.[19] The examples of voluntary behaviour that Plotinus gives in IV.3[27].13 show that he understands the concept in the first of the above two senses

since he compares the descent of soul into body to the sprouting of beard and horns, the passionate desire for sexual union or indeed the unreasoning impulse to perform noble deeds. Aware of the conceptual tension involved in describing the same "event" or "process" as both necessary and voluntary, Plotinus repeatedly emphasizes the impulsive character of the soul's descent. In the early tractate *On the Souls' Descent into Bodies* (*Enn.* IV.8[6].5), defending Plato against a charge of inconsistency which he suspected might be levelled also at himself, Plotinus writes: "there is … no contradiction (*ou diaphōnei*) between the sowing to birth and the descent for the perfection of the All" (ll.1–2).[20] Later, in the tractate *On Difficulties about the Soul I* (*Enn.* IV.3[27].13.17–18), he specified: "the souls go neither willingly nor because they are sent, nor is the voluntary element in their going like deliberate choice (*hekousion*)".[21]

Descent, however, is also decline and Plotinus, always a Platonist, held that "whatever goes to the worse does so unwillingly (cf. *to akousion*)" (*Enn.* IV.8[6].5.8). He ascribed the souls' descent to a flaw (*hamartia*) in their nature.[22] In that context, *hamartia*, one of the densest words in the Greek philosophical vocabulary, does carry negative moral connotations, which may be taken to refer to the souls' *tolma* (audacity) or "wish to belong to themselves" (cf. *to boulēthēnai de heautōn einai*), a *tolma* that causes them to be ignorant of their true nature and to turn away from the higher world of their origin (see e.g. V.I[10].1.1–5). Such *hamartia*, Plotinus took care to specify, can refer to two things, namely the cause (*aitia*) of their descent or the wrongdoings (*kaka drasai*) of which the individual soul is guilty during her sojourn here below (see also I.1[53].9 *passim*). While the soul's *hamartia* is unavoidable and therefore exempt from blame, the wrongdoings committed by incarnate souls are avoidable and blameworthy. To describe them, as will presently be seen, Plotinus relies on the language of morality.

This is the point at which Plotinus' concept of "freedom" becomes central to the discussion. What makes the incarnate human soul, after her necessary descent in the material world, capable of resisting the promptings of corporeality and of turning upwards to Intellect? The answer lies in Plotinus' conception of the role of the *logizomenon* (the discursive faculty) in human souls.[23] In his reinterpretation of Plato's tripartite division of the human soul,[24] Plotinus assigned to the *logizomenon* or middle part (*to meson*) of the soul the role of "managing" (*dioikousa*, *Enn.* II.9[33].2.14) the body and, more generally, to steer a rational course through the vicissitudes of embodied life. Mostly turned outwards, this element processes the data of sense perception, and, when keeping to its median function, uses inferential reasoning to understand the world of sense and guide our way in it. The *logizomenon* of Plotinus' description is a characteristically human capacity, which is "in the middle between two powers, a worse and a better, the worse that of sense perception, the better that of Intellect" (*Enn.* V.3[49].3.38–9; see also *Enn.* IV.8[6].8.15 and *Enn.* I.8[51].2.9–15). But, if the natural role of the *logizomenon* is to mediate between the highest and the lowest part of the human soul, it is not unalterably fixed. Indeed, by being attentive to the intimations of the higher realities that it bears within itself, the *logizomenon* is capable, albeit intermittently, of lifting itself up to the highest part of the soul. So doing, it gains in power as well as in beauty (cf. *Enn.* II.9[33].2.16: *kalliōn kai dunatōtera*) and becomes better able to illuminate "what comes after it". Conversely, by conceding too much to the physical nature, it is prone to let itself be dragged down to the lowest part of the soul. The authority that it has by rights is then compromised and its power weakened. The action-guiding role of the *logizomenon*, as well as its capacity to go either to the better or to the worse, make it the site of human freedom.

From Plotinus' description of the *logizomenon*, it is to be inferred that there can be no freedom for it, or indeed any part of the soul, to go against her nature or indeed to pursue the worse course. Holding, like the Platonic Socrates, that no one would, knowingly and voluntarily, "choose" the worse course,[25] Plotinus wrote: "the real drive of desire of our soul is towards that which is better. When that is present within it, it is fulfilled and at rest" (*Enn.* I.4[46].6.17–18). Human souls whose life here below is in accord with their higher nature enjoy as great a power of self-determination (*to eph' hēmin* or *to autexousion*) as is compatible with their embodied condition (see e.g. *Enn.* I.4[46].6.17). By contrast, souls whose desires lead them away from the good find themselves progressively enslaved to physical nature and alienated from their true self (*Enn.* VI.8[39].2–4). Since erring souls are, to a large extent, the agents of their own enslavement, Plotinus blames them for it, as well as for the "wrong actions" (*kaka drasai*) that their enslavement leads them to perform. Going beyond blame, he turns to philosophical instruction in order to remind them that they belong by nature to the higher world.[26] Should they, however, ignore such instruction or fail to act according to their higher nature, he warns them that punishment for self-forgetfulness is likely to take the form of reincarnation in a lower form of life.[27] The very fact that he made use of such strategies shows that he took them to have exercised a degree of self-determination in their wrongful choice of life.

Let us now take stock and evaluate the consequences for Plotinus' ethics of the two tenets of his philosophy discussed above, namely his conception of the soul as an amphibious reality and his definition of the human will as a capacity for self-determination. The first tenet has it that while the mission of the soul is to minister to the world of sense, her own destiny is in the higher world. The second tenet has it that in actively ministering to the world of sense, the human soul is constrained both by external contingencies and her inner impulses and passions. As a result, her freedom of choice is doubly limited. By contrast, the soul who has purified herself from the passions and taken her distances from earthly commitments is as free as an embodied reality can be.

The tension in Plotinus' ethics, it will now be argued, mirrors the paradoxes in his metaphysics of the soul. There are two strands in the moral advice that he gives to the human soul, the one favouring a modicum of engagement in the world below, the other favouring return to, and contemplation of, the higher realities from which she is emanated. While teaching that it is good for the soul to follow her natural inclination and manage the external world, Plotinus, as will now be seen, is far more often prone to stress that the soul's natural tendency to look after her product is to be held in check if her care for the bodily nature is not to jeopardize her own integrity as a member of the higher world. While occasionally reassuring the soul that no harm need come to her through caring for her inferior, he more often presents the body as an encumbrance which, in admittedly extreme circumstances, may even have to be jeopardized for the sake of preserving the integrity of the soul.[28] As a preliminary step to considering Plotinus' theory of the virtues, let us now turn to two passages in which he assesses differently the risks that embodiment presents for the soul.

Chapter seventeen of *Enn.* IV.3[27] (*On Difficulties about the Soul*) is representative of Plotinus' pessimistic account of the consequences for the soul of too close an engagement with the body.[29] The passage is a vivid description of the progressive dimming of the light given out by descending souls as they approach the earth. At the start of the descent, in the heavenly regions which border directly on the lowest reaches of the Intelligible realm, the radiance is strong, but, as the souls continue their descent, a descent that Plotinus here describes as not being "to their advantage",[30] the light they emit gets dimmer. As a consequence, "the things which are illuminated need more care" and the souls become ever more closely engaged with their product. Having each become associated with a body, they have almost reached the end of their descent. Although possibly unaware of what threatens them from then on, incarnate souls tend to behave like frantic seamen in charge of steering a vessel through a storm. As Plotinus writes:

> just as the steersmen of ships in a storm concentrate more and more on the care of their ships and are unaware that they are *forgetting themselves*, that they are in danger of being *dragged down* with the wreck of the ships, these souls incline downwards more with what is theirs. Then they are held *fettered* with bonds of magic, held fast by their care (*kēdemonia*) for the bodily nature.   (ll. 22–8)

In this sombre and not entirely helpful metaphor, in which the vessel stands for the pilot's body, the impending shipwreck is being considered from two contrasting points of view: that of the pilot, who may also stand for the reader of the passage, and that of Plotinus, who tells the story. While the pilot is exclusively preoccupied with the safeguard of the vessel (or the survival of his body), Plotinus' sole concern is for the pilot's soul. While the pilot takes the vessel to be what needs to be saved from the storm, Plotinus holds that the pilot has misidentified the object he is to care for and that, when he puts his all in an attempt to save it, he acts in ignorance of his true nature.

At this point the metaphor becomes a little confusing: when Plotinus writes that the pilot is in danger "of being dragged down with the wrecks of the ship" (ll. 24–5), he does not mean that the pilot and the ship are one and the same thing, but that the pilot, having mistakenly made common cause with the ship, is now at risk of sinking with it. Fettered as if by bonds of magic, he has lost the inner freedom to resist the promptings of fear and his behaviour is now entirely dictated by the movements of the waves. Instead of caring for what he should care for, namely his soul or higher self, he devotes all his efforts to the safeguard of the physical object with which he is currently associated (ship or body). In the process, he lets himself be immersed in matter. Bodily death, Plotinus claims in this passage, is not the worst misfortune that can befall the steersman – or indeed the reader of the passage.

From the pessimistic account of soul's engagement with body given in this passage a clear ethical conclusion follows: the best life for an incarnate soul to lead is one in which the utmost care is given to that which most deserves it, namely the higher element in the compound. Were the steersman of Plotinus' metaphor to become actively aware of the divine nature of his soul, he would endeavour to separate her, "as far as possible, from his lower nature" (*Enn.* I.2[19].7.24–5; see also *Enn.* V.1[10].3); instead of being wholly absorbed by his care for the vessel (or body), he would reach out to the divine in himself and direct his sight to Intellect.

While it must be emphasized that such bleak warnings against too close an engagement with the body preponderate in the *Enneads*, it should, even so, be recognized that a more optimistic note is occasionally sounded. One such occasion occurs in the tractate *On the*

Descent of Souls into Bodies (*Enn.* IV.8[6]), where Plotinus denies that harm invariably comes to the soul through her association with body: "it is not evil in every way for soul to give body the ability to flourish and to exist, because not every kind of provident care (*pronoia*) for the inferior deprives the being exercising it of its ability to remain in the highest" (2.24–6).

Although the tone is guarded and the point negatively put, the chapters that follow provide groundings for a more positive outlook. In chapter five, having turned his attention from hypostatic Soul to incarnate human souls, Plotinus outlines the beneficial aspects of their descent and embodiment:

> when it is eternally necessary by the law of nature that it [the soul] should do and experience these things [the soul's experience in the outer world] and, descending from that which is above it, it meets the need of something else in its encounter with it, if anyone said that a god sent it down he would not be out of accord with the truth or with himself. (5.10–14)

To substantiate the point, which he clearly regards as important, Plotinus proceeds to make three distinct claims: (1) the soul's descent brings order and beauty (cf. *kosmēsei*) to the world below (ll. 26–7); (2) the soul herself need not be harmed by her descent and the knowledge of evil acquired in the process (ll. 27–9); (3) the soul may even benefit from gaining some *experience* of evil (7.8–17). Let us briefly take these claims in turn.

According to the first claim, as developed in chapters five to seven of the tractate, the beneficial action of soul on the world below would appear to be of a mostly aesthetic nature. So much is suggested by Plotinus' choice of words; to the soul, we read, is to be credited the wondrous variety (cf. *tēs poikilias*) of fine things (*ta glaphyra*) in the world of sense as well as the greatest perceptible beauty in it (*to en aisthētōi kalliston*). The very existence of such beauty, he explains, is a direct result of soul's descent, a descent which makes it possible for her to unfold powers that would otherwise have remained hidden and unknown, and to give everything in the physical universe a share in the nature of the good. One might have expected Plotinus at this point to mention that the beneficial action of soul in the outer world includes practical activities prompted by concern for the welfare of fellow embodied souls. But he does not do so, and we must take it as highly significant that there should be no mention of "other-related" norms and activities in the one tractate he devoted to outlining the beneficial aspects of the descent of soul into body.

Claims two and three are focused on the soul and the effect that her sojourn in the physical world may have upon her. Plotinus argues, not only that it is possible for the soul to remain unharmed by the knowledge of evil acquired through her descent, but also that she may actually be benefited by it. Although surprising at first, the two claims are consonant with the optimistic tone of the tractate as a whole. They also constitute the first expression of a point of doctrine on which Plotinus would never vary afterwards, namely that the soul in us cannot be permanently harmed by too close an engagement with the material world.

The steps of the argument are as follows. Having first drawn attention to the soul's beneficial action on the world below, Plotinus repeats the familiar point that her care for it must go only so far and no further, on pain of jeopardizing her well-being. He then draws a distinction which turns out to be crucial for the understanding of the rest of the tractate, the distinction between wise and weak souls. Wise souls are those who, while joined to a body, yet succeed in maintaining themselves in universal soul and share in the royal command that she exercises over the world below (4.5–9). Theirs is the right course; they descend, but do not fall. Weak souls, by contrast, sink deep into the body to which they are joined, fret over it, allow themselves to be caught in its fetters and come to act by sense rather than intellect. They are the fallen souls; having become ignorant of their true nature, they have isolated themselves from universal soul.

Fallen souls, however, need not remain fallen, since, in Plotinus' view, evil is power-less to impair the soul in any fundamental way. Although he regards moral evil, namely "the evil that men do",[31] as a serious risk for human souls, he consistently stresses that, however deeply engulfed in the material world a soul has allowed herself to become, she cannot altogether lose the "transcendent something (*hyperechon ti*)" that she holds within (*Enn.* IV.8[6].4.31 and 8.18). In appropriate conditions, therefore, and given the right motivation, such a soul can, through the cultivation of her transcendent element, loosen the fetters – mostly self-made – that bind her to the world below. This point of doctrine constitutes the background against which the puzzling claims proffered in chapters five and seven of the tractate are to be understood.

In these chapters, Plotinus reassures the human soul that, although she must be wary of the ever-present risk of moral evil, the risk could never be fatal; while some rare souls are able to withstand it altogether, others emerge stronger from a brief experience of it. It is at that point that Plotinus puts forward the claim that, by escaping quickly enough from the quagmire below, some human souls can remain altogether unharmed by acquiring the knowledge of evil "if it [the soul] escapes quickly enough it has come to no harm (*ouden beblaptai*) by acquiring a knowledge of evil (*gnōsin kakou*) and coming to know (*gnousa*) the nature of wickedness (*physin kakias*)" (*Enn.* IV.8[6].5.27–9, trans. Armstrong, modified).[32]

These lines raise several large questions: how could a self-professed Platonist conceive of evil as an object of knowledge? Furthermore, assuming that the evil in question is moral, as opposed to metaphysical, how would a soul acquire such knowledge without her vision being clouded as a result? Lastly, on the assumption that the exceptional soul mentioned in the passage is the "perfect soul" described in a later tractate (*Enn.* I.8[51].4.25–8), a soul who "neither sees nor approaches anything undefined and unmeasured and evil", the ques-tion arises as to how a human being could reach adulthood while remaining altogether untouched by evil.[33] However, since these questions are only tangentially related to the problem at issue, the claim made in the above-quoted lines will have to remain unravelled in the present context.

In chapter seven, Plotinus returns to the issue and, this time, the message is less paradoxi-cal. He now seeks to assuage any annoyance that the soul may feel for associating too eagerly with the world of sense. He tells her that, since her metaphysical role is to straddle the divide between the divine and the sensible realms, she should not be "vexed with herself" (*ouk aganaktēteon autēn heautēi*, 7. 4) for giving to the perceptible world "something … of what she has in herself and taking back (*antilambanein*) something from it in return" (7.8–9, trans. Armstrong, modified). He reassures the weaker soul that even though it would be to her true advantage to be turned to the intelligible world, there are, even so, benefits to be drawn from tarrying in the world of sense. From her association with the body, he writes, she might derive not indeed a "knowledge of evil", but an "*experience* of evil":

> If it [the soul] does not use only its safe part in governing the universe, but with great eagerness plunges into the interior and does not stay with the whole; especially as it is possible for it to emerge again having acquired the whole story of what it saw and experienced here (*entautha*) and learnt what it is like to be There (*ekei*), and by the comparison … learning, in a way more clearly, the better things. For the experience of evil (*tou kakou peira*) is a clearer knowledge of the Good (*gnōsis enargestera*) for those whose power is too weak to know evil with clear intellectual certainty (cf. *epistēmēi*) before experiencing it.   (7.9–17)

For weaker yet suitably disposed souls, Plotinus here avers optimistically, some experience of the deficiencies of evil can make the Good shine out all the more by comparison. This presupposes that the weaker souls in question have not become entirely alienated from the divine world of their origins, but have retained, through their 'transcendent element', what Plotinus calls "an intelligent desire" (cf. *orexei noerai*, 4.1) to return to the higher realities. If, as seems likely, such is Plotinus' meaning, the question now arises as to how "intelligent desire" should be rekindled or fostered in those souls.

Ethics comes to occupy centre stage against the background of the distinction between, on the one hand, exceptional souls who are able to know evil with clear intellectual certainty without experiencing it and, on the other hand, weaker-minded souls who need to experience evil to gain a clearer knowledge of the Good. To understand this somewhat confusing distinction, we need to turn to the tractates that Plotinus devoted to questions of ethics, as the subject had been understood since Aristotle.

THE VIRTUES

Plotinus' reinterpretation of the distinction between demotic and purificatory virtues that he had found in Plato is far more significant than is commonly realized.[34]

Not all ways of practising the virtues, so Plato had claimed in the *Phaedo* (68c–69a), are equally valid. When the virtues are inculcated "by habit and training" (*Phd.* 82b2) and practised out of a prudential desire to lead as trouble-free or pleasurable an earthly existence as possible, they are appropriately called "simple-minded" (*euēthē*, *Phd.* 65e5) or "demotic and political" (*dēmotikē kai politikē*, *Phd.* 82a12–b1) and dismissed as mere appearances of virtue. When, by contrast, they are a result of "philosophy and understanding" (*philosophias te kai nou*, *Phd.* 82b3), and are practised out of deference to the immortal element in us and the desire to keep it as immune as possible from bodily contamination (*Phd.* 67c6–7), they are appropriately classified as modes of "purification" (*katharsis*, *Phd.* 67c5). In the *Republic*, the austere implications of the distinction first drawn in the *Phaedo* were to be toned down, if only to take account of the lengthy process of selection and formation of the future guardians, a process which would require that the civic virtues be inculcated in the souls of all young citizens, regardless of their future status in the ideal republic. But, even in the context of the *Republic*, the aspersions that Plato had earlier cast on the civic manner of practising the virtues would not disappear entirely. While he assigned the civic virtues to the guards and the producers, in conformity with their class and calling, he expected that those selected for the guardianship of the city would progress from the civic to the purificatory virtues and, in the process, become as godlike as a human being can be.[35]

In the tractate *On Virtues* (*Enn.* I.2[19]) Plotinus proceeded to rehabilitate the civic virtues. Against the master who had denied that they could make us godlike (3.9–10), he argued that "it is unreasonable (*alogon*) to suppose that we are not made godlike in any way by the civic virtues, but that likeness comes from the greater ones" (1.23–6). The specific contribution of the civic virtues to the life of the embodied soul, he continued, is:

> genuinely [to] set us in order and make us better by giving limit and measure to our desires, and generally by putting measure into the passions; and they abolish false opinions, by what is altogether better and by the fact of limitation, and by the exclusion of the unmeasured and indefinite in accord with their measuredness; and they are themselves limited and clearly defined. And so far as they are a measure which forms the matter of the soul, they are made like the measure There (*ekei*) and have a trace (*ichnos*) of the Best There.   (2.14–20, trans. Armstrong, modified)

So reinterpreted, the civic virtues exert their regulatory influence at the point at which the soul interacts with the material world. This they do in two ways, which are not mutually exclusive. They restrain or curb affections originating in the bodily part of the compound and lessening, therefore, the hold that these affections have on the soul, make it easier for her to resist their demands and maintain her independence. They also abolish false opinions and uncriticized mental images and thereby moderate or altogether extinguish the affections that arise out of them.[36]

How do the civic virtues achieve this? The emphasis that Plotinus places on measure and limitation in the above-quoted lines strongly suggests that he regards the civic virtues as ethical manifestations of the operation in us of the *logizomenon*, whose function, as seen above, is to mediate between the higher and the lower part of the soul. By bringing reasoned thought and order to our lives, the *logizomenon* ensures that each element in the soul plays its allotted part, with reason exercising its rule over passion and appetite and thereby training the irrational part (*to alogon*) into habits of easy compliance. So doing, the *logizomenon* enables the embodied soul to evaluate rationally, and react fittingly to, the adventitious and ever-changing circumstances in which she finds herself in the world of sense.[37] An embodied soul in whom the *logizomenon* functions as it should is a soul who possesses the civic virtues of courage, moderation, practical wisdom and justice, understood as so many dispositions (*diatheseis*) to ensure the harmonious interaction between the plurality of her parts. Lastly, by taming the passions and replacing prejudiced opinion by reasoned judgement, the civic virtues enlarge the domain of what is in our power (*to eph' hēmin*).

However, if the civic virtues play a valuable role in the life of the embodied soul, it is nonetheless only a propaedeutic one. If they set her on the road to godlikeness by sustaining, or reactivating, the "transcendent something" (*hyperechon ti*) (see p. 407 *supra*) that lies within herself, they only take her part of the way. If they "build up"[38] her freedom, they cannot ensure her independence from the external factors in the outer world which, by definition, lie outside her control.[39] To that extent, the civic virtues cannot but be a preliminary stage in a process of purification that must go further and deeper, if it is to succeed in dissociating, so far as possible, the soul from the body to which she is temporarily joined and in making her capable of fulfilling her destiny in the higher world. Their function, beyond guiding the embodied soul in her dealings with the lower world, is to alert her to the traces of the higher realities that she bears within herself and, in so doing, to awaken her to her true nature, and foster her desire to return to her priors.

Does this mean, therefore, that the function of the civic virtues, ideally, is to make themselves redundant by giving way to the purificatory virtues which alone can guide the soul to the true object of her aspiration? The polemics recorded in § "The problem" above stem, for the most part, from the different interpretations that scholars have put on the few passages in which Plotinus considers the question. We shall turn to these passages shortly.

To progress beyond the civic virtues, the embodied soul must "draw together to itself in a sort of place of its own away from the body" (5.4–5). Loosening the ties that bind her to the world below, she must withdraw from the "perceptible sounds" that emanate from it and, by "turning her power of apprehension inwards", make it accessible to "the voices from on high" (adapted from *Enn.* V.I[10].12.13–20). Striving to make herself immune to the pull of pleasure and pain, the soul must do all she can to lessen the impact that passion, emotion and irrational desire would otherwise have upon her as a whole. Rather than simply taming, or training, the irrational part, the higher part of the soul must seek to purify it, so as to make it as "like" herself as possible, and thereby avoid making the incarnate soul into a "spirit who is double" (5.21–31; see also 6.5–11). Once completed, the process of integration of the inferior into the superior will ensure, not only that the embodied soul avoids "culpable error" (*hamartia*), but also, more importantly, that she becomes "godlike" (6.1–3). The virtues of such a soul, rather than fostering harmony between the plurality of her parts, are best described as the kind of dispositions that a unity has to itself:

> the higher justice in the soul is its activity towards intellect, its self-control is its inward turning to intellect, its courage is its freedom from affections, according to the likeness of that to which it looks which is free from affections by nature: this freedom from affections in the soul comes from virtue, to prevent her sharing in the affections of her inferior companion.   (6.23–7)

In setting the soul free from both bodily affections and the tyranny of ever-changing and often unpredictable external circumstances, the purificatory virtues give their possessors as great a power of self-determination (*to autexousion*) as a human being can hope to enjoy.

As can be seen, Plotinus did not regard the civic and the purificatory virtues as different in kind, as Plato had done in the *Phaedo*, but as constituting stages – or degrees – in a process of purification whose ultimate aim is to render the soul in us capable of achieving the kind of mystical union described in IV.8[6].1. Plotinus' conception of virtue as constituting a scale explains why, outside the tractate *On Virtues*, he rarely specifies whether it is the civic or the purificatory virtues that he is referring to.

If the two sets of virtues constitute a scale of moral and spiritual progression leading the embodied soul to her optimal state of being, must it be concluded that the possession of the purificatory virtues renders otiose the practice of the civic ones? Plotinus' answer to this crucial question, as recorded in the tractate *On Virtues*, is less clear than might be wished. On the one hand, he tells us that it is a matter of necessity (*ex anagkēs*, 7.11) that whoever possesses the higher virtues possesses the lower ones "potentially" (*dynamei*, *ibid.*), although perhaps not "in act" (*energeiai*, l.13). On the other hand, he keenly stresses that a man who has reached the higher level will not choose to return to the life he has left behind, preferring instead to follow the "higher principles and different measures" that Intellect gives to those who have rendered themselves capable of receiving them (*Enn.* I.2[19].7.21–2; I.3[20].5.1–2). Such a man, he writes:

> will altogether (*holōs*) separate himself, as far as possible, from his bodily nature and will altogether (*holōs*) dissociate himself from the life of the good man (*ton anthropou bion ton tou agathou*), which civic virtue recommends. He will leave that life behind and choose another, the life of the gods; for it is to them, not to good men, that we are to be made like.   (7.23–8, trans. Armstrong, modified)

This is a key passage for the understanding of Plotinus' conception of the role of virtue in the best life (cf. *zōēn ten aristēn*, *Enn.* IV.8[6].1.4) for a human being to lead. While he recognizes that the separation of the soul from the body can only be "so far as possible", the doctrine of the inviolability of the soul *qua* soul enables him to argue that the ideal of godlikeness can be achieved while the soul is in the body and, therefore, that *eudaimonia* can be reached without the direct participation of the body.[40] When engaged in the contemplation of the higher realities, the possessor of the purificatory virtues, Plotinus here tells us, leaves behind the "life of the good man"; being at one with his higher self, he shares "the life of the gods". Engaging in the highest activity of which human beings are capable, such a man has become, not only as self-determining, but also as *eudaimōn*, as an embodied being can be.

According to the moral norms implied in the above-quoted lines, those who are capable of leading the "life of the gods" will rightly choose it in preference to the "life of the good man". Once more, therefore, the question arises as to whether the Plotinian good life is a life aimed at the higher realities and unperturbed by active participation in the lives of other human beings at either the personal or the civic level. In the hope of bringing further elements of answer to the question, I now turn to two passages in which Plotinus arguably adopts a less uncompromising position than in the texts so far discussed.

The first and, by far, the most significant passage occurs in the context of a discussion of human freedom in the tractate *On Free Will and the Will of the One* (*Enn.* VI.8[39]). In chapter five of that tractate Plotinus argues that no virtuous action undertaken in response to adventitious circumstances in the outer world can be free in the full sense of the term, since neither the occasion for performing it nor its final outcome are within the agent's control. So much, he proceeds to claim, accounts for virtue's reluctance to be compelled (*anagkazomenēs*) "to cope with what turns up" (*pros to prospipton … ergazesthai*, 5.13) in the outer world:

> if someone gave virtue itself the choice whether it would like in order to be active that there should be wars, that it might be brave, and that there should be injustice that it might define what is just and set things in order, and poverty, that it might display its liberality, or to stay quiet because everything was well, it would choose to rest from its practical activities because nothing needed its curative action (*oudenos therapeias deomenou*), as if a physician, for instance Hippocrates, were to wish that nobody needed his skill.   (*Enn.* VI.8[39].5.13–20)

This quasi-prosopopaeic passage, in which Plotinus takes it upon himself to speak in virtue's name, shows that he does allot her a role, albeit a modest one, in dealing with a range
of conditions in the outer world such as war, injustice and poverty. Intruding into the life
of the virtuous agent, such circumstances compel him to actualize the civic virtues that
had lain dormant in him since he attained the purificatory ones.[41] Although it is right that
the virtuous agent should do so, the reactive nature of his intervention inevitably reduces
the extent of "what is in his power".[42] Just as a physician prescribes a course of treatment
(*therapeia*) to deal with an illness or an accident, virtue does not shy away from doing what
it can to alleviate, or to rectify, such desperate states of affairs in the world below.[43] Plotinus'
use of the metaphor of therapy, as well as his comparison of virtue to a somewhat reluctant
physician, are highly significant. Although the virtuous agent, like the responsible physician, will not refuse to intervene whenever he perceives that there is a need to be met, he
will not, even so, seek to do any more than undertake curative action.[44] Indeed, from the
examples given above, it seems clear that Plotinus did not envisage that virtue would, or
should, seek to prevent – as opposed to curing – the future occurrence of external calami-
ties by devising or implementing economic and political strategies to forestall their occurrence.[45] Although modern readers may find this a curious omission on Plotinus' part, his
position is fully consonant with his metaphysics.[46] The conception of virtue as "a kind of
other intellect (*nous*) … which intellectualises the soul" (5.34–6) commits him to the view
that the life of action, however worthy, cannot but be second best to the life of contemplation; while the former keeps the soul anchored in the world below, the latter lifts her above
the contingencies of embodied existence and enables her to share in the godlike activity
of Intellect. However, as the above-quoted lines show, this did not prevent Plotinus from
conceding that contemplation might, on occasion, have to be interrupted or postponed in
order to enable virtue to deal with calamitous events and circumstances in the outer world.

A second passage in which Plotinus arguably shows himself to be favourably disposed
to the life of action in the outer world comes from the tractate *On the Good or the One*
(*Enn.* VI.9[9]). As mentioned in § "The problem" above, the passage has recently benefited from a detailed analysis on the part of Dominic O'Meara, who claims to have found
in it evidence that Plotinus considered civic engagement to be a worthy by-product of
communion with the highest reality (D. O'Meara 2003: 74–6). The passage has a strong
prescriptive flavour unusual in the *Enneads*: having explained how the soul must prepare
herself for mystical communion, Plotinus outlines the responsibility incumbent upon
those who have achieved the vision they were aiming at:

> the soul *must* let go of all outward things and turn altogether to what is within, and
> not be inclined to any outward thing, but ignoring all things … and even ignoring
> itself, come to be in contemplation of that One, and having been in its company
> and had, so to put it, sufficient converse with it, come and announce, if it could, to
> another that transcendent union. *Perhaps* also it was because Minos attained this
> kind of union that he was said in the story to be "the familiar friend of Zeus", and
> it was in remembering this that he laid down laws in its image (cf. *eidōla*), being
> filled full of lawgiving by the divine touch (*plēroumenos*). Or, because he considers
> that even the affairs of the city are unworthy of his attention, he therefore wants to
> remain above always; this is liable to happen to one who has seen much.
>
> (7.16–28, trans. Armstrong, modified)[47]

Plotinus is here freely adapting Plato's allusion in the opening lines of the *Laws* (1.624b) to the legendary Cretan king's lawmaking activities.[48] Conceivably, he is also alluding to his own mystical experience of "waking out of the body", as he recounted it in a passage that Porphyry would later place at the opening of *Enn.* IV.8[6]. But, if he is, a crucial difference between the two passages is to be noted: while the notion of obligation is not even mentioned in the autobiographical passage, it features centrally in the above-quoted lines, to which we now turn.

The first part of the passage, up to the mention of Minos in l.23, is semantically straightforward. The first three infinitives governed by the impersonal verb *dei* ("must"), which serve to describe the steps that a would-be visionary must take in order to achieve a "transcendent union" (*tēn ekei synousian*), all refer to points of doctrine well rehearsed in the *Enneads*. The fourth infinitive, with its attendant proviso, states that the successful visionary has an obligation to "announce" his transcendent vision to another. Aware that no obligation is binding unless it can actually be discharged, Plotinus takes care to note that only "if he can" (*ei dynaito*) should the visionary tell others what he has seen. Plotinus does not specify the form that such an announcement must take, and it is conceivable that it might consist merely in the kind of record he provided in IV.8[6].1 of his own mystical experience. That, of course, does not exclude the possibility that the announcement be of a more robust or practical nature, as suggested by the tentative introduction (cf. *hoian isōs*) of the example of Minos at this point. As a result of "being filled by the divine touch", Plotinus now speculates, Minos may have turned to lawmaking as a reflection (cf. *eidōla*) of his communion with the divine forms. Although the meaning of the passage is not in doubt, it remains unclear whether Plotinus is fully committed to the possibility illustrated by the example or whether he is simply making one of his frequent and dutiful allusions to Plato. The very vagueness of the allusion, which shows that in this case Plotinus had not bothered to check the Platonic text, suggests that the latter possibility is more likely.

As testified by successive attempts to emend the text, the passage becomes unclear with the last sentence, the difficulty being that of identifying the subject of *ethelei* in l. 27. Is it Minos or some other person? If, like recent translators, who mostly accept van Winden's emendation,[49] one takes Minos to be the subject of *ethelei*, a logical tangle ensues in so far as this last sentence in effect empties the *dei* of the binding force that Plotinus had given it in the first. Indeed, if Minos is the person who "may think even civic matters unworthy of him" (*ē kai ta politika ouk axia hautou nomisas*), the two sentences, taken together, commit Plotinus to the absurd view that unwillingness to descend to the political arena constitutes a valid exemption clause to the duty, as earlier stated, of announcing one's vision to others. If, on the other hand, one takes the subject of *ethelei* to be some other person, who, unlike Minos, refuses to engage in the affairs of the city so as to spend all his time contemplating, the two sentences express a genuine disjunction. Plotinus' position would then be that a successful visionary may choose either to come (*hēkein*) and announce his vision to others – as Minos perhaps did – or "to remain (*menein*) always above" on the ground that civic activities are not worthy of his attention. Which is the better way of reading the text? While the first reading would seem to provide a smoother way of reading the lines, the second has the principle of charity on its side. Unfortunately, the issue is not hermeneutically neutral, in so far as one's choice of reading is likely to reflect the position one takes on the nature of Plotinus' ethics.

Wisely disregarding the problem of ascertaining the contribution that the second sentence makes to the argument, O'Meara turns to a later tractate for substantiation of his thesis that Plotinus regards political engagement as a valid way of disseminating the knowledge gained through a unitive experience of the highest order:

> Men ... when their power of contemplation weakens, make action a shadow of contemplation and reasoning. Because contemplation is not enough for them, since their souls are weak and they are not able to grasp the vision sufficiently, and therefore are not filled with it (*plēroumenoi*), but still long to see it, they are carried into action, so as to see what they cannot see with their intellect. When they make something, then, it is because they want to see their object themselves and also because they want others to be aware of it and contemplate it, when their project is realised in practice as well as possible. Everywhere we shall find that making (*poiēsin*) and action (*praxin*) are either a weakening (*astheneian*) or a consequence (*parakolouthēma*) of contemplation; a weakening, if the doer or maker had nothing in view beyond the thing done, a consequence if he had another prior object of contemplation better than what he made. For who, if he is able to contemplate what is truly real will deliberately go after its image (*eidōlon*)? (*Enn.* III.8[30].4.31–44)

Although O'Meara's choice of text may initially surprise in so far as lines 31 to 35 and 43 to 44 are often quoted in support of the view that Plotinus dismissed the life of action as inferior to the life of contemplation,[50] lines 36 to 43 do, as he claims, make the point that action and production can be valid consequences of contemplation. Having drawn attention to the few parallels, verbal and non-verbal, between this passage and the one quoted previously, O'Meara proceeds to draw substantive inferences from the combination of the two. Plotinus' claim that action and production can follow from contemplation, so O'Meara tells us, "corresponds to the example of Minos in *Enn.* VI.9". Generalizing the point, O'Meara then concludes: "*Thus* political action, as indeed all action, may arise as a result that accompanies the fulfilment of philosophical knowledge" (D. O'Meara 2003: 75, emphasis added).

O'Meara's interpretation of these two passages, for all its ingenuity, calls for reservations. First, he plays down the tentative manner in which Plotinus presents Minos as a visionary who *may* (cf. *hoian isōs*, *Enn.* VI.9[9].7.23) have turned to law-making as a result of his converse with Zeus. Second, he ignores the fact that there is no mention whatsoever of civic activities in the context of the second passage he adduces as evidence for his thesis. Indeed, the argument of *Enn.* III.8[30] as a whole is aimed at showing that although contemplation is the true goal of the soul, not all souls are capable of it and lesser souls, be it Nature or human beings, have to turn to action (*praxis*) or production (*poiēsis*) in order to maintain a precarious hold on what they have seen but dimly. Unlike fully fledged contemplation, which constitutes its own end, weaker or unsteady forms of contemplation have to be sustained by activities which produce tangible results in the external world, results which stem from their producers' desire to "see their object [i.e. that which they have made] themselves" and to make others "be aware of it and contemplate it" (*Enn.* III.8[30].4.37–8). As suggested by the reference, earlier in the chapter, to the productive activity of Nature from whose weak contemplation issue "the lines which bound bodies", Plotinus is here more likely to be expressing an idea that will be developed more fully in the tractate *On Intelligible Beauty* (*Enn.* V.8[31].1), which immediately follows in the chronological order. There, in seemingly open disagreement with Plato, Plotinus writes that "the arts (cf. *tas technas*) do not simply imitate what they see, but they run back up to the forming principles from which nature derives" (ll. 35–6). Yet, striking though the disagreement on this point appears to be between the two philosophers, Plotinus does not depart from the Platonic position as radically as it might seem, since he takes care to add that although artworks may translate the artist's vision of *logoi* in the soul, the status of the works as material objects makes them ontologically inferior to, and less beautiful than, the principles from which they derive. Even in the highly favourable cases of Minos' laws or Pheidias' Zeus, the vision translated in, or for, the external world is of lesser value than pure contemplation that sustains itself independently of external means. Taken within the context of the whole of the *Enneads*, therefore, the two passages selected by O'Meara do not, it seems to me, constitute sufficient evidence that Plotinus believed that, other things being equal, political action could constitute as valid a "fulfilment of political knowledge" as pure contemplation unaccompanied by action.

Could a more modest conclusion than O'Meara's own be drawn? Could it be inferred from the passages discussed above that Plotinus does recognize that, in some admittedly rare circumstances, it is appropriate that action should take precedence over contemplation, and that the production of artifacts can be a way of expressing intelligibles contemplated from within the soul? It can, but only to a modest extent. The passage from *Enn.* VI.8[39].5, as discussed above (pp. 411–12), shows Plotinus to be willing to concede that in the event of war, famine or gross injustice in the world below, virtue would compromise her independence and undertake curative action. The passage from *Enn.* VI.9[9].7 shows that he was not so doctrinaire as to refuse to envisage the possibility that civic engagement, which by definition is concerned with the needs and entitlements of others, might be a valuable way for a visionary of giving weaker souls a share in his vision of the higher reality. As for the passage from *Enn.* III.8[30].4, whose ethical significance is negligible, it simply makes the point that production can be directly related to contemplation, a point that Plotinus later clarifies by reference to the plastic arts. Although the first two passages, taken together, do usefully correct the assumption that Plotinus' ethics is uncompromisingly otherworldly, they should not be taken to ground a conclusion that the rest of the *Enneads* invalidate. The fact that, even in these passages, Plotinus takes care to emphasize that virtue's engagement in the outer world would be hesitant or downright reluctant confirms that the otherworldly strand dominates his ethical reflections. Under normal circumstances, he held, those who are capable of discerning the light above will not be content to devote their time and energy to improving conditions in the darkness below.

Unlike Plato, therefore, Plotinus would not compel philosophers and visionaries to return to the Cave. From the available evidence it seems that he did not even seek to prepare for public life those who attended the *synousiai* he held in Rome for almost thirty years. Admittedly, as Porphyry reports in the *Vita Plotini*, he did at one time hope that a city of philosophers, Platonopolis, could be founded in the vicinity of Rome (Porphyry, *Plot.*, 12). But then Porphyry also tells us in an earlier chapter of the *Vita* that Plotinus tried to divert (*anastellein*) Zethus, a close friend of his and a valued member of the school, from embarking on the political career to which he was drawn (*ibid.*: 7.17–21).

To judge by the more reliable evidence of his own writings, Plotinus' overriding aim was to give members of his audience a stake in the system of philosophy he was developing and to motivate them to lead their life according to the principles laid in it. This he sought to achieve by opening the *synousiai* to all those who cared to attend them, irrespective of age, gender or depth of philosophical training, and by a method of instruction best described as interactive. His writings show him to have actively "philosophized" in front of his audience, either in response to the questions or objections he encouraged them to raise or through his own engagement with the views of other philosophers. Such pedagogic style, with its distinct hortatory element, was well suited to promoting philosophy as a practice or, as a famous title goes, as "a way of life".[51] To members of his circle, he was a *maître à penser*, who relied on the considerable suasive power of his style to add seductiveness to the philosophical arguments by which he sought to induce them to turn their life around (*epistrephein*) into a direction opposite (*eis ta enantia*) to the one they had so far been heading towards (*Enn.* V.I[10].1.23). His choice of metaphors, almost invariably apt, drew them into the spirit of his philosophy. So much is testified by his use of the metaphor of stillness, to which we now, very briefly, turn.

Plotinus' mostly commendatory use of *hēsychia* and its cognates, not only to describe the higher levels of reality, but also to characterize the inner state which most becomes the human soul, tells us a great deal about his ethical thinking. To convey the value of stillness, he drew a sharp contrast between, on the one hand, what is still, tranquil, quiet, abiding, undisturbed or gathered into itself, and, on the other, what is moving, agitated, unquiet, busy, clamouring or otherwise disturbed. The polarity between the two clusters of concepts is vividly conveyed in the following lines:

> the soul which comes from the divine was quiet (*hēsychos*), standing in itself according to its character; but the body, in a tumult (*thoryboumenon*) because of its weakness, flying away itself and battered by the flows from outside, first itself cried out to the community of the living thing and imparted its disturbance (*tarachēn*) to the whole. It is like when in an assembly the elders of the people sit in quiet consideration (*eph' hēsychōi synnoiai*), and the disorderly populace, demanding food and complaining of other sufferings, throws the whole assembly into an ugly tumult (*eis thorybon aschēmona*).   (*Enn* VI.4[22].15.18–26)[52]

The normative implications of these lines are unmistakable: the body must be brought to order if it is not to be for the soul an occasion of self-alienation by imparting its inherent weakness and instability to the compound. As seen above, the function of the virtues is to induce stillness in the embodied soul by bringing limit and measure to all the desires and passions that come to her through the body. Stillness, once achieved, enables the soul to gather unto herself, turn inwards and focus her attention on "the voices from on high" which sound within her (*ibid.*: 12.19–20). In using this particular metaphor Plotinus was relying on the positive connotations that stillness as tranquillity had for his audience in order to reinforce a conclusion he had elsewhere reached by abstract argument, namely that the best life for a human being to lead is a life of attentiveness to, and contemplation of, the higher realities. Such a life, inevitably solitary for the most part,[53] would mostly rule out active involvement in practical affairs.

CONCLUSION

I have argued above that the seemingly interminable nature of the debates generated by Plotinus' ethics is a reflection, not only of the assumptions on the nature of ethics that many a modern scholar has brought to the issue, but also of the presence of two strands in Plotinus' account of Soul's engagement with the material world. Once it is realized that the assumptions in question are anachronistic projections onto a philosophy to which they are profoundly alien, Plotinus' ethics can be seen for what it is, namely a guide to the soul in us, pointing the way she must go if she is to lead a "perfect and true life". The need for such a guide stems from the temptable and therefore peccable character of the human soul, which Plotinus describes as poised between her mission in the world below and her destiny in the world above. Unsurprisingly, the ethical reflections that Plotinus drew from his conception of the soul as an amphibious reality show a degree of variation which, in turn, goes a long way towards explaining why the nature of his ethics should have given rise to the scholarly disagreements identified in § "The problem" above. At times, Plotinus assures the incarnate soul that it is appropriate for her to give the body to which she is joined the ability to flourish and, when necessary, to engage in the affairs of men. More often, however, as we saw, he presents the body as the soul's alien garb and advises her to give it all it needs, but not all it wants. Only so will the soul in us, he claims, be able to preserve her integrity and return to the higher realities to which she belongs. In line with the moral norms that he had built into his concept of selfhood, Plotinus presented self-regard, understood as the disposition to honour the highest element in oneself, as the prime condition of virtue and the first step towards the ideal of godlikeness.

ACKNOWLEDGEMENTS

This long chapter is, in more ways than one, the result of conversations and discussions held over the years with a number of scholars, including Luc Brisson, John Dillon, Peter Herissone-Kelly, Deepa Majumdar, Denis O'Brien, Pauliina Remes, Svetla Slaveva-Griffin and the late Steven Strange. John Dillon, Denis O'Brien and Christian Tornau have all made judicious comments on the penultimate draft, most of which I have gratefully taken into account. Pauliina Remes and Svetla Slaveva-Griffin have proved to be ideal editors, being flexible and patient, mindful of their contributors' other commitments and problems while remaining utterly committed to the excellence of the volume. Let all of them be warmly thanked.

NOTES

1. Dillon (1996b: 323, 318). See also Dillon (2007: 132–3). Flamand, in his introduction to his translation and commentary of the tractate *On Virtues* (*Traités* 7–21, Brisson & Pradeau 2003: 419), expresses the same view. "Plotinus' ethics", he writes, "is somewhat disconcerting for the modern reader … neither on the theoretical nor even on the practical level does the tractate present an ethics oriented to the relation of self to others" (my trans.).
2. Bodéüs (1983: 259, my trans.). Intriguingly, Bodéüs grounds his argument in a reading of the very tractate (*Enn.* I.4[46]), in which Schniewind (2003), as will be seen below, professes to find ethical norms of an "other-regarding" nature.
3. Rist (1967: 167). See also Baltzly (2004), who argues that, after Plotinus, Proclus did much "to put human beings in general and ethics in particular back into the world" (*ibid.*: 303) and that the ideal of godlikeness, as he conceived it, "takes on a much more human form than it does in Plotinus" (*ibid.*: 319).
4. A. Smith (1999: 227, 232). Passages selected in support of this interpretation include *Enn.* VI.4[22].15.35–8 and IV.3[27].4. See also A. Smith (2004) and McGroarty (2006: 194).

5. D. O'Meara (2003: 76): the Plotinian passage in question, which is discussed further in § "The virtues" below, is *Enn.* VI.9[9].7.16–28.

6. One cannot but wonder whether the fact that Porphyry, by his own account, was in Sicily when Plotinus wrote *Enn.* I.4[46] weakens Schniewind's interpretive hypothesis.

7. It may be that in formulating this hypothesis Schniewind is adapting Porphyry's division (*Plot.* 7) of the listeners who attended the *synousiai* in Plotinus' school into three categories, namely those who led a money-making life (such as Serapion), those who engaged in politics (such as Rogatianus) and those who devoted themselves to philosophy, such as Amelius, Eustochius and Porphyry himself. For the historical context of such classifications, see Joly (1956) and Brisson *et al.* (1992: 11, 226–36).

8. In this brief review of attempts to find in Plotinus an ethic of concern for the world of sense, there is no space available to include more precisely targeted aspects of the *Enneads*, such as *Enn.* IV.3[27].9 by ecologically minded Plotinian scholars. In recent years Michael Wagner (2002a) and Kevin Corrigan (2009b), more specifically, have claimed that Neoplatonic concepts such as those of *synaptic logos* (*Enn.* III.3[48].4), *physis* as living contemplation (*Enn.* III.8[30].7), and life conceived as an organic force, can assist us in rethinking the relationship between humankind and nature, in the sense in which ecologists currently understand nature. See also T. M. Robinson & Westra (2002) as well as Corrigan (Chapter 24), above.

9. Most twentieth-century forms of ethical anti-foundationalism derive from the so-called Hume's guillotine ("no ought from an is", *A Treatise of Human Nature*, bk III, 1). Rist (1976) had already called attention to crucial differences between Plotinus' ethical views and those of most post-Humean moral philosophers. Schniewind (2003), too, alludes to contemporary ethical anti-foundationalism, but her account of it misfires in so far as she writes that "it is not admitted that 'what is' can be deduced from 'what ought to be'" ("l'on n'admet pas que l'être (*to be*) puisse être déduit du devoir-être (*ought*)") (*ibid.*: 17). It is, of course, the other way round: what Hume and his followers warn us against is the attempt to deduct norms (i.e. "what ought to be") from facts ("what is").

10. As argued by e.g. Singer (1959: 202) and Williams (1985: 181–2).

11. The example of promise-keeping best illustrates this point: when promiser and promisee are different persons, no conceptual difficulties need be encountered in either the making of a promise or the releasing of the promiser by the promisee; when, on the other hand, the promiser and the promisee are one and the same person, both the act of promising and that of releasing the promiser from his obligation appear to be conceptually confused. For a useful account of contemporary objections to the notion of self-regarding duty, see Denis (2001).

12. Examples of duties to self mediated through duties to others would include the duty, on the part of parents, to keep themselves healthy for the sake of their dependent children as well as the more generally conceived duty to cultivate one's talents for the sake of the benefits they might bring to others.

13. Each of these aspects of Plotinus' metaphysics generates complex exegetical and philosophical problems, which are discussed in other chapters of this volume.

14. As Plotinus puts the point in *Enn.* IV.3[27].13.30–32. The issue is pellucidly analysed in Leroux (1996), to whom I am here indebted.

15. *Enn.* IV.8[6].4.32; the phrase was made famous by Inge (1929: vol. 1, 257), to whom it is often ascribed.

16. So much is clear from the discussion of human freedom in VI.8[39].1.33–4: "everything is a voluntary act (*hekousion*) which we do without being forced to and with knowledge [of what we are doing], and in our power which we are also competent to do".

17. The secondary literature on the issue, most of which also considers the problem of accounting for the origin of matter in Plotinus' monistic system, is too vast to be listed here. For a particularly lucid account of the issue, see Rist (1961, 1965) and O'Brien (1971, 1977); for dissenting views, see Schwyzer (1973), Corrigan (1986), Narbonne (1992 and Chapter 15 in the present volume) and Phillips (2009); for a critique of the dissenting views, see O'Brien (1996, 2011–12, and forthcoming) and Lavaud (in his commentary of tractate *Enn.* IV.8[6] for Brisson & Pradeau [2002–10: 264]). I am here indebted to both Rist and O'Brien who seem to me to have had the better of the controversy. Because the issue is not directly germane to my present concern, I shall not here test for consistency the various statements in which Plotinus describes the manner in which Soul descends. For a detailed analysis of the passages in question, see O'Brien (1977, 1993).

18. For the same point, couched in almost identical terms, see also *Enn.* IV.8[6].5.

19. For Plotinus' concept of action, see note 18 *supra* as well as Remes (Chapter 28), below.

20. Except when otherwise indicated, all quotations from the *Enneads* are in Armstrong's translation, with occasional modifications, flagged as such.

21. I here follow the reading of the manuscripts, not the emendation proposed by Theiler (1962) and adopted by O'Brien (1977: 408–10).

22. *Enn.* IV.8[6].5.17–18. The translation of *hamartia* into modern vernaculars raises well-known difficulties. I here adopt MacKenna's rendering ("flaw"), in preference to Armstrong's ("sin") and Fleet's ("error") on the ground that it best conveys Plotinus' view that the fact that soul's nature and destiny are in the higher world does not preclude the presence of an imperfection in her nature.

23. Also called *to dianoētikon* or *dianoia*. For a study of the diverse appellations of the middle part of the soul, see Blumenthal (1971a: 100–105), to whom I am here indebted.

24. For a clear expression of Plotinus' reinterpretation of Plato on this point, see *Enn.* II.9[33].2; V.3[49].3.

25. In Horn's (2007: 169) apt summary of Plotinus' theory of the will, "The will is not free because of its power to decide arbitrarily, but because of its possession of the faculty to act according to reason. It is not a two-way power but a faculty to adopt the good."

26. Such instruction is provided throughout V.1[10].

27. On reincarnation into a lower form of life as punishment for wrongdoings committed during embodied life, see e.g. *Enn.* IV.8[6].5.16–24; III.4[15].2; III.2[47].13. On Plotinus' views on reincarnation in general, see Rich (1957).

28. *Enn.* VI.8[39].6; for a detailed analysis of the passage, see Stern-Gillet (2013).

29. Since the theme is a recurrent one, other passages could have been selected, in particular I.7[54].3.19–22, in which Plotinus gives us his last and, one presumes, most carefully thought-out advice on the issue: "life in a body is an evil in itself, but the soul comes into good by its virtue, by not living the life of the compound but separating itself even now".

30. In MacKenna's felicitous translation, the souls are "not themselves the better for the depth to which they have penetrated".

31. In e.g. *Enn.* IV.8[6].5 and *Enn.* I.8[51].5, Plotinus uses various expressions to denote metaphysical (or cosmological) evil, which he distinguishes from moral evil. While the first kind has to do with the (necessary) descent of soul and the generation of matter, the second kind comprises the (avoidable) wrongdoings (*kaka drasai*, *Enn.* IV.8[6].5.18), for which embodied souls can be held responsible. To render as closely as possible Plotinus' expression *tēn kakian hēn anthrōpoi echousin* (*Enn.* I.8[51].5.31–2), I borrow Shakespeare's expression "the evil that men do" (*Julius Caesar*, Act III, sc. 2).

32. See also "there is an escape from the evils in the soul for those who are capable of it, though not all men are" (*Enn.* I.8[51].5.29–30).

33. Plotinus' claim in the tractate *On Dialectic* (*Enn.* I.3[20].1.9, 3.8) that the philosopher, as conceived by Plato, "goes the upward way by nature" and is "by nature virtuous" is equally puzzling in view of the long process of education to which Plato would subject the future guardians of the ideal state. However, the allusion, whether justifiable or not, is too undeveloped to shed light on Plotinus' claim in the above lines.

34. To take but one example: in the otherwise excellent commentary of *Enn.* I.2[19] by J.-M. Flamand (Brisson & Pradeau 2003) there is no discussion of doctrinal divergences on this particular point between Plato and Plotinus.

35. As shown by David Sedley (1999), to whom I am here indebted, the ideal of being made godlike maintains a presence in the *Republic* (518d–e and 613a–b) and later dialogues.

36. For a description of this particular action of the civic virtues on the soul in us, see *Enn.* III.6[26].4–5.

37. As described in I.3[20].6.8–10 and VI.8[39].5.13–19.

38. To render *kataskeuazein* in *Enn.* VI.8[39].5.32.

39. *Enn.* VI.8[39].2.35–7: "everything in the sphere of action, even if reason is dominant, is mixed and cannot have being in our power in a pure state".

40. *Enn.* I.4[46].14.4–7: "It is absurd to maintain that well-being (*eudaimonia*) extends as far as the living body, since well-being is the good life, which is concerned with soul and is an activity of soul, and not of all of it".

41. *Enn.* I.2[19].7.11–13, as discussed earlier in the present section.

42. For the unmistakable Stoic flavour of the lines, see Graeser (1972: 121–2), Eliasson (2008: ch. 6, esp. 6.2.2, pp. 190–206) and Lavaud (Brisson & Pradeau 2007: 178, 243 sqq).

43. *Pace* Annas (1999: 68), who claims that the possessor of the higher, purificatory, virtues "will not activate the lower virtues although he has them potentially".

44. Just how detached the virtuous agent (*ho spoudaios*) is from outward circumstances comes out clearly in the tractate *On Well-Being* (*Enn*. I.4[46.].11.12–14): "He would like all men to prosper and no one to be subject to any sort of evil; but if this does not happen, he is all the same well off (*eudaimōn*)." See also *Enn*. I.5[36].10. *passim*, as commented on by Ciapalo (1997). As Gerson (1994: 202) well said: "In so far as this man [the man of higher virtue] is required to don the role of incarnate moral agent he will, so to speak, recreate an image of true virtue. But his dissociation from this life is such that he does not unqualifiedly desire to perform such acts, nor does he desire the occasion for their performance or even any particular outcome."

45. The issue is dealt with at greater length in Stern-Gillet (2009). See also Bene (2013: 145–7).

46. After noting the Stoic flavour of these lines and relating them to *Enn*. VI.8[39].4.9, Graeser (1972: 122) aptly comments that "the empirical world cannot, *sub specie aeternitatis*, be a concern of the real self, for the metaphysical self, to use this Kantian term, is not intrinsically related to πρᾶξις, i.e., to situations externally necessitated in which a decision has to be made.The soul, so it seems, would rather not act at all and not commit itself to any further state of alienation but would prefer to actualise its genuine state of being through contemplative acts."

47. "πάντων τῶν ἔξω ἀφεμένην (sc. τὴν ψυχήν) δεῖ ἐπιστραφῆναι πρὸς τὸ εἴσω πάντη, μὴ πρός τι τῶν ἔξω κεκλίσθαι, ἀλλὰ ἀγνοήσαντα τὰ πάντα καὶ πρὸ τοῦ μὲν τῇ διαθέσει, τότε δὲ καὶ τοῖς εἴδεσιν, ἀγνοήσαντα δὲ καὶ αὑτὸν ἐν τῇ θέᾳ ἐκείνου γενέσθαι, κἀκείνῳ συγγενόμενον καὶ ἱκανῶς οἷον ὁμιλήσαντα ἥκειν ἀγγέλλοντα, εἰ δύναιτο, καὶ ἄλλῳ τὴν ἐκεῖ συνουσίαν· οἵαν ἴσως καὶ Μίνως ποιούμενος ὀαριστὴς τοῦ Διὸς ἐφημίσθη εἶναι, ἧς μεμνημένος εἴδωλα αὐτῆς τοὺς νόμους ἐτίθει τῇ τοῦ θείου ἐπαφῇ εἰς νόμων πληρούμενος θέσιν. Ἢ καὶ τὰ πολιτικὰ οὐκ ἄξια αὐτοῦ νομίσας ἀεὶ ἐθέλει μένειν ἄνω, ὅπερ καὶ τῷ πολὺ ἰδόντι ἂν πάθημα". I adopt van Winden's emendation of the manuscript reading, *nomisasa ei*, into *nomisas aei* (1962: 173).

48. Discussing the origin of the laws of Sparta and Crete, the Athenian Stranger asks Megillus the Spartan and Cleinias the Cretan: "Do you then, like Homer, say that Minos used to go every ninth year to hold converse with his father Zeus, and that he was guided by his divine oracles in laying down the laws for your cities?" (624a7–10, trans. Bury).

49. As do Armstrong (1966–88), P. Hadot (1994), D. O'Meara (1999) and Fronterotta (in Brisson & Pradeau 2003). MacKenna (1956) and Bréhier (1954) as well as D. O'Meara (2003) keep to the manuscript reading.

50. See, for example, Armstrong's *ad loc.* comment: "Plotinus is so deeply convinced of the inferiority of the material world that he has to represent the activity of soul in forming material things as an activity of the lowest form of soul and due to its weakness in contemplation; hence the comparison with the substitute activities of uncontemplative men."

51. P. Hadot (1995). As also noted by Goulet-Cazé (in Brisson *et al.* 1982: 234): "For them [Plotinus' audience] philosophy was not in the main a body of knowledge to be learned or a mere object of study, but an opportunity to choose a way of life" (my trans.). On Plotinus' style of teaching, see also Vassilopoulou (2003).

52. For interesting comments on these lines, see Karfík (2013).

53. As already noted by Armstrong (1976: 194).

26

Plotinus on founding freedom in *Ennead* VI.8[39]

Bernard Collette-Dučić

To Lambros Couloubaritsis, with respect and gratitude

It is commonly assumed that Plotinus was not particularly interested in ethical and practical matters and that the goal he set for the achievement of happiness was essentially contemplative and otherworldly. We owe this assumption to a selection of some passages in Plotinus' *Enneads* and also to a very influential article by Dillon, "An Ethics for the Late Antique Sage" (Dillon 1996b; for Plotinus' ethics, see Schniewind 2003). The impact of such a reading of Plotinus is that the metaphysical part of his philosophy (broadly speaking, the two first hypostases: the Intellect and the One) is often taken as having little or no significance regarding the way a sage, in his view, should act "here below".[1]

If there is one text among the central texts of the *Enneads* that challenges the above interpretation,[2] or at least the unfortunate consequence one may draw from it that a metaphysical enquiry is of little help for our understanding of more mundane matters, it is certainly *Enn.* VI.8[39].[3] Its official topic, according to its title, is "the voluntary and the will of the One". So, right from the start, we are confronted with a curious *mélange de genres* where the questions of the voluntary and the will, traditionally confined to ethics, are here being ascribed a new domain, that of the One, which is in Plotinus the very first metaphysical principle of everything.

Although the first chapter of the treatise, in line with its title, asks whether one should ascribe to God (the One) or the other gods (presumably lower gods[4]) such things as "what is in one's power" (*to eph' hēmin*; cf. *Enn.* VI.8[39].1.1–11) or, more generally, freedom (*eleutheria*), it quickly becomes obvious that such an enquiry is not the final goal of the treatise but rather the path one has to follow in order to found *our* human freedom. Indeed, not only does Plotinus start his enquiry with the case of human beings, but the reason why he is at some point bound to address the question of freedom in the case of the Intellect, and subsequently in that of the One, is because these hypostases are *principles* in which human freedom appears eventually to be *founded*. The point is well made by Sylvain Delcomminette, who is developing an interpretation initially put forward by Trouillard:

The foundation in question here is not an external foundation of freedom, but rather its centre, that animates freedom from within. Indeed, gods are not for Plotinus entities foreign to us: although radically transcendent to our common experience, they are at the same time what is the most within us. In Plotinus, as wrote Trouillard, the problem of transcendence "is not the problem of the other (*de l'autre*), but that of 'being selfer than oneself' (*plus soi que soi*)". For our self (*notre moi*) is itself laid out in tiers (*étagé*), and coincides at its upper levels with the founding principles of everything else. Therefore, to enquire into the freedom of the gods is to enquire into the very heart of our freedom.

(Delcomminette forthcoming)

The whole enterprise of *Enn.* VI.8[39] should therefore be dubbed "foundational" and its main interrogation spelled out as follows: in what principle(s) should human freedom be founded for this freedom to be possible?

My purpose in this chapter is not to provide a full review of *Enn.* VI.8[39], but rather to try to clarify the main features of the doctrine of freedom that Plotinus is presenting there. I have chosen to present Plotinus' position within a broader context, in order to show what he owes to the Greek philosophical tradition (in particular to the Stoa) that has somehow paved the way for his own understanding of freedom. Finally, I shall reflect on the reasons why, according to Plotinus, the One must eventually be thought as remaining beyond freedom and why freedom should be located in the Intellect rather than in the One.

TWO ANCIENT CONCEPTIONS OF FREEDOM

Before entering into the details of Plotinus' doctrine of freedom it may be useful to try to locate it on a broader map. In the ancient philosophical tradition, one can distinguish between two main conceptions of freedom: one libertarian and one (more or less) deterministic. In his remarkable introduction to Alexander's *de Fato*, Sharples noted that "for the Stoics and the Neoplatonists, [contrary to what is the case for Alexander and the Peripatetics,] freedom is located not in the possibility for alternatives but precisely in choosing the most rational course of action" (Sharples [1983] 2003: 22). The affinity between the Stoics and the Neoplatonists (in particular Plotinus), which Sharples rightly acknowledges here, is significant indeed and may eventually help us to understand better Plotinus' own particular stance on freedom.

From a libertarian point of view, one endorsed by Alexander and which Plotinus clearly rejects,[5] freedom[6] is something utterly incompatible with determinism and takes the form of a power or capacity for opposite courses of actions:[7] one is free only if, at least at some early point in one's life,[8] one has been able to make a free choice between, say, following goodness and virtue or following vice.[9]

For the Stoics, on the other hand, who were determinists who held that everything happens according to fate,[10] freedom is not hindered by external or even internal determinations.[11] Indeed, in their view fate is nothing but God himself, who happens to be also assimilated to providence on account of his essential goodness and of his concern regarding everything that is part of the world (particularly human beings). Because God is also for the Stoics both immanent to the world and identified with right reason, everything that happens to men (i.e. fate) is to be taken as "what is best", even if the good of it might not be immediately obvious to them. One can, for instance, initially fail to see what good there is in falling severely sick or in having one's best friend taken away from you. But if one understands, the Stoics say, that everything that happens is the most rational thing that can possibly happen, and that rationality is goodness, then one should also welcome these apparently unfortunate events. This is the famous *amor fati* doctrine, to which we shall return in the course of the next section.

One difficulty with the Stoic doctrine is to understand why I should feel that what is good for the whole world is also good for me. Indeed, it may be part of God's plan that I shall fall sick and die young for the sake of the good of the world itself (God may work in mysterious ways but at least I do not doubt they are the best), but why should I take the good of the whole to be relevant *to me*? The question raised here and which will be of central importance to Plotinus, as will be revealed later, is that of the relationship between one's particular and individual good and the good of the whole. In a nutshell, the Stoic reply to that difficulty consists in reminding us, first, that we are parts of the world and that the good of the parts ultimately lies in the good of the whole in the sense that parts are for the sake of the whole.[12] Second, since the world itself is nothing but God and God is right reason, then men, being parts of God, have also a share in God's perfect reason. Thus the Stoics said that man's reason or *hēgēmonikon* is a "detached fragment" or *apospasma* of God (cf. Diogenes Laertius 7.143). In that sense, not only are we parts of God, but we do share the very same nature, namely reason. For these reasons there is no essential difference between the good of the whole and our particular good.[13]

KNOWLEDGE, MASTERSHIP AND THE WILL

Now where exactly does Plotinus stand in regard to these two conceptions of freedom? In order to make a non-superficial assessment, we need to focus on some notions that Plotinus himself recognizes as essential to what he thinks freedom is. From the very beginning of *Enn*. VI.8[39], we see him putting the emphasis on three notions, namely knowledge, mastership and the will. Introduced in the first chapter, they regularly reappear throughout the rest of the treatise and, as will be shown below, can all be traced back to the Stoic doctrine of freedom. This, of course, does not make Plotinus' account of freedom a Stoic one, but helps to show with which philosophical tradition he sides on this subject.

The requirement of knowledge

First, like the Stoics,[14] Plotinus holds that freedom is achieved only through right reason; that is, *knowledge*. Significant here is Plotinus' critique of Aristotle's understanding of what is voluntary (*hekousion*). According to the latter, in order to be "voluntary" an act must be done in the awareness of the particulars that are involved (cf. Aristotle, *EN* 3.1.1110b33–1111a1). For instance, one cannot say that I voluntarily murdered my father if I was not aware that it was actually my father. Plotinus, clearly resorting to Socrates' conviction that no one does wrong voluntarily, claims that the knowledge one must have is not simply a particular one but also a more general and even universal one:[15]

> Certainly the knowledge involved in a voluntary act must not only apply in the particular circumstances but also generally. For why is the action involuntary (*akousion*) if one does not know that it is a close relative, but not involuntary if one does not know that one ought not to do it? Is it because one ought to have learnt that? [But n]ot knowing that one ought to have learnt it is not voluntary, nor is what leads one way away from learning.   (*Enn.* VI.8[39].1.39–44)

There is no reason, Plotinus explains, that one should say an act is not voluntary when it is done in ignorance of the particulars (here, not knowing that the person murdered was in fact a close relative) but voluntary when the ignorance concerns more generally the fact that one ought not to murder another person. One may object that "one ought to have learnt" that in the first place, in the sense that it is one's responsibility to learn such a general knowledge. But for that, Plotinus says, one would have had to know that one had to learn it and failing to know *that* is also involuntary (see Delcomminette [forthcoming] for further comments). This criticism of Aristotle's concept of *hekousion* plays a major role in Plotinus' more general account of freedom, as it will eventually lead him to show that freedom lies in (universal) *knowledge*, hence that it should be essentially located in the second hypostases or Intellect (cf. *Enn.* VI.8[39].2.35).

The requirement of mastership

Technically speaking, however, Plotinus continues, we should remark that an act that is voluntary is not necessarily an act that is in "our power" (*eph' hēmin*). The difference between the two is that when we say that something is in our power, we mean that we are *masters* over it:

> For what is voluntary (*hekousion*) is everything that we do without being forced to and with knowledge, whereas what is in our power (*eph' hēmin*) is what we do when we are also masters (*kyrioi*). And both may often coincide, even if their definition is different; but sometimes they might be discordant; for instance, if one were master of killing [another man], it would not be a voluntary act when one did so if one did not know that this man was one's father.   (*Enn.* VI.8[39].1.33–8)

According to Plotinus, what is *hekousion*, even when it is correctly understood as requiring universal rather than simply particular knowledge, is insufficient to account for what is *eph' hēmin*. Indeed, freedom is not only a matter of knowing but also of mastering. In order that my killing of my father is voluntary, I need to know that it is my father that I am about to kill and that killing is indeed a bad thing to do. But even if nobody forces me to commit this act and I have the right knowledge about it, there is no way I can carry it out if I have no mastership over (killing) my father. If, for example, my father is protected and hidden on a remote island and I have no access to him, I am in no position of killing him: he is simply out of reach and killing him is not in my power.[16]

As is plain from the rest of the treatise, Plotinus takes "master" (*kyrios*) as the opposite of "slave" (*doulos*). The idea of presenting moral freedom in the light of the master/slave relationship is certainly not infrequent in ancient texts, but it is fair to say that it is in the Stoa that it was initially developed.[17] It is actually at the heart of the Stoic conception of freedom: "The Stoics say: only he [sc. the virtuous man] is free (*eleutheron*), but the bad are slaves (*doulous*). For freedom is *exousia* over one's own business (*exousian autopragias*), but slavery is the privation of one's own business (*sterēsin autopragias*)" (Diogenes Laertius 7.121, my translation).

As will be discussed in the final section below, the Stoics define freedom as an *exousia*, the domain of which is *autopragia*. *Autopragia* is a rare word in ancient philosophical texts and is mainly used only by the Stoics.[18] It is loosely translated as "autonomous" (Garnsey [1996] 2001) or "independent action" (Erskine 1990). Commentators generally ignore the fact that the word was initially used by Chrysippus as a synonym for Plato's minding-one's-own-business (*to ta autou prattein*).[19] We should therefore read the prefix *auto-* in *autopragia* as referring not simply to the autonomous capacity for action, but also to the special and *limited domain* over which humans are masters and in which *only* they are indeed free. This limitation and its recognition are the key of Stoic freedom as documented in Epictetus' presentation of *eph' hēmin*, which encapsulates the essentials of the Stoic original:[20]

> Of things that are, some are in our power (*ta men estin eph' hēmin*), and others are not (*ta de ouk eph' hēmin*). In our power are judgements, impulsions, desire, aversion, in a word, whatever is our own business; not in our power are the body, property, reputation, offices, in a word, whatever is not our own business. And the things in our power are by nature free, not subject to restraint nor hindrance; but the things not in our power are weak, slavish, subject to restraint, alien.
>
> (*Ench.* 1.1–2, my trans.)

Here we can distinctively see how Epictetus' *to eph' hēmin* is grounded in the recognition of a distinction between two domains: there are things that are *ours* and it is our business to care about them; and there are things that are *not ours* (they are called "alien" by Epictetus) and it is not our business to mind about them. The secret of happiness and freedom is to never confuse these two domains: for only things that are ours are by nature free, whereas things that are not ours are by nature hindered and slavish. The domain of things that are ours is eventually called *prohairesis* by Epictetus, which he takes to be what each of us truly *is*.[21]

We can observe a similar train of thought in Plotinus who, in *Enn.* VI.8[39], progressively circumscribes the domain of freedom to what is *internal* to us and finally to *what we truly are*. One first important step of this approach is his recognition that actions are external to us (*exōthen*, *Enn.* VI.8[39].4.9), and therefore that we should exclude them from the domain of what is in our power (the same is done in regard to the body, as discussed below in relation to *Enn.* VI.8[39].12.4–7). This leads Plotinus to conceive of virtue, held by Plato to be *adespoton* or without master, as essentially contemplative, actually "another intellect":

> In what way then are we saying that being good is in our power and "virtue has no master" (*adespoton tēn aretēn*)? … Because when virtue comes to be in us it provides us with freedom and with being in our power (*to eleutheron kai to eph' hēmin*) and does not allow us to be any more slaves (*doulous*) of what we were enslaved before. If then virtue is a kind of other intellect, a state which in a way intellectualises the

soul, again, being in our power does not belong to the realm of action but in intellect
at rest from actions.   (*Enn.* VI.8[39].5.30–37; cf. Plato, *R.* 617e)

Like Epictetus, here we find Plotinus distinguishing between two domains, one within
us, and one without, and locating (see *Enn.* VI.8[39].1.36–7) freedom and what is in our
power *within* ourselves, namely, in his case, in the intellect.[22]

In Plotinus, intellect is not simply a faculty but a principle or hypostasis of our soul.
This means that it is not simply something that we possess, along with other faculties, but
what we truly belong to, even what we are. Much influenced by Aristotle, his conception
is that Intellect is essentially identical to its object, namely Being or *ousia*.[23] Therefore, by
making the Intellect the domain of human freedom, Plotinus also asserts that freedom
lies in Being; that is, in what we truly are:[24]

> Each one of us, in respect of his body, is far from *ousia* (*porrō an eiē ousias*), but in
> respect of the soul, that is, of what we most are we participate in *ousia* (*metechomen
> ousias*) and are a particular kind of *ousia* (*esmen tis ousia*), which means that we
> are in some sense a composite of *ousia* and difference (*syntheton ti ek diaphoras kai
> ousias*). We are not then *ousia* in the strict and proper sense (*oukoun kyriōs ousia*)
> or absolute *ousia* (*oud' autoousia*); and for this reason we are not masters of our
> own *ousia* (*oude kyrioi tēs autōn ousias*). For in some way *ousia* is one thing and we
> are another (*ousia kai hēmeis allo*) and we are not masters of our own *ousia* (*kyrioi
> ouch hēmeis tēs autōn ousias*), but *ousia*, the very thing itself, is master of us (*ousia
> auto hēmōn*), given that this also adds the difference.   (*Enn.* VI.8[39].12.4–11)

In this passage, Plotinus makes two apparently different claims about what we truly are.
In one sense, what we are is soul rather than body, but, in another sense, it is *ousia* itself.
The reason for this is that the realization that we are not our body does not simply lead to
the recognition that soul is what we most are, but to a form of purification of the soul itself
until we reach *what the soul really is*. Such purification means that we should not identify
ourselves with the lower irrational part of the soul. We should not, therefore, make *ours*
the desires of the spirit and of the appetitive parts. For these lower irrational parts of the
soul are so because they partake in the body. We should therefore rather identify ourselves
with the upper part of the soul, and in particular with the intellect.

Similarly to what we have seen in Epictetus, as long as we continue to identify ourselves
with what we are not, namely the body, we remain in a state of slavery. Indeed, instead of
being master of ourselves, hence of our *ousia*, it is rather we that are enslaved to it. But
how are we exactly to understand such enslavement? In a manner that recalls the famous
image of the god of Glaucus in Plato's *Republic*,[25] Plotinus presents the compound of soul
and body as the result of the addition of a difference to the original *ousia*. The difference
in question has a double meaning. On the one hand, it is presented as a logical (or specific)
difference, one that if added to a given genus, produces a species. Hence Plotinus' presentation of the compound of soul and body is as "a particular kind of *ousia*" (*tis ousia*).
But this understanding of what the added difference is is insufficient and even misleading,
because it suggests that, by being a particular kind of *ousia*, we are also therefore *ousiai*.
But Plotinus says that we are *not*: "We are not then *ousia* in the strict and proper sense
(*oukoun kyriōs ousia*) or absolute *ousia* (*oud' autoousia*)." *Diaphora* in the present context,

then, must also have the sense of *otherness*: the addition of the difference (namely body) to the original *ousia* produces a form of estrangement or alienation;[26] because of the difference, we are not any more what we truly are.

It is only if we identify ourselves with our soul rather than with the body that we can free ourselves and therefore become masters:

> But since in some way we are that which is master of us (*kyrion hēmōn hēmeis pōs esmen*), in this way, all the same, even here below we can be called masters of ourselves (*autōn kyrioi*). For[27] what is absolutely, what is *ousia* in itself, and which is not other than its own *ousia*, is also master of what it is here below, being no longer referred to something else, in that it is and in that it is *ousia*.
>
> (*Enn.* VI.8[39].12.11–16)

Plotinus here makes the important point that the freedom that is being achieved by our identification with our soul is not some otherworldly freedom. The only way we can gain our freedom and become masters ourselves "here below" is by identifying ourselves with what truly is, namely *ousia*. Indeed, we saw in the previous passage that it is the *ousia* that masters us, and by "us" Plotinus meant the very compound of soul and body. So, by recognizing *ousia* as our true self and therefore identifying us with it, we similarly become masters of ourselves.

The requirement of a will

Let us now come to the third and most important notion, that of will.[28] It is actually the first of the three to be introduced by Plotinus, as a conclusion to a passage where Plotinus tries to decipher what we really mean when we speak of what is in our power:

> What then do we have in our minds when we speak of "being in our power" (*to eph' hēmin*), and why are we trying to find out? I myself think that, when we are pushed around among opposing chances and compulsions and strong assaults of passions possessing our soul, we acknowledge all these things as our masters (*kyria*) and are enslaved to them (*douleuontes autois*) and carried wherever they take us, and so are in doubt whether we are not nothing (*ouden esmen*) and nothing is in our power (*oude ti estin eph' hēmin*), on the assumption that whatever we might do when not enslaved to chances or compulsions or strong passions because we wished it and with nothing opposing our wishes, this would be in our power. But if this is so, our conception of what is in our power (*ennoia tou eph' hēmin*) would be something enslaved to our will (*boulēsei*) and would come to pass (or not) to the extent to which we wished it.
>
> (*Enn.* VI.8[39].1.21–33)

The passage makes heavy use of the master/slave relationship which we have recognized above as indeed essential to Plotinus' idea of freedom. Being free or having things that are "in our power" is only achievable through us being (or becoming) masters. We have seen that freedom thus understood converges towards our true nature and somehow the same seems to be implied here when Plotinus is equating having nothing in our power (i.e. not being free) with being nothing. The assumption is that we are only as long as we are free precisely because what we are coincides with the very domain of our freedom.

Now, knowing that freedom requires mastership is one thing and knowing what in us should master is another. The function of this passage is precisely to provide an answer for this distinction: what should master is our *will* (*boulēsis*). What helps us to get to this recognition is that when we dread that we are nothing (that nothing is in our power) is when we feel that our *will* is unable to exercise itself. In other words, we have this precon- ception (*ennoia*), according to Plotinus, that freedom is essentially a question of will and that if there are to be things that are in our power, they must be somehow "enslaved to our will"; that is, they must be in a position where nothing can prevent us from master- ing them.[29]

Before entering more into Plotinus' account of the will, let us compare his passage with the opening lines of Epictetus' *On Freedom*: "Free (*eleutheros*) is the person who lives as he wishes and cannot be coerced, impeded or compelled, whose impulses cannot be thwarted, who always gets what he desires and never has to experience what he would avoid" (*Dissertationes* 4.1, trans. Dobbin). It is difficult not to see the striking similari- ties between Plotinus'*ennoia* of freedom and this central text of Epictetus. In both cases, freedom is defined as living "as one wishes", and is presented as the opposite of being coerced or thwarted in any possible way, which is another way to assert that freedom lies in being a master as opposed to a slave.

Epictetus' placement of freedom in our will is probably original to him, even if there are precedents going back as far as Zeno, who is reported to have emphasized the incoercible nature of the sage's will: "Sooner will you sink an inflated bladder than compel any virtu- ous man to do against his will anything that he does not wish."[30] Furthermore, Epictetus' decision of making the sage's will the very place of freedom is to be understood as a natural development of the well-established Stoic doctrine that the only way one can avoid being compelled and thus become free is *to wish* that "everything that happens" actually happens. And everything that happens, as we have already explained, is only another way to refer to fate, hence to God himself. This thesis (the *amor fati* doctrine) was famously expressed by the Stoics through the simile of a dog tied to a moving cart:

> They too [Zeno and Chrysippus] affirmed that everything is fated, with the fol- lowing model. When a dog is tied to a cart, *if it wants* to follow, it is pulled and follows, making its authority over itself coincide with necessity, but *if it does not want* to follow, it will be compelled in any case. So it is with men too: even if they do not want to, they will be compelled in any case to follow what is destined.
> (Hippolytus, *Haer.* 1.21 = *SVF* II.975, trans. Long and Sedley;
> cf. Cleanthes, *apud* Epictetus, *Ench.* 53 = *SVF* I.527)

The passage emphasizes that it is actually through our *will* that we can avoid the constraints and limitations of the nonetheless unavoidable determination of fate. Both Epictetus and the first Stoics also connect such a will with the sage or good man only. In other words, the will is the location of freedom only if correctly oriented: that is, in order that one may achieve whatever one wills and thus be free, one must will what God has ordained.

Now, there is maybe a further explanation of why Epictetus chooses to present freedom in the form of a will and that is because the Stoics appear to have attributed a will to God himself by positing that "everything that happens happens according to God's *will*".[31] Also, they do not qualitatively differentiate between man's reason and God's. It is therefore likely that Epictetus attempts to mark off a further correspondence between man and god by granting men a will that is in some sense *the same* as God's. And indeed he is famous for asserting that "not even Zeus can conquer my will (*prohairesin*)!"[32] By that, he certainly does not try to weaken God's will, only to reaffirm that *our human freedom is as incoercible as that of God*. And if it is so, it is precisely because our will (if we are sages) is nothing but God's.[33]

I think the above analysis is sufficient for us to understand what Plotinus' essential link between freedom and will ultimately owes to the Stoics. Like them, he also eventually ascribes a will to God himself (i.e. to the One as will be discussed below), and makes the One's will the very principle of freedom. We shall, however, see that one must somehow qualify this connection between the One and freedom since, truly, the One is beyond freedom, hence beyond will itself. In any case, one cannot but see that Plotinus' own decision to ascribe (if for the sake of persuasion, *Enn.* VI.8[39].12.2) a will to the One accounts for the very recognition that our freedom, defined in terms of a will in the first chapter of the treatise, must ultimately be founded upon God's will.

Now why is it exactly so? Why should we take freedom, our freedom, as a will that is founded in God's or the One's will? To answer this question, we must first understand better the role played by the One in Plotinus' conception of freedom. Contrary to the Peripatetic view of freedom advocated by Alexander, Plotinus' freedom is not a matter of being able to choose freely between two opposite courses of action, one good, one bad, but a matter of seeking after the *good* and ultimately possessing it. Indeed, for Plotinus there is no way one can be free if one chooses the wrong, evil path:[34]

> That is enslaved (*douleuei*) which is not master of its going to the good (*ho mē kyrion estin epi to agathon elthein*), but, since something stronger than it stands over it, it is enslaved to that (*douleuon ekeinōi*) and led away from its own goods. For it is for this reason that slavery is ill spoken of, not where one has no *exousia* to go to the bad, but where one has no *exousia* to go to one's own good but is led away to the good of another.   (*Enn.* VI.8[39].4.17–22)

Typically, a master/slave relationship supposes that the slave is called so because he is prevented by his master from attaining his own good; indeed, when one is a slave, the good that is sought to secure, is not one's own, but the master's. A slave never achieves his own good because his desires are ill-directed; that is, not directed towards *his* own good. Conversely, one is free if one both correctly directs one's desire and eventually gets one's own good. Now, in Plotinus, the One is not simply the first principle of everything, it is also the Good of every subsequent being. Of course, the One could not be my own good if it were alien to me and this is why it is said to lie at *the very inner centre* of my being, even beyond the Intellect:

> If we ever see in ourselves a nature of this kind (i.e. the One's) which shares nothing with the other things which are attached to us[35] by which we have to experience whatever happens by chance (for all the other things which belong to us are enslaved to and exposed to chances, and come to us in a way by chance), but this

alone has self-mastery (*to kyrion auto*) and authority over itself (*to autexousion*) by the act of a light that has the form of good and is good, and is greater than that which belongs to Intellect. And this act does not possess its superiority over the Intellect on account of something brought in from outside. Surely, when we ascend to this [light] and become this alone and let the rest go, what can we say of it except that we are more than free (*pleon ē eleutheroi*) and more than independent (*pleon ē autexousioi*)?   (*Enn.* VI.8[39].15.14–23)

Continuing Glaucus' theme that what is truly ours is what lies within us beyond any external and thus alien addition (*Enn.* VI.8[39].12.4–11), here Plotinus locates the One in our inner self, making it not simply a good, but *our very own good*, one that we must seek after if we want to free ourselves from what ties us to external and enslaving conditions.

One important fact about the foundational role of the One regarding human freedom is therefore that the One is our *own* good (rather than somebody else's) and that, since one is free when one is able to seek after one's own good, then the One becomes an essential condition for our freedom: it is the very *object* of our will.[36] But there is more than that. Plotinus' insistence on presenting our freedom in terms of a will and his ascription of a will (if only for the sake of persuasion) to the One strongly suggests that the very possession of the good (through our inner ascent to the One) is a matter of having our will coincide with God's will. The One is not simply the object of our will but must also be *a kind of model for the will itself*. This, I believe, is confirmed in the following: "If we were to grant acts to him, and ascribe his acts to what is like his will – for it does not act unwillingly – and his acts are like his being, his will and his substance will be the same thing" (Plotinus, *Enn.* VI.8[39].13.5–8).

Since the One is *beyond* any form of multiplicity, one should not ascribe to it anything that may produce, by its very addition, a duality. However, if, for the sake of persuading a refractory soul – like the one addressed in *Enn.* VI.8[39].12.2 – we concede to grant acts or activities (*energeiai*) to the One, then we have to grant to the One what is like (*hoion*) a will too: indeed, if we are to represent the One acting in some way or another, his acting cannot be unwilling. Now, we have seen that what the will wants or desires is the good. But the One is the good: what is like (*hoion*) his being, which is a pure act (i.e. an act unmixed with potency), is the good. Contrary to the Intellect, however, the One does not simply eternally possess the good but is actually fully identical to it: *what is like his will and what is like his being are one and the same*. The will of the One (i.e. the sort of will that the One somehow embodies) is a will of oneself where there is no difference left between the will and the self:

It is not possible to apprehend him without the will to be by his own agency what he is: coinciding with himself, he wants to be himself and he is what he wants. His will and himself are one (*hē thelēsis kai autos hen*), and his unity is not diminished since there is no difference between, on the one hand, himself happening to be as he is, and, on the other, what he would have wished to be. For what could he have wished to be except this which he is? For even if we assumed that he could choose to become what he wished, and it was possible for him to change his own nature into something else, he would not wish to become something else, or blame himself for being what he is by necessity, this "being himself" (*autos einai*) which he always willed and wills. For the nature of the Good *is* in reality the will of himself, a self not corrupted nor following his own nature, but choosing himself, because there was nothing else at all that he might be drawn to.   (*Enn.* VI.8[39].13.28–40)

The will of the One is a will that is directed to oneself in such a way that there is no difference, no otherness left between the will and the self. Such a perfect will is free as it supplants any form of alienation, such as being what you are by chance (*Enn.* VI.8[39].13.32), by necessity (*Enn.* VI.8[39].13.36) or by nature (*Enn.* VI.8[39].13.39).[37] Indeed, any of these forms introduces a disparity between what one wishes to be and what one actually is: since it is in the nature of the will to be a master (as shown above), a will cannot ever be satisfied with something that ultimately is not in his power.

We can now see that the foundational role of the One regarding our freedom is not limited to that of being the object of the will: the One is actually the will itself, the perfect expression of what *a free will* must be. This double function can be seen in the following passage: "As long as each individual did not have the Good, it wished something else, but in that it possesses the Good, it wills itself. And neither is this kind of presence by chance nor is its being (*ousia*) outside its will, and it is by this Good that its being is defined and by this that it belongs to itself" (*Enn.* VI.8[39].13.20–24).

On the one hand, one can see that the One is the object of our will, since the One is the Good and the Good is what our will wants. At the same time, identifying ourselves with the One (possessing the good that we will) is achieved only through *a certain form of will*, a will that is *directed to ourselves*. In other words, our will can be fulfilled only if we somehow imitate the will of the One, a will that never seeks after what is alien and outside. Our identification with the One, by which we finally come to possess our *own* good, is ultimately a matter of recognizing what we truly are, what defines us, as opposed to what we mistakenly think we are. We are not our body. We are not any action that we may undertake. We are not anything that is external and material and, in that respect, *what we are is our will*, since the will is what is most immaterial and inner, like the One.

FREEDOM AS BEING MADE FREE

Plotinus' attribution of a will (hence of freedom) to the One is always qualified. We should speak only of what is like (*hoion*) a will when we discuss the will of the One, exactly as when we speak of what is like (*hoion*) his *ousia*. The reason is that, strictly speaking, the One is *beyond* freedom. In Plotinus' view, the true realm of freedom is not that of the first principle, but of a lower principle: the Intellect (we have seen that knowledge is indeed a requirement for freedom). It is important to reflect on this distinction. What difference does it make for our understanding of what freedom is to locate it ultimately in the Intellect rather than in the One? The following passage, in which Plotinus explains how the Intellect has been made free by the One, gives us a decisive clue: "For, again, it (i.e. the Intellect) has been let go into self-mastery in that it is primarily related to Being. That (i.e. the One), then, which has made Being free, which is clearly of a nature to make free and can be called free-maker (*eleutheropoion*) – to what could it be a slave, if it is even in any way permitted to utter this word?" (*Enn.* VI.8[39].12.16–20).

The essential point here is that if we cannot imagine the One to be enslaved in any sort of way, it is not because the One is free, but rather because it is the principle of freedom. Strictly speaking, the One is not free, rather what makes other things free. Among these things, one finds first of all the Intellect itself, because the Intellect is primarily related to Being or *ousia*, and we have indeed seen that freedom is a matter of finding out what we truly *are*.

The reason why the One is not, in a strict sense, free, but rather the principle of freedom, has also to do with the way in which Plotinus conceives freedom and which once again recalls the Stoic understanding of it, as will be demonstrated below. Freedom is mastership. But mastership is a contrary term, opposed to slavery. In other words, it is not possible to conceive freedom as a simple term, since it is always at the same time negatively defined by its opposite. Each time we think of being free, according to Plotinus, we think of it as being a master of some subjected and enslaved other thing. Remember how Plotinus defined the *eph' hēmin*: "our conception of what is in our power would be something *enslaved* to our will" (*Enn.* VI.8[39].1.31–2). The essential connection of freedom with mastership makes the notion of freedom unsuitable to the One, since the One is beyond any form of otherness and difference.

But is there not a difficulty here? How can Plotinus conceive true freedom as mastership and locate it in a *secondary* principle like the Intellect? How can the Intellect be truly free if it is not the first principle? Should we not say that the One, superior to the Intellect as it is, is the master of the Intellect, hence that Intellect is enslaved? No. For mastership is not just a matter of power (*dynamis*). One can have limited power and still be free. In fact, mastership precisely supposes the idea of a limited realm of power, since mastership is only achievable over *oneself* (as opposed to other things). It is only when we have detached our *self* from external inessential additions that we reach what we truly are or *ousia*, which is Intellect. The One is not a master in regard to Intellect. Rather, it is the good that the Intellect always possesses and on the account of which is free:

> And even if Intellect does have another principle (i.e. the One), it is not outside it, but it is in the Good. And if it is according to the Good, it is much more in its own power and free; since one seeks freedom and being for the sake of the Good. If then it is active according to the Good, it would be still more in its power; for it possesses already the object of his sight, towards which it is directed and from which it comes, while remaining in itself, which is the best way for it to be in itself, if it is directed towards it.   (*Enn.* VI.8[39].4.32–40)

The superiority of the One over the Intellect does not make the One a master of Intellect or the Intellect a slave of the One. It is rather a condition for the Intellect to be free: by directing its sight (i.e. its will) towards the One, Intellect is in fact concentrating itself on its *own* good and is then freed (in anticipation, so to say) from other possible enslaving conditions into which Intellect would necessarily fall, if it were to direct its sight in the opposite direction.

The characterization of the One as a liberator or a free-maker and the reluctance of Plotinus to ascribe freedom and *eph' hēmin* to it shed some light on his general under-standing of freedom. It teaches us that *freedom*, in his view, *is always the result of liberation* (be it anticipatively or not) and that only he who has been made so is free. Here again, it is important to acknowledge what Plotinus owes to the philosophical tradition with which he sides on this subject. For the Stoics, too, freedom is something that is granted or imparted and thus always implies some superior principle that is ultimately responsible for it. Let us return for a second to their definition of freedom as *exousia autopragias* and try to elucidate the meaning of the term *exousia*, a word that is also used by Plotinus (in *Enn.* VI.8[39].4.20 and 7.38) and which is present in the important notion of *autexousia* he constantly employs.[38] A testimony from Origen shows such an *exousia*, for the Stoics, to be divinely bestowed upon men: "According to what they say, … the wise man alone and every wise man is free and has received from the divine law a licence over his own business (*exousian autopragian*), and they define this licence a lawful power of administration" (Origen, *Commentary on John* 2.16.112.4–8 = *SVF* III.544).

Exousia is a certain power, or rather a certain authority, and thus we could translate *exousia autopragias* as the authority one has over one's own business. But since it is bestowed by divine law, that is, by God himself,[39] it is better to render it by *licence*, a word that advantageously captures the essential link of the Stoic *exousia* with freedom. By definition, a licence is a legal authorization bestowed to somebody by a superior authority. Now, this understanding of freedom as a sort of *licence* shows that for the Stoics, as for Plotinus, freedom cannot be conceived without a superior authority or power responsible for its bestowal. Freedom cannot be ascribed to the first principle or God who is responsible for granting it.

There is no reason to suspect Origen of Christianizing the original Stoic doctrine, for we find in Epictetus a perfect illustration of the same idea: "the gods", he says, "have put in our power (*eph' hēmin*) only the supreme and most masterful thing, the power of making correct use of impressions", a power thanks to which "one will never be impeded, never thwarted" (*Dissertationes* 1.1.7–13).

Like Plotinus' One, Epictetus' Zeus is depicted as the principle responsible for human beings to be (ontologically) free, not in the sense that he makes us once and for all free, but in that he endows us with a power to free ourselves, the power which the early Stoics called *exousia* or licence. The only condition for its fulfilment is that we care for what is ours and flee from what is alien and external. The key to freedom lies, for Epictetus as for Plotinus, in finding out what we truly are; that is, in our identification with this part of the divine that is *in* us and which *defines* us.[40]

CONCLUSION

Plotinus' doctrine of freedom, although undeniably extremely original and perfectly in tune with the main principles of his own metaphysics, is nevertheless deeply rooted in the Greek philosophical tradition that preceded him. I have tried to show how the three main concepts Plotinus uses to characterize the *ennoia* of freedom or *to eph' hēmin*, namely knowledge, mastership and the will, all point towards the Stoic conception of freedom. These, I believe, are not simply superficial contact points between two systems of thought but, quite the contrary, uncontroversial signs of a deep and general agreement regarding the very nature of freedom: that it lies in goodness and in knowing oneself. I have recalled how the Stoic doctrine of freedom historically came to embody one of the two main ancient Greek conceptions of freedom, the other being the one defended by the Peripatetic school, in particular by its most powerful advocate, Alexander of Aphrodisias.[41] Given that Alexander's main opponents were the Stoics, one can see why Plotinus chose to side so willingly with them in order to defeat a view about freedom which he uncompromisingly rejected.[42]

ACKNOWLEDGEMENTS

My very great thanks to Sylvain Delcomminette, Svetla Slaveva-Griffin and Pauliina Remes for reading the first draft and for their helpful suggestions. I also thank an anonymous reader for detailed and valuable comments.

NOTES

1. For instance, in *Enn.* I.2[19].3, he endorses the famous "assimilation to God" notion of the *Theaetetus* (176b), according to which the philosopher's *telos* is to flee from earthly concerns and concentrate only on contemplation. He also dedicates a full treatise to the question of contemplation: *Enn.* III.8[30].
2. For an attempt to show that the perfect life of the Plotinian *spoudaios* includes both contemplation and action, see Collette-Dučić (2011–12).
3. The edition used is Henry & Schwyzer (1983). English translations of Plotinus' text are from Armstrong (1966–88), amended or adapted. For a full commentary of *Enn.* VI.8[39], see Leroux (1990). For a critical review of Leroux's work, see D. O'Meara (1992). An excellent French translation and helpful notes are provided by Lavaud (2007). On freedom in Plotinus, see Leroux (1996) and Ousager (2004).
4. In chapter 1, the identity of these other gods is left unspecified, but in the course of the rest of the treatise it seems that he has in mind some sort of intermediary gods, in which one finds the Intellect (and maybe also therefore the multiple particular intellects that compose it).
5. See in particular *Enn.* VI.8[39].4.17–22, discussed below.
6. One must be warned here that, contrary to what the above quotation from Sharples may suggest, Alexander's doctrine is not directly concerned with freedom, but rather *moral responsibility*. However, it is likely that other philosophers have interpreted his stance about the conditions for human responsibility as also a stance on the question of human freedom. This has to do with the shift of meaning of the expression "*eph' hēmin*" which, in Aristotle and Alexander, refers primarily to human responsibility whereas in Stoicism, starting at least with Epictetus, it refers to human freedom (see below, note 20). Plotinus' use of the expression in *Enn.* VI.8[39] is in line with Epictetus. For Sharples' use of the word "freedom", see his own clarification ([1983] 2003: 9).
7. Cf. Alexander of Aphrodisias, *Fat.* 196.25 [Bruns] and, more generally, ch. 12. For this kind of "indeterminist freedom", see Bobzien (1998: 278).
8. This qualification is added by Alexander to prevent the obvious objection that it would be impossible for the good person to choose anything but the right course of action or for the bad person the opposite. What matters, explains Alexander, is that the person that has now become good or bad (which are stable if not irreversible features of his nature) has initially had the capacity to make a free choice: "Granting to them [the Stoics] that virtues and vices cannot be lost, we might perhaps take [the point] in a more obvious way by saying that it is in this respect that dispositions depend on those who possess them, [namely] in so far as, before they acquired them, it was in their power also not to acquire them" (*Fat.* 197.3–7 [Bruns], hereinafter trans. Sharples).
9. The choices in question do not necessarily have to be between good and evil actions, but the contrast with the second sort of freedom is clearer if presented this way.
10. In antiquity, the Stoics were taken to hold a very strong and materialistic version of determinism according to which each event is determined by an antecedent cause and "the movements of our minds are nothing more than instruments for carrying out determined decisions since it is necessary that they be performed through us" (Calcidius, *in Ti.* clx–clxi = *SVF* II.943, trans. Long).
11. For the issue regarding the compatibility of determinism with freedom and moral responsibility in Stoicism, see Long ([1971]1996b). For the Stoic doctrine of fate, see Long & Sedley (1987: 333–43) and Salles (2009).

12. Alexander, *Fat.* 192.25–8: "Fate itself, Nature, and the reason according to which the whole is organised, they assert to be god; it is present in all that is and comes to be, and in this way employs the individual nature of every thing (χρωμένην ἀπάντων τῶν ὄντων τῇ οἰκείᾳ φύσει) for the organisation of the whole (πρὸς τὴν τοῦ παντὸς οἰκονομίαν)."

13. Cf. Marcus Aurelius, *Meditations* 5.8.4.1–4, who urges us to "consider the doing and perfecting of what the universal Nature decrees in the same light as [our] health" (trans. Long 2002).

14. The Stoics notoriously asserted that only the virtuous man is free (cf. Diogenes Laertius 7.33) and that virtues are themselves sciences (cf. Plutarch, *de Virtute Morali* 2.441a = *SVF* I.201).

15. See, for instance, Plato, *Prt.* 352c2–7 and 358b6–c1. For an analysis of this doctrine, see Segvic (2000).

16. Of course, I supply much here. Plotinus only speaks of "being master of killing". Could he not simply mean that I am not *competent* in the field of killing other people? (This is actually how Armstrong understands and translates *kyrios* here.) But if so, it would go somehow against the distinction he aims to make, i.e. that knowledge is not enough to account for what is in our power. In fact, if we look at the other numerous occurrences of *kyrios* in the treatise, we see that a master is one that has power over his subject, who is *free* to do whatever he *wills* with his subject. Conversely, one who is the subject of a master is in many respects his slave: he is helpless and cannot avoid anything that may happen to him because of his master. Examples of that over which we have no mastership are *phantasiai*, occurring to "children, wild animals and madmen" (*Enn.* VI.8[39].2.6–8), and the success or accomplishment of one's actions (*Enn.* VI.8[39].5.5). Even if this understanding of *kyrios* can also account for one's competence in a given science or art, Plotinus' example is certainly better served if we understand that it is not simply the knowledge of killing that one ought to "master", but the intended target of the killing itself.

17. Cf. Bobzien (1998: 340): "All testimonies on Stoic freedom (*eleutheria*), without exception, belong to ethics and politics. 'Freedom' and being 'free' are typically contrasted with 'slavery' (*douleia*) and being a 'slave' (*doulos*), and the philosophical use of the concepts in ethics seems to have taken its origin from the analogy with politics and public life, as in Zeno's *Republic*. … Most sources make the point that the sage is (truly) free whereas common mortals are all (truly) slaves." On this topic, see also Erskine (1990: 43–63) and Garnsey ([1996] 2001: 17–19, 128–52).

18. For a fuller account, see Collette-Dučić (2011). For the meaning of *autopragia*, see also M. Frede (2011: 68–9).

19. Plutarch, *de Stoicorum Repugnantiis* 20.1043a–b [Cherniss]: "The work on *Ways of Living* is a single treatise in four books. In the fourth of these [Chrysippus] says that the sage is unmeddlesome (ἀπράγμονά) and retiring (ἰδιοπράγμονα) and minds his own business (τὰ αὑτοῦ πράττειν). These are his words: 'For I think that the prudent man is unmeddlesome (ἀπράγμονα) and unofficious (ὀλιγοπράγμονα) and that he minds his own business (τὰ αὑτοῦ πράττειν), minding one's own business and unofficiousness being alike matters of decency (ὁμοίως τῆς τ' αὐτοπραγίας καὶ τῆς ὀλιγοπραγμοσύνης ἀστείων ὄντων)'" (trans. Cherniss). Cf. Plato's definition of justice in *R.* 433a–b: "And further, we have often heard it said and often said ourselves that justice consists in minding your own business (τὸ τὰ αὑτοῦ πράττειν) and not meddling in the business of others (μὴ πολυπραγμονεῖν)" (trans. Lee).

20. Epictetus' *to eph' hēmin* is not to be confused with the use of this expression by the first Stoics. In Epictetus, the notion is essentially ethical and linked to freedom, whereas in the Early Stoa it is used in the context of moral responsibility. On this, see Bobzien (1998: 276–90, 331–8, 341–3) and Gourinat (2007). For a comparative study of the meaning of *to eph' hēmin* in Plotinus and others, cf. Eliasson (2008).

21. See Epictetus, *Dissertationes* 3.5.1–3, where *prohairesis* and *hēgemonikon* (the leading part of the soul for the Stoics) are equivalents. In other contexts, *prohairesis* refers to one's essential occupation (*epitēdeuma*) (*Dissertationes* 3.23.4–6). On these occurrences and the meanings of *prohairesis* in Epictetus, see Sorabji (2007) and Gourinat (2005).

22. See also *Enn.* VI.8[39].6.4–7: "[We claim that] virtue and the intellect have the mastery (κύρια) and that we should refer being in our power and freedom to them."

23. For a good assessment of what Plotinus owes to Aristotle's conception of God as Intellect (in *Metaphysics* 12), see Nyvlt (2012: 215–32). Cf. *Enn.* V.3[49].5.21–3: "Contemplation must be identical to what is contemplated and Intellect to the intelligible." On the historical background of this doctrine, see Armstrong (1957) and Pépin (1956). For a good recent treatement of this doctrine, see Emilsson (2007: 124–75).

24. On selfhood and inwardness in Plotinus, see Remes (2007, 2008a).

25. *R.* 611c6–b6: "We see [the soul] in the state of that of Glaucus the sea-god, and its original nature is as difficult to see as his was after long immersion had broken and worn away and deformed his limbs, and

covered more like a monster than what he really was. That is the sort of state we see the soul reduced to by countless evils."

26. In Plotinus, soul's fall into the body is understood as a form of particularization, literally a process of "becoming a part". For attachment to the body as the reason behind this fall, see Collette-Dučić (2010) and O'Brien (1977).

27. Contrary to many translators, I do not follow Theiler's emendation (οὗ instead of ὅ, *Enn.* VI.8[39].12.14) that splits the whole passage in two and leaves the first line unexplained. My reading owes much here to Lavaud (2007: n. 219).

28. An excellent analysis of this notion is provided by M. Frede (2011: esp. 19–30, 66–88, 125–52).

29. *Ennoia* in the sense of notion or preconception is of Epicurean and Stoic origins: see Long & Sedley (1987: vol. I, 252–3).

30. *Apud* Philo of Alexandria, *Quod Omnis Probus Liber sit* 97 (trans. Garnsey [1996] 2001: 133).

31. Cyril of Alexandria, *Contra Julianum* III.625c (= frag. 3 [Grant 1964]; cf. Alexander of Aphrodisias, *de Providentia* 5.1–9 [Ruland 1976]).

32. Cf. Epictetus, *Dissertationes* 1.1.23. We should note that the word *prohairesis* (sometimes also translated by "choice") used here, a word that plays such a programmatic part in Epictetus' philosophy, was initially defined by the early Stoics as a kind of will (*boulēsis*): cf. Stobaeus, *Anth.* II.7.9a, p. 87.14–22 [Wachsmuth] = *SVF* III.173, where *prohairesis* is defined as "a choice before a choice (αἵρεσιν πρὸ αἱρέσεως)", and a choice defined as "a *will* that results from a reasoning (βούλησιν ἐξ ἀναλογισμοῦ)". For a commentary of this definition, see again Gourinat (2005).

33. On the importance of the identification of our will with God's in the history of thought, see M. Frede (2011: 126).

34. On Plotinus' criticism of Alexander's conception of freedom, see M. Frede (2011: 142).

35. The phrase συνήρτηται ἡμῖν somehow recalls the use of προστίθησιν in *Enn.* VI.8[39].12.11.

36. *Enn.* VI.8[39].6.38–9: Ἡ γὰρ βούλησις θέλει τὸ ἀγαθόν ("the will wants the good").

37. These three forms of alienation are already mentioned in *Enn.* VI.8[39].1.21–33.

38. Some Plotinian scholars have defended the view that Plotinus' use of *exousia* is related to his controversy with the Gnostics. See in particular the arguments of Narbonne (2011: 139–41).

39. For the identification of God and Law in the Stoa, see Diogenes Laertius 7.87–9.

40. Since the condition of our liberation is the recognition that the *exousia* we have been granted with is only a licence over things that are ours (i.e. over ourselves), then it is understandable why, in the expression of freedom, the term *exousia* seems to have been historically more or less supplanted by that of *autexousia*. For the connection between the two terms, see Bobzien (1998: 335–6).

41. Plotinus' criticism of Alexander's thought in *Enn.* VI.8[39] is well recognized; see in particular D. O'Meara (1992) and Lavaud (2007).

42. By saying that, I do not mean that Alexander is the only (unnamed) target of Plotinus in *Enn.* VI.8[39]. Some have argued that the main objection (the so-called *tolmēros logos*) brought up against Plotinus' own doctrine of freedom, in chapter 7, is of gnostic origin. The most recent advocate of this interpretation is Narbonne (2011c) and the hypothesis is well discussed in Leroux (1990: 106–23). I do not feel competent enough to pass judgement on this identification. I do think however that not enough has been done to clarify the many ties Plotinus' account of freedom has with the Greek philosophical tradition in general, and I hope this essay will be helpful in this respect.

27

Freedom, providence and fate

Peter Adamson

Few issues interested late ancient philosophers as much as providence and its relation to fate and human freedom. Already in the generations leading up to Plotinus, Alexander of Aphrodisias wrote treatises entitled *On Fate* and *On Providence*. In this same period various "Middle" Platonists articulated a distinction between fate and providence that was still used by some of the latest pagan Neoplatonist thinkers. Plotinus wrote treatises that Porphyry saw fit to title *On Fate* (*Enn.* III.1[3]) and *On Providence* (*Enn.* III.2–3[47–8]), not to mention the treatise called *On the Voluntary and the Will of the One* (*Enn.* VI.8[39]), one of Plotinus' greatest works. Comments on the *Republic* by Porphyry have come down to us with the title *On What is Up to Us*. His student Iamblichus wrote letters on the subject of fate, preserved only as fragments, and discussed the topic in *On Mysteries*. Proclus, known above all for his commentaries on Plato and his Euclidean treatment of Neoplatonism, the *Elements of Theology*, also wrote two independent works on providence (three if one counts *On Evil*, which belongs to the same group). At about the same time, the Alexandrian Neoplatonist Hierocles also wrote a treatise *On Providence*. This is without even delving into the treatments of providence found in ancient Christian authors, which are of course influenced by Hellenic philosophical sources.

Thus we have plenty of material to work with in asking the questions of the present chapter: how did Neoplatonists conceive of providence and fate? What role did they leave for human autonomy in light of their commitment to providence? What conditions did they think needed to be satisfied for humans to possess autonomy? Along the way, we will also get a sense of why late ancient Platonists were so obsessed with these issues. Part of the reason is that providence and determinism had already been hotly debated in the preceding Hellenistic era. To take up these questions was, in particular, to position oneself relative to the Stoics. This is an explicit motive of Alexander's *On Fate*. Even as Stoicism faded into history, astrological determinism remained a threat to human autonomy. Plotinus worries about this in several treatises, and Proclus' *On Providence* is aimed at a determinist interlocutor, Theodore the Engineer, who may have been influenced by

Stoicism and astrology (Steel 2007: 2, 14). But the Platonists' continuing fascination with providence and fate suggests that there was more at stake here than refuting determinist opponents. Rather, the issue proved to be a useful way to explore central difficulties inherent to Neoplatonism itself. One of these was the difficulty of how the gods relate to the physical cosmos. Are they to blame for evils found in the sublunary world? Do they even pay attention to particular events in that world? Another was the problem of whether embodied human souls are entirely trapped within the physical realm. As we will see at the end of this chapter, both of these puzzles were made more pressing still by passages in the dialogues of Plato, especially that *locus classicus* for the Platonic view of providence and freedom, the Myth of Er.

FATE AND PROVIDENCE

The god is superior to necessity.
(Iamblichus, *Myst.* 3.18, trans. Clarke *et al.* 2003)

A range of "Middle" Platonist authors, including Alcinous, Apuleius and Pseudo-Plutarch, distinguish fate (*heimarmenē*) from providence (*pronoia*).[1] Providence is a higher cause than fate, and embraces fate within its scope. Pseudo-Plutarch (*On Fate*) further distinguishes providence into three types, exercised respectively by the creator god (the Demiurge of the *Timaeus*), the heavenly gods, and *daimones*.[2] But as this subdivision shows, the basic notion is that providence proceeds from divine or other superhuman entities. The providence exercised by the highest divinities influences and bestows beneficial order not only on the physical cosmos, but also on lower supernatural beings. Fate, by contrast, is limited to the physical world. The other main claim about fate in Middle Platonism is that it is conditional. A "fated law" (cf. *Ti.* 41e) has the form: anyone who does X will undergo Y. This is meant to ensure that human actions are subject to fate, in the sense that even remote and unforeseen consequences of our actions are ineluctably fated. On the other hand, the account attempts to leave room for human autonomy, because the initial action that leads to the fated consequences is "up to" the human agent. A classic (in every sense) example might be Oedipus' sorry end, which is initially triggered by his decision to kill a man at a crossroads.

In his treatise *On Fate*, Alexander of Aphrodisias likewise restricts fate to the physical realm, but he does not adopt the idea of fate as a conditional law.[3] For Alexander, fate must be an efficient cause, which acts for the sake of something, and is operative always or for the most part (§4–5). In fact, fate ought to be characterized by immutability and necessity. Alexander proposes that we can satisfy these demands by identifying fate with nature. It is fate, for example, that ensures the propagation of all eternal species through generations of forebears and offspring. Alexander's conception of fate is in sharp contrast to that of the Middle Platonists. Whereas they saw fate as being concerned with the consequences of human action, Alexander argues that human actions (along with chance events, §8) constitute a different kind of event entirely. This is shown by the fact that nature or fate acts always or for the most part, whereas human actions are "up to" or "in the power of" human agents. We cannot presume that a given human agent in a given situation will perform a given action (e.g. the virtuous action rather than the vicious action, or even a minor movement like raising the eyebrows: §9, and for the point more generally, §12), the way we can presume that a pregnant horse will give birth to a foal, or that fire will give rise to heat.

On the other hand, Alexander agrees again with the Platonists in distinguishing fate from providence, and seeing fate as causally posterior to providence. His *On Providence*, lost in Greek but extant in two Arabic versions, argues that providence is exercised by the divine movers of the heavenly spheres, using these spheres as instruments to bring about a well-ordered sublunary world.[4] This idea has clear affinities with astrology, something exploited by philosophers writing in Arabic who drew on the treatise (Adamson 2007: 181–206). But Alexander's objective in *On Providence* is not to show that particular events in our world are intended by the gods. To the contrary, he believes that it would be impossible and inappropriate for the gods to direct their concern to multiple events in our world (*Fat.* 17–21; 65). Rather, the heavenly gods exercise providence universally, guaranteeing a world order in which natural species are eternally preserved, but not bestowing their attention on particular members of those species (*Fat.* 67). To put this point another way, providence brings about nature or fate, but not the individual events or substances that fall under the scope of nature or fate.

Something else the Middle Platonists and Alexander have in common is a desire to refute the Stoics. This is made especially explicit in Alexander's *On Fate*, which criticizes the Stoics at length. Different though they may be, the Platonist and Peripatetic theories share an advantage over the Stoic conception of providence. The Stoics see divine providence as a force immanent within this world, and reduce all things to this single cause. The anti-Stoic views instead allow providence to govern all things (albeit only in a general way, in the case of Alexander) without making all other causes mere instruments of providence. This is possible in part because both Alexander and the Platonists, rejecting the physicalism of the Stoics, postulate immaterial causes. It is noteworthy that Alexander, no less than the Platonists, wants to associate providence with the divine, and fate with physical things. Because the Stoics trace all causation back to the single divine source, they can be accused of saddling God with the blame for evils and imperfections. Avoiding this is clearly in Alexander's mind when he distances the gods from particulars. The Platonist conception of fate avoids blaming the gods by making suffering the well-deserved consequence of human actions. Furthermore, the Stoic "single-cause" theory supposedly provides no basis for distinguishing human action from the workings of fate or providence. As Plotinus will later put it when criticizing the deterministic theories of Stoics and astrologers (*Enn.* III.1[3].5), they make humans to be nothing more than stones that have been set rolling. The anti-Stoic theories, by contrast, give human actions a special status to ensure that, even if our actions are within the realm of fate, they are not determined by fate.

The contrast between fate and providence was remarkably durable in the Platonist tradition. In his great treatise *On Providence* Plotinus sounds very like a Middle Platonist when he says that the providence of all things is one: "but it is fate starting from what is worse, whereas up above it is just providence" (*Enn.* III.3[48].5, my trans.). One letter Iamblichus wrote on fate says that "fate exists by virtue of the existence of providence, and it derives its existence from it".[5] Proclus in his own *On Providence* (extant in Latin) similarly remarks that "providence is to be distinguished from fate (*providentia differat a fato*), as god differs from what is divine".[6] He also provides an etymological account in support of the contrast. The word *pronoia* indicates that providence comes from the highest principle, the Good, which is prior (*pro*) to intellect (*nous*), whereas *heimarmenē* relates fate to the idea of *heirmos*, that is, the "connection" between things in the corporeal world (Steel 2007: 44, 46). The same etymology is offered by Hierocles.[7]

Among these authors it is Hierocles who most clearly operates with the Middle Platonist idea that fate is the meting out of punishment (or "justice": *dikē*) for previous human actions. Providence meanwhile ensures the distribution of fated punishments (*Prov.* codex 214.4; 251.6, 14). This is not to say that fate is restricted to the consequences of human action. It also includes all things that happen to irrational animals,[8] and in general fate is simply the good order of the cosmos (*On the Golden Verses* 11.27). But Hierocles is most interested in fate as applied to human actions, actions which are not themselves caused by fate. Rather, as Hierocles puts it, "choices are in our power, while the just consequences of our choices lie with the ethereal beings" (*Prov.* 251.11). He gives the analogy of a murderer, who willingly chooses to commit murder but certainly does not willingly choose the punishment given him by a judge (*On the Golden Verses* 11.11–12).

Hierocles here makes the point that the judge's punishment is "primarily" handed down to the murderer, but only "accidentally" directed at this individual man. For the judge punishes him in so far as he is a murderer, not in so far as he is this individual. This may seem to suggest that the judge – and by analogy, divine providence – pays no heed to individuals and only cares about general laws, like Alexander's divine causes. But elsewhere Hierocles says explicitly that "providence among men is directed to each individual" (*On the Golden Verses* 11.33, trans. Schibli). The apparent contradiction can be resolved in light of Hierocles' use of the word "primarily". "Primarily" providence is directed towards the satisfaction of universal laws. Only "secondarily" does it affect certain people who subject themselves to the laws of fate through their choices.[9] Thus the gods can punish them without being arbitrary.

As I say, Hierocles is unusually explicit among Neoplatonists in describing fate as (in part) a kind of conditional necessity regarding human actions. But the idea did not disappear between the second and fifth centuries. Plotinus, for instance, writes that no one can escape the "law of the universe" and that when souls fall into error "justice (*dikē*) follows" (*Enn.* III.2[47].4). Plotinus' student Porphyry gives us an analogy that works in much the same way as Hierocles' case of the murderer (*On What is Up to Us*, frag. 271 [Smith]). He wishes to illustrate that "fate is like the prescriptions of laws, it itself being a law" (trans. Wilberding). Porphyry's example is a thief, who is not forced by the law to steal but must suffer punishment if he does. On the other hand, we just saw that Hierocles associates fate not only with the results of human actions, but also with the cosmic order in general. This is only one example of the close connection drawn by Neoplatonists between nature and fate. In one passage Proclus actually identifies the two, writing that fate is "the nature of this world, an incorporeal substance … it moves bodies from the inside and not from the outside, moving everything according to time and connecting the movements of all things that are dissociated in time and place" (*Prov.* 12, trans. Steel).[10] Iamblichus is more nuanced when he says, in the only surviving fragment from one of his letters on fate, that "the substance of fate is entirely *within* nature (*sympasa estin en tēi physei*)".[11]

This brings us to another central Neoplatonic idea about fate: it is limited to the natural, corporeal world, unlike divine providence which governs all things.[12] So although humans are always entirely within the care of providence, we exist beyond the scope of fate with that part of ourselves that is immaterial. Only in so far as we have bodies and bodily existence do we fall under fate. Unfortunately, most humans are benighted enough that they live only at the level of the physical world. Their limited perspective means that they are in effect entirely within fate, whereas wiser people who are cognizant of immaterial reality are subject to it only by virtue of their lower, bodily selves. Plotinus thus writes:

> We must flee from here and separate ourselves from additional accretions (*tōn prosgegenēmenōn*), not being the composite, an ensouled body in which the bodily nature is more in control (*kratei*)… but the other soul, which is outside, has a movement towards what is higher and towards the noble and divine, which nobody can control (*kratei*). … Otherwise, deprived of this soul, one lives within the scope of fate (*zēi en heimarmenēi*).   (*Enn*. II.3[52].9.19–28, my trans.)

This is a radical version of earlier attempts to safeguard a role for human autonomy, while also accepting that fate is without exception efficacious within its proper sphere.

FREEDOM FROM NECESSITY

> The immaterial is the free.
>
> (Plotinus, *Enn*. VI.8[39].6)

The Neoplatonists are thus committed to what may seem a surprising view, namely that one has a choice about whether or not one will be entirely subject to fate.[13] The wrong path is to identify oneself with the lower soul and the body, in which case one surrenders to determination by external causes. Proclus describes this option succinctly: "when rendered corporeal, we are necessarily led by fate (*corporati ex necessitate a fato ducimur*)" (*Prov*. 21). The other option is of course to liberate oneself from body and thus from necessity and fate. Different Neoplatonists give different accounts of how such liberation can occur. Plotinus, notoriously, thinks that a part of every soul remains always attached to intellect. For Iamblichus, by contrast, souls (or perhaps only impure souls[14]) require the intervention of theurgy to achieve liberation. In *On Mysteries* 8.7, he speaks of this theurgic process in terms of the gods "freeing us from fate".

The Neoplatonist account has several virtues. It integrates the earlier accounts of fate with fundamental Neoplatonist ethical precepts. It also explains and critiques the link between determinism and materialism in Stoicism: the Stoics were always bound to wind up as determinists, since they mistake their bodies for their true selves. Another advantage, never one to be overlooked in Neoplatonism, is that it makes good exegetical sense of Plato, in this case offering an account of the *Timaeus*' contrast between intellect and necessity (cf. in Plotinus, e.g. *Enn*. III.2[47].2). The passage from *On Mysteries* just mentioned alludes to the *Timaeus*, when Iamblichus writes that only the gods, "ruling over necessity (*tēs anangkēs archontes*) through intellectual persuasion, release us from evils laid in store for us from fate" (*Myst*. 8.7). Proclus makes the point still more explicit when, in a gloss on *Timaeus* 48a, he aligns Plato's contrast with the traditional distinction between fate and providence (albeit that providence is strictly seen as transcending intellect):

> Plato calls "necessity" the moving cause of the bodies, which he calls "fate" in other texts. … There is no choice (*electio*) in bodies. … Thus Plato set necessity to preside

over the coming to be of bodies ... but he removed intellect from it, ordering it to rule over necessity. If, then, providence is above intellect, it is evident that it rules over (*principatur*) intellect and over all those things that fall under necessity, and that necessity rules only over the things that fall under it.

(Prov. 13, trans. Steel, modified)

Notice that, like the Middle Platonists and Alexander, the Neoplatonists have managed to link fate to necessity while also insisting that we retain autonomy in the face of this necessity. For the Middle Platonists, the necessity was qualified by being only conditional on original choices. For Alexander, human choices are simply outside the framework of fate, which is natural necessity. For Neoplatonists, our freedom from necessity lies in a life of immaterial, intellectual activity achieved through philosophy (or theurgy).

Now we must confront an objection. The Neoplatonist account explains that we are exempt from necessity (*anangkē*) in so far as we are souls that transcend body, and hence transcend nature, fate and necessity. But what good does it do us to transcend fate, if we are still subject to providence? We have just seen Proclus, for instance, saying that providence even "rules over" intellect. This fits well with his aforementioned etymology of *pronoia* ("before intellect"). But it also shows that we humans inevitably fall under the rule of providence, given that we are ourselves below intellect or, at best, at the level of intellect. The difficulty emerges nicely in the following passage from Hierocles: "There are three possibilities in what concerns us: that everything is the result of necessity, that nothing is, that everything happens with or without necessity alternatively. ... They are equally absurd and equally destructive of all providence" (*Prov.* 251.11). Surely, if divine providence rules all things and fate does not, then it is divine providence and not fate that threatens to make all things necessary. Hierocles tries to solve the problem by insisting that our choices are up to us, with providence merely guaranteeing that these choices will be punished or rewarded appropriately through the mechanism of fate. But if providence includes all things, it is hard to see why the original choices themselves should escape necessitation – not by fate, but by providence itself.[15]

Neoplatonists might hope to solve this problem by exploiting the notion that the soul is, as Plotinus puts it, "on the horizon" of the sensible and intelligible realms (*Enn.* IV.4[28].3), and "amphibious" (IV.8[6].4), capable of living in both. The soul is by its nature neither doomed to succumb to body and "necessity" nor to fly upwards to intellect – it has a choice between the two. This point is made with particular emphasis by Proclus:

The intellectual life must be opposed to sense perception, as it is immaterial, separate and self-activating. To this life we must attribute choice (*electio*), which may tend to both sides, upwards and downwards, towards the intellect from which it originated and towards sense perception which it generated. Sense perception, however, and all forms of life together with the bodies are without choice. (*Prov.* 44)

The gist of this response is that in so far as we are separate from body we have a choice (a power for "self-activation") which is irreducibly in the power of the chooser. It is determined by neither providence nor fate. When we choose to identify with the body, to go downwards rather than upwards, we are thenceforth deprived of choice and subject to fate. This is comparable to the original, un-fated choice in the Middle Platonic theory, which once made subjects the chooser to necessary consequences. We will explore this response further when we look at Neoplatonic treatments of the Myth of Er.

But first, let us dwell on the irony of the situation just envisaged. It seems to be tantamount to the following: you are given the opportunity either to (a) submit to the control of an external agent (here, the body and its necessity) or (b) unswervingly devote the rest of your life to intellectual contemplation. Would you really say, in this situation, that you would be "free" in choosing option (b)? After all, the only other alternative is option (a), which involves giving up one's very capacity for choice. Looked at from this point of view, the choice facing the amphibious soul hardly looks like a choice at all, because one of the options brings with it utter slavery. Even the other, preferable option looks like merely submitting to the rule of providence, which is what we originally worried would compromise our autonomy. Arguably, the situation described by Proclus is a choice between enslavement by the body and rule by the gods. The only choice is which master to serve.

A powerful answer to this difficulty is offered by Plotinus in *Enn.* VI.8[39] (see Chapter 26, by Collette-Dučić). His goal is to explain the sense in which anything is "up to" the gods or "in their power". Characteristically, though, he begins lower down in the system by considering what it means for something to be "up to us *(eph' hēmin)*" in the case of human souls.[16] Plotinus provides a careful and lengthy analysis of the meaning of this phrase, and how it relates to terms like "self-determination *(autexousion)*", "wish *(boulēsis)*", "freedom *(eleutheron)*" and the "voluntary *(hekousion)*". I will not pretend to give an adequate recounting of his analysis here, but make only a few points germane to our difficulty. First, Plotinus seems to hold consistently throughout VI.8[39] that something is "up to me" only if I am "in charge *(kyrios)*" with regard to that thing. Thus he says, right at the outset, that when we are subject to "opposed fortunes and necessities" we judge these things to be our "masters *(kyria)*" and ourselves "enslaved *(douleuontes)*" to them (*Enn.* VI.8[39].1.23–30). Tellingly, when he alludes to the conditions Aristotle requires for an action to be voluntary – it must be done not under compulsion *(bia)* or out of ignorance – Plotinus adds that we must "be in charge of what we do *(kyrioi praxai)*" (VI.8[39].1.34).

Plotinus elucidates this notion of being "in charge" by contrasting it to the situation where we are influenced by "what is outside". As he says, "how can we be in charge when we are being led?" (*Enn.* VI.8[39].2.19). Plotinus worries that even our own desires and wishes could threaten to take away our control – the paradigm case being an action performed in thrall to bodily appetites. Correspondingly, an action that is wholly "up to" the agent would be one where the agent was entirely free from external compulsion. This has the significant consequence that Plotinus' notion of autonomy (the "up to us", "being in charge", etc.) does not require the presence of alternative possibilities. He makes this point when he worries that a higher principle, like intellect, will lack freedom *(eleutheron)* if it always performs the same activity by its very nature. He responds:

> Where there is no compulsion to follow another, how can one speak of slavery? How could something borne towards the good be under compulsion, since its desire for the good will be voluntary if it knows that it is good and goes to it as good? For the involuntary is a leading away from the good and towards the compulsory. … It is for this reason that slavery is ill spoken of, not where one has no power to go to the bad, but where one has no power to go to one's own good but is led away to the good of another.   (*Enn.* VI.8[39].4.11–22, trans. Armstrong)

Here again, in the last phrase, we have the idea that autonomy or freedom is compromised not by the absence of multiple options, but by the threat of determination from outside.[17] This conveniently sets up Plotinus to argue that the One itself has "self-determination (*to autexousion*)" in the strongest possible sense, because nothing influences it in any way whatsoever (e.g. VI.8[39].7.42–5).

This seems a good response to the objection that the option of enslaving oneself is not a genuine one – Plotinus can simply say that the absence of genuine options need not impair our freedom. But is there not still the difficulty that in choosing the right path of intellectual life, the soul would merely submit to a better, but still external, master – the source of divine providence? Plotinus has an answer ready here too: the divine is not really external to the soul, but is the soul's true identity. Thus, at least in *Enn.* VI.8, Plotinus does not identify soul's freedom with a choice between "up and down" that is available to it because of its immateriality. Rather, he says that the soul *becomes* free (*ginetai eleuthera*) when it rises upwards towards the Good, by means of intellect (VI.8[39].7.1–2). For Plotinus, we become free by becoming truly ourselves.[18]

One might speculate that this position is available to Plotinus in a way that it is not to later figures like Iamblichus and Proclus. After all, they reject the doctrine of the undescended soul. They might therefore be more reluctant to say that the source of providence simply *is* the soul's true self. In fact it is even worse than this, because, as we saw, Proclus says that providence (*pro-noia*) comes from *before* intellect; that is, from the Good itself. So to avoid the idea that soul is determined "from the outside" by providence, we might need to contemplate the prospect of identifying the soul, or some aspect of soul, with the Good. Here we are in danger of wading into deep metaphysical waters. For current purposes, I will simply note that Iamblichus' rejection of the undescended soul does not prevent him from agreeing with Plotinus that soul is fully free, not in so far as it can choose between body and intellect, but in so far as it chooses the latter option:

> [The substance of soul] contains within itself self-determined and independent life. And insofar as it gives itself to the realm of generation and subjects itself to the motion of the cosmos (*tēn tou pantos phoran*), thus far also it is drawn beneath the sway of fate and is enslaved to the necessities of nature (*douleuei tais tēs physeōs anangkais*). But insofar, on the other hand, as it exercises its intellectual activity, activity that is really left free from everything and independent in its choices, thus far it voluntarily "does its own" and lays hold of what is divine.
>
> (*Letter* 8, frag. 2, trans. Dillon & Polleichtner, modified)

NEOPLATONISTS ON THE MYTH OF ER

> Virtue has no master … god is blameless.
>
> (Plato, *R.* 617e, my trans.)

The Neoplatonists have a mostly well-deserved reputation for being selective readers of Plato. In part because of their philosophical concerns and in part because of their school curriculum, they concentrate more on certain dialogues, and on certain passages within those dialogues, at the expense of others. When it comes to fate, providence and freedom, the *Timaeus* is seen as a particularly important text, as we have seen already. Book X of the *Laws* is also central to Neoplatonic discussions. But in this final section I want to look at a third favourite text related to these themes: the Myth of Er, which concludes the tenth and final book of the *Republic* (614b–621d).[19]

The Myth recounts a vision of the afterlife seen by a man named Er, who came back from the brink of death after falling in battle. He sees souls returning from their thousand-year sojourns, either below the earth where they have received recompense (*dikē*, 615a) for misdeeds, or in heaven where they have been rewarded for good deeds. He proceeds with these souls to witness the structure of the cosmos, which revolves on a spindle seated in the lap of the goddess Necessity (*Anangkē*, 617b). The three daughters of Necessity, the Fates, are also in attendance, and the system regulating the apportionment of earthly lives to the souls is explained by the representative of one of the Fates, Lachesis (617d–e). The souls randomly receive lots which set the order in which they will choose their next lives. The representative informs them that they will be bound to their chosen lives by necessity (*ex anangkēs*, 617e) through the offices of a guardian spirit or *daimon*. Still, the choice of life itself is up to them. He later adds that even those who choose last will still have good lives available to them (619b). Thus, despite the element of necessitation, "virtue has no master (*adespoton*); each person has it more or less depending on whether he honors it or not. The blame belongs to the chooser; god is blameless (*aitia helomenou, theosanaitios*)" (617e, my trans.).

Er then watches as the souls make their choices. The first rashly picks a life distinguished by its tyrannical power, not noticing the tragedies that will befall him: in accordance with fate (*heimarmenē*), he will eat his own children. Souls that were humans become animals, and vice versa. The representative's promise that the holder of the final lot can still choose well is borne out by the soul who was Odysseus. He goes last and carefully selects a quiet and peaceful life (620c). Many of the choices, including this final one, are explained with reference to the souls' previous experiences. But, as Socrates makes clear in a speech of his own (618b–619b) that he dramatically inserts into his account of the rules governing the choice of lives, it is philosophy that provides the surest preparation for choosing well. For philosophy teaches us to value a life for its degree of justice – to "honour virtue", in the words of the representative. This is the preferable choice both while we are alive and in light of the prospect of punishment in the hereafter (618e).

One does not need to be a Neoplatonist to think that this Myth is of great importance for the themes of providence, fate and freedom. It seems to anticipate several of the ideas we have seen above; for instance, that suffering in this life is requital for earlier bad choices. Of course, this is no coincidence. The Middle Platonist idea of fate as a conditional law was always intended, in part, as an interpretation of this passage in the *Republic*.[20] Many of the tendencies we have observed in Neoplatonist authors are likewise anticipated in the Myth. For instance, the Myth can provide a basis for integrating astrology with philosophical accounts of providence, given that Necessity presides over heavenly motion as well as the dispensation of lives. The Myth also upholds three ideas dear to our Neoplatonist authors: there is divine oversight of all things that happen to humans; despite this, humans are autonomous and hence responsible ("the blame belongs to the chooser"); therefore, the gods are blameless.

Another striking implication of the Myth, bound to fascinate any Neoplatonist, is that the power of choice is exercised above all when the soul is disembodied. In fact, the Myth might well be read as saying that souls *only* get a chance to choose how their lives will go at this moment before they have been reborn into bodies.[21] Once this choice has been made, a *daimon* will make sure that the chosen life unfolds as foreordained, for good or ill. Thus the rash soul who goes first and chooses the life of the child-eating tyrant can no longer avoid this fate once he is born. Neoplatonists who engage with the Myth – and pretty well all of them do – have mixed feelings about this implication of Er's vision. On the one hand, it fits nicely with the idea we explored in the previous section: embodiment is linked to necessitation, and freedom of choice to freedom from the body. On the other hand, they tend to balk at the suggestion that choice, or morally significant choice, can only occur prior to birth. Indeed, that would undermine their insistence that we can, even during our embodied lives, wrench ourselves away from bodily concerns and choose a life of philosophical contemplation.

Among the authors we have been considering, Hierocles seems most attracted to the idea that significant choice occurs solely before birth. Photius, the Christian author who is our source for *On Providence*,[22] in fact summarizes Hierocles' position as follows:

> The great argument on which [Hierocles] counts most is human souls' existence before this life and interchange of bodies (*probiotē kai metensōmatōsis*)… he thinks that through it he can confirm divine providence, establish the "up to us" and self-mastery (*to eph' hēmin kai autodespoton*), and so actually serve the [idea of] fate (*heimarmenē*) that is so dear to him.   (*Bibliotheca* 214.6)

The word *autodespoton* is presumably a reminiscence of the Myth of Er's claim that virtue is *adespoton*. If so, it is one of several allusions to the Myth scattered throughout the evidence concerning Hierocles. The allusions are particularly dense in the last part of Photius' summary of *On Providence*:

> Each one of us obtains by the decision of our judicial *daimones* the life deserved on the basis of our previous lives. In this life everything (*panta*) has been included: ancestry, city, father, mother, the moment of conception, such-and-such a body, the modes of behaviour and various fortunes (*tychai*) that belong to life, the manner and appointed hour of our death. And there is a *daimon* whose role it is to guard and fulfil these things. … The ordinances of providence, the judgements of the daemons, the lots of our lives, the requitals for ancient sins, and other factors determine both the moment and manner of our death. Thus both chosen actions and apparent chance events are connected to the fate of each of us and fulfil the recompense that is deserved. … Human choices are corrected by the laws of fate which the Demiurge has ordained for our souls.   (251.29, 31)

Elsewhere, Hierocles also emphasizes the Myth's theme that the gods are blameless for what we suffer.[23]

There seems to be a tension between Hierocles' talk of choice (*prohairesis*) and his emphasis that our lives unfold in a way that is preordained, and guaranteed by daemonic action. Hierocles seems almost to revel in the apparent paradox when he remarks, "we say that even as one is allotted (*klērousthai*) one's life, one chooses it" (251.15). In light of Photius' claim that the cycle of reincarnation was pivotal in Hierocles' account, the difficulty might be resolved as follows. Our present lives are indeed preordained, perhaps even down to the smallest detail (note Hierocles' use of the word *panta* – albeit that this could perhaps mean the entire context in which we choose). But in line with the Middle Platonist doctrine of fate, all this is divine recompense for previous choices. Those choices were made freely, and if we chose badly we are punished justly for it. Hence we and not the gods are to be blamed for what we suffer, as stated in the Myth. One might object that if the relevant choices were made in previous lives that were also subject to fate, then those choices too should have been preordained, so that the puzzle remains unsolved (a complaint made by Schibli [2002: 135–6]). But Hierocles may be adhering more closely to the Myth, and thinking of a choice of lives that occured after our previous earthly incarnation and before the present one. This is suggested by Photius' phrase "existence before this life and interchange of bodies" in the quotation from 214.6 above. On the other hand, Photius presents Hierocles as speaking of "the life deserved on the basis of our *previous lives*" in the quotation from 251.29. Still, if Hierocles does think that souls choose their next lives before being embodied, that would fit nicely with the Neoplatonic conviction that we exercise choice above all before birth, when we are free of the body.

Other Neoplatonists, though, would be unhappy about locating all significant human freedom at a moment of disembodiment. A particularly clear case is Porphyry, whose treatment of the Myth of Er is preserved by another Christian anthologist, John Stobaeus, and given the title *On What is Up to Us*.[24] Porphyry squarely addresses the threat posed to human autonomy by Plato's teaching in the Myth. He writes that the Myth "seems at risk of doing away with the 'up to us (*to eph' hēmin*)' and in general with our so-called self-determination (*to autexousion*)". He then explains: "Since these things have been assigned (*epikeklōsmenōn*) as well as necessitated and ratified by the Fates and Lethe and Necessity, with a *daimon* accompanying them and standing guard over their fate, of what could we be in charge (*kyrioi*)? And how is it still the case that 'virtue has no master'?" (frag. 268). Porphyry's question shows that he will not be satisfied by saying that our lives have been chosen in advance by us, before we were born. For the necessitation of the Fates, the guarding of the *daimon*, and so on are subsequent to that choice of lives. Rather, he worries that we will be deprived of control *during* this chosen life.

His solution is an innovative one. There are two kinds of choice available to the soul. The first, and more significant, choice is made prior to embodiment when the general form of existence – the "first life" – is selected by the soul. At this stage the soul decides whether it will be a human or a non-human animal, for instance, and whether it will inhabit a male or female body. But there remains scope for control within this life:

> The whole meaning of Plato's theory seems to be something like this: souls, prior to falling into bodies and different lives, have the power of self-determination for choosing (*helesthai*) this or that life, which they are to live out with a certain life-form and a body appropriate to that life-form. For it is up to them to choose the life of a lion or of a man. That power of self-determination, however, is hindered as soon as they fall into one of these kinds of lives. Once they have gone down into bodies and become souls of living things instead of unconfined souls, they bear [only] the power of self-determination that is appropriate to the constitution of that living thing. (Frag. 270)

The "constitution (*kataskeuē*)" of the soul removes some of the soul's power of self-deter-mination, especially if it comes to reside in a non-human animal body which will force it to live "along a single track (*monotropon*)". But souls in human bodies retain "more range of movement (*polykinēton*)", and apparently every soul has at least some residual power of self-determination, except for those humans who are totally given over to vice (frag. 268). Despite this twofold complexity in Porphyry's account, he anticipates Hierocles in associating the Myth with the standard teaching on fate as divine retribution for the soul's choices.[25]

It is worth pausing to consider how Porphyry's position compares to what we saw in Plotinus, for whom self-determination and *to eph' hēmin* are to do with causal control, and not the presence of multiple possibilites. It is striking that Porphyry too initially formu-lates the difficulty in terms of being *kyrios* ("in charge"), which suggests that his concerns are the same as his master's. On the other hand, both the first and second choices of lives have to do with selecting from among alternatives. (Lion or man? If man, then virtu-ous or vicious?) It would seem, however, that the choice between alternatives matters to Porphyry not as such, but because it is an indication of causal control. This is suggested by his remarks on the stars and their relation to our chosen lives. He is enough of a believer in astrology that he thinks our lives can be predicted, at least in part, using our natal horoscopes. But Porphyry insists that the stars' positions at our births only "signify", and do not "necessitate", the events of our future lives (frag. 271). This is not because he wants to say that the stars leave open multiple possible futures. To the contrary, as this fragment goes on, Porphyry says explicitly that the choice of first life is immutable once it has been made. Rather, the contrast between signification and necessitation is intended to preserve the point that it is the souls, not the stars, that are to be identified as the *causes* of the first lives.[26] Furthermore, thanks to the possibility of a "second choice" the souls remain caus-ally efficacious even after they have been born.

Porphyry's meticulous exegesis of the Myth of Er suggests that it was read carefully in Plotinus' school. This is confirmed by the fact that Plotinus devoted a short treatise to it: *Enneads* III.4[15], titled by Porphyry *On Our Allotted (eilēchotos) Daimon*. The opening chapter already raises a key theme of the treatise, namely "being in control" or "being dominant" (*kratein*). In humans, soul generates the faculty of growth but "controls" or "dominates" it, whereas in plants, the growth faculty "is in control, because it has become, as it were, alone (*kratei hoion monē genomenē*)" (*Enn.* III.4[15].1.5). Plotinus moves from plants to animals in chapter 2, quoting Plato's *Phaedrus* to the effect that soul appears in different forms (*en allois eidesin*, *Phdr.* 246b) as a way of introducing the topic of human–animal transmigration. In humans there is a struggle between the lower aspects of growth and sense-perception, and a better aspect which is rational. Again Plotinus describes this struggle as one over "control", but adds that the rational aspect of soul needs not only to control the lower parts but to "flee upwards". Those who live rationally become human in their next incarnation; others will receive animal forms or even plant forms as appropriate to the way they have lived this time around (*Enn.* III.4[15].2.16–30).

All this provides a natural introduction to a discussion of the Myth of Er, which itself becomes dominant in the rest of the treatise. As suggested by the title chosen by Porphyry, Plotinus is particularly interested in the status of the guiding *daimon* mentioned in the Myth. He identifies this as whatever is immediately superior to the operative aspect (*to energēsan*) of each soul – in other words, whichever aspect has dominated the soul in its previous incarnation. For instance, if someone lives by sense-perception, the rational aspect of the soul (*to logikon*) will be his *daimon*. By choosing our life during this incarnation (e.g. by choosing to live a life devoted to sensation), we also choose our *daimon*. Plotinus' view is characteristically optimistic: each of us, no matter how debased, has a higher aspect which is leading him or her on to improve their rank within the order of things. But the lower aspect can refuse to be led. It too is a *daimon* – after all, there can be bad *daimones* as well – and if it "takes control" it can lead a human down into the life of a beast. Hence the soul can become anything from bodily to divine, depending on whether it is led by its lower or upper *daimon*; that is, the worse aspect that has dominated the soul in the past or the better aspect that would lead it to higher things (*Enn.* III.4[15].3.5–16).

This brings Plotinus to what seems the critical question of the treatise, and indeed the critical question for any interpretation of the Myth (cf. Porphyry's similar puzzle in *On What is Up to Us*): "if [the soul] chooses the *daimon* there [before entering the body], and chooses its life, then how could it still be in charge (*kyrioi*)?" Plotinus gives an explicitly de-mythologizing answer:

> The so-called "choice (*hairesis*)" there is a riddle (*ainittetai*) for the soul's universal and ever-present will (*prohairesis*) and disposition (*diathesis*). If, however, the soul's will is in charge (*kyria*), and that part has control (*kratei*) which is ready from the previous lives, then the body is in no way to blame (*aition*) for evil [that comes] to him. (*Enn.* III.4[15].5.2–6, my trans.)

In other words, the (descended) soul is already good or bad when it comes into the body, because its previous lives have prepared it either to succumb to the body or to resist it. For this reason, even a substandard body will not thwart the soul if it is good. The point of the Myth is not – as it might seem – that souls are somehow deprived of control in this life. Rather, Plato's message is precisely that souls always have mastery (*to kyrion*). The *daimon* which is leading or supervising the soul is not controlling it from the outside – which would, as we recall from *Enn.* VI.8[39], compromise the soul's autonomy and freedom – and this for two reasons, both of which were established earlier in the treatise. First, the *daimon* is not actually "operative (*energōn*)", but is the aspect superior and adjacent to the operative aspect of soul. Second, the *daimon* is not in fact outside the soul completely, since it too belongs to soul, albeit not to the soul in so far as it leads this or that life (*Enn.* III.4[15].5.19–22).

To spell this out in more concrete terms, the man who is living a life dedicated to sensible pleasure is to be held responsible for that life, both because he has "chosen" it by living in a similar way in previous incarnations, and because he ought to avail himself of the influence of his better *daimon* (which in his case is the rational aspect of his soul). By contrast, the sage (*ho spoudaios*) is the one who allows his higher aspect to become active (*energei*); the *daimon* is not an external force "acting in concert with him (*synergounta*)" (*Enn.* III.4[15].6.1–3). Again, this would compromise the sage's autonomy. The upshot is that the soul's current disposition has been chosen by the soul in previous lives and is still being chosen all the time. This is not to say that everything is up to the soul, or even that everything that comes to the soul is necessarily deserved. Plotinus does not, like Hierocles, seem wedded to the thought that suffering in this life is a punishment for what has come before. He does speak of *dikē* (*Enn.* III.4[15].6.17), but only as something that occurs between death and rebirth (in fact he contrasts *dikē* to *bios* – punishment is not the same thing as incarnated life).

Regarding the turns of fortune that do befall us in this life, Plotinus instead offers a masterful (and very Greek) analogy. Perhaps thinking of the "ship of state" image in the *Republic*, Plotinus says that the spindle of Necessity places us into the cosmos as if in a boat. A passenger will be moved along with a boat when it is tossed by a storm, yet one can also move about "by oneself (*par autou*)" even on a storm-tossed boat. Likewise, each soul experiences threats to its autonomy, but remains responsible for itself. Plotinus concludes his treatise with an almost comically lapidary summary of the way various souls react to bodily events in various ways: "Different things, then, happen to different people, either because the same things befall them, or different things. Or the same things happen to people who are not the same, even if the things that befall them are different. That's how fate is (*touiouton gar hē heimarmenē*)" (*Enn* III.4[15].6.57–60, my trans.).

Elsewhere (in the much later *On Providence*), Plotinus does suggest that events in our lives may be recompense for deeds "in previous cycles (*pros tas prosthen periodous*)" (*Enn.* III.2[47].13.2–3). He illustrates this with chilling examples: matricides will be born as women so that they can be killed by their sons, and rapists will be born as women so that they may be raped. But here in *Enn.* III.4[15], Plotinus tends to shrug off earthly events as being nothing to us. This difference is more one of emphasis than doctrine. When divine providence is in focus, he is keen to show that the gods send no evils without justification. When he considers human autonomy, he is keen to show that bodily evils do not impair that autonomy. These are really just two sides of the core lesson of the Myth: responsibility lies not with the gods, but with us.[27]

The numerous tensions that beset Neoplatonic treatments of freedom, providence and fate are, then, already prefigured in the Myth of Er. Among these tensions, the most philosophically interesting one concerns the very question of how to conceive freedom or autonomy. Sometimes Neoplatonists depict freedom as something the soul *achieves* by turning away from body and towards intellect (as at *Enn.* VI.8[39].7, quoted above). At other times, freedom appears to belong to the soul by its very nature, because it has a choice whether to turn towards body or soul (as at Proclus, *Prov.* 44; for a classic statement of the choice, see *Enn.* V.1[10].1). The first of these two conceptions, with its assimilation of freedom to secure rational commitment, owes more than a little to Stoic compatibilism. The second, with its emphasis on a genuine option that confronts the soul, is more libertarian. The Myth of Er, with its dramatic vision of a choice between many possible lives, can support this libertarian view of freedom.[28] Yet as we have seen, it depicts the choice as occurring before birth – rather cold comfort, now that we are embodied. On the other hand, in his speech within the Myth Socrates claims that it is still within our power here and now to change our long-term fate by living a life of philosophy. This is hard to square with the all-encompassing choice made by the souls before birth. So if the Neoplatonists sometimes seem conflicted in their understanding of freedom, that may just show that they were good Platonists after all.

ACKNOWLEDGEMENTS

I am grateful for helpful comments from the editors, an anonymous referee, and Chris Noble.

NOTES

1. On this see e.g. Dillon (1996a), Dragona-Monachou (1994), Mansfeld (1999), Boys-Stones (2007b).
2. On *daimones* or demons in Plato and his heirs, see Timotin (2012).
3. For this work see Sharples ([1983] 2003), and for discussion D. Frede (1982), Sharples (2007). Cited by section numbers from Sharples ([1983] 2003).
4. Arabic text with German translation in Ruland (1976). Also available in French: Thillet (2003) and Italian: Fazzo & Zonta (1998). For discussion see Fazzo & Wiesner (1993), Sharples (1982). Cited by page number from Ruland.
5. Fragment 4 of Letter 8 (*To Macedonius*, the most extensively preserved letter on this topic); translation from Dillon & Polleichtner (2009). See further Taormina & Piccione (2010).
6. Translation from Steel (2007: 48). For the text and French translation see also Isaac (2003).
7. *On Providence*, codex 214.5, text and English translation in Schibli (2002). On Hierocles see also P. Hadot (2004).
8. *On Providence* 251.13, 30; *Commentary on the Golden Verses*, also in Schibli (2002: 11.28–32). Cf. Schibli's discussion at *ibid.*: 143.
9. See Schibli (2002: 229 n.18). Cf. Aristotle's example of the builder who accidentally produces health, because he also happens to be a doctor (*Metaph.* 6.2).
10. This may seem to bring Proclus' view into line with that of Alexander, but the two authors are separated by their different conceptions of nature. Proclus in fact criticizes Alexander for assimilating fate to nature when the latter is conceived of as the nature of individual animals and plants. See Proclus, *in Ti.* 3.272, cited by Schibli (2002: 153 n. 79).
11. *Letter* 12, *To Sopater on Fate*, ed. in Dillon & Polleichtner (2009), my translation and emphasis.
12. This relates to the idea that providence is universal, and fate particular, in so far as it is only at the corporeal level that we have multiple particulars that fall under the same kind. The position of souls here is rather ambiguous, in so far as each soul relates to a particular body, yet the souls themselves are incorporeal and, especially for Plotinus, keep a foothold in the intelligible realm. This helps to explain why they are able to submit to the particular workings of fate or to be guided by the universal rule of providence.
13. By contrast the Stoic view was that we are subjected to fate in any case, and either go along gladly or not. This is illustrated with the analogy of a dog tied to a cart, which either trots along obediently behind or is dragged unwillingly (see Long & Sedley 1987: 62A).
14. For this debate see van den Berg (1997) and Finamore (1997).
15. Schibli (2002: 135) likewise worries that Hierocles cannot really explain how it is that human souls are able to *initiate* causal sequences.
16. On the previous history of this concept and its meaning in Plotinus, see Eliasson (2008).
17. We can summarize this result by saying that for Plotinus, modal necessity (the lack of alternative possibilities) need not impair freedom; what impairs freedom is "necessity (*anangkē*)" in the sense of a requirement that was not of the agent's choosing, or that the agent might have reason to regret. I have explored this sense of "necessity", which can be traced back to Plato, in Adamson (2011).
18. The same holds at the level of intellect, except that it is eternally identical with its own objects and thus free of any need to seek itself. In this respect the intellect has permanently the sort of autonomy soul is trying to achieve – albeit that it remains dependent on the One, and thus lacks the One's utter autonomy and self-sufficiency.
19. On this and other eschatological myths in Plato see Annas (1982), Halliwell (1988), Partenie (2009).
20. See e.g. Alcinous, *Didaskalikos* 26, which explicitly connects the conditional theory of fate to the choice of lives made by a soul, and then paraphrases the Myth by adding that "the soul has no master (*adespoton*)" (trans. Dillon).
21. Socrates' interpolated speech seems to support this reading: he begins by saying that "the *entire* risk for mankind occurs here (*entha ... ho pas kindynos anthrōpōi*)" at the moment of the choice of lives (618b, emphasis added). Translators tend to avoid this implication by rendering *pas* more figuratively. Shorey has "the supreme hazard" (Hamilton & Cairns 1961), and Grube & Reeve have "the greatest danger of all" (J. M. Cooper 1997), both of which suggest that there remains scope for other significant choices, albeit not ones that are of such momentous importance.
22. Translations taken from Schibli (2002), with some modifications.
23. *On the Golden Verses* 9.8.19-20.

24. Translations taken from Wilberding (2011), with some modifications, and cited by fragment number from A. Smith (1993).
25. Cf. his example of the thief (frag. 271), already discussed above.
26. Indeed, with his contrast between signification and necessitation, Porphyry presumably has in mind the same contrast made by Plotinus when he says, at the beginning of *Enneads* II.3[52], that the stars merely signify (*sēmainei*) but do not actually cause (*poiei*) events in our lower world. On this see Adamson (2008), and for the contrast more generally Long (1982).
27. Unfortunately I do not have the space here to deal with the longest and most complex treatment of the Myth of Er in the Neoplatonic corpus – Proclus' sixteenth essay on the *Republic*, which is devoted entirely to the Myth. But see note 28 for one interesting passage.
28. For instance, Proclus says explicitly that if the soul can select only one life it will not have genuine choice, since choice requires preferring one object over another (*in R.* 16.262).

28

Action, reasoning and the highest good

Pauliina Remes

Ancient ethical theories are, as it is often pointed out, agent-centred. Instead of explaining morality in terms of actions and their circumstances, ancient philosophers start with the agent, her dispositions and knowledge, and her ethical character (Annas 1981: 157–8). While it might be true that to recognize a just action is in some sense prior to recognizing a just agent, a just agent is something over and above the sum of her actions (or their consequences, for that matter). In one epistemological order of priority, actions may well come first. From this it does not follow, however, that the causal-ontological order of priority would be the same. Quite the contrary, ancient philosophers think that in order to deeply understand – and to generate – just actions, we need to have a proper grasp of the thing that produces the actions, the agent. Action guidance calls for understanding which kinds of psychological outlook lead to which kinds of action. It is for this reason that character-formation is of utmost importance in eudaimonist ethics. You shape your life through improving your character, not primarily by concentrating on the qualities or consequences of your actions. The promoting of virtuous activity happens through promoting a virtuous soul. Yet the very same notion of character-formation brings the importance of actions right back to the picture: our characters are formed by our activities, by things we do, and by our choices and decisions to engage in certain things and refrain from others. The relationship between action and its causal origin becomes thereby complicated: it is a two-way street.

It seems, further, that ancient philosophy includes a strand of thinking that values internal – rational or theoretical – activity above action that happens in the external world, in the social and moral sphere. This is connected to the question of the highest good. Pretty much all ancient philosophers agreed that, first, there is a shared human nature, an essence of which people can know through philosophizing about it. Second, fulfilment of that nature leads to human flourishing (*eudaimonia*) (one seminal study on this is Annas 1993). In theory one should, therefore, be able to figure out the kind of activity that is most properly human, and attain happiness through living a life in accordance with it. The quest for happiness becomes a search for an activity (or set of activities?) that would be higher and more perfect than other activities. While acting in our social environment is the natural and indispensable framework of human beings, pure reasoning is sometimes suggested as this ultimate *telos* of human life. Reason is distinctive of human beings, as well as the means by which the shaping of our character and the organization of good things in our life (and in the society) are done thoughtfully. Theoretical thinking in itself is understood as both intrinsically pleasurable as well as invulnerable to surroundings, and hence more valuable than other pleasurable activities dependent upon external circumstances.

Thereby the role of actions is again challenged, but now in a different way. In a life of something less than a perfectly wise and virtuous person, the role of actions can be highly important. They are the means by which this person both achieves and communicates her virtue. From the point of view of the goal to become as godlike as possible (Plato, *Tht.* 176b; Sedley 1999), however, their role can be seen as preparatory and instrumental. Conventionally virtuous actions have a place in building a stably virtuous disposition from which truly virtuous actions then unfold.[1] Once fully acquired, intellectual virtue may be expressed through actions, but this expression is no part of the virtue itself. Or so the story goes.

In the history of philosophy, there is also an alternative strand of thinking. This strand suggests a competing value hierarchy between theoretical activity and practical action. According to the philosopher of the golden age of Islamic philosophy, Al-Farabi (872–950/951 CE), for instance, in the development of a philosopher, practical and theoretical virtues come in a different order. The student of philosophy proceeds through preliminary studies in logic and mathematics to the core of philosophy, physics and metaphysics. But the end of philosophy lies elsewhere, in ethical and political philosophy. The previous studies enable the philosopher *to act* in the way that she is supposed to act, and it is there that the final goal of the philosopher and her studies lies.[2] Knowledge is completed through actions. Bypassing here any claims about the history of ideas – it is for other scholars to say whether this is a correct picture of Al-Farabi, and whether the Arabic philosophers were influenced, indirectly or directly, by the late ancient materials presented in this chapter[3] – it can be noted that the view to be explicated below has much of the same flavour to it. As we shall see, late Stoicism and Neoplatonism already include a strand of thinking according to which practical activity is, in a certain sense to be explicated below, *that for the sake of which* theoretical studies are undertaken.

In what follows, I will begin by briefly discussing the classical Platonic and Aristotelian sources for the discussion of the highest, supreme good. This involves various suggestions on the kind of human activities the highest good possibly consists of, the sources elevating, occasionally, theoretical activity above practical life. In order to assess these claims, it is further necessary to raise the question of the general role of the highest good in a given ethical theory. What does it mean to say that something or other is a highest good? Is the highest good a single, better activity among other activities, or perhaps something else, something that governs other activities? What implications do claims about the highest good have for choosing different kinds of activities? This is followed by an exposition of the same discussions, situated within and to some extent radicalized by Neoplatonic metaphysics, in the writings of Plotinus (204/5–70 CE). The picture emerging from the *Enneads* seems to promote contemplation, for several reasons, clearly above practical engagement in the world. The concluding part will be on the competing strand of thinking that originates in the Stoic Epictetus (55–135 CE), and is explored, and to an extent adopted, by the late Neoplatonic philosopher Simplicius (*floruit* 530–50 CE). The less well-known materials and novel claims about them concern Simplicius' commentary on Epictetus' *Enchiridion*, the so-called *Manual* or *Handbook*,[4] and the views expressed there of character formation and the final end of philosophy.

PLATONIC-ARISTOTELIAN BACKGROUND

One of Plato's crucial significances for ethical thinking lies in making moral psychology essential for virtue. In book 3 of the *Republic*, Plato internalizes virtues: virtues are proper relationships between different motivations, reason's control and moderation of the appetitive and other a-rational drives (e.g. *R*. 441–2). This also leads to the centrality of character-formation. The task of everyone aspiring to virtue is to make his or her soul as harmonious as possible, so that each part of the soul takes care of its own task (*R*. 433a), creating a balanced state of the soul, a kind of mental health. For Plato, famously, reason has a central role to play in not merely understanding and striving for goodness, but also governing the soul so that what is truly good would motivate the person as a whole (*R*. 442c). As regards the place of action in this picture, it has a double role. First, for Plato, actions are internally caused (*Phdr*. 245e4–6). Generally, Platonic causes are understandable and intelligible without reference to effects but not vice versa. This would seem to imply that explicating the internal activities or states of the soul is central for action explanation (Emilsson 2012). This agent-centred view suggests that actions unfold from the soul, following its states. Virtuous soul gives rise to virtuous actions.[5]

Second, Plato also leaves room for action in the formation of the virtuous soul. In his view, just actions produce justice in the soul, while unjust actions promote injustice in the soul (*R*. 444c). The whole political programme of the *Republic* rests on the idea that a surrounding society has a large role in the formation of our characters, and that certain activities promote virtue in soul. While true virtue only belongs to the one who has an internally balanced and virtuous soul, acting in conventionally virtuous or socially learned ways helps shape the soul towards that goal.

There is a recent challenge to the prevailing notion of agent-centredness in Plato's *Republic*. The new interpretation understands the relationship of virtuous action and the state of the soul differently. What some passages seem to indicate is that virtuous action is an action that promotes virtue upon the soul; that is, that promoting inner virtue is essentially what it means to act virtuously (e.g. *R*. 443e). The virtuousness of an action would thus depend on the virtue of the soul in a different way. It would not be an automatic unfolding from a virtuous state, but, rather, defined through its causal effects on the state of the soul: that which promotes virtue in soul can be called a virtuous action.[6] If this reading were correct, the significance of actions for character-shaping would be further emphasized. However, the view still belongs to the overall understanding in which the role of actions is understood through their connection to the inner state of virtuous soul. Indeed, this reading seems to accentuate a certain instrumentality connected to actions: their virtuousness is not assessed by their success in guiding us in the moral realm of other people, but by their impact on the state of the soul.

Assuming that a good enough society and education came miraculously to be, and a gifted enough individual took the search for virtue and happiness seriously, what lies at the end of her path? After the preparatory activities have been successfully concluded, what will the Platonically wise person do? How will she lead her life? Just as the role of the best and most proper part of the human being, the rational motivation, is twofold, that is, both to rule and to contemplate the good, the task of the guardians of the ideal state is double: to rule the city and to engage in theoretical philosophizing. This, as such, is an inclusive picture that combines theoretical activity with practical activities. It is through the recognition of the highest good that reason can fashion a best possible life for the soul as a whole, for the person. The guardians of Plato's Kallipolis are good rulers because of their knowledge of the good, because of their ability for theoretical thinking, including mathematics. But a well-known dilemma in the *Republic* shows that there is some ambivalence as regards the co-existence of practical and theoretical reasoning. Namely it is stated that these same guardians will have to be forced to rule. If they could choose their lifestyle without any compulsion, they would prefer theoretical studies. Pure contemplation would render them most perfect pleasure and happiness, while political engagement necessarily entails disturbances to such peaceful activities, as well as dependencies on things external to one's own self (516e; 517c; 519c; 520e; 539e). Several different solutions have been suggested to remedy this,[7] but for our purposes it is enough to note that there seems to be an ambivalence that does not easily dissolve.

Two other Platonic dialogues are relevant for our theme. In the *Theaetetus*, the goal of human life is famously described as "becoming as godlike as possible" (*homoiōsis theōi kata to dynaton*, *Tht.* 176b1). This involves living as justly as possible, becoming just and pure, with understanding. Other forms of wisdom and ability are considered more profane (*Tht.* 176c).[8] The emphasis of this discussion is, however, on justice and morality, not solely on reason or intellectual achievements. It thereby remains an option that when done justly, many different activities could be considered godlike. The picture given in the *Philebus* is even closer to the ground: the discussants are looking for a good that would be final or end-like (*teleon*) and sufficient (*hikanon*). They attest that neither the life of reason nor the life of pleasure qualify as the highest good, because each requires something else beyond itself, and thus does not qualify as sufficient, nor final, in the required sense. The best life has to be a mixture of these (*Phlb.* 22a–d). Goodness, in turn, is the harmony and proportion that applies to the relationships of the components. Rather than being a sum of the components, it is actually neither, but the constitution that secures their proper relations (see e.g. J. Cooper 2003). The *Philebus*, then, gives a highly inclusivist picture of the final good.

Aristotle continues this discussion, sharing with Plato the overall idea of reason's central role in the good life. Happiness comes from actualizing the unique, rational function of human beings (*EN* 1097b24–1098a21). Further, he promotes character-formation as essential: since the good is, for him, not one thing over and above activities and persons, but always someone's good, or the particular good of a particular activity, striving for a virtuous state of the soul becomes crucial. Ethics is not about giving people rationally realized rules of conduct. It is about shaping one's character to be such that it can reason the good for itself and for the community in differing circumstances and in a variety of activities. This shaping happens in a lengthy process and starts in childhood, as Aristotle explicates in *Nicomachean Ethics* (1.1–2). While intellectual excellence increases as a result of teaching, other excellences of character are built through habituation. Acting in our dealings with human beings builds firm dispositions of behaviour. The issue of what kind of habituation leads into just and good dispositions becomes crucial, and Aristotle connects this discussion to, among others, his notion of moderateness.

Interpreting Aristotle further encounters related, although not the same, problems about ambivalence as we find in Plato. In the *Nicomachean Ethics*, Aristotle defines the highest or chief good, whatever that turns out to be, as the most complete (*teleion*) of human ends, chosen only for its own sake and never for anything else. It is whatever is desirable without qualification, in itself. This kind of good is also self-sufficient (*autarkes*): it makes life desirable even in isolation. It is the end of our actions, or practical undertakings (*EN* 1094a18–19; 1097a15–b21).[9] Having claimed, famously, that happiness (*eudaimonia*) qualifies as such an end, he goes on in later books to specify what kind of life this could be. In the last book, book 10, two kinds of life are mentioned. The highest is the life of reflection (*nous*), the aspect that is divine in us (10.7); the second highest that of the excellences in us that are most properly human, connected to the compound of body and soul (10.8). Aristotle thus identifies both specifically human excellences and those that are "divine", and goes on to suggest that we should try to become as immortal as is possible for human beings (*eph' hoson endechetai athanatizein*; *EN* 1177b33).

These remarks have given rise to two interpretations about the good life: the inclusivist and the intellectualist, or "dominant" ("monist"), one. The inclusivist reading says that the final goal is a set of different kinds of activities, not any one activity on its own. Happy life involves the actualization of virtues/excellences other than intellectual, such as courage, for instance (*EN* 1097b1–4).[10] This down-to-earth approach suits well Aristotle's view that things like wealth and origin have their own bearing upon happiness – that happiness cannot be, even in an ideal case, entirely internally controlled (e.g. *EN* 1101a15). The intellectualist emphasis arises from the call to overcome our human nature and to engage in divine activity: from the specification of the highest life as that of the life of *nous* in book 10 (6–7). It gets support from comments in which the reflective activity is described as invulnerable to the worldly surroundings. As an activity it is, among other things, independent of the presence of other people, unlike practical projects (*EN* 1177a30–b1). The dominant reading comes in different varieties, but many are not radically intellectualist. They underline, rather, the close relationship between practical and theoretical thinking. While pure contemplation for longer periods is not possible for a human being, a human may approximate an immortal god through the use of practical reason in the moral life.[11] The dominant reading thus admits the primacy of reflection, but says that even if the final good were some one kind of activity, this one element would not be that in which a human being should exclusively engage. Rather, the notion of primacy involved means that it dominates the whole life "in the logical sense of typifying it" (Broadie 1991: 26; 2007: 113–83). You are not advised to turn your back on all other aspects of human life. Activities of different kinds are organized around a single dominant goal that gives the life overall the special character that it has.

The literature on Aristotle on good is vast, but here we need only to draw attention to two things: first, that there is a dispute over what precisely Aristotle says about the constituents and structure of the good life, and, second, that this dispute has raised the question of what is meant by the highest, final kind of life. The discussion suggests that finality need not be taken as an answer to the question "Which activity should you try to engage in as much as is humanly possible?" What is sought for is not only, or perhaps primarily, an answer to the kind of activity that in itself is most pleasant, final and good, but, rather, a kind of good that renders life good in the most complete way. When an ancient philosopher talks about a final, highest or supreme good, he may be intending a search for an activity that should dominate and organize other activities towards an overall good life. This way even the intellectualist, "dominant" or "monistic" interpretation can be more inclusive than one might think.

PLOTINUS: THE NEOPLATONIC PROBLEM ARISES

As regards Plotinus, we have four different discussions in the *Enneads* relevant to the theme at hand:

(1) metaphysical background;
(2) theory of virtues;
(3) discussion of "up to us" (*eph' hēmin*);
(4) some comments about action, its purpose and role in life, and its value.

Let us treat these in turn.

(1) In all brevity, Neoplatonic metaphysics can be said to be a system of priority and dependence relations in which everything has a place in a layered hierarchy that these relations give rise to. What is higher up in this system always has more causal relevance: the cause is more powerful than the effect, in the sense of being both simpler and more universal (see e.g. D. O'Meara 1996). This hierarchy further coincides with one about perfection and goodness: anything closer to the highest cause on top of the hierarchy, the One, is also closer to unity, perfection and goodness (e.g. Gerson 2013). As regards action explanation, we can see how nicely the ancient way of promoting the status of the soul as explanatorily more important than the characteristics of action already fits into this outlook. Plotinus, accordingly, situates action as a causal unfolding of the soul, its external activity (as suggested by A. Smith 2005). Thereby we know two central things about action: first, its status *vis-à-vis* the hierarchy of being and goodness as a whole: it must be further removed from goodness and power than soul's own proper, or internal, activities, like thinking; second, that it is causally dependent upon the soul: action-description follows, in the Platonic fashion, the description of the state of the soul. From virtuous soul come virtuous actions.

(2) One of the Neoplatonic ethical particularities is their hierarchy of virtues, connected to their overall layered understanding of reality. In its most simple and original form, this means a twofold distinction between political and purificatory virtue. Plotinus posits at least two levels or grades of virtue,[12] which have different relations to action. The role of the so-called political or civic virtues (*aretai politikai*) is to give order to desires and guide the agent in her normal, everyday life. Practical wisdom is connected to discursive reason, courage to emotions, reasonableness consists of a sort of agreement and harmony of passion and reason, and justice makes each of these parts take care of their own task within the whole (e.g. *R.* 433a; *Enn.* I.2[19].1.16–21). Together all of these virtues are connected to control and command within the motivations and powers of the soul, internalizing Platonic notions even further, and despite their name, have little directly to do with the *polis* or with any social relationships.[13] These virtues would, however, still suggest a kind

of *metriopatheia*: the person lives in the realm of action and very much in and through the body, but ruled by reason. Such an agent is self-controlled and practically wise, and has only moderate passions. Above the political virtues are the purificatory or contemplative virtues (*katharseis*). At that stage, the soul is wholly directed to the intelligible realm and to the contemplation of forms, as well as separated and purified from the body. It has something that resembles the Stoic ideal of life without emotions, *apatheia*, rather than *metriopatheia* (*Enn.* I.2[19].6.19–28, 5.4–7).[14]

The theory raises the problem of the relationship between the two kinds of virtue. In general, the role of actions in character-formation seems inherently problematic, given that the causal relations are top-down. Actions would seem to be capable, at best, of clearing the ground for the inner activity to display itself – they should not be involved in making a true causal difference on the soul or its states. This means troubles for any view on habituation.[15] Moving from the political to katharctic level is also the point where interpretations start to diverge from one another: according to one interpretation, once you attain the higher virtue, you can disregard the lower ones entirely. In its most radical form, this would entail inactivity in the sphere of other people, and thereby leaving behind as unnecessary not just the lower, political virtues, but any virtue in action. Political or civic virtues would be a transitory step in the moral and cognitive development, and the reformed contemplative life of higher virtues would come to share little with the virtuous life understood as virtuous action in everyday situations and circumstances.[16] A sage would, in so far as it is possible for an embodied being, withdraw from practical activity. According to an alternative reading, the political virtues retain their role, but get reformed in the development. Obviously a fully virtuous sage does not need to struggle for control of emotions, for instance. He is internally harmonious. He continues, however, living in a changing world and among other people, and the virtuousness of his soul gets expressed in this life through something that looks very much like political virtues (D. O'Meara 2003: 42–4). His virtuousness is not merely an inner state. This inner state has a natural or inherent relationship to the external world.

In Plotinus we find again an ambivalence as regards the role of normal human activities in happiness and goodness. Some rhetorically powerful passages seem to suggest that a person who attains the highest good avoids, as far as possible, meddling with the world, its dependencies and rapidly changing circumstances (e.g. *Enn.* VI.9[9].7.26–8). He will not be moved, for instance, by human misery, for he understands, in a Stoic fashion, its cosmological and providential role (*Enn.* III.2[47].13). Other considerations give a more inclusive view: the goodness and virtue of the sage cannot but unfold itself in good and virtuous action. Moreover, the sage would seem to be described not as a hermit, but as someone in possession of social virtues (*Enn.* I.4[46].15.22–5; 1.6[1].5.9–17).[17]

(3) Even though there are good reasons to interpret Plotinus' theory of virtues in the latter, more inclusive light, there are other strong considerations in favour of a more radically intellectualist interpretation of Plotinus as regards action. One of them is his discussion on what is and is not in human power. He adopts the originally Stoic discussion of what is "up to us" (*eph' hēmin*), following relatively closely the Stoics, especially Epictetus. The Stoics famously put many aspects of the everyday human life in a class of indifferents (*adiaphora*). Many of them, like a good marriage or a healthy, long life, may be preferred, but they do not constitute happiness, which is constituted solely by virtue. Epictetus summarizes his version of this idea by saying that "our own doings" are

conception (*hypolēpsis*), impulse (*hormē*), desire (*orexis*) and aversion (*ekklisis*), while other than or outside of our own doings are our body, our property, reputation, office, and so on (Epictetus, *Ench.* 1; *Diss.* 4.12.15–19).[18] Broadly taken, then, in our power belongs only our soul's own impulses, states and stances, and nothing in the external world. Plotinus repeats the same idea, contending that in the realm of action, pure "up to us" is not possible. As Peter Adamson shows in Chapter 27, the bodily realm is one of necessity and fate, leaving only the immaterial free or properly autonomous. In our power are our inner activities proper to the soul. For Plotinus, only purely theoretical contemplation (*noein*) is in no way dependent upon the external world (e.g. *Enn.* VI.8[39].2.33–7). The significance of this for the discussion on the role of action in the final good is dire: anything dependent upon the external world cannot be in our power, and thereby constitutive of true, invulnerable happiness. Self-sufficiency cannot be attained within normal action.

(4) At this point, Plotinus' explicit utterances about the relationship between theoretical reasoning, or contemplation (*noein, theorein*), and action should come as no surprise. He asserts that actions and ways of life are made beautiful by dispositions of soul, and that happiness concerns this inner good and virtuous state of the soul rather than actions (*Enn.* I.5[36].10.10–15; I.6[1].6.27–30). Happiness is connected, first and foremost, to noetic contemplation (*Enn.* I.4[46].3–4) because this is closest to the true goodness of the One (see Gerson 2013). What gives action self-determination is the inner activity of virtue, namely thought and contemplation (*Enn.* VI.8[39].6.19–24). Moreover, the *telos* of actions (*praxeis*), Plotinus says, is knowledge (*gnōsis*) and their driving force is a desire of knowledge (*ephesis gnōseōs*; *Enn.* III.8[30].7.3–5). Action, he says, is for the sake of contemplation and that which is contemplated (*heneka theōrias kai theōrēmatos*; *Enn.* III.8[30].6.1–4).

What does Plotinus mean by these last remarks about contemplation as an end? Can he really be intending to say that we act in order to contemplate better or more? To this the answer is yes, but with heavy qualifications on what it means to contemplate. Plotinus' claim that action is always for the sake of contemplation, or for the *telos* of knowledge, is not a claim about some one activity the sole immersion in which would make us happier than other kinds of life – although this view is obviously not precluded by these remarks, and may indeed be close to what he thought. In this context, he is making a claim, again, about priority and posteriority relations, and defending the Platonic view according to which intelligible higher principles are always prior to sensible instantiations, things or happenings. Actions are both ontologically and for their psychological explanation heavily dependent upon intelligible principles, principles that both make them to be, and give them their intelligibility and directionality.[19]

Yet it cannot be denied that Plotinus also sounds as if he would think that action is not only ontologically and psychologically posterior, but of less value, and therefore also less desirable as a constituent of human life. The following passage is clear enough about his values:

> Men, too, when their power of contemplation weakens, make action (*praxis*) a shadow of contemplation and reasoning. Because contemplation is not enough for them, since their souls are weak and they are not able to grasp the vision sufficiently, and therefore are not filled with it, but still long to see it, they are carried into action, so as to see what they cannot see with their intellect. When they make

something, then, it is because they want to see their object themselves and also because they want others to be aware of it and contemplate it, when their project is realised in practice as well as possible. Everywhere we shall find that making (*poiēsis*) and action (*praxis*) are either a weakening or a consequence of contemplation; a weakening, if the doer or maker had nothing in view beyond the thing done, a consequence if he had another prior object of contemplation better than what he had made. For who, if he is able to contemplate what is truly real will deliberately go after its image (*eidōlon*)? The duller children, too, are evidence of this, who are incapable of learning and contemplative studies and turn to crafts and manual work.   (*Enn.* III.8[30].4.29–47, trans. Armstrong)[20]

Despite the beauty and ethical as well as therapeutical significance virtuous action can have, according to the passage, it, too, will fall under what Plotinus thinks of as *effects* of contemplation; that is, as things on a lower plane and of less value than the causes.[21] This is entirely in line with his causal system which can be established from other contexts. There is no question here about which way the order of primacy goes, since it follows unfailingly the order of metaphysical causation: from top down.[22] The passage suggests, further, that there would be two different ways of achieving the same end: the possession of intelligible principles. One is the theoretical activity proper. The other is action, which is done in order to try to realize and clarify the intelligible principle in the soul. The former is clearly the better, more desirable option. In the embodied, less than perfect reality, the latter option is more common, and further dominates the life of those who are cognitively not gifted enough for the first option. The position of action becomes derivative and instrumental: in the great scheme of things, it is an *eidōlon* done in order to approximate contemplation and true possession of intelligible principles.

According to Plotinus, then, the order of priority is emphatically such that the theoretical activity is the higher one, and all other activities, be they productions or makings, lower. Contemplation is more final, more self-sufficient, and more desirable. The significance of this should, however, be neither misunderstood, nor overstated. First, we have seen that Plotinus' claims are not formulated as an answer to a worry over which kind of activity one should devote one's time to. They belong, rather, to his metaphysics and psychology. That both are infested with notions about value has implications for that very same worry, but the discussion is not motivated by a search for some one activity worth devoting oneself to exclusively. Second, from other sources we may gather that contemplation gives practical reasoning its strength, and thus its role as a *telos* is to improve also on practical and discursive reasoning of the life of the composite (e.g. the example of generalship, *Enn.* V.9[5].11.21) (see Remes forthcoming b). Interestingly, and probably true to Plato's spirit, Plotinus contends that reason (*logos*) makes a great difference to acting. Human acting can be driven externally, following the necessities imposed on it from outside. When, however, "in its impulse it has as director its own pure and untroubled reason, then this impulse alone is to be said to be in our own power and free" (*Enn.* III.1[3].9.9–12; cf. *Enn.* II.3[52].9.12–18). In the best of embodied lives, contemplation unfolds as approximations of freedom and virtuousness in the realm of normal action.

SIMPLICIUS AND EPICTETUS' *HANDBOOK*: PRACTICAL ACTION AS AN END

In the Neoplatonic curriculum, it was customary to start with Aristotle's works that were considered as a propaedeutic to Plato, and only then to proceed to Plato, starting first from the easier dialogues and then concluding the reading list with more challenging dialogues such as the *Parmenides* and the *Timaeus*. What the Platonic curriculum apparently lacked was some guidelines about *practical* ethical issues, that is, the way in which Platonic dialectic could guide human beings in the realm of action and other people.[23] The *lacuna* was filled with a somewhat surprising source from the camps of Neoplatonists' adversaries in many issues: the Stoics. Namely (as also noted by Baltussen [Chapter 7], above) what the Neoplatonists recommended for reading was Epictetus' *Handbook*, with its very practical advice on how to behave in private as well as in public, for example, in public baths. On the one hand, then, the curriculum testifies of a hierarchical order of reading, of philosophical works and subject matters, in which action, as something that happens in the lower levels of being, has no significant place. On the other hand, there is a recognition of this very lack being a problem, and an attempt to fix the situation with a work of Stoic origin.

On closer examination, the Neoplatonists' approval of Epictetus as a philosophical educator is not that startling: the Stoicism Epictetus propounds is so practical that many of the theoretical issues that formed the main disagreements between the Neoplatonists and the Stoics are not discussed in the work at all.[24] On several issues concerning human nature and good life the Stoics and Platonists agreed. Within the much-discussed issue of emotions, Stoics and Neoplatonists were the hardliners, advocating eradication instead of moderation (see e.g. Knuuttila 2004: 5–110). Epictetus' view of the body, its pleasures and value is very close to Plotinus' teachings about the topic: the body is not a real part of the self, for the true self is reason, that which assents and denies its assent to appearances (e.g. *Ench.* 1; 9; 41). Although serious disagreements between Epictetan and Neoplatonic approaches to ethics remain, Epictetus' work and the values it propounds are sufficiently close to those of the Neoplatonists, and since his *Handbook*, furthermore, shows emotional power and practical applicability (see T. Brennan 2002) that were not easy to surpass, it was adopted as a course book.[25]

As Simplicius says in the introduction to his commentary, the point of Epictetus' *Handbook* was not so much in providing a systematic study of any area of philosophy than in "rousing the rational soul to the maintenance of its proper value". The book was entitled as "a handbook because it ought always to be at hand or ready for those who want to live well" (*in Epict. Ench.* 1.26–7; 2.20–23). As a literary device it uses short precepts rather than treatises. This also sets the tone of the commentary in so far as Simplicius proceeds by explicating and clarifying the precepts. He does, however, also incorporate them into his overall ethical-psychological framework. Nor is this a work simply or primarily for a beginner: as Ilsetraut and Pierre Hadot (2004) have remarked, even the *Handbook* itself is not immediately transparent to someone with no or very little studies in philosophy. Moreover, the commentary goes into details and sometimes presupposes other parts of Neoplatonic philosophy. Yet given the nature of the commented work, as concerned mainly with practical matters and moral psychology, any expectation of finding a full-fledged theory of what action is for is not met. *Pragma* and *ergon*, the words Simplicius uses for something like action, only come in towards the end of the commentary, in the context of Epictetus' exhortation not to leave one single day or a single action unused in the quest for moral self-improvement.

The overall taste we get from the *Handbook*, and from Simplicius' commentary on it, as regards action is very different from the one visible in Plotinus. In general, the later Neoplatonists seem to take more seriously Plato's suggestions in the *Republic* that acting virtuously not merely follows souls' virtuous disposition but also promotes the virtue in the soul (see e.g. D. O'Meara 2003: 48). In the very beginning of the commentary, Simplicius identifies as one objective of Epictetus' work the theme of putting words into practice (*in Epict. Ench.* 1.22; see I. Hadot & P. Hadot 2004: 64–5). This view becomes apparent when Simplicius comments on Epictetus' warning not to lose a single day or even a single action but start acting virtuously *now* (*Ench.* 51; Simplicius, *in Epict. Ench.* 135.1). Epictetus is not just counselling people to take virtue seriously. He directs his word of warning to those who keep on looking for good moral guidance and learning moral theories. His point is that if one is adult, one should not wait until one has become a perfect sage but put one's learning into action as soon as possible. Simplicius clarifies this account further by saying that there is a danger in merely trying to acquire a more virtuous state of the soul: this attempt at *becoming* a more virtuous person may gradually turn into laziness and negligence. If one has already made some progress in philosophy, the learned ethical and logical theorems should be put into practice without delay (*in Epict. Ench.* 135.4; 135.49–52).

One explicit reason for preferring acting virtuously to merely talking or philosophizing about virtue is given. Earlier in the same work Simplicius has accepted Epictetus' view that putting the theorems into action is, in fact, better than teaching them. "At a dinner party, don't talk about the right way to eat; instead, eat the right way" (*Ench.* 46; Simplicius, *in Epict. Ench.* 130.43–4). Teaching, and thus also teaching virtue, often involves the aspect of showing off, of flaunting what one knows in front of other people, and thereby has more to do with caring for what people think of oneself than with true love of truth and goodness. Acting according to the virtuous teaching is safer in this respect. Simplicius repeats and explicates on Epictetus' analogue: sheep do not show their shepherd how much they have eaten by vomiting, but by digesting what they have eaten, and by producing milk and wool as a result. "What you should display", Simplicius says, "are not the words but the deeds (*erga*) that stem from the words when they have been digested and have nourished your condition" (*in Epict. Ench.* 131.35–8).

This approach already seems to preclude the idea that one could be virtuous just by entertaining ethical theorems, without putting them into action. But there is a weaker and a stronger reading of this claim. According to the weaker reading, the whole business discussed concentrates on the life of people that are less than sages – the intended audience is not ordinary people disinterested in philosophy, nor full-fledged sages, but imperfect people working on the project of self-improvement (*in Epict. Ench.* 133.28–40; as also stated in the introduction: 2.30–3.2). Thereby it is quite possible that virtuous actions are necessary merely as a preparatory phase, because without actions the whole process of becoming virtuous cannot be completed. According to this view, theoretical activity alone cannot make the soul virtuous: the process has to be supplemented with virtuous actions. The stronger view claims that virtuous actions are not merely a path or an instrument of becoming virtuous: they are constitutive of what it means to be virtuous. It is this latter view that I take to be the view propounded by Epictetus, and at least recognized if not adopted by Simplicius, for reasons that will become clear below. For now, let us keep these alternatives in mind.

Simplicius next explicates Epictetus' idea that destroying or preserving moral progress hinges upon each single day, even upon each single action (*in Epict. Ench.* 135.49–136.9). Let us use a figure famous in Finland, called Turmiolan Tommi (the equivalent, roughly, of something like "Dennis from the village of Deprivation"), used by teetotallers in the nineteenth century to warn of the dangers of drinking, to stand as an example. The argument personified by Tommi was, more or less, that drinking one cup of liquor will necessarily take one on a path which leads, with inevitable force, down the ladder towards alcoholism. From the moment the first cup is emptied, we can see how, in the end, one loses one's job, home and wife, and one's children are driven to the streets. Something rather close to this is also Simplicius' line: the progress towards right reason and the virtuous state of the soul is destroyed gradually so that the first neglected virtuous action already decreases the stability one has acquired, resulting in more probability that the next virtuous action is also neglected, and so on until all the progress one has made is destroyed. However, perhaps unlike the case of the alcoholic's addiction, the reverse is also true. Every new action done in the spirit of good ethical theorems one has learned contributes to the progress, thus making each new step towards the right direction easier and more likely (*in Epict. Ench.* 135.48–136.9). This gives us a rudimentary picture of how moral dispositions to act are acquired as well as destroyed. It also appeals to the phenomenal or experiential difficulty of taking the first step, of launching something new, and the experience of relative ease in continuing the activity once the first steps are taken. Every single action constitutes our developing character in time: each of them leaves a mark on the soul, making us either well or ill disposed with respect to the next action, and the next with respect to the act immediately following, and so forth.

While we find some marks of a similar idea of gradual degradation in Plotinus (*Enn.* III.2[47].4.36–44),[26] the weight this theory gives to a single token action is un-Plotinian. For Plotinus, acting in the world is always tied to the contingencies and necessities of the sensible, material realm and its impact on the soul is questionable and at the very least limited. Simplicius' positive take on the Aristotelian–Epictetan ideas on habituation is best understood within the context of a significant doctrinal change that happened after Plotinus. The later Neoplatonic philosophers rejected Plotinus' idea that each human being encloses a perfect, divine intellect not unlike the Intellect (e.g. *Enn.* V.3[49].6; IV.8[6].8.1–3). While we may not be conscious of our impersonal but individual intellect, it is the entity that explains our cognitive capacities and claim to knowledge. It also creates a divine and immutable core within human being. The later Neoplatonists separated humanity and divinity more clearly by postulating a soul that is no longer inviolable in its superior heights (e.g. Proclus, *ET* 211). No part of it is perfectly intellectual and beyond the causal order of the universe. We may surmise that with this move, action must also have gained weight as a philosophical topic: since action is essential for human beings as embodied creatures in the world rather than gods or semi-gods, its study must be directly revelatory of our own nature. Moreover, we are now entitled to assume that action perhaps has some power to affect the soul, and not just the bodily dispositions. Soul becomes something that not merely causes things in its surroundings, but also undergoes changes in the world. Even though actions would not constitute goodness, they can have a significant role in one's moral and rational progress.

Even more startling, however, is the way in which Epictetus and his commentator describe the relations between what he calls the method of logic and the application of theorems, especially the way in which the order of priority between the two is made. In some sense understanding the theorems is primary, but in another actions are those *for the sake of* which the theorems are contemplated. In the passage Simplicius is quoting from Epictetus' *Handbook*, Epictetus states a clear hierarchy of value within philosophy, and it is worth quoting in full:

> The first and most necessary topic in philosophy is the one that concerns applying the theorems (*chrēseōs tōn theōrēmatōn*), e.g. not lying. The second topic concerns proofs, e.g. why it is that one must not lie. The third is the one that makes the proofs secure and explicit, e.g. why does that constitute a proof? After all, what is a proof? What is consequence? What is incompatibility? What is the true and the false?
>
> So the third topic is necessary on the account of the second, and the second on account of the first. But the one that is the most necessary is the first one and that is the one we should dwell on. Yet we do the opposite; we spend our time with the third one and direct our entire effort towards it and completely fail to attend to the first one. That is why we lie, though we have ready to hand a theory showing how to construct a proof that we should not lie. (*Ench.* 52, trans. Brittain & Brennan)

Epictetus' point hits the professional philosophers where it really hurts. For it seems, indeed, to be the case that no amount of studies on logic or ethics will necessarily or inevitably lead into moral or even rational behaviour. If it did, the philosophy departments around the world would be far better organized and governed than any other departments, without the kind of scheming and immoral behaviour that we sometimes do meet in these havens. So there is something more to be done, more emphasis to be put in virtuous acting and not merely theorizing.[27]

Commenting on this, Simplicius elaborates on three levels: (1) application of theorems, as not lying (*tēs chrēseōs tōn theōrēmatōn, in Epict. Ench.* 136.32–3); (2) immediate proofs for action (e.g. why is it that one must not lie; *ho tēs apodeixeōs, ho meta aitias apodeiknys, hoti dei tauta prattein*); (3) "that which makes proofs secure", namely what he calls logic (what constitutes a proof? What is a consequence? What are truth and falsity?). All of these three are necessary, but the first one, the application of theorems in action, is the most necessary one, and the necessity of the others is dependent and parasitic upon it (*in Epict. Ench.* 136.30–137.1). For Simplicius to report this without any indication of disagreement is already a doctrinally interesting move. In itself, the idea of a socially and politically active sage is, of course, entirely Platonic, and several Neoplatonists had views about the "descent back to the cave" (D. O'Meara 2003: 73–86). But Epictetus as interpreted here seems to go further. The point is put so strongly that it could endanger the role of contemplation in the Neoplatonic system and make it *instrumental* for action rather than an end in itself.

The question that must now be raised brings us back to the weak and the strong readings. According to the former, virtuous acting is an instrument of reaching wisdom and virtue, and thereby happiness; according to the latter, it is a constitutive part of it. That Epictetus would intend the latter seems to be implied, first, by the overall look of Stoicism. That virtue is knowledge does not mean, for them, that we should merely theorize, but that a rational, knowledgeable man knows that he is first and foremost his reason, and that having correctly identified himself with reason, he knows how to use appearances, when to assent and when not to assent to them (Long & Sedley 1987: 59; 60H). This is precisely what is confirmed by Epictetus. The point of philosophy is not in trying to understand, for instance, Chrysippus' words, but in trying to "apply the precepts" and to "show deeds (*erga*) that are similar and in harmony with the words" (*Ench.* 49).

Does Simplicus in his own comments merely report Epictetus' view or does he also adopt the stronger version? At first sight it looks as if he only recapitulates the same point in different wording, explicating further what kinds of activity the different levels consist of and what their relations are. He also ends the *Handbook* by saying that these were his elucidations of the teachings of Epictetus (as opposed to claiming the ideas for himself; *in Epict. Ench.* 138.16–17). However, besides the fact that he chose to write a commentary on this particular work – thus deeming it interesting and worth commenting on – there are two significant developments. First, as a good commentator, Simplicius has truly understood something about what he is commenting, and his remarks on the relationship between action and theory go beyond the text, helping to understand what Epictetus is doing. For instance, on the matter of why commenting Chrysippus is of less value than acting in accordance with his views, Simplicius explicates the goal of philosophy as follows. When a human being seeks his good, he wants to discover his own nature and what befits that nature to do and suffer. This, for example, is that this nature is a rational life, using the body as an instrument, and that he must adapt his desire and aversion to its perfection (*in Epict. Ench.* 134.4–9). Simplicius thus connects Epictetus' claim to the Stoic ethical exhortation to live in accordance with nature. For a human life, this is life in accordance with reason, and the actualization, rightly, of such activities that are proper to it – the soul's inner powers of conception, impulse, desire and aversion. In learning and studying Chrysippus' teachings, a person uses only the first of these, and remains, as Simplicius says, a grammarian. Becoming a philosopher means that this learning is supplemented with applying the precepts, and thereby living – assenting and inclining – in accordance with one's nature (cf. *in Epict. Ench.* 134.9–24).

Further, there are interesting choices – and changes – of vocabulary. While Epictetus talks about applying the precepts or theorems (*chrēsthai tois parēggelmenois* at 49; *chrēsis tōn theōrēmatōn* at 52), Simplicius adds that this application amounts to "partaking of their goodness" (*tou agathou autōn meteschon* at *in Epict. Ench.* 134.17), suggesting a Platonic framework of participation. Where Epictetus claims that we do the theoretical activities "on account of" (*dia touton*) the first level, namely the application of them, Simplicius adds that they are "for the sake of" it (*toutou heneka*). "It is on account of and for the sake of this that we take on the other parts" (136.51–2). He even calls application a goal, *telos* (*kai houtos estin ho anagkaiotatos, kai to telos hopou pauesthai dei*; 136.49–50). Simplicius may not be changing the theory in any significant way, but what he does is startling in terms of rendering the idea in Aristotelian and Neoplatonic terms. This involves understanding the application of precepts in the framework of teleology: action itself is the final cause (*Ph.* 2.3) of human beings, that for the sake of which theoretical activities are done, that for the sake of which human beings ultimately exist. They exist in order to actualize goodness and virtue in the sensible realm, not in order to know its principles, the beautiful structure of the universe, or anything like that. Within a practical discipline like ethics, action is the aim through which we can also understand why theoretical activities matter. The Aristotelian terminology[28] enforces Epictetus' hierarchy further, suggesting a subordination of the understanding of the "why" of the other activities to (virtuous) action as their ultimate end. The distinction intended is no longer merely between idle theorizing and living the theory learned. Simplicius' point seems to be that theorizing over the higher principles that govern truth and falsity, as well as logic (proofs and demonstrations), is done in order to act better.

Moreover, that the theory is not merely translated, as it were, into Aristotelian philosophical terminology and framework, is testified by a slightly earlier passage where Simplicius states that: "For just as things up there are the origin (*archai*) of things here, and the preconditioning we receive from there is a great help, so too things here are the origin and predisposition for things up there. All of life is one, and the life you live is one, alternating between here and there" (*in Epict. Ench.* 135.36–40, trans. Brittain & Brennan). This passage incorporates Stoic and Aristotelian claims finally into the Neoplatonic worldview. The "here"/"there" (*entautha-ekei*) distinction is the familiar Plotinian and Neoplatonic way of referring to the higher metaphysical hypostases (Soul, Intellect, One) as opposed to the level of the sensible. In orthodox "Plotinianism", the higher levels are always the origins (*archai*) of everything in the sensible. Simplicius takes this overall picture of layered metaphysics to be true, but contends that there is another order of priority, and one in which the sensible is prior to the intelligible. Acting in the sensible and bodily existence is some kind of *origin* of goodness and virtue: although their principle must in some sense be God and the divine layers of metaphysics, in another sense it is the actual life in the corporeal world that is prior. It is temporally prior, because, as we have seen, virtuous acts create moral dispositions, and they are, thus, prior preparations for true virtue and goodness. Yet if the language of "*archē*" and "for the sake of which" is taken seriously, it is also prior in some stronger sense of value or ethical significance. It is the purpose of life.

The commentary, it is true, is designed for progressors, not for sages. Is the sage's ultimate purpose of life different from that of the progressor's? As regards embodied life, it doesn't have to be. That action is in one sense the chief goal of life does not need to mean that theoretical work, through which the Neoplatonist approaches the higher levels of existence, would turn out to be instrumental. Rather, for a human being action is a final end in one sense of the word, in so far as we are embodied composites acting in the world. If I may borrow Sarah Broadie's formulation quoted earlier, now in a reverse sense, virtuous action "logically typifies" the different aspects of embodied human existence. What gives human beings their particularity is not only their rationality, but their capacity of rational, intentional action. Just as the final good in Aristotle does not have to mean that an ideally happy person would engage exclusively in contemplation, lifting application of theorems to a final end does not mean that we should cease to contemplate, and instead run around acting as much as possible. In an ideal case, theoretical reasonings are not disconnected from the ability to act. Acting as typical for embodied human beings also typifies their reasonings: it connects these reasonings with the human nature as intentional agents. From intelligible principles follow also the transcendental justifications of our actions.

The sage, of course, need not read through any exhortations to apply the precepts, any more than he has to read and memorize the precepts themselves. He both understands them and naturally, as well as effortlessly, lives according to them. Temporarily, the sage may also surpass his embodied nature and truly become like God, or at any rate Intellect. In doing so, he may well attain a level that lies beyond not just action, but even logic, a higher contemplation, even spiritual unity with divinity. The connected experiences of goodness and truth would presumably surpass everything else, action included. But this cannot be an exhaustive picture of a sage and his *telos* in this life, because he, too, is an embodied creature.

Finally, there is one indication that Simplicius may not be going entirely against Plotinus. Note the way the former said, above, that "All of life is one, and the life you live is one, alternating between here and there" (*in Epict. Ench.* 135.40). This recalls what Plotinus says in the treatise on *Nature and Contemplation*, right after he has proclaimed that the truest life is to live by thought, *theoria*. Namely, he goes on to say that the truest life is life by thought, and this is the same as truest thought, and the truest thought lives, and that contemplation and the object of contemplation is living and life, and the two together are one (*Enn.* III.8[30].8.26–30) – that is, if one takes seriously the claim that the truest kind of life is not merely contemplation but the object of contemplation, one gets a much more inclusive view of what the ultimate goal of human life is. It is not just to contemplate the intelligible principles, but also to become them, to embrace them. Thereby one embraces the whole intelligible structure of the universe, inclusive of those principles that make it alive. In that sense even life is included in the objects of contemplation.

ORDERS OF PRIORITY

Neoplatonic philosophy, one may well argue, is essentially about orders of priority. In its original, Plotinian form it postulates a metaphysical hierarchy in which the higher is always prior and not dependent upon the latter. Goodness and beauty follow this hierarchy so that the ontological hierarchy is also a hierarchy of value. In this picture, the sensible is not unqualifiedly evil, but it does amount to imperfection. It is always understood as a realm of fading order, understanding, unity, goodness and beauty, the unblemished principles of which are in the higher, intelligible realm. But this is not an exhaustive picture of priority and posteriority relations in Neoplatonism. For Plotinus, the sensible comes first in an epistemic and therapeutic sense. The intelligible principles, of course, coincide with truth and both make knowledge possible and explain it, but the cognitive and therapeutic processes of human beings towards knowledge and goodness start by using and systematizing experiences and memory-imprints of the particulars, as well as by doing virtuous actions. In knowledge acquisition the starting points are in this limited but important sense in the sensible, in a way not entirely unlike the Aristotelian distinction between things "better known to us" and "better known by nature".[29] In his commentary of the *Handbook*, Simplicius complements Neoplatonism by challenging the exclusivity of the top-down order of priority in another, crucial way. By lifting actions to a status of "that for the sake of which" he creates an ethical order of priority opposite to the Neoplatonic hierarchy of metaphysics and value, arguing that it is this new two-directional hierarchy that actually creates one unified life and universe. While it may well be the case that the ethical order of priority is more limited than the metaphysical one, in the sense of not reaching to the highest levels of existence, nor beyond being, in this universe and embodied existence, the life and actions of human beings are not just productions of higher levels but that for the sake of which the understanding of those very same levels has value. Even if it turned out to be the case that much in this emphasis on action is Stoic rather than Simplicius' own, proper view, its lengthy exposition and interpretation by Simplicius enrich considerably our view of the Neoplatonic ethical discussions.

ACKNOWLEDGEMENTS

As usual, I have benefited from the various comments of the people in Uppsala and Helsinki seminars, as well as, on this particular chapter, the Budapest ancient philosophy community (especially László Bene and Péter Lautner), in a two-day seminar in the autumn of 2011. I am deeply grateful, further, to Dominic O'Meara and Svetla Slaveva-Griffin as well as the anonymous referee for invaluable comments on earlier written versions, and to Suzanne Stern-Gillet on numerous discussions on Plotinus' ethics.

NOTES

1. One issue that cannot be discussed here is the widespread ideal of unity of virtues, the idea that virtues are interconnected in such a way that one who has one of them has to have them all. This obviously makes virtue hard to acquire, and the idea of a single virtuous action, disconnected from a virtuous overall character, impossible. For unity of virtues, see e.g. Penner (1973).
2. Al-Farabi in Najjar (1986 : 97–8). I am relying here entirely on a new PhD thesis by Janne Mattila (2011: esp. 189–92).
3. Al-Farabi's Neoplatonist leanings have, of course, been noted by others: see e.g. D. O'Meara (2003: 185–97).
4. I have used (and sometimes modified) the translation of Brittain & T. Brennan (2002) and the I. Hadot edition (1996). The references are to the Dübner pagination used in the margins of the English translation.
5. This is the predominant picture found in, among others, Julia Annas' classic (1981: 157).
6. Everson (2011). This view is anticipated by Sachs (1963: 152): "acting justly is to be understood as acting in a way which will produce the condition of justice in the soul".
7. In this discussion, I have learned a great deal from Olof Pettersson. For discussion, and plenty of references to literature on the question, cf. Pettersson (2013: 88–107).
8. In Annas (1999: 52–71), Julia Annas challenges the ideal of godlikeness in the *Theaetetus* and its Neoplatonic aftermath.
9. I have benefited extensively from both the translation and the commentary of Broadie & Rowe (2002).
10. For example, J. Cooper (1986: 1–76, 144–77); Nussbaum (1986: 318–54); Irwin (1991).
11. For example, Richardson Lear (2004: *passim* but see e.g. p. 92). See also Kraut (1989).
12. For example, Trouillard (1955: 167–203); Dillon (1983); Gerson (1994: 201–2); Saffrey & Segonds (2001); D. O'Meara (2003: 40–43).
13. The theory has its basis in the internalization of justice in the *Republic*. For a discussion of internalized virtues already in Plato, cf. Emilsson (2012).
14. As John Dillon (1983) has pointed out, the notion of grades of virtue is Plotinus' clever postulation to dissolve a problem inherent in Plato. By positing grades, he accommodates Plato's different accounts (*Tht.* 176a–b. Cf. *Phd.* 82a on *dēmotikē kai politikē*, and *R.* 430c on *politikē*).
15. I aim not to suggest that Plotinus was uninterested in the phenomenon, nor that he simply could not solve it. He often depicts therapy as stripping away rather than building up dispositions. What I suggest is that given the kind of metaphysics committed to, the issue is bound to be complicated.
16. Paul Plass (1982), for example, talks of "radical deprecation of conventional virtue". John Dillon (1996b) has been influential and much discussed. Richard Sorabji, whose interpretation is based not just on Plotinus but also on Porphyry, points out that an otherworldly goal evidently calls for worldly wisdom: see Sorabji (2004–2005: vol. 1, 340).
17. I have explored some of this more fully in Remes (2006).
18. For *adiaphora* and *eph' hēmin*, see e.g. Long & Sedley (1987: 58); Long (2002: 212–19).
19. I discuss Plotinus' view on action in more detail in a forthcoming article (Remes forthcoming a). On human action as part of the contemplation of Nature, see Wildberg (2009).
20. This passage is discussed by Vassilopoulos (Chapter 30), below. I interpret it more closely in Remes (forthcoming a).
21. And as Emilsson (2012) points out, this picture also has the repercussion that the causes can be understood without a reference to the effects, i.e. that states of soul can be understood and adequately described and explained without taking the actions into account.

22. For the repercussions of the descent of the soul in the body, see Stern-Gillet (Chapter 25), above.

23. The new research has amply shown that there is such a thing as Neoplatonic ethics, and even politics (cf. e.g. the works of Alexandrine Schniewind and Dominic O'Meara), and hence this lack concerns particularly practical, "applied" ethics. For curricula, see Tarrant (Chapter 2), above.

24. For example, the question of the basic nature of being (Stoics: matter; Platonists: intelligible forms) need not arise.

25. One point of interest in Simplicius' commentary is whether and how he chooses to amend, interpret and explain the *Handbook* so that it would reflect and be compatible with the main lines of Neoplatonic thought. Another is the way in which Simplicius weaves together not merely Stoics and Neoplatonism, but Aristotle. Simplicius is one of the sources of the so-called agreement doctrine according to which, despite superficial differences, there is a fundamental agreement between Plato and Aristotle (*in Cat.* 7.28–32), and it will be interesting to see if and how his take on action reveals the agreement.

26. I owe this reference to Dominic O'Meara. Christian Tornau pointed out to me also a possible Stoic background: trying to limit vice, that is, to engage in it only to a small degree, is as possible as it is for a man who has jumped headlong from a promontory at Leukas to stop the fall at will: Cicero, *Tusc.* 4.18.41.

27. Seneca discusses the relationship between precepts and doctrines, the former being specific recommendations for either token or type situations, the latter the generic parts of a philosophical system that ground the former (Long & Sedley 1987: 66 I–J). He also argues for their mutual utility, but without making the more radical point of Epictetus about application and its role as the most necessary part of philosophy.

28. Simplicius' Aristotelianizing interpretation may well, too, be pointing back towards *Magna Moralia*. The position of the *Magna Moralia* seems to be that while theoretical activity clearly is the highest activity, it makes no sense to talk of happiness, or of things more generally belonging within the practical discipline of ethics, without the idea of putting the virtues acquired into action. Putting virtues into use and activity is crucial, for a man in sleep all his life could not be considered happy, no matter how virtuous a state of the soul he had (1184b32–33; 1185a9–13; 1208a31–b2; 1190a34–1190b6; 1197a32–7).

29. For example, Aristotle, *Metaph.* 1029b3–12. This is an issue I wish later to explore more fully, but there are cases in Plotinus in which he starts the enquiry not merely from a method very much like the Aristotelian use of *endoxa* (as argued by Strange [1994]), but more generally from human experience and level (e.g. *Enn.* I.3[20].1–4; III.7[45].1). The major difference lies in the role the Platonists give to the innate abilities of the soul in organizing these experiences: without rational abilities the experiences would probably not be organized in any structured way.

29

Political theory

Dominic J. O'Meara

It has long been believed that Neoplatonist philosophers had no interest in political theory or philosophy. On the contrary, their lack of concern with worldly affairs, their striving to transcend material existence must mean, it has been thought, that they can have no place in their philosophy for political matters. In view of this common opinion, it might be better to begin with some preliminary distinctions which, although obvious enough, need to be kept clearly in mind, if we are to avoid misunderstandings and confusions which typically arise in connection with the very idea of a political theory in Neoplatonism. We need to distinguish first between political theory and political involvement. One may be interested in political questions on the theoretical level, without getting involved in political action (an example of this would be Plato, for part of his life), just as one can be politically active without having any interest in the theoretical issues at stake (no examples needed here!): to have a political theory is not necessarily to be a politician (and vice versa). However, we can expect a political theory to include reflection on the nature of political action and on the conditions in which this action may take place. This chapter will be concerned exclusively with political *theory* as found in Neoplatonist philosophers, not with the separate question as to the extent to which these philosophers may or may not have been active in politics. A further source of confusion is the expression "political philosophy", which today can be taken to mean something quite different from what it meant in ancient philosophy. This chapter will be concerned exclusively with political philosophy as it was conceived in antiquity: we will survey what the concept meant for Neoplatonist philosophers, how political philosophy was thought to relate to other parts of philosophy, and what its objects and finality were in relation to philosophy as a whole.

"POLITICAL SCIENCE" AS A PART OF PHILOSOPHY

The concept of a "political art (*technē*)" is introduced in Plato's *Euthydemus* as being identical with a "royal art": it is an expertise which rules over other arts and makes men wise, good and happy.[1] However, the search for such an art in the dialogue does not go very far. "Political art" reappears in the *Gorgias* (464b–465c), as an expertise promoting the good of the soul and which divides into two branches: legislative and judicial. This art, in its two branches, is contrasted with its counterfeits, which aim at pleasure, not the good, seeking only to flatter: sophistry and rhetoric. In the *Republic*, the philosopher-kings of the ideal state promote the good of the state, taking their model from the transcendent Forms, the Good, Justice, Beauty, Moderation, and so on (R. 500d–501c). Their science is referred to as "dialectic" (R. 511c). But what is the relation, we may ask, of dialectic to the political art of the *Euthydemus* and *Gorgias*? Is it the same, or is it different? If different, what is the relation between the two? Towards the end of his life, Plato returned to the concept of "political art" or "science" in the *Statesman*. Here, as before, "political science (*epistēmē*)", identified also as "royal science", is a ruling (architectonic)[2] expertise promoting the good of the state by ruling over and coordinating subordinate skills (jurisdiction, rhetoric, military expertise) which contribute to the "weaving" of citizens together in a harmonious whole.[3] "Political science", in the *Statesman*, does not appear to be identical with "dialectic" as defined in another dialogue of the same period, the *Sophist* (253ce), but the relations between them remain unclear (see El Murr 2009). "Political science" is the name given by Aristotle to the practical science concerned with the human good, happiness (*eudaimonia*), of the *Nicomachean Ethics* (1.2). This science is called "political" because "even if [the good] is the same for a single person and for a city, the good of the city is something greater and more complete" (*EN* 1094a26–b10). As in Plato, Aristotle's political science is architectonic. As a practical science, it is distinguished from theoretical science, autonomous but also in some way making use of other sciences. Elsewhere, Aristotle criticizes Plato for treating the practical science dealing with the individual, the household and the state as if it were one and the same (*Pol.* 1.1), and, in the ancient Aristotelian tradition, we find that practical philosophy is divided into three sciences: political science (the state), "economics" (the household) and ethics (the individual) (Moraux 1984: 452).

It has been necessary briefly to recall these ideas in Plato and Aristotle, since they are of fundamental importance to the way in which "political science" was understood in the Neoplatonist schools of late antiquity. Already in the Platonism of the first centuries CE, we find that philosophy was seen as being divided, along Aristotelian lines, into practical and theoretical sciences, the practical sciences including politics, economics and ethics, the theoretical sciences including physics, mathematics and metaphysics (or "theology").[4] Plotinus himself does not appear to have been very concerned with such matters.[5] But the division of philosophy into three practical and three theoretical sciences becomes common in later Platonism. We find it in Iamblichus and in Proclus, and it becomes the standard way of organizing the teaching of Platonic philosophy among the late Alexandrian Neoplatonists.[6] What this means is that "political science" was seen as a distinct branch of Platonic philosophy, to be taught and read in the schools.

However, the recognition of "political science" as a branch of philosophy involves a number of questions and problems: What is the domain specific to political science, as compared to the other branches of practical philosophy, economics and ethics? How does political science relate to the theoretical sciences? What texts of Plato should be read as pertinent to political science? What is the place and function of political science in relation to the overall aim of Platonic philosophy, the "assimilation to god as far as possible"?[7]

THE DOMAIN OF POLITICAL SCIENCE

We might begin with a description of political science that Olympiodorus offered his students in sixth-century Alexandria, when commenting on a passage of Plato's *Alcibiades I* (124d–126c), at the beginning of the lecture course on Plato. Olympiodorus describes "political science"[8] as dealing with "things to be done (*prakta*)", all actions that are aimed at what is better. This is its matter, whereas its form is that of ruling over humans, not by blows, as if they were animals,[9] but as humans who enter into mutual agreements. Political science guides and makes use of specific skills in its ruling, and rules on the basis of practical wisdom (*phronēsis*), not of theoretical wisdom (*sophia*), having as its goal like-mindedness (*homonoia*) and love (*storgē; physikē philia*) whereby citizens live together as if they were one family.[10] Let us fill out this description, beginning with the "matter", or domain, covered by political science, moving then to its activity as ruling, to the practical wisdom it uses and to the goal it seeks to achieve.

The domain of "things to be done" concerns the life of soul as involved with bodily existence, as can be seen from Olympiodorus' mention, a little earlier (177.14–16), of the definition of man as "rational soul using body as an instrument" (*Alc.* 129e–130c). This definition concerns man as "political" and as acquiring "political virtue", as compared to higher levels of the life of the soul, which no longer involve bodily existence and which correspond to higher levels in the hierarchy of virtues (purificatory, theoretical, and so on).[11] In coming into relation to body, soul can manage or mismanage this relation, can use or misuse body. This will concern both lower psychic states arising for each soul in its connection with body (in particular material desires and emotions), one's attitude to and use of one's body, one's relations to others, on this level, and in general to the events of the corporeal world. The world in which actions (*prakta*) take place is therefore the material world, a world governed by fate.[12] External events and circumstances can bring us to act, as souls. If our actions, as stemming from our rational soul, are autonomous, yet as taking place in the world, they are heteronomous: they are subject to other forces, to another law, natural law, to "chance" (as an aspect of fate), and they must fit in with these forces. Thus, for example, when we act, we act *in time*, and in so doing, we must take account of this, choosing the right moment, the right occasion (*kairos*), for our action. Such moments are dictated by the temporal sequence of the rule of fate, a sequence into which our acts will fit, successfully or not. The situation can be compared to that of a doctor who must find the moment appropriate for his intervention, as this moment is determined in the evolution of a disease.[13]

This delimitation of the domain of political science may seem far too broad, but it can become more focused if we add the following considerations. Political science is architectonic in that it makes use of and guides subordinate expertises and crafts. Various productive crafts and social expertises cover specific parts of the general domain of our incorporated lives. But what they make and do is coordinated and integrated as part of a greater good by the ruling science. This greater good might be described as moral, as the human good (*eudaimonia*), the goal of political science, in Plato, in Aristotle and in Neoplatonism (see above, § "'Political science' as a part of philosophy", and below, § "Practical wisdom"). Furthermore, the relation of individual soul to body, in particular to psychic states arising in relation to body, involves an order that Neoplatonists, following Plato's analogy between soul and city in the *Republic*, described as an "inner republic". The order (virtue) or disorder (vice) of the "inner republic" of the soul is not unrelated to the order or disorder of the city or state: corrupt souls produce evil states and evil states corrupt souls.[14] The link between individual souls in the material world varies in Neoplatonism. In Plotinus, soul's relation to body seems somewhat loose (even if it can become disastrous) and material concerns appear to be of minor importance. What matters more is the community of souls (see below, § "Earthly and heavenly cities"), which soul can join in seeking the good in the transcendent life of Intellect. However, Iamblichus and his Neoplatonist successors laid much more emphasis on the importance of soul's relation to the body and on the role of the body in the welfare of the soul (see above, Chapter 18 by Finamore; D. O'Meara 2003: 39). As a consequence, the political context and its material concerns become much more important in promoting the human good. Iamblichus indeed recalls Plato's suggestion of an organic relation between individual and community: the individual, as part, is saved in the whole and as part of the whole.[15] This view is repeated by Proclus and defended in detail against Aristotle's criticisms of it.[16]

LAW

Following Plato's *Gorgias*, Neoplatonists divided political science into two branches: legislative and judicial. These branches are not equal. Rather, legislation is primary, since it concerns the formulation of laws, whereas the judiciary is secondary, since it presupposes the laws, which it protects by correcting deviations from them (see D. O'Meara 2003: 56–8). Some aspects of the legislative branch will be noted in this and in the following section (on the judicial branch see D. O'Meara 2003: 106–15).

Plato's playful etymology of the word "law" (*nomos*) as the "disposition of intellect (*tou nou dianomē*)" in the *Laws* (714a1–2) is interpreted by Proclus as expressing a determination of reason which is inspired by a transcendent reality (*in R.* 1.238.22–239.9; *in Alc.* 220.18–221.5). We will come back later (§ "Practical wisdom") to this relation as a determination of practical wisdom derived from a transcendent, theoretical wisdom. For the moment, we may note that law is a source of order in cities which promotes virtue and thus the common good of citizens. It is in these terms that Iamblichus justifies[17] the words of Pindar that law is the "king of all", a saying quoted in Plato's *Gorgias* (484b). This sovereignty of law reminds us of the prominence of law in the good city-state proposed in Plato's *Laws*, where the highest officers are referred to as the "guardians of the law" (752d–755b), a function to which Iamblichus refers after having emphasized the importance of law.

As regards the order brought by law to cities and states, we might consider constitutional order as fundamental. The Neoplatonists recall on this subject Plato's descriptions of constitutional types in the *Republic*: the aristocratic (or monarchic) type characterizing the ideal city of *Republic* books 2–3, and the series of increasingly degraded types described in books 8 and 9: timocracy, oligarchy, democracy and tyranny.[18] Following

Plato's example, Neoplatonists express a preference for the aristocratic-monarchic type.[19] However, it should be stressed that the "aristocracy" involved is one of virtue and knowledge, not of power, blood or money: an ideal city should be ruled by philosophers who are morally and intellectually perfect and thus qualified for this rule. At the opposite end, as the most degraded type of rule, is tyranny, a constitutional type with which Simplicius identified the Roman imperial rule of Domitian and, in his own time, of Justinian.[20] But could there ever exist perfect philosophers who would be qualified and have the possibility to exert monarchical rule?

Under the influence of a passage in Plato's *Laws* (739b–e), later Neoplatonists[21] distinguished between the ideal city of the *Republic* (characterized for them by the sharing of everything) and that of the *Laws* (in which some private property is admitted) as being a distinction between a "non-hypothetical" and a "hypothetical" ideal; that is, a distinction between an ideal that is not limited by pre-conditions ("hypotheses", e.g. the particular backgrounds, characters and education of citizens, specific geographical conditions, etc.) and one that is. The good city elaborated in Plato's *Laws*, a "second-best" ideal, is "hypothetical": it takes account of the human need for family life, private property, the sharing of power, whereas that of the *Republic*, in particular as regards its rulers, does not. The *Laws* passage speaks of the highest ideal, a city where all is shared in common, as a city "of gods or children of the gods" (739d). This seems to suggest that the ideal constitutional type for *humans* would be that of the "second-best" project of the *Laws*; that is, a mixed constitution combining monarchic/aristocratic and democratic components. The theory of a mixed constitution can also be found in a Pseudo-Pythagorean text (attributed to Archytas), *On Law and Justice*, which is used by Boethius, and in an anonymous sixth-century dialogue *On Political Science*, which shows strong Neoplatonic influence (see D. O'Meara 2003: 105, 181–2).

PRACTICAL WISDOM

Olympiodorus, in his description of political science (see above, § "The domain of political science"), links this science to practical wisdom (*phronēsis*), which he contrasts with theoretical wisdom (*sophia*). The contrast originates in Aristotle's distinction between the kind of knowledge used in practical action and that found in theoretical sciences such as mathematics. The Aristotelian distinction seems to be directed against a Platonic view suggesting that the highest theoretical knowledge, dialectic, is the basis of political action, a view illustrated by the image, in Plato's *Republic* (500e–501b), of philosopher-kings who "paint" a copy, on the "canvas" of the city, of the transcendent Forms. However, we have also noted that, in the *Statesman* and *Sophist*, Plato does not appear to identify dialectic and political science. How then does political science relate to higher theoretical knowledge, for Plato's Neoplatonic heirs? How does practical wisdom relate to theoretical wisdom?

A view reminding us of that described in the *Republic* can be found in Plotinus:

> Having been in [the One's] company and had, so to put it, sufficient converse with it, [the soul must] come and announce, if it could, to another that transcendent union. Perhaps also it was because Minos attained this kind of union that he was

said in the story to be the familiar friend of Zeus, and it was in remembering this that he laid down laws in its image, being filled with lawgiving by the divine contact. Or, also, [the soul] may think political matters unworthy of it and want to remain always above, this is liable to happen to one who has seen much.

(*Enn.* VI.9[9].7.20–28, trans. Armstrong, slightly modified)

The "story" is told in the *Minos* (319b–320b) and the *Laws* (624a), but the passage reminds us also of the philosopher-kings of the *Republic* who ascend to the knowledge of the Good (with which Plotinus identifies his first principle, the One) and then must descend – one senses their reluctance – from the vision of light to the cave of politics, where they make an image of what they saw. Plato's philosopher-king who makes an image of a higher vision can be found, more explicitly, in Iamblichus and Hierocles,[22] and corresponds, as a particular case, to the general metaphysics of the Good in Neoplatonism, which has the Good express itself in a series of descending images: as the divine Intellect, in Plotinus, is an out-flowing multiple determinate expression of the Good, so is Soul an image and expression of Intellect, and so is the world a product of the goodness and knowledge of soul. A political imitation of the transcendent would then just be a particular case of the good and rational order which soul brings to the world.

We will meet a passage in Plotinus below (§ "Earthly and heavenly cities") where soul is said, in its relation to body, to be inspired by the higher city to which it originally belongs that of the intelligible world. In later Neoplatonism, as the structure of transcendent reality, on the one hand, became ever more complicated, and as soul, on the other hand, became more and more enmeshed in bodily existence and thus distant from the highest levels of being, the models inspiring soul in its political action could be less lofty. The nearest, most accessible of such models is provided by the physical world which is characterized by a cosmic order, a natural law, that human law can imitate, as suggested already in Plato's *Timaeus*.[23] This cosmic order reflects mathematical principles which can also inspire political order.[24] The divine source of cosmic order, the Demiurge, can also function as a political model. Proclus identifies no less than three such demiurges: Zeus, Dionysus and Adonis (*in R.* 2.8.15–23). These demiurges are placed at the lower end of the hierarchy of transcendent reality and correspond respectively to models of the highest ideal city of Plato's *Republic* and of the second- and third-best cities mentioned in the *Laws* (739b–e). Proclus' statesman seems dependent, then, for his inspiration on the lower ranks of a supra-celestial bureaucracy of byzantine complexity, as compared with the relatively direct converse of Plotinus' philosopher with Intellect and the One.

This dependence of political science on models taken from the domain of theoretical science (physics, mathematics and metaphysics) does not, however, mean the fusion of practical and theoretical wisdom. Practical wisdom involves account being taken of the corporeal world in which actions take place, the particulars of place and time involved. Olympiodorus expresses the situation as follows:

The statesman (*politikos*)…draws his conclusions from a universal major premise based on reflection and from a particular minor [premise], because he uses the body as an instrument and is therefore concerned with actions, and actions are particular, and the particular is individual, so that the statesman depends on one particular premise for his conclusion.   (*in Phd.* 4.4, trans. Westerink)

The universal premises of the statesman are innate truths (*logoi*; see *in Phd.* 4.3) deriving from theoretical wisdom; the particular premises are his knowledge of material conditions in which action takes place; and the conclusions he draws, in this practical syllogism, include, as we can see from a similar passage in Proclus, his actions (*in Alc.* 95.19–23). In considering particular situations, practical wisdom will demand deliberation such as that suggested in a passage in Plotinus:

> The other virtues apply reasoning to particular experiences and actions, but practical wisdom is a kind of further reasoning (*epilogismos*)[25] concerned more with the universal; it considers questions of mutual implication [of the virtues], and whether to refrain from action, now or later, or whether an entirely different course would be better.   (*Enn.* I.3[20].6.9–13, trans. Armstrong, slightly modified)

The "other virtues" to which Plotinus refers seem to be in particular the other cardinal virtues, courage, moderation and justice, which, with practical wisdom, constitute what Plotinus elsewhere calls the "political" virtues: each of these virtues involves practical reasoning (see *Enn.* I.2[19].1.17–21). However, practical wisdom is a more general reasoning, presiding over and guiding the other virtues. As Iamblichus puts it, "practical wisdom leads the virtues and makes use of them all, like an intellectual eye, arranging well their ranks and measures and opportune dispositions".[26] Practical action, at any rate, does not simply flow directly from theoretical wisdom: it requires practical reasoning, an appropriate knowledge and reflection on the material particularities in which action must fit.[27]

THE GOAL OF POLITICAL SCIENCE

The goal of political science, according to Olympiodorus' account, is to achieve like-mindedness and love or friendship uniting citizens as if members of a harmonious family. In taking up items in the passage from the *Alcibiades* that he is explaining, Olympiodorus includes major themes of Plato's *Republic*, where the ideal city is also designed to achieve a common good, a maximum of harmony, unity and friendship. This common good, which can also be described as happiness, is therefore the goal reached by the ideal city, a goal for which we find the expression "political happiness" in later Neoplatonic texts (Proclus, *in R.* 1.26.30–27.6 ; Olympiodorus, *in Grg.* 178.10–11).

However, political science, like the political virtue which it promotes, occupies a lower level in a hierarchy of sciences and types of virtue, a hierarchy that transcends corporeal existence, extending to higher levels of life for soul taken in itself, to which correspond the theoretical sciences and virtues, and leading even further, beyond the level of science, in the direction of union with the One. This is the ultimate goal of philosophy. If philosophy aims at "assimilation to god as far as possible", the divine, even if spread over ever-extending levels of transcendence, is the true objective of philosophy. Philosophy ultimately seeks to make us not good humans, but gods (*Enn.* I.2[19].7.26–8). However, divine assimilation involves various stages, of which political virtue represents a preliminary, indispensable step: to become gods, we must first become good humans (Hierocles, *in CA* 6.19–21). Political virtue must be acquired for access to higher virtues. So, we can conclude, political science and its goal, "political happiness", are subordinate to the higher parts and goals of philosophy. Political science can create the conditions in which souls may acquire political virtues. But this is an early stage, not the final goal, of the philosophical search. The good of the *polis* is not the goal of philosophy, as it may have been, to a greater degree at least, in Plato.

If the goal of political science is to promote political virtues and political happiness in souls as a preparatory stage for their ascent to higher levels of life, to divine life, once these souls have made the ascent, they may wish, as did Plotinus' Minos, to descend, communicating their vision of divine life in legislation. In doing this they would be following the natural inclination of soul to communicate its goodness and knowledge in ordering material existence. If this were to be done in politics, in cities and states, then such action, inspired by divine life and being in its image, could be described as a divinization of the material existence of souls.[28] Developing a theme to be found in Stoic philosophers such as Epictetus (see his *Discourses* 2.14.9–13), later Neoplatonists, describing the assimilation of the philosopher to the divine as an imitation of the divine, find two activities of the divine which the philosopher should imitate: knowledge and providential action. As the divine knows all things and takes providential care of the world, so also should the philosopher attain knowledge (theoretical philosophy) and take care of others (practical philosophy), for example, in the political sphere, in legislative and judicial action.[29]

EARTHLY AND HEAVENLY CITIES

Olympiodorus' description of the goal of political science includes the mention of a love or friendship linking citizens as if members of a family. But what is the importance of this friendship to the soul that wishes to ascend, going beyond the level of political virtue? When describing political virtue, Plotinus refers just to the "inner republic" of the soul (*Enn.* I.2[19].1.17–21): the outer republic – relations with other embodied souls – seems less important. This is also the case when Plotinus compares states of soul with constitutional types, following the analogy suggested in Plato's *Republic*:

> And in the worst kind of man there is the common[30] and his human nature is composed of everything in the manner of a bad political constitution; in the middling man it is as it is in the city in which some good can prevail as the popular (*demotikē*) constitution is not entirely out of control; but in the better kind of man the kind of life is aristocratic; his human nature is already escaping from the common [the ensouled body] and giving itself over to the better sort. But in the best man, the man who separates himself, the ruling principle is one, and the order comes from this to the rest. It is as if there were a double city, one above and one composed of the lower elements set in order by the powers above.
> (*Enn.* IV.4[28].17.26–36, trans. Armstrong, slightly modified)

The best man, here, both is a member of a higher city, the intelligible world (as we will see in a moment), and makes a second city of his embodied existence to the extent that his rational soul exercises monarchical rule, like the philosopher-kings of the *Republic*, over the lower elements of *his* embodied nature. However, Plotinus himself could not have been concerned exclusively with his own inner republic (see Schniewind 2005; Remes 2006).

His domestic life, as reported by Porphyry in the *Life of Plotinus*, and his philosophical teaching, as reflected in the *Enneads*, suggest a care for the material concerns of others and a community of souls – the different voices who speak in his treatises – in search of the Good. Plotinus' unrealized project of a city, Platonopolis, to be run according to "Plato's laws",[31] may have aimed at establishing a more perfect community of like-mindedness and friendship (to use Olympiodorus' terms) in which souls could seek their goal.[32]

Beginning with Porphyry, Plotinus' Neoplatonic heirs also include the outer republic in describing the political virtues[33] and they pay more attention, in their teaching, to the themes of political science, as this chapter shows. An example of this can be seen in the idealized portrait of Pythagoras given in Iamblichus' *On the Pythagorean Life*, where political science, political virtue, legislation, the reform of cities, and communities based on like-mindedness and friendship (*philia*) are very much present.

Plotinus suggests that soul is a member of a higher city. We can relate this first to the hypostasis of Soul, a rational nature which is both one and many, a community in which each individual soul is part of the whole, in which each part is united to each other part, without losing its identity, in which the whole is in each part.[34] Soul is an expression of Intellect which is also, more intensively, a unity in multiplicity, a community which Plotinus compares with a city:

> For there, in Intellect, we have on the one hand Intellect ... and on the other [hand] individual intellects ... as if, supposing that a city had a soul and included other beings with souls, the soul of the city would be more complete and powerful, but there would certainly be nothing to prevent the others from being the same kind of thing.   (*Enn.* IV.8[6].3.16–19, trans. Armstrong)[35]

Soul derives from Intellect: this is its "fatherland", which it has forgotten, alienating itself in its fascination with things of inferior value, material things, admiring them and despising itself, like the degraded souls of Plato's *Republic* book 8.[36]

Proclus, in referring to the intelligible world, refers to the Empedoclean principle of friendship (*philia*): a divine friendship, an intelligible love (*erōs noētos*), characterizes the unity of the intelligible. It is to this intelligible love that lower sharings and likeness of mind can be referred (*in Prm.* 723.5–724.8; *in Ti.* I.18.1–6). Simplicius, indeed, sees in our experience of friendship, as the sharing of all things in common, a revelation of this higher unity (*in Epict. Ench.* 88.1–89.17). Embodied soul, experiencing true friendship, can remember and return to the transcendent community from which it came. Such friendship, as sharing all in common, characterizes an ideal constitution (above, § "Law"), whereas other constitutions, based on material desires, alienate soul and correspond to its degradation (Damascius, *Isid.*, frags 30, 30a; D. O'Meara forthcoming).

THE PLACE OF THE PHILOSOPHER IN THE CITY

In an interesting section of his *Commentary on Epictetus' Handbook*, Simplicius discusses the question of the place of the philosopher in the city, in a way that allows us to see how the Neoplatonist philosopher of late antiquity would have conceived of his position in the society of his time.[37] Simplicius sees the function of the philosopher as being that of the

"beneficent care of all men, as far as possible"; that is, the providential care noted above
(§ "The goal of political science"). This involves "humanizing" his fellow-citizens; that
is, promoting the "political virtues" among them, the virtues that make of them good
humans (*in Epict. Ench.* 32.164–72; see D. O'Meara 2011). But in what capacity can he
do this? Simplicius distinguishes here between two situations: that obtaining in a good
state and that in an evil state. In a good state the philosopher (the true philosopher!) will
assume the functions of ruler (given his qualifications) and of other high offices in the
state: counsellor, general (if he has the relevant experience), judge. However, in an evil
state the philosopher will exclude himself and be excluded from public affairs, since he
will not conform to the material values which dominate in evil states. Simplicius sees two
possibilities for the philosopher in this situation. One possibility is exile: that suffered by
Epictetus under Domitian's rule and, we might add, that known by Simplicius himself,
Damascius and other members of the school at Athens, when they took refuge in Persia,
after 529, at the court of Chosroes. But if the philosopher does not go into exile – and could
there be a good state to which he could go?[38] – but must stay, then Simplicius recommends
(*in Epict.* 193–4) that he "hide himself, as if avoiding a sandstorm behind a little wall": the
image is taken from Plato's *Republic* (496d). It is as if the conditions which prevailed when
Socrates was condemned to death, as Plato saw them, also applied, for the philosopher, in
the reign of the emperor Justinian. In hiding himself, however, the philosopher neither
gives up his function of "beneficent care" for others, nor compromises himself: he will
pursue his work of "humanizing" among "family, friends, and all citizens, if there might
happen some good action in need of his collaboration" (*in Epict.* 196–7). In other words,
if excluded from official functions in an evil state, the philosopher will act unofficially, as
far as possible, working for the good, avoiding bringing harm to others. Simplicius suggests that the philosopher will exercise some caution in all this, but will not allow himself
to be compromised and corrupted in his values and choice of life. Reading between the
lines, we can see that the hidden philosopher may not escape persecution and even death.
Damascius, Simplicius' teacher, in his *Life of Isidore*, tells the stories of pagans who resisted,
were tortured or killed (the famous example is that of the assassination of Hypatia), or
compromised themselves and betrayed their values. Perhaps the most obvious area where
the philosopher could realize his care of others was that of the philosophical school, a
community of family and friends, where, in reading texts together, political virtues could
be practised and higher levels of the philosophical life could be reached.

TEXTS

What texts would one have read in the Neoplatonic schools in relation to the study of
political science? If we consider first the curriculum followed by the later Neoplatonic
schools, we can identify, in the second and main cycle of the curriculum, devoted to the
study of Plato, the *Gorgias* as the primary text to be studied. A reflection of study of the
Gorgias can be found in Olympiodorus' commentary on the dialogue, but there were
of course other, earlier commentaries which are no longer extant, in particular those
of Hierocles and of Proclus. The *Gorgias* was read as the second text of the cycle, being
preceded by the *Alcibiades*, which some Neoplatonists also considered as relevant for
political virtue (see Olympiodorus, *in Alc.* 4.15–21, citing Damascius). We can still read

the commentaries of Proclus and Olympiodorus on this dialogue. More diligent students would also read, on this subject, Plato's *Republic* (too long, it seems, to serve as a basic text). The commentaries by Porphyry, Syrianus and Damascius on the *Republic* do not survive, but we can read Proclus' series of essays on different parts of the *Republic*.[39] We also hear of commentaries on Plato's *Laws*, no longer extant, by Syrianus and Damascius. At any rate, the *Republic* and *Laws*, as indeed Plato's *Statesman*, are used when the themes of political science are discussed, as we have seen above.

Before starting the study of Plato, the student in the later Neoplatonist school would be expected to do a preparatory course of reading in Aristotle and this would include, for ambitious students like Proclus, Aristotle's ethics and politics (Marinus, *Life of Proclus*, chs 13, 14). Proclus indeed defends Plato against the criticisms directed at him by Aristotle in the *Politics*. But there is little sign that the *Politics* was much read in the schools. The teachers mention not only the *Politics*, but also the Aristotelian collection of *Constitutions*, but it is probable that this is scholastic diligence, not necessarily reflecting real acquaintance on the part of students or their teachers (see D. O'Meara 2008)! Some fragments still survive of Porphyry's commentary on Aristotle's *Nicomachean Ethics*.

The Aristotelian cycle would itself be preceded by an initial edification in ethical and political virtues, by means of the study of the Pythagorean *Golden Verses*, commented on by Hierocles, or of Epictetus' *Handbook*, commented on by Simplicius. Here also themes relating to political science could come up, as they could in two texts of Isocrates (*To Nicocles* and *Nicocles*), the study of which is attested for later Neoplatonic schools (Hoffmann 2000: 611–12).

Besides the commentaries on authoritative texts that have survived, we can also read today other Neoplatonic works relevant to political science. Some of Iamblichus' letters, those to Dyscolius and to Agrippa, appear to be "mirrors of princes" addressed to influential politicians, as is a letter directed by Sopatros (II), son of Iamblichus' pupil Sopatros (I), to his brother Himerius.[40] Synesius' *On Kingship* is also a "mirror of princes". Furthermore, much can be found in Julian the Emperor's discourses and correspondence. A particularly fascinating document is the anonymous dialogue *On Political Science* of the sixth century, which is profoundly Neoplatonic in inspiration and reflects, through the proposal of a political ideal, on problems characterizing the latter part of Justinian's reign.[41]

Returning to Plotinus, we find little in his treatises that concerns political science. The treatises do not correspond to the full extent of his teaching – of which Amelius made one hundred volumes of notes – but probably are a complete collection of his formal compositions. In these treatises, the emphasis is put on access to the higher stages of philosophical progress, beyond the level of political virtue: on purification, on self-knowledge and ascent to the life of Intellect. This is perhaps not surprising: it corresponds to the difference between Plotinus and later Neoplatonists on the subject of the importance of the embodied life for soul (see above, Chapter 18 by Finamore; D. O'Meara 2003: 39).[42]

NOTES

1. *Euthd.* 291c, 292c–e; see also *Prt.* 319a.
2. Plato compares this science to that of an architect, or master-builder (*architectōn*), who coordinates and controls the work of various subsidiary crafts contributing to a building project (*Plt.* 259e–261a).
3. Plato's "statesman" (*politikos*) is the bearer of political science, not to be confused therefore with the

modern concept of the politician. Thus, one is a *politikos* in virtue of possessing political science, even in private life, whether or not this science is brought to use (*Plt.* 259b).

4. Alcinous, *Handbook of Platonism*, ch. 3 (where the Aristotelian division of philosophy is combined with the Hellenistic division of philosophy into ethics, physics and logic).

5. But he does refer to a division of sciences in *Enn.* I.3[20].6 and to practical sciences (rhetoric, military expertise, economics and "royal" art) in *Enn.* V.9[5].11.21–6.

6. Iamblichus, *Comm. Math.* chs 15 and 30; in *VP* 6, 32, Iamblichus describes Pythagoras as having communicated "the best *politeia*", among much other knowledge, to mankind (cf. Prometheus in the myth of Plato's *Prt.* 322b–c); Proclus, *in Euc.* 22.1–24.20; *in Ti.* I.32.1–15. For further references see Dörrie & Baltes (1987–2008: vol. 4, sections 215–16, with notes).

7. The definition of the aim of philosophy as "assimilation to god" is taken by the Platonists from Plato's *Theaetetus* (176b); see D. O'Meara (2003: 31–2, 36–9); Männlein-Robert (2013).

8. *In Alc.* 178.1–179.10; see Proclus, *in Alc.* 202.4–203.16. "Political science" is not named as such in the passage of the *Alcibiades*.

9. Olympiodorus cites Plato's *Critias* (109c1). The point is made in Plato's *Statesman* that humans are not appropriately ruled as if they were a herd of animals; such a rule would be that either of a god or of a tyrant (*Plt.* 275c–276e).

10. The reference here is to the community of guardians of Plato: *R.* 461d.

11. On the hierarchy of virtues see above, Chapter 28 by Remes; Marinus, *Life of Proclus* [Saffrey & Segonds], Introduction, 69–98.

12. See also Simplicius, *in Cat.* 318.18–19 and above, Chapter 27 by Adamson, on the Neoplatonic concept of fate.

13. See Proclus, *in Alc.* 120.12–121.26; *de Prov.* 34.25–30; *de Decem Dub.* 51. For more discussion of these themes, see D. O'Meara (2003: 133–6).

14. Proclus, *in R.* I.210.4–211.3, 217.7–16 (see MacIsaac 2009); Damascius, *Isid.*, frag. 109; on the corruption of souls by evil states see Simplicius, *in Epict. Ench.* 32.225–9 (inspired by Plato, *R.* 494b–495b, 497b).

15. Iamblichus, *Letter to Dyscolius* (Stob. *Anth.* IV.222.14–18 = Taormina & Piccione 2010: 324).

16. Proclus, *in R.* Essay 17. For discussion of Proclus' answer to Aristotle, see Stalley (1995) and Narbonne (2003).

17. In a letter to Agrippa, in Stobaeus, *Anth.* IV.223.14–24 (= Taormina & Piccione 2010: 328).

18. Proclus, *in Ti.* III.282.8–21; Olympiodorus, *in Grg.* 14.8–21; Pseudo-Elias, *in Porph.* 22.10–11. Olympiodorus (*in Grg.* 221.11–17), citing Ammonius, points out that for Plato (*R.* 445c–e) aristocracy and monarchy do not essentially differ: what matters is that rule be exercised by whoever has the philosophical competence, whether the ruler be one or several in number.

19. See Plotinus, *Enn.* IV.4[28].17.24–36 (quoted below in § "Earthly and heavenly cities"); Olymp., *in Grg.* 221.1–17.

20. See below, § "The place of the philosopher in the city"; Saffrey (2000: 212–14). On tyranny see Proclus, *in R.* 2.176.11–15.

21. Proclus, *in R.* 1.9.17–11.4; Anonymous, *Prolegomena to Platonic Philosophy* 26.45–58.

22. Iamblichus, *Letter to Asphalius*, Stobaeus, *Anth.* III.201.17–202.17 (= Taormina & Piccione 2010: 310); Hierocles, *On Providence*, in Photius, *Bibl.* 251.464b (trans. in Schibli [2002: 353]).

23. *Ti.* 90b–d; Proclus, *in R.* 2.3.5–10; 99.10–100.28.

24. Iamblichus, *Comm. Math.* chs 15 (56.4–8) and 30 (91.27–92.6); Proclus, *in Euc.* 23.12–24.20.

25. This rare term, used only once in Plotinus, is of Epicurean origin, where it signifies a more general inference drawn from experience.

26. Letter to Asphalius, in Stobaeus, *Anth.* III.201.17–202.17 (= Taormina & Piccione 2010: 310).

27. See Schibli (2002: 85–8, and his notes on Hierocles at 213–18) for more discussion of practical wisdom and its inspiration in Aristotle's ethics; Simplicius, *in Cat.* 318.19–21.

28. See Plato, *R.* 501b–c, quoted by Iamblichus in a letter (above, note 22).

29. Ammonius, *in Porph.* 3.8–19; Pseudo-Elias, *in Porph.* 18.9–10. These ideas are already to be found in Plotinus; see Song (2009).

30. *To koinon*: i.e. what arises in the ensouled body, as described a few lines before (*Enn.* IV.4[28].20–23).

31. Porphyry, *Plot.* 12. The report recalls a similar project attributed to Plato in Diogenes Laertius, *Lives* 3.21.

32. The theme of friendship and love in Neoplatonism has been generally neglected, but see now Staab (2002: 426–34), Schramm (2013), D'Andrès (2010).

33. Porphyry, *Sent.* 32.23.4–8 ; Macrobius, *Somn. Scip.* 1.8.8; Marinus, *Procl.* 14–17.

34. *Enn.* VI.4[22].4.35–44; IV.3[27].2; V.8[31].4. On the undescended soul in Plotinus, see *Enn.* IV.8[6].8 and above, Chapter 20 by Aubry.

35. On the transcendent community of souls, see D. O'Meara (2002).

36. *R.* 551a, 553d; Plotinus, *Enn.* V.1[10].1.1–15; D. O'Meara (forthcoming).

37. Simplicius, *in Epict. Ench.* 32.163–234; I summarize here the analysis of the text proposed in D. O'Meara (2004).

38. The Christian historian Agathias (*Hist.* 2.30) mocked the Athenian philosophers who emigrated to Persia for thinking that they would find there an ideal republic like Plato's. But one may doubt that they were so naïve.

39. Notice, for example, Essay 1, containing *prolegomena* to the reading of the *Republic*: Proclus insists that the aim of the text is to deal *both* with justice in the soul *and* with constitutions of city-states; one aspect is not to be preferred to the detriment of the other. Most of Essay 1, dealing largely with constitutional types (see *in R.* 1.6.12–21), has been lost in the manuscript transmission. Essays 8–9 deal with the question of the equality of women and men in education and virtue (the basis for Plato's revolutionary inclusion of women among the rulers of the ideal state): Proclus adopts a characteristically scholastic and conservative approach (see Longo 2002; D. O'Meara 2003: 83–6). Essay 17 responds to Aristotle's criticisms in *Politics* book 2 of the *Republic*: here also, only the first pages of the essay have been preserved.

40. See O'Meara & Schamp (2006), which includes a French translation of Sopatros' letter.

41. See D. O'Meara (2003: 171–84); MacCoull (2006).The anonymous dialogue has been translated into English by Bell (2009), who provides extensive historical notes.

42. This section summarizes information that is collected in D. O'Meara (2003: 65–8), where further references can be found.

30

Plotinus' aesthetics: in defence of the lifelike

Panayiota Vassilopoulou

PLOTINUS' AESTHETICS

Does Plotinus have an aesthetics and/or a philosophy of art? If we start from a naïve conception of aesthetics as a philosophical discourse on beauty – its nature, our experience of it, our interest in it, our judgements concerning it – the *Enneads* provide ample evidence for an affirmative answer. Plotinus discusses beauty in many contexts, including two treatises explicitly dedicated to it, *On Beauty*, I.6[1], and *On Intelligible Beauty*, V.8[31], and he does so because he considers beauty an essential characteristic of reality and our experience.[1] The importance Plotinus attaches to beauty is indicated by the wide extension he attributes to the term: every object of human experience, including natural things, animals and human beings, technological products, works of art, moral and cognitive practices and their results, can be appreciated from the point of view of beauty.[2] This usage reflects common ancient Greek linguistic habits, but even the proper philosophical objects of Plotinus' thought (the One, the Intellect, the Soul, or the universe as a whole), which obviously transcend ordinary experience, are approached systematically through their relation to beauty and deployed to provide a metaphysical account of the presence of beauty in the sensible world.[3]

With regard to philosophy of art, the evidence is ambiguous. Although there are no treatises explicitly dedicated to the creation and reception of works of art, Plotinus discusses the function of the artist and the nature of the work of art in many contexts. These brief discussions do not amount to a comprehensive or detailed philosophy of art; moreover, their incidental nature and general tenor, as well as some of their claims, suggest that Plotinus did not attach much significance to art. It is clear that Plotinus, who lived in an age when philosophers could be openly proud of being philosophers, had no problem in sometimes contrasting philosophy as a "serious" (*spoudaia*) pursuit to a conception of artistic activity as producing "toys (*paignia*) not worth much" (*Enn.* IV.3[27].10.18). Yet, even in such contexts, Plotinus situates art firmly within life, since life "does not rest from ceaselessly making beautiful and shapely living toys" (*Enn.* III.2[47].15.32–3) and places art at the same level as any other human activity, because, apart from philosophy, "the rest of humanity is a toy" (*Enn.* III.2[47].15.54–5). I shall revisit this issue, but at present I should indicate that Plotinus' scattered remarks do give us a sense of what he would consider a successful work of art; moreover, by situating artistic creativity within the broader context of the fundamental theoretical, practical and affective possibilities of human interaction with reality, they offer the outline for a philosophical account of the existence, purpose and value of art.

These observations lead to two further comments about the manner of Plotinus' engagement with beauty and art. The first is that even when dealing with passages that clearly focus on aesthetic issues, one cannot make much sense of them without referring to the metaphysical background they reflect. Plotinus' aesthetics is not a detached account of the relevant experience without explicit philosophical presuppositions, but rather a systematically motivated part of his philosophy, closely integrated with his metaphysics, epistemology and psychology. Accordingly, his views on beauty and art do not aim to describe historically given artistic practices, but are offered in a normative perspective shaped by specific ontological commitments. Moreover, his philosophy as a whole seems characterized by an aesthetic orientation, in a sense that transcends the concrete issue of art. This orientation issues from his fundamental conception of reality as a hierarchy of levels – the One, the Intellect, the Soul, the material world – each of which can be considered as an "image" of the one above, the lower level generated by the higher one as its reflection, striving to become through its own activity like the higher one. The material world (which, properly speaking, does not constitute a distinct ontological level but is "in the soul") is grasped as the image of an intelligible model generated through the productive activity of the Soul. As a result, aesthetically pregnant notions like creation, imagination, imitation or presentation perform crucial functions in wider contexts, in ways that often defy the distinction between the literal and the metaphorical. Plotinus' reliance on the paradigm of art for the articulation of fundamental tenets of his thought indicates that his influence on the tradition of aesthetics may not just derive from his explicit discussions of aesthetic issues, but could be the result of an appropriation of its overall content.

It comes as no surprise, then, that Plotinus has been credited with an innovative and more attractive interpretation of the role of art and artists than his predecessors, especially Plato.[4] This interpretation is thought to have influenced or inspired subsequent theories of art and artistic practices: links between Plotinus' aesthetics and various forms of art have been recurrently explored in connection with the art of late antiquity, the Byzantine period, the Renaissance, or even contemporary trends like abstract or conceptual art.[5] But these remarks also shed some light on the claim that Plotinus did not have an aesthetics in the modern sense of the term, and thus any talk about it would be a misleading anachronism.[6] The claim can be understood in different ways. If by "aesthetics in the modern sense" we understand a project like the contemporary discipline of aesthetics, where the explicit aim is the philosophical discussion of beauty or art with a minimum of general philosophical presuppositions, then it is true that Plotinus does not have an aesthetics, for the same reasons that, say, Kant, Hegel or Nietzsche did not have one either. If by "aesthetics in the modern sense", following Baumgarten's original definition of the term, we understand the study of an object strictly confined within sensory experience, then Plotinus does not have an aesthetics (but, once again, neither do Kant nor Hegel in their engagement with beauty or art). If by "aesthetics in the modern sense" we understand a philosophical examination of art or beauty based on whatever common ideas underlie the work of the thinkers of the eighteenth and nineteenth centuries, such as a modern conception of subjectivity, or a new understanding of the function of imagination, or the invention of a "system" of arts,[7] then again Plotinus does not have an aesthetics, but in this case one cannot help but share the concern expressed by Stephen Halliwell that,

> of all the branches of philosophy, it is only aesthetics, it seems, whose own prac-
> titioners are commonly tempted to equate the history of their discipline with the
> discovery of its supposedly "pure" truths. No approach of this kind would make
> much sense for, say, the history of metaphysics, epistemology, or ethics, or the pure
> philosophy of mind, in all of which it seems necessary to acknowledge a history
> that embraces substantially, even radically, different ways of thinking, rather than
> making any one set of ideas definitional of the subject itself.   (2002: 11–12)

In this sense, the claim that Plotinus does have an aesthetics goes against both the con-temporary understanding of aesthetics as a separate discipline that can pursue its aims independently of wider philosophical articulations and the tendency to equate aesthetics as such with modern aesthetics. These two points are not independent. If we credit Kant with the definitive philosophical articulation of modern aesthetics, one of its constitu-tive moments is the radical separation between the claims of the true, the good and the beautiful. Kant articulated this separation from within a comprehensive philosophical system and noted the epistemological and moral implications of the aesthetic domain; nevertheless, it is this articulation that created the possibility for a separate discipline of aesthetics. Plotinus, obviously, does not share this starting point, since for him the true, the good and the beautiful are intimately connected and thus there is a continuum between cognition or theory and practice, whether moral or artistic.[8] But it is important to note that this separation, already questioned by the German Idealists and Romantics or Nietzsche, may be also historically overcome in the practices that guide artistic crea-tion and reception today, and thus any 'modern' aesthetics based on the assumption of autonomous aesthetic values may be already obsolete. As Arthur Danto notes in his 1984 essay on "The End Of Art",

> If we look at the art of our recent past …, what we see is something which depends
> more and more upon theory for its existence as art. … But there is another feature
> exhibited by these late productions which is that the objects approach zero as
> their theory approaches infinity, so that virtually all there is at the end *is* theory,
> art having finally become vaporized in a dazzle of pure thought about itself, and
> remaining, as it were, solely as the object of its own theoretical consciousness …
> [F]or the object in which the artwork consists is so irradiated by theoretical con-
> sciousness that the division between object and subject is all but overcome, and it
> little matters whether art is philosophy in action or philosophy is art in thought.
> (1986: 111–13)

What is striking about this passage for anyone familiar with Plotinus' views on art is that it seems to describe equally well both the conditions of a Hegelian end of art (where "end" signifies the closure of a historical period in which art has an important independent function; this is the sense in which Danto offers his description) and the substance of a Plotinian end of art (where "end" stands for the purpose, the *telos*, which art should serve). If, as Danto's remarks suggest, this is an important problem for art today, Plotinus' articulation of it, however distant from our modern presuppositions, may still be relevant. The aim of the reflections that follow is to present an overview of Plotinus' philosophy of art from the point of view of the problem of the relation between theory and practice, or philosophy and art. As we shall see, a promising starting point in this direction, which however has been relatively neglected in the literature, is offered by the notions of "life" and "lifelikeness" which Plotinus seems to accentuate in his account of beauty.

THE LIFELIKE

A philosophy of art needs to coordinate three related issues: artistic creation, the work of art and aesthetic reception. What distinguishes artistic creation from other forms of human practice? What distinguishes the work of art from other human artefacts? What distinguishes aesthetic experience from other forms of human experience? If the enquiry is embedded within a broader framework of aesthetics, which allows that there are objects of aesthetic experience that are not works of art, then the emphasis shifts to the latter two questions, of which the former needs to be correspondingly broadened: What makes an object appropriate for aesthetic appreciation?[9] These issues can be approached from various perspectives, but what marks the philosophical approach, and this is as true for Plato or Plotinus as it is for Kant or Hegel, is the attempt to elucidate these questions in terms of the interests and objects of philosophy itself.

Plotinus does not think that beauty, which, for him, is what makes an object appropriate for aesthetic appreciation and is thus his central aesthetic category or value, comes into being exclusively through the work of artists. One could claim that his interest is directed primarily at the experience of beautiful objects of any kind and only secondarily at the specific issues raised by artistic creation and works of art.[10] This is true to the extent that the existence of non-artificial beauty, whether sensible or intelligible, and our reaction to it are of special systematic importance for Plotinus' philosophy.[11] However, it would be a mistake to draw a sharp distinction here between the natural and the artificial. On the one hand, artistic creation is fully "natural" for Plotinus, because the activity of artists is explicated within the same metaphysical context that accounts for the existence of natural beauty without any radical break between nature and history and, thus, the work of art exists as "naturally" as any other beautiful object. On the other hand, what underlies the existence of any form of beauty is an activity of metaphysical principles that is at least partly to be conceptualized with the help of the paradigm of art, whether that of a craftsman or an artist.[12]

The first question to consider, therefore, concerns the work of art, and in particular the issue of its success and its evaluation: how can we conceive and judge the excellence of a work of art? Obviously, the short response would be in terms of beauty, since the apprehension of beauty is both what initially captivates us and makes us concentrate on the work of art as well as the final purpose of aesthetic experience.[13] We are led, then, to the question of the elucidation of the nature of beauty, and a good starting point is provided by the following passage from the treatise *The Forms and the Good*, VI.7[38]:

> So here below also beauty is what illuminates good proportions rather than the good proportions themselves, and this is what is lovable. For why is there more light of beauty on a living face, but only a trace of it on a dead one, even if its flesh and its proportions are not yet wasted away? And are not the more lifelike (*dzōtikōtera*) statues the more beautiful ones, even if the others are better proportioned? And is not an uglier living man more beautiful than the man in a statue?
>
> (*Enn.* VI.7[38].22.24–32)

The immediate suggestion is that beauty does not depend essentially on any of the factors ordinarily thought to shape the aesthetic reception of an object, such as its symmetry, proportions or, more generally, its sensible form or material qualities. The claim that these factors are neither sufficient nor necessary conditions for beauty, since they cannot be considered as its cause or principle, is made by Plotinus in *Enn.* I.6[1] and his arguments in support of it have been discussed in Plotinian scholarship (see Anton 1964; Kuisma 2003: 163–5; Darras-Worms 2007: 123–36). One consideration that Plotinus raises here is that the same body appears sometimes beautiful and sometimes not beautiful, presumably while its structure and composition remain unaffected (*Enn.* I.6[1].1.15–17, 38–40). Under the assumption that these variations in judgement are not entirely due to subjective factors, this fact seems to imply that in beautiful bodies, "being bodies is one thing, their being beautiful is another" (*Enn.* I.6[1].1.16–17), which, in terms of the particular aesthetic position that Plotinus discusses, means that "being beautiful is something else over and above good proportion and good proportion is beautiful because of something else" (1.39–41). It is in this context that the notion of "lifelikeness" or "liveliness" (*to zōtikon*) is introduced in the attempt to capture this "something else" that transcends every determinate sensible characteristic of the object, the "grace" (*charis*) or "light" (*phengos*) (*Enn.* VI.7[38].22.24) which is responsible for making the sensible form of an object lovable to its beholder.

At one level, the notion of lifelikeness operates as an aesthetic predicate, enabling us to articulate our aesthetic response to different objects, and to compare and evaluate these objects accordingly. A work of art could be considered more "lifelike", and hence better, the more faithfully or realistically it represents the physical entity it portrays.[14] The well-known anecdote of the contest between Zeuxis and Parrhasius illustrates this notion (Pliny, *Natural History* 35.65): Zeuxis' painting was so realistic as to deceive the birds who took his painted grapes for real and pecked at them; yet Parrhasius was the winner because he deceived Zeuxis himself, who tried to lift a curtain in order to see Parrhasius' work behind it only to realize that the curtain itself was the masterpiece. As the anecdote indicates, this notion of lifelikeness is associated with the idea of some form of deception that underlies the spectator's strong engagement with a successful work of art; given Plato's hostility towards this aspect of artistic creation, it seems unlikely that Plotinus had this in mind when praising lifelikeness.[15] But there are other aspects of this traditional aesthetic theme that are more congenial to Plotinus' use of the term. In some cases, the idea of a vivid artistic representation merges with that of expression: if the point of the work is to evoke a certain response in its viewer, such that the viewer would engage with the work as if it were alive, the representation should not be just "realistic" in a formal sense (if at all), but should express internal contents that can motivate and sustain this kind of engagement. As Socrates puts it in Xenophon's *Memorabilia* (3.10.1–8) in the typical case of a human statue, if "the appearance of being alive (*to zōtikon phainesthai*) is what most enchants (*psychagōgei*) people who look at statues", then "the sculptor must represent the activity of the soul in his figures" or "imitate the character of the soul", a task that goes beyond any formal or material considerations, since this character itself "has neither symmetry nor colour [...], and it is not even visible at all".

I thus claim provisionally that a "lifelike" work of art would need to have the appearance of having a soul, to intimate the presence of soul beneath its visible form, in such a way that another soul (that of the spectator) can sense or recognize an affinity with it.[16] This fits with the claim, explicitly made by Plotinus (in *Enn.* I.6[1].6.25–30, quoted above in note 3), that it is the soul that makes a sensible body beautiful, by its presence (or appearance of its presence) and its beauty; it also corresponds to a conception of the soul as the principle of life, namely as the organizing and formative force behind all kinds of movements and changes we can observe in the natural world (see e.g. *Enn.* IV.7[2].9 or *Enn.* VI.2[43].6).

This claim would also explain Plotinus' account of aesthetic experience as an essentially reflective one in which, beyond any bodily pleasures or affections, the soul "sees something akin to it or a trace of its kindred reality" and is thus "delighted and thrilled and returns to itself (*anapherei pros heautēn*) and remembers itself" (*Enn.* I.6[1].2.9–11). This enables us to elucidate the mixed way in which Plotinus uses the term from a categorical point of view, a usage that underlines the wide extension of the term "beautiful" noted earlier. If lifelikeness functioned as a distinct, purely aesthetic, category, one could imagine that some statues might be more beautiful than a living human being; in more general terms, that the norms of the aesthetic semblance would be independent of the norms of the real and circumscribe an autonomous aesthetic realm. However, as the passage from *Enn.* VI.7 indicates, for Plotinus the living is always more beautiful than the dead or the artificial, presumably under the assumption of a categorical continuum in which appearing to have a soul can be compared with actually having a soul and be found ontologically inferior.[17] On the other hand, if a living face can sometimes appear beautiful and others not so, as Plotinus claims in *Enn.* I.6, the mere fact of being alive in the biological sense is not to be considered identical with being beautiful. A living being, and similarly a work of art, can be more or less attractive, or "lifelike", in different circumstances to the extent that its visible form (a) intimates more vividly the presence of soul, and (b) reveals in the appropriate way the presence of a beautiful soul, since, certainly, souls can be ugly, or less beautiful, too (see *Enn.* I.6[1].5.26–58).[18] In this sense, one can talk about lifelikeness as a *relatively* autonomous aesthetic category, measuring the extent to which the sensible form of an object in a given condition facilitates or hinders the recognition of its ensouled nature.

Since the soul itself is not visible, from a strictly empirical point of view, the recognition of a living human being would not be very different from that of a "fully" lifelike statue: in both cases, the soul of the observer (which knows itself also in other ways) has to "guess" the presence of the other soul ("sense" its affinity to it) through the evidence afforded by the sensible form of the body in front of it.[19] This similarity can be explained from a metaphysical point of view if we take into account Plotinus' claim that the term "life" is not univocal, but "is used in many different senses, distinguished according to the rank of the things to which it is applied" (*Enn.* I.4[46].3.19–20). The primary sense, "the perfect, true, real life", refers to the life lived by the Intellect; the "other lives are incomplete, traces of life, not perfect or pure and no more life than its opposite" (ll. 33–6). Now, if all these other lives are "images" (*eidōla, indalmata*) of the life of the Intellect, there is nothing in principle that prevents us from adding to this list of metaphors another entry, and talk about the "life" of a "lifelike" work of art.[20]

The nature of this "life", as well as our motivation for adopting this way of talking, need elaboration; but here it suffices to highlight that Plotinus' refusal to circumscribe an aesthetic domain proper rests precisely on an "aesthetic" understanding of ordinary life. If, from a metaphysical perspective, the life of a plant and an animal are already forms of "lifelikeness", that is, presentations of (a real, intelligible) life to be distinguished or evaluated as presentations (aesthetically) in terms of their difference in "clarity or dimness" (*tranotēti kai amydrotēti*) (*Enn.* II.3[52].9.22), we have a way to order all forms of lifelikeness in terms of their distance from real life, but we have no reason to categorically separate one kind of lifelikeness from another. In this sense, if we wish to understand what it would mean for a work of art to be lifelike, we need to ascend to the level of the Intellect and examine the (real) life it lives, in which "beauty is just beauty, because it is not in what is not beautiful" (*Enn.* VI.8[39].4.14–15).

The most vivid description of the life of the Plotinian Intellect can be found in chapter 4 of his treatise *On Intelligible Beauty, Enn.* V.8[31]. There are three aspects of this account that are of particular interest to the present discussion (for a broader exploration of these themes, see Beierwaltes 1985: 38–64). The first concerns the self-sufficiency of (the life of) the Intellect that underlies the idea of its perfection. Despite the Intellect's metaphysical dependency on the One, its activity is fully self-grounded, self-directed and self-contained. As Plotinus puts it, "the thing itself is Intellect and its ground is Intellect" (*Enn.* V.8[31].4.18–19), which can be taken to mean that the Intellect is both the cause and the end of itself, capable of exercising its proper immanent activity without any kind of awareness of deficiency or lack within itself that would necessitate the recognition of something exterior to itself to be desired, sought or obtained. In this sense, "its good will not be something brought in from the outside" (*Enn.* I.4[46].3.28–9); in contemporary terms, the Intellect contains within itself the norm of its life and activity. Second, the nature of this activity is contemplation, a purely intellectual activity that, despite the duality of a subject and object presupposed by every form of intellection, amounts to a form of self-constitution in a thorough identity between subject and object, thinking and being. The Intellect as a mind brings its intelligible objects into being, *creates* these objects, by thinking these; but at the same time it is nothing over and above the thinking of these objects, it is itself thinking itself (*Enn.* V.9[5].5.12–13, 7.12–13; V.3[49].5.43–7). This thinking is not of the discursive variety familiar to human beings, in which the object of thought must be sought and obtained through conceptual or argumentative elaborations (*Enn.* V.9[5].7.10–11), leading to mental chains of associations formed by "letting some things go and attending to others" (*Enn.* V.1[10].4.19). Rather it is fully intuitive, the continuous and undisturbed presence of the objects of thought (the continuous presence of the Intellect to itself), and regardless of its content and complexity, "is not composed of theorems, but one thing as a whole" (*Enn.* V.8[31].5.6–7), in which "everything and all things are clear to the inmost part of anything" (*Enn.* V.8[31].4.5), arranged, so to speak, in a transparent and unified network grasped immediately in all its distinctions and without any opaque remainders. Accordingly, this thought experiences no resistance, requires no effort, is not punctuated by distinct moments of achievement, and is thus not subject to the sequence of lack, desire, effort, achievement, pleasure, satiety. As a result, "there is a lack of satisfaction there in the sense that fullness does not cause contempt for that which has produced it: for that which sees goes on seeing still more, and, perceiving its own infinity and that of what it sees, follows its own" (*Enn.* V.8[31].4.31–3). Finally, what from a subjective point of view appears as an intuitive form of thought, from an objective point of view corresponds to a maximally unified multiplicity or diversity in which the relation between whole and parts loses any real ontological significance (as much as the whole determines the parts, the parts determine the whole) and becomes almost an inconsequential oscillation between foreground and background. Although "a different kind of being stands out in each" distinct intelligible object, "each comes only from the whole [and not from another part] and is part and whole at once: it has the appearance of a part, but a penetrating look sees the whole in it" (*Enn.* V.8[31].4.23–5; see also *Enn.* III.2[47].1.27–36).

This is the real or true life lived by the Intellect. And when Plotinus tries to sum it up, taking his cue from a phrase in Plato's *Phaedo*, he talks about "exceedingly blessed spectators" contemplating things that "are like images seen by their own light" (*Enn.* V.8[31].4.42–4), not abstract propositions, but "beautiful images [...] images not painted but real" (5.20–24). Given what has been said about the nature of the Intellect, it should be added that images and spectators are identical, since in this case "the seer does not differ in any way from the seen" (*Enn.* V.3[49].5.4–5), despite the "distance" implied in the very notion of contemplation.

This brief presentation of the fundamental characteristics of the life of the Intellect is, I think, enough to show how productive it could be to take seriously Plotinus' claim that a successful work of art must be lifelike and to try to understand this lifelikeness analogically on the basis of the account of the real life of the Intellect. Consider, first, the aspect of self-sufficiency. To claim that a successful work of art must be (or appear to be) self-sufficient would mean, in the most straightforward sense, that it must be a complete whole, a totality in which there is no evident lack or deficiency of any kind. Depending on the kind of art one has in mind, this requirement can be specified in a variety of ways, some of these obvious, for example, a story must have a beginning and an end, and some more subtle, for example, Socrates' claim in the *Phaedrus* (264c) that a speech must be like a living creature. It may even be pursued in antithetical directions – for example, one direction could take us to an "aesthetics of the fragment", in which the work of art is valued as a fragment constructed in such a way that allows for the imaginative reconstruction of a relevant totality, while another to a Wagnerian project of a total work of art that would result from the fusion of different forms of art. In another, perhaps less obvious sense, the requirement of self-sufficiency would mean that the work of art must be self-contained in that it would appear able to answer, as it were, all the questions or issues that it is capable of raising. Why is this shape red? Why does X die on p. 324? If, in order to respond to questions like these, one would have to go outside the work to reality or to other works, one would think that the work has failed precisely because it needs something external in order to be understood. Finally, in the most fundamental and comprehensive sense, the successful work of art must be self-sufficient in that it must appear to contain within itself the norm of itself, in the sense of establishing the point of view from which it should be appreciated or evaluated.

If we now turn our attention to the question of the formal structure of a beautiful object or a successful work of art, we are on relatively firmer ground, since Plotinus himself has drawn explicitly the implications of lifelikeness in this respect. A piece of matter or, more generally, a sensible multiplicity, becomes beautiful to the extent that, through the creative intervention of the soul (and this applies both to natural and artificial beauty), it is shaped by form: "The form, then, approaches and composes that which is to come into being from many parts into a single ordered whole; it brings it into a completed unity and makes it one by agreement of its parts; for since it is one itself, that which is shaped by it must also be one as far as a thing can be which is composed of many parts" (*Enn.* V.6[24].2.19–23).

This passage makes clear how Plotinus understands sensible beauty (what we should strictly speaking call "beautylikeness", beauty that exists in something that is not itself beautiful) through an analogical transference of the characteristics of the structure of the Intellect: the object must approximate as much as possible the fully unified diversity of the Intellect in which every part is the whole and the whole is each of its parts. Keeping in mind this particular aspect of the unity of the Intellect helps us understand why Plotinus is against any conception of beauty in terms of sensible form (proportion, harmony or symmetry), even if, obviously, the formative power to which the sensible material is submitted causes the emergence of such formal qualities. The problem is that a purely formal approach would inevitably locate beauty exclusively on the whole, granting it thus primacy over the parts. In such a case, the parts, obeying a principle of division of labour, would contribute to this beauty, but they need not themselves be beautiful. But if in the metaphysical background lies the idea of a structure in which every part "is part and whole at once" or the demand for a maximum and thus homogeneous unification of reality, then Plotinus can indeed claim, perhaps against the verdict of most empirically oriented aesthetic theorists, that "a beautiful whole can certainly not be composed of ugly parts; all the parts must have beauty" (*Enn.* I.6[1].1.29–30).[21]

Since this claim appears problematic in a variety of ways,[22] it may be interesting to refer briefly to the way in which the problem of the whole–part relation in a beautiful object is posed by a much later thinker, Friedrich Schiller, who, in addition to his strong philosophical commitments, has an intimate connection with artistic practice. As the *Letters on Aesthetic Education* indicate (§6), Schiller was critical of the modern principle of the division of labour in its social expression, precisely because it hinders the existence of complete and unified individuals. When faced with the corresponding aesthetic problem, Schiller, like Plotinus, refuses to "sacrifice" the part for the whole, not in the name of a classical demand for unity, but in that of a modern demand for freedom: "Beauty ... regards all things as ends in themselves and will not permit one to serve as the purpose of another. ... Everyone is a free citizen and has the same rights as the most noble in the world of aesthetics, coercion may not take place even for the sake of the whole" (*Kallias* 170).

Schiller understands beauty as "freedom in appearance", that is, "self-determination of a thing insofar as it is available to intuition" (*Kallias* 154); thus his refusal to "coerce" the parts corresponds to the claim that a beautiful whole cannot be made of ugly parts. On the other hand, Schiller knows that "it is necessary for every great composition that the particular restrict itself to let the whole reach its effect"; his way out of the problem is to claim that "if this restriction by the particular is at once the effect of its freedom, that is, if it posits the whole itself, the composition is beautiful" (*Kallias* 171). Notice how close Schiller's position is to Plotinus', given his positive conception of freedom as self-determination: in a beautiful whole, every significant part must "replicate" the whole, in the sense of appearing equally beautiful (self-determined, "containing its good in itself", "lifelike") with the whole. Of course, both Plotinus (*Enn.* V.9[5].2.13–14) and Schiller (*Kallias* 155) are aware that a sensible object cannot be really self-determined in this sense.

There are, in fact, several points of similarity between important themes of the modern aesthetic tradition, especially in the line originating in Kant, and the Plotinian claims we have been exploring. In the *Critique of Judgement*, one may single out the idea that the successful work of art (the work of genius) contains indeed its own norm of being, of course not ontologically or empirically, but in terms of its exemplary function as a concrete standard from which the rules that guide its appreciation must be reflectively abstracted (§46–7).[23] Or one may point out that when the aesthetic experience is famously protected from the intrusion of any real (theoretical or practical) interests of the subject through the notion of a disinterested satisfaction (§2) and is grounded on the notion of a free and harmonious play of the cognitive capacities of understanding and imagination (§9), the result is an intellectual activity that "has a causality in itself, namely that of maintaining the state of the representation of the mind and the occupation of the cognitive powers without a further aim" (§12.222). Consequently, "we linger over the consideration of the beautiful because this consideration strengthens and reproduces itself" (§12.222), which seems like a finite approximation of the infinite activity of the Intellect.

These points of comparison could be multiplied, and indeed show, if necessary, that even if modern aesthetics constitutes in some sense a radical break, classical themes (not necessarily elaborated as part of an aesthetics) did not suddenly disappear but may have even held key roles in the new configuration. If there is a fundamental point of continuity here, one may try to locate it in the fascination felt by an anthropological structure (call it an individual soul or a finite subject) for certain objects that display a kind of self-sufficiency (a lifelikeness) that goes against everything that can be ascertained about their reality. The extension of this set of objects changes over time (the cosmos was obviously such an object for Plotinus and the ancients, in a way that it is not for us today), as do the philosophical descriptions aiming at capturing their nature, in ways that reflect the changes in the conception of the reality against which the claims of these objects are measured or explained: from Plotinus' intelligible reality, which indeed possesses the self-sufficiency of real life, to Kant's scientific physical universe of the *Critique of Pure Reason* in which nothing can really possess any kind of self-sufficiency. However, at least from Plato to Nietzsche, one can trace a line of philosophical reflection investigating the claims of these objects, and this could be called aesthetics in an appropriately broad sense.

ARTISTIC CREATION

The previous section has given, I hope, a sense of what a successful work of art or a beautiful object is supposed to be for Plotinus, and as I tried to show, Plotinus' account has a double aspect corresponding to two senses of the term "lifelike": a sensible object that (a) attracts the soul in a certain immediate way grounded on the affinity that the soul feels for it[24] by (b) being unified in a certain way through the presence of form. This duality is explicitly recognized by Plotinus in a short discussion of sensible beauty in *Enn.* V.9[5]: "What then is it which makes a body beautiful? In one way it is the presence of beauty, in another the soul." However, in this passage the soul enters the picture not as the spectator, but as the artist: it is the soul that "moulded [the body] and put this particular form in it" (*Enn.* V.9[5].2.17–18). Thus, we move on to the issue of artistic creativity, an issue that concerns particularly the soul, since the soul is the proximate creator of sensible beauty in all its natural or artificial forms. What, then, distinguishes artistic creation from other forms of human practice? And, in particular, what is the value, if any, of this particular form of human creativity?

In order to tackle this issue, we need to start from Plotinus' ambivalence towards production or creation, as this is expressed in his metaphysics. Plotinus' valuation of practice, in the broad sense of any fully or partially intentional practical activity of making or doing that involves some kind of effort for the accomplishment of its objective, is generally negative, because any such activity can be motivated only by some felt lack or deficiency and is thus an index of ontological inferiority. As he puts it, talking about the Intellect's purely self-contained and perfectly transparent theoretical activity: "For what reason could it have for making, since it is deficient in nothing? ... Being able to make something by itself is the characteristic of something that is not altogether in a good state" (*Enn.* III.2[47].1.37–9; V.3[49].6.39–40, 12.33). In a philosophical system where the norm of being is unity and self-sufficiency, this valuation is to be expected. The obvious problem, then, is why reality is not exhausted in the self-sufficient intelligible world, but includes the soul, the sensible world, and everything that this world contains. In order to respond to this problem, Plotinus introduces a dynamic creative element in his ontology and incorporates it into a general principle of being: reality unfolds hierarchically, from the One, through the Intellect and the Soul, to the objects of the sensible world, because every being, both as a hypostasis and as an individual, "makes" (produces, generates) what comes ontologically after it. This natural tendency of every being "to produce what comes after it and to unfold itself" (*Enn.* IV.8[6].6.8–9) leads to a different kind of productive activity which, according to Plotinus, does not originate in lack, but is the manifestation of a plenitude of power or a state of perfection (*Enn.* V.1[10].6.38; V.4[7].1.28–9) that results from the theoretical activity of each being.[25] This spontaneous productive overflow does not have a global aim, but merely moves towards an eventual point of exhaustion of the original power, as it becomes diffused in its various (de)gradations (*Enn.* II.9[33].8.24–6; IV.8[6].6.13–16). However, its local effect is to generate around each creative entity a familiar environment, a familiarity that Plotinus understands in terms of the similarity between an image and its original. "The snow does not only keep its cold inside itself"; in the same way, "all existing things, as long as they remain in being, necessarily produce from their own substances, in dependence of their present power, a surrounding reality directed to what is outside them, a kind of image of the archetypes from which it was produced" (*Enn.* V.1[10].6.31–34; see also *Enn.* V.4[7].1.24–42 or *Enn.* IV.3[27].10.35–6).[26]

With the appropriate specifications, all these points can be applied to the soul. Its creation or image, the familiar place it provides for itself in order to unfold ontologically, is, of course, the sensible world, as a whole (the universe is the creation of the cosmic soul) and severally (every sensible object is either a product of the formative action of the soul *qua* nature or an artificial creation of some individual human soul). The condition that determines the resources and the objectives of the creative project of the soul is its mediating position in the overall hierarchy of reality. Since the proper domain of the soul is the "in between" (*Enn.* III.9[13].3.15) or the "frontier" (*Enn.* IV.4[28].3.11) that separates (and unites) the intelligible and the sensible realm, souls are effectively "amphibious, compelled to live by turns the life there, and the life here" (*Enn.* IV.8[6].4.32–5), intelligible entities that nevertheless must "be able to participate in the sensible" (7.3), in order to bring them into contact and ensure that "nothing is a long way off or far from anything else" (*Enn.* IV.3[27].11.22–3).²⁷ Accordingly, their task consists in shaping the sensible world in ways that reflect its intelligible origin, a task that Plotinus presents as a form of creative "translation" or "interpretation" (*hermeneutikē*):

> This [cosmic] soul gives the edge of itself which borders on this [visible] sun to this [intelligible] sun, and makes a connection of it to the divine realm through the medium of itself, and acts as an interpreter of what comes from this sun to the intelligible sun and from the intelligible sun to this sun, in so far as this sun does reach the intelligible sun through soul.
>
> (*Enn.* IV.3[27].11.17–22; see also *Enn.* I.2[19].3.30)

Against this metaphysical background, we may now consider how Plotinus construes the relation between the theoretical and practical capacities and activities of human beings. Plotinus' understanding of this relation is captured by the claims that "some wisdom makes all the things which have come into being, whether they are products of art or nature" (*Enn.* V.8[31].5.1–3) and that "action is for the sake of contemplation and vision, so that for men of action, too, contemplation is the goal" (*Enn.* III.8[30].6.1–2). In other words, practice is thoroughly subordinated to theory: every practical activity must be always conditioned and guided by the appropriate theoretical cognition, while its sole purpose is the theoretical appropriation of its product; in this sense practical activity cannot possess any independent objectives or value.²⁸ Accordingly, with respect to the presence or absence of a contemplative origin of a creative instance, Plotinus distinguishes between two kinds of creative activity, which we may call the "strong" and the "weak" kinds: "Everywhere we shall find that making and action are either a weakening or a consequence of contemplation: a weakening, if the doer or maker had nothing in view beyond the thing done, a consequence if he had another prior object of contemplation better than what he made" (*Enn.* III.8[30].4.40–44).

Within this framework, there are two problems we have to face with regard to artistic creativity: (1) Is the work of an artist a form of "strong" or "weak" creation, as Plotinus' description of the latter seems to indicate?²⁹ In other words, do artists know in some sense what they are making, are they guided by some prior access to the truth of their work, or do they create their work in order to address their inability to contemplate and provide themselves with a substitute object of theoretical vision? Moreover, even if we assume that artistic creation can be a form of "strong" creation, we would have to tackle a more fundamental question: (2) What is the point of artistic practice, namely why someone who "is able to contemplate what is truly real will deliberately go after its image"? (ll. 44–5).

These considerations seem to undermine the claims of artistic practice in comparison to those of theoretical activity; the case against art, as it were, becomes even stronger when we examine the issue in the perspective established by the distinction between art and nature. In this respect, Plotinus claims that "art is posterior to it [the soul *qua* "nature"], and imitates it by making dim and weak imitations, little toys of little value, using a variety of devices to create an image of nature" (*Enn.* IV.3[27].10.17–19; see also *Enn.* III.8[30].5.6–10). This claim could be understood as a criticism of art along traditional Platonic lines: if artistic creation amounts to the mere imitation of the objects of the sensible world, then its products are inferior, since they are further removed from the intelligible reality. However, it could also be understood in Plotinian terms, on the basis of the difference between the creative activity of the soul *qua* cosmic soul or nature and any individual human soul. Whereas the latter will typically involve perplexity, deliberation, planning, discursive and instrumental reasoning, and effort in the actual execution, the former will be the spontaneous result of an immediately available intuitive knowledge, without "fuss" or "toil" (*Enn.* V.8[31].7.24–5).[30] In this sense, the question of the relative valuation of the natural versus the artistic brings us back to the issue of the relation between contemplation and practice: (3) Is nature always a "stronger" creator than art?

In response to these three questions, and in defence of artistic creativity, we should point out that Plotinus did explicitly accept the possibility of a "strong" form of artistic creation. In a well-known passage, he asserts:

> But if anyone despises the arts because they produce their works by imitating nature, we must tell him, first, that natural things are imitations too. Then he must know that the arts do not simply imitate what they see, but they run back up to the forming principles from which nature derives; then also that they do a great deal by themselves, and, since they possess beauty, they make up what is defective in things. For Pheidias too did not make his Zeus from any model perceived by the senses, but understood what Zeus would look like if he wanted to make himself visible.   (*Enn.* V.8[31].1.32–41)[31]

This passage seems to meet several of the challenges that I have identified so far. The fundamental point is that artistic practices are acknowledged as fully legitimate elements of the domain of sensible reality and assigned equal importance with every other natural or human activity occurring in this domain. With respect to the Platonic heritage of Plotinus, the promotion of the status enjoyed by art is made possible by the assertion that the intelligible models that guide, consciously or unconsciously, the productive activity of soul *qua* nature are available to the individual soul of the artists directly and independently of their sensory access to the empirical world. In this sense, art remains imitative in the philosophical sense in which everything except the One is imitative for Plotinus, but the artist, as in the modern conception of genius, is not condemned to the superfluous imitation of *natura naturata*, but can proceed from the same starting point occupied by *natura naturans*, since this is also a soul and "the same vision is in every soul" (*Enn.* III.8[30].5.32). One implication of this position is that, if the term "representational" denotes the art that aims to present objects as they appear in the sensible world, then, for Plotinus, art is essentially symbolic or conceptual, in the sense that it aims at presenting meanings (*noēmata*) rather than things. Despite their sensible constitution, artistic presentations are not homogeneous to their apparent objects and do not obey the norms of sensibility. Rather, and in compliance with the general creative mandate of the soul, they should be understood as "metaphors", "translations", "symbols" or "interpretations" of intelligible contents in sensible terms, a fact that accounts for their apparent normative self-sufficiency: Pheidias' Zeus is to be judged in itself (in the perspective of the "metaphor" it establishes) and not in terms of human physiology. Another implication is that Plotinus' understanding conforms to an idealistic conception of the work of art, in which the "real" work is not the external product of artistic activity (which, given its material nature, will be a defective realization of the conception of the artist), but rather the "art", that is, the contemplative achievement, in the mind of the artist that guides the creative activity.[32] Finally, in this context, Plotinus can qualify his categorical denial that the artificially "lifelike" can be more beautiful than the living (*Enn.* VI.7[38].22.30–32) and envisage the possibility of works of art in which the mastery of form over matter would exceed the relevant capacities of nature, resulting in a local intensification or enrichment of intelligibility, or else, a stronger "metaphorical" connection with the intelligible domain.

And yet, even if art is a "strong" form of creation, possibly even "stronger" than nature,[33] we are still left with the second question raised above: why someone who "is able to con-template what is truly real will deliberately go after its image" (*Enn.* III.8[30].4.44–5). To explore this final question, I return to a passage that is generally overlooked in the relevant literature but which has preoccupied me in the past, with the intention of further elucidat-ing its relevance to Plotinus' aesthetics.[34] In this passage, Plotinus describes the activity of the mysterious "sages of old", who appear several times in the *Enneads*:

> And I think that the sages of old, those who wanted the gods to be present to them, created temples and statues by looking back at the nature of the All, having in mind that the nature of the soul is in all directions ductile, but it [the nature of soul] would be the easiest thing to receive [or retain], if one were to make something attractive to it that would be able to receive a share of it. (*Enn.* IV.3[27].11.1–8)[35]

In the context of the discussion so far, the evidence contained in this passage points to an understanding of the sages as artists or, given their legendary status, as exemplary artists: (a) their activity is the result of a conscious desire and decision, and hence belongs to the order of art, and not nature; (b) their aim, like Pheidias' in the passage quoted earlier, was to make the gods present to them, "gods" signifying here the "beautiful images in [the intelligible] world, of the kind which someone imagined to exist in the soul of the wise man, images not painted but real" (*Enn.* V.8[31].5.20–24); (c) their project involved the creation of statues and temples; and (d) it was guided by a "looking back at the nature of the All"; that is, an attempt to appropriate reflectively the original access of the cosmic soul to the intelligible world, as a result of which the cosmic soul itself, in ordering the universe, "had constructed in the world statues of gods, dwellings of men, and other place for other creatures" (*Enn.* IV.3[27].10.27–9).

The work of these paradigmatic artists becomes possible through a fundamental char-acteristic of the soul: the soul is "ductile in all directions" (*pantachou ... euagōgon*), which should be understood in a number of active and passive registers associated with the verb *agein* (lead, carry, conduct; thus "to enchant" or *psychagōgein*, typically associated with the response to a work of art). The soul is "easily led"; but it is also a conductive medium con-necting without obstructions the intelligible with the sensible realm (*Enn.* IV.3[27].11.17), it can control and lead bodies to the state it wants (l. 20), and, in particular, it can "lead things to a likeness with itself" (l. 35). In these terms, the complex undertaking of the sages can be described as follows: the sages, being souls themselves, must through their art and effort lead an object to a certain likeness with the soul ("animate" it, make it "lifelike"), so that the soul, easily led, will be attracted to it by recognizing its affinity with it, so that, in the vicinity of these objects, the gods can be present to the sages through the conductive passageway created by the intense concentration of the attracted soul.

This way of presenting artistic creation suggests a way of capturing its specificity. Within the perspective of the soul, the work of art acquires a privileged status as the only sensible object deliberately and exclusively made for the sake of the soul itself. At a first level, this means that the work of art is explicitly made in order to attract the soul, for its pleasure or enchantment; since this is a pleasure in self-recognition, the work may be considered as soul's inanimate counterpart. Pursuing an analogy with the Intellect, we could say that the work of art constitutes the proper object of soul: in the way that the Intellect creates the intelligibles in order to live its proper life as a thinker thinking these, the soul creates the works of art in order to live its proper life as an interpreter interpreting these. This activity of interpretation sustains the life that the work of art lives, saving it from collapsing into its temporality and materiality; it also suggests another sense in which a work of art can be more "lifelike" than a living thing. The works of art, as sensible passages of the gods, are those objects in which the soul recognizes its own peculiar predicament, which is neither its involvement with matter nor the serene contemplation of the objects of the Intellect, but precisely its amphibious and self-effacing task.

On this basis, we may respond to our final question: those of us who are "able to contemplate what is truly real" can certainly "work unceasingly" on their internal statue (*Enn.* I.6[1].9.13), with the aim of visiting the gods face to face, so to speak, in their own intelligible temples and sanctuaries of *Enn.* V.1[10].6 or *Enn.* VI.9[9].11, instead of undertaking the uncertain endeavour of extending invitations to them through the creation of beautiful temples and statues of our own. But what the activity of the "sages of old" (who, as sages of a legendary past, are superior to both philosophers and artists) suggests is the possibility of a life for the soul, a human life, in which we are not forced to make a choice between thinking what we have not created (*qua* philosophers) and creating what we have not thought (*qua* artists). Going back to Danto's comments, we may thus envisage an "end" of art in which "the objects approach zero as their theory approaches infinity" and "the object in which the artwork consists is so irradiated by theoretical consciousness that the division between object and subject is all but overcome". In Plotinian terms, this may initially seem like a reality in which the skills of the soul as an interpreter would have become superfluous, but it may be more appropriately considered as a reality in which the soul has fulfilled its self-effacing task of creative interpretation so well that indeed "nothing is a long way off or far from anything else" (*Enn.* IV.3[27].11.21–2), where *all* that matters is that "art is philosophy in action or philosophy is art in thought".

ACKNOWLEDGEMENTS

I would like to thank Daniel Whistler, Michael McGhee and the anonymous reviewer for their suggestions, as well as the editors for their warm support and patience.

NOTES

1. Plotinus' text used is that of Henry & Schwyzer (1964–82), and translations follow, with minor revisions, Armstrong (1966–88).
2. For the extension of the term "beautiful" (τὸ καλόν), see *Enn.* I.6[1].1 and V.9[5].2 and the brief remarks of Kuisma (2003: 43–5).
3. Consider, for example, the following typical statement: "And first we must posit beauty which is also the good; from this immediately comes intellect, which is beauty; and soul is given beauty by intellect.

Everything else is beautiful by the shaping of soul, the beauties in actions and in ways of life. And soul makes beautiful the bodies which are spoken of as beautiful" (*Enn.* I.6[1].6.25–30).

4. For a concise discussion of this claim, see Rich (1960).

5. Two recent collections of essays that study the influence of Neoplatonic aesthetics are De Girolami Cheney & Hendrix (2004) and Lobsien & Olk (2007); for the late antiquity and Byzantine context, see Walter (1984); for Plotinus' influence on medieval aesthetics, see Grabar (1945); for connections with modern and contemporary art, see Beierwaltes (2002a) and Alexandrakis (2002); for the place of Plotinus in the classical tradition of art conceived as mimesis, see Halliwell (2002: 313–23).

6. See Stern-Gillet (2000: 63 and n. 69 for further references to similar views): "The reason, as I hope to have shown above, is that Plotinus had no aesthetics in the sense in which this term is generally understood since the eighteenth century. It is therefore appropriate to stop looking for an aesthetics in a philosophy that, in all other respects, is richly systematic" (my translation from the French); see also Kuisma (2003: 65–6).

7. For a brief discussion of the origins of modern aesthetics, see Guyer (2004).

8. "For this reason being is longed for because it is the same as beauty, and beauty is lovable because it is being" (V.8[31].9.41–2). There are, of course, certain complications in the relation between the Good (*qua* the One) and the beautiful; see V.5[32].12, VI.7[38].22, and VI.7[38].32.31–4.

9. I am assuming here that aesthetics is broader than philosophy of art in the sense outlined above. The relation between the two becomes more complicated if one thinks that the creation and reception of works of art raise issues that transcend the framework of the aesthetic experience of natural objects.

10. Thus, after discussing extensively Plotinus' reflections on art, Kuisma notes: "The foregoing chapters should have substantiated the view that Plotinus was not an enthusiast of art, art criticism, or art theory" (Kuisma 2003: 148).

11. Hence, for example, Plotinus' persistent claim that the universe as a whole, the natural cosmos, is beautiful (see e.g. *Enn.* II.9[33].16.48–56; III.8[30].11.29–30; V.8[31].8.21–2) is clearly motivated by his philosophical polemics against the Gnostics, regardless of any personal experience that may underlie it.

12. See, among many other passages, *Enn.* II.3[52].18.13–15, where the Intellect is called "δημιουργός" and the cosmic soul "ποιητὴς ἔσχατος". The extensive presence of the paradigm of art in Plotinus' work, a legacy from the Platonic *Timaeus* that Plotinus transformed in significant ways, is documented in Ferwerda (1965: 139–58).

13. Beauty is what "attracts the gaze of those who look at something and turns and draws them to it and makes them enjoy the sight" (*Enn.* I.6[1].1.18–19); for a vivid description of the effects of beauty on the soul of the beholder, see *Enn.* I.6[1].4.13–18. Even if one considers the experience of sensible beauty as a merely instrumental step towards the appreciation of intelligible beauty (as e.g. in *Enn.* V.9[5].2.1–10), the experience of the latter, an inseparable aspect of contemplation, is clearly an end in itself.

14. For a brief overview of the presence of this theme in ancient Greek literature, see Halliwell (2002: 20–21).

15. See e.g. *Republic* 10.598b–c, where Plato claims polemically that such a deception is relevant only in the case of "children and stupid adults".

16. This claim should not be understood in a modern sense, in which what is intimated by the work is the individual subjectivity of the artist belonging to a radically different order of being from that of the material work. Plotinus' universe is thoroughly animated; as a result, even a stone is ensouled (see e.g. *Enn.* IV.4[28].22, 27) and the boundaries between "being made by a soul" and "having a soul" are not sharp.

17. As we shall see below, this may not be Plotinus' last word on the potency of artificial beauty.

18. Given Plotinus' understanding of the aesthetic reaction and judgement in terms of a "fitting together" between the object and the soul (claimed in general terms in *Enn.* I.6[1].2.4–5 and specified as an agreement between the sensible or external form of the object and the mental or internal form possessed by the soul in *Enn.* I.6[1].3.1–9), the recognition of beauty presupposes also a beautiful soul on the judging side (see also *Enn.* V.5[32].12.9–12).

19. The possibility of "fully" lifelike statues had been registered in ancient Greek imagination (e.g. in the story of the Telchines, mythical workers of metal capable of creating "works of art in the likeness of beings that lived and moved" [Pindar, *Ol.* 7.52]).

20. Including, in order of rank, the life lived by the Soul as a hypostasis and the lives lived by various kinds of embodied souls, i.e. human beings, animals, plants, even "inanimate" objects like stones. As the life of the Soul is an image of the life of the Intellect, the lives of these embodied entities are images of the life of the Soul (*Enn.* II.3[52].9.23; IV.3[27].10.40).

21. This strong association of beauty with unity raises the possibility that, in metaphysical terms, beauty should be located at the level of the One and not at that of the Intellect. For a good discussion of this issue, see Stern-Gillet (2000a); whether this metaphysical adjustment has any implications for sensible beauty is an issue that I cannot pursue here.

22. From a logical point of view, one could accuse Plotinus of a fallacy of division, uncritically transferring the predicate "beautiful" from the whole to the parts; from a methodological point of view, one may consider Plotinus' claim as an example of a metaphysically motivated assertion that overlooks the relevant empirical evidence. Lloyd Gerson, in his brief discussion of Plotinus' position in Gerson (1994: 213–14), raises some of these issues, but does not resolve them, because, although he notes that through the domination of form "the parts are brought into a unity, presumably the complex unity that is naturally understood as symmetry" (213), he does not take into account the requirement that each part must "replicate" the whole in the relevant sense.

23. The entire *Critique of Judgement* can be considered as Kant's attempt to come to terms with these objects of our experience that appear, contrary to the ontological conditions imposed by the categorical structure of reality, to contain within themselves the norm of their constitution or activity, an "inscrutable property", to which "perhaps one comes closer … if one calls it an analogue of life" (§65 374). It is important to remember that the third *Critique* is a book in two parts, and, as much as it achieves the establishment of an autonomous aesthetic domain, it also brings together, under the concept of reflective judgement, all these "lifelike" sensible objects, natural and artificial, that Plotinus would consider as candidates for beauty.

24. "[Beauty] is something which we become aware of even at first glance; the soul speaks of it as if it understood it, recognises and welcomes it and as it were adapts itself to it" (*Enn.* I.6[1].2.2–4).

25. For concise descriptions of this process, see *Enn.* V.2[11].1.8–23 or V.1[10].6.40–55. The general metaphysical distinction between an "internal" (self-constitutive) and an "external" (productive) activity of each being is discussed in Schroeder (1980); Gerson (1994: 23–37); Emilsson (2007: 22–68); and, with special reference to the soul, Kalligas (2000: 31–5).

26. In terms of this hierarchy, a work of art is "lifelike" and yet different from an ordinary living being in the sense that "in every rational principle, its last and lowest manifestation springs from contemplation, and is contemplation in the sense of being contemplated" (*Enn.* III.8[30].3.6–7). To say that something "springs from contemplation and is contemplation" is to say that it is "lifelike"; to say that it is limited in "being contemplated" means that, as it itself cannot contemplate, it lacks the power to create, and thus cannot continue the productive chain of being. For another way of expressing the difference between works of art and living things, see *Enn.* VI.4[22].10.5–11.

27. The intermediate and mediating position of the soul is stressed by Plotinus throughout the *Enneads*; see e.g. *Enn.* III.6[26].14.22–4; III.9[13].3.2–3; IV.8[6].7.6–9; V.8[31].7.12–16.

28. See also *Enn.* III.8[30].7.8–10: "[the active beings] had as their goal in making, not makings or actions, but the finished object of contemplation".

29. "Because contemplation is not enough for them, since their souls are weak and they are not able to grasp the vision sufficiently … but still long to see it, they are carried into action, so as to see what they cannot see with their intellect. When they make something, then, it is because they want to see their object themselves and also because they want others to be aware of it and contemplate it, when their project is realised in practice as well as possible" (*Enn.* III.8[30].4.32–5).

30. Obviously, there are important differences between the "highest" and the "lowest" "part of the Soul of the All" (*Enn.* IV.3[27].4.28), namely the cosmic soul and the immanent soul of nature. However, there are important similarities in the form of their creative activity, captured in the formulation above and pointing to a continuity with the productive activity of the Intellect; see *Enn.* V.8[31].7; IV.4[28].11–13; IV.3[27].11.8–14; III.3[48].3.13–17; II.9[33].12.12–24.

31. This fascinating passage has generated a lot of discussion in the literature. The immediate exegetical problem concerns the identity of the one who "despises the arts": does Plotinus have in mind some Platonists (or Gnostics or Christians) of his own time, or Plato himself? More broadly: is Plotinus' claim a critical response to Plato's hostile depreciation of art in the *Republic* and elsewhere? For a discussion of the issue, see Rich (1960) and Kuisma (2003: 96–131), where further references to ancient sources and scholarly literature can be found.

32. See *Enn.* V.8[31].1.16–31, 2.14–21; III.8[30].2.10–14, 5.6–10, 22–4. In these passages, the point is presented as a corollary of the general principle that the cause is ontologically superior to the effect: if the

form in the mind of the artist is the cause of the beauty of the work, then the form will be more beautiful than the work. The resulting position is similar to that put forward by Collingwood, who claims that, "the work of art may be completely created as a thing whose place is in the artist's mind" (Collingwood 1938: 130).

33. "Stronger" in the "local" sense indicated above; globally, the creative superiority of the cosmic soul and its immanent counterpart ("nature") is clearly asserted by Plotinus in *Enn.* III.9[13].7.

34. For a more expanded version of what I will be summarizing here, see Vassilopoulou (2005).

35. Apart from this passage, the "sages of old" appear also in *Enn.* V.1[10].6.4, III.6[26].19 and V.8[31].6.

Legacy

INTRODUCTION

When does Neoplatonism end? While the closure of Plato's Academy in Athens in 529 CE may have some institutional entitlement of an end of a period, this, as has often been pointed out, is nowhere near the end of Neoplatonism. Geographically, Neoplatonic philosophers continued their work, especially in Alexandria, as did even the Athenians in exile in Persia, and, to be judged from the sheer volume of Simplicius' works written after the exile, there was no interruption in terms of literary work on their return to the Christian empire.[1] How about the last pagan Neoplatonic head of the school in Alexandria, then, Damascius (*c*.460–540 CE)? Could we end the Neoplatonic school of thought with him? Or with some other, less-known pagan Neoplatonist active after him? If paganism is used as a condition for being a proper Neoplatonist, do we automatically rule out Damascius' Christian partner in debate, John Philoponus, and his clear Neoplatonic leanings? The problem with these questions is, as has been pointed out in many contexts, that they presuppose that Neoplatonism is a school with clearly defined geographical, religious, doctrinal and chronological limits. But ideas and movements, of course, do not work this way. They are fluid collections of shared assumptions, approaches and intuitions, sometimes strengthened with common written documents considered helpful, worth going back to, or even authoritative. In the case of Neoplatonism, even the transmission and working with such texts – the Classical and Hellenistic philosophical heritage, the *Chaldaean Oracles*, as well as other works that the Neoplatonists read and commented – testifies of this same flexibility. While certain key commitments, like the idea of the One as the unified source of everything, are shared, as we have seen in Part II, they bring together very different thinkers and writers, expanded over a period of several hundreds of years.

As was established in Part I, the borderline between the Neoplatonists and their predecessors is already hazy (see M. Frede 1987), and we should expect nothing less than a similar indeterminacy at the other end of late antiquity, when it turns, gradually, into the medieval period. Neoplatonism does not disappear, it is transformed and subsumed in the ways of thinking we now entitle "medieval". This poses an immediate challenge to scholarship. What we witness are gradual rather than abrupt changes, combined with the indisputable emergence of new elements and ways of thinking, especially in the form of the advancing monotheistic religions, both in the East and in the West. There is one change that, while perhaps not abrupt, is nonetheless sharp: the authoritative texts are changed into the sacred Scriptures of Christian and Islamic canons. Platonic philosophy, and its predominant interpretation in this period, Neoplatonism, is both a patient and an agent in this intellectual uprise. On the one hand, it has to be adapted to suit even better the religious commitments dictated in the Scriptures; on the other hand, it will turn spiritual stories, dogmatic statements, religious teachings and other non-philosophical approaches into Christian and Islamic philosophy proper. We shall be considering the earliest phases of these developments.

In his "Neoplatonism and Christianity in the West", Moran (Chapter 31) traces the Christian religious movement from its early history as one among Judaic sects to the heavily Neoplatonically influenced ideology of St Augustine (354–430 CE), following the influence of Pseudo-Dionysius the Areopagite (*floruit c*.500 CE), all the way to Johannes Eriugena (*c*.790/800–*c*.877 CE). Here we see some of the main challenges involved in combining Christian thinking with ancient, and Platonic, philosophy. The attack launched by Tertullian on dialectic and pagan eloquence brings to the fore the uneasy relationship between argument and faith, which was to preoccupy medieval philosophers for centuries to come. Any hints at the "eternal", as opposed to "created", existence of soul, or the possibility of transmigration of the souls, needed to be abolished. But in the Neoplatonic variety, there is also much that immediately appeals to a mind tuned to Christian thinking, not least the two following central ideas: the causal role of the One within metaphysics and the cosmos, and the divine, immaterial and immortal nature of the soul.[2] As Moran puts it below (p. 512), Neoplatonism "provided an intellectual architecture for articulating theological insights into the nature of the infinite God, the nature of the procession of the Word, the meaning of the Trinity, the nature of creation, and the relation between the soul and the divine".

In the early Eastern or Byzantine church, Neoplatonism is visible particularly in the thinking of the fourth-century Cappadocian Fathers, Basil the Great (330–79 CE), Gregory of Nyssa (c.332–95 CE) and Gregory of Nazianzus (329–389 CE) (for the early Byzantine Neoplatonism, see also Ierodiakonou & Zografidis 2010). In "Neoplatonism and Christianity in the East: philosophical and theological challenges for bishops" (Chapter 32), Dimitrov cross-illuminates the thinking of one of these, Gregory of Nyssa, with Synesius of Cyrene (c.373–c.414 CE), a near contemporary and also a bishop, and a disciple of the late Neoplatonic teachers of Alexandria. Dimitrov's discussion concentrates on three major debates characterizing the continuous efforts at reconciling Christian faith with Neoplatonic philosophy: the soul, the resurrection of the body, and the eternity of the world. How do the ideas of the soul's descent and ascent to and from the body fit into the Christian dogma of soul as created after the body, and the resurrection of both soul and the body? How do we deal with the pagan commitment to the eternity of the world in a context that assumes and insists on the creation of that same world by a God?

While the Christian developments of ancient thought are a self-evident part of all general expositions of the history of Western philosophy and ideas, there is a long-standing neglect of the Arabic and Jewish tradition and transmission. Happily, this neglect has recently given way to a more wholesale understanding of our intellectual heritage (for Islamic philosophy, see also D'Ancona 2010). The interpretations, for example, of soul by Avicenna and Averroes – or, rather, Ibn Sīnā and Ibn Rushd – have made their way into mainstream scholarship. It is no longer possible to exclude the influential readings of thinkers writing in Arabic or Hebrew. In "Islamic and Jewish Neoplatonisms" (Chapter 33), Pessin guides us to the main figures, sources and traits of Neoplatonism in Islamic and Jewish medieval authors, as well as to the dividing questions and dogmas between them and ancient, pagan Neoplatonisms. Besides providing this missing link in the history of philosophy and ideas, however, Pessin invites the reader to consider the potential apophatic and prescriptive nature of all Neoplatonic writings, a way of writing that seeks the ethical and spiritual transformation of the reader. By interlacing the texts of Plotinus and those of Jewish and Arabic Neoplatonists, Pessin reveals several points of contact. Not only are there doctrinal similarities: there is also a shared sense of direction, of becoming a good person, of emulating God, the origin of goodness in the world.

Can we be now content, and say that Neoplatonism, while still existing as a part of Jewish, Christian and Islamic medieval thinking, comes to an end when the medieval period gains its full bloom and gradually ends itself, and that Neoplatonism must give space to other strands of thinking, and ultimately to modern ideas that loom at the end of this period? Even here there cannot be any strict border. Many later medieval thinkers are relevant for the new fates of Neoplatonism, even if they cannot be treated within the confines of this study. The Neoplatonic legacy in Renaissance, or in, say, Cambridge Platonism, in Schelling and German idealism more generally, or American Transcendentalism, are, with good reason, thriving research areas with more and more recently acquired emphasis.[3] We will leave it as a task for other volumes and studies to go into the details of both the intricacies of the medieval combination of religion and Plato, and of later developments still bearing recognizable insights of the Neoplatonic philosophers.

NOTES

1. One much discussed and contested suggestion is that they worked in Harran near the border of the Persian empire: see Tardieu (1986).
2. That is, the Christians and the Neoplatonists, while disagreeing about the soul's beginning (eternal or created), agreed upon its capacity of transgressing the other limit, that of death.
3. For the Renaissance, early modern and modern period see e.g. Celenza (2007); Hutton & Hedley (2008); there are, further, ongoing research projects by C. Mercer; for German idealism, see e.g. Beierwaltes (2002b, 2004); for American transcendentalism, see e.g. Bregman (1990).

31

Neoplatonism and Christianity in the West

Dermot Moran

Christianity began as a breakaway sect within Judaism. As such, it was one of a number of reform movements in Judea. Initially, it was a religious millenarian movement, possibly with some political ambition, but without a developed philosophical outlook. The Roman historian Tacitus (56–117 CE) reported the existence of Christians in the empire in the time of Nero. He wrote that "Christus, from whom the name is derived, was executed at the hands of the procurator Pontius Pilatus" (*Annals* 15.44, trans. Bettenson) and goes on to describe the persecution of the Christians (see Bettenson 1975: 2). The immediate followers of Jesus do not appear to have had any great degree of literacy or sophisticated training in theology. Gradually, however, early Christianity evolved in the context of the vibrant local cultures within the Roman Empire. As Christianity spread, Greek and Roman temples were taken over and adapted, often involving rebuilding, for Christian worship, and existing images and symbols were adapted and absorbed into the new religion. The Roman calendar and ceremonial dress, for instance, was taken over by Christianity. Nevertheless, Christianity left its distinctive mark and completely transformed the inherited Classical tradition.

A similar oscillation between the old and the new took place at the intellectual level as the Christians developed an intellectual language to articulate their beliefs and to convert pagans. The first significant event in this long process of acculturation was the translation of texts of the Hebrew Old Testament into Greek – the so-called "translation of the seventy interpreters" (*Septuagint*) ordered by the Egyptian pharaoh Ptolemy II and carried out in Alexandria in the second century BCE (see Pietersma & Wright 2007). This translation allowed traditional Jewish wisdom to circulate in the Roman Empire, and indeed the Greek texts of the Septuagint were drawn on by Jesus' own Apostles and by the Early Church Fathers. Clearly, the Jewish insistence on the one God was a direct challenge to pagan polytheism, as were the ideas of a holy text, a covenant between the divine and humans, and the idea of a sacral history. The early Christians were able to point to many features in Platonism that seemed to anticipate their own conception of the divine, as, for instance, "father and maker of all the universe" (*Ti.* 28C) who desires to create out of goodness.

Already in the immediate pre-Christian era, religious scholars in the Greek-speaking city of Alexandria explored the meaning of the Jewish sacred writings using the grammatical and philosophical techniques of the Greek philosophers, drawing parallels between the creation accounts in Genesis (see Runia 2001) and the cosmology of Plato's *Timaeus* (See Runia 1986; Dillon 1988). Philo Judaeus (*c.*15 BCE–50 CE), a Hellenized Alexandrian Jew, who had apparently no influence on the Jewish tradition, read the *Septuagint* and applied Platonic and Stoic ideas to articulate his notion of the unchangeability, eternity and transcendence of God, and of the changeable nature of human beings (see Goodenough 1963; Chadwick 1967; Williamson 1989; Troiani 2003). God is true being and "He Who Is" (Exodus 3:4). Humans are made in the image and likeness of God and aim to achieve "assimilation" (*homoiōsis*) with God. Moreover, God operates through the *logos* or the rational principle. God first created an intelligible world akin to the Platonic forms and thereafter the sensible world. One can hear the echoes of the Platonic tradition, especially in Philo's discussion of the nature of the human soul (see Dillon 2009). I am here relying on my 2003 article.

The earliest Christian writers, notably the Roman citizen of Jewish origin St Paul (5–67 CE), who had a dramatic conversion to Christianity, show a marked hostility towards philosophy, which they interpreted as pagan wisdom. Thus Paul contrasted Greek philosophy as arrogant foolishness with the wisdom and truth of Jesus. Nevertheless, he absorbed philosophical conceptions current in his time and his epistles contain allusions to Platonic and Stoic philosophical ideas, such as the concept of the "inner man" (*esō anthrōpos*) found in the Second Letter to the Corinthians 4:16 (which echoes Plato's *Republic* 9.589a–b), the concept of natural law in the Second Letter to the Romans, the discussion of immortality in the Second Letter to the Corinthians 3–5, the concept of the "pneumatic body" (*sōma pneumatikon*; see Van Kooten 2009; also Heckel 1993) in the First Letter to the Corinthians 15, or the claim that existence of God may be proved by natural reason from the examination of natural things (Romans 1:20), a text much cited by medieval Christian philosophers. Indeed, St Paul refers to Christ as wisdom using the Greek word for wisdom (*sophia*) in I Corinthians 1:24.[1]

The early Christians were struggling to define their own new insights in terms of the philosophical systems and ideas available at that time. They initially proselytized in the Greek language, the lingua franca of the early Roman Empire, and inevitably the Greek intellectual world began to shine through in their writings, most famously in the Prologue to the Gospel of John whose opening sentence "In the Beginning was the Word" (*en archē ēn ho logos*) is undoubtedly a phrase heavily resonant with the philosophical ideas of "*archē*" (source, principle, origin) and "*logos*" (word, reason, rationale) as well as echoing the opening of Genesis. John's conception of the *logos* which became flesh and who is a person and the messiah is radically different from the impersonal *logos* of Philo, although the *logos* does play the same functional role in both writers.

Later, the so-called Christian Apologists – for instance, Justin Martyr (100–*c.*165 CE) (see Parvis & Foster 2007) – were quick to invoke the *logos* of Greek philosophy as a vehicle for spreading the Good News of the Gospels. Justin Martyr recounts that he initially sought wisdom from the Stoics, Peripatetics and Platonists, before being won over to the God of Scripture and to the person of Jesus Christ (see van Winden 1971; Barnard 1997). For

Justin Martyr the *logos* which runs through all things is to be identified with Jesus, the Son of God. This marks a radical departure from all late Hellenic pagan thought.

The absorption of Greek culture into Christianity did not go ahead without some opposition. Tertullian (*c*.160–*c*.225 CE), who was born in Carthage and was one of the first Christian apologists to write in Latin (he is often called "the father of Latin Christianity"), questioned the uncritical use of Greek philosophy in Christian texts (see Osborn 1997; Sider 2001). He famously posed the question in his *On Prescription against Heretics*, ch. 7: what has Athens to do with Jerusalem, what has philosophy to do with faith? He wrote:

> What indeed has Athens to do with Jerusalem? What concord is there between the Academy and the Church? What between heretics and Christians? Our instruction comes from "the porch of Solomon", who had himself taught that "the Lord should be sought in simplicity of heart". Away with all attempts to produce a mottled Christianity of Stoic, Platonic, and dialectic composition! We want no curious disputation after possessing Christ Jesus, no inquisition after enjoying the gospel! With our faith, we desire no further belief.
>
> (Tertullian, *de Praescriptione haereticorum* 7)

For Tertullian, it was sufficient for the Christian to have *faith* (*pistis, fides*) – the believer had no need of pagan eloquence and philosophy. Yet, Tertullian himself was not immune to philosophy.[2] Thus, for instance, in *Against Praxeas* (*adversus Praxean*) he conceived of God as a kind of vaporous material spirit (Greek: *pneuma*) in the manner of the Stoics, and in his *de Anima* he conceived of the soul as a kind of material substance (following the Stoics) opposing the Platonic conception of the soul as completely immaterial and as "unborn". Tertullian criticizes Plato's denigration of the senses and rejects the idea that "memory loss" occurs (as Plato claimed) with the entrance of the soul into the body. For Tertullian, body and soul are created together and death is the separation of soul from the body.

Various versions of late Platonism (a loose progression of ideas often including Stoic and Hermetic elements is to be found in both Middle Platonism and Neoplatonism) continued to provide the intellectual backdrop for early Christian scholars in the Roman Empire.[3] Thus the hugely influential Christian philosopher and theologian Origen (*c*.184–*c*.254 CE), working in Alexandria, is deeply Platonist in outlook and even Porphyry acknowledges his familiarity with Greek philosophy. Origen was attempting to articulate and define the tenets of Christianity over and against the writings and preaching of the Gnostics. He was regarded as the great theologian of the age (see Crouzel 1989), and his *On First Principles* (Greek: *Peri Archōn*; translated by Rufinus as *de Principiis*; see Butterworth 1973) had widespread influence. Origen's homilies and scriptural commentaries circulated widely in the Middle Ages. However, Origen was condemned – specifically, for his views on *apocatastasis*, the universal restoration of all souls to the divine by the Fifth Ecumenical Council – and the medieval Latin West tended to treat him with some suspicion although his influence is everywhere. To illustrate Origen's way of interpreting scriptural teaching in relation to Platonism, one could refer to his discussion of the kinds of bodies that humans will have after the resurrection of the dead (*de Principiis* 2.10.1–4.38). Basing his comments on St Paul's First Letter to the Corinthians (1 Cor. 15:44), Origen argues that most people do not have a sophisticated understanding of the meaning of the spiritual domain or of the nature of the resurrected body. For Origen it seems absurd that this body will be of actual flesh and blood; rather it will be changed and transformed, something that later Christian Platonists will also emphasize. Elsewhere he distinguishes between the material body and the spiritual body and claims that there is progress from one body into the other. In *de Principiis* Origen offers the image of a seed which when sown must die and be transformed in order that the new life emerge. Origen maintains that the body possesses a certain inborn "principle" (*insita ratio, de Principiis* 2.10.3) or "seminal reason" (*logos spermatikos, ratio seminalis*) which is not corrupted and which survives in the new state. In general, Origen refers to the body as the garment of the soul, a Platonic metaphor that also occurs in Plotinus' *Enneads* I.6[1].7, and sees this as changeable depending on the location of the soul: the soul needs a garment suitable to it.

The early Christian Fathers were concerned to express the unity, eternity and transcendence of God, the creation of the universe and – against the Platonists – the *creation* of the human soul rather than its unborn eternity. The doctrine of the Trinity also began to be defended by Tertullian and others at this time, and the articulation of this doctrine became an important theological task through to St Augustine (who makes liberal use of Neoplatonic triads to illustrate the workings of the Trinity). Furthermore, the Christian apologists began to produce arguments against any doctrine of the transmigration of souls such as might be found in the Platonists following the Pythagoreans. Thus Tertullian's *de Anima* offers rigorous arguments for the rejection of transmigration of souls into other humans – or indeed, as found in Empedocles (and indeed, entertained playfully in Plato's *Phaedo*), into animals.

The Christian Fathers were generally struggling against various pagan doctrines associated loosely with Stoics, Aristotelians and Platonists. But a new intellectual movement arose in the third century which, while pagan, had a striking appeal for Christians. "Neoplatonism", as it came to be called, is normally associated with the philosopher Plotinus (*c*.204–70 CE) (see Rist 1967; Gerson 1994, 1996; Remes 2007), his student Porphyry (*c*.234–*c*.305 CE) and with a line of pagan philosophers extending to Proclus (*c*.412–85 CE), the last head of the Platonic School at Athens. In fact, it is clear that a strong pagan tradition informed by Neoplatonism ran parallel to and contended with Christianity for several centuries, and the pagan Neoplatonists were regarded as sages and ascetic holy men (see Edwards 2000). Neoplatonism offered a kind of template that was adopted in one form or another by all Christian philosophers in the period from St Augustine to Anselm (i.e. prior to the revival of Aristotle in the Latin West). A distinctly Christian version of Neoplatonism evolved in the Greek Cappadocian Fathers (Basil, Gregory of Nyssa, Gregory Nazianzus), St Ambrose of Milan and the African-born Roman senator Marius Victorinus, as well as the Christian texts of Boethius which included his *On the Trinity*. Boethius outlines a typical Neoplatonic hierarchy of principles in his *On the Consolation of Philosophy*.

Both Neoplatonism and Christianity were essentially spiritual philosophies that opposed what they understood to be the materialism of the Stoics. They maintained the transcendent nature of the One as the source and origin of the visible universe. They further defended the divine origin of the soul and its desire to return to the One from which it came. The body and the world of the senses are regarded as distractions and impediments to achieving this unity with the One. Both Neoplatonism and Christianity advocated spiritual practices to purify the soul, leading ultimately to deification.

Various attempts were made to re-establish paganism, most notably by the emperor Julian "the Apostate" (Dodds 1965), and the progressive Christianization of Europe was not without its regressions and interruptions. However, Neoplatonism was seen as in many ways being very acceptable to Christians. Plotinus (c.204–70 CE) in particular was regarded as sympathetic to Christianity and was translated into Latin by the Roman senator and convert to Christianity Marius Victorinus. Porphyry (234–c.305 CE), on the other hand, had explicitly written works, for example, *Against the Christians* (*adversus Christianos*, which survives only in fragmentary form), criticizing Christians and their biblical interpretations (see Berchman 2005). We now know of this work only from the references to it in works attacking it, by Christian writers such as Arnobius, Lactantius, Eusebius, Jerome, Augustine and others. Even his adversaries acknowledged that Porphyry was well versed in the Bible, but he criticizes it for historical inconsistencies, and even moral improprieties. There were also some fierce clashes between pagan Neoplatonists and Christian zealots, the most notorious of which was the murder of the female Neoplatonist philosopher Hypatia (c.350–415 CE) (Dzielska 1996), head of the academy in Alexandria, by followers of the Christian St Cyril, bishop of Alexandria. Later it seems that Proclus had Christian students (Steel 2010; Chlup 2012), and it is likely that the Christian writer who wrote under the pseudonym of Dionysius Areopagite was a student of Proclus. He certainly transmitted Proclus' ideas in a new Christian garb. Proclus' writings tended to offer support to various theological interpretations drawn on by the Christians (see Dodds 1963; Morrow & Dillon 1987). The Christians tended to regard Neoplatonism as a somewhat composite doctrine that provided an intellectual architecture for articulating theological insights into the nature of the infinite God, the nature of the procession of the Word, the meaning of the Trinity, the nature of creation, and the relation between the soul and the divine. There are several key features of any Neoplatonic account that have to be taken into consideration by Christian interpreters. Primarily there is the doctrine of the One (*to hen*) as the unique unknowable and unspeakable transcendent source of all things. This "One", drawing on an amalgam of arguments originally found in Plato's *Parmenides*, is itself the principle of unity in all other things, while remaining in itself, above everything. The One is transcendent and unknowable: unknown even to itself, as Eriugena puts it, following Plotinus. For the pagan Middle Platonists it was unclear whether this One had self-consciousness or whether it was even above this distinction between thinker and thought. From Plotinus onward, for instance, in Porphyry, Iamblichus, Syrianus, Proclus and Damascius, some form of consciousness is admitted in the One (Bussanich 1988).

All other things are what they are because of the One. They too are unities (*henades*) and they move because they want to be "one with the one". The pagan Neoplatonists postulated all kinds of unities and intermediary principles in the succession from the One, and the Christians reinterpreted these often as angelic intelligences but not gods. Moreover, this infinite One must be understood as creator of all things, "father of all". That which follows from the One is engendered by the One. The One overflows because of its own infinite, superabundant goodness and generosity. In this sense, it is identified with the Platonic form of the Good (*to agathon*) as found in Plato's *Republic*. The Christians would interpret this superabundance as equivalent to boundless love.

The One – as the Good – is "beyond being" (*epekeina tēs ousias*: Plato, *R*. 509b). Its first manifestation is Intellect or Mind (*nous*), which is identified by Christians with the *logos* and with Jesus Christ. Pagan Platonism has a further emanation of Intellect into "Soul" (*psychē*) which itself generates the body of the world and thereafter all material things. By the twelfth century Neoplatonic Christians were unhappy to posit the idea of a "World

Soul" (*anima mundi*) but Eriugena has no difficulty in accepting that the finite created cosmos emanates from intellect and soul (understood often as to be identified with the Holy Spirit as the third person or "hypostasis" of the Trinity).

The aim of all things and the explicit aim of Neoplatonic meditation or contemplation (*theōria*) is becoming one (*henōsis*). There is an "outgoing" (*proodos, exitus*) of all things from the One and a corresponding "return" (*epistrophē, reditus*) of all things to the One. There is no separate principle opposed to the One. Matter is at best an emanation from soul. There is therefore no reality to evil and matter also cannot be an ultimate principle. Christian Neoplatonists never think of this outgoing as a necessary emanation (it is of course the case that Plotinus did not think of the descent from the One as a necessary emanation either, but the Christians like to emphasize divine freedom and love in creation); rather it is because of the boundless freedom, generosity and grace of the One that it seeks to mirror itself in all the levels that follow from it. Thus the universe carries a certain image or trace of the divine. Indeed, for Christian Neoplatonists – and in relation to his theory of creation we might include Thomas Aquinas as a Platonist here – the term *emanatio* is frequently used as a synonym for *creatio*, and the kind of necessary relation which holds between creation and Creator is one-sided: necessary from the point of view of the dependent created being; neither necessary for, nor even known by, the Creator whose Oneness transcends all relation to anything outside itself. Other things come into being by participating in the One. The divine will is a kind of open invitation for things to come into being in order to emulate it.

Both Neoplatonism and Christianity were strongly committed to the divine origin of the soul, its immateriality and its immortality, but disagreed on the issue of its uncreated nature. In this regard, both Christian and Neoplatonist opposed the Gnostics and the Manichees with their dualist cosmological vision of a world governed by both light and dark forces. Both also were ascetic movements – Plotinus did not want his portrait painted (image of an image) – and there was also a certain disdain for, or at least devaluation of, the physical world. Salvation (*theōsis* for the Greek Christians; *deificatio* for the Latins – literally becoming divine, divinization) was conceived as unity with God (Russell 2004). For Eriugena, following the Greek Christian tradition, this deification is rare: most beings return to God but only a few (St Paul, John the Evangelist, Moses) are "rapt up in the third heaven" and actually become one with God.

Of course, the most prominent figure in the articulation of intellectual Christianity in the Latin West was St Augustine of Hippo (354–430 CE), and his writings, especially the *Confessions, On Christian Doctrine, The City of God, On the Literal Meaning of Genesis* and *On the Trinity* had a major impact in the Latin West for the following thousand years. He was familiar with the writings of Marius Victorinus (*floruit* 350 CE) (see S. A. Cooper 2005: 16–40; also M. T. Clark 1981), a Roman senator from Africa and another convert to Christianity, as well as with the views of his teacher, bishop Ambrose of Milan. Marius Victorinus had translated Plotinus' *Enneads* into Latin and maintained a Neoplatonic outlook in his defence of the Trinity and of the nature of the divine as "above being". According to his *Confessions* (*Confessiones* 7.9.13 and 7.20.26),[4] St Augustine's conversion to Christianity was influenced by his reading of what he terms the "books of the Platonists" (*libri platonicorum, Confessiones* 7.9) – most likely Marius Victorinus' translations of Plotinus and Porphyry, although Augustine does not tell us whose texts they were – texts which convinced Augustine that truth was incorporeal, and that God was eternal, unchanging, the cause of all things – in his mind paralleling truths revealed in St Paul's epistles (on the nature of the *libri platonicorum*, see Cary 2000: 33–8). One of the great lessons that Augustine learns from these Neoplatonists (and this theme is distinctively Plotinian) is the inner connection between the soul and the divine and that the journey inwards is also the journey upwards to the divine. Late nineteenth-century scholars originally saw Augustine as a thinker who converted first to Neoplatonism and then somewhat later to Christianity, but the modern consensus is that Augustine was through and through a Christian Platonist although he began to clarify for himself – especially in his *Retractions* (*Retractationes, c.*426 CE), which are essentially restatements rather than withdrawals – those doctrines of Christianity which directly conflicted with classical Platonism.

St Augustine was masterful in his manner of incorporating pagan thought into a thoroughly Christian outlook and carefully refining it througout his life, including offering various self-criticisms and reformulations (see Rist 1994; King 2005: 213–26). While it is not clear what Plotinus thought of the One as having mind or consciousness in some special elevated sense, it is certain that Christian Neoplatonism with its personal God and Trinitarian doctrine does allow that the One is *at least* Mind; and, to say that it is not Mind is really to say that it is more than Mind. This is clearly Augustine's position in *de Trinitate* book 15, where, following John 4:24, God is understood as "spirit" and credited with life and mental perception and understanding:

> But the life which God is senses and understands all things (*sentit atque intelligit omnia*), and senses with mind (*et sentit mente*) not with body, because God is spirit. God does not sense through a body like animals which have bodies, for he does not consist of body and soul. And thus this simple nature (*simplex illa natura*) senses as it understands, understands as it senses, and its sensing and understanding are identical. (*de Trinitate* 15.2.7, trans. Hill)

According to Augustine, for example, all created things bear the stamp of their maker and display traces (*vestigia*) of the divine Trinity. Creatures testify to their very dependency on the divine. As he puts it, each creature cries out: "God made me" (*Deus me fecit*). For Augustine, Christ is the very incarnation of eternal wisdom, and true philosophy meant the love of Christ. Augustine follows St Paul, who in I Corinthians 1.20 contrasted the worldly wisdom or "foolishness" of Greek pagan philosophy with Christian wisdom. St Paul claims that God would destroy the "wisdom of the wise". Augustine expands on this idea: true wisdom cannot merely be knowledge of earthly, temporal things but actually must be the desire for eternal things. For Augustine, the philosopher seeks to transcend the world and not solely to know it; otherwise his knowledge is vain and empty, mere *vana curiositas*. For Augustine, particularly in early works such as *Of True Religion* (*de Vera Religione*, trans. Burleigh), true religion and true philosophy were one and the same, and by philosophy here he meant Platonism. In the same work (*de Vera Religione* IV.7), Augustine claimed one need only change a few words to see how closely Plato resembled Christianity. In his *City of God* (*de Civitate Dei* [Dyson]) Plato is portrayed as the philosopher closest to Christianity (see also Wetzel 2012). For instance, Plato had defined philosophy as the love of God (*de Civitate Dei* 8.11). For Augustine, furthermore, the positive legacy of Plato and others should be integrated into Christian culture, just as the "spoils of the Egyptians" were taken with them by the Israelites as they fled their captivity in Egypt. Augustine writes in *On Christian Doctrine*:

> If those who are called philosophers, especially the Platonists, have said things which are indeed true and are well accommodated to our faith, they should not be feared; rather, what they have said should be taken from them as from unjust possessors and converted to our use. Just as the Egyptians had not only idols and grave burdens which the people of Israel detested and avoided, so also they had vases and ornaments of gold and silver and clothing which the Israelites took with them secretly when they fled, as if to put them to a better use.
>
> (*de Doctrina Christiana* 2.40.60)[5]

Having initially adopted Neoplatonism in a somewhat uncritical manner, as a way of overcoming his earlier scepticism and Manichaeism, St Augustine gradually began to see the limitation of the Neoplatonic outlook especially in articulating central tenets of Christianity such as the incarnation of the Word and the resurrection of the body. As he details in his *Retractions* (trans. Brogan), Augustine came to realize that Neoplatonism, while enormously important as an antidote to materialism and dualism (e.g. the Manichees), could not countenance the concept of the Divine becoming human, in the sense of taking on a physical corruptible body. Neoplatonism also had a tendency to downplay the importance of the temporal order and Augustine, who realized that part of the message of Christianity was the idea of history as a progress towards the divine, recognized that a genuine Christian philosophy must see time and history as real and indeed as playing a crucial role in the divine plan for the salvation of humans (see, for instance, *de Civitate Dei* 22).

Another important source of Christian Platonism especially into the Middle Ages was the corpus of writings purporting to be authored by Dionysius, St Paul's convert at Athens as mentioned in the Acts of the Apostles. These texts were in reality pious forgeries produced by a sixth-century Christian follower of the Neoplatonist Proclus. They are now referred to as the works of Pseudo-Dionysius the Areopagite (*floruit c.*500 CE) (Louth 1989). Because of their provenance – they are considered more or less as ancient and authentic as the Gospels themselves – they had extraordinary influence on Christian philosophers from the ninth-century John Scottus Eriugena to Thomas Aquinas and Robert Grosseteste (who both wrote commentaries on Dionysius), as well as on later medieval mystics such as Meister Eckhart and Nicolas of Cusa, whose outlook continued to be Neoplatonic in inspiration (see Dillon & Klitenic 2007). The Dionysian writings were eventually exposed as forgeries by the Renaissance humanist Lorenzo Valla.

The Dionysian corpus consists of four treatises and a number of letters (trans. Luibhéid; see Perl 2008). Dionysius' *The Divine Names* (*de Divinis Nominibus*) examines scriptural and philosophical appellations for the divine and argues that they all fail to fully express the nature of the highest being, who is nameless, beyond all names. Names are really processions from the divinity and do not reach the divinity itself. Negations, in fact, express the nature of the divine more accurately than affirmations. This theme is expressed even more radically in the *Mystical Theology*, which had enormous influence on the later medieval mystical tradition, transmitting to the Latin West the Platonism of the *Parmenides* in the form of negative theology. Dionysius maintains that God is unknowable and yet all things in the world are somehow traces of their unknowable cause. God is the being of all things. Dionysius furthermore states in his *Celestial Hierarchy* that "the being of all things is the divinity above being" (*to gar einai pantōn estin hē hyper to einai theotēs*, *Patrologia Graeca* [*PG*] 3.177d), a phrase that will be repeated by Eriugena.

Dionysius had an enormous influence on Albert the Great, Aquinas, Bonaventure and Grosseteste among others, particularly his concept of the self-diffusion of the good (*bonum diffusivum sui*), his principle that all things have being through being one, and his notion that the being of all things is the "above being" (*super esse; hyper ousias*) of the divinity (*esse omnium est superesse divinitatis*, as Eriugena translates it).[6] Eriugena also takes from Dionysius the idea of the act of creation as akin to the sun spreading its rays equally in all directions. The comparison of the One to the sun is found in many Neoplatonists including, for instance, Iamblichus, *de Mysteriis* I.12 and in Proclus, *ET* 122, 140, 189.

Dionysius' main translator (until the thirteenth century) and important disciple was an Irish philosopher named John who also signed himself, in one manuscript, "Eriugena" (meaning "Irish-born"). This Johannes (*c.*790/800–*c.*877 CE) was identified in local correspondence as an "Irishman" (*scottus*) and so gradually he came to be known as "Johannes Scottus", the Irishman named John. He also became known by the name "Eriugena" and by the nineteenth century, historians of philosophy began to refer to him as Johannes Scottus Eriugena (or "Scotus Erigena"). Scottus Eriugena was the leading thinker of the Carolingian *renovatio*.[7] Born somewhere in Ireland, and with an extraordinary reputation for learning, he first emerged in the written historical record as a theological disputant, scholar and teacher (*magister*) at the largely itinerant court of Charles the Bald,[8] which moved around various monastic and royal centres in the Île de France region (see Contreni 1978). Eriugena is first mentioned as a liberal arts scholar, but was then engaged in 850 as a theological disputant in a debate over predestination. Following some difficulties with ecclesiastical authorities over his *On Predestination* (*de Praedestinatione*; see M. Brennan 1998), he re-emerged as a translator of Greek Christian texts, specifically the works of Dionysius the Areopagite. However, his most original and creative philosophical work is to be found in his extraordinary cosmological dialogue, *Periphyseon* (also known as *de Divisione Naturae*, *c.*862–*c.*867 [Floss]).[9] The *Periphyseon* (literally "on natures") is a "study of nature" (*physiologia*, *PP* IV.741c). The two participants in the dialogue – named simply as "teacher" (*Nutritor*) and "student" or "disciple" (*Alumnus*) – discourse on the "totality of all things" (*universitas rerum*); that is, everything gathered under the name "universal nature" (*universalis natura*, *PP* II.525b). In the course of the dialogue, the "philosopher" (*philosophus*) and "theologian" (*theologus*) is also presented as a "cosmologist" (*sapiens mundi*) or "physicist" (*fisicus*) conducting an "inquiry into natures" (*inquisitio naturarum*, *PP* II.608c), guided by "nature, the teacher herself" (*natura ipsa magistra*, *PP* II.608d). As part of this enquiry, a *Hexaemeron* or account of the six days of creation is included, which is based in a large part on St Augustine's *On the Literal Meaning of Genesis* (*de Genesi ad Litteram*), written between 401 and 415, which offers a detailed discussion of creation.

In this grand theological and cosmological *system*, Eriugena offers a novel definition of nature as the "general name for all things that are and all things that are not" (*est igitur natura generale nomen, ut diximus, omnium quae sunt et quae non sunt*, *PP* I.441a). Nature in this sense explicitly *includes* "both God and the creature" (*deus et creatura*, *PP* II.524d), and this has led to accusations of pantheism; indeed, the *Periphyseon* was condemned along with other works in the thirteenth century.[10] But Eriugena thinks of created nature as a manifestation of the hidden divine Nature. God and nature are thought as ultimately one (the hidden and revealed sides of the same divine power) and are not to be considered as separated (*a seipsis distantia*, *PP* III.678c). Thus Eriugena says: "For when you say that it [the divine nature] creates itself the true meaning is nothing else but that it is establishing the natures of things. For the creation of itself, that is, the manifestation of itself in something, is surely that by which all things subsist" (*PP* I.455a–b). Indeed, nature is the manifestation of the divine, more or less the incarnation of the divine. Accordingly, nature also encapsulates the transcendence, unknowability and darkness of the divine. Eriugena then sets out to explain how nature includes "all that is and all that is not" (*ea quae sunt et ea quae non sunt*), both being and non-being, both God and creation. Eriugena even thinks, following Dionysius, that God can be called "nothing" (*nihilum*) and He is called so because He is "nothing through excellence" (*nihil per excellentiam*) rather than "through privation" (*per privationem*). The claim that God is a transcendent nothingness links Eriugena to Meister Eckhart in the later Middle Ages.

In the course of the *Periphyseon*, Eriugena gives an account of the nature of the divine One, its cosmic outgoing into created nature and its return into its own hidden depth in strongly Neoplatonic terms, drawing on Dionysius and also, especially, on the Greek Christian theologian Maximus Confessor, several of whose writings (e.g. *Ambigua ad Iohannem*) Eriugena knew and even translated. Maximus, especially, is Eriugena's source for much of his discussion of the stages of the return of all created things to the divine (see Petrov 2002). Moreover, and here he is following Gregory of Nyssa, according to the principle that human nature is made in the *imago et similitudo dei*, all created things are contained in human nature, which itself undergoes a process of outgoing and return to its source in the divine mind. Part of the power of Eriugena's cosmology lies in its radical anthropology (see Otten 1991; Stock 1967).

Eriugena's Platonism is so all-pervasive that it prompted more than one nineteenth-century scholar to conclude that he must have had direct knowledge of the writings of Plotinus or Proclus. In 1927, for instance, Téchert (1927) thought she had identified the direct influence of Plotinus in Eriugena based on a comparison of doctrines and technical expressions, but Eriugena's biographer Maïeul Cappuyns (1933) has shown that the expressions and doctrines can be found generally in the Christian Neoplatonic tradition, especially in Basil and Gregory of Nyssa (see Rist 2000), with whom Eriugena was familiar. The French historian Barthélemy Hauréau (1812–96) called Eriugena "the Proclus of the West" (Hauréau 1872), and Stephen Gersh has explored the Proclean influence in Eriugena (which, of course, comes not directly but through the writings of Dionysius) (see Gersh 1978). Strictly speaking, Eriugena does not draw directly from Plato, Plotinus, Porphyry or Proclus, but rather from the Christian Platonist tradition of Marius Victorinus, Augustine, Boethius (among the Latin authors), and Gregory of Nyssa, Basil, Dionysius the Areopagite and Maximus Confessor, from the Greek Christian tradition.

Eriugena, even leaving aside his own speculative theological works, would be important as a transmitter of Platonism precisely because of his work as a translator. He translated the *Corpus Dionysii*, the revered manuscript of which had been presented to the King of Francia Louis the Pious by the Byzantine emperor Michael the Stammerer and which had earlier been given an unsatisfactory translation by Hilduin.[11] He subsequently rendered into Latin Gregory of Nyssa's short treatise *de Hominis Opificio* (which he called *de Imagine*), Maximus Confessor's *Ambigua ad Iohannem*, and *Quaestiones ad Thalassium*, and possibly other works. Skilfully interweaving his text with these authorities, Eriugena still manages to develop his own highly original cosmology in his *Periphyseon* as an analysis of "nature" and of "those things that are and those that are not".

In the *Periphyseon* Eriugena confidently expounds an extraordinarily consistent system that is both Neoplatonic and Christian, and for him, the two never come into contrast or opposition. Thus in the *Homilia*, he is able to say in a Platonic manner that man receives his body from this world but his soul from another world. He never entertains Augustine's worries about the possibility of conflict between Neoplatonic doctrine and Christian teaching on such matters as the pre-existence of the soul, the nature of creation and salvation, or the meaning of nature and grace. Eriugena's main concern is in fact to integrate into a single coherent system the diverse Neoplatonisms he received from Greek and Latin anthorities (see e.g. *PP* IV.504c–505b) and to communicate this integrated system as the truth of Christianity and the meaning of nature itself. He frequently cites Augustine and Dionysius together, showing that they agree.

Eriugena's encounter with the writings of Dionysius and the Greek Eastern Christian tradition transformed his outlook and led him to interpret St Augustine in a more radically spiritual and immaterialist manner, especially in relation to the nature of the resurrected body, which for Eriugena will be purely spiritual. Eriugena now directed his philosophical study at constructing a vast synthesis of the learning of Greek East and Latin West, reconciling Augustine with Dionysius, Ambrose with Gregory of Nyssa. Eriugena saw no contradictions between these versions of Christian metaphysics: for him, there were merely differences of emphasis and differences of approach. After all, Scripture has as many meanings as there are colours in a peacock's tail and cosmological speculations may be entertained so long as they do not directly contradict Scripture.

Eriugena's point of departure is novel. He sets out by defining his area of investigation as *nature*, which for him includes, as we have seen above, both God and creation.[12] Universal nature, as he calls it, includes not only being (material, spiritual) but also those things which escape the intellect because of their superiority to it (e.g. God transcends the mind). From this beginning he is able to sketch out the four possible logical options offered by considering nature in relation to creation. We can, he says, conceive of nature as uncreated and creating (i.e. God as creator), as created and creating (i.e. the Platonic ideas or "Primary Causes" (*causae primordiales*), as Eriugena calls them, upon which the created world is modelled and from which it is derived), as created and not creating (the visible spatio-temporal world, which is what we usually mean by the term *nature*), and as uncreated and uncreating (nature as unrelated to creation: i.e. either pure nothingness or else God considered apart from creation). These four divisions of nature express, for Eriugena, successive *moments* in the being of God and the world, related according to the Neoplatonic sequence of procession and return. Eriugena's God is above being. Eriugena, following Dionysius, thinks of the Good, which is prior to being, as responsible for the movement from non-being to being:

> Therefore if the creator through his goodness brought all things out of nothing so that they might be, the aspect of goodness-in-itself must necessarily precede the aspect of being through itself. For goodness does not come through essence but essence comes through goodness (*non enim per essentiam introducta est bonitas set per bonitatem introducta est essentia*).   (*PP* III.627c–d)

God is "beyond being", "beyond essence", and can even be characterized, Eriugena insists, as "nothingness" (*nihilum, PP* III.685a) and the "negation of essence" (*negatio essentiae, PP* I.462b). Eriugena writes: "For when it is said: 'It is superessential', this can be understood by me as nothing other but a negation of essence (*nam cum dicitur: superessentialis est, nil aliud mihi datur intelligi quam negatio essentiae*)" (*PP* I.462b).

God, for Eriugena, is "not this nor that nor anything" (*nec hoc nec illud nec ullum ille est, PP* I.510c); a formula that will be developed also by Meister Eckhart.

When God creates the world, He wills the Primary Causes into being and these causes are conceived of as contained in the Word or *verbum*, the utterance (*clamor*) of which gives rise to creation. The primary causes in their turn "flow forth" into their effects, which gives rise to the spatio-temporal world of creatures in all their particularity. These effects are themselves unproductive of anything lower and depend totally upon their causes to which they revert or return. According to the Neoplatonists, all effects depend on and return towards their causes. Proclus inspired Dionysius in this regard, and Eriugena follows the latter. The effect is nothing other than the manifestation of the cause. Thus in *Periphyseon* book III, Eriugena says that the creature conceived as cause is not other than the creature conceived as effect (see *PP* III.693a–b). In this regard, the effect is said to "remain in" the cause and to seek to return to it (see Gersh 1977, 1978). The highest form of return or reversion of an effect upon a cause is the manner in which the thoughts produced by the intellect return to contemplate their own nature and the nature of the intellect that produced them. This self-conscious dialectic is the best example of Neoplatonic causation and reversion. In fact, in his return of all things to the One, Eriugena will say that cause and effect are one and the same (*PP* III.693b) and that whatever may be predicated of the cause may also be predicated of the effect (*PP* III.646c). Below this region of created effects lies the realm of *non-being*.[13] Ultimately, however, when the cycle of procession of causes into effects has terminated and all the effects have returned to rest in their causes, then the cycle of creation is complete and the absolute non-being of the fourth level becomes indistinguishable from the manner of existence of the inaccessible One.

Although this brief description of the cycle of nature conveys the impression of a temporal sequence, Eriugena more properly conceives of the four "levels" or "divisions" of nature as four aspects or ways of viewing (he calls them *theōriai* or "contemplations", *contemplationes*) the absolute unity of the One. The four divisions of nature are ways in which the human rational mind orders the manifest appearances of this world in relation to the One which, above time and space, is their origin.[14]

Eriugena's metaphysics, then, is an attempt to elucidate the Christian understanding of the creation through the understanding of the dynamics of the One as developed by Neoplatonist philosophers.The Christian Neoplatonists generally exploited the parallels between the biblical myth of creation and the Platonic understanding of the dependence of this imperfect world upon the perfect realm of the forms (or causes) and ultimately on the One itself. The Christian Platonists, whom Eriugena read in the original Greek and many of whom he translated for the first time into Latin (e.g. Maximus), conceived of God more or less in the manner in which Plotinus conceives of the One (developed from the concepts of the One in the hypotheses of Plato's dialogue *Parmenides*). Especially in the post-Plotinian tradition, for example, in Pseudo-Dionysius, this One is above being, beyond the good, beyond the realm of intellect or the intellectual light, dwelling in an inaccessible darkness, unknowable and unfathomable. This conception of God (as wholly transcendent) satisfied the Greek demand that God should be unsullied by the world, even to the extent of not knowing about it. At the same time all other beings flow forth from the One and depend on it for their existence. All things achieve their identity by attempting to imitate the primal unity of the One at a lower level. Everything that exists is a unity of some kind, and the more integrated is the unity, the closer does the thing come to the One. Thus the lower-level unities imitate the higher and the whole chain or procession of being is linked together by a pattern of imitation and striving upwards by which each thing tries to become more self-integrated. The One, itself, of course, is unaffected by this striving. The result of this striving is that the world must be seen as possessing a triadic structure of unity–procession–return.

This Neoplatonic metaphysics struck the Christians as aptly expressive of the truth of Christian revelation in two ways. First, the triadic structure paralleled the paradise–fall–salvation sequence of Christian myth. All creatures were originally one with God in paradise, then they fell through the sin of Adam (which the Neoplatonists and Eriugena see as a disruption of the original unity in which man's total consciousness was centred on God, brought about by man turning his gaze upon himself, thus giving rise to the phenomenon of human self-consciousness). The aim to achieve salvation is understood as a process through which man will recover his primordial unity with God by purifying his self-conscious activity until it is once again God-centred. The second parallel with the Neoplatonic triad is expressed by the nature of the One itself, since for the Christians the One is also a Trinity. According to Eriugena, God is in Himself hidden and unknown, dwelling in inaccessible darkness; but when He utters the Word which gives rise to creation, He makes himself manifest at the same time in the Person of the Word, the second Person of the Trinity. This movement of self-manifestation from darkness to light is understood by Eriugena as a procession similar in kind to the procession of things from the One.[15] The second procession from the Son to the Holy Spirit is understood by Eriugena as overseeing the procession of the primary causes (contained in the Son as *verbum* and *sapientia*) into their spatio-temporal effects, and of course at the same time is responsible for the reversion of those effects upon their causes.[16]

From the Greeks, then, Eriugena inherited a very unusual theory of creation. Creation is to be understood as the self-manifestation of God, the process by which He makes His hidden nature manifest.[17] As such it is a timeless event, inseparable from the Trinitarian procession from Father to Son. The whole of the created universe is to be understood as unfolding within the Trinity; at no stage is creation to be seen as an alienation or separation of things from God. If the Fall had not taken place, it is implied, all things including man would have evolved in their own mysterious manner in the bosom of God Himself. Eriugena's God is not static but dynamic, manifesting, unfolding and explicating Himself in spirals of divine history. The Fall, however, disrupts this cycle. For Eriugena the Fall, like the creation of all things, is a timeless event that takes place within the godhead.

Eriugena maintains that, in its prelapsarian condition, human nature was originally one with God, indistinguishable from Him, omnipotent and omniscient like Him, because human nature was the perfect image of God, and, following Gregory of Nyssa, Eriugena maintains that the image is in all respects likes its archetype "except in number". Eriugena has an account of the Fall that makes it take place at an epistemological level. Human nature became obsessed with its own self-image and self-consciousness and sought to impose human rather than divine meanings on things. Eriugena has no time for more literal interpretations of the Bible that sought to blame the devil or Eve for original sin. All human beings are separate from God so long as their free wills are self-centred rather than directed towards the infinite, endless will of God. Eriugena elevates human nature to the highest position in the cosmos under God. In Greek, God's boundlessness is expressed by the term *anarchos*, which means without limit or without ruling principle:[18] "So the human replica of the Divine Essence is not bound by any fixed limit any more than the Divine Essence in Whose Image it is made" (*PP* IV.772a).

And again:

> For if human nature had not sinned but had adhered unchangeably to Him Who had created her, she would certainly have been omnipotent. For whatever in nature she wished to happen would necessarily happen, since she would wish for nothing else to happen save that which she understood that her Creator wished to happen.   (*PP* IV.778b)

Eriugena took this doctrine of the potential omnipotence and omniscience of human nature from the Greek writers, notably Gregory of Nyssa. In the *Periphyseon*, Eriugena quotes long passages from Gregory of Nyssa's tract *de Hominis Opificio* (*Peri kataskeuēs anthrōpou*, which Eriugena himself translated as *de Imagine*), amounting to almost 80 per cent of the whole text, a work which explained the concept of human nature as made in God's image in terms of the complete identity between image and archetype. For Gregory, as Eriugena constantly emphasizes, an image resembled its archetype or exemplar in *all* aspects; they differ only in being numerically distinct. Thus, in *Periphyseon* book IV Eriugena quotes at length from Gregory of Nyssa's *On the Image of Man* XVII.44.177d–185d [Laplace & Daniélou]. The following excerpt is significant. Eriugena writes in his rendering of Gregory:

> For if God is the plenitude of good things (*plenitude bonorum*), and man is an image of God, the image must resemble the Primal Exemplar in this respect also, that it is the plenitude of all good. … In this respect also it is the image, in that it is free from all necessity, and is subjected to no natural or material authority but possesses in itself a will which is capable of obtaining its desires.   (*PP* IV.796a–b)

As the image of God, human nature mirrors God's perfect freedom and power. For Eriugena, the transcendence of God is mirrored by the transcendence of human nature above the rest of creation. God is always an unknown darkness above the world: it cannot be said *what* He is. But what about human nature? Can one understand the essence of human nature? If human will is really infinite and boundless then perhaps it is equally impossible to say what man is, and indeed that is Eriugena's conclusion. Human nature (exactly like divine nature) can know *that it is*, but not *what it is*.

A Neoplatonic outlook continued to dominate European thought from the sixth to twelfth centuries, until, in the thirteenth and fourteenth centuries, new Aristotelian texts, often through Arabic intermediaries, became available and were studied in the newly founded universities at Paris, Bologna, Oxford and elsewhere. This new interest in Aristotle was such that, although Plato's *Timaeus* was widely lectured on during the twelfth and early thirteenth centuries, by 1255 it was no longer required reading at the University of

Paris. Medieval Neoplatonism continued to maintain a dualistic opposition of the divine and temporal worlds, with the sensible world patterned on unchanging immaterial forms, often expressed as numbers. It also affirms the soul's immortality and direct knowledge of intelligible truths, combined with a suspicion of the mortal body and a distrust of the evidence of the senses. Interest in Plato re-emerged in the Italian Renaissance with the availability of genuine works of Plato, Plotinus and Proclus. Nevertheless, through Pseudo-Dionysius in particular, Platonism reverberates in many thirteenth-century authors, especially in theology. Eriugena's consistent Neoplatonism was revived by Meister Eckhart and Nicholas of Cusa (1401–64) in the fourteenth and fifteenth centuries. This new form of Neoplatonism was strengthened by greater familiarity with Plato's dialogues as well as by the rediscovery of the works of Proclus. Cusanus regularly characterizes his own Platonism as stemming from Dionysius and before him from Plato. He also draws on Dionysius' commentators, including his Latin translators, especially Eriugena (who he calls "Johannes Scotigena"),[19] Albertus Magnus' *Commentary on the Divine Names*,[20] Robert Grosseteste (whose translations of Dionysius' *Mystical Theology* and *Celestial Hierarchy* he owned in manuscript), Thomas Gallus and Meister Eckhart.

Cusanus reads Dionysius as a Christian practitioner of dialectic in the tradition stemming from Plato's *Parmenides*.[21] He also quotes Proclus' *Commentary on Parmenides*[22] to the effect that Plato denied that predications can be made of the first principle, just as Dionysius prefers negative to affirmative theology (*de Beryllo* 12). Cusanus writes: "The great Dionysius imitates Plato" (*de Beryllo* 27, trans. Hopkins 1998) and in his *Apologia doctae ignorantiae* (1449): "The divine Dionysius imitated Plato to such an extent that he is quite frequently found to have cited Plato's words in series" (*Apologia* 10, see Hopkins 1984: esp. 97–118) (Moran 2007).

Thus Neoplatonism continued to have a significant role in Christian theology to the very dawn of modernity. Indeed, there is a new outbreak of Christian Neoplatonism with the so-called Cambridge Platonists in the seventeenth century (see Rogers *et al.* 1997; Hutton 2002).

NOTES

1. For a recent provocative discussion of St Paul and philosophy, see Caputo & Alcoff (2009). See also Maccoby (1986, 1991). Maccoby claims that St Paul more or less invented Christianity as a religion; this is a view that has been challenged but there is no doubt that St Paul shaped the manner Christianity developed in a decisive way.
2. For more evidence of this characteristic ambivalence towards Greek philosophy found among early Christian writers, see Beierwaltes (1998: esp. pp. 7–24).
3. For recent discussions of the term "Platonism" and "Neoplatonism", see Gersh (2006). See also Moran (1998: 431–9), Dillon (1996a), Remes (2008b).
4. Pine-Coffin (1961: 154). For a discussion, see J. J. O'Meara (1954) and O'Donnell (2006).
5. Trans. Robertson. This is an idea frequently found among ancient Christian writers, perhaps beginning with Origen's "Letter to Gregory Thaumaturgus".
6. For an excellent study of Eriugena's translation of Dionysius, *Versio Dionysii*, see Budde (2011). One of Budde's main points is that Eriugena finds a doctrine of creation which he can express in Dionysian terms, although Dionysius himself is almost silent on the concept of creation.
7. On Eriugena's life, see Moran (1989: 35–47). Johannes Scottus signs his epistolary dedication to his translation of the works of Dionysius with the pen-name "Eriugena". Eriugena corrected and extended the earlier translation of Dionsyius by Hilduin and challenges anyone who doubts his translation to check the Greek (see *Patrologia Latina* 122.1032c).

8. See M. Brennan (1986). Eriugena's name is absent from the *Annals of St Bertin*, which recorded life at the court of King Charles the Bald. The earliest references to him record certain medicinal recipes attributed to him. However, John "the Irishman" is referred to by Prudentius in his *de Praedestinatione* (851) as a follower of Pelagius (*Patrologia Latina* 115.1011b), who alone "Ireland sent to Gaul" (*Patrologia Latina* 115.1194a). He is mentioned by Bishop Pardulus (as quoted by Remigius) as "that Irishman, who is in the king's palace, named John" (*Scotum illum qui est in palatio regis, Joannem nomine, Patrologia Latina* 121.1052a).

9. There is a new edition by Jeauneau (1996–2003). The *Periphyseon* is cited according to the following editions: book 1: Sheldon-Williams (1968); book 2: Sheldon-Williams (1972); book 3, Sheldon-Williams (1981); book 4: Jeauneau (1995). The English translation is by I. P. Sheldon-Williams and J. J. O'Meara, published in Sheldon-Williams (1987). *Periphyseon* will be cited hereafter as "*PP*" followed by the book number (in Roman numerals) and the *Patrologia Latina* page number and paragraph letter in line with the traditional way of citing Eriugena's works.

10. Moran (1990). The thirteenth-century condemnations of Eriugena refer specifically to the doctrine that God is "the form of all things" (*forma omnium*), a doctrine associated in its most radical statement with Almericus of Bène (who died *c.*1206). Another associated doctrine, that God is the "matter of all things" (*materia omnium*), was supposedly defended by David of Dinant. Eriugena does call God *forma omnium* at *Periphyseon* I.499d, but follows immediately by saying that God is also without form and beyond form. In other words, in keeping with Eriugena's affirmative and negative theologies, the statement must be both affirmed and denied (*PP* I.500b). In fact, the phrases *forma omnium* and *forma formarum* are already found in Augustine, who uses them to describe the divine nature.

11. On Eriugena's translation of Dionysius, see Harrington (2004: 22–8). Harrington (*ibid.*: 24) points out that in translating Dionysius, Eriugena makes some changes, including expressing the merging of the mind with God as a *theoria* or *speculatio* rather than a non-cognitive "onrush" or interaction with the divine theophany or divine ray (see *PL* 122.1116c).

12. This abrupt introduction of the difficult concept of "non-being" or "nothing" is characteristic of Eriugena's style. Actually, non-being (*nihil*) is understood by him in two main ways: (a) non-being signifies total absence of any substance, and (b) non-being signifies those things which the intellect cannot comprehend within its own categories. Thus God, conceived of as transcending the mind, cannot be described by our category of substance or existence, and he thus may be said to be non-being. Eriugena complicates these two basic meanings in his dialogue by suggesting that those things which are merely potential (still immanent in the Primary Causes or seminal reasons) may be said to be non-being.

13. Strictly speaking of course, this realm of non-being does not *exist*, it is really a privation of being, and Eriugena terms it *nihil per privationem* to distinguish it from the non-being of God which he calls *nihil per excellentiam*. See Sheldon-Williams (1981: 5–10).

14. Time is understood by Eriugena, in the manner of the Platonists, as an illusory form of existence, scarcely fully real. Eriugena went much further than Augustine in his analysis of time, and makes it merely a category of the human mind in its fallen state. Once the return of man to a state of grace or deification has been achieved then time will have a new mystical significance, expressing the endless nature of the human circulation around the divine; see Moran (2002).

15. "Do you not see how the Creator of the whole universe takes the first place? … For in Him are all things immutably and essentially and He is the division and collection of the universal creature, and genus and species and whole and part. … For the monad also is the beginning of numbers and the leader of their progression, and from it the plurality of all numbers begins and in it is consummated the return and collection of the same" (*PP* III.621b–c). Eriugena does not clearly distinguish the creation of all things in their causes and the generation of the Word, and indeed the two are one for him, since the Word is the coming together in wisdom of the principles of all things: "For to the human intellect which Christ assumed all the intellectual essences adhere" (*PP* II.542a–b). The Cappadocian Fathers and Augustine would have taken exception to this claim which, for them, would have implied a subordinationism. Eriugena is, on the contrary, willing to proclaim boldly the identity between the One and what is subsequent to the One.

16. The Holy Spirit acts as a kind of individuating principle in Eriugena's scheme. Eriugena conceives of Him mythically as brooding over and hatching the cosmic egg: "For the Holy Spirit fermented … the primordial causes which the Father had made in the beginning, that is, in his Son, so that they might proceed into

those things of which they are the causes. For to this end are eggs fermented by birds, from whom this metaphor is drawn" (*PP* II.554b–c).

17. God's act of self-manifestation is at the same time the creation all things: "For the creation of itself, that is, the manifestation of itself in something, is surely that by which all things subsist" (*PP* I.455b).

18. Eriugena frequently stresses that God is "without beginning" (*anarchos*): "*Deus autem anarchos, hoc est sine principio*" (*PP* I.516a).

19. Besides Eriugena's translations of Dionysius, Cusanus, at the very least, was familiar with *Periphyseon* book I, which he owned in manuscript (British Museum Codex Additivus 11035) and annotated, as well as the *Clavis Physicae* of Honorius Augustodunensis (Paris Bib. Nat. cod. lat. 6734), a compendium of Eriugenian excerpts, and the homily *Vox Spiritualis* (under the name of Origen).

20. Albertus Magnus also commented on Dionysius' *Divine Names* in his *Super Dionysium de Divinis Nominibus*, *Opera Omnia* vols 36 and 37 [Simon], which Cusanus cites in his *de Beryllo* 17.

21. Paradoxically, Cusanus anticipates the great Renaissance scholar Lorenzo Valla, who eventually unmasked the pseudonymous nature of the Dionysian corpus, with his independent recognition of the close doctrinal proximity between Proclus and Dionysius. For Cusanus, however, it was simply that Proclus and Dionysius were both sages who knew the truth.

22. See *in Prm.* VI.1075 (trans. Morrow & Dillon): "So then it is more proper to reveal the incomprehensible and indefinable cause which is the One through negations."

32

Neoplatonism and Christianity in the East: philosophical and theological challenges for bishops

Dimitar Y. Dimitrov

Gregory of Nyssa and Synesius of Cyrene do not form a traditional pair in the history of Neoplatonism and Christianity, but they are, nevertheless, two representatives of Christian thought in the Greek-speaking world of the late fourth and the early fifth century. Both of them received a good, if not excellent, education. As Christians, they were sometimes attacked for their alleged inclination towards Hellenic culture and style, and furthermore were accused of abandoning *the grace from above* in favour of secular learning. Both were regarded as elitarian in a sense, although they became, willingly or not, shepherds of the souls in their bishoprics, the Cappadocian Nyssa and Cyrenaican Ptolemais, respectively. As bishops, they also passed through turbulent times. Why, then, are they rarely, if ever, juxtaposed together?

Gregory (*c*.335–*c*.395) was one of the Cappadocian Fathers, considered to be a teacher of the Church *par excellence* and an important figure in Greek patristics. There were, however, suspicions that, in comparison with the others, he readily made concessions to Hellenic learning and to Platonism in particular. As shall be seen below, this observation is debatable. Considered sometimes as a child of the Second Sophistic, he was influenced by Plato, with the qualification that a form of Stoicizing Platonism is often recognized in his writings.[1] This is perhaps a result of the literary culture and education in which he was immersed since his youth, as well as of his open interest in philosophy and anthropology. Gregory was, however, very conscious not to cite directly the sources he used, nor to fill his writings with names from the past. He was more of a philosopher than Basil or Athanasius of Alexandria, and more spiritually open to discussing different natural and philosophical questions when compared to Gregory of Nazianzus, for example. In this vein, some parallels between the creativity with which he and Origen, whose influence on the Cappadocians is a well-known fact, deal with spiritual questions will transpire below.

On the other side is Synesius of Cyrene (*c*.370–*c*.413), who in the past was viewed as an unoriginal philosopher, a kind of dilettante, who did not succeed in solving the controversial issues between Christianity and Neoplatonism; even worse, he did not even recognize them. Although later scholars have been more charitable towards him, they have continued to bring up the arguments from Synesius' *Letter* 105 as evidence for his pagan or at least crypto-pagan views, which deviated considerably from the Christian concepts of the day.[2] These arguments have been further scrutinized so as to yield a more complex cluster of problems (Marrou 1963). The posed questions were difficult to solve, indeed, and they were the key problems dividing pagan and Christian views, yet they could not be disposed of even by the Church in Synesius' lifetime. The charge of paganism thus seems to be impetuous. What is recognized in the more recent literature is Synesius' appurtenance to Christianity and the Church, although not without acknowledging the oddity of his case.[3]

The goal of the present chapter is to analyse the views of Gregory and Synesius on souls, resurrection and the eternity of the world, in the context of their diverse Christian and Hellenic intellectual milieu. Some references to the elusive personality of Nemesius of Emesa, the author of *de Natura Hominis*, will be made as well. This examination will shed new light on possible links between the Christian and the Platonic philosophical culture of the day, but also on conflicts and differences which seem to be insurmountable for both sides. The proponents of each side shared the hard task of representing philosophical truths as cornerstones of faith to devoted masses often not educated enough, or, conversely, ready to learn, argue and ask inconvenient questions loudly and without restraint.

The famous *Letter* 105 is a good starting point.[4] In 410, under the insistence of the citizens of Ptolemais and with the decisive role of the Alexandrian Patriarch Theophilus, Synesius was appointed to the bishopric office. It was at least partly a political decision, with Synesius being a prominent citizen as well as a highly educated person. Hypatia of Alexandria, the pagan philosopher, killed by the Christian mob in Alexandria in 415, was his most beloved teacher. (It was obviously not so unusual at that time for a Christian to study under the guidance of a pagan teacher.) As an avid pursuer of free time in which to study (*scholē*) and hunt, Synesius was rather reluctant to accept the post in those difficult times for the Church and the Empire. From his position as an intellectual, Synesius was frank and bold to proclaim that he would deal with philosophy at home and "mythologize in public" (*exō philomythos eimi didaskōn, Letter* 105: 188.17–189.1). In the *Letter* he proceeds to list his three philosophical and theological objections against the main Christian doctrines, which are traditionally cited as evidence of his pagan Neoplatonic aspirations. His principal objection concerns the origin of the soul, the eternity of the world, and the resurrection. That Synesius undoubtedly raises questions to Theophilus is obvious, but does he set forth positions as well? And if there are such positions, what exactly are they?

After explaining why he would accept the bishopric with such apprehension and reluctance, but also with a strong notion of duty and dignity, Synesius moves to the *difficillimae quaestiones*. "It is difficult," he admits, "if not quite impossible, that views should be shaken, which have entered the soul through knowledge to the point of demonstration" (*Letter* 105: 188.1–3). After such a definite stand on the importance of the rational and "scientific" methods, the future bishop of Ptolemais states the following, no less important but regularly neglected, observation: "You know that philosophy rejects many of these convictions which are cherished by the common people" (*Letter* 105: 188.3–5). Immediately after this, he formulates his first objection: "For my part I can never persuade myself that the soul is of more recent origin than the body."[5]

Plato had already postulated the immortality of soul and the Neoplatonists had further expanded and defended his view. According to Plotinus, all souls inhabit the intelligible realm before a part of them (the lower part) descends into bodies, while the higher unde-scending part remains in the intelligible realm and contemplates the unchangeable world of ideas. The soul is immortal, and, after the death of the body it has ensouled, it ascends or moves to another body (discussed in his *Enn.* IV.1–7). What does it mean, then, for a man educated in the traditional course of "pagan" philosophy to accept that the soul is created after the body?[6] It surely means to place the highest principle of life on the same footing with or even as posterior to the material world. This is one of the main pagan objections against the Christian theory of Creation.[7]

Without explicitly adopting the idea of the immortality of the soul, Synesius is never-theless attached to the Neoplatonic views about it. The influence of Plotinus and Porphyry is visible in his writings. Probably through them, rather than directly, he was exposed to the philosophy of Aristotle, Plato and the Stoics, while, in Hypatia's school, he was acquainted with Neopythagoreanism. In his *de Providentia*, he states that unlike bodies, souls, because their generative source is different, are not produced by material parents. Furthermore, they descend from two distinctive sources (unspecified in the text) which explains their principal differences here, on earth (*de Providentia* I.2). By drawing a con-nection between soul's higher generative sources and its earthly permutations, Synesius infuses Plotinus' understanding of souls inhabiting the intelligible realm with certain dualistic overtones.

If we can detect something like a theory of soul in Synesius, it is mostly developed in *de Insomniis* and in his hymns. He believes in souls' descent into bodies and their possible ascent towards the intelligible. For him, soul has a specific structure: there is a division between the "first soul" (*prōtē psychē*) keeping something of the divine in itself, and the "carrying pneuma" (*ochēma, pneuma*), its envelope, the vehicle, the outer door or the door-keeper of the soul proper. The outer part of the soul possesses sensual abilities. When this envelope is clean and ethereal, it can easily bring the soul up, but when polluted by the material world, it becomes heavy and oriented downwards. Once fallen in matter, soul should do everything in its power to ascend again to its divine source. Often, for Synesius, even the misfortunes of the material world can act as stimuli for ascension (*de Insomniis* 6–7, based on Porphyry's *Sententiae*, mainly chapters 16 and 32).[8] If we compare this account with its Neoplatonic sources, we can discern a notable change, not so much in the evaluation of matter, which remains rather negative, but in the possibility of salvation. The individual acts of ascent can finish in a universal salvation through Christ's descent as its guarantee (see Vollenweider 1984: 155–60, 173–6 on *positiven Abstiegs*).

All the hymns of Synesius, therefore, were devoted to the general idea of rising up the author's soul from the bonds of the material existence to the higher spheres of the Divine. They are Christian in their essence, although they sounded pagan and Platonic. As a prison for the soul, matter is perilous and it should be avoided. In the third hymn of his collec-tion, Synesius invokes the Father to have mercy on his soul and not to allow the soul, once escaped, to return into the body (3.375–80). Here it is not clear if Synesius presumes the possibility of *metempsychōsis* or just repudiates the bodily existence. The very expression of "the soul fleeing the body" (*sōma phygoisan*) echoes Porphyry's *omne corpus fugiendum*, criticized by Augustine in *de Civitate Dei* (10.29; 22.25–8). In the hymns, however, the descent of the Divine (the Son, the Holy Spirit) is presented not so much as a diminution and degradation reaching into the darkest corners (*eschata*) of matter, but rather as an act of God's Will to save His creatures from the material bonds. Synesius does not debase the Holy Spirit to the level of the *Chaldaean* World Soul, which he obviously knows well, but prefers to represent it as a hypostasis equal to the other two (the Creator and His Son). Keeping in mind the different purpose of his writings, we can still safely suppose that Synesius' traditional outlook on souls and matter is shaped mostly by his contact with the views of Plotinus, Porphyry and the *Chaldaean Oracles* through his philosophical training in Alexandria and its intellectual milieu. It also tentatively transpires in his explanation of the Christian faith that he had already cherished at that time, if not since his youth.

Let us return to Synesius' objection, in *Letter* 105, namely that he does not accept the view of the post-corporeal creation of soul. That he means *after* is obvious from his word choice of "posteriorly created" (*hysterogenē*). This objection enlists Synesius in the long dispute about the origin and the fate of souls, of their descent from and ascent to God. In this context we should, however, notice an important detail. His disagreement with the thesis of the post-corporeal origin of souls leaves open a loophole for two possible inter-pretations: (a) that he has been defending the pre-existence of souls; and (b) that he has been inclined to accept the simultaneous act of creation for both body and soul.

Regarding the first possibility, Volkmann is the first, to my knowledge, to suggest a possible thread of Origen's influence on Synesius.[9] I acknowledge, however, the difficulty of tracing word-for-word parallels between the two. Volkmann's view is further made problematic by the uncertainty surrounding Origen's original teaching in general.[10] In addition, what we know from *de Principiis* is that the main reason for souls' descent is free will, which does not fit well with Synesius' philosophy (and theology), where the topic of free will is treated rather sparingly. Further, Origen obviously does not subscribe to the idea that the intelligible realm exists autonomously; that is, independently of imagination (*de Principiis* 2.3.6). That makes him rather independent of Plato, while Synesius kept nearly intact the Neoplatonic acceptance of the intelligible sphere as the realm of pure Essence and Truth.

The problems started from the interpretation of Genesis 2:7, especially in light of the Neoplatonic way of thinking and argumentation. There was a need for the Christian theologians and preachers, who "took into armament" the Neoplatonic imagery and ter-minology, to explain the biblical statement in a proper way. In general, the idea of the pre-existence of souls, which scholars ascribe to Origen, could be an attempt to react, in a situation where the theological system is still underdeveloped, against two popular trends in the Christian thought concerning soul's origin, namely *traducianism* (or *generation-ism*) and *creationism*.[11] We know that the question was not completely clarified until late in the Middle Ages, if not even beyond. It was a weak point in traducianism, anyway, to reject the Platonic *descent* and to accept the soul as being created through sexual activity and generation. Creationism provokes, namely, a certain uneasiness combined with the presupposition that the soul is a non-corporeal substance being put into body. Nemesius of Emesa was indirectly engaged in the dispute, defending the immortality and incor-porality of souls. If the individual soul enters and grows in an already created embryo, we have to accept – as Nemesius observes – the premise that the soul, created in body, is actually created *after* the body. To be created after the body would mean a lower quality and even a corporeal essence. It would presuppose mortality (*de Natura Hominis* II.46 [Morani]). Such a thesis, however, seems to be far from the truth for the basic Christian tenets. Eunomius (the leader of an extreme Arian wing in the late fourth century) will have to admit that – continues Nemesius in his attack – either the soul is mortal or it is not created in body. According to the traducianist (labelled sometimes as generationist) view, developed by Tertullian in the Latin tradition and also popular in the Greek-speaking world, souls are born one from another, like bodies, and thus are transferred from the parents to their children. For Nemesius, the main propagator of the "middle way", soul is imperishable, immortal, combined with body indivisibly and non-transferrable (*de Natura* 2.45–54; 3.57).[12] Soul logically pre-exists body so that it is not the soul which was closed in the body, but rather the opposite. Thus, the bishop of Emesa, Synesius' contemporary, became an extreme supporter of the thesis for an autonomous and leading role of the soul. Origen and Nemesius, although divided by approximately two centuries, reached, in their fight against the extremes of traducianism and creationism, quite similar conclusions presuming the pre-existence of souls. Even Augustine of Hippo shows, in his *Retractationes* and elsewhere, doubts when discussing the origin of souls and their binding with bodies. With Synesius, he also finds this question the *difficillima quaestio*.[13]

Let us now turn to Gregory of Nyssa who was forced, by the actual questions of the day, repeatedly to address the problems of soul and resurrection in his writings. In fact, he developed – in disputes with pagans as well as with the followers of Eunomius and Apollinaris – what we may consider a system of views concerning specifically the human soul. The main gist of this system, although inconsistent and often evading categorical solutions, could be summarized as this.[14] Soul is a created essence, alive and rational, non-spatial and in the same time providing the body – a mixture of organs – with life, unity and sense-perception. Gregory is not ready to accept the notion of soul's pre-existence implied in the idea of its immortality, since it contradicts the idea of Creation. Believing strongly in the spiritual principle of the soul in the World, however, he assumes in *de Hominis* (24.213b) that the higher intellectual part of the soul originates from the Divine and is a constituting principle of the Creation. Appealing to the immortality of God, he argues that the soul receives eternal life with resurrection only through the grace of God, and not as an immortal entity by itself. What soul has *is* immortality through God's will and the resurrection, but not immortality *per se*.

His explanation of the resurrection is based on the premise that the soul, an indivisible and non-dimensional entity itself, unifies the elements, notwithstanding the distance between them, and thus keeps together the dissolute. The soul–body union could last so long as there is nature ready to accept it (*de Anima* 31b–c). Soul is spiritual and non-material by nature, but through the senses it is mixed with matter and incorporated (*de Hominis* 14.173d–176b). Movements and the development of bodies depend on soul, otherwise they lose motion and die. Soul, or rather its rational aspect, is the "real" soul; the others, that is, the vital force common for both humans and animals, is no more than a semblance (*de Hominis* 15.176c–177c).

When discussing soul's parts, Gregory examines it from different perspectives and thus leaves room for numerous considerations. According to him, human nature includes three parts, which are controlled by the individual soul. The product of this is some kind of composite, constituted of a material/natural part (in plants), a sensible part (in animals), and an intellectual part, or all three of the parts, in one (in man) (*de Hominis* 8.145c–d). A few chapters later, he again enumerates the three parts as nutritional, sensitive and rational (chapter 14). He envisions the mind (*nous*) as the highest among them, and the very essence of the human soul *per se*. Thus a certain tri-unity is formed of mind, soul and body, in which mind is given pre-eminence. Besides the Aristotelian division, the strong Platonic overtones can be heard in the emphasis on the primary role of the rational part, and the idea of other parts being dependent semblances or unfoldings of that part.

Gregory also supposes that lower bodily natures could put mind and soul into their service, somehow lowering the status of the latter. The irrational part of soul is formed last, after the soul enters the body and lives with and in it. Gregory's understanding of soul's "failure" as a result of its inclination towards the body resonates with Synesius' view of soul's polluted breath (*pneuma*) which lowers the divine into the morass of material existence. We see another parallel between the two thinkers again in the case of the "phantastic" abilities of the soul. Gregory supposes that the irrational disposition in soul incites phantastic imagination in dreams (*de Hominis* 13.173). Synesius tries to explain the very possibility of dreams in more detail, mostly holding the fantastic *pneuma*, or *ochēma*, the imperfect breath/vehicle, responsible for the visions, which are sometimes confused before reaching the rational core of the higher soul for proper analysis (Kissling 1922; Aujoulat 1983, 1984; Dickie 2002). There are many similarities between Gregory and Synesius in explaining the phenomena of soul's failure, irrationality and dreams, but while the former tries to escape from the traditional imagery, the latter fully embraces it.

Gregory is far more positive in his evaluation of the place of matter in the order of existence than Synesius. For him, matter is created and thus a receptacle of soul as a unique mode of salvation. Without the free will of the human being – a composite of body and soul – the salvation would be virtually impossible. The view of the Cappadocians, and especially that of Gregory, on evil as accidental and as a lack of good is well known and closer to Plotinus than that of Synesius, implied by a certain dualism in his thought, supposing even the existence of evil *per se* (on evil and matter in Plotinus, see O'Brien 1996). In his insistence on the existence of free will, Gregory also differs from the Neoplatonists' acceptance of evil as immanent in nature, thus parting from Synesius as well, the latter being prone to reject matter as the abode of demons and evil spirits. Although in *Oratio Catechetica* Gregory points to the devil's jealousy as the reason for sin, human nature becomes sinful because the primordial sin mingles with matter and mind (chapter 6). In what is probably Gregory's work, *Life of Macrina*, the author exhibits some most critical comments about matter, and Platonic allusions of the body as the soul's tomb and the passions as prison for the soul. This work also portrays the general longing for salvation of the soul which is characteristic for that particular genre. In *de Hominis*, Gregory considers a different line of thought: the embodied life is the only possible way for the human soul to exist before death and resurrection. Evil is just a result of soul's inclination to animal passions and lust. It is subjective and not a universal deviation of behaviour. Gregory views evil as a mixture and not an absolute, while Synesius discerns grades of evil in soul's descent, the lowest of which are the extremes of matter in complete possession by the evil.

Moreover, for Synesius, souls could ascend only through purification, including intellectual activity, while for Gregory, soul's ascent involves spirituality.[15] Gregory is prone, as a "good Cappadocian", to present the soul's ascent from the spiritual rather than from the intellectual point of view. Always ready to follow and investigate the human heart and mind, he offers, in the *Life of Moses*, an example of divinization, a spiritual imitation of the souls' life ascending to God. Synesius, on the other side, looks always at the erratic nature of the soul. In *de Insomniis* he compares the soul to a hired employee who, when falling in love with the serving maid of the boss, decides to stay and work as a slave to his chief, without desire to free himself from the bondage of slavery (chapter 8). The wicked side has some permanency in Synesius, while Gregory regards the evil of the earthly world just as a shadow we have to pass through in order to reach Divine light (*de Hominis* 21). Thus in Gregory not only soul, but the body too could be restored in the state of incorruption and spirituality. The difference between the two could hardly be greater at this particular point.

Gregory's idea of the inseparability of soul and body in their restored state of purity finds stronger conceptual roots in his rejection of the pre-existence of souls:

> If we accept that the soul lives somehow before the body, we will necessarily have to acknowledge that those insane doctrines (*dogmatopoiias*), which put soul in body, have the strength to suggest that it happens because of some vices. Nobody who is sensible enough would admit, moreover, that it happens after birth (*ephysterizein*), so that souls are newer than the created bodies. It is clear for everybody that something inanimate could not contain the moving and growing force in itself. But it is beyond doubt that the embryo in the womb demonstrates growth and movement. Nothing remains than to accept the simultaneous beginning of soul and body.
> (*de Anima et Resurrectione* 125a–c)[16]

Thus, through the words he put in the mouth of his sister Macrina, Gregory defends the simultaneous creation of body and soul. He also gives a detailed account of different critics of the Christian conception of resurrection. In *de Hominis* (especially 9.229b–233b), he restates his concept of the simultaneous creation of body and soul and their mutual existence against the theories of pre-existence (found in Platonism and the works of Origen) and some trends presuming post-existence (exemplified by Methodius of Olympus). To prove his theory, Gregory prefers to use his favourite Pauline example of the seeds, which have all features of the plant into which they later develop. Thus, as a living ensemble, soul exists in the embryo potentially and with time its potentials develop into accidentals.

Synesius, as discussed earlier, also refuses to accept the *post-existence* of the soul in relation to the body. We know well the commitment of both Gregory and Synesius against Eunomius and his followers. Gregory's famous treatises against Eunomius add more conceptual weight to the development of the Christian doctrine of Trinity, while Synesius, as bishop of Ptolemais, acts directly, and with zeal, against the Eunomeans among his congregation. Synesius' hymns are not so much a purported development from paganism to Christianity, but an advance into the Trinitarian topics with strongly anti-Arian sentiment, connected directly with his anti-Eunomean policy. Synesius maintains the Neoplatonic conception of soul's descent into bodies, in accordance with the philosophical methodology of his time, adopting the view straight from the Neoplatonic literature he had read, without explicitly supporting the soul's pre-existence with an argument, and thus entering into contradiction with the "orthodox" Christianity of the day. In that sense, Synesius kept rather a "silent presupposition" about immortality, connecting the soul with its Divine source. His views could also co-exist with the creationist theory, permeating the conceptual efforts of Christianity at the time. Concerning the way in which souls descend into bodies, however, Gregory and Synesius differ considerably, as well as in their evaluation of matter. But they fight together against the heretic view of the possible post-existence of souls, "cherished by the common people" (*Letter* 105: 188.3–5).

Let us return to *Letter* 105. After addressing the body–soul problem, Synesius makes another conceptually vital statement: "Never would I admit that the world and the parts (*t'alla merē*), which make it, must perish in a certain moment."[17] Is the scholar from Cyrene ready to defend the pagan concept of the world's eternity?

The Neoplatonists always energetically rejected the Christian view of the creation of the universe as a single and unique act of God's will. For Neoplatonists, as the pagan followers of ancient cosmogony and Plato, the creation proceeds from itself in eternity, as an out-of-time act of descent from the higher to the lower levels of existence, which is best illustrated by the ontological series of remaining (*monē*), procession (*proodos*) and return (*epistrophē*). The Christian view, however, is quite different: the world has its beginning and end in God and man could be like Him only through His blessing. In the times of Synesius and Gregory, this contradiction becomes an important divisive line between pagan philosophers and Christian theologians, despite the fact that both camps usually shared similar educational and worldly backgrounds.

Within Christian theology itself, this question is far from being solved unanimously. Origen presents ample evidence for the gravity of the dispute. The letter of Emperor Justinian I to the patriarch Menas, concerning *de Principiis* 1.2.10, implies that Origen is disposed to accept some kind of eternity of the world. He supposedly maintains the hypothesis that there are multiple worlds, changing into each other, until a final break in this chain of periodical re-establishments (*apokatastaseis*) occurs.[18] In honour of Origen's intellectual correctness and honest propriety we have to respect the fact that he does not offer a definitive answer to the question, at least not in his extant texts. Instead, he proposes three different, but plausible, hypotheses, without a conclusive commitment to any (*de Princ.* 2.3.6). The first hypothesis allows only for the material world to be definitely destroyed. The second hypothesis entertains the possibility for the material nature to be transformed into some ethereal condition, while the third postulates a full destruction of the world, together with all its elements. Faithful to the primary tenets of Christian theology, Origen is forced, as a result of the lack of an authoritative Christian Creation theory in the third century CE, to borrow from the Platonic theories of emanation, subordination and the "eternal reversal".[19] Being honest regarding his uncertainty, Origen prefers to expose different theories in order to reject the gnostic and Manichaean views alike. Both Gnostics and Manichaeans were active in the third century with concepts such as the vicious Demiurge, founder of the world, the persistence of evil, and salvation through *gnōsis* by escaping the here-in world of evil.

If Synesius defended before Theophilus heretic, and even pagan, views about the world's eternity, and even if, in Origen's spirit, he only exposed his hesitations in a time when the patriarch of Alexandria had started a real war against Origen's followers, why does he not mention the Creation itself, but does mention its (eventual) end? Why does he add, in his objection, the different "parts" that would never be destroyed? And which parts[20] does he have in mind?

According to Marrou, Synesius did express some reservations concerning the possibility of the destruction of the sun, the moon and the stars (Marrou 1963: 147). Does he, rather, mean the eternity of the *noetic* world as opposed to the material world? The latter is a plausible hypothesis, but the laconic character of the statement prevents us from drawing any definitive conclusions. All we can do is to compare this objection with his praise of the Creator and His Creation in the third hymn:

> You, Leader of the worlds, cleaned by any filth, You are the Nature of natures. You warm up the nature, the creation of things mortal, the visible images of eternity, so that even the latest part of this world receives the lot of life in its own turn. The law of God would not allow the filth of the world (*tryga tan kosmou*) to be equal with the heights of heaven. But never will perish completely (*holōs*) what has been put in order in the choir of beings,[21] so far as each one depends on another and all of them taste the benefit from their common existence. From elements destined to death, the eternal circle has been brought to life by Your breath. (Synesius, *Hymni* 3.309–32)[22]

The fragment raises many questions. The influence of Neoplatonism is noticeable, especially the hierarchical structure of beings as a result of the emanative descent. Reading between the lines, we can safely detect in the mention of *beings* Synesius' subtle reference also to *non-beings*, especially since matter is described as *non-being* everywhere in his hymns. From this, it seems that he wants to say that what really exists would never completely perish, since it has in itself a sparkle from the higher entities. However, it is not so easy to interpret the fragment because the text implies that God's breath (*pnoias*) gives life even to the mortal things destined to death (*ollymenōn*); it warms them so that they form an eternal circle (*kyklos aidios*).

De Providentia II.7 offers a clearer interpretation of the *Werdung* of events in the world. "If there is generation in the realm around us, the cause of generation is in the realm above us. It is from this source that the seeds of events arrive here."[23] The events also recur periodically, which gives the wise man opportunity to realize the truth. The idea of such cyclical movement is reminiscent of the Stoic *seminal logoi*, but it also carries connotations of Origen's *apokatastaseis*. We may suppose that those *logoi* are eternal and could therefore refer to the indestructible parts mentioned in the objection in *Letter* 105. At the end of his reflections on the cause of generation and the seeds of the events to come, Synesius is wise enough to call these doctrines myths and allegories, to defend himself against possible accusations for adopting the non-Christian or heretic theory of the *eternal reversal*.[24]

Gregory of Nyssa is less ambiguous than Synesius, and not without originality when it comes to his ideas about the end of the human race and the world we know. He generally holds on to, along with the other Cappadocians, the already established Christian understanding that since the world, created by God, has a beginning, it should logically have an end as well.[25] In *de Hominis* (chapters 23 and 24) he presents as contrary to the Christian faith the ideas about co-eternity and co-existence of matter and the Divine. Among his antagonists, referred to as the "outer philosophers", we can easily recognize pagan thinkers working out ideas from Plato and, especially as regards the eternity of matter, from Aristotle. Even more prominent seem the Manichaean dualists supporting the eternity of matter as a primordial evil principle opposed to God.

Gregory also subscribes to the intriguing theory of the double creation of man, as primordial and terrestrial (*de Hominis* 16, 29).[26] The double creation and double-life theories attempt to overcome the problem of embedding the notion of sin in godlike creatures. This problem is further enhanced by free will. We know that Gregory was not at all alien to the belief in *apokatastasis*, the rebirth of the original status of man before the primordial sin and the fall of the human race. Contrary to Origen, however, Gregory believes in restoration in bodies, although spiritualized and definitely different from the the bodies of this earthly sojourn in sin. These ideas are best illustrated in *de Anima* and *de Instituto Christiano*. His *Oratio Catechetica* (26) even presents a picture alluding to the Stoic *empyrosis* (the concept of a general conflagration leading to a "restart" of the world) by comparing the purification of gold from golden ore to the restoration of the world, in which the sinful and contemptible parts of matter are destroyed and purified into a splendid and superior nature. Thus the return to the primordial purity of man is a result of purging what is bad and has gone astray in a nature that has Divine origin.[27]

The idea of two creations seems also somehow to presuppose the pre-existence of humanity in God's mind; that is, God creates humanity first, as an idea, and not Adam personally who is created as terrestrial and already burdened with the primordial sin envisaged by God. Thus the human being comes to be a medium (*meson*) between God and the material world, and the human race becomes image of God *in toto*, along with every personal human being.[28]

Gregory also insists on the infinity of God, its All-mighty Goodness and incomprehensibility by human mind (Carabine 1992). His use of apophatic discourse purposefully poses restrictions on the human *hybris* of knowing everything by installing the Divine in the Procrustean bed of human definitions and syllogisms.[29] The *apokatastaseis* presuppose some cyclical eruptions in the traditionally linear model, adding a sense of limitlessness and infinity, found in God Himself. The *Life of Moses* demonstrates the inclination of perceiving the spiritual path upwards as something disposed in time, but also repeating itself and ultimately eternal, as stages of reality leading to the perpetual Above.

The dispute over whether the world is eternal or destructible becomes pressing in the fifth and sixth century and provokes numerous polemics, like that of John Philoponus with Proclus against the latter's arguments in favour of the world's eternity. Zacharias Scholasticus is one author within the dispute, engaged in a probably fictitious discussion with his pagan teacher, Ammonius of Alexandria, and with another anonymous opponent, introduced by the name of *Iatrosophist* (Merlan 1968: 193–203). In defence of the Christian theory of Creation and its subsequent end, Zacharias pronounces that "God is good even when destroying the visible world, so far as He does not intend to remove the cosmos away, neither to judge its full destruction, but to transform it and change it to better."[30]

For a Christian and Neoplatonist of Synesius' kind, such a thesis could be more palatable, whereas the idea of the full-scale destruction of the world would have necessarily implied the inevitable destruction of the intelligible forms as well – an absurd proposition for a pupil of the Neoplatonist Hypatia. Around the beginning of the fifth century, this view could still co-exist with the Christian orthodoxy. Synesius' objections lead in the same direction, leaving place for some kind of eternity, reserved for the immortal entities in the cosmos. In Gregory's case, all of his writings and methodology always relate to faith and to the biblical tradition, while they still leave room for the emergence of attractive images and theories from Platonism, Stoicism and Origen. Those images fit with the spirituality of a man longing for the human being's angelic status after the resurrection, when only the possibility for evil will be destroyed, and not the bodies. Through purging, evil signs and phenomena will disappear, leaving place for purified and spiritualized bodies endowed with their divinized souls.

Let us follow Synesius' third objection in *Letter* 105: "As for resurrection, which is an object of common belief, I consider it as a sacred and mysterious allegory, being far from sharing the views of the vulgar crowd thereon."[31] Provoked by both "pagans" (whatever this inaccurate term means) and by such authors as Origen and Methodius of Olympus, Gregory deals with the problem of resurrection in a rather apologetic way. The question is virtually ubiquitous in his works, but three of them are of special importance: the frequently mentioned *de Anima et Resurrectione*, *de Hominis Opificio* and *Oratio Catechetica*. His views, however, have been criticized for inconsistency.[32] One should, however, recognize his intellectual efforts to explain the phenomenon, using "pagan" criticism as a goad and a means for manoeuvring between Origen and Methodius of Olympus. He considers both of them as defenders of truth, but not the whole truth. In *de Anima*, Gregory promotes, like Synesius, a more intellectual approach to the idea of resurrection. This approach is set against the opinions of the uneducated. "The people with insufficiently trained mind, unable to see the good because of their passion for the carnal life, ruin the portion of good, otherwise immanent to their very nature, thus preserving nil of their future life" (*de Anima* 84a, my trans.).

Siding with Synesius in viewing resurrection as a Divine mystery, Gregory does not consider it as completely unexplainable. He often uses his favourite examples from human physiology or agriculture to explain, as clearly as possible, without falling into the debris of complicated terminology, the act of Divine mercy. The main goal of resurrection is the restoration of nature in its initial status (*apokatastasis*).[33] Unlike Origen's teachings, however, Gregory's view is that the resurrection happens in bodies which have been purified from every sin, without sex or age. According to that primordial status, there is no old age, no diseases or misery, nor the evil aspirations of man, since human nature used to be Divine before evil entered it. And how will the elements of a body dead long ago be gathered together for the resurrection? This question had obviously become a *topos* for both the adversaries of Christianity and the opponents of the literal acceptance of resurrection since at least the second century CE, if not from the Apostolic times. Gregory answers it by enlisting the support of St Paul's example of the seed (I Cor. 15.36–44) which, once decomposed in the soil, brings forth new life, so that every seed creates a plant according to its nature. Thus the place of soul, connected also with the *eidos*, is introduced as crucial for the development of every proper nature.

The role of *eidos* in resurrection, developed especially in *de Hominis* (27), follows to a great extent Origen and the Platonic tradition, but with an important novelty of rising above the status of the image. *Eidos* is thus the image – unchangeable, spiritual and intellectual – of the material body, imprinted in the soul. The image/idea does not change, having been shaped in some stable form, notwithstanding any changes that body could pass through. Because of this image, the individual soul keeps its inclination towards the body long after it dissolves into its composing elements, so that, at the time of resurrection, it will be able to recognize and pick up the elements needed for its restoration. To the simple allusions from everyday life and the Platonic concept of *eidos*, Gregory adds examples from the New Testament to illustrate God's omnipotence, to juxtapose them with the petty arguments of the humans.

Revisiting Synesius' statement, we should recognize that it by no means implies a mere refutation of the act of resurrection but, instead, defines it as "a sacred and mysterious allegory". *De Insomniis*, a text with clearly discernible Neoplatonic overtones and mostly based on Porphyry, affirms that principally nothing could impede, in certain conditions, the corporeal substance (*sōmatikēn ousian*) from ascending to higher "regions" or from *resurrecting* (*anastasan*) from its fallen position, and together with the soul reaching the light and the heavenly spheres (ch.10). It is thanks to *eidōlon*, the "ghostly" and debased image of the outer soul, or *pneuma*, that not only the soul, but even the lower physical elements, can enter into contact with the divine. Synesius' idea of the divine image of the corporeal elements resonates strikingly with Gregory's notion of *eidos*. The difference lies in terminology in so far as for Synesius *eidōlon* is an image of the lowest scale, a phantom, which plays a role in the ascent of the material reality. If Synesius disagrees with something concerning resurrection, it is not the essence of the concept, but its rough and vulgarized understanding of dressing oneself, again, in the ordinary, rotting flesh. His intentional defiance of the rogue naturalism in describing the resurrection of the body also shares the pathos of Origen's treatment of the subject in *de Principiis* 2.10.3. Synesius' language is predominantly (Neo)Platonic, but a similar style is also used by Gregory of Nyssa. In describing the resurrection as a recovery of the combination of elements and as a rebuilding of what has already been destroyed, Gregory emphasizes the role of the "God-seeing soul" (*theoeidēs*), striving towards its similar entities, but "covered up by body and nailed in it" (*de Anima* 76a–80a, 89b, 97a–100b). Such Neoplatonic imagery with slight elements of dualistic thinking is discernible in Synesius as well.

If we are to understand Synesius' position, additional details should be taken into consideration. The last twenty years of the fourth century were the "golden period" of the Egyptian monasticism in Nitria and Scetis. Different ideas grew in rank there. Certain Hierax of Leontopolis in the Delta refuted the resurrection of bodies completely. Origen's views concerning resurrection were interpreted in different ways. A particular trend, usually called *anthropomorphism*, became popular among the monks, especially the ones who were illiterate or otherwise insufficiently educated. God was thought to be in a human form and this conception was connected with different *chiliastic* (the doctrine that Jesus will reign on earth for a thousand years) views and expectations. Long before the appearance of the *anthropomorphites* in Egypt there was a temptation to read the text from Genesis literally and thus to presuppose that God has a human form.

There are also different interpretations among Christians, some of which envisioned man to be made in likeness to the *logos*, to Jesus Christ, and not to God the Father, thus dividing Their essence through image or subordinating them. This diversity of interpretations does not even reflect the philosophical tradition outside Christianity. The "outer", non-Christian philosophical and religious thought could accept only the original idea that the image, presumably divine in essence, exists in the intelligible realm, but not as a literal likeness of man to God. Gregory answers to all those possible, and real, objections in an interesting way. As already mentioned above, he presupposes the double creation of man as an ideal image, the celestial Adam, and the terrestrial one, with many features common with the animals, and also subject to sin. God as the Creator is completely identical with the Divine essence, while human beings are created and thus exposed to change. God is connected with eternity, man with time. The image according to God possesses eternal features, but not the second Adam who already exists in times of change and deterioration, and also in times of opportunities for improvement and salvation. The latter are subject to the free will given to this creature that otherwise leans towards the animal order. The idea of double creation, probably influenced by, if not originating from, Philo (*de Opificio*

Mundi 181), but also proposed by St Paul (I Cor. 15.45), grows into an understanding of man as a double creature with reason and intelligence coming from the direct likeness to God and the terrestrial features, including the division into sexes, corresponding to, as we saw, the animal nature after the sin. Thus the problem of man as an image of God is to a great extent solved against any possible accusations connected with the mean, animal-like elements in the human nature. Synesius is more traditionally Hellenic in his attitude towards human nature, stating that only a wise man is akin to God, thus generally defending the principle of the spiritual and intellectual activity as God-kindred.[34]

Towards the last years of Gregory's life and around the time of Synesius' studious years in Alexandria, the problem of the Divine image became acute in Egypt, and not only there. A serious conflict arose between the "intellectuals" and the "villagers" among the monks, a conflict that to a great extent coincided with the traditional misunderstanding between the Copts and the Hellenized (and also Romanized) *foreigners*. In his Pascal letter for the year 399, the patriarch of Alexandria, Theophilus, a friend and supporter of Synesius, ultimately forbade the theory of anthropomorphism as a wrong and heretical infatuation. This letter was accepted openly by the "intellectuals", but unfavourably by the *anthropomorphites* (Chitty 1966: 53–4; Declerck 1984; Meinardus 2003: 53–4). Synesius was a witness of those events and, as far as we know from his *Dio, or How to Live According to His Ideal*, had a clear sight on the Egyptian monasticism. In the aforementioned treatise, the future bishop of Ptolemais shows himself as a man with intellectual affiliations, always with an emphasis on the priority of the rational approach to knowledge and imitation of the Divine. The anthropomorphism together with the overtly graphic physical notions of resurrection are always unacceptable for him, being a part of what he usually calls "vulgar conceptions". That there are many common features between Augustine and Synesius should not come to us as a surprise. Augustine himself confesses that he has thought of God in human form for a long time and only his occupation with philosophy has made him change his wrong view, popular among the ordinary people (*Confessiones* 7.1.1). The man from Cyrene never made such a mistake. He was a loyal Christian, but also an elitarian intellectual, aspiring to be a philosopher more than anything else.[35]

In conclusion, we have no reason to regard the three objections of Synesius in his *Letter* 105 as a testimony for his formal belonging to "paganism", neither can we consider his way of thinking as incompatible with Christianity.[36] It is important to stress, again, that these objections did not stop Theophilus for actively promoting Synesius to be ordained as a bishop. Synesius represents the highly educated intellectual strata in the Christian Church at that time. He was a literary elitist, often using relatively new Judaic and Christian terminology in a combination with Classical, sometimes too archaic, Greek terms in religious and philosophical poetry, including the outdated Doric dialect. People with his educational background were not prone to abandon the Neoplatonic modes of thought and behaviour. In their own enriching way, they took part in the formation of a refined philosophical and theological system, which reached its perfection in the next few centuries. Through his *Hymns* and *Letters*, the intellectual from Cyrene joins the pioneers of the just forming post-Nicaean orthodoxy. His writings reveal not only commitment, but also a deep knowledge of the essence of the problems. Notwithstanding his (Neo)Platonic background and affiliations, Synesius was a Christian, interested in the deep foundations of faith, probably not so profoundly in the pure theology as the Cappadocians were, yet an active supporter of the union between faith, Empire and civilization.

It is difficult, if not impossible, to present a picture of a developed system of theological views in any author from the period under discussion. Their writings are composed in response to a certain problem, or to clarify a certain doctrine, by using different styles, approaches and even sources depending on the purpose of the work. This is true for Synesius and even more for Gregory of Nyssa. Gregory never sounds completely the same, and his style always directly reflects the objectives of his work. It is one thing to attack Eunomius on the doctrine of the hypostases of Trinity, another to defend the co-existence of soul against those presupposing its pre- or post-existence, or to defend in general the Orthodox faith against a many-faced mass of enemies in his *Oratio Catechetica*. Gregory knew the dialogues of Plato, from the *Phaedrus* and the *Timaeus* to the *Sophist* and the *Cratylus*, as well as Plotinus and probably Porphyry. He knew the Stoic tradition and the exegetic style of Philo of Alexandria who came to be his model for writing allegorically. He kept the division between the physical and the intellectual, uncreated Divine essence. Joining the mainstream Neoplatonists, he used the apophatic method to define God as Good and evil as non-entity. And yet, Gregory was not a Neoplatonic philosopher, neither was he eager to be considered one. His Trinitarian theology stands far from the emanational theory of Neoplatonism. Although supporting the non-dimensionality and transcendency of soul and the notion of *eidos* as a constituting factor of keeping dispersed objects together, he did believe in the resurrection in body, not getting upward, out of the body, as in Plotinus (*Enn.* III.6[26].6; IV.8[6].1). For Gregory, physical matter is a part of the Salvation plan, not just an escape of the higher entities from non-being and evil. His view of the soul–body connection is stronger than the Platonic philosophical tradition could ever presume. The ideas of evolutionism, creationism and individuation are not very compatible with the philosophical trends in the so-called "paganism". His anthropocentric spiritualism, together with the central role of free will, is so specifically Christian that it could hardly have any meaning outside his faith.

Both Gregory and Synesius became bishops at a certain time in their lives, to a great extent unwillingly, but with a clear sense of duty. It is difficult to say which one was more successful; their obligations and problems were close to ruining them both.[37] We could add to the same group Nemesius as well, although we know nearly nothing about him, except that he probably had some medical expertise, which could be an additional reason for his election. The three of them belong to the same intellectual type, lacking some of the Christo-centric attitude and warmth characteristic of many other teachers of the Church. Yet they were probably not philosophers *par excellence* either. But they had in common the philosophical adjustment of mind, not completely devoid of practical issues at hand, ready to solve theological problems with the armament of the rational soul, alienated from the uproar of the uneducated crowd.

NOTES

1. For the earlier scholarship, see Cherniss (1930), Daniélou (1944) and Jaeger (1966), together with the writings of von Balthasar (1995) and Meredith (1999). See also the editions of Gregory's writings, namely *Patrologia Graeca*, vols 44–6, along with the Brill series of editions by Jaeger *et al.*(1960–98) onwards, as well as the French translations in *Sources chrétiennes*.
2. I would specially point to the views of Crawford (1901), Lacombrade (1951) and also Bregman (1982) as the most explicit examples of viewing Synesius as a predominantly pagan thinker.

3. Lacombrade (1951); Wallis (1972: 101–5). Bregman (1982) slightly exaggerates Synesius' "pro-pagan" and pro-Platonic inclination and (1997) presents Synesius as "a religious Neoplatonist". Roos (1991) makes a challenging attempt at a psychological portrait; Barbanti (1994: 114–48) emphasizes the pagan language and content of the hymns; Vollenweider (1984) recognizes in Synesius an endeavour to mould a theological system of thought.

4. Hereinafter the English translation of Synesius' letters and hymns is according to Fitzgerald (1926) and Fitzgerald & Milford (1930), with slight alterations and in consultation with Garzya's full edition of Synesius in an Italian translation (1989). References are made to both the older edition of the epistles by Garzya (1979) and the new edition by Garzya & Roques (2003). For *Letter* 105, see Garzya (1979: 184–90).

5. *Letter* 105 188.5–6: Ἀμέλει τὴν ψυχὴν οὐκ ἀξιώσω ποτὲ σώματος ὑστηρογενῆ νομίζειν.

6. I prefer to put "pagan" in quotation marks so far as the notion was used by (some) Christians to denominate their adversaries with quite different origins, profiles and worldviews.

7. See Origen, *Cels.* 5.14; Porphyry, *Chr.* 94; Augustine, *de Civ. Dei* 10.31. See also Genesis 2:7.

8. For Porphyry's *Sententiae*, see the Teubner edition of Lamberz (1975).

9. Volkmann (1869: 208–17). For Gregory of Nyssa' possible indebtedness to Origen, see Ludlow (2002: 45–66) and Meredith (1999: 344–56).

10. We could find a certain kind of "defence" of Origen from the point of orthodoxy in Crouzel (1989) and from the point of his Platonism in Dillon (1992a).

11. Traducianism: the immaterial aspect of human being, the soul, is transmitted through natural generation along with the body; that is, human beings are propagated as whole beings. Creationism: God specially creates a new soul *ex nihilo* when a human being is conceived.

12. *Patrologia Graeca* vol. 40.572–90, 595–6. See also Morani's edition of *de Natura Hominis*.

13. See the medieval solutions and their indebtedness to the late antique tradition in Nauta (1996).

14. Peroli (1997); Meredith (1999: 15–26); M. R. Barnes (2002: 475–90); Moreschini (2004; 2008: esp. 160–210); and see Ayres (2002), concerning the Trinitarian polemic along with a considerable list of literature.

15. In some sense, Synesius shows a form of elitism, which refuses to a great extent salvation to the souls of the uneducated mob estranged from the higher realities.

16. Translation mine. Here Gregory obliquely disputes with a passage from Origen's *Cels.* 3.75. See also Ludlow (2002).

17. *Letter* 105 188.6–7: Τὸν κόσμον οὐ φήσω καὶ τἆλλα μέρη συνδιαφθείρεσθαι.

18. *De Princ.* 1.6.2–3; 2.3.1; 3.5, based on Isaiah 66:22 and Ecclesiastes 1:9–10.

19. See von Ivanka (1992: 110–13); Dillon (1991: xxi; 1992) on the influence of Middle Platonism on Origen and some parallels with the respective interpretations of Proclus two centuries later in the *Elements of Theology*; Stead (1981) on Origen and the Cappadocian Fathers. See also Weber (1962) for the two Origens.

20. *Letter* 105 188.6: Καὶ τἆλλα μέρη.

21. Synesius uses "beings" (ὄντων, gen. pl.), which specifically denote existence as opposed to non-beings.

22. Translation is mine, from the edition of Garzya, with some parallels to Fitzgerald & Milford (1930).

23. Εἰ δὲ γένεσις ἐν τοῖς περὶ ἡμᾶς, αἰτία γενέσεως ἐν τοῖς ὑπὲρ ἡμᾶς, κἀκεῖθεν ἐνταῦθα καθήκει τὰ τῶν συμβαινόντων σπέρματα.

24. Here we could compare Synesius' tentative deliberations on the non-destructibility of the Divine particles, souls included, to Nemesius' opinion that it is unwise to presume the end of everything at the time of completion if one bears in mind the resurrected souls (*de Nat. Hom.* 2.46 [573a]).

25. Basil the Great, *Homiliae in Hexaemeron* 1.4; Gregory of Nyssa, *de Hominis* 23.209b.

26. It is not easy to determine whether the theory is developed under Platonic influence, through Philo, or as a form of homage to Origen.

27. Compare with *de Hominis* 27.228c for a similar example and also with *de Anima* 148a.

28. The ambiguity that all together are an image of God, and that each person also is an image of God was embedded in Gregory's thought – it is a combination of the Neoplatonic idea of humanity as an abstract notion existing in God and the biblical story of the creation of the first individuals. Every individual, however, has something from the Divine idea of humanity *in toto*.

29. For the earlier origins of this method of thinking, see van den Berg (Chapter 16), above.

30. *Discussion with the Iatrosophist* 2.516–729, my trans. See Colonna (1973).

31. *Letter* 105 188.7–9: Τὴν καθωμιλημένην ἀνάστασιν ἱερόν τι καὶ ἀπόρρητον ἥγημαι, καὶ πολλοῦ δέω ταῖς τοῦ πλήθους ὑπολήψεσιν ὁμολογῆσαι.

32. Bynum (1995: 59–86). Dennis (1981) divides Gregory's ideas into two periods, distinguishing between an

early more Platonic or Origenist period and a later period which supports the idea of bodily resurrection. For the philosophical language used by Gregory, see Stead (1976); for the role of the *apokatastasis* theory in the Christianity of the age, see Riggs (2006).

33. *De Anima* 148a; *de Hominis* 25–7; *Oratio Catechetica* 26. For the soul in Plotinus, see also Blumenthal (1993b: III).

34. *De Insomniis* 1: οἰκεῖος θεῷ.

35. This elitarian attitude could be summarized in his rhetorical question in *Letter* 105 (189.5): "What can there be in common between the ordinary people and philosophy?"(Δήμῳ γὰρ δὴ φιλοσοφίᾳ τί πρὸς ἄλληλα).

36 Whether it is possible, if at all, to talk about Christian Platonism, or if it is a technical term for something which does not really exist, see arguments and discussions in de Vogel (1953); Armstrong (1979: xxii); McEvoy (1992); Blumenthal (1993b: i); Stead (1994: 79–159) and Rist (1996: 386–409), among many others.

37. For the different roles and functions of bishops in this period, see Rapp (2005).

33

Islamic and Jewish Neoplatonisms

Sarah Pessin

Following in the tradition of Greek Neoplatonism, Islamic and Jewish Neoplatonisms reflect on the relation between the divine source and the human subject through the intermediation of a number of emanating hypostases (namely one or more universal intellects, and one or more universal souls).[1] Looking at some representative figures, we find among Islamic Neoplatonists such thinkers as al-Kindi, al-Farabi, the *Ikhwān aṣ-Ṣafā'* (the Brethren of Purity), Avicenna (Ibn Sina), Ibn Tufayl and Suhrawardi, and we find among Jewish Neoplatonists such thinkers as Isaac Israeli, Ibn Gabirol, Ibn Ezra, Moses Maimonides, Ibn Ḥasday and Yoḥanan Alemanno. In terms of language, we might note that a good deal of Islamic and Jewish Neoplatonism is written in Arabic (including Judeo-Arabic), though there are also classic works of Islamic Neoplatonism in Persian, and classic works of Jewish Neoplatonism in Hebrew (and Aramaic if one considers the *Zohar* to be part of the Jewish Neoplatonic tradition). The transmission of Greek Neoplatonism into Islamic and Jewish contexts is a complex story suggesting vestiges of Pythagorean, Platonic, Aristotelian, Stoic, Plotinian, Proclean, Pseudo-Empedoclean and other influences, with many details still uncertain. Adding to the complexity, Islamic and Jewish Neoplatonisms also often reveal ideas and imagery drawn from Islamic and Jewish scriptural, legal, theological and mystical traditions.

There are two Arabic texts in particular that play especially central roles in the Greek-into-Arabic transmission, namely the *Theology of Aristotle* and the *Kalām fī maḥḍ al-khair* (*The Book of the Pure Good*). Jointly bringing Greek Neoplatonism into Islamic and Jewish contexts, the *Theology of Aristotle* is an edited version of books IV–VI of Plotinus' *Enneads* (and part of a broader set of "Arabic Plotinus" materials), while the *Kalām fī maḥḍ al-khair* is an edited version of parts of Proclus' *Elements of Theology* (and lives on as the *Liber de Causis* (*Book of Causes*) in its later Latin reception).[2]

Turning to philosophical-theological content, we may note that like Greek Neoplatonists, Islamic and Jewish Neoplatonists envision a processive emanation at the heart of reality, alongside a jointly epistemological and ethical call to "return to Intellect", which is to say, to strive towards wisdom and goodness. That said, we may point to five *prima facie* points of difference (or at least differences in conceptual emphasis) between Islamic and Jewish Neoplatonism on the one hand and Greek Neoplatonism on the other; considering Islamic and Jewish Neoplatonisms, we may note that:

1. They sometimes engage the language of creation (in ways that Greek Neoplatonism does not), including the language of "Divine Will", especially in describing the relationship between God and the first being/s.
2. They describe God in terms of pure being and – with exceptions in such texts at the *Theology of Aristotle* and *Kalām fī maḥḍ al-khair* – in terms of pure intellect (as opposed to the emphasis on the One's being *beyond* being and intellect that we find, for example, in Plotinus).
3. They sometimes speak of a first Intellect outside of God as a "first created being".
4. They sometimes speak of an additional principle of "first matter" (sometimes in addition to "first form") before even the onset of Intellect (see § "Matter's dual identity").
5. They envision the "return to Intellect" in terms of an "*ittiṣāl*" (literally, "conjunction") between the human intellect and the cosmic universal intellect. This "conjunction" is sometimes with a first intellect outside of God, and sometimes – as in cases of more Aristotelianized Neoplatonic Islamic and Jewish thinkers – with a tenth intellect outside God (itself known as the "Active Intellect", and based [at least in some interpretive sense] on Aristotle's remarks at *de Anima* 3.5).[3]

By way of introduction, it is also important to bear in mind that in their engagement with the very essence of being, all Neoplatonists dance and wrestle with language, giving voice to a range of creative and difficult metaphors and conjuring up a range of creative and difficult imageries. Self-consciously aware of the limits of human reason, and self-consciously aware that their spatio-temporal metaphors mean to convey truths which are neither spatial nor temporal, the Neoplatonist overtly enters into an apophatic register, using language to draw us closer to ultimate truths while at the same time beckoning to language's inadequacies to the task at hand. For this reason, it is especially critical for any reader of Neoplatonism – Greek, Islamic, Jewish or otherwise – to take special care to avoid drawing too-quick conclusions about a given Neoplatonist's beliefs from a surface consideration of their language. Mindful of the apophatic undertone of the Neoplatonic enterprise, it is advisable to adopt a spirit of humility when approaching these texts, avoiding calcified (and/or overly simplistic) final conclusions about metaphorical claims that aim to engage the very deepest truths of human and divine life. In this spirit, when setting out to interpret any text of Neoplatonism, it is worth considering (a) whether there is an underlying prescriptive force in even the apparently descriptive accounts of cosmo-ontology, (b) to what extent Neoplatonic texts are aimed at enacting transformational experiences in their readers, and (c) what implications the answers to these questions ought to have for how we ultimately interpret these texts.

While this chapter does not explore these questions,[4] it does traverse some of the paths of Islamic and Jewish Neoplatonisms from the following starting points:

- Creation, emanation, divine will and divine sovereignty;
- On the threefold process of emanation;

- Three paradoxes of descent;
  - God without jealousy: on the paradox of unity's bounty (or: On God's descent);
  - Audacious servitude and rhetorics of rebellion and redemption: on the paradox of soul (or: On soul's descent);
  - Lights and shadows: on the paradox of emanation (or: On reality's descent);
- Turning and returning;
- Love, desire, being;
- Matter's dual identity; and
- On the goal of being a good person.

CREATION, EMANATION, DIVINE WILL AND DIVINE SOVEREIGNTY

We have already noted that Islamic and Jewish Neoplatonisms are often contrasted with Greek Neoplatonism for their emphasis on God's role as a creator. However, among those Islamic and Jewish Neoplatonists who talk of creation, it is often, if not always, the case that creation is consistent with (or simply refers to) standard Greek emanation.[5] For example, the *Theology of Aristotle* speaks of God as a creator and as a reality that "gushes forth",[6] going on to emphasize that God's act of creation (a) is not in time, and (b) is not a reasoned activity (and is in that respect not an act of choice), but is rather something that arises "merely by the fact of his being".[7] In the *Theology of Aristotle*, the act of creation is itself the emanation of being from God, seen first and foremost in the emanation of Intellect from God.

In this spirit, we ought to approach Islamic and Jewish Neoplatonisms with a starting sense that claims of creation can be perfectly consistent with claims of emanation, and that there would be – for most of these thinkers – nothing impious or odd in jointly holding that God and the world are co-eternal, that being eternally emanates from God, *and* that God is the sovereign Creator. Supporting this generally fluid set of intuitions about creation, emanation and divine sovereignty, we might note that within Islamic tradition, the *Quran* describes God's creation sometimes in ways that suggest creation *ex nihilo*, but sometimes in ways that suggest creation *ex aliquo* (thus suggesting the eternal co-existence with God of other realities), and within the Jewish tradition, the Hebrew Bible's opening claim about creation (Genesis 1:1) carries with it a wealth of Rabbinic, Midrashic, mystical and philosophical interpretations, many of which overtly read "creation" as an eternal (and in some cases, an eternally emanating) process. As such, in Islamic and Jewish contexts, "creation" need not imply a beginning in time, need not imply a choice between alternatives, need not imply the absence of other co-eternal realities, and can – for any or all of these reasons – be read perfectly consistently in terms of an eternal process, an eternal process co-eternal with other realities, and even an eternal process of emanation.[8]

In such contexts, divine sovereignty is best thought of in terms of: (a) God's eternal role as the ontological root and sustaining cause of the world's being and of the being of all beings, and (b) the eternally undiminished power and presence of God in the being of all beings even in spite of the many intermediaries involved in the process. As the ontological (as opposed to temporal) source of being in all beings, the Sovereign Emanating God of (some) Islamic and Jewish Neoplatonisms eternally gives forth His goodness. Moving a step *away from* various "orthodox"[9] senses of creation, the Sovereign Emanating God of (some) Islamic and Jewish Neoplatonisms can't help but overflow His Goodness forward

and is in this respect unlike the God of Augustine and al-Ghazali, whose theologies of creation and Divine Will emphasize a kind of divine "freedom to choose between alternatives"
(a philosophical idea associated with *proairesis* or *al-ikhtiyār*).[10] Moving a step *closer to*
various "orthodox" senses of creation, the Sovereign Emanating God of (some) Islamic and
Jewish Neoplatonisms is a cause of being, and is in this respect unlike Aristotle's eternal
First Unmoved Mover who is only a cause of change and motion.

The idea of God's sovereignty as an ontological (as opposed to temporal) grounding
role can be found in many Islamic and Jewish Neoplatonic contexts, including Avicenna's
description of God as the Necessary of Existence upon whom all non-God beings rely for
their existence (see *The Metaphysics of al-Shifā'* I.6–7; Marmura 2005: 29–38). The idea of
God's sovereignty as an undiminished presence can be found in many Islamic and Jewish
Neoplatonic contexts, including the *Kalām fī maḥḍ al-khair*: after depicting God as the
unity of "Pure Being" (or "Being Only") who gives being to all things and life to all living
things "by way of creation"[11] (an act also described as the "infusing" of things with goodness), God's causal power is described as undiminishing, and His power in all things is
described as complete *even in light of the mediation of intermediaries*. God's power is seen
as permeating all things as He is, *qua* first cause, the source of all being and goodness.[12]

In spite of the fact that such Neoplatonic texts as the *Theology of Aristotle* present
creation and divine sovereignty alongside talk of eternal emanation, scholars nonetheless
often read Neoplatonic claims about creation – and about Divine Will – as indicating the
rejection of Plotinian divine emanation. Examples of this can be seen in the history of
scholarship on Isaac Israeli and Solomon Ibn Gabirol.[13] In opposition to this scholarly
trend, I have argued elsewhere for reading creation in Israeli and Divine Will in Ibn
Gabirol as perfectly consistent with – and as in fact illustrative of – Plotinian emanation
in these Jewish Neoplatonic thinkers (Pessin 2012b, 2013, 2014).

ON THE THREEFOLD PROCESS OF EMANATION

Following on a blend of emanationist imagery in *Enneads* IV–VI,[14] the *Theology of Aristotle*
envisions God as the emanating good who pours forward into an emanating Intellect.[15]
This image – together with the use of the Arabic term "*fayḍ*" (emanation, overflow) – features prominently in Islamic and Jewish Neoplatonism.

The process of emanation in its Greek as well as its Islamic and Jewish contexts carries
at least three threefold elements. First, there is the Neoplatonic triad of hypostases, namely
the One (or God), Universal Intellect (and in more Aristotelianized Neoplatonic schools of
Islamic and Jewish philosophy, ten Intellects), and Soul (and in some Islamic and Jewish
contexts, three Souls). Second, there is also the somewhat more subtle tripart description
of the emanatory unfolding from any one level of reality to the next in a way that often
emphasizes three causal "moments" of each reality (often categorized – and amplified
within Proclean Greek Neoplatonism – in terms of Remaining, Procession and Reversion)
(see Gersh 1978; for application to Ibn Gabirol, see Pessin 2013). Third, we find emphasis
on "three moments" in the particular move from God's pure unity to the unity of Intellect.
This can be seen in Plotinus' own description of the rise of Intellect from the One in terms
of a "first moment" in which Intellect "turns back upon the One and is filled, and becomes
Intellect by looking towards it" which is itself seen in terms of "two moments", namely

Intellect's "halt and turning toward the One" which constitutes being and its "gaze upon the One" which constitutes Intellect (*Enn.* V.2[11].1, trans. Armstrong).

It is in this spirit that we might approach the idea, found in a number of Islamic and Jewish Neoplatonic traditions, of the cosmic overflow in three steps. Turning to al-Farabi, we find:

> The First [i.e. God] is that from which everything which exists comes into exist-ence. … The genesis of that which comes into existence from it takes place by way of an emanation (*fayḍ*), the existence of which is due to the existence of something else, so that the existence of something different from the First emanates from the First's existence.   (al-Farabi, *Perfect State* 1.2.1, trans. Walzer)

Going on to elaborate the unfolding of the universe from God, the First Intellect, al-Farabi describes the emanation of ten Intellects from the First, explaining how the dual intel-lection of each of these Intellects (intellection of its own essence on the one hand, and intellection of God on the other) in turn results in the coming into being of (a) a heaven or celestial sphere, and (b) the Intellect below it:

> From the First emanates the existence of the Second. This Second is, again, an utterly incorporeal substance, and is not in matter. It thinks of its own essence and thinks the First. What it thinks of its own essence is no more than its essence. As a result of its thinking of the First, a third existent follows necessarily from it; and as a result of its substantification in its specific essence, the existence of the First Heaven follows necessarily. The existence of the Third, again, is not in matter, its substance is intellect, and it thinks its own essence and thinks the First. As a result of its substantification in its specific essence, the existence of the sphere of the fixed stars follows necessarily, and as a result of its thinking of the First, a fourth existence follows necessarily.   (al-Farabi, *Perfect State* 2.3.1–2, trans. Walzer)

And so on until we arrive at the last intellect, namely the "Active Intellect" with which the human soul seeks to "conjoin".[16]

We can discern these same tripart themes in a range of Islamic and Jewish Neoplatonisms, sometimes (as above) with a focus on ten Intellects with the lowest of those Intellects as the one to which the human soul aims to connect, and sometimes with a focus instead on the emergence of a "first created Intellect" as the supernal end-goal of the Neoplatonic Return.

THREE PARADOXES OF DESCENT

God without jealousy: on the paradox of unity's bounty (or: On God's descent)

A key concept for Neoplatonists is the paradox of God's unity-with-plurality (what I have elsewhere called the Paradox of Divine Unity; see Pessin 2013). On the one hand, God's purity is a unity of God-with-God. On the other hand, God's purity also involves being a God-with-World, which is to say, God's ownmost radical unity is also the source of the universe's bounty of plurality. This is especially heightened in Islamic and Jewish Neoplatonic contexts where God takes on characteristics of both the Plotinian One and

Intellect: whereas Plotinus talks of the One as a Goodness "above/beyond Being" and above the reality of Intellect, Islamic and Jewish Neoplatonists talk of God in terms of Pure Goodness, Pure Being and – sometimes – Pure Intellect.

Alongside talk of God's unity and talk of His role as the ontological source and sustaining cause of plurality, we find Islamic and Jewish Neoplatonic descriptions of God's relation to plurality (seen first in the unity-plurality of Intellect) in particularly evocative terms of repose and generosity. In this spirit, the *Theology of Aristotle* speaks of the dynamic relation between God's unity and the cosmic plurality in terms of an intense restfulness: "The true One originates the identity (*hūwiyya*) of Intellect because of the intensity of its repose (*shidda sukūnihi*)" (*Theology of Aristotle*, chapter 10, trans. Lewis with my revisions: 293; Arabic at Badawi 1955: 135, ll. 12–13). Pointing us to the loving nature of God in this relation to plurality, al-Farabi emphasizes God's generosity in flowing forth: "Inasmuch as the substance of the First is a substance from which all the existents emanate, while it does not neglect any existence beneath its existence, it is generous, and its generosity is in its substance" (al-Farabi, *On the Perfect State* 1.2, trans. Walzer).

It is arguably in this spirit that Moses Maimonides, in his *Guide of the Perplexed*, reflects repeatedly on God's loving kindness (*ḥesed*). Reflecting further on God's generous nature as giver, Suhrawardi notes:

> Generosity (*al-jūd*) is giving that which is appropriate without any recompense. The one who seeks praise or reward works for a wage, as does the one who seeks to be free of blame and the like. But there is nothing more generous than that which is light in its own reality. By its essence, it reveals itself to and emanates upon every receptive one. The True King is He who possesses the essence of everything but whose essence is possessed by none. He is the Light of Lights.
> (*The Philosophy of Illumination*, part 2, discourse 2, section 5:144;
> Walbridge & Ziai 1999: 96)

Looking at this emphasis on God's grace[17] in these Islamic and Jewish Neoplatonic contexts, we may trace a trajectory to Plato's description of a "God without jealousy" in the *Timaeus*:

> Let us, then, state for what reason becoming and this universe were framed by him who framed them. He was good; and in the good no jealousy (*phthonos*) in any matter can ever arise. So, being without jealousy, he desired that all things should come as near as possible to being like himself.   (*Ti.* 29e, trans. Cornford)

This idea of the gracious giving God follows through into Plotinus' own thought:

> Now when anything else comes to perfection we see that it produces and does not endure to remain by itself, but makes something else. … How then could the most perfect, the first Good, remain in itself as if it grudged (*phthonēsan*) to give of itself?   (*Enn.* V.4[7].1; cf. IV.8[6].6)

Emphasizing the unity of a divine emanating source of being, Plotinus' own text ties together the idea of God's unity with the ideas of God's essential repose and gracious generosity. This tripart sensibility extends across Islamic and Jewish Neoplatonic descriptions of God, and it also extends to their descriptions of Intellect and Soul, as can be seen in the *Theology of Aristotle*'s description of Intellect's giving forth without "fatigue, toil or sadness",[18] and Soul's giving forth "without fatigue or toil".[19]

Sensitive to the paradox of at once embracing God as a pure unity-at-rest-with-Himself and as a pure unity-in-action-towards-plurality, Islamic and Jewish Neoplatonists adopt a range of metaphorical and other apophatic strategies for reflecting on God and being. As we have seen, some employ terms of divine creation (or creation *ex nihilo*), some terms of emanation, and some terms of creation and/as emanation. What is important to consider in approaching any of these terminologies is the extent to which Neoplatonic cosmogenies are, at least in part, apophatic engagements with the paradox of God's unity-with-plurality. As apophatic strategy, Neoplatonic talk of "creation" and/or "emanation" must be read very differently from claims made within the context of, for example, geography where language is used in a more straightforwardly denotative (and non-apophatic) way. Attempts to understand and/or critique Islamic and Jewish Neoplatonic descriptions of creation or emanation must be sensitive to the apophatic nature and end-goals of Neoplatonic language, including cosmogenic language.[20]

Audacious servitude and rhetorics of rebellion and redemption: on the paradox of soul (or: On soul's descent)

Neoplatonists are also deeply moved by the paradoxical human condition that we might, following Armstrong, call "Double Selfhood".[21] Mirroring God's own paradoxical duality as unity-in-unity and unity-in-plurality, the human being is at once rooted in her higher source in Intellect (in this respect she is grounded in unity) and yet she is also far away from that source (in this respect she is grounded in plurality). While more Aristotelian-minded philosophers reduce this insight to a simple claim about potency ("we all have the potential to actualize intellect more fully"), Neoplatonists embrace the claim about rootedness-in-Intellect and distance-from-Intellect as a paradox: we are two opposing selves – we are at once in Intellect and fallen from it. Appreciating the paradoxical approach to selfhood in Neoplatonism allows us also to better appreciate the various linguistic and dialectical strategies that Neoplatonists develop around this topic.

Amplifying this sense of human complexity, we find a dual focus on the state of soul more generally as at once a blessing and a failure. Emphasizing the sense of blessing, we might note the strong emphasis within Neoplatonic emanation contexts on all realities, including souls, being the outpouring of the perfect Universal Intellect (itself born of God Himself). In this sense we may speak of souls in rather elevated – we might even say, redemptive – terms of light, wisdom, unity and perfection. Emphasizing, however, the sense of failure, consider Plotinus on the audacity of souls:

> What is it, then, which has made the souls forget their father, God, and be ignorant of themselves and him, even though they are parts which come from his higher world and altogether belong to it? The beginning of evil for them was audacity (*tolma*) ... and the wishing to belong to themselves.
>
> (*Enn.* V.1[10].1)

In reflecting on the soul's sojourn in the prison of corporeality (a theme already found in Plato, and echoed too in the *Theology of Aristotle*), Plotinus speaks of the soul's audacity: a recalcitrant turning away from God as father. Alongside this emphasis on rebellion, Plotinus also at times talks more neutrally of soul's descent; in this respect, we find what we might call a "rhetoric of rebellion" alongside a far more neutral description of soul's earthly sojourn, itself alongside the overarching redemptive sense that all things are born of Intellect.

Turning to Islamic and Jewish Neoplatonisms, we find an even more pronounced contrast between a "rhetoric of rebellion" on the one hand, and a "rhetoric of redemption" on the other. Looking to the *Theology of Aristotle*, for example, we find descriptions of soul's descent in terms of heedlessness, recklessness, error and sin. On the other hand, we also find the sentiment that God has sent soul to the realm of nature so as to bring to this lower world some vestige of Intellect's own wisdom, beauty and order. Following from God's own goodness and sent by God as part of his own design, soul's descent is described here no longer merely as an act of rebellion, but in lofty, noble, redemptive terms: "We say that, although the noble lordly soul has left her high world and descended to this low world, she did that by an aspect of her high ability and power, in order to give form to and to administer the essence that is after her" (*Theology of Aristotle*, chapter 7, trans. Lewis: 243; Arabic at Badawi 1955: 84, ll. 1–3). In this spirit, soul is described as that which "expend[s] her powers on it [viz. this world] and manifest[s] her resident [or, latent; Ar. *al-sākina*] noble deeds and acts that were within her when she was in the world of Intellect" (*ibid.*: trans. Lewis: 243 with my revisions; Arabic at Badawi 1955: 84, ll. 5–6).

And through an evocative language of overflow and desire that mirrors the very process of divine creation itself, we learn of soul that

> when the soul is filled with light and power and the other virtues, she cannot stand still in herself, because those virtues in her are the awakening of her desire [*al-tashwīq*] for action. So she travels down, not travelling up because Intellect does not need any of her virtues, for it is the cause of her virtues. Since she cannot travel up she travels down and pours forth of her light and her other virtues on whatever is beneath her, and fills this world with light and beauty and splendour.   (*Theology of Aristotle, chapter 7,* trans. Lewis with my revisions: 249;
> Arabic at Badawi 1955: 89, ll. 12–16)

Similarly emphasizing soul's bringing to nature the gift of right guidance, the *Kalām fī maḥḍ al-khair* notes: "For it is characteristic of soul that it give life to bodies, since it infused them with its power, and also [that] it guide them to the right activity" (*Kalām fī maḥḍ al-khair*, prop. 3, trans. Guagliardo *et al.*; for Arabic, see Bardenhewer 1882: 64)

In this respect, the text speaks too of the "noble soul" and its "divine activity"; serving as a conduit between God (mediated by Intellect) and nature, soul infuses nature with something of the higher power, nudging it towards right action by providing it access to the final cause of goodness.

Lights and shadows: on the paradox of emanation (or: On reality's descent)

Alongside the paradoxical encounter with God as pure unity and source of being, the paradoxical encounter with souls as audacious and noble, and the paradoxical encounter with human being as grounded-in-Intellect and fallen-from-Intellect, the Neoplatonist can be understood as seeing the vestige of paradox in the very fabric of being itself. This can be seen (a) in reflections on the *culmination* of emanation – in the natural world – in terms of the reality of form (as a vestige of light) intermingled with matter (as a privative marker of darkness), and (b) in reflections on even the very essence of emanation, even in its very starting moment of Intellect, not only as a downward effluence of light, but also – in a particular subcategory of Islamic and Jewish Neoplatonists – as a downward proliferation of shadows.

The first insight, about form and matter, can be found in all Neoplatonists, and is explored in especially evocative terms in Avicenna's *Ḥayy Ibn Yaqẓān* (*Alive, Son of Awake*). There Avicenna describes the human soul's journey as an eastward journey to the light. Describing a journey to the innermost chamber of the king's palace theorized as a place beyond the easternmost East, the *Ḥayy* imagery develops a strong link between enlightenment, forms, intellect and light: a journey bringing us towards (even if ultimately beyond) the site of sunrise. In this context, darkness is associated with bodies and matter. Whether taken allegorically or symbolically,[22] this Avicennan text resonates with images of light and dark, and links images of light with the goal of enlightenment, form and goodness, and images of darkness with the vicissitudes of embodiment.

In spite of his critiques of Avicennan and other more Aristotelian-inspired thought, Suhrawardi reflects a similar aligning of lights with God and form, and of darkness with body, described by him as a "*barzakh*", or barrier, and also as a veil,[23] an image which resonates with a number of Jewish Neoplatonic descriptions, including Moses Maimonides' description of matter as a "strong veil".[24]

Illustrating our second insight about the very essence of Intellect itself (and as such, emanation itself) as involving darkness, Suhrawardi also uses light *and* dark terms to describe Intellect's turning to reflect upon God, the Light of Lights:

> Its intellection of its dependence is a dark state; but it beholds the Light of Lights and beholds its own essence. ... Thus, by that whereby [an incorporeal light] beholds the Light of Lights, it shadows and darkens itself in comparison to It. ... By the manifestation to itself of its dependence and the darkening of its own essence in its contemplation of the glory of the Light of Lights in relation to itself, a shadow (*ẓill*) results from [the incorporeal light].
>
> (*Philosophy of Illumination*, part 2, discourse 2, section 4:142;
> Walbridge & Ziai 1999: 95)

We also find a sensitivity to the unfolding of spiritual reality (souls and intellects) as a play of light-with-shadows in Isaac Israeli's ninth–tenth-century elaboration of rays and shades:

> the form of nature and its specificality which establishes its essence is brought into being from the shade (*fai'*) of the ... soul and its ray (*shu'ā'*, lit. rays). ... The form of the ... soul is brought into being from the shade of the intellect. Thus it is evident

that the ray and shade of the intellect are the specificity (nau'iya) of the rational soul, the ray and shade of the rational soul are the specificity of the animal soul, the ray and shade of the animal soul are the specificity of the vegetative soul, the ray and shade of the vegetative soul are the specificity of nature. This being so, the intellect is the specificity of all substances, and the form which establishes their essence, as its ray and light, which emanate from its shade, are the fountain (yanbū') of their substantiality and the root ('aṣl) of their forms and specificity. (Isaac Israeli, *The Book of Substances*, trans. Altmann & Stern 1958/2009: 83–4; for Judeo-Arabic, see Stern 1958: 143, ll. 6–13)

Whereas Avicenna's imagery in his *Ḥayy Ibn Yaqẓān* links darkness with corporeality (rooted in corporeal matter and in the privations of form that such matter occasions), Suhrawardi and Israeli link darkness even to the realm of spiritual simples: in the very process of emanation (and even at the level of intellects and souls) we may speak of a combination of lights and shadows. This sense that even spiritual reality is best understood in terms of lights-with-shadows might be said to be an outgrowth of "Pseudo-Empedoclean" tradition (to be addressed in § "Matter's dual identity") which can be seen as rooting the idea of shadows in the spiritual realm through its teaching of a kind of matter that lies between God and Intellect.

TURNING AND RETURNING

Another key theme for Neoplatonists is "Return" or "Reversion", an idea whose upward-directed imagery also gives way to talk of "Ascent". In more Aristotelian texts of Islamic and Jewish Neoplatonism, this Return/Ascent additionally gets described in terms of "conjunction" (ittiṣāl) with Active Intellect (a common medieval Islamic and Jewish Neoplatonic reading of Aristotle's *de Anima* 3.5). Perhaps most clearly highlighting the link between cosmo-ontology and human subjectivity, Neoplatonic Return is a call to self-transformation – an epistemological-ethical call to realign oneself with the knowledge-goodness of Intellect. The Return also draws upon a background sense that this world is a microcosm of the higher world, and that each human soul is a microcosm of Soul, and ultimately of Intellect. Connected to the idea of "Double Selfhood" (see § "Audacious servitude and rhetorics of rebellion and redemption", above), the rhetoric of Return plays on the sense that our own innermost reality is in fact found in the fullness of Intellect; it also plays on the related sense that our innermost reality is a microcosmic mirror of that higher macrocosmic reality. Drawing upon a key Return passage at *Enneads* IV.8[6].1, the *Theology of Aristotle* engages this theme:

Sometimes, I was as it were alone with my soul: I divested myself of my body, put it aside, and was as it were a simple substance without a body. Then I entered into my essence by returning into it free from all things. I was knowledge, knowing and known at the same time. I saw in my essence so much of beauty, loveliness, and splendour that I remained astonished and confused, and I knew that I was a part of the exalted, splendid, divine upper world, and that I was endowed with an active life. When this became clear to myself, I rose in my essence from this world

to the divine world, and I was as it were placed there and attached (*muta'alliq*) to it.
I was above the whole intelligible world and saw myself as if I stood in that exalted
divine position, and beheld there such light and splendour as tongues are unable
to describe and ears are impotent to hear.

(Theology of Aristotle, chapter 1, trans. Altmann & Stern 1958: 191;
see also Lewis 1959: 225; Arabic at Badawi 1955: 22, ll. 1–8)

This theme of Return lies at the heart of all Islamic and Jewish Neoplatonisms. One especially beautiful recounting of the Return – in express combination with the idea of *imitatio
dei* – can be found in Ibn Tufayl's version of *Ḥayy Ibn Yaqẓān*. Ibn Tufayl there offers a
tripart vision of return through a tripart series of imitations (Ibn Tufayl, *Ḥayy Ibn Yaqẓān*,
trans. Kocache 1982: 39–43):

- First, we must imitate the animals whose attention to food and shelter reminds us to
care for our bodies.
- Second, we must imitate the heavens in three respects:
  - Reflecting on the heavens' gracious heating and cooling of the earth, we are reminded
    to care for others beyond just ourselves (an ethical point which reverberates across
    a number of Islamic and Jewish traditions of Return, including the use in Jewish
    sources of the Hebrew term "*devēqūth*" (cleaving) to refer both to the *ittiṣāl* (conjunc-
    tion) with Intellect, as well as to devotion to God through following God's Law).[25]
  - Reflecting on the heavens' pure circular motions, we are reminded to keep ourselves
    clean (and we are also invited to Sufi spinning).
  - Reflecting on the heavens' witnessing of God, we are invited to turn our attention
    to our divine source.
- Finally, Ibn Tufayl speaks of the last imitation, the *imitatio dei* (itself in mystically
inspired terms as a unification with God): reflecting on the transcendent nature of
God's ownmost being, we are led to strive towards pure thinking of being *qua* being, a
thinking that gives way finally to witnessing God's glory and to an annihilation of the
self: "Immersed in this state, he saw what eyes have not seen nor ears heard, neither
has human heart experienced ... [H]e was annihilated beyond his essence and beyond
all other essences and could see within existence nothing but the One, the Living, the
Self-subsisting" (Ibn Tufayl, *Ḥayy Ibn Yaqẓān*, trans. Kocache 1982: 45–6).

Ibn Tufayl goes on to liken this supra-discursive state beyond ordinary reason to inebriation, and mindful of a *noēsis*-beyond-discursivity, he self-reflectively notes:

Explaining the state which he had reached is impossible. Any attempt is like
someone trying to taste a colour and requiring that black, say, is to be sweet or
sour. We shall not leave you, however, entirely without signs which may point to
what he saw of the wonders of that stage – but as an analogy only and not as a
knock on the door of the truth. The only way to verify that state is to reach it.

(Ibn Tufayl, Ḥayy Ibn Yaqẓān, Kocache 1982: 46)[26]

Turning to one other especially creative Return account, we might note how Ibn Gabirol's
version bears the traces of his Pseudo-Empedoclean commitment (see § "Matter's dual

identity") to a pure spiritual matter between God and Intellect: "If you should lift yourself to the first universal matter and are illumined by its shadow, you will then see the most wondrous of wonders. Devote yourself to this … since here lies the meaning for which the human soul exists, and here lies too amazing delight and utmost happiness" (Solomon Ibn Gabirol, *Fons Vitae* 3.56, p. 205, lines 14–18).[27]

In his call to devotion here, as in the context of the *Fons Vitae* more broadly, Ibn Gabirol is sensitive to the interplay of epistemology and ethics in Return, and, as such, to the Arabic language of *ittiṣāl* as at once beckoning to the conjunction of human soul with Intellect and to the Jewish notion of "*devēqūth*" as a devotion to God through righteous living. In this particular passage, Ibn Gabirol also illustrates the unique way in which a Pseudo-Empedoclean commitment to spiritual matter (see § "Matter's dual identity") impacts upon one's Neoplatonic language of Ascent: whereas other Neoplatonists speak of returning to the light of Intellect, Ibn Gabirol, sensitive to the presence of a spiritual matter in the spiritual realm that, as it were, casts a shadow into the downward unfolding of being, speaks of the Return to Intellect in terms of light as well as in terms of shadow. In this sense, Ibn Gabirol's Return passage beckons to the same rays-with-shade impulse that we have seen at play in Suhrawardi and Isaac Israeli (see § "Lights and shadows: on the paradox of emanation"), and in a range of Pseudo-Empedoclean texts of Islamic and Jewish Neoplatonism (see § "Matter's dual identity").

LOVE, DESIRE, BEING

> And for Empedocles Strife (*neikos*) divides, but Love (*philia*) is the One.
> (Plotinus, *Enn.* V.1[10].9)

Plotinus' particular way of recounting Empedocles suggests a link between the ultimate divine source and love. But regardless of whether or not such a link is part of Plotinus' (or Empedocles') worldview, it certainly can be found in a number of later Islamic and Jewish Neoplatonists. Consider Ibn Gabirol's Hebrew poetic reflection on the human–divine connection in a yearning love, with God as the "desire of my desire":

> to whom shall my soul run?
> to the god of my life, the desire of my desire
> and all my soul and all my flesh pine for him …
> … and I palpitate.[28]

Advancing an entire discourse on God as Love, Avicenna (in his *Risālah fi'l-'ishq, Treatise on Love*) theorizes God, *qua* the Pure Good that is the highest Essence and origin of all beings, as both the ultimate subject and object of love (Ibn Sina, *Risālah fi'l-'ishq*, Fackenheim 1945: 214). Avicenna understands God's goodness as identical to love and to being, as he understands God's origination of all beings as the investment into all things of being-*qua*-love (*ibid.*: 213). And in this spirit, Avicenna speaks too of God's desire to share his Goodness-as-Being-as-Love with all creation (*ibid.*: 228). In his reflections on love and being, Avicenna concludes that "In all beings, therefore, love (*al-'ishq*) is either the cause of their being, or being and love are identical in them. It is thus evident that no being is devoid of love" (*ibid*.: 214; see Arabic in Mehren 1891: 5, ll 7–9).

Turning to chapter 8 of the *Theology of Aristotle*, we find the idea that God – as source of Intellect – is the source of love and desire.[29] After showing that the "true love, which is intellectual, unites all things … in an intellectual bond and makes them one so as never to be severed"[30] and that "the whole of that entire world is pure love, containing no variance or antagonism in its being",[31] the *Theology of Aristotle* concludes that: "The upper world is love (*al-maḥabbah*) and life alone, whence are sent forth every life … and union that is not severed" (*Theology of Aristotle*, chapter 8, trans. Lewis 1959: 473; Arabic at Badawi 1955: 99, ll. 7–8).

For the Islamic and Jewish Neoplatonist, love is invested (through the very fact of being) at the core of all beings, and this love is at once born of and directed to God's Pure Goodness.[32]

MATTER'S DUAL IDENTITY

In the history of philosophy, including Islamic and Jewish Neoplatonisms, matter most frequently plays a negative role, a point we have seen above in the association of matter and the occlusion of light. Identified as locus of chaos in Plato's *Timaeus*, as source of evil in Plotinus, and arguably aligned with the lesser of two principles in Aristotle's hylomorphic metaphysics of substance, matter is likened by both Avicenna and Maimonides to an unvirtuous woman. On this theme, Avicenna speaks of the "low-born and blameworthy woman who tries to prevent her ugliness from becoming known" (Ibn Sina, *Risālah fī'l-'ishq*, Fackenheim 1945: 215), and Maimonides draws on the Proverbs 7:6–21 image of the "married harlot" (in particular, see Proverbs 7:10 and 7:19; see Maimonides, *Guide of the Perplexed*, "Introduction to the First Part" and 3.8, trans. Pines 1963: 13, 431): just as the disloyal wife moves from one partner to the next, so too matter takes on one form and then the next. At *Guide* 1.17, Maimonides points to Plato's own likening of matter to a woman in this regard, here emphasizing the fickleness of matter in terms of its rotating through a constant series not only of forms but of privations: "when a form is achieved, the particular privation in question, I mean the privation of the form that is achieved, disappears, and another privation is conjoined with matter; and this goes on for ever [*sic*]" (*Guide of the Perplexed* 1.17, trans. Pines).

Taken in its negative feminine role as compared with form, matter can in this sense be related to the Platonic receptacle as the female "Nurse of Becoming" in contrast to the stable realm of Being with which the male Demiurge is aligned.[33] In addition to connecting matter with the feminine, Avicenna can further be seen as alluding to the *Timaeus* imagery in his description of matter as "*al-maḥall*" (place, or receptacle) in his *Metaphysics* (Ibn Sina; Marmura 2005: 70). Further emphasizing matter in negative terms, Avicenna symbolically links matter in *Ḥayy Ibn Yaqẓān* to the "Hot and Muddy Sea" (an allusion to Quran 18:86) which Avicenna describes as the place where the sun sets, where "Perpetual Darkness reigns", and whose soil is "a desert of salt" (Ibn Sina, *Ḥayy Ibn Yaqẓān*, section 13; Corbin 1960: 142).

In Islamic and Jewish Neoplatonism, one also finds a very different tradition of matter: a tradition of spiritual matter. Categorized by scholars as following a "Pseudo-Empedoclean" tradition (or traditions), and linked by some to the Islamic mysticism of Ibn Masarra (see Asín-Palacios 1978; Stern 1983b), this unique class of texts speaks of a spiritual matter between God and Intellect in the Great Chain of Being. This "*al-'unṣur al-awwal*" is translated variously as prime matter, primal matter, and in my own work as Grounding Element (see Pessin 2013: 23–7), and should not be confused with Aristotelian "prime matter": while Aristotelian prime matter is a principle of bodies, the Pseudo-Empedoclean "*al-'unṣur al-awwal*" is a principle of even spiritual simples (namely all souls and all intellects other than God). Coming as it does "between" God and Intellect in the more standard Neoplatonic cosmic hierarchy, this pure spiritual matter is described at times as a pre-existent existent prior to Intellect, and at times as a constituent principle of souls and intellects. It is in this latter regard that the view gives rise to what later Christian scholastics, in their reading of the *Fons Vitae* of Ibn Gabirol, call "universal hylomorphism", namely the view that all non-God substances – corporeal and spiritual – are matter+form composites (in contrast to Aristotelian hylomorphism according to which only corporeal substances admit of matter+form composition).[34] It might be noted that in a number of Islamic texts, this spiritual matter is described as itself comprised of the dual Empedoclean principles of love and strife, while in a number of Jewish texts it is not itself composite but is instead coupled with a First Form; in this sense, it can be said to emerge in Islamic contexts as the first composite and in Jewish contexts as the first constituent.[35] In the writings of Ibn Gabirol it is likened to the river in the Garden of Eden as well as to the Divine Throne upon which the Glory of God resides. This spiritual matter might suggest links to Pythagorean and Platonic traditions of "Indefinite Dyad",[36] and to Plotinus' own occasional allusions to intelligible matter[37] as a "first moment" of Intellect "before" it receives its being as intellect from the One. As for its relationship to Empedocles, while various Islamic and Jewish texts directly associate the view with Empedocles, scholars have not found any clear link to the writings of Empedocles, and for that reason refer to this set of teachings as "Pseudo-Empedoclean".

Looking back to § "Love, desire, being", it is interesting to note the connections in various Islamic and Jewish contexts between matter and love. Looking to the more standard negative philosophical approaches to matter (as, for example, can be found in Plato, Aristotle, Plotinus and a host of Islamic and Jewish Neoplatonists, including those who additionally speak in positive terms of a spiritual matter), we find descriptions of matter's desire for form in a negative sense: the negative sense at play in Avicenna's and Maimonides' allegorical depiction of matter as a woman of questionable moral character who lusts after one partner and then another. However, turning to the decidedly positive grade of spiritual matter at play in Pseudo-Empedoclean contexts, we find a very different set of associations between matter and love. In the context of Pseudo-Empedoclean texts that describe spiritual matter as itself composed of love and strife, we find a sense of love – related, we might suggest, to the unifying pull of being described in the *Theology of Aristotle*'s and in Avicenna's reflections on love – at the heart of existence coupled with the equally core principle of strife (the source of division). And, in those texts, such as Ibn Gabirol's *Fons Vitae*, in which the spiritual matter is not itself composed of love and strife, we may suggest an even stronger identification of pure matter with love.[38]

ON THE GOAL OF BEING A GOOD PERSON

We end with what is perhaps the starting animating insight for Neoplatonists: it is important to strive to be a good person. We have already seen vestiges of this insight throughout this chapter: we have talked of Return as a jointly epistemological-and-ethical seeking after knowledge-and-goodness, we have seen the dual resonances of *ittiṣāl*/*devēqūth* as the "conjunction" with Intellect and the "devotion" to God by right living, and we have seen the description of soul's descent in terms of her gifting nature with a taste of Intellect's beauty in and through soul's "manifesting her noble deeds and acts" (see § "Audacious servitude and rhetorics of rebellion and redemption"). To these ideas, we might add two background intuitions about *imitatio dei* at the heart of these traditions: to be like God means becoming both wise and good, since (a) God's own Being is identical with both pure wisdom and pure goodness, and relatedly, (b) God – as Creator and/or Emanating Source – is not just a Unity of Being unto Himself; He is, in the purity of His Being, the First Cause of all plurality and is in this sense a generous caregiver who ministers beyond Himself to the Other. In both senses, Islamic and Jewish Neoplatonists strive to emulate God by becoming minds filled with knowledge, and by becoming hearts filled with care, ethically directing us to the care of the world and the people around us in the manner of God's own sharing forth of goodness.

With a deeply intertwined sense of the seamless relationship between ethics, theology and philosophical knowledge-seeking, many Islamic and Jewish Neoplatonists offer express directives for virtue and action inspired by Islamic and Jewish Law alongside Pythagorean, Stoic, Platonic and Aristotelian insights. For example, emphasizing the importance of the "middle path", Suhrawardi describes moderation as "most excellent of virtues",[39] and Maimonides sees the perfection of the Law itself in its "aim[ing] at man's following the path of moderation" (Maimonides, *Eight Chapters*; see Twersky 1972: 371).

In the spirit of this chapter's opening call for methodological humility in our own attempts to understand Neoplatonism, we end this chapter with some insights on the virtue of humility from Suhrawardi and Ibn Gabirol. In his description of God's illuminating effluence, Suhrawardi links the grounding love of all being to humility,[40] in this way opening us to a deep encounter with God, the universe, and our ownmost selfhood in terms of humility. In like spirit, Ibn Gabirol poetically beckons to the grounding of human being (and in this particular poem, a grounding of the human being in her mindful act as poet, or, we might add, scholar) in an utter dependency upon God: a mode of being which, upon reflection, signifies the core of human being in a call to receptive humility (in scholarship, as in living):

> I've made you my refuge and hope –
> who's made me rich and then poor;
> your oneness I sought at the door to the poem,
> so grace your servant, my Lord,
> with the good that you've long laid in store.
> Extend your mercy across me
> And my way with these words will be sure.
> How could my failings distract you so –

who fashioned the world in a void –

…

See now my dread, my Lord,
I stand here before you exposed.[41]

NOTES

1. For additional resources, see Pingree (1980), Goodman (1992), Morewedge (1992), Nasr (1993), Shayegan (1996), Rudavsky (1997), Gutas (1998), Kraemer (2003), Harvey (2004).

2. On the development and transmission of the *Theology of Aristotle*, see Fenton (1986), Kraye *et al.* (1986), Aouad (1989), Langermann (1999), D'Ancona (2001), Adamson (2002); for treatment of the longer and shorter versions of the *Theology of Aristotle*, see Borisov (1929), Pines (1954), Fenton (1986). On the *Kalām fī maḥḍ al-khair* and *Liber de Causis*, see R. C. Taylor (1983, 1986, 1989, 1992), D'Ancona & Taylor (2003).

3. For an overview of the Active Intellect in some of these traditions, see Davidson (1972, 1992), Ivry (2007a, 2007b).

4. To begin thinking about these issues, one might consider P. Hadot (1993, 1995), Corrigan (2005), Rappe (2007) and Pessin (2013) (esp. chapter 9 in which I provide further references for how to engage these kinds of questions).

5. A similar point might be made for Christian Neoplatonists (e.g. Ps. Dionysius, Eriugena, *et al.*), though, in Christian cases, one must consider the possibility that creation/emanation from God to the world is less perfect and less infinite in some important sense than intra-Trinitarian emanation (emanation, that is, between the Father, the Son and the Holy Spirit); no such considerations exist in the case of Greek, Jewish and Islamic Neoplatonisms.

6. *Theology of Aristotle* 10.1; Lewis (1959: 291); see Arabic at Badawi (1955: 134).

7. *Theology of Aristotle* 10.175; Lewis (1959: 391, 393, 395, 437).

8. It might be noted that not all thinkers classified within Islamic and Jewish Neoplatonism would view God's creation in this way; for example, al-Kindi emphasizes that the created world is not eternal; see al-Kindi's *Metaphysics*, Ivry (1974); see also Pormann & Adamson (2012).

9. I here use "orthodox" to loosely refer to the position people take themselves to be representing (or occupying) when they express concern that eternal emanation is not consistent with a particular religion's cosmogeny. I don't myself consider "orthodox" an appropriate title for such a view (as it suggests that the view in question is somehow more basic to the religion than an emanation view), but the view does seem to arise in various primary and secondary materials. I remain perplexed as to why anyone would find emanation to be "less orthodox" a view than some other kind of cosmogenical view within an Islamic or Jewish context.

10. Though it might be noted that in his own Islamic Neoplatonism, Avicenna upholds eternal emanation not only through the language of creation, but even through the language of *al-ikhtiyār*. I am thankful to Jon Hoover for bringing this to my attention; for the relevant passage in Avicenna's *al-Ta'aliqāt*, see Hoover (2007: 71). We might say that for many Islamic and Jewish Neoplatonists, any and all theological language is consistent with eternal emanation.

11. *Kalām fī maḥḍ al-khair*, Prop. 17; Arabic at Bardenhewer (1882: 93); English at Guagliardo *et al.* (1996: 111, Prop. 18 in Latin commentary).

12. See *Kalām fī maḥḍ al-khair*, prop. 4. This emphasis on God's sovereignty – seen in the permeating of God's power – can also be seen in the causal reminder at *Kalām fī maḥḍ al-khair*, prop. 1, trans. Guagliardo *et al.* (1996: 6, with n. 7); Arabic at Bardenhewer (1882: 61).

13. In the case of Israeli, Altmann reads creation as opposing emanation, while H. A. Wolfson reads creation as a type of non-Plotinian emanation: see Wolfson (1973), Altmann (1979); for my response to these readings, and for full references, see Pessin (2003, 2012b, 2013, 2014). In the case of Ibn Gabirol, each of Weisheipl, Gilson, Munk and Husik (and with them, many others) read into his *Fons Vitae* a "Doctrine of Divine Will" which opposes emanation; for full references as well as for my rejection of this reading of Ibn Gabirol (including my replacement of the term "Divine Will" with the term "Divine Desire" for the Arabic *al-irāda*, and my identification of *al-irāda* as demarcating the very process of divine emanation itself) see Pessin (2013: 53–90).

14. Some scholars (e.g. Beierwaltes, F. M. Schroeder, Dörrie) have emphasized the absence of emanation imagery in Greek Neoplatonism as an attempt to avoid any overly materialistic imageries in the description of the One's unfolding (I am thankful to the anonymous reviewer of this chapter for making note of this). That said, it seems that we may indeed point to emanation imagery in Plotinus – e.g. his use of the metaphor of illumination (e.g. *Enn.* V.8[31].10), and his use of languages of flow to describe various aspects of the unfolding process (e.g. *Enn.* III.5[50].3 on the origin of Love in terms of *aporreōn*, III.5[50].9 on Soul's emergence from Intellect in terms of *eisrueis*, VI.9[9].9 on the soul's seeing "the fountain of life" [*pēgē zōēs*, there a reference to the One] and becoming "filled with God" (*plērōtheisa theou*), with the One being there also described in terms of a pouring out (*ekxeomenōn*) that does not diminish). Following undoubtedly on such claims (at least as they appear in *Enneads* IV–VI), the *Theology of Aristotle* edition of Plotinus does read emanation in the Greek source, and emanation emerges as a standard element in traditions of Islamic and Jewish Neoplatonism. The use of emanation imagery, of course, is just imagery – it suggests nothing materialistic (or temporal) about a thinker's theological/ontological worldview.

15. For example, see *Theology of Aristotle* 7.8 on God as the good (*al-khair*) that emanates (English at Lewis 1959 243; Arabic at Badawi 1955: 85, line 9), and see 7.33 on God ("first originator") as emanating (translated by Lewis as "pours forth") light (English at Lewis 1959: 247; Arabic at Badawi 1955: 89, line 7); the language of *fayḍ* underlies these and other claims.

16. This last intellect arisen in the great cosmic chain of being is the Active Intellect, described by al-Farabi here as the "eleventh existence". For al-Farabi, the Active Intellect is – as in other Arabic Aristotelianized Neoplatonic texts – the tenth of the emanated intellects; his description of it as the "eleventh existence" does not challenge that idea, but simply follows from al-Farabi's counting God as the first existence, the first emanated intellect after God as the second existence, and so on until the Active Intellect, which, as the tenth emanated intellect after God, is the "eleventh existence". On the emanation of this Active Intellect, see al-Farabi, *Perfect State* 2.3.9–10, trans. Walzer.

17. In our context, of course, "grace" lacks implications that many readers might associate with it from within Christian contexts.

18. *Theology of Aristotle*, chapter 8; English at Lewis 1959: 407; Arabic at Badawi 1955: 119, line 1.

19. *Ibid.*, chapter 7; English at Lewis 1959: 251; Arabic at Badawi 1955: 91, line 6.

20. For more on the Paradox of Divine Unity, the Neoplatonic strategies for engaging this paradox, and the differences (as such) between "descriptive" language and Neoplatonic apophatic cosmo-ontological talk, see Pessin (2013: esp. chs 8–9).

21. In his notes to the first volume of Plotinus' *Enneads*, Armstrong speaks of Plotinus' "double-self psychology"; see Armstrong (1966–88: vol. 1, 195 n. 1).

22. On the symbolic approach, see Ibn Sina; Corbin (1960); a "symbolic" account is there presented as being beyond a mere allegory where each term simply denotes something that can be reached through reason.

23. Suhrawardi, *Philosophy of Illumination*, part 2, discourse 3, section 2:180; Walbridge & Ziai (1999: 117).

24. Maimonides, *Guide of the Perplexed* 3.9; Pines (1963: 436).

25. For a fuller treatment with sources of this Jewish notion of "*devēqūth*" (with an emphasis on its particular role in Jewish mystical ethics), see Dan (1971); see also Scholem (1971); Schmidt (1995).

26. On the Neoplatonic theme of inebriation, one might compare Plotinus in *Enn.* VI.7[38], and on the idea that one must attain the state to know it, consider too *Enn.* I.6[1] and VI.9[9]; I am thankful to the anonymous reviewer for these points of comparison in Plotinus.

27. For the entire exchange, see *Fons Vitae* 3.56, p. 204, line 13 – 3.57, p. 205, line 18ff. [Baeumker]. For Arabic surrounding text, see Pines (1958: section 2, 47–8). The last line literally says "there" (*ibi*), not "here"; I have used the construction "here lies ... and here too lies" for effect. For another English rendering, see Wedeck (1962: 127–8).

28. From Ibn Gabirol's *reshūt le-nishmath*; my translation. For Hebrew text and another translation, see Zangwill (1923/44: 15). I have included Zangwill's "palpitate" for "*ve-'ahīm*". See also Cole (2001: 121 with notes at 27–45).

29. On the fluid interplay of the concepts of love and desire in this context (and for a sense of some of the Arabic and Hebrew terms at play), see Pessin (2013: 15–22).

30. *Theology of Aristotle*, chapter 8, trans. Lewis (1959: 473); Arabic at Badawi (1955: 99, lines 2–4).

31. *Ibid.*: trans. Lewis (1959: 473); Arabic at Badawi (1955: 99, line 5).

32. On this theme, see also the thirty-sixth treatise of the Brethren of Purity's *Rasā'il*; Fackenheim also references al-Kindi and al-Farabi; see Fackenheim (1945). For the idea of desire as a final cause of motion

(not, as in the cases we are considering, a final cause and origin of existence itself), one might consider the influence of Aristotle's own description, in *Metaphysics* 12, of the divine Unmoved Mover as the object of cosmic desire. One might also consider the impact of Plato's *Symposium* on Greek traditions of Neoplatonism on this topic; we also know that at least parts of the *Symposium* were available in Arabic in al-Kindi's time; see Aouad (1989); Gutas (2012: 855); D'Ancona (2013).

33. For a consideration of themes of femininity in the history of matter (including a positive feminist sense of matter in Ibn Gabirol's Pseudo-Empedoclean tradition), see Pessin (2004).

34. For a fuller sense of this teaching in Latin Christian contexts, one must also consider Augustine's teachings on spiritual matter. For an account of what it means for a substance to reveal "form+matter" in Ibn Gabirol's Neoplatonic context, see Pessin (2013). For a comparison of the hylomorphic ideas found in the Islamic contexts of Avicenna's Aristotelian Neoplatonism on the one hand and the non-Aristotelian Pseudo-Empedocleanism recounted by Shahrastani on the other hand, see Pessin (forthcoming).

35. For an overview of this point, as well as the overarching themes of Pseudo-Empedoclean matter, see Pessin (2013) (including appendix A12). See also Pessin (2004, 2005, forthcoming). For details on the Pseudo-Empedoclean tradition(s), see also: Stern (1954, 1983a), Kaufmann (1899), G. Freudenthal & Brague (2005); for possible links between this tradition and Ibn Masarra, see Asín-Palacios (1978), Stern (1983b).

36. For Aristotle's discussion of the idea in these traditions, see *Metaph.* 1.6 and 1.9; on theme of dyad as related to intelligible matter in Plotinus, see Rist (1962); on themes of dyad and the unlimited in Ibn Gabirol and Iamblichus, see Mathis II (1992), and see also appendix A15 in Pessin (2013).

37. For intelligible matter in Plotinus, see *Enn.* II.4[12].1–5; III.8[30].11; on related images of intellect, see *Enn.* V.3[49].11, VI.7[38].17; on related dyad theme, see *Enn.* V.1[10].5, V.4[7].2, V.5[32].4; see also Rist (1962), Dillon (1992c); on conceptual link to Ibn Gabirol and broader Islamic and Jewish Ps. Empedoclean traditions, see appendix A5 in Pessin (2013).

38. For a fuller investigation of this suggestion in the case of Ibn Gabirol, see Pessin (2004, 2013); for an analysis of "negative", "neutral" and "positive" implications of matter in a range of Jewish medieval philosophy, see Pessin (2009).

39. Suhrawardi, *Philosophy of Illumination*, part 2, discourse 5, section 2:239; Walbridge & Ziai (1999: 146).

40. See *ibid.*, discourse 2, section 157; Walbridge & Ziai (1999: 103).

41. Part of a Hebrew poem by Ibn Gabirol, as translated by Peter Cole (2007: 98).

Contributors

Peter Adamson is Professor of Late Antique and Arabic Philosophy at the Ludwig-Maximilians-Universität München. He has edited numerous volumes on ancient and Arabic philosophy and is the author of *The Arabic Plotinus* (2002), *Al-Kindi* (2007) and *A History of Philosophy Without Any Gaps: Classical Philosophy* (2014).

Vishwa Adluri is Adjunct Associate Professor at Hunter College, New York. He is the author of *Parmenides, Plato and Mortal Philosophy: Return from Transcendence* (2011) and the editor of *Philosophy and Salvation in Greek Religion* (2013). He has also produced a translation of Arbogast Schmitt's *Die Moderne und Platon – Modernity and Plato: Two Paradigms of Rationality* (2012) and a new book on the relationship of contemporary scholarship to ancient Indian thought, *The Nay Science: A History of German Indology* (2014, with J. Bagchee).

Sara Ahbel-Rappe is Professor of Greek and Latin at the University of Michigan, Ann Arbor. She is the author of *Reading Neoplatonism: Non-discursive Thinking in the Texts of Plotinus, Proclus, and Damascius* (2010), *Socrates: A Guide for the Perplexed* (2009), and a translation of Damascius' *Doubts and Solutions Concerning First Principles* (2010). She is also co-editor of *A Companion to Socrates* (2009, with R. Kamtekar).

Gwenaëlle Aubry is a researcher at the CNRS (UPR 76/Centre Jean Pépin). She is the editor of *L'Excellence de la vie: Sur* l'Ethique à Nicomaque *et* l'Ethique à Eudème *d'Aristote* (2002) and *Le moi et l'intériorité* (2008, with F. Ildefonse); and the author of *Plotin: Traité 53 (I, 1)* (2004); *Dieu sans la puissance. Dunamis et* Energeia *chez Aristote et chez Plotin* (2006) and *Porphyre: Sur la manière dont l'embryon reçoit l'âme* (2012, with L. Brisson, M.-H. Congourdeau, F. Hudry *et al.*).

Han Baltussen is Hughes Professor of Classics at the University of Adelaide and Fellow of the Australian Academy of the Humanities. He is the author of *Theophrastus Against the Presocratics and Plato* (2000) and *Philosophy and Exegesis in Simplicius: The Methodology of a Commentator* (2008), editor of *Philosophy, Science and Exegesis in Greek, Latin and Arabic Commentaries* (2004, with P. Adamson and M. Stone) and of *Greek and Roman Consolations: Eight Studies of a Tradition and its Afterlife* (2013), and translator of *Simplicius' Commentary on Aristotle's Physics 1.5–9* (with M. Chase, M. Atkinson and I. Mueller).

Luc Brisson is Director of Research (Emeritus) at the National Centre for Scientific Research (Paris, France). His seminal publications on both Plato and Plotinus, including bibliographies, translations and commentaries, include *Platon, le mots et les mythes* (1982; published in English as *Plato the Myth Maker*, 1999) and *Einführung in die Philosophie des Mythos* I (1996; published in English as *How Philosophers Saved Myths:*

Allegorical Interpretation and Classical Mythology, 2004). He has edited *Platon. Oeuvres completes* (2008) and *Plotin: Traités*, 9 vols (2002–10, with J.-F. Pradeau).

Riccardo Chiaradonna is Associate Professor of Ancient Philosophy at Roma Tre University. He is the author of *Sostanza movimento analogia: Plotino critico di Aristotele* (2002) and *Plotino* (2009), and editor of *Physics and Philosophy of Nature in Greek Neoplatonism* (2009, with F. Trabattoni) and *Universals in Ancient Philosophy* (2013, with G. Galluzzo).

Bernard Collette-Dučić is Professor of Ancient Philosophy at Université Laval. He is the author of *Plotin et l'ordonnancement de l'être* (2007), "Sommeil, éveil et attention chez Plotin" (2011–12), "Le stoïcisme dans l'*Ad Gaurum*" (2011) and "On the Chrysippean thesis that the virtues are *poia*" (2009). He is currently preparing a new translation with commentary of Plotinus' *On Fate* as well as a book on the Stoic conception of Providence.

Kevin Corrigan is Samuel Candler Dobbs Professor of Interdisciplinary Humanities and Director of the Graduate Institute of the Liberal Arts at Emory University. He is the author of *Evagrius and Gregory: Mind, Soul and Body in the Fourth Century* (2009) and *Reason, Faith and Otherness in Neoplatonic and Early Christian Thought* (2013), and editor of *Religion and Philosophy in the Platonic and Neoplatonic Traditions: From Antiquity to the Early Medieval Period (Pagan, Jewish, Christian, Islamic, and Comparative Eastern Perspectives)* (2012, with John D. Turner and Peter Wakefield); *Gnosticism, Platonism and the Late Ancient World: Essays in Honour of John D. Turner* (2001, with T. Rasimus, in collaboration with D. Burns, L. Jenott and Z. Mazur).

Dimitar Y. Dimitrov is Lecturer in Byzantine and Medieval Balkan History and Culture at St Cyril and Methodius University in Veliko Tarnovo, Bulgaria. He is the author of many publications in Bulgarian, including *Pagans and Christians in the IV Century: Modes of Behaviour* (2000), *Philosophy, Culture and Politics in Late Antiquity* (2005, in Bulgarian) and *The Dark Ages of Byzantium* (2005) and a co-author in the general volume *Byzantium and the Byzantine World* (2011).

Franco Ferrari is Professor of Ancient Philosophy at the University of Salerno. He is coordinator of the Editorial Board of the International Plato Studies and member of the Academia Platonica Septima. He is the author of *Dio, idea e materia: la struttura del cosmo in Plutarco di Cheronea* (1995), *I miti di Platone* (2006), *L'esercizio della ragione nel mondo classico* (2005, with P. L. Donini) and the translation with commentary of Plato's *Parmenides* (2004) and *Theaetetus* (2011). With I. Männlein-Robert, he has prepared the section on Middle Platonism in the new edition of *Grundriss der Geschichte der Philosophie* (2015).

John F. Finamore is Professor of Classics at the University of Iowa and the editor of *The International Journal of the Platonic Tradition*. He is the author of *Iamblichus and the Theory of the Vehicle of the Soul* (1985) and *Iamblichus' De Anima: Text, Translation, and Commentary* (2002, with J. M. Dillon).

Lloyd P. Gerson is Professor of Philosophy in the University of Toronto. He is the author, most recently, of *From Plato to Platonism* (2013), a commentary on and translation of Plotinus' treatise V.5, *That the Intelligibles are not External to the Intellect* (2013), *Ancient Epistemology* (2009) and *Aristotle and Other Platonists* (2005). He is the editor of the *Cambridge History of Philosophy in Late Antiquity* (2010).

Jens Halfwassen is Professor of Philosophy and Director of the Seminar of Philosophy at the University of Heidelberg, Member of the Heidelberg Academy of Sciences, and Founding Member of the Academia Platonica Septima Monasteriensis. He is also the editor of *Philosophische Rundschau* (with B. Waldenfels and P. Stekeler-Weithofer). He is the author of *Plotin und der Neuplatonismus* (2004); *Der Aufstieg zum Einen. Untersuchungen zu Platon und Plotin* (1992, 2nd edn 2006); *Geist und Selbstbewusstsein. Studien zu Plotin und Numenios* (1994); *Hegel und der spätantike Neuplatonismus* (1999, 2nd edn 2005).

Péter Lautner is Associate Professor at the Faculty of Humanities and Social Sciences, Pázmány Péter Catholic University, Budapest. He has published widely on Platonic epistemology and theories of the soul, and contributed many volumes to the Ancient Commentators on Aristotle project.

Alessandro Linguiti is Associate Professor of Ancient Philosophy in the Department of History and Cultural Heritage at the University of Siena and a member of the Academia Platonica Septima Monasteriensis. His main publications are *L'ultimo platonismo greco: Principi e conoscenza* (1990); Anonymous, *Commentary on the Parmenides*, in *Corpus dei papiri filosofici greci e latini* III (1995: 63–202); Plotin, *Traité* 36 (I,5) (2007); and Proclo, *Teologia Platonica* (2007, with M. Casaglia).

Marije Martijn is Associate Professor of Ancient and Patristic Philosophy at the VU University Amsterdam. She is author of numerous publications on Proclus, ancient aesthetics and metaphysics among which is *Proclus on Nature: Philosophy of Nature and its Methods in Proclus' Commentary on Plato's Timaeus* (2010).

Dermot Moran is Professor of Philosophy at University College Dublin and Sir Walter Murdoch Adjunct Professor at Murdoch University. He is founding editor of the *International Journal of Philosophical Studies*, and currently President of the International Federation of Philosophical Studies (FISP). He is the author of *The Philosophy of John Scottus Eriugena: A Study of Idealism in the Middle Ages* (1989), *Introduction to Phenomenology* (2000), *Edmund Husserl: Founder of Phenomenology* (2005) and *Husserl's Crisis of the European Sciences: An Introduction* (2012). He has published widely on John Scottus Eriugena, Meister Eckhart and Nicolas of Cusa.

Jean-Marc Narbonne is Professor of Philosophy at Laval University (Quebec). He is responsible for the new edition and translation of Plotinus in the Budé Collection (Collection des Universités de France), and has published extensively on the Neoplatonic tradition, including *Plotinus in Dialogue with the Gnostics* (2011); *Levinas and the Greek Heritage* (2006); *Hénologie, ontologie et ereignis: Plotin – Proclus – Heidegger* (2001); and *La métaphysique de Plotin* (2001).

Dominic J. O'Meara is Professor Emeritus of Metaphysics and Ancient Philosophy, University of Fribourg (Switzerland). His works include: *Pythagoras Revived: Mathematics and Philosophy in Late Antiquity* (1989), *Plotinus: An Introduction to the* Enneads (1993) and *Platonopolis: Platonic Political Philosophy in Late Antiquity* (2003).

Sarah Pessin is Associate Professor of Philosophy and Judaic Studies at the University of Denver. She has published widely in areas of medieval philosophy and Neoplatonism, and is the author of *Ibn Gabirol's Theology of Desire: Matter and Method in Jewish Medieval Neoplatonism* (2013).

Pauliina Remes is University Lecturer in Philosophy at Uppsala University (Sweden). She is the author of *Plotinus on Self: The Philosophy of the "We"* (2007) and *Neoplatonism* (2008), and the editor of *Ancient Philosophy of the Self* (2008, with J. Sihvola) and *Consciousness: From Perception to Reflection in the History of Philosophy* (2007, with S. Heinämaa and V. Lähteenmäki).

Gretchen Reydams-Schils is Professor in the Program of Liberal Studies at the University of Notre Dame, with concurrent appointments in Philosophy and Theology. She is the author of *Demiurge and Providence: Stoic and Platonist Readings of Plato's Timaeus* (1999) and *The Roman Stoics: Self, Responsibility, and Affection* (2005). She is currently working on a monograph about Calcidius.

Frederic M. Schroeder is Professor Emeritus at Queen's University, Kingston, Canada. His publications include *Two Greek Aristotelian Commentators on the Intellect: The De Intellectu attributed to Alexander of Aphrodisias and Themistius' Paraphrase on Aristotle De Anima 3.4–8. Introduction, Translation, Commentary and Notes* (1990, with R. B. Todd) and *Form and Transformation: A Study in the Philosophy of Plotinus* (1992).

Svetla Slaveva-Griffin is Associate Professor of Classics and a core faculty in the History and Philosophy of Science Program at the Florida State University. She has published on a wide range of topics in ancient philosophy, among which is *Plotinus on Number* (2009).

Andrew Smith is Professor Emeritus of Classics, University College Dublin, and Associate Director of the Plato Centre, Trinity College Dublin. His publications include *Porphyry's Place in the Neoplatonic Tradition* (1974), the Teubner edition of Porphyry's fragments (1993) and *Plotinus, Porphyry and Iamblichus: Philosophy and Religion in Neoplatonism* (2011).

Richard Sorabji is an Honorary Fellow of Wolfson College, Oxford. He is author of three books on the history of philosophy of the physical universe, and of six on the history of philosophy of mind and ethics, the last two being *Gandhi and the Stoics: Modern Experiments on Ancient Values* (2012) and *Moral Conscience through the Ages, Fifth Century BCE to the Present* (2014). He is editor of 100 volumes so far in the series *Ancient Commentators on Aristotle*, author of a three-volume Sourcebook on them, and editor of two explanatory books about them with a third in preparation.

Suzanne Stern-Gillet is Professor of Ancient Philosophy at the University of Bolton and Honorary Research Fellow in the Department of Classics and Ancient History at the University of Manchester. She is the author of *Aristotle's Philosophy of Friendship* (1995) and editor of *Reading Ancient Texts*, 2 vols (2007, with K. Corrigan). Her collection on *Ancient and Medieval Concepts of Friendship*, edited with G. Gurtler, is forthcoming. Currently she is working on a monograph on Plato's *Ion* and is preparing a translation and commentary on Plotinus' tractate *On the Virtues* (I.2[19]) for the series *The Enneads of Plotinus*.

Harold Tarrant is an Honorary Professor at the University of Newcastle, Australia. He is the author of *Plato's First Interpreters* (2000), *Recollecting Plato's Meno* (2005), *Proclus' Commentary on Plato's Timaeus: Volume 1, Book 1* (2010) and editor of *Reading Plato in Antiquity* (2006, with D. Baltzly) and *Alcibiades and the Socratic Lover-Educator* (2012, with M. Johnson).

John D. Turner is Cotner Professor of Religious Studies and Charles J. Mach University Professor of Classics and History at the University of Nebraska-Lincoln. He is the author of *Sethian Gnosticism and the Platonic Tradition* (2002), a principal contributor to the English and French language critical editions of seven of the Nag Hammadi texts, and editor of *Platonisms: Ancient, Modern, and Postmodern* (2007, with K. Corrigan) and *Rethinking Plato's Parmenides and its Platonic, Gnostic and Patristic Reception* (2010).

Robbert M. van den Berg is University Lecturer in Ancient Philosophy at Leiden University. His publications include *Proclus' Hymns* (2001) and *Proclus' Commentary on the Cratylus in Context: Ancient Theories of Language and Naming* (2008).

Panayiota Vassilopoulou is Lecturer in the Philosophy Department at the University of Liverpool. She is the editor of *Epistemology in Late Antique Philosophy* (2009, with S. R. L. Clark).

James Wilberding is Professor in Ancient and Medieval Philosophy at the Ruhr University in Bochum, Germany. He is the author of *Plotinus' Cosmology* (2006), *Philoponus: On the Eternity of the World Books 12–18* (2006) and *Porphyry: To Gaurus on How Embryos are Ensouled and On What is in Our Power* (2011), and editor of *Neoplatonism and the Philosophy of Nature* (2012, with C. Horn) and *Philosophical Themes in Galen* (2014, with P. Adamson and R. Hansberger).

Bibliography

ANCIENT AUTHORS

This is a compiled list of editions, collections, commentaries, translations and sourcebooks of ancient authors and texts referred to in the *Handbook*. When there is more than one item per work, the ancient author's works are separated and relevant items are grouped together. When deemed necessary, some items are cross-listed here and in the bibliography of modern authors. Authors' names with the prefix "pseudo-" are alphabetized according to the suggested author's name.

COLLECTIONS AND SOURCEBOOKS
Adorno, F. *et al.* (eds) 1995. *Corpus dei papiri filosofici greci e latini* III: Commentari. Florence: Olschki.

Bettenson, H. (ed.) 1975. *Documents of the Christian Church*, 2nd edn. Oxford: Oxford University Press.

Diels, H. & W. Kranz (eds) 1951–52. *Die Fragmente der Vorsokratiker*, 6th edn, 3 vols. Berlin: Weidmann.

Dillon, J. M. & L. P. Gerson (trans.) 2004. *Neoplatonic Philosophy: Introductory Readings*. Indianapolis, IN: Hackett.

Dörrie, H. & M. Baltes (eds) 1987–2008. *Der Platonismus in der Antike*, 7 vols. Stuttgart: Frommann-Holzboog.

Edelstein, E. J. & L. Edelstein 1945. *Asclepius. Collection and Interpretation of the Testimonies*, 2 vols. Baltimore, MD: Johns Hopkins University Press.

Gioè, A. (ed.) 2002. *Filosofi Medioplatonici del II secolo D. C. Testimonianze e frammenti (Gaio, Albino, Lucio, Nicostrato, Tauro, Severo, Arpocrazione)*. Naples: Bibliopolis.

Long, A. A. & D. N. Sedley (eds) 1987. *The Hellenistic Philosophers*, 2 vols. Cambridge: Cambridge University Press.

Sider, R. D. (ed.) 2001. *Christian and Pagan in the Roman Empire: The Witness of Tertullian*, Selections from the Fathers of the Church Book 2. Washington, DC: Catholic University of America Press.

Sorabji, R. (ed.) 2004–2005. *The Philosophy of the Commentators, 200–600 AD*, vol. 1: *Psychology (with Ethics and Religion)*; vol. 2: *Physics*; vol. 3: *Logic and Metaphysics*. Ithaca, NY: Cornell University Press.

Von Arnim, H. (ed.) 1903–5. *Stoicorum Veterum Fragmenta*, 4 vols. Stuttgart: Teubner.

ALBERTUS MAGNUS
Simon, P. (ed. & trans.) 1972. *Albertus Magnus: Super Dionysium de Divinis Nominibus*, Opera Omnia 36–7. Munster: Aschendorff.

ALBINUS

Reis, B. (ed.) 1999. *Der Platoniker Albinos und sein sogenannter Prologos: Prolegomena, Überlieferungsgeschichte, kritische Edition und Übersetzung*. Wiesbaden: Reichert.

ALCINOUS

Dillon, J. (trans.) 1993. *Alcinous: The Handbook of Platonism*. Oxford: Clarendon Press.
Whittaker, J. (ed.) 1990. *Alkinoos: Enseignement des doctrines de Platon*, trans. P. Louis. Paris: Les Belles Lettres.

ALEXANDER OF APHRODISIAS

de Anima liber
Accattino, P. & P. L. Donini (eds) 1996. *Alessandro di Afrodisia: L'Anima*. Rome: Laterza.
Bergeron, M. & R. Dufour (eds & trans.) 2008. *Alexandre d'Aphrodise: De l'Âme*. Paris: Vrin.
Bruns, I. (ed.) 1887. *Alexandri Aphrodisiensis praeter commentaria scripta minora. De Anima liber cum Mantissa*, Supplementum Aristotelicum 2.1. Berlin: Reimer.
Moraux, P. (ed.) 1942. *Alexandre d'Aphrodise: Exégète de la noétique d'Aristote*. Liège: Bibliothèque de la faculté de philosophie et lettres de l'Université de Liège.
Sharples, R. W. (trans.) 2004. *Alexander of Aphrodisias. Supplement to "On the Soul"*. Ithaca, NY: Cornell University Press.

de Fato
Bruns, I. (ed.) 1892. *De Fato*, Supplementum Aristotelicum 2.1. Berlin: Reimer.
Sharples, R. W. (ed. & trans.) 1983. *Alexander of Aphrodisias: On Fate*. London: Duckworth.

de Intellectu
Schroeder, F. M. & R. B. Todd (trans.) 1990. *Two Greek Aristotelian Commentators on the Intellect. The De Intellectu attributed to Alexander of Aphrodisias and Themistius' Paraphrase of Aristotle De Anima 3.4–8. Introduction*. Toronto: Pontifical Institute of Medieval Studies.

in Aristotelis Analyticorum Priorum librum I
Barnes, J., S. Bobzien, K. Flannery & K. Ierodiakonou (trans.) 1991. *Alexander of Aphrodisias on Aristotle Prior Analytics 1.1–7*. London: Duckworth.

in Aristotelis Metaphysica
Hayduck, M. (ed.) 1891. *Alexandri Aphrodisiensis in Aristotelis Metaphysica commentaria*, Commentaria in Aristotelem Graeca 1. Berlin: Reimer.

in Librum de Sensu
Wendland, P. (ed.) 1901. *Alexandri Aphrodisiensis in Librum de Sensu commentarium*, Commentaria in Aristotelem Graeca 3.1. Berlin: Reimer.

Questiones
Bruns, I. (ed.) 1892. *Alexandri Aphrodisiensis praeter commentaria scripta minora. Quaestiones, de Fato, de Mixtione*, Supplementum Aristotelicum 2.2. Berlin: Reimer.
Sharples, R. W. (trans.) 1994. *Alexander of Aphrodisias: Quaestiones 2.16–3.15*. Ithaca, NY: Cornell University Press.

AL-FARABI

Najjar, F. (ed.) 1986. *Fusul muntaza'a*. Beirut: Dar al-Mashriq.
Walzer, R. 1985. *On the Perfect State (Mabādi' ārā' ahl al-madīnat al-fāḍilah)*, Abū Naṣr Al-Fārābī. Oxford: Clarendon Press.

AL-KINDI

Ivry, A. L. (ed. & trans.) 1974. *Al-Kindī's Metaphysics*. Albany, NY: SUNY Press.
Pormann, P. E. & P. Adamson (eds & trans.) 2012. *The Philosophical Works of al-Kindi*. Oxford: Oxford University Press.

AMMONIUS

in Aristotelis Categorias

Busse, A. (ed.) 1895. *Ammonius in Aristotelis Categorias*, Commentaria in Aristotelem Graeca 4.4. Berlin: Reimer.

Cohen, S. M. & G. B. Matthews (trans.) 1991. *Ammonius: On Aristotle Categories*. Ithaca, NY: Cornell University Press.

in Aristotelis de Interpretatione

Blank, D. (trans.) 1996. *Ammonius: On Aristotle On Interpretation 1–8*. Ithaca, NY: Cornell University Press.

Busse, A. (ed.) 1897. *Ammonius in Aristotelis de Interpretatione commentarius*, Commentaria in Aristotelem Graeca 4.5. Berlin: Reimer.

in Porphyrii Isagogen sive V Voces

Busse, A. (ed.) 1891. *Ammonius in Porphyrii Isagogen sive V Voces*, Commentaria in Aristotelem Graeca 4.3. Berlin: Reimer.

ANONYMOUS COMMENTARY ON PLATO'S PARMENIDES

Bechtle, G. 1999. *The Anonymous Commentary on Plato's Parmenides*. Bern: Paul Haupt.

Linguiti, A. 1995. *Commentarium in Platonis Parmenidem*. In *Corpus dei papiri filosofici greci e latini* III: Commentari, F. Adorno *et al.* (eds), 63–201. Florence: Olschki.

ANONYMOUS COMMENTARY ON PLATO'S THEAETETUS

Bastianini, G. & D. Sedley (eds) 1995. *Anonymous in Tht. (PBerol. inv. 9782)*. In *Corpus dei papiri filosofici greci e latini* III, F. Adorno *et al.* (eds), 227–562. Florence: Olschki.

ANONYMOUS DIALOGUE ON POLITICAL SCIENCE

Mazzucchi, C. (ed. & trans.) 1982. *Menae patricii cum Thoma referendario de scientia politica dialogus*. Milan: Vita e Pensiero.

ANONYMOUS PROLEGOMENA TO PLATONIC PHILOSOPHY

Westerink, L. G. (ed. & trans.) 1962. *Anonymous Prolegomena to Platonic Philosophy*. Amsterdam: North-Holland.

Westerink, L. G., J. Trouillard & A. Segonds (eds & trans.) 1990. *Prolégomènes à la philosophie de Platon*. Paris: Les Belles Lettres.

PSEUDO-ARCHYTAS

Thesleff, H. (ed.) 1965. *The Pythagorean Texts of the Hellenistic Period*. Åbo: Åbo Akademi.

ARISTOTLE

Barnes, J. (ed.) 1984. *Complete Works of Aristotle. The Revised Oxford Translation*, 2 vols. Princeton, NJ: Princeton University Press.

Ross, W. D. (ed.) 1910–52. *The Works of Aristotle*, 12 vols. Oxford: Clarendon Press.

Analytica Priora et Posteriora

Ross, W. D. (ed.) 1968. *Aristotelis Analytica Priora et Posteriora*. Oxford: Clarendon Press.

Categoriae

Ackrill, J. L. (trans.) 1963. *Aristotle: Categories and De Interpretatione*. Oxford: Clarendon Press.

de Anima

Hamlyn, D. W. (trans. & comm.) 1993. *Aristotle: De Anima, Books II and III (with passages from Book I)*. With a Report on Recent Work and a Revised Bibliography by C. Shields. Oxford: Oxford University Press.

de Interpretatione

Ackrill, J. L. (trans.) 1963. *Aristotle: Categories and De Interpretatione*. Oxford: Clarendon Press.

Ethica Nicomachea

Broadie, S. & C. Rowe (trans.) 2002. *Aristotle: Nicomachean Ethics*. Translation, Introduction and Commentary. Oxford: Oxford University Press.

Bywater, I. (ed.) 1962. *Aristotelis Ethica Nicomachea*. Oxford: Clarendon Press.

Fragmenta

Ross, W. D. (ed.) 1955. *Aristotelis Fragmenta Selecta*. Oxford: Clarendon Press.

Metaphysica

Annas, J. (trans.) 1976. *Aristotle's Metaphysics, Books M and N*. Oxford: Clarendon Press.

Frede, M. & G. Patzig (eds & trans.) 1988. *Aristoteles Metaphysik Z: Text, Übersetzung und Kommentar*, 2 vols. Munich: Beck.

Jaeger, W. (ed.) 1957. *Aristotelis Metaphysica*. Oxford: Clarendon Press.

Ross, W. D. (ed.) 1924. *Aristotle: Metaphysics*, 2 vols. Oxford: Clarendon Press.

ATTICUS

Des Places, É. (ed.) 1977. *Atticus: Fragments*. Paris: Les Belles Lettres.

AUGUSTINE OF HIPPO

Brogan, M. I. (trans.) 1968. *St Augustine: The Retractions*. Washington, DC: Catholic University of America Press.

Burleigh, J. H. S. (trans.) 1959. *St Augustine: Of True Religion*. Chicago: Henry Regnery.

Dyson, R. W. (trans.) 1998. *St Augustine: The City of God against the Pagans*. Cambridge: Cambridge University Press.

Hill, E. (trans.) 1991. *St Augustine: The Trinity*. Hyde Park, NY: New City Press.

Pine-Coffin, R. S. (trans.) 1961. *St Augustine: Confessions*. Harmondsworth: Penguin.

Robertson, D. W. (trans.) 1958. *St Augustine: On Christian Doctrine*. New York: Macmillan.

AULUS GELLIUS

Rolfe, J. C. (trans.) 1927. *The Attic Nights of Aulus Gellius*, 3 vols. Cambridge, MA: Harvard University Press.

CALCIDIUS

Den Boeft, J. 1970. *Calcidius on Fate: His Doctrine and Sources*. Leiden: Brill.

Waszink, J. (ed.) 1962. *Timaeus a Calcidio translatus commentarioque instructus*, Corpus Platonicum Medii Aevi, Plato Latinus 4. Leiden: Brill.

CHALDAEAN ORACLES

Des Places, É. (ed. & trans.) 1971. *Oracles Chaldaïques*. Paris: Les Belles Lettres.

CICERO

Moreschini, C. (ed.) 2005. *M. T. Cicero: De finibus bonorum et malorum*. Leipzig: Teubner.

Van Straaten, M. (ed.) 1946. *Panétius, sa vie, ses écrits et sa doctrine avec une édition des fragments*. Amsterdam: H. J. Paris.

CLEMENT

Casey, R. P. (ed.) 1934. *The Excerpta ex Theodoto of Clement of Alexandria*, Studies and Documents 1. London: Christophers.

Migne, J. P. (ed.) 1857–66. *Clementis Alexandrini opera quae extant omnia*, Patrologia Graeca 8 & 9. Paris: Imprimerie Catholique.

PSEUDO-CLEMENT

Rehm, B. & I. Irmscher (eds) 1953. *Die Pseudoklementinen* I. Berlin: Akademie.

CODEX BRUCE

Schmidt, C. & V. MacDermot (eds & trans.) 1978. *The Books of Jeu and the Untitled Text in the Bruce Codex*. Leiden: Brill.

COPTIC GNOSTIC LIBRARY, NAG HAMMADI CODICES

Barry, C., W.-P. Funk, P.-H. Poirier & J. D. Turner (eds) 2000. *Zostrien (NH VIII,1)*. Bibliothèque copte de Nag Hammadi, section "Textes" 24. Quebec: Presses de l'Université Laval.

Funk, W.-P., P.-H. Poirier & J. D. Turner (eds) 2000. *Marsanès (NH X,1)*. Bibliothèque copte de Nag Hammadi, section "Textes" 27. Quebec: Presses de l'Université Laval.

Funk, W.-P., M. Scopello, P.-H. Poirier & J. D. Turner (eds) 2004. *L'Allogène (NH XI,3)*. Bibliothèque copte de Nag Hammadi, section "Textes" 30. Quebec: Presses de l'Université Laval.

Hedrick, C. W. (trans.) 1990. *Nag Hammadi Codices XI, XII and XIII*. The Coptic Gnostic Library, Nag Hammadi Studies 28. English translation, introduction and notes. Leiden: Brill.

Meyer, M. (ed.) 2007. *The Nag Hammadi Scriptures: The International Edition*. San Francisco, CA: HarperOne.

CORPUS HERMETICUM

Festugière, A.-J. (ed. & trans.) 1954. *Hermès Trismégiste. Corpus Hermeticum*, vols 3–4. Paris: Les Belles Lettres.

Nock, A. D. (ed.) & A.-J. Festugière (trans.) 1946. *Hermès Trismégiste. Corpus Hermeticum*, vols 1–2. Paris: Les Belles Lettres.

DAMASCIUS

de Principiis

Ahbel-Rappe, S. (trans.) 2010. *Damascius: Problems and Solutions Concerning First Principles*. New York: Oxford University Press.

Westerink, L. G. & Combès, J. (eds & trans.) 1986–91. *Damascius: Traité des Premiers Principes*, 3 vols. Paris: Les Belles Lettres.

in Platonis Parmenidem

Westerink, L. G, J. Combès, A.-Ph. Segonds & C. Luna (eds & trans.) 1997–2003. *Damascius: Commentaire du Parménide de Platon*, 4 vols. Paris: Les Belles Lettres.

Vita Isidori

Athanassiadi, P. (trans.) 1999. *Damascius: The Philosophical History*. Athens: Apameia Cultural Association.

Zintzen, C. (ed.) 1967. *Vitae Isidori reliquiae*. Hildesheim: Olms.

DAVID

Busse, A. (ed.) 1900. *In Porphyrii Isagogen*, Commentaria in Aristotelem Graeca 18.1. Berlin: Reimer.

DEXIPPUS

Dillon, J. (trans.) 1990. *Dexippus: On Aristotle Categories*. Ithaca, NY: Cornell University Press.

DIOGENES LAERTIUS

Long, H. S. (ed.) 1964. *Diogenes Laertius: Vitae Philosophorum*, 2 vols. Oxford: Clarendon Press.

Marcovich, M. (ed.) 1999–2002. *Diogenis Laertii Vitae Philosophorum*, 3 vols. Stuttgart: Teubner.

PSEUDO-DIONYSIUS THE AREOPAGITE

Hopkins, J. (trans.) 1998. *Nicolas of Cusa: Metaphysical Speculations. Six Latin Texts*. Minneapolis: Arthur J. Banning Press.

Luibhéid, C. (trans.) 1987. *Pseudo-Dionysius: The Complete Works*. New York: Paulist Press.

"ELIAS" VEL PSEUDO-ELIAS

Busse, A. (ed.) 1892. *Eliae in Porphyrii Isagogen et Aristotelis Categorias commentaria*, Commentaria in Aristotelem Graeca 18.1. Berlin: Reimer.

Westerink, L. G. (ed.) 1967. *Pseudo-Elias (Pseudo-David): Lectures on Porphyry's Isagoge*. Amsterdam: North-Holland.

EPICTETUS

Dobbin, R. (trans.) 2008. *Epictetus: Discourses and Selected Writings*. London: Penguin.

Schenkl, H. (ed.) 1916. *Epicteti Dissertationes ab Arriano Digestae*, 2nd edn. Lepzig: Teubner.

EPICURUS

Arrighetti, G. (ed.) 1973. *Epicuro: Opere*, 2nd edn. Turin: Einaudi.

ERIUGENA, JOHN SCOTUS

Brennan, M. (ed.) 1998. *John Scottus Eriugena: Treatise on Divine Predestination*. Notre Dame, IN: University of Notre Dame Press.

Floss, H. J. (ed.) 1853. *Johannis Scoti Opera quae supersunt Omnia*, Patrologia Latina 122. Paris: Migne.

Jeauneau, É. (ed.) 1995. *Johannis Scotti Eriugenae Periphyseon (De Divisione Naturae) Liber Quartus*, J. J. O'Meara and I. P. Sheldon-Williams (trans.) Scriptores Latini Hiberniae 13. Dublin: Institute for Advanced Studies.

Jeauneau, É. (ed.) 1996–2003. *Peryphyseon: Editionem novam a suppositiciis quidem additamentis purgatam, ditatam vero appendice in qua vicissitudines operis synoptice exhibentur*, Corpus Christianorum Continuation Mediaevalis 161–5. Turnhout: Brepols.

Sheldon-Williams, I. P. (ed.) 1968. *John Scotus Eriugena: Periphyseon (De Divisione Naturae) Liber Primus*. Dublin: Institute for Advanced Studies.

Sheldon-Williams, I. P. (ed.) 1972. *John Scotus Eriugena: Periphyseon (De Divisione Naturae) Liber Secundus*. Dublin: Institute for Advanced Studies.

Sheldon-Williams, I. P. (ed.) 1981. *John Scotus Eriugena: Periphyseon (De Divisione Naturae) Liber Tertius*. Dublin: Institute for Advanced Studies.

Sheldon-Williams, I. P. (trans.) 1987. *John Scotus Eriugena: Periphyseon (The Division of Nature)*, books 1-5, revised by J. J. O'Meara. Montreal: Bellarmin.

EUCLID

Heath, T. L. (ed. & trans.) 1956. *Euclid: The Thirteen Books of the Elements*, vol. 1. Translated with introduction and commentary. New York: Dover.

EUNAPIUS

Giangrande, I. (ed.) 1956. *Eunapii Vitae Sophistarum*. Rome: Istituto Poligrafico dello Stato.

EUSEBIUS

Des Places, É. (ed.) 1982–3. *Praeparatio Evangelica*, 2 vols, 2nd edn. Berlin: Akademie.

Lake, K. (trans.) [1926] 2001. *The Ecclesiastical History*, 2 vols. Cambridge, MA: Harvard University Press.

GALEN

Kühn, K. G. (ed.) 1821–1933. *Claudii Galeni opera omnia*, 20 vols. Leipzig: Cnobloch.

Individual works

De Lacy, P. (ed.) 2005. *Galeni de placitis Hippocratis et Platonis*, Corpus Medicorum Graecorum 5.4.1.2. Berlin: Akademie.

Diels, H. (ed.) 1915. *Galeni in Hippocratis prorrheticum I commentaria III*, Corpus Medicorum Graecorum 5.9.2. Berlin: Akademie.

Helmreich, G. (ed.) 1907–9. *Galeni de usu partium libri XVII*, 2 vols. Leipzig: Teubner.

Mewaldt, J. (ed.) 1914. *Galeni in Hippocratis de natura hominis commentaria III*, Corpus Medicorum Graecorum 5.9.1. Berlin: Akademie.

Müller, I. (ed.) 1891. *Quod animi mores corporis temperamenta sequuntur* [QAM]. In *Claudii Galeni Pergameni scripta minora*, vol. 2. Leipzig: Teubner.

Nickel, D. (ed.) 2001. *Galeni de foetuum formatione*, Corpus Medicorum Graecorum 5.3.3. Berlin: Akademie.

Nutton, V. (ed.) 1999. *Galeni de propriis placitis*, Corpus Medicorum Graecorum 5.3.2. Berlin: Akademie.

Schröder, H. O. (ed.) 1934. *Galeni in Platonis Timaeum commentarii fragmenta*. Leipzig: Teubner.

PSEUDO-GALEN

Wagner, H. 1914. *Galeni qui fertur libellus* Εἰ ζῷον τὸ κατὰ γαστρός. Ph.D. dissertation, Marburg.

GREGORY OF NYSSA

Daniélou, J. (ed.) 1941. *Grégoire de Nysse: Contemplation sur la vie de Moïse*. Paris: Cerf.

Jaeger, W., H. Langerbeck, H. Dörrie & H. Hoerner (eds) 1960–98. *Gregorii Nysseni opera*, 10 vols. Leiden: Brill.

Laplace, J. & J. Daniélou (trans.) 1943. *Peri kataskeuēs anthropou (De opificio hominis)*, trans. *La création de l'homme*. Paris: Cerf.

Maraval, P. (ed.) 1971. *Grégoire de Nysse: Vie de sainte Macrine*. Paris: Cerf.

Migne, J.-P. (ed.) 1857–66. *Sancti Patris Nostri Gregorii Episcopi Nysseni opera omnia*, Patrologia Graeca 44–6. Paris: Imprimerie Catholique.

HERMIAS OF ALEXANDRIA

Lucarini, C. M. & C. Moreschini (eds) 2012. *Hermias Alexandrinus: In Platonis Phaedrum scholia*. Berlin: De Gruyter.

HIEROCLES OF ALEXANDRIA

Henry, R. (ed. & trans.) 1959–79. *De fato*. In *Photius, Bibliotheca*. Paris: Les Belles Lettres.

Köhler, F. (ed.) 1974. *In aureum Pythagoreorum carmen commentarius*. Stuttgart: Teubner.

Schibli, H. S. (trans.) 2002. *Hierocles of Alexandria*. Oxford: Oxford University Press.

HIPPOCRATES

Littré, E. 1839–61. *Oeuvres complètes d'Hippocrate*, 10 vols. Paris: Baillière.

Individual works

Joly, R. (ed. & trans.) 1967. *Hippocrate: Du régime (De diaeta)*. Paris: Les Belles Lettres.

Jouanna, J. (ed.) 1996. *Hippocrate. Tome II, 2e Partie: Airs, Eaux, Lieux*. Paris: Les Belles Lettres.

Jouanna, J. (ed.) 2002. *Hippocratis de natura hominis*, Corpus Medicorum Graecorum 1.1.3. Berlin: Akademie.

HIPPOLYTUS

Marcovich, M. (ed.) 1986. *Hippolytus. Refutatio omnium haeresium*, Patristische Texte und Studien 25. Berlin: De Gruyter.

HOMER

Lattimore, R. (trans.) 1972. *The Iliad of Homer*. Chicago, IL: University of Chicago Press.

IAMBLICHUS

de Communi Mathematica Scientia

Festa, N. (ed.) 1891. *Iamblichi de communi mathematica scientia*. Leipzig: Teubner.

de Mysteriis

Clarke, E. C., J. M. Dillon & J. P. Hershbell (trans.) 2003. *Iamblichus: De Mysteriis*. Atlanta, GA: Society of Biblical Literature.

Saffrey, H. D. & A. P. Segonds (eds) 2013. *Jamblique: Réponse à Porphyre (De Mysteriis)*. Paris: Les Belles Lettres.

de Vita Pythagorica

Deubner, L. & U. Klein (eds) 1975. *Iamblichi De Vita Pythagorica Liber*. Leipzig: Teubner.

Dillon, J. & J. Herschbell (eds & trans.) 1991. *Iamblichus. On the Pythagorean Way of Life*. Text, Translation and Notes. Atlanta, GA: Scholars Press.

Epistolae

Wachsmuth, C. & O. Hense (eds) 1884–1923. *Iamblichi Epistolae*. In *Stobaeus, Anthologium*. Berlin: Weidmann.

Fragmenta

Dillon, J. M. (ed.) 1973. *Iamblichi Chalcidensis in Platonis dialogos commentariorum fragmenta*. Leiden: Brill. Reprinted Westbury: Prometheus Trust, 2009.

in Aristotelis de Anima

Finamore, J. F & J. Dillon (eds & trans.) 2002. *Iamblichus: De Anima. Text, Translation, and Commentary*. Leiden: Brill.

Wachsmuth, C. & O. Hense (eds) 1884–1923. *Ioannis Stobaei Anthologium*, 4 vols. Berlin: Weidmann.

in Nicomachi Arithmeticam Introductionem
Pistelli, H. & U. Klein (eds) 1975. *In Nicomachi arithmeticam introductionem*. Stuttgart: Teubner.

PSEUDO-IAMBLICHUS
De Falco, V. & U. Klein (eds) 1975. *[Iamblichi] Theologoumena arithmeticae*. Stuttgart: Teubner.
Waterfield, R. (trans.) 1988. *The Theology of Arithmetic*. Grand Rapids, MI: Phanes Press.

IBN GABIROL (AVICEBRON)
Fons Vitae
Baeumker, C. (ed.) 1982. *Avencebrolis (Ibn Gebirol) Fons Vitae, ex Arabico in Latinum Translatus ab Johanne Hispano et Dominico Gundissalino*. Beiträge zur Geschichte der Philosophie des Mittelalters, Texte und Untersuchungen 1.2. Munster: Aschendorff.
Pines, S. 1958. "*Sēfer 'Arūgat ha-Bōsem: ha-Qeta'īm mī-tōkh Sēfer 'Meqōr Hayyīm'*". *Tarbiẓ* 27: 218–33. Reprinted (with a renumbering of notes from note 22) in S. Pines (1977) *Bēyn Maḥshevet Yisrael le-Maḥshevet ha-'Amīm: Meḥqarīm be-Tōldōt ha-Fīlōsōfiya ha-Yehūdit*, 44–60. Jerusalem: Bialik Institute.

Keter Malkhūt ("Kingdom's Crown," "The Royal Crown") and other poems
Cole, P. 2001. *Selected Poems of Solomon Ibn Gabirol*. Princeton, NJ: Princeton University Press.
Cole, P. 2007. *The Dream of the Poem: Hebrew Poetry from Muslim and Christian Spain, 950–1492*. Princeton, NJ: Princeton University Press.
Lewis, B. 2003. *The Kingly Crown: Keter Malkhut by Solomon Ibn Gabirol*. Introduction and commentary by A. L. Gluck. Notre Dame, IN: University of Notre Dame Press.
Zangwill, I. 1923/44. *Selected Religious Poems of Solomon Ibn Gabirol*. Philadelphia, PA: The Jewish Publication Society of America.

IBN SINA (AVICENNA)
"*Risālah fi'l-'ishq*" (*Treatise on Love*)
Fackenheim, E. (trans.) 1945. "A Treatise on Love by Ibn Sina". *Mediaeval Studies* 7: 208–28.
Mehren, A. F. M. (ed.) 1891. *Traités Mystiques*. Arabic text. Leiden: Brill.

Other works
Corbin, H. (ed.) 1960. *Avicenna and the Visionary Recital*. New York: Pantheon Books.
Marmura, M. E. (ed.) 2005. *The Metaphysics of the Healing: A Parallel English-Arabic Text (Al-Shifā': Al-lIāhīyāt)*. Provo, UT: Brigham Young University Press.
McGinnis, J. (ed.) 2009. *The Physics of the Healing: A Parallel English-Arabic Text (Al-Shifā': Al-Samā' Al-Ṭabī'ī)*, 2 vols. Provo, UT: Brigham Young University Press.

IBN TUFAYL
Kocache, R. 1982. *The Journey of the Soul*. London: The Octagon Press.

IKHWĀN AṢ-ṢAFĀ' (THE BRETHREN OF PURITY)
al-Ziriklī, Khayr al-Dīn (ed.) 1928. *Ikhwān aṣ-Ṣafā' (The Brethren of Purity), Rasā'il*, 4 vols. Cairo: 'Arabīyah Press.

IRENAEUS
Doutreleau, L. & A. Rousseau (eds & trans.) 1965–74. *Irénée de Lyon: Contre les hérésies*, 3 vols. Paris: Cerf.
Harvey, W. W. (ed.) 1857. *Sancti Irenaei episcopi Lugdunensis libri quinque adversus haereses*, 2 vols. Cambridge: Cambridge University Press.

ISAAC BEN SOLOMON IZRAELI
Altmann, A. & S. M. Stern (eds) 1958. *Isaac Israeli*. Oxford: Oxford University Press. Reprinted with introduction by A. Ivry: Chicago, IL: University of Chicago Press, 2009.

JOHN OF ALEXANDRIA

Bell, T. A., D. P. Carpenter, D. W. Schmidt, M. N. Sham, G. I. Vardon & L. G. Westerink (eds) 1997. *Ioannis Alexandrini in Hippocratis de natura pueri commentarium. Anonymi in Hippocratis de natura pueri commentarium*, Corpus Medicorum Graecorum 11.1.4. Berlin: Akademie.

Duffy, J. M. (ed.) 1997. *Ioannis Alexandrini in Hippocratis epidemiarum librum VI commentarii fragmenta*, Corpus Medicorum Graecorum 11.1.4. Berlin: Akademie.

JOHN OF NIKIU

Charles, H. R. (trans.) 1916. *The Chronicle of John, Bishop of Nikiu*. Oxford: Oxford University Press.

JUSTIN MARTYR

Barnard, L. W. (ed.) 1997. *St Justin Martyr: The First and Second Apologies*. Mahwah, NJ: Paulist Press.

Van Winden, J. C. M. (ed.) 1971. *An Early Christian Philosopher: Justin Martyr's Dialogue with Trypho, Chapters One to Nine*, Philosophia Patrum 1. Leiden: Brill.

KALĀM FĪ MAḤḌ AL-KHAIR (AKA LIBER DE CAUSIS)

Badawi, A. (ed.) 1955. *Neoplatonici apud Arabes: Liber (Pseudo-Aristotelis) de expositione bonitatis purae*. Cairo: Maktabat al-nahda al-Misriya.

Bardenhewer, O. (ed.) 1882. *Die pseudo-aristotelische Schrift, Über das reine Gute, bekannt unter dem Namen, Liber de Causis*. Freiberg-im-Breisgau: Herdersche Verlagshandlung.

Guagliardo, V. A., C. Hess & R. C. Taylor (trans.) 1996. *St Thomas Aquinas' Commentary on the Book of Causes*. Washington, DC: Catholic University of America Press.

LIBANIUS

Foerster, R. (ed.) 1915. *Libanii opera*, 8 vols. Leipzig: Teubner.

MACROBIUS

Willis, J. (ed.) 1970. *Commentarii in somnium Scipionis*. Leipzig: Teubner.

MAHĀBHĀRATA

Esnoul, A.-M. 1979. *Nārāyaṇīya Parvan du Mahābhārata. Un texte Pāñcaratra*. Paris: Les Belles Lettres.

Ganguli, K. M. (trans.) 1891. *Mahābhārata, The Mahābhārata of Krishna-Dwaipayana Vyasa Translated into English Prose: Çanti Parva*, 2 vols. Calcutta: Bhārata Press.

Sukthankar, V. S. (ed.) 1933–66. *The Mahābhārata for the First Time Critically Edited*, 19 vols. Pune: Bhandarkar Oriental Research Institute.

MAIMONIDES, MOSES

Munk, S. (ed.) 1931. *Dalālat al-Ḥā'irīn*. Jerusalem: Janovitch.

Pines, S. (trans.) 1963. *The Guide of the Perplexed*, 2 vols. Chicago, IL: University of Chicago Press.

Twersky, I. (ed.) 1972. "Eight Chapters". In *A Maimonides Reader*, 361–86. Springfield, NJ: Behrman House, Inc.

MARINUS

Edwards, M. (trans.) 2000. *Neoplatonic Saints. The Lives of Plotinus and Proclus by their Students*. Liverpool: Liverpool University Press.

Guthrie, K. (trans.) 1925. *The Life of Proclus or Concerning Happiness*. North Yonkers, NY: Platonist Press.

Saffrey, H. D. & A.-Ph. Segonds (eds & trans.) 2001. *Proclus ou sur le bonheur*. Paris: Les Belles Lettres.

MARIUS VICTORINUS

Henry, P. (ed.) & P. Hadot (trans.) 1960. *Marius Victorinus: Traités théologiques sur la Trinité*, vol. 1: Text and translation; vol. 2: Notes, *Sources chrétiennes* 68–9. Paris: Cerf.

MICHAEL OF EPHESUS

Hayduck, M. (ed.) 1903. *Ioannis Philoponi (Michaelis Ephesii) in libros de generatione animalium commentaria*, Corpus Medicorum Graecorum 14.3. Berlin: Reimer.

MICHAEL PSELLUS

Duffy, J. M. & D. J. O'Meara (eds) 1989. *Psellus: Philosophica Minora*, vol. 1. Leipzig: Teubner.
O'Meara, D. J. 1986. "The Excerpts of Iamblichus' *On Pythagoreanism* V–VII in Psellus: Text, Translation, and Notes". In his *Pythagoras Revived: Mathematics and Philosophy in Late Antiquity*, 217–29. Oxford: Clarendon Press.
O'Meara, D. J. (ed.) 1989. *Psellus: Philosophica minora*, vol. 2. Leipzig: Teubner.

MODERATUS

Mullach, F. A. (ed.) 1860. *Fragmenta philosophorum graecorum*. Paris: Didot.

NEMESIUS

Migne, J.-P. (ed.) 1857–66. *Nemesius Emesenus: De natura hominis*, Patrologia Graeca 40. Paris: Imprimerie Catholique.
Morani, M. (ed.) 1987. *Nemesii Emeseni De natura hominis*. Leipzig: Teubner.
Sharples, R. W. & Ph. J. van der Eijk (trans.) 2008. *Nemesius: On the Nature of Man*. Liverpool: Liverpool University Press.

NICOMACHUS OF GERASA

D'Ooge, M. L. (trans.)1926. *Nicomachus of Gerasa: Introduction to Arithmetic*. London: Macmillan.
Hoche, R. (ed.) 1846. *Nicomachi Geraseni arithmetica introductio*. Stuttgart: Teubner.

NUMENIUS

Des Places, É. 1973. *Numénius: Fragments*. Paris: Les Belles Lettres.
Leemans, E.-A. (ed.) 1937. *Studie over den Wijsgeer Numenius van Apamea met Uitgave der Fragmenten*. Brussels: Académie royale de Belgique.

OLYMPIODORUS

in Aristotelis Metaphysica
Stüve, G. (ed.) 1900. *Olympiodori in Aristotelis Metaphysica commentaria*, Commentaria in Aristotelem Graeca 12.2. Berlin: Reimer.

in Platonis Alcibiadem
Westerink, L. G. (trans.) [1956] 1982. *Olympiodorus: Commentary on the First Alcibiades of Plato*. Amsterdam: Hakkert.

in Platonis Gorgiam
Jackson, R., K. Lycos & H. Tarrant (trans.) 1998. *Olympiodorus: Commentary on Plato's Gorgias*. Leiden: Brill.
Westerink, L. G. (ed.) 1970. *Olympiodorus: In Platonis Gorgiam commentaria*. Leipzig: Teubner.

in Platonis Phaedonem
Westerink, L. G. (ed. & trans.) 1976. *The Greek Commentaries on Plato's Phaedo*, vol. 1: *Olympiodorus*. Amsterdam: North-Holland.

ORIGEN

Bader, R. (ed.) 1940. *Der Alethes Logos des Kelsos*. Stuttgart: Kohlhammer.
Butterworth, G. W. (trans.) 1973. *Origen: On First Principles*. Gloucester, MA: Peter Smith.

ORPHIC ARGONAUTICA

Dottin, G. 1930. *Les Argonautiques d'Orphée*. Paris: Les Belles Lettres.

PANAETIUS

Van Straaten, M. (ed.) 1962. *Panaetii Rhodii fragmenta*. Leiden: Brill.

PHANES

Preisendanz, K. & A. Henrichs (eds) 1973–4. *Die griechischen Zauberpapyri*, vols 1–2, 2nd edn. Stuttgart: Teubner.

Quandt, W. (ed.) 1962. *Orphei hymni*, 3rd edn. Berlin: Weidmann.

PHILODEMUS

Mekler, S (ed.) [1902] 1958. *Academicorum philosophorum index Herculanensis*. Berlin: Weidmann.

PHILO OF ALEXANDRIA

Runia, D. T. (ed.) 2001. *Philo of Alexandria: On the Creation of the Cosmos According to Moses*. Introduction, Translation and Commentary, Philo of Alexandria Commentary Series 1. Leiden: Brill.

PHILOPONUS

in Aristotelis de Anima Libros

Charlton, W. (trans.) 2000. *"Philoponus": On Aristotle On the Soul 3.1–8*. Ithaca, NY: Cornell University Press.

Charlton, W. & F. Bossier (trans.) 1991. *Philoponus: On Aristotle on the Intellect (de Anima 3.4-8)*. Ithaca, NY: Cornell University Press.

Van der Eijk, Ph. J. (trans.) 2005. *Philoponus: On Aristotle On the Soul 1.1–2*. Ithaca, NY: Cornell University Press.

Van der Eijk, Ph. J. (trans.) 2006. *Philoponus: On Aristotle On the Soul 1.3–5*. Ithaca, NY: Cornell University Press.

Verbeke, G. (ed.) 1966. *Philoponus: Commentaire sur le De Anima d'Aristote. Traduction de Guillaume de Moerbeke*, Corpus Latinum Commentariorum in Aristotelem Graecorum 3. Paris: Éditions Béatrice-Nauwelaerts.

in Aristotelis Physica

Urmson, J. O. & P. Lettinck 1994. *Philoponus, On Aristotle Physics 5–8 with Simplicius, On Aristotle on the Void*. London: Duckworth.

Vitelli, H. (ed.) 1887–8. *Philoponi in Aristotelis Physica commentaria*, Commentaria in Aristotelem Graeca 16–17. Berlin: Reimer.

On the Astrolabe

Green, H. W. (trans.) 1932. *Treatise on the Astrolabe*. In R. T. Gunther, *The Astrolabes of the World*. Oxford: Clarendon Press. Reprinted London: Holland Press, 1976, 61–81.

Hase, H. (ed.) 1893. *On the Use and Construction of the Astrolabe*. Bonn: Weber. Reprinted in 1839, *Rheinisches Museum für Philologie* 6: 127–71. Trans. into French in 1981 as *Jean Philopon, traité de l'astrolabe*, A.-Ph. Segonds (trans.). Paris: Librairie Alain Brieux.

PHOTIUS

Porson, R. (ed.) 1822. *Photiou tou patriarchou lexeon synagoge*, 2 vols. Cambridge: Cambridge University Press.

PINDAR

Race, W. H. (ed. & trans.) 1997. *Olympian Odes. Pythian Odes*. Cambridge, MA: Harvard University Press.

PLATO

Burnet, J. (ed.) 1900–1907. *Platonis opera*, 5 vols. Oxford: Clarendon Press.

Duke, E. A., W. F. Hicken, W. S. M. Nicoll, D. B. Robinson & J. C. G. Strachan (eds) 1995. *Platonis opera*, vol. 1. Oxford: Clarendon Press.

Cratylus

Ademollo, F. 2011. *The Cratylus of Plato: A Commentary*. Cambridge: Cambridge University Press.

Leges

Bury, R. G. (trans.) 1926. *Plato: Laws*. Cambridge, MA: Harvard University Press.

Meno

Guthrie, W. K. C. (trans.) 1971. *Plato's Meno*. Indianapolis: Bobbs-Merrill.

Phaedrus

Fowler, H. N. (trans.) 1999. *Plato: Euthyphro, Apology, Crito, Phaedo, Phaedrus.* Cambridge, MA: Harvard
   University Press.

Philebus

Frede, D. (trans.) 1993. *Plato: Philebus.* Indianapolis, IN: Hackett.
Frede, D. 1997. *Philebus.* In *Plato: Complete Works,* J. M. Cooper & D. S. Hutchinson (eds). Indianapolis, IN:
   Hackett.

Respublica

Cooper, J. M. (ed.) 1997. *Plato: Complete Works.* Indianapolis, IN: Hackett.
Halliwell, S. (trans.) 1988. *Plato: Republic 10.* Warminster: Aris & Phillips.
Hamilton, E. & H. Cairns (eds) 1961. *Plato: The Collected Dialogues.* Princeton, NJ: Princeton University Press.
Lee, H. P. D. (trans.) 1955. *Plato: The Republic.* London: Penguin.
Shorey, P. (trans.) 1969. *Plato: Republic,* 2 vols. Cambridge, MA: Harvard University Press.
Slings, S. R. (ed.) 2003. *Platonis opera,* vol. 4. Oxford: Clarendon Press.

Sophist

Fowler, H. N. (trans.) 1988. *Plato: Theaetetus. Sophist.* Cambridge, MA: Harvard University Press.

Symposium

Dover, K. (ed.) 1980. *Plato: Symposium.* Cambridge: Cambridge University Press.

Testimonia Platonica

Gaiser, K. (ed.) 1963. *Testimonia Platonica. Quellentexte zur Schule und mündlichen Lehre Platons.* In *Platons
   Ungeschriebene Lehre.* Stuttgart: Klett.

Theaetetus

Cornford, F. M. (trans.) 1935. *Plato's Theory of Knowledge: The Theaetetus and the Sophist.* London: Kegan Paul.

Timaeus

Cornford, F. M. (trans.) [1935] 1997. *Plato: Timaeus.* Indianapolis, IN: Hackett.
Jowett, B. (trans.) 1892. *The Dialogues of Plato,* 5 vols. Oxford: Oxford University Press.
Zeyl, D. (trans.) 2000. *Plato: Timaeus.* Indianapolis, IN: Hackett.

PLINY

Rackham, H. (trans.) 1952. *Pliny: Natural History,* vol. 9. Cambridge, MA: Harvard University Press.

PLOTINUS

Editions, translations and readers
Armstrong, A. H. (trans.) 1966–88. *Plotinus: Enneads,* 7 vols. Cambridge, MA: Harvard University Press.
Bréhier, É. (ed. & trans.) 1924–38. *Plotin: Ennéades,* 7 vols. Paris: Les Belles Lettres.
Bréhier, É. (ed. & trans.) 1954. *Plotin: Ennéad VI,* 2nd edn. Paris: Les Belles Lettres.
Brisson, L. & J.-F. Pradeau (eds) 2002–10. *Plotin: Traités,* 9 vols. Paris: Flammarion.
Cilento, V. (trans.) 1947–9. *Plotino: Enneadi,* 3 vols. Bari: Laterza.
Corrigan, K. 2004. *Reading Plotinus: A Practical Introduction to Neoplatonism.* West Lafayette, IN: Purdue
   University Press.
Harder, R., R. Beutler & W. Theiler (eds) 1956–97. *Plotins Schriften,* 6 vols. Hamburg: Felix Meiner.
Henry, P. & H.-R. Schwyzer (eds) 1951–73. *Plotini opera,* 3 vols *(editio maior).* Paris: Desclée de Brouwer.
Henry, P. & H.-R. Schwyzer (eds) 1964–82. *Plotini opera cum Porphyrii Vita Plotini,* 3 vols *(editio minor).*
   Oxford: Clarendon Press.
Igal, J. 1982, 1985. *Porfirio: Vida de Plotino; Plotino: Enneadas I–II and Plotino: Enneadas III–IV.* Madrid: Gredos.
MacKenna, S. (trans.) 1917. *Plotinus: The Ethical Treatises.* London: Macmillan.
MacKenna, S. 1956. *Plotinus: The Enneads,* 2nd edn, rev. trans. London: Faber.

Individual *Enneads*

Atkinson, M. 1983. *Plotinus: Ennead V, 1: On the Three Principal Hypostases.* Commentary with translation. Oxford: Oxford University Press.

Aubry, G. (trans.) 2004. *Plotin: Traité 53 (I, 1).* Introduction, commentary and notes. Paris: Cerf.

Bertier, J., L. Brisson & A. Charles-Saget *et al.* (eds & trans) 1980. *Plotin: Traité sur les nombres (Ennéade VI 6 [34]).* Paris: Vrin. Reprinted in A. Charles-Saget (ed.) 1982. *L'Architecture du divin: mathématique et philosophie chez Plotin et Proclus.* Paris: Les Belles Lettres.

Brisson, L. (trans.) 2008. *Plotin: Traités 42–44.* In *Plotin: Traités,* L. Brisson & J.-F. Pradeau (eds). Paris: Flammarion.

Bussanich, J. 1988. *The One and its Relation to Intellect in Plotinus: A Commentary on Selected Texts.* Leiden: Brill.

Fleet, B. 1995. *Plotinus: Ennead III.6. On the Impassivity of the Bodiless.* Translation with commentary. Oxford: Clarendon Press.

Fleet, B. 2012. *Plotinus. Ennead IV.8: On the Descent of the Soul into Bodies.* Translation, introduction and commentary. Las Vegas: Parmenides.

Hadot, P. (trans.) 1987. *Plotin. Traité 38 (VI, 7).* Introduction, translation, commentary and notes. Paris: Cerf.

Isnardi Parente, M. (ed. & trans.) 1994. *Plotino: Enneadi VI, 1–3.* Naples: Loffredo.

Lavaud, L. (trans.) 2007. *Plotin: Traité 39.* In *Plotin: Traités,* L. Brisson & J.-F. Pradeau (eds). Paris: Flammarion.

Leroux, G. (ed. & trans.) 1990. *Plotin: Traité sur la liberté et la volonté de l'Un (Ennéade VI, 8 (39)).* Paris: Vrin.

McGroarty, K. 2006. *Plotinus on Eudaimonia: A Commentary on Ennead I.4.* Oxford: Oxford University Press.

Narbonne, J.-M. (ed. & trans.) 1993. *Plotin, Les deux matières (Ennéade II, 4 (12)).* Paris: Vrin.

Narbonne, J.-M. & Ferroni, L. (eds & trans.) 2012. *Plotin: Œuvres complètes. Traité 1 (I, 6) Sur le beau.* Paris: Les Belles Lettres.

PLUTARCH

de Animae Procreatione in Timaeo

Ferrari, F. (ed.) 2002. *Plutarco: La generazione dell'anima nel Timeo.* Naples: D'Auria Editore.

de Iside et Osiride

Babbitt, F. C. (trans.) 1936. *Isis and Osiris.* In *Plutarch: Moralia,* vol. 5. Cambridge, MA: Harvard University Press.

Moralia

Babbitt, F. C. (trans.) 1928. *Plutarch: Moralia,* vol. 2. Cambridge, MA: Harvard University Press.

Cherniss, H. 1976. *Plutarch: On Stoic Self-Contradictions.* In *Plutarch: Moralia,* vol. 13.2. Cambridge, MA: Harvard University Press.

Cherniss, H. & W. C. Helmbold (trans.) 1957. *Plutarch: Moralia,* vol. 12. Cambridge, MA: Harvard University Press.

Fowler, H. N. (trans.) 1936. *Plutarch: Moralia,* vol. 10. Cambridge, MA: Harvard University Press.

Helmbold, W. C. (trans.) 1939. *Plutarch: Moralia,* vol. 6. Cambridge, MA: Harvard University Press.

Sieveking, W. (ed.) [1935] 1971. *Plutarchi Moralia,* vol. 2.3. Leipzig: Teubner.

PSEUDO-PLUTARCH

Mau, J. (ed.) 1971. *Plutarchi moralia,* vol. 5.2.1. Leipzig: Teubner.

PORPHYRY

ad Gaurum

Brisson, L., M.-H. Congourdeau & F. Hudry (eds & trans.) 2012. *Porphyre: Sur la manière dont l'embryon reçoit l'âme.* Paris: Vrin.

Kalbfleisch, K. 1895. *Die neuplatonische fälschlich dem Galen zugeschriebene Schrift* πρὸς Γαῦρον περὶ τοῦ πῶς ἐμψυχοῦνται τὰ ἔμβρυα. Berlin: Verlag der königlichen Akademie der Wissenschaften.

Wilberding, J. (trans.) 2011. *Porphyry: To Gaurus on How Embryos are Ensouled and On What is in Our Power.* London: Bristol Classical Press.

ad Marcellam

Nauck, A. (ed.) 1886. *Porphyrii philosophi platonici opuscula selecta.* Leipzig: Teubner.

adversus Christianos
Berchman, R. M. (trans.) 2005. *Porphyry: Against the Christians*. Leiden: Brill.

de Abstinentia
Clark, G. 2000. *Porphyry: On Abstinence from Killing Animals*. Ithaca, NY: Cornell University Press.

Fragmenta
Smith, A. (ed.) 1993. *Porphyrii philosophi fragmenta*. Stuttgart: Teubner.

in Aristotelis Categorias
Bodéüs, R. (trans.) 2008. *Porphyre: Commentaire aux Catégories d'Aristote*. Translation, introduction and notes. Paris: Vrin.
Strange, S. K. (trans.) 1992. *Porphyry: On Aristotle Categories*. Ithaca, NY: Cornell University Press.

in Platonis Timaeum
Sodano, A. R. (ed.) 1964. *Porphyrii in Platonis Timaeum commentariorum fragmenta*. Naples: privately printed.

in Ptolemaei Harmonica
Düring, I. (ed.) 1932. *Porphyrios Kommentar zur Harmonienlehre des Ptolemaios*. Gothenburg: Elander.

Isagoge
Barnes, J. (trans.) 2003. *Porphyry: Isagoge*. Oxford: Clarendon Press.
Busse, A. (ed.) 1887. *Porphyrii Isagoge et in Aristotelis Categorias commentarium*. Berlin: Reimer.

Quaestionum Homericarum ad Iliadem
Schrader, H. (ed.) 1880. *Porphyrii quaestionum Homericarum ad Iliadem pertinentium reliquiae*. Leipzig: Teubner.

Sententiae
Brisson, L. *et al.* 2005. *Porphyre: Sentences. Études d'introduction, texte grec et traduction française, commentaire*, 2 vols. With English translation by J. M. Dillon. Paris: Vrin.
Dillon, J. M. & L. P. Gerson (trans.) 2004. *Neoplatonic Philosophy: Introductory Readings*. Indianapolis, IN: Hackett.
Lamberz, F. (ed.) 1975. *Porphyry: Sentences*. Leipzig: Teubner.

Vita Plotini
Armstrong, A. H. (trans.) 1966. *Porphyry: On the Life of Plotinus and the Order of His Books*, in *Plotinus: Enneads*, vol 1, 1–87. Cambridge, MA: Harvard University Press.
Brisson, L., M.-O. Goulet Cazé, R. Goulet & D. O'Brien *et al.* (eds) 1982. *Porphyre: La Vie de Plotin*, vol. I. Paris: Vrin.
Brisson, L., M.-O. Goulet Cazé, R. Goulet & D. O'Brien *et al.* (eds) 1992. *Porphyre: La Vie de Plotin*, vol. II. Paris: Vrin.
Edwards, M. J. (trans.) 2000. *Neoplatonic Saints. The Lives of Plotinus and Proclus by their Students*. Liverpool: Liverpool University Press.
Henry, P. & H.-R. Schwyzer (eds) 1964. *Pophyrii Vita Plotini, in Plotini opera*, 3 vols (*editio maior*), vol. 1, 1–38. Paris: Desclée de Brouwer.

Vita Pythagorae
Nauck, A. (ed.) 1886. *Porphyrii philosophi Platonici opuscula selecta*. Leipzig: Teubner.

PRISCIAN
Bywater, I. (ed.) 1886. *Prisciani Lydi quae extant: Metaphrasis in Theophrastum et Solutionum ad Chosroem Liber*. Supplementum Aristotelicum 1.1. Berlin: Reimer.
Huby, P. & C. Steel (trans.) 1997. *Priscian: On Theophrastus on Sense-Perception and Simplicius' On Aristotle's On the Soul 2.5–12*. Ithaca, NY: Cornell University Press.

PROCLUS

de Malorum Subsistentia

Opsomer, J. & C. Steel (trans.) 2003. *Proclus: On the Existence of Evils*. Ithaca, NY: Cornell University Press.

de Providentia et Fato et Eo Quod in Nobis

Isaac, D. (ed. & trans.) 1977–82. *Proclus: Trois études sur la providence*, 3 vols. Paris: Les Belles Lettres.

Steel, C. (trans.) 2007. *Proclus: On Providence*. London: Duckworth.

de Providentia, Libertate, Malo

Boese, H. (ed.) 1960. *Procli Diadochi tria opuscula*. Berlin: De Gruyter.

de Sacrificio et Magia

Bidez, J. (ed.) 1928. *Catalogue des manuscrits alchimiques grecs*, 6 vols. Brussels: Lamertin.

Copenhaver, B. 1988. "Hermes Trismegistus, Proclus, and a Philosophy of Magic". In *Hermeticism and the Renaissance: Intellectual History and the Occult in Early Modern Europe*, I. Merkel & A. G. Debus (eds), 79–110. Washington, DC: Folger Books.

Hymni

Van den Berg, R. M. 2001. *Proclus' Hymns. Essays, Translations, Commentary*. Leiden: Brill.

Vogt, E. (ed.) 1957. *Procli Hymni*. Wiesbaden: Harrassowitz.

in Platonis Alcibiadem

Segonds, A.-Ph. (trans.) 1985–6. *Proclus: Sur le premier Alcibiade de Platon*, 2 vols. Paris: Les Belles Lettres.

in Platonis Cratylum

Duvick, B. (trans.) 2007. *Proclus: On Plato's Cratylus*. Ithaca, NY: Cornell University Press.

Pasquali, G. (ed.) 1908. *Procli Diadochi in Platonis Cratylum commentaria*. Leipzig: Teubner.

in Platonis Parmenidem

Cousin, V. (ed.) 1864. *Procli commentariorum in Platonis Parmenidem*. In *Procli opera inedita*, 617–1244. Paris: Durand.

Morrow, G. R. & J. M. Dillon (trans.) 1987. *Proclus' Commentary on Plato's Parmenides*. Princeton, NJ: Princeton University Press.

Steel, C. (ed.) 2007–9. *Procli in Platonis Parmenidem commentaria*, 3 vols. Oxford: Clarendon Press.

in Platonis Rempublicam

Kroll, W. (ed.) 1899–1901. *Procli Diadochi in Platonis Rem Publicam commentarii*, 2 vols. Leipzig: Teubner.

in Platonis Timaeum

Arnzen, R. (trans.) 2013. "Proclus on Plato's *Timaeus* 89e3–90c7". *Arabic Sciences and Philosophy* 23(1): 1–45.

Diehl, E. 1903–6. *Procli Diadochi In Platonis Timaeum commentaria*, 3 vols. Leipzig: Teubner.

Festugière, A.-J. (trans.) 1966–8. *Proclus: Commentaire sur le Timée*, 5 vols. Paris: Vrin.

Pfaff, F. 1941. "Kommentar des Proklos *Timaios* C. 43 (89e–90c). Aus dem Cod. Arab. Agia Sophia 3725 (pgg. 214–218)". In *Galeni de consuetudinibus*, I. M. Schmutte (ed.), Corpus Medicorum Graecorum Supplementum 3: 53–60. Leipzig: Teubner.

Tarrant, H. & D. Baltzly (eds & trans.) 2007–13. *Proclus' Commentary on Plato's Timaeus*, 5 vols (vol. 2 edited with M. Share & D. T. Runia). Cambridge: Cambridge University Press.

in Primum Euclidis Librum

Friedlein, G. (ed.) 1873. *Procli Diadochi in Primum Euclidis Elementorum librum commentarii*. Leipzig: Teubner.

Morrow, G. R. (trans.) 1970. *A Commentary on the First Book of Euclid's Elements*. Princeton, NJ: Princeton University Press.

Institutio (Elementatio) Theologica
Dodds, E. R. (ed. & trans.) 1963. *Proclus: The Elements of Theology*. Oxford: Clarendon Press.

Institutio Physica
Ritzenfeld, A. (ed.) 1912. *Procli Diadochi Lycii institutio physica*. Leipzig: Teubner.

Theologia Platonica
Saffrey, H. D. & L. G. Westerink (eds & trans.) 1968–97. *Proclus: Théologie platonicienne*, 6 vols. Paris: Les Belles Lettres.

SĒFER YEZĪRAH (*THE BOOK OF FORMATION/CREATION*)
Kaplan, A. 1997. *Sefer Yezirah, The Book of Creation*. Maine: Samuel Weiser Inc.

SEPTUAGINT
Pietersma, A. & B. G. Wright (eds) 2007. *A New English Translation of the Septuagint*. New York: Oxford University Press.

SEXTUS EMPIRICUS
Mutschmann, H. (ed.) 1912. *Pyrrhoniae hypotyposes. Sexti Empirici opera*, vol. 1. Leipzig: Teubner.
Mutschmann, H. & J. Mau (eds) 1914. *Adversus mathematicos. Sexti Empirici opera*, vols. 2 & 3, 2nd edn. Leipzig: Teubner.

SIMPLICIUS
in Aristotelis Categorias
Chase, M. (trans.) 2003. *Simplicius: On Aristotle's Categories 1–4*. Ithaca, NY: Cornell University Press.
De Haas, A. J. & B. Fleet (trans.) 2001. *Simplicius: On Aristotle's Categories 5–6*. Ithaca, NY: Cornell University Press.
Kalbfleisch, C. (ed.) 1907. *Simplicii in Aristotelis Categorias commentarium*, Commentaria in Aristotelem Graeca 8. Berlin: Reimer.
Luna, C. 2001. *Simplicius: Commentaire sur les Catégories d'Aristote. Chapitres 2–4*. Paris: Les Belles Lettres.

in Aristotelis de Caelo
Heiberg, J. L. (ed.) 1884. *Simplicii in Aristotelis de Caelo commentaria*, Commentaria in Aristotelem Graeca 7. Berlin: Reimer.
Mueller, I. (trans.) 2004. *Simplicius: On Aristotle's On the Heavens 2.1–9*. Ithaca, NY: Cornell University Press.

in Aristotelis Physica
Diels, H. (ed.) 1882 & 1895. *Simplicii in Aristotelis Physica commentaria*, Commentaria in Aristotelem Graeca 9–10. Berlin: Reimer.

in Epictetum
Brittain, C. & T. Brennan (eds & trans.) 2002. *Simplicius: On Epictetus' Handbook, Ancient Commentators on Aristotle*. London: Duckworth.
Dübner, F. 1842. *Theophrasti Characteres*. Paris: Didot.
Hadot, I. (ed.) 1996. *Simplicius: Commentaire sur le Manuel d'Epictète*. Leiden: Brill.

in Libros Aristotelis de Anima Commentaria
Blumenthal, H. J. (trans.) 2000. *"Simplicius": On Aristotle's On the Soul 3.1–5*. Ithaca, NY: Cornell University Press.
Hayduck, M. (ed.) 1882. *Simplicii in libros Aristotelis De Anima commentaria*. Berlin: Reimer.
Huby, P. & C. Steel (trans.) 1997. *Priscian: On Theophrastus' On Sense Perception and "Simplicius": On Aristotle's On the Soul 2.5–12*. Ithaca, NY: Cornell University Press.
Urmson, J. O. & P. Lautner (trans.) 1995. *"Simplicius": On Aristotle's On the Soul 1.1–2.4*. Ithaca, NY: Cornell University Press.

SPEUSIPPUS

Isnardi Parente, M. (ed. & trans.) 1980. *Speusippo: Frammenti*. Naples: Bibliopolis.

STEPHANUS OF ALEXANDRIA

Duffy, J. M. (ed. & trans.) 1983. *Stephani Philosophi in Hippocratis prognosticum commentaria III*, Corpus Medicorum Graecorum 11.1.2. Berlin: Akademie.

Westerink, L. G. (ed.) 1985–95. *Stephani Atheniensis in Hippocratis aphorismos commentaria*, Corpus Medicorum Graecorum 11.1.3.1–3. Berlin: Akademie.

STOBAEUS

Wachsmuth, C. 1974. *Ioannis Stobaei Anthologii libri duo priores qui inscribi solent Eclogae Physicae et Ethicae*, 2 vols. Zurich: Weidmann.

Wachsmuth, C. & O. Hense (eds) 1884–1923. *Ioannis Stobaei Anthologium*, 4 vols. Berlin: Weidmann.

SUDA

Adler, A. (ed.) 1928–38. *Suidae Lexicon*, 5 vols. Stuttgart: Teubner.

SUHRAWARDI

Walbridge, J. & H. Ziai (eds) 1999. *The Philosophy of Illumination: A New Critical Edition of the Text of Ḥikmat al-ishrāq*. Provo, UT: Brigham Young University Press.

SYNESIUS OF CYRENE

Fitzgerald, A. (trans.) 1926. *The Letters of Synesius of Cyrene*. Oxford: Oxford University Press.

Fitzgerald, A. & H. Milford (trans.) 1930. *The Essays and Hymns of Synesius of Cyrene*. Oxford: Oxford University Press.

Garzya, A. 1979. *Synesii Cyrenensis Epistolae*. Rome: Officinae poligraficae.

Garzya, A. (ed.) 1989. *Opere di Sinesio di Cirene: Epistole, Operette, Inni*. Turin: Unione tipografico-editrice Torinese.

Garzya, A. & D. Roques (eds & trans.) 2003. *Synésios de Cyrène: Correspondance*. Paris: Les Belles Lettres.

SYRIANUS

Dillon, J. & D. J. O'Meara (eds & trans.) 2006. *Syrianus: On Aristotle Metaphysics 3–4*. Ithaca, NY: Cornell University Press.

Kroll, W. (ed.) 1902. *Syriani in Aristotelis Metaphysica commentaria*, Commentaria in Aristotelem Graeca 7.1. Berlin: Reimer.

Wear, S. K. (ed. & trans.) 2011. *The Teachings of Syrianus on Plato's Timaeus and Parmenides*. Leiden: Brill.

TERTULLIAN

Roberts, A. *et al.* 1976. *Tertullian: The Prescription Against Heretics*. In *Latin Christianity: Its Founder Tertullian*, The Anti-Nicene Fathers vol. 3. Grand Rapids, MI: Eerdmans.

THEOLOGY OF ARISTOTLE

Badawi, A. (ed.) 1955. *Plotinus apud Arabes, Theologia Aristotelis et fragmenta quae supersunt*. Cairo: Maktabat al-nahda al-Misriya.

Lewis, G. L. (trans.) 1959. *Plotiniana Arabica*. In *Plotini opera*, vol. 2, P. Henry & H.-R. Schwyzer (eds). Brussels: Édition universelle.

THEON OF SMYRNA

Hiller, E. (ed.) 1878. *Theo Smyrnaeus: Expositio rerum mathematicarum ad legendum Platonem utilium*. Leipzig: Teubner.

THRASYLLUS

Tarrant, H. (ed.) 1993. *Thrasyllan Platonism*. Ithaca, NY: Cornell University Press.

XENOCRATES
Isnardi Parente, M. (ed.) 1982. *Senocrate—Ermodoro. Frammenti*. Naples: Bibliopolis.

XENOPHON
Marchant, E. C. (ed.) 1946. *Xenophontis opera omnia*. Oxford: Clarendon Press.

ZACHARIAS SCHOLASTICUS
Colonna, M. M. (ed. & trans.) 1973. *Zacaria Scolastico: Ammonio*. Naples: La Buona Stampa.
Gertz, S. (trans.) 2012. *Ammonius*. In *Aeneas of Gaza Theophrastus with Zacharias of Mytilene Ammonius*, S. Gertz, J. Dillon & D. Russell (trans.). London: Bloomsbury.
Kugener, M.-A. 1903. *Vie de Sévère par Zacharie le Scholastique*. Paris: Firmin-Didot.

MODERN AUTHORS

Abramowski, L. 1983. "Nag Hammadi 8,1 'Zostrianos', das Anonymum Brucianum, Plotin Enn. 2,9 (33)". In *Platonismus und Christentum: Festschrift für Heinrich Dörrie*, Jahrbuch für Antike und Christentum 10, H.-D. Blume & F. Mann (eds), 1–10. Munster: Aschendorff.

Abrams, M. H. 1973. *Natural Supernaturalism: Tradition and Revolution in Romantic Literature*. New York: Norton.

Accattino, P. 1992. "Alessandro di Afrodisia e gli astri: l'anima e la luce". *Atti della Accademia delle Scienze di Torino, classe di scienze morali, storiche e filologiche* 126: 39–62.

Ackrill, J. L. 1979. "Aristotle's Definitions of *Psuchē*". In *Articles on Aristotle*, vol. 4: *Psychology and Aesthetics*, J. Barnes, M. Schofield & R. Sorabji (eds), 65–75. London: Duckworth.

Adamson, P. 2002. *The Arabic Plotinus: A Philosophical Study of the Theology of Aristotle*. London: Duckworth.

Adamson, P. 2007. *Al-Kindī*. New York: Oxford University Press.

Adamson, P. 2008. "Plotinus on Astrology". *Oxford Studies in Ancient Philosophy* 35: 265–91.

Adamson, P. 2011. "Making a Virtue of Necessity: *Anangkē* in Plato, Plotinus and Proclus". *Études platoniciennes* 8: 9–30.

Adamson, P., H. Baltussen & M. W. F. Stone (eds) 2004. *Philosophy, Science and Exegesis in Greek, Arabic and Latin Commentaries*, Bulletin of the Institute of Classical Studies Suppl. 83(1–2). London: Institute of Classical Studies.

Adluri, V. 2009. "Warrior and Art Critic: Plato's *Republic* 10". Paper presented at the Seventh Annual Conference of the International Society for Neoplatonic Studies, 18–21 June, Krakow, Poland.

Adluri, V. 2010. "The Critical Edition and its Critics: A Retrospective of *Mahābhārata* Scholarship". *Journal of Vaishnava Studies* 19(2): 1–21.

Adluri, V. 2012a. "*Ascensio ad Deum*: Garuḍa and Onto-Theologic Praxis in the Mahābhārata". Paper presented at the 2012 Annual Meeting of the American Academy of Religions, 17 November, Chicago.

Adluri, V. 2012b. Review of A. J. Nicholson, *Unifying Hinduism: Philosophy and Identity in Indian Intellectual History*. *Humanities and Social Sciences Online* (H-Net), www.h-net.org/reviews/showrev.php?id=32207 (accessed January 2014).

Adluri, V. (ed.) 2013. *Philosophy and Salvation in Greek Religion*. Berlin: De Gruyter.

Adluri, V. forthcoming. "Philosophical Aspects of *Bhakti* in the *Nārāyaṇīya*". In *Papers of the 15th World Sanskrit Conference*, A. Hiltebeitel (ed.). Delhi: Rashtriya Sanskrit Sansthan.

Adluri, V. & J. Bagchee 2014. *The Nay Science: A History of German Indology*. New York: Oxford University Press.

Adorno, F. *et al.* (eds) 1995. *Corpus dei papiri filosofici greci e latini* III: *Commentari*. Florence: Olschki.

Alexandrakis, A. 2002. "Does Modern Art Reflect Plotinus' Notion of Beauty?" In *Neoplatonism and Contemporary Thought*, 2, R. Baine Harris (ed.), 231–42. Albany, NY: SUNY Press.

Altmann, A. 1979. "Creation and Emanation in Isaac Israeli: A Reappraisal". In *Studies in Medieval Jewish History and Literature*, 1, I. Twersky (ed.), 1–15. Cambridge, MA: Harvard University Press.

Angelus Silesius, J. 1986. *Cherubinischer Wandersmann oder Geistreiche Sinn- und Schlußreime*, L. Gnädiger (ed.) (based on Glatz 1675). Zurich: Manesse.

Annas, J. 1976. *Aristotle's Metaphysics, Books M and N*. Oxford: Clarendon Press.

Annas, J. 1981. *An Introduction to Plato's Republic*. Oxford: Oxford University Press.

Annas, J. 1982. "Plato's Myths of Judgement". *Phronesis* 27: 119–43.

Annas, J. 1993. *The Morality of Happiness*. Oxford: Oxford University Press.

Annas, J. 1999. *Platonic Ethics, Old and New*. Ithaca, NY: Cornell University Press.

Anton, J. P. 1964. "Plotinus' Refutation of Beauty as Symmetry". *Journal of Aesthetics and Art Criticism* 23: 233–7.

Aouad, M. 1989. "La *Théologie d'Aristote* et autres textes du Plotinus Arabus". In *Dictionnaire des philosophes antiques*, I. R. Goulet (ed.), 541–90. Paris: CNRS Éditions.

Armstrong, A. H. 1936. "Plotinus and India". *Classical Quarterly* 30(1): 22–8.

Armstrong, A. H. 1957. "The Background of the Doctrine 'That the intelligibles are not outside Intellect'". In *Les Sources de Plotin*, Entretiens sur l'Antiquité Classique 5, P. Henry, E. R. Dodds *et al.* (eds), 393–425. Geneva: Fondation Hardt.

Armstrong, A. H. (ed.) 1967. *The Cambridge History of Later Greek and Early Mediaeval Philosophy*. Cambridge: Cambridge University Press.

Armstrong, A. H. 1976. "The Apprehension of Divinity in the Self and Cosmos in Plotinus". In *The Significance of Neoplatonism*, R. Baine Harris (ed.), 187–98. Albany, NY: SUNY Press.

Armstrong, A. H. 1977. "Form, Individual and Person in Plotinus". *Dionysus* 1: 49–68.

Armstrong, A. H. 1978. "Gnosis and Greek Philosophy". In *Gnosis: Festschrift für Hans Jonas*, B. Aland (ed.), 87–124. Göttingen: Vandenhoeck & Ruprecht.

Armstrong, A. H. 1979. *Plotinian and Christian Studies*. London: Variorum.

Armstrong, A. H. & R. R. Ravindra 1982. "*Buddhi* in the *Bhagavadgītā* and *Psyché* in Plotinus". See Baine Harris (1982), 63–86.

Arnou, R. 1921. *Le Désir de Dieu dans la philosophie de Plotin*. Paris: Alcan.

Arpe, C. 1941. "Substantia". *Philologus* 94: 65–78.

Asín Palacios, M. 1978. *The Mystical Philosophy of Ibn Masarra and His Followers*. Leiden: Brill.

Athanassiadi, A. (trans.) 1999. *Damascius: The Philosophical History*. Oxford: Oxbow Books.

Attridge, H. W. 1991. "Gnostic Platonism". In *Proceedings of the Boston Colloquium in Ancient Philosophy* 7, J. C. Cleary (ed.), 1–29, 36–41. Lanham, MD: University Press of America.

Aubry, G. 2006. *Dieu sans la puissance. Dunamis et Energeia chez Aristote et chez Plotin*. Paris: Vrin.

Aubry, G. 2007. "Conscience, pensée et connaissance de soi selon Plotin: le double héritage de l'*Alcibiade* et du *Charmide*". *Études platoniciennes* 4: 163–81.

Aubry, G. 2008a. "Individuation, particularisation et détermination selon Plotin". *Phronesis* 53: 271–89.

Aubry, G. 2008b. "Capacité et convenance: la fonction de la notion d'*epitēdeiotēs* dans la théorie porphyrienne de l'embryon". In *L'embryon: Formation et animation*, L. Brisson, M.-H. Congourdeau & J.-L. Solère (eds), 139–55. Paris: Vrin.

Aubry, G. 2008c. "Un moi sans identité? Le *hēmeis* plotinien". In *Le moi et l'intériorité*, G. Aubry & F. Ildefonse (eds), 107–27. Paris: Vrin.

Aubry, G. 2012. "Procession et sécession: la problème de la descente de l'âme en *Enn.* IV, 8 (6)". *ΦΙΛΟΣΟΦΙΑ* 42: 270–79.

Aubry, G. & F. Ildefonse (eds) 2008. *Le moi et l'intériorité*. Paris: Vrin.

Aujoulat, N. 1983. "Les avatars de la *phantasia* dans le *Traité des songes* de Synésios de Cyrène I". *Koinonia* 7: 157–77.

Aujoulat, N. 1984. "Les avatars de la *phantasia* dans le *Traité des songes* de Synésios de Cyrène II". *Koinonia* 8: 33–55.

Ayres, L. 2002. "On Not Three People: The Fundamental Themes of Gregory of Nyssa's Trinitarian Theology as seen in *To Ablabius: On Not Three Gods*". *Modern Theology* 18(4): 445–74.

Baeumker, C. 1890. *Das Problem der Materie in der griechischen Philosophie*. Münster: Aschendorff.

Baier, K. 1965. *The Moral Point of View: A Rational Basis for Ethics*. New York: Random House.

Baine Harris, R. (ed.) 1982. *Neoplatonism and Indian Thought*. Albany, NY: SUNY Press.

Baltussen, H. 2002. "Philology or Philosophy? Simplicius on the Use of Quotations". In *Epea and Grammata: Oral and Written Communication in Ancient Greece*, I. Worthington & J. Foley (eds), 173–189. Leiden: Brill.

Baltussen, H. 2004. "Plato *Protagoras* 340–48: Commentary in the Making?" See Adamson, Baltussen & Stone (2004), 21–35.

Baltussen, H. 2007. "From Polemic to Exegesis: The Ancient Philosophical Commentary". In *Genres in Philosophy*, J. Lavery (ed.). *Poetics Today* 28(2): 247–81.

Baltussen, H. 2008. *Philosophy and Exegesis in Simplicius: The Methodology of a Commentator*. London: Duckworth.

Baltussen, H. 2009. "Simplicius and the Subversion of Authority". *Antiquorum Philosophia: An International Journal* 3: 121–36.

Baltussen, H. 2010. "Simplicius of Cilicia". See Gerson (2010), vol. 2, 711–32.

Baltzly, D. 2004. "The Virtues and 'Becoming like God': Alcinous to Proclus". *Oxford Studies in Ancient Philosophy* 26: 297–321.

Baltzly, D. (trans.) 2007. *Proclus: Commentary on Plato's Timaeus 3, Book 3, Part 1*. Cambridge: Cambridge University Press.

Baltzly, D. 2009. "Gaia Gets to Know Herself: Proclus on the World's Self-Perception". *Phronesis* 54: 261–85.

Baltzly, D. 2011. Review of *Proclus on Nature* by M. Martin. *Bryn Mawr Classical Review*, http://bmcr.brynmawr.edu/2011/2011-04-42.html (accessed January 2014).

Barbanti, M. di Pasquale 1994. *Filosofia e cultura in Sinesio di Cirene*. Florence: La Nuova Italia.

Barnard, L.W. (ed.) 1997. *St Justin Martyr: The First and Second Apologies*, Ancient Christian Writers. Mahwah, NJ: Paulist Press.

Barnes, J. 1983. "Immaterial Causes". *Oxford Studies in Ancient Philosophy* 1: 169–82.

Barnes, J. 1992. "Metacommentary". *Oxford Studies in Ancient Philosophy* 10: 267–81.

Barnes, J. 1999. "Introduction to Aspasius". In *Aspasius: The Earliest Extant Commentary on Aristotle's Ethics*, A. Alberti & R. W. Sharples (eds), 1–50. Berlin: De Gruyter.

Barnes, J. 2005. "Les Catégories et les *Catégories*". In *Les Catégories et leur histoire*, O. Bruun & L. Corti (eds), 11–80. Paris: Vrin.

Barnes, J. 2008. "'There Was an Old Person from Tyre'. Critical Notice of George Karamanolis & Anne Sheppard (eds), *Studies on Porphyry*". *Rhizai* 5: 127–51.

Barnes, J. 2009. "Feliciano's Translation of Dexippus". *International Journal of the Classical Tradition* 16: 523–31.

Barnes, J., S. Bobzien, K. Flannery & K. Ierodiakonou (trans.) 1991. *Alexander of Aphrodisias on Aristotle Prior Analytics 1.1–7*. Translation and notes. London: Duckworth.

Barnes, M. R. 2002. "Divine Unity and the Divided Self: Gregory of Nyssa's Trinitarian Theology in its Psychological Context". *Modern Theology* 18(4): 475–96.

Bazán, B. C. 1973. "L'authenticité du 'de intellectu' attribué à Alexandre d'Aphrodise". *Revue philosophique de Louvain* 71: 468–87.

Beaney, M. 2003. "Analysis". In *Stanford Encyclopedia of Philosophy*, E. N. Zalta (ed.). http://plato.stanford.edu/archives/win2012/entries/analysis/ (accessed October 2013).

Beauchamp, T. L. & R. G. Frey (eds) 2011. *The Oxford Handbook of Animal Ethics*. Oxford: Oxford University Press.

Becchi, F. 1983. "Aspasio e i peripatetici posteriori: La formula definitioria della passione". *Prometheus* 9: 83–104.

Bechtle, G. 2000. "The Question of Being and the Dating of the Anonymous Parmenides Commentary". *Ancient Philosophy* 20(2): 393–414.

Bechtle, G. 2006. "Über die Mittelstellung und Einheit des Seelisch-Mathematischen im Späteren Platonismus". In *Iamblichus. Aspekte Seiner Philosophie Und Wissenschaftskonzeption*, G. Bechtle (ed.), 15–41. Sankt Augustin: Academia Verlag.

Bechtle, G. & D. J. O'Meara (eds) 2000. *La philosophie des mathématiques de l'antiquité tardive*. Fribourg: Éditions Universitaires Fribourg.

Beierwaltes, W. 1961. "Die Metaphysik des Lichtes in der Philosophie Plotins". *Zeitschriften für philosophische Forschung* 15: 334–62.

Beierwaltes, W. 1969. *Platonismus in der Philosophie des Mittelalters*. Darmstadt: Wissenschaflische Buchgesellschaft.

Beierwaltes, W. 1979. *Proklos: Grundzüge Seiner Metaphysik*, 2nd edn. Frankfurt: Klostermann.

Beierwaltes, W. 1985. *Denken des Einen: Studien zur neuplatonischen Philosophie und ihrer Wirkungsgeschichte*. Frankfurt: Klostermann.

Beierwaltes, W. 1998. *Platonismus in Christentum*. Frankfurt: Klostermann.

Beierwaltes, W. 2001. *Das wahre Selbst. Studien zu Plotins Begriff des Geistes und des Einen*. Frankfurt: Klostermann.

Beierwaltes, W. 2002a. "Some Remarks about the Difficulties in Realizing Neoplatonic Thought in Contemporary Philosophy and Art". In *Neoplatonism and Contemporary Thought*, 2, R. Baine Harris (ed.), 269–84. Albany, NY: SUNY Press.

Beierwaltes, W. 2002b. "The Legacy of Neoplatonism in F. W. J. Schelling's Thought". *International Journal of Philosophical Studies* 10(4): 393–428.

Beierwaltes, W. 2004. *Platonismus und Idealismus*. Frankfurt: Klostermann.

Beierwaltes, W. 2007. "Das 'Systematische' in der Philosophie des Proklos". In *Procliana*, W. Beierwaltes (ed.), 65–84. Frankfurt: Klostermann.

Bell, P. 2009. *Three Political Voices from the Age of Justinian: Agapetus, Advice to the Emperor. Dialogue on Political Science. Paul the Silentiary, Description of Hagia Sophia*. Liverpool: Liverpool University Press.

Bene, L. 2013. "Ethics and Metaphysics in Plotinus". In *Plato Revived: Essays on Ancient Platonism in Honour of Dominic J. O'Meara*, F. Karfík & E. Song (eds), 141–61. Berlin: De Gruyter.

Bergeron, M. & R. Dufour (eds & trans.) 2008. *Alexandre d'Aphrodise: De l'Âme*. Paris: Vrin.

Bergson, H. 2011. "Le problème de la personnalité (Gifford Lectures, Édimbourg, 1914)". In *Henri Bergson: Écrits philosophiques*, F. Worms (ed.), 418–39. Paris: PUF.

Bernard, W. 1987. "Philoponus on Self-Awareness". In *Philoponus and the Rejection of Aristotelian Science*, R. Sorabji (ed.), 154–63. London: Duckworth.

Betegh, G. 2004. *The Derveni Papyrus: Cosmology, Theology and Interpretation*. Cambridge: Cambridge University Press.

Bettenson, H. (ed.) 1975. *Documents of the Christian Church*, 2nd edn. Oxford: Oxford University Press.

Betti, A., W. R. De Jong & M. Martijn (eds) 2011. "The Classical Model of Science II: The Axiomatic Method, the Order of Concepts and the Hierarchy of Sciences: An Introduction". Special issue, *Synthese* 183(1): 1–5.

Biardeau, M. 1968. "Études de mythologie hindoue (I): Cosmogonies purāṇiques". *Bulletin de l'École française d'Extrême-Orient* 54: 19–45.

Biardeau, M. 1989. *Hinduism: The Anthropology of a Civilization*, R. Nice (trans.) Delhi: Oxford University Press.

Biardeau, M. 1991. "Nara et Nārāyaṇa". *Wiener Zeitschrift für die Kunde Südasiens* 35: 75–108.

Biardeau, M. & C. Malamoud 1976. *Le sacrifice dans l'Inde ancienne*. Paris: Presses Universitaires de France.

Blank, D. 2010. "Ammonius Hermeiou and His School". See Gerson (2010), vol. 2, 654–66.

Blank, D. 2011. "Ammonius". In *Stanford Encyclopedia of Philosophy*, E. N. Zalta (ed.). http://plato.stanford.edu/archives/win2012/entries/ammonius/ (accessed January 2014).

Blumenthal, H. J. 1966. "Did Plotinus Believe in Ideas of Individuals?" *Phronesis* 11: 61–80.

Blumenthal, H. J. 1971a. *Plotinus' Psychology. His Doctrines of the Embodied Soul*. The Hague: Martinus Nijhoff.

Blumenthal, H. J. 1971b. "Soul, World-Soul and Individual Soul in Plotinus". In *Le Néoplatonisme, Colloques internationaux du CNRS à Royaumont du 9 au 13 juin 1969*, 55–63. Paris: CNRS Éeditions.

Blumenthal, H. J. 1972. "Aristotle in the Service of Platonism". *International Philosophical Quarterly* 12: 340–64.

Blumenthal, H. J. 1975. "Plutarch's Exposition of the *De Anima* and the Psychology of Proclus". In *De Iamblique à Proclus*, 123–47. Geneva: Fondation Hardt.

Blumenthal, H. J. 1982. "The Psychology of (?) Simplicius' Commentary on the *De Anima*". In *Soul and the Structure of Being in Late Neoplatonism: Syrianus, Proclus, and Simplicius*, H. J. Blumenthal & A. C. Lloyd (eds), 73–93. Liverpool: Liverpool University Press.

Blumenthal, H. J. 1987. "Plotinus in the Light of Twenty Years' Scholarship, 1951–1971". In *Aufstieg und Niedergang der Römischen Welt* 2.36.1, W. Haase (ed.), 528–70. Berlin: De Gruyter.

Blumenthal, H. J. 1990. "Neoplatonic Elements in the *De Anima* Commentaries". See Sorabji (1990), 305–24.

Blumenthal, H. J. 1993a. "*Nous* and Soul in Plotinus: Some Problems of Demarcation". In *Soul and Intellect: Studies in Plotinus and Later Neoplatonism*, 203–19. Aldershot: Variorum.

Blumenthal, H. J. 1993b. *Soul and Intellect: Studies in Plotinus and Later Neoplatonism*. Aldershot: Variorum.

Blumenthal, H. J. 1996a. *Aristotle and Neoplatonism in Late Antiquity: Interpretations of the De anima*. London: Duckworth.

Blumenthal, H. J. 1996b. "On Soul and Intellect". See Gerson (1996), 82–104.

Blumenthal, H. J. 1998. "The History and Destiny of the Individual Soul in Plotinus". In *Retour, repentir et constitution de soi*, A. Charles-Saget (ed.), 114–32. Paris: Vrin.

Blumenthal, H. J. 2000. "*Simplicius*": On Aristotle On the Soul 3.1–5. London: Duckworth.

Bobzien, S. 1998. *Determinism and Freedom in Stoic Philosophy*. Oxford: Clarendon Press.

Bodéüs, R. 1983. "L'autre Homme de Plotin". *Phronesis* 28: 256–64.

Böhlig, A. 1981. "Triad und Trinität". In *The Rediscovery of Gnosticism: Proceedings of the International Conference on Gnosticism at Yale, March 28–31, 1978*. Vol. 2: *Sethian Gnosticism*, Supplements to *Numen* 41, B. Layton (ed.), 617–34. Leiden: Brill.

Bonazzi, M. 2003. *Academici e Platonici: Il dibattito antico sullo scetticismo di Platone*. Milan: LED.

Bonazzi, M. 2005. "Eudoro di Alessandria alle origini del platonismo imperiale". In *L'eredità platonica. Studi sul platonismo da Arcesilao a Proclo*, M. Bonazzi & V. Celluprica (eds), 115–60. Naples: Bibliopolis.

Bonazzi, M. & J. Opsomer (eds) 2009. *The Origins of the Platonic System. Platonisms of the Early Empire and their Philosophical Contexts*. Leuven: Peeters.

Borisov, A. 1929. "The Arabic Original of the Work Called 'Theology of Aristotle'" (in Russian). *Zapiski Kollegii Vostokovedov* 5: 83–98.

Bos, A. P. 1984. "World Views in Collision: Plotinus, Gnostics, and Christians". In *Plotinus amid Gnostics and Christians, Papers Presented at the Plotinus Symposium Held at the Free University, Amsterdam, on 25 January 1984*, D. T. Runia (ed.), 11–28. Amsterdam: Free University Press.

Bos, A. P. 1994. "Cosmic and Meta-Cosmic Theology in Greek Philosophy and Gnosticism". In *Hellenization Revisited: Shaping a Christian Response within the Greco-Roman World*, W.-E. Helleman (ed.), 1–21. New York: University Press of America.

Boys-Stones, G. R. 2001. *Post-Hellenistic Philosophy*. Oxford: Oxford University Press.

Boys-Stones, G. R. 2007a. "Physiognomy and Ancient Psychological Theory". In *Seeing the Face, Seeing the Soul*, S. Swain (ed.), 19–124. Oxford: Oxford University Press.

Boys-Stones, G. R. 2007b. "'Middle' Platonists on Fate and Human Autonomy". In *Greek and Roman Philosophy 100 BC–200 AD*, vol. 2, R. W. Sharples & R. Sorabji (eds), 431–47. London: Institute of Classical Studies.

Brakke, D. 2010. *The Gnostics: Myth, Ritual, and Diversity in Early Christianity*. Cambridge, MA: Harvard University Press.

Bregman, J. 1982. *Synesius of Cyrene: Philosopher-Bishop*. Berkeley, CA: University of California Press.

Bregman, J. 1990. "The Neoplatonic Revival in North America". *Hermathena: A Trinity College Dublin Review* 149: 99–119.

Bregman, J. 1997. "The Christian Platonism of A. H. Armstrong and Synesius". See Cleary (1997), 536–49.

Bréhier, É. 1924. *Plotin: Ennéades I*, Introduction. Paris: Les Belles Lettres.

Bréhier, É. 1955. "Images plotiniennes, images bergsonniennes". In his *Études de philosophie antique*, 292–307. Paris: PUF.

Bréhier, É. 1958. *The Philosophy of Plotinus*, J. Thomas (trans.). Chicago, IL: University of Chicago Press. Originally published in French. See Bréhier [1928] 1961.

Bréhier, É. [1928] 1961. *La philosophie de Plotin*, 3rd edn. Paris: Vrin.

Brennan, M. 1986. "Materials for the Biography of Johannes Scottus Eriugena". *Studi medievali*, 3rd Series, 27(1): 413–60.

Brennan, T. 2002. "Introduction". In *Simplicius: On Epictetus' Handbook*, Ancient Commentators on Aristotle, C. Brittain & T. Brennan (eds), 1–26. London: Duckworth.

Breton, S. 1969. *Philosophie et mathématique chez Proclus: suivi de Principes philosophiques des mathématiques par N. Hartmann*. Paris: Beauchesne.

Brisson, L. 1992. "Une édition d'Eustochius?" In *La vie de Plotin*, 2, L. Brisson, M.-O. Goulet Cazé & D. O'Brien (eds), 65–76. Paris: Vrin.

Brisson, L. 1999. "*Logos et Logoi* chez Plotin: leur nature et leur rôle". *Cahiers philosophiques de Strasbourg* 8: 87–108.

Brisson, L. 2000. "Entre physique et métaphysique. Le terme ὄγκος chez Plotin, dans ses rapports avec la matière (ὕλη) et le corps (σῶμα)". See Fattal (2000), 87–111.

Brisson, L. 2004. *How Philosophers Saved Myths: Allegorical Interpretation and Classical Mythology*, C. Tihanyi (trans.). French original 1996. Chicago, IL: University of Chicago Press.

Brisson, L. 2006. "The Doctrine of Degrees of Virtue in the Neoplatonists: An Analysis of Porphyry's *Sentence 32*, Its Antecedents, and Its Heritage". In *Reading Plato in Antiquity*, H. Tarrant & D. Baltzly (eds), 89–106. London: Duckworth.

Brisson, L., M.-O. Goulet Cazé, R. Goulet & D. O'Brien *et al.* 1982. *Porphyre: La Vie de Plotin*, 1. Paris: Vrin.

Brisson, L., M.-O. Goulet Cazé, R. Goulet & D. O'Brien *et al.* 1992. *Porphyre: La Vie de Plotin*, 2. Paris: Vrin.

Brisson, L., M.-H. Congourdeau & J.-L. Solère (eds) 2008. *L'embryon: Formation et animation*. Paris: Vrin.

Broadie, S. 1991. *Ethics with Aristotle*. Oxford: Oxford University Press.

Broadie, S. 2007. *Aristotle and Beyond: Essays on Metaphysics and Ethics*. Cambridge: Cambridge University Press.

Broadie, S. 2010. "Divine and Natural Causation in the *Timaeus*: The Case of Mortal Animals". In *La scienza e le cause a partire dalla Metafisica di Aristotele*, F. Fronterotta (ed.), 73–92. Naples: Bibliopolis.

Brucker, J. 1742–67. *Historia Critica Philosophiae*. Leipzig: Breitkopf.

Brunschwig, J. 1983. "Aristote et l'effet Perrichon". In *La Passion de la raison: Hommage à Ferdinand Alquié*, J.-L. Marion (ed.), 361–77. Paris: PUF.

Brunschwig, J. 1996. "La déconstruction du 'Connais-toi toi-même' dans l'*Alcibiade Majeur*". In *Réflexions contemporaines sur l'antiquité classique*, Recherches sur la philosophie et le langage 18, M.-L. Desclos (ed.), 61–84. Grenoble: Université Pierre-Mendès-France.

Budde, T. R. 2011. *The Versio Dionysii of John Scottus Eriugena: A Study of the Manuscript Tradition and Influence of Eriugena's Translation of the Corpus Areopagiticum from the Ninth through the Twelfth Century*. Toronto: Centre for Medieval Studies.

Bulmer-Thomas, I. 1983. "Plato's Theory of Number". *Classical Quarterly* 33(2): 375–84.

Burkert, W. 1972. *Lore and Science in Ancient Pythagoreanism*, E. L. Minar, Jr. (trans.). Cambridge, MA: Harvard University Press.

Burnyeat, M. F. 1987. "Platonism and Mathematics: A Prelude to Discussion". In *Mathematik und Metaphysik*, A. Graeser (ed.), 213–40. Bern: Haupt.

Bussanich, J. 1988. *The One and its Relation to Intellect in Plotinus: A Commentary on Selected Texts*. Leiden: Brill.

Bussanich, J. 1990. "The Invulnerability of Goodness in the Ethics and Psychology of Plotinus". *Proceedings of the Boston Area Colloquium in Ancient Philosophy* 6: 151–84.

Butler, E. 2005. "Polytheism and Individuality in the Henadic Manifold". *Dionysius* 23: 83–104.

Butler, E. 2008. "The Gods and Being in Proclus". *Dionysius* 26: 93–114.

Bynum, C. W. 1995. *The Resurrection of the Body*. New York: Columbia University Press.

Campbell, G. 2008. "'And Bright Was the Flame of Their Friendship' (Empedocles B130): Humans, Animals, Justice, and Friendship, in Lucretius and Empedocles". *Leeds International Classical Studies* 7(4): 1–23.

Cappuyns, M. 1933. *Jean Scott Erigéne: sa vie, son oeuvre, sa pensée*. Louvain: Abbaye du Mont César.

Caputo, J. D. & L. M. Alcoff (eds) 2009. *St Paul Among the Philosophers*. Bloomington, IN: Indiana University Press.

Carabine, D. 1992. "Gregory of Nyssa on the Incomprehensibility of God". See Finan & Twomey (1992), 79–99.

Cary, P. 2000. *Augustine's Invention of the Inner Self: The Legacy of a Christian Platonist*. Oxford: Oxford University Press.

Cassin, B. & J.-L. Labarrière (eds) 2000. *L'animal dans l'antiquité*. Paris: Vrin.

Caston, V. 2012. "Higher-Order Awareness in Alexander of Aphodisias". *Bulletin of the Institute for Classical Studies* 55: 31–49.

Catana, L. 2013. "The Origin of the Division between Middle Platonism and Neoplatonism". *Apeiron* 46(2): 166–200.

Celenza, C. S. 2007. "The Platonic Revival". In *The Cambridge Companion to Renaissance Philosophy*, J. Hankins (ed.), 72–96. Cambridge: Cambridge University Press.

Chadwick, H. 1967. "Philo". See Armstrong (1967), 137–57.

Chaniotis, A. 2004. "Epigraphic Evidence for the Philosopher Alexander of Aphrodisias". *Bulletin of the Institute for Classical Studies* 47: 79–81.

Charlton, W. (trans.) 2000. "*Philoponus*". On Aristotle On the Soul 3.1–8. London: Duckworth.

Cherniss, H. 1930. *The Platonism of Gregory of Nyssa*. Berkeley, CA: University of California Press.

Chiaradonna, R. 2002. *Sostanza movimento analogia: Plotino critico di Aristotele*. Naples: Bibliopolis.

Chiaradonna, R. 2003. "Il tempo misura del movimento? Plotino e Aristotele (*Enn.* III 7 [45])". In *Platone e la tradizione platonica. Studi di filosofia antica*, M. Bonazzi & F. Trabattoni (eds), 221–50. Milan: LED.

Chiaradonna, R. 2007a. "Porphyry's Views on the Immanent Incorporeals". In *Studies on Porphyry, Bulletin of the Institute of Classical Studies* Suppl. 98, G. Karamanolis & A. Sheppard (eds), 35–49. London: Institute of Classical Studies.

Chiaradonna, R. 2007b. "Porphyry and Iamblichus on Universals and Synonymous Predication". *Documenti e studi sulla tradizione filosofica medievale* 18: 123–40.

Chiaradonna, R. 2008a. "Hylémorphisme et causalité des intelligibles: Plotin et Alexandre d'Aphrodise". *Études philosophiques* 2008(3): 379–97.

Chiaradonna, R. 2008b. "What is Porphyry's Isagoge?" *Documenti e studi sulla tradizione filosofica medievale* 19: 1–30.

Chiaradonna, R. 2008c. "Plotino: il 'noi' e il NOUS (*Enn.* V, 3 (49) 8, 37–57)". In *Le moi et l'intériorité*, G. Aubry & F. Ildefonse (eds), 277–93. Paris: Vrin.

Chiaradonna, R. 2009a. "Autour d'Eudore: Les débuts de l'exégèse des *Catégories* dans le moyen platonisme".

In *The Origins of the Platonic System. Platonisms of the Early Empire and their Philosophical Contexts*, M. Bonazzi & J. Opsomer (eds), 89–111. Leuven: Peeters.

Chiaradonna, R. 2009b. *Plotino*. Rome: Carocci.

Chiaradonna, R. 2011. "Plotino e la scienza dell'essere". In *Plato, Aristotle or Both? Dialogues between Platonism and Aristotelianism in Antiquity*, Th. Bénatoüil, E. Maffi & F. Trabattoni (eds), 117–37. Hildesheim: Olms.

Chiaradonna, R. 2012a. "Neoplatonismo e atto di essere: A margine dell'interpretazione di Cornelio Fabro". In *Crisi e destino della filosofia: Studi su Cornelio Fabro*, A. Acerbi (ed.), 123–38. Rome: EDUSC.

Chiaradonna, R. 2012b. "Plotinus' Account of the Cognitive Powers of the Soul: Sense-Perception and Discursive Thought". *Topoi* 31(2): 191–207.

Chiaradonna, R. & F. Trabattoni (eds) 2009. *Physics and Philosophy of Nature in Greek Neoplatonism*. Leiden: Brill.

Chiaradonna, R., M. Rashed & D. Sedley 2013. "A Rediscovered *Categories* Commentary". *Oxford Studies in Ancient Philosophy* 44: 129–94.

Chitty, D. J. 1966. *The Desert A City*. Oxford: Blackwell.

Chlup, R. 2012. *Proclus: An Introduction*. Cambridge: Cambridge University Press.

Ciapalo, R. T. 1997. "The Relation of Plotinian *Eudaimonia* to the Life of the Serious Man in Treatise I.4 [46]". *American Catholic Philosophical Quarterly* 71(3): 489–98.

Ciapalo, R. T. 2002. "The Oriental Influences upon Plotinus' Thought: An Assessment of the Controversy between Bréhier and Rist on the Soul's Relation to the One". In *Neoplatonism and Indian Philosophy*, P. M. Gregorios (ed.), 71–81. Albany, NY: SUNY Press.

Clark, M. T. 1981. "The Neoplatonism of Marius Victorinus the Christian". In *Neoplatonism and Early Christian Thought: Essays in Honour of A. H. Armstrong*, H. J. Blumenthal & R. A. Markus (eds), 153–9. London: Variorum.

Clark, S. 2011. "Animals in Classical and Late Antique Philosophy". In *The Oxford Handbook of Animal Ethics*, T. L. Beauchamp & R. G. Frey (eds), 35–60. Oxford: Oxford University Press.

Cleary, J. J. (ed.) 1997. *The Perennial Tradition of Neoplatonism*. Leuven: Leuven University Press.

Cleary, J. J. 2000a. "The Role of Mathematics in Proclus' Theology". In *Proclus et La Théologie Platonicienne*, A. Segonds & C. Steel (eds), 65–90. Leuven: Leuven University Press.

Cleary, J. J. 2000b. "Proclus' Philosophy of Mathematics". See Bechtle & O'Meara (2000), 85–101.

Cleary, J. J. 2006. "Proclus as a Reader of Plato's *Timaeus*". In *Reading Plato in Antiquity*, H. Tarrant & D. Baltzly (eds), 135–50. London: Duckworth.

Cole, P. 2001. *Selected Poems of Solomon Ibn Gabirol*. Princeton, NJ: Princeton University Press.

Cole, P. 2007. *The Dream of the Poem: Hebrew Poetry from Muslim and Christian Spain, 950–1492*. Princeton, NJ: Princeton University Press.

Collette-Dučić, B. 2010. "Becoming a Part. The Case of Attachment in Plotinus". In *Conversations Platonic and Neoplatonic: Intellect, Soul, and Nature*, J. Finamore & R. Berchman (eds), 115–130. St Augustin: Academia Verlag.

Collette-Dučić, B. 2011. "Stoïcisme et tyrannie au Ier siècle de notre ère. De l'action libre à l'action singulière". In *L'émergence de l'individu entre formes substantielles et droits essentiels. Contextes historiques et enjeux sociologiques des processus d'individuation de l'antiquité à nos jours*, A. Ruelle (ed.), 91–115. Brussels: Presses des FUSL.

Collette-Dučić, B. 2011–12. "Sommeil, éveil et attention chez Plotin". *Chôra – Revue d'études anciennes et médiévales* 9–10: 259–81.

Collingwood, R. G. 1938. *The Principles of Art*. Oxford: Oxford University Press.

Contreni, J. J. 1978. *The Cathedral School of Laon from 850 to 930: Its Manuscripts and Masters*, Münchener Beiträge zur Mediavistik und Renaissance-Forschung 29. Munich: Arbeo-Gesellschaft.

Cooper, J. 1986. *Reason and Human Good in Aristotle*. Indianapolis, IN: Hackett.

Cooper, J. 2003. "Plato and Aristotle on 'Finality' and '(Self)-Sufficiency'". In *Plato and Aristotle's Ethics*, R. Heinaman (ed.), 117–47. London: Ashgate.

Cooper, S. A. 2005. "The Life and Times of Marius Victorinus". In *Marius Victorinus' Commentary on Galatians*, Introduction, Translation, and Notes, Oxford Early Christian Studies, 16–40. Oxford: Oxford University Press.

Corbin, H. 1960. *Avicenna and the Visionary Recital*. New York: Pantheon Books.

Corbin, H. 1969. *Alone with the Alone: Creative Imagination in the Sufism of Ibn 'Arabi*, R. Manheim (trans.). Princeton, NJ: Princeton University Press. Originally published in 1958 in French as *L'imagination créatrice dans le Soufisme d'Ibn 'Arabi*. Paris: Flammarion.

Corcoran, S. 2005. "Learning Law". Paper presented at the conference "The Alexandrian Philosophy School of the 6th Century", Institute of Classical Studies, 18–19 April, University of London.

Cornford, F. M. [1935] 1997. *Plato's Cosmology: The Timaeus of Plato*. Indianapolis, IN: Hackett.

Corrigan, K. 1986. "Is there More than One Generation of Matter in the *Enneads?" Phronesis* 31: 167–81.

Corrigan, K. 1996a. *Plotinus' Theory of Matter-Evil and the Question of Substance: Plato, Aristotle and Alexander of Aphrodisias*. Leuven: Peeters.

Corrigan, K. 1996b. "Essence and Existence in the *Enneads*". See Gerson (1996), 105–29.

Corrigan, K. 2000. "Platonism and Gnosticism: The Anonymous Commentary on the Parmenides: Middle or Neoplatonic?" In *Gnosticism and Later Platonism: Themes, Figures, and Texts*, Society of Biblical Literature Symposium Series 12, J. D. Turner & R. Majercik (eds), 141–78. Atlanta, GA: Society of Biblical Literature.

Corrigan, K. 2001. "Positive and Negative Matter in Later Platonism: The Uncovering of Plotinus' Dialogue with the Gnostics". In *Gnosticism and Later Platonism: Themes, Figures, and Texts*, Society of Biblical Literature Symposium Series 12, J. D. Turner & R. Majercik (eds), 19–56. Atlanta, GA: Society of Biblical Literature.

Corrigan, K. 2005. *Reading Plotinus: A Practical Introduction to Neoplatonism*. West Lafayette, IN: Purdue University Press.

Corrigan, K. 2009a. *Evagrius and Gregory: Mind, Soul and Body in the 4th Century*. Aldershot: Ashgate Press.

Corrigan, K. 2009b. "Ecology's Future Debt to Plotinus and Neoplatonism". In *Late Antique Epistemology: Other Ways to Truth*, P. Vassilopoulou & S. R. L. Clark (eds), 250–72. London: Palgrave Macmillan.

Corrigan, K. 2012. "Religion and Philosophy in the Platonic Tradition". In *Religion and Philosophy in the Platonic and Neoplatonic Traditions, from Antiquity to the Early Medieval Period*, K. Corrigan, J. D. Turner & P. Wakefield (eds), 19–34. Sankt Augustin: Academia Verlag.

Corrigan, K. & M. Harrington 2004. "Pseudo-Dionysius the Areopagite". In *Stanford Encyclopedia of Philosophy*, E. N. Zalta (ed.). http://plato.stanford.edu/archives/spr2014/entries/pseudo-dionysius-areopagite/ (accessed January 2014).

Corrigan, K. & J. D. Turner 2012. "Plotinus and the Gnostics: The Peculiar Impact of the Tripartite Tractate and Later Works". Paper presented at the annual meeting of the International Society for Neoplatonic Studies, 22 June, Cagliari, Italy.

Crawford, W. S. 1901. *Synesius the Hellene*. London: Rivingstons.

Cribiore, R. 2005. "The School of Alexandria and the Rivalry Between Rhetoric and Philosophy". Paper presented at the conference "The Alexandrian Philosophy School of the 6th Century", Institute of Classical Studies, 18–19 April, University of London.

Cribiore, R. "The Conflict between Rhetoric and Philosophy and Zacharias' Ammonius", in preparation.

Crouzel, H. 1989. *Origen: The Life and Thought of the First Great Theologian*, A. S. Worrall (trans.). Edinburgh: T & T Clark.

Dan, J. 1971. "Devekut". In *Encyclopaedia Judaica*, C. Roth (ed.), vol. 5, 628–9. Jerusalem: Encyclopaedia Judaica/New York: Macmillan.

D'Ancona, C. 2000. "Syrianus dans la tradition exégétique de la *Métaphysique* d'Aristote". In *Le commentaire: entre tradition et innovation: actes du Colloque international de l'Institut des traditions textuelles (Paris et Villejuif, 22–25 septembre 1999)*, M.-O. Goulet Cazé & T. Dorandi (eds), 311–27. Paris: Vrin.

D'Ancona, C. 2001. "Pseudo 'Theology of Aristotle', Chapter I: Structure and Composition". *Oriens* 36: 78–112.

D'Ancona, C. 2002. "Commenting on Aristotle: From Late Antiquity to the Arab Aristotelianism". See Geerlings & Schulz (2002), 201–51.

D'Ancona, C. 2003. *Plotino. La discesa dell'anima nei corpi* (Enn. IV 8 (6)). *Plotiniana Arabica* (Pseudo-Teologia di Aristotele, *cap. 1 e 7*; "Detti del Sapiente Greco"). Padua: Il Poligrafo.

D'Ancona, C. 2005. "Les *Sentences* de Porphyre entre les *Ennéades* de Plotin". In *Porphyre: Sentences*, 1, L. Brisson (ed.), 139–274. Paris: Vrin.

D'Ancona, C. 2007. "Deux traités plotiniens chez Eusèbe de Césarée". In *The Libraries of the Neoplatonists*, Philosophia Antiqua 107, C. D'Ancona (ed.), 63–97. Leiden: Brill.

D'Ancona, C. 2010. "The Origins of Islamic Philosophy". See Gerson (2010), vol. 2, 869–94.

D'Ancona, C. 2013. "Greek Sources in Arabic and Islamic Philosophy". In *Stanford Encyclopedia of Philosophy*, E. N. Zalta (ed.). http://plato.stanford.edu/archives/win2013/entries/arabic-islamic-greek/ (accessed January 2014).

D'Ancona, C. & R. C. Taylor 2003. "*Le Liber de Causis*". In *Dictionnaire des philosophes antiques, Supplément*, R. Goulet (ed.), 599–647. Paris: CNRS Éditions.

D'Andrès, N. 2010. *Socrate Néoplatonicien. Une science de l'amour dans le commentaire de Proclus au prologue de l'Alcibiade.* Unpublished Ph.D. thesis, University of Geneva.

Daniélou, J. 1944. *Platonisme et théologie mystique: Essai sur la doctrine spirituelle de saint Grégoire de Nysse.* Paris: Aubier.

Danto, A. C. 1986. *The Philosophical Disenfranchisement of Art.* New York: Columbia University Press.

Darras-Worms, A. 2007. *Plotin. Traité 1 I, 6.* Paris: Cerf.

Davidson, H. A. 1972. "Alfarabi and Avicenna on the Active Intellect". *Viator* 3: 109–78.

Davidson, H. A. 1992. *Alfarabi, Avicenna, and Averroes on Intellect: Their Cosmologies, Theories of the Active Intellect and Theories of Human Intellect.* Oxford: Oxford University Press.

De Angelis, F. (ed.) 2010. *Spaces of Justice in the Roman World.* Leiden: Brill.

De Girolami Cheney, L. & J. Hendrix (eds) 2004. *Neoplatonic Aesthetics: Music, Literature, & the Visual Arts.* New York: Peter Lang.

De Haas, F. A. J. 2001. "Did Plotinus and Porphyry Disagree on Aristotle's *Categories*?" *Phronesis* 46: 492–526.

De Haas, F. A. J. 2010. "Priscian of Lydia and Pseudo-Simplicius on the Soul". See Gerson (2010), vol. 2, 756–63.

De Haas, F. A. J. 2011. "Principles, Conversion, and Circular Proof. The Reception of an Academic Debate in Proclus and Philoponus". In *Plato, Aristotle, or Both? Dialogues Between Platonism and Aristotelianism in Antiquity*, T. Bénatouïl, E. Maffi & F. Trabattoni (eds), 215–40. Hildesheim: Olms.

De Jong, W. R. & A. Betti 2010. "The Classical Model of Science: A Millennia-Old Model of Scientific Rationality". *Synthese* 174(2): 185–203.

De Risi, V. 2012. "Plotino e la Rivoluzione scientifica. La presenza delle *Enneadi* nell'epistemologia leibniziana dello spazio fenomenico". In *Il platonismo e le scienze*, R. Chiaradonna (ed.), 143–63. Rome: Carocci.

De Vogel, C. J. 1953. "On the Neoplatonic Character of Platonism and the Platonic Character of Neoplatonism". *Mind* 62(245): 43–64.

Declerck, J. 1984. "Théophile d'Alexandrie contre Origène". *Byzantion* 54: 495–507.

Delcomminette, S. forthcoming. "Plotin et le problème de la fondation de la liberté". In *Foundations of Ancient Ethics / Grundlagen der antiken Ethik*, J. Hardy & G. Rudebusch (eds). Göttingen: Vandenhoeck & Ruprecht.

Denis, L. 2001. *Moral Self-Regard: Duties to Oneself in Kant's Moral Theory.* New York: Routledge.

Dennis, T. J. 1981. "Gregory on the Resurrection of the Body". In *The Easter Sermons of Gregory of Nyssa*, Patristic Monographs Series 9, A. Spira & C. Klock (eds), 55–74. Philadelphia, PA: Patristic Foundation.

Derda, T., T. Markiewicz & E. Wipszycka (eds) 2007. *Alexandria: The Auditoria of Kom el-Dikka and Late Antique Education. Journal of Juristic Papyrology* Supplement 8.

Deussen, P. (trans.) 1897. *Sechzig Upanischads des Veda.* Leipzig: Brockhaus.

"devekut", s.v. 1996. *Encyclopaedia Judaica*, vol. 5, 1598–9. Jerusalem: Keter Publishing. www.jewishvirtual-library.org/jsource/judaica/ejud_0002_0005_0_05173.html (accessed January 2014).

Dickie, M. W. 2002. "Synesius, *de Insomniis* 2–3 Terzaghi and Plotinus, *Enneades* 2.3.7 and 4.4.40–44". *Symbolae Osloenses* 77: 165–74.

Dillon, J. 1972. "Iamblichus and the Origin of the Doctrine of Henads". *Phronesis* 17: 102–6.

Dillon, J. (ed.) 1973. *Iamblichi Chalcidensis in Platonis dialogos commentariorum fragmenta.* Leiden: Brill.

Dillon, J. 1983. "Plotinus, Philo and Origen on the Grades of Virtue". In *Platonismus und Christentum*, H.-D. Blume & F. Mann (eds), 92–105. Münster: Aschendorff.

Dillon, J. 1984. "Speusippus in Iamblichus". *Phronesis* 29(3): 325–32.

Dillon, J. 1987. "Iamblichus of Chalcis". In *Aufstieg und Niedergang der Römischen Welt* 2.36.2, W. Haase (ed.), 862–909. Berlin: De Gruyter.

Dillon, J. 1988. "Philo of Alexandria and the *Timaeus* of Plato". *Journal of the History of Philosophy* 26(4): 658–60.

Dillon, J. 1990. *The Golden Chain: Studies in the Development of Platonism and Christianity.* Aldershot: Variorum.

Dillon, J. 1992a. "Origen and Plotinus: The Platonic Influence on Early Christianity". See Finan & Twomey (1992), 7–26.

Dillon, J. 1992b. "Plotinus at Work on Platonism". *Greece & Rome* 39(2): 189–204.

Dillon, J. 1992c. "Solomon Ibn Gabirol's Doctrine of Intelligible Matter". In *Neoplatonism and Jewish Thought*, L. E. Goodman (ed.), 43–59. Albany, NY: SUNY Press.

Dillon, J. 1993. "Iamblichus and Henads Again". In *The Divine Iamblichus*, H. J. Blumenthal & E. C. Clark (eds), 48–54. London: Bristol Classical Press.

Dillon, J. 1994. "Calcidius". In *Dictionnaire des philosophes antiques* 2, R. Goulet (ed.), 156–7. Paris: CNRS.

Dillon, J. 1996a. *The Middle Platonists: A Study of Platonism, 80 BC to AD 220*, 2nd edn. Ithaca, NY: Cornell University Press.

Dillon, J. 1996b. "An Ethic for the Late Antique Sage". See Gerson (1996), 315–35.

Dillon, J. 1997. "Iamblichus' *Noera Theōria* of Aristotle's *Categories*". *Syllecta Classica* 8: 65–77.

Dillon, J. 2003. *The Heirs of Plato: A Study of the Old Academy (347–274 BC)*. Oxford: Clarendon Press.

Dillon, J. 2007. "The Freedom of the Caged Bird". *Philosophia* 37: 124–33.

Dillon, J. 2009. "Philo of Alexandria and Platonist Psychology". In *The Afterlife of the Platonic Soul: Reflections of Platonic Psychology in the Monotheistic Religions*, M. Elkaisy-Friemuth & J. M. Dillon (eds), 17–24. Leiden: Brill.

Dillon, J. & S. Klitenic. 2007. *Dionysius the Areopagite and the Neoplatonist Tradition: Despoiling the Hellenes*, Ashgate Studies in Philosophy and Theology in Late Antiquity. Aldershot: Ashgate.

Dillon, J. & W. Polleichtner. 2009. *Iamblichus of Chalcis: The Letters*. Atlanta, GA: Society of Biblical Literature.

Dillon, J., D. Russell & S. Gertz (trans.) 2012. *Aeneas of Gaza, Theophrastus with Zacharias of Mytilene, Ammonius*. London: Bloomsbury.

Dodds, E. R. 1928. "The Parmenides of Plato and the Origin of the Neoplatonic 'One'". *Classical Quarterly* 22: 129–42.

Dodds, E. R. 1960. "Tradition and Personal Achievement in the Philosophy of Plotinus". *Journal of Roman Studies* 50: 1–7.

Dodds, E. R. 1965. *Pagan and Christian in an Age of Anxiety*. Cambridge: Cambridge University Press.

Donini, P. 1970. "L'anima e gli elementi nel *de anima* di Alessandro di Afrodisia". *Atti della Accademia delle Scienze del Torino* 105: 61–107.

Donini, P. 1974. *Tre studi sull' Aristotelismo nel II secolo D. C.* Turin: Paravia.

Donini, P. 1982. *Le scuole, l'anima, l'impero: La filosofia antica da Antioco a Plotino*. Turin: Rosenberg & Sellier.

Dorandi, T. 1991. "Den Antiken Autoren über die Schulter geschaut: Arbeitsweise und Autographie bei den antiken Schriftstellern". *Zeitschrift für Papyrologie und Epigrafik* 87: 11–33.

Dragona-Monachou, M. 1994. "Divine Providence in the Philosophy of the Empire". In *Aufstieg und Niedergang der römischen Welt* 2.36.7, W. Hasse (ed.), 4417–90. Berlin: De Gruyter.

Drews, A. 1907. *Plotin und der Untergang der antiken Weltanschauung*. Jena: Diederichs.

Duffy, J. M. 1984. "Byzantine Medicine in the Sixth and Seventh Centuries: Aspects of Teaching and Practice". *Dumbarton Oaks Papers* 38: 21–7.

Duysinx, F. 1969. "Asclépiodote et le monocorde". *Antiquité classique* 38: 447–58.

Dzielska, M. 1996. *Hypatia of Alexandria*, Revealing Antiquity 8, F. Lyra (trans). Cambridge, MA: Harvard University Press.

Ebbesen, S. 1990. "Porphyry's Legacy to Logic: A Reconstruction". See Sorabji (1990), 141–71.

Edelstein, L. 1937. "Greek Medicine in its Relation to Religion and Magic". *Bulletin of the History of Medicine* 5: 201–46.

Edwards, M. J. (ed.) 2000. *Neoplatonic Saints: The Lives of Plotinus and Proclus by Their Students*. Liverpool: Liverpool University Press.

El Murr, D. 2009. "Politics and Dialectic in Plato's *Statesman*". *Proceedings of the Boston Area Colloquium in Ancient Philosophy* 25: 109–35.

Eliasson, E. 2008. *The Notion of That Which Depends on Us in Plotinus and its Background*. Leiden: Brill.

Emilsson, E. K. 1988. *Plotinus on Sense-Perception: A Philosophical Study*. Cambridge: Cambridge University Press.

Emilsson, E. K. 2007. *Plotinus on Intellect*. Oxford: Clarendon Press.

Emilsson, E. K. 2012. "Plotinus and Plato on Action". In *Plato and the Divided Self*, R. Barney, T. Brennan & C. Brittain (eds), 350–67. Cambridge: Cambridge University Press.

Erbse, H. 1960. *Beiträge zur Überlieferung der Iliasscholien*. Munich: Beck.

Erismann, C. 2011. *L'homme commun: La genèse du réalisme ontologique durant le haut Moyen Âge*. Paris: Vrin.

Erskine, A. 1990. *The Hellenistic Stoa: Political Thought and Action*. London: Duckworth.

Evangeliou, C. 1988. *Aristotle's Categories and Porphyry*. Leiden: Brill.

Everson, S. 2011. "Justice and Just Action in Plato's *Republic*". In *Episteme, etc. Essays in Honour of Jonathan Barnes*, B. Morrison & K. Ierodiakonou (eds), 249–76. Oxford: Oxford University Press.

Fackenheim, E. 1945. "A Treatise on Love by Ibn Sina". *Mediaeval Studies* 7: 208–28.

Falcon, A. 2011. "Filosofia della natura". In *Filosofia tardoantica*, R. Chiaradonna (ed.), 155–71. Rome: Carocci.

Falcon, A. 2012. *Aristotelianism in the First Century BCE*. Cambridge: Cambridge University Press.

Fattal, M. 1998. *"Logos" et image chez Plotin*. Paris: L'Harmattan.

Fattal, M. (ed.) 2000. *Études sur Plotin*. Paris: L'Harmattan.

Fazzo, S. 1999. "Philology and Philosophy in the Margin of Early Printed Editions of the Ancient Greek Commentators on Aristotle, with Special Reference to Copies Held in the Biblioteca Nazionale Braidense, Milan". In *Philosophy in the Sixteenth and Seventeenth Centuries: Conversations with Aristotle*, C. Blackwell & S. Kusukawa (eds), 48–75. Aldershot: Ashgate.

Fazzo, S. & H. Wiesner 1993. "Alexander of Aphrodisias in the Kindi Circle and in al-Kindī's Cosmology". *Arabic Sciences and Philosophy* 3: 119–53.

Fazzo, S. & M. Zonta 1998. *Alessandro di Afrodisia: La Provvidenza*. Milan: Rizzoli.

Fenton, P. 1986. "The Arabic and Hebrew Versions of the *Theology of Aristotle*". See Kraye, Ryan & Schmitt (eds) (1986), 241–64.

Ferber, R. 1989. *Platos Idee des Guten*, 2nd edn. Sankt Augustin: Academia Verlag.

Ferrari, F. 2002. "Motivi platonici e motivi aristotelici nella concezione della doppia energeia dell'Uno in Plotino". In *Henosis kai philia, unione e amicizia. Omaggio a Francesco Romano*, M. Barbanti, G. R. Giardina, P. Manganaro and E. Berti (eds), 375–88. Catania: CUECM.

Ferrari, F. 2010. "Esegesi, commento e sistema nel medioplatonismo". In *Argumenta in dialogos Platonis 1: Platoninterpretation und ihre Hermeneutik von der Antike bis zum Beginn des 19. Jahrhunderts*, A. Netschke-Hentschke (ed.), 51–76. Basel: Schwabe.

Ferrari, F. 2012. "L'esegesi medioplatonica del *Timeo*: metodi, finalità, risultati". In *Il Timeo: Esegesi greche, arabe, latine*, F. Celia & A. Ulacco (eds), 81–131. Pisa: Pisa University Press.

Ferrari, G. R. F. 2007. "The Three-Part Soul". In *The Cambridge Companion to Plato's* Republic, G. R. F. Ferrari (ed.), 165–201. Cambridge: Cambridge University Press.

Ferwerda, R. 1965. *La signification des images et des métaphores dans la pensée de Plotin*. Groningen: Wolters.

Festugière, A. J. 1963. "Modes de composition des commentaries de Proclus". *Museum Helveticum* 20: 77–100.

Festugière, A. J. 1969. "L'ordre de lecture des dialogues de Platon aux Ve/VIe siècles". *Museum Helveticum* 26(4): 281–96.

Festugière, A. J. 1986. *La Révélation d'Hermès Trismégiste* 2, 2nd edn. Paris: Les Belles Lettres.

Field, H. H. 1980. *Science without Numbers: A Defense of Nominalism*. Princeton, NJ: Princeton University Press.

Finamore, J. F. 1985. *Iamblichus and the Theory of the Vehicle of the Soul*. Chico, CA: Scholars Press.

Finamore, J. F. 1997. "The Rational Soul in Iamblichus' Philosophy". *Syllecta Classica* 8: 163–76.

Finamore, J. F. 2005. "The Tripartite Soul in Plato's *Republic*". In *History of Platonism: Plato Redivivus*, J. F. Finamore & R. Berchman (eds), 35–51. New Orleans: University Press of the South.

Finamore, J. F. 2009. "Iamblichus and the Intermediate Nature of the Human Soul". In *Perspectives sur le Néoplatonisme*, J.-M. Narbonne & M. Achard (eds), 123–36. Québec: Presses de l'Université Laval.

Finamore, J. F. 2010. "Iamblichus' Interpretation of *Parmenides*' Third Hypothesis". In *Plato's Parmenides and Its Heritage: Volume II: Reception in Patristic, Gnostic, and Christian Neoplatonic Texts*, J. D. Turner & K. Corrigan (eds), 119–32. Atlanta, GA: Society of Biblical Literature.

Finamore, J. F. 2011. "Themistius on Soul and Intellect in Aristotle's *De Anima*". *Proceedings of the Boston Area Colloquium on Ancient Philosophy* 26: 1–23.

Finamore, J. F. 2013. "Iamblichus, Theurgy, and the Soul's Ascent". In *Philosophy and Salvation in Greek Religion*, V. Adluri (ed.), 262–76. Berlin: De Gruyter.

Finamore, J. F. & J. M. Dillon (eds) 2002. *Iamblichus De Anima*. Text, translation, and commentary. Leiden: Brill.

Finan, T. & V. Twomey (eds) 1992. *The Relationship Between Neoplatonism and Christianity*. Dublin: Four Courts Press.

Fineman, M. 2008. "The Vulnerable Subject: Anchoring Equality in the Human Condition". *Yale Journal of Law and Feminism* 20(1), Emory Public Law Research Paper No. 8-40, http://ssrn.com/abstract=1131407 (accessed January 2014).

Finkelberg, A. 1996. "Plato's Method in the *Timaeus*". *American Journal of Philology* 117: 191–209.

Fleming, R. 2005. "Learning Medicine 1". Paper presented at the conference "The Alexandrian Philosophy School of the 6th Century", Institute of Classical Studies, 18–19 April, University of London.

Föllinger, S. 1999. "Biologie in der Spätantike". In *Geschichte der Mathematik und der Naturwissenschaften in der Antike 1. Biologie*, G. Wöhrle (ed.), 253–81. Stuttgart: Franz Steiner.

Fortier, S. 2008. "The Relationship of the Kantian and Proclan Conceptions of Evil". *Dionysius* 26: 175–92.

Foucault, M. 2001. *L'Herméneutique du sujet, Cours au Collège de France, 1981–1982*. Paris: Hautes-Études-Gallimard-Seuil.

Frede, D. 1982. "The Dramatization of Determinism: Alexander of Aphrodisias' *De Fato*". *Phronesis* 27: 276–98.

Frede, M. 1987 "Numenius". In *Aufstieg und Niedergang der Römischen Welt* 36.2, W. Haase (ed.), 1034–75. Berlin: De Gruyter.

Frede, M. 1999. "The Stoic Conception of the Good". In *Topics in Stoic Philosophy*, K. Ierodiakonou (ed.), 71–94. Oxford: Clarendon Press.

Frede, M. 2003. "Galen's Theology". In *Galien et la philosophie. Entretiens sur l'antiquité classique* 49, J. Barnes & J. Jouanna (eds), 74–129. Vandoeuvres-Genève: Librarie Droz.

Frede, M. 2011. *A Free Will: Origins of the Notion in Ancient Thought*. Berkeley, CA: University of California Press.

Frede, M. & G. Patzig 1988. *Aristoteles Metaphysik Z: Text, Übersetzung und Kommentar*, 2 vols. Munich: Beck.

Frege, G. 1950. *The Foundations of Arithmetic*, J. L Austin (trans.). New York: Philosophical Library.

Freudenthal, G. & R. Brague 2005. "Ni Empédocle, ni Plotin. Pour le dossier du Pseudo-Empédocle arabe". In *Agonistes: Essays in Honour of Denis O'Brien*, J. Dillon & M. Dixsaut (eds), 267–83. Aldershot: Ashgate.

Freudenthal, J. 1896. "Asklepiodotos 11". In *RE* 2(4): 1641–2.

Gabriel, M. 2009. *Skeptizismus und Idealismus in der Antike*. Frankfurt: Suhrkamp.

Gadamer, H.-G. 1978. *Die Idee des Guten zwischen Plato und Aristoteles*. Heidelberg: Carl Winter Universitätsverlag.

Gadamer, H.-G. 1986. *The Idea of the Good in Platonic-Aristotelian Philosophy*, P. C. Smith (trans.). New Haven, CT: Yale University Press. For original, see Gadamer (1978).

Garnsey, P. [1996] 2001. *Ideas of Slavery from Aristotle to Augustine*. Cambridge: Cambridge University Press.

Geerlings, W. & C. Schulz (eds) 2002. *Der Kommentar in Antike und Mittelalter. Beiträge zu seiner Erforschung*. Leiden: Brill.

Gersh, S. 1973. *Kinēsis Akinētos: A Study of Spiritual Motion in the Philosophy of Proclus*, Philosophia Antiqua 26. Leiden: Brill.

Gersh, S. 1977. "*Per se ipsum*: The Problem of Immediate and Mediate Causation in Eriugena and his Neoplatonic Predecessors". In *Jean Scot Erigène et l'histoire de la philosophie*, R. Roques (ed.), 367–77. Paris: CNRS.

Gersh, S.1978. *From Iamblichus to Eriugena: An Investigation of the Prehistory and Evolution of the Pseudo-Dionysian Tradition*. Leiden: Brill.

Gersh, S. 2006. "Platonism, Platonic Tradition". In *The Encyclopedia of Philosophy*, 2nd edn, D. M. Borchert (ed.). Detroit: Macmillan Reference.

Gerson, L. P. 1994. *Plotinus*. London: Routledge.

Gerson, L. P. (ed.) 1996. *The Cambridge Companion to Plotinus*. Cambridge: Cambridge University Press.

Gerson, L. P. 1997a. "*Epistrophe pros heauton*: History and Meaning". *Documenti e studi sulla tradizione filosofica medievale* 8: 1–32.

Gerson, L. P. 1997b. "Introspection, Self-Reflexivity, and the Essence of Thinking according to Plotinus". See Cleary (1997), 153–73.

Gerson, L. P. 2005a. "What is Platonism?" *Journal of the History of Philosophy* 43(3): 253–76.

Gerson, L. P. 2005b. *Aristotle and Other Platonists*. Ithaca, NY: Cornell University Press.

Gerson, L. P. 2009. *Ancient Epistemology*. Cambridge: Cambridge University Press.

Gerson, L. P. (ed.) 2010. *The Cambridge History of Philosophy in Late Antiquity*, 2 vols. Cambridge: Cambridge University Press.

Gerson, L. P. 2013. "Platonic Ethics". In *The Oxford Handbook of the History of Ethics*, Roger Crisp (ed.), 129–46. Oxford: Oxford University Press.

Gerson, L. P. forthcoming. "Plotinus on Happiness". In *Happiness in Ancient Philosophical Thinking and Contemporary Ethics*, P. Destrée & Ch. Rapp (eds).

Gerson, L. P. & M. Martijn forthcoming. "Proclus' System". In *Proclus*, P. d'Hoine & M. Martijn (eds). Oxford: Oxford University Press.

Gibb, H. A. R. (ed.) 1954. *The Encyclopaedia of Islam*. Leiden: Brill.

Gibson, R. K. 2002. "'Cf. E.g.': A Typology of 'Parallels' and the Function of Commentaries on Latin Poetry". In *The Classical Commentary: Histories, Practices, Theory*, R. K. Gibson & C. S. Kraus (eds), 331–57. Leiden: Brill.

Gilhus, I. S. 2006. *Animals, Gods and Humans: Changing Attitudes to Animals in Greek, Roman and Early Christian Ideas*. London: Routledge.

Gill, C., T. Whitmarsh & J. Wilkins (eds) 2009. *Galen and the World of Knowledge*. Cambridge: Cambridge University Press.

Glei, R. 1999. "Lux Regiomontana. Der kategorische Imperativ in Ciceros De officiis". *Bochumer Philosophisches Jahrbuch für Antike und Mittelalter* 4: 49–61.

Glucker, J. 1978. *Antiochus and the Late Academy*. Göttingen: Vandenhoeck & Ruprecht.

Gonzalez, F. J. 1998. *Dialectic and Dialogue: Plato's Practice of Philosophical Inquiry*. Evanston, IL: Northwestern University Press.

Goodenough, E. R. 1963. *An Introduction to Philo Judaeus*, 2nd edn. rev. New York: Barnes & Noble.

Goodman, L. E. (ed.) 1992. *Neoplatonism and Jewish Thought*. Albany, NY: SUNY Press.

Goulet, R. (ed.) 1989–2012. *Dictionnaire des philosophes antiques*, 5 vols & 1 suppl. to date. Paris: CNRS.

Goulet Cazé, M.-O. 1982. "L'édition d'Eustochius". In *Porphyre: La Vie de Plotin*, 1, L. Brisson, M.-O. Goulet Cazé & D. O'Brien (eds), 289–94. Paris: Vrin.

Goulet Cazé, M.-O. 1992. "Answer to Brisson". In *Porphyre: La Vie de Plotin*, 2, L. Brisson, M.-O. Goulet Cazé & D. O'Brien (eds), 71–6. Paris: Vrin.

Gourinat, J.-B. 2005. "La *prohairesis* chez Épictète: décision, volonté ou 'personne morale'?" *Philosophie antique* 5: 93–133.

Gourinat, J.-B. 2007. "In nostra potestate". *Lexis* 25: 143–50.

Grabar, A. 1945. "Plotin et les origines de l'esthétique médiévale". *Cahiers archéologiques* 1:15–34.

Graeser, A. 1972. *Plotinus and the Stoics: A Preliminary Study*. Leiden: Brill.

Grant, R. M. 1964. "Greek Literature in the Treatise *De Trinitate* and Cyril *Contra Julianum*". *Journal of Theological Studies* 15: 265–79.

Gregorios, P. M. 2002. "Does Geography Condition Philosophy? On Going Beyond the Occidental–Oriental Distinction". In *Neoplatonism and Indian Philosophy*, P. M. Gregorios (ed.), 13–30. Albany, NY: SUNY Press.

Griffin, M. 2012. "What Does Aristotle Categorize? Semantics and the Early Peripatetic Reading of the *Categories*". *Bulletin of the Institute of Classical Studies* 55: 65–108.

Griffin, M. forthcoming. *The Reception of Aristotle's Categories, c. 80 BC to AD 220*. Oxford: Clarendon Press.

Gritti, E. 2008. *Proclo. Dialettica, anima, esegesi*. Milan: LED.

Grmek, M. D. 1992. "Les maladies et la mort de Plotin". In *Porphyre: La Vie de Plotin* 2, L. Brisson, M.-O. Goulet Cazé & D. O'Brien (eds), 335–53. Paris: Vrin.

Gurtler, G. M. 2005. "Plotinus on the Soul". *Ancient Philosophy* 25(1): 231–4.

Gutas, D. 1998. *Greek Thought, Arabic Culture*. London: Routledge.

Gutas, D. 2012. "*Platon. Tradition arabe*". In *Dictionnaire des philosophes antiques*, R. Goulet (ed.), 845–63. Paris: CNRS Éditions.

Guthrie, W. K. C. 1978. *A History of Greek Philosophy*, 5. Cambridge: Cambridge University Press.

Guyer, P. 2004. "The Origins of Modern Aesthetics: 1711–35". In *The Blackwell Guide to Aesthetics*, P. Kivy (ed.), 15–44. Oxford: Blackwell.

Guyomarc'h, G. 2008. "Le visage du divin: La forme pure selon Alexandre d'Aphrodise". *Études philosophiques* 2008(3): 323–41.

Haas, C. 1997. *Alexandria in Late Antiquity: Topography and Social Conflict*. Baltimore, MD: Johns Hopkins University Press.

Hadot, I. 1978. *Le Problème du Néoplatonisme Alexandrin: Hiéroclès et Simplicius*. Paris: Études augustiniennes.

Hadot, I. 1982. "La doctrine de Simplicius sur l'âme raisonnable humaine dans le commentaire sur le *Manuel d'Épictète*". In *Soul and the Structure of Being in Late Neoplatonism: Syrianus, Proclus, and Simplicius*, H. J. Blumenthal & A. C. Lloyd (eds), 46–72. Liverpool: Liverpool University Press.

Hadot, I. (ed.) 1987. *Simplicius: Sa vie, son oeuvre, sa survie*. Berlin: De Gruyter.

Hadot, I. 1990. "The Life and Work of Simplicius in Greek and Arabic Sources". See Sorabji (1990), 275–303.

Hadot, I. 1997. "Aspects de la théorie de la perception chez les néoplatoniciens: sensation (αἴσθησις), sensation commune (κοινὴ αἴσθησις), sensibles communs (κοινὰ αἰσθητά) et conscience de soi (συναίσθησις)". *Documenti e studi sulla tradizione filosofica medievale* 7–8: 33–87.

Hadot, I. 2001. *Simplicius: Commentaire sur les Catégories d'Aristote, Chapître 1*. Leiden: Brill.

Hadot, I. 2002. "Simplicius or Priscianus? On the Author of the Commentary on Aristotle's *De Anima* (CAG 11): A Methodological Study". *Mnemosyne* 50(2): 159–99.

Hadot, I. & P. Hadot 2004. *Apprendre à philosopher dans l'antiquité: L'enseignement du "Manuel d'Épictète" et son commentaire néoplatonicien*. Paris: Librairie Général Française.

Hadot, P. 1968. *Porphyre et Victorinus*, 2 vols. Paris: Études augustiniennes.

Hadot, P. 1973. "L'être et l'étant dans le Néoplatonisme". *Revue de théologie et de philosophie* 2: 101–13. Reprinted in P. Hadot 1999. *Plotin, Porphyre: Études néoplatoniciennes*. Paris: Les Belles Lettres.

Hadot, P. 1974. "L'harmonie des philosophies de Plotin et d'Aristote selon Porphyre dans le commentaire de Dexippe sur les *Catégories*". In *Plotino e il Neoplatonismo in Oriente e in Occidente*, 32–47. Rome: Accademia nazionale dei Lincei. English translation in R. Sorabji (ed.) 1990. *Aristotle Transformed: The Ancient Commentators and Their Influence*, 125–40. London: Duckworth. Reprinted in P. Hadot, 1999. *Plotin, Porphyre: Études néoplatoniciennes*. Paris: Les Belles Lettres.

Hadot, P. 1976. "Le mythe de Narcisse et son interprétation par Plotin". *Nouvelle revue de psychanalyse* 13: 81–108.

Hadot, P. 1979. "Les divisions des parties de la philosophie dans l'antiquité". *Museum Helveticum* 36: 201–23.

Hadot, P. 1980. "Les niveaux de conscience dans les états mystiques selon Plotin". *Journal de psychologie* 2–3: 243–66.

Hadot, P. 1981a. "Ouranos, Kronos and Zeus in Plotinus' treatise against the Gnostics". In *Neoplatonism and Early Christian Thought. Essays in Honour of A. H. Armstrong*, H. J. Blumenthal & R. A. Markus (eds), 124–37. Aldershot: Variorum.

Hadot, P. 1981b. *Exercices spirituels et philosophie antique*, Collection des études augustiniennes. Série antiquité 88. Paris: Études augustiniennes.

Hadot, P. 1986. "Neoplatonist Spirituality: Plotinus and Porphyry". In *Classical Mediterranean Spirituality*, A. H. Armstrong (ed.), 230–49. New York: Crossroad.

Hadot, P. (trans.) 1987. *Plotin. Traité 38* (VI, 7). Introduction, Translation, Commentary and Notes. Paris: Cerf.

Hadot, P. 1993. *Plotinus, or, The Simplicity of Vision*, M. Chase (trans.). Chicago, IL: University of Chicago Press. For French original, see P. Hadot ([1963] 1997).

Hadot, P. 1994. *Plotin: Traité 9* (VI.9). Paris: Cerf.

Hadot, P. 1995. *Philosophy as a Way of Life: Spiritual Exercises from Socrates to Foucault*, M. Chase (trans.). Malden, MA: Blackwell. Translation of the French original (1981b).

Hadot, P. [1963] 1997. *Plotin ou la simplicité du regard*. Paris: Folio & Gallimard. For English translation, see P. Hadot (1993).

Hadot, P. 1999. *Plotin, Porphyre. Études néoplatoniciennes*. Paris: Les Belles Lettres.

Hadot, P. 2004. *Le voile d'Isis. Essai sur l'histoire de l'idée de nature*. Paris: Gallimard.

Halfwassen, J. 1992. *Der Aufstieg zum Einen. Untersuchungen zu Platon und Plotin*. Stuttgart: Teubner.

Halfwassen, J. 1996. "Das Eine als Einheit und Dreiheit". *Rheinisches Museum* 139: 52–83.

Halfwassen, J. 2002. "Sein als uneingeschränkte Fülle. Zur Vorgeschichte des ontologischen Gottesbeweises im antiken Platonismus". *Zeitschrift für philosophische Forschung* 56: 497–516.

Halfwassen, J. 2004. *Plotin und der Neuplatonismus*. Munich: Beck.

Halliwell, S. 1988. *Plato: Republic 10*. Warminster: Aris & Phillips.

Halliwell, S. 2002. *The Aesthetics of Mimesis: Ancient Texts and Modern Problems*. Princeton, NJ: Princeton University Press.

Hammond, N. G. L. 1987. "A Papyrus Commentary on Alexander's Balkan Campaign". *Journal of Greek, Roman and Byzantine Studies* 28: 331–47.

Hanson, A. E. 1987. "The Eight Months' Child and the Etiquette of Birth: *Obsit Omen!*" *Bulletin of the History of Medicine* 61(4): 589–602.

Harari, O. 2008. "Proclus' Account of Explanatory Demonstrations in Mathematics and its Context". *Archiv für Geschichte der Philosophie* 90(2): 137–64.

Harrington, L. M. 2004. *A Thirteenth-Century Textbook of Mystical Theology at the University of Paris*, Dallas Medieval Texts and Translations 4. Leuven: Peeters.

Harvey, S. 2004. "Islamic Philosophy and Jewish Philosophy". In *The Cambridge Companion to Arabic Philosophy*, P. Adamson & R. C. Taylor (eds), 349–69. Cambridge: Cambridge University Press.

Hatab, L. J. "Plotinus and the Upaniṣads". See Baine Harris (1982), 27–43.

Hathaway, R. 1969. *Hierarchy and the Definition of Order in the Letters of Pseudo-Dionysius*. The Hague: Nijhoff.

Hathaway, R. 1982. "The Anatomy of a Neoplatonist Metaphysical Proof". In *The Structure of Being: A Neoplatonist Approach*, R. Baine Harris (ed.), 122–36. Albany, NY: SUNY Press.

Hauréau, B. 1872. *Histoire de la philosophie scolastique, 1: De Charlemagne à la fin du XII siècle*. Paris: Durand & Pedone-Lauriel.

Havelock, E. A. [1966] 1982. "Preliteracy and the Presocratics". In *The Literate Revolution in Greece and its Cultural Consequences*, E. A. Havelock (ed.), 220–60. Princeton, NJ: Princeton University Press. (= 1966, *Bulletin of the Institute of Classical Studies* 13: 44–67.)

Heath, J. 2005. *The Talking Greeks: Speech, Animals, and the Other in Homer, Aeschylus, and Plato*. Cambridge: Cambridge University Press.

Heckel, T. K. 1993. *Der innere Mensch: die paulinische Verarbeitung eines platonischen Motivs.* Tübingen: Mohr Siebeck.

Heiser, J. H. 1991. *Logos and Language in the Philosophy of Plotinus.* Lewiston, NY: Mellen.

Helbig, M. O. 2000. "La fortune des commentaires de Proclus sur le premier livre des 'Éléments' d'Euclide à l'époque de Galilée". See Bechtle & O'Meara (2000), 173–93.

Helmig, C. 2006. "Die atmende Form in der Materie – Einige Überlegungen zum ἔνυλον εἶδος in der Philosophie des Proklos". See Perkams & Piccione (2006), 259–78.

Helmig, C. 2007. "The Relationship Between Forms and Numbers in Nicomachus' *Introduction to Arithmetic*". In *Platonic Pythagoras*, M. Bonazzi & C. Steel (eds), 127–46. Turnhout: Brepols.

Helmig, C. 2012. *Concept-Formation in the Platonic Tradition.* Berlin: De Gruyter.

Henry, P. 1938. *Études plotiniennes, vol. 1: Les états du texte de Plotin.* Brussels: Édition Universelle.

Herling, B. L. 2009. *The German Gītā: Hermeneutics and Discipline in the German Reception of Indian Thought, 1778-1831.* New York: Routledge.

Hicks, R. D. 1907. *Aristotle De Anima.* Cambridge: Cambridge University Press.

Hiltebeitel, A. 2011a. "The Nārāyaṇa and Early Reading Communities of the Mahābhārata". In *Reading the Fifth Veda: Studies on the Mahābhārata, Essays by Alf Hiltebeitel*, 1, V. Adluri & J. Bagchee (eds), 187–220. Leiden: Brill.

Hiltebeitel, A. 2011b. "Two Kṛṣṇas on One Chariot: Upaniṣadic Imagery and Epic Mythology". In *Reading the Fifth Veda: Studies on the Mahābhārata, Essays by Alf Hiltebeitel* vol. 1, V. Adluri & J. Bagchee (eds), 485–512. Leiden: Brill.

Hiltebeitel, A. 2012. "The *Mahābhārata* and the Stories Some People Tell about It: Part 1". *Exemplar* 1(2): 2–26.

Hinske, N. 1974. "Horizont". In *Historisches Wörterbuch der Philosophie*, 3, J. Ritter (ed.), 1187–94. Darmstadt: Wissenschaftliche Buchgesellschaft.

Hoffmann, P. 1987. "Aspects de la polémique de Simplicius contre Philopon". In *Simplicius: Sa vie, son oeuvre, sa survie*, I. Hadot (ed.), 183–221. Berlin: De Gruyter.

Hoffmann, P. 2000. "Bibliothèques et formes du livre à la fin de l'antiquité. Le témoignage de la littérature néoplatonicienne des Ve et VIe siècles". In *I manoscritti greci tra riflessione e dibattito*, G. Prato (ed.), 601–32. Florence: Gonnelli.

Hoover, J. 2007. *Ibn Taymiyya's Theodicy of Perpetual Optimism.* Leiden: Brill.

Hopkins, J. 1984. *Nicholas of Cusa's Debate with John Wenck. A Translation and Appraisal of De Ignota Litteratura and Apologia Doctae Ignorantiae.* Minneapolis, MN: Banning.

Horn, C. 1995a. *Plotin über Sein, Zahl und Einheit.* Stuttgart: Teubner.

Horn, C. 1995b. "Der platonische 'Parmenides' und die Möglichkeiten seiner prinzipientheoretischen Interpretation". *Antike und Abendland* 41: 95–114.

Horn, C. 2007. "The Concept of Will in Plotinus". In *Reading Ancient Texts, vol. 2: Aristotle and Neoplatonism*, S. Stern-Gillet & K. Corrigan (eds), 153–78. Leiden: Brill.

Huber, G. 1955. *Das Sein und das Absolute. Studien zur Geschichte der ontologischen Problematik in der spätantiken Philosophie.* Basel: Verlag für Recht und Gesellschaft.

Hubler, N. J. 2005. "The Perils of Self-Perception: Explanations of Apperception in the Greek Commentaries on Aristotle". *Review of Metaphysics* 59: 287–311.

Huby, P. 1993. "Priscian of Lydia as Evidence for Iamblichus". In *The Divine Iamblichus: Philosopher and Man of Gods*, H. J. Blumenthal & E. G. Clark (eds), 5–12. Bristol: Bristol Classical Press.

Hume, D. 1739-40. *A Treatise of Human Nature: Being an Attempt to Introduce the Experiential Method of Reasoning into Moral Subjects.* Vols 1–2, London: London Noon. Vol. 3, London: Thomas Longman.

Hutton, S. 2002. "The Cambridge Platonists". In *Blackwell Companion to Early Modern Philosophy*, S. Nadler (ed.), 308–19. Oxford: Blackwell.

Hutton, S. & D. Hedley (eds) 2008. *Platonism at the Origins of Modernity.* Dordrecht: Springer.

Ierodiakonou, K. 2009a. "Some Observations on Michael of Ephesus' Comments on *Nicomachean Ethics* X". In *Medieval Greek Commentaries on the Nicomachean Ethics*, C. E. Barber & D. Jenkins (eds), 185–202. Leiden: Brill.

Ierodiakonou, K. 2009b. "Syrianus on Scientific Knowledge and Demonstration". In *Syrianus et la métaphysique de l'antiquité tardive: actes du colloque international, Université de Gèneve, 29 Septembre-1er Octobre 2006*, A. Longo (ed.), 401–22. Naples: Bibliopolis.

Ierodiakonou, K. & G. Zografidis 2010. "Early Byzantine Philosophy". See Gerson (2010), 843–68.

Inge, R. 1929. *The Philosophy of Plotinus*, 2 vols, 3rd edn. London: Longmans, Green & Co.

Irwin, T. 1991. "The Structure of Aristotelian Happiness". *Ethics* 101: 382–90.

Ivry, A. L. 2007a. "Conjunction in and of Maimonides and Averroes". In *Averroes et les averroïsmes juif et latin: actes du colloque international, Paris, 16–18 juin 2005*, J.-B. Brenet (ed.), 231–47. Turnhout: Brepols.

Ivry, A. L. 2007b. "Getting to Know Thee: Conjuction and Conformity in Averroes' and Maimonides' Philosophy". In *Adaptations and Innovations: Studies on the Interaction Between Jewish and Islamic Thought and Literature from the Early Middle Ages to the Late Twentieth Century, Dedicated to Professor Joel L. Kraemer*, Y. T. Langermann & J. Stern (eds), 143–56. Leuven: Peeters.

Jaeger, W. 1966. *Gregor von Nyssa's Lehre von Heiligen Geist*. Leiden: Brill.

Johansen, T. K. 2004. *Plato's Natural Philosophy*. Cambridge: Cambridge University Press.

Joly, R. 1956. *Le Thème philosophique des genres de vie dans l'antiquité classique*. Brussels: Académie Royale de Belgique.

Jonas, H. 1934–93. *Gnosis und spätantiker Geist*, Forschungen zur Religion und Literatur des Alten und Neuen Testaments n.F. 33, 2 vols, K. Rudolph (ed.). Göttingen: Vandenheock & Ruprecht.

Jones, R. M. 1916. *The Platonism of Plutarch*. Menasha, WI: Collegiate Press.

Jufresa, M. 1981. "Basilides, A Path to Plotinus". *Vigiliae Christianae* 35: 1–15.

Kahn, C. 1976. "Why Existence Does Not Emerge as a Distinct Concept in Greek Philosophy". *Archiv für Geschichte der Philosophie* 58: 323–34. Reprinted in his *Essays on Being*, 62–74. Oxford: Clarendon Press, 2002.

Kahn, C. 2003. "Writing Philosophy". In *Written Texts and the Rise of Literate Culture in Ancient Greece*, H. Yunis (ed.) , 139–61. Cambridge: Cambridge University Press.

Kalligas, P. 1997. "Forms of Individuals in Plotinus: A Re-Examination". *Phronesis* 42(2): 206–27.

Kalligas, P. 2000. "Living Body, Soul, and Virtue in the Philosophy of Plotinus". *Dionysius* 18: 25–38.

Kalligas, P. 2011. "The Structure of Appearances: Plotinus on the Constitution of Sensible Objects". *Philosophical Quarterly* 61: 762–82.

Kalligas, P. 2012. "*Eiskrisis*, Or the Presence of the Soul in the Body: A Plotinian Conundrum". *Ancient Philosophy* 32: 147–65.

Kane, P. V. 1930–62. *A History of Dharmaśāstra*, 5 vols. Poona: Bhandarkar Oriental Research Institute.

Kant, I. 1902. *Gesammelte Schriften*, Berlin-Brandenburgische Akademie der Wissenschaften. Berlin: De Gruyter.

Kant, I. 2002. *Critique of the Power of Judgment*, P. Guyer (ed. & trans.). Cambridge: Cambridge University Press.

Kapparis, K. 2002. *Abortion in the Ancient World*. London: Duckworth.

Karamanolis, G. 2004. "Porphyry: The First Platonist Commentator on Aristotle". See Adamson, Baltussen & Stone (2004), 97–120.

Karamanolis, G. 2006. *Plato and Aristotle in Agreement? Platonists on Aristotle from Antiochus to Porphyry*. Oxford: Oxford University Press.

Karamanolis, G. 2009. "Plotinus on Quality and Immanent Form". See Chiaradonna & Trabattoni (2009), 79–100.

Karamanolis, G. & A. Sheppard (eds) 2007. *Studies on Porphyry, Bulletin of the Institute of Classical Studies* Suppl. 98. London: Institute of Classical Studies.

Karfik, F. 2013. "*Dēmogerontes*: L'image de l'assemblée dans les *Ennéades* VI, 4[22],15". In *Plato Revived: Essays on Ancient Platonism in Honour of Dominic J. O'Meara*, F. Karfik & E. Song (eds), 85–95. Berlin: De Gruyter.

Katz, J. 1954. "Plotinus and the Gnostics". *Journal of the History of Ideas* 15(2): 289–98.

Kaufmann, D. 1899. *Studien über Salomon Ibn Gabirol (Jahresberichte der Landes-Rabbinerschule zu Budapest für das Schuljahr 1898/99)*. Budapest. Reprinted New York: Arno Press, 1980; also in *Die Spuren al-Batlajūsi's, Studien Über Salomon ibn Gabirol und Die Sinne*. London: Gregg International Publishers, 1972.

Keyser, P. T. 1997. "Science and Magic in Galen's Recipes (Sympathy and Efficacy)". In *Galen on Pharmacology*, A. Debru (ed.), 175–98. Leiden: Brill.

Keyser, P. T. & G. L. Irby-Massie (eds) 2008. *The Encyclopedia of Ancient Natural Scientists*. London: Routledge.

King, P. 2005. "Augustine's Encounter with Neoplatonism". *The Modern Schoolman: A Quarterly Journal of Philosophy* 82(3): 213–26.

Kissling, R. C. 1922. "The ὄχημα-πνεῦμα of the Neo-Platonists and the *de Insomniis* of Synesius of Cyrene". *American Journal of Philology* 43(4): 318–30.

Klostermaier, K. K. 2007. *A Survey of Hinduism*. Albany, NY: SUNY Press.

Knuuttila, S. 2004. *Emotions in Ancient and Medieval Philosophy*. Oxford: Oxford University Press.

Kobusch, T. 1976. *Studien zur Philosophie des Hierokles von Alexandrien: Untersuchungen zum christlichen Neuplatonismus*. Munich: Johannes Berchmans Verlag.

Koch, I. 2013. "L'exégèse Plotinienne des dialogues". In *Lire les dialogues, mais lesquels et en quel ordre: Définitions du corpus et interprétations de Platon*, A. Balansard & I. Koch (eds), 59–84. Sankt Augustin: Academia Verlag.

Köckert, C. 2009. *Christliche Kosmologie und kaiserzeitliche Philosophie: Die Auslegung des Schöpfungsberichtes bei Origines, Basilius und Gregor von Nyssa vor dem Hintergrund kaiserzeitlicher Timaeus-Interpretationen.* Tübingen: Mohr Siebeck.

Kotzia-Panteli, P. 2000. "ΕΝΝΟΗΜΑΤΙΚΟΣ und ΟΥΣΙΩΔΗΣ ΛΟΓΟΣ as exegetisches Begriffspaar". *Philologus* 144: 45–61.

Kraemer, J. L. 2003. "The Islamic Context of Medieval Jewish Philosophy". In *The Cambridge Companion to Medieval Jewish Philosophy*, D. H. Frank & O. Leaman (eds), 38–68. Cambridge: Cambridge University Press.

Krämer, H. J. 1973. "Aristoteles und die akademische Eidoslehre. Zur Geschichte des Universalienproblems im Platonismus". *Archiv für Geschichte der Philosophie* 55: 119–90.

Krämer, H. J. 1990. *Plato and the Foundations of Metaphysics*, J. R. Catan (ed. & trans.). Albany, NY: SUNY Press.

Kraut, R. 1989. *Aristotle on the Human Good.* Princeton, NJ: Princeton University Press.

Kraye, J., W. F. Ryan & C. B. Schmitt (eds) 1986. *Pseudo-Aristotle in the Middle Ages: The Theology and Other Texts.* London: The Warburg Institute.

Kudlien, F. 1968. "The Third Century AD – A Blank Spot in the History of Medicine?" In *Medicine, Science and Culture: Historical Essays in Honor of Owsei Temkin*, L. G. Stevenson & R. P. Multhauf (eds), 25–34. Baltimore, MD: Johns Hopkins Press.

Kühn, W. 2009. *Quel savoir après le scepticisme: Plotin et ses prédécesseurs sur la connaissance de soi.* Histoire des doctrines de l'antiquité classique 37. Paris: Vrin.

Kuiper, F. B. J. 1979. *Varuṇa and Viduṣāka: On the Origin of the Sanskrit Drama.* Amsterdam: North Holland.

Kuisma, O. 2003. *Art or Experience: A Study on Plotinus' Aesthetics.* Helsinki: Societas Scientiarum Fennica.

Lacombrade, C. 1951. *Synésios de Cyrène: hellène et chrétien.* Paris: Les Belles Lettres.

Lacrosse, J. 2001. "La rêve indien de Plotin et Porphyry". *Revue de philosophie ancienne* 19(1): 79–97.

Lamberz, E. 1987. "Proklos und die Form des philosophischen Kommentars". In *Proclus: Lecteur et interprète des anciens*, J. Pépin & H. D. Saffrey (eds), 1–20. Paris: CNRS.

Langermann, Y. T. 1999. "A New Hebrew Passage from the *Theology of Aristotle* and its Significance". *Arabic Sciences and Philosophy* 9: 247–59.

Larsen, B. D. 1972. *Jamblique de Chalcis. Exégète et philosophe*, 2 vols. Aarhus: Universitetsforlage.

Lautner, P. 1992. "Philoponus, *In De Anima III*: Quest for an Author". *Classical Quarterly* 42: 510–22.

Lautner, P. 2000. "Plutarch of Athens on κοινὴ αἴσθησις and *phantasia*". *Ancient Philosophy* 20: 425–47.

Lautner, P. 2006. "Some Clarifications on Proclus' Fourfold Division of Sense-Perception in the *Timaeus* Commentary". See Perkams & Piccione (2006), 117–35.

Lavaud, L. 2002. "Structure et thèmes du *Traité 49*". In *La Connaissance de soi. Études sur le Traité 49 de Plotin*, M. Dixsaut (ed.), 179–207. Paris: Vrin.

Lavaud, L. 2008. *D'une métaphysique à l'autre. Figures de l'altérité dans la philosophie de Plotin.* Paris: Vrin.

Lefebvre, D. 2008. "Le commentaire d'Alexandre d'Aphrodise à *Métaphysique*, A, 9, 990 a 34–b8. Sur le nombre et l'objet des idées". *Études philosophiques* 2008(3): 305–22.

Leng, M. 2010. *Mathematics and Reality.* Oxford: Oxford University Press.

Lernould, A. 2001. *Physique et théologie. Lecture du* Timée *de Platon par Proclus.* Villeneuve d'Ascq (Nord): Presses Universitaires du Septentrion.

Lernould, A. (ed.) 2010. *Études sur le commentaire de Proclus au Premier Livre Des Éléments d'Euclide.* Villeneuve d'Ascq: Presses Universitaires du Septentrion.

Lernould, A. 2011. "De la logique à la théologie. Les preuves démonstratives dans le *Timée* de Platon selon Proclus". In *Argument from Hypothesis in Ancient Philosophy*, A. Longo & D. del Forno (eds), 383–411. Naples: Bibliopolis.

Leroux, G. 1990. *Traité sur la liberté et la volonté de l'Un.* Paris: Vrin.

Leroux, G. 1996. "Human Freedom in the Thought of Plotinus". See Gerson (1996), 292–314.

Lettinck, P. 1994. *Philoponus, On Aristotle's* Physics 5–8 *with Simplicius, On Aristotle on the Void*, P. L. & J. O. Urmson (trans.). London: Duckworth.

Lévy, C. 2003. "Cicero and the *Timaeus*". In *Plato's Timaeus as Cultural Icon*, G. Reydams-Schils (ed.), 95–110. Notre Dame: University of Notre Dame Press.

Linguiti, A. 2007. "La materia dei corpi: sullo pseudoilomorfismo plotiniano". *Quaestio* 7: 105–22.

Linguiti, A. 2009. "*Physis* as *Heimarmene*: On Some Fundamental Principles of the Neoplatonic Philosophy of Nature". See Chiaradonna & Trabattoni (2009), 173–88.

Lloyd, A. C. 1962. "Genus, Species and Ordered Series in Aristotle". *Phronesis* 7: 67–90.

Lloyd, A. C. 1964. "*Nosce Teipsum* and *Conscientia*". *Archiv für Geschichte der Philosophie* 46: 188–200.

Lloyd, A. C. 1969-70. "Non-Discursive Thought – An Enigma of Greek Philosophy". *Proceedings of the Aristotelian Society* 70: 261–74.

Lloyd, A. C. 1976. "The Principle that the Cause is Greater than its Effect". *Phronesis* 31: 146–56.

Lloyd, A. C. 1987. "Plotinus on the Genesis of Thought and Existence". *Oxford Studies in Ancient Philosophy* 5: 155–86.

Lloyd, A. C. 1990. *The Anatomy of Neoplatonism*. Oxford: Clarendon Press.

Lloyd, G. E. R. 2005. "Mathematics as a Model of Method in Galen". In *Philosophy and the Sciences in Antiquity*, R. W. Sharples (ed.), 110–30. Aldershot: Ashgate.

Lobsien, V. O. & K. Olk (eds) 2007. *Neuplatonismus und Ästhetik. Zur Transformationsgeschichte des Schönen*. Berlin: De Gruyter.

Lohr, C. H. 1986. "The Pseudo-Aristotelian *Liber de Causis* and Latin Theories of Science in the Twelfth and Thirteenth Centuries". See Kraye, Ryan & Schmitt (1986), 53–62.

Long, A. A. 1982. "Astrology: Arguments Pro and Contra". In *Science and Speculation: Studies in Hellenistic Theory and Practice*, J. Barnes, J. Brunschwig, M. Burnyeat & M. Schofield (eds), 165–92. Cambridge: Cambridge University Press.

Long, A. A. 1996a. *Stoic Studies*. Cambridge: Cambridge University Press.

Long, A. A. [1971] 1996b. "Freedom and Determinism in the Stoic Theory of Human Action". In *Problems in Stoicism*, A. A. Long (ed.), 173–99. London: Athlone Press.

Long, A. A. 2002. *Epictetus. A Stoic and Socratic Guide to Life*. Oxford: Oxford University Press.

Longo, A. 2002. "Gli argomenti di Teodoro di Asine sull'educazione comune di uomini e donne nel Commento alla *Repubblica* di Proclo (I, 253–255 Kroll)". *Elenchos* 23: 51–73. Reprinted in her *Amicus Plato*, 63–83. Milan: Mimesis, 2007.

Longo, A. 2010. "Syrianus". See Gerson (2010), vol. 2, 616–29.

Lorenz, H. 2006. "The Analysis of the Soul in Plato's *Republic*". In *The Blackwell Guide to Plato's Republic*, G. Santas (ed.), 146–65. Malden, MA: Blackwell.

Louth, A. 1989. *Denys the Areopagite*. London: Geoffrey Chapman.

Lowry, J. M. P. 1980. *The Logical Principles of Proclus' Στοιχείωσις Θεολογική as Systematic Ground of the Cosmos*. Amsterdam: Rodopi.

Ludlow, M. 2002. "Theology and Allegory: Origen and Gregory of Nyssa on the Unity and Diversity of Scripture". *International Journal of Systematic Theology* 4(1): 45–66.

Łukasiewicz, J. 1951. *Aristotle's Syllogistic from the Standpoint of Modern Formal Logic*. Oxford: Clarendon.

Mabbett, I. W. 1983. "The Symbolism of Mount Meru". *History of Religions* 23(1): 64–83.

Maccoby, H. 1986. *The Mythmaker: Paul and the Invention of Christianity*. New York: Harper & Row.

Maccoby, H. 1991. *Paul and Hellenism*. London: SCM Press.

MacCoull, L. 2006. "Menas and Thomas: Notes on the *Dialogus de scientia politica*". *Greek, Roman, and Byzantine Studies* 46: 301–13.

MacIsaac, G. 2009. "The Soul and the Virtues in Proclus' *Commentary on the Republic of Plato*". *Philosophie antique* 9: 115–43.

MacPhail, J. A. Jr. 2011. *Porphyry's "Homeric Questions" on the "Iliad"*. Text, Translation, and Commentary. Berlin: De Gruyter.

Maggi, C. 2009. *Plotino Sui numeri. Enneade VI 6 [34]*. Naples: Università degli Studi suor Orsola Benincasa.

Maggi, C. 2010. *Sinfonia matematica. Aporie e soluzioni in Platone, Aristotele, Plotino, Giamblico*. Naples: Loffredo Editore.

Maggi, C. 2012. "Iamblichus on Mathematical Entities". In *Iamblichus and the Foundations of Late Platonism*, E. Afonasin, J. M. Dillon & J. F. Finamore (eds), 75–89. Leiden: Brill.

Majcherek, G. 2004. "Excavations and Preservation Work 2002/2003". *Polish Archaeology in the Mediterranean* 15: 25–38.

Majcherek, G. & W. Kolataj 2003. "Alexandria, Excavations and Preservation Work, 2001/2". *Polish Archaeology in the Mediterranean* 14: 19–31.

Männlein-Robert, I. 2013. "Tugend, Flucht und Ekstase: zur ὁμοίωσις θεῷ in Kaiserzeit und Spätantike". In *Ethik des antiken Platonismus*, C. Pietsch (ed.), 99–111. Stuttgart: Franz Steiner.

Männlein-Robert, I. & F. Ferrari forthcoming. *Mittelplatonismus und Neupythagoreismus*, Überweg, Die Philosophie der Antike 5: Philosophie der Kaiserzeit und der Spätantike, C. Horn, C. Riedweg and D. Wyrwa (eds). Basel: Schwabe.

Manolea, C. P. 2004. *The Homeric Tradition in Syrianus*. Thessaloniki: Stamoulis.

Mansfeld, J. 1986. "Aristotle, Plato, and the Pre-Platonic Doxography and Chronography". In *Storiografia e dossografia*, E. Cambiano (ed.), 1–59. Turin: Tirrenia.

Mansfeld, J. 1994. *Prolegomena: Questions to be Settled before the Study of an Author, or a Text*. Leiden: Brill.

Mansfeld, J. 1999. "Alcinous on Fate and Providence". In *Traditions of Platonism*, J. Cleary (ed.), 139–50. Aldershot: Ashgate.

Marrou, H.-I. 1963. "Synesius of Cyrene and Alexandrian Neoplatonism". In *The Conflict Between Paganism and Christianity in the Fourth Century*, A. Momigliano (ed.), 126–50. Oxford: Clarendon Press.

Martijn, M. 2010a. *Proclus on Nature: Philosophy of Nature and its Methods in Proclus' Commentary on Plato's Timaeus*, Philosophia Antiqua 121. Leiden: Brill.

Martijn, M. 2010b. "Why Beauty is Truth in All We Know: Aesthetics and Mimesis in Neoplatonic Science". *Proceedings of the Boston Area Colloquium in Ancient Philosophy* 25: 69–92.

Martijn, M. 2010c. "Proclus on the Order of Philosophy of Nature". *Synthese* 174(2): 205–23.

Martindale, J. R. 1980. *The Prosopography of the Later Roman Empire*, 2. Cambridge: Cambridge University Press.

Mathis II, C. K. 1992. "Parallel Structures in the Metaphysics of Iamblichus and Ibn Gabirol". In *Neoplatonism and Jewish Thought*, L. E. Goodman (ed.), 61–76. Albany, NY: SUNY Press.

Mattila, J. 2011. *Philosophy as a Path to Happiness: Attainment of Happiness in Arabic Peripatetic and Ismaili Philosophy*. PhD dissertation. Helsinki: University of Helsinki Print.

Mazur, B. 2003. *Imagining Numbers*. New York: Farrar Straus Giroux.

Mazur, Z. 2005. "Primordial Self-Reversion and the Gnostic Background of Plotinian Procession". Paper presented at the International Society for Neoplatonic Studies Annual Meeting, June, New Orleans.

Mazur, Z. 2010. "The Platonizing Sethian Gnostic Background of Plotinus' Mysticism". Ph.D. dissertation, University of Chicago.

Mazur, Z. 2013. "The Platonizing Sethian Interpretation of Plato's *Sophist*". In *Practicing Gnosis: Ritual, Magic, Theurgy, and Liturgy in Nag Hammadi, Manichaean and Other Late Antique Literature. Essays in Honor of Birger A. Pearson*, Nag Hammadi and Manichaean Studies, A. D. DeConick, G. Shaw & J. D. Turner (eds), 469–93. Leiden: Brill.

McCarty, W. 2002. "A Network with a Thousand Entrances: Commentary in an Electronic Age?" In *The Classical Commentary: Histories, Practices, Theory*, R. K. Gibson & C. S. Kraus (eds), 359–403. Leiden: Brill.

McEvoy, J. J. 1992. "Neoplatonism and Christianity: Influence, Syncretism or Discernment". See Finan & Twomey (1992), 155–70.

McGroarty, K. 2006. *Plotinus on Eudaimonia: A Commentary on Ennead I 4*. Oxford: Oxford University Press.

Meinardus, O. F. A. 2003. *Monks and Monasteries of the Egyptian Deserts*, 5th edn. Cairo: The American University in Cairo Press.

Meredith, A. S. J. 1999. *Gregory of Nyssa*. London: Routledge.

Merlan, P. 1953. *From Platonism to Neoplatonism*. The Hague: Nijhoff.

Merlan, P. 1967. "Greek Philosophy from Plato to Plotinus". See Armstrong (1967), 14–132.

Merlan, P. 1968. "Ammonius Hermiae, Zacharias Scholasticus and Boethius". *Greek, Roman, and Byzantine Studies* 9(2): 193–203.

Merlan, P. 1969. *Monopsychism, Mysticism, Metaconsciousness. Problems of the Soul in the Neoaristotelian and Neoplatonic Tradition*. The Hague: Martinus Nijhoff.

Mesyats, S. 2012. "Iamblichus' Exegesis of Parmenides' Hypotheses and His Doctrine of Divine Henads". In *Iamblichus and the Foundations of Late Platonism*, E. Afonasin, J. M. Dillon & J. F. Finamore (eds), 151–75. Leiden: Brill.

Metzger, N. forthcoming. "Dämon oder Krankheit? Der Alpdruck in der frühbyzantinischer Medizin". *Das Mittelalter*.

Miller, M. 1986. *Plato's Parmenides: The Conversion of the Soul*. Princeton, NJ: Princeton University Press.

Monier-Williams, M. 1899. *A Sanskrit–English Dictionary*. Oxford: Clarendon Press.

Moran, D. 1989. *The Philosophy of John Scottus Eriugena: A Study of Idealism in the Middle Ages*. Cambridge: Cambridge University Press.

Moran, D. 1990. "Pantheism from John Scottus Eriugena to Nicholas of Cusa". *American Catholic Philosophical Quarterly* 64(1): 131–52.

Moran, D. 1998. "Platonism, Medieval". In *The Routledge Encyclopedia of Philosophy* 7, E. Craig (ed.), 431–9. London: Routledge.

Moran, D. 2002. "Time and Eternity in the *Periphyseon*". In *History and Eschatology in John Scottus Eriugena and His Time. Proceedings of the Tenth International Conference of the Society for the Promotion of Eriugena Studies*, J. McEvoy & M. Dunne (eds), 487–507. Leuven: Leuven University Press.

Moran, D. 2003. "Medieval Philosophy: From Augustine to Nicolas of Cusa". In *Fundamentals of Philosophy*, J. Shand (ed.), 155–203. London: Routledge.

Moran, D. 2007. "Nicholas of Cusa (1401–1464): Platonism at the Dawn of Modernity". In *Platonism at the Origins of Modernity: Studies on Platonism and Early Modern Philosophy*, D. Hedley & S. Hutton (eds), 9–29. Dordrecht: Springer.

Moraux, P. 1942. *Alexandre d'Aphrodise: Exégète de la noétique d'Aristote*. Liège: Bibliothèque de la faculté de philosophie et lettres de l'Université de Liège.

Moraux, P. 1973. *Der Aristotelismus bei den Griechen I*. Berlin: De Gruyter.

Moraux, P. 1978. "Le 'De Anima' dans la tradition grecque. Quelques aspects de l'interprétation du traité du Théophraste à Thémistius". In *Aristotle on Mind and The Senses. Proceedings of the Seventh Symposium Aristotelicum*, G. E. R. Lloyd & G. E. L. Owen (eds), 281–324. Cambridge: Cambridge University Press.

Moraux, P. 1984. *Der Aristotelismus bei den Griechen von Andronikos bis Alexander von Aphrodisias* 2. Berlin: De Gruyter.

Morel, P.-M. 1999. "Individualité et identité de l'âme humaine chez Plotin". *Cahiers philosophiques de Strasbourg* 8: 53–66.

Morel, P.-M. 2002. "La sensation, messagère de l'âme. Plotin, V, 3 [49], 3". In *La connaissance de soi. Études sur le traité 49 de Plotin*, M. Dixsaut (ed.), 209–28. Paris: Vrin.

Moreschini, C. 2004. *Storia della filosofia patristica*. Brescia: Morcelliana.

Moreschini, C. 2008. *I Padri cappadoci: storia, letteratura, teologia*. Rome: Città Nuova.

Morewedge, P. (ed.) 1992. *Neoplatonism and Islamic Thought*. Albany, NY: SUNY Press.

Most, G. W. (ed.) 1999. *Commentaries – Kommentare*, Aporemata 4. Göttingen: Vandenhoeck & Rupprecht.

Mueller, I. 2000. "Syrianus and the Concept of Mathematical Number". See Bechtle & O'Meara (2000), 71–83.

Mullins, E. 2011. *Roman Provence*. Oxford: Signal Books.

Narbonne, J.-M. 1992. "Le non-être chez Plotin et la tradition grecque". *Revue de philosophie ancienne* 12: 115–33.

Narbonne, J.-M. 1994. *La Métaphysique de Plotin*. Paris: Vrin.

Narbonne, J.-M. 2003. "De l'un matière à l'un forme. La réponse de Proclus à la critique aristotélicienne de l'unité du politique dans la *République* de Platon (*In Remp.* II, 361–368)". In *Pensées de l'Un dans la tradition métaphysique occidentale* (Festschrift Werner Beierwaltes), J.-M. Narbonne & A. Reckermann (eds), 3–25. Paris: Vrin.

Narbonne, J.-M. 2006. "Plotinus and the Gnostics on the Generation of Matter (33 [II 9], 12 and 51 [I 8], 14)". *Dionysius* 24: 45–64.

Narbonne, J.-M. 2007. "La controverse à propos de la génération de la matière chez Plotin: L'énigme résolue?" *Quaestio* 7(1): 123–63.

Narbonne, J.-M. 2008. "L'énigme de la non-descente partielle de l'âme chez Plotin: la piste gnostique/hermétique de l'ΟΜΟΟΥΣΙΟΣ". *Laval théologique et philosophique* 64: 691–708.

Narbonne, J.-M. 2009. "Plotinus on the Generation of Matter". *International Journal of the Platonic Tradition* 3: 103–37.

Narbonne, J.-M. 2011. *Plotinus in Dialogue with the Gnostics*. Ancient Mediterranean and Medieval Texts: Studies in Platonism, Neoplatonism, and the Platonic Tradition 11. Leiden: Brill.

Nasr, S. H. 1993. *An Introduction to Islamic Cosmological Doctrines*. Albany, NY: SUNY Press.

Nauta, L. 1996. "The Preexistence of the Soul in Medieval Thought". *Recherches de théologie ancienne et médiévale* 63: 93–135.

Nehamas, A. 1990. "Eristic, Antilogic, Sophistic, Dialectic: Plato's Demarcation of Philosophy from Sophistry". *History of Philosophy Quarterly* 7: 3–16.

Netz, R. 1999. "Proclus' Division of the Mathematical Proposition into Parts: How and Why Was it Formulated?" *Classical Quarterly* 49: 282–303.

Newmyer, S. 2006. *Animals, Rights and Reason in Plutarch and Modern Ethics.* London: Routledge.

Nikulin, D. 1998a. "Foundations of Arithmetic in Plotinus: *Enn.* VI.6 [34] on the Structure and the Constitution of Number". *Methexis* 11: 85–102.

Nikulin, D. 1998b. "The One and the Many in Plotinus". *Hermes* 126: 326–40.

Nikulin, D. 2002. *Matter, Imagination and Geometry: Ontology, Natural Philosophy and Mathematics in Plotinus, Proclus and Descartes.* Aldershot: Ashgate.

Nikulin, D. 2003. "*Physica More Geometrico Demonstrata*: Natural Philosophy in Proclus and Aristotle". *Proceedings of the Boston Area Colloquium in Ancient Philosophy* 18: 183–221.

Nikulin, D. 2005. "Unity and Individuation of the Soul in Plotinus". In *Studi sull'anima in Plotino*, R. Chiaradonna (ed.), 277–304. Naples: Bibliopolis.

Nussbaum, M. 1986. *The Fragility of Goodness.* Cambridge: Cambridge University Press.

Nussbaum, M. 2000. *Women and Human Development: The Capabilities Approach.* Cambridge: Cambridge University Press.

Nussbaum, M. 2003. "Capabilities as Fundamental Entitlements: Sen and Social Justice". *Feminist Economics* 9(2–3): 33–59.

Nussbaum, M. 2006. *Frontiers of Justice: Disability, Nationality, Species Membership.* Cambridge, MA: Harvard University Press.

Nutton, V. 2004. *Ancient Medicine.* London: Routledge.

Nyvlt, M. J. 2012. *Aristotle and Plotinus on the Intellect: Monism and Dualism Revisited.* Lanham, MD: Lexington Books.

O'Brien, D. 1971. "Plotinus on Evil. A Study of Matter and the Soul in Plotinus' Conception of Human Evil". In *Le Néoplatonism, Colloques internationaux du CNRS à Royaumont du 9 au 13 juin 1969*, 113–46. Paris: CNRS.

O'Brien, D. 1977. "Le volontaire et la nécessité: réflexions sur la descente de l'âme dans la philosophie de Plotin". *Revue philosophique de la France et de l'étranger* 167: 401–22.

O'Brien, D. 1996. "Plotinus on Matter and Evil". See Gerson (1996), 171–95.

O'Brien, D. 1998. "Proclus on the Existence of Evil". *Proceedings of the Boston Area Colloquium in Ancient Philosophy* 14: 83–102.

O'Brien, D. 1999. "La matière chez Plotin: son origine, sa nature". *Phronesis* 44(1): 45–71.

O'Brien, D. 2011–12. "Plotinus on the Making of Matter: The Identity of Darkness", Parts I–III. *International Journal of the Platonic Tradition* 5(1): 6–57; 5(2): 209–61; 6(1): 27–80.

O'Daly, G. 1973. *Plotinus' Philosophy of the Self.* Shannon: Irish University Press.

O'Donnell, J. 2006. *Augustine: A New Biography.* New York: Harper Perennial Books.

O'Meara, D. 1975. *Structures hiérarchiques dans la pensée de Plotin*, Philosophia Antiqua 27. Leiden: Brill.

O'Meara, D. 1988. "Proclus' First Prologue to Euclid: The Problem of its Major Source". In *Gonimos: Neoplatonic and Byzantine Studies Presented to Leendert G. Westerink at 75*, J. Duffy & J. Peradotto (eds), 49–59. Buffalo, NY: Arethusa.

O'Meara, D. 1989. *Pythagoras Revived: Mathematics and Philosophy in Late Antiquity.* Oxford: Clarendon Press.

O'Meara, D. 1992. "The Freedom of the One". *Phronesis* 37: 343–9.

O'Meara, D. 1996. "The Hierarchical Ordering of Reality in Plotinus". See Gerson (1996), 66–81.

O'Meara, D. 1999. "Neoplatonist Conceptions of the Philosopher-King". In *Plato and Platonism*, Studies in Philosophy and the History of Philosophy 33, J. M. Van Ophuijsen (ed.), 278–329. Washington, DC: Catholic University of America Press.

O'Meara, D. 2000. "La science métaphysique (ou théologie) de Proclus comme exercice spirituel". In *Proclus et la Théologie Platonicienne*, A.-Ph. Segonds & C. Steel (eds), 279–90. Leuven: Leuven University Press.

O'Meara, D. 2002. "Neoplatonic Cosmopolitanism". In *Henosis kai philia, unione e amicizia. Omaggio a Francesco Romano*, M. Barbanti, G. R. Giardina, P. Manganaro & E. Berti (eds), 311–15. Catania: CUECM.

O'Meara, D. 2003. *Platonopolis: Platonic Political Philosophy in Late Antiquity.* Oxford: Clarendon Press.

O'Meara, D. 2004. "Simplicius on the Place of the Philosopher in the City". In *The Greek Strand in Islamic Political Thought, Mélanges de l'Université Saint-Joseph* 57, E. Gannagé, P. Crone, M. Aouad, D. Gutas & E. Schütrumpf (eds), 89–98. Beirut: Université de Saint-Joseph.

O'Meara, D. 2005. "The Metaphysics of Evil in Plotinus: Problems and Solutions". In *Essays in Honour of D. O'Brien*, J. M. Dillon & M. Dixsaut (eds), 179–85. Aldershot: Ashgate.

O'Meara, D. 2008. "Spätantike und Byzanz: Neuplatonische Rezeption – Michael von Ephesos". In *Politischer*

Aristotelismus. Die Rezeption der aristotelischen Politik *von der Antike bis zum 19. Jahrhundert*, C. Horn & A. Neschke-Hentschke (eds), 42–52. Stuttgart: Metzler.

O'Meara, D. 2011. "ΑΝΘΡΩΠΟΠΟΙΟΣ". In *Mots Médiévaux offerts à Ruedi Imbach*, I. Atucha, D. Calma, C. König-Pralong & I. Zavattero (eds), 99–103. Porto: Fédération internationale des instituts d'études médiévales.

O'Meara, D. forthcoming. "Souls and Cities in Late Ancient Platonic Philosophy".

O'Meara, D. & J. Schamp 2006. *Miroirs de prince de l'Empire romain au IVe siècle*. Fribourg: Academic Press.

O'Meara, J. J. 1954. *The Young Augustine: The Growth of St Augustine's Mind up to his Conversion*. London: Longmans, Green.

Oeing-Hanhoff, L. 1971. "Analyse/Synthese". In *Historisches Wörterbuch der Philosophie*, 1, J. Ritter (ed.), 232–48. Darmstadt: Wissenschaftliche Buchgesellschaft.

Oldenberg, H. 1906. "Indische und klassische Philologie". *Neue Jahrbücher für das klassische Altertum, Geschichte und deutsche Literatur und für Pädagogik* 17: 1–9.

Oldenberg, H. 1915. *Die Lehre der Upanishaden und die Anfänge des Buddhismus*. Göttingen: Vandenhoeck & Ruprecht.

Ong, W. 1982. *Orality and Literacy: The Technologizing of the Word*. London: Methuen.

Opsomer, J. 1998. *In Search of the Truth: Academic Tendencies in Middle Platonism*. Brussels: Paleis der Academiën.

Opsomer, J. 2001. "Proclus vs. Plotinus on Matter (*De mal. subs.* 30-7)". *Phronesis* 46(2): 154–88.

Opsomer, J. 2005. "The Demiurges in Early Imperial Platonism". In *Gott und die Götter bei Plutarch*, R. Hirsh-Luipold (ed.), 51–99. Berlin: De Gruyter.

Opsomer, J. 2006a. "Proclus et le statut ontologique de l'âme plotinienne". *Études platoniciennes* 3: 195–207.

Opsomer, J. 2006b. "Was sind irrationale Seelen?" See Perkams & Piccione (2006), 136–66.

Opsomer, J. 2007. "Some Problems with Plotinus' Theory of Matter/Evil. An Ancient Debate Continued". *Quaestio* 7: 165–89.

Opsomer, J. 2009. "The Integration of Aristotelian Physics in a Neoplatonic Context: Proclus on Movers and Indivisibility". See Chiaradonna & Trabattoni (2009), 189–229.

Opsomer, J. 2013. "Proclus, Syrianus and Damascius". In *Routledge Companion to Ancient Philosophy*, J. Warren & F. Sheffield (eds), 626–42. London: Routledge.

Opsomer, J. forthcoming. "The Natural World". In P. d'Hoine & M. Martijn (eds), *All from One: A Guide to Proclus*. Oxford: Oxford University Press.

Opsomer, J. & C. Steel (trans.) 2003. *Proclus: On the Existence of Evils*. Ithaca, NY: Cornell University Press.

Osborn, E. F. 1997. *Tertullian, First Theologian of the West*. Cambridge: Cambridge University Press.

Osborne, C. 2007. *Dumb Beasts and Dead Philosophers: Humanity and the Humane in Ancient Philosophy and Literature*. Oxford: Clarendon Press.

Otten, W. 1991. *The Anthropology of John Scottus Eriugena*. Leiden: Brill.

Ousager, A. 2004. *Plotinus, on Selfhood, Freedom and Politics*. Aarhus: Aarhus University Press.

Pagel, W. 1985. *Religion and Neoplatonism in Renaissance Medicine*. London: Variorum.

Pahta, P. 1998. *Medieval Embryology in the Vernacular: The Case of De spermate*. Helsinki: Société Néophilologique.

Papadis, D. 1991a. "'L'intellect agent' selon Alexandre d'Aphrodisias". *Revue de philosophie ancienne* 9: 133–51.

Papadis, D. 1991b. *Die Seelenlehre bei Alexander von Aphrodisias*. Bern: Peter Lang.

Partenie, C. (ed.) 2009. *Plato's Myths*. Cambridge: Cambridge University Press.

Parvis, S. & P. Foster (eds) 2007. *Justin Martyr and His Worlds*. Minneapolis: Fortress Press.

Pearson, B. A. 1984. "Gnosticism as Platonism: With Special Reference to Marsanes (NHC 10.1)". *Harvard Theological Review* 77: 55–74.

Penner, T. 1973. "The Unity of Virtue". *Philosophical Review* 82: 35–6.

Pépin, J. 1956. "Éléments pour une histoire de la relation entre l'intelligence et l'intelligible chez Platon et dans le néoplatonisme". *Revue philosophique de la France et de l'étranger* 81: 39–64.

Peramatzis, M. 2008. "Aristotle's Notion of Priority in Nature and Substance". *Oxford Studies in Ancient Philosophy* 35: 187–247.

Perkams, M. 2005. "Priscian of Lydia. Commentator on the *De anima* in the tradition of Iamblichus". *Mnemosyne* 58: 510–30.

Perkams, M. 2006. "An Innovation by Proclus. The Theory of the Substantial Diversity of the Human Soul". See Perkams & Piccione (2006), 167–85.

Perkams, M. 2008. *Selbstbewusstsein in der Spätantike. Die neuplatonische Kommentare zu Aristoteles'* De anima, Quellen und Studien zur Philosophie 85. Berlin: De Gruyter.

Perkams, M. & R. M. Piccione (eds) 2006. *Proklos: Methode, Seelenlehre, Metaphysik.* Leiden: Brill.

Perl, E. D. 2008. *Theophany: The Neoplatonic Philosophy of Dionysius the Areopagite.* Albany, NY: SUNY.

Peroli, E. 1997. "Gregory of Nyssa and the Neoplatonic Doctrine of the Soul". *Vigiliae Christianae* 51(2): 117–39.

Pessin, S. 2003. "Jewish Neoplatonism: Being Above Being and Divine Emanation in Solomon Ibn Gabirol and Isaac Israeli". In *The Cambridge Companion to Medieval Jewish Philosophy*, D. Frank & O. Leaman (eds), 91–110. Cambridge: Cambridge University Press.

Pessin, S. 2004. "Loss, Presence, and Gabirol's Desire: Medieval Jewish Philosophy and the Possibility of a Feminist Ground". In *Women and Gender in Jewish Philosophy*, H. Tirosh-Samuelson (ed.), 27–50. Bloomington, IN: Indiana University Press.

Pessin, S. 2005. "The Manifest Image: Revealing the Hidden in Halevi, Saadya and Gabirol". In *History of Platonism: Plato Redivivus*, R. M. Berchman & J. F. Finamore (eds), 253–70. New Orleans: University Press of the South.

Pessin, S. 2009. "Matter, Form and the Corporeal World". In *The Cambridge History of Jewish Philosophy: From Antiquity to the Seventeenth Century*, T. Rudavsky & S. Nadler (eds), 269–301. Cambridge: Cambridge University Press.

Pessin, S. 2012a. "Divine Presence, Divine Absence and the Plotinian Apophatic Dialectic: Reinterpreting 'Creation and Emanation' in Isaac Israeli". In *Religion and Philosophy in the Platonic and Neoplatonic Traditions: From Antiquity to the Early Medieval Period*, K. Corrigan, J. D. Turner & P. Wakefield (eds), 133–49. Berlin: Akademie.

Pessin, S. 2012b. "On the Possibility of a Hidden Christian Will: Methodological Pitfalls in the Study of Medieval Jewish Philosophy". In *Encountering the Medieval in Modern Jewish Thought*, A. Hughes & J. Diamond (eds), 52–94. Leiden: Brill.

Pessin, S. 2013. *Ibn Gabirol's Theology of Desire: Matter and Method in Jewish Medieval Neoplatonism.* Cambridge: Cambridge University Press.

Pessin, S. 2014. "Solomon Ibn Gabirol [Avicebron]". In *Stanford Encyclopedia of Philosophy*, E. N. Zalta (ed.), http://plato.stanford.edu/archives/sum2014/entries/ibn-.-gabirol/ (accessed January 2014).

Pessin, S. forthcoming. "Islamic Hylomorphisms". In *The Routledge Companion to Islamic Philosophy*, R. Taylor & L. X. López-Farjeat (eds). New York: Routledge.

Petit, A. 1999. "Forme et individualité dans le système plotinien". *Cahiers philosophiques de Strasbourg* 8: 109–22.

Petrov, V. 2002. "*Theoriae* of the Return in John Scottus' Eschatology". In *History and Eschatology in John Scottus Eriugena and His Time. Proceedings of the 10th Conference of the SPES, Maynooth and Dublin, August 16–20, 2000*, J. McEvoy & M. Dunne (eds), 527–79. Leuven: Leuven University Press.

Petrucci, F. 2009. "Riargomentare il platonismo: L'esegesi di Platone nell'*Expositio* di Teone di Smirne". *Elenchos* 30: 293–327.

Pettersson, O. 2013. *A Multiform Desire: A Study of Appetite in Plato's* Timaeus, Republic *and* Phaedrus. Ph.D. thesis. Uppsala: Uppsala University Press.

Phillips, J. 2007. *Order from Disorder: Proclus' Doctrine of Evil and its Roots in Ancient Platonism.* Leiden: Brill.

Phillips, J. 2009. "Plotinus on the Generation of Matter". *International Journal of the Platonic Tradition* 3(2): 103–37.

Pincock, C. 2012. *Mathematics and Scientific Representation.* Oxford: Oxford University Press.

Pines, S. 1954. "La longue recension de la *Théologie d'Aristote* dans ses rapports avec la doctrine ismaélienne". *Revue des études islamiques* 22: 8–20.

Pingree, D. 1980. "Some of the Sources of the Ghayat al-Hakim". *Journal of the Warburg and Courtauld Institutes* 43: 1–15.

Plass, P. 1982. "Plotinus' Ethical Theory". *Illinois Classical Studies* 7: 241–59.

Pormann, P. E. 2003. "Jean le Grammairien et le *De sectis* dans la littérature médicale d'Alexandrie". In *Galenismo e medicina tardoantica fonti greche, latine e arabe*, I. Garofalo & A. Roselli (eds), 233–63. Naples: AION.

Praechter, K. 1906. "Review of *Michaelis Ephesii In libros De partibus animalium commentaria*". *Göttingische gelehrte Anzeigen* 168: 861–907.

Praechter, K. 1909. *Die Philosophie des Altertums: Grundriss der Geschichte der Philosophie.* Berlin: Mittler.

Puech, H.-C. 1960. "Plotin et les Gnostiques". In *Les Sources de Plotin: dix exposés et discussions*, Entretiens sur l'antiquité classique 5, E. R. Dodds *et al.* (eds), 161–74; "Discussion", 175–90. Geneva: Fondation Hardt.

Quine, van O. W. 1960. *Word & Object*. Cambridge, MA: MIT Press.

Radke, G. 2003. *Die Theorie der Zahl im Platonismus*. Tubingen: Francke Verlag.

Rapp, C. 2005. *Holy Bishops in Late Antiquity*. Berkeley, CA: University of California Press.

Rappe, S. 1996. "Self-Knowledge and Subjectivity in the *Enneads*". See Gerson (1996), 250–74.

Rappe, S. 2000. *Reading Neoplatonism: Non-Discursive Thinking in the Texts of Plotinus, Proclus, and Damascius*. Cambridge: Cambridge University Press.

Rashed, M. 1997. "A 'New' Text of Alexander on the Soul's Motion". In *Aristotle and After, Bulletin of the Institute of Classical Studies* Suppl. 68, R. Sorabji (ed.), 181–95. London: Institute of Classical Studies.

Rashed, M. 2007. *Essentialisme. Alexandre d'Aphrodise entre logique, physique et cosmologie*. Berlin: De Gruyter.

Rashed, M. 2013. "Boethus' Aristotelian Ontology". In *Plato, Aristotle and Pythagoras in the First Century BC*, M. Schofield (ed.), 53–77. Cambridge: Cambridge University Press.

Remes, P. 2005. "Plotinus on the Unity and Identity of Changing Particulars". *Oxford Studies in Ancient Philosophy* 28: 273–301.

Remes, P. 2006. "Plotinus' Ethics of Disinterested Interest". *Journal of the History of Philosophy* 44: 1–23.

Remes, P. 2007. *Plotinus on Self: The Philosophy of the "We"*. Cambridge: Cambridge University Press.

Remes, P. 2008a. "Inwardness and Infinity of Selfhood: From Plotinus to Augustinus". In *Ancient Philosophy of the Self*, P. Remes & J. Sihvola (eds), 155–76. New York: Springer.

Remes, P. 2008b. *Neoplatonism*. Stocksfield: Acumen.

Remes, P. forthcoming a. "Plotinus on Action". In *Understanding Agency*, T. Ekenberg & L. Halldenius (eds).

Remes, P. forthcoming b. "Plotinus on *Phronēsis*".

Remes, P. & J. Sihvola (eds) 2008. *Ancient Philosophy of the Self*. Dordrecht: Springer.

Reydams-Schils, G. 1999. *Demiurge and Providence: Stoic and Platonist Readings of Plato's Timaeus*. Turnhout: Brepols.

Reydams-Schils, G. 2002. "Philo of Alexandria on Stoic and Platonist Psycho-Physiology: The Socratic Higher Ground". *Ancient Philosophy* 22: 125–47.

Reydams-Schils, G. 2006. "Calcidius on the Human and the World-Soul, and Middle-Platonist Psychology". *Apeiron* 39(2): 177–200.

Reydams-Schils, G. 2011. "Authority and Agency in Stoicism". *Greek, Roman, and Byzantine Studies* 51: 296–322.

Reydams-Schils, G. 2013. "The Academy, the Stoics, and Cicero on Plato's *Timaeus*". In *Plato and the Stoics*, A. Long (ed.), 29–58. Cambridge: Cambridge University Press.

Rich, A. N. M. 1957. "Reincarnation in Plotinus". *Mnemosyne* 10(3): 232–8.

Rich, A. N. M. 1960. "Plotinus and the Theory of Artistic Imitation". *Mnemosyne* 13: 233–9.

Richardson, N. J. 1975. "Homeric Professors in the Age of the Sophists". *Proceedings of the Cambridge Philological Society* 21: 65–81.

Richardson, N. J. 1992. "Aristotle's Reading of Homer and its Background". In *Homer's Ancient Readers: The Hermeneutics of Greek Epic's Earliest Readers*, K. Lamberton & J. J. Keaney (eds), 30–40. Princeton, NJ: Princeton University Press.

Richardson, N. J. 1993. "Aristotle and Hellenistic Scholarship". In *La Philologie Grecque à l'époque Hellénistique et Romaine*, Entretiens Fondation Hardt 40, F. Montanari (ed.), 7–28, 29–38 (discussion). Vandoeuvres-Genève: Fondation Hardt.

Richardson Lear, G. 2004. *Happy Lives and the Highest Good: An Essay in Aristotle's Nicomachean Ethics*. Princeton, NJ: Princeton University Press.

Riggs, C. 2006. "*Apokatastasis* and the Search for Religious Identity in Patristic Salvation History". In *Religious Identity in Late Antiquity*, R. M. Frakes & E. DePalma Digeser (eds), 84–102. Toronto: Edgar Kent Publishers.

Rilke, R. M. 1963. *Duino Elegies*, B. Leishman & S. Spender (trans.). London: Hogarth Press.

Rist, J. 1961. "Plotinus on Matter and Evil". *Phronesis* 6: 154–66.

Rist, J. 1962. "The Indefinite Dyad and Intelligible Matter in Plotinus". *Classical Quarterly* 12(1): 99–107.

Rist, J. 1963. "Forms of Individuals in Plotinus". *Classical Quarterly* 13: 223–31.

Rist, J. 1965. "Monism: Plotinus and some Predecessors". *Harvard Studies in Classical Philology* 69: 329–44.

Rist, J. 1966a. "Notes on Aristotle *De Anima* 3.5". *Classical Philology* 6: 8–19. Reprinted in J. P. Anton & G. L. Kustas (eds) 1971. *Essays in Ancient Greek Philosophy*, 505–21. Albany, NY: SUNY Press.

Rist, J. 1966b. "On Tracking Alexander of Aphrodisias". *Archiv für Geschichte der Philosophie* 48: 82–90.

Rist, J. 1967. *Plotinus: The Road to Reality*. Cambridge: Cambridge University Press.

Rist, J. 1970. "Ideas of Individuals: A Reply to Dr Blumenthal". *Revue internationale de philosophie* 92(2): 298–303.

Rist, J. 1976. "Plotinus and Moral Obligation". In *Studies in Neoplatonism vol. 1: The Significance of Neoplatonism*, R. Baine Harris (ed.), 217–33. Norfolk, VA: Old Dominion University Press.

Rist, J. 1994. *Augustine: Ancient Thought Baptized*. Cambridge: Cambridge University Press.

Rist, J. 1996. "Plotinus and Christian Philosophy". See Gerson (1996), 386–413.

Rist, J. 2000. "On the Platonism of Gregory of Nyssa". *Hermathena* 169: 129–52.

Robinson, J. M. 1977. "The *Three Steles of Seth* and the Gnostics of Plotinus". In *Proceedings of the International Colloquium on Gnosticism, Stockholm, August 20–25, 1973*. Kungl. Vitterhets Historie ock Antikvitets Akademiens Handlingar, Filologisk-filosofiska serien 17, G. Widengren (ed.), 132–42. Stockholm: Almqvist & Wiksell.

Robinson, T. M. & L. Westra (eds) 2002. *Thinking about the Environment: Our Debt to the Classical and Medieval Past*. Lanham, MD: Lexington Books.

Rodier, D. F. T. 1982. "Meditative States in the Abhidharma and in Pseudo-Dionysus". See Baine Harris (1982), 121–36.

Rodiewicz, E. 1991. "Remains of a Chryselephantine Statue in Alexandria". *Bulletin de la Société archéologique d'Alexandrie* 44: 119–30.

Rogers, G. A. J., J.-M. Vienne & Y.-C. Zarka (eds) 1997. *The Cambridge Platonists in Philosophical Context: Politics, Metaphysics and Religion*. Dordrecht: Kluwer Academic Publishers.

Roos, B.-A. 1991. *Synesius of Cyrene: A Study in His Personality*. Lund: Lund University Press.

Rosán, L. J. 1949. *The Philosophy of Proclus: The Final Phase of Ancient Thought*. New York: Cosmos.

Rosán, L. J. 1982. "Proclus and the *Tejobindu Upaniṣad*". See Baine Harris (1982), 45–62.

Roueché, C. 1989. *Aphrodisias in Late Antiquity*, Journal of Roman Studies Monograph 5. London: Society for the Promotion of Roman Studies.

Roueché, M. 1999. "Did Medical Students Study Philosophy in Alexandria?" *Bulletin of the Institute of Classical Studies* 43: 153–69.

Rudavsky, T. M. 1997. "Medieval Jewish Neoplatonism". In *History of Jewish Philosophy*, D. H. Frank & O. Leaman (eds), 149–87. London: Routledge.

Ruland, H.-J. 1976. *Die arabische Fassungen von zwei Schriften des Alexander von Aphrodisias: Über die Vorsehung und Über das liberum arbitrium*. Ph.D. thesis, University of Saarbrücken.

Runia, D. 1986. *Philo of Alexandria and the* Timaeus *of Plato*. Leiden: Brill.

Runia, D. 1997. "The Literary and Philosophical Status of *Timaeus'* Prooemium". In *Interpreting the* Timaeus-Critias, *Proceedings of the IV Symposium Platonicum Selected Papers*, T. Calvo & L. Brisson (eds), 101–18. Sankt Augustin: Academia Verlag.

Runia, D. (ed.) 2001. *Philo of Alexandria: On the Creation of the Cosmos According to Moses. Introduction, Translation and Commentary*, Philo of Alexandria Commentary Series 1. Leiden: Brill.

Russell, N. 2004. *The Doctrine of Deification in the Greek Patristic Tradition*, Oxford Early Christian Studies. Oxford: Oxford University Press.

Rutten, C. 1956. "La doctrine des deux actes dans la philosophie de Plotin". *Revue philosophique de la France et de l'étranger* 146: 100–106.

Sachs, D. 1963. "A Fallacy in Plato's *Republic*". *Philosophical Review* 72(2): 141–58.

Saffrey, H. D. 1984. "La *Théologie platonicienne* de Proclus, fruit de l'exégèse du *Parménide*". *Revue de théologie et de philosophie* 116: 1–12.

Saffrey, H. D. 1987. "Comment Syrianus, le maître de l'école néoplatonicienne d'Athènes, considerait-il Aristote?" In *Aristoteles: Werk und Wirkung. Paul Moraux gewidmet*, 2, J. Wiesner (ed.), 205–14. Berlin: De Gruyter.

Saffrey, H. D. 1992. "Accorder entre elles les traditions théologiques: une caractéristique du Néoplatonisme Athénien". In *On Proclus and his Influence in Medieval Philosophy*, E. P. Bos & P. A. Meijer (eds), 35–50. Leiden: Brill.

Saffrey, H. D. 2000. "Le thème du malheur des temps chez les derniers philosophes néoplatoniciens". In *Le néoplatonisme après Plotin*, H. D. Saffrey (ed.), 207–17. Paris: Vrin.

Saffrey, H. D. & A. P. Segonds (eds & trans) 2001. *Proclus, ou sur le bonheur*, Collection des universités de France. Paris: Les Belles Lettres.

Saffrey, H. D. & A. P. Segonds (eds) 2013. *Jamblique: Réponse à Porphyre (De Mysteriis)*. Paris: Les Belles Lettres.

Salles, R. (ed.) 2009. *God and Cosmos in Stoicism*. Oxford: Oxford University Press.

Santa Cruz, M. I. 1997. "L'exégèse Plotinienne des ΜΕΓΙΣΤΑ ΓΕΝΗ du *Sophiste* de Platon". See Cleary (1997), 105–18.

Schäfer, C. 2002. *"Unde malum?": die Frage nach dem Woher des Bösen bei Plotin, Augustinus und Dionysius.* Würzburg: Königshausen & Neumann.

Schäublin, C. 1977. *"Homerum ex Homero". Museum Helveticum* 34: 221–7.

Schiaparelli, A. 2009. "Plotinus on Dialectic". *Archiv für Geschichte der Philosophie* 91: 253–87.

Schiaparelli, A. 2010. "Essence and Cause in Plotinus' *Ennead* VI.7 [38] 2: An Outline of Some Problems". In *Definition in Greek Philosophy*, D. Charles (ed.), 467–92. Oxford: Clarendon Press.

Schibli, H. 2002. *Hierocles of Alexandria.* Oxford: Oxford University Press.

Schiller, F. 2003. "Kallias or Concerning Beauty: Letters to Gottfried Körner". In *Classic and Romantic German Aesthetics*, J. M. Bernstein (ed.), 145–84. Cambridge: Cambridge University Press.

Schmidt, G. G. 1995. "'Cleaving to God' through the Ages: An Historical Analysis of the Jewish Concept of 'Devekut'". *Mystics Quarterly* 21(4): 103–20.

Schmitt, A. 2012. *Modernity and Plato: Two Paradigms of Rationality*, V. Adluri (trans.). Rochester, NY: Camden House.

Schniewind, A. 2000. "Quelles conditions pour une éthique plotinienne? Prescription et description dans les *Ennéades*". See Fattal (2000), 47–75.

Schniewind, A. 2003. *L'éthique du sage chez Plotin: le paradigme du spoudaios.* Paris: Vrin.

Schniewind, A. 2005. "The Social Concern of the Plotinian Sage". In *The Philosopher and Society in Late Antiquity*, A. Smith (ed.), 51–64. Swansea: The Classical Press of Wales.

Scholem, G. 1971. "*Devekut*, or Communion with God". In *The Messianic Idea in Judaism: And Other Essays on Jewish Spirituality*, G. Scholem (ed.), 203–27. New York: Schocken Books.

Schramm, M. 2013. *Freundschaft im Neuplatonismus. Politisches Denken und Sozialphilosophie von Plotin bis Kaiser Julian.* Berlin: De Gruyter.

Schreiner, P. (ed.) 1997. *Nārāyaṇīya-Studien. Purāṇa Research Publications.* Wiesbaden: Harrassowitz.

Schroeder, F. M. 1980. "Representation and Reflection in Plotinus". *Dionysius* 4: 37–60.

Schroeder, F. M. 1981. "The Analogy of the Active Intellect to Light in the *De Anima* of Alexander of Aphrodisias". *Hermes* 109: 215–25.

Schroeder, F. M. 1982. "The Potential or Material Intellect and the Authorship of the *De Intellectu*: A Reply to B. C. Bazán". *Symbolae Osloenses* 57: 115–25.

Schroeder, F. M. 1984. "Light and the Active Intellect in Alexander and Plotinus". *Hermes* 112: 239–48.

Schroeder, F. M. 1986. "Conversion and Consciousness in Plotinus '*Enneads*' 5, 1 [10], 7". *Hermes* 114: 186–96.

Schroeder, F. M. 1992. *Form and Transformation: A Study in the Philosophy of Plotinus.* Montreal: McGill-Queen's Press.

Schroeder, F. M. 1997a. "The Provenance of the *De Intellectu* attributed to Alexander of Aphrodisias". *Documenti e studi sulla tradizione filosofica medievale* 8: 105–20.

Schroeder, F. M. 1997b. "Plotinus and Aristotle on the Good Life". See Cleary (1997), 207–20.

Schroeder, F. M. 2010. "Review of Bergeron and Dufour". *Classical Review* 60: 84–6.

Schroeder, F. M. & R. B. Todd 2008. "The *De Intellectu* Revisited". *Laval théologique et philosophique* 64(3): 663–80.

Schwyzer, H.-R. 1951. "Plotinos". In *Paulys Realenzyklopädie der klassischen Altertumswissenschaft* 21(1): 471–592. Stuttgart: Druckenmüller. With supplement notes in 1978, *Paulys Realenzyklopädie der klassischen Altertumswissenschaft*, Suppl. 15: 321–23. Munich: Druckenmüller.

Schwyzer, H.-R. 1960. "Bewusst und Unbewusst bei Plotin". In *Les sources de Plotin*, Entretiens sur l'antiquité classique 5, P. Henry, E. R. Dodds *et al.* (eds), 341–90. Geneva: Hardt Foundation.

Schwyzer, H.-R. 1970. "Plotin und Platons *Philebos*". *Revue internationale de philosophie* 92: 81–93.

Schwyzer, H.-R. 1973. "Zu Plotins Deutung der sogenannten platonischen Materie". In *Zetesis. Festschrift E. de Strijcker*, 266–80. Antwerp: De Nederlandsche Boekhandel.

Sedley, D. 1985. "The Stoic Theory of Universals". *Southern Journal of Philosophy* 23: 87–92.

Sedley, D. 1997. "Plato's *Auctoritas* and the Rebirth of Commentary Tradition". In *Philosophia Togata II: Plato and Aristotle at Rome*, J. Barnes & M. Griffin (eds), 110–19. Oxford: Clarendon Press.

Sedley, D. 1999. "The Ideal of Godlikeness". In *Plato 2. Ethics Politics, Religion and the Soul*, Oxford Readings in Philosophy, G. Fine (ed.), 309–28. Oxford: Oxford University Press.

Sedley, D. 2005. "Empedocles' Life Cycles". In *The Empedoclean Cosmos: Structure, Process and the Question of Cyclicity*, A. Pierris (ed.), 331–71. Patras: Institute for Philosophical Research.

Sedley, D. 2009. "A Thrasyllan Interpretation of Plato's *Theaetetus*". *Oxyrhynchus Papyri* 73: 65–71.

Sedley, D. 2012. *The Philosophy of Antiochus.* Cambridge: Cambridge University Press.

Segvic, H. 2000. "No One Errs Willingly: The Meaning of Socratic Intellectualism". *Oxford Studies in Ancient Philosophy* 19: 1–45.

Serres, M. 1982. *Hermes: Literature, Science, Philosophy*, J. V. Harari & D. F. Bell (eds). Baltimore, MD: Johns Hopkins University Press.

Sharma, I. C. 1982. "The Plotinian One and the Concept of *Paramapuruṣa* in the *Bhagavadgītā*". See Baine Harris (1982), 87–100.

Sharples, R. W. 1982. "Alexander of Aphrodisias on Providence: Two Problems". *Classical Quarterly* 32: 198–211.

Sharples, R. W. [1983] 2003. *Alexander of Aphrodisias: On Fate*. London: Duckworth.

Sharples, R. W. 1987. "Alexander of Aphrodisias: Scholasticism and Innovation". In *Aufstieg und Niedergang der Römischen Welt* 2.36.2, W. Hasse (ed.), 1176–243. Berlin: De Gruyter.

Sharples, R. W. (trans. & notes) 1994. *Alexander of Aphrodisias, Quaestiones 2.16–3.15*. London: Duckworth.

Sharples, R. W. 2002. "Alexander of Aphrodisias and the End of Aristotelian Theology". In *Metaphysik und Religion. Zur Signatur des spätantiken Denkens. Akten des Internationalen Kongresses vom 13.-17. März 2001 in Würzburg*, T. Kobusch & M. Erler. (eds), 1–21. Munich: Saur.

Sharples, R. W. (trans.) 2004. *Alexander of Aphrodisias. Supplement to "On the Soul"*. Ithaca, NY: Cornell University Press.

Sharples, R. W. 2007. "Peripatetics on Fate and Providence". In Sharples and Sorabji (2007), 595–605.

Sharples, R. W. 2010. *Peripatetic Philosophy, 200 BC to AD 200: An Introduction and Collection of Sources in Translation*. Cambridge: Cambridge University Press.

Sharples, R. W. & R. Sorabji (eds) 2007. *Greek and Roman Philosophy 100 BC–200 AD*, 2 vols. London: Institute of Classical Studies.

Shaw, G. 1995. *Theurgy and the Soul: The Neoplatonism of Iamblichus*. University Park, PN: Pennsylvania State University Press.

Shaw, G. 1999. "*Eros* and *Arithmos*: Pythagorean Theurgy in Iamblichus and Plotinus". *Ancient Philosophy* 19: 121–43.

Shayegan, Y. 1996. "The Transmission of Greek Philosophy into the Islamic World". In *History of Islamic Philosophy*, S. H. Nasr & O. Leaman (eds), 98–104. London: Routledge.

Sheldon-Williams, I. P. 1981. "Introduction". In *Iohannis Scotti Eriugenae Periphyseon (De Divisione Naturae)* 3, I. P. Sheldon-Williams & J. J. O'Meara (eds), 5–10. Dublin: Dublin Institute for Advanced Studies.

Sheppard, A. 1997. "*Phantasia* and Mathematical Projection in Iamblichus". *Syllecta Classica* 8: 113–20.

Sider, R. D. (ed.) 2001. *Christian and Pagan in the Roman Empire: The Witness of Tertullian*, Selections from the Fathers of the Church Book 2. Washington, DC: Catholic University of America Press.

Singer, M. G. 1959. "On Duties to Oneself". *Ethics* 69: 202–5.

Sinnige, Th. G. 1984. "Gnostic Influences in the Early Works of Plotinus and in Augustine". In *Plotinus amid Gnostics and Christians: Papers Presented at the Plotinus Symposium Held at the Free University, Amsterdam, on 25 January 1984*, D. T. Runia (ed.), 73–97. Amsterdam: Free University Press.

Siorvanes, L. 1996. *Proclus: Neo-Platonic Philosophy and Science*. Edinburgh: Edinburgh University Press.

Skliris, D. 2008. "The Theory of Evil in Proclus: Proclus' Theodicy as a Completion of Plotinus' Monism". *Philotheos* 8: 137–59.

Slaveva-Griffin, S. 2009. *Plotinus on Number*. Oxford: Clarendon Press.

Slaveva-Griffin, S. 2010. "Medicine in the Life and Works of Plotinus". *Proceedings of the Langford Latin Seminar* 14: 93–117.

Slaveva-Griffin, S. 2014. "Tracing the Untraceable: Plotinian Motifs in the Pseudo-Galenic *De Spermate*". In *Neoplatonic Questions*, J. M. Zamora (ed.), 9–42. Berlin: Logos.

Sluiter, I. 2000. "The Dialectics of Genre: Some Aspects of Secondary Literature and Genre in Antiquity". In *Matrices of Genre: Authors, Canons and Society*, M. Depew & D. Obbink (eds), 183–203. Cambridge, MA: Harvard University Press.

Smith, A. 1974. *Porphyry's Place in the Neoplatonic Tradition: A Study in Post-Plotinian Neoplatonism*. The Hague: Nijhoff.

Smith, A. 1992. "Reason and Experience in Plotinus". In *At the Heart of the Real*, F. O'Rourke (ed.), 21–30. Dublin: Irish Academic Press. Reprinted in his *Plotinus, Porphyry and Iamblichus: Philosophy and Religion in Neoplatonism*. Aldershot: Variorum, 2011.

Smith, A. 1993. *Porphyrii Philosophii Fragmenta*. Stuttgart: Teubner.

Smith, A. 1999. "The Significance of Practical Ethics for Plotinus". In *The Perennial Traditions of Neoplatonism*, J. J. Cleary (ed.), 227–36. Aldershot: Ashgate.

Smith, A. 2004. "Plotinus on Ideas between Plato and Aristotle". In *Aristotle on Plato: The Metaphysical Question*, A. P. Pierris (ed.), 93–108. Patras: Institute for Philosophical Research.

Smith, A. 2005. "Action and Contemplation in Plotinus". In *The Philosopher and Society in Late Antiquity: Essays in Honour of Peter Brown*, A. Smith (ed.), 65–72. Swansea: The Classical Press of Wales.

Smith, R. B. E. 1995. *Julian's Gods: Religion and Philosophy in the Thought and Action of Julian the Apostate*. London: Routledge.

Smith, R. R. R. 1990. "Late Roman Philosopher Portraits from Aphrodisias". *Journal of Roman Studies* 80: 127–55.

Snyder, H. G. 2000. *Teachers and Texts in the Ancient World: Philosophers, Jews and Christians*. London: Routledge.

Solmsen, F. 1961. "Greek Philosophy and the Discovery of the Nerves". *Museum Helveticum* 18: 150–97.

Song, E. 2009. "The Ethics of Descent in Plotinus". *Hermathena* 187: 27–48.

Sorabji, R. 1980. *Necessity, Cause and Blame*. London: Duckworth.

Sorabji, R. 1982. "Myths about Non-propositional Thought". In *Language and Logos*, M. Schofield & M. Nussbaum (eds), 295–314. Cambridge: Cambridge University Press.

Sorabji, R. 1983. *Time, Creation and the Continuum*. London: Duckworth.

Sorabji, R. 1988. *Matter, Space and Motion*. London: Duckworth.

Sorabji, R. (ed.) 1990. *Aristotle Transformed: The Ancient Commentators and Their Influence*. London: Duckworth. (2nd edn London: Bloomsbury, forthcoming 2014.)

Sorabji, R. 1993. *Animal Minds and Human Morals: The Origins of the Western Debate*. Ithaca, NY: Cornell University Press.

Sorabji, R. 2004–2005. *Four Hundred Years of Transition: The Philosophy of the Commentators, 200–600 AD: A Sourcebook, vol. 1: Psychology; vol 2: Physics; vol. 3: Logic and Metaphysics.* Vols 1 and 3, Ithaca, NY: Cornell University Press, 2005. Vol. 2, London: Duckworth, 2004.

Sorabji, R. 2005. "Divine Names and Sordid Deals in Ammonius' Alexandria". In *The Philosopher and Society in Late Antiquity*, A. Smith (ed.), 203–13. Cardiff: University of Wales Press.

Sorabji, R. 2006. *Self: Ancient and Modern Insights about Individuality, Life, and Death*. Oxford: Clarendon Press.

Sorabji, R. 2007. "Epictetus on *proairesis* and Self". In *The Philosophy of Epictetus*, T. Scaltsas & A. S. Mason (eds), 87–98. Oxford: Oxford University Press.

Sorabji, R. (ed.) 2010. *Philoponus and the Rejection of Aristotelian Science, Bulletin of the Institute of Classical Studies* Suppl. 103. London: University of London.

Sprague, R. K. 1972. "A Parallel with '*De Anima*' III.5". *Phronesis* 17: 250–51.

Srinivasan, D. 1979. "Early Vaiṣṇava Imagery: Caturvyūha and Variant Forms". *Archives of Asian Art* 32: 39–54.

Staab, G. 2002. *Pythagoras in der Spätantike. Studien zu De Vita Pythagorica des Iamblichos von Chalkis*. Munich-Leipzig: Saur.

Stalley, R. 1995. "The Unity of the State: Plato, Aristotle and Proclus". *Polis* 14: 129–49.

Stamatellos, G. 2007. *Plotinus and the Presocratics*. Albany, NY: SUNY Press.

Stead, G. C. 1976. "Ontology and Terminology in Gregory of Nyssa". In *Gregor von Nyssa und die Philosophie*, H. Dörrie, M. Altenburger & U. Schramm (eds), 107–27. Leiden: Brill.

Stead, G. C. 1981. "Individual Personality in Origen and the Cappadocian Fathers". In *Arché e Telos. L'antropologia di Origine e di Gregorio di Nissa*, Studia Patristica Mediolanensia 12, 170–91. Milan: Studia Patristica Mediolanensia.

Stead, G. C. 1994. *Philosophy in Christian Antiquity*. Cambridge: Cambridge University Press.

Steel, C. 1978. *The Changing Self: A Study on the Soul in Later Neoplatonism: Iamblichus, Damascius and Priscianus*. Brussels: Paleis der Academiën.

Steel, C. 1987. "L'anagogie par les apories". In *Proclus et son influence. Actes du Colloque de Neuchâtel (juin 1985)*, J. Bos & G. Seel (eds), 101–28. Zurich: Éditions du Grand Midi.

Steel, C. 1997a. "Breathing Thought. Proclus on the Innate Knowledge of the Soul". See Cleary (1997), 293–309.

Steel, C. 1997b. *Priscian: On Theophrastus' On Sense Perception and "Simplicius": On Aristotle's On the Soul 2.5–12*, P. Huby & C. Steel (trans.). London: Duckworth.

Steel, C. 1998. "Proclus on the Existence of Evil". *Proceedings of the Boston Area Colloquium in Ancient Philosophy* 14: 83–102.

Steel, C. 2002a. "Neoplatonic Sources in the Commentaries on the *Nicomachean Ethics* by Eustratius and Michael of Ephesus". *Bulletin de philosophie médiévale* 44: 51–7.

Steel, C. 2002b. "Neoplatonic versus Stoic Causality: The Case of the Sustaining Cause ('*sunektikon*')". In *La causalità*, C. Esposito & P. Porro (eds), *Quaestio* 2: 77–93.

Steel, C. 2003. "Why Should we Prefer Plato's *Timaeus* to Aristotle's *Physics*? Proclus' Critique of Aristotle's Causal Explanation of the Physical World". In *Ancient Approaches to Plato's* Timaeus, *Bulletin of the Institute of Classical Studies* Suppl. 78, R. W. Sharples & A. Sheppard (eds), 175–87. London: Institute of Classical Studies.

Steel, C. 2004. "Proklos über Selbstreflexion und Selbstbegründung". See Perkams & Piccione (2006), 230–55.

Steel, C. 2007. *Proclus: On Providence*. London: Duckworth.

Steel, C. 2010. "Proclus". In *The Cambridge History of Philosophy in Late Antiquity*, L. P. Gerson (ed.), 630–53. Cambridge: Cambridge University Press.

Steiner, G. 2005. *Anthropocentrism and its Discontents: The Moral Status of Animals in the History of Western Philosophy*. Pittsburgh: University of Pittsburgh Press.

Stern, S. M. 1954. "*Anbaduklis*". In *Encyclopedia of Islam*, 2nd edn, H. A. R. Gibb (ed.). Leiden: Brill.

Stern, S. M. 1983a. "Ibn Ḥasday's Neoplatonist". In *Medieval Arabic and Hebrew Thought*, F. W. Zimmerman (ed.), 58–120. London: Variorum Reprints.

Stern, S. M. 1983b. "Ibn Masarra – A Myth?" In *Medieval Arabic and Hebrew Thought*, F. W. Zimmerman (ed.). London: Variorum Reprints.

Stern-Gillet, S. 2000a. "Le Principe du beau chez Plotin: Réflexions sur *Enneas* VI. 7.32 et 33". *Phronesis* 45: 38–63.

Stern-Gillet, S. 2000b. "Singularité et resemblance: le portrait refuse". In *Études sur Plotin*, M. Fattal (ed.), 13–47. Paris: L'Harmattan.

Stern-Gillet, S. 2009. "Dual Selfhood and Self-Perfection in the *Enneads*". *Epoché* 13(2): 331–45.

Stern-Gillet, S. 2013. "When Virtue Bids Us Abandon Life (*Ennead* VI 8 [39] 6, 14–26)". *Plato Revived: Essays on Ancient Platonism in Honour of Dominic J. O'Meara*, F. Karfik & E. Song (eds), 182–98. Berlin: De Gruyter.

Stern-Gillet, S. & K. Corrigan (eds) 2007. *Reading Ancient Texts. Volume I: Presocratics and Plato; Volume II: Aristotle and Neoplatonism. Essays in Honour of Denis O'Brien*. Leiden: Brill.

Stock, B. 1967. "The Philosophical Anthropology of Johannes Scottus Eriugena". *Studi medievali* 3(8): 1–57.

Strange, S. K. 1987. "Plotinus, Porphyry, and the Neoplatonic Interpretation of the *Categories*". In *Aufstieg und Niedergang der Römischen Welt* 2.36.2, W. Hasse (ed.), 955–74. Berlin: De Gruyter.

Strange, S. K. 1994. "Plotinus on the Nature of Time and Eternity". In *Aristotle in Late Antiquity*, Studies in Philosophy and the History of Philosophy 27, L. P. Schrenk (ed.), 22–53. Washington, DC: Catholic University of America Press.

Strohmaier, G. 2003. "Der Kommentar des Johannes Grammaticus zu Galen, *De usu partium* (Buch 11), in einer unikalen Gothaer Handschrift". In *Hellas im Islam. Interdisziplinäre Studien zur Ikonographie, Wissenschaft und Religionsgeschichte*, G. Strohmaier (ed.), 109–12. Wiesbaden: Harrassowitz.

Szabó, Á. 1965. "Anfänge der Euklidischen Axiomensystems". In *Zur Geschichte der Griechischen Mathematik*, O. Becker (ed.), 355–461. Darmstadt: Wissenschaftliche Buchgesellschaft.

Szlezák, T. 1979. *Platon und Aristoteles in der Nuslehre Plotins*. Basel: Schwabe.

Szlezák, T. 2010. "The Indefinite Dyad in Sextus Empiricus's Report (*Adversus Mathematicos* 10.248–283) and Plato's *Parmenides*". In *Plato's Parmenides and its Heritage*, 1, J. D. Turner & K. Corrigan (eds), 79–91. Atlanta, GA: Society of Biblical Literature.

Taormina, D. 1989. *Plutarco di Atene. L' Uno, l' Anima, le Forme. Saggio introduttivo, fonti, traduzione e commento*. Catania: Università di Catania.

Taormina, D. 1993. "Le *dunameis* dell'anima. Psicologia ed etica in Giamblico". In *The Divine Iamblichus: Philosopher and Man of Gods*, H. J. Blumenthal & G. Clark (eds), 30–47. London: Bristol Classical Press.

Taormina, D. 1999. *Jamblique, critique de Plotin et de Porphyre: Quatre études*. Paris: Vrin.

Taormina, D. & R. Piccione (eds) 2010. *Giamblico. I frammenti dalle epistole. Introduzione, testo, traduzione e commento*. Naples: Bibilopolis.

Tarán, L. 1987. "The Text of Simplicius' Commentary on Aristotle's *Physics*". In *Simplicius: Sa vie, son oeuvre, sa survie*, I. Hadot (ed.), 246–66. Berlin: De Gruyter.

Tardieu, M. 1986. "Sâbiens coraniques et 'Sâbiens' de Harrân". *Journal asiatique* 274: 1–44.

Tardieu, M. 1990. *Les paysages reliques. Routes et haltes syriennes d'Isidore à Simplicius*. Leuven: Peeters.

Tardieu, M. 1996. "Recherches sur la formation de l'*Apocalypse* de Zostrien et les sources de Marius Victorinus". *Res Orientales* 9: 7–114.

Tardieu, M. 2005. "Plotin citateur du Zostrien". Paper presented at the Colloquium on "Thèmes et problèmes du traité 33 de Plotin contre les Gnostiques", 7–8 June, Collège de France, Paris.

Tarrant, H. 1983. "Middle Platonism and the *Seventh Epistle*". *Phronesis* 28: 75–103.

Tarrant, H. 1993. *Thrasyllan Platonism*. Ithaca, NY: Cornell University Press.

Tarrant, H. 1997. "*Politike Eudaimonia*: Olympiodorus on Plato's *Republic*". In *Plato's Political Thought and Contemporary Political Theory* 2, K. Boudouris (ed.), 200–207. Athens: International Center for Greek Philosophy and Culture.

Tarrant, H. 2011. *From the Old Academy to Later Neo-Platonism*. Farnham: Ashgate.

Taylor, A. E. 1918. "The Philosophy of Proclus". *Proceedings of the Aristotelian Society* 18: 600–635.

Taylor, C. 1989. *Sources of the Self*. Cambridge, MA: Harvard University Press.

Taylor, R. C. 1983. "The *Liber de Causis*: A Preliminary List of Extant MSS". *Bulletin de philosophie médiévale* 25: 63–84.

Taylor, R. C. 1986. "The *Kalām fī maḥḍ al-khair* (*Liber de causis*) in the Islamic Philosophical Milieu". See Kraye, Ryan & Schmitt (1986), 37–42.

Taylor, R. C. 1989. "Remarks on the Latin Text and the Translator of the *Kalām fī maḥḍ al-khair/Liber de causis*". *Bulletin de philosophie medieval* 31: 75–102.

Taylor, R. C. 1992. "A Critical Analysis of the Structure of the *Kalam fī mahd al-khair* (*Liber de causis*)". In *Neoplatonism and Islamic Thought*, P. Morewedge (ed.), 11–40. Albany, NY: SUNY Press.

Téchert, M. 1927. "Le plotinisme dans le système de J. Scot Erigène". *Revue néoscolastique de philosophie* 28: 28–68.

Temkin, O. 1991. *Hippocrates in a World of Pagans and Christians*. Baltimore: Johns Hopkins University Press.

Temkin, O. & C. L. Temkin (eds) [1967] 1987. *Ancient Medicine: Selected Papers of Ludwig Edelstein*, 2nd edn. Baltimore, MD: Johns Hopkins University Press.

Theiler, W. 1934. *Die Vorbereitung des Neuplatonismus*. Berlin: Weidmann.

Thillet, P. 2003. *Alexandre d'Aphrodise: Traité de la providence*. Lagrasse: Verdier.

Thomas, R. 1992. *Literacy and Orality in Ancient Greece*. Cambridge: Cambridge University Press.

Thomassen, E. 2007. *The Tripartite Tractate*. In *The Nag Hammadi Scriptures: The International Edition*, M. Meyer (ed), 57–101. New York: HarperOne.

Tieleman, T. 1996. *Galen and Chrysippus on the Soul: Argument and Refutation in the De Placitis, Books II–III*. Leiden: Brill.

Tieleman, T. 1998. "Plotinus on the Seat of the Soul: Reverberations of Galen and Alexander in *Enn*. IV, 3 [27], 23". *Phronesis* 43(4): 306–25.

Timotin, A. 2012. *La démonologie platonicienne. Histoire de la notion de Daimon de Platon aux derniers néoplatoniciens*. Leiden: Brill.

Todd, R. B. 1977. "Galenic Medical Ideas in the Greek Aristotelian Commentators". *Symbolae Osloenses* 52: 117–34.

Todd, R. B. 1984. "Philosophy and Medicine in John Philoponus' Commentary on Aristotle's *De Anima*". *Dumbarton Oaks Papers* 38: 103–10.

Tornau, C. 2007. "Bemerkungen zu Stephanus von Alexandria, Plotinus und Plutarch von Athen". *Elenchos* 28: 105–27.

Tornau, C. 2009. "Qu'est-ce qu'un individu?" *Études philosophiques* 3: 332–60.

Tournaire, R. 1996. "La classification des existants selon Victorin l'Africain". *Bulletin de l'Association Guillaume Budé* 1: 55–63.

Tripathi, C. L. 1982. "The Influence of Indian Philosophy on Neoplatonism". See Baine Harris (1982), 273–92.

Troiani, L. 2003. "Philo of Alexandria and Christianity at its Origins". In *Italian Studies on Philo of Alexandria*, F. Calabi (ed.), 9–24. Leiden: Brill.

Trouillard, J. 1955. *La purification plotinienne*. Paris: Presses Universitaires de France.

Tuominen, M. 2009. *The Ancient Commentators on Plato and Aristotle*. Berkeley, CA: University of California Press.

Turnbull, R. G. 1998. *The Parmenides and Plato's Late Philosophy*. Toronto: University of Toronto Press.

Turner, D. 1995. *The Darkness of God: Negativity in Christian Mysticism*. Cambridge: Cambridge University Press.

Turner, J. D. 1980. "The Gnostic Threefold Path to Enlightenment: The Ascent of Mind and the Descent of Wisdom". *Novum Testamentum* 22(1980): 324–51.

Turner, J. D. 1986. "Sethian Gnosticism: A Literary History". In *Nag Hammadi, Gnosticism and Early Christianity*, C. W. Hedrick & R. Hodgson (eds), 55–86. Peabody, MA: Hendrickson Publishers.

Turner, J. D. 2000a. "Introduction"; "Commentary". In *Zostrien (NH VIII, 1)*, Bibliothèque copte de Nag Hammadi, section "Textes" 24, C. Barry, W.-P. Funk, P.-H. Poirier & J. D. Turner (eds), 32–225; 483–662. Québec: Presses de l'Université Laval.

Turner, J. D. 2000b. "Introduction"; "Commentaire" (with P.-H. Poirier). In *Marsanès (NH X,1)*, Bibliothèque copte de Nag Hammadi, section "Textes" 27, W.-P. Funk, P.-H. Poirier & J. D. Turner (eds), 1–248; 363–469.

Québec: Presses de l'Université Laval.

Turner, J. D. 2001. *Sethian Gnosticism and the Platonic Tradition*, Bibliothèque copte de Nag Hammadi 6. Québec: Presses de l'Université Laval.

Turner, J. D. 2004. "Introduction". In *L'Allogène (NH XI,3)*, Bibliothèque copte de Nag Hammadi, section "Textes" 30, W.-P. Funk, Madeleine Scopello, P.-H. Poirier & J. D. Turner (eds), 14–210. Québec: Presses de l'Université Laval.

Turner, J. D. 2006. "The Gnostic Sethians and Middle Platonism: Interpretations of the *Timaeus* and *Parmenides*". *Vigiliae Christianae* 60: 9–64.

Turner, J. D. 2007. "Victorinus, *Parmenides* Commentaries and the Platonizing Sethian Treatises". In *Platonisms, Ancient, Modern and Postmodern*, Ancient Mediterranean and Medieval Texts and Contexts: Academic Studies in History, Philosophy, Religion and Culture: History of Philosophy, K. Corrigan & J. D. Turner (eds), 55–96. Leiden: Brill.

Turner, J. D. & K. Corrigan 2010. *Plato's Parmenides and its Heritage*, 2 vols. Atlanta, GA: Society for Biblical Literature.

Twersky, I. (ed.) 1972. *A Maimonides Reader*. Springfield, NJ: Behrman House, Inc.

Van Atten, M. 2012. "Kant and Real Numbers". In *Epistemology versus Ontology: Essays on the Philosophy and Foundations of Mathematics in Honour of Per Martin-Löf Dybjer*, P. Lindström, S. Palmgren & E. Sundholm (eds), 3–23. Dordrecht: Springer.

Van den Berg, R. M. 1997. "Proclus, *In Platonis Timaeum Commentarii* 3.333.28ff.: The Myth of the Winged Charioteer according to Iamblichus and Proclus". *Syllecta Classica* 8: 149–62.

Van den Berg, R. M. 2004. "Smoothing over the Differences: Proclus and Ammonius on Plato's *Cratylus* and Aristotle's *De Interpretatione*". In Adamson *et al.* (2004), 191–201.

Van den Berg, R. M. 2008. *Proclus' Commentary on the* Cratylus *in Context: Ancient Theories of Language and Naming*. Leiden: Brill.

Van den Berg, R. M. 2010. "*Procheirisis*: Porphyry *Sent.* 16 and Plotinus on the Similes of the Waxen Block and the Aviary". *International Journal of the Platonic Tradition* 4: 163–80.

Van Kooten, G. H. 2009. "St Paul on Soul, Spirit and the Inner Man". In *The Afterlife of the Platonic Soul*, M. Elkaisy-Friemuth & J. M. Dillon (eds), 25–44. Leiden: Brill.

Van Riel, G. 1997. "Iamblichus and the *Philebus* of Plato". *Syllecta Classica* 8: 31–46.

Van Riel, G. 2001. "Horizontalism or Verticalism? Proclus vs Plotinus on the Procession of Matter". *Phronesis* 46: 129–53.

Van Winden, J. C. M. 1962. "A Crucial Passage in Plotinus, *Enn.* VI 9,7". *Mnemosyne*, 4th Series, 15(2): 173.

Vassilopoulou, P. 2003. "From a Feminist Perspective: Plotinus on Teaching and Learning Philosophy". *Women: A Cultural Review* 14(2): 130–43.

Vassilopoulou, P. 2005. "Sages of Old, Artists Anew: Plotinus' *Enneads* IV.3.[27].11". *Classical Bulletin* 81: 35–49.

Verbeke, G. 1997. "Individual Consciousness in Neoplatonism". See Cleary (1997), 135–52.

Vernant, J.-P. 1989. "L'Individu dans la cité". In his *L'Individu, la mort, l'amour. Soi-même et l'autre en Grèce ancienne*, 214–16. Paris: Gallimard.

Vitrac, B. & D. Rabouin 2010. "Sur le passage mathématique de l'*Épinomis* (990c–992a): Signification et postérité". *Philosophie antique* 10: 5–39.

Vlastos, G. 1981. "The Individual as Object of Love in Plato". In *Platonic Studies*, 2nd edn, 3–42. Princeton, NJ: Princeton University Press.

Volk, R. 1990. *Der medizinische Inhalt der Schriften des Michael Psellos*. PhD dissertation, Munich: Institut für Byzantinistik und neugriechische Philologie der Ludwig-Maximilians Universität.

Volkmann, R. 1869. *Synesius von Cyrene*. Berlin: Ebeling & Plahn.

Vollenweider, S. 1984. *Neuplatonische und christliche Theologie bei Synesios von Kyrene*. Göttingen: Vandenhoeck & Ruprecht.

Von Balthasar, H. U. 1995. *Presence and Thought: Essay on the Religious Philosophy of Gregory of Nyssa*. San Francisco, CA: Communio Books/Ignatius Press.

Von Ivanka, E. 1992. *Platonismo cristiano*. Milan: Vita e Pensiero.

Von Staden, H. 1989. *Herophilus: The Art of Medicine in Early Alexandria*. Cambridge: Cambridge University Press.

Von Staden, H. 1995. "Anatomy as Rhetoric: Galen on Dissection and Persuasion". *Journal of the History of Medicine and Allied Sciences* 50: 47–66.

Wagner, M. F. 1982a. "Plotinus' World". *Dionysius* 6: 13–42.

Wagner, M. F. 1982b. "Vertical Causation in Plotinus". In *The Structure of Being*, R. Baine Harris (ed.), 51–72. Albany, NY: SUNY Press.

Wagner, M. F. 1985. "Realism and the Foundations of Science in Plotinus". *Ancient Philosophy* 5: 269–92.

Wagner, M. F. 1986. "Plotinus' Idealism and the Problem of Matter in *Enneads* VI 4 and 5". *Dionysius* 10: 57–63.

Wagner, M. F. 1996. "Plotinus on the Nature of Physical Reality". See Gerson (1996), 130–70.

Wagner, M. F. 2002a. "Plotinus, Nature, and the Scientific Spirit". See Wagner (2002b), 277–329.

Wagner, M. F. (ed.) 2002b. *Neoplatonism and Nature*. Albany, NY: SUNY Press.

Wallis, R. T. 1972. *Neoplatonism*. London: Duckworth. 2nd edn 1995.

Wallis, R. T. 1982. "Phraseology and Imagery in Plotinus and Indian Thought". See Baine Harris (1982), 101–20.

Walter, C. 1984. "Expressionism and Hellenism. A Note on Stylistic Tendencies in Byzantine Figurative Art from *Spätantike* to the Macedonian 'Renaissance'". *Revue des études byzantines* 42: 265–87.

Warnock, G. J. 1971. *The Object of Morality*. London: Methuen.

Warren, E. 1964. "Consciousness in Plotinus". *Phronesis* 9: 83–98.

Watt, W. M. 1972. *The Influence of Islam on Medieval Europe*. Edinburgh: Edinburgh University Press.

Watts, E. 2004. "Justinian, Malalas, and the End of Athenian Philosophical Teaching in AD 529". *Journal of Roman Studies* 94: 168–82.

Watts, E. 2006. *City and School in Late Antiquity: Athens and Alexandria*. Berkeley, CA: University of California Press.

Watts, E. 2009. "The Enduring Legacy of the Iatrosophist Gessius". *Greek, Roman, and Byzantine Studies* 49: 113–33.

Watts, E. 2010. *Riot in Alexandria*. Berkeley, CA: University of California Press.

Wear, S. K. 2011. *The Teachings of Syrianus on Plato's Timaeus and Parmenides*. Leiden: Brill.

Weber, K. O. 1962. *Origenes der Neoplatoniker*. Munich: Beck.

Wedeck, H. E. (trans.) 1962. *The Fountain of Life*. New York: Philosophical Library. Reprinted as *Solomon Ibn Gabirol, The Fountain of Life*. Breinigsville, PA: Bibliobazaar, 2008.

Westerink, L. G. 1959. "Excerpte aus Proklos' Enneadenkommentar bei Psellos". *Byzantinische Zeitschrift* 52: 1–10.

Westerink, L. G. 1964. "Philosophy and Medicine in Late Antiquity". *Janus* 51: 169–77.

Westerink, L. G. 1967. *Pseudo-Elias: Lectures on Porphyry's Isagoge*. Amsterdam: North-Holland.

Westerink, L. G. 1977. *The Greek Commentaries on Plato's Phaedo. Volume II, Damascius*, Verhandelingen der Koninklijke Nederlandse Akademie van Wetenschappen, Afd. Letterkunde, Nieuwe Reeks 93. Amsterdam: North-Holland.

Westerink, L. G. 1990. "Anonymous Prolegomena to Platonic Philosophy". See Sorabji (1990), 328–36.

Westerink, L. G., J. Trouillard & A. Segonds (eds) 1990. *Prolégomènes à la philosophie de Platon*. Paris: Budé.

Westra, L. 1987. "Proclus' Ascent of the Soul Towards the One in the *Elements of Theology*: Is It Plotinian?" In *Proclus et son influence: Actes du colloque de Neuchâtel, juin 1985*, G. Bos & G. Seel (eds), 193–237. Zurich: Éditions du Grand Midi.

Wetzel, J. (ed.) 2012. *Augustine's City of God: A Critical Guide*. Cambridge: Cambridge University Press.

Whitehead, A. N. 1979. *Process and Reality*. New York: Free Press.

Wilberding, J. 2008. "Porphyry and Plotinus on the Seed". *Phronesis* 53: 406–32.

Wilberding, J. 2011. *Porphyry: To Gaurus on How Embryos are Ensouled, and On What is in Our Power*. London: Bristol Classical Press.

Wilberding, J. & C. Horn (eds) 2012. *Neoplatonism and the Philosophy of Nature*. Oxford: Oxford University Press.

Wildberg, C. 2009. "A World of Thoughts: Plotinus on Nature and Contemplation (*Enn*. III.8. [30] 1–6)". See Chiaradonna & Trabattoni (2009), 121–43.

Williams, B. 1985. *Ethics and the Limits of Philosophy*. Cambridge, MA: Harvard University Press.

Williamson, R. 1989. *Jews in the Hellenistic World: Philo*. Cambridge: Cambridge University Press.

Wilson, N. G. 1969. "*Philologia Perennis*", review of Pfeiffer 1968. *Classical Review* 19: 370–72.

Witt, R. E. 1931. "The Plotinian *Logos* and its Stoic Basis". *Classical Quarterly* 25: 103–11.

Wittgenstein, L. 1953. *Philosophical Investigations*, G. E. M. Anscombe & R. Rhees (eds), G. E. M. Anscombe (trans.). Oxford: Blackwell.

Wöhrle, G. 1990. *Studien zur Theorie der antiken Gesundheitslehre*. Stuttgart: Steiner.

Wolfson, H. A. 1973. "The Meaning of *ex nihilo* in Isaac Israeli". In his *Studies in the History of Philosophy and Religion*, 1, I. Twersky & G. H. Williams (eds), 222–33. Cambridge, MA: Harvard University Press.

Wolska-Conus, W. 1989. "Stéphanos d'Athènes et Stéphanos d'Alexandrie. Essai d'identification et de biographie". In *Revue des études byzantines* 47: 5–89.

Wolska-Conus, W. 1992. "Les Commentaires de Stéphanos d'Athènes et au *Prognostikon* et aux *Aphorismes* d'Hippocrate: De Galien à la pratique scholaire Alexandrine". *Revue des études byzantines* 50: 5–86.

Wolters, A. W. 1982. "A Survey of Modern Scholarly Opinion on Plotinus and Indian Thought." See Baine Harris (1982), 293–308.

Wurm, K. 1973. *Substanz und Qualität. Ein Beitrag zur Interpretation der Plotinischen Traktate VI 1, 2 und 3.* Berlin: De Gruyter.

Yunis, H. (ed.) 2003. *Written Texts and the Rise of Literate Culture in Ancient Greece.* Cambridge: Cambridge University Press.

Zambon, M. 2002. *Porphyre et le moyen-platonisme.* Paris: Vrin.

Zeller, E. 1868. *Die Philosophie der Griechen in ihrer geschichtlichen Entwicklung* 3.2, 2nd edn. Leipzig: Fues's Verlag.

Index of passages cited

General index